Business Analytics
Descriptive • Predictive • Prescriptive

Jeffrey D. Camm
Wake Forest University

James J. Cochran
University of Alabama

Michael J. Fry
University of Cincinnati

Jeffrey W. Ohlmann
University of Iowa

 Cengage

Australia • Brazil • Canada • Mexico • Singapore • United Kingdom • United States

Business Analytics,
Fourth Edition
Jeffrey D. Camm, James J. Cochran,
Michael J. Fry, Jeffrey W. Ohlmann

Senior Vice President, Higher Education & Skills
Product: Erin Joyner

Product Director: Jason Fremder

Senior Product Manager: Aaron Arnsparger

Senior Content Manager: Conor Allen

Product Assistant: Maggie Russo

Marketing Manager: Chris Walz

Senior Learning Designer: Brandon Foltz

Digital Delivery Lead: Mark Hopkinson

Intellectual Property Analyst: Ashley Maynard

Intellectual Property Project Manager: Kelli
Besse

Production Service: MPS Limited

Senior Project Manager, MPS Limited:
Santosh Pandey

Art Director: Chris Doughman

Text Designer: Beckmeyer Design

Cover Designer: Beckmeyer Design

Cover Image: iStockPhoto.com/tawanlubfah

For product information and technology assistance, contact us at
Cengage Customer & Sales Support, 1-800-354-9706
or support.cengage.com.

For permission to use material from this text or product, submit all
requests online at **www.copyright.com**.

Library of Congress Control Number: 2019921119

ISBN: 978-0-357-13178-7

Loose-leaf Edition
ISBN: 978-0-357-13179-4

Cengage
200 Pier 4 Boulevard
Boston, MA 02210
USA

Cengage is a leading provider of customized learning solutions
with employees residing in nearly 40 different countries and sales in more
than 125 countries around the world. Find your local representative at:
www.cengage.com.

To learn more about Cengage platforms and services, register or access your
online learning solution, or purchase materials for your course,
visit **www.cengage.com.**

Printed in Mexico
Print Number: 07   Print Year: 2022

Brief Contents

Contents

Contents

Jeffrey D. Camm. is the Inmar Presidential Chair and Associate Dean of Business Analytics in the School of Business at Wake Forest University. Born in Cincinnati, Ohio, he holds a B.S. from Xavier University (Ohio) and a Ph.D. from Clemson University. Prior to joining the faculty at Wake Forest, he was on the faculty of the University of Cincinnati. He has also been a visiting scholar at Stanford University and a visiting professor of business administration at the Tuck School of Business at Dartmouth College.

Dr. Camm has published over 40 papers in the general area of optimization applied to problems in operations management and marketing. He has published his research in *Science, Management Science, Operations Research, Interfaces,* and other professional journals. Dr. Camm was named the Dornoff Fellow of Teaching Excellence at the University of Cincinnati and he was the 2006 recipient of the INFORMS Prize for the Teaching of Operations Research Practice. A firm believer in practicing what he preaches, he has served as an operations research consultant to numerous companies and government agencies. From 2005 to 2010 he served as editor-in-chief of *Interfaces.* In 2016, Professor Camm received the George E. Kimball Medal for service to the operations research profession, and in 2017 he was named an INFORMS Fellow.

James J. Cochran. James J. Cochran is Associate Dean for Research, Professor of Applied Statistics and the Rogers-Spivey Faculty Fellow at The University of Alabama. Born in Dayton, Ohio, he earned his B.S., M.S., and M.B.A. from Wright State University and his Ph.D. from the University of Cincinnati. He has been at The University of Alabama since 2014 and has been a visiting scholar at Stanford University, Universidad de Talca, the University of South Africa and Pole Universitaire Leonard de Vinci.

Dr. Cochran has published more than 40 papers in the development and application of operations research and statistical methods. He has published in several journals, including *Management Science, The American Statistician, Communications in Statistics—Theory and Methods, Annals of Operations Research, European Journal of Operational Research, Journal of Combinatorial Optimization, Interfaces,* and *Statistics and Probability Letters.* He received the 2008 INFORMS Prize for the Teaching of Operations Research Practice, 2010 Mu Sigma Rho Statistical Education Award and 2016 Waller Distinguished Teaching Career Award from the American Statistical Association. Dr. Cochran was elected to the International Statistics Institute in 2005, named a Fellow of the American Statistical Association in 2011, and named a Fellow of INFORMS in 2017. He also received the Founders Award in 2014 and the Karl E. Peace Award in 2015 from the American Statistical Association, and he received the INFORMS President's Award in 2019.

A strong advocate for effective operations research and statistics education as a means of improving the quality of applications to real problems, Dr. Cochran has chaired teaching effectiveness workshops around the globe. He has served as an operations research consultant to numerous companies and not-for-profit organizations. He served as editor-in-chief of *INFORMS Transactions on Education* and is on the editorial board of *INFORMS Journal of Applied Analytics, International Transactions in Operational Research,* and *Significance.*

Michael J. Fry. Michael J. Fry is Professor of Operations, Business Analytics, and Information Systems (OBAIS) and Academic Director of the Center for Business Analytics in the Carl H. Lindner College of Business at the University of Cincinnati. Born in Killeen, Texas, he earned a B.S. from Texas A&M University, and M.S.E. and Ph.D. degrees from the University of Michigan. He has been at the University of Cincinnati since 2002, where he served as Department Head from 2014 to 2018 and has been named a Lindner Research Fellow. He has also been a visiting professor at Cornell University and at the University of British Columbia.

Professor Fry has published more than 25 research papers in journals such as *Operations Research, Manufacturing & Service Operations Management, Transportation Science, Naval Research Logistics, IIE Transactions, Critical Care Medicine*, and *Interfaces*. He serves on editorial boards for journals such as *Production and Operations Management, INFORMS Journal of Applied Analytics* (formerly *Interfaces*), and *Journal of Quantitative Analysis in Sports*. His research interests are in applying analytics to the areas of supply chain management, sports, and public-policy operations. He has worked with many different organizations for his research, including Dell, Inc., Starbucks Coffee Company, Great American Insurance Group, the Cincinnati Fire Department, the State of Ohio Election Commission, the Cincinnati Bengals, and the Cincinnati Zoo & Botanical Gardens. In 2008, he was named a finalist for the Daniel H. Wagner Prize for Excellence in Operations Research Practice, and he has been recognized for both his research and teaching excellence at the University of Cincinnati. In 2019, he led the team that was awarded the INFORMS UPS George D. Smith Prize on behalf of the OBAIS Department at the University of Cincinnati.

Jeffrey W. Ohlmann. Jeffrey W. Ohlmann is Associate Professor of Business Analytics and Huneke Research Fellow in the Tippie College of Business at the University of Iowa. Born in Valentine, Nebraska, he earned a B.S. from the University of Nebraska, and M.S. and Ph.D. degrees from the University of Michigan. He has been at the University of Iowa since 2003.

Professor Ohlmann's research on the modeling and solution of decision-making problems has produced more than two dozen research papers in journals such as *Operations Research, Mathematics of Operations Research, INFORMS Journal on Computing, Transportation Science*, and the *European Journal of Operational Research*. He has collaborated with companies such as Transfreight, LeanCor, Cargill, the Hamilton County Board of Elections, and three National Football League franchises. Because of the relevance of his work to industry, he was bestowed the George B. Dantzig Dissertation Award and was recognized as a finalist for the Daniel H. Wagner Prize for Excellence in Operations Research Practice.

Preface

B *usiness Analytics* 4E is designed to introduce the concept of business analytics to undergraduate and graduate students. This edition builds upon what was one of the first collections of materials that are essential to the growing field of business analytics. In Chapter 1, we present an overview of business analytics and our approach to the material in this textbook. In simple terms, business analytics helps business professionals make better decisions based on data. We discuss models for summarizing, visualizing, and understanding useful information from historical data in Chapters 2 through 6. Chapters 7 through 9 introduce methods for both gaining insights from historical data and predicting possible future outcomes. Chapter 10 covers the use of spreadsheets for examining data and building decision models. In Chapter 11, we demonstrate how to explicitly introduce uncertainty into spreadsheet models through the use of Monte Carlo simulation. In Chapters 12 through 14, we discuss optimization models to help decision makers choose the best decision based on the available data. Chapter 15 is an overview of decision analysis approaches for incorporating a decision maker's views about risk into decision making. In Appendix A we present optional material for students who need to learn the basics of using Microsoft Excel. The use of databases and manipulating data in Microsoft Access is discussed in Appendix B. Appendixes in many chapters illustrate the use of additional software tools such as R, JMP Pro and Tableau to apply analytics methods.

This textbook can be used by students who have previously taken a course on basic statistical methods as well as students who have not had a prior course in statistics. *Business Analytics* 4E is also amenable to a two-course sequence in business statistics and analytics. All statistical concepts contained in this textbook are presented from a business analytics perspective using practical business examples. Chapters 2, 4, 6, and 7 provide an introduction to basic statistical concepts that form the foundation for more advanced analytics methods. Chapters 3, 5, and 9 cover additional topics of data visualization and data mining that are not traditionally part of most introductory business statistics courses, but they are exceedingly important and commonly used in current business environments. Chapter 10 and Appendix A provide the foundational knowledge students need to use Microsoft Excel for analytics applications. Chapters 11 through 15 build upon this spreadsheet knowledge to present additional topics that are used by many organizations that are leaders in the use of prescriptive analytics to improve decision making.

Updates in the Fourth Edition

The fourth edition of *Business Analytics* is a major revision. We have added online appendixes for many topics in Chapters 1 through 9 that introduce the use of R, the exceptionally popular open-source software for analytics. *Business Analytics* 4E also includes an appendix to Chapter 3 introducing the powerful data visualization software Tableau. We have further enhanced our data mining chapters to allow instructors to choose their preferred means of teaching this material in terms of software usage. We have expanded the number of conceptual homework problems in both Chapters 5 and 9 to increase the number of opportunities for students learn about data mining and solve problems without the use of data mining software. Additionally, we now include online appendixes on using JMP Pro and R for teaching data mining so that instructors can choose their favored way of teaching this material. Other changes in this edition include an expanded discussion of binary variables for integer optimization in Chapter 13, an additional example in Chapter 11 for Monte Carlo simulation, and new and revised homework problems and cases.

- **Tableau Appendix for Data Visualization.** Chapter 3 now includes a new appendix that introduces the use of the software Tableau for data visualization. Tableau is a very powerful software for creating meaningful data visualizations that can be used to display, and to analyze, data. The appendix includes step-by-step directions for generating many of the charts used in Chapters 2 and 3 in Tableau.

- **Incorporation of R.** R is an exceptionally powerful open-source software that is widely used for a variety of statistical and analytics methods. We now include online appendixes that introduce the use of R for many of the topics covered in Chapters 1 through 9, including data visualization and data mining. These appendixes include step-by-step directions for using R to implement the methods described in these chapters. To facilitate the use of R, we introduce RStudio, an open-source integrated development environment (IDE) that provides a menu-driven interface for R. For Chapters 5 and 9 that cover data mining, we introduce the use of Rattle, a library package providing a graphical-user interface for R specifically tailored for data mining functionality. The use of RStudio and Rattle eases the learning curve of using R so that students can focus on learning the methods and interpreting the output.

- **Updates for Data Mining Chapters.** Chapters 5 and 9 have received extensive updates. We have moved the Descriptive Data Mining chapter to Chapter 5 so that it is located after our chapter on Probability. This allows us to use probability concepts such as conditional probability to explain association rule measures. Additional content on text mining and further discussion of ways to measure distance between observations have been added to a reorganized Descriptive Data Mining chapter. Descriptions of cross-validation approaches, methods of addressing class imbalanced data, and out-of-bag estimation in ensemble methods have been added to Chapter 9 on Predictive Data Mining. The end-of-chapter problems in Chapters 5 and 9 have been revised and generalized to accommodate the use of a wide range of data mining software. To allow instructors to choose different software for use with these chapters, we have created online appendixes for both JMP Pro and R. JMP has introduced a new version of its software (JMP Pro 14) since the previous edition of this textbook, so we have updated our JMP Pro output and step-by-step instructions to reflect changes in this software. We have also written online appendixes for Chapters 5 and 9 that use R and the graphical-user interface Rattle to introduce topics from these chapters to students. The use of Rattle removes some of the more difficult line-by-line coding in R to perform many common data mining techniques so that students can concentrate on learning the methods rather than coding syntax. For some data mining techniques that are not available in Rattle, we show how to accomplish these methods using R code. And for all of our textbook examples, we include the exact R code that can be used to solve the examples. We have also added homework problems to Chapters 5 and 9 that can be solved without using any specialized software. This allows instructors to cover the basics of data mining without introducing any additional software. The online appendixes for Chapters 5 and 9 also include JMP Pro and R specific instructions for how to solve the end-of-chapter problems and cases using JMP Pro and R. Problem and case solutions using both JMP Pro and R are also available to instructors.

- **Additional Simulation Model Example.** We have added an additional example of a simulation model in Chapter 11. This new example helps bridge the gap in the difficultly levels of the previous examples. The new example also gives students additional information on how to build and interpret simulation models.

- **New Cases.** *Business Analytics* 4E includes nine new end-of-chapter cases that allow students to work on more extensive problems related to the chapter material and work with larger data sets. We have also written two new cases that require the use of material from multiple chapters. This helps students understand the connections between the material in different chapters and is more representative of analytics projects in practice where the methods used are often not limited to a single type.

- **Legal and Ethical Issues Related to Analytics and Big Data.** Chapter 1 now includes a section that discusses legal and ethical issues related to analytics and the use of big data. This section discusses legal issues related to the protection of data as well as ethical issues related to the misuse and unintended consequences of analytics applications.

- **New End-of-Chapter Problems.** The fourth edition of this textbook includes more than 20 new problems. We have also revised many of the existing problems to update and improve clarity. Each end-of-chapter problem now also includes a short header to make the application of the exercise more clear. As we have done in past editions, Excel solution files are available to instructors for problems that require the use of Excel. For problems that require the use of software in the data-mining chapters (Chapters 5 and 9), we include solutions for both JMP Pro and R/Rattle.

Continued Features and Pedagogy

In the fourth edition of this textbook, we continue to offer all of the features that have been successful in the first two editions. Some of the specific features that we use in this textbook are listed below.

- **Integration of Microsoft Excel:** Excel has been thoroughly integrated throughout this textbook. For many methodologies, we provide instructions for how to perform calculations both by hand and with Excel. In other cases where realistic models are practical only with the use of a spreadsheet, we focus on the use of Excel to describe the methods to be used.

- **Notes and Comments:** At the end of many sections, we provide Notes and Comments to give the student additional insights about the methods presented in that section. These insights include comments on the limitations of the presented methods, recommendations for applications, and other matters. Additionally, margin notes are used throughout the textbook to provide additional insights and tips related to the specific material being discussed.

- **Analytics in Action:** Each chapter contains an Analytics in Action article. Several of these have been updated and replaced for the fourth edition. These articles present interesting examples of the use of business analytics in practice. The examples are drawn from many different organizations in a variety of areas including healthcare, finance, manufacturing, marketing, and others.

- **DATAfiles and MODELfiles:** All data sets used as examples and in student exercises are also provided online on the companion site as files available for download by the student. DATAfiles are Excel files (or .csv files for easy import into JMP Pro and R/Rattle) that contain data needed for the examples and problems given in the textbook. MODELfiles contain additional modeling features such as extensive use of Excel formulas or the use of Excel Solver, JMP Pro, or R.

- **Problems and Cases:** With the exception of Chapter 1, each chapter contains an extensive selection of problems to help the student master the material presented in that chapter. The problems vary in difficulty and most relate to specific examples of the use of business analytics in practice. Answers to even-numbered problems are provided in an online supplement for student access. With the exception of Chapter 1, each chapter also includes at least one in-depth case study that connects many of the different methods introduced in the chapter. The case studies are designed to be more open-ended than the chapter problems, but enough detail is provided to give the student some direction in solving the cases. New to the fourth edition is the inclusion of two cases that require the use of material from multiple chapters in the text to better illustrate how concepts from different chapters relate to each other.

MindTap

MindTap is a customizable digital course solution that includes an interactive eBook, autograded exercises from the textbook, algorithmic practice problems with solutions feedback, Exploring Analytics visualizations, Adaptive Test Prep, and more! MindTap is also where instructors and users can find the online appendixes for JMP Pro and R/Rattle. All of these materials offer students better access to resources to understand the materials within the course. For more information on MindTap, please contact your Cengage representative.

WebAssign

Prepare for class with confidence using WebAssign from Cengage. This online learning platform fuels practice, so students can truly absorb what you learn – and are better prepared come test time. Videos, Problem Walk-Throughs, and End-of-Chapter problems and cases with instant feedback help them understand the important concepts, while instant grading allows you and them to see where they stand in class. Class Insights allows students to see what topics they have mastered and which they are struggling with, helping them identify where to spend extra time. Study Smarter with WebAssign.

For Students

Online resources are available to help the student work more efficiently. The resources can be accessed through **www.cengage.com/decisionsciences/camm/ba/4e**.

- **R, RStudio, and Rattle:** R, RStudio, and Rattle are open-source software, so they are free to download. *Business Analytics* 4E includes step-by-step instructions for downloading these software.

- **JMP Pro:** Many universities have site licenses of SAS Institute's JMP Pro software on both Mac and Windows. These are typically offered through your university's software licensing administrator. Faculty may contact the JMP Academic team to find out if their universities have a license or to request a complementary instructor copy at www.jmp .com/contact-academic. For institutions without a site license, students may rent a 6- or 12-month license for JMP at www.onthehub.com/jmp.

- **Data Files:** A complete download of all data files associated with this text.

For Instructors

Instructor resources are available to adopters on the Instructor Companion Site, which can be found and accessed at **www.cengage.com/decisionsciences/camm/ba/4e** including:

- **Solutions Manual:** The Solutions Manual, prepared by the authors, includes solutions for all problems in the text. It is available online as well as print. Excel solution files are available to instructors for those problems that require the use of Excel. Solutions for Chapters 5 and 9 are available using both JMP Pro and R/Rattle for data mining problems.

- **Solutions to Case Problems:** These are also prepared by the authors and contain solutions to all case problems presented in the text. Case solutions for Chapters 5 and 9 are provided using both JMP Pro and R/Rattle. Extensive case solutions are also provided for the new multi-chapter cases that draw on material from multiple chapters.

- **PowerPoint Presentation Slides:** The presentation slides contain a teaching outline that incorporates figures to complement instructor lectures.

- **Test Bank:** Cengage Learning Testing Powered by Cognero is a flexible, online system that allows you to:

  - author, edit, and manage test bank content from multiple Cengage Learning solutions,
  - create multiple test versions in an instant, and
  - deliver tests from your Learning Management System (LMS), your classroom, or wherever you want.

Acknowledgments

We would like to acknowledge the work of reviewers and users who have provided comments and suggestions for improvement of this text. Thanks to:

Rafael Becerril Arreola
University of South Carolina

Matthew D. Bailey
Bucknell University

Phillip Beaver
University of Denver

M. Khurrum S. Bhutta
Ohio University

Paolo Catasti
Virginia Commonwealth University

Q B. Chung
Villanova University

Elizabeth A. Denny
University of Kentucky

Mike Taein Eom
University of Portland

Yvette Njan Essounga
Fayetteville State University

Lawrence V. Fulton
Texas State University

Tom Groleau
Carthage College

James F. Hoelscher
Lincoln Memorial University

Eric Huggins
Fort Lewis College

Faizul Huq
Ohio University

Marco Lam
York College of Pennsylvania

Thomas Lee
University of California, Berkeley

Roger Myerson
Northwestern University

Ram Pakath
University of Kentucky

Susan Palocsay
James Madison University

Andy Shogan
University of California, Berkeley

Dothan Truong
Embry-Riddle Aeronautical University

Kai Wang
Wake Technical Community College
Ed Wasil
American University

Ed Winkofsky
University of Cincinnati

A special thanks goes to our associates from business and industry who supplied the Analytics in Action features. We recognize them individually by a credit line in each of the articles. We are also indebted to our senior product manager, Aaron Arnsparger; our Senior Content Manager, Conor Allen; senior learning designer, Brandon Foltz; digital delivery lead, Mark Hopkinson; and our senior project manager at MPS Limited, Santosh Pandey, for their editorial counsel and support during the preparation of this text.

Jeffrey D. Camm
James J. Cochran
Michael J. Fry
Jeffrey W. Ohlmann

Chapter 1

Introduction

CONTENTS

You apply for a loan for the first time. How does the bank assess the riskiness of the loan it might make to you? How does Amazon.com know which books and other products to recommend to you when you log in to their web site? How do airlines determine what price to quote to you when you are shopping for a plane ticket? How can doctors better diagnose and treat you when you are ill or injured?

You may be applying for a loan for the first time, but millions of people around the world have applied for loans before. Many of these loan recipients have paid back their loans in full and on time, but some have not. The bank wants to know whether you are more like those who have paid back their loans or more like those who defaulted. By comparing your credit history, financial situation, and other factors to the vast database of previous loan recipients, the bank can effectively assess how likely you are to default on a loan.

Similarly, Amazon.com has access to data on millions of purchases made by customers on its web site. Amazon.com examines your previous purchases, the products you have viewed, and any product recommendations you have provided. Amazon.com then searches through its huge database for customers who are similar to you in terms of product purchases, recommendations, and interests. Once similar customers have been identified, their purchases form the basis of the recommendations given to you.

Prices for airline tickets are frequently updated. The price quoted to you for a flight between New York and San Francisco today could be very different from the price that will be quoted tomorrow. These changes happen because airlines use a pricing strategy known as revenue management. Revenue management works by examining vast amounts of data on past airline customer purchases and using these data to forecast future purchases. These forecasts are then fed into sophisticated optimization algorithms that determine the optimal price to charge for a particular flight and when to change that price. Revenue management has resulted in substantial increases in airline revenues.

Finally, consider the case of being evaluated by a doctor for a potentially serious medical issue. Hundreds of medical papers may describe research studies done on patients facing similar diagnoses, and thousands of data points exist on their outcomes. However, it is extremely unlikely that your doctor has read every one of these research papers or is aware of all previous patient outcomes. Instead of relying only on her medical training and knowledge gained from her limited set of previous patients, wouldn't it be better for your doctor to have access to the expertise and patient histories of thousands of doctors around the world?

A group of IBM computer scientists initiated a project to develop a new decision technology to help in answering these types of questions. That technology is called Watson, named after the founder of IBM, Thomas J. Watson. The team at IBM focused on one aim: How the vast amounts of data now available on the Internet can be used to make more data-driven, smarter decisions. Watson is an example of the exploding field of **artificial intelligence (AI)**. Broadly speaking, AI is the use of data and computers to make decisions that would have in the past required human intelligence. Often, the computer software mimics the way we understand the human brain functions.

Watson became a household name in 2011, when it famously won the television game show, *Jeopardy!* Since that proof of concept in 2011, IBM has reached agreements with the health insurance provider WellPoint (now part of Anthem), the financial services company Citibank, Memorial Sloan-Kettering Cancer Center, and automobile manufacturer General Motors to apply Watson to the decision problems that they face.

Watson is a system of computing hardware, high-speed data processing, and analytical algorithms that are combined to make data-based recommendations. As more and more data are collected, Watson has the capability to learn over time. In simple terms, according to IBM, Watson gathers hundreds of thousands of possible solutions from a huge data bank, evaluates them using analytical techniques, and proposes only the best solutions for consideration. Watson provides not just a single solution, but rather a range of good solutions with a confidence level for each.

For example, at a data center in Virginia, to the delight of doctors and patients, Watson is already being used to speed up the approval of medical procedures. Citibank is beginning to explore how to use Watson to better serve its customers, and cancer specialists at more than a dozen hospitals in North America are using Watson to assist with the diagnosis and treatment of patients.[1]

This book is concerned with data-driven decision making and the use of analytical approaches in the decision-making process. Three developments spurred recent explosive growth in the use of analytical methods in business applications. First, technological advances—such as improved point-of-sale scanner technology and the collection of data through e-commerce and social networks, data obtained by sensors on all kinds of mechanical devices such as aircraft engines, automobiles, and farm machinery through the so-called Internet of Things and data generated from personal electronic devices—produce incredible amounts of data for businesses. Naturally, businesses want to use these data to improve the efficiency and profitability of their operations, better understand their customers, price their products more effectively, and gain a competitive advantage. Second, ongoing research has resulted in numerous methodological developments, including advances in computational approaches to effectively handle and explore massive amounts of data, faster algorithms for optimization and simulation, and more effective approaches for visualizing data. Third, these methodological developments were paired with an explosion in computing power and storage capability. Better computing hardware, parallel computing, and, more recently, cloud computing (the remote use of hardware and software over the Internet) have enabled businesses to solve big problems more quickly and more accurately than ever before.

In summary, the availability of massive amounts of data, improvements in analytic methodologies, and substantial increases in computing power have all come together to result in a dramatic upsurge in the use of analytical methods in business and a reliance on the discipline that is the focus of this text: business analytics. As stated in the Preface, the purpose of this text is to provide students with a sound conceptual understanding of the role that business analytics plays in the decision-making process. To reinforce the applications orientation of the text and to provide a better understanding of the variety of applications in which analytical methods have been used successfully, Analytics in Action articles are presented throughout the book. Each Analytics in Action article summarizes an application of analytical methods in practice.

1.1 Decision Making

It is the responsibility of managers to plan, coordinate, organize, and lead their organizations to better performance. Ultimately, managers' responsibilities require that they make strategic, tactical, or operational decisions. **Strategic decisions** involve higher-level issues concerned with the overall direction of the organization; these decisions define the organization's overall goals and aspirations for the future. Strategic decisions are usually the domain of higher-level executives and have a time horizon of three to five years. **Tactical decisions** concern how the organization should achieve the goals and objectives set by its strategy, and they are usually the responsibility of midlevel management. Tactical decisions usually span a year and thus are revisited annually or even every six months. **Operational decisions** affect how the firm is run from day to day; they are the domain of operations managers, who are the closest to the customer.

Consider the case of the Thoroughbred Running Company (TRC). Historically, TRC had been a catalog-based retail seller of running shoes and apparel. TRC sales revenues grew quickly as it changed its emphasis from catalog-based sales to Internet-based sales. Recently, TRC decided that it should also establish retail stores in the malls and downtown areas of major cities. This strategic decision will take the firm in a new direction that it hopes will complement its Internet-based strategy. TRC middle managers will therefore have to make a variety of tactical decisions in support of this strategic decision, including

---

[1] "IBM's Watson Is Learning Its Way to Saving Lives," Fastcompany web site, December 8, 2012; H. Landi, "IBM Watson Health Touts Recent Studies Showing AI Improves How Physicians Treat Cancer," FierceHealthcare web site, June 4, 2019.

how many new stores to open this year, where to open these new stores, how many distribution centers will be needed to support the new stores, and where to locate these distribution centers. Operations managers in the stores will need to make day-to-day decisions regarding, for instance, how many pairs of each model and size of shoes to order from the distribution centers and how to schedule their sales personnel's work time.

Regardless of the level within the firm, *decision making* can be defined as the following process:

1. Identify and define the problem.
2. Determine the criteria that will be used to evaluate alternative solutions.
3. Determine the set of alternative solutions.
4. Evaluate the alternatives.
5. Choose an alternative.

Step 1 of decision making, identifying and defining the problem, is the most critical. Only if the problem is well-defined, with clear metrics of success or failure (step 2), can a proper approach for solving the problem (steps 3 and 4) be devised. Decision making concludes with the choice of one of the alternatives (step 5).

There are a number of approaches to making decisions: tradition ("We've always done it this way"), intuition ("gut feeling"), and rules of thumb ("As the restaurant owner, I schedule twice the number of waiters and cooks on holidays"). The power of each of these approaches should not be underestimated. Managerial experience and intuition are valuable inputs to making decisions, but what if relevant data were available to help us make more informed decisions? With the vast amounts of data now generated and stored electronically, it is estimated that the amount of data stored by businesses more than doubles every two years. How can managers convert these data into knowledge that they can use to be more efficient and effective in managing their businesses?

1.2 Business Analytics Defined

What makes decision making difficult and challenging? Uncertainty is probably the number one challenge. If we knew how much the demand will be for our product, we could do a much better job of planning and scheduling production. If we knew exactly how long each step in a project will take to be completed, we could better predict the project's cost and completion date. If we knew how stocks will perform, investing would be a lot easier.

Another factor that makes decision making difficult is that we often face such an enormous number of alternatives that we cannot evaluate them all. What is the best combination of stocks to help me meet my financial objectives? What is the best product line for a company that wants to maximize its market share? How should an airline price its tickets so as to maximize revenue?

Some firms and industries use the simpler term, analytics. Analytics is often thought of as a broader category than business analytics, encompassing the use of analytical techniques in the sciences and engineering as well. In this text, we use business analytics and analytics synonymously.

Business analytics is the scientific process of transforming data into insight for making better decisions.[2] Business analytics is used for data-driven or fact-based decision making, which is often seen as more objective than other alternatives for decision making.

As we shall see, the tools of business analytics can aid decision making by creating insights from data, by improving our ability to more accurately forecast for planning, by helping us quantify risk, and by yielding better alternatives through analysis and optimization. A study based on a large sample of firms that was conducted by researchers at MIT's Sloan School of Management and the University of Pennsylvania concluded that firms guided by data-driven decision making have higher productivity and market value and increased output and profitability.[3]

---

[2]We adopt the definition of analytics developed by the Institute for Operations Research and the Management Sciences (INFORMS).

[3]E. Brynjolfsson, L. M. Hitt, and H. H. Kim, "Strength in Numbers: How Does Data-Driven Decisionmaking Affect Firm Performance?" Thirty-Second International Conference on Information Systems, Shanghai, China, December 2011.

1.3 A Categorization of Analytical Methods and Models

Business analytics can involve anything from simple reports to the most advanced optimization techniques (methods for finding the best course of action). Analytics is generally thought to comprise three broad categories of techniques: descriptive analytics, predictive analytics, and prescriptive analytics.

Descriptive Analytics

Descriptive analytics encompasses the set of techniques that describes what has happened in the past. Examples are data queries, reports, descriptive statistics, data visualization including data dashboards, some data-mining techniques, and basic what-if spreadsheet models.

Appendix B, at the end of this book, describes how to use Microsoft Access to conduct data queries.

A **data query** is a request for information with certain characteristics from a database. For example, a query to a manufacturing plant's database might be for all records of shipments to a particular distribution center during the month of March. This query provides descriptive information about these shipments: the number of shipments, how much was included in each shipment, the date each shipment was sent, and so on. A report summarizing relevant historical information for management might be conveyed by the use of descriptive statistics (means, measures of variation, etc.) and data-visualization tools (tables, charts, and maps). Simple descriptive statistics and data-visualization techniques can be used to find patterns or relationships in a large database.

Data dashboards are collections of tables, charts, maps, and summary statistics that are updated as new data become available. Dashboards are used to help management monitor specific aspects of the company's performance related to their decision-making responsibilities. For corporate-level managers, daily data dashboards might summarize sales by region, current inventory levels, and other company-wide metrics; front-line managers may view dashboards that contain metrics related to staffing levels, local inventory levels, and short-term sales forecasts.

Data mining is the use of analytical techniques for better understanding patterns and relationships that exist in large data sets. For example, by analyzing text on social network platforms like Twitter, data-mining techniques (including cluster analysis and sentiment analysis) are used by companies to better understand their customers. By categorizing certain words as positive or negative and keeping track of how often those words appear in tweets, a company like Apple can better understand how its customers are feeling about a product like the Apple Watch.

Predictive Analytics

Predictive analytics consists of techniques that use models constructed from past data to predict the future or ascertain the impact of one variable on another. For example, past data on product sales may be used to construct a mathematical model to predict future sales. This mode can factor in the product's growth trajectory and seasonality based on past patterns. A packaged-food manufacturer may use point-of-sale scanner data from retail outlets to help in estimating the lift in unit sales due to coupons or sales events. Survey data and past purchase behavior may be used to help predict the market share of a new product. All of these are applications of predictive analytics.

Linear regression, time series analysis, some data-mining techniques, and simulation, often referred to as risk analysis, all fall under the banner of predictive analytics. We discuss all of these techniques in greater detail later in this text.

Data mining, previously discussed as a descriptive analytics tool, is also often used in predictive analytics. For example, a large grocery store chain might be interested in developing a targeted marketing campaign that offers a discount coupon on potato chips. By studying historical point-of-sale data, the store may be able to use data mining to predict which customers are the most likely to respond to an offer on discounted chips by purchasing higher-margin items such as beer or soft drinks in addition to the chips, thus increasing the store's overall revenue.

Simulation involves the use of probability and statistics to construct a computer model to study the impact of uncertainty on a decision. For example, banks often use simulation to model investment and default risk in order to stress-test financial models. Simulation is also often used in the pharmaceutical industry to assess the risk of introducing a new drug.

Prescriptive Analytics

Prescriptive analytics differs from descriptive and predictive analytics in that **prescriptive analytics** indicates a course of action to take; that is, the output of a prescriptive model is a decision. Predictive models provide a forecast or prediction, but do not provide a decision. However, a forecast or prediction, when combined with a rule, becomes a prescriptive model. For example, we may develop a model to predict the probability that a person will default on a loan. If we create a rule that says if the estimated probability of default is more than 0.6, we should not award a loan, now the predictive model, coupled with the rule is prescriptive analytics. These types of prescriptive models that rely on a rule or set of rules are often referred to as **rule-based models**.

Other examples of prescriptive analytics are portfolio models in finance, supply network design models in operations, and price-markdown models in retailing. Portfolio models use historical investment return data to determine which mix of investments will yield the highest expected return while controlling or limiting exposure to risk. Supply-network design models provide plant and distribution center locations that will minimize costs while still meeting customer service requirements. Given historical data, retail price markdown models yield revenue-maximizing discount levels and the timing of discount offers when goods have not sold as planned. All of these models are known as **optimization models**, that is, models that give the best decision subject to the constraints of the situation.

Another type of modeling in the prescriptive analytics category is **simulation optimization** which combines the use of probability and statistics to model uncertainty with optimization techniques to find good decisions in highly complex and highly uncertain settings. Finally, the techniques of **decision analysis** can be used to develop an optimal strategy when a decision maker is faced with several decision alternatives and an uncertain set of future events. Decision analysis also employs **utility theory**, which assigns values to outcomes based on the decision maker's attitude toward risk, loss, and other factors.

In this text we cover all three areas of business analytics: descriptive, predictive, and prescriptive. Table 1.1 shows how the chapters cover the three categories.

1.4 Big Data

On any given day, 500 million tweets and 294 billion e-mails are sent, 95 million photos and videos are shared on Instagram, 350 million photos are posted on Facebook, and 3.5 billion searches are made with Google.[4] It is through technology that we have truly been thrust into the data age. Because data can now be collected electronically, the available amounts of it are staggering. The Internet, cell phones, retail checkout scanners, surveillance video, and sensors on everything from aircraft to cars to bridges allow us to collect and store vast amounts of data in real time.

In the midst of all of this data collection, the term *big data* has been created. There is no universally accepted definition of big data. However, probably the most accepted and most general definition is that **big data** is any set of data that is too large or too complex to be handled by standard data-processing techniques and typical desktop software. IBM describes the phenomenon of big data through the four Vs: volume, velocity, variety, and veracity, as shown in Figure 1.1.[5]

---

[4]J. Desjardins, "How Much Data Is Generated Each Day?" Visual Capitalist web site, April 15, 2019.

[5]IBM web site: www.ibmbigdatahub.com/sites/default/files/infographic_file/4-Vs-of-big-data.jpg.

TABLE 1.1	Coverage of Business Analytics Topics in This Text			
Chapter	Title	Descriptive	Predictive	Prescriptive
1	Introduction	●	●	●
2	Descriptive Statistics	●		
3	Data Visualization	●		
4	Probability: An Introduction to Modeling Uncertainty	●		
5	Descriptive Data Mining	●		
6	Statistical Inference	●		
7	Linear Regression		●	
8	Time Series and Forecasting		●	
9	Predictive Data Mining		●	
10	Spreadsheet Models	●	●	●
11	Monte Carlo Simulation		●	●
12	Linear Optimization Models			●
13	Integer Linear Optimization Models			●
14	Nonlinear Optimization Models			●
15	Decision Analysis			●

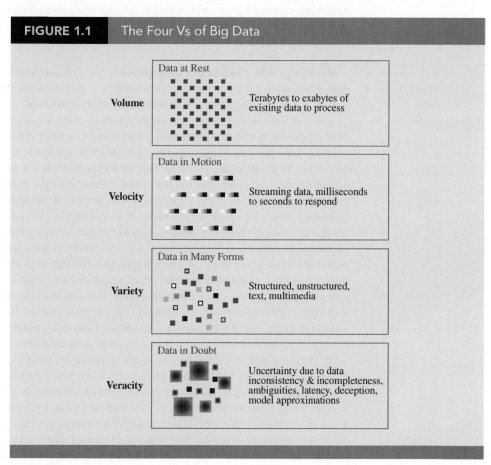

| FIGURE 1.1 | The Four Vs of Big Data |

Volume — Data at Rest — Terabytes to exabytes of existing data to process

Velocity — Data in Motion — Streaming data, milliseconds to seconds to respond

Variety — Data in Many Forms — Structured, unstructured, text, multimedia

Veracity — Data in Doubt — Uncertainty due to data inconsistency & incompleteness, ambiguities, latency, deception, model approximations

Source: IBM.

Volume

Because data are collected electronically, we are able to collect more of it. To be useful, these data must be stored, and this storage has led to vast quantities of data. Many companies now store in excess of 100 terabytes of data (a terabyte is 1,024 gigabytes).

Velocity

Real-time capture and analysis of data present unique challenges both in how data are stored, and the speed with which those data can be analyzed for decision making. For example, the New York Stock Exchange collects 1 terabyte of data in a single trading session, and having current data and real-time rules for trades and predictive modeling are important for managing stock portfolios.

Variety

In addition to the sheer volume and speed with which companies now collect data, more complicated types of data are now available and are proving to be of great value to businesses. Text data are collected by monitoring what is being said about a company's products or services on social media platforms such as Twitter. Audio data are collected from service calls (on a service call, you will often hear "this call may be monitored for quality control"). Video data collected by in-store video cameras are used to analyze shopping behavior. Analyzing information generated by these nontraditional sources is more complicated in part because of the processing required to transform the data into a numerical form that can be analyzed.

Veracity

Veracity has to do with how much uncertainty is in the data. For example, the data could have many missing values, which makes reliable analysis a challenge. Inconsistencies in units of measure and the lack of reliability of responses in terms of bias also increase the complexity of the data.

Businesses have realized that understanding big data can lead to a competitive advantage. Although big data represents opportunities, it also presents challenges in terms of data storage and processing, security, and available analytical talent.

The four Vs indicate that big data creates challenges in terms of how these complex data can be captured, stored, and processed; secured; and then analyzed. Traditional databases more or less assume that data fit into nice rows and columns, but that is not always the case with big data. Also, the sheer volume (the first V) often means that it is not possible to store all of the data on a single computer. This has led to new technologies like **Hadoop**—an open-source programming environment that supports big data processing through distributed storage and distributed processing on clusters of computers. Essentially, Hadoop provides a divide-and-conquer approach to handling massive amounts of data, dividing the storage and processing over multiple computers. **MapReduce** is a programming model used within Hadoop that performs the two major steps for which it is named: the map step and the reduce step. The map step divides the data into manageable subsets and distributes it to the computers in the cluster (often termed nodes) for storing and processing. The reduce step collects answers from the nodes and combines them into an answer to the original problem. Technologies like Hadoop and MapReduce, paired with relatively inexpensive computer power, enable cost-effective processing of big data; otherwise, in some cases, processing might not even be possible.

While some sources of big data are publicly available (Twitter, weather data, etc.), much of it is private information. Medical records, bank account information, and credit card transactions, for example, are all highly confidential and must be protected from computer hackers. **Data security**, the protection of stored data from destructive forces or unauthorized users, is of critical importance to companies. For example, credit card transactions are potentially very useful for understanding consumer behavior, but compromise of these data could lead to unauthorized use of the credit card or identity theft. A 2016 study of 383 companies in 12 countries conducted by the Ponemon Institute and IBM found that the average cost of a data breach is \$3.86 million.[6] Companies such as Target, Anthem, JPMorgan Chase, Yahoo!, Facebook, Marriott, Equifax, and Home Depot have faced major data breaches costing millions of dollars.

The complexities of the 4 Vs have increased the demand for analysts, but a shortage of qualified analysts has made hiring more challenging. More companies are searching for **data scientists**, who know how to effectively process and analyze massive amounts of data because they are well trained in both computer science and statistics. Next we discuss three examples of how companies are collecting big data for competitive advantage.

Kroger Understands Its Customers[7] Kroger is the largest retail grocery chain in the United States. It sends over 11 million pieces of direct mail to its customers each quarter. The quarterly mailers each contain 12 coupons that are tailored to each household based on several years of shopping data obtained through its customer loyalty card program. By collecting and analyzing consumer behavior at the individual household level, and better matching its coupon offers to shopper interests, Kroger has been able to realize a far higher redemption rate on its coupons. In the six-week period following distribution of the mailers, over 70% of households redeem at least one coupon, leading to an estimated coupon revenue of \$10 billion for Kroger.

MagicBand at Disney[8] The Walt Disney Company offers a wristband to visitors to its Orlando, Florida, Disney World theme park. Known as the MagicBand, the wristband contains technology that can transmit more than 40 feet and can be used to track each visitor's location in the park in real time. The band can link to information that allows Disney to better serve its visitors. For example, prior to the trip to Disney World, a visitor might be asked to fill out a survey on his or her birth date and favorite rides, characters, and restaurant table type and location. This information, linked to the MagicBand, can allow Disney employees using smartphones to greet you by name as you arrive, offer you products they know you prefer, wish you a happy birthday, have your favorite characters show up as you wait in line or have lunch at your favorite table. The MagicBand can be linked to your credit card, so there is no need to carry cash or a credit card. And during your visit, your movement throughout the park can be tracked and the data can be analyzed to better serve you during your next visit to the park.

General Electric and the Internet of Things[9] The **Internet of Things (IoT)** is the technology that allows data, collected from sensors in all types of machines, to be sent over the Internet to repositories where it can be stored and analyzed. This ability to collect data from products has enabled the companies that produce and sell those products to better serve their customers and offer new services based on analytics. For example, each day General Electric (GE) gathers nearly 50 million pieces of data from 10 million sensors on medical equipment and aircraft engines it has sold to customers throughout the world. In the case of aircraft engines, through a service agreement with its customers, GE collects data each time an airplane powered by its engines takes off and lands. By analyzing these data, GE can better predict when maintenance is needed, which helps customers avoid unplanned maintenance and downtime and helps ensure safe operation. GE can also use the data to better control how the plane is flown, leading to a decrease in fuel cost by flying more efficiently. GE spun off a new company called GE Digital 2.0 which operates as a stand-alone company focused on software that leverages IoT data. In 2018, GE announced that it would spin off a new company from its existing GE Digital business that will focus on industrial IoT applications.

Although big data is clearly one of the drivers for the strong demand for analytics, it is important to understand that, in some sense, big data issues are a subset of analytics. Many very valuable applications of analytics do not involve big data, but rather traditional data sets that are very manageable by traditional database and analytics software. The key to

---

[6]S. Shepard, "The Average Cost of a Data Breach," Security Today web site, July 17, 2018.

[7]Based on "Kroger Knows Your Shopping Patterns Better than You Do," Forbes.com, October 23, 2013.

[8]Based on "Disney's \$1 Billion Bet on a Magical Wristband," Wired.com, March 10, 2015.

[9]Based on "G.E. Opens Its Big Data Platform," NYTimes.com, October 9, 2014; "GE Announces New Industrial IoT Software Business," Forbes web site, December 14, 2018.

analytics is that it provides useful insights and better decision making using the data that are available—whether those data are "big" or "small."

1.5 Business Analytics in Practice

Business analytics involves tools as simple as reports and graphs to those that are as sophisticated as optimization, data mining, and simulation. In practice, companies that apply analytics often follow a trajectory similar to that shown in Figure 1.2. Organizations start with basic analytics in the lower left. As they realize the advantages of these analytic techniques, they often progress to more sophisticated techniques in an effort to reap the derived competitive advantage. Therefore, predictive and prescriptive analytics are some-times referred to as **advanced analytics**. Not all companies reach that level of usage, but those that embrace analytics as a competitive strategy often do.

Analytics has been applied in virtually all sectors of business and government. Organizations such as Procter & Gamble, IBM, UPS, Netflix, Amazon.com, Google, the Internal Revenue Service, and General Electric have embraced analytics to solve important problems or to achieve a competitive advantage. In this section, we briefly discuss some of the types of applications of analytics by application area.

Financial Analytics

Applications of analytics in finance are numerous and pervasive. Predictive models are used to forecast financial performance, to assess the risk of investment portfolios and projects, and to construct financial instruments such as derivatives. Prescriptive models are used to construct optimal portfolios of investments, to allocate assets, and to create optimal capital budgeting plans. For example, Europcar, the leading rental car company in Europe, uses forecasting models, simulation and optimization to predict demand, assess risk, and optimize the use of its fleet. It's models are implemented via a decision support system used in nine countries in Europe and has led to higher utilization of its fleet, decreased costs, and increased profitability.[10] Simulation is also often used to assess risk in the financial sector; one example is the deployment by Hypo Real Estate International of simulation models to successfully manage commercial real estate risk.[11]

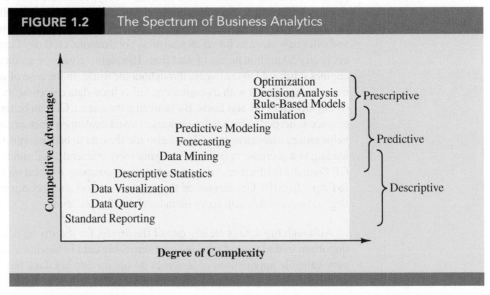

FIGURE 1.2	The Spectrum of Business Analytics

Source: Adapted from SAS.

[10]J. Guillen et al., "Europcar Integrates Forecasting, Simulation, and Optimization Techniques in a Capacity and Revenue Management System," *INFORMS Journal on Applied Analytics*, 49, no. 1 (January–February 2019).

[11]Y. Jafry, C. Marrison, and U. Umkehrer-Neudeck, "Hypo International Strengthens Risk Management with a Large-Scale, Secure Spreadsheet-Management Framework," *Interfaces* 38, no. 4 (July–August 2008).

Human Resource (HR) Analytics

A relatively new area of application for analytics is the management of an organization's human resources. The HR function is charged with ensuring that the organization (1) has the mix of skill sets necessary to meet its needs, (2) is hiring the highest-quality talent and providing an environment that retains it, and (3) achieves its organizational diversity goals. Google refers to its HR Analytics function as "people analytics." Google has analyzed substantial data on their own employees to determine the characteristics of great leaders, to assess factors that contribute to productivity, and to evaluate potential new hires. Google also uses predictive analytics to continually update their forecast of future employee turnover and retention.[12]

Marketing Analytics

Marketing is one of the fastest-growing areas for the application of analytics. A better understanding of consumer behavior through the use of scanner data and data generated from social media has led to an increased interest in marketing analytics. As a result, descriptive, predictive, and prescriptive analytics are all heavily used in marketing. A better understanding of consumer behavior through analytics leads to the better use of advertising budgets, more effective pricing strategies, improved forecasting of demand, improved product-line management, and increased customer satisfaction and loyalty. For example, Turner Broadcasting System Inc. uses forecasting and optimization models to create more-targeted audiences and to better schedule commercials for its advertising partners. The use of these models has led to an increase in Turner year-over-year advertising revenue of 186% and, at the same time, dramatically increased sales for the advertisers. Those advertisers that chose to benchmark found an increase in sales of $118 million.[13]

In another example of high-impact marketing analytics, automobile manufacturer Chrysler teamed with J.D. Power and Associates to develop an innovative set of predictive models to support its pricing decisions for automobiles. These models help Chrysler to better understand the ramifications of proposed pricing structures (a combination of manufacturer's suggested retail price, interest rate offers, and rebates) and, as a result, to improve its pricing decisions. The models have generated an estimated annual savings of $500 million.[14]

Health Care Analytics

The use of analytics in health care is on the increase because of pressure to simultaneously control costs and provide more effective treatment. Descriptive, predictive, and prescriptive analytics are used to improve patient, staff, and facility scheduling; patient flow; purchasing; and inventory control. A study by McKinsey Global Institute (MGI) and McKinsey & Company[15] estimates that the health care system in the United States could save more than $300 billion per year by better utilizing analytics; these savings are approximately the equivalent of the entire gross domestic product of countries such as Finland, Singapore, and Ireland.

The use of prescriptive analytics for diagnosis and treatment is relatively new, but it may prove to be the most important application of analytics in health care. For example, a group of scientists in Georgia used predictive models and optimization to develop personalized treatment for diabetes. They developed a predictive model that uses fluid dynamics and patient monitoring data to establish the relationship between drug dosage and drug effect at the individual level. This alleviates the need for more invasive procedures to monitor drug concentration. Then they used an optimization model that takes output from the predictive model to determine how an

[12]J. Sullivan, "How Google Is Using People Analytics to Completely Reinvent HR," Talent Management and HR web site, February 26, 2013.

[13]J. A. Carbajal, P. Williams, A. Popescu, and W. Chaar, "Turner Blazes a Trail for Audience Targeting on Television with Operations Research and Advanced Analytics," *INFORMS Journal on Applied Analytics,* 49, no. 1 (January–February 2019).

[14]J. Silva-Risso et al., "Chrysler and J. D. Power: Pioneering Scientific Price Customization in the Automobile Industry," *Interfaces* 38, no. 1 (January–February 2008).

[15]J. Manyika et al., "Big Data: The Next Frontier for Innovation, Competition and Productivity," McKinsey Global Institute Report, 2011.

individual achieves better glycemic control using less dosage. Using the models results in about a 39% savings in hospital costs, which equates to about $40,880 per patient.[16]

Supply Chain Analytics

The core service of companies such as UPS and FedEx is the efficient delivery of goods, and analytics has long been used to achieve efficiency. The optimal sorting of goods, vehicle and staff scheduling, and vehicle routing are all key to profitability for logistics companies such as UPS and FedEx.

Companies can benefit from better inventory and processing control and more efficient supply chains. Analytic tools used in this area span the entire spectrum of analytics. For example, the women's apparel manufacturer Bernard Claus, Inc. has successfully used descriptive analytics to provide its managers a visual representation of the status of its supply chain.[17] ConAgra Foods uses predictive and prescriptive analytics to better plan capacity utilization by incorporating the inherent uncertainty in commodities pricing. ConAgra realized a 100% return on its investment in analytics in under three months—an unheard of result for a major technology investment.[18]

Analytics for Government and Nonprofits

Government agencies and other nonprofits have used analytics to drive out inefficiencies and increase the effectiveness and accountability of programs. Indeed, much of advanced analytics has its roots in the U.S. and English military dating back to World War II. Today, the use of analytics in government is becoming pervasive in everything from elections to tax collection. For example, the New York State Department of Taxation and Finance has worked with IBM to use prescriptive analytics in the development of a more effective approach to tax collection. The result was an increase in collections from delinquent payers of $83 million over two years.[19] The U.S. Internal Revenue Service has used data mining to identify patterns that distinguish questionable annual personal income tax filings. In one application, the IRS combines its data on individual taxpayers with data received from banks, on mortgage payments made by those taxpayers. When taxpayers report a mortgage payment that is unrealistically high relative to their reported taxable income, they are flagged as possible underreporters of taxable income. The filing is then further scrutinized and may trigger an audit.

Likewise, nonprofit agencies have used analytics to ensure their effectiveness and accountability to their donors and clients. Catholic Relief Services (CRS) is the official international humanitarian agency of the U.S. Catholic community. The CRS mission is to provide relief for the victims of both natural and human-made disasters and to help people in need around the world through its health, educational, and agricultural programs. CRS uses an analytical spreadsheet model to assist in the allocation of its annual budget based on the impact that its various relief efforts and programs will have in different countries.[20]

Sports Analytics

The use of analytics in sports has gained considerable notoriety since 2003 when renowned author Michael Lewis published *Moneyball*. Lewis' book tells the story of how the Oakland Athletics used an analytical approach to player evaluation in order to assemble a competitive team with a limited budget. The use of analytics for player evaluation and on-field strategy is now common, especially in professional sports. Professional sports teams use analytics to assess players for the amateur drafts and to decide how much to offer players in contract negotiations;[21]

---

[16]E. Lee et al., "Outcome-Driven Personalized Treatment Design for Managing Diabetes," *Interfaces*, 48, no. 5 (September–October 2018).

[17]T. H. Davenport, ed., *Enterprise Analytics* (Upper Saddle River, NJ: Pearson Education Inc., 2013).

[18]"ConAgra Mills: Up-to-the-Minute Insights Drive Smarter Selling Decisions and Big Improvements in Capacity Utilization," IBM Smarter Planet Leadership Series. Available at: www.ibm.com/smarterplanet/us/en/leadership /conagra/, retrieved December 1, 2012.

[19]G. Miller et al., "Tax Collection Optimization for New York State," *Interfaces* 42, no. 1 (January–February 2013).

[20]I. Gamvros, R. Nidel, and S. Raghavan, "Investment Analysis and Budget Allocation at Catholic Relief Services," *Interfaces* 36, no. 5 (September–October 2006).

[21]N. Streib, S. J. Young, and J. Sokol, "A Major League Baseball Team Uses Operations Research to Improve Draft Preparation," *Interfaces* 42, no. 2 (March–April 2012).

professional motorcycle racing teams use sophisticated optimization for gearbox design to gain competitive advantage;[22] and teams use analytics to assist with on-field decisions such as which pitchers to use in various games of a Major League Baseball playoff series.

The use of analytics for off-the-field business decisions is also increasing rapidly. Ensuring customer satisfaction is important for any company, and fans are the customers of sports teams. The Cleveland Indians professional baseball team used a type of predictive modeling known as conjoint analysis to design its premium seating offerings at Progressive Field based on fan survey data. Using prescriptive analytics, franchises across several major sports dynamically adjust ticket prices throughout the season to reflect the relative attractiveness and potential demand for each game.

Web Analytics

Web analytics is the analysis of online activity, which includes, but is not limited to, visits to web sites and social media sites such as Facebook and LinkedIn. Web analytics obviously has huge implications for promoting and selling products and services via the Internet. Leading companies apply descriptive and advanced analytics to data collected in online experiments to determine the best way to configure web sites, position ads, and utilize social networks for the promotion of products and services. Online experimentation involves exposing various subgroups to different versions of a web site and tracking the results. Because of the massive pool of Internet users, experiments can be conducted without risking the disruption of the overall business of the company. Such experiments are proving to be invaluable because they enable the company to use trial-and-error in determining statistically what makes a difference in their web site traffic and sales.

1.6 Legal and Ethical Issues in the Use of Data and Analytics

With the advent of big data and the dramatic increase in the use of analytics and data science to improve decision making, increased attention has been paid to ethical concerns around data privacy and the ethical use of models based on data.

As businesses routinely collect data about their customers, they have an obligation to protect the data and to not misuse that data. Clients and customers have an obligation to understand the trade-offs between allowing their data to be collected and used, and the benefits they accrue from allowing a company to collect and use that data. For example, many companies have loyalty cards that collect data on customer purchases. In return for the benefits of using a loyalty card, typically discounted prices, customers must agree to allow the company to collect and use the data on purchases. An agreement must be signed between the customer and the company, and the agreement must specify what data will be collected and how it will be used. For example, the agreement might say that all scanned purchases will be collected with the date, time, location, and card number, but that the company agrees to only use that data internally to the company and to not give or sell that data to outside firms or individuals. The company then has an ethical obligation to uphold that agreement and make every effort to ensure that the data are protected from any type of unauthorized access. Unauthorized access of data is known as a data breach. Data breaches are a major concern for all companies in the digital age. A study by IBM and the Ponemon Institute estimated that the average cost of a data breach is $3.86 million.

Data privacy laws are designed to protect individuals' data from being used against their wishes. One of the strictest data privacy laws is the General Data Protection Regulation (GDPR) which went into effect in the European Union in May 2018. The law stipulates that the request for consent to use an individual's data must be easily understood and accessible, the intended uses of the data must be specified, and it must be easy to withdraw consent. The law also stipulates that an individual has a right to a copy of their data and the right "to be forgotten," that is, the right to demand that their data be erased. It is the

---

[22]J. Amoros, L. F. Escudero, J. F. Monge, J. V. Segura, and O. Reinoso, "TEAM ASPAR Uses Binary Optimization to Obtain Optimal Gearbox Ratios in Motorcycle Racing," *Interfaces* 42, no. 2 (March–April 2012).

responsibility of analytics professionals, indeed, anyone who handles or stores data, to understand the laws associated with the collection, storage, and use of individuals' data.

Ethical issues that arise in the use of data and analytics are just as important as the legal issues. Analytics professionals have a responsibility to behave ethically, which includes protecting data, being transparent about the data and how it was collected, and what it does and does not contain. Analysts must be transparent about the methods used to analyze the data and any assumptions that have to be made for the methods used. Finally, analysts must provide valid conclusions and understandable recommendations to their clients.

Intentionally using data and analytics for unethical purposes is clearly unethical. For example, using analytics to identify whom to target for fraud is of course inherently unethical because the goal itself is an unethical objective. Intentionally using biased data to achieve a goal is likewise inherently unethical. Misleading a client by misrepresenting results is clearly unethical.

For example, consider the case of an airline that runs an advertisement that "84% of business fliers to Chicago prefer that airline over its competitors." Such a statement is valid if the airline randomly surveyed business fliers across all airlines with a destination of Chicago. But, if for convenience, the airline surveyed only its own customers, the survey would be biased, and the claim would be misleading because fliers on other airlines were not surveyed. Indeed, if anything, the only conclusion one can legitimately draw from the biased sample of its own customers would be that 84% of that airlines' own customers preferred that airline and 16% of its own customers actually preferred another airline![23]

In her book, *Weapons of Math Destruction*, author Cathy O'Neil discusses how algorithms and models can be unintentionally biased.[24] For example, consider an analyst who is building a credit risk model for awarding loans. The location of the home of the applicant might be a variable that is correlated with other variables like income and ethnicity. Income is perhaps a relevant variable for determining the amount of a loan, but ethnicity is not. A model using home location could therefore lead to unintentional bias in the credit risk model. It is the analysts' responsibility to make sure this type of model bias and data bias do not become a part of the model.

Researcher and opinion writer Zeynep Tufecki[25] examines so-called "unintended consequences" of analytics, and particularly of machine learning and recommendation engines. Tufecki has pointed out that many Internet sites that use recommendation engines often suggest more extreme content, in terms of political views and conspiracy theories, to users based on their past viewing history. Tufecki and others theorize that this is because the machine learning algorithms being used have identified that more extreme content increases users' viewing time on the site, which is often the objective function being maximized by the machine learning algorithm. Therefore, while it is not the intention of the algorithm to promote more extreme views and disseminate false information, this may be the unintended consequence of using a machine learning algorithm that maximizes users' viewing time on the site. Analysts and decision makers must be aware of potential unintended consequences of their models, and they must decide how to react to these consequences once they are discovered.

Several organizations, including the American Statistical Association (ASA) and the Institute for Operations Research and the Management Sciences (INFORMS), provide ethical guidelines for analysts. In their "Ethical Guidelines for Statistical Practice,"[26] the ASA uses the term *statistician* throughout, but states that this "includes all practitioners of statistics and quantitative sciences—regardless of job title or field of degree— comprising statisticians at all levels of the profession and members of other professions who utilize and report statistical analyses and their applications." Their guidelines

---

[23]A. Barnett, "Misapplications Reviews: Newswatch," *Interfaces* 14, no. 6 (November–December 1984).

[24]C. O'Neil, *Weapons of Math Destruction, How Big Data Increases Inequality and Threatens Democracy* (New York: Crown Publishing, 2016).

[25]Z. Tufecki. "YouTube, the Great Radicalizer," *The New York Times*, March 10, 2018.

[26]Ethical Guidelines for Statistical Practice, the American Statistical Association, April 14, 2018.

state that "Good statistical practice is fundamentally based on transparent assumptions, reproducible results, and valid interpretations." More details are given in eight different sections of the guidelines and we encourage you to read and familiarize yourself with these guidelines.

INFORMS is a professional society focused on operations research and the management sciences, including analytics. INFORMS offers an analytics certification called CAP—certified analytics professional. All candidates for CAP are required to comply with the code of ethics/conduct provided by INFORMS.[27] The INFORMS CAP guidelines state, "In general, analytics professionals are obliged to conduct their professional activities responsibly, with particular attention to the values of consistency, respect for individuals, autonomy of all, integrity, justice, utility and competence." INFORMS also offers a set of Ethics Guidelines for its members, which covers ethical behavior for analytics professionals in three domains: Society, Organizations (businesses, government, nonprofit organization, and universities), and the Profession (operations research and analytics).[28] As these guidelines are fairly easy to understand and at the same time fairly comprehensive, we list them here in Table 1.2 and encourage you as a user/provider of analytics to make them your guiding principles.

TABLE 1.2	INFORMS Ethics Guidelines

Relative to Society

Analytics professionals should aspire to be:

- **Accountable** for their professional actions and the impact of their work.
- **Forthcoming** about their assumptions, interests, sponsors, motivations, limitations, and potential conflicts of interest.
- **Honest** in reporting their results, even when they fail to yield the desired outcome.
- **Objective** in their assessments of facts, irrespective of their opinions or beliefs.
- **Respectful** of the viewpoints and the values of others.
- **Responsible** for undertaking research and projects that provide positive benefits by advancing our scientific understanding, contributing to organizational improvements, and supporting social good.

Relative to Organizations

Analytics professionals should aspire to be:

- **Accurate** in our assertions, reports, and presentations.
- **Alert** to possible unintended or negative consequences that our results and recommendations may have on others.
- **Informed** of advances and developments in the fields relevant to our work.
- **Questioning** of whether there are more effective and efficient ways to reach a goal.
- **Realistic** in our claims of achievable results, and in acknowledging when the best course of action may be to terminate a project.
- **Rigorous** by adhering to proper professional practices in the development and reporting of our work.

Relative to the Profession

Analytics professionals should aspire to be:

- **Cooperative** by sharing best practices, information, and ideas with colleagues, young professionals, and students.
- **Impartial** in our praise or criticism of others and their accomplishments, setting aside personal interests.
- **Inclusive** of all colleagues, and rejecting discrimination and harassment in any form.
- **Tolerant** of well-conducted research and well-reasoned results, which may differ from our own findings or opinions.
- **Truthful** in providing attribution when our work draws from the ideas of others.
- **Vigilant** by speaking out against actions that are damaging to the profession

[27]Certified Analytics Professional Code of Ethics/Conduct. Available at www.certifiedanalytics.org/ethics.php.

[28]INFORMS Ethics Guidelines. Available at www.informs.org/About-INFORMS/Governance/INFORMS-Ethics-Guidelines.

SUMMARY

This introductory chapter began with a discussion of decision making. Decision making can be defined as the following process: (1) identify and define the problem, (2) determine the criteria that will be used to evaluate alternative solutions, (3) determine the set of alternative solutions, (4) evaluate the alternatives, and (5) choose an alternative. Decisions may be strategic (high level, concerned with the overall direction of the business), tactical (mid-level, concerned with how to achieve the strategic goals of the business), or operational (day-to-day decisions that must be made to run the company).

Uncertainty and an overwhelming number of alternatives are two key factors that make decision making difficult. Business analytics approaches can assist by identifying and mitigating uncertainty and by prescribing the best course of action from a very large number of alternatives. In short, business analytics can help us make better-informed decisions.

There are three categories of analytics: descriptive, predictive, and prescriptive. Descriptive analytics describes what has happened and includes tools such as reports, data visualization, data dashboards, descriptive statistics, and some data-mining techniques. Predictive analytics consists of techniques that use past data to predict future events or ascertain the impact of one variable on another. These techniques include regression, data mining, forecasting, and simulation. Prescriptive analytics uses data to determine a course of action. This class of analytical techniques includes rule-based models, simulation, decision analysis, and optimization. Descriptive and predictive analytics can help us better understand the uncertainty and risk associated with our decision alternatives. Predictive and prescriptive analytics, also often referred to as advanced analytics, can help us make the best decision when facing a myriad of alternatives.

Big data is a set of data that is too large or too complex to be handled by standard data-processing techniques or typical desktop software. The increasing prevalence of big data is leading to an increase in the use of analytics. The Internet, retail scanners, and cell phones are making huge amounts of data available to companies, and these companies want to better understand these data. Business analytics helps them understand these data and use them to make better decisions.

We also discussed various application areas of analytics. Our discussion focused on financial analytics, human resource analytics, marketing analytics, health care analytics, supply chain analytics, analytics for government and nonprofit organizations, sports analytics, and web analytics. However, the use of analytics is rapidly spreading to other sectors, industries, and functional areas of organizations. We concluded this chapter with a discussion of legal and ethical issues in the use of data and analytics, a topic that should be of great importance to all practitioners and consumers of analytics. Each remaining chapter in this text will provide a real-world vignette in which business analytics is applied to a problem faced by a real organization.

GLOSSARY

Artificial Intelligence (AI) The use of data and computers to make decisions that would have in the past required human intelligence.

Advanced analytics Predictive and prescriptive analytics.

Big data Any set of data that is too large or too complex to be handled by standard data-processing techniques and typical desktop software.

Business analytics The scientific process of transforming data into insight for making better decisions.

Data dashboard A collection of tables, charts, and maps to help management monitor selected aspects of the company's performance.

Data mining The use of analytical techniques for better understanding patterns and relationships that exist in large data sets.

Data query A request for information with certain characteristics from a database.

Data scientists Analysts trained in both computer science and statistics who know how to effectively process and analyze massive amounts of data.

Data security Protecting stored data from destructive forces or unauthorized users.

Decision analysis A technique used to develop an optimal strategy when a decision maker is faced with several decision alternatives and an uncertain set of future events.

Descriptive analytics Analytical tools that describe what has happened.

Hadoop An open-source programming environment that supports big data processing through distributed storage and distributed processing on clusters of computers.

Internet of Things (IoT) The technology that allows data collected from sensors in all types of machines to be sent over the Internet to repositories where it can be stored and analyzed.

MapReduce Programming model used within Hadoop that performs the two major steps for which it is named: the map step and the reduce step. The map step divides the data into manageable subsets and distributes it to the computers in the cluster for storing and processing. The reduce step collects answers from the nodes and combines them into an answer to the original problem.

Operational decisions A decision concerned with how the organization is run from day to day.

Optimization models A mathematical model that gives the best decision, subject to the situation's constraints.

Predictive analytics Techniques that use models constructed from past data to predict the future or to ascertain the impact of one variable on another.

Prescriptive analytics Techniques that analyze input data and yield a best course of action.

Rule-based model A prescriptive model that is based on a rule or set of rules.

Simulation The use of probability and statistics to construct a computer model to study the impact of uncertainty on the decision at hand.

Simulation optimization The use of probability and statistics to model uncertainty, combined with optimization techniques, to find good decisions in highly complex and highly uncertain settings.

Strategic decision A decision that involves higher-level issues and that is concerned with the overall direction of the organization, defining the overall goals and aspirations for the organization's future.

Tactical decision A decision concerned with how the organization should achieve the goals and objectives set by its strategy.

Utility theory The study of the total worth or relative desirability of a particular outcome that reflects the decision maker's attitude toward a collection of factors such as profit, loss, and risk.

Chapter 2

Descriptive Statistics

CONTENTS

ANALYTICS IN ACTION

U.S. Census Bureau

The U.S. Census Bureau is part of the Department of Commerce. The U.S. Census Bureau collects data related to the population and economy of the United States using a variety of methods and for many purposes. These data are essential to many government and business decisions.

Probably the best-known data collected by the U.S. Census Bureau is the decennial census, which is an effort to count the total U.S. population. Collecting these data is a huge undertaking involving mailings, door-to-door visits, and other methods. The decennial census collects categorical data such as the sex and race of the respondents, as well as quantitative data such as the number of people living in the household. The data collected in the decennial census are used to determine the number of representatives assigned to each state, the number of Electoral College votes apportioned to each state, and how federal government funding is divided among communities.

The U.S. Census Bureau also administers the Current Population Survey (CPS). The CPS is a cross-sectional monthly survey of a sample of 60,000 households used to estimate employment and unemployment rates in different geographic areas. The CPS has been administered since 1940, so an extensive time series of employment and unemployment data

now exists. These data drive government policies such as job assistance programs. The estimated unemployment rates are watched closely as an overall indicator of the health of the U.S. economy.

The data collected by the U.S. Census Bureau are also very useful to businesses. Retailers use data on population changes in different areas to plan new store openings. Mail-order catalog companies use the demographic data when designing targeted marketing campaigns. In many cases, businesses combine the data collected by the U.S. Census Bureau with their own data on customer behavior to plan strategies and to identify potential customers. The data collected by the U.S. Census Bureau is publicly available and can be downloaded from its web site.

In this chapter, we first explain the need to collect and analyze data and identify some common sources of data. Then we discuss the types of data that you may encounter in practice and present several numerical measures for summarizing data. We cover some common ways of manipulating and summarizing data using spreadsheets. We then develop numerical summary measures for data sets consisting of a single variable. When a data set contains more than one variable, the same numerical measures can be computed separately for each variable. In the two-variable case, we also develop measures of the relationship between the variables.

2.1 Overview of Using Data: Definitions and Goals

Data are the facts and figures collected, analyzed, and summarized for presentation and interpretation. Table 2.1 shows a data set containing information for stocks in the Dow Jones Industrial Index (or simply "the Dow") on June 25, 2019. The Dow is tracked by many financial advisors and investors as an indication of the state of the overall financial markets and the economy in the United States. The share prices for the 30 companies listed in Table 2.1 are the basis for computing the Dow Jones Industrial Average (DJI), which is tracked continuously by virtually every financial publication. The index is named for Charles Dow and Edward Jones who first began calculating the DJI in 1896.

A characteristic or a quantity of interest that can take on different values is known as a **variable**; for the data in Table 2.1, the variables are Symbol, Industry, Share Price, and

TABLE 2.1	Data for Dow Jones Industrial Index Companies			
Company	Symbol	Industry	Share Price ($)	Volume
Apple	AAPL	Technology	195.57	21,060,685
American Express	AXP	Financial	123.16	2,387,770
Boeing	BA	Manufacturing	369.32	3,002,708
Caterpillar	CAT	Manufacturing	133.71	3,747,782
Cisco Systems	CSCO	Technology	56.08	25,533,426
Chevron Corporation	CVX	Chemical, Oil, and Gas	123.64	4,705,879
Disney	DIS	Entertainment	139.94	14,670,995
Dow, Inc.	DOW	Chemical, Oil, and Gas	49.69	4,002,257
Goldman Sachs	GS	Financial	196.06	1,828,219
The Home Depot	HD	Retail	204.74	3,583,573
IBM	IBM	Technology	138.36	2,797,803
Intel	INTC	Technology	46.85	16,658,127
Johnson & Johnson	JNJ	Pharmaceuticals	144.24	7,516,973
JPMorgan Chase	JPM	Banking	107.76	18,654,861
Coca-Cola	KO	Food and Drink	51.76	11,517,843
McDonald's	MCD	Food and Drink	205.71	3,017,625
3M	MMM	Conglomerate	172.03	2,730,927
Merck	MRK	Pharmaceuticals	85.24	8,909,750
Microsoft	MSFT	Technology	133.43	33,328,420
Nike	NKE	Consumer Goods	82.62	7,335,836
Pfizer	PFE	Pharmaceuticals	43.76	26,952,088
Procter & Gamble	PG	Consumer Goods	111.72	6,795,912
Travelers	TRV	Insurance	153.13	1,295,768
UnitedHealth Group	UNH	Healthcare	247.66	3,178,942
United Technologies	UTX	Conglomerate	129.02	2,790,767
Visa	V	Financial	171.28	9,897,832
Verizon	VZ	Telecommunications	58.00	10,554,753
Walgreens Boots Alliance	WBA	Retail	52.95	8,535,442
Wal-Mart	WMT	Retail	110.72	6,104,935
ExxonMobil	XOM	Chemical, Oil, and Gas	76.27	9,722,688

Volume. An **observation** is a set of values corresponding to a set of variables; each row in Table 2.1 corresponds to an observation.

Practically every problem (and opportunity) that an organization (or individual) faces is concerned with the impact of the possible values of relevant variables on the business outcome. Thus, we are concerned with how the value of a variable can vary; **variation** is the difference in a variable measured over observations (time, customers, items, etc.).

The role of descriptive analytics is to collect and analyze data to gain a better understanding of variation and its impact on the business setting. The values of some variables are under direct control of the decision maker (these are often called decision variables). The values of other variables may fluctuate with uncertainty because of factors outside the direct control of the decision maker. In general, a quantity whose values are not known with certainty is called a **random variable, or uncertain variable**. When we collect data, we are gathering past observed values, or realizations of a variable. By collecting these past realizations of one or more variables, our goal is to learn more about the variation of a particular business situation.

Decision variables used in optimization models are covered in Chapters 12, 13, and 14. Random variables are covered in greater detail in Chapters 4 and 11.

2.2 Types of Data

Population and Sample Data

To ensure that the companies in the Dow form a representative sample, companies are periodically added and removed from the Dow. It is possible that the companies in the Dow today have changed from what is shown in Table 2.1.

Data can be categorized in several ways based on how they are collected and the type collected. In many cases, it is not feasible to collect data from the **population** of all elements of interest. In such instances, we collect data from a subset of the population known as a **sample**. For example, with the thousands of publicly traded companies in the United States, tracking and analyzing all of these stocks every day would be too time consuming and expensive. The Dow represents a sample of 30 stocks of large public companies based in the United States, and it is often interpreted to represent the larger population of all publicly traded companies. It is very important to collect sample data that are representative of the population data so that generalizations can be made from them. In most cases (although not true of the Dow), a representative sample can be gathered by **random sampling** from the population data. Dealing with populations and samples can introduce subtle differences in how we calculate and interpret summary statistics. In almost all practical applications of business analytics, we will be dealing with sample data.

Quantitative and Categorical Data

Data are considered **quantitative data** if numeric and arithmetic operations, such as addition, subtraction, multiplication, and division, can be performed on them. For instance, we can sum the values for Volume in the Dow data in Table 2.1 to calculate a total volume of all shares traded by companies included in the Dow. If arithmetic operations cannot be performed on the data, they are considered **categorical data**. We can summarize categorical data by counting the number of observations or computing the proportions of observations in each category. For instance, the data in the Industry column in Table 2.1 are categorical. We can count the number of companies in the Dow that are in the telecommunications industry. Table 2.1 shows three companies in the financial industry: American Express, Goldman Sachs, and Visa. We cannot perform arithmetic operations on the data in the Industry column.

Cross-Sectional and Time Series Data

For statistical analysis, it is important to distinguish between cross-sectional data and time series data. **Cross-sectional data** are collected from several entities at the same, or approximately the same, point in time. The data in Table 2.1 are cross-sectional because they describe the 30 companies that comprise the Dow at the same point in time (June 2019). **Time series data** are collected over several time periods. Graphs of time series data are frequently found in business and economic publications. Such graphs help analysts understand what happened in the past, identify trends over time, and project future levels for the time series. For example, the graph of the time series in Figure 2.1 shows the DJI value from January 2006 to May 2019. The figure illustrates that the DJI limbed to above 14,000 in 2007. However, the financial crisis in 2008 led to a significant decline in the DJI to between 6,000 and 7,000 by 2009. Since 2009, the DJI has been generally increasing and topped 26,000 in 2019.

Sources of Data

Data necessary to analyze a business problem or opportunity can often be obtained with an appropriate study; such statistical studies can be classified as either experimental or observational. In an *experimental study*, a variable of interest is first identified. Then one or more other variables are identified and controlled or manipulated to obtain data about how these variables influence the variable of interest. For example, if a pharmaceutical firm conducts an experiment to learn about how a new drug affects blood pressure, then blood pressure is the variable of interest. The dosage level of the new drug is another variable that is hoped to have a causal effect on blood pressure. To obtain data about the effect of

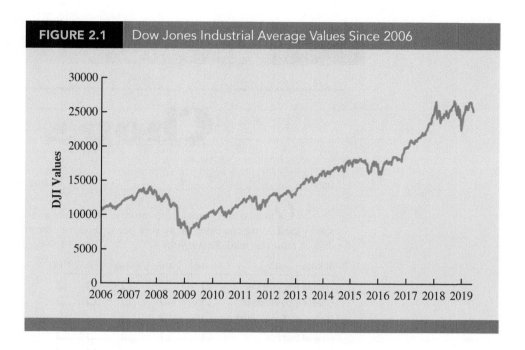

FIGURE 2.1 Dow Jones Industrial Average Values Since 2006

the new drug, researchers select a sample of individuals. The dosage level of the new drug is controlled by giving different dosages to the different groups of individuals. Before and after the study, data on blood pressure are collected for each group. Statistical analysis of these experimental data can help determine how the new drug affects blood pressure.

Nonexperimental, or *observational*, *studies* make no attempt to control the variables of interest. A survey is perhaps the most common type of observational study. For instance, in a personal interview survey, research questions are first identified. Then a questionnaire is designed and administered to a sample of individuals. Some restaurants use observational studies to obtain data about customer opinions with regard to the quality of food, quality of service, atmosphere, and so on. A customer opinion questionnaire used by Chops City Grill in Naples, Florida, is shown in Figure 2.2. Note that the customers who fill out the questionnaire are asked to provide ratings for 12 variables, including overall experience, the greeting by hostess, the table visit by the manager, overall service, and so on. The response categories of excellent, good, average, fair, and poor provide categorical data that enable Chops City Grill management to maintain high standards for the restaurant's food and service.

In some cases, the data needed for a particular application exist from an experimental or observational study that has already been conducted. For example, companies maintain a variety of databases about their employees, customers, and business operations. Data on employee salaries, ages, and years of experience can usually be obtained from internal personnel records. Other internal records contain data on sales, advertising expenditures, distribution costs, inventory levels, and production quantities. Most companies also maintain detailed data about their customers.

In Chapter 15 we discuss methods for determining the value of additional information that can be provided by collecting data.

Anyone who wants to use data and statistical analysis to aid in decision making must be aware of the time and cost required to obtain the data. The use of existing data sources is desirable when data must be obtained in a relatively short period of time. If important data are not readily available from a reliable existing source, the additional time and cost involved in obtaining the data must be taken into account. In all cases, the decision maker should consider the potential contribution of the statistical analysis to the decision-making process. The cost of data acquisition and the subsequent statistical analysis should not exceed the savings generated by using the information to make a better decision.

FIGURE 2.2   Customer Opinion Questionnaire Used by Chops City Grill Restaurant

Chops
CITY GRILL

Date: _____   Server Name: _____

*O*ur customers are our top priority. Please take a moment to fill out our survey card, so we can better serve your needs. You may return this card to the front desk or return by mail. Thank you!

SERVICE SURVEY	Excellent	Good	Average	Fair	Poor
Overall Experience	❑	❑	❑	❑	❑
Greeting by Hostess	❑	❑	❑	❑	❑
Manager (Table Visit)	❑	❑	❑	❑	❑
Overall Service	❑	❑	❑	❑	❑
Professionalism	❑	❑	❑	❑	❑
Menu Knowledge	❑	❑	❑	❑	❑
Friendliness	❑	❑	❑	❑	❑
Wine Selection	❑	❑	❑	❑	❑
Menu Selection	❑	❑	❑	❑	❑
Food Quality	❑	❑	❑	❑	❑
Food Presentation	❑	❑	❑	❑	❑
Value for $ Spent	❑	❑	❑	❑	❑

What comments could you give us to improve our restaurant?

_____

_____

_____

Thank you, we appreciate your comments. —The staff of Chops City Grill.

NOTES + COMMENTS

1. Organizations that specialize in collecting and maintaining data make available substantial amounts of business and economic data. Companies can access these external data sources through leasing arrangements or by purchase. Dun & Bradstreet, Bloomberg, and Dow Jones & Company are three firms that provide extensive business database services to clients. Nielsen and Ipsos are two companies that have built successful businesses collecting and processing data that they sell to advertisers and product manufacturers. Data are also available from a variety of industry associations and special-interest organizations.

2. Government agencies are another important source of existing data. For instance, the web site data.gov was launched by the U.S. government in 2009 to make it easier for the public to access data collected by the U.S. federal government. The data.gov web site includes over 150,000 data sets from a variety of U.S. federal departments and agencies, but many other federal agencies maintain their own web sites and data repositories. Many state and local governments are also now providing data sets online. As examples, the states of California and Texas maintain open data portals at data.ca.gov and data.texas.gov, respectively. New York City's open data web site is opendata.cityofnewyork.us and the city of Cincinnati, Ohio, is at data.cincinnati-oh.gov. In general, the Internet is an important source of data and statistical information. One can obtain access to stock quotes, meal prices at restaurants, salary data, and a wide array of other information simply by performing an Internet search.

2.3 Modifying Data in Excel

Projects often involve so much data that it is difficult to analyze all of the data at once. In this section, we examine methods for summarizing and manipulating data using Excel to make the data more manageable and to develop insights.

Sorting and Filtering Data in Excel

Excel contains many useful features for sorting and filtering data so that one can more easily identify patterns. Table 2.2 contains data on the 20 top-selling passenger-car automobiles in the United States in February 2019. The table shows the model and manufacturer of each automobile as well as the sales for the model in February 2019 and February 2018.

Figure 2.3 shows the data from Table 2.2 entered into an Excel spreadsheet, and the percent change in sales for each model from February 2018 to February 2019 has been calculated. This is done by entering the formula *=(D2-E2)/E2* in cell F2 and then copying the contents of this cell to cells F3 to F20.

Suppose that we want to sort these automobiles by February 2018 sales instead of by February 2019 sales. To do this, we use Excel's Sort function, as shown in the following steps.

Step 1. Select cells A1:F21
Step 2. Click the **Data** tab in the Ribbon
Step 3. Click **Sort** in the **Sort & Filter** group

DATA *file*

Top20Cars2019

TABLE 2.2	20 Top-Selling Automobiles in United States in February 2019			
Rank (by February 2019 Sales)	Manufacturer	Model	Sales (February 2019)	Sales (February 2018)
1	Toyota	Corolla	29,016	25,021
2	Toyota	Camry	24,267	30,865
3	Honda	Civic	22,979	25,816
4	Honda	Accord	20,254	19,753
5	Nissan	Sentra	17,072	17,148
6	Nissan	Altima	16,216	19,703
7	Ford	Fusion	13,163	16,721
8	Chevrolet	Malibu	10,799	11,890
9	Hyundai	Elantra	10,304	15,724
10	Kia	Soul	8,592	6,631
11	Chevrolet	Cruze	7,361	12,875
12	Nissan	Versa	7,410	7,196
13	Volkswagen	Jetta	7,109	4,592
14	Kia	Optima	7,212	6,402
15	Kia	Forte	6,953	7,662
16	Hyundai	Sonata	6,481	6,700
17	Tesla	Model 3	5,750	2,485
18	Dodge	Charger	6,547	7,568
19	Ford	Mustang	5,342	5,800
20	Ford	Fiesta	5,035	3,559

Source: *Manufacturers and Automotive News Data Center.*

FIGURE 2.3   Data for 20 Top-Selling Automobiles Entered into Excel with Percent Change in Sales from 2018

	A	B	C	D	E	F
1	Rank (by February 2019 Sales)	Manufacturer	Model	Sales (February 2019)	Sales (February 2018)	Percent Change in Sales from 2018
2	1	Toyota	Corolla	29016	25021	16.0%
3	2	Toyota	Camry	24267	30865	-21.4%
4	3	Honda	Civic	22979	25816	-11.0%
5	4	Honda	Accord	20254	19753	2.5%
6	5	Nissan	Sentra	17072	17148	-0.4%
7	6	Nissan	Altima	16216	19703	-17.7%
8	7	Ford	Fusion	13163	16721	-21.3%
9	8	Chevrolet Cruze	Malibu	10799	11890	-9.2%
10	9	Hyundai	Elantra	10304	15724	-34.5%
11	10	Kia	Soul	8592	6631	29.6%
12	11	Chevrolet	Cruze	7361	12875	-42.8%
13	12	Nissan	Versa	7410	7196	3.0%
14	13	Volkswagen	Jetta	7109	4592	54.8%
15	14	Kia	Optima	7212	6402	12.7%
16	15	Kia	Forte	6953	7662	-9.3%
17	16	Hyundai	Sonata	6481	6700	-3.3%
18	17	Tesla	Model 3	5750	2485	131.4%
19	18	Dodge	Charger	6547	7568	-13.5%
20	19	Ford	Mustang	5342	5800	-7.9%
21	20	Ford	Fiesta	5035	3559	41.5%

Step 4. Select the check box for **My data has headers**
Step 5. In the first **Sort by** dropdown menu, select **Sales (February 2018)**
Step 6. In the **Order** dropdown menu, select **Largest to Smallest** (see Figure 2.4)
Step 7. Click **OK**

The result of using Excel's Sort function for the February 2018 data is shown in Figure 2.5. Now we can easily see that, although the Toyota Corolla was the best-selling automobile in February 2019, both the Toyota Camry and the Honda Civic outsold the Toyota Corolla in February 2018. Note that while we sorted on Sales (February 2018), which is in column E, the data in all other columns are adjusted accordingly.

Now let's suppose that we are interested only in seeing the sales of models made by Nissan. We can do this using Excel's Filter function:

Step 1. Select cells A1:F21
Step 2. Click the **Data** tab in the Ribbon
Step 3. Click **Filter** in the **Sort & Filter** group
Step 4. Click on the **Filter Arrow** ▼ in column B, next to **Manufacturer**
Step 5. If all choices are checked, you can easily deselect all choices by unchecking (**Select All**). Then select only the check box for **Nissan**.
Step 6. Click **OK**

The result is a display of only the data for models made by Nissan (see Figure 2.6). We now see that of the 20 top-selling models in February 2019, Nissan made three of them: the Altima, the Sentra, and the Versa. We can further filter the data by choosing the down arrows in the other columns. We can make all data visible again by clicking on the down arrow in column B and checking (**Select All**) and clicking **OK**, or by clicking **Filter** in the **Sort & Filter** Group again from the **Data** tab.

FIGURE 2.4 Using Excel's Sort Function to Sort the Top-Selling Automobiles Data

	A	B	C	D	E	F
1	Rank (by February 2019 Sales)	Manufacturer	Model	Sales (February 2019)	Sales (February 2018)	Percent Change in Sales from 2018
2	1	Toyota	Corolla	29016	25021	15.97%
3	2	Toyota	Camry	24267	30865	-21.38%
4	3	Honda	Civic	22979	25816	-10.99%
5	4	Hon				
6	5	Niss				
7	6	Niss				
8	7	Ford				
9	8	Che				
10	9	Hyu				
11	10	Kia				
12	11	Che				
13	12	Niss				
14	13	Volk				
15	14	Kia				
16	15	Kia				
17	16	Hyu	Sonata			
18	17	Tesla	Model 3	5750	2485	131.39%
19	18	Dodge	Charger	6547	7568	-13.49%
20	19	Ford	Mustang	5342	5800	-7.90%
21	20	Ford	Fiesta	5035	3559	41.47%

FIGURE 2.5 Top-Selling Automobiles Data Sorted by Sales in February 2018 Sales

	A	B	C	D	E	F
1	Rank (by February 2019 Sales)	Manufacturer	Model	Sales (February 2019)	Sales (February 2018)	Percent Change in Sales from 2018
2	2	Toyota	Camry	24267	30865	-21.38%
3	3	Honda	Civic	22979	25816	-10.99%
4	1	Toyota	Corolla	29016	25021	15.97%
5	4	Honda	Accord	20254	19753	2.54%
6	6	Nissan	Altima	16216	19703	-17.70%
7	5	Nissan	Sentra	17072	17148	-0.44%
8	7	Ford	Fusion	13163	16721	-21.28%
9	9	Hyundai	Elantra	10304	15724	-34.47%
10	11	Chevrolet	Cruze	7361	12875	-42.83%
11	8	Chevrolet Cruze	Malibu	10799	11890	-9.18%
12	15	Kia	Forte	6953	7662	-9.25%
13	18	Dodge	Charger	6547	7568	-13.49%
14	12	Nissan	Versa	7410	7196	2.97%
15	16	Hyundai	Sonata	6481	6700	-3.27%
16	10	Kia	Soul	8592	6631	29.57%
17	14	Kia	Optima	7212	6402	12.65%
18	19	Ford	Mustang	5342	5800	-7.90%
19	13	Volkswagen	Jetta	7109	4592	54.81%
20	20	Ford	Fiesta	5035	3559	41.47%
21	17	Tesla	Model 3	5750	2485	131.39%

FIGURE 2.6   Top-Selling Automobiles Data Filtered to Show Only Automobiles Manufactured by Nissan

	A	B	C	D	E	F
1	Rank (by February 2019 Sales) ▾	Manufacturer ▾	Model ▾	Sales (February 2019) ▾	Sales (February 2018) ▾	Percent Change in Sales from 2018 ▾
6	5	Nissan	Sentra	17072	17148	-0.44%
7	6	Nissan	Altima	16216	19703	-17.70%
12	12	Nissan	Versa	7410	7196	2.97%

Conditional Formatting of Data in Excel

Conditional formatting in Excel can make it easy to identify data that satisfy certain conditions in a data set. For instance, suppose that we wanted to quickly identify the automobile models in Table 2.2 for which sales had decreased from February 2018 to February 2019. We can quickly highlight these models:

Step 1.   Starting with the original data shown in Figure 2.3, select cells F1:F21
Step 2.   Click the **Home** tab in the Ribbon
Step 3.   Click **Conditional Formatting** in the **Styles** group
Step 4.   Select **Highlight Cells Rules**, and click **Less Than . . .** from the dropdown menu
Step 5.   Enter *0%* in the **Format cells that are LESS THAN:** box
Step 6.   Click **OK**

The results are shown in Figure 2.7. Here we see that the models with decreasing sales (for example, Toyota Camry, Honda Civic, Nissan Sentra, Nissan Altima) are now

FIGURE 2.7   Using Conditional Formatting in Excel to Highlight Automobiles with Declining Sales from February 2018

	A	B	C	D	E	F
1	Rank (by February 2019 Sales)	Manufacturer	Model	Sales (February 2019)	Sales (February 2018)	Percent Change in Sales from 2018
2	1	Toyota	Corolla	29016	25021	15.97%
3	2	Toyota	Camry	24267	30865	-21.38%
4	3	Honda	Civic	22979	25816	-10.99%
5	4	Honda	Accord	20254	19753	2.54%
6	5	Nissan	Sentra	17072	17148	-0.44%
7	6	Nissan	Altima	16216	19703	-17.70%
8	7	Ford	Fusion	13163	16721	-21.28%
9	8	Chevrolet Cruze	Malibu	10799	11890	-9.18%
10	9	Hyundai	Elantra	10304	15724	-34.47%
11	10	Kia	Soul	8592	6631	29.57%
12	12	Nissan	Versa	7410	7196	2.97%
13	11	Chevrolet	Cruze	7361	12875	-42.83%
14	14	Kia	Optima	7212	6402	12.65%
15	13	Volkswagen	Jetta	7109	4592	54.81%
16	15	Kia	Forte	6953	7662	-9.25%
17	18	Dodge	Charger	6547	7568	-13.49%
18	16	Hyundai	Sonata	6481	6700	-3.27%
19	17	Tesla	Model 3	5750	2485	131.39%
20	19	Ford	Mustang	5342	5800	-7.90%
21	20	Ford	Fiesta	5035	3559	41.47%

clearly visible. Note that Excel's Conditional Formatting function offers tremendous flexibility. Instead of highlighting only models with decreasing sales, we could instead choose **Data Bars** from the **Conditional Formatting** dropdown menu in the **Styles** Group of the **Home** tab in the Ribbon. The result of using the **Blue Data Bar Gradient Fill** option is shown in Figure 2.8. Data bars are essentially a bar chart input into the cells that shows the magnitude of the cell values. The widths of the bars in this display are comparable to the values of the variable for which the bars have been drawn; a value of 20 creates a bar twice as wide as that for a value of 10. Negative values are shown to the left side of the axis; positive values are shown to the right. Cells with negative values are shaded in red, and those with positive values are shaded in blue. Again, we can easily see which models had decreasing sales, but Data Bars also provide us with a visual representation of the magnitude of the change in sales. Many other Conditional Formatting options are available in Excel.

The **Quick Analysis** button in Excel appears just outside the bottom-right corner of a group of selected cells whenever you select multiple cells. Clicking the **Quick Analysis** button gives you shortcuts for Conditional Formatting, adding Data Bars, and other operations. Clicking on this button gives you the options shown in Figure 2.9 for **Formatting**. Note that there are also tabs for **Charts**, **Totals**, **Tables**, and **Sparklines**.

Bar charts and other graphical presentations will be covered in detail in Chapter 3. We will see other uses for Conditional Formatting in Excel in Chapter 3.

FIGURE 2.8 Using Conditional Formatting in Excel to Generate Data Bars for the Top-Selling Automobiles Data

	A	B	C	D	E	F
1	Rank (by February 2019 Sales)	Manufacturer	Model	Sales (February 2019)	Sales (February 2018)	Percent Change in Sales from 2018
2	1	Toyota	Corolla	29016	25021	15.97%
3	2	Toyota	Camry	24267	30865	-21.38%
4	3	Honda	Civic	22979	25816	-10.99%
5	4	Honda	Accord	20254	19753	2.54%
6	5	Nissan	Sentra	17072	17148	-0.44%
7	6	Nissan	Altima	16216	19703	-17.70%
8	7	Ford	Fusion	13163	16721	-21.28%
9	8	Chevrolet Cruze	Malibu	10799	11890	-9.18%
10	9	Hyundai	Elantra	10304	15724	-34.47%
11	10	Kia	Soul	8592	6631	29.57%
12	12	Nissan	Versa	7410	7196	2.97%
13	11	Chevrolet	Cruze	7361	12875	-42.83%
14	14	Kia	Optima	7212	6402	12.65%
15	13	Volkswagen	Jetta	7109	4592	54.81%
16	15	Kia	Forte	6953	7662	-9.25%
17	18	Dodge	Charger	6547	7568	-13.49%
18	16	Hyundai	Sonata	6481	6700	-3.27%
19	17	Tesla	Model 3	5750	2485	131.39%
20	19	Ford	Mustang	5342	5800	-7.90%
21	20	Ford	Fiesta	5035	3559	41.47%

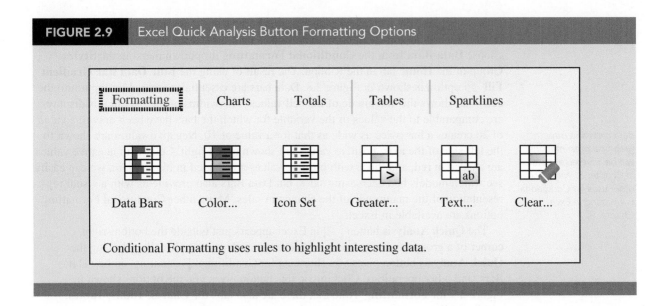

FIGURE 2.9	Excel Quick Analysis Button Formatting Options

Formatting | Charts | Totals | Tables | Sparklines

Data Bars | Color... | Icon Set | Greater... | Text... | Clear...

Conditional Formatting uses rules to highlight interesting data.

2.4 Creating Distributions from Data

Distributions help summarize many characteristics of a data set by describing how often certain values for a variable appear in that data set. Distributions can be created for both categorical and quantitative data, and they assist the analyst in gauging variation.

Frequency Distributions for Categorical Data

Bins for categorical data are also referred to as classes.

It is often useful to create a frequency distribution for a data set. A **frequency distribution** is a summary of data that shows the number (frequency) of observations in each of several nonoverlapping classes, typically referred to as **bins**. Consider the data in Table 2.3, taken

DATA *file*

SoftDrinks

TABLE 2.3	Data from a Sample of 50 Soft Drink Purchases	
Coca-Cola	Sprite	Pepsi
Diet Coke	Coca-Cola	Coca-Cola
Pepsi	Diet Coke	Coca-Cola
Diet Coke	Coca-Cola	Coca-Cola
Coca-Cola	Diet Coke	Pepsi
Coca-Cola	Coca-Cola	Dr. Pepper
Dr. Pepper	Sprite	Coca-Cola
Diet Coke	Pepsi	Diet Coke
Pepsi	Coca-Cola	Pepsi
Pepsi	Coca-Cola	Pepsi
Coca-Cola	Coca-Cola	Pepsi
Dr. Pepper	Pepsi	Pepsi
Sprite	Coca-Cola	Coca-Cola
Coca-Cola	Sprite	Dr. Pepper
Diet Coke	Dr. Pepper	Pepsi
Coca-Cola	Pepsi	Sprite
Coca-Cola	Diet Coke	

from a sample of 50 soft drink purchases. Each purchase is for one of five popular soft drinks, which define the five bins: Coca-Cola, Diet Coke, Dr. Pepper, Pepsi, and Sprite.

To develop a frequency distribution for these data, we count the number of times each soft drink appears in Table 2.3. Coca-Cola appears 19 times, Diet Coke appears 8 times, Dr. Pepper appears 5 times, Pepsi appears 13 times, and Sprite appears 5 times. These counts are summarized in the frequency distribution in Table 2.4. This frequency distribution provides a summary of how the 50 soft drink purchases are distributed across the 5 soft drinks. This summary offers more insight than the original data shown in Table 2.3. The frequency distribution shows that Coca-Cola is the leader, Pepsi is second, Diet Coke is third, and Sprite and Dr. Pepper are tied for fourth. The frequency distribution thus summarizes information about the popularity of the five soft drinks.

See Appendix A for more information on absolute versus relative references in Excel.

We can use Excel to calculate the frequency of categorical observations occurring in a data set using the COUNTIF function. Figure 2.10 shows the sample of 50 soft drink purchases in an Excel spreadsheet. Column D contains the five different soft drink categories as the bins. In cell E2, we enter the formula $=COUNTIF(\$A\$2:\$B\$26, D2)$, where A2:B26 is the range for the sample data, and D2 is the bin (Coca-Cola) that we are trying to match. The COUNTIF function in Excel counts the number of times a certain value appears in the indicated range. In this case we want to count the number of times Coca-Cola appears in the sample data. The result is a value of 19 in cell E2, indicating that Coca-Cola appears 19 times in the sample data. We can copy the formula from cell E2 to cells E3 to E6 to get frequency counts for Diet Coke, Pepsi, Dr. Pepper, and Sprite. By using the absolute reference $\$A\$2:\$B\$26$ in our formula, Excel always searches the same sample data for the values we want when we copy the formula.

Relative Frequency and Percent Frequency Distributions

A frequency distribution shows the number (frequency) of items in each of several nonoverlapping bins. However, we are often interested in the proportion, or percentage, of items in each bin. The *relative frequency* of a bin equals the fraction or proportion of items belonging to a class. For a data set with n observations, the relative frequency of each bin can be determined as follows:

The percent frequency of a bin is the relative frequency multiplied by 100.

$$\text{Relative frequency of a bin} = \frac{\text{Frequency of the bin}}{n}$$

A **relative frequency distribution** is a tabular summary of data showing the relative frequency for each bin. A **percent frequency distribution** summarizes the percent frequency of the data for each bin. Table 2.5 shows a relative frequency distribution and a percent frequency distribution for the soft drink data. Using the data from Table 2.4, we see that the relative frequency for Coca-Cola is 19/50 = 0.38, the relative frequency for Diet Coke is 8/50 = 0.16, and so on. From the percent frequency distribution, we see that 38% of the purchases were Coca-Cola, 16% were Diet Coke, and so on. We can also note that 38% + 26% + 16% = 80% of the purchases were the top three soft drinks.

A percent frequency distribution can be used to provide estimates of the relative likelihoods of different values for a random variable. So, by constructing a percent frequency

TABLE 2.4	Frequency Distribution of Soft Drink Purchases
Soft Drink	**Frequency**
Coca-Cola	19
Diet Coke	8
Dr. Pepper	5
Pepsi	13
Sprite	5
Total	50

FIGURE 2.10		Creating a Frequency Distribution for Soft Drinks Data in Excel			

◢	A	B	C	D	E
1	**Sample Data**			**Bins**	
2	Coca-Cola	Coca-Cola		**Coca-Cola**	19
3	Diet Coke	Sprite		**Diet Coke**	8
4	Pepsi	Pepsi		**Dr. Pepper**	5
5	Diet Coke	Coca-Cola		**Pepsi**	13
6	Coca-Cola	Pepsi		**Sprite**	5
7	Coca-Cola	Sprite			
8	Dr. Pepper	Dr. Pepper			
9	Diet Coke	Pepsi			
10	Pepsi	Diet Coke			
11	Pepsi	Pepsi			
12	Coca-Cola	Coca-Cola			
13	Dr. Pepper	Coca-Cola			
14	Sprite	Diet Coke			
15	Coca-Cola	Pepsi			
16	Diet Coke	Pepsi			
17	Coca-Cola	Pepsi			
18	Coca-Cola	Coca-Cola			
19	Diet Coke	Dr. Pepper			
20	Coca-Cola	Sprite			
21	Coca-Cola	Coca-Cola			
22	Coca-Cola	Coca-Cola			
23	Sprite	Pepsi			
24	Coca-Cola	Dr. Pepper			
25	Coca-Cola	Pepsi			
26	Diet Coke	Pepsi			

TABLE 2.5	Relative Frequency and Percent Frequency Distributions of Soft Drink Purchases	
Soft Drink	**Relative Frequency**	**Percent Frequency (%)**
Coca-Cola	0.38	38
Diet Coke	0.16	16
Dr. Pepper	0.10	10
Pepsi	0.26	26
Sprite	0.10	10
Total	1.00	100

distribution from observations of a random variable, we can estimate the probability distribution that characterizes its variability. For example, the volume of soft drinks sold by a concession stand at an upcoming concert may not be known with certainty. However, if the data used to construct Table 2.5 are representative of the concession stand's customer population, then the concession stand manager can use this information to determine the appropriate volume of each type of soft drink.

Frequency Distributions for Quantitative Data

We can also create frequency distributions for quantitative data, but we must be more careful in defining the nonoverlapping bins to be used in the frequency distribution. For

DATA *file*

AuditTime

TABLE 2.6	Year-End Audit Times (Days)		
12	14	19	18
15	15	18	17
20	27	22	23
22	21	33	28
14	18	16	13

example, consider the quantitative data in Table 2.6. These data show the time in days required to complete year-end audits for a sample of 20 clients of Sanderson and Clifford, a small public accounting firm. The three steps necessary to define the classes for a frequency distribution with quantitative data are as follows:

1. Determine the number of nonoverlapping bins.
2. Determine the width of each bin.
3. Determine the bin limits.

Let us demonstrate these steps by developing a frequency distribution for the audit time data shown in Table 2.6.

Number of Bins   Bins are formed by specifying the ranges used to group the data. As a general guideline, we recommend using from 5 to 20 bins. For a small number of data items, as few as five or six bins may be used to summarize the data. For a larger number of data items, more bins are usually required. The goal is to use enough bins to show the variation in the data, but not so many that some contain only a few data items. Because the number of data items in Table 2.6 is relatively small ($n = 20$), we chose to develop a frequency distribution with five bins.

Width of the Bins   Second, choose a width for the bins. As a general guideline, we recommend that the width be the same for each bin. Thus, the choices of the number of bins and the width of bins are not independent decisions. A larger number of bins means a smaller bin width and vice versa. To determine an approximate bin width, we begin by identifying the largest and smallest data values. Then, with the desired number of bins specified, we can use the following expression to determine the approximate bin width.

APPROXIMATE BIN WIDTH

$$\frac{\text{Largest data value} - \text{smallest data value}}{\text{Number of bins}} \qquad (2.1)$$

The approximate bin width given by equation (2.1) can be rounded to a more convenient value based on the preference of the person developing the frequency distribution. For example, an approximate bin width of 9.28 might be rounded to 10 simply because 10 is a more convenient bin width to use in presenting a frequency distribution.

For the data involving the year-end audit times, the largest data value is 33, and the smallest data value is 12. Because we decided to summarize the data with five classes, using equation (2.1) provides an approximate bin width of $(33 - 12)/5 = 4.2$. We therefore decided to round up and use a bin width of five days in the frequency distribution.

In practice, the number of bins and the appropriate class width are determined by trial and error. Once a possible number of bins are chosen, equation (2.1) is used to find the approximate class width. The process can be repeated for a different number of bins.

Ultimately, the analyst judges the combination of the number of bins and bin width that provides the best frequency distribution for summarizing the data.

For the audit time data in Table 2.6, after deciding to use five bins, each with a width of five days, the next task is to specify the bin limits for each of the classes.

Bin Limits Bin limits must be chosen so that each data item belongs to one and only one class. The lower bin limit identifies the smallest possible data value assigned to the bin. The upper bin limit identifies the largest possible data value assigned to the class. In developing frequency distributions for qualitative data, we did not need to specify bin limits because each data item naturally fell into a separate bin. But with quantitative data, such as the audit times in Table 2.6, bin limits are necessary to determine where each data value belongs.

Although an audit time of 12 days is actually the smallest observation in our data, we have chosen a lower bin limit of 10 simply for convenience. The lowest bin limit should include the smallest observation, and the highest bin limit should include the largest observation.

Using the audit time data in Table 2.6, we selected 10 days as the lower bin limit and 14 days as the upper bin limit for the first class. This bin is denoted 10–14 in Table 2.7. The smallest data value, 12, is included in the 10–14 bin. We then selected 15 days as the lower bin limit and 19 days as the upper bin limit of the next class. We continued defining the lower and upper bin limits to obtain a total of five classes: 10–14, 15–19, 20–24, 25–29, and 30–34. The largest data value, 33, is included in the 30–34 bin. The difference between the upper bin limits of adjacent bins is the bin width. Using the first two upper bin limits of 14 and 19, we see that the bin width is $19 - 14 = 5$.

With the number of bins, bin width, and bin limits determined, a frequency distribution can be obtained by counting the number of data values belonging to each bin. For example, the data in Table 2.6 show that four values—12, 14, 14, and 13—belong to the 10–14 bin. Thus, the frequency for the 10–14 bin is 4. Continuing this counting process for the 15–19, 20–24, 25–29, and 30–34 bins provides the frequency distribution shown in Table 2.7. Using this frequency distribution, we can observe the following:

- The most frequently occurring audit times are in the bin of 15–19 days. Eight of the 20 audit times are in this bin.
- Only one audit required 30 or more days.

Other conclusions are possible, depending on the interests of the person viewing the frequency distribution. The value of a frequency distribution is that it provides insights about the data that are not easily obtained by viewing the data in their original unorganized form. Table 2.7 also shows the relative frequency distribution and percent frequency distribution for the audit time data. Note that 0.40 of the audits, or 40%, required from 15 to 19 days. Only 0.05 of the audits, or 5%, required 30 or more days. Again, additional interpretations and insights can be obtained by using Table 2.7.

We define the relative frequency and percent frequency distributions for quantitative data in the same manner as for qualitative data.

Frequency distributions for quantitative data can also be created using Excel. Figure 2.11 shows the data from Table 2.6 entered into an Excel Worksheet. The sample of 20 audit times is contained in cells A2:A21. The upper limits of the defined bins are in cells C2:C6.

DATA *file*

AuditTime

TABLE 2.7	Frequency, Relative Frequency, and Percent Frequency Distributions for the Audit Time Data		
Audit Times (days)	**Frequency**	**Relative Frequency**	**Percent Frequency**
10–14	4	0.20	20
15–19	8	0.40	40
20–24	5	0.25	25
25–29	2	0.10	10
30–34	1	0.05	5

FIGURE 2.11   Using Excel to Generate a Frequency Distribution for Audit Times Data

We can use the FREQUENCY function in Excel to count the number of observations in each bin.

*Pressing **CTRL+SHIFT+ ENTER** in Excel indicates that the function should return an array of values.*

Step 1. Select cells D2:D6
Step 2. Type the formula =*FREQUENCY(A2:A21, C2:C6)*. The range A2:A21 defines the data set, and the range C2:C6 defines the bins.
Step 3. Press **CTRL+SHIFT+ENTER** after typing the formula in Step 2

Because these were the cells selected in Step 1 above (see Figure 2.11), Excel will then fill in the values for the number of observations in each bin in cells D2 through D6.

Histograms

A common graphical presentation of quantitative data is a **histogram**. This graphical summary can be prepared for data previously summarized in either a frequency, a relative frequency, or a percent frequency distribution. A histogram is constructed by placing the variable of interest on the horizontal axis and the selected frequency measure (absolute frequency, relative frequency, or percent frequency) on the vertical axis. The frequency measure of each class is shown by drawing a rectangle whose base is the class limits on the horizontal axis and whose height is the corresponding frequency measure.

Figure 2.12 is a histogram for the audit time data. Note that the class with the greatest frequency is shown by the rectangle appearing above the class of 15–19 days. The height of the rectangle shows that the frequency of this class is 8. A histogram for the relative or percent frequency distribution of these data would look the same as the histogram in

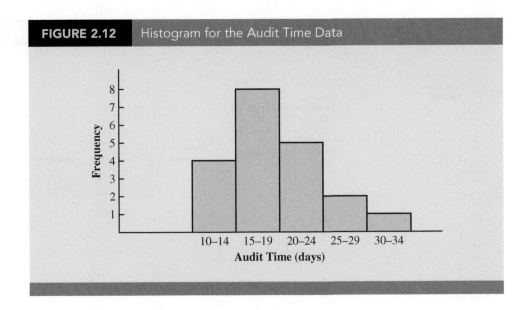

FIGURE 2.12 Histogram for the Audit Time Data

Figure 2.12, with the exception that the vertical axis would be labeled with relative or percent frequency values.

Histograms can be created in Excel using the Data Analysis ToolPak. We will use the sample of 20 year-end audit times and the bins defined in Table 2.7 to create a histogram using the Data Analysis ToolPak. As before, we begin with an Excel Worksheet in which the sample of 20 audit times is contained in cells A2:A21, and the upper limits of the bins defined in Table 2.7 are in cells C2:C6 (see Figure 2.11).

Step 1. Click the **Data** tab in the Ribbon
Step 2. Click **Data Analysis** in the **Analyze** group
Step 3. When the **Data Analysis** dialog box opens, choose **Histogram** from the list of **Analysis Tools**, and click **OK**
   In the **Input Range:** box, enter *A2:A21*
   In the **Bin Range:** box, enter *C2:C6*
   Under **Output Options:**, select **New Worksheet Ply:**
   Select the check box for **Chart Output** (see Figure 2.13)
   Click **OK**

The text "10-14" in cell A2 can be entered in Excel as '10-14. The single quote indicates to Excel that this should be treated as text rather than a numerical or date value.

The histogram created by Excel for these data is shown in Figure 2.14. We have modified the bin ranges in column A by typing the values shown in Figure 2.14 into cells A2:A6 so that the chart created by Excel shows both the lower and upper limits for each bin. We have also removed the gaps between the columns in the histogram in Excel to match the traditional format of histograms. To remove the gaps between the columns in the histogram created by Excel, follow these steps:

Step 1. Right-click on one of the columns in the histogram
   Select **Format Data Series...**
Step 2. When the **Format Data Series** pane opens, click the **Series Options** button, ▮▮▮
   Set the **Gap Width** to 0%

One of the most important uses of a histogram is to provide information about the shape, or form, of a distribution. **Skewness**, or the lack of symmetry, is an important characteristic of the shape of a distribution. Figure 2.15 contains four histograms constructed from relative frequency distributions that exhibit different patterns of skewness. Panel A shows the histogram for a set of data moderately skewed to the left. A histogram is said to

FIGURE 2.13	Creating a Histogram for the Audit Time Data Using Data Analysis ToolPak in Excel

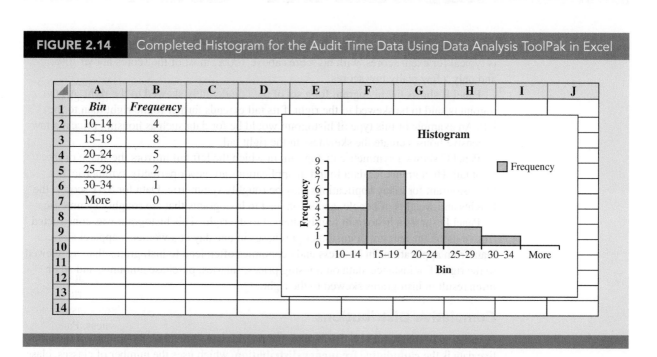

FIGURE 2.14	Completed Histogram for the Audit Time Data Using Data Analysis ToolPak in Excel

	A	B	C	D	E	F	G	H	I	J
1	*Bin*	*Frequency*								
2	10–14	4								
3	15–19	8								
4	20–24	5								
5	25–29	2								
6	30–34	1								
7	More	0								
8										
9										
10										
11										
12										
13										
14										

FIGURE 2.15   Histograms Showing Distributions with Different Levels of Skewness

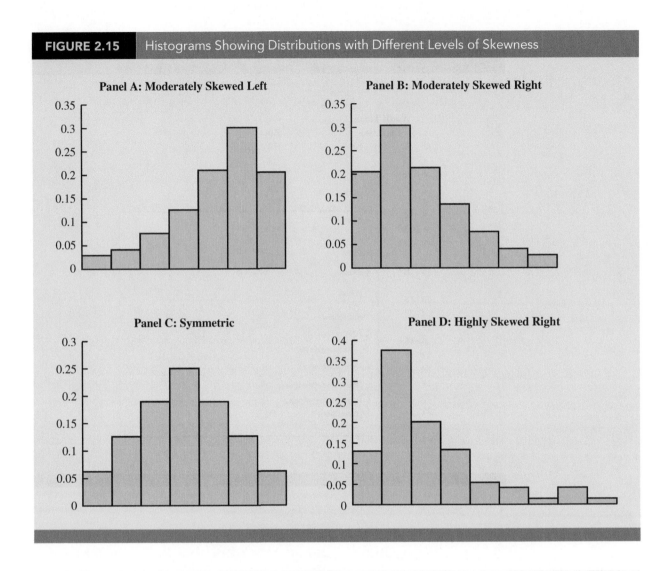

be skewed to the left if its tail extends farther to the left than to the right. This histogram is typical for exam scores, with no scores above 100%, most of the scores above 70%, and only a few really low scores.

Panel B shows the histogram for a set of data moderately skewed to the right. A histogram is said to be skewed to the right if its tail extends farther to the right than to the left. An example of this type of histogram would be for data such as housing prices; a few expensive houses create the skewness in the right tail.

Panel C shows a symmetric histogram, in which the left tail mirrors the shape of the right tail. Histograms for data found in applications are never perfectly symmetric, but the histogram for many applications may be roughly symmetric. Data for SAT scores, the heights and weights of people, and so on lead to histograms that are roughly symmetric.

Panel D shows a histogram highly skewed to the right. This histogram was constructed from data on the amount of customer purchases in one day at a women's apparel store. Data from applications in business and economics often lead to histograms that are skewed to the right. For instance, data on housing prices, salaries, purchase amounts, and so on often result in histograms skewed to the right.

Cumulative Distributions

A variation of the frequency distribution that provides another tabular summary of quantitative data is the **cumulative frequency distribution**, which uses the number of classes, class widths, and class limits developed for the frequency distribution. However, rather than showing the frequency of each class, the cumulative frequency distribution shows the number of data items with values less than or equal to the upper class limit of each class. The first two columns of Table 2.8 provide the cumulative frequency distribution for the audit time data.

To understand how the cumulative frequencies are determined, consider the class with the description "Less than or equal to 24." The cumulative frequency for this class is simply the sum of the frequencies for all classes with data values less than or equal to 24. For the frequency distribution in Table 2.7, the sum of the frequencies for classes 10–14, 15–19, and 20–24 indicates that $4 + 8 + 5 = 17$ data values are less than or equal to 24. Hence, the cumulative frequency for this class is 17. In addition, the cumulative frequency distribution in Table 2.8 shows that four audits were completed in 14 days or less and that 19 audits were completed in 29 days or less.

As a final point, a cumulative relative frequency distribution shows the proportion of data items, and a cumulative percent frequency distribution shows the percentage of data items with values less than or equal to the upper limit of each class. The cumulative relative frequency distribution can be computed either by summing the relative frequencies in the relative frequency distribution or by dividing the cumulative frequencies by the total number of items. Using the latter approach, we found the cumulative relative frequencies in column 3 of Table 2.8 by dividing the cumulative frequencies in column 2 by the total number of items ($n = 20$). The cumulative percent frequencies were again computed by multiplying the relative frequencies by 100. The cumulative relative and percent frequency distributions show that 0.85 of the audits, or 85%, were completed in 24 days or less, 0.95 of the audits, or 95%, were completed in 29 days or less, and so on.

TABLE 2.8	Cumulative Frequency, Cumulative Relative Frequency, and Cumulative Percent Frequency Distributions for the Audit Time Data		
Audit Time (days)	**Cumulative Frequency**	**Cumulative Relative Frequency**	**Cumulative Percent Frequency**
Less than or equal to 14	4	0.20	20
Less than or equal to 19	12	0.60	60
Less than or equal to 24	17	0.85	85
Less than or equal to 29	19	0.95	95
Less than or equal to 34	20	1.00	100

NOTES + COMMENTS

1. If Data Analysis does not appear in your Analyze group then you need to include the Data Analysis ToolPak Add-In. To do so, click on the **File** tab in the Ribbon and choose **Options**. When the **Excel Options** dialog box opens, click **Add-Ins**. At the bottom of the **Excel Options** dialog box, where it says **Manage: Excel Add-ins**, click **Go**…. Select the check box for **Analysis ToolPak**, and click **OK**.

2. Distributions are often used when discussing concepts related to probability and simulation because they are used to describe uncertainty. In Chapter 4 we will discuss probability distributions, and then in Chapter 11 we will revisit distributions when we introduce simulation models.

3. In more recent versions of Excel, histograms can also be created using the new Histogram chart which can be found by clicking on the **Insert** tab in the Ribbon, clicking **Insert Statistic Chart** ▪ ▾ in the **Charts** group and selecting **Histogram**. Excel automatically chooses the number of bins and bin sizes. These values can be changed using **Format Axis**, but the functionality is more limited than the steps we provide in this section to create your own histogram.

2.5 Measures of Location

Mean (Arithmetic Mean)

The most commonly used measure of location is the **mean (arithmetic mean)**, or average value, for a variable. The mean provides a measure of central location for the data. If the data are for a sample (typically the case), the mean is denoted by $\bar{x}$. The sample mean is a point estimate of the (typically unknown) population mean for the variable of interest. If the data for the entire population are available, the population mean is computed in the same manner, but denoted by the Greek letter μ.

In statistical formulas, it is customary to denote the value of variable x for the first observation by x_1, the value of variable x for the second observation by x_2, and so on. In general, the value of variable x for the ith observation is denoted by x_i. For a sample with n observations, the formula for the sample mean is as follows.

If the data set is not a sample, but is the entire population with N observations, the population mean is computed directly by:

$$\mu = \frac{\Sigma x_i}{N}.$$

SAMPLE MEAN

$$\bar{x} = \frac{\Sigma x_i}{n} = \frac{x_1 + x_2 + \cdots + x_n}{n} \qquad (2.2)$$

To illustrate the computation of a sample mean, suppose a sample of home sales is taken for a suburb of Cincinnati, Ohio. Table 2.9 shows the collected data. The mean home selling price for the sample of 12 home sales is

$$
\begin{aligned}
\bar{x} &= \frac{\Sigma x_i}{n} = \frac{x_1 + x_2 + \cdots + x_{12}}{12} \\
&= \frac{138,000 + 254,000 + \cdots + 456,250}{12} \\
&= \frac{2,639,250}{12} = 219,937.50
\end{aligned}
$$

The mean can be found in Excel using the AVERAGE function. Figure 2.16 shows the Home Sales data from Table 2.9 in an Excel spreadsheet. The value for the mean in cell E2 is calculated using the formula $= AVERAGE(B2:B13)$.

DATA *file*

HomeSales

TABLE 2.9	Data on Home Sales in a Cincinnati, Ohio, Suburb
Home Sale	**Selling Price ($)**
1	138,000
2	254,000
3	186,000
4	257,500
5	108,000
6	254,000
7	138,000
8	298,000
9	199,500
10	208,000
11	142,000
12	456,250

FIGURE 2.16	Calculating the Mean, Median, and Modes for the Home Sales Data Using Excel

	A	B	C	D	E
1	**Home Sale**	**Selling Price ($)**			
2	1	138,000		**Mean:**	=AVERAGE(B2:B13)
3	2	254,000		**Median:**	=MEDIAN(B2:B13)
4	3	186,000		**Mode 1:**	=MODE.MULT(B2:B13)
5	4	257,500		**Mode 2:**	=MODE.MULT(B2:B13)
6	5	108,000			
7	6	254,000			
8	7	138,000			
9	8	298,000			
10	9	199,500			
11	10	208,000			
12	11	142,000			
13	12	456,250			

	A	B	C	D	E
1	**Home Sale**	**Selling Price ($)**			
2	1	138,000		**Mean:**	$ 219,937.50
3	2	254,000		**Median:**	$ 203,750.00
4	3	186,000		**Mode 1:**	$ 138,000.00
5	4	257,500		**Mode 2:**	$ 254,000.00
6	5	108,000			
7	6	254,000			
8	7	138,000			
9	8	298,000			
10	9	199,500			
11	10	208,000			
12	11	142,000			
13	12	456,250			

Median

The **median**, another measure of central location, is the value in the middle when the data are arranged in ascending order (smallest to largest value). With an odd number of observations, the median is the middle value. An even number of observations has no single middle value. In this case, we follow convention and define the median as the average of the values for the middle two observations.

Let us apply this definition to compute the median class size for a sample of five college classes. Arranging the data in ascending order provides the following list:

$$32 \quad 42 \quad 46 \quad 46 \quad 54$$

Because $n = 5$ is odd, the median is the middle value. Thus, the median class size is 46 students. Even though this data set contains two observations with values of 46, each observation is treated separately when we arrange the data in ascending order.

Suppose we also compute the median value for the 12 home sales in Table 2.9. We first arrange the data in ascending order.

108,000 138,000 138,000 142,000 186,000 199,500 208,000 254,000 254,000 257,500 298,000 456,250

Middle Two Values

Because $n = 12$ is even, the median is the average of the middle two values: 199,500 and 208,000.

$$\text{Median} = \frac{199{,}500 + 208{,}000}{2} = 203{,}750$$

The median of a data set can be found in Excel using the function MEDIAN. In Figure 2.16, the value for the median in cell E3 is found using the formula =*MEDIAN(B2:B13)*.

Although the mean is the more commonly used measure of central location, in some situations the median is preferred. The mean is influenced by extremely small and large data values. Notice that the median is smaller than the mean in Figure 2.16. This is because the one large value of $456,250 in our data set inflates the mean but does not have the same effect on the median. Notice also that the median would remain unchanged if we replaced the $456,250 with a sales price of $1.5 million. In this case, the median selling price would remain $203,750, but the mean would increase to $306,916.67. If you were looking to buy a home in this suburb, the median gives a better indication of the central selling price of the homes there. We can generalize, saying that whenever a data set contains extreme values or is severely skewed, the median is often the preferred measure of central location.

Mode

A third measure of location, the **mode**, is the value that occurs most frequently in a data set. To illustrate the identification of the mode, consider the sample of five class sizes.

32   42   46   46   54

The only value that occurs more than once is 46. Because this value, occurring with a frequency of 2, has the greatest frequency, it is the mode. To find the mode for a data set with only one most often occurring value in Excel, we use the MODE.SNGL function.

Occasionally the greatest frequency occurs at two or more different values, in which case more than one mode exists. If data contain at least two modes, we say that they are *multimodal*. A special case of multimodal data occurs when the data contain exactly two modes; in such cases we say that the data are *bimodal*. In multimodal cases when there are more than two modes, the mode is almost never reported because listing three or more modes is not particularly helpful in describing a location for the data. Also, if no value in the data occurs more than once, we say the data have no mode.

The Excel MODE.SNGL function will return only a single most-often-occurring value. For multimodal distributions, we must use the MODE.MULT command in Excel to return more than one mode. For example, two selling prices occur twice in Table 2.9: $138,000 and $254,000. Hence, these data are bimodal. To find both of the modes in Excel, we take these steps:

*We must press **CTRL+SHIFT+ENTER** because the MODE.MULT function returns an array of values.*

Step 1. Select cells E4 and E5
Step 2. Type the formula =*MODE.MULT(B2:B13)*
Step 3. Press **CTRL+SHIFT+ENTER** after typing the formula in Step 2.

Excel enters the values for both modes of this data set in cells E4 and E5: $138,000 and $254,000.

Geometric Mean

The **geometric mean** is a measure of location that is calculated by finding the nth root of the product of n values. The general formula for the sample geometric mean, denoted $\bar{x}_g$, follows.

The geometric mean for a population is computed similarly but is defined as μ_g to denote that it is computed using the entire population.

SAMPLE GEOMETRIC MEAN

$$\bar{x}_g = \sqrt[n]{(x_1)(x_2)\cdots(x_n)} = [(x_1)(x_2)\cdots(x_n)]^{1/n} \tag{2.3}$$

The geometric mean is often used in analyzing growth rates in financial data. In these types of situations, the arithmetic mean or average value will provide misleading results.

To illustrate the use of the geometric mean, consider Table 2.10, which shows the percentage annual returns, or growth rates, for a mutual fund over the past 10 years. Suppose we want to compute how much $100 invested in the fund at the beginning of year 1 would be worth at the end of year 10. We start by computing the balance in the fund at the end of year 1. Because the percentage annual return for year 1 was -22.1%, the balance in the fund at the end of year 1 would be

$$\$100 - 0.221(\$100) = \$100(1 - 0.221) = \$100(0.779) = \$77.90$$

The growth factor for each year is 1 plus 0.01 times the percentage return. A growth factor less than 1 indicates negative growth, whereas a growth factor greater than 1 indicates positive growth. The growth factor cannot be less than zero.

We refer to 0.779 as the **growth factor** for year 1 in Table 2.10. We can compute the balance at the end of year 1 by multiplying the value invested in the fund at the beginning of year 1 by the growth factor for year 1: $\$100(0.779) = \$77.90$.

The balance in the fund at the end of year 1, $77.90, now becomes the beginning balance in year 2. So, with a percentage annual return for year 2 of 28.7%, the balance at the end of year 2 would be

$$\$77.90 + 0.287(\$77.90) = \$77.90(1 + 0.287) = \$77.90(1.287) = \$100.26$$

Note that 1.287 is the growth factor for year 2. By substituting $100(0.779) for $77.90, we see that the balance in the fund at the end of year 2 is

$$\$100(0.779)(1.287) = \$100.26$$

In other words, the balance at the end of year 2 is just the initial investment at the beginning of year 1 times the product of the first two growth factors. This result can be generalized to show that the balance at the end of year 10 is the initial investment times the product of all 10 growth factors.

$$\$100[(0.779)(1.287)(1.109)(1.049)(1.158)(1.055)(0.630)(1.265)(1.151)(1.021)]$$
$$= \$100(1.335) = \$133.45$$

So a $100 investment in the fund at the beginning of year 1 would be worth $133.45 at the end of year 10. Note that the product of the 10 growth factors is 1.335. Thus, we can compute the balance at the end of year 10 for any amount of money invested at the beginning of year 1 by multiplying the value of the initial investment by 1.335. For instance, an initial investment of $2,500 at the beginning of year 1 would be worth $2,500(1.335), or approximately $3,337.50, at the end of year 10.

DATA *file*

MutualFundReturns

TABLE 2.10	Percentage Annual Returns and Growth Factors for the Mutual Fund Data	
Year	**Return (%)**	**Growth Factor**
1	−22.1	0.779
2	28.7	1.287
3	10.9	1.109
4	4.9	1.049
5	15.8	1.158
6	5.5	1.055
7	−37.0	0.630
8	26.5	1.265
9	15.1	1.151
10	2.1	1.021

What was the mean percentage annual return or mean rate of growth for this investment over the 10-year period? The geometric mean of the 10 growth factors can be used to answer this question. Because the product of the 10 growth factors is 1.335, the geometric mean is the 10th root of 1.335, or

$$\bar{x}_g = \sqrt[10]{1.335} = 1.029$$

The geometric mean tells us that annual returns grew at an average annual rate of $(1.029 - 1)$ 100, or 2.9%. In other words, with an average annual growth rate of 2.9%, a \$100 investment in the fund at the beginning of year 1 would grow to $\$100(1.029)^{10} = \$133.09$ at the end of 10 years. We can use Excel to calculate the geometric mean for the data in Table 2.10 by using the function GEOMEAN. In Figure 2.17, the value for the geometric mean in cell C13 is found using the formula $=GEOMEAN(C2:C11)$.

It is important to understand that the arithmetic mean of the percentage annual returns does not provide the mean annual growth rate for this investment. The sum of the 10 percentage annual returns in Table 2.10 is 50.4. Thus, the arithmetic mean of the 10 percentage returns is 50.4/10 = 5.04%. A salesperson might try to convince you to invest in this fund by stating that the mean annual percentage return was 5.04%. Such a statement is not only misleading, it is inaccurate. A mean annual percentage return of 5.04% corresponds to an average growth factor of 1.0504. So, if the average growth factor were really 1.0504, \$100 invested in the fund at the beginning of year 1 would have grown to $\$100(1.0504)^{10} = \$163.51$ at the end of 10 years. But, using the 10 annual percentage returns in Table 2.10, we showed that an initial \$100 investment is worth \$133.09 at the end of 10 years. The salesperson's claim that the mean annual percentage return is 5.04% grossly overstates the true growth for this mutual fund. The problem is that the arithmetic mean is appropriate only for an additive process. For a multiplicative process, such as applications involving growth rates, the geometric mean is the appropriate measure of location.

While the application of the geometric mean to problems in finance, investments, and banking is particularly common, the geometric mean should be applied any time you want to determine the mean rate of change over several successive periods. Other common applications include changes in the populations of species, crop yields, pollution levels, and birth and death rates. The geometric mean can also be applied to changes that occur over any number

FIGURE 2.17   Calculating the Geometric Mean for the Mutual Fund Data Using Excel

	A	B	C	D
1	Year	Return (%)	Growth Factor	
2	1	−22.1	0.779	
3	2	28.7	1.287	
4	3	10.9	1.109	
5	4	4.9	1.049	
6	5	15.8	1.158	
7	6	5.5	1.055	
8	7	−37.0	0.630	
9	8	26.5	1.265	
10	9	15.1	1.151	
11	10	2.1	1.021	
12				
13		**Geometric Mean:**	1.029	
14				

of successive periods of any length. In addition to annual changes, the geometric mean is often applied to find the mean rate of change over quarters, months, weeks, and even days.

2.6 Measures of Variability

In addition to measures of location, it is often desirable to consider measures of variability, or dispersion. For example, suppose that you are considering two financial funds. Both funds require a $1,000 annual investment. Table 2.11 shows the annual payouts for Fund A and Fund B for $1,000 investments over the past 20 years. Fund A has paid out exactly $1,100 each year for an initial $1,000 investment. Fund B has had many different payouts, but the mean payout over the previous 20 years is also $1,100. But would you consider the payouts of Fund A and Fund B to be equivalent? Clearly, the answer is no. The difference between the two funds is due to variability.

Figure 2.18 shows a histogram for the payouts received from Funds A and B. Although the mean payout is the same for the two funds, their histograms differ in that the payouts associated with Fund B have greater variability. Sometimes the payouts are considerably larger than the mean, and sometimes they are considerably smaller. In this section, we present several different ways to measure variability.

Range

The simplest measure of variability is the **range**. The range can be found by subtracting the smallest value from the largest value in a data set. Let us return to the home sales data set to demonstrate the calculation of range. Refer to the data from home sales prices in Table 2.9. The largest home sales price is $456,250, and the smallest is $108,000. The range is $456,250 − $108,000 = $348,250.

TABLE 2.11	Annual Payouts for Two Different Investment Funds	
Year	**Fund A ($)**	**Fund B ($)**
1	1,100	700
2	1,100	2,500
3	1,100	1,200
4	1,100	1,550
5	1,100	1,300
6	1,100	800
7	1,100	300
8	1,100	1,600
9	1,100	1,500
10	1,100	350
11	1,100	460
12	1,100	890
13	1,100	1,050
14	1,100	800
15	1,100	1,150
16	1,100	1,200
17	1,100	1,800
18	1,100	100
19	1,100	1,750
20	1,100	1,000
Mean	1,100	1,100

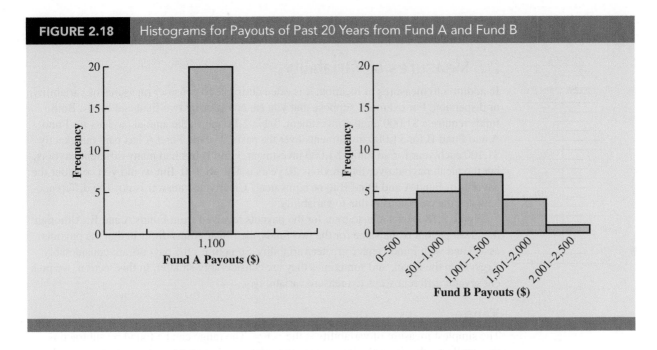

FIGURE 2.18 Histograms for Payouts of Past 20 Years from Fund A and Fund B

Although the range is the easiest of the measures of variability to compute, it is seldom used as the only measure. The reason is that the range is based on only two of the observations and thus is highly influenced by extreme values. If, for example, we replace the selling price of $456,250 with $1.5 million, the range would be $1,500,000 − $108,000 = $1,392,000. This large value for the range would not be especially descriptive of the variability in the data because 11 of the 12 home selling prices are between $108,000 and $298,000.

The range can be calculated in Excel using the MAX and MIN functions. The range value in cell E7 of Figure 2.19 calculates the range using the formula =*MAX(B2:B13) − MIN(B2:B13)*. This subtracts the smallest value in the range B2:B13 from the largest value in the range B2:B13.

Variance

The **variance** is a measure of variability that utilizes all the data. The variance is based on the *deviation about the mean*, which is the difference between the value of each observation (x_i) and the mean. For a sample, a deviation of an observation about the mean is written ($x_i - \bar{x}$). In the computation of the variance, the deviations about the mean are squared.

In most statistical applications, the data being analyzed are for a sample. When we compute a sample variance, we are often interested in using it to estimate the population variance, σ^2. Although a detailed explanation is beyond the scope of this text, for a random sample, it can be shown that, if the sum of the squared deviations about the sample mean is divided by $n - 1$, and not n, the resulting sample variance provides an unbiased estimate of the population variance.[1]

For this reason, the sample variance, denoted by s^2, is defined as follows:

If the data are for a population, the population variance, σ^2, can be computed directly (rather than estimated by the sample variance). For a population of N observations and with μ denoting the population mean, population variance is computed by $\sigma^2 = \frac{\Sigma(x_i - \mu)^2}{N}$.

SAMPLE VARIANCE

$$s^2 = \frac{\Sigma(x_i - \bar{x})^2}{n - 1} \tag{2.4}$$

[1]Unbiased means that if we take a large number of independent random samples of the same size from the population and calculate the sample variance for each sample, the average of these sample variances will tend to be equal to the population variance.

FIGURE 2.19   Calculating Variability Measures for the Home Sales Data in Excel

	A	B	C	D	E
1	Home Sale	Selling Price ($)			
2	1	138000		Mean:	=AVERAGE(B2:B13)
3	2	254000		Median:	=MEDIAN(B2:B13)
4	3	186000		Mode 1:	=MODE.MULT(B2:B13)
5	4	257500		Mode 2:	=MODE.MULT(B2:B13)
6	5	108000			
7	6	254000		Range:	=MAX(B2:B13)-MIN(B2:B13)
8	7	138000		Variance:	=VAR.S(B2:B13)
9	8	298000		Standard Deviation:	=STDEV.S(B2:B13)
10	9	199500			
11	10	208000		Coefficient of Variation:	=E9/E2
12	11	142000			
13	12	456250		85th Percentile:	=PERCENTILE.EXC(B2:B13,0.85)
14					
15				1st Quartile:	=QUARTILE.EXC(B2:B13,1)
16				2nd Quartile:	=QUARTILE.EXC(B2:B13,2)
17				3rd Quartile:	=QUARTILE.EXC(B2:B13,3)
18					
19				IQR:	=E17-E15

	A	B	C	D	E
1	Home Sale	Selling Price ($)			
2	1	138000		Mean:	$ 219,937.50
3	2	254000		Median:	$ 203,750.00
4	3	186000		Mode 1:	$ 138,000.00
5	4	257500		Mode 2:	$ 254,000.00
6	5	108000			
7	6	254000		Range:	$ 348,250.00
8	7	138000		Variance:	9037501420
9	8	298000		Standard Deviation:	$ 95,065.77
10	9	199500			
11	10	208000		Coefficient of Variation:	43.22%
12	11	142000			
13	12	456250		85th Percentile:	$ 305,912.50
14					
15				1st Quartile:	$ 139,000.00
16				2nd Quartile:	$ 203,750.00
17				3rd Quartile:	$ 256,625.00
18					
19				IQR:	$ 117,625.00

To illustrate the computation of the sample variance, we will use the data on class size from page 41 for the sample of five college classes. A summary of the data, including the computation of the deviations about the mean and the squared deviations about the mean, is shown in Table 2.12. The sum of squared deviations about the mean is $\Sigma(x_i - \bar{x})^2 = 256$. Hence, with $n - 1 = 4$, the sample variance is

$$s^2 = \frac{\Sigma(x_i - \bar{x})^2}{n - 1} = \frac{256}{4} = 64$$

Note that the units of variance are squared. For instance, the sample variance for our calculation is $s^2 = 64\,(\text{students})^2$. In Excel, you can find the variance for sample data using the VAR.S function. Figure 2.19 shows the data for home sales examined in the previous section. The variance in cell E8 is calculated using the formula $=VAR.S(B2:B13)$. Excel calculates the variance of the sample of 12 home sales to be 9,037,501,420.

Standard Deviation

The **standard deviation** is defined to be the positive square root of the variance. We use s to denote the sample standard deviation and σ to denote the population standard deviation. The sample standard deviation, s, is a point estimate of the population standard deviation, σ, and is derived from the sample variance in the following way:

SAMPLE STANDARD DEVIATION

$$s = \sqrt{s^2} \qquad\qquad (2.5)$$

TABLE 2.12	Computation of Deviations and Squared Deviations About the Mean for the Class Size Data		
Number of Students in Class (x_i)	Mean Class Size ($\bar{x}$)	Deviation About the Mean ($x_i - \bar{x}$)	Squared Deviation About the Mean ($x_i - \bar{x}$)^2
46	44	2	4
54	44	10	100
42	44	−2	4
46	44	2	4
32	44	−12	144
		$\Sigma(x_i - \bar{x}) = 0$	$\Sigma(x_i - \bar{x})^2 = 256$

If the data are for a population, the population standard deviation σ is obtained by taking the positive square root of the population variance: $\sigma = \sqrt{\sigma^2}$. To calculate the population variance and population standard deviation in Excel, we use the functions =VAR.P and =STDEV.P.

The sample variance for the sample of class sizes in five college classes is $s^2 = 64$. Thus, the sample standard deviation is $s = \sqrt{64} = 8$.

Recall that the units associated with the variance are squared and that it is difficult to interpret the meaning of squared units. Because the standard deviation is the square root of the variance, the units of the variance, (students)^2 in our example, are converted to students in the standard deviation. In other words, the standard deviation is measured in the same units as the original data. For this reason, the standard deviation is more easily compared to the mean and other statistics that are measured in the same units as the original data.

Figure 2.19 shows the Excel calculation for the sample standard deviation of the home sales data, which can be calculated using Excel's STDEV.S function. The sample standard deviation in cell E9 is calculated using the formula =STDEV.S(B2:B13). Excel calculates the sample standard deviation for the home sales to be $95,065.77.

Coefficient of Variation

In some situations we may be interested in a descriptive statistic that indicates how large the standard deviation is relative to the mean. This measure is called the **coefficient of variation** and is usually expressed as a percentage.

COEFFICIENT OF VARIATION

$$\left(\frac{\text{Standard deviation}}{\text{Mean}} \times 100 \right)\% \tag{2.6}$$

For the class size data on page 41, we found a sample mean of 44 and a sample standard deviation of 8. The coefficient of variation is $(8/44 \times 100) = 18.2\%$. In words, the coefficient of variation tells us that the sample standard deviation is 18.2% of the value of the sample mean. The coefficient of variation for the home sales data is shown in Figure 2.19. It is calculated in cell E11 using the formula =E9/E2, which divides the standard deviation by the mean. The coefficient of variation for the home sales data is 43.22%. In general, the coefficient of variation is a useful statistic for comparing the relative variability of different variables, each with different standard deviations and different means.

2.7 Analyzing Distributions

In Section 2.4 we demonstrated how to create frequency, relative, and cumulative distributions for data sets. Distributions are very useful for interpreting and analyzing data. A distribution describes the overall variability of the observed values of a variable. In this section we introduce additional ways of analyzing distributions.

Percentiles

A **percentile** is the value of a variable at which a specified (approximate) percentage of observations are below that value. The pth percentile tells us the point in the data where approximately $p\%$ of the observations have values less than the pth percentile; hence, approximately $(100 - p)\%$ of the observations have values greater than the pth percentile.

Colleges and universities frequently report admission test scores in terms of percentiles. For instance, suppose an applicant obtains a raw score of 54 on the verbal portion of an admission test. How this student performed in relation to other students taking the same test may not be readily apparent. However, if the raw score of 54 corresponds to the 70th percentile, we know that approximately 70% of the students scored lower than this individual, and approximately 30% of the students scored higher.

Several procedures can be used to compute the location of the pth percentile using sample data. All provide similar values, especially for large data sets. The procedure we show here is the procedure used by Excel's PERCENTILE.EXC function as well as several other statistical software packages.

To calculate the pth percentile for a data set containing n observations we must first arrange the data in ascending order (smallest value to largest value). The smallest value is in position 1, the next smallest value is in position 2, and so on. The location of the pth percentile, denoted by L_p, is computed using the following equation:

LOCATION OF THE pth PERCENTILE

$$L_p = \frac{p}{100}(n + 1) \tag{2.7}$$

Once we find the position of the value of the pth percentile, we have the information we need to calculate the pth percentile.

To illustrate the computation of the pth percentile, let us compute the 85th percentile for the home sales data in Table 2.9. We begin by arranging the sample of 12 starting salaries in ascending order.

108,000	138,000	138,000	142,000	186,000	199,500	208,000	254,000	254,000	257,500	298,000	456,250
Position 1	2	3	4	5	6	7	8	9	10	11	12

The position of each observation in the sorted data is shown directly below its value. For instance, the smallest value (108,000) is in position 1, the next smallest value (138,000) is in position 2, and so on. Using equation (2.7) with $p = 85$ and $n = 12$, the location of the 85th percentile is

$$L_{85} = \frac{p}{100}(n + 1) = \left(\frac{85}{100}\right)(12 + 1) = 11.05$$

The interpretation of $L_{85} = 11.05$ is that the 85th percentile is 5% of the way between the value in position 11 and the value in position 12. In other words, the 85th percentile is the value in position 11 (298,000) plus 0.05 times the difference between the value in position 12 (456,250) and the value in position 11 (298,000). Thus, the 85th percentile is

$$85\text{th percentile} = 298{,}000 + 0.05(456{,}250 - 298{,}000) = 298{,}000 + 0.05(158{,}250)$$
$$= 305{,}912.50$$

Therefore, \$305,912.50 represents the 85th percentile of the home sales data.

The pth percentile can also be calculated in Excel using the function PERCENTILE.EXC. Figure 2.19 shows the Excel calculation for the 85th percentile of the home sales data. The value in cell E13 is calculated using the formula =*PERCENTILE.EXC(B2:B13,0.85)*; B2:B13 defines the data set for which we are calculating a percentile, and 0.85 defines the percentile of interest.

Quartiles

It is often desirable to divide data into four parts, with each part containing approximately one-fourth, or 25 percent, of the observations. These division points are referred to as the **quartiles** and are defined as follows:

Q_1 = first quartile, or 25th percentile
Q_2 = second quartile, or 50th percentile (also the median)
Q_3 = third quartile, or 75th percentile

To demonstrate quartiles, the home sales data are again arranged in ascending order.

108,000 138,000 138,000 142,000 186,000 199,500 208,000 254,000 254,000 257,500 298,000 456,250

Position 1   2   3   4   5   6   7   8   9   10   11   12

We already identified Q2, the second quartile (median), as 203,750. To find Q1 and Q3 we must find the 25th and 75th percentiles.

For Q1,

$$L_{25} = \frac{p}{100}(n + 1) = \left(\frac{25}{100}\right)(12 + 1) = 3.25$$

$$25\text{th percentile} = 138,000 + 0.25(142,000 - 138,000) = 138,000 + 0.25(4,000)$$
$$= 139,000$$

For Q3,

$$L_{75} = \frac{p}{100}(n + 1) = \left(\frac{75}{100}\right)(12 + 1) = 9.75$$

$$75\text{th percentile} = 254,000 + 0.75(257,500 - 254,000) = 254,000 + 0.75(3,500)$$
$$= 256,625$$

Therefore, the 25th percentile for the home sales data is $139,000 and the 75th percentile is $256,625.

The quartiles divide the home sales data into four parts, with each part containing 25% of the observations.

108,000	142,000	208,000	257,500
138,000	186,000	254,000	298,000
138,000	199,500	254,000	456,250

$Q_1 = 139,000$ $Q_2 = 203,750$ $Q_3 = 256,625$

The difference between the third and first quartiles is often referred to as the **interquartile range**, or IQR. For the home sales data, IQR = $Q_3 - Q_1$ = 256,625 − 139,000 = 117,625. Because it excludes the smallest and largest 25% of values in the data, the IQR is a useful measure of variation for data that have extreme values or are highly skewed.

A quartile can be computed in Excel using the function QUARTILE.EXC. Figure 2.19 shows the calculations for first, second, and third quartiles for the home sales data. The formula used in cell E15 is =*QUARTILE.EXC(B2:B13,1)*. The range B2:B13 defines the data set, and 1 indicates that we want to compute the first quartile. Cells E16 and E17 use similar formulas to compute the second and third quartiles.

z-Scores

A **z-score** allows us to measure the relative location of a value in the data set. More specifically, a z-score helps us determine how far a particular value is from the mean relative to the data set's standard deviation. Suppose we have a sample of n observations, with the values denoted by $x_1, x_2, \ldots, x_n$. In addition, assume that the sample mean, $\bar{x}$, and the sample standard deviation, s, are already computed. Associated with each value, x_i, is another value called its z-score. Equation (2.8) shows how the z-score is computed for each x_i:

z-SCORE

$$z_i = \frac{x_i - \bar{x}}{s} \tag{2.8}$$

where

z_i = the z-score for x_i
$\bar{x}$ = the sample mean
s = the sample standard deviation

The z-score is often called the *standardized value*. The z-score, z_i, can be interpreted as the number of standard deviations, x_i, from the mean. For example, $z_1 = 1.2$ indicates that x_1 is 1.2 standard deviations greater than the sample mean. Similarly, $z_2 = -0.5$ indicates that x_2 is 0.5, or 1/2, standard deviation less than the sample mean. A z-score greater than zero occurs for observations with a value greater than the mean, and a z-score less than zero occurs for observations with a value less than the mean. A z-score of zero indicates that the value of the observation is equal to the mean.

The z-scores for the class size data are computed in Table 2.13. Recall the previously computed sample mean, $\bar{x} = 44$, and sample standard deviation, $s = 8$. The z-score of -1.50 for the fifth observation shows that it is farthest from the mean; it is 1.50 standard deviations below the mean.

The z-score can be calculated in Excel using the function STANDARDIZE. Figure 2.20 demonstrates the use of the STANDARDIZE function to compute z-scores for the home sales data. To calculate the z-scores, we must provide the mean and standard deviation for the data set in the arguments of the STANDARDIZE function. For instance, the z-score in cell C2 is calculated with the formula =*STANDARDIZE(B2, $B$15, $B$16)*, where cell B15 contains the mean of the home sales data and cell B16 contains the standard deviation of the home sales data. We can then copy and paste this formula into cells C3:C13.

Empirical Rule

When the distribution of data exhibits a symmetric bell-shaped distribution, as shown in Figure 2.21, the **empirical rule** can be used to determine the percentage of data values that are within a specified number of standard deviations of the mean. Many, but not all, distributions of data found in practice exhibit a symmetric bell-shaped distribution.

TABLE 2.13	z-Scores for the Class Size Data	
No. of Students in Class (x_i)	**Deviation About the Mean ($x_i - \bar{x}$)**	**z-Score $\left(\dfrac{x_i - \bar{x}}{s} \right)$**
46	2	2/8 = 0.25
54	10	10/8 = 1.25
42	−2	−2/8 = −0.25
46	2	2/8 = 0.25
32	−12	−12/8 = −1.50

FIGURE 2.20	Calculating z-Scores for the Home Sales Data in Excel

◢	A	B	C
1	**Home Sale**	**Selling Price ($)**	**z-Score**
2	1	138000	=STANDARDIZE(B2,$B$15,$B$16)
3	2	254000	=STANDARDIZE(B3,$B$15,$B$16)
4	3	186000	=STANDARDIZE(B4,$B$15,$B$16)
5	4	257500	=STANDARDIZE(B5,$B$15,$B$16)
6	5	108000	=STANDARDIZE(B6,$B$15,$B$16)
7	6	254000	=STANDARDIZE(B7,$B$15,$B$16)
8	7	138000	=STANDARDIZE(B8,$B$15,$B$16)
9	8	298000	=STANDARDIZE(B9,$B$15,$B$16)
10	9	199500	=STANDARDIZE(B10,$B$15,$B$16)
11	10	208000	=STANDARDIZE(B11,$B$15,$B$16)
12	11	142000	=STANDARDIZE(B12,$B$15,$B$16)
13	12	456250	=STANDARDIZE(B13,$B$15,$B$16)
14			
15	**Mean:**	=AVERAGE(B2:B13)	
16	**Standard Deviation:**	=STDEV.S(B2:B13)	

◢	A	B	C
1	**Home Sale**	**Selling Price ($)**	**z-Score**
2	1	138,000	−0.862
3	2	254,000	0.358
4	3	186,000	−0.357
5	4	257,500	0.395
6	5	108,000	−1.177
7	6	254,000	0.358
8	7	138,000	−0.862
9	8	298,000	0.821
10	9	199,500	−0.215
11	10	208,000	−0.126
12	11	142,000	−0.820
13	12	456,250	2.486
14			
15	**Mean:**	$ 219,937.50	
16	**Standard Deviation:**	$ 95,065.77	

FIGURE 2.21	A Symmetric Bell-Shaped Distribution

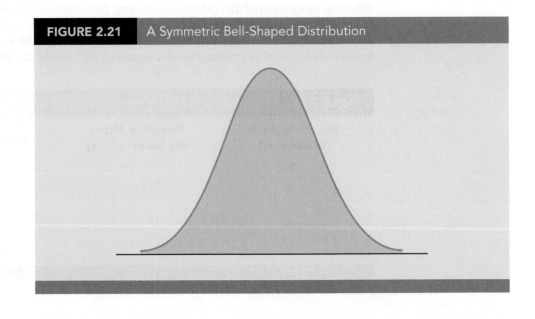

> **EMPIRICAL RULE**
>
> For data having a bell-shaped distribution:
>
> - Approximately 68% of the data values will be within 1 standard deviation of the mean.
> - Approximately 95% of the data values will be within 2 standard deviations of the mean.
> - Almost all of the data values will be within 3 standard deviations of the mean.

The height of adult males in the United States has a bell-shaped distribution similar to that shown in Figure 2.21, with a mean of approximately 69.5 inches and standard deviation of approximately 3 inches. Using the empirical rule, we can draw the following conclusions.

- Approximately 68% of adult males in the United States have heights between $69.5 - 3 = 66.5$ and $69.5 + 3 = 72.5$ inches.
- Approximately 95% of adult males in the United States have heights between 63.5 and 75.5 inches.
- Almost all adult males in the United States have heights between 60.5 and 78.5 inches.

Identifying Outliers

Sometimes a data set will have one or more observations with unusually large or unusually small values. These extreme values are called **outliers**. Experienced statisticians take steps to identify outliers and then review each one carefully. An outlier may be a data value that has been incorrectly recorded; if so, it can be corrected before the data are analyzed further. An outlier may also be from an observation that doesn't belong to the population we are studying and was incorrectly included in the data set; if so, it can be removed. Finally, an outlier may be an unusual data value that has been recorded correctly and is a member of the population we are studying. In such cases, the observation should remain.

Standardized values (z-scores) can be used to identify outliers. Recall that the empirical rule allows us to conclude that for data with a bell-shaped distribution, almost all the data values will be within 3 standard deviations of the mean. Hence, in using z-scores to identify outliers, we recommend treating any data value with a z-score less than -3 or greater than $+3$ as an outlier. Such data values can then be reviewed to determine their accuracy and whether they belong in the data set.

Boxplots

A **boxplot** is a graphical summary of the distribution of data. A boxplot is developed from the quartiles for a data set. Figure 2.22 is a boxplot for the home sales data. Here are the steps used to construct the boxplot:

Boxplots are also known as box-and-whisker plots.

1. A box is drawn with the ends of the box located at the first and third quartiles. For the home sales data, $Q1 = 139{,}000$ and $Q3 = 256{,}625$. This box contains the middle 50% of the data.
2. A vertical line is drawn in the box at the location of the median (203,750 for the home sales data).
3. By using the interquartile range, IQR $= Q3 - Q1$, limits are located. The limits for the boxplot are 1.5(IQR) below $Q1$ and 1.5(IQR) above $Q3$. For the home sales data, IQR $= Q3 - Q1 = 256{,}625 - 139{,}000 = 117{,}625$. Thus, the limits are $139{,}000 - 1.5(117{,}625) = -37{,}437.5$ and $256{,}625 + 1.5(117{,}625) = 433{,}062.5$. Data outside these limits are considered outliers.
4. The dashed lines in Figure 2.22 are called *whiskers*. The whiskers are drawn from the ends of the box to the smallest and largest values inside the limits computed in Step 3. Thus, the whiskers end at home sales values of 108,000 and 298,000.

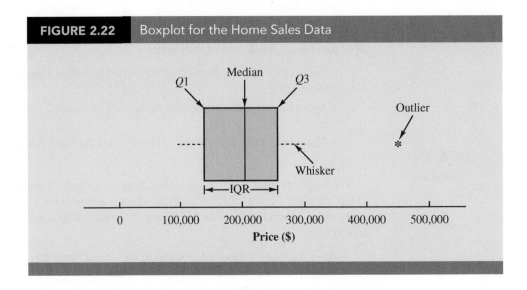

FIGURE 2.22   Boxplot for the Home Sales Data

*Clearly, we would not
expect a home sales price
less than 0, so we could
also define the lower limit
here to be $0.*

5. Finally, the location of each outlier is shown with an asterisk (*). In Figure 2.22, we see one outlier, 456,250.

Boxplots are also very useful for comparing different data sets. For instance, if we want to compare home sales from several different communities, we could create boxplots for recent home sales in each community. An example of such boxplots is shown in Figure 2.23.

What can we learn from these boxplots? The most expensive houses appear to be in Shadyside and the cheapest houses in Hamilton. The median home sales price in Groton is about the same as the median home sales price in Irving. However, home sales prices in Irving have much greater variability. Homes appear to be selling in Irving for many different prices, from very low to very high. Home sales prices have the least variation in Groton and Hamilton. The only outlier that appears in these boxplots is for home sales in Groton. However, note that most homes sell for very similar prices in Groton, so the selling price does not have to be too far from the median to be considered an outlier.

*Boxplots can be drawn
horizontally or vertically.
Figure 2.22 shows a
horizontal boxplot, and
Figure 2.23 shows vertical
boxplots.*

FIGURE 2.23   Boxplots Comparing Home Sales Prices in Different Communities

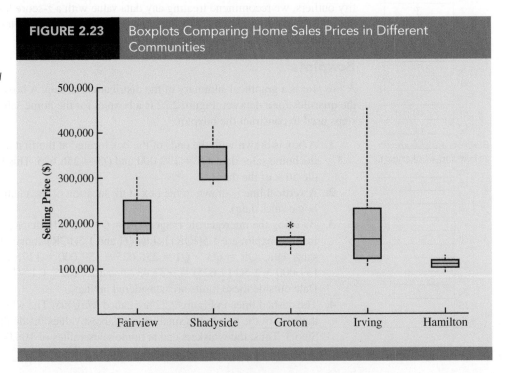

Note that boxplots use a different definition of an outlier than what we described for using *z*-scores because the distribution of the data in a boxplot is not assumed to follow a bell-shaped curve. However, the interpretation is the same. The outliers in a boxplot are extreme values that should be investigated to ensure data accuracy.

The step-by-step directions below illustrate how to create boxplots in Excel for both a single variable and multiple variables. First we will create a boxplot for a single variable using the *HomeSales* file.

DATA *file*

HomeSales

Step 1. Select cells B1:B13
Step 2. Click the **Insert** tab on the Ribbon
Click the **Insert Statistic Chart** button in the **Charts** group
Choose the **Box and Whisker** chart from the drop-down menu

The resulting boxplot created in Excel is shown in Figure 2.24. Comparing this figure to Figure 2.22, we see that all the important elements of a boxplot are generated here. Excel orients the boxplot vertically, and by default it also includes a marker for the mean.

Next we will use the *HomeSalesComparison* file to create boxplots in Excel for multiple variables similar to what is shown in Figure 2.26.

Step 1. Select cells B1:F11
Step 2. Click the **Insert** tab on the Ribbon
Click the **Insert Statistic Chart** button in the **Charts** group
Choose the **Box and Whisker** chart from the drop-down menu

DATA *file*

HomeSalesComparison

The boxplot created in Excel is shown in Figure 2.25. Excel again orients the boxplot vertically. The different selling locations are shown in the Legend at the top of the figure, and different colors are used for each boxplot.

FIGURE 2.24 Boxplot Created in Excel for Home Sales Data

	A	B
1	Home Sale	Selling Price ($)
2	1	138000
3	2	254000
4	3	186000
5	4	257500
6	5	108000
7	6	254000
8	7	138000
9	8	298000
10	9	199500
11	10	208000
12	11	142000
13	12	456250

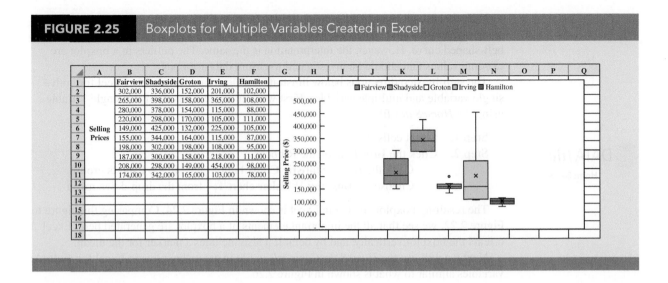

FIGURE 2.25   Boxplots for Multiple Variables Created in Excel

1. The empirical rule applies only to distributions that have an approximately bell-shaped distribution because it is based on properties of the normal probability distribution, which we will discuss in Chapter 4. For distributions that do not have a bell-shaped distribution, one can use Chebyshev's theorem to make statements about the proportion of data values that must be within a specified number of standard deviations of the mean. Chebyshev's theorem states that at least $\left(1 - \dfrac{1}{z^2}\right)$ × 100% of the data values must be within z standard deviations of the mean, where z is any value greater than 1.

2. The ability to create boxplots in Excel is only available in more recent versions of Excel. Unfortunately, there is no easy way to generate boxplots in older versions of Excel that do not have the Insert Statistic Chart button.

3. Note that the boxplot in Figure 2.24 has been formatted using Excel's Chart Elements button. These options will be discussed in more detail in Chapter 3. We have also added the text descriptions of the different elements of the boxplot.

2.8 Measures of Association Between Two Variables

Thus far, we have examined numerical methods used to summarize the data for one variable at a time. Often a manager or decision maker is interested in the relationship between two variables. In this section, we present covariance and correlation as descriptive measures of the relationship between two variables. To illustrate these concepts, we consider the case of the sales manager of Queensland Amusement Park, who is in charge of ordering bottled water to be purchased by park customers. The sales manager believes that daily bottled water sales in the summer are related to the outdoor temperature. Table 2.14 shows data for high temperatures and bottled water sales for 14 summer days. The data have been sorted by high temperature from lowest value to highest value.

Scatter Charts

A scatter chart is also known as a scatter diagram or a scatter plot.

A **scatter chart** is a useful graph for analyzing the relationship between two variables. Figure 2.26 shows a scatter chart for sales of bottled water versus the high temperature experienced on 14 consecutive days. The scatter chart in the figure suggests that higher

TABLE 2.14	Data for Bottled Water Sales at Queensland Amusement Park for a Sample of 14 Summer Days
High Temperature (°F)	**Bottled Water Sales (Cases)**
78	23
79	22
80	24
80	22
82	24
83	26
85	27
86	25
87	28
87	26
88	29
88	30
90	31
92	31

DATA *file*

BottledWater

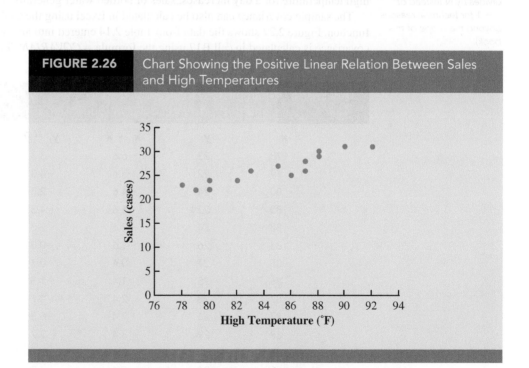

FIGURE 2.26	Chart Showing the Positive Linear Relation Between Sales and High Temperatures

Scatter charts are covered in Chapter 3.

daily high temperatures are associated with higher bottled water sales. This is an example of a positive relationship, because when one variable (high temperature) increases, the other variable (sales of bottled water) generally also increases. The scatter chart also suggests that a straight line could be used as an approximation for the relationship between high temperature and sales of bottled water.

Covariance

Covariance is a descriptive measure of the linear association between two variables. For a sample of size n with the observations (x_1, y_1), (x_2, y_2), and so on, the sample covariance is defined as follows:

DATA *file*

BottledWater

SAMPLE COVARIANCE

$$s_{xy} = \frac{\Sigma(x_i - \bar{x})(y_i - \bar{y})}{n - 1} \tag{2.9}$$

If data consist of a population of N observations, the population covariance σ_{xy} is computed by:

$$\sigma_{xy} = \frac{\Sigma(x_i - \mu_x)\Sigma(y_i - \mu_y)}{N}.$$

Note that this equation is similar to equation (2.8), but uses population parameters instead of sample estimates (and divides by N instead of n − 1 for technical reasons beyond the scope of this book).

This formula pairs each x_i with a y_i. We then sum the products obtained by multiplying the deviation of each x_i from its sample mean $(x_i - \bar{x})$ by the deviation of the corresponding y_i from its sample mean $(y_i - \bar{y})$; this sum is then divided by $n - 1$.

To measure the strength of the linear relationship between the high temperature x and the sales of bottled water y at Queensland, we use equation (2.9) to compute the sample covariance. The calculations in Table 2.15 show the computation $\Sigma(x_i - \bar{x})(y_i - \bar{y})$. Note that for our calculations, $\bar{x} = 84.6$ and $\bar{y} = 26.3$.

The covariance calculated in Table 2.15 is $s_{xy} = 12.8$. Because the covariance is greater than 0, it indicates a positive relationship between the high temperature and sales of bottled water. This verifies the relationship we saw in the scatter chart in Figure 2.26 that as the high temperature for a day increases, sales of bottled water generally increase.

The sample covariance can also be calculated in Excel using the COVARIANCE.S function. Figure 2.27 shows the data from Table 2.14 entered into an Excel Worksheet. The covariance is calculated in cell B17 using the formula = *COVARIANCE.S(A2:A15, B2:B15)*.

TABLE 2.15	Sample Covariance Calculations for Daily High Temperature and Bottled Water Sales at Queensland Amusement Park				
	x_i	y_i	$x_i - \bar{x}$	$y_i - \bar{y}$	$(x_i - \bar{x})(y_i - \bar{y})$
	78	23	−6.6	−3.3	21.78
	79	22	−5.6	−4.3	24.08
	80	24	−4.6	−2.3	10.58
	80	22	−4.6	−4.3	19.78
	82	24	−2.6	−2.3	5.98
	83	26	−1.6	−0.3	0.48
	85	27	0.4	0.7	0.28
	86	25	1.4	−1.3	−1.82
	87	28	2.4	1.7	4.08
	87	26	2.4	−0.3	−0.72
	88	29	3.4	2.7	9.18
	88	30	3.4	3.7	12.58
	90	31	5.4	4.7	25.38
	92	31	7.4	4.7	34.78
Totals	1,185	368	0.6	−0.2	166.42

$$\bar{x} = 84.6$$
$$\bar{y} = 26.3$$
$$s_{xy} = \frac{\Sigma(x_i - \bar{x})(y_i - \bar{y})}{n - 1} = \frac{166.42}{14 - 1} = 12.8$$

FIGURE 2.27	Calculating Covariance and Correlation Coefficient for Bottled Water Sales Using Excel

	A	B
1	High Temperature (°F)	Bottled Water Sales (cases)
2	78	23
3	79	22
4	80	24
5	80	22
6	82	24
7	83	26
8	85	27
9	86	25
10	87	28
11	87	26
12	88	29
13	88	30
14	90	31
15	92	31
16		
17	Covariance:	=COVARIANCE.S(A2:A15,B2:B15)
18	Correlation Coefficient:	=CORREL(A2:A15,B2:B15)

	A	B
1	High Temperature (°F)	Bottled Water Sales (cases)
2	78	23
3	79	22
4	80	24
5	80	22
6	82	24
7	83	26
8	85	27
9	86	25
10	87	28
11	87	26
12	88	29
13	88	30
14	90	31
15	92	31
16		
17	Covariance:	12.80
18	Correlation Coefficient:	0.93

A2:A15 defines the range for the x variable (high temperature), and B2:B15 defines the range for the y variable (sales of bottled water).

For the bottled water, the covariance is positive, indicating that higher temperatures (x) are associated with higher sales (y). If the covariance is near 0, then the x and y variables are not linearly related. If the covariance is less than 0, then the x and y variables are negatively related, which means that as x increases, y generally decreases. Figure 2.28 demonstrates several possible scatter charts and their associated covariance values.

One problem with using covariance is that the magnitude of the covariance value is difficult to interpret. Larger s_{xy} values do not necessarily mean a stronger linear relationship because the units of covariance depend on the units of x and y. For example, suppose we are interested in the relationship between height x and weight y for individuals. Clearly the strength of the relationship should be the same whether we measure height in feet or inches. Measuring the height in inches, however, gives us much larger numerical values for $(x_i - \bar{x})$ than when we measure height in feet. Thus, with height measured in inches, we would obtain a larger value for the numerator $\Sigma(x_i - \bar{x})(y_i - \bar{y})$ in equation (2.9)—and hence a larger covariance—when in fact the relationship does not change.

FIGURE 2.28   Scatter Charts and Associated Covariance Values for Different Variable Relationships

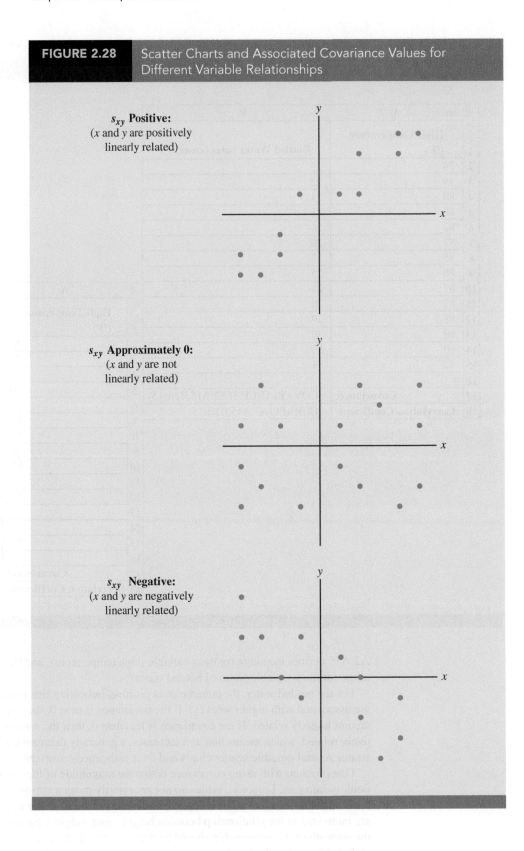

If data are a population, the population correlation coefficient is computed by $\rho_{xy} = \dfrac{\sigma_{xy}}{\sigma_x \sigma_y}$. Note that this is similar to equation (2.10) but uses population parameters instead of sample estimates.

Correlation Coefficient

The **correlation coefficient** measures the relationship between two variables, and, unlike covariance, the relationship between two variables is not affected by the units of measurement for x and y. For sample data, the correlation coefficient is defined as follows:

SAMPLE CORRELATION COEFFICIENT

$$r_{xy} = \frac{s_{xy}}{s_x s_y} \tag{2.10}$$

where

$$
\begin{aligned}
r_{xy} &= \text{sample correlation coefficient} \\
s_{xy} &= \text{sample covariance} \\
s_x &= \text{sample standard deviation of } x \\
s_y &= \text{sample standard deviation of } y
\end{aligned}
$$

The sample correlation coefficient is computed by dividing the sample covariance by the product of the sample standard deviation of x and the sample standard deviation of y. This scales the correlation coefficient so that it will always take values between -1 and $+1$.

Let us now compute the sample correlation coefficient for bottled water sales at Queensland Amusement Park. Recall that we calculated $s_{xy} = 12.8$ using equation (2.9). Using data in Table 2.14, we can compute sample standard deviations for x and y.

$$s_x = \sqrt{\frac{\Sigma(x_i - \bar{x})^2}{n - 1}} = 4.36$$

$$s_y = \sqrt{\frac{\Sigma(y_i - \bar{y})^2}{n - 1}} = 3.15$$

The sample correlation coefficient is computed from equation (2.10) as follows:

$$r_{xy} = \frac{s_{xy}}{s_x s_y} = \frac{12.8}{(4.36)(3.15)} = 0.93$$

The correlation coefficient can take only values between -1 and $+1$. Correlation coefficient values near 0 indicate no linear relationship between the x and y variables. Correlation coefficients greater than 0 indicate a positive linear relationship between the x and y variables. The closer the correlation coefficient is to $+1$, the closer the x and y values are to forming a straight line that trends upward to the right (positive slope). Correlation coefficients less than 0 indicate a negative linear relationship between the x and y variables. The closer the correlation coefficient is to -1, the closer the x and y values are to forming a straight line with negative slope. Because $r_{xy} = 0.93$ for the bottled water, we know that there is a very strong positive linear relationship between these two variables. As we can see in Figure 2.26, one could draw a straight line with a positive slope that would be very close to all of the data points in the scatter chart.

Because the correlation coefficient defined here measures only the strength of the linear relationship between two quantitative variables, it is possible for the correlation coefficient to be near zero, suggesting no linear relationship, when the relationship between the two variables is nonlinear. For example, the scatter chart in Figure 2.29 shows the relationship between the amount spent by a small retail store for environmental control (heating and cooling) and the daily high outside temperature for 100 consecutive days.

The sample correlation coefficient for these data is $r_{xy} = -0.007$ and indicates that there is no linear relationship between the two variables. However, Figure 2.29 provides strong visual evidence of a nonlinear relationship. That is, we can see that as the daily high

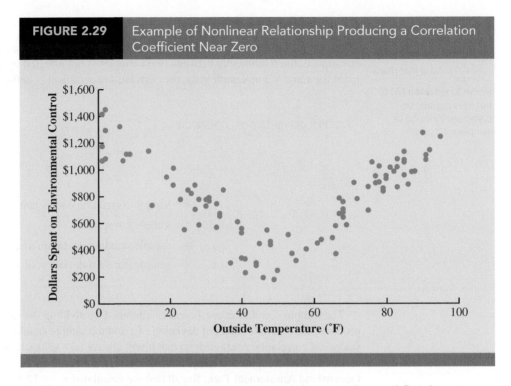

FIGURE 2.29   Example of Nonlinear Relationship Producing a Correlation Coefficient Near Zero

outside temperature increases, the money spent on environmental control first decreases as less heating is required and then increases as greater cooling is required.

We can compute correlation coefficients using the Excel function CORREL. The correlation coefficient in Figure 2.27 is computed in cell B18 for the sales of bottled water using the formula =*CORREL(A2:A15, B2:B15)*, where A2:A15 defines the range for the *x* variable and B2:B15 defines the range for the *y* variable.

NOTES + COMMENTS

1. The correlation coefficient discussed in this chapter was developed by Karl Pearson and is sometimes referred to as Pearson product moment correlation coefficient. It is appropriate for use only with two quantitative variables. A variety of alternatives, such as the Spearman rank-correlation coefficient, exist to measure the association of categorical variables. The Spearman rank-correlation coefficient is discussed in Chapter 11.

2. Correlation measures only the association between two variables. A large positive or large negative correlation coefficient does not indicate that a change in the value of one of the two variables *causes* a change in the value of the other variable.

2.9 Data Cleansing

The data in a data set are often said to be "dirty" and "raw" before they have been put into a form that is best suited for investigation, analysis, and modeling. Data preparation makes heavy use of the descriptive statistics and data-visualization methods to gain an understanding of the data. Common tasks in data preparation include treating missing data, identifying erroneous data and outliers, and defining the appropriate way to represent variables.

Missing Data

Data sets commonly include observations with missing values for one or more variables. In some cases missing data naturally occur; these are called **legitimately missing data**. For example, respondents to a survey may be asked if they belong to a fraternity or a sorority, and then in the next question are asked how long they have belonged to a fraternity or a sorority. If a respondent does not belong to a fraternity or a sorority, she or he should skip the ensuing question about how long. Generally no remedial action is taken for legitimately missing data.

In other cases missing data occur for different reasons; these are called **illegitimately missing data**. These cases can result for a variety of reasons, such as a respondent electing not to answer a question that she or he is expected to answer, a respondent dropping out of a study before its completion, or sensors or other electronic data collection equipment failing during a study. Remedial action is considered for illegitimately missing data. The primary options for addressing such missing data are (1) to discard observations (rows) with any missing values, (2) to discard any variable (column) with missing values, (3) to fill in missing entries with estimated values, or (4) to apply a data-mining algorithm (such as classification and regression trees) that can handle missing values.

Deciding on a strategy for dealing with missing data requires some understanding of why the data are missing and the potential impact these missing values might have on an analysis. If the tendency for an observation to be missing the value for some variable is entirely random, then whether data are missing does not depend on either the value of the missing data or the value of any other variable in the data. In such cases the missing value is called **missing completely at random** (MCAR). For example, if missing value for a question on a survey is completely unrelated to the value that is missing and is also completely unrelated to the value of any other question on the survey, the missing value is MCAR.

However, the occurrence of some missing values may not be completely at random. If the tendency for an observation to be missing a value for some variable is related to the value of some other variable(s) in the data, the missing value is called **missing at random** (MAR). For data that is MAR, the reason for the missing values may determine its importance. For example if the responses to one survey question collected by a specific employee were lost due to a data entry error, then the treatment of the missing data may be less critical. However, in a health care study, suppose observations corresponding to patient visits are missing the results of diagnostic tests whenever the doctor deems the patient too sick to undergo the procedure. In this case, the absence of a variable measurement actually provides additional information about the patient's condition, which may be helpful in understanding other relationships in the data.

A third category of missing data is **missing not at random** (MNAR). Data is MNAR if the tendency for the value of a variable to be missing is related to the value that is missing. For example, survey respondents with high incomes may be less inclined than respondents with lower incomes to respond to the question on annual income, and so these missing data for annual income are MNAR.

Understanding which of these three categories—MCAR, MAR, and MNAR—missing values fall into is critical in determining how to handle missing data. If a variable has observations for which the missing values are MCAR or MAR and only a relatively small number of observations are missing values, the observations that are missing values can be ignored. We will certainly lose information if the observations that are missing values for the variable are ignored, but the results of an analysis of the data will not be biased by the missing values.

If a variable has observations for which the missing values are MNAR, the observation with missing values cannot be ignored because any analysis that includes the variable with MNAR values will be biased. If the variable with MNAR values is thought to be redundant with another variable in the data for which there are few or no missing values, removing the MNAR variable from consideration may be an option. In particular, if the MNAR variable is highly correlated with another variable that is known for a majority of observations, the loss of information may be minimal.

Whether the missing values are MCAR, MAR, or MNAR, the first course of action when faced with missing values is to try to determine the actual value that is missing by examining the source of the data or logically determining the likely value that is missing. If the missing values cannot be determined and ignoring missing values or removing a variable with missing values from consideration is not an option, **imputation** (systematic replacement of missing values with values that seems reasonable) may be useful. Options for replacing the missing entries for a variable include replacing the missing value with the variable's mode, mean, or median. Imputing values in this manner is truly valid only if variable values are MCAR; otherwise, we may be introducing misleading information into the data. If missing values are particularly troublesome and MAR, it may be possible to build a model to predict a variable with missing values and then to use these predictions in place of the missing entries. How to deal with missing values is fairly subjective, and caution must be used to not induce bias by replacing missing values.

Blakely Tires

Blakely Tires is a U.S. producer of automobile tires. In an attempt to learn about the conditions of its tires on automobiles in Texas, the company has obtained information for each of the four tires from 116 automobiles with Blakely brand tires that have been collected through recent state automobile inspection facilities in Texas. The data obtained by Blakely includes the position of the tire on the automobile (left front, left rear, right front, right rear), age of the tire, mileage on the tire, and depth of the remaining tread on the tire. Before Blakely management attempts to learn more about its tires on automobiles in Texas, it wants to assess the quality of these data.

The tread depth of a tire is a vertical measurement between the top of the tread rubber to the bottom of the tire's deepest grooves, and is measured in 32nds of an inch in the United States. New Blakely brand tires have a tread depth of 10/32nds of an inch, and a tire's tread depth is considered insufficient if it is 2/32nds of an inch or less. Shallow tread depth is dangerous as it results in poor traction and so makes steering the automobile more difficult. Blakely's tires generally last for four to five years or 40,000 to 60,000 miles.

We begin assessing the quality of these data by determining which (if any) observations have missing values for any of the variables in the *TreadWear* data. We can do so using Excel's COUNTBLANK function. After opening the file *TreadWear*

DATA *file*

TreadWear

Step 1. Enter the heading *# of Missing Values* in cell G2
Step 2. Enter the heading *Life of Tire (Months)* in cell H1
Step 3. Enter *=COUNTBLANK(C2:C457)* in cell H2

The result in cell H2 shows that none of the observations in these data is missing its value for Life of Tire.

By repeating this process for the remaining quantitative variables in the data (Tread Depth and Miles) in columns I and J, we determine that there are no missing values for Tread Depth and one missing value for Miles. The first few rows of the resulting Excel spreadsheet is provided in Figure 2.30.

Next we sort all of Blakely's data on Miles from smallest to largest value to determine which observation is missing its value of this variable. Excel's sort procedure will list all observations with missing values for the sort variable, Miles, as the last observations in the sorted data.

FIGURE 2.30   Portion of Excel Spreadsheet Showing Number of Missing Values for Variables in *TreadWear* Data

	A	B	C	D	E	F	G	H	I	J
1	ID Number	Position on Automobile	Life of Tire (Months)	Tread Depth	Miles			Life of Tire (Months)	Tread Depth	Miles
2	13391487	LR	58.4	2.2	2805		# of Missing Values	0	0	1
3	21678308	LR	17.3	8.3	39371					
4	18414311	RR	16.5	8.6	13367					
5	19778103	RR	8.2	9.8	1931					
6	16355454	RR	13.7	8.9	23992					
7	8952817	LR	52.8	3.0	48961					
8	6559652	RR	14.7	8.8	4585					

We can see in Figure 2.31 that the value of Miles is missing from the left front tire of the automobile with ID Number 3354942. Because only one of the 456 observations is missing its value for Miles, this is likely MCAR and so ignoring the observation would not likely bias any analysis we wish to undertake with these data. However, we may be able to salvage this observation by logically determining a reasonable value to substitute for this missing value. It is sensible to suspect that the value of Miles for the left front tire of the automobile with the ID Number 3354942 would be identical to the value of miles for the other three tires on this automobile, so we sort all the data on ID number and scroll through the data to find the four tires that belong to the automobile with the ID Number 3354942.

Figure 2.32 shows that the value of Miles for the other three tires on the automobile with the ID Number 3354942 is 33,254, so this may be a reasonable value for the Miles of the left front tire of the automobile with the ID Number 3354942. However, before substituting this value for the missing value of the left front tire of the automobile with ID Number 3354942, we should attempt to ascertain (if possible) that this value is valid—there are legitimate reasons why a driver might replace a single tire. In this instance we will assume that the correct value of Miles for the left front tire on the automobile with the ID Number 3354942 is 33,254 and substitute that number in the appropriate cell of the spreadsheet.

Occasionally missing values in a data set are indicated with a unique value, such as 9999999. Be sure to check to see if a unique value is being used to indicate a missing value in the data.

FIGURE 2.31   Portion of Excel Spreadsheet Showing *TreadWear* Data Sorted on Miles from Lowest to Highest Value

Note that we have hidden rows 5 through 454.

	A	B	C	D	E	F	G	H	I	J
1	ID Number	Position on Automobile	Life of Tire (Months)	Tread Depth	Miles			Life of Tire (Months)	Tread Depth	Miles
2	15890813	LF	16.1	8.6	206		# of Missing Values	0	0	1
3	15890813	LR	16.1	8.6	206					
4	15890813	RF	16.1	8.6	206					
455	9306585	RR	45.4	4.1	107237					
456	9306585	LF	45.4	4.1	107237					
457	3354942	LF	17.1	8.5						

FIGURE 2.32   Portion of Excel Spreadsheet Showing *TreadWear* Data Sorted from Lowest to Highest by ID Number

54	3121851	LR	17.1	8.4	21378
55	3121851	RR	17.1	8.4	21378
56	3121851	RF	17.1	8.4	21378
57	3121851	LF	17.1	8.5	21378
58	3354942	LF	17.1	8.5	
59	3354942	RF	21.4	7.7	33254
60	3354942	RR	21.4	7.8	33254
61	3354942	LR	21.4	7.7	33254
62	3374739	RR	73.3	0.2	57313
63	3574739	RF	73.3	0.2	57313
64	3574739	LF	73.3	0.2	57313
65	3574739	LR	73.3	0.2	57313

Identification of Erroneous Outliers and Other Erroneous Values

Examining the variables in the data set by use of summary statistics, frequency distributions, bar charts and histograms, z-scores, scatter charts, correlation coefficients, and other tools can uncover data-quality issues and outliers. For example, finding the minimum or maximum value for Tread Depth in the *TreadWear* data may reveal unrealistic values—perhaps even negative values—for Tread Depth, which would indicate a problem for the value of Tread Depth for any such observation.

It is important to note here that many software, including Excel, ignore missing values when calculating various summary statistics such as the mean, standard deviation, minimum, and maximum. However, if missing values in a data set are indicated with a unique value (such as 9999999), these values may be used by software when calculating various summary statistics such as the mean, standard deviation, minimum, and maximum. Both cases can result in misleading values for summary statistics, which is why many analysts prefer to deal with missing data issues prior to using summary statistics to attempt to identify erroneous outliers and other erroneous values in the data.

We again consider the Blakely tire data. We calculate the mean and standard deviation of each variable (age of the tire, mileage on the tire, and depth of the remaining tread on the tire) to assess whether values of these variable are reasonable in general.

Return to the file *TreadWear* and complete the following steps:

Step 1. Enter the heading *Mean* in cell G3
Step 2. Enter the heading *Standard Deviation* in cell G4
Step 3. Enter *=AVERAGE(C2:C457)* in cell H3
Step 4. Enter *=STDEV.S(C2:C457)* in cell H4

The results in cells H3 and H4 show that the mean and standard deviation for life of tires are 23.8 months and 31.83 months, respectively. These values appear to be reasonable for the life of tires in months.

If you do not have good information on what are reasonable values for a variable, you can use z-scores to identify outliers to be investigated.

By repeating this process for the remaining variables in the data (Tread Depth and Miles) in columns I and J, we determine that the mean and standard deviation for tread depth are 7.62/12ths of an inch and 2.47/12ths of an inch, respectively, and the mean and standard deviation for miles are 25,440.22 and 23,600.21, respectively. These values appear to be reasonable for tread depth and miles. The results of this analysis are provided in Figure 2.33.

Summary statistics only provide an overall perspective on the data. We also need to attempt to determine if there are any erroneous individual values for our three variables. We start by finding the minimum and maximum values for each variable.

Return again to the file *TreadWear* and complete the following steps:

Step 1. Enter the heading *Minimum* in cell G5
Step 2. Enter the heading *Maximum* in cell G6
Step 3. Enter *=MIN(C2:C457)* in cell H5
Step 4. Enter *=MAX(C2:C457)* in cell H6

The results in cells H5 and H6 show that the minimum and maximum values for Life of Tires (Months) are 1.8 months and 601.0, respectively. The minimum value of life of tires in months appears to be reasonable, but the maximum (which is equal to slightly over 50 years) is not a reasonable value for Life of Tires (Months). In order to identify the automobile with this extreme value, we again sort the entire data set on Life of Tire (Months) and scroll to the last few rows of the data.

We see in Figure 2.34 that the observation with Life of Tire (Months) value of 601.0 is the left rear tire from the automobile with ID Number 8696859. Also note that the left rear tire of the automobile with ID Number 2122934 has a suspiciously high value for Life of Tire (Months) of 111. Sorting the data by ID Number and scrolling until we find the four tires from the automobile with ID Number 8696859, we find the value for Life of Tire (Months) for the other three tires from this automobile is 60.1. This suggests that the

FIGURE 2.33	Portion of Excel Spreadsheet Showing the Mean and Standard Deviation for Each Variable in the *TreadWear* Data

	A	B	C	D	E	F	G	H	I	J
1	ID Number	Position on Automobile	Life of Tire (Months)	Tread Depth	Miles			Life of Tire (Months)	Tread Depth	Miles
2	80441	LR	19.0	8.1	37419		# of Missing Values	0	0	1
3	80441	LF	19.0	8.1	37419		Mean	23.80	7.68	25440.22
4	80441	RR	19.0	8.2	37419		Standard Deviation	31.82	2.62	23600.21
5	80441	RF	19.0	8.1	37419					
6	95990	RR	8.6	9.7	5670					
7	95990	LR	8.6	9.7	5670					
8	95990	LF	8.6	9.7	5670					

FIGURE 2.34	Portion of Excel Spreadsheet Showing the *TreadWear* Data Sorted on Life of Tires (Months) from Lowest to Highest Value

	A	B	C	D	E	F	G	H	I	J
1	ID Number	Position on Automobile	Life of Tire (Months)	Tread Depth	Miles			Life of Tire (Months)	Tread Depth	Miles
2	9091771	RF	1.8	10.8	2917		# of Missing Values	0	0	1
3	9091771	RR	1.8	10.7	2917		Mean	23.80	7.68	25440.22
4	9091771	LF	1.8	10.7	2917		Standard Deviation	31.82	2.62	23600.21
5	7712178	LF	2.1	10.7	2186		Minimum	1.8		
6	7712178	RR	2.1	10.7	2186		Maximum	601.0		
452	3574739	RR	73.3	0.2	57313					
453	3574739	LF	73.3	0.2	57313					
454	3574739	LR	73.3	0.2	57313					
455	3574739	LR	73.3	0.2	57313					
456	2122934	LR	111.0	9.3	21000					
457	8696859	LR	601.0	2.0	26129					

decimal for Life of Tire (Months) for this automobile's left rear tire value is in the wrong place. Scrolling to find the four tires from the automobile with ID Number 2122934, we find the value for Life of Tire (Months) for the other three tires from this automobile is 11.1, which suggests that the decimal for Life of Tire (Months) for this automobile's left rear tire value is also misplaced. Both of these erroneous entries can now be corrected.

By repeating this process for the remaining variables in the data (Tread Depth and Miles) in columns I and J, we determine that the minimum and maximum values for Tread Depth are 0.0/12ths of an inch and 16.7/12ths of an inch, respectively, and the minimum and maximum values for Miles are 206.0 and 107237.0, respectively. Neither the minimum nor the maximum value for Tread Depth is reasonable; a tire with no tread would not be drivable, and the maximum value for tire depth in the data actually exceeds the tread depth on new Blakely brand tires. The minimum value for Miles is reasonable, but the maximum value is not. A similar investigation should be made into these values to determine if they are in error and if so, what might be the correct value.

Not all erroneous values in a data set are extreme; these erroneous values are much more difficult to find. However, if the variable with suspected erroneous values has a relatively strong relationship with another variable in the data, we can use this knowledge to look for erroneous values. Here we will consider the variables Tread Depth and Miles; because more miles driven should lead to less tread depth on an automobile tire, we expect these two variables to have a negative relationship. A scatter chart will enable us to see whether any of the tires in the data set have values for Tread Depth and Miles that are counter to this expectation.

The red ellipse in Figure 2.35 shows the region in which the points representing Tread Depth and Miles would generally be expected to lie on this scatter plot. The points that lie outside of this ellipse have values for at least one of these variables that is inconsistent with the negative relationship exhibited by the points inside the ellipse. If we position the cursor over one of the points outside the ellipse, Excel will generate a pop-up box that shows that the values of Tread Depth and Miles for this point are 1.0 and 1472.1, respectively. The tire represented by this point has very little tread and has been driven relatively few miles, which suggests that the value of one or both of these two variables for this tire may be inaccurate and should be investigated.

Closer examination of outliers and potential erroneous values may reveal an error or a need for further investigation to determine whether the observation is relevant to the current analysis. A conservative approach is to create two data sets, one with and one without outliers and potentially erroneous values, and then construct a model on both data sets. If a model's implications depend on the inclusion or exclusion of outliers and erroneous values, then you should spend additional time to track down the cause of the outliers.

Variable Representation

In many data-mining applications, it may be prohibitive to analyze the data because of the number of variables recorded. In such cases, the analyst may have to first identify variables that can be safely omitted from further analysis before proceeding with a data-mining technique. **Dimension reduction** is the process of removing variables from the analysis without losing crucial information. One simple method for reducing the number of

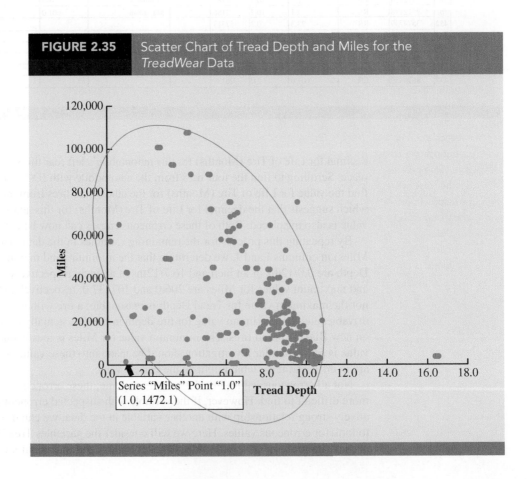

FIGURE 2.35 Scatter Chart of Tread Depth and Miles for the *TreadWear* Data

variables is to examine pairwise correlations to detect variables or groups of variables that may supply similar information. Such variables can be aggregated or removed to allow more parsimonious model development.

A critical part of data mining is determining how to represent the measurements of the variables and which variables to consider. The treatment of categorical variables is particularly important. Typically, it is best to encode categorical variables with 0–1 dummy variables. Consider a data set that contains the variable Language to track the language preference of callers to a call center. The variable Language with the possible values of English, German, and Spanish would be replaced with three binary variables called English, German, and Spanish. An entry of German would be captured using a 0 for the English dummy variable, a 1 for the German dummy variable, and a 0 for the Spanish dummy variable. Using 0–1 dummy variables to encode categorical variables with many different categories results in a large number of variables. In these cases, the use of Pivot-Tables is helpful in identifying categories that are similar and can possibly be combined to reduce the number of 0–1 dummy variables. For example, some categorical variables (zip code, product model number) may have many possible categories such that, for the purpose of model building, there is no substantive difference between multiple categories, and therefore the number of categories may be reduced by combining categories.

Often data sets contain variables that, considered separately, are not particularly insightful but that, when appropriately combined, result in a new variable that reveals an important relationship. Financial data supplying information on stock price and company earnings may be as useful as the derived variable representing the price/earnings (PE) ratio. A variable tabulating the dollars spent by a household on groceries may not be interesting because this value may depend on the size of the household. Instead, considering the *proportion* of total household spending on groceries may be more informative.

NOTES + COMMENTS

1. Many of the data visualization tools described in Chapter 3 can be used to aid in data cleansing.

2. In some cases, it may be desirable to transform a numerical variable into categories. For example, if we wish to analyze the circumstances in which a numerical outcome variable exceeds a certain value, it may be helpful to create a binary categorical variable that is 1 for observations with the variable value greater than the threshold and 0 otherwise. In another case, if a variable has a skewed distribution, it may be helpful to categorize the values into quantiles.

3. Most dedicated statistical software packages provide functionality to apply a more sophisticated dimension-reduction approach called principal components analysis. Principal components analysis creates a collection of metavariables (components) that are weighted sums of the original variables. These components are not correlated with each other, and often only a few of them are needed to convey the same information as the large set of original variables. In many cases, only one or two components are necessary to explain the majority of the variance in the original variables. Then the analyst can continue to build a data-mining model using just a few of the most explanatory components rather than the entire set of original variables. Although principal components analysis can reduce the number of variables in this manner, it may be harder to explain the results of the model because the interpretation of a component that is a linear combination of variables can be unintuitive.

SUMMARY

In this chapter we have provided an introduction to descriptive statistics that can be used to summarize data. We began by explaining the need for data collection, defining the types of data one may encounter, and providing a few commonly used sources for finding data. We presented several useful functions for modifying data in Excel, such as sorting and filtering to aid in data analysis.

We introduced the concept of a distribution and explained how to generate frequency, relative, percent, and cumulative distributions for data. We also demonstrated the use of histograms as a way to visualize the distribution of data. We then introduced measures of location for a distribution of data such as mean, median, mode, and geometric mean, as well as measures of variability such as range, variance, standard deviation, coefficient of variation, and interquartile range. We presented additional measures for analyzing a distribution of data including percentiles, quartiles, and z-scores. We showed that boxplots are effective for visualizing a distribution.

We discussed measures of association between two variables. Scatter plots allow one to visualize the relationship between variables. Covariance and the correlation coefficient summarize the linear relationship between variables into a single number.

We also introduced methods for data cleansing. Analysts typically spend large amounts of their time trying to understand and cleanse raw data before applying analytics models. We discussed methods for identifying missing data and how to deal with missing data values and outliers.

GLOSSARY

Bins The nonoverlapping groupings of data used to create a frequency distribution. Bins for categorical data are also known as classes.

Boxplot A graphical summary of data based on the quartiles of a distribution.

Categorical data Data for which categories of like items are identified by labels or names. Arithmetic operations cannot be performed on categorical data.

Coefficient of variation A measure of relative variability computed by dividing the standard deviation by the mean and multiplying by 100.

Correlation coefficient A standardized measure of linear association between two variables that takes on values between -1 and $+1$. Values near -1 indicate a strong negative linear relationship, values near $+1$ indicate a strong positive linear relationship, and values near zero indicate the lack of a linear relationship.

Covariance A measure of linear association between two variables. Positive values indicate a positive relationship; negative values indicate a negative relationship.

Cross-sectional data Data collected at the same or approximately the same point in time.

Cumulative frequency distribution A tabular summary of quantitative data showing the number of data values that are less than or equal to the upper class limit of each bin.

Data The facts and figures collected, analyzed, and summarized for presentation and interpretation.

Dimension reduction The process of removing variables from the analysis without losing crucial information.

Empirical rule A rule that can be used to compute the percentage of data values that must be within 1, 2, or 3 standard deviations of the mean for data that exhibit a bell-shaped distribution.

Frequency distribution A tabular summary of data showing the number (frequency) of data values in each of several nonoverlapping bins.

Geometric mean A measure of central location that is calculated by finding the nth root of the product of n values.

Growth factor The percentage increase of a value over a period of time is calculated using the formula (growth factor $-$ 1). A growth factor less than 1 indicates negative growth, whereas a growth factor greater than 1 indicates positive growth. The growth factor cannot be less than zero.

Histogram A graphical presentation of a frequency distribution, relative frequency distribution, or percent frequency distribution of quantitative data constructed by placing the bin intervals on the horizontal axis and the frequencies, relative frequencies, or percent frequencies on the vertical axis.

Illegitimately missing data Missing data that do not occur naturally.

Imputation Systematic replacement of missing values with values that seem reasonable.

Interquartile range The difference between the third and first quartiles.

Legitimately missing data Missing data that occur naturally.

Mean (arithmetic mean) A measure of central location computed by summing the data values and dividing by the number of observations.

Median A measure of central location provided by the value in the middle when the data are arranged in ascending order.

Missing at random (MAR) The tendency for an observation to be missing a value of some variable is related to the value of some other variable(s) in the data.

Missing completely at random (MCAR) The tendency for an observation to be missing a value of some variable is entirely random.

Missing not at random (MNAR) The tendency for an observation to be missing a value of some variable is related to the missing value.

Mode A measure of central location defined as the value that occurs with greatest frequency.

Observation A set of values corresponding to a set of variables.

Outliers An unusually large or unusually small data value.

Percent frequency distribution A tabular summary of data showing the percentage of data values in each of several nonoverlapping bins.

Percentile A value such that approximately $p\%$ of the observations have values less than the pth percentile; hence, approximately $(100 - p)\%$ of the observations have values greater than the pth percentile. The 50th percentile is the median.

Population The set of all elements of interest in a particular study.

Quantitative data Data for which numerical values are used to indicate magnitude, such as how many or how much. Arithmetic operations such as addition, subtraction, and multiplication can be performed on quantitative data.

Quartiles The 25th, 50th, and 75th percentiles, referred to as the first quartile, second quartile (median), and third quartile, respectively. The quartiles can be used to divide a data set into four parts, with each part containing approximately 25% of the data.

Random sampling Collecting a sample that ensures that (1) each element selected comes from the same population and (2) each element is selected independently.

Random variable, or uncertain variable A quantity whose values are not known with certainty.

Range A measure of variability defined to be the largest value minus the smallest value.

Relative frequency distribution A tabular summary of data showing the fraction or proportion of data values in each of several nonoverlapping bins.

Sample A subset of the population.

Scatter chart A graphical presentation of the relationship between two quantitative variables. One variable is shown on the horizontal axis and the other on the vertical axis (**scatter chart or scatter plot**).

Skewness A measure of the lack of symmetry in a distribution.

Standard deviation A measure of variability computed by taking the positive square root of the variance.

Time series data Data that are collected over a period of time (minutes, hours, days, months, years, etc.).

Variable A characteristic or quantity of interest that can take on different values.

Variance A measure of variability based on the squared deviations of the data values about the mean.

Variation Differences in values of a variable over observations.

z-score A value computed by dividing the deviation about the mean $(x_i - x)$ by the standard deviation s. A z-score is referred to as a standardized value and denotes the number of standard deviations that x_i is from the mean.

PROBLEMS

1. ***Wall Street Journal* Subscriber Characteristics.** A *Wall Street Journal* subscriber survey asked 46 questions about subscriber characteristics and interests. State whether each of the following questions provides categorical or quantitative data.
   a. What is your age?
   b. Are you male or female?

    c. When did you first start reading the *WSJ*? High school, college, early career, midcareer, late career, or retirement?

    d. How long have you been in your present job or position?

    e. What type of vehicle are you considering for your next purchase? Nine response categories include sedan, sports car, SUV, minivan, and so on.

2. **Gross Domestic Products.** The following table contains a partial list of countries, the continents on which they are located, and their respective gross domestic products (GDPs) in U.S. dollars. A list of 125 countries and their GDPs is contained in the file *GDPlist*.

GDPlist

Country	Continent	GDP (Millions of US$)
Afghanistan	Asia	18,181
Albania	Europe	12,847
Algeria	Africa	190,709
Angola	Africa	100,948
Argentina	South America	447,644
Australia	Oceania	1,488,221
Austria	Europe	419,243
Azerbaijan	Europe	62,321
Bahrain	Asia	26,108
Bangladesh	Asia	113,032
Belarus	Europe	55,483
Belgium	Europe	513,396
Bolivia	South America	24,604
Bosnia and Herzegovina	Europe	17,965
Botswana	Africa	17,570

    a. Sort the countries in *GDPlist* from largest to smallest GDP. What are the top 10 countries according to GDP?

    b. Filter the countries to display only the countries located in Africa. What are the top 5 countries located in Africa according to GDP?

    c. What are the top 5 countries by GDP that are located in Europe?

3. **On-Time Performance of Logistics Companies.** Ohio Logistics manages the logistical activities for firms by matching companies that need products shipped with carriers that can provide the best rates and best service for the companies. Ohio Logistics is very concerned that its carriers deliver their customers' material on time, so it carefully monitors the percentage of on-time deliveries. The following table contains a list of the carriers used by Ohio Logistics and the corresponding on-time percentages for the current and previous years.

Carriers

Carrier	Previous Year On-Time Deliveries (%)	Current Year On-Time Deliveries (%)
Blue Box Shipping	88.4	94.8
Cheetah LLC	89.3	91.8
Granite State Carriers	81.8	87.6
Honsin Limited	74.2	80.1

Carrier	Previous Year On-Time Deliveries (%)	Current Year On-Time Deliveries (%)
Jones Brothers	68.9	82.8
Minuteman Company	91.0	84.2
Rapid Response	78.8	70.9
Smith Logistics	84.3	88.7
Super Freight	92.1	86.8

a. Sort the carriers in descending order by their current year's percentage of on-time deliveries. Which carrier is providing the best service in the current year? Which carrier is providing the worst service in the current year?

b. Calculate the change in percentage of on-time deliveries from the previous to the current year for each carrier. Use Excel's conditional formatting to highlight the carriers whose on-time percentage decreased from the previous year to the current year.

c. Use Excel's conditional formatting tool to create data bars for the change in percentage of on-time deliveries from the previous year to the current year for each carrier calculated in part b.

d. Which carriers should Ohio Logistics try to use in the future? Why?

4. **Relative Frequency Distribution.** A partial relative frequency distribution is given.

Class	Relative Frequency
A	0.22
B	0.18
C	0.40
D	

a. What is the relative frequency of class D?

b. The total sample size is 200. What is the frequency of class D?

c. Show the frequency distribution.

d. Show the percent frequency distribution.

5. **Most Visited Web Sites.** In a recent report, the top five most-visited English-language web sites were google.com (GOOG), facebook.com (FB), youtube.com (YT), yahoo.com (YAH), and wikipedia.com (WIKI). The most-visited web sites for a sample of 50 Internet users are shown in the following table:

WebSites

YAH	WIKI	YT	WIKI	GOOG
YT	YAH	GOOG	GOOG	GOOG
WIKI	GOOG	YAH	YAH	YAH
YAH	YT	GOOG	YT	YAH
GOOG	FB	FB	WIKI	GOOG
GOOG	GOOG	FB	FB	WIKI
FB	YAH	YT	YAH	YAH
YT	GOOG	YAH	FB	FB
WIKI	GOOG	YAH	WIKI	WIKI
YAH	YT	GOOG	GOOG	WIKI

a. Are these data categorical or quantitative?

b. Provide frequency and percent frequency distributions.

c. On the basis of the sample, which web site is most frequently the most-often-visited web site for Internet users? Which is second?

6. **CEO Time in Meetings.** In a study of how chief executive officers (CEOs) spend their days, it was found that CEOs spend an average of about 18 hours per week in meetings, not including conference calls, business meals, and public events. Shown here are the times spent per week in meetings (hours) for a sample of 25 CEOs:

DATA*file*
CEOtime

14	15	18	23	15
19	20	13	15	23
23	21	15	20	21
16	15	18	18	19
19	22	23	21	12

a. What is the least amount of time a CEO spent per week in meetings in this sample? The highest?
b. Use a class width of 2 hours to prepare a frequency distribution and a percent frequency distribution for the data.
c. Prepare a histogram and comment on the shape of the distribution.

DATA*file*
BBB

7. **Complaints Reported to BBB.** Consumer complaints are frequently reported to the Better Business Bureau. Industries with the most complaints to the Better Business Bureau are often banks, cable and satellite television companies, collection agencies, cellular phone providers, and new car dealerships. The results for a sample of 200 complaints are in the file *BBB*.
a. Show the frequency and percent frequency of complaints by industry.
b. Which industry had the highest number of complaints?
c. Comment on the percentage frequency distribution for complaints.

8. **Busiest North American Airports.** Based on the total passenger traffic, the airports in the following list are the 20 busiest airports in North America in 2018 (*The World Almanac*).

DATA*file*
Airports

Airport (Airport Code)	Total Passengers (Million)
Boston Logan (BOS)	36.3
Charlotte Douglas (CLT)	44.4
Chicago O'Hare (ORD)	78
Dallas/Ft. Worth (DFW)	65.7
Denver (DEN)	58.3
Detroit Metropolitan (DTW)	34.4
Hartsfield-Jackson Atlanta (ATL)	104.2
Houston George Bush (IAH)	41.6
Las Vegas McCarran (LAS)	47.5
Los Angeles (LAX)	80.9
Miami (MIA)	44.6
Minneapolis/St. Paul (MSP)	37.4
New York John F. Kennedy (JFK)	59.1
Newark Liberty (EWR)	40.6
Orlando (MCO)	41.9
Philadelphia (PHL)	36.4
Phoenix Sky Harbor (PHX)	43.3
San Francisco (SFO)	53.1
Seattle-Tacoma (SEA)	45.7
Toronto Pearson (YYZ)	44.3

a. Which is busiest airport in terms of total passenger traffic? Which is the least busy airport in terms of total passenger traffic?
b. Using a class width of 10, develop a frequency distribution of the data starting with 30–39.9, 40–49.9, 50–59.9, and so on.
c. Prepare a histogram. Interpret the histogram.

9. **Relative and Percent Frequency Distributions.** Consider the following data:

DATA *file*

Frequency

14	24	18	22
19	18	16	22
24	17	15	16
19	23	24	16
16	26	21	16
20	22	16	12
24	23	19	25
20	25	21	19
21	25	23	24
22	19	20	20

a. Develop a frequency distribution using classes of 12–14, 15–17, 18–20, 21–23, and 24–26.
b. Develop a relative frequency distribution and a percent frequency distribution using the classes in part a.

10. **Cumulative Frequency Distribution.** Consider the following frequency distribution.

Class	Frequency
10–19	10
20–29	14
30–39	17
40–49	7
50–59	2

Construct a cumulative frequency distribution.

11. **Repair Shop Waiting Times.** The owner of an automobile repair shop studied the waiting times for customers who arrive at the shop for an oil change. The following data with waiting times in minutes were collected over a one-month period.

DATA *file*

RepairShop

2   5   10   12   4   4   5   17   11   8   9   8   12   21   6   8   7   13   18   3

Using classes of 0–4, 5–9, and so on, show the following:
a. The frequency distribution
b. The relative frequency distribution
c. The cumulative frequency distribution
d. The cumulative relative frequency distribution
e. The proportion of customers needing an oil change who wait 9 minutes or less

12. **Largest University Endowments.** University endowments are financial assets that are donated by supporters to be used to provide income to universities. There is a large discrepancy in the size of university endowments. The following table provides a listing of many of the universities that have the largest endowments as reported by the National Association of College and University Business Officers in 2017.

DATA *file*

Endowments

University	Endowment Amount ($ Billion)	University	Endowment Amount ($ Billion)
Amherst College	2.2	Smith College	1.8
Boston College	2.3	Stanford University	24.8
Boston University	2.0	Swarthmore College	2.0
Brown University	3.2	Texas A&M University	11.6
California Institute of Technology	2.6	Tufts University	1.7
		University of California	9.8
Carnegie Mellon University	2.2	University of California, Berkeley	1.8
Case Western Reserve University	1.8	University of California, Los Angeles	2.1
Columbia University	10.0	University of Chicago	7.5
Cornell University	6.8	University of Illinois	2.6
Dartmouth College	5.0	University of Michigan	10.9
Duke University	7.9	University of Minnesota	3.5
Emory University	6.9	University of North Carolina at Chapel Hill	3.0
George Washington University	1.7	University of Notre Dame	9.4
Georgetown University	1.7	University of Oklahoma	1.6
Georgia Institute of Technology	2.0	University of Pennsylvania	12.2
		University of Pittsburgh	3.9
Grinnell College	1.9	University of Richmond	2.4
Harvard University	36.0	University of Rochester	2.1
Indiana University	2.2	University of Southern California	5.1
Johns Hopkins University	3.8		
Massachusetts Institute of Technology	15.0	University of Texas	26.5
		University of Virginia	8.6
Michigan State University	2.7	University of Washington	2.5
New York University	4.0	University of Wisconsin–Madison	2.7
Northwestern University	10.4		
Ohio State University	4.3	Vanderbilt University	4.1
Pennsylvania State University	4.0	Virginia Commonwealth University	1.8
Pomona College	2.2	Washington University in St. Louis	7.9
Princeton University	23.8		
Purdue University	2.4	Wellesley College	1.9
Rice University	5.8	Williams College	2.5
Rockefeller University	2.0	Yale University	27.2

Summarize the data by constructing the following:
a. A frequency distribution (classes 0–1.9, 2.0–3.9, 4.0–5.9, 6.0–7.9, and so on).
b. A relative frequency distribution.
c. A cumulative frequency distribution.
d. A cumulative relative frequency distribution.
e. What do these distributions tell you about the endowments of universities?
f. Show a histogram. Comment on the shape of the distribution.
g. What is the largest university endowment and which university holds it?

13. **Computing Mean and Median.** Consider a sample with data values of 10, 20, 12, 17, and 16.
    a. Compute the mean and median.
    b. Consider a sample with data values 10, 20, 12, 17, 16, and 12. How would you expect the mean and median for these sample data to compare to the mean and median for part a (higher, lower, or the same)? Compute the mean and median for the sample data 10, 20, 12, 17, 16, and 12.

14. **Computing Percentiles.** Consider a sample with data values of 27, 25, 20, 15, 30, 34, 28, and 25. Compute the 20th, 25th, 65th, and 75th percentiles.

15. **Computing Mean, Median, and Mode.** Consider a sample with data values of 53, 55, 70, 58, 64, 57, 53, 69, 57, 68, and 53. Compute the mean, median, and mode.

16. **Mean Annual Growth Rate of Asset.** If an asset declines in value from $5,000 to $3,500 over nine years, what is the mean annual growth rate in the asset's value over these nine years?

17. **Comparing Mutual Fund Investments.** Suppose that you initially invested $10,000 in the Stivers mutual fund and $5,000 in the Trippi mutual fund. The value of each investment at the end of each subsequent year is provided in the table:

DATA *file*

StiversTrippi

Year	Stivers ($)	Trippi ($)
1	11,000	5,600
2	12,000	6,300
3	13,000	6,900
4	14,000	7,600
5	15,000	8,500
6	16,000	9,200
7	17,000	9,900
8	18,000	10,600

Which of the two mutual funds performed better over this time period?

18. **Commute Times.** The average time that Americans commute to work is 27.7 minutes (*Sterling's Best Places*). The average commute times in minutes for 48 cities are as follows:

DATA *file*

CommuteTimes

City	Time	City	Time	City	Time
Albuquerque	23.3	Jacksonville	26.2	Phoenix	28.3
Atlanta	28.3	Kansas City	23.4	Pittsburgh	25.0
Austin	24.6	Las Vegas	28.4	Portland	26.4
Baltimore	32.1	Little Rock	20.1	Providence	23.6
Boston	31.7	Los Angeles	32.2	Richmond	23.4
Charlotte	25.8	Louisville	21.4	Sacramento	25.8
Chicago	38.1	Memphis	23.8	Salt Lake City	20.2
Cincinnati	24.9	Miami	30.7	San Antonio	26.1
Cleveland	26.8	Milwaukee	24.8	San Diego	24.8
Columbus	23.4	Minneapolis	23.6	San Francisco	32.6
Dallas	28.5	Nashville	25.3	San Jose	28.5
Denver	28.1	New Orleans	31.7	Seattle	27.3
Detroit	29.3	New York	43.8	St. Louis	26.8
El Paso	24.4	Oklahoma City	22.0	Tucson	24.0
Fresno	23.0	Orlando	27.1	Tulsa	20.1
Indianapolis	24.8	Philadelphia	34.2	Washington, D.C.	32.8

a. What is the mean commute time for these 48 cities?
b. What is the median commute time for these 48 cities?
c. What is the mode for these 48 cities?
d. What is the variance and standard deviation of commute times for these 48 cities?
e. What is the third quartile of commute times for these 48 cities?

19. **Patient Waiting Times.** Suppose that the average waiting time for a patient at a physician's office is just over 29 minutes. To address the issue of long patient wait times, some physicians' offices are using wait-tracking systems to notify patients of expected wait times. Patients can adjust their arrival times based on this information and spend less time in waiting rooms. The following data show wait times (in minutes) for a sample of patients at offices that do not have a wait-tracking system and wait times for a sample of patients at offices with such systems.

PatientWaits

Without Wait-Tracking System	With Wait-Tracking System
24	31
67	11
17	14
20	18
31	12
44	37
12	9
23	13
16	12
37	15

a. What are the mean and median patient wait times for offices with a wait-tracking system? What are the mean and median patient wait times for offices without a wait-tracking system?
b. What are the variance and standard deviation of patient wait times for offices with a wait-tracking system? What are the variance and standard deviation of patient wait times for visits to offices without a wait-tracking system?
c. Create a boxplot for patient wait times for offices without a wait-tracking system.
d. Create a boxplot for patient wait times for offices with a wait-tracking system.
e. Do offices with a wait-tracking system have shorter patient wait times than offices without a wait-tracking system? Explain.

20. **Number of Hours Worked per Week by Teachers.** According to the National Education Association (NEA), teachers generally spend more than 40 hours each week working on instructional duties. The following data show the number of hours worked per week for a sample of 13 high school science teachers and a sample of 11 high school English teachers.

Teachers

High school science teachers 53 56 54 54 55 58 49 61 54 54 52 53 54
High school English teachers 52 47 50 46 47 48 49 46 55 44 47

a. What is the median number of hours worked per week for the sample of 13 high school science teachers?
b. What is the median number of hours worked per week for the sample of 11 high school English teachers?
c. Create a boxplot for the number of hours worked for high school science teachers.
d. Create a boxplot for the number of hours worked for high school English teachers.
e. Comment on the differences between the boxplots for science and English teachers.

DATA *file*

PatientWaits

21. **z-Scores for Patient Waiting Times.** Return to the waiting times given for the physician's office in Problem 19.
    a. Considering only offices *without* a wait-tracking system, what is the z-score for the 10th patient in the sample (wait time = 37 minutes)?
    b. Considering only offices *with* a wait-tracking system, what is the z-score for the 6th patient in the sample (wait time = 37 minutes)? How does this z-score compare with the z-score you calculated for part a?
    c. Based on z-scores, do the data for offices without a wait-tracking system contain any outliers? Based on z-scores, do the data for offices without a wait-tracking system contain any outliers?

22. **Amount of Sleep per Night.** The results of a national survey showed that on average adults sleep 6.9 hours per night. Suppose that the standard deviation is 1.2 hours and that the number of hours of sleep follows a bell-shaped distribution.
    a. Use the empirical rule to calculate the percentage of individuals who sleep between 4.5 and 9.3 hours per day.
    b. What is the z-score for an adult who sleeps 8 hours per night?
    c. What is the z-score for an adult who sleeps 6 hours per night?

23. **GMAT Exam Scores.** The Graduate Management Admission Test (GMAT) is a standardized exam used by many universities as part of the assessment for admission to graduate study in business. The average GMAT score is 547 (Magoosh web site). Assume that GMAT scores are bell-shaped with a standard deviation of 100.
    a. What percentage of GMAT scores are 647 or higher?
    b. What percentage of GMAT scores are 747 or higher?
    c. What percentage of GMAT scores are between 447 and 547?
    d. What percentage of GMAT scores are between 347 and 647?

24. **Scatter Chart.** Five observations taken for two variables follow.

x_i	4	6	11	3	16
y_i	50	50	40	60	30

    a. Develop a scatter chart with x on the horizontal axis.
    b. What does the scatter chart developed in part a indicate about the relationship between the two variables?
    c. Compute and interpret the sample covariance.
    d. Compute and interpret the sample correlation coefficient.

25. **Company Profits and Market Cap.** The scatter chart in the following figure was created using sample data for profits and market capitalizations from a sample of firms in the Fortune 500.

DATA *file*

Fortune500

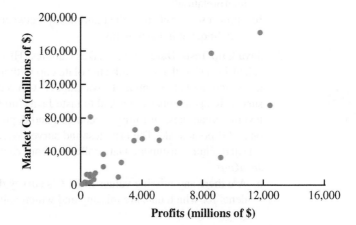

a. Discuss what the scatter chart indicates about the relationship between profits and market capitalization?

b. The data used to produce this are contained in the file *Fortune500*. Calculate the covariance between profits and market capitalization. Discuss what the covariance indicates about the relationship between profits and market capitalization?

c. Calculate the correlation coefficient between profits and market capitalization. What does the correlation coefficient indicate about the relationship between profits and market capitalization?

26. **Jobless Rate and Percent of Delinquent Loans.** The economic downturn in 2008–2009 resulted in the loss of jobs and an increase in delinquent loans for housing. In projecting where the real estate market was headed in the coming year, economists studied the relationship between the jobless rate and the percentage of delinquent loans. The expectation was that if the jobless rate continued to increase, there would also be an increase in the percentage of delinquent loans. The following data show the jobless rate and the delinquent loan percentage for 27 major real estate markets.

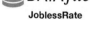

DATA *file*

JoblessRate

Metro Area	Jobless Rate (%)	Delinquent Loans (%)	Metro Area	Jobless Rate (%)	Delinquent Loans (%)
Atlanta	7.1	7.02	New York	6.2	5.78
Boston	5.2	5.31	Orange County	6.3	6.08
Charlotte	7.8	5.38	Orlando	7.0	10.05
Chicago	7.8	5.40	Philadelphia	6.2	4.75
Dallas	5.8	5.00	Phoenix	5.5	7.22
Denver	5.8	4.07	Portland	6.5	3.79
Detroit	9.3	6.53	Raleigh	6.0	3.62
Houston	5.7	5.57	Sacramento	8.3	9.24
Jacksonville	7.3	6.99	St. Louis	7.5	4.40
Las Vegas	7.6	11.12	San Diego	7.1	6.91
Los Angeles	8.2	7.56	San Francisco	6.8	5.57
Miami	7.1	12.11	Seattle	5.5	3.87
Minneapolis	6.3	4.39	Tampa	7.5	8.42
Nashville	6.6	4.78			

Source: *The Wall Street Journal, January 27, 2009.*

a. Compute the correlation coefficient. Is there a positive correlation between the jobless rate and the percentage of delinquent housing loans? What is your interpretation?

b. Show a scatter chart of the relationship between the jobless rate and the percentage of delinquent housing loans.

27. **Java Cup Taste Data.** Huron Lakes Candies (HLC) has developed a new candy bar called Java Cup that is a milk chocolate cup with a coffee-cream center. In order to assess the market potential of Java Cup, HLC has developed a taste test and follow-up survey. Respondents were asked to taste Java Cup and then rate Java Cup's taste, texture, creaminess of filling, sweetness, and depth of the chocolate flavor of the cup on a 100-point scale. The taste test and survey were administered to 217 randomly selected adult consumers. Data collected from each respondent are provided in the file *JavaCup*.

DATA *file*

JavaCup

a. Are there any missing values in HLC's survey data? If so, identify the respondents for which data are missing and which values are missing for each of these respondents.

b. Are there any values in HLC's survey data that appear to be erroneous? If so, identify the respondents for which data appear to be erroneous and which values appear to be erroneous for each of these respondents.

AttendMLB

28. **Major League Baseball Attendance.** Marilyn Marshall, a professor of sports economics, has obtained a data set of home attendance for each of the 30 major league baseball franchises for each season from 2010 through 2016. Dr. Marshall suspects the data, provided in the file *AttendMLB*, is in need of a thorough cleansing. You should also find a reliable source of Major League Baseball attendance for each franchise between 2010 and 2016 to use to help you identify appropriate imputation values for data missing in the *AttendMLB* file.

a. Are there any missing values in Dr. Marshall's data? If so, identify the teams and seasons for which data are missing and which values are missing for each of these teams and seasons. Use the reliable source of Major League Baseball Attendance for each franchise between 2010 and 2016 you have found to find the correct value in each instance.

b. Are there any values in Dr. Marshall's data that appear to be erroneous? If so, identify the teams and seasons for which data appear to be erroneous and which values appear to be erroneous for each of these teams and seasons. Use the reliable source of Major League Baseball Attendance for each franchise between 2010 and 2016 you have found to find the correct value in each instance.

CASE PROBLEM 1: HEAVENLY CHOCOLATES WEB SITE TRANSACTIONS

Heavenly Chocolates manufactures and sells quality chocolate products at its plant and retail store located in Saratoga Springs, New York. Two years ago, the company developed a web site and began selling its products over the Internet. Web site sales have exceeded the company's expectations, and management is now considering strategies to increase sales even further. To learn more about the web site customers, a sample of 50 Heavenly Chocolates transactions was selected from the previous month's sales. Data showing the day of the week each transaction was made, the type of browser the customer used, the time spent on the web site, the number of web pages viewed, and the amount spent by each of the 50 customers are contained in the file *HeavenlyChocolates*. A portion of the data is shown in the table that follows:

HeavenlyChocolates

Customer	Day	Browser	Time (min)	Pages Viewed	Amount Spent ($)
1	Mon	Chrome	12.0	4	54.52
2	Wed	Other	19.5	6	94.90
3	Mon	Chrome	8.5	4	26.68
4	Tue	Firefox	11.4	2	44.73
5	Wed	Chrome	11.3	4	66.27
6	Sat	Firefox	10.5	6	67.80
7	Sun	Chrome	11.4	2	36.04
.	.	.	.	.	.
.	.	.	.	.	.
.	.	.	.	.	.
48	Fri	Chrome	9.7	5	103.15
49	Mon	Other	7.3	6	52.15
50	Fri	Chrome	13.4	3	98.75

Heavenly Chocolates would like to use the sample data to determine whether online shoppers who spend more time and view more pages also spend more money during their visit to the web site. The company would also like to investigate the effect that the day of the week and the type of browser have on sales.

Managerial Report

Use the methods of descriptive statistics to learn about the customers who visit the Heavenly Chocolates web site. Include the following in your report.

1. Graphical and numerical summaries for the length of time the shopper spends on the web site, the number of pages viewed, and the mean amount spent per transaction. Discuss what you learn about Heavenly Chocolates' online shoppers from these numerical summaries.
2. Summarize the frequency, the total dollars spent, and the mean amount spent per transaction for each day of week. Discuss the observations you can make about Heavenly Chocolates' business based on the day of the week?
3. Summarize the frequency, the total dollars spent, and the mean amount spent per transaction for each type of browser. Discuss the observations you can make about Heavenly Chocolates' business based on the type of browser?
4. Develop a scatter chart, and compute the sample correlation coefficient to explore the relationship between the time spent on the web site and the dollar amount spent. Use the horizontal axis for the time spent on the web site. Discuss your findings.
5. Develop a scatter chart, and compute the sample correlation coefficient to explore the relationship between the number of web pages viewed and the amount spent. Use the horizontal axis for the number of web pages viewed. Discuss your findings.
6. Develop a scatter chart, and compute the sample correlation coefficient to explore the relationship between the time spent on the web site and the number of pages viewed. Use the horizontal axis to represent the number of pages viewed. Discuss your findings.

CASE PROBLEM 2: AFRICAN ELEPHANT POPULATIONS

Although millions of elephants once roamed across Africa, by the mid-1980s elephant populations in African nations had been devastated by poaching. Elephants are important to African ecosystems. In tropical forests, elephants create clearings in the canopy that encourage new tree growth. In savannas, elephants reduce bush cover to create an environment that is favorable to browsing and grazing animals. In addition, the seeds of many plant species depend on passing through an elephant's digestive tract before germination.

The status of the elephant now varies greatly across the continent. In some nations, strong measures have been taken to effectively protect elephant populations; for example, Kenya has destroyed over five tons of elephant ivory confiscated from poachers in an attempt to deter the growth of illegal ivory trade (Associated Press, July 20, 2011). In other nations the elephant populations remain in danger due to poaching for meat and ivory, loss of habitat, and conflict with humans. The table below shows elephant populations for several African nations in 1979, 1989, 2007, and 2012 (ElephantDatabase.org web site).

The David Sheldrick Wildlife Trust was established in 1977 to honor the memory of naturalist David Leslie William Sheldrick, who founded Warden of Tsavo East National Park in Kenya and headed the Planning Unit of the Wildlife Conservation and Management Department in that country. Management of the Sheldrick Trust would like to know what these data indicate about elephant populations in various African countries since 1979.

AfricanElephants

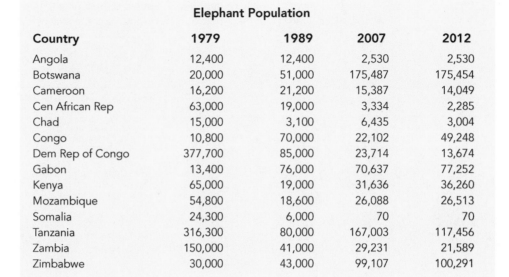

Country	Elephant Population 1979	1989	2007	2012
Angola	12,400	12,400	2,530	2,530
Botswana	20,000	51,000	175,487	175,454
Cameroon	16,200	21,200	15,387	14,049
Cen African Rep	63,000	19,000	3,334	2,285
Chad	15,000	3,100	6,435	3,004
Congo	10,800	70,000	22,102	49,248
Dem Rep of Congo	377,700	85,000	23,714	13,674
Gabon	13,400	76,000	70,637	77,252
Kenya	65,000	19,000	31,636	36,260
Mozambique	54,800	18,600	26,088	26,513
Somalia	24,300	6,000	70	70
Tanzania	316,300	80,000	167,003	117,456
Zambia	150,000	41,000	29,231	21,589
Zimbabwe	30,000	43,000	99,107	100,291

Managerial Report

Use methods of descriptive statistics to summarize the data and comment on changes in elephant populations since 1979. Include the following in your report.

1. Use the geometric mean calculation to find the mean annual change in elephant population for each country in the 10 years from 1979 to 1989, and a discussion of which countries saw the largest changes in elephant population over this 10-year period.
2. Use the geometric mean calculation to find the mean annual change in elephant population for each country in the 18 years from 1989 to 2007, and a discussion of which countries saw the largest changes in elephant population over this 18-year period.
3. Use the geometric mean calculation to find the mean annual change in elephant population for each country in the 5 years from 2007 to 2012, and a discussion of which countries saw the largest changes in elephant population over this 5-year period.
4. Create a multiple boxplot graph that includes boxplots of the elephant population observations in each year (1979, 1989, 2007, 2012). Use these boxplots and the results of your analyses in points 1 through 3 above to comment on how the populations of elephants have changed during these time periods.

Chapter 3

Data Visualization

CONTENTS

ANALYTICS IN ACTION:
CINCINNATI ZOO & BOTANICAL GARDEN

ANALYTICS IN ACTION

Cincinnati Zoo & Botanical Garden[1]

The Cincinnati Zoo & Botanical Garden, located in Cincinnati, Ohio, is one of the oldest zoos in the United States. In 2019, it was named the best zoo in North America by *USA Today*. To improve decision making by becoming more data-driven, management decided they needed to link the various facets of their business and provide nontechnical managers and executives with an intuitive way to better understand their data. A complicating factor is that when the zoo is busy, managers are expected to be on the grounds interacting with guests, checking on operations, and dealing with issues as they arise or anticipating them. Therefore, being able to monitor what is happening in real time was a key factor in

deciding what to do. Zoo management concluded that a data-visualization strategy was needed to address the problem.

Because of its ease of use, real-time updating capability, and iPad compatibility, the Cincinnati Zoo decided to implement its data-visualization strategy using IBM's Cognos advanced data-visualization software. Using this software, the Cincinnati Zoo developed the set of charts shown in Figure 3.1 (known as a data dashboard) to enable management to track the following key measures of performance:

- Item analysis (sales volumes and sales dollars by location within the zoo)
- Geoanalytics (using maps and displays of where the day's visitors are spending their time at the zoo)
- Customer spending

[1]The authors are indebted to John Lucas of the Cincinnati Zoo & Botanical Garden for providing this application.

| **FIGURE 3.1** | Data Dashboard for the Cincinnati Zoo |

- Cashier sales performance
- Sales and attendance data versus weather patterns
- Performance of the zoo's loyalty rewards program

An iPad mobile application was also developed to enable the zoo's managers to be out on the grounds and still see and anticipate occurrences in real time. The Cincinnati Zoo's iPad application, shown in Figure 3.2, provides managers with access to the following information:

- Real-time attendance data, including what types of guests are coming to the zoo (members, non-members, school groups, and so on)

- Real-time analysis showing which locations are busiest and which items are selling the fastest inside the zoo
- Real-time geographical representation of where the zoo's visitors live

Having access to the data shown in Figures 3.1 and 3.2 allows the zoo managers to make better decisions about staffing levels, which items to stock based on weather and other conditions, and how to better target advertising based on geodemographics.

The impact that data visualization has had on the zoo has been substantial. Within the first year of use, the system was directly responsible for revenue growth of over $500,000, increased visitation to the zoo, enhanced customer service, and reduced marketing costs.

FIGURE 3.2   The Cincinnati Zoo iPad Data Dashboard

The first step in trying to interpret data is often to visualize it in some way. Data visualization can be as simple as creating a summary table, or it could require generating charts to help interpret, analyze, and learn from the data. Data visualization is very helpful for identifying data errors and for reducing the size of your data set by highlighting important relationships and trends.

Data visualization is also important in conveying your analysis to others. Although business analytics is about making better decisions, in many cases, the ultimate decision maker is not the person who analyzes the data. Therefore, the person analyzing the data has to make the analysis simple for others to understand. Proper data-visualization techniques greatly improve the ability of the decision maker to interpret the analysis easily.

In this chapter we discuss some general concepts related to data visualization to help you analyze data and convey your analysis to others. We cover specifics dealing with how to design tables and charts, as well as the most commonly used charts, and present an overview of some more advanced charts. We also introduce the concept of data dashboards and geographic information systems (GISs). Our detailed examples use Excel to generate tables and charts, and we discuss several software packages that can be used for advanced data visualization.

3.1 Overview of Data Visualization

Decades of research studies in psychology and other fields show that the human mind can process visual images such as charts much faster than it can interpret rows of numbers. However, these same studies also show that the human mind has certain limitations in its ability to interpret visual images and that some images are better at conveying information than others. The goal of this chapter is to introduce some of the most common forms of visualizing data and demonstrate when each form is appropriate.

Microsoft Excel is a ubiquitous tool used in business for basic data visualization. Software tools such as Excel make it easy for anyone to create many standard examples of data visualization. However, as discussed in this chapter, the default settings for tables and charts created with Excel can be altered to increase clarity. New types of software that are dedicated to data visualization have appeared recently. We focus our techniques on Excel in this chapter, but we also mention some of these more advanced software packages for specific data-visualization uses.

Effective Design Techniques

One of the most helpful ideas for creating effective tables and charts for data visualization is the idea of the **data-ink ratio**, first described by Edward R. Tufte in 2001 in his book *The Visual Display of Quantitative Information*. The data-ink ratio measures the proportion of what Tufte terms "data-ink" to the total amount of ink used in a table or chart. Data-ink is the ink used in a table or chart that is necessary to convey the meaning of the data to the audience. Non-data-ink is ink used in a table or chart that serves no useful purpose in conveying the data to the audience.

Let us consider the case of Gossamer Industries, a firm that produces fine silk clothing products. Gossamer is interested in tracking the sales of one of its most popular items, a particular style of women's scarf. Table 3.1 and Figure 3.3 provide examples of a table and chart with low data-ink ratios used to display sales of this style of women's scarf. The data used in this table and figure represent product sales by day. Both of these examples are similar to tables and charts generated with Excel using common default settings. In Table 3.1, most of the grid lines serve no useful purpose. Likewise, in Figure 3.3, the horizontal lines in the chart also add little additional information. In both cases, most of these lines can be deleted without reducing the information conveyed. However, an important piece of information is missing from Figure 3.3: labels for axes. Axes should always be labeled in a chart unless both the meaning and unit of measure are obvious.

TABLE 3.1	Example of a Low Data-Ink Ratio Table		
Scarf Sales			
Day	**Sales (units)**	**Day**	**Sales (units)**
1	150	11	170
2	170	12	160
3	140	13	290
4	150	14	200
5	180	15	210
6	180	16	110
7	210	17	90
8	230	18	140
9	140	19	150
10	200	20	230

Table 3.2 shows a modified table in which all grid lines have been deleted except for those around the title of the table. Deleting the grid lines in Table 3.1 increases the data-ink ratio because a larger proportion of the ink in the table is used to convey the information (the actual numbers). Similarly, deleting the unnecessary horizontal lines in Figure 3.4 increases the data-ink ratio. Note that deleting these horizontal lines and removing (or reducing the size of) the markers at each data point can make it more difficult to determine the exact values plotted in the chart. However, as we discuss later, a simple chart is not the most effective way of presenting data when the audience needs to know exact values; in these cases, it is better to use a table.

In many cases, white space in a table or a chart can improve readability. This principle is similar to the idea of increasing the data-ink ratio. Consider Table 3.2 and Figure 3.4. Removing the unnecessary lines has increased the "white space," making it easier to read both the table and the chart. The fundamental idea in creating effective tables and charts is to make them as simple as possible in conveying information to the reader.

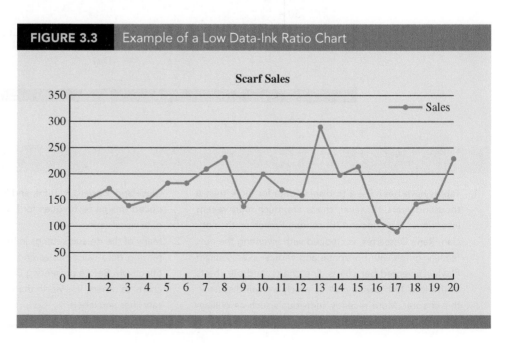

FIGURE 3.3   Example of a Low Data-Ink Ratio Chart

TABLE 3.2   Increasing the Data-Ink Ratio by Removing Unnecessary Gridlines

Scarf Sales			
Day	Sales (units)	Day	Sales (units)
1	150	11	170
2	170	12	160
3	140	13	290
4	150	14	200
5	180	15	210
6	180	16	110
7	210	17	90
8	230	18	140
9	140	19	150
10	200	20	230

FIGURE 3.4   Increasing the Data-Ink Ratio by Adding Labels to Axes and Removing Unnecessary Lines and Labels

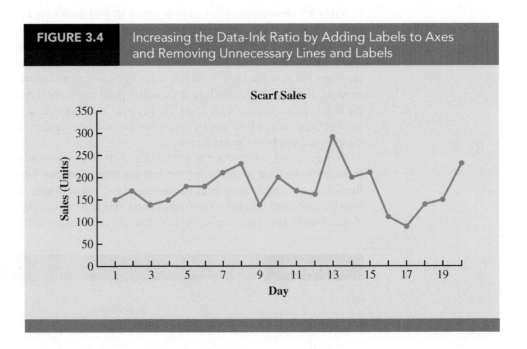

NOTES + COMMENTS

1. Tables have been used to display data for more than a thousand years. However, charts are much more recent inventions. The famous 17th-century French mathematician, René Descartes, is credited with inventing the now familiar graph with horizontal and vertical axes. William Playfair invented bar charts, line charts, and pie charts in the late 18th century, all of which we will discuss in this chapter. More recently, individuals such as William Cleveland, Edward R. Tufte, and Stephen Few have introduced design techniques for both clarity and beauty in data visualization.

2. Many of the default settings in Excel are not ideal for displaying data using tables and charts that communicate effectively. Before presenting Excel-generated tables and charts to others, it is worth the effort to remove unnecessary lines and labels.

TABLE 3.3	Table Showing Exact Values for Costs and Revenues by Month for Gossamer Industries						
	Month						
	1	**2**	**3**	**4**	**5**	**6**	**Total**
Costs ($)	48,123	56,458	64,125	52,158	54,718	50,985	326,567
Revenues ($)	64,124	66,128	67,125	48,178	51,785	55,687	353,027

3.2 Tables

The first decision in displaying data is whether a table or a chart will be more effective. In general, charts can often convey information faster and easier to readers, but in some cases a table is more appropriate. Tables should be used when the

1. reader needs to refer to specific numerical values.
2. reader needs to make precise comparisons between different values and not just relative comparisons.
3. values being displayed have different units or very different magnitudes.

When the accounting department of Gossamer Industries is summarizing the company's annual data for completion of its federal tax forms, the specific numbers corresponding to revenues and expenses are important and not just the relative values. Therefore, these data should be presented in a table similar to Table 3.3.

Similarly, if it is important to know by exactly how much revenues exceed expenses each month, then this would also be better presented as a table rather than as a line chart as seen in Figure 3.5. Notice that it is very difficult to determine the monthly revenues and costs in Figure 3.5. We could add these values using data labels, but they would clutter the figure. The preferred solution is to combine the chart with the table into a single figure, as in Figure 3.6, to allow the reader to easily see the monthly changes in revenues and costs while also being able to refer to the exact numerical values.

Now suppose that you wish to display data on revenues, costs, and head count for each month. Costs and revenues are measured in dollars, but head count is measured in number of employees. Although all these values can be displayed on a line chart using multiple

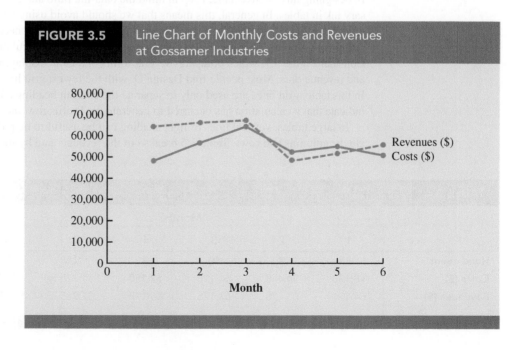

FIGURE 3.5 Line Chart of Monthly Costs and Revenues at Gossamer Industries

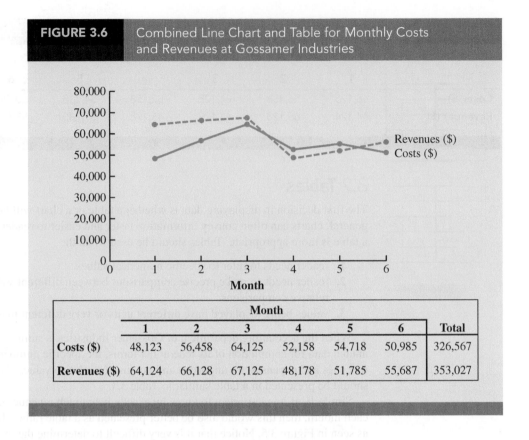

FIGURE 3.6 Combined Line Chart and Table for Monthly Costs and Revenues at Gossamer Industries

				Month			
	1	**2**	**3**	**4**	**5**	**6**	**Total**
Costs ($)	48,123	56,458	64,125	52,158	54,718	50,985	326,567
Revenues ($)	64,124	66,128	67,125	48,178	51,785	55,687	353,027

vertical axes, this is generally not recommended. Because the values have widely different magnitudes (costs and revenues are in the tens of thousands, whereas head count is approximately 10 each month), it would be difficult to interpret changes on a single chart. Therefore, a table similar to Table 3.4 is recommended.

Table Design Principles

In designing an effective table, keep in mind the data-ink ratio and avoid the use of unnecessary ink in tables. In general, this means that we should avoid using vertical lines in a table unless they are necessary for clarity. Horizontal lines are generally necessary only for separating column titles from data values or when indicating that a calculation has taken place. Consider Figure 3.7, which compares several forms of a table displaying Gossamer's costs and revenue data. Most people find Design D, with the fewest grid lines, easiest to read. In this table, grid lines are used only to separate the column headings from the data and to indicate that a calculation has occurred to generate the Profits row and the Total column.

In large tables, vertical lines or light shading can be useful to help the reader differentiate the columns and rows. Table 3.5 breaks out the revenue data by location for nine cities

TABLE 3.4 Table Displaying Head Count, Costs, and Revenues at Gossamer Industries

			Month				
	1	**2**	**3**	**4**	**5**	**6**	**Total**
Head count	8	9	10	9	9	9	
Costs ($)	48,123	56,458	64,125	52,158	54,718	50,985	326,567
Revenues ($)	64,124	66,128	67,125	48,178	51,785	55,687	353,027

FIGURE 3.7	Comparing Different Table Designs

Design A:

	Month						
	1	**2**	**3**	**4**	**5**	**6**	**Total**
Costs ($)	48,123	56,458	64,125	52,158	54,718	50,985	326,567
Revenues ($)	64,124	66,128	67,125	48,178	51,785	55,687	353,027
Profits ($)	16,001	9,670	3,000	(3,980)	(2,933)	4,702	26,460

Design C:

	Month						
	1	**2**	**3**	**4**	**5**	**6**	**Total**
Costs ($)	48,123	56,458	64,125	52,158	54,718	50,985	326,567
Revenues ($)	64,124	66,128	67,125	48,178	51,785	55,687	353,027
Profits ($)	16,001	9,670	3,000	(3,980)	(2,933)	4,702	26,460

Design B:

	Month						
	1	**2**	**3**	**4**	**5**	**6**	**Total**
Costs ($)	48,123	56,458	64,125	52,158	54,718	50,985	326,567
Revenues ($)	64,124	66,128	67,125	48,178	51,785	55,687	353,027
Profits ($)	16,001	9,670	3,000	(3,980)	(2,933)	4,702	26,460

Design D:

	Month						
	1	**2**	**3**	**4**	**5**	**6**	**Total**
Costs ($)	48,123	56,458	64,125	52,158	54,718	50,985	326,567
Revenues ($)	64,124	66,128	67,125	48,178	51,785	55,687	353,027
Profits ($)	16,001	9,670	3,000	(3,980)	(2,933)	4,702	26,460

and shows 12 months of revenue and cost data. In Table 3.5, every other column has been lightly shaded. This helps the reader quickly scan the table to see which values correspond with each month. The horizontal line between the revenue for Academy and the Total row helps the reader differentiate the revenue data for each location and indicates that a calculation has taken place to generate the totals by month. If one wanted to highlight the differences among locations, the shading could be done for every other row instead of every other column.

We depart from these guidelines in some figures and tables in this textbook to more closely match Excel's output.

Notice also the alignment of the text and numbers in Table 3.5. Columns of numerical values in a table should usually be right-aligned; that is, the final digit of each number should be aligned in the column. This makes it easy to see differences in the magnitude of values. If you are showing digits to the right of the decimal point, all values should include the same number of digits to the right of the decimal. Also, use only the number of digits that are necessary to convey the meaning in comparing the values; there is no need to include additional digits if they are not meaningful for comparisons. In many business applications, we report financial values, in which case we often round to the nearest dollar or include two digits to the right of the decimal if such precision is necessary. Additional digits to the right of the decimal are usually unnecessary. For extremely large numbers, we may prefer to display data rounded to the nearest thousand, ten thousand, or even million. For instance, if we need to include, say, $3,457,982 and $10,124,390 in a table when exact dollar values are not necessary, we could write these as 3.458 and 10.124 and indicate that all values in the table are in units of $1,000,000.

It is generally best to left-align text values within a column in a table, as in the Revenues by Location (the first) column of Table 3.5. In some cases, you may prefer to center text, but you should do this only if the text values are all approximately the same length. Otherwise, aligning the first letter of each data entry promotes readability. Column headings should either match the alignment of the data in the columns or be centered over the values, as in Table 3.5.

Crosstabulation

Types of data such as categorical and quantitative are discussed in Chapter 2.

A useful type of table for describing data of two variables is a **crosstabulation**, which provides a tabular summary of data for two variables. To illustrate, consider the following application based on data from Zagat's Restaurant Review. Data on the quality rating, meal price, and the usual wait time for a table during peak hours were collected for a sample of 300 Los Angeles area restaurants. Table 3.6 shows the data for the first 10 restaurants.

TABLE 3.5 Larger Table Showing Revenues by Location for 12 Months of Data

Revenues by Location ($)	1	2	3	4	5	6	7	8	9	10	11	12	Total
Temple	8,987	8,595	8,958	6,718	8,066	8,574	8,701	9,490	9,610	9,262	9,875	11,058	107,895
Killeen	8,212	9,143	8,714	6,869	8,150	8,891	8,766	9,193	9,603	10,374	10,456	10,982	109,353
Waco	11,603	12,063	11,173	9,622	8,912	9,553	11,943	12,947	12,925	14,050	14,300	13,877	142,967
Belton	7,671	7,617	7,896	6,899	7,877	6,621	7,765	7,720	7,824	7,938	7,943	7,047	90,819
Granger	7,642	7,744	7,836	5,833	6,002	6,728	7,848	7,717	7,646	7,620	7,728	8,013	88,357
Harker Heights	5,257	5,326	4,998	4,304	4,106	4,980	5,084	5,061	5,186	5,179	4,955	5,326	59,763
Gatesville	5,316	5,245	5,056	3,317	3,852	4,026	5,135	5,132	5,052	5,271	5,304	5,154	57,859
Lampasas	5,266	5,129	5,022	3,022	3,088	4,289	5,110	5,073	4,978	5,343	4,984	5,315	56,620
Academy	4,170	5,266	7,472	1,594	1,732	2,025	8,772	1,956	3,304	3,090	3,579	2,487	45,446
Total	64,124	66,128	67,125	48,178	51,785	55,687	69,125	64,288	66,128	68,128	69,125	69,258	759,079
Costs ($)	48,123	56,458	64,125	52,158	54,718	50,985	57,898	62,050	65,215	61,819	67,828	69,558	710,935

Month

TABLE 3.6	Quality Rating and Meal Price for 300 Los Angeles Restaurants		
Restaurant	**Quality Rating**	**Meal Price ($)**	**Wait Time (min)**
1	Good	18	5
2	Very Good	22	6
3	Good	28	1
4	Excellent	38	74
5	Very Good	33	6
6	Good	28	5
7	Very Good	19	11
8	Very Good	11	9
9	Very Good	23	13
10	Good	13	1

DATA*file*

Restaurant

Quality ratings are an example of categorical data, and meal prices are an example of quantitative data.

For now, we will limit our consideration to the quality-rating and meal-price variables. A crosstabulation of the data for quality rating and meal price is shown in Table 3.7. The left and top margin labels define the classes for the two variables. In the left margin, the row labels (Good, Very Good, and Excellent) correspond to the three classes of the quality-rating variable. In the top margin, the column labels ($10–19, $20–29, $30–39, and $40–49) correspond to the four classes (or bins) of the meal-price variable. Each restaurant in the sample provides a quality rating and a meal price. Thus, each restaurant in the sample is associated with a cell appearing in one of the rows and one of the columns of the crosstabulation. For example, restaurant 5 is identified as having a very good quality rating and a meal price of $33. This restaurant belongs to the cell in row 2 and column 3. In constructing a crosstabulation, we simply count the number of restaurants that belong to each of the cells in the crosstabulation.

Table 3.7 shows that the greatest number of restaurants in the sample (64) have a very good rating and a meal price in the $20–29 range. Only two restaurants have an excellent rating and a meal price in the $10–19 range. Similar interpretations of the other frequencies can be made. In addition, note that the right and bottom margins of the crosstabulation give the frequencies of quality rating and meal price separately. From the right margin, we see that data on quality ratings show 84 good restaurants, 150 very good restaurants, and 66 excellent restaurants. Similarly, the bottom margin shows the counts for the meal price variable. The value of 300 in the bottom-right corner of the table indicates that 300 restaurants were included in this data set.

TABLE 3.7	Crosstabulation of Quality Rating and Meal Price for 300 Los Angeles Restaurants				
	Meal Price				
Quality Rating	**$10–19**	**$20–29**	**$30–39**	**$40–49**	**Total**
Good	42	40	2	0	84
Very Good	34	64	46	6	150
Excellent	2	14	28	22	66
Total	78	118	76	28	300

PivotTables in Excel

A crosstabulation in Microsoft Excel is known as a **PivotTable**. We will first look at a simple example of how Excel's PivotTable is used to create a crosstabulation of the Zagat's restaurant data shown previously. Figure 3.8 illustrates a portion of the data contained in the file *Restaurant*; the data for the 300 restaurants in the sample have been entered into cells B2:D301.

To create a PivotTable in Excel, we follow these steps:

DATA*file*

Restaurant

Step 1. Click the **Insert** tab on the Ribbon
Step 2. Click **PivotTable** in the **Tables** group
Step 3. When the **Create PivotTable** dialog box appears:
　　　　　Choose **Select a table or range**
　　　　　Enter *A1:D301* in the **Table/Range:** box
　　　　　Select **New Worksheet** as the location for the PivotTable Report
　　　　　Click **OK**

The resulting initial PivotTable Field List and PivotTable Report are shown in Figure 3.9.

Each of the four columns in Figure 3.8 [Restaurant, Quality Rating, Meal Price ($), and Wait Time (min)] is considered a field by Excel. Fields may be chosen to represent rows, columns, or values in the body of the PivotTable Report. The following steps show how to use Excel's PivotTable Field List to assign the Quality Rating field to the rows, the Meal Price ($) field to the columns, and the Restaurant field to the body of the PivotTable report.

DATA*file*

Restaurant

FIGURE 3.8	Excel Worksheet Containing Restaurant Data

	A	**B**	**C**	**D**
1	Restaurant	Quality Rating	Meal Price ($)	Wait Time (min)
2	1	Good	18	5
3	2	Very Good	22	6
4	3	Good	28	1
5	4	Excellent	38	74
6	5	Very Good	33	6
7	6	Good	28	5
8	7	Very Good	19	11
9	8	Very Good	11	9
10	9	Very Good	23	13
11	10	Good	13	1
12	11	Very Good	33	18
13	12	Very Good	44	7
14	13	Excellent	42	18
15	14	Excellent	34	46
16	15	Good	25	0
17	16	Good	22	3
18	17	Good	26	3
19	18	Excellent	17	36
20	19	Very Good	30	7
21	20	Good	19	3
22	21	Very Good	33	10
23	22	Very Good	22	14
24	23	Excellent	32	27
25	24	Excellent	33	80
26	25	Very Good	34	9

FIGURE 3.9   Initial PivotTable Field List and PivotTable Field Report for the Restaurant Data

Step 4.   In the **PivotTable Fields** task pane, go to **Drag fields between areas below:**
 Drag the **Quality Rating** field to the **ROWS** area
 Drag the **Meal Price ($)** field to the **COLUMNS** area
 Drag the **Restaurant** field to the **VALUES** area
Step 5.   Click on **Sum of Restaurant** in the **VALUES** area
Step 6.   Select **Value Field Settings** from the list of options
Step 7.   When the **Value Field Settings** dialog box appears:
 Under **Summarize value field by**, select **Count**
 Click **OK**

Figure 3.10 shows the completed PivotTable Field List and a portion of the PivotTable worksheet as it now appears.

To complete the PivotTable, we need to group the columns representing meal prices and place the row labels for quality rating in the proper order:

Step 8.   Right-click in cell B4 or any other cell containing a meal price column label
Step 9.   Select **Group** from the list of options
Step 10.   When the **Grouping** dialog box appears:
 Enter *10* in the **Starting at:** box
 Enter *49* in the **Ending at:** box
 Enter *10* in the **By:** box
 Click **OK**
Step 11.   Right-click on "Excellent" in cell A5
Step 12.   Select **Move** and click **Move "Excellent" to End**

The final PivotTable, shown in Figure 3.11, provides the same information as the crosstabulation in Table 3.7.

The values in Figure 3.11 can be interpreted as the frequencies of the data. For instance, row 8 provides the frequency distribution for the data over the quantitative variable of meal price. Seventy-eight restaurants have meal prices of $10 to $19. Column F provides the frequency distribution for the data over the categorical variable of quality.

FIGURE 3.10   Completed PivotTable Field List and a Portion of the PivotTable Report for the Restaurant Data (Columns H:AK Are Hidden)

Count of Restaurant	Columns Labels ▾	10	11	12	13	14	15	47	48	Grand Total
Row Labels ▾										
Excellent					1			2	2	66
Good		6	4	3	3	2	4			84
Very Good		1	4	3	5	6	1		1	150
Grand Total		7	8	6	9	8	5	2	3	300

PivotTable Fields   ▾ ✕

Choose fields to add to report:

☑ **Restaurant**
☑ **Quality Rating**
☑ **Meal Price ($)**
☐ Wait Time (min)

MORE TABLES...

Drag fields between areas below:

▼ FILTERS

▦ COLUMNS
Meal Price ($)   ▾

▦ ROWS
Quality Rating   ▾

Σ VALUES
Count of Restaur... ▾

FIGURE 3.11   Final PivotTable Report for the Restaurant Data

Count of Restaurant	Column Labels ▾	10–19	20–29	30–39	40–49	Grand Total
Row Labels ▾						
Good		42	40	2		84
Very Good		34	64	46	6	150
Excellent		2	14	28	22	66
Grand Total		78	118	76	28	300

PivotTable Fields   ▾ ✕

Choose fields to add to report:

☑ **Restaurant**
☑ **Quality Rating**
☑ **Meal Price ($)**
☐ Wait Time (min)

MORE TABLES...

Drag fields between areas below:

▼ FILTERS

▦ COLUMNS
Meal Price ($)   ▾

▦ ROWS
Quality Rating   ▾

Σ VALUES
Count of Restaur... ▾

A total of 150 restaurants have a quality rating of Very Good. We can also use a PivotTable to create percent frequency distributions, as shown in the following steps:

Step 1. To invoke the **PivotTable Fields** task pane, select any cell in the pivot table

Step 2. In the **PivotTable Fields** task pane, click the **Count of Restaurant** in the **VALUES** area

Step 3. Select **Value Field Settings . . .** from the list of options

Step 4. When the **Value Field Settings** dialog box appears, click the tab for **Show Values As**

Step 5. In the **Show values as** area, select **% of Grand Total** from the drop-down menu
Click **OK**

Figure 3.12 displays the percent frequency distribution for the Restaurant data as a PivotTable. The figure indicates that 50% of the restaurants are in the Very Good quality category and that 26% have meal prices between $10 and $19.

PivotTables in Excel are interactive, and they may be used to display statistics other than a simple count of items. As an illustration, we can easily modify the PivotTable in Figure 3.11 to display summary information on wait times instead of meal prices.

Step 1. To invoke the **PivotTable Fields** task pane, select any cell in the pivot table

Step 2. In the **PivotTable Fields** task pane, click the **Count of Restaurant** field in the **VALUES** area
Select **Remove Field**

Step 3. Drag the **Wait Time (min)** to the **VALUES** area

Step 4. Click on **Sum of Wait Time (min)** in the **VALUES** area

Step 5. Select **Value Field Settings...** from the list of options

Step 6. When the **Value Field Settings** dialog box appears:
Under **Summarize value field by**, select **Average**
Click **Number Format**
In the **Category:** area, select **Number**
Enter *1* for **Decimal places:**
Click **OK**
When the **Value Field Settings** dialog box reappears, click **OK**

FIGURE 3.12 Percent Frequency Distribution as a PivotTable for the Restaurant Data

	A	B	C	D	E	F	G
1							
2							
3	Count of Restaurant	Column					
4	Row Labels	Labels 10–19	20–29	30–39	40–49	Grand Total	
5	Good	14.00%	13.33%	0.67%	0.00%	28.00%	
6	Very Good	11.33%	21.33%	15.33%	2.00%	50.00%	
7	Excellent	0.67%	4.67%	9.33%	7.33%	22.00%	
8	Grand Total	26.00%	39.33%	25.33%	9.33%	100.00%	
9							
10							
11							
12							
13							
16							
15							
16							
17							
18							

PivotTable Fields

Choose fields to add to report:

☑ Restaurant
☑ Quality Rating
☑ Meal Price ($)
☐ Wait Time (min)

MORE TABLES...

Drag fields between areas below:

▼ FILTERS   ▦ COLUMNS
                 Meal Price ($)

▦ ROWS   Σ VALUES
Quality Rating   Count of Restaurant

The completed PivotTable appears in Figure 3.13. This PivotTable replaces the counts of restaurants with values for the average wait time for a table at a restaurant for each grouping of meal prices ($10–19, $20–29, $30–39, and $40–49). For instance, cell B7 indicates that the average wait time for a table at an Excellent restaurant with a meal price of $10–19 is 25.5 minutes. Column F displays the total average wait times for tables in each quality rating category. We see that Excellent restaurants have the longest average wait of 35.2 minutes and that Good restaurants have an average wait time of only 2.5 minutes. Finally, cell D7 shows us that the longest wait times can be expected at Excellent restaurants with meal prices in the $30–39 range (34 minutes).

*You can also filter data in a PivotTable by dragging the field that you want to filter to the **FILTERS** area in the **PivotTable Fields**.*

We can also examine only a portion of the data in a PivotTable using the Filter option in Excel. To Filter data in a PivotTable, click on the **Filter Arrow** ▼ next to **Row Labels** or **Column Labels** and then uncheck the values that you want to remove from the PivotTable. For example, we could click on the arrow next to Row Labels and then uncheck the Good value to examine only Very Good and Excellent restaurants.

Recommended PivotTables in Excel

Excel also has the ability to recommend PivotTables for your data set. To illustrate Recommended PivotTables in Excel, we return to the restaurant data in Figure 3.8. To create a Recommended PivotTable, follow the steps below using the file *Restaurant*.

Hovering your pointer over the different options will display the full name of each option, as shown in Figure 3.14.

Step 1. Select any cell in table of data (for example, cell A1)
Step 2. Click the **Insert** tab on the Ribbon
Step 3. Click **Recommended PivotTables** in the **Tables** group
Step 4. When the **Recommended PivotTables** dialog box appears:
Select the **Count of Restaurant, Sum of Wait Time (min), Sum of Meal Price ($) by Quality Rating** option (see Figure 3.14)
Click **OK**

The steps above will create the PivotTable shown in Figure 3.15 on a new Worksheet. The Recommended PivotTables tool in Excel is useful for quickly creating commonly used PivotTables for a data set, but note that it may not give you the option to create the

FIGURE 3.13   PivotTable Report for the Restaurant Data with Average Wait Times Added

	A	B	C	D	E	F	G
1							
2							
3	Average of Wait Time (min) Column	▼					
4	Row Labels ▼	Labels 10–19	20–29	30–39	40–49	Grand Total	
5	Good	2.6	2.5	0.5		2.5	
6	Very Good	12.6	12.6	12.0	10.0	12.3	
7	Excellent	25.5	29.1	34.0	32.3	32.1	
8	Grand Total	7.6	11.1	19.8	27.5	13.9	
9							
10							
11							
12							
13							
16							
15							
16							
17							

PivotTable Fields

Choose fields to add to report:
☐ Restaurant
☑ Quality Rating
☑ Meal Price ($)
☑ Wait Time (min)

Drag fields between areas below:

▼ FILTERS   ▦ COLUMNS
                   Meal Price ($)   ▼

▦ ROWS   Σ VALUES
Quality Rating ▼ Average of Wait Time (... ▼

FIGURE 3.14 Recommended PivotTables Dialog Box in Excel

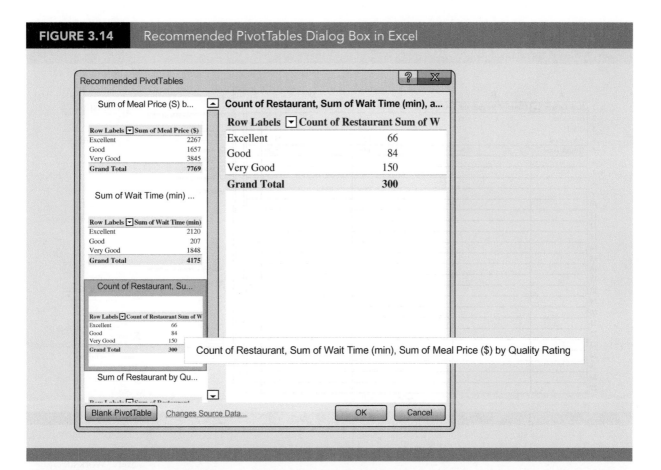

FIGURE 3.15 Default PivotTable Created for Restaurant Data Using Excel's Recommended PivotTables Tool

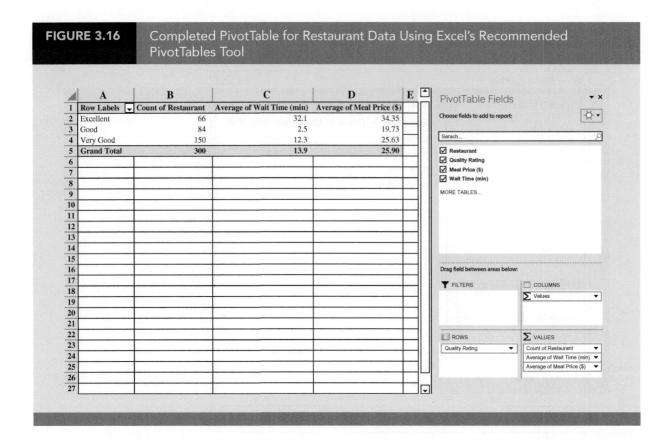

FIGURE 3.16 Completed PivotTable for Restaurant Data Using Excel's Recommended PivotTables Tool

exact PivotTable that will be of the most use for your data analysis. Displaying the sum of wait times and the sum of meal prices within each quality-rating category, as shown in Figure 3.15, is not particularly useful here; the average wait times and average meal prices within each quality-rating category would be more useful to us. But we can easily modify the PivotTable in Figure 3.14 to show the average values by selecting any cell in the PivotTable to invoke the **PivotTable Fields** task pane, clicking on **Sum of Wait Time (min)** and then **Sum of Meal Price ($)**, and using the **Value Field Settings…** to change the **Summarize value field by** option to **Average**. The finished PivotTable is shown in Figure 3.16.

3.3 Charts

Charts (or graphs) are visual methods for displaying data. In this section, we introduce some of the most commonly used charts to display and analyze data including scatter charts, line charts, and bar charts. Excel is the most commonly used software package for creating simple charts. We explain how to use Excel to create scatter charts, line charts, sparklines, bar charts, bubble charts, and heat maps.

Scatter Charts

A **scatter chart** is a graphical presentation of the relationship between two quantitative variables. As an illustration, consider the advertising/sales relationship for an electronics store in San Francisco. On 10 occasions during the past three months, the store used weekend television commercials to promote sales at its stores. The managers want to investigate whether a relationship exists between the number of commercials shown and sales at the store the following week. Sample data for the 10 weeks, with sales in hundreds of dollars, are shown in Table 3.8.

TABLE 3.8	Sample Data for the San Francisco Electronics Store	
	No. of Commercials	**Sales ($100s)**
Week	*x*	*y*
1	2	50
2	5	57
3	1	41
4	3	54
5	4	54
6	1	38
7	5	63
8	3	48
9	4	59
10	2	46

DATA *file*

Electronics

We will use the data from Table 3.8 to create a scatter chart using Excel's chart tools and the data in the file *Electronics*:

Step 1. Select cells B2:C11
Step 2. Click the **Insert** tab in the Ribbon
Step 3. Click the **Insert Scatter (X,Y) or Bubble Chart** button ⊞ ▾ in the **Charts** group

Hovering the pointer over the chart type buttons in Excel will display the names of the buttons and short descriptions of the types of chart.

Step 4. When the list of scatter chart subtypes appears, click the **Scatter** button
Step 5. Click the **Design** tab under the **Chart Tools** Ribbon
Step 6. Click **Add Chart Element** in the **Chart Layouts** group
Select **Chart Title**, and click **Above Chart**
Click on the text box above the chart, and replace the text with *Scatter Chart for the San Francisco Electronics Store*
Step 7. Click **Add Chart Element** in the **Chart Layouts** group
Select **Axis Title**, and click **Primary Horizontal**
Click on the text box under the horizontal axis, and replace "Axis Title" with *Number of Commercials*
Step 8. Click **Add Chart Element** in the **Chart Layouts** group
Select **Axis Title,** and click **Primary Vertical**
Click on the text box next to the vertical axis, and replace "Axis Title" with *Sales ($100s)*

Steps 9 and 10 are optional, but they improve the chart's readability. We would want to retain the gridlines only if they helped the reader to determine more precisely where data points are located relative to certain values on the horizontal and/or vertical axes.

Step 9. Right-click on one of the horizontal grid lines in the body of the chart, and click **Delete**
Step 10. Right-click on one of the vertical grid lines in the body of the chart, and click **Delete**

We can also use Excel to add a trendline to the scatter chart. A **trendline** is a line that provides an approximation of the relationship between the variables. To add a linear trendline using Excel, we use the following steps:

Step 1. Right-click on one of the data points in the scatter chart, and select **Add Trendline…**
Step 2. When the **Format Trendline** task pane appears, select **Linear** under **Trendline Options**

Figure 3.17 shows the scatter chart and linear trendline created with Excel for the data in Table 3.8. The number of commercials (*x*) is shown on the horizontal axis, and sales (*y*)

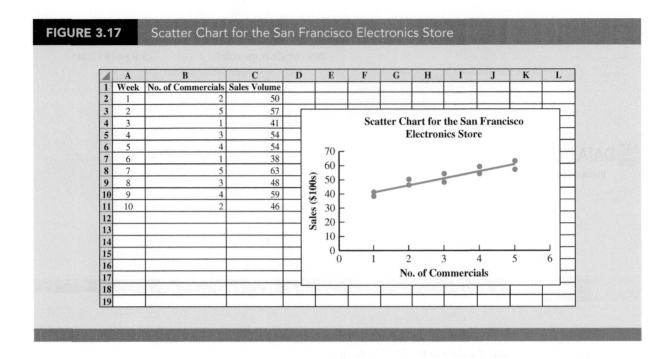

FIGURE 3.17   Scatter Chart for the San Francisco Electronics Store

are shown on the vertical axis. For week 1, $x = 2$ and $y = 50$. A point is plotted on the scatter chart at those coordinates; similar points are plotted for the other nine weeks. Note that during two of the weeks, one commercial was shown, during two of the weeks, two commercials were shown, and so on.

Scatter charts are often referred to as scatter plots or scatter diagrams.

The completed scatter chart in Figure 3.17 indicates a positive linear relationship (or positive correlation) between the number of commercials and sales: Higher sales are associated with a higher number of commercials. The linear relationship is not perfect because not all of the points are on a straight line. However, the general pattern of the points and the trendline suggest that the overall relationship is positive. This implies that the covariance between sales and commercials is positive and that the correlation coefficient between these two variables is between 0 and +1.

Chapter 2 introduces scatter charts and relates them to the concepts of covariance and correlation.

The **Chart Buttons** in Excel allow users to quickly modify and format charts. Three buttons appear next to a chart whenever you click on a chart to make it active. Clicking on the **Chart Elements** button ➕ brings up a list of check boxes to quickly add and remove axes, axis titles, chart titles, data labels, trendlines, and more. Clicking on the **Chart Styles** button 🖌 allows the user to quickly choose from many preformatted styles to change the look of the chart. Clicking on the **Chart Filter** button ▼ allows the user to select the data to be included in the chart. The Chart Filter button is very useful for performing additional data analysis.

Recommended Charts in Excel

Similar to the ability to recommend PivotTables, Excel has the ability to recommend charts for a given data set. The steps below demonstrate the Recommended Charts tool in Excel for the *Electronics* data.

DATA *file*

Electronics

Step 1.   Select cells B2:C11

Step 2:   Click the **Insert** tab in the Ribbon

Step 3:   Click the **Recommended Charts** button in the **Charts** group

Step 4:   When the **Insert Chart** dialog box appears, select the **Scatter** option (see Figure 3.18)
Click **OK**

These steps create the basic scatter chart that can then be formatted (using the Chart Buttons or Chart Tools Ribbon) to create the completed scatter chart shown in Figure 3.17. Note that the Recommended Charts tool gives several possible recommendations for the electronics data in Figure 3.18. These recommendations include scatter charts, line charts, and bar charts, which will be covered later in this chapter. Excel's Recommended Charts tool generally does a good job of interpreting your data and providing recommended charts, but take care to ensure that the selected chart is meaningful and follows good design practice.

Line Charts

A line chart for time series data is often called a time series plot.

Line charts are similar to scatter charts, but a line connects the points in the chart. Line charts are very useful for time series data collected over a period of time (minutes, hours, days, years, etc.). As an example, Kirkland Industries sells air compressors to manufacturing companies. Table 3.9 contains total sales amounts (in $100s) for air compressors during

FIGURE 3.18   Insert Chart Dialog Box from Recommended Charts Tool in Excel

TABLE 3.9	Monthly Sales Data of Air Compressors at Kirkland Industries
Month	**Sales ($100s)**
Jan	135
Feb	145
Mar	175
Apr	180
May	160
Jun	135
Jul	210
Aug	175
Sep	160
Oct	120
Nov	115
Dec	120

DATA *file*

Kirkland

each month in the most recent calendar year. Figure 3.19 displays a scatter chart and a line chart created in Excel for these sales data. The line chart connects the points of the scatter chart. The addition of lines between the points suggests continuity, and it is easier for the reader to interpret changes over time.

To create the line chart in Figure 3.19 in Excel, we follow these steps:

Step 1. Select cells A2:B13
Step 2. Click the **Insert** tab on the Ribbon
Step 3. Click the **Insert Line Chart** button in the **Charts** group
Step 4. When the list of line chart subtypes appears, click the **Line with Markers** button under **2-D Line**

This creates a line chart for sales with a basic layout and minimum formatting
Step 5. Select the line chart that was just created to reveal the **Chart Buttons**

In the line chart in Figure 3.19, we have kept the markers at each data point. This is a matter of personal taste, but removing the markers tends to suggest that the data are continuous when in fact we have only one data point per month.

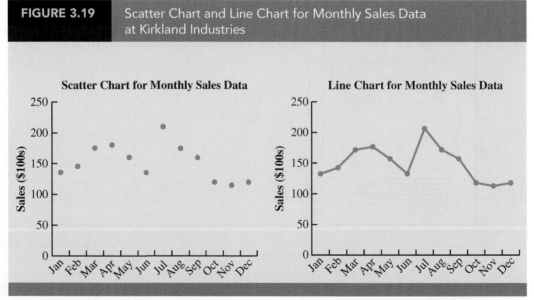

FIGURE 3.19	Scatter Chart and Line Chart for Monthly Sales Data at Kirkland Industries

Step 6. Click the **Chart Elements** button ⊞
 Select the check boxes for **Axes**, **Axis Titles**, and **Chart Title**
 Deselect the check box for **Gridlines**
 Click on the text box next to the vertical axis, and replace "Axis Title" with *Sales ($100s)*
 Click on the text box next to the horizontal axis and replace "Axis Title" with *Month*
 Click on the text box above the chart, and replace "Sales ($100s)" with *Line Chart for Monthly Sales Data*

*Because the gridlines do not add any meaningful information here, we do not select the check box for **Gridlines** in **Chart Elements**, as it increases the data-ink ratio.*

Figure 3.20 shows the line chart created in Excel along with the selected options for the Chart Elements button.

Line charts can also be used to graph multiple lines. Suppose we want to break out Kirkland's sales data by region (North and South), as shown in Table 3.10. We can create a line chart in Excel that shows sales in both regions, as in Figure 3.21 by following similar steps but selecting cells A2:C14 in the file *KirklandRegional* before creating the line chart. Figure 3.21 shows an interesting pattern. Sales in both the North and the South regions seemed to follow the same increasing/decreasing pattern until October. Starting in October, sales in the North continued to decrease while sales in the South increased. We would probably want to investigate any changes that occurred in the North region around October.

A special type of line chart is a **sparkline**, which is a minimalist type of line chart that can be placed directly into a cell in Excel. Sparklines contain no axes; they display only the line for the data. Sparklines take up very little space, and they can be effectively used to provide information on overall trends for time series data. Figure 3.22 illustrates the use of sparklines in Excel for the regional sales data. To create a sparkline in Excel:

DATA *file*
KirklandRegional

Step 1. Click the **Insert** tab on the Ribbon
Step 2. Click **Line** in the **Sparklines** group

FIGURE 3.20 Line Chart and Excel's Chart Elements Button Options for Monthly Sales Data at Kirkland Industries

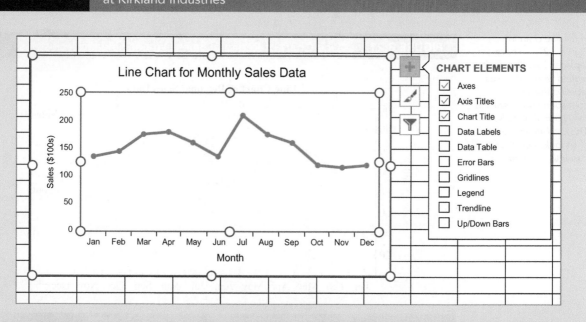

TABLE 3.10	Regional Sales Data by Month for Air Compressors at Kirkland Industries		
		Sales ($100s)	
Month	North		South
Jan	95		40
Feb	100		45
Mar	120		55
Apr	115		65
May	100		60
Jun	85		50
Jul	135		75
Aug	110		65
Sep	100		60
Oct	50		70
Nov	40		75
Dec	40		80

DATA *file*

KirklandRegional

Step 3. When the **Create Sparklines** dialog box appears:
Enter *B3:B14* in the **Data Range:** box
Enter *B15* in the **Location Range:** box
Click **OK**

Step 4. Copy cell B15 to cell C15

The sparklines in cells B15 and C15 do not indicate the magnitude of sales in the North and the South regions, but they do show the overall trend for these data. Sales in the North appear to be decreasing and sales in the South increasing overall. Because sparklines are input directly into the cell in Excel, we can also type text directly into the same cell that will then be overlaid on the sparkline, or we can add shading to the cell, which will appear as the background. In Figure 3.22, we have shaded cells B15 and C15 to highlight the sparklines. As can be seen, sparklines provide an efficient and simple way to display basic information about a time series.

In the line chart in Figure 3.21, we have replaced Excel's default legend with text boxes labeling the lines corresponding to sales in the North and the South. This can often make the chart look cleaner and easier to interpret.

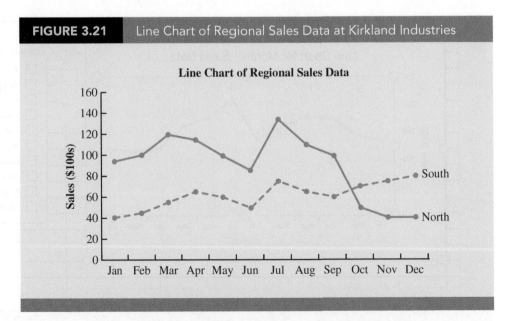

FIGURE 3.21   Line Chart of Regional Sales Data at Kirkland Industries

FIGURE 3.22 Sparklines for the Regional Sales Data at Kirkland Industries

▲	A	B	C	D	E	F	G	H	I
1		Sales ($100s)							
2	Month	North	South						
3	Jan	95	40						
4	Feb	100	45						
5	Mar	120	55						
6	Apr	115	65						
7	May	100	60						
8	Jun	85	50						
9	Jul	135	75						
10	Aug	110	65						
11	Sep	100	60						
12	Oct	50	70						
13	Nov	40	75						
14	Dec	40	80						
15									

Create Sparklines

Choose the data that you want

Data Range: B3:B14

Choose where you want the sparklines to be placed

Location Range: B15

OK   Cancel

Bar Charts and Column Charts

DATA *file*

AccountsManaged

Bar charts and column charts provide a graphical summary of categorical data. **Bar charts** use horizontal bars to display the magnitude of the quantitative variable. **Column charts** use vertical bars to display the magnitude of the quantitative variable. Bar and column charts are very helpful in making comparisons between categorical variables. Consider a regional supervisor who wants to examine the number of accounts being handled by each manager. Figure 3.23 shows a bar chart created in Excel displaying these data. To create this bar chart in Excel:

Step 1. Select cells A2:B9
Step 2. Click the **Insert** tab on the Ribbon
Step 3. Click the **Insert Column or Bar Chart** button ▾ in the **Charts** group
Step 4. When the list of bar chart subtypes appears:

Click the **Clustered Bar** button in the **2-D Bar** section

Step 5. Select the bar chart that was just created to reveal the **Chart Buttons**
Step 6. Click the **Chart Elements** button ⊞

Select the check boxes for **Axes**, **Axis Titles**, and **Chart Title**
Deselect the check box for **Gridlines**
Click on the text box next to the vertical axis, and replace "Axis Title" with *Accounts Managed*
Click on the text box next to the vertical axis, and replace "Axis Title" with *Manager*
Click on the text box above the chart, and replace "Chart Title" with *Bar Chart of Accounts Managed*

From Figure 3.23 we can see that Gentry manages the greatest number of accounts and Williams the fewest. We can make this bar chart even easier to read by ordering the results by the number of accounts managed. We can do this with the following steps:

Step 1. Select cells A1:B9
Step 2. Right-click any of the cells A1:B9

Select **Sort**
Click **Custom Sort**

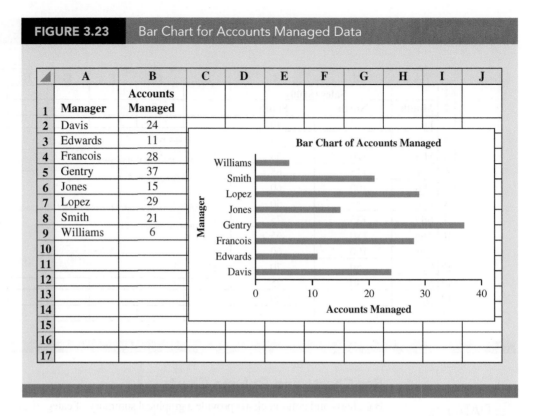

FIGURE 3.23   Bar Chart for Accounts Managed Data

Step 3. When the **Sort** dialog box appears:
Make sure that the check box for **My data has headers** is checked
Select **Accounts Managed** in the **Sort by** box under **Column**
Select **Smallest to Largest** under **Order**
Click **OK**

In the completed bar chart in Excel, shown in Figure 3.24, we can easily compare the relative number of accounts managed for all managers. However, note that it is difficult to interpret from the bar chart exactly how many accounts are assigned to each manager. If this information is necessary, these data are better presented as a table or by adding data labels to the bar chart, as in Figure 3.25, which is created in Excel using the following steps:

Step 1. Select the chart to reveal the **Chart Buttons**
Step 2. Click the **Chart Elements** button ⊞

Alternatively, you can add Data Labels by right-clicking on a bar in the chart and selecting ***Add Data Labels****.*

Select the check box for **Data Labels**

This adds labels of the number of accounts managed to the end of each bar so that the reader can easily look up exact values displayed in the bar chart.

A Note on Pie Charts and Three-Dimensional Charts

Pie charts are another common form of chart used to compare categorical data. However, many experts argue that pie charts are inferior to bar charts for comparing data. The pie chart in Figure 3.26 displays the data for the number of accounts managed in Figure 3.23. Visually, it is still relatively easy to see that Gentry has the greatest number of accounts and that Williams has the fewest. However, it is difficult to say whether Lopez or Francois has more accounts. Research has shown that people find it very difficult to perceive differences in area. Compare Figure 3.26 to Figure 3.24. Making visual comparisons is much easier in the bar chart than in the pie chart (particularly when using a limited number of colors for differentiation). Therefore, we recommend against using pie charts in most situations and suggest instead using bar charts for comparing categorical data.

FIGURE 3.24   Sorted Bar Chart for Accounts Managed Data

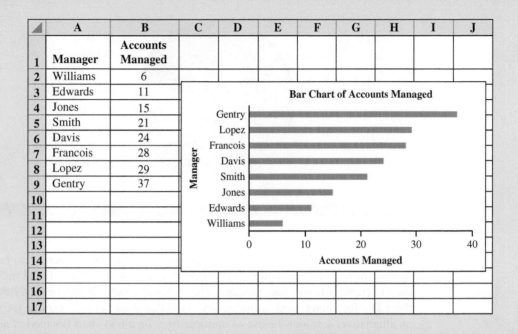

FIGURE 3.25   Bar Chart with Data Labels for Accounts Managed Data

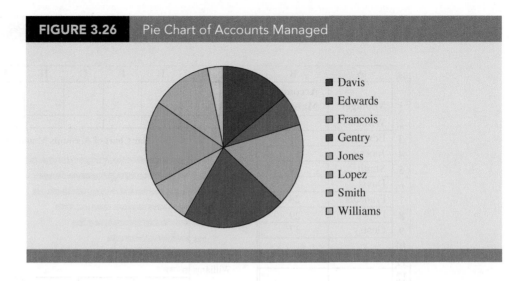

FIGURE 3.26   Pie Chart of Accounts Managed

■ Davis
■ Edwards
□ Francois
■ Gentry
□ Jones
■ Lopez
□ Smith
□ Williams

Because of the difficulty in visually comparing area, many experts also recommend against the use of three-dimensional (3-D) charts in most settings. Excel makes it very easy to create 3-D bar, line, pie, and other types of charts. In most cases, however, the 3-D effect simply adds unnecessary detail that does not help explain the data. As an alternative, consider the use of multiple lines on a line chart (instead of adding a z-axis), employing multiple charts, or creating bubble charts in which the size of the bubble can represent the z-axis value. Never use a 3-D chart when a two-dimensional chart will suffice.

Bubble Charts

A **bubble chart** is a graphical means of visualizing three variables in a two-dimensional graph and is therefore sometimes a preferred alternative to a 3-D graph. Suppose that we want to compare the number of billionaires in various countries. Table 3.11 provides a sample of six countries, showing, for each country, the number of billionaires per 10 million residents, the per capita income, and the total number of billionaires. We can create a bubble chart using Excel to further examine these data:

DATA *file*

Billionaires

Step 1.   Select cells B2:D7
Step 2.   Click the **Insert** tab on the Ribbon
Step 3.   In the **Charts** group, click **Insert Scatter (X,Y) or Bubble Chart**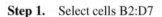

In the **Bubble** subgroup, click **Bubble**

Step 4.   Select the chart that was just created to reveal the **Chart Buttons**

TABLE 3.11   Sample Data on Billionaires per Country

Country	Billionaires per 10M Residents	Per Capita Income	No. of Billionaires
United States	54.7	$54,600	1,764
China	1.5	$12,880	213
Germany	12.5	$45,888	103
India	0.7	$ 5,855	90
Russia	6.2	$24,850	88
Mexico	1.2	$17,881	15

Step 5.   Click the **Chart Elements** button ➕

      Select the check boxes for **Axes**, **Axis Titles**, **Chart Title** and **Data Labels**. **Deselect** the check box for **Gridlines**.
      Click on the text box under the horizontal axis, and replace "Axis Title" with *Billionaires per 10 Million Residents*
      Click on the text box next to the vertical axis, and replace "Axis Title" with *Per Capita Income*
      Click on the text box above the chart, and replace "Chart Title" with *Billionaires by Country*

Step 6.   Double-click on one of the Data Labels in the chart (e.g., the "$54,600" next to the largest bubble in the chart) to reveal the **Format Data Labels** task pane

Step 7.   In the **Format Data Labels** task pane, click the **Label Options** icon ▮▮▮ and open the **Label Options** area
      Under **Label Contains**, select **Value from Cells** and click the **Select Range...** button
      When the **Data Label Range** dialog box opens, select cells A2:A8 in the Worksheet
      Click **OK**

Step 8.   In the **Format Data Labels** task pane, deselect **Y Value** under **Label Contains**, and select **Right** under **Label Position**

The completed bubble chart appears in Figure 3.27. This size of each bubble in Figure 3.27 is proportionate to the number of billionaires in that country. The per capita income and billionaires per 10 million residents is displayed on the vertical and horizontal axes. This chart shows us that the United States has the most billionaires and the highest number of billionaires per 10 million residents. We can also see that China has quite a few billionaires but with much lower per capita income and much lower billionaires per 10 million residents (because of China's much larger population). Germany, Russia, and India all appear to have similar numbers of billionaires, but the per capita income and billionaires per 10 million residents are very different for each country. Bubble charts can be very effective for comparing categorical variables on two different quantitative values.

Heat Maps

A **heat map** is a two-dimensional graphical representation of data that uses different shades of color to indicate magnitude. Figure 3.28 shows a heat map indicating the magnitude of changes for a metric called same-store sales, which are commonly used in the retail industry to measure trends in sales. The cells shaded red in Figure 3.28 indicate declining same-store sales for the month, and cells shaded blue indicate increasing same-store sales for the month. Column N in Figure 3.28 also contains sparklines for the same-store sales data.
    Figure 3.28 can be created in Excel by following these steps:

DATA *file*

SameStoreSales

Step 1.   Select cells B2:M17
Step 2.   Click the **Home** tab on the Ribbon
Step 3.   Click **Conditional Formatting** in the **Styles** group
      Select **Color Scales** and click on **Blue–White–Red Color Scale**

To add the sparklines in column N, we use the following steps:

Step 4.   Select cell N2
Step 5.   Click the **Insert** tab on the Ribbon
Step 6.   Click **Line** in the **Sparklines** group
Step 7.   When the **Create Sparklines** dialog box appears:
      Enter *B2:M2* in the **Data Range:** box
      Enter *N2* in the **Location Range:** box
      Click **OK**
Step 8.   Copy cell N2 to N3:N17

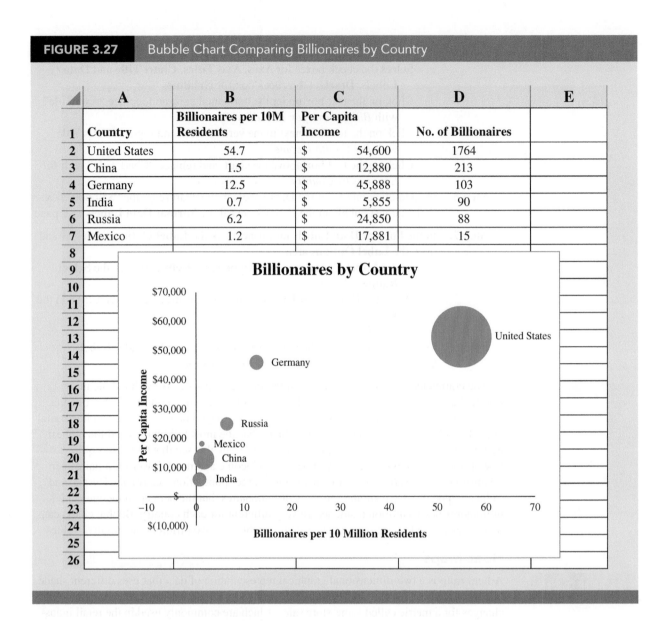

FIGURE 3.27   Bubble Chart Comparing Billionaires by Country

	A	B	C		D	E
1	Country	Billionaires per 10M Residents	Per Capita Income		No. of Billionaires	
2	United States	54.7	$	54,600	1764	
3	China	1.5	$	12,880	213	
4	Germany	12.5	$	45,888	103	
5	India	0.7	$	5,855	90	
6	Russia	6.2	$	24,850	88	
7	Mexico	1.2	$	17,881	15	

*Both the heat map and the sparklines described here can also be created using the **Quick Analysis** button. To display this button, select cells B2:M17. The **Quick Analysis** button will appear at the bottom right of the selected cells. Click the button to display options for heat maps, sparklines, and other data-analysis tools.*

The heat map in Figure 3.28 helps the reader to easily identify trends and patterns. We can see that Austin has had positive increases throughout the year, while Pittsburgh has had consistently negative same-store sales results. Same-store sales at Cincinnati started the year negative but then became increasingly positive after May. In addition, we can differentiate between strong positive increases in Austin and less substantial positive increases in Chicago by means of color shadings. A sales manager could use the heat map in Figure 3.28 to identify stores that may require intervention and stores that may be used as models. Heat maps can be used effectively to convey data over different areas, across time, or both, as seen here.

Because heat maps depend strongly on the use of color to convey information, one must be careful to make sure that the colors can be easily differentiated and that they do not become overwhelming. To avoid problems with interpreting differences in color, we can add sparklines as shown in column N of Figure 3.28. The sparklines clearly show the overall trend (increasing or decreasing) for each location. However, we cannot gauge

	A	B	C	D	E	F	G	H	I	J	K	L	M	N
1		JAN	FEB	MAR	APR	MAY	JUN	JUL	AUG	SEP	OCT	NOV	DEC	SPARKLINES
2	St. Louis	–2%	–1%	–1%	0%	2%	4%	3%	5%	6%	7%	8%	8%	
3	Phoenix	5%	4%	4%	2%	2%	–2%	–5%	–8%	–6%	–5%	–7%	–8%	
4	Albany	–5%	–6%	–4%	–5%	–2%	–5%	–5%	–3%	–1%	–2%	–1%	–2%	
5	Austin	16%	15%	15%	16%	18%	17%	14%	15%	16%	19%	18%	16%	
6	Cincinnati	–9%	–6%	–7%	–3%	3%	6%	8%	11%	10%	11%	13%	11%	
7	San Francisco	2%	4%	5%	8%	4%	2%	4%	3%	1%	–1%	1%	2%	
8	Seattle	7%	7%	8%	7%	5%	4%	2%	0%	–2%	–4%	–6%	–5%	
9	Chicago	5%	3%	2%	6%	8%	7%	8%	5%	8%	10%	9%	8%	
10	Atlanta	12%	14%	13%	17%	12%	11%	8%	7%	7%	8%	5%	3%	
11	Miami	2%	3%	0%	1%	–1%	–4%	–6%	–8%	–11%	–13%	–11%	–10%	
12	Minneapolis	–6%	–6%	–8%	–5%	–6%	–5%	–5%	–7%	–5%	–2%	–1%	–2%	
13	Denver	5%	4%	1%	1%	2%	3%	1%	–1%	0%	1%	2%	3%	
14	Salt Lake City	7%	7%	7%	13%	12%	8%	5%	9%	10%	9%	7%	6%	
15	Raleigh	4%	2%	0%	5%	4%	3%	5%	5%	9%	11%	8%	6%	
16	Boston	–5%	–5%	–3%	4%	–5%	–4%	–3%	–1%	1%	2%	3%	5%	
17	Pittsburgh	–6%	–6%	–4%	–5%	–3%	–3%	–1%	–2%	–2%	–1%	–2%	–1%	

differences in the magnitudes of increases and decreases among locations using sparklines. The combination of a heat map and sparklines here is a particularly effective way to show both trend and magnitude.

KirklandRegional

Additional Charts for Multiple Variables

Figure 3.29 provides an alternative display for the regional sales data of air compressors for Kirkland Industries. The figure uses a **stacked-column chart** to display the North and the South regional sales data previously shown in a line chart in Figure 3.21. We could also

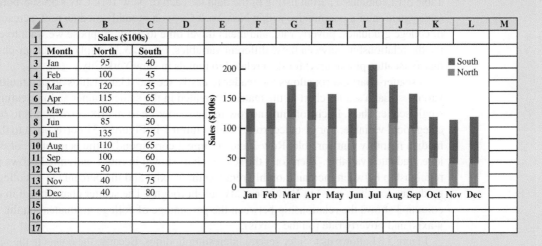

	A	B	C
1		Sales ($100s)	
2	Month	North	South
3	Jan	95	40
4	Feb	100	45
5	Mar	120	55
6	Apr	115	65
7	May	100	60
8	Jun	85	50
9	Jul	135	75
10	Aug	110	65
11	Sep	100	60
12	Oct	50	70
13	Nov	40	75
14	Dec	40	80

use a stacked-bar chart to display the same data by using horizontal bars instead of vertical. To create the stacked-column chart shown in Figure 3.29, we use the following steps:

*Note that here we have not included the additional steps for formatting the chart in Excel using the **Chart Elements** button, but the steps are similar to those used to create the previous charts.*

Step 1.   Select cells A2:C14
Step 2.   Click the **Insert** tab on the Ribbon
Step 3.   In the **Charts** group, click the **Insert Column or Bar Chart** button ▮▮ ▾
Select **Stacked Column** ▮▮ under **2-D Column**

Stacked-column and stacked-bar charts allow the reader to compare the relative values of quantitative variables for the same category in a bar chart. However, these charts suffer from the same difficulties as pie charts because the human eye has difficulty perceiving small differences in areas. As a result, experts often recommend against the use of stacked-column and stacked-bar charts for more than a couple of quantitative variables in each category. An alternative chart for these same data is called a **clustered-column (or clustered-bar) chart**. It is created in Excel following the same steps but selecting **Clustered Column** under the **2-D Column** in Step 3. Clustered-column and clustered-bar charts are often superior to stacked-column and stacked-bar charts for comparing quantitative variables, but they can become cluttered for more than a few quantitative variables per category.

Clustered-column (bar) charts are also referred to as side-by-side-column (bar) charts.

An alternative that is often preferred to both stacked and clustered charts, particularly when many quantitative variables need to be displayed, is to use multiple charts. For the regional sales data, we would include two column charts: one for sales in the North and one for sales in the South. For additional regions, we would simply add additional column charts. To facilitate comparisons between the data displayed in each chart, it is important to maintain consistent axes from one chart to another. The categorical variables should be listed in the same order in each chart, and the axis for the quantitative variable should have the same range. For instance, the vertical axis for both North and South sales starts at 0 and ends at 140. This makes it easy to see that, in most months, the North region has greater sales. Figure 3.30 compares the approaches using stacked-, clustered-, and multiple-bar charts for the regional sales data.

Figure 3.30 shows that the multiple-column charts require considerably more space than the stacked- and clustered-column charts. However, when comparing many quantitative variables, using multiple charts can often be superior even if each chart must be made smaller. Stacked-column and stacked-bar charts should be used only when comparing a few quantitative variables and when there are large differences in the relative values of the quantitative variables within the category.

An especially useful chart for displaying multiple variables is the **scatter-chart matrix**. Table 3.12 contains a partial listing of the data for each of New York City's 55 sub-boroughs (a designation of a community within New York City) on monthly median rent, percentage of college graduates, poverty rate, and mean travel time to work. Suppose we want to examine the relationship between these different variables. Figure 3.31 displays a scatter-chart matrix (scatter-plot matrix) for data related to rentals in New York City.

A scatter-chart matrix allows the reader to easily see the relationships among multiple variables. Each scatter chart in the matrix is created in the same manner as for creating a single scatter chart. Each column and row in the scatter-chart matrix corresponds to one categorical variable. For instance, row 1 and column 1 in Figure 3.31 correspond to the median monthly rent variable. Row 2 and column 2 correspond to the percentage of college graduates variable. Therefore, the scatter chart shown in row 1, column 2 shows the relationship between median monthly rent (on the y-axis) and the percentage of college graduates (on the x-axis) in New York City sub-boroughs. The scatter chart shown in row 2, column 3 shows the relationship between the percentage of college graduates (on the y-axis) and poverty rate (on the x-axis).

Figure 3.31 allows us to infer several interesting findings. Because the points in the scatter chart in row 1, column 2 generally get higher moving from left to right, this tells us that sub-boroughs with higher percentages of college graduates appear to have higher median monthly rents. The scatter chart in row 1, column 3 indicates that sub-boroughs with higher

FIGURE 3.30   Comparing Stacked-, Clustered-, and Multiple-Column Charts for the Regional Sales Data for Kirkland Industries

Stacked-Column Chart:

Clustered-Column Chart:

Multiple-Column Charts:

TABLE 3.12   Rental Data for New York City Sub-Boroughs

DATA *file*

NYCityData

Area (Sub-Borough)	Median Monthly Rent ($)	Percentage College Graduates (%)	Poverty Rate (%)	Travel Time (min)
Astoria	1,106	36.8	15.9	35.4
Bay Ridge	1,082	34.3	15.6	41.9
Bayside/Little Neck	1,243	41.3	7.6	40.6
Bedford Stuyvesant	822	21.0	34.2	40.5
Bensonhurst	876	17.7	14.4	44.0
Borough Park	980	26.0	27.6	35.3
Brooklyn Heights/ Fort Greene	1,086	55.3	17.4	34.5
Brownsville/ Ocean Hill	714	11.6	36.0	40.3
Bushwick	945	13.3	33.5	35.5
Central Harlem	665	30.6	27.1	25.0
Chelsea/Clinton/ Midtown	1,624	66.1	12.7	43.7
Coney Island	786	27.2	20.0	46.3
⋮	⋮	⋮	⋮	⋮

The scatter charts along the diagonal in a scatter-chart matrix (e.g., in row 1, column 1 and in row 2, column 2) display the relationship between a variable and itself. Therefore, the points in these scatter charts will always fall along a straight line at a 45-degree angle, as shown in Figure 3.31.

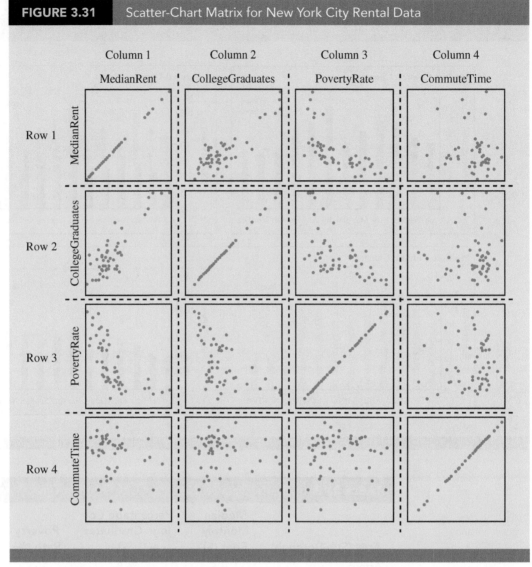

FIGURE 3.31   Scatter-Chart Matrix for New York City Rental Data

We demonstrate how to create scatter-chart matrixes in several different software packages in the online appendix.

poverty rates appear to have lower median monthly rents. The data in row 2, column 3 show that sub-boroughs with higher poverty rates tend to have lower percentages of college graduates. The scatter charts in column 4 show that the relationships between the mean travel time and the other categorical variables are not as clear as relationships in other columns.

The scatter-chart matrix is very useful in analyzing relationships among variables. Unfortunately, it is not possible to generate a scatter-chart matrix using standard Excel functions. Each scatter chart must be created individually in Excel using the data from those two variables to be displayed on the chart.

PivotCharts in Excel

DATA *file*

Restaurant

To summarize and analyze data with both a crosstabulation and charting, Excel pairs **PivotCharts** with PivotTables. Using the restaurant data introduced in Table 3.7 and Figure 3.7, we can create a PivotChart by taking the following steps:

Step 1.   Click the **Insert** tab on the Ribbon
Step 2.   In the **Charts** group, select **PivotChart**
Step 3.   When the **Create PivotChart** dialog box appears:
          Choose **Select a Table or Range**

Enter *A1:D301* in the **Table/Range:** box

Select **New Worksheet** as the location for the PivotTable Report

Click **OK**

Step 4.   In the **PivotChart Fields** area, under **Choose fields to add to report:**

Drag the **Quality Rating** field to the **AXIS (CATEGORIES)** area

Drag the **Meal Price ($)** field to the **LEGEND (SERIES)** area

Drag the **Wait Time (min)** field to the **VALUES** area

Step 5.   Click on **Sum of Wait Time (min)** in the **Values** area

Step 6.   Select **Value Field Settings…** from the list of options that appear

Step 7.   When the **Value Field Settings** dialog box appears:

Under **Summarize value field by**, select **Average**

Click **Number Format**

In the **Category:** box, select **Number**

Enter *1* for **Decimal places:**

Click **OK**

When the **Value Field Settings** dialog box reappears, click **OK**

Step 8.   Right-click in cell B2 or any cell containing a meal price column label

Step 9.   Select **Group** from the list of options that appears

Step 10. When the **Grouping** dialog box appears:

Enter *10* in the **Starting at:** box

Enter *49* in the **Ending at:** box

Enter *10* in the **By:** box

Click **OK**

Step 11. Right-click on "Excellent" in cell A5

Step 12. Select **Move** and click **Move "Excellent" to End**

The completed PivotTable and PivotChart appear in Figure 3.32. The PivotChart is a clustered-column chart whose column heights correspond to the average wait times and are clustered into the categorical groupings of Good, Very Good, and Excellent. The columns

*Like PivotTables, PivotCharts are interactive. You can use the arrows on the axes and legend labels to change the categorical data being displayed. For example, you can click on the **Quality Rating** horizontal axis label (see Figure 3.32) and choose to look at only Very Good and Excellent restaurants, or you can click on the **Meal Price ($)** legend label and choose to view only certain meal price categories.*

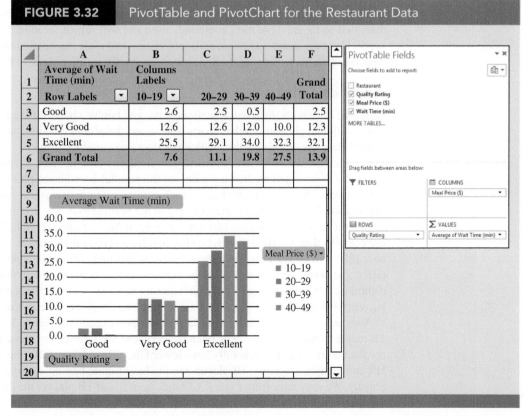

FIGURE 3.32   PivotTable and PivotChart for the Restaurant Data

are different colors to differentiate the wait times at restaurants in the various meal price ranges. Figure 3.32 shows that Excellent restaurants have longer wait times than Good and Very Good restaurants. We also see that Excellent restaurants in the price range of $30–$39 have the longest wait times. The PivotChart displays the same information as that of the PivotTable in Figure 3.13, but the column chart used here makes it easier to compare the restaurants based on quality rating and meal price.

N O T E S   +   C O M M E N T S

1. Excel assumes that line charts will be used to graph only time series data. The Line Chart tool in Excel is the most intuitive for creating charts that include text entries for the horizontal axis (e.g., the month labels of Jan, Feb, Mar, etc. for the monthly sales data in Figure 3.19). When the horizontal axis represents numerical values (1, 2, 3, etc.), then it is easiest to go to the **Charts** group under the **Insert** tab in the Ribbon, click the **Insert Scatter (X,Y) or Bubble Chart** button ▚ ▼, and then select the **Scatter with Straight Lines and Markers** button ⬭.

2. Color is frequently used to differentiate elements in a chart. However, be wary of the use of color to differentiate for several reasons: (1) Many people are color-blind and may not be able to differentiate colors. (2) Many charts are printed in black and white as handouts, which reduces or eliminates the impact of color. (3) The use of too many colors in a chart can make the chart appear too busy and distract or even confuse the reader. In many cases, it is preferable to differentiate chart elements with dashed lines, patterns, or labels.

3. Histograms and boxplots (discussed in Chapter 2 in relation to analyzing distributions) are other effective data-visualization tools for summarizing the distribution of data.

3.4 Advanced Data Visualization

In this chapter, we have presented only some of the most basic ideas for using data visualization effectively both to analyze data and to communicate data analysis to others. The charts discussed so far are those most commonly used and will suffice for most data-visualization needs. However, many additional concepts, charts, and tools can be used to improve your data-visualization techniques. In this section we briefly mention some of them.

Advanced Charts

Although line charts, bar charts, scatter charts, and bubble charts suffice for most data-visualization applications, other charts can be very helpful in certain situations. One type of helpful chart for examining data with more than two variables is the **parallel-coordinates plot**, which includes a different vertical axis for each variable. Each observation in the data set is represented by drawing a line on the parallel-coordinates plot connecting each vertical axis. The height of the line on each vertical axis represents the value taken by that observation for the variable corresponding to the vertical axis. For instance, Figure 3.33 displays a parallel coordinates plot for a sample of Major League Baseball players. The figure contains data for 10 players who play first base (1B) and 10 players who play second base (2B). For each player, the leftmost vertical axis plots his total number of home runs (HR). The center vertical axis plots the player's total number of stolen bases (SB), and the rightmost vertical axis plots the player's batting average. Various colors differentiate 1B players from 2B players (1B players are in blue and 2B players are in red).

We can make several interesting statements upon examining Figure 3.33. The sample of 1B players tend to hit lots of HR but have very few SB. Conversely, the sample of 2B players steal more bases but generally have fewer HR, although some 2B players have many HR and many SB. Finally, 1B players tend to have higher batting averages (AVG) than 2B players. We may infer from Figure 3.33 that the traits of 1B players may be different from

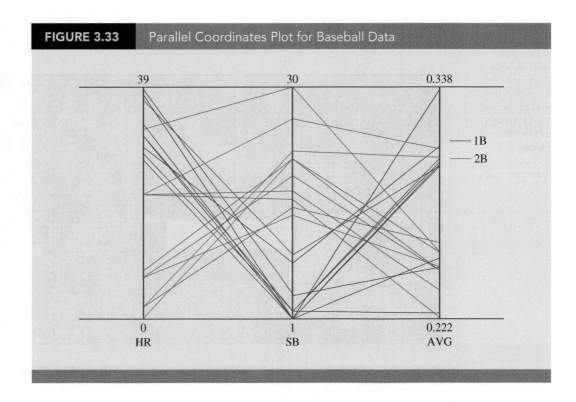

FIGURE 3.33 Parallel Coordinates Plot for Baseball Data

those of 2B players. In general, this statement is true. Players at 1B tend to be offensive stars who hit for power and average, whereas players at 2B are often faster and more agile in order to handle the defensive responsibilities of the position (traits that are not common in strong HR hitters). Parallel-coordinates plots, in which you can differentiate categorical variable values using color as in Figure 3.33, can be very helpful in identifying common traits across multiple dimensions.

A **treemap** is useful for visualizing hierarchical data along multiple dimensions. Smart-Money's Map of the Market, shown in Figure 3.34, is a treemap for analyzing stock market performance. In the Map of the Market, each rectangle represents a particular company (Apple, Inc. is highlighted in Figure 3.34). The color of the rectangle represents the overall performance of the company's stock over the previous 52 weeks. The Map of the Market is also divided into market sectors (Health Care, Financials, Oil & Gas, etc.). The size of each company's rectangle provides information on the company's market capitalization size relative to the market sector and the entire market. Figure 3.34 shows that Apple has a very large market capitalization relative to other firms in the Technology sector and that it has performed exceptionally well over the previous 52 weeks. An investor can use the treemap in Figure 3.34 to quickly get an idea of the performance of individual companies relative to other companies in their market sector as well as the performance of entire market sectors relative to other sectors.

Excel allows the user to create treemap charts. The step-by-step directions below explain how to create a treemap in Excel for the top-100 global companies based on 2014 market value using data in the file *Global100*. In this file we provide the continent where the company is headquartered in column A, the country headquarters in column B, the name of the company in column C, and the market value in column D. For the treemap to display properly in Excel, the data should be sorted by column A, "Continent," which is the highest level of the hierarchy.

Note that the treemap chart is not available in older versions of Excel.

Step 1. Select cells A1: D101

Step 2. Click **Insert** on the Ribbon

Click on the **Insert Hierarchy Chart** button in the **Charts** group

Select **Treemap** from the drop-down menu

The Map of the Market is based on work done by Professor Ben Shneiderman and students at the University of Maryland Human–Computer Interaction Lab.

FIGURE 3.34   SmartMoney's Map of the Market as an Example of a Treemap

DATA *file*

Global100

Step 3. When the treemap chart appears, right-click on the treemap portion of the chart
Select **Format Data Series…** in the pop-up menu
When the **Format Data Series** task pane opens, select **Banner**

Figure 3.35 shows the completed treemap created with Excel. Selecting **Banner** in Step 3 places the name of each continent as a banner title within the treemap. Each continent is also

FIGURE 3.35   Treemap Created in Excel for Top 100 Global Companies Data

	A	B	C	D	E	F	G	H	I	J	K	L	M	N	O	P	Q
1	Continent	Country	Company	Market Value (Billions US $)													
2	Asia	China	Agricultural Bank of China	141.1													
3	Asia	China	Bank of China	124.2													
4	Asia	China	China Construction Bank	174.4													
5	Asia	China	ICBC	215.6													
6	Asia	China	PetroChina	202													
7	Asia	China	Sinopec-China Petroleum	94.7													
8	Asia	China	Tencent Holdings	135.4													
9	Asia	Hong Kong	China Mobile	184.6													
10	Asia	Japan	Softbank	91.2													
11	Asia	Japan	Toyota Motor	193.5													
12	Asia	Russia	Gazprom	88.8													
13	Asia	Saudi Arabia	Saudi Basic Industries	94.4													
14	Asia	South Korea	Samsung Electronics	186.5													
15	Asia	Taiwan	Taiwan Semiconductor	102													
16	Australia	Australia	ANZ	83.9													
17	Australia	Australia	BHP Billiton	182.3													
18	Australia	Australia	Commonwealth Bank	114.5													
19	Australia	Australia	Westpac Banking Group	99													
20	Europe	Belgium	Anheuser-Busch InBev	171.2													
21	Europe	Denmark	Novo Nordisk	119.6													
22	Europe	France	BNP Paribas	98.6													
23	Europe	France	L'OrÃ©al Group	98.7													
24	Europe	France	Sanofi	137.1													
25	Europe	France	Total	149.8													
26	Europe	Germany	BASF	102.3													
27	Europe	Germany	Bayer	111.3													
28	Europe	Germany	BMW Group	83.4													
29	Europe	Germany	Daimler	102.9													

assigned a different color within the treemap. From this figure we can see that North America has more top-100 companies than any other continent, followed by Europe and then Asia. The size of the rectangles for each company in the treemap represents their relative market value. We can see that Apple, ExxonMobile, Google, and Microsoft have the four highest market values. Australia has only four companies in the top 100 and South America has two. Africa and Antarctica have no companies in the top 100. Hovering your pointer over one of the companies in the treemap will display the market value for that company.

Geographic Information Systems Charts

Consider the case of the Cincinnati Zoo & Botanical Garden, which derives much of its revenue from selling annual memberships to customers. The Cincinnati Zoo would like to better understand where its current members are located. Figure 3.36 displays a map of the Cincinnati, Ohio, metropolitan area showing the relative concentrations of Cincinnati Zoo members. The more darkly shaded areas represent areas with a greater number of members. Figure 3.36 is an example of the output from a **geographic information system (GIS)**, which merges maps and statistics to present data collected over different geographic areas. Displaying geographic data on a map can often help in interpreting data and observing patterns.

A GIS chart such as that shown in Figure 3.36 is an example of geoanalytics, the use of data by geographical area or some other form of spatial referencing to generate insights.

The GIS chart in Figure 3.36 combines a heat map and a geographical map to help the reader analyze this data set. From the figure we can see that a high concentration of zoo members in a band to the northeast of the zoo that includes the cities of Mason and

FIGURE 3.36   GIS Chart for Cincinnati Zoo Member Data

Hamilton (circled). Also, a high concentration of zoo members lies to the southwest of the zoo around the city of Florence. These observations could prompt the zoo manager to identify the shared characteristics of the populations of Mason, Hamilton, and Florence to learn what is leading them to be zoo members. If these characteristics can be identified, the manager can then try to identify other nearby populations that share these characteristics as potential markets for increasing the number of zoo members.

More recent versions of Excel have a feature called 3D Maps that allows the user to create interactive GIS-type charts. This tool is quite powerful, and the full capabilities are beyond the scope of this text. The step-by-step directions below show an example using data from the World Bank on gross domestic product (GDP) for countries around the world.

3D Maps is not available in older versions of Excel.

DATA *file*

WorldGDP 2014

Step 1.   Select cells A1:C191

Step 2.   Click the **Insert** tab on the Ribbon

Click the **3D Map** button in the **Tours** group

Select **Open 3D Maps.** This will open a new Excel window that displays a world map (see Figure 3.37)

Step 3.   Drag **GDP 2014 (Billions US $)** from the **Field List** to the **Height** box in the **Data** area of the **Layer 1** task pane.

Click the **Change the visualization to Region** button in the **Data** area of the **Layer 1** task pane.

Step 4.   Click **Layer Options** in the **Layer 1** task pane.

Change the **Color** to a dark red color to give the countries more differentiation on the world map.

FIGURE 3.37   Initial Window Opened by Clicking on 3D Map Button in Excel for World GDP Data

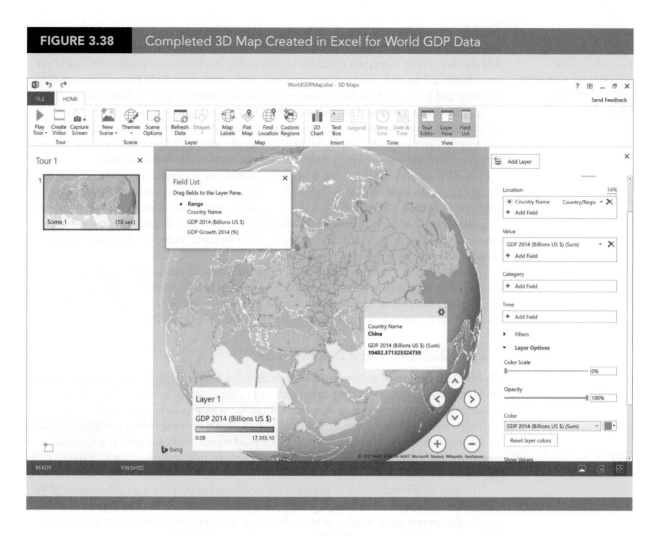

FIGURE 3.38 Completed 3D Map Created in Excel for World GDP Data

The completed GIS chart is shown in Figure 3.38. You can now click and drag the world map to view different parts of the world. Figure 3.38 shows much of Europe and Asia. The countries with the darker shading have higher GDPs. We can see that China has a very dark shading indicating very high GDP relative to other countries. Russia and Germany have slightly darker shadings than other countries shown indicating that Russia and China have higher GDPs than most other countries, but lower GDPs than China. If you hover over a country, it will display the Country Name and GDP 2014 (Billions US $) in a pop-up window. In Figure 3.38 we have hovered over China to display its GDP.

3.5 Data Dashboards

A **data dashboard** is a data-visualization tool that illustrates multiple metrics and automatically updates these metrics as new data become available. It is like an automobile's dashboard instrumentation that provides information on the vehicle's current speed, fuel level, and engine temperature so that a driver can assess current operating conditions and take effective action. Similarly, a data dashboard provides the important metrics that managers need to quickly assess the performance of their organization and react accordingly. In this section we provide guidelines for creating effective data dashboards and an example application.

Principles of Effective Data Dashboards

In an automobile dashboard, values such as current speed, fuel level, and oil pressure are displayed to give the driver a quick overview of current operating characteristics. In a

Key performance indicators are sometimes referred to as key performance metrics (KPMs).

business, the equivalent values are often indicative of the business's current operating characteristics, such as its financial position, the inventory on hand, customer service metrics, and the like. These values are typically known as **key performance indicators (KPIs)**. A data dashboard should provide timely summary information on KPIs that are important to the user, and it should do so in a manner that informs rather than overwhelms its user.

Ideally, a data dashboard should present all KPIs as a single screen that a user can quickly scan to understand the business's current state of operations. Rather than requiring the user to scroll vertically and horizontally to see the entire dashboard, it is better to create multiple dashboards so that each dashboard can be viewed on a single screen.

The KPIs displayed in the data dashboard should convey meaning to its user and be related to the decisions the user makes. For example, the data dashboard for a marketing manager may have KPIs related to current sales measures and sales by region, while the data dashboard for a Chief Financial Officer should provide information on the current financial standing of the company, including cash on hand, current debt obligations, and so on.

A data dashboard should call attention to unusual measures that may require attention, but not in an overwhelming way. Color should be used to call attention to specific values to differentiate categorical variables, but the use of color should be restrained. Too many different or too bright colors make the presentation distracting and difficult to read.

Applications of Data Dashboards

To illustrate the use of a data dashboard in decision making, we discuss an application involving the Grogan Oil Company which has offices located in three cities in Texas: Austin (its headquarters), Houston, and Dallas. Grogan's Information Technology (IT) call center, located in Austin, handles calls from employees regarding computer-related problems involving software, Internet, and e-mail issues. For example, if a Grogan employee in Dallas has a computer software problem, the employee can call the IT call center for assistance.

The data dashboard shown in Figure 3.39, developed to monitor the performance of the call center, combines several displays to track the call center's KPIs. The data presented are for the current shift, which started at 8:00 a.m. The stacked column chart in the upper left-hand corner shows the call volume for each type of problem (software, Internet, or email) over time. This chart shows that call volume is heavier during the first few hours of the shift, calls concerning email issues appear to decrease over time, and volume of calls regarding software issues are highest at midmorning.

The column chart in the upper right-hand corner of the dashboard shows the percentage of time that call center employees spent on each type of problem or were idle (not working on a call). These top two charts are important displays in determining optimal staffing levels. For instance, knowing the call mix and how stressed the system is, as measured by percentage of idle time, can help the IT manager make sure that enough call center employees are available with the right level of expertise.

The clustered-bar chart in the middle right of the dashboard shows the call volume by type of problem for each of Grogan's offices. This allows the IT manager to quickly identify whether there is a particular type of problem by location. For example, the office in Austin seems to be reporting a relatively high number of issues with e-mail. If the source of the problem can be identified quickly, then the problem might be resolved quickly for many users all at once. Also, note that a relatively high number of software problems are coming from the Dallas office. In this case, the Dallas office is installing new software, resulting in more calls to the IT call center. Having been alerted to this by the Dallas office last week, the IT manager knew that calls coming from the Dallas office would spike, so the manager proactively increased staffing levels to handle the expected increase in calls.

For each unresolved case that was received more than 15 minutes ago, the bar chart shown in the middle left of the data dashboard displays the length of time for which each

FIGURE 3.39   Data Dashboard for the Grogan Oil Information Technology Call Center

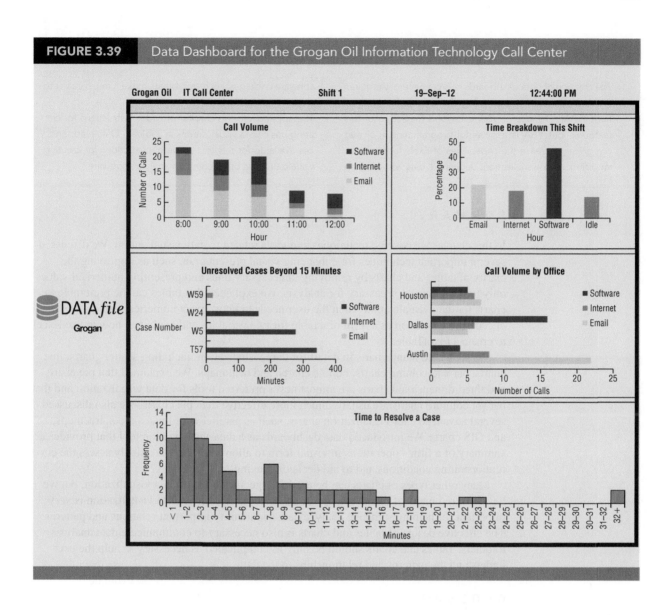

Chapter 2 discusses the construction of frequency distributions for quantitative and categorical data.

case has been unresolved. This chart enables Grogan to quickly monitor the key problem cases and decide whether additional resources may be needed to resolve them. The worst case, T57, has been unresolved for over 300 minutes and is actually left over from the previous shift. Finally, the chart in the bottom panel shows the length of time required for resolved cases during the current shift. This chart is an example of a frequency distribution for quantitative data.

Throughout the dashboard, a consistent color coding scheme is used for problem type (E-mail, Software, and Internet). Other dashboard designs are certainly possible, and improvements could certainly be made to the design shown in Figure 3.39. However, what is important is that information is clearly communicated so that managers can improve their decision making.

The Grogan Oil data dashboard presents data at the operational level, is updated in real time, and is used for operational decisions such as staffing levels. Data dashboards may also be used at the tactical and strategic levels of management. For example, a sales manager could monitor sales by salesperson, by region, by product, and by customer. This would alert the sales manager to changes in sales patterns. At the highest level, a more strategic dashboard would allow upper management to quickly assess the financial health of the company by monitoring more aggregate financial, service-level, and capacity-utilization information.

NOTES + COMMENTS

1. The creation of data dashboards in Excel generally requires the use of macros written using Visual Basic for Applications (VBA). The use of VBA is beyond the scope of this textbook, but VBA is a powerful programming tool that can greatly increase the capabilities of Excel for analytics, including data visualization. Dedicated data visualization software packages, such as Tableau, make it much easier to create data dashboards.

2. The appendix to this chapter provides instructions for creating basic data visualizations in Tableau. Online appendices available for this text provide instructions for creating visualizations in other common analytics software.

SUMMARY

In this chapter we covered techniques and tools related to data visualization. We discussed several important techniques for enhancing visual presentation, such as improving the clarity of tables and charts by removing unnecessary lines and presenting numerical values only to the precision necessary for analysis. We explained that tables can be preferable to charts for data visualization when the user needs to know exact numerical values. We introduced crosstabulation as a form of a table for two variables and explained how to use Excel to create a PivotTable.

We presented many charts in detail for data visualization, including scatter charts, line charts, bar and column charts, bubble charts, and heat maps. We explained that pie charts and three-dimensional charts are almost never preferred tools for data visualization and that bar (or column) charts are usually much more effective than pie charts. We also discussed several advanced data-visualization charts, such as parallel-coordinates plots, treemaps, and GIS charts. We introduced data dashboards as a data-visualization tool that provides a summary of a firm's operations in visual form to allow managers to quickly assess the current operating conditions and to aid decision making.

Many other types of charts can be used for specific forms of data visualization, but we have covered many of the most-popular and most-useful ones. Data visualization is very important for helping someone analyze data and identify important relations and patterns. The effective design of tables and charts is also necessary to communicate data analysis to others. Tables and charts should be only as complicated as necessary to help the user understand the patterns and relationships in the data.

GLOSSARY

Bar chart A graphical presentation that uses horizontal bars to display the magnitude of quantitative data. Each bar typically represents a class of a categorical variable.

Bubble chart A graphical presentation used to visualize three variables in a two-dimensional graph. The two axes represent two variables, and the magnitude of the third variable is given by the size of the bubble.

Chart A visual method for displaying data; also called a graph or a figure.

Clustered-column (or clustered-bar) chart A special type of column (bar) chart in which multiple bars are clustered in the same class to compare multiple variables; also known as a side-by-side-column (bar) chart.

Column chart A graphical presentation that uses vertical bars to display the magnitude of quantitative data. Each bar typically represents a class of a categorical variable.

Crosstabulation A tabular summary of data for two variables. The classes of one variable are represented by the rows; the classes for the other variable are represented by the columns.

Data dashboard A data-visualization tool that updates in real time and gives multiple outputs.

Data-ink ratio The ratio of the amount of ink used in a table or chart that is necessary to convey information to the total amount of ink used in the table and chart. Ink used that is not necessary to convey information reduces the data-ink ratio.

Geographic information system (GIS) A system that merges maps and statistics to present data collected over different geographies.

Heat map A two-dimensional graphical presentation of data in which color shadings indicate magnitudes.

Key performance indicator (KPI) A metric that is crucial for understanding the current performance of an organization; also known as a key performance metric (KPM).

Line chart A graphical presentation of time series data in which the data points are connected by a line.

Parallel-coordinates plot A graphical presentation used to examine more than two variables in which each variable is represented by a different vertical axis. Each observation in a data set is plotted in a parallel-coordinates plot by drawing a line between the values of each variable for the observation.

Pie chart A graphical presentation used to compare categorical data. Because of difficulties in comparing relative areas on a pie chart, these charts are not recommended. Bar or column charts are generally superior to pie charts for comparing categorical data.

PivotChart A graphical presentation created in Excel that functions similarly to a PivotTable.

PivotTable An interactive crosstabulation created in Excel.

Scatter chart A graphical presentation of the relationship between two quantitative variables. One variable is shown on the horizontal axis and the other on the vertical axis.

Scatter-chart matrix A graphical presentation that uses multiple scatter charts arranged as a matrix to illustrate the relationships among multiple variables.

Sparkline A special type of line chart that indicates the trend of data but not magnitude. A sparkline does not include axes or labels.

Stacked-column chart A special type of column (bar) chart in which multiple variables appear on the same bar.

Treemap A graphical presentation that is useful for visualizing hierarchical data along multiple dimensions. A treemap groups data according to the classes of a categorical variable and uses rectangles whose size relates to the magnitude of a quantitative variable.

Trendline A line that provides an approximation of the relationship between variables in a chart.

PROBLEMS

1. **Sales Performance Bonuses.** A sales manager is trying to determine appropriate sales performance bonuses for her team this year. The following table contains the data relevant to determining the bonuses, but it is not easy to read and interpret. Reformat the table to improve readability and to help the sales manager make her decisions about bonuses.

DATA*file*

SalesBonuses

Salesperson	Total Sales ($)	Average Performance Bonus Previous Years ($)	Customer Accounts	Years with Company
Smith, Michael	325,000.78	12,499.3452	124	14
Yu, Joe	13,678.21	239.9434	9	7
Reeves, Bill	452,359.19	21,987.2462	175	21
Hamilton, Joshua	87,423.91	7,642.9011	28	3
Harper, Derek	87,654.21	1,250.1393	21	4
Quinn, Dorothy	234,091.39	14,567.9833	48	9
Graves, Lorrie	379,401.94	27,981.4432	121	12
Sun, Yi	31,733.59	672.9111	7	1
Thompson, Nicole	127,845.22	13,322.9713	17	3

2. **Gross Domestic Product Values.** The following table shows an example of gross domestic product values for five countries over six years in equivalent U.S. dollars ($).

Gross Domestic Product (in US $)						
Country	Year 1	Year 2	Year 3	Year 4	Year 5	Year 6
Albania	7,385,937,423	8,105,580,293	9,650,128,750	11,592,303,225	10,781,921,975	10,569,204,154
Argentina	169,725,491,092	198,012,474,920	241,037,555,661	301,259,040,110	285,070,994,754	339,604,450,702
Australia	704,453,444,387	758,320,889,024	916,931,817,944	982,991,358,955	934,168,969,952	1,178,776,680,167
Austria	272,865,358,404	290,682,488,352	336,840,690,493	375,777,347,214	344,514,388,622	341,440,991,770
Belgium	335,571,307,765	355,372,712,266	408,482,592,257	451,663,134,614	421,433,351,959	416,534,140,346

DATA *file*

GDPYears

a. How could you improve the readability of this table?
b. The file *GDPYears* contains sample data from the United Nations Statistics Division on 30 countries and their GDP values from Year 1 to Year 6 in US $. Create a table that provides all these data for a user. Format the table to make it as easy to read as possible.

Hint: It is generally not important for the user to know GDP to an exact dollar figure. It is typical to present GDP values in millions or billions of dollars.

3. **Monthly Revenue Data.** The following table provides monthly revenue values for Tedstar, Inc., a company that sells valves to large industrial firms. The monthly revenue data have been graphed using a line chart in the following figure.

Month	Jan	Feb	Mar	Apr	May	Jun	Jul	Aug	Sep	Oct	Nov	Dec
Revenue ($)	145,869	123,576	143,298	178,505	186,850	192,850	134,500	145,286	154,285	148,523	139,600	148,235

DATA *file*

Tedstar

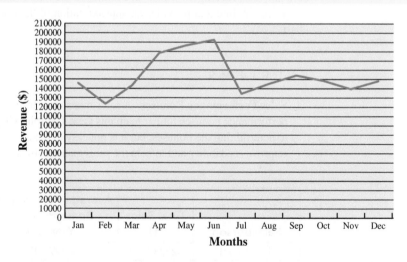

a. What are the problems with the layout and display of this line chart?
b. Create a new line chart for the monthly revenue data at Tedstar, Inc. Format the chart to make it easy to read and interpret.

DATA *file*

MajorSalary

4. **Business Graduates Salaries.** In the file *MajorSalary*, data have been collected from 111 College of Business graduates on their monthly starting salaries. The graduates include students majoring in management, finance, accounting, information systems, and marketing. Create a PivotTable in Excel to display the number of graduates in each major and the average monthly starting salary for students in each major.
a. Which major has the greatest number of graduates?

b. Which major has the highest average starting monthly salary?

c. Use the PivotTable to determine the major of the student with the highest overall starting monthly salary. What is the major of the student with the lowest overall starting monthly salary?

5. **Top U.S. Franchises.** *Entrepreneur* magazine ranks franchises. Among the factors that the magazine uses in its rankings are growth rate, number of locations, start-up costs, and financial stability. A recent ranking listed the top 20 U.S. franchises and the number of locations as follows:

Franchise	Number of U.S. Locations	Franchise	Number of U.S. Locations
Hampton Inns	1,864	Jan-Pro Franchising Intl. Inc.	12,394
ampm	3,183	Hardee's	1,901
McDonald's	32,805	Pizza Hut Inc.	13,281
7-Eleven Inc.	37,496	Kumon Math & Reading Centers	25,199
Supercuts	2,130	Dunkin' Donuts	9,947
Days Inn	1,877	KFC Corp.	16,224
Vanguard Cleaning Systems	2,155	Jazzercise Inc.	7,683
Servpro	1,572	Anytime Fitness	1,618
Subway	34,871	Matco Tools	1,431
Denny's Inc.	1,668	Stratus Building Solutions	5,018

DATA*file*

Franchises

These data can be found in the file *Franchises*. Create a PivotTable to summarize these data using classes 0–9,999, 10,000–19,999, 20,000–29,999, and 30,000–39,999 to answer the following questions. (*Hint:* Use Number of U.S. Locations as the COLUMNS, and use Count of Number of U.S. Locations as the VALUES in the PivotTable.)

a. How many franchises have between 0 and 9,999 locations?

b. How many franchises have more than 30,000 locations?

DATA*file*

MutualFunds

6. **Mutual Funds Data.** The file *MutualFunds* contains a data set with information for 45 mutual funds that are part of the *Morningstar Funds 500*. The data set includes the following five variables:

> *Fund Type:* The type of fund, labeled DE (Domestic Equity), IE (International Equity), and FI (Fixed Income)
>
> *Net Asset Value ($):* The closing price per share
>
> *Five-Year Average Return (%):* The average annual return for the fund over the past five years
>
> *Expense Ratio (%):* The percentage of assets deducted each fiscal year for fund expenses
>
> *Morningstar Rank:* The risk adjusted star rating for each fund; Morningstar ranks go from a low of 1 Star to a high of 5 Stars.

Note that Excel may display the column headings as 0–10, 10–20, 20–30, etc., but they should be interpreted as 0–9.99, 10–19.99, 20–29.99, etc.

a. Prepare a PivotTable that gives the frequency count of the data by Fund Type (rows) and the five-year average annual return (columns). Use classes of 0–9.99, 10–19.99, 20–29.99, 30–39.99, 40–49.99, and 50–59.99 for the Five-Year Average Return (%).

b. What conclusions can you draw about the fund type and the average return over the past five years?

DATA*file*

TaxData

7. **Tax Data by County.** The file *TaxData* contains information from federal tax returns filed in 2007 for all counties in the United States (3,142 counties in total). Create a PivotTable in Excel to answer the questions below. The PivotTable should have State Abbreviation as Row Labels. The Values in the PivotTable should be the sum of adjusted gross income for each state.

a. Sort the PivotTable data to display the states with the smallest sum of adjusted gross income on top and the largest on the bottom. Which state had the smallest sum of adjusted gross income? What is the total adjusted gross income for federal tax returns filed in this state with the smallest total adjusted gross income? (*Hint:* To sort data in a PivotTable in Excel, right-click any cell in the PivotTable that contains the data you want to sort, and select **Sort**.)

b. Add the County Name to the Row Labels in the PivotTable. Sort the County Names by Sum of Adjusted Gross Income with the lowest values on the top and the highest values on the bottom. Filter the Row Labels so that only the state of Texas is displayed. Which county had the smallest sum of adjusted gross income in the state of Texas? Which county had the largest sum of adjusted gross income in the state of Texas?

c. Click on **Sum of Adjusted Gross Income** in the **Values** area of the PivotTable in Excel. Click **Value Field Settings…**. Click the tab for **Show Values As**. In the **Show values as** box, select **% of Parent Row Total**. Click **OK**. This displays the adjusted gross income reported by each county as a percentage of the total state adjusted gross income. Which county has the highest percentage adjusted gross income in the state of Texas? What is this percentage?

d. Remove the filter on the Row Labels to display data for all states. What percentage of total adjusted gross income in the United States was provided by the state of New York?

FDICBankFailures

8. **Federally Insured Bank Failures.** The file *FDICBankFailures* contains data on failures of federally insured banks between 2000 and 2012. Create a PivotTable in Excel to answer the following questions. The PivotTable should group the closing dates of the banks into yearly bins and display the counts of bank closures each year in columns of Excel. Row labels should include the bank locations and allow for grouping the locations into states or viewing by city. You should also sort the PivotTable so that the states with the greatest number of total bank failures between 2000 and 2012 appear at the top of the PivotTable.

a. Which state had the greatest number of federally insured bank closings between 2000 and 2012?

b. How many bank closings occurred in the state of Nevada (NV) in 2010? In what cities did these bank closings occur?

c. Use the PivotTable's filter capability to view only bank closings in California (CA), Florida (FL), Texas (TX), and New York (NY) for the years 2009 through 2012. What is the total number of bank closings in these states between 2009 and 2012?

d. Using the filtered PivotTable from part c, what city in Florida had the greatest number of bank closings between 2009 and 2012? How many bank closings occurred in this city?

e. Create a PivotChart to display a column chart that shows the total number of bank closings in each year from 2000 through 2012 in the state of Florida. Adjust the formatting of this column chart so that it best conveys the data. What does this column chart suggest about bank closings between 2000 and 2012 in Florida? Discuss.

(*Hint:* You may have to switch the row and column labels in the PivotChart to get the best presentation for your PivotChart.)

9. **Scatter Chart and Trendline.** The following 20 observations are for two quantitative variables, *x* and *y*.

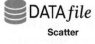

Scatter

Observation	x	y	Observation	x	y
1	−22	22	11	−37	48
2	−33	49	12	34	−29
3	2	8	13	9	−18
4	29	−16	14	−33	31
5	−13	10	15	20	−16
6	21	−28	16	−3	14
7	−13	27	17	−15	18
8	−23	35	18	12	17
9	14	−5	19	−20	−11
10	3	−3	20	−7	−22

a. Create a scatter chart for these 20 observations.

b. Fit a linear trendline to the 20 observations. What can you say about the relationship between the two quantitative variables?

DATA *file*

Fortune500

10. **Profits and Market Capitalizations.** The file *Fortune500* contains data for profits and market capitalizations from a recent sample of firms in the Fortune 500.

a. Prepare a scatter diagram to show the relationship between the variables Market Capitalization and Profit in which Market Capitalization is on the vertical axis and Profit is on the horizontal axis. Comment on any relationship between the variables.

b. Create a trendline for the relationship between Market Capitalization and Profit. What does the trendline indicate about this relationship?

11. **Vehicle Production Data.** The International Organization of Motor Vehicle Manufacturers (officially known as the Organisation Internationale des Constructeurs d'Automobiles, OICA) provides data on worldwide vehicle production by manufacturer. The following table shows vehicle production numbers for four different manufacturers for five recent years. Data are in millions of vehicles.

DATA *file*

AutoProduction

	Production (Millions of vehicles)				
Manufacturer	**Year 1**	**Year 2**	**Year 3**	**Year 4**	**Year 5**
Toyota	8.04	8.53	9.24	7.23	8.56
GM	8.97	9.35	8.28	6.46	8.48
Volkswagen	5.68	6.27	6.44	6.07	7.34
Hyundai	2.51	2.62	2.78	4.65	5.76

a. Construct a line chart for the time series data for years 1 through 5 showing the number of vehicles manufactured by each automotive company. Show the time series for all four manufacturers on the same graph.

b. What does the line chart indicate about vehicle production amounts from years 1 through 5? Discuss.

c. Construct a clustered-bar chart showing vehicles produced by automobile manufacturer using the year 1 through 5 data. Represent the years of production along the horizontal axis, and cluster the production amounts for the four manufacturers in each year. Which company is the leading manufacturer in each year?

12. **Price of Gasoline.** The following table contains time series data for regular gasoline prices in the United States for 36 consecutive months:

DATA *file*

GasPrices

Month	Price ($)	Month	Price ($)	Month	Price ($)
1	2.27	13	2.84	25	3.91
2	2.63	14	2.73	26	3.68
3	2.53	15	2.73	27	3.65
4	2.62	16	2.73	28	3.64
5	2.55	17	2.71	29	3.61
6	2.55	18	2.80	30	3.45
7	2.65	19	2.86	31	3.38
8	2.61	20	2.99	32	3.27
9	2.72	21	3.10	33	3.38
10	2.64	22	3.21	34	3.58
11	2.77	23	3.56	35	3.85
12	2.85	24	3.80	36	3.90

a. Create a line chart for these time series data. What interpretations can you make about the average price per gallon of conventional regular gasoline over these 36 months?

b. Fit a linear trendline to the data. What does the trendline indicate about the price of gasoline over these 36 months?

13. **Term Life Insurance.** The following table contains sales totals for the top six term life insurance salespeople at American Insurance.

Salesperson	Contracts Sold
Harish	24
David	41
Kristina	19
Steven	23
Tim	53
Mona	39

a. Create a column chart to display the information in the table above. Format the column chart to best display the data by adding axes labels, a chart title, etc.

b. Sort the values in Excel so that the column chart is ordered from most contracts sold to fewest.

c. Insert data labels to display the number of contracts sold for each salesperson above the columns in the column chart created in part a.

14. **Pie Chart Alternatives.** The total number of term life insurance contracts sold in Problem 13 is 199. The following pie chart shows the percentages of contracts sold by each salesperson.

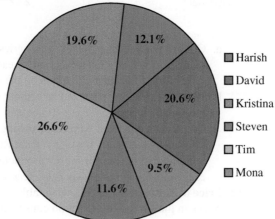

a. What are the problems with using a pie chart to display these data?

b. What type of chart would be preferred for displaying the data in this pie chart?

c. Use a different type of chart to display the percentage of contracts sold by each salesperson that conveys the data better than the pie chart. Format the chart and add data labels to improve the chart's readability.

15. **Engine Type Preference.** An automotive company is considering the introduction of a new model of sports car that will be available in four-cylinder and six-cylinder engine types. A sample of customers who were interested in this new model were asked to indicate their preference for an engine type for the new model of automobile. The customers were also asked to indicate their preference for exterior color from four choices: red, black, green, and white. Consider the following data regarding the customer responses:

	Four Cylinders	Six Cylinders
Red	143	857
Black	200	800
Green	321	679
White	420	580

a. Construct a clustered-column chart with exterior color as the horizontal variable.

b. What can we infer from the clustered-bar chart in part a?

16. **Smartphone Ownership.** Consider the following survey results regarding smartphone ownership by age:

DATA*file*

SmartPhone

Age Category	Smartphone (%)	Other Cell Phone (%)	No Cell Phone (%)
18–24	49	46	5
25–34	58	35	7
35–44	44	45	11
45–54	28	58	14
55–64	22	59	19
65+	11	45	44

a. Construct a stacked-column chart to display the survey data on type of cell-phone ownership. Use Age Category as the variable on the horizontal axis.

b. Construct a clustered column chart to display the survey data. Use Age Category as the variable on the horizontal axis.

c. What can you infer about the relationship between age and smartphone ownership from the column charts in parts a and b? Which column chart (stacked or clustered) is best for interpreting this relationship? Why?

17. **Store Manager Tasks.** The Northwest regional manager of Logan Outdoor Equipment Company has conducted a study to determine how her store managers are allocating their time. A study was undertaken over three weeks that collected the following data related to the percentage of time each store manager spent on the tasks of attending required meetings, preparing business reports, customer interaction, and being idle. The results of the data collection appear in the following table:

DATA*file*

Logan

		Attending Required Meetings (%)	Tasks Preparing Business Reports (%)	Customer Interaction (%)	Idle (%)
	Seattle	32	17	37	14
	Portland	52	11	24	13
Locations	Bend	18	11	52	19
	Missoula	21	6	43	30
	Boise	12	14	64	10
	Olympia	17	12	54	17

a. Create a stacked-bar chart with locations along the vertical axis. Reformat the bar chart to best display these data by adding axis labels, a chart title, and so on.

b. Create a clustered-bar chart with locations along the vertical axis and clusters of tasks. Reformat the bar chart to best display these data by adding axis labels, a chart title, and the like.

c. Create multiple bar charts in which each location becomes a single bar chart showing the percentage of time spent on tasks. Reformat the bar charts to best display these data by adding axis labels, a chart title, and so forth.

d. Which form of bar chart (stacked, clustered, or multiple) is preferable for these data? Why?

e. What can we infer about the differences among how store managers are allocating their time at the different locations?

18. **R&D Project Portfolio.** The Ajax Company uses a portfolio approach to manage their research and development (R&D) projects. Ajax wants to keep a mix of projects to balance the expected return and risk profiles of their R&D activities. Consider a situation in which Ajax has six R&D projects as characterized in the table. Each project is given an expected rate of return and a risk assessment, which is a value between 1 and 10, where

1 is the least risky and 10 is the most risky. Ajax would like to visualize their current R&D projects to keep track of the overall risk and return of their R&D portfolio.

DATA *file*

Ajax

Project	Expected Rate of Return (%)	Risk Estimate	Capital Invested (Millions $)
1	12.6	6.8	6.4
2	14.8	6.2	45.8
3	9.2	4.2	9.2
4	6.1	6.2	17.2
5	21.4	8.2	34.2
6	7.5	3.2	14.8

a. Create a bubble chart in which the expected rate of return is along the horizontal axis, the risk estimate is on the vertical axis, and the size of the bubbles represents the amount of capital invested. Format this chart for best presentation by adding axis labels and labeling each bubble with the project number.

b. The efficient frontier of R&D projects represents the set of projects that have the highest expected rate of return for a given level of risk. In other words, any project that has a smaller expected rate of return for an equivalent, or higher, risk estimate cannot be on the efficient frontier. From the bubble chart in part a, which projects appear to be located on the efficient frontier?

DATA *file*

SurveyResults

19. **Marketing Survey Results.** Heat maps can be very useful for identifying missing data values in moderate to large data sets. The file *SurveyResults* contains the responses from a marketing survey: 108 individuals responded to the survey of 10 questions. Respondents provided answers of 1, 2, 3, 4, or 5 to each question, corresponding to the overall satisfaction on 10 different dimensions of quality. However, not all respondents answered every question.

a. To find the missing data values, create a heat map in Excel that shades the empty cells a different color. Use Excel's Conditional Formatting function to create this heat map. *Hint:* Click on **Conditional Formatting** in the **Styles** group in the **Home** tab. Select **Highlight Cells Rules** and click **More Rules….** Then enter **Blanks** in the **Format only cells with:** box. Select a format for these blank cells that will make them obviously stand out.

b. For each question, which respondents did not provide answers? Which question has the highest nonresponse rate?

20. **Revenues of Web Development Companies.** The following table shows monthly revenue for six different web development companies.

DATA *file*

WebDevelop

Company	Revenue ($)					
	Jan	Feb	Mar	Apr	May	Jun
Blue Sky Media	8,995	9,285	11,555	9,530	11,230	13,600
Innovate Technologies	18,250	16,870	19,580	17,260	18,290	16,250
Timmler Company	8,480	7,650	7,023	6,540	5,700	4,930
Accelerate, Inc.	28,325	27,580	23,450	22,500	20,800	19,800
Allen and Davis, LLC	4,580	6,420	6,780	7,520	8,370	10,100
Smith Ventures	17,500	16,850	20,185	18,950	17,520	18,580

a. Use Excel to create sparklines for sales at each company.

b. Which companies have generally decreasing revenues over the six months? Which company has exhibited the most consistent growth over the six months? Which companies have revenues that are both increasing and decreasing over the six months?

c. Use Excel to create a heat map for the revenue of the six companies. Do you find the heat map or the sparklines to be better at communicating the trend of revenues over the six months for each company? Why?

21. **NFL Attendance.** Below is a sample of the data in the file *NFLAttendance* which contains the 32 teams in the National Football League, their conference affiliation, their division, and their average home attendance.

DATA *file*

NFLAttendance

Conference	Division	Team	Average Home Attendance
AFC	West	Oakland	54,584
AFC	West	Los Angeles Chargers	57,024
NFC	North	Chicago	60,368
AFC	North	Cincinnati	60,511
NFC	South	Tampa Bay	60,624
NFC	North	Detroit	60,792
AFC	South	Jacksonville	61,915

a. Create a treemap using these data that separates the teams into their conference affiliations (NFC and AFC) and uses size to represent each team's average home attendance. Note that you will need to sort the data in Excel by Conference to properly create a treemap.

b. Create a sorted bar chart that compares the average home attendance for each team.

c. Comment on the advantages and disadvantages of each type of chart for these data. Which chart best displays these data and why?

22. **Global 100 Companies.** For this problem we will use the data in the file *Global100* that was referenced in Section 3.4 as an example for creating a treemap. Here we will use these data to create a GIS chart. A portion of the data contained in *Global100* is shown below.

DATA *file*

Global100

Continent	Country	Company	Market Value (Billions US $)
Asia	China	Agricultural Bank of China	141.1
Asia	China	Bank of China	124.2
Asia	China	China Construction Bank	174.4
Asia	China	ICBC	215.6
Asia	China	PetroChina	202.0
Asia	China	Sinopec-China Petroleum	94.7
Asia	China	Tencent Holdings	135.4
Asia	Hong Kong	China Mobile	184.6
Asia	Japan	Softbank	91.2
Asia	Japan	Toyota Motor	193.5

Use Excel to create a GIS chart that (1) displays the Market Value of companies in different countries as a heat map; (2) allows you to filter the results so that you can choose to add and remove specific continents in your GIS chart; and (3) uses text labels to display which companies are located in each country. To do this you will need to create a **3D Map** in Excel. You will then need to click the **Change the visualization to Region** button, and then add **Country** to the **Location** box (and remove **Continent** from the **Location** box if it appears there), add **Continent** to the **Filters** box and add **Market Value (Billions US $)** to the **Value** box. Under **Layer Options**, you will also need to **Customize** the **Data Card** to include **Company** as a **Field** for the **Custom Tooltip**.

a. Display the results of the GIS chart for companies in Europe only. Which country in Europe has the highest total Market Value for Global 100 companies in that country? What is the total market value for Global 100 companies in that country?

b. Add North America in addition to Europe for continents to be displayed. How does the heat map for Europe change? Why does it change in this way?

23. **Online Customers versus In-Store Customers.** Zeitler's Department Stores sells its products online and through traditional brick-and-mortar stores. The following

parallel-coordinates plot displays data from a sample of 20 customers who purchased clothing from Zeitler's either online or in-store. The data include variables for the customer's age, annual income, and the distance from the customer's home to the nearest Zeitler's store. According to the parallel-coordinates plot, how are online customers differentiated from in-store customers?

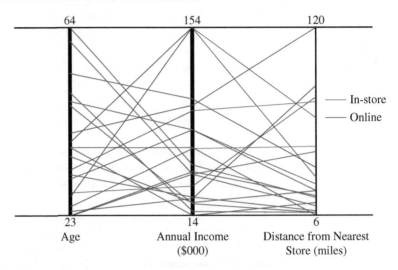

Problem 24 requires the use of software outside native Excel.

ZeitlersElectronics

24. **Customers Who Purchase Electronic Equipment.** The file *ZeitlersElectronics* contains data on customers who purchased electronic equipment either online or in-store from Zeitler's Department Stores.
   a. Create a parallel-coordinates plot for these data. Include vertical axes for the customer's age, annual income, and distance from nearest store. Color the lines by the type of purchase made by the customer (online or in-store).
   b. How does this parallel-coordinates plot compare to the one shown in Problem 23 for clothing purchases? Does the division between online and in-store purchasing habits for customers buying electronics equipment appear to be the same as for customers buying clothing?
   c. Parallel-coordinates plots are very useful for interacting with your data to perform analysis. Filter the parallel-coordinates plot so that only customers whose homes are more than 40 miles from the nearest store are displayed. What do you learn from the parallel-coordinates plot about these customers?

25. **Radiological Imaging Services Clinics.** Aurora Radiological Services is a health care clinic that provides radiological imaging services (such as MRIs, X-rays, and CAT scans) to patients. It is part of Front Range Medical Systems that operates clinics throughout the state of Colorado.
   a. What type of key performance indicators and other information would be appropriate to display on a data dashboard to assist the Aurora clinic's manager in making daily staffing decisions for the clinic?
   b. What type of key performance indicators and other information would be appropriate to display on a data dashboard for the CEO of Front Range Medical Systems who oversees the operation of multiple radiological imaging clinics?

26. **Customers Ordering by Phone.** Bravman Clothing sells high-end clothing products online and through phone orders. Bravman Clothing has taken a sample of 25 customers who placed orders by phone. The file *Bravman* contains data for each customer purchase, including the wait time the customer experienced when he or she called, the customer's purchase amount, the customer's age, and the customer's credit score. Bravman Clothing would like to analyze these data to try to learn more about their phone customers.
   a. Create a scatter-chart matrix for these data. Include the variables wait time, purchase amount, customer age, and credit score.
   b. What can you infer about the relationships between these variables from the scatter-chart matrix?

Problem 26 requires the use of software outside native Excel.

Bravman

CASE PROBLEM 1: PELICAN STORES

Pelican Stores, a division of National Clothing, is a chain of women's apparel stores operating throughout the country. The chain recently ran a promotion in which discount coupons were sent to customers of other National Clothing stores. Data collected for a sample of 100 in-store credit card transactions at Pelican Stores during one day while the promotion was running are contained in the file *PelicanStores*. Table 3.13 shows a portion of the data set. The Proprietary Card method of payment refers to charges made using a National Clothing charge card. Customers who made a purchase using a discount coupon are referred to as promotional customers and customers who made a purchase but did not use a discount coupon are referred to as regular customers. Because the promotional coupons were not sent to regular Pelican Stores customers, management considers the sales made to people presenting the promotional coupons as sales it would not otherwise make. Of course, Pelican also hopes that the promotional customers will continue to shop at its stores.

Most of the variables shown in Table 3.13 are self-explanatory, but two of the variables require some clarification.

Items   The total number of items purchased
Net Sales   The total amount ($) charged to the credit card

Pelican's management would like to use this sample data to learn about its customer base and to evaluate the promotion involving discount coupons.

DATA *file*

PelicanStores

TABLE 3.13				Data for a Sample of 100 Credit Card Purchases at Pelican Stores			
Customer	Type of Customer	Items	Net Sales	Method of Payment	Gender	Marital Status	Age
1	Regular	1	39.50	Discover	Male	Married	32
2	Promotional	1	102.40	Proprietary Card	Female	Married	36
3	Regular	1	22.50	Proprietary Card	Female	Married	32
4	Promotional	5	100.40	Proprietary Card	Female	Married	28
5	Regular	2	54.00	MasterCard	Female	Married	34
.	.	.	.	.	.	.	.
.	.	.	.	.	.	.	.
.	.	.	.	.	.	.	.
96	Regular	1	39.50	MasterCard	Female	Married	44
97	Promotional	9	253.00	Proprietary Card	Female	Married	30
98	Promotional	10	287.59	Proprietary Card	Female	Married	52
99	Promotional	2	47.60	Proprietary Card	Female	Married	30
100	Promotional	1	28.44	Proprietary Card	Female	Married	44

Managerial Report

Use the tabular and graphical methods of descriptive statistics to help management develop a customer profile and to evaluate the promotional campaign. At a minimum, your report should include the following:

Percent frequency distributions were introduced in Section 2.4. You can use Excel to create percent frequency distributions using PivotTables.

1. Percent frequency distributions for each of the key variables: number of items purchased, net sales, method of payment, gender, marital status, and age.
2. A sorted bar chart showing the number of customer purchases attributable to the method of payment.
3. A crosstabulation of type of customer (regular or promotional) versus net sales. Comment on any similarities of differences observed.

4. A scatter chart to explore the relationship between net sales and customer age.
5. A chart to examine whether the relationship between net sales and age depends on the marital status of the customer.
6. A side-by-side bar chart to examine the method of payment by customer type (regular or promotional). Comment on any differences you observe between the methods of payments used by the different types of customers.

CASE PROBLEM 2: MOVIE THEATER RELEASES

The movie industry is a competitive business. More than 50 studios produce hundreds of new movies for theater release each year, and the financial success of each movie varies considerably. The opening weekend gross sales ($ millions), the total gross sales ($ millions), the number of theaters the movie was shown in, and the number of weeks the movie was in release are common variables used to measure the success of a movie released to theaters. Data collected for the top 100 theater movies released in 2016 are contained in the file *Movies2016* (Box Office Mojo website). Table 3.14 shows the data for the first 10 movies in this file.

Managerial Report

Use the tabular and graphical methods of descriptive statistics to learn how these variables contribute to the success of a motion picture. Include the following in your report.

1. Tabular and graphical summaries for each of the four variables along with a discussion of what each summary tells us about the movies that are released to theaters.
2. A scatter diagram to explore the relationship between Total Gross Sales and Opening Weekend Gross Sales. Discuss.
3. A scatter diagram to explore the relationship between Total Gross Sales and Number of Theaters. Discuss.
4. A scatter diagram to explore the relationship between Total Gross Sales and Number of Weeks in Release. Discuss.

DATA*file*

Movies2016

TABLE 3.14	Performance Data for Ten 2016 Movies Released to Theaters			
Movie Title	Opening Gross Sales ($ Million)	Total Gross Sales ($ Million)	Number of Theaters	Weeks in Release
Rogue One: A Star Wars Story	155.08	532.18	4,157	20
Finding Dory	135.06	486.30	4,305	25
Captain America: Civil War	179.14	408.08	4,226	20
The Secret Life of Pets	104.35	368.38	4,381	25
The Jungle Book	103.26	364.00	4,144	24
Deadpool	132.43	363.07	3,856	18
Zootopia	75.06	341.27	3,959	22
Batman v Superman: Dawn of Justice	166.01	330.36	4,256	12
Suicide Squad	133.6	325.10	4,255	14
Sing	35.26	270.40	4,029	20

Data Visualization in Tableau Appendix

In this appendix, we introduce the use of Tableau Desktop software for visualizing data. Tableau allows for easy creation of a variety of charts and interactive visualizations of data. Tableau is particularly useful for creating interactive visualizations that allow a user to sort, filter, and otherwise explore data.

Connecting to a Data File in Tableau

Tableau can connect with many different types of data files for use in creating data visualizations. When you open Tableau Desktop, you should see a screen similar to Figure Tableau 3.1. This is the Tableau Desktop Home Screen. The Connect section allows you to connect to many different data file types. The Open section allows you to open sample data sets provided by Tableau and the Discover section provides information on ways to use Tableau.

Tableau can open different types of data files including Excel files, text files, database files and many others. We will use the steps below and the file *Electronics* to illustrate how we can connect to an Excel file in Tableau.

| FIGURE TABLEAU 3.1 | Tableau Desktop Home Screen |

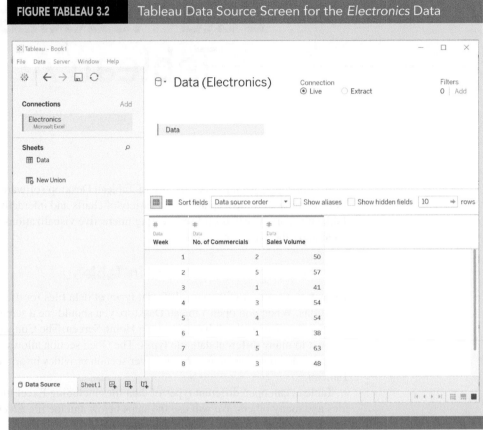

FIGURE TABLEAU 3.2   Tableau Data Source Screen for the *Electronics* Data

*Each worksheet contained in the Excel file will be listed in the **Sheets** area on the left of the dialog box. Tableau can connect to multiple data locations, but you must combine the data locations into a table using the **New Union** function.*

DATA *file*

Electronics

Step 1. Click the **File** tab in the Tableau Ribbon and select **Open…**

Step 2. When the **Open** dialog box appears, navigate to the location of the *Electronics.xlsx* file.

Select the *Electronics.xlsx* file, and click **Open**

Steps 1 and 2 above will open the Tableau Data Source screen shown in Figure Tableau 3.2. This screen shows a preview of the data file to which Tableau is currently connected. From the top of Figure Tableau 3.2 we see that Tableau is connected to the data file *Electronics* using a Live Connection. This means that as the data file is updated, these updates will be reflected in any visualizations created using Tableau. Alternatively, Tableau can use an Extract Connection, in which case all data from the file would be extracted, and any visualizations created in Tableau would not be updated as the data in the file is changed. The lower portion of the Tableau Data Source screen shows a preview of the data file to which Tableau is connected. From Figure Tableau 3.2, we see the columns from the file *Electronics* are titled "Week", "No. of Commercials," and "Sales Volume," and we see the first 8 observations for these data.

NOTES + COMMENTS

1. To update the visualizations created in Tableau from a Live Connection, first save any changes in the original data file. Then click **Data** in the Tableau Ribbon and select **Data** (*name of data file*), and click **Refresh**.

2. Tableau saves files as Tableau Workbooks with the file extension .twb. To save a file in Tableau, click the **File** tab in the Ribbon and select **Save**. Tableau workbooks can be viewed by users who either have a licensed copy of Tableau or the free Tableau Reader that allows users to only view visualizations created with Tableau.

Creating a Scatter Chart in Tableau

We will use the file *Electronics* and the steps below to create a scatter chart similar to the one shown in Figure 3.17.

Step 1. Click the **Sheet 1** tab at the bottom of Tableau Data Source screen (see Figure Tableau 3.2). This will open a Tableau sheet as shown in Figure Tableau 3.3

Step 2. Drag **No. of Commercials** from the **Measures** area to the **Columns** area to set number of commercials as the horizontal axis value

Drag **Sales Volume** from the **Measures** area to the **Rows** area to set sales volume as the vertical axis value

Note that after Step 2, Tableau will display only a single circle in the chart as shown in Figure Tableau 3.4. This is because Tableau is currently plotting the SUM of the No. of Commercials versus the SUM of the Sales Volume. In Step 3, we will force Tableau to plot the values for No. of Commercials and Sales Volume by week. We do this by indicating that the level of detail that Tableau should plot is given by the Dimension of Week.

Step 3. Drag **Week** from the **Dimensions** area to the **Detail** box [⠿ Detail] in the **Marks** area to set the level of detail to weeks

Step 4. Right-click the scatter chart for **Sheet 1**

Select **Trend Lines** and click **Show Trend Lines**

Steps 1 through 4 will create the scatter chart with trendline shown in Figure Tableau 3.5.

The green # signs next to Week, No. of Commercials, Sales Volume, etc. indicate that Tableau has identified these variables as continuous numerical values. Blue # signs indicate discrete numerical values; Abc indicates text values. These value types can be changed by right-clicking on the variable and selecting Convert or Change Data Type.

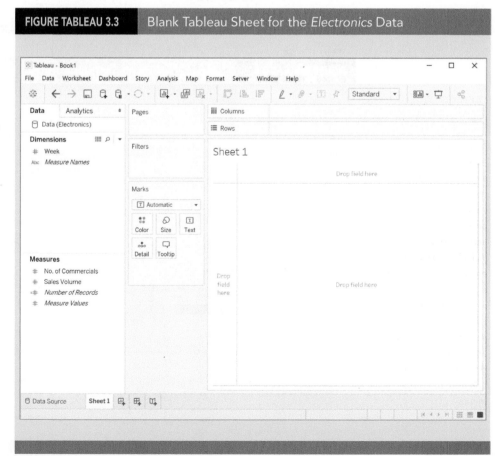

FIGURE TABLEAU 3.3   Blank Tableau Sheet for the *Electronics* Data

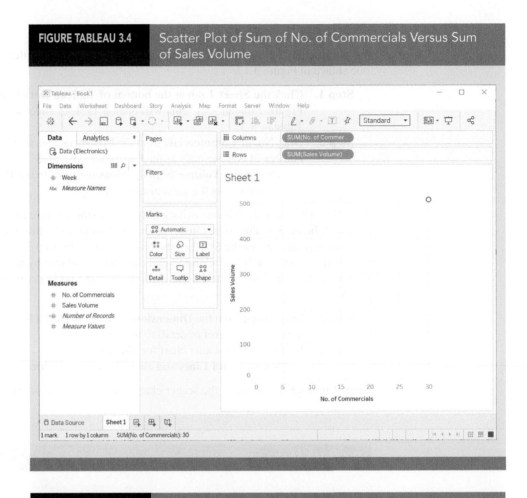

FIGURE TABLEAU 3.4   Scatter Plot of Sum of No. of Commercials Versus Sum of Sales Volume

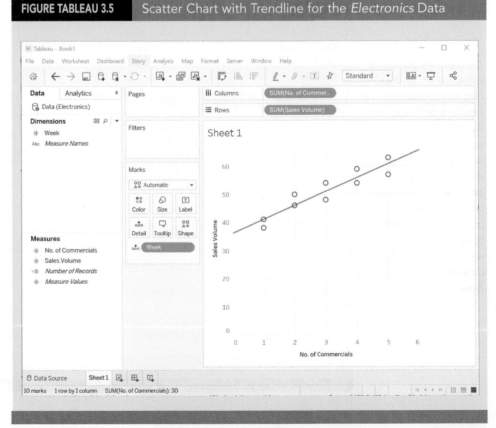

FIGURE TABLEAU 3.5   Scatter Chart with Trendline for the *Electronics* Data

*Note the setting of Automatic in the Marks area. Tableau attempts to choose the best type of visualization for your data based on the Dimensions and Measures that you include. Tableau generally does a very good job of choosing the best visualization, but you can change this by clicking on **Automatic** in the **Marks** area and choosing a different type of visualization from the drop-down menu.*

Creating a Line Chart in Tableau

We will now show how to create a line chart in Tableau similar to that shown in Figure 3.21 using the file *KirklandRegional* and the steps below. You will first need to connect to the *KirklandRegional* Excel file by opening a new Tableau sheet (click **File** in the Tableau Ribbon and select **New**) and then following the steps in the Connecting to a Data File in Tableau section at the beginning of this chapter appendix to connect to the *KirklandRegional* Excel file.

Once you connect to the *KirklandRegional* Excel file, the Tableau Data Source screen will appear similar to Figure Tableau 3.6. Note that the current column titles are incorrect. It shows "F1" as the title of Column 1, "Sales ($100s)" as the title of Column 2 and "F3" as the title of Column 3. The actual column titles are shown in the second row: "Month", "North" and "South". Tableau provides an easy-to-use tool known as Data Interpreter that can clean many common data errors such as these. Click the check box for **Use Data Interpreter** in the **Sheets** area. This will alter the column names to be "Month", "North" and "South". We can then use the steps below to create a line chart similar to Figure 3.21.

DATA *file*

KirklandRegional

Step 1. Click the **Sheet 1** tab at the bottom of the Tableau Data Source screen to open a new Tableau Sheet

Step 2. Drag **Month** from the **Dimensions** area to the **Columns** area to set month as the horizontal axis value

Drag **North** from the **Measures** area to the **Rows** area to set sales amounts in the North region as the vertical axis value

Drag **South** from the **Measures** area to the **Rows** area to set sales amounts in the South region as the vertical axis value

Step 3. Change the chart type in the drop-down menu of the **Marks** area from **Automatic** to **Line**

This creates the line charts shown in Figure Tableau 3.7. Step 4 will put both line charts on the same axis.

Step 4. Drag **SUM(South)** from the **Rows** area to the **North** vertical axis area of the line chart (see Figure Tableau 3.7) to put both North and South on the same axis

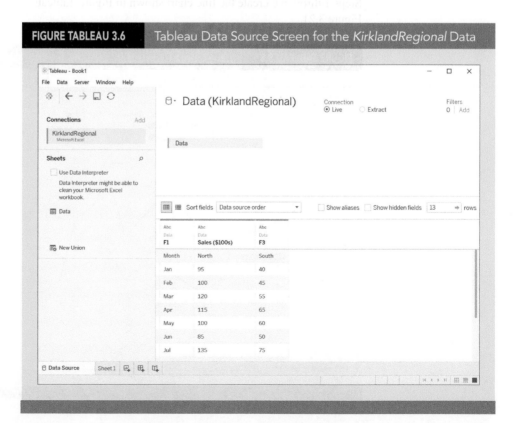

| FIGURE TABLEAU 3.6 | Tableau Data Source Screen for the *KirklandRegional* Data |

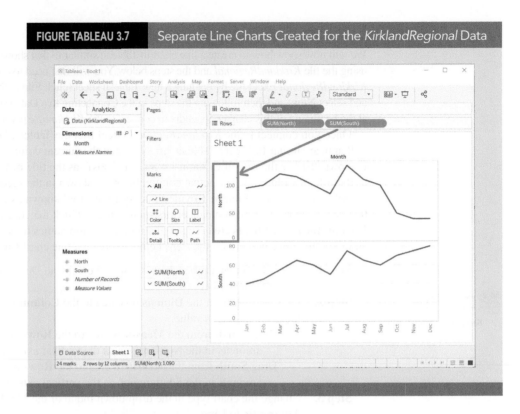

FIGURE TABLEAU 3.7   Separate Line Charts Created for the *KirklandRegional* Data

Step 5.   Right-click on the **Value** label on the vertical axis of the line chart
Select **Edit Axis…**
Step 6.   When the **Edit Axis [Measure Values]** dialog box appears, change the **Title** in the **Axis Titles** area to *Sales ($100s)*
Click **Apply** and then click **OK**

Steps 1 through 6 create the line chart shown in Figure Tableau 3.8 which is similar to Figure 3.21.

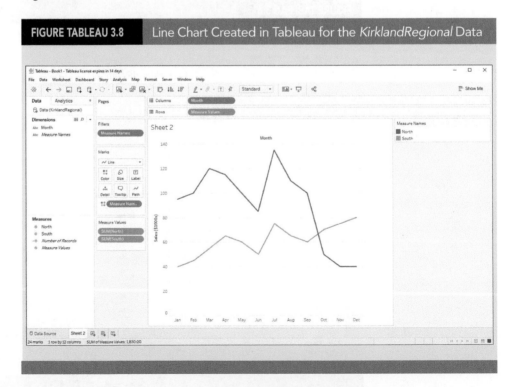

FIGURE TABLEAU 3.8   Line Chart Created in Tableau for the *KirklandRegional* Data

Creating a Bar Chart in Tableau

We will now show how to create a bar chart in Tableau similar to that shown in Figure 3.25 using the file *AccountsManaged* and the steps below. You will first need to connect to the *AccountsManaged* Excel file by opening a new Tableau sheet (click **File** in the Tableau Ribbon and select **New**) and then following the steps in the Connecting to a Data File in Tableau section at the beginning of this chapter appendix to connect to the *AccountsManaged* Excel file.

DATA *file*

AccountsManaged

If you reverse Step 2 to put Manager in the Columns area and Accounts Managed in the Rows area, this will create a vertical column chart rather than the horizontal bar chart.

Step 1. Click the **Sheet 1** tab at the bottom of the Tableau Data Source screen to open a new Tableau Sheet

Step 2. Drag **Accounts Managed** from the **Measures** area to the **Columns** area to set this as the horizontal axis value

Drag **Manager** from the **Dimensions** area to the **Rows** area to set this as the vertical axis value

Step 3. Click the **Sort Manager descending by Accounts Managed** button just below the Tableau Ribbon to sort the bar chart by decreasing number of accounts managed

Step 4. Drag **Accounts Managed** from the **Measures** area to the **Label** button in the **Marks** area to add data labels to the bars corresponding to the number of accounts managed for each manager

Steps 1 through 4 create the bar chart shown in Figure Tableau 3.9.

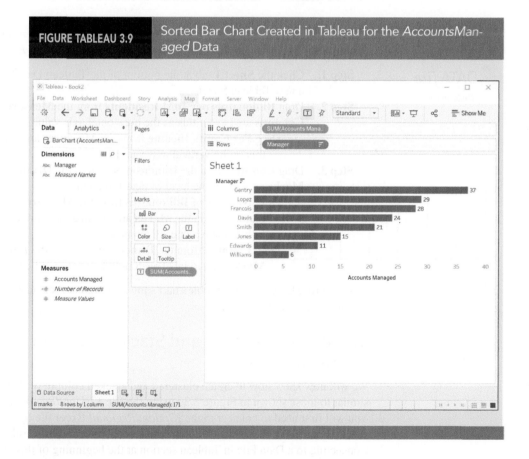

FIGURE TABLEAU 3.9   Sorted Bar Chart Created in Tableau for the *AccountsManaged* Data

Creating a Bubble Chart in Tableau

We will now show how to create a bubble chart in Tableau similar to that shown in Figure 3.27 using the file *Billionaires* and the steps below. You will first need to connect to the *Billionaires* Excel file by opening a new Tableau sheet (click **File** in the Tableau Ribbon

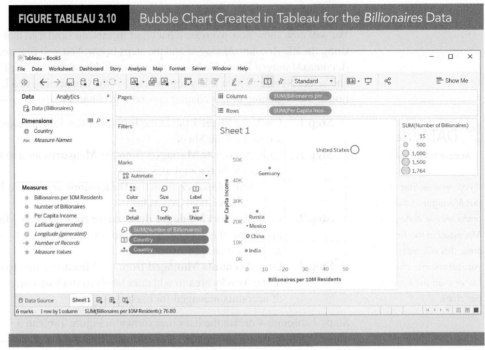

FIGURE TABLEAU 3.10   Bubble Chart Created in Tableau for the *Billionaires* Data

You may notice that Tableau has added variables in the Measures section for Latitude (generated) and Longitude (generated). Whenever Tableau recognizes a geographic variable (country name, state name, etc.) it automatically generates the corresponding latitudes and longitudes so that the values can be plotted on maps.

and select **New**) and then following the steps in the Connecting to a Data File in Tableau section at the beginning of this chapter appendix to connect to the *Billionaires* Excel file.

Billionaires

Step 1. Click the **Sheet 1** tab at the bottom of the Tableau Data Source screen to open a new Tableau Sheet

Step 2. Drag **Billionaires per 10M Residents** from the **Measures** area to the **Columns** area to set this as the horizontal axis value

Drag **Per Capita Income** from the **Measures** area to the **Rows** area to set this as the vertical axis value

Step 3. Drag **Country** from the **Dimensions** area to the **Detail** button [Detail] in the **Marks** area to set the level of detail to countries

Drag **Number of Billionaires** from the **Measures** area to the **Size** button [Size] in the **Marks** area to size the bubbles based on the number of billionaires in each country

Drag **Country** from the **Dimensions** area to the **Label** button [Label] in the **Marks** area to label each bubble by name of country

Steps 1 through 3 create the bubble chart shown in Figure Tableau 3.10 which is similar to the chart shown in Figure 3.27.

Creating a Clustered and Stacked Column Charts in Tableau

We will now show how to create clustered and stacked column (or bar) charts in Tableau similar to those shown in Figure 3.30 using the file *KirklandRegional* and the steps below. You will first need to connect to the *KirklandRegional* Excel file by opening a new Tableau sheet (click **File** in the Tableau Ribbon and select **New**) and then following the steps in the Connecting to a Data File in Tableau section at the beginning of this chapter appendix to connect to the *KirklandRegional* Excel file.

KirklandRegional

Step 1. Click the check box for **Use Data Interpreter** in the **Sheets** area of the Tableau Data Source screen to alter the column names to be "Month", "North" and "South".

If you reverse Step 3 to put Month in the Rows area and North and South in the Columns area, this will create a horizontal bar chart rather than a vertical column chart.

Step 2. Click the **Sheet 1** tab at the bottom of the Tableau Data Source screen to open a new Tableau Sheet

Step 3. Drag **Month** from the **Dimensions** area to the **Columns** area to set month as the horizontal axis value

   Drag **North** from the **Measures** area to the **Rows** area to set sales amounts in the North region as the vertical axis value

   Drag **South** from the **Measures** area to the **Rows** area to set sales amounts in the South region as the vertical axis value

Step 4. Drag **SUM(South)** from the **Rows** area to the **North** label of the vertical bar chart (see Figure Tableau 3.11) to put both column charts on the same axis

Step 5. Drag **Measure Names** from the **Dimensions** area to the **Color** button 🔲 Color in the **Marks** area to change the color of the columns based on the Measure names

Step 6. Right-click on the **Value** label on the vertical axis of the column chart

   Select **Edit Axis…**

Step 7. When the **Edit Axis [Measure Values]** dialog box appears:

   Change the **Title** in the **Axis Titles** area to *Sales ($100s)*

   Click **Apply** and then click **OK**

This creates the clustered column chart as shown in Figure Tableau 3.12. Step 8 changes the clustered column chart to a stacked column chart.

Step 8. Drag **Measure Names** from the **Columns** area back to the **Dimensions** area

Step 8 removes Measure Names from Columns and forces Tableau to display both North and South regions on the same column as shown in Figure Tableau 3.13.

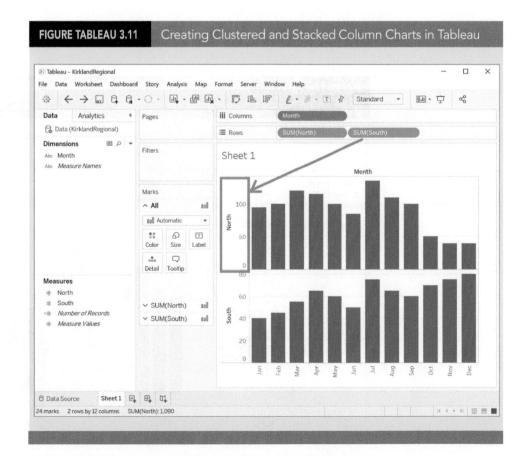

FIGURE TABLEAU 3.11   Creating Clustered and Stacked Column Charts in Tableau

FIGURE TABLEAU 3.12   Clustered Column Chart Created in Tableau for the *KirklandRegional* Data

FIGURE TABLEAU 3.13   Stacked Column Chart Created in Tableau for the *KirklandRegional* Data

Creating a Scatter-Chart Matrix in Tableau

We will now show how to create a scatter-chart matrix in Tableau similar to that shown in Figure 3.31 using the file *NYCityData* and the steps below. You will first need to connect to the *NYCityData* Excel file by opening a new Tableau sheet (click **File** in the Tableau Ribbon and select **New**) and then following the steps in the Connecting to a Data File in Tableau section at the beginning of this chapter appendix to connect to the *NYCityData* Excel file.

DATA *file*

NYCityData

Step 1. Click the **Sheet 1** tab at the bottom of the Tableau Data Source screen to open a new Tableau Sheet

Step 2. Drag **Median Monthly Rent ($), Percentage College Graduates (%), Poverty Rate (%),** and **Travel Time (min)** from the **Measures** area to the **Columns** area to add each of these variables to the horizontal axis

Drag **Median Monthly Rent ($), Percentage College Graduates (%), Poverty Rate (%),** and **Travel Time (min)** from the **Measures** area to the **Rows** area to add each of these variables to the vertical axis

Step 3. Drag **Area (Sub-Borough)** from the **Dimensions** area to the **Detail** button ⚬⚬⚬ Detail in the **Marks** area to set the level of detail to Area

Step 4. Click the **Shape** button ▦ Shape in the **Marks** area and select the filled circle ● to replace the empty circles with filled circles in the scatter charts

Click the **Size** button ◌ Size in the **Marks** area and adjust the slider ├─■──────── to make the filled circles smaller in the scatter charts

Steps 1 through 4 create the scatter-chart matrix shown in Figure Tableau 3.14 which is similar to that shown in Figure 3.31.

FIGURE TABLEAU 3.14 Scatter-Chart Matrix Created in Tableau using the *NYCityData*

Creating a Treemap in Tableau

We will now show how to create a treemap in Tableau, similar to that shown in Figure 3.35 using the file *Global100* and the steps below. You will first need to connect to the *Global100* Excel file by opening a new Tableau sheet (click **File** in the Tableau Ribbon and select **New**) and then following the steps in the Connecting to a Data File in Tableau section at the beginning of this chapter appendix to connect to the *Global100* Excel file.

Step 1. Click the **Sheet 1** tab at the bottom of the Tableau Data Source screen to open a new Tableau Sheet

Step 2. Drag **Market Value (Billions US $)** from the **Measures** area to the **Size** button [Size] in the **Marks** area to use the relative market value as the rectangle size measure in the treemap

Step 3. Drag **Company** from the **Dimensions** area to the **Label** button [Label] in the **Marks** area to label each rectangle with the name of the company

Step 4. Drag **Continent** from the **Dimensions** area to the **Color** button [Color] to color the treemap by continent location of each company

*You can edit the appearance of the Tooltip by clicking on the **Tooltip** button [Tooltip] in the **Marks** area.*

Steps 1 through 4 create the treemap shown in Figure Tableau 3.15 which is similar to that shown in Figure 3.35. Note that hovering the pointer over any rectangle (even those where space constraints prevent the company name from appearing) shows the Tooltip which contains the Company Name, Continent of Location, and Market Value.

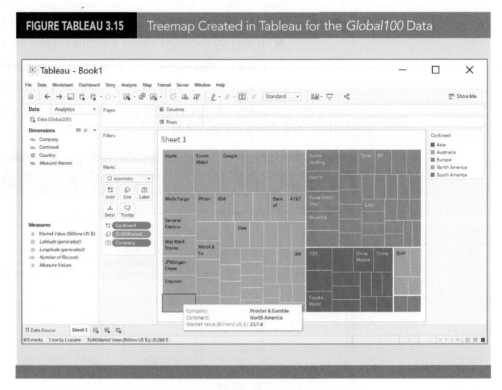

FIGURE TABLEAU 3.15   Treemap Created in Tableau for the *Global100* Data

Creating a GIS Chart in Tableau

We will now show how to create a GIS chart (map) in Tableau similar to that shown in Figure 3.38 using the file *WorldGDP2014* and the steps below. You will first need to connect to the *WorldGDP2014* Excel file by opening a new Tableau sheet (click **File** in the Tableau Ribbon and select **New**) and then following the steps in the Connecting to a Data File in Tableau section at the beginning of this chapter appendix to connect to the *WorldGDP2014* Excel file.

Step 1. Click the **Sheet 1** tab at the bottom of the Tableau Data Source screen to open a new Tableau Sheet

Step 2. Drag **Longitude (generated)** from the **Measures** area to the **Columns** area
Drag **Latitude (generated)** from the **Measures** area to the **Rows** area

This will generate a map in the chart area.

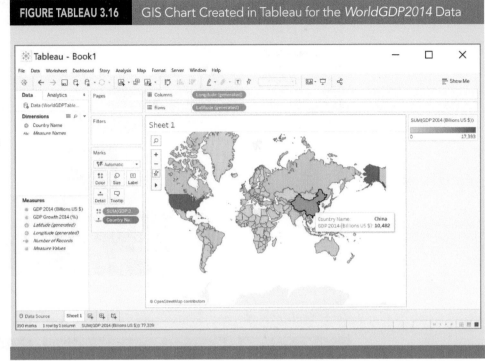

FIGURE TABLEAU 3.16   GIS Chart Created in Tableau for the *WorldGDP2014* Data

You can also generate a map using the Tableau Show Me tool by dragging Country Name from the Dimensions area to the Rows area, clicking the Show Me button **Show Me** *and then selecting the Filled Map icon* *.*

Step 3. Drag **Country Name** from the **Dimensions** area to the **Detail** button in the **Marks** area to set the level of detail to Country

Step 4. Drag **GDP 2014 (Billions US $)** from the **Measures** area to the **Color** button

 in the **Marks** area to color the map based on the relative GDP 2014 values in each country

Step 5. Click the **Color** button and choose **Edit Colors…**

Change the color drop-down from **Automatic** to **Red** to more closely match the shadings in Figure 3.38

Click **Apply** and then click **OK**

Steps 1 through 5 create the GIS chart shown in Figure Tableau 3.16 which is similar to Figure 3.38.

Creating Histograms and Boxplots in Tableau

We can also use Tableau to create several of the visualizations introduced in Chapter 2 for descriptive statistics, namely histograms and boxplots. We will begin by showing how to create a histogram in Tableau using the file *AuditTime* and the steps below. You will first need to connect to the *AuditTime* Excel file by opening a new Tableau sheet (click **File** in the Tableau Ribbon and select **New**) and then following the steps in the Connecting to a Data File in Tableau section at the beginning of this chapter appendix to connect to the *AuditTime* Excel file.

DATA *file*

AuditTime

Step 1. Click the **Sheet 1** tab at the bottom of the Tableau Data Source screen to open a new Tableau Sheet

Step 2. Drag **Audit Times (in Days)** from the **Measures** area to the **Rows** area

Step 3. Click the **Show Me** button **Show Me** and select the **Histogram** icon to generate the default histogram

Step 4. Right-click **Audit Times (in Days) (bin)** in the **Dimensions** area and select **Edit…**

Step 5. When the **Edit Bins [Audit Times (in Days)]** dialog box appears:

Change the **Size of bins:** to 5

Click **OK**

FIGURE TABLEAU 3.17 Histogram Created in Tableau for the *AuditTime* Data

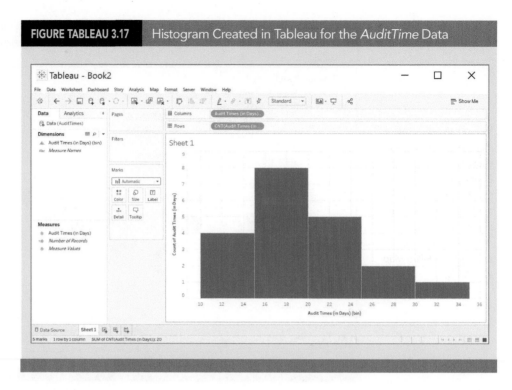

Steps 1 through 5 create the histogram shown in Figure Tableau 3.17 which matches the histogram in Figure 2.12.

We will now show how to create boxplots in Tableau for multiple variables similar to those shown in Figure 2.25 using the file *HomeSalesStacked* and the steps below. Note that we are using what is known as a "stacked" version of the home sales comparison data to Connect to Tableau.[1] You will first need to connect to the *HomeSalesStacked* Excel file by opening a new Tableau sheet (click **File** in the Tableau Ribbon and select **New**) and then following the steps in the Connecting to a Data File in Tableau section at the beginning of this chapter appendix to connect to the *HomeSalesStacked* Excel file.

DATA *file*

HomeSalesStacked

Step 1. Click the **Sheet 1** tab at the bottom of the Tableau Data Source screen to open a new Tableau Sheet

Step 2. Drag **Selling Price ($)** from the **Measures** area to the **Rows** area

Steps 1 and 2 create the bar chart shown in Figure Tableau 3.18. To create a boxplot, we need to disaggregate the data, which is what we do in Step 3.

Step 3. Click the **Analysis** tab in the Tableau Ribbon and uncheck **Aggregate Measures** to disaggregate the Selling Price ($) values (see Figure Tableau 3.19)

We can now use Tableau's Show Me tool to create the boxplot.

Step 4. Click the **Show Me** button ☰ Show Me and select the **box-and-whisker** icon to generate the default boxplot

Step 5. Drag **Location** from the **Dimensions** area to the **Columns** area

Steps 1 through 5 create the completed multiple variable boxplot shown in Figure Tableau 3.20. This figure is similar to the boxplots shown in Figure 2.25, but you may notice that the whiskers are different in Figure Tableau 3.19 than in Figure 2.25. This is because Tableau uses slightly different definitions for these values than Excel.

---

[1] A "stacked" data file means that the values for all groups (for example, locations in these data) are in a single column and each row represents a single observation (or record). This type of data file is common in databases, and most statistical analysis software expects data in this format. However, to create the multiple boxplots in Excel in Chapter 2 we had to use the "unstacked" data file *HomeSalesComparison*. The data is the same in files *HomeSalesComparison* and *HomeSalesStacked*, but arranged differently.

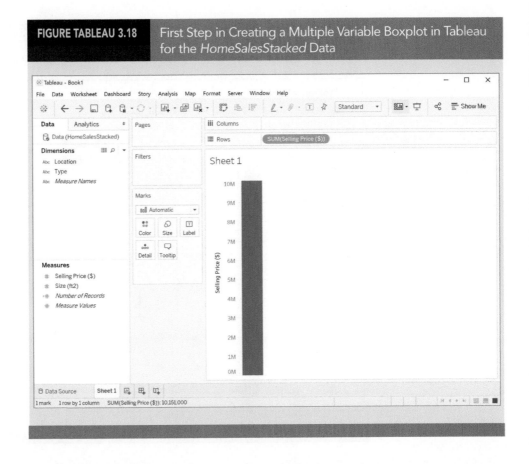

FIGURE TABLEAU 3.18 First Step in Creating a Multiple Variable Boxplot in Tableau for the *HomeSalesStacked* Data

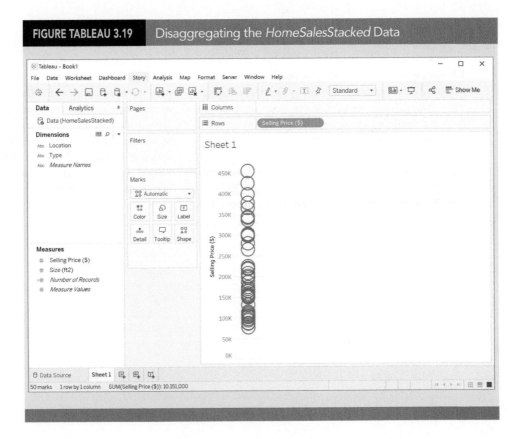

FIGURE TABLEAU 3.19 Disaggregating the *HomeSalesStacked* Data

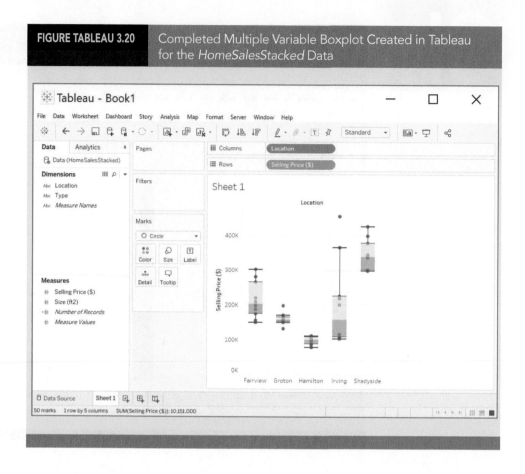

FIGURE TABLEAU 3.20   Completed Multiple Variable Boxplot Created in Tableau for the *HomeSalesStacked* Data

NOTES + COMMENTS

1. Tableau can create many additional visualizations for data including bullet graphs, violin plots, Gantt charts, and many others. These are beyond the scope of this textbook, but the References section in the textbook contains several excellent references for learning more about using Tableau for data visualization.

2. Tableau makes it very easy to create Data Dashboards from multiple charts. To create a Dashboard in Tableau, click **Dashboard** in the Tableau Ribbon and select **New Dashboard**. You can then drag individual Tableau Sheets from the **Sheets** area to the **Drop sheets here** area and arrange them into a single Dashboard.

3. Tableau includes a Presentation Mode that provides better visualizations of the charts and Dashboards created. To access Presentation Mode, click **Window** in the Tableau Ribbon and select **Presentation Mode**. To exit Presentation Mode, press the **Esc** key.

Chapter 4

Probability: An Introduction to Modeling Uncertainty

ANALYTICS IN ACTION

National Aeronautics and Space Administration*

WASHINGTON, D.C.

The National Aeronautics and Space Administration (NASA) is the U.S. government agency that is responsible for the U.S. civilian space program and for aeronautics and aerospace research. NASA is best known for its manned space exploration; its mission statement is to "drive advances in science, technology, aeronautics, and space exploration to enhance knowledge, education, innovation, economic vitality and stewardship of Earth." With more than 17,000 employees, NASA oversees many different space-based missions including work on the International Space Station, exploration beyond our solar system with the Hubble telescope, and planning for possible future astronaut missions to the moon and Mars.

Although NASA's primary mission is space exploration, its expertise has been called on in assisting countries and organizations throughout the world in nonspace endeavors. In one such situation, the San José copper and gold mine in Copiapó, Chile, caved in, trapping 33 men more than 2,000 feet underground. It was important to bring the men safely to the surface as quickly as possible, but it was also imperative that the rescue effort be carefully designed and implemented to save as many miners as possible. The Chilean government asked NASA to provide assistance in developing a rescue method. NASA sent a four-person team consisting of an engineer with expertise

in vehicle design, two physicians, and a psychologist with knowledge about issues of long-term confinement.

The probability of success and the failure of various other rescue methods was prominent in the thoughts of everyone involved. Since no historical data were available to apply to this unique rescue situation, NASA scientists developed subjective probability estimates for the success and failure of various rescue methods based on similar circumstances experienced by astronauts returning from short- and long-term space missions. The probability estimates provided by NASA guided officials in the selection of a rescue method and provided insight as to how the miners would survive the ascent in a rescue cage. The rescue method designed by the Chilean officials in consultation with the NASA team resulted in the construction of 13-foot-long, 924-pound steel rescue capsule that would be used to bring up the miners one at a time. All miners were rescued, with the last emerging 68 days after the cave-in occurred.

In this chapter, you will learn about probability as well as how to compute and interpret probabilities for a variety of situations. The basic relationships of probability, conditional probability, and Bayes' theorem will be covered. We will also discuss the concepts of random variables and probability distributions and illustrate the use of some of the more common discrete and continuous probability distributions.

*The authors are indebted to Dr. Michael Duncan and Clinton Cragg at NASA for providing this Analytics in Action.

The concept of identifying uncertainty in data was introduced in Chapters 2 and 3 through descriptive statistics and data-visualization techniques, respectively. In this chapter, we expand on our discussion of modeling uncertainty by formalizing the concept of probability and introducing the concept of probability distributions.

Uncertainty is an ever-present fact of life for decision makers, and much time and effort are spent trying to plan for, and respond to, uncertainty. Consider the CEO who has to make decisions about marketing budgets and production amounts using forecasted demands. Or consider the financial analyst who must determine how to build a client's portfolio of stocks and bonds when the rates of return for these investments are not known with certainty. In many business scenarios, data are available to provide information on possible outcomes for some decisions, but the exact outcome from a given decision is almost never known with certainty because many factors are outside the control of the decision maker (e.g., actions taken by competitors, the weather).

Probability is the numerical measure of the likelihood that an event will occur.[1] Therefore, it can be used as a measure of the uncertainty associated with an event. This measure of uncertainty is often communicated through a probability distribution. Probability distributions are extremely helpful in providing additional information about an

[1]Note that there are several different possible definitions of probability, depending on the method used to assign probabilities. This includes the classical definition, the relative frequency definition, and the subjective definition of probability. In this text, we most often use the relative frequency definition of probability, which assumes that probabilities are based on empirical data. For a more thorough discussion of the different possible definitions of probability see Chapter 4 of Anderson, Sweeney, Williams, Camm, Cochran, Fry, and Ohlmann, *An Introduction to Statistics for Business and Economics*, 14e (2020).

event, and as we will see in later chapters in this textbook, they can be used to help a decision maker evaluate possible actions and determine the best course of action.

4.1 Events and Probabilities

In discussing probabilities, we start by defining a **random experiment** as a process that generates well-defined outcomes. Several examples of random experiments and their associated outcomes are shown in Table 4.1.

By specifying all possible outcomes, we identify the **sample space** for a random experiment. Consider the first random experiment in Table 4.1—a coin toss. The possible outcomes are head and tail. If we let S denote the sample space, we can use the following notation to describe the sample space.

$$S = \{\text{Head, Tail}\}$$

Suppose we consider the second random experiment in Table 4.1—rolling a die. The possible experimental outcomes, defined as the number of dots appearing on the upward face of the die, are the six points in the sample space for this random experiment.

$$S = \{1, 2, 3, 4, 5, 6\}$$

Outcomes and events form the foundation of the study of probability. Formally, an **event** is defined as a collection of outcomes. For example, consider the case of an expansion project being undertaken by California Power & Light Company (CP&L). CP&L is starting a project designed to increase the generating capacity of one of its plants in Southern California. An analysis of similar construction projects indicates that the possible completion times for the project are 8, 9, 10, 11, and 12 months. Each of these possible completion times represents a possible outcome for this project. Table 4.2 shows the number of past construction projects that required 8, 9, 10, 11, and 12 months.

Let us assume that the CP&L project manager is interested in completing the project in 10 months or less. Referring to Table 4.2, we see that three possible outcomes (8 months, 9 months, and 10 months) provide completion times of 10 months or less. Letting C denote the event that the project is completed in 10 months or less, we write:

$$C = \{8, 9, 10\}$$

Event C is said to occur if *any one* of these outcomes occurs.

A variety of additional events can be defined for the CP&L project:

L = The event that the project is completed in *less than* 10 months = $\{8, 9\}$

M = The event that the project is completed in *more than* 10 months = $\{11, 12\}$

In each case, the event must be identified as a collection of outcomes for the random experiment.

TABLE 4.1	Random Experiments and Experimental Outcomes
Random Experiment	**Experimental Outcomes**
Toss a coin	Head, tail
Roll a die	1, 2, 3, 4, 5, 6
Conduct a sales call	Purchase, no purchase
Hold a particular share of stock for one year	Price of stock goes up, price of stock goes down, no change in stock price
Reduce price of product	Demand goes up, demand goes down, no change in demand

TABLE 4.2	Completion Times for 40 CP&L Projects	
Completion Time (months)	No. of Past Projects Having This Completion Time	Probability of Outcome
8	6	6/40 = 0.15
9	10	10/40 = 0.25
10	12	12/40 = 0.30
11	6	6/40 = 0.15
12	6	6/40 = 0.15
Total	40	1.00

The **probability of an event** is equal to the sum of the probabilities of outcomes for the event. Using this definition and given the probabilities of outcomes shown in Table 4.2, we can now calculate the probability of the event $C = \{8, 9, 10\}$. The probability of event C, denoted $P(C)$, is given by

$$P(C) = P(8) + P(9) + P(10) = 0.15 + 0.25 + 0.30 = 0.70$$

Similarly, because the event that the project is completed in less than 10 months is given by $L = \{8, 9\}$, the probability of this event is given by

$$P(L) = P(8) + P(9) = 0.15 + 0.25 = 0.40$$

Finally, for the event that the project is completed in more than 10 months, we have $M = \{11, 12\}$ and thus

$$P(M) = P(11) + P(12) = 0.15 + 0.15 = 0.30$$

Using these probability results, we can now tell CP&L management that there is a 0.70 probability that the project will be completed in 10 months or less, a 0.40 probability that it will be completed in less than 10 months, and a 0.30 probability that it will be completed in more than 10 months.

4.2 Some Basic Relationships of Probability

Complement of an Event

The complement of event A is sometimes written as $\bar{A}$ or A' in other textbooks.

Given an event A, the **complement of A** is defined to be the event consisting of all outcomes that are *not* in A. The complement of A is denoted by A^C. Figure 4.1 shows what is known as a **Venn diagram**, which illustrates the concept of a complement. The rectangular area represents the sample space for the random experiment and, as such, contains all possible outcomes. The circle represents event A and contains only the outcomes that belong to A. The shaded region of the rectangle contains all outcomes not in event A and is by definition the complement of A.

In any probability application, either event A or its complement A^C must occur. Therefore, we have

$$P(A) + P(A^C) = 1$$

Solving for $P(A)$, we obtain the following result:

COMPUTING PROBABILITY USING THE COMPLEMENT

$$P(A) = 1 - P(A^C) \tag{4.1}$$

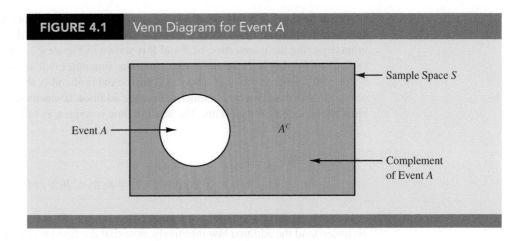

FIGURE 4.1   Venn Diagram for Event A

Equation (4.1) shows that the probability of an event A can be computed easily if the probability of its complement, $P(A^C)$, is known.

As an example, consider the case of a sales manager who, after reviewing sales reports, states that 80% of new customer contacts result in no sale. By allowing A to denote the event of a sale and A^C to denote the event of no sale, the manager is stating that $P(A^C) = 0.80$. Using equation (4.1), we see that

$$P(A) = 1 - P(A^C) = 1 - 0.80 = 0.20$$

We can conclude that a new customer contact has a 0.20 probability of resulting in a sale.

Addition Law

The addition law is helpful when we are interested in knowing the probability that at least one of two events will occur. That is, with events A and B we are interested in knowing the probability that event A or event B occurs or both events occur.

Before we present the addition law, we need to discuss two concepts related to the combination of events: the *union* of events and the *intersection* of events. Given two events A and B, the **union of A and B** is defined as the event containing all outcomes belonging to A or B or both. The union of A and B is denoted by $A \cup B$.

The Venn diagram in Figure 4.2 depicts the union of A and B. Note that one circle contains all the outcomes in A and the other all the outcomes in B. The fact that the circles overlap indicates that some outcomes are contained in both A and B.

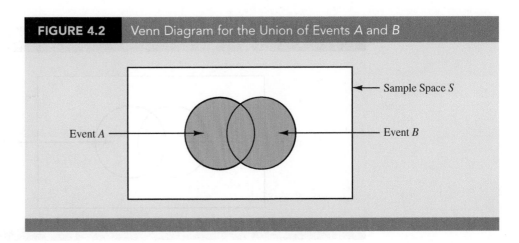

FIGURE 4.2   Venn Diagram for the Union of Events A and B

The definition of the **intersection of A and B** is the event containing the outcomes that belong to both A and B. The intersection of A and B is denoted by $A \cap B$. The Venn diagram depicting the intersection of A and B is shown in Figure 4.3. The area in which the two circles overlap is the intersection; it contains outcomes that are in both A and B.

The **addition law** provides a way to compute the probability that event A or event B occurs or both events occur. In other words, the addition law is used to compute the probability of the union of two events. The addition law is written as follows:

ADDITION LAW

$$P(A \cup B) = P(A) + P(B) - P(A \cap B) \tag{4.2}$$

To understand the addition law intuitively, note that the first two terms in the addition law, $P(A) + P(B)$, account for all the sample points in $A \cup B$. However, because the sample points in the intersection $A \cap B$ are in both A and B, when we compute $P(A) + P(B)$, we are in effect counting each of the sample points in $A \cap B$ twice. We correct for this double counting by subtracting $P(A \cap B)$.

As an example of the addition law, consider a study conducted by the human resources manager of a major computer software company. The study showed that 30% of the employees who left the firm within two years did so primarily because they were dissatisfied with their salary, 20% left because they were dissatisfied with their work assignments, and 12% of the former employees indicated dissatisfaction with *both* their salary and their work assignments. What is the probability that an employee who leaves within two years does so because of dissatisfaction with salary, dissatisfaction with the work assignment, or both?

Let

$$S = \text{the event that the employee leaves because of salary}$$
$$W = \text{the event that the employee leaves because of work assignment}$$

We can also think of this probability in the following manner: What proportion of employees either left because of salary or left because of work assignment?

From the survey results, we have $P(S) = 0.30$, $P(W) = 0.20$, and $P(S \cap W) = 0.12$. Using the addition law from equation (4.2), we have

$$P(S \cup W) = P(S) + P(W) - P(S \cap W) = 0.30 + 0.20 - 0.12 = 0.38$$

This calculation tells us that there is a 0.38 probability that an employee will leave for salary or work assignment reasons.

Before we conclude our discussion of the addition law, let us consider a special case that arises for **mutually exclusive events**. Events A and B are mutually exclusive if the occurrence of one event precludes the occurrence of the other. Thus, a requirement for A and B

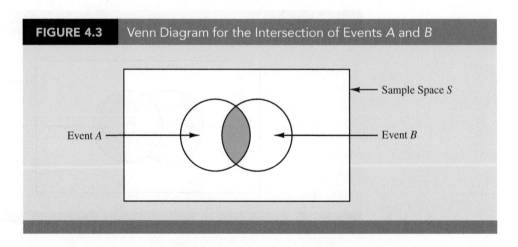

FIGURE 4.3   Venn Diagram for the Intersection of Events A and B

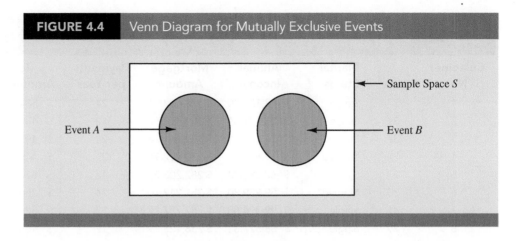

FIGURE 4.4 Venn Diagram for Mutually Exclusive Events

to be mutually exclusive is that their intersection must contain no sample points. The Venn diagram depicting two mutually exclusive events A and B is shown in Figure 4.4. In this case $P(A \cap B) = 0$ and the addition law can be written as follows:

ADDITION LAW FOR MUTUALLY EXCLUSIVE EVENTS

$$P(A \cup B) = P(A) + P(B)$$

More generally, two events are said to be mutually exclusive if the events have no outcomes in common.

NOTES + COMMENTS

The addition law can be extended beyond two events. For example, the addition law for three events A, B, and C is $P(A \cup B \cup C) = P(A) + P(B) + P(C) - P(A \cap B) - P(A \cap C) -$ $P(B \cap C) + P(A \cap B \cap C)$. Similar logic can be used to derive the expressions for the addition law for more than three events.

4.3 Conditional Probability

Often, the probability of one event is dependent on whether some related event has already occurred. Suppose we have an event A with probability $P(A)$. If we learn that a related event, denoted by B, has already occurred, we take advantage of this information by calculating a new probability for event A. This new probability of event A is called a **conditional probability** and is written $P(A \mid B)$. The notation | indicates that we are considering the probability of event A *given* the condition that event B has occurred. Hence, the notation $P(A \mid B)$ reads "the probability of A given B."

To illustrate the idea of conditional probability, consider a bank that is interested in the mortgage default risk for its home mortgage customers. Table 4.3 shows the first 25 records of the 300 home mortgage customers at Lancaster Savings and Loan, a company that specializes in high-risk subprime lending. Some of these home mortgage customers have defaulted on their mortgages and others have continued to make on-time payments. These data include the age of the customer at the time of mortgage origination, the marital status of the customer (single or married), the annual income of the customer, the mortgage amount, the number of payments made by the customer per year on the mortgage, the total amount paid by the customer over the lifetime of the mortgage, and whether or not the customer defaulted on her or his mortgage.

TABLE 4.3		Subset of Data from 300 Home Mortgages of Customers at Lancaster Savings and Loan					
Customer No.	Age	Marital Status	Annual Income	Mortgage Amount	Payments per Year	Total Amount Paid	Default on Mortgage?
1	37	Single	$172,125.70	$473,402.96	24	$581,885.13	Yes
2	31	Single	$108,571.04	$300,468.60	12	$489,320.38	No
3	37	Married	$124,136.41	$330,664.24	24	$493,541.93	Yes
4	24	Married	$79,614.04	$230,222.94	24	$449,682.09	Yes
5	27	Single	$68,087.33	$282,203.53	12	$520,581.82	No
6	30	Married	$59,959.80	$251,242.70	24	$356,711.58	Yes
7	41	Single	$99,394.05	$282,737.29	12	$524,053.46	No
8	29	Single	$38,527.35	$238,125.19	12	$468,595.99	No
9	31	Married	$112,078.62	$297,133.24	24	$399,617.40	Yes
10	36	Single	$224,899.71	$622,578.74	12	$1,233,002.14	No
11	31	Married	$27,945.36	$215,440.31	24	$285,900.10	Yes
12	40	Single	$48,929.74	$252,885.10	12	$336,574.63	No
13	39	Married	$82,810.92	$183,045.16	12	$262,537.23	No
14	31	Single	$68,216.88	$165,309.34	12	$253,633.17	No
15	40	Single	$59,141.13	$220,176.18	12	$424,749.80	No
16	45	Married	$72,568.89	$233,146.91	12	$356,363.93	No
17	32	Married	$101,140.43	$245,360.02	24	$388,429.41	Yes
18	37	Married	$124,876.53	$320,401.04	4	$360,783.45	Yes
19	32	Married	$133,093.15	$494,395.63	12	$861,874.67	No
20	32	Single	$85,268.67	$159,010.33	12	$308,656.11	No
21	37	Single	$92,314.96	$249,547.14	24	$342,339.27	Yes
22	29	Married	$120,876.13	$308,618.37	12	$472,668.98	No
23	24	Single	$86,294.13	$258,321.78	24	$380,347.56	Yes
24	32	Married	$216,748.68	$634,609.61	24	$915,640.13	Yes
25	44	Single	$46,389.75	$194,770.91	12	$385,288.86	No

Lancaster Savings and Loan is interested in whether the probability of a customer defaulting on a mortgage differs by marital status. Let

S = event that a customer is single
M = event that a customer is married
D = event that a customer defaulted on his or her mortgage
D^C = event that a customer did not default on his or her mortgage

Table 4.4 shows a crosstabulation for two events that can be derived from the Lancaster Savings and Loan mortgage data.

Chapter 3 discusses PivotTables in more detail.

Note that we can easily create Table 4.4 in Excel using a PivotTable by using the following steps:

Step 1. In the *Values* worksheet of *MortgageDefaultData* file
　　　　Click the **Insert** tab on the Ribbon
Step 2. Click **PivotTable** in the **Tables** group
Step 3. When the **Create PivotTable** dialog box appears:
　　　　Choose **Select a Table or Range**
　　　　Enter *A1:H301* in the **Table/Range:** box

MortgageDefaultData

Select **New Worksheet** as the location for the PivotTable Report
Click **OK**

Step 4. In the **PivotTable Fields** area go to **Drag fields between areas below:**
Drag the **Marital Status** field to the **ROWS** area
Drag the **Default on Mortgage?** field to the **COLUMNS** area
Drag the **Customer Number** field to the **VALUES** area

Step 4. Click on **Sum of Customer Number** in the **VALUES** area and select **Value Field Settings**

Step 6. When the **Value Field Settings** dialog box appears:
Under **Summarize value field by**, select **Count**

These steps produce the PivotTable shown in Figure 4.5.

TABLE 4.4	Crosstabulation of Marital Status and if Customer Defaults on Mortgage		
Marital Status	**No Default**	**Default**	**Total**
Married	64	79	143
Single	116	41	157
Total	180	120	300

FIGURE 4.5	PivotTable for Marital Status and Whether Customer Defaults on Mortgage

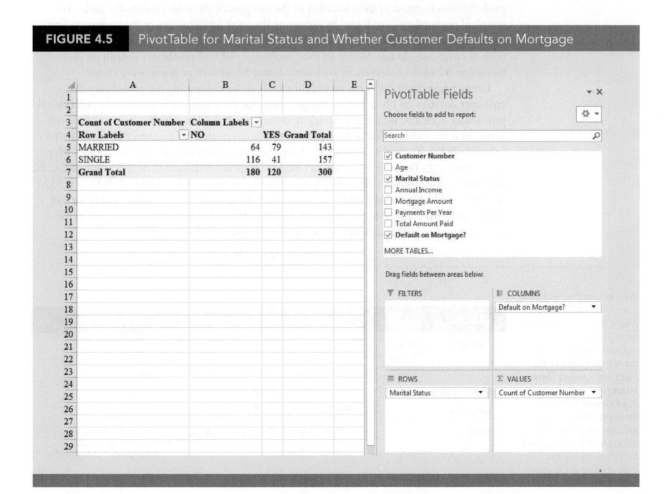

From Table 4.4 or Figure 4.5, the probability that a customer defaults on his or her mortgage is 120/300 = 0.4. The probability that a customer does not default on his or her mortgage is 1 − 0.4 = 0.6 (or 180/300 = 0.6). But is this probability different for married customers as compared with single customers? Conditional probability allows us to answer this question.

We can also think of this joint probability in the following manner: What proportion of all customers is both married and defaulted on their loans?

But first, let us answer a related question: What is the probability that a randomly selected customer does not default on his or her mortgage and the customer is married? The probability that a randomly selected customer is married and the customer defaults on his or her mortgage is written as $P(M \cap D)$. This probability is calculated as $P(M \cap D) = \frac{79}{300} = 0.2633$.

Similarly,

$P(M \cap D^C) = \frac{64}{300} = 0.2133$ is the probability that a randomly selected customer is married and that the customer does not default on his or her mortgage.

$P(S \cap D) = \frac{41}{300} = 0.1367$ is the probability that a randomly selected customer is single and that the customer defaults on his or her mortgage.

$P(S \cap D^C) = \frac{116}{300} = 0.3867$ is the probability that a randomly selected customer is single and that the customer does not default on his or her mortgage.

Because each of these values gives the probability of the intersection of two events, these probabilities are called **joint probabilities**. Table 4.5, which provides a summary of the probability information for customer defaults on mortgages, is referred to as a joint probability table.

The values in the Total column and Total row (the margins) of Table 4.5 provide the probabilities of each event separately. That is, $P(M) = 0.4766$, $P(S) = 0.5234$, $P(D^C) = 0.6000$, and $P(D) = 0.4000$. These probabilities are referred to as **marginal probabilities** because of their location in the margins of the joint probability table. The marginal probabilities are found by summing the joint probabilities in the corresponding row or column of the joint probability table. From the marginal probabilities, we see that 60% of customers do not default on their mortgage, 40% of customers default on their mortgage, 47.66% of customers are married, and 52.34% of customers are single.

Let us begin the conditional probability analysis by computing the probability that a customer defaults on his or her mortgage given that the customer is married. In conditional probability notation, we are attempting to determine $P(D \mid M)$, which is read as "the probability that the customer defaults on the mortgage given that the customer is married." To calculate $P(D \mid M)$, first we note that we are concerned only with the 143 customers who are married (M). Because 79 of the 143 married customers defaulted on their mortgages, the probability of a customer defaulting given that the customer is married is 79/143 = 0.5524. In other words, given that a customer is married, there is a 55.24% chance that he or she will default. Note also that the conditional probability $P(D \mid M)$ can be computed as the ratio of the joint probability $P(D \cap M)$ to the marginal probability $P(M)$.

$$P(D \mid M) = \frac{P(D \cap M)}{P(M)} = \frac{0.2633}{0.4766} = 0.5524$$

*We can use the PivotTable from Figure 4.5 to easily create the joint probability table in Excel. To do so, right-click on any of the numerical values in the PivotTable, select **Show Values As**, and choose **% of Grand Total**. The resulting values, which are percentages of the total, can then be divided by 100 to create the probabilities in the joint probability table.*

TABLE 4.5	Joint Probability Table for Customer Mortgage Prepayments		
Joint Probabilities			
	No Default (D^C)	Default (D)	Total
Married (M)	0.2133	0.2633	0.4766
Single (S)	0.3867	0.1367	0.5234
Total	0.6000	0.4000	1.0000

Marginal Probabilities

The fact that a conditional probability can be computed as the ratio of a joint probability to a marginal probability provides the following general formula for conditional probability calculations for two events A and B.

CONDITIONAL PROBABILITY

$$P(A \mid B) = \frac{P(A \cap B)}{P(B)} \tag{4.3}$$

or

$$P(B \mid A) = \frac{P(A \cap B)}{P(A)} \tag{4.4}$$

We have already determined that the probability a customer who is married will default is 0.5524. How does this compare to a customer who is single? That is, we want to find $P(D \mid S)$. From equation (4.3), we can compute $P(D \mid S)$ as

$$P(D \mid S) = \frac{P(D \cap S)}{P(S)} = \frac{0.1367}{0.5234} = 0.2611$$

In other words, the chance that a customer will default if the customer is single is 26.11%. This is substantially less than the chance of default if the customer is married.

Note that we could also answer this question using the Excel PivotTable in Figure 4.5. We can calculate these conditional probabilities by right-clicking on any numerical value in the body of the PivotTable and then selecting **Show Values As** and choosing **% of Row Total**. The modified Excel PivotTable is shown in Figure 4.6.

FIGURE 4.6   Using Excel PivotTable to Calculate Conditional Probabilities

By calculating the **% of Row Total**, the Excel PivotTable in Figure 4.6 shows that 55.24% of married customers defaulted on mortgages, but only 26.11% of single customers defaulted.

Independent Events

Note that in our example, $P(D) = 0.4000$, $P(D \mid M) = 0.5524$, and $P(D \mid S) = 0.2611$. So the probability that a customer defaults is influenced by whether the customer is married or single. Because $P(D \mid M) \neq P(D)$, we say that events D and M are dependent. However, if the probability of event D is not changed by the existence of event M—that is, if $P(D \mid M) = P(D)$—then we would say that events D and M are **independent events**. This is summarized for two events A and B as follows:

INDEPENDENT EVENTS

Two events A and B are independent if

$$P(A \mid B) = P(A) \qquad (4.5)$$

or

$$P(B \mid A) = P(B) \qquad (4.6)$$

Otherwise, the events are dependent.

Multiplication Law

The multiplication law can be used to calculate the probability of the intersection of two events. The multiplication law is based on the definition of conditional probability. Solving equations (4.3) and (4.4) for $P(A \cap B)$, we obtain the **multiplication law**.

MULTIPLICATION LAW

$$P(A \cap B) = P(B)P(A \mid B) \qquad (4.7)$$

or

$$P(A \cap B) = P(A)P(B \mid A) \qquad (4.8)$$

To illustrate the use of the multiplication law, we will calculate the probability that a customer defaults on his or her mortgage and the customer is married, $P(D \cap M)$. From equation (4.7), this is calculated as $P(D \cap M) = P(M)P(D \mid M)$.

From Table 4.5 we know that $P(M) = 0.4766$, and from our previous calculations we know that the conditional probability $P(D \mid M) = 0.5524$. Therefore,

$$P(D \cap M) = P(M)P(D \mid M) = (0.4766)(0.5524) = 0.2633$$

This value matches the value shown for $P(D \cap M)$ in Table 4.5. The multiplication law is useful when we know conditional probabilities but do not know the joint probabilities.

Consider the special case in which events A and B are independent. From equations (4.5) and (4.6), $P(A \mid B) = P(A)$ and $P(B \mid A) = P(B)$. Using these equations to simplify equations (4.7) and (4.8) for this special case, we obtain the following multiplication law for independent events.

MULTIPLICATION LAW FOR INDEPENDENT EVENTS

$$P(A \cap B) = P(A)P(B) \qquad (4.9)$$

To compute the probability of the intersection of two independent events, we simply multiply the probabilities of each event.

Bayes' Theorem

Revising probabilities when new information is obtained is an important aspect of probability analysis. Often, we begin the analysis with initial or **prior probability** estimates for specific events of interest. Then, from sources such as a sample survey or a product test, we obtain additional information about the events. Given this new information, we update the prior probability values by calculating revised probabilities, referred to as **posterior probabilities**. **Bayes' theorem** provides a means for making these probability calculations.

Bayes' theorem is also discussed in Chapter 15 in the context of decision analysis.

As an application of Bayes' theorem, consider a manufacturing firm that receives shipments of parts from two different suppliers. Let A_1 denote the event that the part is from supplier 1 and let A_2 denote the event that a part is from supplier 2. Currently, 65% of the parts purchased by the company are from supplier 1 and the remaining 35% are from supplier 2. Hence, if a part is selected at random, we would assign the prior probabilities $P(A_1) = 0.65$ and $P(A_2) = 0.35$.

The quality of the purchased parts varies according to their source. Historical data suggest that the quality ratings of the two suppliers are as shown in Table 4.6.

If we let G be the event that a part is good and we let B be the event that a part is bad, the information in Table 4.6 enables us to calculate the following conditional probability values:

$$P(G \mid A_1) = 0.98 \qquad P(B \mid A_1) = 0.02$$
$$P(G \mid A_2) = 0.95 \qquad P(B \mid A_2) = 0.05$$

Figure 4.7 shows a diagram that depicts the process of the firm receiving a part from one of the two suppliers and then discovering that the part is good or bad as a two-step random experiment. We see that four outcomes are possible; two correspond to the part being good and two correspond to the part being bad.

Each of the outcomes is the intersection of two events, so we can use the multiplication rule to compute the probabilities. For instance,

$$P(A_1, G) = P(A_1 \cap G) = P(A_1)P(G \mid A_1)$$

The process of computing these joint probabilities can be depicted in what is called a probability tree (see Figure 4.8). From left to right through the tree, the probabilities for each branch at step 1 are prior probabilities and the probabilities for each branch at step 2 are conditional probabilities. To find the probability of each experimental outcome, simply multiply the probabilities on the branches leading to the outcome. Each of these joint probabilities is shown in Figure 4.8 along with the known probabilities for each branch.

Now suppose that the parts from the two suppliers are used in the firm's manufacturing process and that a machine breaks down while attempting the process using a bad part. Given the information that the part is bad, what is the probability that it came from supplier 1 and what is the probability that it came from supplier 2? With the information in the probability tree (Figure 4.8), Bayes' theorem can be used to answer these questions.

For the case in which there are only two events (A_1 and A_2), Bayes' theorem can be written as follows:

BAYES' THEOREM (TWO-EVENT CASE)

$$P(A_1 \mid B) = \frac{P(A_1)P(B \mid A_1)}{P(A_1)P(B \mid A_1) + P(A_2)P(B \mid A_2)} \tag{4.10}$$

$$P(A_2 \mid B) = \frac{P(A_2)P(B \mid A_2)}{P(A_1)P(B \mid A_1) + P(A_2)P(B \mid A_2)} \tag{4.11}$$

TABLE 4.6	Historical Quality Levels for Two Suppliers	
	% Good Parts	**% Bad Parts**
Supplier 1	98	2
Supplier 2	95	5

FIGURE 4.7   Diagram for Two-Supplier Example

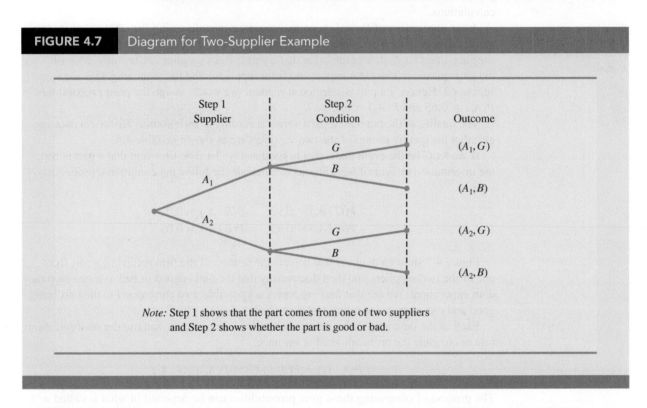

Note: Step 1 shows that the part comes from one of two suppliers
and Step 2 shows whether the part is good or bad.

FIGURE 4.8   Probability Tree for Two-Supplier Example

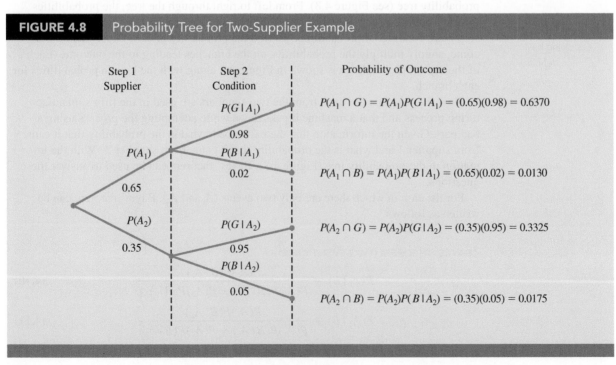

Using equation (4.10) and the probability values provided in Figure 4.8, we have

$$P(A_1 \mid B) = \frac{P(A_1)P(B \mid A_1)}{P(A_1)P(B \mid A_1) + P(A_2)P(B \mid A_2)}$$

$$= \frac{(0.65)(0.02)}{(0.65)(0.02) + (0.35)(0.05)} = \frac{0.0130}{0.0130 + 0.0175}$$

$$= \frac{0.0130}{0.0305} = 0.4262$$

Using equation (4.11), we find $P(A_2 \mid B)$ as

$$P(A_2 \mid B) = \frac{P(A_2)P(B \mid A_2)}{P(A_2)P(B \mid A_1) + P(A_2)P(B \mid A_2)}$$

$$= \frac{(0.35)(0.05)}{(0.65)(0.02) + (0.35)(0.05)} = \frac{0.0175}{0.0130 + 0.0175}$$

$$= \frac{0.0175}{0.0305} = 0.5738$$

Note that in this application we started with a probability of 0.65 that a part selected at random was from supplier 1. However, given information that the part is bad, the probability that the part is from supplier 1 drops to 0.4262. In fact, if the part is bad, the chance is better than 50–50 that it came from supplier 2; that is, $P(A_2 \mid B) = 0.5738$.

Bayes' theorem is applicable when events for which we want to compute posterior probabilities are mutually exclusive and their union is the entire sample space. For the case of n mutually exclusive events $A_1, A_2, \ldots, A_n$, whose union is the entire sample space, Bayes' theorem can be used to compute any posterior probability $P(A_i \mid B)$ as shown in equation (4.12).

If the union of events is the entire sample space, the events are said to be collectively exhaustive.

BAYES' THEOREM

$$P(A_i \mid B) = \frac{P(A_i)P(B \mid A_i)}{P(A_1)P(B \mid A_1) + P(A_2)P(B \mid A_2) + \cdots + P(A_n)P(B \mid A_n)} \qquad (4.12)$$

NOTES + COMMENTS

By applying basic algebra we can derive the multiplication law from the definition of conditional probability. For two events A and B, the probability of A given B is $P(A \mid B) = \dfrac{P(A \cap B)}{P(B)}$. If we multiply both sides of this expression by $P(B)$, the $P(B)$ in the numerator and denominator on the right side of the expression will cancel and we are left with $P(A \mid B)P(B) = P(A \cap B)$, which is the multiplication law.

4.4 Random Variables

Chapter 2 introduces the concept of random variables and the use of data to describe them.

In probability terms, a **random variable** is a numerical description of the outcome of a random experiment. Because the outcome of a random experiment is not known with certainty, a random variable can be thought of as a quantity whose value is not known with certainty. A random variable can be classified as being either discrete or continuous depending on the numerical values it can assume.

Discrete Random Variables

A random variable that can take on only specified discrete values is referred to as a **discrete random variable**. Table 4.7 provides examples of discrete random variables.

Returning to our example of Lancaster Savings and Loan, we can define a random variable x to indicate whether or not a customer defaults on his or her mortgage. As previously

TABLE 4.7	Examples of Discrete Random Variables	
Random Experiment	**Random Variable (x)**	**Possible Values for the Random Variable**
Flip a coin	Face of coin showing	1 if heads; 0 if tails
Roll a die	Number of dots showing on top of die	1, 2, 3, 4, 5, 6
Contact five customers	Number of customers who place an order	0, 1, 2, 3, 4, 5
Operate a health care clinic for one day	Number of patients who arrive	0, 1, 2, 3, ...
Offer a customer the choice of two products	Product chosen by customer	0 if none; 1 if choose product A; 2 if choose product B

stated, the values of a random variable must be numerical, so we can define random variable x such that $x = 1$ if the customer defaults on his or her mortgage and $x = 0$ if the customer does not default on his or her mortgage. An additional random variable, y, could indicate whether the customer is married or single. For instance, we can define random variable y such that $y = 1$ if the customer is married and $y = 0$ if the customer is single. Yet another random variable, z, could be defined as the number of mortgage payments per year made by the customer. For instance, a customer who makes monthly payments would make $z = 12$ payments per year, a customer who makes payments quarterly would make $z = 4$ payments per year.

Table 4.8 repeats the joint probability table for the Lancaster Savings and Loan data, but this time with the values labeled as random variables.

Continuous Random Variables

A random variable that may assume any numerical value in an interval or collection of intervals is called a **continuous random variable**. Technically, relatively few random variables are truly continuous; these include values related to time, weight, distance, and temperature. An example of a continuous random variable is $x =$ the time between consecutive incoming calls to a call center. This random variable can take on any value $x > 0$ such as $x = 1.26$ minutes, $x = 2.571$ minutes, or $x = 4.3333$ minutes. Table 4.9 provides examples of continuous random variables.

As illustrated by the final example in Table 4.9, many discrete random variables have a large number of potential outcomes and so can be effectively modeled as continuous random variables. Consider our Lancaster Savings and Loan example. We can define a random variable $x =$ total amount paid by customer over the lifetime of the mortgage. Because we typically measure financial values only to two decimal places, one could consider this a discrete random variable. However, because in any practical interval there are many possible values for this random variable, then it is usually appropriate to model the amount as a continuous random variable.

TABLE 4.8	Joint Probability Table for Customer Mortgage Prepayments		
	No Default (x = 0)	**Default (x = 1)**	**f(y)**
Married (y = 1)	0.2133	0.2633	0.4766
Single (y = 0)	0.3867	0.1367	0.5234
f(x)	0.6000	0.4000	1.0000

TABLE 4.9	Examples of Continuous Random Variables	

Random Experiment	Random Variable (*x*)	Possible Values for the Random Variable
Customer visits a web page	Time customer spends on web page in minutes	$x \geq 0$
Fill a soft drink can (max capacity = 12.1 ounces)	Number of ounces	$0 \leq x \leq 12.1$
Test a new chemical process	Temperature when the desired reaction takes place (min temperature = 150°F; max temperature = 212°F)	$150 \leq x \leq 212$
Invest $10,000 in the stock market	Value of investment after one year	$x \geq 0$

NOTES + COMMENTS

1. In this section we again use the relative frequency method to assign probabilities for the Lancaster Savings and Loan example. Technically, the concept of random variables applies only to populations; probabilities that are found using sample data are only estimates of the true probabilities. However, larger samples generate more reliable estimated probabilities, so if we have a large enough data set (as we are assuming here for the Lancaster Savings and Loan data), then we can treat the data as if they are from a population and the relative frequency method is appropriate to assign probabilities to the outcomes.

2. Random variables can be used to represent uncertain future values. Chapter 11 explains how random variables can be used in simulation models to evaluate business decisions in the presence of uncertainty.

4.5 Discrete Probability Distributions

The **probability distribution** for a random variable describes the range and relative likelihood of possible values for a random variable. For a discrete random variable *x*, the probability distribution is defined by a **probability mass function**, denoted by *f(x)*. The probability mass function provides the probability for each value of the random variable.

Returning to our example of mortgage defaults, consider the data shown in Table 4.3 for Lancaster Savings and Loan and the associated joint probability table in Table 4.8. From Table 4.8, we see that $f(0) = 0.6$ and $f(1) = 0.4$. Note that these values satisfy the required conditions of a discrete probability distribution that (1) $f(x) \geq 0$ and (2) $\Sigma f(x) = 1$.

We can also present probability distributions graphically. In Figure 4.9, the values of the random variable *x* are shown on the horizontal axis and the probability associated with these values is shown on the vertical axis.

Custom Discrete Probability Distribution

A probability distribution that is generated from observations such as that shown in Figure 4.9 is called an **empirical probability distribution**. This particular empirical probability distribution is considered a custom discrete distribution because it is discrete and the possible values of the random variable have different values.

A **custom discrete probability distribution** is very useful for describing different possible scenarios that have different probabilities of occurring. The probabilities associated with each scenario can be generated using either the subjective method or the relative frequency method. Using a subjective method, probabilities are based on experience or intuition when little relevant data are available. If sufficient data exist, the relative frequency method can be used to determine probabilities. Consider the random variable describing the number of payments made per year by a randomly chosen customer. Table 4.10 presents a summary of the number of payments made per year by the 300 home mortgage

FIGURE 4.9	Graphical Representation of the Probability Distribution for Whether a Customer Defaults on a Mortgage

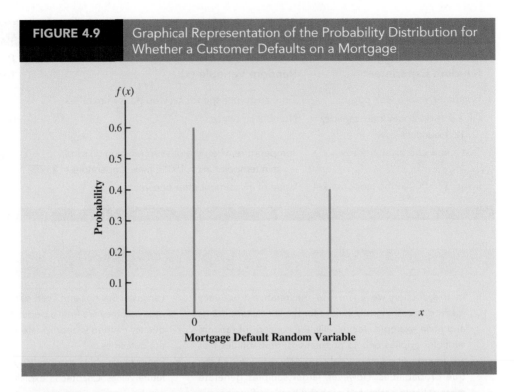

TABLE 4.10	Summary Table of Number of Payments Made per Year

| | Number of Payments Made per Year | | | |
	x = 4	**x = 12**	**x = 24**	**Total**
Number of observations	45	180	75	300
f(x)	0.15	0.60	0.25	

customers. This table shows us that 45 customers made quarterly payments ($x = 4$), 180 customers made monthly payments ($x = 12$), and 75 customers made two payments each month ($x = 24$). We can then calculate $f(4) = 45/300 = 0.15$, $f(12) = 180/300 = 0.60$, and $f(24) = 75/300 = 0.25$. In other words, the probability that a randomly selected customer makes 4 payments per year is 0.15, the probability that a randomly selected customer makes 12 payments per year is 0.60, and the probability that a randomly selected customer makes 24 payments per year is 0.25.

We can write this probability distribution as a function in the following manner:

$$f(x) = \begin{cases} 0.15 \text{ if } x = 4 \\ 0.60 \text{ if } x = 12 \\ 0.25 \text{ if } x = 24 \\ 0 \quad \text{otherwise} \end{cases}$$

This probability mass function tells us in a convenient way that $f(x) = 0.15$ when $x = 4$ (the probability that the random variable $x = 4$ is 0.15); $f(x) = 0.60$ when $x = 12$ (the probability that the random variable $x = 12$ is 0.60); $f(x) = 0.25$ when $x = 24$ (the probability that the random variable $x = 24$ is 0.25); and $f(x) = 0$ when x is any other value (there is zero probability that the random variable x is some value other than 4, 12, or 24).

Note that we can also create Table 4.10 in Excel using a PivotTable as shown in Figure 4.10.

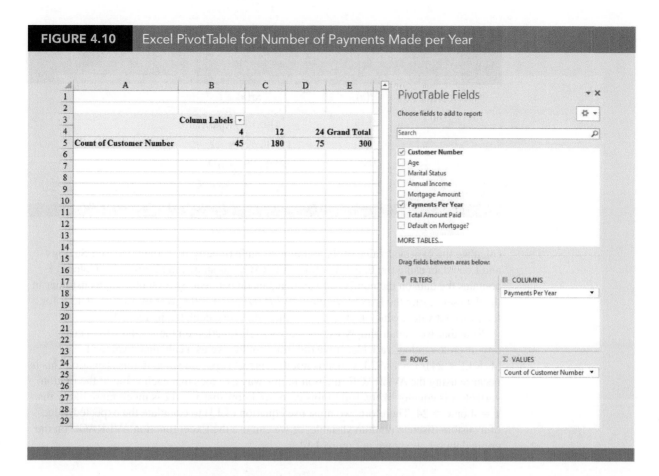

FIGURE 4.10   Excel PivotTable for Number of Payments Made per Year

Expected Value and Variance

Chapter 2 discusses the computation of the mean of a random variable based on data.

The **expected value**, or mean, of a random variable is a measure of the central location for the random variable. It is the weighted average of the values of the random variable, where the weights are the probabilities. The formula for the expected value of a discrete random variable x follows:

EXPECTED VALUE OF A DISCRETE RANDOM VARIABLE

$$E(x) = \mu = \Sigma x f(x) \tag{4.13}$$

Both the notations $E(x)$ and μ are used to denote the expected value of a random variable. Equation (4.13) shows that to compute the expected value of a discrete random variable, we must multiply each value of the random variable by the corresponding probability $f(x)$ and then add the resulting products. Table 4.11 calculates the expected value of the number of payments made by a mortgage customer in a year. The sum of the entries in the $xf(x)$ column shows that the expected value is 13.8 payments per year. Therefore, if Lancaster Savings and Loan signs up a new mortgage customer, the expected number of payments per year made by this new customer is 13.8. Obviously, no customer will make exactly 13.8 payments per year, but this value represents our expectation for the number of payments per year made by a new customer absent any other information about the new customer. Some customers will make fewer payments (4 or 12 per year), some customers will make more payments (24 per year), but 13.8 represents the expected number of payments per year based on the probabilities calculated in Table 4.10.

The SUMPRODUCT function in Excel can easily be used to calculate the expected value for a discrete random variable. This is illustrated in Figure 4.11. We can also

TABLE 4.11	Calculation of the Expected Value for Number of Payments Made per Year by a Lancaster Savings and Loan Mortgage Customer	

x	$f(x)$	$xf(x)$
4	0.15	$(4)(0.15) = 0.6$
12	0.60	$(12)(0.60) = 7.2$
24	0.25	$(24)(0.25) = 6.0$
		$13.8 \longleftarrow E(x) = \mu = \sum xf(x)$

calculate the expected value of the random variable directly from the Lancaster Savings and Loan data using the Excel function AVERAGE, as shown in Figure 4.12. Column F contains the data on the number of payments made per year by each mortgage customer in the data set. Using the Excel formula *=AVERAGE(F2:F301)* gives us a value of 13.8 for the expected value, which is the same as the value we calculated in Table 4.11.

Note that we cannot simply use the AVERAGE function on the x values for a custom discrete random variable. If we did, this would give us a calculated value of $(4 + 12 + 24)/3 = 13.333$, which is not the correct expected value in this scenario. This is because using the AVERAGE function in this way assumes that each value of the random variable x is equally likely. But in this case, we know that $x = 12$ is much more likely than $x = 4$ or $x = 24$. Therefore, we must use equation (4.13) to calculate the expected value of a custom discrete random variable, or we can use the Excel function AVERAGE on the entire data set, as shown in Figure 4.12.

FIGURE 4.11	Using Excel SUMPRODUCT Function to Calculate the Expected Value for Number of Payments Made per Year by a Lancaster Savings and Loan Mortgage Customer	

	A	B	C	D
1	x	$f(x)$		
2	4	0.15		
3	12	0.6		
4	24	0.25		
5				
6	**Expected Value:**	=SUMPRODUCT(A2:A4,B2:B4)		
7				
8				
9				
10				

	A	B	C	D
1	x	$f(x)$		
2	4	0.15		
3	12	0.60		
4	24	0.25		
5				
6	**Expected Value:**	13.8		
7				
8				
9				
10				

FIGURE 4.12	Excel Calculation of the Expected Value for Number of Payments Made per Year by a Lancaster Savings and Loan Mortgage Customer

	A	B	C	D	E	F	G	H
1	Customer Number	Age	Marital Status	Annual Income	Mortgage Amount	Payments Per Year	Total Amount Paid	Prepay Mortgage?
2	1	37	SINGLE	172125.7	473402.96	24	581885.13	YES
3	2	31	SINGLE	108571.04	300468.6	12	489320.38	NO
4	3	37	MARRIED	124136.41	330664.24	24	493541.93	YES
5	4	24	MARRIED	79614.04	230222.94	24	449682.09	YES
6	5	27	SINGLE	68087.33	282203.53	12	520581.82	NO
296	295	37	MARRIED	84791.08	179676.63	24	256361.65	YES
297	296	33	MARRIED	83498.89	235907.5	12	437145.85	NO
298	297	41	SINGLE	16597.53	151972.2	4	171289.87	YES
299	298	30	SINGLE	49293.95	186043.13	12	376694.27	NO
300	299	35	SINGLE	84241.8	194417.84	12	352597.79	NO
301	300	31	MARRIED	94428.15	264175.55	24	434102.49	YES
302								
304					Expected Value:	=AVERAGE(F2:F301)		
305					Variance:	=VAR.P(F2:F301)		
306					Standard Deviation:	=STDEV.P(F2:F301)		

	A	B	C	D	E	F	G	H
1	Customer Number	Age	Marital Status	Annual Income	Mortgage Amount	Payments Per Year	Total Amount Paid	Prepay Mortgage?
2	1	37	SINGLE	$ 172,125.70	$ 473,402.96	24	$ 581,885.13	YES
3	2	31	SINGLE	$ 108,571.04	$ 300,468.60	12	$ 489,320.38	NO
4	3	37	MARRIED	$ 124,136.41	$ 330,664.24	24	$ 493,541.93	YES
5	4	24	MARRIED	$ 79,614.04	$ 230,222.94	24	$ 449,682.09	YES
6	5	27	SINGLE	$ 68,087.33	$ 282,203.53	12	$ 520,581.82	NO
296	295	37	MARRIED	$ 84,791.08	$ 179,676.63	24	$ 256,361.65	YES
297	296	33	MARRIED	$ 83,498.89	$ 235,907.50	12	$ 437,145.85	NO
298	297	41	SINGLE	$ 16,597.53	$ 151,972.20	4	$ 171,289.87	YES
299	298	30	SINGLE	$ 49,293.95	$ 186,043.13	12	$ 376,694.27	NO
300	299	35	SINGLE	$ 84,241.80	$ 194,417.84	12	$ 352,597.79	NO
301	300	31	MARRIED	$ 94,428.15	$ 264,175.55	24	$ 434,102.49	YES
302								
304					Expected Value:	13.8		
305					Variance:	42.360		
306					Standard Deviation:	6.508		

Chapter 2 discusses the computation of the variance of a random variable based on data.

Variance is a measure of variability in the values of a random variable. It is a weighted average of the squared deviations of a random variable from its mean where the weights are the probabilities. Below we define the formula for calculating the variance of a discrete random variable.

VARIANCE OF A DISCRETE RANDOM VARIABLE

$$\text{Var}(x) = \sigma^2 = \Sigma(x - \mu)^2 f(x) \qquad (4.14)$$

As equation (4.14) shows, an essential part of the variance formula is the deviation, $x - \mu$, which measures how far a particular value of the random variable is from the expected value, or mean, μ. In computing the variance of a random variable, the deviations are squared and then weighted by the corresponding value of the probability mass function. The sum of these weighted squared deviations for all values of the random variable is referred to as the *variance*. The notations Var(x) and σ^2 are both used to denote the variance of a random variable.

The calculation of the variance of the number of payments made per year by a mortgage customer is summarized in Table 4.12. We see that the variance is 42.360. The **standard deviation**, σ, is defined as the positive square root of the variance. Thus, the standard deviation for the number of payments made per year by a mortgage customer is $\sqrt{42.360} = 6.508$.

Chapter 2 discusses the computation of the standard deviation of a random variable based on data.

The Excel function SUMPRODUCT can be used to easily calculate equation (4.14) for a custom discrete random variable. We illustrate the use of the SUMPRODUCT function to calculate variance in Figure 4.13.

We can also use Excel to find the variance directly from the data when the values in the data occur with relative frequencies that correspond to the probability distribution of the random variable. Cell F305 in Figure 4.12 shows that we use the Excel formula =VAR.P(F2:F301)

TABLE 4.12	Calculation of the Variance for Number of Payments Made per Year by a Lancaster Savings and Loan Mortgage Customer		
x	$x - \mu$	$f(x)$	$(x - \mu)^2 f(x)$
4	$4 - 13.8 = -9.8$	0.15	$(-9.8)^{2^*} 0.15 = 15.606$
12	$12 - 13.8 = -1.8$	0.60	$(-1.8)^{2^*} 0.60 = 2.904$
21	$21 - 13.8 = 10.2$	0.25	$(10.2)^{2^*} 0.25 = 24.010$
			$\overline{42.360} \leftarrow \sigma^2 = \sum (x - \mu)^2 f(x)$

FIGURE 4.13	Excel Calculation of the Variance for Number of Payments Made per Year by a Lancaster Savings and Loan Mortgage Customer

	A	B	C	D
1	x	$f(x)$	$(x - \mu)^2$	
2	4	0.15	=(A2-$B$6)^2	
3	12	0.6	=(A3-$B$6)^2	
4	24	0.25	=(A4-$B$6)^2	
5				
6	Expected Value:	=SUMPRODUCT(A2:A4,B2:B4)		
7				
8	Variance:	=SUMPRODUCT(B2:B4,C2:C4)		
9				
10	Stadard Deviation:	=SQRT(B8)		

	A	B	C	D
1	x	$f(x)$	$(x - \mu)^2$	
2	4	0.15	96.04	
3	12	0.60	3.24	
4	24	0.25	104.04	
5				
6	Expected Value:	13.8		
7				
8	Variance:	42.360		
9				
10	Stadard Deviation:	6.508		

Note that here we are using the Excel functions VAR.P and STDEV.P rather than VAR.S and STDEV.S. This is because we are assuming that the sample of 300 Lancaster Savings and Loan mortgage customers is a perfect representation of the population.

to calculate the variance from the complete data. This formula gives us a value of 42.360, which is the same as that calculated in Table 4.12 and Figure 4.13. Similarly, we can use the formula $=STDEV.P(F2:F301)$ to calculate the standard deviation of 6.508.

As with the AVERAGE function and expected value, we cannot use the Excel functions VAR.P and STDEV.P directly on the x values to calculate the variance and standard deviation of a custom discrete random variable if the x values are not equally likely to occur. Instead we must either use the formula from equation (4.14) or use the Excel functions on the entire data set as shown in Figure 4.12.

Discrete Uniform Probability Distribution

When the possible values of the probability mass function, $f(x)$, are all equal, then the probability distribution is a **discrete uniform probability distribution**. For instance, the values that result from rolling a single fair die is an example of a discrete uniform distribution because the possible outcomes $y = 1$, $y = 2$, $y = 3$, $y = 4$, $y = 5$, and $y = 6$ all have the same values $f(1) = f(2) = f(3) = f(4) = f(5) = f(6) = 1/6$. The general form of the probability mass function for a discrete uniform probability distribution is as follows:

DISCRETE UNIFORM PROBABILITY MASS FUNCTION

$$f(x) = 1/n \tag{4.15}$$

---

where n = the number of unique values that may be assumed by the random variable.

Binomial Probability Distribution

As an example of the use of the binomial probability distribution, consider an online specialty clothing company called Martin's. Martin's commonly sends out targeted e-mails to its best customers notifying them about special discounts that are available only to the recipients of the e-mail. The e-mail contains a link that takes the customer directly to a web page for the discounted item. The exact number of customers who will click on the link is obviously unknown, but from previous data, Martin's estimates that the probability that a customer clicks on the link in the e-mail is 0.30. Martin's is interested in knowing more about the probabilities associated with one, two, three, etc. customers clicking on the link in the targeted e-mail.

The probability distribution related to the number of customers who click on the targeted e-mail link can be described using a **binomial probability distribution**. A binomial probability distribution is a discrete probability distribution that can be used to describe many situations in which a fixed number (n) of repeated identical and independent trials has two, and only two, possible outcomes. In general terms, we refer to these two possible outcomes as either a success or a failure. A success occurs with probability p in each trial and a failure occurs with probability $1 - p$ in each trial. In the Martin's example, the "trial" refers to a customer receiving the targeted e-mail. We will define a success as a customer clicking on the e-mail link ($p = 0.30$) and a failure as a customer not clicking on the link ($1 - p = 0.70$). The binomial probability distribution can then be used to calculate the probability of a given number of successes (customers who click on the e-mail link) out of a given number of independent trials (number of e-mails sent to customers). Other examples that can often be described by a binomial probability distribution include counting the number of heads resulting from flipping a coin 20 times, the number of customers who click on a particular advertisement link on web site in a day, the number of days on which a particular financial stock increases in value over a month, and the number of nondefective parts produced in a batch.

Equation (4.16) provides the probability mass function for a binomial random variable that calculates the probability of x successes in n independent events.

Whether or not a customer clicks on the link is an example of what is known as a Bernoulli trial—a trial in which (1) there are two possible outcomes, success or failure, and (2) the probability of success is the same every time the trial is executed. The probability distribution related to the number of successes in a set of n independent Bernoulli trials can be described by a binomial probability distribution.

BINOMIAL PROBABILITY MASS FUNCTION

$$f(x) = \left(\begin{array}{c} n \\ x \end{array} \right) p^x (1 - p)^{(n - x)}$$

where

$$x = \text{the number of successes}$$
$$p = \text{the probability of a success on one trial} \tag{4.16}$$
$$n = \text{the number of trials}$$
$$f(x) = \text{the probability of } x \text{ successes in } n \text{ trials}$$

and

$$\left(\begin{array}{c} n \\ x \end{array} \right) = \frac{n!}{x!(n - x)!}$$

$n!$ is read as "n factorial," and $n! = n \times n - 1 \times n - 2 \times \cdots \times 2 \times 1$. For example, $4! = 4 \times 3 \times 2 \times 1 = 24$. The Excel formula $=FACT(n)$ can be used to calculate n factorial.

In the Martin's example, use equation (4.16) to compute the probability that out of three customers who receive the e-mail (1) no customer clicks on the link; (2) exactly one customer clicks on the link; (3) exactly two customers click on the link; and (4) all three customers click on the link. The calculations are summarized in Table 4.13, which gives the probability distribution of the number of customers who click on the targeted e-mail link. Figure 4.14 is a graph of this probability distribution. Table 4.13 and Figure 4.14 show that the highest probability is associated with exactly one customer clicking on the Martin's targeted e-mail link and the lowest probability is associated with all three customers clicking on the link.

Because the outcomes in the Martin's example are mutually exclusive, we can easily use these results to answer interesting questions about various events. For example, using the information in Table 4.13, the probability that no more than one customer clicks on the link is $P(x \leq 1) = P(x = 0) + P(x = 1) = 0.343 + 0.441 = 0.784$.

TABLE 4.13	Probability Distribution for the Number of Customers Who Click on the Link in the Martin's Targeted E-Mail
x	**f(x)**
0	$\dfrac{3!}{0!3!}(0.30)^0(0.70)^3 = 0.343$
1	$\dfrac{3!}{1!2!}(0.30)^1(0.70)^2 = 0.441$
2	$\dfrac{3!}{2!1!}(0.30)^2(0.70)^1 = 0.189$
3	$\dfrac{3!}{3!0!}(0.30)^3(0.70)^0 = \dfrac{0.027}{1.000}$

FIGURE 4.14	Graphical Representation of the Probability Distribution for the Number of Customers Who Click on the Link in the Martin's Targeted E-Mail

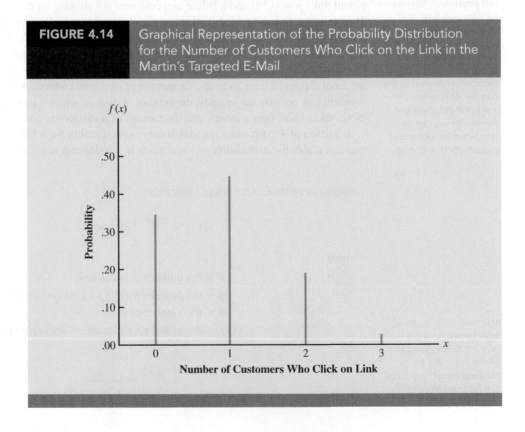

If we consider a scenario in which 10 customers receive the targeted e-mail, the binomial probability mass function given by equation (4.16) is still applicable. If we want to find the probability that exactly 4 of the 10 customers click on the link and $p = 0.30$, then we calculate:

$$f(4) = \frac{10!}{4!6!}(0.30)^4(0.70)^6 = 0.2001$$

In Excel we can use the BINOM.DIST function to compute binomial probabilities. Figure 4.15 reproduces the Excel calculations from Table 4.13 for the Martin's problem with three customers.

The BINOM.DIST function in Excel has four input values: the first is the value of x, the second is the value of n, the third is the value of p, and the fourth is FALSE or TRUE. We choose FALSE for the fourth input if a probability mass function value $f(x)$ is desired, and TRUE if a cumulative probability is desired. The formula $=BINOM.DIST(A5,\$D\$1:\$D\$2,FALSE)$ has been entered into cell B5 to compute the probability of 0 successes in three trials, $f(0)$. Figure 4.15 shows that this value is 0.343, the same as in Table 4.13.

Cells C5:C8 show the cumulative probability distribution values for this example. Note that these values are computed in Excel by entering TRUE as the fourth input in the BINOM.DIST. The cumulative probability for x using a binomial distribution is the probability of x or fewer successes out of n trials. Cell C5 computes the cumulative probability for $x = 0$, which is the same as the probability for $x = 0$ because the probability of 0 successes is the same as the probability of 0 or fewer successes. Cell C7 computes the cumulative probability for $x = 2$ using the formula $=BINOM.DIST(A7,\$D\$1,\$D\$2,TRUE)$. This value is 0.973, meaning that the probability that two or fewer customers click on the targeted e-mail link is 0.973. Note that the value 0.973 simply corresponds to $f(0) + f(1) + f(2) = 0.343 + 0.441 + 0.189 = 0.973$ because it is the probability of two or fewer customers clicking on the link, which could be zero customers, one customer, or two customers.

FIGURE 4.15   Excel Worksheet for Computing Binomial Probabilities of the Number of Customers Who Make a Purchase at Martin's

	A	B	C	D
1			**Number of Trials (*n*):** 3	
2			**Probability of Success (*p*):** 0.3	
3				
4	*x*	*f(x)*	**Cumulative Probability**	
5	0	=BINOM.DIST(A5,$D$1,$D$2,FALSE)	=BINOM.DIST(A5,$D$1,$D$2,TRUE)	
6	1	=BINOM.DIST(A6,$D$1,$D$2,FALSE)	=BINOM.DIST(A6,$D$1,$D$2,TRUE)	
7	2	=BINOM.DIST(A7,$D$1,$D$2,FALSE)	=BINOM.DIST(A7,$D$1,$D$2,TRUE)	
8	3	=BINOM.DIST(A8,$D$1,$D$2,FALSE)	=BINOM.DIST(A8,$D$1,$D$2,TRUE)	

	A	B	C	D
1			**Number of Trials (*n*):**	3
2			**Probability of Success (*p*):**	0.3
3				
4	*x*	*f(x)*	**Cumulative Probability**	
5	0	0.343	0.343	
6	1	0.441	0.784	
7	2	0.189	0.973	
8	3	0.027	1.000	

Poisson Probability Distribution

In this section, we consider a discrete random variable that is often useful in estimating the number of occurrences of an event over a specified interval of time or space. For example, the random variable of interest might be the number of patients who arrive at a health care clinic in 1 hour, the number of computer-server failures in a month, the number of repairs needed in 10 miles of highway, or the number of leaks in 100 miles of pipeline. If the following two properties are satisfied, the number of occurrences is a random variable that is described by the **Poisson probability distribution**: (1) the probability of an occurrence is the same for any two intervals (of time or space) of equal length; and (2) the occurrence or nonoccurrence in any interval (of time or space) is independent of the occurrence or nonoccurrence in any other interval.

The Poisson probability mass function is defined by equation (4.17).

POISSON PROBABILITY MASS FUNCTION

The number e is a mathematical constant that is the base of the natural logarithm. Although it is an irrational number, 2.71828 is a sufficient approximation for our purposes.

$$f(x) = \frac{\mu^x e^{-\mu}}{x!} \qquad\qquad (4.17)$$

where

$f(x) =$ the probability of x occurrences in an interval
$\mu =$ expected value or mean number of occurrences in an interval
$e \approx 2.71828$

For the Poisson probability distribution, x is a discrete random variable that indicates the number of occurrences in the interval. Since there is no stated upper limit for the number of occurrences, the probability mass function $f(x)$ is applicable for values $x = 0, 1, 2, \ldots$ without limit. In practical applications, x will eventually become large enough so that $f(x)$ is approximately zero and the probability of any larger values of x becomes negligible.

Suppose that we are interested in the number of patients who arrive at the emergency room of a large hospital during a 15-minute period on weekday mornings. Obviously, we do not know exactly how many patients will arrive at the emergency room in any defined interval of time, so the value of this variable is uncertain. It is important for administrators at the hospital to understand the probabilities associated with the number of arriving patients, as this information will have an impact on staffing decisions such as how many nurses and doctors to hire. It will also provide insight into possible wait times for patients to be seen once they arrive at the emergency room. If we can assume that the probability of a patient arriving is the same for any two periods of equal length during this 15-minute period and that the arrival or nonarrival of a patient in any period is independent of the arrival or nonarrival in any other period during the 15-minute period, the Poisson probability mass function is applicable. Suppose these assumptions are satisfied and an analysis of historical data shows that the average number of patients arriving during a 15-minute period of time is 10; in this case, the following probability mass function applies:

$$f(x) = \frac{10^x e^{-10}}{x!}$$

The random variable here is $x =$ number of patients arriving at the emergency room during any 15-minute period.

If the hospital's management team wants to know the probability of exactly five arrivals during 15 minutes, we would set $x = 5$ and obtain:

$$\text{Probability of exactly 5 arrivals in 15 minutes} = f(5) = \frac{10^5 e^{-10}}{5!} = 0.0378$$

In the preceding example, the mean of the Poisson distribution is $\mu = 10$ arrivals per 15-minute period. A property of the Poisson distribution is that the mean of the distribution and the variance of the distribution are *always equal*. Thus, the variance for the number of arrivals during all 15-minute periods is $\sigma^2 = 10$, and so the standard deviation is $\sigma = \sqrt{10} = 3.16$. Our illustration involves a 15-minute period, but other amounts of time can be used. Suppose we want to compute the probability of one arrival during a 3-minute period. Because 10 is the expected number of arrivals during a 15-minute period, we see that $10/15 = 2/3$ is the expected number of arrivals during a 1-minute period and that $(2/3)(3\,\text{minutes}) = 2$ is the expected number of arrivals during a 3-minute period. Thus, the probability of x arrivals during a 3-minute period with $\mu = 2$ is given by the following Poisson probability mass function:

$$f(x) = \frac{2^x e^{-2}}{x!}$$

The probability of one arrival during a 3-minute period is calculated as follows:

$$\text{Probability of exactly 1 arrival in 3 minutes} = f(1) = \frac{2^1 e^{-2}}{1!} = 0.2707$$

One might expect that because $(5\,\text{arrivals})/5 = 1\,\text{arrival}$ and $(15\,\text{minutes})/5 = 3\,\text{minutes}$, we would get the same probability for one arrival during a 3-minute period as we do for five arrivals during a 15-minute period. Earlier we computed the probability of five arrivals during a 15-minute period as 0.0378. However, note that the probability of one arrival during a 3-minute period is 0.2707, which is not the same. When computing a Poisson probability for a different time interval, we must first convert the mean arrival rate to the period of interest and then compute the probability.

In Excel we can use the POISSON.DIST function to compute Poisson probabilities. Figure 4.16 shows how to calculate the probabilities of patient arrivals at the emergency room if patients arrive at a mean rate of 10 per 15-minute interval.

FIGURE 4.16   Excel Worksheet for Computing Poisson Probabilities of the Number of Patients Arriving at the Emergency Room

The POISSON.DIST function in Excel has three input values: the first is the value of x, the second is the mean of the Poisson distribution, and the third is FALSE or TRUE. We choose FALSE for the third input if a probability mass function value $f(x)$ is desired, and TRUE if a cumulative probability is desired. The formula $=POISSON.DIST(A4,\$D\$1,FALSE)$ has been entered into cell B4 to compute the probability of 0 occurrences, $f(0)$. Figure 4.16 shows that this value (to four decimal places) is 0.0000, which means that it is highly unlikely (probability near 0) that we will have 0 patient arrivals during a 15-minute interval. The value in cell B12 shows that the probability that there will be exactly eight arrivals during a 15-minute interval is 0.1126.

The cumulative probability for x using a Poisson distribution is the probability of x or fewer occurrences during the interval. Cell C4 computes the cumulative probability for $x = 0$, which is the same as the probability for $x = 0$ because the probability of 0 occurrences is the same as the probability of 0 or fewer occurrences. Cell C12 computes the cumulative probability for $x = 8$ using the formula $=POISSON.DIST(A12,\$D\$1,TRUE)$. This value is 0.3328, meaning that the probability that eight or fewer patients arrive during a 15-minute interval is 0.3328. This value corresponds to

$$f(0) + f(1) + f(2) + \cdots + f(7) + f(8) = 0.0000 + 0.0005 + 0.0023 + \cdots$$
$$+ 0.0901 + 0.1126 = 0.3328$$

Let us illustrate an application not involving time intervals in which the Poisson distribution is useful. Suppose we want to determine the occurrence of major defects in a highway one month after it has been resurfaced. We assume that the probability of a defect is the same for any two highway intervals of equal length and that the occurrence or nonoccurrence of a defect in any one interval is independent of the occurrence or nonoccurrence of a defect in any other interval. Hence, the Poisson distribution can be applied.

Suppose we learn that major defects one month after resurfacing occur at the average rate of two per mile. Let us find the probability of no major defects in a particular 3-mile section of the highway. Because we are interested in an interval with a length of 3 miles, $\mu = (2 \text{ defects/mile})(3 \text{ miles}) = 6$ represents the expected number of major defects over the 3-mile section of highway. Using equation (4.17), the probability of no major defects is

$$f(0) = \frac{6^0 e^{-6}}{0!} = 0.0025.$$ Thus, it is unlikely that no major defects will occur in the 3-mile section. In fact, this example indicates a $1 - 0.0025 = 0.9975$ probability of at least one major defect in the 3-mile highway section.

NOTES + COMMENTS

1. If sample data are used to estimate the probabilities of a custom discrete distribution, equation (4.13) yields the sample mean $\bar{x}$ rather than the population mean μ. However, as the sample size increases, the sample generally becomes more representative of the population and the sample mean $\bar{x}$ converges to the population mean μ. In this chapter we have assumed that the sample of 300 Lancaster Savings and Loan mortgage customers is sufficiently large to be representative of the population of mortgage customers at Lancaster Savings and Loan.

2. We can use the Excel function AVERAGE only to compute the expected value of a custom discrete random variable when the values in the data occur with relative frequencies that correspond to the probability distribution of the

random variable. If this assumption is not satisfied, then the estimate of the expected value with the AVERAGE function will be inaccurate. In practice, this assumption is satisfied with an increasing degree of accuracy as the size of the sample is increased. Otherwise, we must use equation (4.13) to calculate the expected value for a custom discrete random variable.

3. If sample data are used to estimate the probabilities for a custom discrete distribution, equation (4.14) yields the sample variance s^2 rather than the population variance σ^2. However, as the sample size increases the sample generally becomes more representative of the population and the sample variance s^2 converges to the population variance σ^2.

4.6 Continuous Probability Distributions

In the preceding section we discussed discrete random variables and their probability distributions. In this section we consider continuous random variables. Specifically, we discuss some of the more useful continuous probability distributions for analytics models: the uniform, the triangular, the normal, and the exponential.

A fundamental difference separates discrete and continuous random variables in terms of how probabilities are computed. For a discrete random variable, the probability mass function $f(x)$ provides the probability that the random variable assumes a particular value. With continuous random variables, the counterpart of the probability mass function is the **probability density function**, also denoted by $f(x)$. The difference is that the probability density function does not directly provide probabilities. However, the area under the graph of $f(x)$ corresponding to a given interval does provide the probability that the continuous random variable x assumes a value in that interval. So when we compute probabilities for continuous random variables, we are computing the probability that the random variable assumes any value in an interval. Because the area under the graph of $f(x)$ at any particular point is zero, one of the implications of the definition of probability for continuous random variables is that the probability of any particular value of the random variable is zero.

Uniform Probability Distribution

Consider the random variable x representing the flight time of an airplane traveling from Chicago to New York. The exact flight time from Chicago to New York is uncertain because it can be affected by weather (headwinds or storms), flight traffic patterns, and other factors that cannot be known with certainty. It is important to characterize the uncertainty associated with the flight time because this can have an impact on connecting flights and how we construct our overall flight schedule. Suppose the flight time can be any value in the interval from 120 minutes to 140 minutes. Because the random variable x can assume any value in that interval, x is a continuous rather than a discrete random variable. Let us assume that sufficient actual flight data are available to conclude that the probability of a flight time within any interval of a given length is the same as the probability of a flight time within any other interval of the same length that is contained in the larger interval from 120 to 140 minutes. With every interval of a given length being equally likely, the random variable x is said to have a **uniform probability distribution**. The probability density function, which defines the uniform distribution for the flight-time random variable, is:

$$f(x) = \begin{cases} 1/20 & \text{for } 120 \le x \le 140 \\ 0 & \text{elsewhere} \end{cases}$$

Figure 4.17 shows a graph of this probability density function.

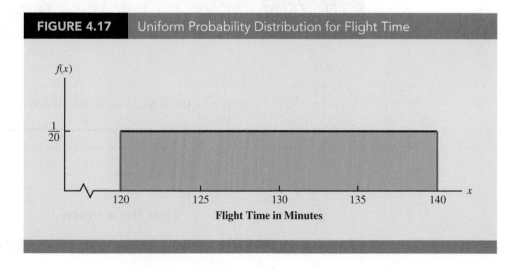

FIGURE 4.17   Uniform Probability Distribution for Flight Time

In general, the uniform probability density function for a random variable x is defined by the following formula:

UNIFORM PROBABILITY DENSITY FUNCTION

$$f(x) = \begin{cases} \dfrac{1}{b-a} & \text{for } a \leq x \leq b \\ 0 & \text{elsewhere} \end{cases} \qquad \textbf{(4.18)}$$

For the flight-time random variable, $a = 120$ and $b = 140$.

For a continuous random variable, we consider probability only in terms of the likelihood that a random variable assumes a value within a specified interval. In the flight time example, an acceptable probability question is: What is the probability that the flight time is between 120 and 130 minutes? That is, what is $P(120 \leq x \leq 130)$?

To answer this question, consider the area under the graph of $f(x)$ in the interval from 120 to 130 (see Figure 4.18). The area is rectangular, and the area of a rectangle is simply the width multiplied by the height. With the width of the interval equal to $130 - 120 = 10$ and the height equal to the value of the probability density function $f(x) = 1/20$, we have area = width $\times$ height = $10(1/20) = 10/20 = 0.50$.

The area under the graph of $f(x)$ and probability are identical for all continuous random variables. Once a probability density function $f(x)$ is identified, the probability that x takes a value between some lower value x_1 and some higher value x_2 can be found by computing the area under the graph of $f(x)$ over the interval from x_1 to x_2.

Given the uniform distribution for flight time and using the interpretation of area as probability, we can answer any number of probability questions about flight times. For example:

- What is the probability of a flight time between 128 and 136 minutes? The width of the interval is $136 - 128 = 8$. With the uniform height of $f(x) = 1/20$, we see that $P(128 \leq x \leq 136) = 8(1/20) = 0.40$.
- What is the probability of a flight time between 118 and 123 minutes? The width of the interval is $123 - 118 = 5$, but the height is $f(x) = 0$ for $118 \leq x < 120$ and $f(x) = 1/20$ for $120 \leq x \leq 123$, so we have that $P(118 \leq x \leq 123) = P(118 \leq x < 120) + P(120 \leq x \leq 123) = 2(0) + 3(1/20) = 0.15$.

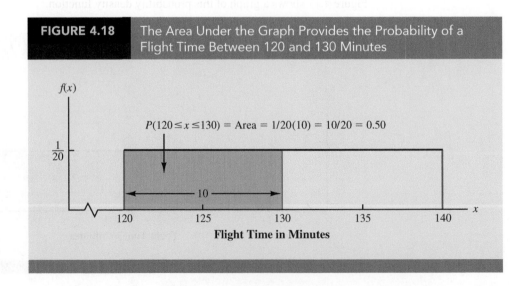

FIGURE 4.18   The Area Under the Graph Provides the Probability of a Flight Time Between 120 and 130 Minutes

$P(120 \leq x \leq 130)$ = Area = 1/20(10) = 10/20 = 0.50

Flight Time in Minutes

Note that $P(120 \leq x \leq 140) = 20(1/20) = 1$; that is, the total area under the graph of $f(x)$ is equal to 1. This property holds for all continuous probability distributions and is the analog of the condition that the sum of the probabilities must equal 1 for a discrete probability mass function.

Note also that because we know that the height of the graph of $f(x)$ for a uniform distribution is $\dfrac{1}{b-a}$ for $a \leq x \leq b$, then the area under the graph of $f(x)$ for a uniform distribution evaluated from a to a point x_0 when $a \leq x_0 \leq b$ is width $\times$ height $= (x_0 - a) \times (b - a)$. This value provides the cumulative probability of obtaining a value for a uniform random variable of less than or equal to some specific value denoted by x_0 and the formula is given in equation (4.19).

UNIFORM DISTRIBUTION: CUMULATIVE PROBABILITIES

$$P(x \leq x_0) = \frac{x_0 - a}{b - a} \text{ for } a \leq x_0 \leq b \qquad \text{(4.19)}$$

The calculation of the expected value and variance for a continuous random variable is analogous to that for a discrete random variable. However, because the computational procedure involves integral calculus, we do not show the calculations here.

For the uniform continuous probability distribution introduced in this section, the formulas for the expected value and variance are as follows:

$$E(x) = \frac{a + b}{2}$$

$$\text{Var}(x) = \frac{(b - a)^2}{12}$$

In these formulas, a is the minimum value and b is the maximum value that the random variable may assume.

Applying these formulas to the uniform distribution for flight times from Chicago to New York, we obtain

$$E(x) = \frac{(120 + 140)}{2} = 130$$

$$\text{Var}(x) = \frac{(140 - 120)^2}{12} = 33.33$$

The standard deviation of flight times can be found by taking the square root of the variance. Thus, for flight times from Chicago to New York, $\sigma = \sqrt{33.33} = 5.77$ minutes.

Triangular Probability Distribution

The triangular probability distribution is useful when only subjective probability estimates are available. There are many situations for which we do not have sufficient data and only subjective estimates of possible values are available. In the **triangular probability distribution**, we need only to specify the minimum possible value a, the maximum possible value b, and the most likely value (or mode) of the distribution m. If these values can be knowledgeably estimated for a continuous random variable by a subject-matter expert, then as an approximation of the actual probability density function, we can assume that the triangular distribution applies.

Consider a situation in which a project manager is attempting to estimate the time that will be required to complete an initial assessment of the capital project of constructing a new corporate headquarters. The assessment process includes completing environmental-impact studies, procuring the required permits, and lining up all the contractors and subcontractors needed to complete the project. There is considerable uncertainty regarding the duration of these tasks, and generally little or no historical data are available to help estimate the probability distribution for the time required for this assessment process.

Suppose that we are able to discuss this project with several subject-matter experts who have worked on similar projects. From these expert opinions and our own experience, we estimate that the minimum required time for the initial assessment phase is six months and that the worst-case estimate is that this phase could require 24 months if we are delayed in the permit process or if the results from the environmental-impact studies require additional action. While a time of six months represents a best case and 24 months a worst case, the consensus is that the most likely amount of time required for the initial assessment phase of the project is 12 months. From these estimates, we can use a triangular distribution as an approximation for the probability density function for the time required for the initial assessment phase of constructing a new corporate headquarters.

Figure 4.19 shows the probability density function for this triangular distribution. Note that the probability density function is a triangular shape.

The general form of the triangular probability density function is as follows:

TRIANGULAR PROBABILITY DENSITY FUNCTION

$$f(x) = \begin{cases} \dfrac{2(x-a)}{(b-a)(m-a)} & \text{for } a \leq x \leq m \\[2mm] \dfrac{2(b-x)}{(b-a)(b-m)} & \text{for } m < x \leq b \end{cases} \tag{4.20}$$

where

a = minimum value
b = maximum value
m = mode

In the example of the time required to complete the initial assessment phase of constructing a new corporate headquarters, the minimum value a is six months, the maximum value b is 24 months, and the mode m is 12 months. As with the explanation given for the uniform distribution above, we can calculate probabilities by using the area under the graph of $f(x)$. We can calculate the probability that the time required is less than 12 months by finding the area under the graph of $f(x)$ from $x = 6$ to $x = 12$ as shown in Figure 4.19.

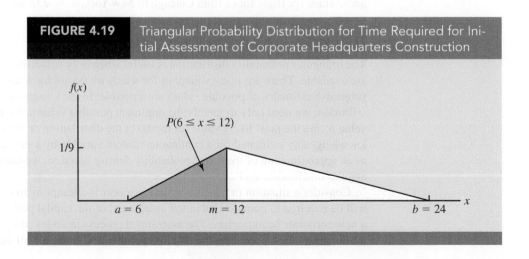

FIGURE 4.19   Triangular Probability Distribution for Time Required for Initial Assessment of Corporate Headquarters Construction

The geometry required to find this area for any given value is slightly more complex than that required to find the area for a uniform distribution, but the resulting formula for a triangular distribution is relatively simple:

TRIANGULAR DISTRIBUTION: CUMULATIVE PROBABILITIES

$$P(x \leq x_0) = \begin{cases} \dfrac{(x_0 - a)^2}{(b - a)(m - a)} & \text{for } a \leq x_0 \leq m \\[4mm] 1 - \dfrac{(b - x_0)^2}{(b - a)(b - m)} & \text{for } m < x_0 \leq b \end{cases}$$ **(4.21)**

Equation (4.21) provides the cumulative probability of obtaining a value for a triangular random variable of less than or equal to some specific value denoted by x_0.

To calculate $P(x \leq 12)$ we use equation (4.20) with $a = 6$, $b = 24$, $m = 12$, and $x_0 = 12$.

$$P(x \leq 12) = \frac{(12 - 6)^2}{(24 - 6)(12 - 6)} = 0.3333$$

Thus, the probability that the assessment phase of the project requires less than 12 months is 0.3333. We can also calculate the probability that the project requires more than 10 months, but less than or equal to 18 months by subtracting $P(x \leq 10)$ from $P(x \leq 18)$. This is shown graphically in Figure 4.20. The calculations are as follows:

$$P(x \leq 18) - P(x \leq 10) = \left[1 - \frac{(24 - 18)^2}{(24 - 6)(24 - 12)} \right] - \left[\frac{(10 - 6)^2}{(24 - 6)(10 - 6)} \right] = 0.6111$$

Thus, the probability that the assessment phase of the project requires at least 10 months but less than 18 months is 0.6111.

Normal Probability Distribution

One of the most useful probability distributions for describing a continuous random variable is the **normal probability distribution**. The normal distribution has been used in a wide variety of practical applications in which the random variables are heights and weights of people, test scores, scientific measurements, amounts of rainfall, and other similar values. It is also widely used in business applications to describe uncertain quantities such as demand for products, the rate of return for stocks and bonds, and the time it takes to manufacture a part or complete many types of service-oriented activities such as medical surgeries and consulting engagements.

FIGURE 4.20 Triangular Distribution to Determine $P(10 \leq x \leq 18) = P(x \leq 18) - P(x \leq 10)$

The form, or shape, of the normal distribution is illustrated by the bell-shaped normal curve in Figure 4.21.

The probability density function that defines the bell-shaped curve of the normal distribution follows.

NORMAL PROBABILITY DENSITY FUNCTION

$$f(x) = \frac{1}{\sigma\sqrt{2\pi}} e^{-(x-\mu)^2/2\sigma^2}$$

(4.22)

where

$$\mu = \text{mean}$$
$$\sigma = \text{standard deviation}$$
$$\pi \approx 3.14159$$
$$e \approx 2.71828$$

Although π and e are irrational numbers, 3.14159 and 2.71828, respectively, are sufficient approximations for our purposes.

We make several observations about the characteristics of the normal distribution.

1. The entire family of normal distributions is differentiated by two parameters: the mean μ and the standard deviation σ. The mean and standard deviation are often referred to as the location and shape parameters of the normal distribution, respectively.
2. The highest point on the normal curve is at the mean, which is also the median and mode of the distribution.
3. The mean of the distribution can be any numerical value: negative, zero, or positive. Three normal distributions with the same standard deviation but three different means (-10, 0, and 20) are shown in Figure 4.22.

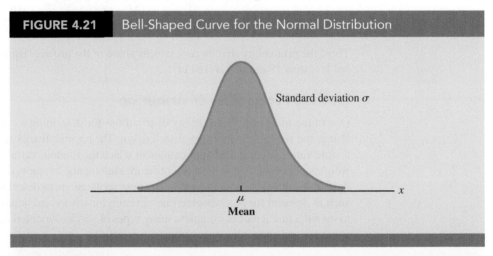

FIGURE 4.21   Bell-Shaped Curve for the Normal Distribution

FIGURE 4.22   Three Normal Distributions with the Same Standard Deviation but Different Means ($\mu = -10$, $\mu = 0$, $\mu = 20$)

4. The normal distribution is symmetric, with the shape of the normal curve to the left of the mean a mirror image of the shape of the normal curve to the right of the mean.

5. The tails of the normal curve extend to infinity in both directions and theoretically never touch the horizontal axis. Because it is symmetric, the normal distribution is not skewed; its skewness measure is zero.

6. The standard deviation determines how flat and wide the normal curve is. Larger values of the standard deviation result in wider, flatter curves, showing more variability in the data. More variability corresponds to greater uncertainty. Two normal distributions with the same mean but with different standard deviations are shown in Figure 4.23.

7. Probabilities for the normal random variable are given by areas under the normal curve. The total area under the curve for the normal distribution is 1. Because the distribution is symmetric, the area under the curve to the left of the mean is 0.50 and the area under the curve to the right of the mean is 0.50.

8. The percentages of values in some commonly used intervals are as follows:

    a. 68.3% of the values of a normal random variable are within plus or minus one standard deviation of its mean.

    b. 95.4% of the values of a normal random variable are within plus or minus two standard deviations of its mean.

    c. 99.7% of the values of a normal random variable are within plus or minus three standard deviations of its mean.

These percentages are the basis for the empirical rule discussed in Section 2.7.

Figure 4.24 shows properties (a), (b), and (c) graphically.

We turn now to an application of the normal probability distribution. Suppose Grear Aircraft Engines sells aircraft engines to commercial airlines. Grear is offering a new performance-based sales contract in which Grear will guarantee that its engines will provide a certain amount of lifetime flight hours subject to the airline purchasing a preventive-maintenance service plan that is also provided by Grear. Grear believes that this performance-based contract will lead to additional sales as well as additional income from providing the associated preventive maintenance and servicing.

From extensive flight testing and computer simulations, Grear's engineering group has estimated that if their engines receive proper parts replacement and preventive maintenance, the mean lifetime flight hours achieved is normally distributed with a mean $\mu = 36,500$ hours and standard deviation $\sigma = 5,000$ hours. Grear would like to know what percentage of its aircraft engines will be expected to last more than 40,000 hours. In other words, what is the probability that the aircraft lifetime flight hours x will exceed 40,000? This question can be answered by finding the area of the darkly shaded region in Figure 4.25.

FIGURE 4.23 Two Normal Distributions with the Same Mean but Different Standard Deviations ($\sigma = 5$, $\sigma = 10$)

FIGURE 4.24 Areas Under the Curve for Any Normal Distribution

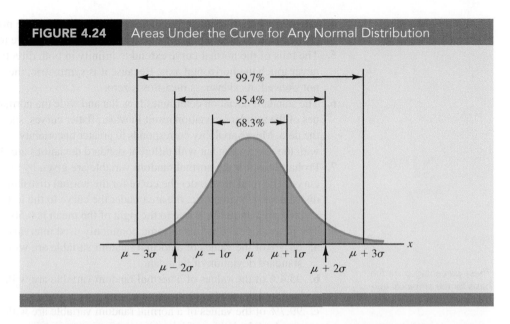

FIGURE 4.25 Grear Aircraft Engines Lifetime Flight Hours Distribution

The Excel function NORM.DIST can be used to compute the area under the curve for a normal probability distribution. The NORM.DIST function has four input values. The first is the value of interest corresponding to the probability you want to calculate, the second is the mean of the normal distribution, the third is the standard deviation of the normal distribution, and the fourth is TRUE or FALSE. We enter TRUE for the fourth input if we want the cumulative distribution function and FALSE if we want the probability density function.

Figure 4.26 shows how we can answer the question of interest for Grear using Excel—in cell B5, we use the formula =NORM.DIST(40,000, $B$1, $B$2, TRUE). Cell B1 contains the mean of the normal distribution and cell B2 contains the standard deviation. Because we want to know the area under the curve, we want the cumulative distribution function, so we use TRUE as the fourth input value in the formula. This formula provides a value of 0.7580 in cell B5. But note that this corresponds to $P(x \leq 40,000) = 0.7580$. In other words, this gives us the area under the curve to the left of $x = 40,000$ in Figure 4.25, and we are interested in the area under the curve to the right of $x = 40,000$. To find this value, we simply use $1 - 0.7580 = 0.2420$ (cell B6). Thus, 0.2420 is the probability that x will exceed 40,000 hours. We can conclude that about 24.2% of aircraft engines will exceed 40,000 lifetime flight hours.

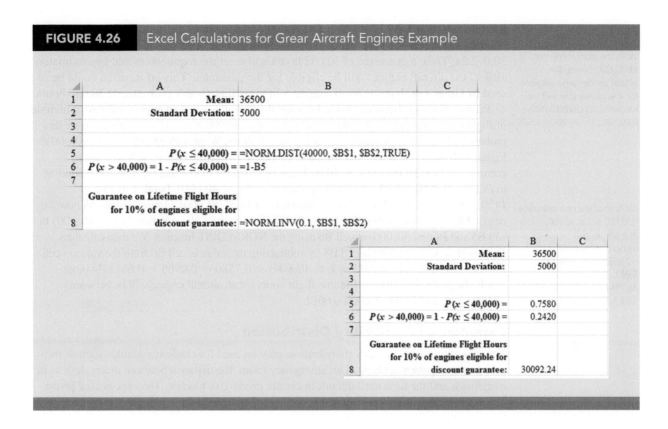

FIGURE 4.26   Excel Calculations for Grear Aircraft Engines Example

Let us now assume that Grear is considering a guarantee that will provide a discount on a replacement aircraft engine if the original engine does not meet the lifetime-flight-hour guarantee. How many lifetime flight hours should Grear guarantee if Grear wants no more than 10% of aircraft engines to be eligible for the discount guarantee? This question is interpreted graphically in Figure 4.27.

According to Figure 4.27, the area under the curve to the left of the unknown guarantee on lifetime flight hours must be 0.10. To find the appropriate value using Excel, we use the function NORM.INV. The NORM.INV function has three input values. The first is the probability of interest, the second is mean of the normal distribution, and the third is the standard deviation of the normal distribution. Figure 4.26 shows how we can use Excel to answer Grear's question about a guarantee on lifetime flight hours. In cell B8 we use the

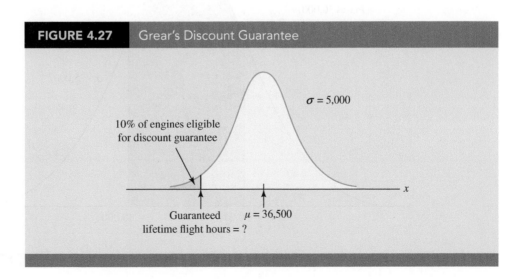

FIGURE 4.27   Grear's Discount Guarantee

With the guarantee set at 30,000 hours, the actual percentage eligible for the guarantee will be =NORM.DIST(30000,36500, 5000,TRUE) = 0.0968, or 9.68%

formula $=NORM.INV(0.10, \$B\$1, \$B\$2)$, where the mean of the normal distribution is contained in cell B1 and the standard deviation in cell B2. This provides a value of 30,092.24. Thus, a guarantee of 30,092 hours will meet the requirement that approximately 10% of the aircraft engines will be eligible for the guarantee. This information could be used by Grear's analytics team to suggest a lifetime flight hours guarantee of 30,000 hours.

Perhaps Grear is also interested in knowing the probability that an engine will have a lifetime of flight hours greater than 30,000 hours but less than 40,000 hours. How do we calculate this probability? First, we can restate this question as follows. What is $P(30,000 \le x \le 40,000)$? Figure 4.28 shows the area under the curve needed to answer this question. The area that corresponds to $P(30,000 \le x \le 40.000)$ can be found by subtracting the area corresponding to $P(x \le 30,000)$ from the area corresponding to $P(x \le 40,000)$. In other words,

Note that we can calculate $P(30,000 \le x \le 40,000)$ in a single cell using the formula =NORM.DIST(40000, $\$B\$1, \$B\$2, TRUE) –$ NORM.DIST(30000, $\$B\$1, \$B\$2, TRUE).

$P(30,000 \le x \le 40,000) = P(x \le 40,000) - P(x \le 30,000)$. Figure 4.29 shows how we can find the value for $P(30,000 \le x \le 40,000)$ using Excel. We calculate $P(x \le 40,000)$ in cell B5 and $P(x \le 30,000)$ in cell B6 using the NORM.DIST function. We then calculate $P(30,000 \le x \le 40,000)$ in cell B8 by subtracting the value in cell B6 from the value in cell B5. This tells us that $P(30,000 \le x \le 40,000) = 0.7580 - 0.0968 = 0.6612$. In other words, the probability that the lifetime flight hours for an aircraft engine will be between 30,000 hours and 40,000 hours is 0.6612.

Exponential Probability Distribution

The **exponential probability distribution** may be used for random variables such as the time between patient arrivals at an emergency room, the distance between major defects in a highway, and the time until default in certain credit-risk models. The exponential probability density function is as follows:

FIGURE 4.28   Graph Showing the Area Under the Curve Corresponding to $P(30,000 \le x \le 40,000)$ in the Grear Aircraft Engines Example

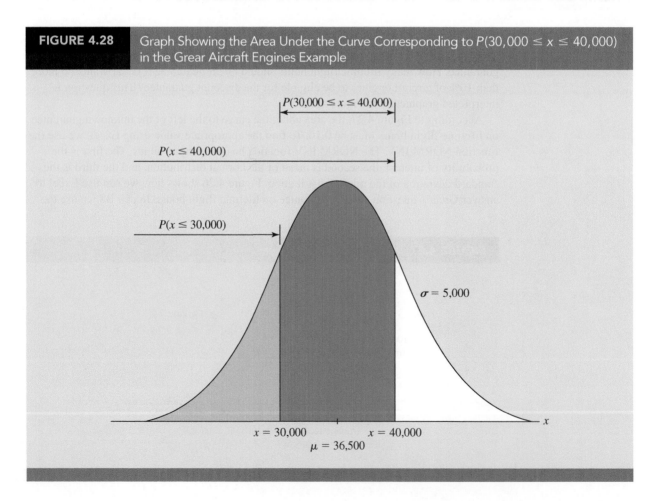

FIGURE 4.29   Using Excel to Find $P(30,000 \le x \le 40.000)$ in the Grear Aircraft Engines Example

	A	B	C
1	Mean:	36500	
2	Standard Deviation:	5000	
3			
4			
5	$P\,(x \le 40{,}000) =$	=NORM.DIST(40000, $B$1, $B$2,TRUE)	
6	$P\,(x \le 30{,}000) =$	=NORM.DIST(30000, $B$1, $B$2,TRUE)	
7			
8	$P\,(30{,}000 \le x \le 40{,}000)$ $= P\,(x \le 40{,}000) - P\,(x \le 30{,}000) =$	=B5-B6	

	A	B	C
1	Mean:	36500	
2	Standard Deviation:	5000	
3			
4			
5	$P\,(x \le 40{,}000) =$	0.7580	
6	$P\,(x \le 30{,}000) =$	0.0968	
7			
8	$P\,(30{,}000 \le x \le 40{,}000)$ $= P\,(x \le 40{,}000) - P\,(x \le 30{,}000) =$	0.6612	

EXPONENTIAL PROBABILITY DENSITY FUNCTION

$$f(x) = \frac{1}{\mu} e^{-x/\mu} \quad \text{for } x \ge 0 \tag{4.23}$$

where

μ = expected value or mean
e = 2.71828

As an example, suppose that x represents the time between business loan defaults for a particular lending agency. If the mean, or average, time between loan defaults is 15 months ($\mu = 15$), the appropriate density function for x is

$$f(x) = \frac{1}{15} e^{-x/15}$$

Figure 4.30 is the graph of this probability density function.

As with any continuous probability distribution, the area under the curve corresponding to an interval provides the probability that the random variable assumes a value in that interval. In the time between loan defaults example, the probability that the time between two defaults is six months or less, $P(x \le 6)$, is defined to be the area under the curve in Figure 4.30 from $x = 0$ to $x = 6$. Similarly, the probability that the time between defaults will be 18 months or less, $P(x \le 18)$, is the area under the curve from $x = 0$ to $x = 18$. Note also that the probability that the time between defaults will be between 6 months and 18 months, $P(6 \le x \le 18)$, is given by the area under the curve from $x = 6$ to $x = 18$.

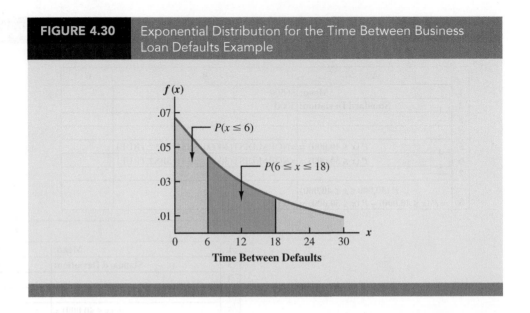

FIGURE 4.30   Exponential Distribution for the Time Between Business Loan Defaults Example

To compute exponential probabilities such as those just described, we use the following formula, which provides the cumulative probability of obtaining a value for the exponential random variable of less than or equal to some specific value denoted by x_0.

EXPONENTIAL DISTRIBUTION: CUMULATIVE PROBABILITIES

$$P(x \leq x_0) = 1 - e^{-x_0/\mu} \qquad (4.24)$$

For the time between defaults example, $x =$ time between business loan defaults in months and $\mu = 15$ months. Using equation (4.24),

$$P(x \leq x_0) = 1 - e^{-x_0/15}$$

Hence, the probability that the time between two defaults is six months or less is:

$$P(x \leq 6) = 1 - e^{-6/15} = 0.3297$$

Using equation (4.24), we calculate the probability that the time between defaults is 18 months or less:

$$P(x \leq 18) = 1 - e^{-18/15} = 0.6988$$

Thus, the probability that the time between two business loan defaults is between 6 months and 18 months is equal to $0.6988 - 0.3297 = 0.3691$. Probabilities for any other interval can be computed similarly.

Figure 4.31 shows how we can calculate these values for an exponential distribution in Excel using the function EXPON.DIST. The EXPON.DIST function has three inputs: the first input is x, the second input is $1/m$, and the third input is TRUE or FALSE. An input of TRUE for the third input provides the cumulative distribution function value and FALSE provides the probability density function value. Cell B3 calculates $P(x \leq 18)$ using the formula =EXPON.DIST(18, 1/$B$1, TRUE), where cell B1 contains the mean of the exponential distribution. Cell B4 calculates the value for $P(x \leq 6)$ and cell B5 calculates the value for $P(6 \leq x \leq 18) = P(x \leq 18) - P(x \leq 6)$ by subtracting the value in cell B4 from the value in cell B3.

We can calculate $P(6 \leq x \leq 18)$ in a single cell using the formula =EXPON.DIST(18, 1/$B$1, TRUE) - EXPON.DIST(6, 1/$B$1, TRUE).

FIGURE 4.31	Using Excel to Calculate $P(6 \leq x \leq 18)$ for the Time Between Business Loan Defaults Example

◢	A	B	C
1	Mean, μ =	15	
2			
3	$P(x \leq 18)$ =	=EXPON.DIST(18,1/$B$1, TRUE)	
4	$P(x \leq 6)$ =	=EXPON.DIST(6,1/$B$1, TRUE)	
5	$P(6 \leq x \leq 18) = P(x \leq 18) - P(x \leq 6)$ =	=B3-B4	

◢	A	B	C
1	Mean, μ =	15	
2			
3	$P(x \leq 18)$ =	0.6988	
4	$P(x \leq 6)$ =	0.3297	
5	$P(6 \leq x \leq 18) = P(x \leq 18) - P(x \leq 6)$ =	0.3691	

NOTES + COMMENTS

1. The way we describe probabilities is different for a discrete random variable than it is for a continuous random variable. For discrete random variables, we can talk about the probability of the random variable assuming a particular value. For continuous random variables, we can only talk about the probability of the random variable assuming a value within a given interval.

2. To see more clearly why the height of a probability density function is not a probability, think about a random variable with the following uniform probability distribution:

$$f(x) = \begin{cases} 2 & \text{for } 0 \leq x \leq 0.5 \\ 0 & \text{elsewhere} \end{cases}$$

The height of the probability density function, $f(x)$, is 2 for values of x between 0 and 0.5. However, we know that probabilities can never be greater than 1. Thus, we see that $f(x)$ cannot be interpreted as the probability of x.

3. The standard normal distribution is the special case of the normal distribution for which the mean is 0 and the standard deviation is 1. This is useful because probabilities for all normal distributions can be computed using the standard normal distribution. We can convert any normal random variable x with mean μ and standard deviation σ to the standard normal random variable z by using the formula $z = \dfrac{x - \mu}{\sigma}$. We interpret z as the number of standard deviations that the normal random variable x is from its mean μ. Then we can use a table of standard normal probability distributions to find the area under the curve using z and the standard normal probability table. Excel contains special functions for the standard normal distribution: NORM.S.DIST and NORM.S.INV. The function NORM.S.DIST is similar to the function NORM.DIST, but it requires only two input values: the value of interest for calculating the probability and TRUE or FALSE, depending on whether you are interested in finding the probability density or the cumulative distribution function. NORM.S.INV is similar to the NORM.INV function, but it requires only the single input of the probability of interest. Both NORM.S.DIST and NORM.S.INV do not need the additional parameters because they assume a mean of 0 and standard deviation of 1 for the standard normal distribution.

4. A property of the exponential distribution is that the mean and the standard deviation are equal to each other.

5. The continuous exponential distribution is related to the discrete Poisson distribution. If the Poisson distribution provides an appropriate description of the number of occurrences per interval, the exponential distribution provides a description of the length of the interval between occurrences. This relationship often arises in queueing applications in which, if arrivals follow a Poisson distribution, the time between arrivals must follow an exponential distribution.

6. Chapter 11 explains how values for discrete and continuous random variables can be generated in Excel for use in simulation models.

SUMMARY

In this chapter we introduced the concept of probability as a means of understanding and measuring uncertainty. Uncertainty is a factor in virtually all business decisions, thus an understanding of probability is essential to modeling such decisions and improving the decision-making process.

We introduced some basic relationships in probability including the concepts of outcomes, events, and calculations of related probabilities. We introduced the concept of conditional probability and discussed how to calculate posterior probabilities from prior probabilities using Bayes' theorem. We then discussed both discrete and continuous random variables as well as some of the more common probability distributions related to these types of random variables. These probability distributions included the custom discrete, discrete uniform, binomial, and Poisson probability distributions for discrete random variables, as well as the uniform, triangular, normal, and exponential probability distributions for continuous random variables. We also discussed the concepts of the expected value (mean) and variance of a random variable.

Probability is used in many chapters that follow in this textbook. In Chapter 5, various measures for showing the strength of association rules are based on probability and conditional probability concepts. Random variables and probability distributions will be seen again in Chapter 6 when we discuss the use of statistical inference to draw conclusions about a population from sample data. In Chapter 7, we will see that the normal distribution is fundamentally involved when we discuss regression analysis as a way of estimating relationships between variables. Chapter 11 demonstrates the use of a variety of probability distributions in simulation models to evaluate the impact of uncertainty on decision-making. Conditional probability and Bayes' theorem will be discussed again in Chapter 15 in the context of decision analysis. It is very important to have a basic understanding of probability, such as is provided in this chapter, as you continue to improve your skills in business analytics.

GLOSSARY

Addition law A probability law used to compute the probability of the union of events. For two events A and B, the addition law is $P(A \cup B) = P(A) + P(B) - P(A \cap B)$. For two mutually exclusive events, $P(A \cap B) = 0$, so $P(A \cup B) = P(A) + P(B)$.

Bayes' theorem A method used to compute posterior probabilities.

Binomial probability distribution A probability distribution for a discrete random variable showing the probability of x successes in n trials.

Complement of A The event consisting of all outcomes that are not in A.

Conditional probability The probability of an event given that another event has already occurred. The conditional probability of A given B is $P(A \mid B) = \dfrac{P(A \cap B)}{P(B)}$.

Continuous random variable A random variable that may assume any numerical value in an interval or collection of intervals. An interval can include negative and positive infinity.

Custom discrete probability distribution A probability distribution for a discrete random variable for which each value x_i that the random variable assumes is associated with a defined probability $f(x_i)$.

Discrete random variable A random variable that can take on only specified discrete values.

Discrete uniform probability distribution A probability distribution in which each possible value of the discrete random variable has the same probability.

Empirical probability distribution A probability distribution for which the relative frequency method is used to assign probabilities.

Event A collection of outcomes.

Expected value A measure of the central location, or mean, of a random variable.

Exponential probability distribution A continuous probability distribution that is useful in computing probabilities for the time it takes to complete a task or the time between arrivals. The mean and standard deviation for an exponential probability distribution are equal to each other.

Independent events Two events A and B are independent if $P(A \mid B) = P(A)$ or $P(B \mid A) = P(B)$; the events do not influence each other.

Intersection of A and B The event containing the outcomes belonging to both A and B. The intersection of A and B is denoted $A \cap B$.

Joint probabilities The probability of two events both occurring; in other words, the probability of the intersection of two events.

Marginal probabilities The values in the margins of a joint probability table that provide the probabilities of each event separately.

Multiplication law A law used to compute the probability of the intersection of events. For two events A and B, the multiplication law is $P(A \cap B) = P(B)P(A \mid B)$ or $P(A \cap B) = P(A)P(B \mid A)$. For two independent events, it reduces to $P(A \cap B) = P(A)P(B)$.

Mutually exclusive events Events that have no outcomes in common; $A \cap B$ is empty and $P(A \cap B) = 0$.

Normal probability distribution A continuous probability distribution in which the probability density function is bell shaped and determined by its mean μ and standard deviation σ.

Poisson probability distribution A probability distribution for a discrete random variable showing the probability of x occurrences of an event over a specified interval of time or space.

Posterior probabilities Revised probabilities of events based on additional information.

Prior probability Initial estimate of the probabilities of events.

Probability A numerical measure of the likelihood that an event will occur.

Probability density function A function used to compute probabilities for a continuous random variable. The area under the graph of a probability density function over an interval represents probability.

Probability distribution A description of how probabilities are distributed over the values of a random variable.

Probability mass function A function, denoted by $f(x)$, that provides the probability that x assumes a particular value for a discrete random variable.

Probability of an event Equal to the sum of the probabilities of outcomes for the event.

Random experiment A process that generates well-defined experimental outcomes. On any single repetition or trial, the outcome that occurs is determined by chance.

Random variables A numerical description of the outcome of an experiment.

Sample space The set of all outcomes.

Standard deviation Positive square root of the variance.

Triangular probability distribution A continuous probability distribution in which the probability density function is shaped like a triangle defined by the minimum possible value a, the maximum possible value b, and the most likely value m. A triangular probability distribution is often used when only subjective estimates are available for the minimum, maximum, and most likely values.

Uniform probability distribution A continuous probability distribution for which the probability that the random variable will assume a value in any interval is the same for each interval of equal length.

Union of A and B The event containing the outcomes belonging to A or B or both. The union of A and B is denoted by $A \cup B$.

Variance A measure of the variability, or dispersion, of a random variable.

Venn diagram A graphical representation of the sample space and operations involving events, in which the sample space is represented by a rectangle and events are represented as circles within the sample space.

PROBLEMS

1. **Airline Performance Measures.** On-time arrivals, lost baggage, and customer complaints are three measures that are typically used to measure the quality of service being offered by airlines. Suppose that the following values represent the on-time arrival percentage, amount of lost baggage, and customer complaints for 10 U.S. airlines.

Airline	On-Time Arrivals (%)	Mishandled Baggage per 1,000 Passengers	Customer Complaints per 1,000 Passengers
Virgin America	83.5	0.87	1.50
JetBlue	79.1	1.88	0.79
AirTran Airways	87.1	1.58	0.91
Delta Air Lines	86.5	2.10	0.73
Alaska Airlines	87.5	2.93	0.51
Frontier Airlines	77.9	2.22	1.05
Southwest Airlines	83.1	3.08	0.25
US Airways	85.9	2.14	1.74
American Airlines	76.9	2.92	1.80
United Airlines	77.4	3.87	4.24

   a. Based on the data above, if you randomly choose a Delta Air Lines flight, what is the probability that this individual flight will have an on-time arrival?

   b. If you randomly choose 1 of the 10 airlines for a follow-up study on airline quality ratings, what is the probability that you will choose an airline with less than two mishandled baggage reports per 1,000 passengers?

   c. If you randomly choose 1 of the 10 airlines for a follow-up study on airline quality ratings, what is the probability that you will choose an airline with more than one customer complaint per 1,000 passengers?

   d. What is the probability that a randomly selected AirTran Airways flight will not arrive on time?

2. **Rolling a Pair of Dice.** Consider the random experiment of rolling a pair of dice. Suppose that we are interested in the sum of the face values showing on the dice.

   a. How many outcomes are possible?

   b. List the outcomes.

   c. What is the probability of obtaining a value of 7?

   d. What is the probability of obtaining a value of 9 or greater?

3. **Ivy League College Admissions.** Suppose that for a recent admissions class, an Ivy League college received 2,851 applications for early admission. Of this group, it admitted 1,033 students early, rejected 854 outright, and deferred 964 to the regular admission pool for further consideration. In the past, this school has admitted 18% of the deferred early admission applicants during the regular admission process. Counting the students admitted early and the students admitted during the regular admission process, the total class size was 2,375. Let E, R, and D represent the events that a student who applies for early admission is admitted early, rejected outright, or deferred to the regular admissions pool.

   a. Use the data to estimate $P(E)$, $P(R)$, and $P(D)$.

   b. Are events E and D mutually exclusive? Find $P(E \cap D)$.

   c. For the 2,375 students who were admitted, what is the probability that a randomly selected student was accepted during early admission?

   d. Suppose a student applies for early admission. What is the probability that the student will be admitted for early admission or be deferred and later admitted during the regular admission process?

4. **Two Events, A and B.** Suppose that we have two events, A and B, with $P(A) = 0.50$, $P(B) = 0.60$, and $P(A \cap B) = 0.40$.
   a. Find $P(A \mid B)$.
   b. Find $P(B \mid A)$.
   c. Are A and B independent? Why or why not?

5. **Intent to Pursue MBA.** Students taking the Graduate Management Admissions Test (GMAT) were asked about their undergraduate major and intent to pursue their MBA as a full-time or part-time student. A summary of their responses is as follows:

		\multicolumn{4}{c}{Undergraduate Major}
		Business	Engineering	Other	Totals
Intended	Full-Time	352	197	251	800
Enrollment	Part-Time	150	161	194	505
Status	Totals	502	358	445	1,305

   a. Develop a joint probability table for these data.
   b. Use the marginal probabilities of undergraduate major (business, engineering, or other) to comment on which undergraduate major produces the most potential MBA students.
   c. If a student intends to attend classes full time in pursuit of an MBA degree, what is the probability that the student was an undergraduate engineering major?
   d. If a student was an undergraduate business major, what is the probability that the student intends to attend classes full time in pursuit of an MBA degree?
   e. Let F denote the event that the student intends to attend classes full time in pursuit of an MBA degree, and let B denote the event that the student was an undergraduate business major. Are events F and B independent? Justify your answer.

6. **Student Loans and College Degrees.** More than 40 million Americans are estimated to have at least one outstanding student loan to help pay college expenses (CNNMoney web site). Not all of these graduates pay back their debt in satisfactory fashion. Suppose that the following joint probability table shows the probabilities of student loan status and whether or not the student had received a college degree.

		\multicolumn{2}{c}{College Degree}	
		Yes	No	
Loan	Satisfactory	0.26	0.24	0.50
Status	Delinquent	0.16	0.34	0.50
		0.42	0.58	

   a. What is the probability that a student with a student loan had received a college degree?
   b. What is the probability that a student with a student loan had not received a college degree?
   c. Given that the student has received a college degree, what is the probability that the student has a delinquent loan?
   d. Given that the student has not received a college degree, what is the probability that the student has a delinquent loan?
   e. What is the impact of dropping out of college without a degree for students who have a student loan?

DATA *file*

OptilyticsLLC

7. **Senior Data Scientist Position Applicants.** The Human Resources Manager for Optilytics LLC is evaluating applications for the position of Senior Data Scientist. The file *OptilyticsLLC* presents summary data of the applicants for the position.

a. Use a PivotTable in Excel to create a joint probability table showing the probabilities associated with a randomly selected applicant's sex and highest degree
achieved. Use this joint probability table to answer the questions below.

b. What are the marginal probabilities? What do they tell you about the probabilities
associated with the sex of applicants and highest degree completed by applicants?

c. If the applicant is female, what is the probability that the highest degree completed
by the applicant is a PhD?

d. If the highest degree completed by the applicant is a bachelor's degree, what is the
probability that the applicant is male?

e. What is the probability that a randomly selected applicant will be a male whose
highest completed degree is a PhD?

8. **U.S. Household Incomes.** The U.S. Census Bureau is a leading source of quantitative
data related to the people and economy of the United States. The crosstabulation below
represents the number of households (thousands) and the household income by the
highest level of education for the head of household (U.S. Census Bureau web site).
Use this crosstabulation to answer the following questions.

Highest Level of Education	Household Income				
	Under $25,000	$25,000 to $49,999	$50,000 to $99,999	$100,000 and Over	Total
High school graduate	9,880	9,970	9,441	3,482	32,773
Bachelor's degree	2,484	4,164	7,666	7,817	22,131
Master's degree	685	1,205	3,019	4,094	9,003
Doctoral degree	79	160	422	1,076	1,737
Total	13,128	15,499	20,548	16,469	65,644

a. Develop a joint probability table.

b. What is the probability the head of one of these households has a master's degree or
higher education?

c. What is the probability a household is headed by someone with a high school
diploma earning $100,000 or more?

d. What is the probability one of these households has an income below $25,000?

e. What is the probability a household is headed by someone with a bachelor's degree
earning less than $25,000?

f. Are household income and educational level independent?

9. **Probability of Homes Selling.** Cooper Realty is a small real estate company located
in Albany, New York, that specializes primarily in residential listings. The company
recently became interested in determining the likelihood of one of its listings being
sold within a certain number of days. An analysis of company sales of 800 homes in
previous years produced the following data.

Initial Asking Price	Days Listed Until Sold			
	Under 30	31–90	Over 90	Total
Under $150,000	50	40	10	100
$150,000–$199,999	20	150	80	250
$200,000–$250,000	20	280	100	400
Over $250,000	10	30	10	50
Total	100	500	200	800

a. If A is defined as the event that a home is listed for more than 90 days before being
sold, estimate the probability of A.

b. If B is defined as the event that the initial asking price is under $150,000, estimate the probability of B.

c. What is the probability of $A \cap B$?

d. Assuming that a contract was just signed to list a home with an initial asking price of less than $150,000, what is the probability that the home will take Cooper Realty more than 90 days to sell?

e. Are events A and B independent?

10. **Computing Probabilities.** The prior probabilities for events A_1 and A_2 are $P(A_1) = 0.40$ and $P(A_2) = 0.60$. It is also known that $P(A_1 \cap A_2) = 0$. Suppose $P(B \mid A_1) = 0.20$ and $P(B \mid A_2) = 0.05$.

a. Are A_1 and A_2 mutually exclusive? Explain.

b. Compute $P(A_1 \cap B)$ and $P(A_2 \cap B)$.

c. Compute $P(B)$.

d. Apply Bayes' theorem to compute $P(A_1 \mid B)$ and $P(A_2 \mid B)$.

11. **Credit Card Defaults.** A local bank reviewed its credit-card policy with the intention of recalling some of its credit cards. In the past, approximately 5% of cardholders defaulted, leaving the bank unable to collect the outstanding balance. Hence, management established a prior probability of 0.05 that any particular cardholder will default. The bank also found that the probability of missing a monthly payment is 0.20 for customers who do not default. Of course, the probability of missing a monthly payment for those who default is 1.

a. Given that a customer missed a monthly payment, compute the posterior probability that the customer will default.

b. The bank would like to recall its credit card if the probability that a customer will default is greater than 0.20. Should the bank recall its credit card if the customer misses a monthly payment? Why or why not?

12. **Prostate Cancer Screening.** According to a 2018 article in *Esquire* magazine, approximately 70% of males over age 70 will develop cancerous cells in their prostate. Prostate cancer is second only to skin cancer as the most common form of cancer for males in the United States. One of the most common tests for the detection of prostate cancer is the prostate-specific antigen (PSA) test. However, this test is known to have a high false-positive rate (tests that come back positive for cancer when no cancer is present). Suppose there is a .02 probability that a male patient has prostate cancer before testing. The probability of a false-positive test is .75, and the probability of a false-negative (no indication of cancer when cancer is actually present) is .20.

a. What is the probability that the male patient has prostate cancer if the PSA test comes back positive?

b. What is the probability that the male patient has prostate cancer if the PSA test comes back negative?

c. For older men, the prior probability of having cancer increases. Suppose that the prior probability of the male patient is .3 rather than .02. What is the probability that the male patient has prostate cancer if the PSA test comes back positive? What is the probability that the male patient has prostate cancer if the PSA test comes back negative?

d. What can you infer about the PSA test from the results of parts (a), (b), and (c)?

13. **Finding Oil in Alaska.** An oil company purchased an option on land in Alaska. Preliminary geologic studies assigned the following prior probabilities.

$$P(\text{high-quality oil}) = 0.50$$
$$P(\text{medium-quality oil}) = 0.20$$
$$P(\text{no oil}) = 0.30$$

a. What is the probability of finding oil?

b. After 200 feet of drilling on the first well, a soil test is taken. The probabilities of finding the particular type of soil identified by the test are as follows.

$$P(\text{soil} \mid \text{high-quality oil}) = 0.20$$
$$P(\text{soil} \mid \text{medium-quality oil}) = 0.80$$
$$P(\text{soil} \mid \text{no oil}) = 0.20$$

How should the firm interpret the soil test? What are the revised probabilities, and what is the new probability of finding oil?

14. **Unemployment Data.** Suppose the following data represent the number of persons unemployed for a given number of months in Killeen, Texas. The values in the first column show the number of months unemployed and the values in the second column show the corresponding number of unemployed persons.

Months Unemployed	Number Unemployed
1	1,029
2	1,686
3	2,269
4	2,675
5	3,487
6	4,652
7	4,145
8	3,587
9	2,325
10	1,120

Let x be a random variable indicating the number of months a randomly selected person is unemployed.

a. Use the data to develop an empirical discrete probability distribution for x.

b. Show that your probability distribution satisfies the conditions for a valid discrete probability distribution.

c. What is the probability that a person is unemployed for two months or less? Unemployed for more than two months?

d. What is the probability that a person is unemployed for more than six months?

15. **Information Systems Job Satisfaction.** The percent frequency distributions of job satisfaction scores for a sample of information systems (IS) senior executives and middle managers are as follows. The scores range from a low of 1 (very dissatisfied) to a high of 5 (very satisfied).

Job Satisfaction Score	IS Senior Executives (%)	IS Middle Managers (%)
1	5	4
2	9	10
3	3	12
4	42	46
5	41	28

a. Develop a probability distribution for the job satisfaction score of a randomly selected senior executive.

b. Develop a probability distribution for the job satisfaction score of a randomly selected middle manager.

c. What is the probability that a randomly selected senior executive will report a job satisfaction score of 4 or 5?

d. What is the probability that a randomly selected middle manager is very satisfied?

e. Compare the overall job satisfaction of senior executives and middle managers.

16. **Expectation and Variance of a Random Variable.** The following table provides a probability distribution for the random variable y.

y	f(y)
2	0.20
4	0.30
7	0.40
8	0.10

   a. Compute $E(y)$.
   b. Compute Var(y) and σ.

17. **Damage Claims at an Insurance Company.** The probability distribution for damage claims paid by the Newton Automobile Insurance Company on collision insurance is as follows.

Payment ($)	Probability
0	0.85
500	0.04
1,000	0.04
3,000	0.03
5,000	0.02
8,000	0.01
10,000	0.01

   a. Use the expected collision payment to determine the collision insurance premium that would enable the company to break even.
   b. The insurance company charges an annual rate of $520 for the collision coverage. What is the expected value of the collision policy for a policyholder? (*Hint:* It is the expected payments from the company minus the cost of coverage.) Why does the policyholder purchase a collision policy with this expected value?

18. **Plant Expansion Decision.** The J.R. Ryland Computer Company is considering a plant expansion to enable the company to begin production of a new computer product. The company's president must determine whether to make the expansion a medium- or large-scale project. Demand for the new product is uncertain, which for planning purposes may be low demand, medium demand, or high demand. The probability estimates for demand are 0.20, 0.50, and 0.30, respectively. Letting x and y indicate the annual profit in thousands of dollars, the firm's planners developed the following profit forecasts for the medium- and large-scale expansion projects.

		Medium-Scale Expansion Profit		Large-Scale Expansion Profit	
		x	f(x)	y	f(y)
	Low	50	0.20	0	0.20
Demand	Medium	150	0.50	100	0.50
	High	200	0.30	300	0.30

   a. Compute the expected value for the profit associated with the two expansion alternatives. Which decision is preferred for the objective of maximizing the expected profit?
   b. Compute the variance for the profit associated with the two expansion alternatives. Which decision is preferred for the objective of minimizing the risk or uncertainty?

19. **Binomial Distribution Calculations.** Consider a binomial experiment with $n = 10$ and $p = 0.10$.
    a. Compute $f(0)$.
    b. Compute $f(2)$.
    c. Compute $P(x \leq 2)$.
    d. Compute $P(x \geq 1)$.
    e. Compute $E(x)$.
    f. Compute $\text{Var}(x)$ and σ.

20. **Acceptance Sampling.** Many companies use a quality control technique called acceptance sampling to monitor incoming shipments of parts, raw materials, and so on. In the electronics industry, component parts are commonly shipped from suppliers in large lots. Inspection of a sample of n components can be viewed as the n trials of a binomial experiment. The outcome for each component tested (trial) will be that the component is classified as good or defective. Reynolds Electronics accepts a lot from a particular supplier if the defective components in the lot do not exceed 1%. Suppose a random sample of five items from a recent shipment is tested.
    a. Assume that 1% of the shipment is defective. Compute the probability that no items in the sample are defective.
    b. Assume that 1% of the shipment is defective. Compute the probability that exactly one item in the sample is defective.
    c. What is the probability of observing one or more defective items in the sample if 1% of the shipment is defective?
    d. Would you feel comfortable accepting the shipment if one item was found to be defective? Why or why not?

21. **Introductory Statistics Course Withdrawals.** A university found that 20% of its students withdraw without completing the introductory statistics course. Assume that 20 students registered for the course.
    a. Compute the probability that two or fewer will withdraw.
    b. Compute the probability that exactly four will withdraw.
    c. Compute the probability that more than three will withdraw.
    d. Compute the expected number of withdrawals.

22. **Poisson Distribution Calculations.** Consider a Poisson distribution with $\mu = 3$.
    a. Write the appropriate Poisson probability mass function.
    b. Compute $f(2)$.
    c. Compute $f(1)$.
    d. Compute $P(x \geq 2)$.

23. **911 Calls.** Emergency 911 calls to a small municipality in Idaho come in at the rate of one every 2 minutes. Assume that the number of 911 calls is a random variable that can be described by the Poisson distribution.
    a. What is the expected number of 911 calls in 1 hour?
    b. What is the probability of three 911 calls in 5 minutes?
    c. What is the probability of no 911 calls during a 5-minute period?

24. **Small Business Failures.** A regional director responsible for business development in the state of Pennsylvania is concerned about the number of small business failures. If the mean number of small business failures per month is 10, what is the probability that exactly 4 small businesses will fail during a given month? Assume that the probability of a failure is the same for any two months and that the occurrence or nonoccurrence of a failure in any month is independent of failures in any other month.

25. **Uniform Distribution Calculations.** The random variable x is known to be uniformly distributed between 10 and 20.
    a. Show the graph of the probability density function.
    b. Compute $P(x < 15)$.
    c. Compute $P(12 \leq x \leq 18)$.
    d. Compute $E(x)$.
    e. Compute $\text{Var}(x)$.

26. **RAND Function in Excel.** Most computer languages include a function that can be used to generate random numbers. In Excel, the RAND function can be used to generate random numbers between 0 and 1. If we let x denote a random number generated using RAND, then x is a continuous random variable with the following probability density function:

$$f(x) = \begin{cases} 1 & \text{for } 0 \le x \le 1 \\ 0 & \text{elsewhere} \end{cases}$$

a. Graph the probability density function.
b. What is the probability of generating a random number between 0.25 and 0.75?
c. What is the probability of generating a random number with a value less than or equal to 0.30?
d. What is the probability of generating a random number with a value greater than 0.60?
e. Generate 50 random numbers by entering =RAND() into 50 cells of an Excel worksheet.
f. Compute the mean and standard deviation for the random numbers in part (e).

27. **Bidding on a Piece of Land.** Suppose we are interested in bidding on a piece of land and we know one other bidder is interested. The seller announced that the highest bid in excess of $10,000 will be accepted. Assume that the competitor's bid x is a random variable that is uniformly distributed between $10,000 and $15,000.

a. Suppose you bid $12,000. What is the probability that your bid will be accepted?
b. Suppose you bid $14,000. What is the probability that your bid will be accepted?
c. What amount should you bid to maximize the probability that you get the property?
d. Suppose you know someone who is willing to pay you $16,000 for the property. Would you consider bidding less than the amount in part (c)? Why or why not?

28. **Triangular Distribution Calculations.** A random variable has a triangular probability density function with $a = 50$, $b = 375$, and $m = 250$.

a. Sketch the probability distribution function for this random variable. Label the points $a = 50$, $b = 375$, and $m = 250$ on the x-axis.
b. What is the probability that the random variable will assume a value between 50 and 250?
c. What is the probability that the random variable will assume a value greater than 300?

29. **Project Completion Time.** The Siler Construction Company is about to bid on a new industrial construction project. To formulate their bid, the company needs to estimate the time required for the project. Based on past experience, management expects that the project will require at least 24 months, and could take as long as 48 months if there are complications. The most likely scenario is that the project will require 30 months.

a. Assume that the actual time for the project can be approximated using a triangular probability distribution. What is the probability that the project will take less than 30 months?
b. What is the probability that the project will take between 28 and 32 months?
c. To submit a competitive bid, the company believes that if the project takes more than 36 months, then the company will lose money on the project. Management does not want to bid on the project if there is greater than a 25% chance that they will lose money on this project. Should the company bid on this project?

30. **Large-Cap Stock Fund Returns.** Suppose that the return for a particular large-cap stock fund is normally distributed with a mean of 14.4% and standard deviation of 4.4%.

a. What is the probability that the large-cap stock fund has a return of at least 20%?
b. What is the probability that the large-cap stock fund has a return of 10% or less?

31. **IQ Scores and Mensa.** A person must score in the upper 2% of the population on an IQ test to qualify for membership in Mensa, the international high IQ society. If IQ scores are normally distributed with a mean of 100 and a standard deviation of 15, what score must a person have to qualify for Mensa?

32. **Web Site Traffic.** Assume that the traffic to the web site of Smiley's People, Inc., which sells customized T-shirts, follows a normal distribution, with a mean of 4.5 million visitors per day and a standard deviation of 820,000 visitors per day.
    a. What is the probability that the web site has fewer than 5 million visitors in a single day?
    b. What is the probability that the web site has 3 million or more visitors in a single day?
    c. What is the probability that the web site has between 3 million and 4 million visitors in a single day?
    d. Assume that 85% of the time, the Smiley's People web servers can handle the daily web traffic volume without purchasing additional server capacity. What is the amount of web traffic that will require Smiley's People to purchase additional server capacity?

33. **Probability of Defect.** Suppose that Motorola uses the normal distribution to determine the probability of defects and the number of defects in a particular production process. Assume that the production process manufactures items with a mean weight of 10 ounces. Calculate the probability of a defect and the suspected number of defects for a 1,000-unit production run in the following situations.
    a. The process standard deviation is 0.15, and the process control is set at plus or minus one standard deviation. Units with weights less than 9.85 or greater than 10.15 ounces will be classified as defects.
    b. Through process design improvements, the process standard deviation can be reduced to 0.05. Assume that the process control remains the same, with weights less than 9.85 or greater than 10.15 ounces being classified as defects.
    c. What is the advantage of reducing process variation, thereby causing process control limits to be at a greater number of standard deviations from the mean?

34. **Exponential Distribution Calculations.** Consider the following exponential probability density function:

$$f(x) = \frac{1}{3}e^{-x/3} \quad \text{for } x \geq 0$$

    a. Write the formula for $P(x \leq x_0)$.
    b. Find $P(x \leq 2)$.
    c. Find $P(x \geq 3)$.
    d. Find $P(x \leq 5)$.
    e. Find $P(2 \leq x \leq 5)$.

35. **Vehicle Arrivals at an Intersection.** The time between arrivals of vehicles at a particular intersection follows an exponential probability distribution with a mean of 12 seconds.
    a. Sketch this exponential probability distribution.
    b. What is the probability that the arrival time between vehicles is 12 seconds or less?
    c. What is the probability that the arrival time between vehicles is 6 seconds or less?
    d. What is the probability of 30 or more seconds between vehicle arrivals?

36. **Time Spent Playing *World of Warcraft*.** Suppose that the time spent by players in a single session on the *World of Warcraft* multiplayer online role-playing game follows an exponential distribution with a mean of 38.3 minutes.
    a. Write the exponential probability distribution function for the time spent by players on a single session of *World of Warcraft*.
    b. What is the probability that a player will spend between 20 and 40 minutes on a single session of *World of Warcraft*?
    c. What is the probability that a player will spend more than 1 hour on a single session of *World of Warcraft*?

CASE PROBLEM 1: HAMILTON COUNTY JUDGES

Hamilton County judges try thousands of cases per year. In an overwhelming majority of the cases disposed, the verdict stands as rendered. However, some cases are appealed, and of those appealed, some of the cases are reversed. Kristen DelGuzzi of the *Cincinnati Enquirer* newspaper conducted a study of cases handled by Hamilton County judges over a three-year period. Shown in the table below are the results for 182,908 cases handled (disposed) by 38 judges in Common Pleas Court, Domestic Relations Court, and Municipal Court. Two of the judges (Dinkelacker and Hogan) did not serve in the same court for the entire three-year period.

The purpose of the newspaper's study was to evaluate the performance of the judges. Appeals are often the result of mistakes made by judges, and the newspaper wanted to know which judges were doing a good job and which were making too many mistakes. You are called in to assist in the data analysis. Use your knowledge of probability and conditional probability to help with the ranking of the judges. You also may be able to analyze the likelihood of appeal and reversal for cases handled by different courts.

Total Cases Disposed, Appealed, and Reversed in Hamilton County Courts

Common Pleas Court

Judge	Total Cases Disposed	Appealed Cases	Reversed Cases
Fred Cartolano	3,037	137	12
Thomas Crush	3,372	119	10
Patrick Dinkelacker	1,258	44	8
Timothy Hogan	1,954	60	7
Robert Kraft	3,138	127	7
William Mathews	2,264	91	18
William Morrissey	3,032	121	22
Norbert Nadel	2,959	131	20
Arthur Ney, Jr.	3,219	125	14
Richard Niehaus	3,353	137	16
Thomas Nurre	3,000	121	6
John O'Connor	2,969	129	12
Robert Ruehlman	3,205	145	18
J. Howard Sundermann	955	60	10
Ann Marie Tracey	3,141	127	13
Ralph Winkler	3,089	88	6
Total	43,945	1,762	199

Domestic Relations Court

Judge	Total Cases Disposed	Appealed Cases	Reversed Cases
Penelope Cunningham	2,729	7	1
Patrick Dinkelacker	6,001	19	4
Deborah Gaines	8,799	48	9
Ronald Panioto	12,970	32	3
Total	30,499	106	17

Municipal Court			
Judge	Total Cases Disposed	Appealed Cases	Reversed Cases
Mike Allen	6,149	43	4
Nadine Allen	7,812	34	6
Timothy Black	7,954	41	6
David Davis	7,736	43	5
Leslie Isaiah Gaines	5,282	35	13
Karla Grady	5,253	6	0
Deidra Hair	2,532	5	0
Dennis Helmick	7,900	29	5
Timothy Hogan	2,308	13	2
James Patrick Kenney	2,798	6	1
Joseph Luebbers	4,698	25	8
William Mallory	8,277	38	9
Melba Marsh	8,219	34	7
Beth Mattingly	2,971	13	1
Albert Mestemaker	4,975	28	9
Mark Painter	2,239	7	3
Jack Rosen	7,790	41	13
Mark Schweikert	5,403	33	6
David Stockdale	5,371	22	4
John A. West	2,797	4	2
Total	108,464	500	104

Managerial Report

Prepare a report with your rankings of the judges. Also, include an analysis of the likelihood of appeal and case reversal in the three courts. At a minimum, your report should include the following:

1. The probability of cases being appealed and reversed in the three different courts.
2. The probability of a case being appealed for each judge.
3. The probability of a case being reversed for each judge.
4. The probability of reversal given an appeal for each judge.
5. Rank the judges within each court. State the criteria you used and provide a rationale for your choice.

CASE PROBLEM 2: McNEIL'S AUTO MALL

Harriet McNeil, proprietor of McNeil's Auto Mall, believes that it is good business for her automobile dealership to have more customers on the lot than can be served, as she believes this creates an impression that demand for the automobiles on her lot is high. However, she also understands that if there are far more customers on the lot than can be served by her salespeople, her dealership may lose sales to customers who become frustrated and leave without making a purchase.

Ms. McNeil is primarily concerned about the staffing of salespeople on her lot on Saturday mornings (8:00 A.M. to noon), which are the busiest time of the week for McNeil's Auto Mall. On Saturday mornings, an average of 6.8 customers arrive per hour. The customers arrive randomly at a constant rate throughout the morning, and a salesperson spends an average of one hour with a customer. Ms. McNeil's experience has led her to conclude that if there are two more customers on her lot than can be served at any time on a Saturday morning, her automobile dealership achieves the optimal balance of creating an impression of high demand without losing too many customers who become frustrated and leave without making a purchase.

Ms. McNeil now wants to determine how many salespeople she should have on her lot on Saturday mornings in order to achieve her goal of having two more customers on her lot than can be served at any time. She understands that occasionally the number of customers on her lot will exceed the number of salespersons by more than two, and she is willing to accept such an occurrence no more than 10% of the time.

Managerial Report

Ms. McNeil has asked you to determine the number of salespersons she should have on her lot on Saturday mornings in order to satisfy her criteria. In answering Ms. McNeil's question, consider the following three questions:

1. How is the number of customers who arrive in the lot on a Saturday morning distributed?
2. Suppose Ms. McNeil currently uses five salespeople on her lot on Saturday morning. Using the probability distribution you identified in (1), what is the probability that the number of customers who arrive on her lot will exceed the number of salespersons by more than two? Does her current Saturday morning employment strategy satisfy her stated objective? Why or why not?
3. What is the minimum number of salespeople Ms. McNeil should have on her lot on Saturday mornings to achieve her objective?

CASE PROBLEM 3: GEBHARDT ELECTRONICS

Gebhardt Electronics produces a wide variety of transformers that it sells directly to manufacturers of electronics equipment. For one component used in several models of its transformers, Gebhardt uses a 1-meter length of 0.20 mm diameter solid wire made of pure Oxygen-Free Electronic (OFE) copper. A flaw in the wire reduces its conductivity and increases the likelihood it will break, and this critical component is difficult to reach and repair after a transformer has been constructed. Therefore, Gebhardt wants to use primarily flawless lengths of wire in making this component. The company is willing to accept no more than a 1 in 20 chance that a 1-meter length taken from a spool will be flawless. Gebhardt also occasionally uses smaller pieces of the same wire in the manufacture of other components, so the 1-meter segments to be used for this component are essentially taken randomly from a long spool of 0.20 mm diameter solid OFE copper wire.

Gebhardt is now considering a new supplier for copper wire. This supplier claims that its spools of 0.20 mm diameter solid OFE copper wire average 127 centimeters between flaws. Gebhardt now must determine whether the new supply will be satisfactory if the supplier's claim is valid.

Managerial Report

In making this assessment for Gebhardt Electronics, consider the following three questions:

1. If the new supplier does provide spools of 0.20 mm solid OFE copper wire that average 127 centimeters between flaws, how is the length of wire between two consecutive flaws distributed?
2. Using the probability distribution you identified in (1), what is the probability that Gebhardt's criteria will be met (i.e., a 1 in 20 chance that a randomly selected 1-meter segment of wire provided by the new supplier will be flawless)?
3. In centimeters, what is the minimum mean length between consecutive flaws that would result in satisfaction of Gebhardt's criteria?
4. In centimeters, what is the minimum mean length between consecutive flaws that would result in a 1 in 100 chance that a randomly selected 1-meter segment of wire provided by the new supplier will be flawless?

Chapter 5

Descriptive Data Mining

CONTENTS

ANALYTICS IN ACTION:
ADVICE FROM A MACHINE

Advice from a Machine[1]

The proliferation of data and increase in computing power have sparked the development of automated *recommender systems*, which provide consumers with suggestions for movies, music, books, clothes, restaurants, dating, and whom to follow on Twitter. The sophisticated, proprietary algorithms guiding recommender systems measure the degree of similarity between users or items to identify recommendations of potential interest to a user.

Netflix, a company that provides media content via DVD-by-mail and Internet streaming, provides its users with recommendations for movies and television shows based on each user's expressed interests and feedback on previously viewed content. As its business has shifted from renting DVDs by mail to streaming content online, Netflix has been able to track its customers' viewing behavior more closely. This allows Netflix's recommendations to account for differences in viewing behavior based on the day of the week,

the time of day, the device used (computer, phone, television), and even the viewing location.

The use of recommender systems is prevalent in e-commerce. Using attributes detailed by the Music Genome Project, Pandora Internet Radio plays songs with properties similar to songs that a user "likes." In the online dating world, web sites such as eHarmony, Match.com, and OKCupid use different "formulas" to take into account hundreds of different behavioral traits to propose date "matches." Stitch Fix, a personal shopping service, combines recommendation algorithms and human input from its fashion experts to match its inventory of fashion items to its clients.

———
[1]"The Science Behind the Netflix Algorithms that Decide What You'll Watch Next," http://www.wired.com/2013/08/qq_netflix-algorithm. Retrieved on August 7, 2013; E. Colson, "Using Human and Machine Processing in Recommendation Systems," *First AAAI Conference on Human Computation and Crowdsourcing* (2013); K. Zhao, X. Wang, M. Yu, and B. Gao, "User Recommendation in Reciprocal and Bipartite Social Networks—A Case Study of Online Dating," *IEEE Intelligent Systems* 29, no. 2 (2014).

Over the past few decades, technological advances have led to a dramatic increase in the amount of recorded data. The use of smartphones, radio-frequency identification (RFID) tags, electronic sensors, credit cards, and the Internet has facilitated the collection of data from phone conversations, e-mails, business transactions, product and customer tracking, business transactions, and web browsing. The increase in the use of data-mining techniques in business has been caused largely by three events: the explosion in the amount of data being produced and electronically tracked, the ability to electronically warehouse these data, and the affordability of computer power to analyze the data. In this chapter, we discuss the analysis of large quantities of data in order to gain insight on customers and to uncover patterns to improve business processes.

We define an **observation**, or **record**, as the set of recorded values of variables associated with a single entity. An observation is often displayed as a row of values in a spreadsheet or database in which the columns correspond to the variables. For example, in a university's database of alumni, an observation may correspond to an alumnus's age, gender, marital status, employer, position title, as well as size and frequency of donations to the university.

Predictive data mining is discussed in Chapter 9.

In this chapter, we focus on descriptive data-mining methods, also called **unsupervised learning** techniques. In an unsupervised learning application, there is no outcome variable to predict; rather, the goal is to use the variable values to identify relationships between observations. Unsupervised learning approaches can be thought of as high-dimensional descriptive analytics because they are designed to describe patterns and relationships in large data sets with many observations of many variables. Without an explicit outcome (or one that is objectively known), there is no definitive measure of accuracy. Instead, qualitative assessments, such as how well the results match expert judgment, are used to assess and compare the results from an unsupervised learning method.

5.1 Cluster Analysis

The goal of clustering is to organize observations into similar groups based on the observed variables. As part of the data preparation step of a larger data analysis project, clustering can be employed to identify variables or observations that can be aggregated or removed from consideration. Cluster analysis is commonly used in marketing to divide consumers into different homogeneous groups, a process known as **market segmentation**. Identifying different clusters of consumers allows a firm to tailor marketing strategies for each segment. Cluster analysis can also be used to identify outliers, which in a manufacturing setting may represent quality-control problems and in financial transactions may represent fraudulent activity.

In this section, we consider the use of cluster analysis to assist a company called Know Thy Customer (KTC), a financial advising company that provides personalized financial advice to its clients. As a basis for developing this tailored advising, KTC would like to segment its customers into several groups (or clusters) so that the customers within a group are similar with respect to key characteristics and are dissimilar to customers that are not in the group. For each customer, KTC has an observation consisting of the following variables:

DemoKTC

Age	= age of the customer in whole years
Female	= 1 if female, 0 if not
Income	= annual income in dollars
Married	= 1 if married, 0 if not
Children	= number of children
Loan	= 1 if customer has a car loan, 0 if not
Mortgage	= 1 if customer has a mortgage, 0 if not

We present two clustering methods using a small sample of data from KTC. First, we consider *k*-means clustering, a method which iteratively assigns each observation to one of *k* clusters in an attempt to achieve clusters that contain observations as similar to each other as possible. Second, we consider agglomerative **hierarchical clustering** which starts with each observation belonging to its own cluster and then sequentially merges the most similar clusters to create a series of nested clusters. Because both methods rely upon measuring the dissimilarity between observations, we first discuss how to calculate distance between observations.

Measuring Distance Between Observations

The goal of cluster analysis is to group observations into clusters such that observations within a cluster are similar and observations in different clusters are dissimilar. Therefore, to formalize this process, we need explicit measurements of dissimilarity or, conversely, similarity. Some metrics track similarity between observations, and a clustering method using such a metric would seek to maximize the similarity between observations. Other metrics measure dissimilarity, or distance, between observations, and a clustering method using one of these metrics would seek to minimize the distance between observations in a cluster.

When observations include numerical variables, **Euclidean distance** is a common method to measure dissimilarity between observations. Let observations $u = (u_1, u_2, \ldots, u_q)$ and $v = (v_1, v_2, \ldots, v_q)$ each comprise measurements of q variables. The Euclidean distance between observations u and v is

$$d_{uv}^{\text{euclid}} = \sqrt{(u_1 - v_1)^2 + (u_2 - v_2)^2 + \cdots + (u_q - v_q)^2}$$

Figure 5.1 depicts Euclidean distance for two observations consisting of two variables ($q = 2$). Euclidean distance becomes smaller as a pair of observations become more similar with respect to their variable values. Euclidean distance is highly influenced by the scale on which variables are measured. For example, consider the task of clustering customers on the basis of the variables Age and Income. Let observation $u = (23, \$20,375)$ correspond to a 23-year-old customer with an annual income of \$20,375 and observation

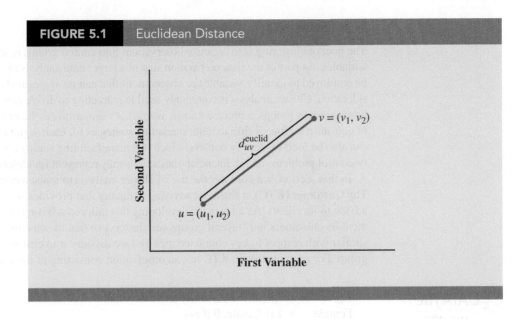

| **FIGURE 5.1** | Euclidean Distance |

$v = (48, \$19{,}475)$ correspond to a 48-year-old with an annual income of \$19,475. As measured by Euclidean distance, the dissimilarity between these two observations is

$$d_{uv}^{\text{euclid}} = \sqrt{(23 - 48)^2 + (20{,}375 - 19{,}475)^2} = \sqrt{625 + 810{,}000} = 900$$

Refer to Chapter 2 for a discussion of z-scores.

Thus, we see that when using the raw variable values, the amount of dissimilarity between observations is dominated by the Income variable because of the difference in the magnitude of the measurements. Therefore, it is common to standardize the units of each variable j of each observation u. One common standardization technique is to replace the variable values of each observation with the respective z-scores. For example, u_j, the value of the jth variable in observation u, is replaced with:

$$z(u_j) = \frac{u_j - \text{average value of } j\text{th variable}}{\text{standard deviation of } j\text{th variable}}$$

Suppose that the variable has a sample mean of 46 and a sample standard deviation of 13. Also, suppose that the Income variable has a sample mean of 28,012 and sample standard deviation of 13,703. Then, the standardized (or normalized) values of observations u and v are $(-1.77, -0.56)$ and $(0.15, -0.62)$, respectively. The Euclidean distance between these two observations based on standardized values is

$$(\text{standardized}) \; d_{uv}^{\text{euclid}} = \sqrt{(-1.77 - 0.15)^2 + (-0.56 - (-0.62))^2}$$
$$= \sqrt{3.6864 + 0.0036} = 1.92$$

Based on standardized variable values, we observe that observations u and v are actually much more different in age than in income. The conversion of the data to z-scores also makes it easier to identify outlier measurements, which can distort the Euclidean distance between observations due to the squaring of the differences in variable values under the square root. Depending on the business goal of the clustering task and the cause of the outlier value, the identification of an outlier may suggest the removal of the corresponding observation, the correction of the outlier value, or the uncovering of an interesting insight corresponding to the outlier observation.

Manhattan distance is a dissimilarity measure that is more robust to outliers than Euclidean distance. The Manhattan distance between observations u and v is

$$d_{uv}^{\text{man}} = |u_1 - v_1| + |u_2 - v_2| + \cdots + |u_q - v_q|$$

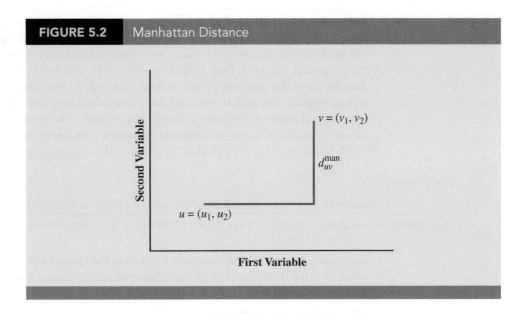

FIGURE 5.2 Manhattan Distance

Figure 5.2 depicts the Manhattan distance for two observations consisting of two variables ($q = 2$). From Figure 5.2, we observe that the Manhattan distance between two observations is the sum of the lengths of the perpendicular line segments connecting observations u and v. In contrast to Euclidean distance, which corresponds to the straight-line "as the crow flies" segment between two observations, Manhattan distance corresponds to the distance as if travelled along rectangular city blocks.

The Manhattan distance between the standardized observations $u = (-1.77, -0.56)$ and $v = (0.15, -0.62)$ is

$$d_{uv}^{man} = |-1.77 - 0.15| + |-0.56 - (-0.62)| = 1.92 + 0.06 = 1.98$$

After conversion to z-scores, unequal weighting of variables can also be considered by multiplying the variables of each observation by a selected set of weights. For instance, after standardizing the units on customer observations so that income and age are expressed as their respective z-scores (instead of expressed in dollars and years), we can multiply the income z-scores by 2 if we wish to treat income with twice the importance of age. In other words, standardizing removes bias due to the difference in measurement units, and variable weighting allows the analyst to introduce any desired bias based on the business context.

When clustering observations solely on the basis of categorical variables encoded as 0–1 (or dummy variables), a better measure of similarity between two observations can be achieved by counting the number of variables with matching values. The simplest overlap measure is called the **matching coefficient** and is computed as follows:

MATCHING COEFFICIENT

$$\frac{\text{number of variables with matching values for observations } u \text{ and } v}{\text{total number of variables}}$$

Subtracting the matching coefficient from 1 results in a distance measure for binary variables. The **matching distance** between observations u and v (consisting entirely of binary variables) is

$$d_{uv}^{match} = 1 - \text{matching coefficient}$$

$$= \frac{\text{total number of variables}}{\text{total number of variables}} - \frac{\text{number of variables with matching values}}{\text{total number of variables}}$$

$$= \frac{\text{number of variables with mismatching values}}{\text{total number of variables}}$$

One weakness of the matching coefficient is that if two observations both have a "0" value for a categorical variable, this is counted as a sign of similarity between the two observations. However, matching "0" values do not necessarily imply similarity. For instance, if the categorical variable is Own A Minivan, then a "0" value in two different observations does not mean that these two people own the same type of car; it means only that neither owns a minivan. The analyst must then determine if "not owning a minivan" constitutes a meaningful notion of similarity between observations in the business context. To avoid misstating similarity due to the absence of a feature, a similarity measure called **Jaccard's coefficient** does not count matching "0" values and is computed as follows:

JACCARD'S COEFFICIENT

$$\frac{\text{number of variables with matching "1" values for observations } u \text{ and } v}{(\text{total number of variables}) - (\text{number of variables with matching "0" values for observations } u \text{ and } v)}$$

Subtracting Jaccard's coefficient from 1 results in the Jaccard distance measure for binary variables. That is, the **Jaccard distance** between observations u and v (consisting entirely of binary variables) is

$$d_{uv}^{jac} = 1 - \text{Jaccard's coefficient}$$

$$= 1 - \frac{\text{number of variables with matching "1"}}{(\text{total number of variables}) - (\text{number of variables with matching "0"})}$$

$$= \frac{(\text{total number of variables}) - (\text{number of variables with matching "0"})}{(\text{total number of variables}) - (\text{number of variables with matching "0"})}$$

$$- \frac{\text{number of variables with matching "1"}}{(\text{total number of variables}) - (\text{number of variables with matching "0"})}$$

$$= \frac{\text{number of variables with mismatching values}}{\text{total number of variables} - \text{number of variables with matching "0"}}$$

For five customer observations from the file *DemoKTC*, Table 5.1 contains observations of the binary variables Female, Married, Loan, and Mortgage and the dissimilarity matrixes based on the matching distance and Jaccard's distance, respectively. Based on the matching distance, Observation 1 and Observation 4 are more similar (0.25) than Observation 2 and Observation 3 (0.5) because 3 out of 4 variable values match between Observation 1 and Observation 4 versus just 2 matching values out of 4 for Observation 2 and Observation 3. However, based on Jaccard's distance, Observation 1 and Observation 4 are equally similar (0.5) as Observation 2 and Observation 3 (0.5) as Jaccard's coefficient discards the matching zero values for the Loan and Mortgage variables for Observation 1 and Observation 4. In the context of this example, choice of the matching distance or Jaccard's distance depends on whether KTC believes that matching 0 entries imply similarity or not. That is, KTC must gauge whether meaningful similarity is implied if a pair of observations are not female, not married, do not have a car loan, or do not have a mortgage.

k-Means Clustering

When considering observations consisting entirely of numerical observations, an approach called *k*-means clustering is commonly used to organize observations into similar groups. In *k*-means clustering, the analyst must specify the number of clusters, *k*. Given a value of *k*, the *k*-means algorithm begins by randomly assigning each observation to one of the *k* clusters. After all observations have been assigned to a cluster, the resulting cluster centroids are calculated (these cluster centroids are the "means" of *k*-means clustering). Using the updated cluster centroids, all observations are reassigned to the cluster with the closest

TABLE 5.1	Comparison of Distance Matrixes for Observations with Binary Variables			
Observation	Female	Married	Loan	Mortgage
1	1	0	0	0
2	0	1	1	1
3	1	1	1	0
4	1	1	0	0
5	1	1	0	0
Matrix of Matching Distances					
Observation	1	2	3	4	5
1	0				
2	1	0			
3	0.5	0.5	0		
4	0.25	0.75	0.25	0	
5	0.25	0.75	0.25	0	0
Matrix of Jaccard Distances					
Observation	1	2	3	4	5
1	0				
2	1	0			
3	0.667	0.5	0		
4	0.5	0.75	0.333	0	
5	0.5	0.75	0.333	0	0

DATAfile

DemoKTC

centroid (where Euclidean distance is the standard metric). The algorithm repeats this process (calculate cluster centroid, assign each observation to the cluster with nearest centroid) until there is no change in the clusters or a specified maximum number of iterations is reached.

As an unsupervised learning technique, cluster analysis is not guided by any explicit measure of accuracy, and thus the notion of a "good" clustering is subjective and is dependent on what the analyst hopes the cluster analysis will uncover. Regardless, one can measure the strength of a cluster by comparing the average distance between observations within the same cluster to the average distance between observations in different pairs of clusters. One rule of thumb is that the ratio of average between-cluster distance to average within-cluster distance should exceed 1.0 for useful clusters. If there is a wide disparity in the cluster strength across a collection of k clusters, it may be possible to find a better clustering of the data by removing all the observations of the strong clusters, and then continuing the clustering process on the remaining observations.

To illustrate k-means clustering, we consider a 3-means clustering of a small sample of KTC's customer data in the file *DemoKTC*. Figure 5.3 shows three clusters based on customer income and age. Cluster 1 is characterized by relatively younger, lower-income customers (Cluster 1's centroid is at [32.58, $20,364]). Cluster 2 is characterized by relatively older, higher-income customers (Cluster 2's centroid is at [57.88, $47,729]). Cluster 3 is characterized by relatively older, lower-income customers (Cluster 3's centroid is at [52.50, $21,416]). As visually corroborated by Figure 5.3, Table 5.2 shows that Cluster 2 is the smallest, but most heterogeneous cluster. We also observe that Cluster 1 is the largest cluster and Cluster 3 is the most homogeneous cluster. Table 5.3 displays the average distance between observations in different pairs of clusters to demonstrate how distinct the clusters are from each other. Cluster 1 and Cluster 2 are the most distinct from each other. To evaluate the strength of the clusters, we compare the average distance within

FIGURE 5.3	Clustering Observations by Age and Income Using *k*-Means Clustering with $k = 3$

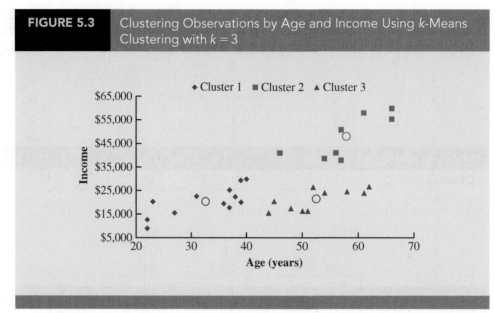

TABLE 5.2	Average Distances Within Clusters	
	No. of Observations	Average Distance Between Observations in Cluster
Cluster 1	12	0.886
Cluster 2	8	1.051
Cluster 3	10	0.731

TABLE 5.3	Average Distances Between Clusters		
	Cluster 1	Cluster 2	Cluster 3
Cluster 1	0	2.812	1.629
Cluster 2	2.812	0	2.054
Cluster 3	1.629	2.054	0

each cluster (Table 5.2) to the average distances between clusters (Table 5.3). For example, although Cluster 2 is the most heterogeneous, with an average distance between observations of 1.051, comparing this to the average distance between Cluster 2 observations and Cluster 3 observations (2.054) reveals that on average an observation in Cluster 2 is approximately 1.95 times closer to Cluster 2 observations than Cluster 3 observations. In general, a clustering becomes more distinct as the ratio of the average between-distance to the average within-distance increases. Although qualitative considerations should take priority in evaluating clusters, using the ratios of the average between-cluster distance and the average within-cluster distance provides some guidance in evaluating a set of clusters.

If the number of clusters, *k*, is not clearly established by the context of the business problem, the *k*-means clustering algorithm can be repeated for several values of *k* to identify promising values. A common approach to quickly compare the effect of *k* is to consider its impact on the total sum of squared deviations from the observations to their assigned cluster centroid. In Figure 5.4, we visualize the effect of varying the number of clusters (*k* = 1, . . ., 6). In this figure, the blue curve connects the total sums of squared deviations for the

| FIGURE 5.4 | Total Sum of Squared Deviations for Various Number of Clusters |

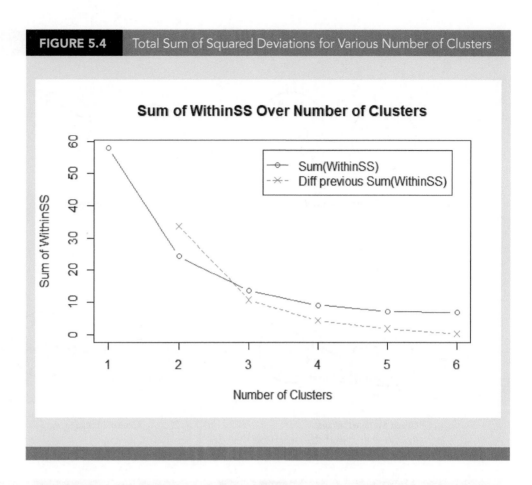

various values of k. The red curve depicts the decrease in the total sum of squared deviations that occurs when increasing the number of clusters from $k-1$ to k.

We observe from Figure 5.4 that as the number of clusters increases, the total sum of squared deviations decreases. Indeed, if we allow the number of clusters be equal to the number of observations this sum of squared deviations is zero. Of course, placing each observation in its own cluster provides no insight into the similarity between observations, so minimizing the total sum of squared deviations is not the goal. Figure 5.4 shows there is a large decrease in the total sum of squared deviation when k increases from 1 to 2, but the marginal decrease in the total sum of squared deviations decreases for further increases in k. From this plot, we see that the most promising values of k are 2, 3, or 4. The sets of clusters for these values of k should be examined more closely. In particular, an "elbow" occurs at $k = 3$, as this is the point beyond which the marginal decrease in the total sum of squared deviations flattens, suggesting this may be a good choice.

Hierarchical Clustering and Measuring Dissimilarity Between Clusters

An alternative to partitioning observations with the k-means approach is an agglomerative hierarchical clustering approach that starts with each observation in its own cluster and then iteratively combines the two clusters that are the least dissimilar (most similar) into a single cluster. Each iteration corresponds to an increased level of aggregation by decreasing the number of distinct clusters. Hierarchical clustering determines the dissimilarity of two clusters by considering the distance between the observations in first cluster and the observations in the second cluster. Given a way to measure distance between observations (e.g., Euclidean distance, Manhattan distance, matching distance, Jaccard distance), there are several agglomeration methods for comparing observations in two clusters to obtain a cluster dissimilarity measure. Using Euclidean distance to illustrate, Figure 5.5 provides a two-dimensional depiction of four agglomeration methods we will discuss.

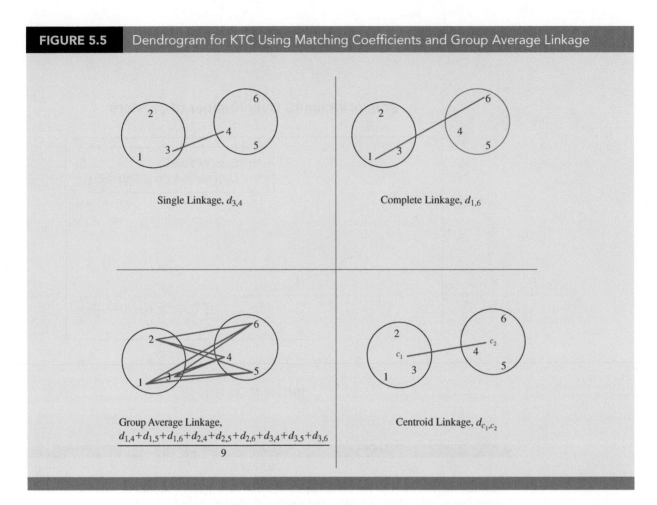

Single Linkage, $d_{3,4}$

Complete Linkage, $d_{1,6}$

Group Average Linkage,
$$\frac{d_{1,4}+d_{1,5}+d_{1,6}+d_{2,4}+d_{2,5}+d_{2,6}+d_{3,4}+d_{3,5}+d_{3,6}}{9}$$

Centroid Linkage, d_{c_1,c_2}

When using the **single linkage** agglomeration method, the dissimilarity between two clusters is defined by the distance between the pair of observations (one from each cluster) that are the most similar. Thus, single linkage will consider two clusters to be close if an observation in one of the clusters is close to at least one observation in the other cluster. However, a cluster formed by merging two clusters that are close with respect to single linkage may also consist of pairs of observations that are very different. The reason is that there is no consideration of how different an observation may be from other observations in a cluster as long as it is similar to at least one observation in that cluster. Thus, in two dimensions (variables), single linkage clustering can result in long, elongated clusters rather than compact, circular clusters.

The **complete linkage** agglomeration method defines the dissimilarity between two clusters as the distance between the pair of observations (one from each cluster) that are the most different. Thus, complete linkage will consider two clusters to be close if their most-different pair of observations are close. This method produces clusters such that all member observations of a cluster are relatively close to each other. The clusters produced by complete linkage have approximately equal diameters. However, complete linkage clustering can be distorted by outlier observations.

The single linkage and complete linkage methods define between-cluster dissimilarity based on the single pair of observations in two different clusters that are most similar or least similar. In contrast, the **group average linkage** agglomeration method defines the dissimilarity between two clusters to be the average distance computed over *all* pairs of observations between the two clusters. If Cluster 1 consists of n_1 observations and Cluster 2 consists of n_2 observations, the dissimilarity of these clusters would be the average of $n_1 \times n_2$ distances. This method produces clusters that are less dominated by the dissimilarity between single pairs of observations. The **median linkage** method is analogous to group average linkage except that it uses the median distance (not the average) computed over all pairs of observations between the two clusters. The use of the median reduces the effect of outliers.

Centroid linkage uses the averaging concept of cluster centroids to define between-cluster dissimilarity. The centroid for cluster k, denoted as c_k, is found by calculating the average value for each variable across all observations in a cluster; that is, a centroid is the average observation of a cluster. The dissimilarity between cluster k and cluster j is then defined as the distance between the centroids c_k and c_j.

Ward's method for merging clusters is based on the notion that representing a cluster with its centroid can be viewed as a loss of information in the sense that the individual differences in the observations within the cluster are not be captured by the cluster centroid. For a pair of clusters under consideration for aggregation, Ward's method computes the centroid of the resulting merged cluster and then calculates the sum of squared distances between this centroid and each observation in the union of the two clusters. At each iteration, Ward's method merges the pair of clusters with the smallest value of this dissimilarity measure. As a result, hierarchical clustering using Ward's method results in a sequence of aggregated clusters that minimizes this loss of information between the individual observation level and the cluster centroid level.

Similar to group average linkage, **McQuitty's method** for merging clusters also defines the dissimilarity between two clusters on averaging, but computes the average in a different manner. To illustrate, suppose at an iteration cluster A and cluster B are the most similar over the entire set of clusters and therefore merged into cluster AB. For the next iteration, the dissimilarity between cluster AB and any other cluster C is updated as ((dissimilarity between A and C) + (dissimilarity between B and C)) ÷ 2. This is different than group average linkage because this calculation is a simple average of two dissimilarity measures rather than calculating the average dissimilarity over all pairs of observations between cluster AB and cluster C. By always computing the average dissimilarity between two clusters as a simple average of the two component dissimilarity measures, McQuitty's method is implicitly placing different weights on the distances between the individual observations whereas in group average linkage the distance between each pair of observations between two clusters is weighted equally.

DATA *file*

DemoKTC

Returning to our example, KTC is interested in developing customer segments based on gender, marital status, whether the customer is repaying a car loan, and whether the customer is repaying a mortgage. Using data in the file *DemoKTC*, we base the clusters on a collection of 0–1 categorical variables (Female, Married, Loan, and Mortgage). We use the matching distance to measure dissimilarity between observations and the group average linkage agglomeration method to measure similarity between clusters. The choice of the matching distance (over Jaccard's distance) is reasonable because a pair of customers that both have an entry of zero for any of these four variables implies some degree of similarity. For example, two customers that both have zero entries for Mortgage means that neither has the significant debt associated with a mortgage.

Figure 5.6 depicts a **dendrogram** to visually summarize the output from a hierarchical clustering using matching distance to measure dissimilarity between observations and the group average linkage agglomeration method to measure dissimilarity between clusters. A dendrogram is a chart that depicts the set of nested clusters resulting at each step of aggregation. The horizontal axis of the dendrogram lists the observation indexes. The vertical axis of the dendrogram represents the dissimilarity (distance) resulting from a merger of two different groups of observations. Each blue horizontal line in the dendrogram represents a merger of two (or more) clusters, where the observations composing the merged clusters are connected to the blue horizontal line with a blue vertical line.

For example, the blue horizontal line connecting observations 4, 5, 6, 11, 19, and 28 conveys that these six observations are grouped together and the resulting cluster has a dissimilarity measure of 0. A dissimilarity of 0 results from this merger because these six observations have identical values for the Female, Married, Loan, and Mortgage variables. In this case, each of these six observations corresponds to a married female with no car loan and no mortgage. Following the blue vertical line up from the cluster of {4, 5, 6, 11, 19, 28}, another blue horizontal line connects this cluster with the cluster consisting solely of observation 1. Thus, the cluster {4, 5, 6, 11, 19, 28} and cluster {1} are merged resulting in a dissimilarity of 0.25. The dissimilarity of 0.25 results from this merger because

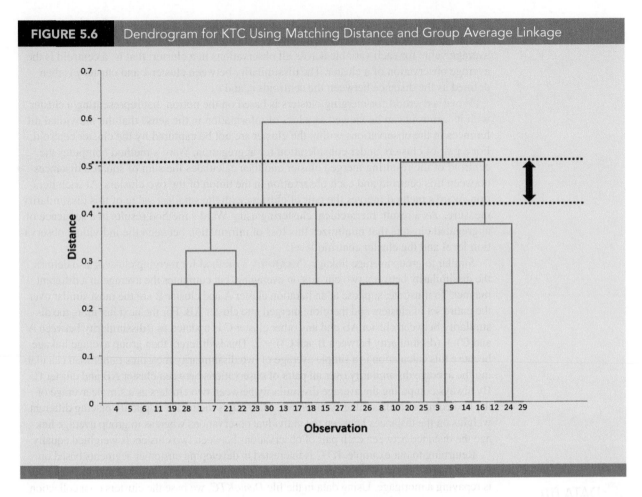

FIGURE 5.6 Dendrogram for KTC Using Matching Distance and Group Average Linkage

observation 1 differs in one out of the four categorical variable values; observation 1 is an *unmarried* female with no car loan and no mortgage.

To interpret a dendrogram at a specific level of aggregation, it is helpful to visualize a horizontal line such as one of the black dashed lines we have drawn across Figure 5.6. The bottom horizontal black dashed line intersects with the vertical branches in the dendrogram three times; each intersection corresponds to a cluster containing the observations connected by the vertical branch that is intersected. The composition of these three clusters is

Cluster 1: {4, 5, 6, 11, 19, 28, 1, 7, 21, 22, 23, 30, 13, 17, 18, 15, 27}
   = 10 out of 17 female, 15 out of 17 married, no car loans, 5 out of 17 with mortgages

Cluster 2: {2, 26, 8, 10, 20, 25}
   = all males with car loans, 5 out of 6 married, 2 out of 6 with mortgages

Cluster 3: {3, 9, 14, 16, 12, 24, 29}
   = all females with car loans, 4 out of 7 married, 5 out of 7 with mortgages

These clusters segment KTC's customers into three groups that could possibly indicate varying levels of responsibility—an important factor to consider when providing financial advice.

The nested construction of the hierarchical clusters allows KTC to identify different numbers of clusters and assess (often qualitatively) the implications. By sliding a horizontal line up or down the vertical axis of a dendrogram and observing the intersection of the horizontal line with the vertical dendrogram branches, an analyst can extract varying numbers of clusters. Note that sliding up to the position of the top horizontal black line in Figure 5.6 results in merging cluster 2 with cluster 3 into a single, more dissimilar, cluster. The vertical distance between the points of agglomeration is the "cost" of merging clusters in terms of decreased homogeneity within clusters. Thus, vertically elongated portions of the dendrogram represent mergers of more dissimilar clusters, and vertically compact portions of the dendrogram represent mergers of more similar clusters. A cluster's durability (or strength) can be measured by the difference between the distance value at which a cluster is originally formed and the distance value at which it is merged with another cluster. Figure 5.6 shows that the cluster consisting of {12, 24, 29} (single females with car loans and mortgages) is a very durable cluster in this example because the vertical line for this cluster is very long before it is merged with another cluster.

Hierarchical Clustering versus *k*-Means Clustering

Hierarchical clustering is a good choice in situations in which you want to easily examine solutions with a wide range of clusters. Hierarchical clusters are also convenient if you want to observe how clusters are nested. However, hierarchical clustering can be very sensitive to outliers, and clusters may change dramatically if observations are eliminated from (or added to) the data set. Hierarchical clustering may be less appropriate option as the number of the observations in the data set grows large as the procedure is relatively computationally expensive (starting with each observation in its own cluster).

The *k*-means approach is a good option for clustering data on the basis of numerical variables, and is computationally efficient enough to handle an increasingly large number of observations. Recall that *k*-means clustering partitions the observations, which is appropriate if you are trying to summarize the data with *k* "average" observations that describe the data with the minimum amount of error. However, *k*-means clustering is generally not appropriate for categorical or ordinal data, for which an "average" is not meaningful.

For both hierarchical and *k*-means clustering, the selection of variables on which to base the clustering process is a critical aspect. Clustering should be based on a parsimonious set of variables, determined through a combination of context knowledge and experimentation with various variable combinations, that reveal interesting patterns in the data. As the number of variables upon which distance between observations is computed increases, all observations tend to become equidistant. That is, as the number of variables considered in a clustering approach increases, the distances between pairs of observations get larger (distance can only increase when adding variables to the calculation), but the relative differences in the distances between pairs of observations tend to get smaller.

NOTES + COMMENTS

1. Clustering observations based on both numerical and categorical variables (mixed data) can be challenging. Dissimilarity between observations with numerical variables is commonly computed using Euclidean distance. However, Euclidean distance is not well defined for categorical variables as the magnitude of the Euclidean distance measure between two category values will depend on the numerical encoding of the categories. There are elaborate methods beyond the scope of this book to try to address the challenge of clustering mixed data.

   Using the methods introduced in this section, there are two alternative approaches to clustering mixed data. The first approach is to decompose the clustering into two steps. The first step applies hierarchical clustering of the observations only on categorical variables using an appropriate measure (matching distance or Jaccard's distance) to identify a set of "first-step" clusters. The second step is to apply *k*-means clustering (or hierarchical clustering again) separately to each of these "first-step" clusters using only the numerical variables. This decomposition approach is not fail-safe as it fixes clusters with respect to one variable type before clustering with respect to the other variable type, but it does allow the analyst to identify how the observations are similar or different with respect to the two variable types.

   A second approach to clustering mixed data is to numerically encode the categorical values (e.g., binary coding, ordinal coding) and then to standardize both the categorical and numerical variable values. To reflect relative importance of the variables, the analyst may experiment with various weightings of the variables and apply hierarchical or *k*-means clustering. This approach is very experimental and the variable weights are subjective.

2. When dealing with mixed data, instead of standardizing the variable values by replacing them with the corresponding z-scores, it a common to scale the numerical variable values between 0 and 1 so that they have values on same scale as the binary-encoded categorical variables. To achieve this, u_j, the value of the *j*th variable in observation *u*, is replaced with:

$$b(u_j) = \frac{(u_j - \text{minimum value of } j\text{th variable})}{(\text{maximum value of } j\text{th variable} - \text{minimum value of } j\text{th variable})}$$

5.2 Association Rules

In marketing, analyzing consumer behavior can lead to insights regarding the placement and promotion of products. Specifically, marketers are interested in examining transaction data on customer purchases to identify the products commonly purchased together. Bar-code scanners facilitate the collection of retail transaction data, and membership in a customer's loyalty program can further associate the transaction with a specific customer. In this section, we discuss the development of probabilistic if–then statements, called **association rules**, which convey the likelihood of certain items being purchased together. Although association rules are an important tool in **market basket analysis**, they are also applicable to disciplines other than marketing. For example, association rules can assist medical researchers in understanding which treatments have been commonly prescribed to certain patient symptoms (and the resulting effects).

Hy-Vee grocery store would like to gain insight into its customers' purchase patterns to possibly improve its in-aisle product placement and cross-product promotions. Table 5.4 contains a small sample of data in which each transaction comprises the items purchased by a shopper in a single visit to a Hy-Vee. An example of an association rule from this data would be "if {bread, jelly}, then {peanut butter}," meaning that "if a transaction includes bread and jelly, then it also includes peanut butter." The collection of items (or item set) corresponding to the *if* portion of the rule, {bread, jelly}, is called the **antecedent**. The item set corresponding to the *then* portion of the rule, {peanut butter}, is called the **consequent**.

Typically, only association rules for which the consequent consists of a single item are considered because these are more actionable. Although the number of possible association rules can be overwhelming, we typically investigate only association rules that involve antecedent and consequent item sets that occur together frequently. To formalize the notion of "frequent," we define the **support** of an item set as the percentage of transactions in the data that include that item set. In Table 5.4, the support of {bread, jelly} is 4/10 = 0.4. For a transaction randomly selected from the data set displayed in Table 5.4, the probability of it containing the item set {bread, jelly} is 0.4. The potential impact of an association rule is often governed by the number of transactions it may affect, which is measured by computing the support of the item set consisting of the union of its antecedent and consequent. Investigating the rule "if {bread, jelly}, then {peanut butter}" from Table 5.4, we see the support of {bread, jelly, peanut butter} is 0.2. For a transaction randomly selected from the data set displayed in Table 5.4, the probability of it containing the item set {bread, jelly, peanut butter} is 0.2. By only considering rules involving item sets with a support above a minimum level, inexplicable rules capturing random noise in the data can generally be avoided. A rule of thumb is to

Support is also sometimes expressed as the number (or count) of total transactions in the data containing an item set.

The data in Table 5.4 are in item list format; that is, each transaction row corresponds to a list of item names. Alternatively, the data can be represented in binary matrix format, in which each row is a transaction record and the columns correspond to each distinct item. A third approach is to store the data in stacked form in which each row is an ordered pair; the first entry is the transaction number and the second entry is the item.

TABLE 5.4	Shopping-Cart Transactions
Transaction	**Shopping Cart**
1	bread, peanut butter, milk, fruit, jelly
2	bread, jelly, soda, potato chips, milk, fruit, vegetables, peanut butter
3	whipped cream, fruit, chocolate sauce, beer
4	steak, jelly, soda, potato chips, bread, fruit
5	jelly, soda, peanut butter, milk, fruit
6	jelly, soda, potato chips, milk, bread, fruit
7	fruit, soda, potato chips, milk
8	fruit, soda, peanut butter, milk
9	fruit, cheese, yogurt
10	yogurt, vegetables, beer

consider only association rules with a support of at least 20% of the total number of transactions. If an item set is particularly valuable and represents a lucrative opportunity, then the minimum support used to filter the rules can be lowered.

A property of a reliable association rule is that, given a transaction contains the antecedent item set, there is a high probability that it contains the consequent item set. This conditional probability of P(consequent item set | antecedent item set) is called the **confidence** of a rule, and is computed as

The definition of confidence follows from the definition of conditional probability discussed in Chapter 4.

CONFIDENCE

$$P(\text{consequent} \mid \text{antecedent}) = \frac{P(\text{consequent and antecedent})}{P(\text{antecedent})}$$

$$= \frac{\text{support of}\{\text{consequent and antecedent}\}}{\text{support of antecedent}}$$

Although high value of confidence suggests a rule in which the consequent is frequently true when the antecedent is true, a high value of confidence can be misleading. For example, if the support of the consequent is high—that is, the item set corresponding to the *then* part is very frequent—then the confidence of the association rule could be high even if there is little or no association between the items. In Table 5.4, the rule "if {cheese}, then {fruit}" has a confidence of 1.0 (or 100%). This is misleading because {fruit} is a frequent item; *almost any* rule with {fruit} as the consequent will have high confidence. Therefore, to evaluate the efficiency of a rule, we need to compare the P(consequent | antecedent) to the P(consequent) to determine how much more likely the consequent item set is given the antecedent item set versus just the overall (unconditional) likelihood that a transaction contains the consequent. The ratio of the P(consequent | antecedent) to P(consequent) is called the **lift ratio** of the rule and is computed as:

LIFT RATIO

$$\frac{P(\text{consequent} \mid \text{antecedent})}{P(\text{consequent})} = \frac{P(\text{consequent and antecedent})}{P(\text{consequent}) \times P(\text{antecedent})}$$

$$= \frac{\text{confidence of rule}}{\text{support of consequent}}$$

Thus, the lift ratio represents how effective an association rule is at identifying transactions in which the consequent item set occurs versus a randomly selected transaction. A lift ratio greater than one suggests that there is some usefulness to the rule and that it is better at identifying cases when the consequent occurs than having no rule at all. From the definition of lift ratio, we see that the denominator contains the probability of a transaction containing the consequent set multiplied by the probability of a transaction containing the antecedent set. This product of probabilities is equivalent to the expected likelihood of a transaction containing both the consequent item set and antecedent item set if these item sets were independent. In other words, a lift ratio greater than one suggests that the level of association between the antecedent and consequent is higher than would be expected if these item sets were independent.

For the data in Table 5.4, the rule "if {bread, jelly}, then {peanut butter}" has confidence = 2/4 = 0.5 and lift ratio = 0.5/0.4 = 1.25. In other words, a customer who purchased both bread and jelly is 25% more likely to have purchased peanut butter than a randomly selected customer.

The utility of a rule depends on both its support and its lift ratio. Although a high lift ratio suggests that the rule is very efficient at finding when the consequent occurs,

TABLE 5.5	Association Rules for Hy-Vee					
Antecedent (A)	Consequent (C)	Support for A	Support for C	Support for A & C	Confidence	Lift Ratio
Bread	Fruit, Jelly	0.40	0.50	0.40	1.00	2.00
Bread	Jelly	0.40	0.50	0.40	1.00	2.00
Bread, Fruit	Jelly	0.40	0.50	0.40	1.00	2.00
Fruit, Jelly	Bread	0.50	0.40	0.40	0.80	2.00
Jelly	Bread	0.50	0.40	0.40	0.80	2.00
Jelly	Bread, Fruit	0.50	0.40	0.40	0.80	2.00
Fruit, Potato Chips	Soda	0.40	0.60	0.40	1.00	1.67
Peanut Butter	Milk	0.40	0.40	0.60	1.00	1.67
Peanut Butter	Milk, Fruit	0.40	0.60	0.40	1.00	1.67
Peanut Butter, Fruit	Milk	0.40	0.60	0.40	1.00	1.67
Potato Chips	Fruit, Soda	0.40	0.60	0.40	1.00	1.67
Potato Chips	Soda	0.40	0.60	0.40	1.00	1.67
Fruit, Soda	Potato Chips	0.60	0.40	0.40	0.67	1.67
Milk	Peanut Butter	0.60	0.40	0.40	0.67	1.67
Milk	Peanut Butter, Fruit	0.60	0.40	0.40	0.67	1.67
Milk, Fruit	Peanut Butter	0.60	0.40	0.40	0.67	1.67
Soda	Fruit, Potato Chips	0.60	0.40	0.40	0.67	1.67
Soda	Potato Chips	0.60	0.40	0.40	0.67	1.67
Fruit, Soda	Milk	0.60	0.60	0.50	0.83	1.39
Milk	Fruit, Soda	0.60	0.60	0.50	0.83	1.39
Milk	Soda	0.60	0.60	0.50	0.83	1.39
Milk, Fruit	Soda	0.60	0.60	0.50	0.83	1.39
Soda	Milk	0.60	0.60	0.50	0.83	1.39
Soda	Milk, Fruit	0.60	0.60	0.50	0.83	1.39

if it has a very low support, the rule may not be as useful as another rule that has a lower lift ratio but affects a large number of transactions (as demonstrated by a high support). However, an association rule with a high lift ratio and low support may still be useful if the consequent represents a very valuable opportunity.

Based on the data in Table 5.4, Table 5.5 shows the list of association rules that achieve a lift ratio of at least 1.39 while satisfying a minimum support of 40% and a minimum confidence of 50%. The top rules in Table 5.5 suggest that bread, fruit, and jelly are commonly associated items. For example, the fourth rule listed in Table 5.5 states, "If Fruit and Jelly are purchased, then Bread is also purchased." Perhaps Hy-Vee could consider a promotion and/or product placement to leverage this perceived relationship.

DATA_file_

HyVeeDemoBinary
HyVeeDemoStacked

Evaluating Association Rules

Although explicit measures such as support, confidence, and lift ratio can help filter association rules, an association rule is ultimately judged on how actionable it is and how well it explains the relationship between item sets. For example, suppose Walmart mined its transactional data to uncover strong evidence of the association rule, "If a customer purchases a Barbie doll, then a customer also purchases a candy bar." Walmart could leverage this relationship in product placement decisions as well as in advertisements and promotions, perhaps by placing a high-margin candy-bar display near the Barbie dolls. However, we must be aware that association rule analysis often results in obvious relationships such as "If a customer purchases hamburger patties, then a customer also purchases hamburger buns," which may be true but provide no new insight. Association rules with a weak support measure often are inexplicable. For an association rule to be useful, it must be well supported *and* explain an important previously unknown relationship. The support of an association rule can generally be improved by basing it on less specific antecedent and consequent item sets. Unfortunately, association rules based on less specific item sets tend to yield less insight. Adjusting the data by aggregating items into more general categories (or splitting items into more specific categories) so that items occur in roughly the same number of transactions often yields better association rules.

5.3 Text Mining

Every day, nearly 500 million tweets are published on the online social network service Twitter. Many of these tweets contain important clues about how Twitter users value a company's products and services. Some tweets might sing the praises of a product; others might complain about low-quality service. Furthermore, Twitter users vary greatly in the number of followers (some have thousands of followers and others just a few) and therefore these users have varying degrees of influence. Data-savvy companies can use social media data to improve their products and services. Online reviews on web sites such as Amazon and Yelp provide data on how customers feel about products and services.

However, the data in these examples are not numerical. The data are text: words, phrases, sentences, and paragraphs. Text, like numerical data, may contain information that can help solve problems and lead to better decisions. **Text mining** is the process of extracting useful information from text data. In this section, we discuss text mining, how it is different from data mining of numerical data, and how it can be useful for decision making.

Text data is often referred to as **unstructured data** because in its raw form, it cannot be stored in a traditional structured database (with observations in rows and variables in columns). Audio and video data are also examples of unstructured data. Data mining with text data is more challenging than data mining with traditional numerical data, because it requires more preprocessing to convert the text to a format amenable for analysis. However, once the text data has been converted to numerical data, we can apply the data mining methods discussed earlier in this chapter. We begin with a small example which illustrates how text data can be converted to numerical data and then analyzed. Then we will provide more in-depth discussion of text-mining concepts and preprocessing procedures.

Voice of the Customer at Triad Airline

Triad Airlines is a regional commuter airline. Through its voice of the customer program, Triad solicits feedback from its customers through a follow-up e-mail the day after the customer has completed a flight. The e-mail survey asks the customer to rate various aspects of the flight and asks the respondent to type comments into a dialog box in the e-mail.

In addition to the quantitative feedback from the ratings, the comments entered by the respondents need to be analyzed so that Triad can better understand its customers' specific concerns and respond in an appropriate manner. Table 5.6 contains a small training sample of these comments we will use to illustrate how descriptive text mining can be used in this business context. In the text mining domain, a contiguous piece of text is referred to as a **document**. A document can be a single sentence or an entire book, depending on how the text is organized for analysis. Each document is composed of individual **terms**, which often correspond to words. In general, a collection of text documents to be analyzed is called a **corpus**. In the Triad Airline example, our corpus consists of 10 documents, where each document is a single customer's comments.

Triad's management would like to categorize these customer comments into groups whose member comments share similar characteristics so that a focused solution team can be assigned to each group of comments.

Preprocessing text can be viewed as representation engineering. To be analyzed, text data needs to be converted to structured data (rows and columns of numerical data) so that the tools of descriptive statistics, data visualization, and data mining can be applied. Considering each document as an observation (row in a data set), we wish to represent the text in

TABLE 5.6	Ten Respondents' Comments for Triad Airlines

Comments

The wi-fi service was horrible. It was slow and cut off several times.

My seat was uncomfortable.

My flight was delayed 2 hours for no apparent reason.

My seat would not recline.

The man at the ticket counter was rude. Service was horrible.

The flight attendant was rude. Service was bad.

My flight was delayed with no explanation.

My drink spilled when the guy in front of me reclined his seat.

My flight was canceled.

The arm rest of my seat was nasty.

Triad

the document with variables (or columns in a data set). One common approach, called **bag of words**, treats every document as just a collection of individual words (or terms). Bag of words is a simple (but often effective) approach that ignores natural language processing aspects such as grammar, word order, and sentence structure. In bag of words, we can think of converting a group of documents into a matrix of rows and columns where the rows correspond to a document and the columns correspond to a particular word. In Triad's case, a document is a single respondent's comment. A **presence/absence or binary document-term matrix** is a matrix with the rows representing documents and the columns representing words, and the entries in the columns indicating either the presence or the absence of a particular word in a particular document (1 = present and 0 = not present).

Creating the list of terms to use in the presence/absence matrix can be a complicated matter. Too many terms results in a matrix with many columns, which may be difficult to manage and could yield meaningless results. Too few terms may miss important relationships. Often, term frequency along with the problem context are used as a guide. We discuss this in more detail in the next section. In Triad's case, management used word frequency and the context of having a goal of satisfied customers to come up with the following list of terms they feel are relevant for categorizing the respondent's comments: delayed, flight, horrible, recline, rude, seat, and service.

If the document-term matrix is transposed (so that the terms are in the rows and the documents are in the columns), the resulting matrix is referred to as a term-document matrix

As shown in Table 5.7, these seven terms correspond to the columns of the presence/absence document-term matrix and the rows correspond to the 10 documents. Each matrix entry indicates whether or not a column's term appears in the document corresponding to the row. For example, a 1 entry in the first row and third column means that the term "horrible" appears in document 1. A zero entry in the third row and fourth column means that the term "recline" does not appear in document 3.

Having converted the text to numerical data, we can apply clustering. In this case, because we have binary presence-absence data, we apply hierarchical clustering. Observing that the absence of a term in two different documents does not imply similarity between the documents, we select Jaccard's distance to measure dissimilarity between observations (documents). To measure dissimilarity between clusters, we use the complete linkage agglomeration method. At the level of three clusters, hierarchical clustering results in the following groups of documents:

Cluster 1:   {1, 5, 6}   = documents discussing service issues

Cluster 2:   {2, 4, 8, 10} = documents discussing seat issues

Cluster 3:   {3, 7, 9}   = documents discussing schedule issues

With these three clusters defined, management can assign an expert team to each of these clusters to directly address the concerns of its customers.

TABLE 5.7	The Presence/Absence Document-Term Matrix for Triad Airlines						
	Term						
Document	**Delayed**	**Flight**	**Horrible**	**Recline**	**Rude**	**Seat**	**Service**
1	0	0	1	0	0	0	1
2	0	0	0	0	0	1	0
3	1	1	0	0	0	0	0
4	0	0	0	1	0	1	0
5	0	0	1	0	1	0	1
6	0	1	0	0	1	0	1
7	1	1	0	0	0	0	0
8	0	0	0	1	0	1	0
9	0	1	0	0	0	0	0
10	0	0	0	0	0	1	0

Preprocessing Text Data for Analysis

In general, the text mining process converts unstructured text into numerical data and applies data mining techniques. For the Triad example, we converted the text documents into a document-term matrix and then applied hierarchical clustering to gain insight on the different types of comments. In this section, we present a more detailed discussion of terminology and methods used in preprocessing text data into numerical data for analysis.

Converting documents to a document-term matrix is not a simple task. Obviously, which terms become the headers of the columns of the document-term matrix can greatly impact the analysis. **Tokenization** is the process of dividing text into separate terms, referred to as tokens. The process of identifying tokens is not straightforward and involves **term normalization**, a set of natural language processing techniques to map text into a standardized form. First, symbols and punctuations must be removed from the document and all letters should be converted to lowercase. For example, "Awesome!", "awesome," and "#Awesome" should all be converted to "awesome." Likewise, different forms of the same word, such as "stacking," "stacked," and "stack" probably should not be considered as distinct terms. **Stemming**, the process of converting a word to its stem or root word, would drop the "ing" and "ed" suffixes and place only "stack" in the list of terms to be tracked.

The goal of preprocessing is to generate a list of most relevant terms that is sufficiently small so as to lend itself to analysis. In addition to stemming, frequency can be used to eliminate words from consideration as tokens. For example, if a term occurs very frequently in every document in the corpus, then it probably will not be very useful and can be eliminated from consideration. Text mining software contains procedures to automatically remove **stopwords**, very common words in English (or whatever language is being analyzed), such as "the," "and," and "of." Similarly, low-frequency words probably will not be very useful as tokens. Another technique for reducing the consideration set for tokens is to consolidate a set of words that are synonyms. For example, "courteous," "cordial," and "polite" might be best represented as a single token, "polite."

In addition to automated stemming and text reduction via frequency and synonyms, most text-mining software gives the user the ability to manually specify terms to include or exclude as tokens. Also, the use of slang, humor, irony, and sarcasm can cause interpretation problems and might require more sophisticated data cleansing and subjective intervention on the part of the analyst to avoid misinterpretation.

Data preprocessing parses the original text data down to the set of tokens deemed relevant for the topic being studied. Based on these tokens, a presence/absence document-term matrix such as in Table 5.7 can be generated.

When the documents in a corpus contain many more words than the brief comments in the Triad Airline example, and when the *frequency* of word occurrence is important to the context of the business problem, preprocessing can be used to develop a **frequency document-term matrix**. A frequency document-term matrix is a matrix whose rows represent documents and columns represent tokens, and the entries in the matrix are the frequency of occurrence of each token in each document. We illustrate this in the following example.

Movie Reviews

A new action film has been released and we now have a sample of 10 reviews from movie critics. Using preprocessing techniques, including text reduction by synonyms, we have reduced the number of tokens to only two: "great" and "terrible." Table 5.8 displays the corresponding frequency document-term matrix. As Table 5.8 shows, the token "great" appears four times in Document 7. Reviewing the entire table, we observe that five is the maximum frequency of a token in a document and zero is the minimum frequency.

To demonstrate the analysis of a frequency document-term matrix with descriptive data mining, we apply k-means clustering with $k = 2$ to the frequency document-term matrix to obtain the two clusters in Figure 5.7. Cluster 1 contains reviews that tend to be negative

TABLE 5.8	The Frequency Document-Term Matrix for Movie Reviews	
	Term	
Document	**Great**	**Terrible**
1	5	0
2	5	1
3	5	1
4	3	3
5	5	1
6	0	5
7	4	1
8	5	3
9	1	3
10	1	2

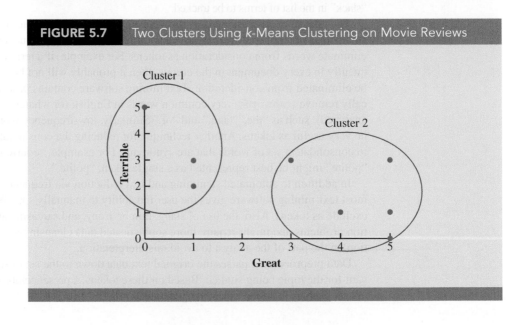

FIGURE 5.7   Two Clusters Using k-Means Clustering on Movie Reviews

and Cluster 2 contains reviews that tend to be positive. We note that the Observation (3, 3) corresponds to the balanced review of Document 4; based on this small corpus, the balanced review is more similar to the positive reviews than the negative reviews, suggesting that the negative reviews may tend to be more extreme.

Table 5.8 shows the raw counts (frequencies) of terms. When documents in a corpus substantially vary in length (number of terms), it is common to adjust for document length by dividing the raw term frequencies by the total number of terms in the document.

Term frequency (whether based on raw count or relative frequency to account for document length) is a text mining measure that pertains to an individual document. For a particular document, an analyst may also be interested how unique a term is relative to the other documents in the corpus. As previously mentioned, it is common to impose lower and upper limits on the term frequencies to filter out terms that are extremely rare or extremely common. In addition to those mechanisms, an analyst may be interested in weighting terms based on their distribution over the corpus. The logic is that the fewer the documents in which a term occurs, the more likely it is to be potentially insightful to the analysis of the documents it does occur in.

A popular measure for weighting terms based on frequency and uniqueness is **term frequency times inverse document frequency (TFIDF)**. The TFIDF of a term t in document d is computed as follows:

$$TFIDF(t, d) = \text{term frequency} \times \text{inverse document frequency}$$

$$= (\text{number of times term } t \text{ appears in document } d)$$

$$\times \left[1 + \log\left(\frac{\text{total number of documents in corpus}}{\text{number of documents containing term } t} \right) \right]$$

The inverse document frequency portion of the TFIDF calculation gives a boost to terms for being unique. Thus, using $TFIDF(t, d)$ more highly scores a term t that frequently appears in document d and does not appear frequently in other documents. Thus, basing a document-term matrix on TFIDF can make the unique terms (with respect to their frequency) more pronounced. For five different possible term frequencies of term t in a document d (represented by $TF(t,d)$), Figure 5.8 displays the

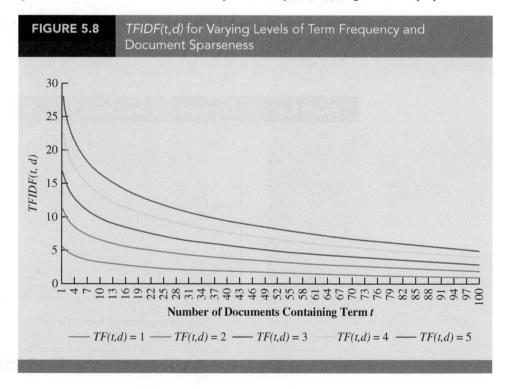

FIGURE 5.8 *TFIDF(t,d)* for Varying Levels of Term Frequency and Document Sparseness

TFIDF(t,d) value as the number of total documents containing the term *t* ranges from one document to 100 documents (in a corpus of 100 documents).

Computing Dissimilarity Between Documents

After preprocessing text and the conversion of a corpus into a frequency document-term matrix (based on raw frequency, relative frequency, or TFIDF), the notion of distance between observations discussed earlier in this chapter applies. In this case, the distance between observations corresponds to the dissimilarity between documents. To measure the dissimilarity between text documents, **cosine distance** is commonly used. Cosine distance is computed by:

$$d_{uv}^{\cos} = 1 - \frac{u_1 \times v_1 + \cdots + u_q \times v_q}{\sqrt{u_1^2 + \cdots u_q^2}\sqrt{v_1^2 + \cdots v_q^2}}$$

The cosine distance between document 3 and document 10 in Table 5.8 is:

$$d_{uv}^{\cos} = 1 - \frac{5 \times 1 + 1 \times 2}{\sqrt{5^2 + 1^2}\sqrt{1^2 + 2^2}} = 0.386$$

To visualize the cosine distance between two observations, in this case (5, 1) and (1, 2), Figure 5.9 represents these observations as vectors emanating from the origin. The cosine distance between two observations is equivalent to the cosine of the angle (measured in radians) between their corresponding vectors. Cosine distance can be particularly useful for analyzing a frequency document-term matrix because the angle between two observation vectors does not depend on the magnitude of the variables (making it different than distance measures discussed earlier in this chapter). This allows cosine distance to measure dissimilarity in frequency patterns rather than frequency magnitude. For instance, the cosine distance between the observation (10, 2) and observation (1, 2) is the same as the cosine distance between (5, 1) and (1, 2).

Word Clouds

A **word cloud** is a visual representation of a document or set of documents in which the size of the word is proportional to the frequency with which the word appears. Figure 5.10 displays a word cloud of Chapter 1 of this textbook.

FIGURE 5.9   Visualization of Cosine Distance

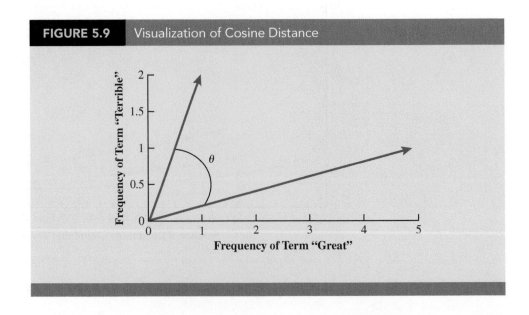

FIGURE 5.10   A Word Cloud of Chapter 1 of this Text

As can be seen from this word cloud, analytics and data are used most frequently in Chapter 1. Other more frequently mentioned words are decision, models, prescriptive, and predictive. The word cloud gives a quick visual sense of what the document's content. Using word clouds on tweets, for example, can provide insight on trending topics.

SUMMARY

We have introduced descriptive data-mining methods and related concepts. After introducing how to measure the similarity of individual observations, we presented two methods for grouping observations based on the similarity of their respective variable values: hierarchical clustering and k-means clustering. Agglomerative hierarchical clustering begins with each observation in its own cluster and iteratively aggregates clusters using a specified agglomeration method. We described several of these agglomeration methods and discussed their features. In k-means clustering, the analyst specifies k, the number of clusters, and observations then are placed into these clusters in an attempt to minimize the dissimilarity within the clusters. We concluded our discussion of clustering with a comparison of hierarchical clustering and k-means clustering.

We then introduced association rules and explained their use for identifying patterns across transactions, particularly in retail data. We defined the concepts of support count, confidence, and lift ratio, and we described their utility in gleaning actionable insight from association rules.

Finally, we discussed the text-mining process. Text is first preprocessed by deriving a smaller set of tokens from the larger set of words contained in a collection of documents. The tokenized text data is then converted into a presence/absence document-term matrix or a frequency document-term matrix. We then demonstrated the application of hierarchical clustering on a binary document-term matrix and k-means clustering on a frequency document-term matrix to glean insight from the underlying text data.

GLOSSARY

Antecedent The item set corresponding to the *if* portion of an if–then association rule.

Association rule An if–then statement describing the relationship between item sets.

Bag of words An approach for processing text into a structured row-column data format in which documents correspond to row observations and words (or more specifically, terms) correspond to column variables.

Binary document-term matrix A matrix with the rows representing documents (units of text) and the columns representing terms (words or word roots), and the entries in the columns indicating either the presence or absence of a particular term in a particular document (1 = present and 0 = not present).

Centroid linkage Method of calculating dissimilarity between clusters by considering the two centroids of the respective clusters.

Complete linkage Measure of calculating dissimilarity between clusters by considering only the two most dissimilar observations between the two clusters.

Confidence The conditional probability that the consequent of an association rule occurs given the antecedent occurs.

Consequent The item set corresponding to the *then* portion of an if–then association rule.

Corpus A collection of documents to be analyzed.

Cosine distance A measure of dissimilarity between two observations often used on frequency data derived from text because it is unaffected by the magnitude of the frequency and instead measures differences in frequency patterns.

Dendrogram A tree diagram used to illustrate the sequence of nested clusters produced by hierarchical clustering.

Document A piece of text, which can range from a single sentence to an entire book depending on the scope of the corresponding corpus.

Euclidean distance Geometric measure of dissimilarity between observations based on the Pythagorean theorem.

Frequency document-term matrix A matrix whose rows represent documents (units of text) and columns represent terms (words or word roots), and the entries in the matrix are the number of times each term occurs in each document.

Group average linkage Measure of calculating dissimilarity between clusters by considering the distance between each pair of observations between two clusters.

Hierarchical clustering Process of agglomerating observations into a series of nested groups based on a measure of similarity.

Jaccard's coefficient Measure of similarity between observations consisting solely of binary categorical variables that considers only matches of nonzero entries.

Jaccard distance Measure of dissimilarity between observations based on Jaccard's coefficient.

k-means clustering Process of organizing observations into one of k groups based on a measure of similarity (typically Euclidean distance).

Lift ratio The ratio of the performance of a data mining model measured against the performance of a random choice. In the context of association rules, the lift ratio is the ratio of the probability of the consequent occurring in a transaction that satisfies the antecedent versus the probability that the consequent occurs in a randomly selected transaction.

Manhattan distance Measure of dissimilarity between two observations based on the sum of the absolute differences in each variable dimensions.

Market basket analysis Analysis of items frequently co-occurring in transactions (such as purchases).

Market segmentation The partitioning of customers into groups that share common characteristics so that a business may target customers within a group with a tailored marketing strategy.

Matching coefficient Measure of similarity between observations based on the number of matching values of categorical variables.

Matching distance Measure of dissimilarity between observations based on the matching coefficient.

McQuitty's method Measure that computes the dissimilarity introduced by merging clusters A and B by, for each other cluster C, averaging the distance between A and C and the distance between B and C and summing these average distances.

Median linkage Method that computes the similarity between two clusters as the median of the similarities between each pair of observations in the two clusters.

Observation (record) A set of observed values of variables associated with a single entity, often displayed as a row in a spreadsheet or database.

Presence/absence document-term matrix A matrix with the rows representing documents and the columns representing words, and the entries in the columns indicating either the presence or the absence of a particular word in a particular document (1 = present and 0 = not present).

Sentiment analysis The process of clustering/categorizing comments or reviews as positive, negative, or neutral.

Single linkage Measure of calculating dissimilarity between clusters by considering only the two most similar observations between the two clusters.

Stemming The process of converting a word to its stem or root word.

Stopwords Common words in a language that are removed in the pre-processing of text

Support The percentage of transactions in which a collection of items occurs together in a transaction data set.

Term The most basic unit of text comprising a document, typically corresponding to a word or word stem.

Term frequency times inverse document frequency (TFIDF) Text mining measure which accounts for term frequency and the uniqueness of a term in a document relative to other documents in a corpus.

Term normalization A set of natural language processing techniques to map text into a standardized form.

Text mining The process of extracting useful information from text data.

Tokenization The process of dividing text into separate terms, referred to as tokens.

Unsupervised learning Category of data-mining techniques in which an algorithm explains relationships without an outcome variable to guide the process.

Unstructured data Data, such as text, audio, or video, that cannot be stored in a traditional structured database.

Ward's method Procedure that partitions observations in a manner to obtain clusters with the least amount of information loss due to the aggregation.

Word cloud A visualization of text data based on word frequencies in a document or set of documents.

PROBLEMS

Problems 1 through 10 and Case Problem 1 do not require the use of data mining software and focus on knowledge of concepts and basic calculations.

Problems 11 through 23 and Case Problem 2 require the use of data mining software. If using R/Rattle to solve these problems, refer to Appendix: *R/Rattle Settings to Solve Chapter 5 Problems*. If using JMP Pro to solve these problems, refer to Appendix: *JMP Pro Settings to Solve Chapter 5 Problems*.

1. **k-Means Clustering of Wines.** Amanda Boleyn, an entrepreneur who recently sold her start-up for a multi-million-dollar sum, is looking for alternate investments for her newfound fortune. She is considering an investment in wine, similar to how some people invest in rare coins and fine art. To educate herself on the properties of fine wine, she has collected data on 13 different characteristics of 178 wines. Amanda has applied k-means clustering to this data for $k = 1, \ldots, 10$ and generated the following plot of total sums of squared deviations. After analyzing this plot, Amanda generates summaries for $k = 2$, 3, and 4. Which value of k is the most appropriate to categorize these wines? Justify your choice with calculations.

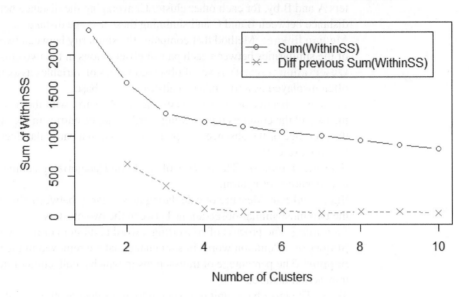

Sum of WithinSS Over Number of Clusters

k = 2		Inter-Cluster Distances
	Cluster 1	Cluster 2
Cluster 1	0	5.640
Cluster 2	5.640	0

Within-Cluster Summary

	Size	Average Distance
Cluster 1	87	4.003
Cluster 2	91	4.260
Total	178	4.134

k = 3		Inter-Cluster Distances	
	Cluster 1	Cluster 2	Cluster 3
Cluster 1	0	5.147	6.078
Cluster 2	5.147	0	5.432
Cluster 3	6.078	5.432	0

Within-Cluster Summary

	Size	Average Distance
Cluster 1	62	3.355
Cluster 2	65	3.999
Cluster 3	51	3.483
Total	178	3.627

k = 4		Inter-Cluster Distances		
	Cluster 1	Cluster 2	Cluster 3	Cluster 4
Cluster 1	0	5.255	6.070	4.853
Cluster 2	5.255	0	5.136	4.789
Cluster 3	6.070	5.136	0	6.074
Cluster 4	4.853	4.789	6.074	0

Within-Cluster Summary		
	Size	Average Distance
Cluster 1	56	3.024
Cluster 2	45	3.490
Cluster 3	49	3.426
Cluster 4	28	4.580
Total	178	3.498

2. **Distance to Centroid Calculation for Wine Clusters.** Jay Gatsby categorizes wines into one of three clusters. The centroids of these clusters, describing the average characteristics of a wine in each cluster, are listed in the following table.

Characteristic	Cluster 1	Cluster 2	Cluster 3
Alcohol	0.819	0.164	−0.937
Malic Acid	−0.329	0.869	−0.368
Ash	0.248	0.186	−0.393
Alkalinity	−0.677	0.523	0.249
Magnesium	0.643	−0.075	−0.573
Phenols	0.825	0.977	−0.034
Flavanoids	0.896	−1.212	0.083
Nonflavanoids	−0.595	0.724	0.009
Proanthocyanins	0.619	−0.778	0.010
Color Intensity	0.135	0.939	−0.881
Hue	0.497	−1.162	0.437
Dilution	0.744	−1.289	0.295
Proline	1.117	−0.406	−0.776

Jay has recently discovered a new wine from the Piedmont region of Italy with the following characteristics. In which cluster of wines should he place this new wine? Justify your choice with appropriate calculations.

Characteristic	
Alcohol	−1.023
Malic Acid	−0.480
Ash	0.049
Alkalinity	0.600
Magnesium	−1.242
Phenols	1.094
Flavanoids	0.001
Nonflavanoids	0.548
Proanthocyanins	−0.229
Color Intensity	−0.797
Hue	0.711
Dilution	−0.425
Proline	0.010

3. **Outliers' Impact on Clustering.** Sol & Nieve is a sporting good and outdoor gear retailer that operates in North America and Central America. In an attempt to characterize its stores (and re-assess Sol & Nieve's supply chain operations), Gustavo Esposito is analyzing sales in 22 regions for its two primary product lines: sol (beach-oriented apparel) and nieve (mountain-oriented apparel). Gustavo has generated the following output for k-means clustering for $k = 2, 3, 4$ (output reported in standardized units). Which value of k is the most appropriate for these data? How should Gustavo interpret the results to characterize the clusters?

$k = 2$

Inter-Cluster Distances

	Cluster 1	Cluster 2
Cluster 1	0	2.215
Cluster 2	2.215	0

	Within-Cluster Summary		**Centroid (Original Units)**	
	Size	Average Distance	Sol	Nieve
Cluster 1	11	0.655	25.148	6.695
Cluster 2	11	0.685	6.340	25.276

$k = 3$

Inter-Cluster Distances

	Cluster 1	Cluster 2	Cluster 3
Cluster 1	0	4.603	1.977
Cluster 2	4.603	0	3.076
Cluster 3	1.977	3.076	0

	Within-Cluster Summary		**Centroid (Original Units)**	
	Size	Average Distance	Sol	Nieve
Cluster 1	11	0.655	25.148	6.695
Cluster 2	1	0	6.500	60.000
Cluster 3	10	0.154	6.324	22.932

$k = 4$

Inter-Cluster Distances

	Cluster 1	Cluster 2	Cluster 3	Cluster 4
Cluster 1	0	4.458	3.060	6.064
Cluster 2	4.458	0	1.728	3.076
Cluster 3	3.060	1.728	0	4.457
Cluster 4	6.064	3.076	4.457	0

	Within-Cluster Summary		**Centroid (Original Units)**	
	Size	Average Distance	Sol	Nieve
Cluster 1	1	0	60.000	6.500
Cluster 2	10	0.154	6.324	22.932
Cluster 3	10	0.120	20.099	6.715
Cluster 4	1	0	6.500	60.000

4. **Cluster Shapes for k-Means versus Single Linkage.** Heidi Zahn is a human resources manager currently reviewing data on 98 employees. In the data, each observation consists of an employee's age and an employee's performance rating.
   a. Heidi applied k-means clustering with $k = 2$ to the data and generated the following plot to visualize the clusters. Based on this plot, qualitatively characterize the two clusters of employees categorized by the k-means approach.

k-Means Clustering Solution with $k = 2$

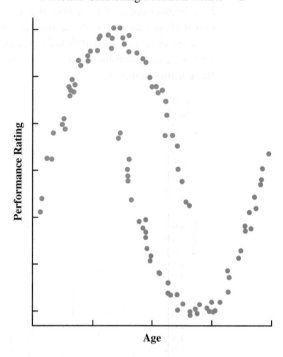

b. For a comparison, Heidi applied hierarchical clustering with the Euclidean distance and single linkage to the data and generated the following plot based on the level of agglomeration with two clusters. Based on this plot, qualitatively characterize the two clusters of employees categorized by the hierarchical approach.

c. Which of the two approaches (*k*-means clustering from part (a) or hierarchical clustering from part (b)) would you recommend?

Hierarchical Clustering Solution Using Euclidean
Distance and Single Linkage

5. **Dendrogram of Utility Companies.** The regulation of electric and gas utilities is an important public policy question affecting consumer's choice and cost of energy

provider. To inform deliberation on public policy, data on eight numerical variables have been collected for a group of energy companies. To summarize the data, hierarchical clustering has been executed using Euclidean distance to measure dissimilarity between observations and Ward's method as the agglomeration method. Based on the following dendrogram, what is the most appropriate number of clusters to organize these utility companies?

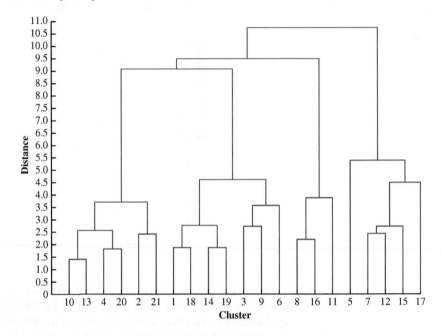

6. **Complete Linkage Clustering of Utility Companies.** In an effort to inform political leaders and economists discussing the deregulation of electric and gas utilities, data on eight numerical variables from utility companies have been grouped using hierarchical clustering based on Euclidean distance to measure dissimilarity between observations and complete linkage as the agglomeration method.

   a. Based on the following dendrogram, what is the most appropriate number of clusters to organize these utility companies?

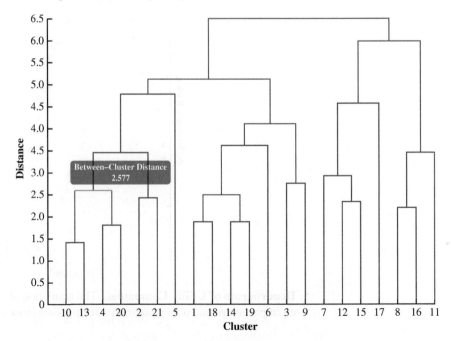

b. Using the following data on the Observations 10, 13, 4, and 20, confirm that the complete linkage distance between the cluster containing {10, 13} and the cluster containing {4, 20} is 2.577 units as displayed in the dendrogram.

	Observation			
	10	**13**	**4**	**20**
Income/Debt	0.032	0.195	−0.510	0.466
Return	0.741	0.875	0.207	0.474
Cost	0.700	0.748	−0.004	−0.490
Load	−0.892	−0.735	−0.219	0.655
Peak	−0.173	1.013	−0.943	0.083
Sales	−0.693	−0.489	−0.702	−0.458
Percent Nuclear	1.620	2.275	1.328	1.733
Total Fuel Costs	−0.863	−1.035	−0.724	−0.721

7. **Interpreting Merge Steps from a Dendrogram.** From 1946 to 1990, the Big Ten Conference consisted of the University of Illinois, Indiana University, University of Iowa, University of Michigan, Michigan State University, University of Minnesota, Northwestern University, Ohio State University, Purdue University, and University of Wisconsin. In 1990, the conference added Pennsylvania State University. In 2011, the conference added the University of Nebraska. In 2014, the University of Maryland and Rutgers University were added to the conference with speculation of more schools being added in the future.

   Based on the football stadium capacity, latitude, longitude, and enrollment, the Big Ten commissioner is curious how a clustering algorithm would suggest the conference expand beyond its current 14 members. To represent the 14 member schools as an entity, each variable value for the 14 schools of the Big Ten Conference has been replaced with the respective variable median over these 10 schools. Using Euclidean distance to measure dissimilarity between observations, hierarchical clustering with complete linkage generates the following dendrogram. Describe the next three stages of conference expansion plan suggested by the dendrogram.

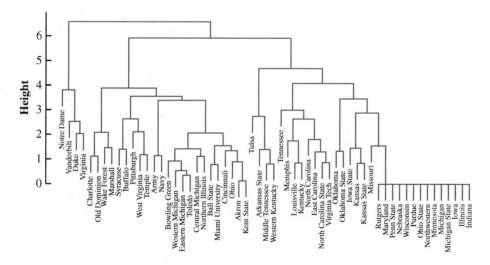

8. **Comparing Different Linkage Methods.** The Football Bowl Subdivision (FBS) level of the National Collegiate Athletic Association (NCAA) consists of over 100 schools. Most of these schools belong to one of several conferences, or collections of schools, that compete with each other on a regular basis in collegiate sports.

Suppose the NCAA has commissioned a study that will propose the formation of conferences based on the similarities of constituent schools. If the NCAA cares only about geographic proximity of schools when determining conferences, it could use hierarchical clustering based on the schools' latitude and longitude values and Euclidean distance to compute dissimilarity between observations. The following charts and tables illustrate the 10-cluster solutions when using various linkage methods (group average, Ward's method, complete, and centroid) to determine clusters of schools to be assigned to conferences using hierarchical clustering. Compare and contrast the resulting clusters created using each of these different linkage methods for hierarchical clustering.

Group Average Linkage Clusters

● Cluster 1 ● Cluster 2 ● Cluster 3 ● Cluster 4 ● Cluster 5
● Cluster 6 ● Cluster 7 ● Cluster 8 ● Cluster 9 ● Cluster 10

Row Labels	▾Count of School	Min of Latitude2	Max of Latitude	Min of Longitude2	Max of Longitude2
1	7	38.9	41.7	−111.9	−104.8
2	6	36.2	39.4	−122.3	−115.3
3	8	31.8	35.1	−118.4	−106.4
4	6	43.6	47.6	−123.1	−116.2
5	43	38.0	43.6	−96.7	−71.0
6	1	45.0	45.0	−93.3	−93.3
7	30	31.8	38.0	−97.5	−76.2
8	18	29.5	33.2	−98.5	−88.1
9	7	25.8	30.5	−84.3	−80.1
10	1	19.7	19.7	−155.1	−155.1
Grand Total	**127**	**19.7**	**47.6**	**−155.1**	**−71.0**

Ward's Method Clusters

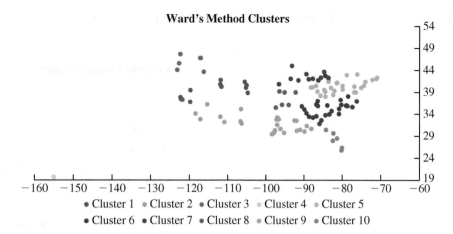

Cluster	⏷Count of School	Min of Latitude	Max of Latitude	Min of Longitude	Max of Longitude
1	12	36.8	41.7	122.3	104.8
2	9	31.8	36.2	−118.4	−106.4
3	6	43.6	47.6	−123.1	−116.2
4	1	19.7	19.7	−155.1	−155.1
5	28	38.0	43.0	−88.3	−71.0
6	13	10.8	45.0	−96.7	−83.6
7	20	31.8	38.0	−90.7	−70.2
8	7	35.5	39.2	−97.5	−92.3
9	18	29.5	33.2	−98.5	−88.1
10	7	25.8	30.5	−84.3	−80.1
Grand Total	127	19.7	47.6	−155.1	−71.0

Complete Linkage

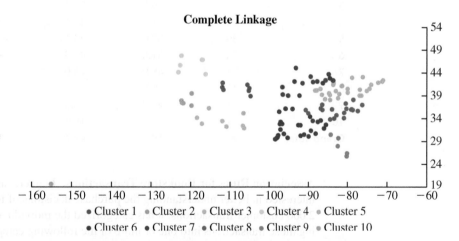

Cluster	⏷Count of School	Min of Latitude	Max of Latitude	Min of Longitude	Max of Longitude
1	7	38.9	41.7	−111.9	−104.8
2	5	36.8	39.2	−122.3	−119.7
3	9	31.8	36.2	−118.4	−106.4
4	6	43.6	47.6	−123.1	−116.2
5	28	38.0	43.0	−88.3	−71.0
6	16	39.0	45.0	−96.7	−83.6
7	28	29.5	36.1	−98.5	−85.5
8	20	33.8	38.0	−90.7	−76.2
9	7	25.8	30.5	−84.3	−80.1
10	1	19.7	19.7	−155.1	−155.1
Grand Total	127	19.7	47.6	−155.1	−71.0

Centroid Linkage Clusters

Cluster	▾ Count of School	Min of Latitude	Max of Latitude	Min of Longitude	Max of Longitude
1	7	38.9	41.7	−111.9	−104.8
2	8	31.8	35.1	−118.4	−106.4
3	6	36.2	39.4	−122.3	−115.3
4	6	43.6	47.6	−123.1	−116.2
5	39	38.0	43.6	−93.6	−71.0
6	34	31.8	40.8	−97.5	−76.2
7	1	45.0	45.0	−93.3	−93.3
8	18	29.5	33.2	−98.5	−88.1
9	7	25.8	30.5	−84.3	−80.1
10	1	19.7	19.7	−155.1	−155.1
Grand Total	**127**	**19.7**	**47.6**	**−155.1**	**−71.0**

9. **Association Rules for Bookstore Transactions.** Leggere, an Internet book retailer, is interested in better understanding the purchase decisions of its customers. For a set of 2,000 customer transactions, it has categorized the individual book purchases comprising those transactions into one or more of the following categories: Novels, Willa Bean series, Cooking Books, Bob Villa Do-It-Yourself, Youth Fantasy, Art Books, Biography, Cooking Books by Mossimo Bottura, Harry Potter series, Florence Art Books, and Titian Art Books. Leggere has conducted association rules analysis on this data set and would like to analyze the output. Based on a minimum support of 200 transactions and a minimum confidence of 50%, the table below shows the top 10 rules with respect to lift ratio.

   a. Explain why the top rule "If customer buys a Bottura cooking book, then they buy a cooking book," is not helpful even though it has the largest lift and 100% confidence.

   b. Explain how the confidence of 52.99% and lift ratio of 2.20 was computed for the rule "If a customer buys a cooking book and a biography book, then they buy an art book." Interpret these quantities.

   c. Based on these top 10 rules, what general insight can Leggere gain on the purchase habits of these customers?

d. What will be the effect on the rules generated if Leggere decreases the minimum support and reruns the association rules analysis?

e. What will be the effect on the rules generated if Leggere decreases the minimum confidence and reruns the association rules analysis?

Antecedent	Consequent	Support for A & C	Confidence	Lift Ratio
BotturaCooking	Cooking	0.227	1.00	1.16
Cooking, BobVilla	Art	0.205	0.54	1.12
Cooking, Art	Biography	0.204	0.61	1.10
Cooking, Biography	Art	0.204	0.53	1.10
Youth Fantasy	Novels, Cooking	0.245	0.55	1.075
Cooking, Art	BobVilla	0.205	0.61	1.055
Cooking, BobVilla	Biography	0.218	0.58	1.04
Biography	Novels, Cooking	0.293	0.53	1.035
Novels, Cooking	Biography	0.293	0.57	1.035
Art	Novels, Cooking	0.249	0.52	1.01

10. **Association Rules on Congressional Voting Records.** Freelance reporter Irwin Fletcher is examining the historical voting records of members of the U.S. Congress. For 175 representatives, Irwin has collected the voting record (yes or no) on 16 pieces of legislation. To examine the relationship between representatives' votes on different issues, Irwin has conducted an association rules analysis with a minimum support of 40% and a minimum confidence of 90%.

The data included the following bills:

Budget: approve federal budget resolution

Contras: aid for Nicaraguan contra rebels

El_Salvador: aid to El Salvador

Missile: funding for M-X missile program

Physician: freeze physician fees

Religious: equal access to all religious groups at schools

Satellite: ban on anti-satellite weapons testing

The following table shows the top five rules with respect to lift ratio. The table displays representatives' decisions in a "bill-vote" format. For example, "Contras-y" indicates that the representative voted yes on a bill to support the Nicaraguan Contra rebels and "Physician-n" indicates a no vote on a bill to freeze physician fees.

Antecedent	Consequent	Support for A&C	Confidence	Lift Ratio
Contras-y, Physician-n, Satellite-y	El_Salvador-n	0.40	0.95	1.98
Contras-y, Missile-y	El_Salvador-n	0.40	0.40	1.90
Contras-y, Physician-n	El_Salvador-n	0.44	0.91	1.90
Missile-n, Religious-y	El_Salvador-y	0.40	0.93	1.79
Budget-y, Contras-y, Physician-n	El_Salvador-n	0.41	0.90	1.89

Problems 11 through 23 require the use of data mining software such as R or JMP Pro to solve. There are two versions (.csv and .xlsx) of the DATAfiles for these problems. Use the .csv file as input if using R and use the .xlsx file as input if using JMP Pro.

DATA file

DemoKTC

DATA file

FBS

a. Interpret the lift ratio of the first rule in the table.

b. What is the probability that a representative votes no on El Salvador aid given that they vote yes to aid to Nicaraguan Contra rebels and yes to the M-X missile program?

c. What is the probability that a representative votes no on El Salvador aid given that they vote no to the M-X missile program and yes to equal access to religious groups in schools?

d. What is the probability that a randomly selected representative votes yes on El Salvador aid?

11. **k-Means Clustering of Bank Customers.** Apply k-means clustering with values of $k = 2, 3, 4,$ and 5 to cluster the data in *DemoKTC* based on the Age, Income, and Children variables. Normalize the values of the input variables to adjust for the different magnitudes of the variables. How many clusters do you recommend? Why?

12. **Hierarchical Clustering on Binary Variables.** Using matching distance to compute dissimilarity between observations, apply hierarchical clustering employing group average linkage to the data in *DemoKTC* to create three clusters based on the Female, Married, Loan, and Mortgage variables. Report the characteristics of each cluster including the total number of customers in each cluster as well as the number of customers who are female, the number of customers who are married, the number of customers with a car loan, and the number of customers with a mortgage in each cluster. How would you describe each cluster?

13. **Clustering Colleges with k-Means.** The Football Bowl Subdivision (FBS) level of the National Collegiate Athletic Association (NCAA) consists of over 100 schools. Most of these schools belong to one of several conferences, or collections of schools, that compete with each other on a regular basis in collegiate sports. Suppose the NCAA has commissioned a study that will propose the formation of conferences based on the similarities of the constituent schools. The file *FBS* contains data on schools that belong to the Football Bowl Subdivision. Each row in this file contains information on a school. The variables include football stadium capacity, latitude, longitude, athletic department revenue, endowment, and undergraduate enrollment.

a. Apply k-means clustering with $k = 10$ using football stadium capacity, latitude, longitude, endowment, and enrollment as variables. Normalize the input variables to adjust for the different magnitudes of the variables. Analyze the resultant clusters. What is the smallest cluster? What is the least dense cluster (as measured by the average distance in the cluster)? What makes the least dense cluster so diverse?

b. What problems do you see with the plan for defining the school membership of the 10 conferences directly with the 10 clusters?

c. Repeat part (a), but this time do not normalize the values of the input variables. Analyze the resultant clusters. How and why do they differ from those in part (a)? Identify the dominating factor(s) in the formation of these new clusters.

14. **Grouping Colleges with Hierarchical Clustering.** Refer to the clustering problem involving the file *FBS* described in Problem 13. Using Euclidean distance to compute dissimilarity between observations, apply hierarchical clustering employing Ward's method with 10 clusters using football stadium capacity, latitude, longitude, endowment, and enrollment as variables. Normalize the values of the input variables to adjust for the different magnitudes of the variables.

a. Compute the cluster centers for the clusters created by the hierarchical clustering.

b. Identify the cluster with the largest average football stadium capacity. Using all the variables, how would you characterize this cluster?

c. Examine the smallest cluster. What makes this cluster unique?

15. **Cluster Comparison of Single Linkage to Group Average Linking.** Refer to the clustering problem involving the file *FBS* described in Problem 13. Using Euclidean distance to compute dissimilarity between observations, apply hierarchical clustering with 10 clusters using latitude and longitude as variables. Execute the clustering two times—once with single linkage and once with group average linkage. Compute the

cluster sizes and visualize the clusters by creating a scatter plot with longitude as the *x*-variable and latitude as the *y*-variable. Compare the results of the two approaches.

BigBlue

16. ***k*-Means Clustering of Employees.** IBM employs a network of expert analytics consultants for various projects. To help it determine how to distribute its bonuses, IBM wants to form groups of employees with similar performance according to key performance metrics. Each observation (corresponding to an employee) in the file *BigBlue* consists of values for UsageRate which corresponds to the proportion of time that the employee has been actively working on high-priority projects, Recognition which is the number of projects for which the employee was specifically requested, and Leader which is the number of projects on which the employee has served as project leader. Apply *k*-means clustering with values of $k = 2$ to 7. Normalize the values of the input variables to adjust for the different magnitudes of the variables. How many clusters do you recommend to categorize the employees? Why?

Sandler

17. ***k*-Means Clustering of Sandler Movies.** Attracted by the possible returns from a portfolio of movies, hedge funds have invested in the movie industry by financially backing individual films and/or studios. The hedge fund Star Ventures is currently conducting some research involving movies involving Adam Sandler, an American actor, screenwriter, and film producer. As a first step, Star Ventures would like to cluster Adam Sandler movies based on their gross box office returns and movie critic ratings. Using the data in the file *Sandler*, apply *k*-means clustering with $k = 3$ to characterize three different types of Adam Sandler movies. Base the clusters on the variables Rating and Box. Rating corresponds to movie ratings provided by critics (a higher score represents a movie receiving better reviews). Box represents the gross box office earnings in 2015 dollars. Normalize the values of the input variables to adjust for the different magnitudes of the variables. Report the characteristics of each cluster including a count of movies, the average rating of movies, and the average box office earnings of movies in each cluster. How would you describe the movies in each cluster?

TraderJoes

18. ***k*-Means Clustering of Trader Joe's Stores.** Josephine Mater works for the supply-chain analytics division of Trader Joe's, a national chain of specialty grocery stores. Trader Joe's is considering a redesign of its supply chain. Josephine knows that Trader Joe's uses frequent truck shipments from its distribution centers to its retail stores. To keep costs low, retail stores are typically located near a distribution center. The file *TraderJoes* contains data on the location of Trader Joe's retail stores. Josephine would like to use *k*-means clustering with $k = 8$ to estimate the preferred locations for a proposal to use eight distribution centers to support its retail stores. If Trader Joe's establishes eight distribution centers, how many retail stores does the *k*-means approach suggest assigning to each distribution center? What are the drawbacks to directly applying this solution to assign retail stores to distribution centers?

AppleCartBinary
AppleCartStacked

19. **Association Rules of iStore Transactions.** Apple Inc. tracks online transactions at its iStore and is interested in learning about the purchase patterns of its customers in order to provide recommendations as a customer browses its web site. A sample of the "shopping cart" data resides in the files *AppleCartBinary* and *AppleCartStacked*. Use a minimum support of 10% of the total number of transactions and a minimum confidence of 50% to generate a list of association rules.
   a. Interpret what the rule with the largest lift ratio is saying about the relationship between the antecedent item set and consequent item set.
   b. Interpret the confidence of the rule with the largest lift ratio.
   c. Interpret the lift ratio of the rule with the largest lift ratio.
   d. Review the top 15 rules and summarize what the rules suggest.

CookieMonsterBinary
CookieMonsterStacked

20. **Association Rules of Browser Histories.** Cookie Monster Inc. is a company that specializes in the development of software that tracks web browsing history of individuals. Cookie Monster Inc. is interested in analyzing its data to gain insight on the online behavior of individuals. A sample of browser histories is provided in the files *CookieMonsterBinary* and *CookieMonsterStacked* that indicate which websites were visited by which customers. Use a

minimum support of 4% of the transactions (800 of the 20,000 total transactions) and a minimum confidence of 50% to generate a list of association rules.

a. Based on the top 14 rules, which three web sites appear in the association rules with the largest lift ratio?

b. Identify the association rule with the largest lift ratio that also has Pinterest as the antecedent. What is the consequent web site in this rule?

c. Interpret the confidence of the rule from part (b). While the antecedent and consequent are not necessarily chronological, what does this rule suggest?

d. Identify the association rule with the largest lift ratio that also has TheEveryGirl as the antecedent. What is the consequent web site in this rule?

e. Interpret the lift ratio of the rule from part (d).

21. **Association Rules of Grocery Store Transactions.** A grocery store introducing items from Italy is interested in analyzing buying trends of these new "international" items, namely prosciutto, Peroni, risotto, and gelato. The files *GroceryStoreList* and *GroceryStoreStacked* provide data on a collection of transactions in item-list format.

DATA *file*
GroceryStoreList
GroceryStoreStacked

a. Use a minimum support of 10% of the transactions (100 of the 1,000 total transactions) and a minimum confidence of 50% to generate a list of association rules. How many rules satisfy this criterion?

b. Use a minimum support of 25% of the transactions (250 of the 1,000 total transactions) and a minimum confidence of 50% to generate a list of association rules. How many rules satisfy this criterion? Why may the grocery store want to increase the minimum support required for their analysis? What is the risk of increasing the minimum support required?

c. Using the list of rules from part (b), consider the rule with the largest lift ratio that also involves an Italian item. Interpret what this rule is saying about the relationship between the antecedent item set and consequent item set.

d. Interpret the confidence of the rule with the largest lift ratio that also involves an Italian item.

e. Interpret the lift ratio of the rule with the largest lift ratio that also involves an Italian item.

f. What insight can the grocery store obtain about its purchasers of the Italian fare?

22. **Text Mining of Tweets.** Companies can learn a lot about customer experiences by monitoring the social media web site Twitter. The file *AirlineTweets* contains a sample of 36 tweets of an airline's customers. Normalize the terms by using stemming and generate frequency and binary document-term matrices.

DATA *file*
AirlineTweets

a. What are the five most common terms occurring in these tweets? How often does each term appear?

b. Using Jaccard's distance to compute dissimilarity between observations, apply hierarchical clustering employing Ward's linkage method to yield three clusters on the binary document-term matrix using the following tokens as variables: agent, attend, bag, damag, and rude. How many documents are in each cluster? Give a description of each cluster.

c. How could management use the results obtained in part (b)?

Source: Kaggle web site

23. **Text Mining of Yelp Reviews.** The online review service Yelp helps millions of consumers find the goods and services they seek. To help consumers make more-informed choices, Yelp includes over 120 million reviews. The file *YelpItalian* contains a sample of 21 reviews for an Italian restaurant. Normalize the terms by using stemming and a generate frequency and binary document-term matrices.

DATA *file*
YelpItalian

a. What are the five most common terms in these reviews? How often does each term appear?

b. Using Jaccard's distance to compute dissimilarity between observations, apply hierarchical clustering employing Ward's linkage method to yield two clusters from the binary document-term matrix using all five of the most common terms from the reviews. How many documents are in each cluster? Give a description of each cluster.

Case Problem 1 does not require the use of data mining software (such as R/Rattle or JMP Pro), but the use of Excel is recommended.

CASE PROBLEM 1: BIG TEN EXPANSION

DATA *file*

BigTenExpand

From 1946 to 1990, the Big Ten Conference consisted of the University of Illinois, Indiana University, University of Iowa, University of Michigan, Michigan State University, University of Minnesota, Northwestern University, Ohio State University, Purdue University, and University of Wisconsin. In 1990, the conference added Pennsylvania State University. In 2011, the conference added the University of Nebraska. In 2014, the University of Maryland and Rutgers University were added to the conference with speculation of more schools being added in the future.

The file *BigTenExpand* contains data on the football stadium capacity, latitude, longitude, endowment, and enrollment of 59 National Collegiate Athletic Association (NCAA) Football Bowl Subdivision (FBS) schools. Treat the 10 schools that were members of the Big Ten from 1946 to 1990 as being in a cluster and the other 49 schools as each being in their own cluster.

1. Using Euclidean distance to measure dissimilarity between observations, determine which school (in its own cluster of one) that hierarchical clustering with complete linkage would recommend integrating into the Big Ten Conference. That is, which school is the most similar with respect to complete linkage to the cluster of ten schools that were members of the Big Ten from 1946 to 1990?

2. Add the single school identified in (1) to create a cluster of 11 schools representing a hypothetical Big Ten Conference. Repeat the calculations to identify the school most similar with respect to complete linkage to this new cluster of 11 schools.

3. Add the school identified in (2) to create a cluster of 12 schools representing a hypothetical Big Ten Conference. Repeat the calculations to identify the school most similar with respect to complete linkage to this new cluster of 12 schools.

4. Add the school identified in (3) to create a cluster of 13 schools representing a hypothetical Big Ten Conference. Repeat the calculations to identify the school most similar with respect to complete linkage to this new cluster of 13 schools. Add this school to create a 14-school cluster.

5. How does the hypothetical 14-team cluster created in (4) compare to the actual 14-team Big Ten Conference? For both the hypothetical 14-team Big Ten Conference and the actual 14-team Big Ten Conference, compute the cluster centroid, the distance from each cluster member to the cluster centroid, and average distance between the observations in the cluster. What do you observe when comparing these two clusters? Which cluster has the smaller average distance between observations? Is this surprising? Explain.

CASE PROBLEM 2: KNOW THY CUSTOMER

DATA *file*

KnowThyCustomer

Know Thy Customer (KTC) is a financial consulting company that provides personalized financial advice to its clients. As a basis for developing this tailored advising, KTC would like to segment its customers into several representative groups based on key characteristics. Peyton Blake, the director of KTC's fledgling analytics division, plans to establish the set of representative customer profiles based on 600 customer records in the file *KnowThyCustomer*. Each customer record contains data on age, gender, annual income, marital status, number of children, whether the customer has a car loan, and whether the customer has a home mortgage. KTC's market research staff has determined that these seven characteristics should form the basis of the customer clustering.

Peyton has invited a summer intern, Danny Riles, into her office so they can discuss how to proceed. As they review the data on the computer screen, Peyton's brow furrows as she realizes that this task may not be trivial. The data contains both categorical variables (Female, Married, Car, and Mortgage) and numerical variables (Age, Income, and Children).

1. Using Manhattan distance to compute dissimilarity between observations, apply hierarchical clustering on all seven variables, experimenting with using complete linkage and group average linkage. Normalize the values of the input variables. Recommend a

set of customer profiles (clusters). Describe these clusters according to their "average" characteristics. Why might hierarchical clustering not be a good method to use for these seven variables?

2. Apply a two-step approach:

a. Using matching distance to compute dissimilarity between observations, employ hierarchical clustering with group average linkage to produce four clusters using the variables Female, Married, Loan, and Mortgage.

b. Based on the clusters from part (a), split the original 600 observations into four separate data sets as suggested by the four clusters from part (a). For each of these four data sets, apply k-means clustering with $k = 2$ using Age, Income, and Children as variables. Normalize the values of the input variables. This will generate a total of eight clusters. Describe these eight clusters according to their "average" characteristics. What benefit does this two-step clustering approach have over just using hierarchical clustering on all seven variables as in part (1) or just using k-means clustering on all seven variables? What weakness does it have?

Chapter 6

Statistical Inference

CONTENTS

ANALYTICS IN ACTION

John Morrell & Company*

CINCINNATI OHIO

John Morrell & Company, which was established in England in 1827, is considered the oldest continuously operating meat manufacturer in the United States. It is a wholly owned and independently managed subsidiary of Smithfield Foods, Smithfield, Virginia. John Morrell & Company offers an extensive product line of processed meats and fresh pork to consumers under 13 regional brands, including John Morrell, E-Z-Cut, Tobin's First Prize, Dinner Bell, Hunter, Kretschmar, Rath, Rodeo, Shenson, Farmers Hickory Brand, Iowa Quality, and Peyton's. Each regional brand enjoys high brand recognition and loyalty among consumers.

Market research at Morrell provides management with up-to-date information on the company's various products and how the products compare with competing brands of similar products. In order to compare a beef pot roast made by Morrell to similar beef products from two major competitors, Morrell asked a random sample of consumers to indicate how the products rated in terms of taste, appearance, aroma, and overall preference.

In Morrell's independent taste-test study, a sample of 224 consumers in Cincinnati, Milwaukee, and Los Angeles was chosen. Of these 224 consumers, 150 preferred the beef pot roast made by Morrell. Based on these results, Morrell estimates that the population proportion that prefers Morrell's beef pot roast is $\bar{p} = 150/224 = 0.67$. Recognizing that this estimate is subject to sampling error, Morrell calculates the 95% confidence interval for the population proportion that prefers Morrell's beef pot roast to be 0.6080 to 0.7312.

Morrell then turned its attention to whether these sample data support the conclusion that Morrell's beef pot roast is the preferred choice of more than 50% of the consumer population. Letting p indicate the proportion of the population that prefers Morrell's product, the hypothesis test for the research question is as follows:

$$H_0: p \leq 0.50$$
$$H_a: p > 0.50$$

The null hypothesis H_0 indicates the preference for Morrell's product is less than or equal to 50%. If the sample data support rejecting H_0 in favor of the alternative hypothesis H_a, Morrell will draw the research conclusion that in a three-product comparison, its beef pot roast is preferred by more than 50% of the consumer population. Using statistical hypothesis testing procedures, the null hypothesis H_0 was rejected. The study provided statistical evidence supporting H_a and the conclusion that the Morrell product is preferred by more than 50% of the consumer population.

In this chapter, you will learn about simple random sampling and the sample selection process. In addition, you will learn how statistics such as the sample mean and sample proportion are used to estimate parameters such as the population mean and population proportion. The concept of a sampling distribution will be introduced and used to compute the margins of error associated with sample estimates. You will then learn how to use this information to construct and interpret interval estimates of a population mean and a population proportion. We then discuss how to formulate hypotheses and how to conduct tests such as the one used by Morrell. You will learn how to use sample data to determine whether or not a hypothesis should be rejected.

*The authors are indebted to Marty Butler, Vice President of Marketing, John Morrell, for providing this Analytics in Action.

Refer to Chapter 2 for a fundamental overview of data and descriptive statistics.

When collecting data, we usually want to learn about some characteristic(s) of the population, the collection of all the elements of interest, from which we are collecting that data. In order to know about some characteristic of a population with certainty, we must collect data from every element in the population of interest; such an effort is referred to as a **census**. However, there are many potential difficulties associated with taking a census:

- A census may be expensive; if resources are limited, it may not be feasible to take a census.
- A census may be time consuming; if the data need be collected quickly, a census may not be suitable.
- A census may be misleading; if the population is changing quickly, by the time a census is completed the data may be obsolete.

- A census may be unnecessary; if perfect information about the characteristic(s) of the population of interest is not required, a census may be excessive.
- A census may be impractical; if observations are destructive, taking a census would destroy the population of interest.

In order to overcome the potential difficulties associated with taking a census, we may decide to take a sample (a subset of the population) and subsequently use the sample data we collect to make inferences and answer research questions about the population of interest. Therefore, the objective of sampling is to gather data from a subset of the population that is as similar as possible to the entire population, so that what we learn from the sample data accurately reflects what we want to understand about the entire population. When we use the sample data we have collected to make estimates of or draw conclusions about one or more characteristics of a population (the value of one or more parameters), we are using the process of **statistical inference**.

A sample that is similar to the population from which it has been drawn is said to be representative of the population.

Sampling is done in a wide variety of research settings. Let us begin our discussion of statistical inference by citing two examples in which sampling was used to answer a research question about a population.

1. Members of a political party in Texas are considering giving their support to a particular candidate for election to the U.S. Senate, and party leaders want to estimate the proportion of registered voters in the state that favor the candidate. A sample of 400 registered voters in Texas is selected, and 160 of those voters indicate a preference for the candidate. Thus, an estimate of proportion of the population of registered voters who favor the candidate is $160/400 = 0.40$.

2. A tire manufacturer is considering production of a new tire designed to provide an increase in lifetime mileage over the firm's current line of tires. To estimate the mean useful life of the new tires, the manufacturer produced a sample of 120 tires for testing. The test results provided a sample mean of 36,500 miles. Hence, an estimate of the mean useful life for the population of new tires is 36,500 miles.

A sample mean provides an estimate of a population mean, and a sample proportion provides an estimate of a population proportion. With estimates such as these, some estimation error can be expected. This chapter provides the basis for determining how large that error might be.

It is important to realize that sample results provide only *estimates* of the values of the corresponding population characteristics. We do not expect exactly 0.40, or 40%, of the population of registered voters to favor the candidate, nor do we expect the sample mean of 36,500 miles to exactly equal the mean lifetime mileage for the population of all new tires produced. The reason is simply that the sample contains only a portion of the population and cannot be expected to perfectly replicate the population. Some error, or deviation of the sample from the population, is to be expected. With proper sampling methods, the sample results will provide "good" estimates of the population parameters. But how good can we expect the sample results to be? Fortunately, statistical procedures are available for answering this question.

Let us define some of the terms used in sampling. The **sampled population** is the population from which the sample is drawn, and a **frame** is a list of the elements from which the sample will be selected. In the first example, the sampled population is all registered voters in Texas, and the frame is a list of all the registered voters. Because the number of registered voters in Texas is a finite number, the first example is an illustration of sampling from a finite population.

The sampled population for the tire mileage example is more difficult to define because the sample of 120 tires was obtained from a production process at a particular point in time. We can think of the sampled population as the conceptual population of all the tires that could have been made by the production process at that particular point in time. In this sense, the sampled population is considered infinite, making it impossible to construct a frame from which to draw the sample.

In this chapter, we show how simple random sampling can be used to select a sample from a finite population and we describe how a random sample can be taken from an infinite population that is generated by an ongoing process. We then discuss how data obtained from a sample can be used to compute estimates of a population mean, a population standard deviation, and a population proportion. In addition, we introduce the important concept of a sampling distribution. As we will show, knowledge of the appropriate sampling distribution enables us to make statements about how close the sample estimates are to the corresponding population parameters, to compute the margins of error associated with these sample estimates, and to construct and interpret interval estimates. We then discuss how to formulate hypotheses and how to use sample data to conduct tests of a population means and a population proportion.

6.1 Selecting a Sample

The director of personnel for Electronics Associates, Inc. (EAI) has been assigned the task of developing a profile of the company's 2,500 employees. The characteristics to be identified include the mean annual salary for the employees and the proportion of employees having completed the company's management training program.

DATA*file*

EAI

Using the 2,500 employees as the population for this study, we can find the annual salary and the training program status for each individual by referring to the firm's personnel records. The data set containing this information for all 2,500 employees in the population is in the file *EAI*.

A measurable factor that defines a characteristic of a population, process, or system is called a **parameter**. For EAI, the population mean annual salary μ, the population standard deviation of annual salaries σ, and the population proportion p of employees who completed the training program are of interest to us. Using the EAI data, we compute the population mean and the population standard deviation for the annual salary data.

Chapter 2 discusses the computation of the mean and standard deviation of a population.

$$\text{Population mean:} \quad \mu = \$71,800$$

$$\text{Population standard deviation:} \quad \sigma = \$4,000$$

The data for the training program status show that 1,500 of the 2,500 employees completed the training program. Letting p denote the proportion of the population that completed the training program, we see that $p = 1,500/2,500 = 0.60$. The population mean annual salary ($\mu = \$71,800$), the population standard deviation of annual salary ($\sigma = \$4,000$), and the population proportion that completed the training program ($p = 0.60$) are parameters of the population of EAI employees.

Often the cost of collecting information from a sample is substantially less than the cost of taking a census. Especially when personal interviews must be conducted to collect the information.

Now suppose that the necessary information on all the EAI employees was not readily available in the company's database. The question we must consider is how the firm's director of personnel can obtain estimates of the population parameters by using a sample of employees rather than all 2,500 employees in the population. Suppose that a sample of 30 employees will be used. Clearly, the time and the cost of developing a profile would be substantially less for 30 employees than for the entire population. If the personnel director could be assured that a sample of 30 employees would provide adequate information about the population of 2,500 employees, working with a sample would be preferable to working with the entire population. Let us explore the possibility of using a sample for the EAI study by first considering how we can identify a sample of 30 employees.

Sampling from a Finite Population

Statisticians recommend selecting a probability sample when sampling from a finite population because a probability sample allows you to make valid statistical inferences about the population. The simplest type of probability sample is one in which each sample of size n has the same probability of being selected. It is called a simple random sample. A simple random sample of size n from a finite population of size N is defined as follows.

SIMPLE RANDOM SAMPLE (FINITE POPULATION)

A **simple random sample** of size n from a finite population of size N is a sample selected such that each possible sample of size n has the same probability of being selected.

The random numbers generated using Excel's RAND function follow a uniform probability distribution between 0 and 1.

Procedures used to select a simple random sample from a finite population are based on the use of random numbers. We can use Excel's RAND function to generate a random number between 0 and 1 by entering the formula $=RAND()$ into any cell in a worksheet. The number generated is called a random number because the mathematical procedure used by the RAND function guarantees that every number between 0 and 1 has the same probability of being selected. Let us see how these random numbers can be used to select a simple random sample.

Our procedure for selecting a simple random sample of size n from a population of size N involves two steps.

Excel's Sort procedure is especially useful for identifying the n elements assigned the n smallest random numbers.

Step 1. Assign a random number to each element of the population.
Step 2. Select the n elements corresponding to the n smallest random numbers.

Because each set of n elements in the population has the same probability of being assigned the n smallest random numbers, each set of n elements has the same probability of being selected for the sample. If we select the sample using this two-step procedure, every sample of size n has the same probability of being selected; thus, the sample selected satisfies the definition of a simple random sample.

Let us consider the process of selecting a simple random sample of 30 EAI employees from the population of 2,500. We begin by generating 2,500 random numbers, one for each employee in the population. Then we select 30 employees corresponding to the 30 smallest random numbers as our sample. Refer to Figure 6.1 as we describe the steps involved.

Step 1. In cell D1, enter the text *Random Numbers*
Step 2. In cells D2:D2501, enter the formula *=RAND()*
Step 3. Select the cell range D2:D2501
Step 4. In the **Home** tab in the Ribbon:

The random numbers generated by executing these steps will vary; therefore, results will not match Figure 6.1.

   Click **Copy** in the **Clipboard** group
   Click the arrow below **Paste** in the **Clipboard** group. When the **Paste** window appears, click **Values** in the **Paste Values** area
   Press the **Esc** key
Step 5. Select cells A1:D2501
Step 6. In the **Data** tab on the Ribbon, click **Sort** in the **Sort & Filter** group
Step 7. When the **Sort** dialog box appears:
   Select the check box for **My data has headers**
   In the first **Sort by** dropdown menu, select **Random Numbers**
   Click **OK**

After completing these steps we obtain a worksheet like the one shown on the right in Figure 6.1. The employees listed in rows 2–31 are the ones corresponding to the smallest 30 random numbers that were generated. Hence, this group of 30 employees is a simple random sample. Note that the random numbers shown on the right in Figure 6.1 are in ascending order, and that the employees are not in their original order. For instance, employee 812 in the population is associated with the smallest random number and is the first element in the sample, and employee 13 in the population (see row 14 of the worksheet on the left) has been included as the 22nd observation in the sample (row 23 of the worksheet on the right).

Sampling from an Infinite Population

Sometimes we want to select a sample from a population, but the population is infinitely large or the elements of the population are being generated by an ongoing process for which there is no limit on the number of elements that can be generated. Thus, it is not possible to develop a list of all the elements in the population. This is considered the infinite population case. With an infinite population, we cannot select a simple random sample because we cannot construct a frame consisting of all the elements. In the infinite population case, statisticians recommend selecting what is called a random sample.

RANDOM SAMPLE (INFINITE POPULATION)

A **random sample** of size n from an infinite population is a sample selected such that the following conditions are satisfied.

1. Each element selected comes from the same population.
2. Each element is selected independently.

FIGURE 6.1	Using Excel to Select a Simple Random Sample

	A	B	C	D	E	F	G
1	Employee	Annual Salary	Training Program	Random Numbers			
2	1	75769.50	No	0.613872			
3	2	70823.00	Yes	0.473204			
4	3	68408.20	No	0.549011			
5	4	69787.50	No	0.047482			
6	5	72801.60	Yes	0.531085			
7	6	71767.70	No	0.994296			
8	7	78346.60	Yes	0.189065			
9	8	66670.20	No	0.020714			
10	9	70246.80	Yes	0.647318			
11	10	71255.00	No	0.524341			
12	11	72546.60	No	0.764998			
13	12	69512.50	Yes	0.255244			
14	13	71753.00	No	0.010923			
15	14	73547.10	No	0.238003			
16	15	68052.20	No	0.635675			
17	16	64652.50	Yes	0.177294			
18	17	71764.90	Yes	0.415097			
19	18	65187.80	Yes	0.883440			
20	19	69867.50	Yes	0.476824			
21	20	73706.30	Yes	0.101065			
22	21	72039.50	Yes	0.775323			
23	22	72973.60	No	0.011729			
24	23	73372.50	No	0.762026			
25	24	74592.00	Yes	0.066344			
26	25	75738.10	Yes	0.776766			
27	26	72975.10	Yes	0.828493			
28	27	72386.20	Yes	0.841532			
29	28	71051.60	Yes	0.899427			
30	29	72095.60	Yes	0.486284			
31	30	64956.50	No	0.264628			
32							

The formula in cells D2:D2501 is = RAND().

Note: Rows 32–2501 are not shown.

	A	B	C	D
1	Employee	Annual Salary	Training Program	Random Numbers
2	812	69094.30	Yes	0.000193
3	1411	73263.90	Yes	0.000484
4	1795	69643.50	Yes	0.002641
5	2095	69894.90	Yes	0.002763
6	1235	67621.60	No	0.002940
7	744	75924.00	Yes	0.002977
8	470	69092.30	Yes	0.003182
9	1606	71404.40	Yes	0.003448
10	1744	70957.70	Yes	0.004203
11	179	75109.70	Yes	0.005293
12	1387	65922.60	Yes	0.005709
13	1782	77268.40	No	0.005729
14	1006	75688.80	Yes	0.005796
15	278	71564.70	No	0.005966
16	1850	76188.20	No	0.006250
17	844	71766.00	Yes	0.006708
18	2028	72541.30	No	0.007767
19	1654	64980.00	Yes	0.008095
20	444	71932.60	Yes	0.009686
21	556	72973.00	Yes	0.009711
22	2449	65120.90	Yes	0.010595
23	13	71753.00	Yes	0.010923
24	2187	74391.80	No	0.011364
25	1633	70164.20	No	0.011603
26	22	72973.60	No	0.011729
27	1530	70241.30	No	0.013570
28	820	72793.90	No	0.013669
29	1258	70979.40	Yes	0.014042
30	2349	75860.90	Yes	0.014532
31	1698	77309.10	No	0.014539
32				

Care and judgment must be exercised in implementing the selection process for obtaining a random sample from an infinite population. Each case may require a different selection procedure. Let us consider two examples to see what we mean by the conditions: (1) Each element selected comes from the same population, and (2) each element is selected independently.

A common quality-control application involves a production process for which there is no limit on the number of elements that can be produced. The conceptual population from which we are sampling is all the elements that could be produced (not just the ones that are produced) by the ongoing production process. Because we cannot develop a list of all the elements that could be produced, the population is considered infinite. To be more specific, let us consider a production line designed to fill boxes with breakfast cereal to a mean weight of 24 ounces per box. Samples of 12 boxes filled by this process are periodically selected by a quality-control inspector to determine if the process is operating properly or whether, perhaps, a machine malfunction has caused the process to begin underfilling or overfilling the boxes.

With a production operation such as this, the biggest concern in selecting a random sample is to make sure that condition 1, the sampled elements are selected from the same population, is satisfied. To ensure that this condition is satisfied, the boxes must be selected at approximately the same point in time. This way the inspector avoids the possibility of selecting some boxes when the process is operating properly and other boxes when the process is not operating properly and is underfilling or overfilling the boxes. With a production process such as this, the second condition, each element is selected independently, is satisfied by designing the production process so that each box of cereal is filled independently. With this assumption, the quality-control inspector need only worry about satisfying the same population condition.

As another example of selecting a random sample from an infinite population, consider the population of customers arriving at a fast-food restaurant. Suppose an employee is asked to select and interview a sample of customers in order to develop a profile of customers who visit the restaurant. The customer-arrival process is ongoing, and there is no way to obtain a list of all customers in the population. So, for practical purposes, the population for this ongoing process is considered infinite. As long as a sampling procedure is designed so that all the elements in the sample are customers of the restaurant and they are selected independently, a random sample will be obtained. In this case, the employee collecting the sample needs to select the sample from people who come into the restaurant and make a purchase to ensure that the same population condition is satisfied. If, for instance, the person selected for the sample is someone who came into the restaurant just to use the restroom, that person would not be a customer and the same population condition would be violated. So, as long as the interviewer selects the sample from people making a purchase at the restaurant, condition 1 is satisfied. Ensuring that the customers are selected independently can be more difficult.

The purpose of the second condition of the random sample selection procedure (each element is selected independently) is to prevent selection bias. In this case, selection bias would occur if the interviewer were free to select customers for the sample arbitrarily. The interviewer might feel more comfortable selecting customers in a particular age group and might avoid customers in other age groups. Selection bias would also occur if the interviewer selected a group of five customers who entered the restaurant together and asked all of them to participate in the sample. Such a group of customers would be likely to exhibit similar characteristics, which might provide misleading information about the population of customers. Selection bias such as this can be avoided by ensuring that the selection of a particular customer does not influence the selection of any other customer. In other words, the elements (customers) are selected independently.

McDonald's, a fast-food restaurant chain, implemented a random sampling procedure for this situation. The sampling procedure was based on the fact that some customers presented discount coupons. Whenever a customer presented a discount coupon, the next customer served was asked to complete a customer profile questionnaire. Because arriving customers presented discount coupons randomly and independently of other customers, this sampling procedure ensured that customers were selected independently. As a result, the sample satisfied the requirements of a random sample from an infinite population.

Situations involving sampling from an infinite population are usually associated with a process that operates over time. Examples include parts being manufactured on a production line, repeated experimental trials in a laboratory, transactions occurring at a bank, telephone calls arriving at a technical support center, and customers entering a retail store. In each case, the situation may be viewed as a process that generates elements from an infinite population. As long as the sampled elements are selected from the same population and are selected independently, the sample is considered a random sample from an infinite population.

N O T E S   +   C O M M E N T S

1. In this section we have been careful to define two types of samples: a simple random sample from a finite population and a random sample from an infinite population. In the remainder of the text, we will generally refer to both of these as either a *random sample* or simply a *sample*. We will not make a distinction of the sample being a "simple" random sample unless it is necessary for the exercise or discussion.

2. Statisticians who specialize in sample surveys from finite populations use sampling methods that provide probability samples. With a probability sample, each possible sample has a known probability of selection and a random process is used to select the elements for the sample. Simple random sampling is one of these methods. We use the term *simple* in simple random sampling to clarify that this is the

probability sampling method that ensures that each sample of size n has the same probability of being selected.

3. The number of different simple random samples of size n that can be selected from a finite population of size N is:

$$\frac{N!}{n!(N-n)!}$$

In this formula, $N!$ and $n!$ are the factorial formulas. For the EAI problem with $N = 2,500$ and $n = 30$, this expression can be used to show that approximately 2.75×10^{69} different simple random samples of 30 EAI employees can be obtained.

4. In addition to simple random sampling, other probability sampling methods include the following:
    *   Stratified random sampling—a method in which the population is first divided into homogeneous subgroups or strata and then a simple random sample is taken from each stratum.
    *   Cluster sampling—a method in which the population is first divided into heterogeneous subgroups or clusters and then simple random samples are taken from some or all of the clusters.
    *   Systematic sampling—a method in which we sort the population based on an important characteristic,

randomly select one of the first k elements of the population, and then select every kth element from the population thereafter.

Calculation of sample statistics such as the sample mean $\bar{x}$, the sample standard deviation s, and the sample proportion $\bar{p}$ differ depending on which method of probability sampling is used. See specialized books on sampling such as *Elementary Survey Sampling* (2011) by Scheaffer, Mendenhall, and Ott for more information.

5. Nonprobability sampling methods include the following:
    *   Convenience sampling—a method in which sample elements are selected on the basis of accessibility.
    *   Judgment sampling—a method in which sample elements are selected based on the opinion of the person doing the study.

Although nonprobability samples have the advantages of relatively easy sample selection and data collection, no statistically justified procedure allows a probability analysis or inference about the quality of nonprobability sample results. Statistical methods designed for probability samples should not be applied to a nonprobability sample, and we should be cautious in interpreting the results when a nonprobability sample is used to make inferences about a population.

6.2 Point Estimation

Now that we have described how to select a simple random sample, let us return to the EAI problem. A simple random sample of 30 employees and the corresponding data on annual salary and management training program participation are as shown in Table 6.1. The notation x_1, x_2, and so on is used to denote the annual salary of the first employee in the sample, the annual salary of the second employee in the sample, and so on. Participation in the management training program is indicated by Yes in the management training program column.

To estimate the value of a population parameter, we compute a corresponding characteristic of the sample, referred to as a **sample statistic**. For example, to estimate the population mean μ and the population standard deviation σ for the annual salary of EAI employees, we use the data in Table 6.1 to calculate the corresponding sample statistics: the sample mean and the sample standard deviation s. The sample mean is

Chapter 2 discusses the computation of the mean and standard deviation of a sample.

$$\bar{x} = \frac{\Sigma x_i}{n} = \frac{2,154,420}{30} = \$71,814$$

and the sample standard deviation is

$$s = \sqrt{\frac{\Sigma(x_i - \bar{x})^2}{n-1}} = \sqrt{\frac{325,009,260}{29}} = \$3,384$$

To estimate p, the proportion of employees in the population who completed the management training program, we use the corresponding sample proportion $\bar{p}$. Let x denote the number of employees in the sample who completed the management training program. The data in Table 6.1 show that $x = 19$. Thus, with a sample size of $n = 30$, the sample proportion is

$$\bar{p} = \frac{x}{n} = \frac{19}{30} = 0.63$$

TABLE 6.1	Annual Salary and Training Program Status for a Simple Random Sample of 30 EAI Employees

Annual Salary ($)	Management Training Program	Annual Salary ($)	Management Training Program
$x_1 = 69{,}094.30$	Yes	$x_{16} = 71{,}766.00$	Yes
$x_2 = 73{,}263.90$	Yes	$x_{17} = 72{,}541.30$	No
$x_3 = 69{,}343.50$	Yes	$x_{18} = 64{,}980.00$	Yes
$x_4 = 69{,}894.90$	Yes	$x_{19} = 71{,}932.60$	Yes
$x_5 = 67{,}621.60$	No	$x_{20} = 72{,}973.00$	Yes
$x_6 = 75{,}924.00$	Yes	$x_{21} = 65{,}120.90$	Yes
$x_7 = 69{,}092.30$	Yes	$x_{22} = 71{,}753.00$	Yes
$x_8 = 71{,}404.40$	Yes	$x_{23} = 74{,}391.80$	No
$x_9 = 70{,}957.70$	Yes	$x_{24} = 70{,}164.20$	No
$x_{10} = 75{,}109.70$	Yes	$x_{25} = 72{,}973.60$	No
$x_{11} = 65{,}922.60$	Yes	$x_{26} = 70{,}241.30$	No
$x_{12} = 77{,}268.40$	No	$x_{27} = 72{,}793.90$	No
$x_{13} = 75{,}688.80$	Yes	$x_{28} = 70{,}979.40$	Yes
$x_{14} = 71{,}564.70$	No	$x_{29} = 75{,}860.90$	Yes
$x_{15} = 76{,}188.20$	No	$x_{30} = 77{,}309.10$	No

By making the preceding computations, we perform the statistical procedure called *point estimation*. We refer to the sample mean $\bar{x}$ as the **point estimator** of the population mean μ, the sample standard deviation s as the point estimator of the population standard deviation σ, and the sample proportion $\bar{p}$ as the point estimator of the population proportion p. The numerical value obtained for $\bar{x}$, s, or $\bar{p}$ is called the **point estimate**. Thus, for the simple random sample of 30 EAI employees shown in Table 6.1, $71{,}814 is the point estimate of μ, $3{,}348 is the point estimate of σ, and 0.63 is the point estimate of p. Table 6.2 summarizes the sample results and compares the point estimates to the actual values of the population parameters.

TABLE 6.2	Summary of Point Estimates Obtained from a Simple Random Sample of 30 EAI Employees

Population Parameter	Parameter Value	Point Estimator	Point Estimate
μ = Population mean annual salary	$71,800	$\bar{x}$ = Sample mean annual salary	$71,814
σ = Population standard deviation for annual salary	$4,000	s = Sample standard deviation for annual salary	$3,348
p = Population proportion completing the management training program	0.60	$\bar{p}$ = Sample proportion having completed the management training program	0.63

In Chapter 7, we will show how to construct an interval estimate in order to provide information about how close the point estimate is to the population parameter.

As is evident from Table 6.2, the point estimates differ somewhat from the values of corresponding population parameters. This difference is to be expected because a sample, and not a census of the entire population, is being used to develop the point estimates.

Practical Advice

The subject matter of most of the rest of the book is concerned with statistical inference, of which point estimation is a form. We use a sample statistic to make an inference about a population parameter. When making inferences about a population based on a sample, it is important to have a close correspondence between the sampled population and the target population. The **target population** is the population about which we want to make inferences, while the sampled population is the population from which the sample is actually taken. In this section, we have described the process of drawing a simple random sample from the population of EAI employees and making point estimates of characteristics of that same population. So the sampled population and the target population are identical, which is the desired situation. But in other cases, it is not as easy to obtain a close correspondence between the sampled and target populations.

Consider the case of an amusement park selecting a sample of its customers to learn about characteristics such as age and time spent at the park. Suppose all the sample elements were selected on a day when park attendance was restricted to employees of a large company. Then the sampled population would be composed of employees of that company and members of their families. If the target population we wanted to make inferences about were typical park customers over a typical summer, then we might encounter a significant difference between the sampled population and the target population. In such a case, we would question the validity of the point estimates being made. Park management would be in the best position to know whether a sample taken on a particular day was likely to be representative of the target population.

In summary, whenever a sample is used to make inferences about a population, we should make sure that the study is designed so that the sampled population and the target population are in close agreement. Good judgment is a necessary ingredient of sound statistical practice.

6.3 Sampling Distributions

In the preceding section we said that the sample mean $\bar{x}$ is the point estimator of the population mean μ, and the sample proportion $\bar{p}$ is the point estimator of the population proportion p. For the simple random sample of 30 EAI employees shown in Table 6.1, the point estimate of μ is $\bar{x} = \$71{,}814$ and the point estimate of p is $\bar{p} = 0.63$. Suppose we select another simple random sample of 30 EAI employees and obtain the following point estimates:

$$\text{Sample mean: } \bar{x} = \$72{,}670$$
$$\text{Sample proportion: } \bar{p} = 0.70$$

Note that different values of $\bar{x}$ and $\bar{p}$ were obtained. Indeed, a second simple random sample of 30 EAI employees cannot be expected to provide the same point estimates as the first sample.

Now, suppose we repeat the process of selecting a simple random sample of 30 EAI employees over and over again, each time computing the values of $\bar{x}$ and $\bar{p}$. Table 6.3 contains a portion of the results obtained for 500 simple random samples, and Table 6.4 shows the frequency and relative frequency distributions for the 500 values of $\bar{x}$. Figure 6.2 shows the relative frequency histogram for the $\bar{x}$ values.

A **random variable** is a quantity whose values are not known with certainty. Because the sample mean $\bar{x}$ is a quantity whose values are not known with certainty, the sample mean $\bar{x}$ is a random variable. As a result, just like other random variables, $\bar{x}$ has a mean or expected value, a standard deviation, and a probability distribution. Because the various

TABLE 6.3 Values of $\bar{x}$ and $\bar{p}$ from 500 Simple Random Samples of 30 EAI Employees

Sample Number	Sample Mean ($\bar{x}$)	Sample Proportion ($\bar{p}$)
1	71,814	0.63
2	72,670	0.70
3	71,780	0.67
4	71,588	0.53
.	.	.
.	.	.
.	.	.
500	71,752	0.50

TABLE 6.4 Frequency and Relative Frequency Distributions of $\bar{x}$ from 500 Simple Random Samples of 30 EAI Employees

Mean Annual Salary ($)	Frequency	Relative Frequency
69,500.00–69,999.99	2	0.004
70,000.00–70,499.99	16	0.032
70,500.00–70,999.99	52	0.104
71,000.00–71,499.99	101	0.202
71,500.00–71,999.99	133	0.266
72,000.00–72,499.99	110	0.220
72,500.00–72,999.99	54	0.108
73,000.00–73,499.99	26	0.052
73,500.00–73,999.99	6	0.012
Totals:	500	1.000

Chapter 2 introduces the concept of a random variable, and Chapter 4 discusses properties of random variables and their relationship to probability concepts.

possible values of $\bar{x}$ are the result of different simple random samples, the probability distribution of $\bar{x}$ is called the **sampling distribution** of $\bar{x}$. Knowledge of this sampling distribution and its properties will enable us to make probability statements about how close the sample mean $\bar{x}$ is to the population mean μ.

Let us return to Figure 6.2. We would need to enumerate every possible sample of 30 employees and compute each sample mean to completely determine the sampling distribution of $\bar{x}$. However, the histogram of 500 values of $\bar{x}$ gives an approximation of this sampling distribution. From the approximation we observe the bell-shaped appearance of the distribution. We note that the largest concentration of the $\bar{x}$ values and the mean of the 500 values of $\bar{x}$ is near the population mean $\mu = \$71,800$. We will describe the properties of the sampling distribution of $\bar{x}$ more fully in the next section.

The ability to understand the material in subsequent sections of this chapter depends heavily on the ability to understand and use the sampling distributions presented in this section.

The 500 values of the sample proportion $\bar{p}$ are summarized by the relative frequency histogram in Figure 6.3. As in the case of $\bar{x}$, $\bar{p}$ is a random variable. If every possible sample of size 30 were selected from the population and if a value of $\bar{p}$ were computed for each sample, the resulting probability distribution would be the sampling distribution of $\bar{p}$. The relative frequency histogram of the 500 sample values in Figure 6.3 provides a general idea of the appearance of the sampling distribution of $\bar{p}$.

In practice, we select only one simple random sample from the population. We repeated the sampling process 500 times in this section simply to illustrate that many different

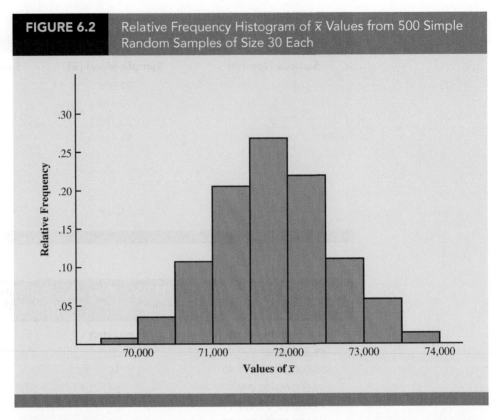

FIGURE 6.2   Relative Frequency Histogram of $\bar{x}$ Values from 500 Simple Random Samples of Size 30 Each

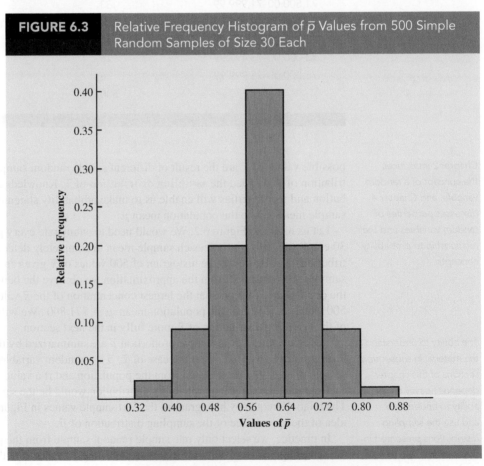

FIGURE 6.3   Relative Frequency Histogram of $\bar{p}$ Values from 500 Simple Random Samples of Size 30 Each

samples are possible and that the different samples generate a variety of values for the sample statistics $\bar{x}$ and $\bar{p}$. The probability distribution of any particular sample statistic is called the sampling distribution of the statistic. Next we discuss the characteristics of the sampling distributions of $\bar{x}$ and $\bar{p}$.

Sampling Distribution of $\bar{x}$

In the previous section we said that the sample mean $\bar{x}$ is a random variable and that its probability distribution is called the sampling distribution of $\bar{x}$.

> **SAMPLING DISTRIBUTION OF $\bar{x}$**
>
> The sampling distribution of $\bar{x}$ is the probability distribution of all possible values of the sample mean $\bar{x}$.

This section describes the properties of the sampling distribution of $\bar{x}$. Just as with other probability distributions we studied, the sampling distribution of $\bar{x}$ has an expected value or mean, a standard deviation, and a characteristic shape or form. Let us begin by considering the mean of all possible $\bar{x}$ values, which is referred to as the expected value of $\bar{x}$.

Expected Value of $\bar{x}$ In the EAI sampling problem we saw that different simple random samples result in a variety of values for the sample mean $\bar{x}$. Because many different values of the random variable $\bar{x}$ are possible, we are often interested in the mean of all possible values of $\bar{x}$ that can be generated by the various simple random samples. The mean of the $\bar{x}$ random variable is the expected value of $\bar{x}$. Let $E(\bar{x})$ represent the expected value of $\bar{x}$ and μ represent the mean of the population from which we are selecting a simple random sample. It can be shown that with simple random sampling, $E(\bar{x})$ and μ are equal.

The expected value of $\bar{x}$ equals the mean of the population from which the sample is selected.

> **EXPECTED VALUE OF $\bar{x}$**
>
> $$E(\bar{x}) = \mu \tag{6.1}$$
>
> where
>
> $$E(\bar{x}) = \text{the expected value of } \bar{x}$$
> $$\mu = \text{the population mean}$$

This result states that with simple random sampling, the expected value or mean of the sampling distribution of $\bar{x}$ is equal to the mean of the population. In Section 6.1 we saw that the mean annual salary for the population of EAI employees is $\mu = \$71,800$. Thus, according to equation (6.1), if we considered all possible samples of size n from the population of EAI employees, the mean of all the corresponding sample means for the EAI study would be equal to $71,800$, the population mean.

When the expected value of a point estimator equals the population parameter, we say the point estimator is **unbiased**. Thus, equation (6.1) states that $\bar{x}$ is an unbiased estimator of the population mean μ.

The term standard error is used in statistical inference to refer to the standard deviation of a point estimator.

Standard Deviation of $\bar{x}$ Let us define the standard deviation of the sampling distribution of $\bar{x}$. We will use the following notation:

$$\sigma_{\bar{x}} = \text{the standard deviation of } \bar{x}, \text{ or the } \textbf{standard error} \text{ of the mean}$$
$$\sigma = \text{the standard deviation of the population}$$
$$n = \text{the sample size}$$
$$N = \text{the population size}$$

It can be shown that the formula for the standard deviation of $\bar{x}$ depends on whether the population is finite or infinite. The two formulas for the standard deviation of $\bar{x}$ follow.

STANDARD DEVIATION OF $\bar{x}$

Finite Population	Infinite Population	

$$\sigma_{\bar{x}} = \sqrt{\frac{N-n}{N-1}}\left(\frac{\sigma}{\sqrt{n}}\right) \qquad\qquad \sigma_{\bar{x}} = \frac{\sigma}{\sqrt{n}} \qquad\qquad \textbf{(6.2)}$$

In comparing the two formulas in equation (6.2), we see that the factor $\sqrt{(N-n)/(N-1)}$ is required for the finite population case but not for the infinite population case. This factor is commonly referred to as the **finite population correction factor**. In many practical sampling situations, we find that the population involved, although finite, is large relative to the sample size. In such cases the finite population correction factor $\sqrt{(N-n)/(N-1)}$ is close to 1. As a result, the difference between the values of the standard deviation of $\bar{x}$ for the finite and infinite populations becomes negligible. Then, $\sigma_{\bar{x}} = \sigma/\sqrt{n}$ becomes a good approximation to the standard deviation of $\bar{x}$ even though the population is finite. In cases where $n/N > 0.05$, the finite population version of equation (6.2) should be used in the computation of $\sigma_{\bar{x}}$. Unless otherwise noted, throughout the text we will assume that the population size is large relative to the sample size, i.e., $n/N \leq 0.05$.

Observe from equation (6.2) that we need to know σ, the standard deviation of the population, in order to compute $\sigma_{\bar{x}}$. That is, the sample-to-sample variability in the point estimator $\bar{x}$, as measured by the standard error $\sigma_{\bar{x}}$, depends on the standard deviation of the population from which the sample is drawn. However, when we are sampling to estimate the population mean with $\bar{x}$, usually the population standard deviation is also unknown. Therefore, we need to estimate the standard deviation of $\bar{x}$ with $s_{\bar{x}}$ using the sample standard deviations as shown in equation (6.3).

ESTIMATED STANDARD DEVIATION OF $\bar{x}$

Finite Population	Infinite Population	

$$s_{\bar{x}} = \sqrt{\frac{N-n}{N-1}}\left(\frac{s}{\sqrt{n}}\right) \qquad\qquad s_{\bar{x}} = \left(\frac{s}{\sqrt{n}}\right) \qquad\qquad \textbf{(6.3)}$$

Let us now return to the EAI example and compute the estimated standard error (standard deviation) of the mean associated with simple random samples of 30 EAI employees. Recall from Table 6.2 that the standard deviation of the sample of 30 EAI employees is $s = 3,348$. In this case, the population is finite ($N = 2,500$), but because $n/N = 30/2,500 = 0.012 < 0.05$, we can ignore the finite population correction factor and compute the estimated standard error as

$$s_{\bar{x}} = \frac{s}{\sqrt{n}} = \frac{3,348}{\sqrt{30}} = 611.3$$

In this case, we happen to know that the standard deviation of the population is actually $\sigma = 4,000$, so the true standard error is

$$\sigma_{\bar{x}} = \frac{\sigma}{\sqrt{n}} = \frac{4,000}{\sqrt{30}} = 730.3$$

The difference between $s_{\bar{x}}$ and $\sigma_{\bar{x}}$ is due to **sampling error**, or the error that results from observing a sample of 30 rather than the entire population of 2,500.

Form of the Sampling Distribution of $\bar{x}$ The preceding results concerning the expected value and standard deviation for the sampling distribution of $\bar{x}$ are applicable for any population. The final step in identifying the characteristics of the sampling distribution of $\bar{x}$ is to determine the form or shape of the sampling distribution. We will consider two cases: (1) The population has a normal distribution; and (2) the population does not have a normal distribution.

Population Has a Normal Distribution In many situations it is reasonable to assume that the population from which we are selecting a random sample has a normal, or nearly normal, distribution. When the population has a normal distribution, the sampling distribution of $\bar{x}$ is normally distributed for any sample size.

Population Does Not Have a Normal Distribution When the population from which we are selecting a random sample does not have a normal distribution, the central limit theorem is helpful in identifying the shape of the sampling distribution of $\bar{x}$. A statement of the central limit theorem as it applies to the sampling distribution of x follows.

CENTRAL LIMIT THEOREM

In selecting random samples of size n from a population, the sampling distribution of the sample mean $\bar{x}$ can be approximated by a *normal distribution* as the sample size becomes large.

Figure 6.4 shows how the central limit theorem works for three different populations; each column refers to one of the populations. The top panel of the figure shows that none of the populations are normally distributed. Population I follows a uniform distribution. Population II is often called the rabbit-eared distribution. It is symmetric, but the more likely values fall in the tails of the distribution. Population III is shaped like the exponential distribution; it is skewed to the right.

The bottom three panels of Figure 6.4 show the shape of the sampling distribution for samples of size $n = 2$, $n = 5$, and $n = 30$. When the sample size is 2, we see that the shape of each sampling distribution is different from the shape of the corresponding population distribution. For samples of size 5, we see that the shapes of the sampling distributions for populations I and II begin to look similar to the shape of a normal distribution. Even though the shape of the sampling distribution for population III begins to look similar to the shape of a normal distribution, some skewness to the right is still present. Finally, for a sample size of 30, the shapes of each of the three sampling distributions are approximately normal.

From a practitioner's standpoint, we often want to know how large the sample size needs to be before the central limit theorem applies and we can assume that the shape of the sampling distribution is approximately normal. Statistical researchers have investigated this question by studying the sampling distribution of $\bar{x}$ for a variety of populations and a variety of sample sizes. General statistical practice is to assume that, for most applications, the sampling distribution of $\bar{x}$ can be approximated by a normal distribution whenever the sample size is 30 or more. In cases in which the population is highly skewed or outliers are present, sample sizes of 50 may be needed.

Sampling Distribution of $\bar{x}$ for the EAI Problem Let us return to the EAI problem where we previously showed that $E(\bar{x}) = \$71,800$ and $\sigma_{\bar{x}} = 730.3$. At this point, we do not have any information about the population distribution; it may or may not be normally distributed. If the population has a normal distribution, the sampling distribution of $\bar{x}$ is normally distributed. If the population does not have a normal distribution, the simple random sample of 30 employees and the central limit theorem enable us to conclude that the sampling distribution of $\bar{x}$ can be approximated by a normal distribution. In either case, we are comfortable proceeding with the conclusion that the sampling distribution of $\bar{x}$ can be described by the normal distribution shown in Figure 6.5. In other words, Figure 6.5 illustrates the distribution of the sample means corresponding to all possible sample sizes of 30 for the EAI study.

FIGURE 6.4   Illustration of the Central Limit Theorem for Three Populations

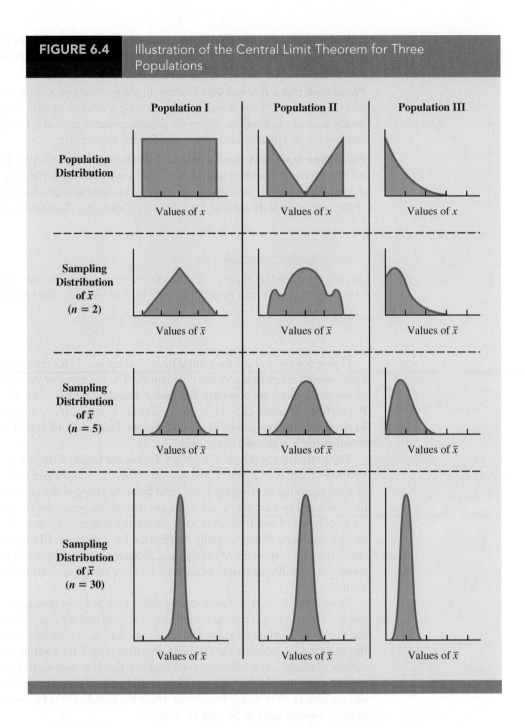

Relationship Between the Sample Size and the Sampling Distribution of $\bar{x}$ Suppose that in the EAI sampling problem we select a simple random sample of 100 EAI employees instead of the 30 originally considered. Intuitively, it would seem that because the larger sample size provides more data, the sample mean based on $n = 100$ would provide a better estimate of the population mean than the sample mean based on $n = 30$. To see how much better, let us consider the relationship between the sample size and the sampling distribution of $\bar{x}$.

First, note that $E(\bar{x}) = \mu$ regardless of the sample size. Thus, the mean of all possible values of $\bar{x}$ is equal to the population mean μ regardless of the sample size μ. However, note that the standard error of the mean, $\sigma_{\bar{x}} = \sigma/\sqrt{n}$, is related to the square root of the sample size. Whenever the sample size is increased, the standard error of the mean $\sigma_{\bar{x}}$

FIGURE 6.5 Sampling Distribution of $\bar{x}$ for the Mean Annual Salary of a Simple Random Sample of 30 EAI Employees

The sampling distribution in Figure 6.5 is a theoretical construct, as typically the population mean and the population standard deviation are not known. Instead, we must estimate these parameters with the sample mean and the sample standard deviation, respectively.

Sampling distribution of $\bar{x}$

$$\sigma_{\bar{x}} = \frac{\sigma}{\sqrt{n}} = \frac{4{,}000}{\sqrt{30}} = 730.3$$

71,800

$E(\bar{x}) = \mu$

decreases. With $n = 30$, the standard error of the mean for the EAI problem is 730.3. However, with the increase in the sample size to $n = 100$, the standard error of the mean is decreased to

$$\sigma_{\bar{x}} = \frac{\sigma}{\sqrt{n}} = \frac{4{,}000}{\sqrt{100}} = 400$$

The sampling distributions of $\bar{x}$ with $n = 30$ and $n = 100$ are shown in Figure 6.6. Because the sampling distribution with $n = 100$ has a smaller standard error, the values of $\bar{x}$ with $n = 100$ have less variation and tend to be closer to the population mean than the values of $\bar{x}$ with $n = 30$.

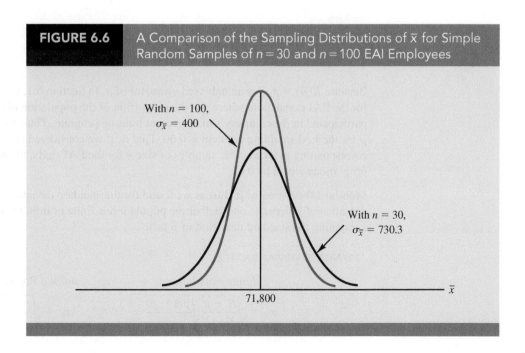

FIGURE 6.6 A Comparison of the Sampling Distributions of $\bar{x}$ for Simple Random Samples of $n = 30$ and $n = 100$ EAI Employees

With $n = 100$, $\sigma_{\bar{x}} = 400$

With $n = 30$, $\sigma_{\bar{x}} = 730.3$

71,800

The important point in this discussion is that as the sample size increases, the standard error of the mean decreases. As a result, a larger sample size will provide a higher probability that the sample mean falls within a specified distance of the population mean. The practical reason we are interested in the sampling distribution of $\bar{x}$ is that it can be used to provide information about how close the sample mean is to the population mean. The concepts of interval estimation and hypothesis testing discussed in Sections 6.4 and 6.5 rely on the properties of sampling distributions.

Sampling Distribution of $\bar{p}$

The sample proportion $\bar{p}$ is the point estimator of the population proportion p. The formula for computing the sample proportion is

$$\bar{p} = \frac{x}{n}$$

where

   x = the number of elements in the sample that possess the characteristic of interest
   n = sample size

As previously noted in this section, the sample proportion $\bar{p}$ is a random variable and its probability distribution is called the sampling distribution of $\bar{p}$.

SAMPLING DISTRIBUTION OF $\bar{p}$

The sampling distribution of $\bar{p}$ is the probability distribution of all possible values of the sample proportion $\bar{p}$.

To determine how close the sample proportion $\bar{p}$ is to the population proportion p, we need to understand the properties of the sampling distribution of $\bar{p}$: the expected value of $\bar{p}$, the standard deviation of $\bar{p}$, and the shape or form of the sampling distribution of $\bar{p}$.

Expected Value of $\bar{p}$ The expected value of $\bar{p}$, the mean of all possible values of $\bar{p}$, is equal to the population proportion p.

EXPECTED VALUE OF $\bar{p}$

$$E(\bar{p}) = p \tag{6.4}$$

where

   $E(\bar{p})$ = the expected value of $\bar{p}$
   p = the population proportion

Because $E(\bar{p}) = p$, $\bar{p}$ is an unbiased estimator of p. In Section 6.1, we noted that $p = 0.60$ for the EAI population, where p is the proportion of the population of employees who participated in the company's management training program. Thus, the expected value of $\bar{p}$ for the EAI sampling problem is 0.60. That is, if we considered the sample proportions corresponding to all possible samples of size n for the EAI study, the mean of these sample proportions would be 0.6.

Standard Deviation of $\bar{p}$ Just as we found for the standard deviation of $\bar{x}$, the standard deviation of $\bar{p}$ depends on whether the population is finite or infinite. The two formulas for computing the standard deviation of $\bar{p}$ follow.

STANDARD DEVIATION OF $\bar{p}$

Finite Population	*Infinite Population*	
$\sigma_{\bar{p}} = \sqrt{\dfrac{N-n}{N-1}}\sqrt{\dfrac{p(1-p)}{n}}$	$\sigma_{\bar{p}} = \sqrt{\dfrac{p(1-p)}{n}}$	(6.5)

Comparing the two formulas in equation (6.5), we see that the only difference is the use of the finite population correction factor $\sqrt{(N - n)/(N - 1)}$.

As was the case with the sample mean $\bar{x}$, the difference between the expressions for the finite population and the infinite population becomes negligible if the size of the finite population is large in comparison to the sample size. We follow the same rule of thumb that we recommended for the sample mean. That is, if the population is finite with $n/N \leq 0.05$, we will use $\sigma_{\bar{p}} = \sqrt{p(1 - p)/n}$. However, if the population is finite with $n/N > 0.05$, the finite population correction factor should be used. Again, unless specifically noted, throughout the text we will assume that the population size is large in relation to the sample size and thus the finite population correction factor is unnecessary.

Earlier in this section, we used the term *standard error of the mean* to refer to the standard deviation of $\bar{x}$. We stated that in general the term *standard error* refers to the standard deviation of a point estimator. Thus, for proportions we use *standard error of the proportion* to refer to the standard deviation of $\bar{p}$. From equation (6.5), we observe that the sample-to-sample variability in the point estimator $\bar{p}$, as measured by the standard error $\sigma_{\bar{p}}$, depends on the population proportion p. However, when we are sampling to compute $\bar{p}$, typically the population proportion is unknown. Therefore, we need to estimate the standard deviation of $\bar{p}$ with $s_{\bar{p}}$ using the sample proportion as shown in equation (6.6).

ESTIMATED STANDARD DEVIATION OF $\bar{p}$

Finite Population	Infinite Population	
$s_{\bar{p}} = \sqrt{\dfrac{N - n}{N - 1}} \sqrt{\dfrac{\bar{p}(1 - \bar{p})}{n}}$	$s_{\bar{p}} = \sqrt{\dfrac{\bar{p}(1 - \bar{p})}{n}}$	**(6.6)**

Let us now return to the EAI example and compute the estimated standard error (standard deviation) of the proportion associated with simple random samples of 30 EAI employees. Recall from Table 6.2 that the sample proportion of EAI employees who completed the management training program is $\bar{p} = 0.63$. Because $n/N = 30/2{,}500 = 0.012 < 0.05$, we can ignore the finite population correction factor and compute the estimated standard error as

$$s_{\bar{p}} = \sqrt{\frac{\bar{p}(1 - \bar{p})}{n}} = \sqrt{\frac{0.63(1 - 0.63)}{30}} = 0.0881$$

In the EAI example, we actually know that the population proportion is $p = 0.6$, so we know that the true standard error is

$$\sigma_{\bar{p}} = \sqrt{\frac{p(1 - p)}{n}} = \sqrt{\frac{0.6(1 - 0.6)}{30}} = 0.0894$$

The difference between $s_{\bar{p}}$ and $\sigma_{\bar{p}}$ is due to sampling error.

Form of the Sampling Distribution of $\bar{p}$ Now that we know the mean and standard deviation of the sampling distribution of $\bar{p}$, the final step is to determine the form or shape of the sampling distribution. The sample proportion is $\bar{p} = x/n$. For a simple random sample from a large population, x is a binomial random variable indicating the number of elements in the sample with the characteristic of interest. Because n is a constant, the probability of x/n is the same as the binomial probability of x, which means that the sampling distribution of $\bar{p}$ is also a discrete probability distribution and that the probability for each value of x/n the same as the binomial probability of the corresponding value of x.

Statisticians have shown that a binomial distribution can be approximated by a normal distribution whenever the sample size is large enough to satisfy the following two conditions:

$$np \geq 5 \quad \text{and} \quad n(1 - p) \geq 5$$

Because the population proportion p is typically unknown in a study, the test to see whether the sampling distribution of $\bar{p}$ can be approximated by a normal distribution is often based on the sample proportion, $n\bar{p} \geq 5$ and $n(1 - \bar{p}) \geq 5$.

Assuming that these two conditions are satisfied, the probability distribution of x in the sample proportion, $\bar{p} = x/n$, can be approximated by a normal distribution. And because n is a constant, the sampling distribution of $\bar{p}$ can also be approximated by a normal distribution. This approximation is stated as follows:

The sampling distribution of $\bar{p}$ can be approximated by a normal distribution whenever $np \geq 5$ and $n(1 - p) \geq 5$.

In practical applications, when an estimate of a population proportion is desired, we find that sample sizes are almost always large enough to permit the use of a normal approximation for the sampling distribution of $\bar{p}$.

Recall that for the EAI sampling problem we know that a sample proportion of employees who participated in the training program is $\bar{p} = 0.63$. With a simple random sample of size 30, we have $n\bar{p} = 30(0.63) = 18.9$ and $n(1 - \bar{p}) = 30(0.37) = 11.1$. Thus, the sampling distribution of $\bar{p}$ can be approximated by a normal distribution shown in Figure 6.7.

Relationship Between Sample Size and the Sampling Distribution of $\bar{p}$ Suppose that in the EAI sampling problem we select a simple random sample of 100 EAI employees instead of the 30 originally considered. Intuitively, it would seem that because the larger sample size provides more data, the sample proportion based on $n = 100$ would provide a better estimate of the population proportion than the sample proportion based on $n = 30$. To see how much better, recall that the standard error of the proportion is 0.0894 when the sample size is $n = 30$. If we increase the sample size to $n = 100$, the standard error of the proportion becomes

$$\sigma_{\bar{p}} = \sqrt{\frac{0.60(1 - 0.60)}{100}} = 0.0490$$

As we observed with the standard deviation of the sampling distribution of $\bar{x}$, increasing the sample size decreases the sample-to-sample variability of the sample proportion. As a result, a larger sample size will provide a higher probability that the sample proportion falls within a specified distance of the population proportion. The practical reason we are

The sampling distribution in Figure 6.7 is a theoretical construct, as typically the population proportion is not known. Instead, we must estimate it with the sample proportion.

FIGURE 6.7   Sampling Distribution of $\bar{p}$ for the Proportion of EAI Employees Who Participated in the Management Training Program

interested in the sampling distribution of $\bar{p}$ is that it can be used to provide information about how close the sample proportion is to the population proportion. The concepts of interval estimation and hypothesis testing discussed in Sections 6.4 and 6.5 rely on the properties of sampling distributions.

6.4 Interval Estimation

In Section 6.2, we stated that a point estimator is a sample statistic used to estimate a population parameter. For instance, the sample mean $\bar{x}$ is a point estimator of the population mean μ and the sample proportion $\bar{p}$ is a point estimator of the population proportion p. Because a point estimator cannot be expected to provide the exact value of the population parameter, **interval estimation** is frequently used to generate an estimate of the value of a population parameter. An **interval estimate** is often computed by adding and subtracting a value, called the **margin of error**, to the point estimate:

$$\text{Point estimate} \pm \text{Margin of error}$$

The purpose of an interval estimate is to provide information about how close the point estimate, provided by the sample, is to the value of the population parameter. In this section, we show how to compute interval estimates of a population mean μ and a population proportion p.

Interval Estimation of the Population Mean

The general form of an interval estimate of a population mean is

$$\bar{x} \pm \text{Margin of error}$$

The sampling distribution of $\bar{x}$ plays a key role in computing this interval estimate.

In Section 6.3 we showed that the sampling distribution of $\bar{x}$ has a mean equal to the population mean ($E(\bar{x}) = \mu$) and a standard deviation equal to the population standard deviation divided by the square root of the sample size ($\sigma_{\bar{x}} = \sigma/\sqrt{n}$). We also showed that for a sufficiently large sample or for a sample taken from a normally distributed population, the sampling distribution of $\bar{x}$ follows a normal distribution. These results for samples of 30 EAI employees are illustrated in Figure 6.5. Because the sampling distribution of $\bar{x}$ shows how values of $\bar{x}$ are distributed around the population mean μ, the sampling distribution of $\bar{x}$ provides information about the possible differences between $\bar{x}$ and μ.

For any normally distributed random variable, 90% of the values lie within 1.645 standard deviations of the mean, 95% of the values lie within 1.960 standard deviations of the mean, and 99% of the values lie within 2.576 standard deviations of the mean. Thus, when the sampling distribution of $\bar{x}$ is normal, 90% of all values of $\bar{x}$ must be within $\pm 1.645\sigma_{\bar{x}}$ of the mean μ, 95% of all values of $\bar{x}$ must be within $\pm 1.96\sigma_{\bar{x}}$ of the mean μ, and 99% of all values of $\bar{x}$ must be within $\pm 2.576\sigma_{\bar{x}}$ of the mean μ.

Figure 6.8 shows what we would expect for values of sample means for 10 independent random samples when the sampling distribution of $\bar{x}$ is normal. Because 90% of all values of $\bar{x}$ are within $\pm 1.645\sigma_{\bar{x}}$ of the mean μ, we expect 9 of the values of $\bar{x}$ for these 10 samples to be within $\pm 1.645\sigma_{\bar{x}}$ of the mean μ. If we repeat this process of collecting 10 samples, our results may not include 9 sample means with values that are within $1.645\sigma_{\bar{x}}$ of the mean μ, but on average, the values of $\bar{x}$ will be within $\pm 1.645\sigma_{\bar{x}}$ of the mean μ for 9 of every 10 samples.

We now want to use what we know about the sampling distribution of $\bar{x}$ to develop an interval estimate of the population mean μ. However, when developing an interval estimate of a population mean μ, we generally do not know the population standard deviation σ, and therefore, we do not know the standard error of $\bar{x}$, $\sigma_{\bar{x}} = \sigma/\sqrt{n}$. In this case, we must use the same sample data to estimate both μ and σ, so we use $s_{\bar{x}} = s/\sqrt{n}$ to estimate the standard error of $\bar{x}$. When we estimate $\sigma_{\bar{x}}$ with $s_{\bar{x}}$, we introduce an additional source of uncertainty about the distribution of values of $\bar{x}$. If the sampling distribution of $\bar{x}$ follows a

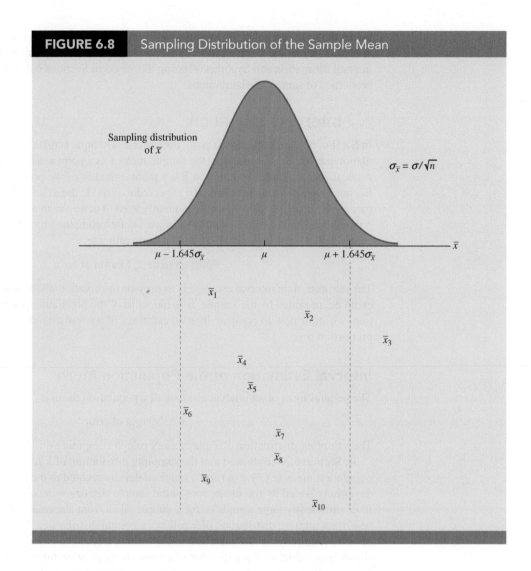

FIGURE 6.8 Sampling Distribution of the Sample Mean

Sampling distribution of $\bar{x}$

$\sigma_{\bar{x}} = \sigma/\sqrt{n}$

$\mu - 1.645\sigma_{\bar{x}}$ μ $\mu + 1.645\sigma_{\bar{x}}$ $\bar{x}$

$\bar{x}_1$
$\bar{x}_2$
$\bar{x}_3$
$\bar{x}_4$
$\bar{x}_5$
$\bar{x}_6$
$\bar{x}_7$
$\bar{x}_8$
$\bar{x}_9$
$\bar{x}_{10}$

normal distribution, we address this additional source of uncertainty by using a probability distribution known as the *t* **distribution**.

The *t* distribution is a family of similar probability distributions; the shape of each specific *t* distribution depends on a parameter referred to as the **degrees of freedom**. The *t* distribution with 1 degree of freedom is unique, as is the *t* distribution with 2 degrees of freedom, the *t* distribution with 3 degrees of freedom, and so on. These *t* distributions are similar in shape to the **standard normal distribution** but are wider; this reflects the additional uncertainty that results from using $s_{\bar{x}}$ to estimate $\sigma_{\bar{x}}$. As the degrees of freedom increase, the difference between $s_{\bar{x}}$ and $\sigma_{\bar{x}}$ decreases and the *t* distribution narrows. Furthermore, because the area under any distribution curve is fixed at 1.0, a narrower *t* distribution will have a higher peak. Thus, as the degrees of freedom increase, the *t* distribution narrows, its peak becomes higher, and it becomes more similar to the standard normal distribution. We can see this in Figure 6.9, which shows *t* distributions with 10 and 20 degrees of freedom as well as the standard normal probability distribution. Note that as with the standard normal distribution, the mean of the *t* distribution is zero.

To use the *t* distribution to compute the margin of error for the EAI example, we consider the *t* distribution with $n - 1 = 30 - 1 = 29$ degrees of freedom. Figure 6.10 shows that for a *t*-distributed random variable with 29 degrees of freedom, 90% of the values are within ± 1.699 standard deviations of the mean and 10% of the values are more than

The standard normal distribution is a normal distribution with a mean of zero and a standard deviation of one. Chapter 5 contains a discussion of the normal distribution and the special case of the standard normal distribution.

Although the mathematical development of the t distribution is based on the assumption that the population from which we are sampling is normally distributed, research shows that the t distribution can be successfully applied in many situations in which the population deviates substantially from a normal distribution.

FIGURE 6.9 Comparison of the Standard Normal Distribution with *t* Distributions with 10 and 20 Degrees of Freedom

FIGURE 6.10 *t* Distribution with 29 Degrees of Freedom

± 1.699 standard deviations away from the mean. Thus, 5% of the values are more than 1.699 standard deviations below the mean and 5% of the values are more than 1.699 standard deviations above the mean. This leads us to use $t_{0.05}$ to denote the value of t for which the area in the upper tail of a t distribution is 0.05. For a t distribution with 29 degrees of freedom, $t_{0.05} = 1.699$.

To see how the difference between the t distribution and the standard normal distribution decreases as the degrees of freedom increase, use Excel's T.INV.2T function to compute $t_{0.05}$ for increasingly larger degrees of freedom (n − 1) and watch the value of $t_{0.05}$ approach 1.645.

We can use Excel's T.INV.2T function to find the value from a t distribution such that a given percentage of the distribution is included in the interval $\pm t$ for any degrees of freedom. For example, suppose again that we want to find the value of t from the t distribution with 29 degrees of freedom such that 90% of the t distribution is included in the interval $-t$ to $+t$. Excel's T.INV.2T function has two inputs: (1) 1 − the proportion of the t distribution that will fall between $-t$ and $+t$, and (2) the degrees of freedom (which in this case is equal to the sample size − 1). For our example, we would enter the formula $= T.INV.2T(1 - 0.90, 30 - 1)$, which computes the value of 1.699. This confirms the data shown in Figure 6.10; for the t distribution with 29 degrees of freedom, $t_{0.05} = 1.699$ and 90% of all values for the t distribution with 29 degrees of freedom will lie between -1.699 and 1.699.

At the beginning of this section, we stated that the general form of an interval estimate of the population mean μ is $\bar{x} \pm$ margin of error. To provide an interpretation for this interval estimate, let us consider the values of $\bar{x}$ that might be obtained if we took 10 independent simple random samples of 30 EAI employees. The first sample might have the mean $\bar{x}_1$ and standard deviation s_1. Figure 6.11 shows that the interval formed by subtracting $1.699 s_1/\sqrt{30}$ from $\bar{x}_1$ and adding $1.699 s_1/\sqrt{30}$ to $\bar{x}_1$ includes the population mean μ. Now consider what happens if the second sample has the mean $\bar{x}_2$ and standard deviation s_2. Although this sample mean differs from the first sample mean, we see in Figure 6.11 that the interval formed by subtracting $1.699 s_2/\sqrt{30}$ from $\bar{x}_2$ and adding $1.699 s_2/\sqrt{30}$ to $\bar{x}_2$ also includes the population mean μ. However, consider the third sample, which has the mean $\bar{x}_3$ and standard deviation s_3. As we see in Figure 6.11, the interval formed by subtracting $1.699 s_3/\sqrt{30}$ from $\bar{x}_3$ and adding $1.699 s_3/\sqrt{30}$ to $\bar{x}_3$ does not include the population mean μ. Because we are using $t_{0.05} = 1.699$ to form this interval, we expect that

FIGURE 6.11 Intervals Formed Around Sample Means from 10 Independent Random Samples

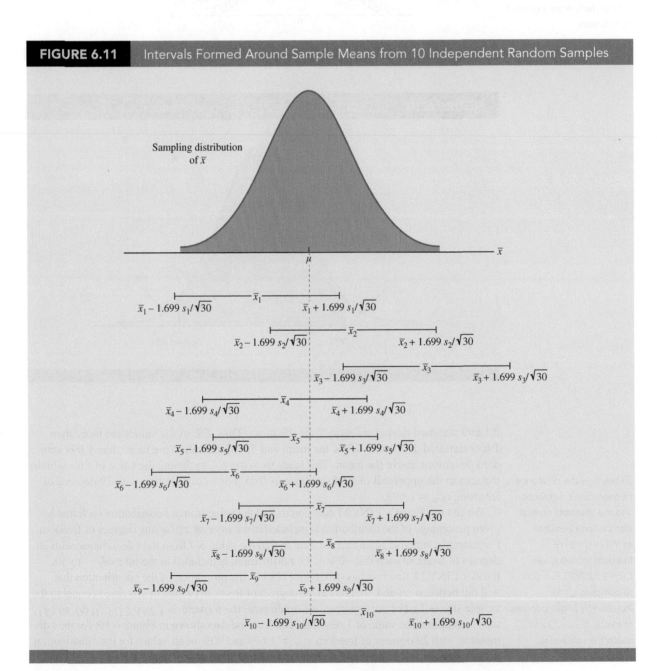

90% of the intervals for our samples will include the population mean μ, and we see in Figure 6.11 that the results for our 10 samples of 30 EAI employees are what we would expect; the intervals for 9 of the 10 samples of $n = 30$ observations in this example include the mean μ. However, it is important to note that if we repeat this process of collecting 10 samples of $n = 30$ EAI employees, we may find that fewer than 9 of the resulting intervals $\bar{x} \pm 1.699 s_{\bar{x}}$ include the mean μ or all 10 of the resulting intervals $\bar{x} \pm 1.699 s_{\bar{x}}$ include the mean μ. However, on average, the resulting intervals $\bar{x} \pm 1.699 s_{\bar{x}}$ for 9 of 10 samples of $n = 30$ observations will include the mean μ.

Now recall that the sample of $n = 30$ EAI employees from Section 6.2 had a sample mean of salary of $\bar{x} = \$71,814$ and sample standard deviation of $s = \$3,340$. Using $\bar{x} \pm 1.699(3,340/\sqrt{30})$ to construct the interval estimate, we obtain $71,814 \pm 1,036$. Thus, the specific interval estimate of μ based on this specific sample is \$70,778 to \$72,850. Because approximately 90% of all the intervals constructed using $\bar{x} \pm 1.699(s/\sqrt{30})$ will contain the population mean, we say that we are approximately 90% confident that the interval \$70,778 to \$72,850 includes the population mean μ. We also say that this interval has been established at the 90% **confidence level**. The value of 0.90 is referred to as the **confidence coefficient**, and the interval \$70,564 to \$73,064 is called the 90% **confidence interval**.

Another term sometimes associated with an interval estimate is the **level of significance**. The level of significance associated with an interval estimate is denoted by the Greek letter α. The level of significance and the confidence coefficient are related as follows:

$$\alpha = \text{level of significance} = 1 - \text{confidence coefficient}$$

The level of significance is the probability that the interval estimation procedure will generate an interval that does not contain μ (such as the third sample in Figure 6.11). For example, the level of significance corresponding to a 0.90 confidence coefficient is $\alpha = 1 - 0.90 = 0.10$.

In general, we use the notation $t_{\alpha/2}$ to represent the value such that there is an area of $\alpha/2$ in the upper tail of the t distribution (see Figure 6.12). If the sampling distribution of $\bar{x}$ is normal, the margin of error for an interval estimate of a population mean μ is

$$t_{\alpha/2} s_{\bar{x}} = t_{\alpha/2} \frac{s}{\sqrt{n}}$$

So if the sampling distribution of $\bar{x}$ is normal, we find the interval estimate of the mean μ by subtracting this margin of error from the sample mean $\bar{x}$ and adding this margin of error to the sample mean $\bar{x}$. Using the notation we have developed, equation (6.7) can be used to find the confidence interval or interval estimate of the population mean μ.

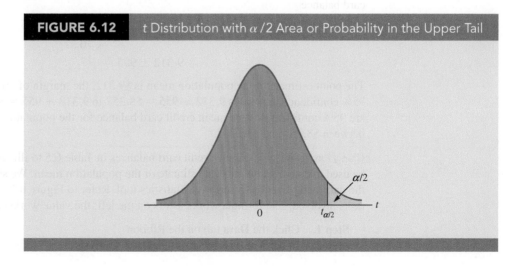

FIGURE 6.12 t Distribution with $\alpha/2$ Area or Probability in the Upper Tail

INTERVAL ESTIMATE OF A POPULATION MEAN

$$\bar{x} \pm t_{\alpha/2}\frac{s}{\sqrt{n}}, \tag{6.7}$$

where s is the sample standard deviation, α is the level of significance, and $t_{\alpha/2}$ is the t value providing an area of $\alpha/2$ in the upper tail of the t distribution with $n - 1$ degrees of freedom.

If we want to find a 95% confidence interval for the mean μ in the EAI example, we again recognize that the degrees of freedom are $30 - 1 = 29$ and then use Excel's T.INV.2T function to find $t_{0.025} = 2.045$. We have seen that $s_{\bar{x}} = 611.3$ in the EAI example, so the margin of error at the 95% level of confidence is $t_{0.025}s_{\bar{x}} = \pm2.045(611.3) = 1,250$. We also know that $\bar{x} = 71,814$ for the EAI example, so the 95% confidence interval is $71,814 \pm 1,250$, or \$70,564 to \$73,064.

It is important to note that a 95% confidence interval does not have a 95% probability of containing the population mean μ. Once constructed, a confidence interval will either contain the population parameter (μ in this EAI example) or not contain the population parameter. If we take several independent samples of the same size from our population and construct a 95% confidence interval for each of these samples, we would expect 95% of these confidence intervals to contain the mean μ. Our 95% confidence interval for the EAI example, \$70,564 to \$73,064, does indeed contain the population mean \$71,800; however, if we took many independent samples of 30 EAI employees and developed a 95% confidence interval for each, we would expect that 5% of these confidence intervals would not include the population mean \$71,800.

To further illustrate the interval estimation procedure, we will consider a study designed to estimate the mean credit card debt for the population of U.S. households. A sample of $n = 70$ households provided the credit card balances shown in Table 6.5. For this situation, no previous estimate of the population standard deviation σ is available. Thus, the sample data must be used to estimate both the population mean and the population standard deviation. Using the data in Table 6.5, we compute the sample mean $\bar{x} = \$9,312$ and the sample standard deviation $s = \$4,007$.

We can use Excel's T.INV.2T function to compute the value of $t_{\alpha/2}$ to use in finding this confidence interval. With a 95% confidence level and $n - 1 = 69$ degrees of freedom, we have that T.INV.2T$(1 - 0.95, 69) = 1.995$, so $t_{\alpha/2} = t_{(1-0.95)/2} = t_{0.025} = 1.995$ for this confidence interval.

We use equation (6.7) to compute an interval estimate of the population mean credit card balance.

$$9,312 \pm 1.995\frac{4,007}{\sqrt{70}}$$

$$9,312 \pm 995$$

The point estimate of the population mean is \$9,312, the margin of error is \$955, and the 95% confidence interval is $9,312 - 955 = \$8,357$ to $9,312 + 955 = \$10,267$. Thus, we are 95% confident that the mean credit card balance for the population of all households is between \$8,357 and \$10,267.

Using Excel We will use the credit card balances in Table 6.5 to illustrate how Excel can be used to construct an interval estimate of the population mean. We start by summarizing the data using Excel's Descriptive Statistics tool. Refer to Figure 6.13 as we describe the tasks involved. The formula worksheet is on the left; the value worksheet is on the right.

Step 1. Click the **Data** tab on the Ribbon
Step 2. In the **Analysis** group, click **Data Analysis**

TABLE 6.5	Credit Card Balances for a Sample of 70 Households				
9,430	14,661	7,159	9,071	9,691	11,032
7,535	12,195	8,137	3,603	11,448	6,525
4,078	10,544	9,467	16,804	8,279	5,239
5,604	13,659	12,595	13,479	5,649	6,195
5,179	7,061	7,917	14,044	11,298	12,584
4,416	6,245	11,346	6,817	4,353	15,415
10,676	13,021	12,806	6,845	3,467	15,917
1,627	9,719	4,972	10,493	6,191	12,591
10,112	2,200	11,356	615	12,851	9,743
6,567	10,746	7,117	13,627	5,337	10,324
13,627	12,744	9,465	12,557	8,372	
18,719	5,742	19,263	6,232	7,445	

DATA*file*

NewBalance

FIGURE 6.13	95% Confidence Interval for Credit Card Balances

	A	B	C	D
1	**NewBalance**		*NewBalance*	
2	9430			
3	7535		Mean	9312
4	4078		Standard Error	478.9281
5	5604		Median	9466
6	5179		Mode	13627
7	4416		Standard Deviation	4007
8	10676		Sample Variance	16056048
9	1627		Kurtosis	−0.2960
10	10112		Skewness	0.1879
11	6567		Range	18648
12	13627		Minimum	615
13	18719		Maximum	19263
14	14661		Sum	651840
15	12195		Count	70
16	10544		Confidence Level(95.0%)	955
17	13659			
18	7061		**Point Estimate**	=D3
19	6245		**Lower Limit**	=D18−D16
20	13021		**Upper Limit**	=D3+D16
70	9743			
71	10324			
72				

	A	B	C	D	E	F
1	**NewBalance**		*NewBalance*			
2	9430					
3	7535		Mean	9312		Point Estimate
4	4078		Standard Error	478.9281		
5	5604		Median	9466		
6	5179		Mode	13627		
7	4416		Standard Deviation	4007		
8	10676		Sample Variance	16056048		
9	1627		Kurtosis	−0.2960		
10	10112		Skewness	0.1879		
11	6567		Range	18648		
12	13627		Minimum	615		
13	18719		Maximum	19263		
14	14661		Sum	651840		
15	12195		Count	70		Margin of Error
16	10544		Confidence Level(95.0%)	955		
17	13659					
18	7061		**Point Estimate**	9312		
19	6245		**Lower Limit**	8357		
20	13021		**Upper Limit**	10267		
70	9743					
71	10324					
72						

Note: Rows 21–69 are hidden.

*If you can't find **Data Analysis** on the **Data** tab, you may need to install the **Analysis Toolpak** add-in (which is included with Excel).*

Step 3. When the **Data Analysis** dialog box appears, choose **Descriptive Statistics** from the list of Analysis Tools

Step 4. When the **Descriptive Statistics** dialog box appears:
  Enter *A1:A71* in the **Input Range** box
  Select **Grouped By Columns**
  Select **Labels in First Row**
  Select **Output Range:**
    Enter *C1* in the **Output Range** box
  Select **Summary Statistics**
  Select **Confidence Level for Mean**
    Enter *95* in the **Confidence Level for Mean** box
  Click **OK**

The margin of error using the t distribution can also be computed with the Excel function CONFIDENCE.T(alpha, s, n), where alpha is the level of significance, s is the sample standard deviation, and n is the sample size.

As Figure 6.13 illustrates, the sample mean ($\bar{x}$) is in cell D3. The margin of error, labeled "Confidence Level(95%)," appears in cell D16. The value worksheet shows $\bar{x} = 9{,}312$ and a margin of error equal to 955.

Cells D18:D20 provide the point estimate and the lower and upper limits for the confidence interval. Because the point estimate is just the sample mean, the formula =D3 is entered into cell D18. To compute the lower limit of the 95% confidence interval, $\bar{x}$ − (margin of error), we enter the formula =D18-D16 into cell D19. To compute the upper limit of the 95% confidence interval, $\bar{x}$ + (margin of error), we enter the formula =D18+D16 into cell D20. The value worksheet shows a lower limit of 8,357 and an upper limit of 10,267. In other words, the 95% confidence interval for the population mean is from 8,357 to 10,267.

Interval Estimation of the Population Proportion

The general form of an interval estimate of a population proportion p is

$$\bar{p} \pm \text{Margin of error}$$

The sampling distribution of $\bar{p}$ plays a key role in computing the margin of error for this interval estimate.

The notation $z_{\alpha/2}$ represents the value such that there is an area of $\alpha/2$ in the upper tail of the standard normal distribution (a normal distribution with a mean of zero and standard deviation of one).

In Section 6.3 we said that the sampling distribution of $\bar{p}$ can be approximated by a normal distribution whenever $np \geq 5$ and $n(1 - p) \geq 5$. Figure 6.14 shows the normal approximation of the sampling distribution of $\bar{p}$. The mean of the sampling distribution of $\bar{p}$ is the population proportion p, and the standard error of $\bar{p}$ is

$$\sigma_{\bar{p}} = \sqrt{\frac{p(1 - p)}{n}} \tag{6.8}$$

Because the sampling distribution of $\bar{p}$ is normally distributed, if we choose $z_{\alpha/2}\sigma_{\bar{p}}$ as the margin of error in an interval estimate of a population proportion, we know that $100(1 - \alpha)\%$ of the intervals generated will contain the true population proportion. But $\sigma_{\bar{p}}$ cannot be used directly in the computation of the margin of error because p will not be known; p is what we are trying to estimate. So we estimate $\sigma_{\bar{p}}$ with $s_{\bar{p}}$ and then the margin of error for an interval estimate of a population proportion is given by

$$\text{Margin of error} = z_{\alpha/2}s_{\bar{p}} = z_{\alpha/2}\sqrt{\frac{\bar{p}(1 - \bar{p})}{n}} \tag{6.9}$$

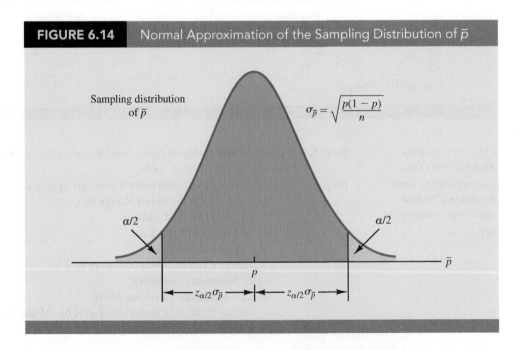

FIGURE 6.14   Normal Approximation of the Sampling Distribution of $\bar{p}$

With this margin of error, the general expression for an interval estimate of a population proportion is as follows.

INTERVAL ESTIMATE OF A POPULATION PROPORTION

$$\overline{p} \pm z_{\alpha/2} \sqrt{\frac{\overline{p}(1 - \overline{p})}{n}}, \qquad (6.10)$$

where α is the level of significance and $z_{\alpha/2}$ is the z value providing an area of $\alpha/2$ in the upper tail of the standard normal distribution.

DATA *file*

TeeTimes

The Excel formula
=NORM.S.INV(1 − α/2)
computes the value of $z_{\alpha/2}$.
For example, for α = 0.05,
$z_{0.025}$ =NORM.S.INV
(1 − .05/2) = 1.96.

The following example illustrates the computation of the margin of error and interval estimate for a population proportion. A national survey of 900 women golfers was conducted to learn how women golfers view their treatment at golf courses in the United States. The survey found that 396 of the women golfers were satisfied with the availability of tee times. Thus, the point estimate of the proportion of the population of women golfers who are satisfied with the availability of tee times is 396/900 = 0.44. Using equation (6.10) and a 95% confidence level:

$$\overline{p} \pm z_{\alpha/2} \sqrt{\frac{\overline{p}(1 - \overline{p})}{n}}$$

$$0.44 \pm 1.96 \sqrt{\frac{0.44(1 - 0.44)}{900}}$$

$$0.44 \pm 0.0324$$

Thus, the margin of error is 0.0324 and the 95% confidence interval estimate of the population proportion is 0.4076 to 0.4724. Using percentages, the survey results enable us to state with 95% confidence that between 40.76% and 47.24% of all women golfers are satisfied with the availability of tee times.

Using Excel Excel can be used to construct an interval estimate of the population proportion of women golfers who are satisfied with the availability of tee times. The responses in the survey were recorded as a Yes or No in the file *TeeTimes* for each woman surveyed. Refer to Figure 6.15 as we describe the tasks involved in constructing a 95% confidence interval. The formula worksheet is on the left; the value worksheet appears on the right.

The file TeeTimes displayed in Figure 6.15 can be used as a template for developing confidence intervals about a population proportion p, by entering new problem data in column A and appropriately adjusting the formulas in column D.

The descriptive statistics we need and the response of interest are provided in cells D3:D6. Because Excel's COUNT function works only with numerical data, we used the COUNTA function in cell D3 to compute the sample size. The response for which we want to develop an interval estimate, *Yes* or *No*, is entered into cell D4. Figure 6.15 shows that *Yes* has been entered into cell D4, indicating that we want to develop an interval estimate of the population proportion of women golfers who are satisfied with the availability of tee times. If we had wanted to develop an interval estimate of the population proportion of women golfers who are not satisfied with the availability of tee times, we would have entered *No* in cell D4. With *Yes* entered in cell D4, the COUNTIF function in cell D5 counts the number of Yes responses in the sample. The sample proportion is then computed in cell D6 by dividing the number of Yes responses in cell D5 by the sample size in cell D3.

Cells D8:D10 are used to compute the appropriate z value. The confidence coefficient (*0.95*) is entered into cell D8 and the level of significance (α) is computed in cell D9 by entering the formula =*1-D8*. The z value corresponding to an upper-tail area of $\alpha/2$ is computed by entering the formula =*NORM.S.INV(1-D9/2)* into cell D10. The value worksheet shows that $z_{0.025} = 1.96$.

Cells D12:D13 provide the estimate of the standard error and the margin of error. In cell D12, we entered the formula =*SQRT(D6*(1-D6)/D3)* to compute the standard error using

FIGURE 6.15   95% Confidence Interval for Survey of Women Golfers

	A	B	C	D
1	Response		Interval Estimate of a Population Proportion	
2	Yes			
3	No		Sample Size	=COUNTA(A2:A901)
4	Yes		Response of Interest	Yes
5	Yes		Count for Response	=COUNTIF(A2:A901,D4)
6	No		Sample Proportion	=D5/D3
7	No			
8	No		Confidence Coefficient	0.95
9	Yes		Level of Significance (alpha)	=1−D8
10	Yes		z Value	=NORM.S.INV(1−D9/2)
11	Yes			
12	No		Standard Error	=SQRT(D6*(1−D6)/D3)
13	No		Margin of Error	=D10*D12
14	Yes			
15	No		Point Estimate	=D6
16	No		Lower Limit	=D15−D13
17	Yes		Upper Limit	=D15+D13
18	No			
900	Yes			
901	Yes			
902				

	A	B	C	D	E	F	G
1	Response		Interval Estimate of a Population Proportion				
2	Yes						
3	No		Sample Size	900		Enter Yes as the	
4	Yes		Response of Interest	Yes		Response of Interest	
5	Yes		Count for Response	396			
6	No		Sample Proportion	0.44			
7	No						
8	No		Confidence Coefficient	0.95			
9	Yes		Level of Significance	0.05			
10	Yes		z Value	1.96			
11	Yes						
12	No		Standard Error	0.0165			
13	No		Margin of Error	0.0324			
14	Yes						
15	No		Point Estimate	0.44			
16	No		Lower Limit	0.4076			
17	Yes		Upper Limit	0.4724			
18	No						
900	Yes						
901	Yes						
902							

the sample proportion and the sample size as inputs. The formula =D10*D12 is entered into cell D13 to compute the margin of error corresponding to equation (6.9).

Cells D15:D17 provide the point estimate and the lower and upper limits for a confidence interval. The point estimate in cell D15 is the sample proportion. The lower and upper limits in cells D16 and D17 are obtained by subtracting and adding the margin of error to the point estimate. We note that the 95% confidence interval for the proportion of women golfers who are satisfied with the availability of tee times is 0.4076 to 0.4724.

NOTES + COMMENTS

1. The reason the number of degrees of freedom associated with the t value in equation (6.7) is $n - 1$ concerns the use of s as an estimate of the population standard deviation σ. The expression for the sample standard deviation is

$$s = \sqrt{\frac{\Sigma(x_i - \bar{x})^2}{n - 1}}.$$

Degrees of freedom refer to the number of independent pieces of information that go into the computation of $\Sigma(x_i - \bar{x})^2$. The n pieces of information involved in computing $\Sigma(x_i - \bar{x})^2$ are as follows: $x_1 - \bar{x}, x_2 - \bar{x}, \ldots, x_n - \bar{x}$. Note that $\Sigma(x_i - \bar{x}) = 0$ for any data set. Thus, only $n - 1$ of the $x_i - \bar{x}$ values are independent; that is, if we know $n - 1$ of the values, the remaining value can be determined exactly by using the condition that the sum of the $x_i - \bar{x}$ values must be 0. Thus, $n - 1$ is the number of degrees of freedom associated with $\Sigma(x_i - \bar{x})^2$ and hence the number of degrees of freedom for the t distribution in equation (6.7).

2. In most applications, a sample size of $n \geq 30$ is adequate when using equation (6.7) to develop an interval estimate of a population mean. However, if the population distribution is highly skewed or contains outliers, most statisticians would recommend increasing the sample size to 50 or more. If the population is not normally distributed but is roughly symmetric, sample sizes as small as 15 can be expected to provide good approximate confidence intervals. With smaller sample sizes, equation (6.7) should be used if the analyst believes, or is willing to assume, that the population distribution is at least approximately normal.

3. What happens to confidence interval estimates of $\bar{x}$ when the population is skewed? Consider a population that is skewed to the right, with large data values stretching the distribution to the right. When such skewness exists, the sample mean x and the sample standard deviation s are positively correlated. Larger values of s tend to be associated with larger values of $\bar{x}$. Thus, when $\bar{x}$ is larger than the population mean, s tends to be larger than σ. This skewness causes the margin of error, $t_{\alpha/2}(s/\sqrt{n})$, to be larger than it would be with σ known. The confidence interval with the larger margin of error tends to include the population mean more often than it would if the true value of σ were used. But when $\bar{x}$ is smaller than the population mean, the correlation between $\bar{x}$ and s causes the margin of error to be small. In this case, the confidence interval with the smaller margin of error tends to miss the population mean

more than it would if we knew σ and used it. For this reason, we recommend using larger sample sizes with highly skewed population distributions.

4. We can find the sample size necessary to provide the desired margin of error at the chosen confidence level. Let E = the desired margin of error. Then
   - the sample size for an interval estimate of a population mean is $n = \dfrac{(z_{\alpha/2})^2 \sigma^2}{E^2}$, where E is the margin of error that the user is willing to accept, and the value of $z_{\alpha/2}$ follows directly from the confidence level to be used in developing the interval estimate.
   - the sample size for an interval estimate of a population proportion is $n = \dfrac{(z_{\alpha/2})^2 p^*(1 - p^*)}{E^2}$, where the planning value p^* can be chosen by use of (i) the sample

proportion from a previous sample of the same or similar units, (ii) a pilot study to select a preliminary sample, (iii) judgment or a "best guess" for the value of p^*, or (iv) if none of the preceding alternatives apply, use of the planning value of $p^* = 0.50$.

5. The desired margin of error for estimating a population proportion is almost always 0.10 or less. In national public opinion polls conducted by organizations such as Gallup and Harris, a 0.03 or 0.04 margin of error is common. With such margins of error, the sample found with $n = \dfrac{(z_{\alpha/2})^2 p^*(1 - p^*)}{E^2}$ will almost always provide a size that is sufficient to satisfy the requirements of $np \geq 5$ and $n(1 - p) \geq 5$ for using a normal distribution as an approximation for the sampling distribution of $\bar{p}$.

6.5 Hypothesis Tests

Throughout this chapter, we have shown how a sample could be used to develop point and interval estimates of population parameters such as the mean μ and the proportion p. In this section, we continue the discussion of statistical inference by showing how hypothesis testing can be used to determine whether a statement about the value of a population parameter should or should not be rejected.

In hypothesis testing, we begin by making a tentative conjecture about a population parameter. This tentative conjecture is called the **null hypothesis** and is denoted by H_0. We then define another hypothesis, called the **alternative hypothesis**, which is the opposite of what is stated in the null hypothesis. The alternative hypothesis is denoted by H_a. The hypothesis testing procedure uses data from a sample to test the validity of the two competing statements about a population that are indicated by H_0 and H_a.

This section shows how hypothesis tests can be conducted about a population mean and a population proportion. We begin by providing examples that illustrate approaches to developing null and alternative hypotheses.

Developing Null and Alternative Hypotheses

It is not always obvious how the null and alternative hypotheses should be formulated. Care must be taken to structure the hypotheses appropriately so that the hypothesis testing conclusion provides the information the researcher or decision maker wants. The context of the situation is very important in determining how the hypotheses should be stated. All hypothesis testing applications involve collecting a random sample and using the sample results to provide evidence for drawing a conclusion. Good questions to consider when formulating the null and alternative hypotheses are, What is the purpose of collecting the sample? What conclusions are we hoping to make?

Learning to formulate hypotheses correctly will take some practice. Expect some initial confusion about the proper choice of the null and alternative hypotheses. The examples in this section are intended to provide guidelines.

In the introduction to this section, we stated that the null hypothesis H_0 is a tentative conjecture about a population parameter such as a population mean or a population proportion. The alternative hypothesis H_a is a statement that is the opposite of what is stated in the null hypothesis. In some situations it is easier to identify the alternative hypothesis first and then develop the null hypothesis. In other situations, it is easier to identify the null hypothesis first and then develop the alternative hypothesis. We will illustrate these situations in the following examples.

The Alternative Hypothesis as a Research Hypothesis Many applications of hypothesis testing involve an attempt to gather evidence in support of a research hypothesis. In these situations, it is often best to begin with the alternative hypothesis and make it the conclusion that the researcher hopes to support. Consider a particular automobile that currently attains a fuel efficiency of 24 miles per gallon for city driving. A product research group has developed a new fuel injection system designed to increase the miles-per-gallon rating. The group will run controlled tests with the new fuel injection system looking for statistical support for the conclusion that the new fuel injection system provides more miles per gallon than the current system.

Several new fuel injection units will be manufactured, installed in test automobiles, and subjected to research-controlled driving conditions. The sample mean miles per gallon for these automobiles will be computed and used in a hypothesis test to determine whether it can be concluded that the new system provides more than 24 miles per gallon. In terms of the population mean miles per gallon μ, the research hypothesis $\mu > 24$ becomes the alternative hypothesis. Since the current system provides an average or mean of 24 miles per gallon, we will make the tentative conjecture that the new system is no better than the current system and choose $\mu \leq 24$ as the null hypothesis. The null and alternative hypotheses are as follows:

$$H_0: \mu \leq 24$$
$$H_a: \mu > 24$$

The conclusion that the research hypothesis is true is made if the sample data provide sufficient evidence to show that the null hypothesis can be rejected.

If the sample results lead to the conclusion to reject H_0, the inference can be made that $H_a: \mu > 24$ is true. The researchers have the statistical support to state that the new fuel injection system increases the mean number of miles per gallon. The production of automobiles with the new fuel injection system should be considered. However, if the sample results lead to the conclusion that H_0 cannot be rejected, the researchers cannot conclude that the new fuel injection system is better than the current system. Production of automobiles with the new fuel injection system on the basis of better gas mileage cannot be justified. Perhaps more research and further testing can be conducted.

Successful companies stay competitive by developing new products, new methods, and new services that are better than what is currently available. Before adopting something new, it is desirable to conduct research to determine whether there is statistical support for the conclusion that the new approach is indeed better. In such cases, the research hypothesis is stated as the alternative hypothesis. For example, a new teaching method is developed that is believed to be better than the current method. The alternative hypothesis is that the new method is better; the null hypothesis is that the new method is no better than the old method. A new sales force bonus plan is developed in an attempt to increase sales. The alternative hypothesis is that the new bonus plan increases sales; the null hypothesis is that the new bonus plan does not increase sales. A new drug is developed with the goal of lowering blood pressure more than an existing drug. The alternative hypothesis is that the new drug lowers blood pressure more than the existing drug; the null hypothesis is that the new drug does not provide lower blood pressure than the existing drug. In each case, rejection of the null hypothesis H_0 provides statistical support for the research hypothesis. We will see many examples of hypothesis tests in research situations such as these throughout this chapter and in the remainder of the text.

The Null Hypothesis as a Conjecture to Be Challenged Of course, not all hypothesis tests involve research hypotheses. In the following discussion we consider applications of hypothesis testing where we begin with a belief or a conjecture that a statement about the value of a population parameter is true. We will then use a hypothesis test to challenge the conjecture and determine whether there is statistical evidence to conclude that the conjecture is incorrect. In these situations, it is helpful to develop the null hypothesis first. The null hypothesis H_0 expresses the belief or conjecture about the value of the population parameter. The alternative hypothesis H_a is that the belief or conjecture is incorrect.

As an example, consider the situation of a manufacturer of soft drink products. The label on a soft drink bottle states that it contains 67.6 fluid ounces. We consider the label correct provided the population mean filling weight for the bottles is *at least* 67.6 fluid ounces. With no reason to believe otherwise, we would give the manufacturer the benefit of the doubt and assume that the statement provided on the label is correct. Thus, in a hypothesis test about the population mean fluid weight per bottle, we would begin with the conjecture that the label is correct and state the null hypothesis as $\mu \geq 67.6$. The challenge to this conjecture would imply that the label is incorrect and the bottles are being underfilled. This challenge would be stated as the alternative hypothesis $\mu < 67.6$. Thus, the null and alternative hypotheses are as follows:

$$H_0: \mu \geq 67.6$$
$$H_a: \mu < 67.6$$

A manufacturer's product information is usually assumed to be true and stated as the null hypothesis. The conclusion that the information is incorrect can be made if the null hypothesis is rejected.

A government agency with the responsibility for validating manufacturing labels could select a sample of soft drink bottles, compute the sample mean filling weight, and use the sample results to test the preceding hypotheses. If the sample results lead to the conclusion to reject H_0, the inference that $H_a: \mu < 67.6$ is true can be made. With this statistical support, the agency is justified in concluding that the label is incorrect and that the bottles are being underfilled. Appropriate action to force the manufacturer to comply with labeling standards would be considered. However, if the sample results indicate H_0 cannot be rejected, the conjecture that the manufacturer's labeling is correct cannot be rejected. With this conclusion, no action would be taken.

Let us now consider a variation of the soft drink bottle-filling example by viewing the same situation from the manufacturer's point of view. The bottle-filling operation has been designed to fill soft drink bottles with 67.6 fluid ounces as stated on the label. The company does not want to underfill the containers because that could result in complaints from customers or, perhaps, a government agency. However, the company does not want to overfill containers either because putting more soft drink than necessary into the containers would be an unnecessary cost. The company's goal would be to adjust the bottle-filling operation so that the population mean filling weight per bottle is 67.6 fluid ounces as specified on the label.

Although this is the company's goal, from time to time any production process can get out of adjustment. If this occurs in our example, underfilling or overfilling of the soft drink bottles will occur. In either case, the company would like to know about it in order to correct the situation by readjusting the bottle-filling operation to result in the designated 67.6 fluid ounces. In this hypothesis testing application, we would begin with the conjecture that the production process is operating correctly and state the null hypothesis as $\mu = 67.6$ fluid ounces. The alternative hypothesis that challenges this conjecture is that $\mu \neq 67.6$, which indicates that either overfilling or underfilling is occurring. The null and alternative hypotheses for the manufacturer's hypothesis test are as follows:

$$H_0: \mu = 67.6$$
$$H_a: \mu \neq 67.6$$

Suppose that the soft drink manufacturer uses a quality-control procedure to periodically select a sample of bottles from the filling operation and computes the sample mean filling weight per bottle. If the sample results lead to the conclusion to reject H_0, the inference is made that $H_a: \mu \neq 67.6$ is true. We conclude that the bottles are not being filled properly and the production process should be adjusted to restore the population mean to 67.6 fluid ounces per bottle. However, if the sample results indicate H_0 cannot be rejected, the conjecture that the manufacturer's bottle-filling operation is functioning properly cannot be rejected. In this case, no further action would be taken and the production operation would continue to run.

The two preceding forms of the soft drink manufacturing hypothesis test show that the null and alternative hypotheses may vary depending on the point of view of the researcher or decision maker. To formulate hypotheses correctly, it is important to understand the context of the situation and to structure the hypotheses to provide the information the researcher or decision maker wants.

Summary of Forms for Null and Alternative Hypotheses The hypothesis tests in this chapter involve two population parameters: the population mean and the population proportion. Depending on the situation, hypothesis tests about a population parameter may take one of three forms: Two use inequalities in the null hypothesis; the third uses an equality in the null hypothesis. For hypothesis tests involving a population mean, we let

μ_0 denote the hypothesized value of the population mean and we must choose one of the following three forms for the hypothesis test:

$$H_0: \mu \geq \mu_0 \qquad H_0: \mu \leq \mu_0 \qquad H_0: \mu = \mu_0$$
$$H_a: \mu < \mu_0 \qquad H_a: \mu > \mu_0 \qquad H_a: \mu \neq \mu_0$$

For reasons that will be clear later, the first two forms are called one-tailed tests. The third form is called a two-tailed test.

In many situations, the choice of H_0 and H_a is not obvious and judgment is necessary to select the proper form. However, as the preceding forms show, the equality part of the expression (either $\geq$, $\leq$, or $=$) *always* appears in the null hypothesis. In selecting the proper form of H_0 and H_a, keep in mind that the alternative hypothesis is often what the test is attempting to establish. Hence, asking whether the user is looking for evidence to support $\mu < \mu_0, \mu > \mu_0$, or $\mu \neq \mu_0$ will help determine H_a.

Type I and Type II Errors

The null and alternative hypotheses are competing statements about the population. Either the null hypothesis H_0 is true or the alternative hypothesis H_a is true, but not both. Ideally the hypothesis testing procedure should lead to the acceptance of H_0 when H_0 is true and the rejection of H_0 when H_a is true. Unfortunately, the correct conclusions are not always possible. Because hypothesis tests are based on sample information, we must allow for the possibility of errors. Table 6.6 illustrates the two kinds of errors that can be made in hypothesis testing.

The first row of Table 6.6 shows what can happen if the conclusion is to accept H_0. If H_0 is true, this conclusion is correct. However, if H_a is true, we made a **Type II error**; that is, we accepted H_0 when it is false. The second row of Table 6.6 shows what can happen if the conclusion is to reject H_0. If H_0 is true, we made a **Type I error**; that is, we rejected H_0 when it is true. However, if H_a is true, rejecting H_0 is correct.

Recall the hypothesis testing illustration in which an automobile product research group developed a new fuel injection system designed to increase the miles-per-gallon rating of a particular automobile. With the current model obtaining an average of 24 miles per gallon, the hypothesis test was formulated as follows:

$$H_0: \mu \leq 24$$
$$H_a: \mu > 24$$

The alternative hypothesis, $H_a: \mu > 24$, indicates that the researchers are looking for sample evidence to support the conclusion that the population mean miles per gallon with the new fuel injection system is greater than 24.

In this application, the Type I error of rejecting H_0 when it is true corresponds to the researchers claiming that the new system improves the miles-per-gallon rating ($\mu > 24$) when in fact the new system is no better than the current system. In contrast, the Type II error of accepting H_0 when it is false corresponds to the researchers concluding that the new system is no better than the current system ($\mu \leq 24$) when in fact the new system improves miles-per-gallon performance.

TABLE 6.6 Errors and Correct Conclusions in Hypothesis Testing

		Population Condition	
		H_0 True	H_a True
Conclusion	**Do Not Reject H_0**	Correct conclusion	Type II error
	Reject H_0	Type I error	Correct conclusion

For the miles-per-gallon rating hypothesis test, the null hypothesis is $H_0: \mu \leq 24$. Suppose the null hypothesis is true as an equality; that is, $\mu = 24$. The probability of making a Type I error when the null hypothesis is true as an equality is called the **level of significance**. Thus, for the miles-per-gallon rating hypothesis test, the level of significance is the probability of rejecting $H_0: \mu \leq 24$ when $\mu = 24$. Because of the importance of this concept, we now restate the definition of level of significance.

The Greek symbol α (alpha) is used to denote the level of significance, and common choices for α are 0.05 and 0.01.

LEVEL OF SIGNIFICANCE

The level of significance is the probability of making a Type I error when the null hypothesis is true as an equality.

In practice, the person responsible for the hypothesis test specifies the level of significance. By selecting α, that person is controlling the probability of making a Type I error. If the cost of making a Type I error is high, small values of α are preferred. If the cost of making a Type I error is not too high, larger values of α are typically used. Applications of hypothesis testing that only control the Type I error are called *significance tests*. Many applications of hypothesis testing are of this type.

Although most applications of hypothesis testing control the probability of making a Type I error, they do not always control the probability of making a Type II error. Hence, if we decide to accept H_0, we cannot determine how confident we can be with that decision. Because of the uncertainty associated with making a Type II error when conducting significance tests, statisticians usually recommend that we use the statement "do not reject H_0" instead of "accept H_0." Using the statement "do not reject H_0" carries the recommendation to withhold both judgment and action. In effect, by not directly accepting H_0, the statistician avoids the risk of making a Type II error. Whenever the probability of making a Type II error has not been determined and controlled, we will not make the statement "accept H_0." In such cases, only two conclusions are possible: *do not reject H_0* or *reject H_0*.

If the sample data are consistent with the null hypothesis H_0, we will follow the practice of concluding "do not reject H_0." This conclusion is preferred over "accept H_0," because the conclusion to accept H_0 puts us at risk of making a Type II error.

Although controlling for a Type II error in hypothesis testing is not common, it can be done. Specialized texts describe procedures for determining and controlling the probability of making a Type II error.[1] If proper controls have been established for this error, action based on the "accept H_0" conclusion can be appropriate.

Hypothesis Test of the Population Mean

In this section, we describe how to conduct hypothesis tests about a population mean for the practical situation in which the sample must be used to develop estimates of both μ and σ. Thus, to conduct a hypothesis test about a population mean, the sample mean $\bar{x}$ is used as an estimate of μ and the sample standard deviation s is used as an estimate of σ.

One-Tailed Test **One-tailed tests** about a population mean take one of the following two forms:

Lower-Tail Test	Upper-Tail Test
$H_0: \mu \geq \mu_0$	$H_0: \mu \leq \mu_0$
$H_a: \mu < \mu_0$	$H_a: \mu > \mu_0$

Let us consider an example involving a lower-tail test.

The Federal Trade Commission (FTC) periodically conducts statistical studies designed to test the claims that manufacturers make about their products. For example, the label on a large can of Hilltop Coffee states that the can contains 3 pounds of coffee. The FTC knows

---

[1]See, for example, D. R. Anderson, D. J. Sweeney, T. A. Williams, J. D. Camm, J. J. Cochran, M. J. Fry, and J. W. Ohlmann *Statistics for Business and Economics*, 14th ed. (Mason, OH: Cengage Learning, 2020).

that Hilltop's production process cannot place exactly 3 pounds of coffee in each can, even if the mean filling weight for the population of all cans filled is 3 pounds per can. However, as long as the population mean filling weight is at least 3 pounds per can, the rights of consumers will be protected. Thus, the FTC interprets the label information on a large can of coffee as a claim by Hilltop that the population mean filling weight is at least 3 pounds per can. We will show how the FTC can check Hilltop's claim by conducting a lower-tail hypothesis test.

The first step is to develop the null and alternative hypotheses for the test. If the population mean filling weight is at least 3 pounds per can, Hilltop's claim is correct. This establishes the null hypothesis for the test. However, if the population mean weight is less than 3 pounds per can, Hilltop's claim is incorrect. This establishes the alternative hypothesis. With μ denoting the population mean filling weight, the null and alternative hypotheses are as follows:

$$H_0: \mu \geq 3$$
$$H_a: \mu < 3$$

Note that the hypothesized value of the population mean is $\mu_0 = 3$.

If the sample data indicate that H_0 cannot be rejected, the statistical evidence does not support the conclusion that a label violation has occurred. Hence, no action should be taken against Hilltop. However, if the sample data indicate that H_0 can be rejected, we will conclude that the alternative hypothesis, $H_a: \mu < 3$, is true. In this case a conclusion of underfilling and a charge of a label violation against Hilltop would be justified.

Coffee

Suppose a sample of 36 cans of coffee is selected and the sample mean $\bar{x}$ is computed as an estimate of the population mean μ. If the value of the sample mean $\bar{x}$ is less than 3 pounds, the sample results will cast doubt on the null hypothesis. What we want to know is how much less than 3 pounds must $\bar{x}$ be before we would be willing to declare the difference significant and risk making a Type I error by falsely accusing Hilltop of a label violation. A key factor in addressing this issue is the value the decision maker selects for the level of significance.

As noted in the preceding section, the level of significance, denoted by α, is the probability of making a Type I error by rejecting H_0 when the null hypothesis is true as an equality. The decision maker must specify the level of significance. If the cost of making a Type I error is high, a small value should be chosen for the level of significance. If the cost is not high, a larger value is more appropriate. In the Hilltop Coffee study, the director of the FTC's testing program made the following statement: "If the company is meeting its weight specifications at $\mu = 3$, I do not want to take action against them. But I am willing to risk a 1% chance of making such an error." From the director's statement, we set the level of significance for the hypothesis test at $\alpha = 0.01$. Thus, we must design the hypothesis test so that the probability of making a Type I error when $\mu = 3$ is 0.01.

For the Hilltop Coffee study, by developing the null and alternative hypotheses and specifying the level of significance for the test, we carry out the first two steps required in conducting every hypothesis test. We are now ready to perform the third step of hypothesis testing: collect the sample data and compute the value of what is called a test statistic.

Test Statistic   From the study of sampling distributions in Section 6.3 we know that as the sample size increases, the sampling distribution of $\bar{x}$ will become normally distributed. Figure 6.16 shows the sampling distribution of $\bar{x}$ when the null hypothesis is true as an equality, that is, when $\mu = \mu_0 = 3$.[2] Note that $\sigma_{\bar{x}}$, the standard error of $\bar{x}$, is estimated by $s_{\bar{x}} = s/\sqrt{n} = 0.17\sqrt{36} = 0.028$. Recall that in Section 6.4, we showed that an interval estimate of a population mean is based on a probability distribution known as the t distribution. The t distribution is similar to the standard normal distribution, but accounts for the additional variability introduced when using a sample to estimate both the population mean and population standard deviation. Hypothesis tests about a population mean are also based on the t distribution. Specifically, if $\bar{x}$ is normally distributed, the sampling distribution of

The standard error of $\bar{x}$ is the standard deviation of the sampling distribution of $\bar{x}$.

$$t = \frac{\bar{x} - \mu_0}{s_{\bar{x}}} = \frac{\bar{x} - \mu_0}{s/\sqrt{n}} = \frac{\bar{x} - 3}{0.028}$$

---

[2]In constructing sampling distributions for hypothesis tests, it is assumed that H_0 is satisfied as an equality.

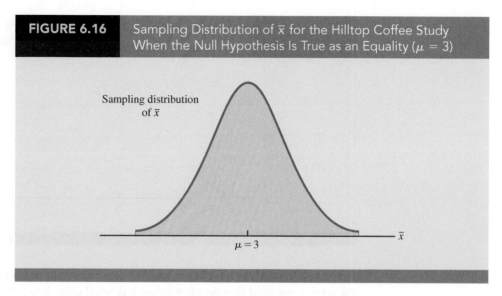

FIGURE 6.16 Sampling Distribution of $\bar{x}$ for the Hilltop Coffee Study When the Null Hypothesis Is True as an Equality ($\mu = 3$)

Sampling distribution of $\bar{x}$

$\mu = 3$

$\bar{x}$

Although the t distribution is based on an conjecture that the population from which we are sampling is normally distributed, research shows that when the sample size is large enough, this conjecture can be relaxed considerably.

is a t distribution with $n - 1$ degrees of freedom. The value of t represents how much the sample mean is above or below the hypothesized value of the population mean as measured in units of the standard error of the sample mean. A value of $t = -1$ means that the value of $\bar{x}$ is 1 standard error below the hypothesized value of the mean, a value of $t = -2$ means that the value of $\bar{x}$ is 2 standard errors below the hypothesized value of the mean, and so on. For this lower-tail hypothesis test, we can use Excel to find the lower-tail probability corresponding to any t value (as we show later in this section). For example, Figure 6.17 illustrates that the lower tail area at $t = -3.00$ is 0.0025. Hence, the probability of obtaining a value of t that is three or more standard errors below the mean is 0.0025. As a result, if the null hypothesis is true (i.e., if the population mean is 3), the probability of obtaining a value of $\bar{x}$ that is 3 or more standard errors below the hypothesized population mean $\mu_0 = 3$ is also 0.0025. Because such a result is unlikely if the null hypothesis is true, this leads us to doubt our null hypothesis.

We use the t-distributed random variable t as a **test statistic** to determine whether $\bar{x}$ deviates from the hypothesized value of μ enough to justify rejecting the null hypothesis. With $s_{\bar{x}} = s/\sqrt{n}$, the test statistic is as follows:

TEST STATISTIC FOR HYPOTHESIS TESTS ABOUT A POPULATION MEAN

$$t = \frac{\bar{x} - \mu_0}{s/\sqrt{n}} \tag{6.11}$$

The key question for a lower-tail test is, How small must the test statistic t be before we choose to reject the null hypothesis? We will draw our conclusion by using the value of the test statistic t to compute a probability called a p **value**.

A small p value indicates that the value of the test statistic is unusual given the conjecture that H_0 is true.

p VALUE

A p value is the probability, assuming that H_0 is true, of obtaining a random sample of size n that results in a test statistic at least as extreme as the one observed in the current sample.

The p value measures the strength of the evidence provided by the sample against the null hypothesis. Smaller p values indicate more evidence against H_0 as they suggest that it is increasingly more unlikely that the sample could occur if the H_0 is true.

Let us see how the p value is computed and used. The value of the test statistic is used to compute the p value. The method used depends on whether the test is a lower-tail, an upper-tail, or a two-tailed test. For a lower-tail test, the p value is the probability of obtaining a value for the test statistic as small as or smaller than that provided by the sample. Thus, to compute the p value for the lower-tail test, we must use the t distribution to find

FIGURE 6.17   Lower-Tail Probability for $t = -3$ from a t Distribution with 35 Degrees of Freedom

the probability that t is less than or equal to the value of the test statistic. After computing the p value, we must then decide whether it is small enough to reject the null hypothesis; as we will show, this decision involves comparing the p value to the level of significance.

Using Excel Excel can be used to conduct one-tailed and two-tailed hypothesis tests about a population mean. The sample data and the test statistic (t) are used to compute three p values: p value (lower tail), p value (upper tail), and p value (two tail). The user can then choose α and draw a conclusion using whichever p value is appropriate for the type of hypothesis test being conducted.

Let's start by showing how to use Excel's T.DIST function to compute a lower-tail p value. The T.DIST function has three inputs; its general form is as follows:

$$=\text{T.DIST(test statistic, degrees of freedom, cumulative).}$$

For the first input, we enter the value of the test statistic; for the second input we enter the degrees of freedom for the associated t distribution; for the third input, we enter *TRUE* to compute the cumulative probability corresponding to a lower-tail p value.

Once the lower-tail p value has been computed, it is easy to compute the upper-tail and the two-tailed p values. The upper-tail p value is 1 minus the lower-tail p value, and the two-tailed p value is two times the smaller of the lower- and upper-tail p values.

Let us now compute the p value for the Hilltop Coffee lower-tail test. Refer to Figure 6.18 as we describe the tasks involved. The formula sheet is in the background and the value worksheet is in the foreground.

MODEL *file*

CoffeeTest

The descriptive statistics needed are provided in cells D4:D6. Excel's COUNT, AVERAGE, and STDEV.S functions compute the sample size, the sample mean, and the sample standard deviation, respectively. The hypothesized value of the population mean (*3*) is entered into cell D8. Using the sample standard deviation as an estimate of the population standard deviation, an estimate of the standard error is obtained in cell D10 by dividing the sample standard deviation in cell D6 by the square root of the sample size in cell D4. The formula *=(D5-D8)/D10* entered into cell D11 computes the value of the test statistic t corresponding to the calculation:

$$t = \frac{\bar{x} - \mu_0}{s/\sqrt{n}} = \frac{2.92 - 3}{0.17/\sqrt{36}} = -2.824$$

The degrees of freedom are computed in cell D12 as the sample size in cell D4 minus 1.

To compute the p value for a lower-tail test, we enter the following formula into cell D14.

$$=T.DIST(D11,D12,TRUE)$$

The p value for an upper-tail test is then computed in cell D15 as 1 minus the p value for the lower-tail test. Finally, the p value for a two-tailed test is computed in cell D16 as

FIGURE 6.18	Hypothesis Test About a Population Mean

◢	A	B	C	D
1	Weight		**Hypothesis Test about a Population Mean**	
2	3.15			
3	2.76			
4	3.18		Sample Size	=COUNT(A2:A37)
5	2.77		Sample Mean	=AVERAGE(A2:A37)
6	2.86		Sample Standard Deviation	=STDEV.S(A2:A37)
7	2.66			
8	2.86		Hypothesized Value	3
9	2.54			
10	3.02		Standard Error	=D6/SQRT(D4)
11	3.13		Test Statistic t	=(D5-D8)/D10
12	2.94		Degrees of Freedom	=D4-1
13	2.74			
14	2.84		p value (Lower Tail)	=T.DIST(D11,D12,TRUE)
15	2.6		p value (Upper Tail)	=1-D14
16	2.94		p value (Two Tail)	=2*MIN(D14,D15)
17	2.93			
18	3.18			
19	2.95			
20	2.86			
21	2.91			
22	2.96			
23	3.14			
24	2.65			
25	2.77			
26	2.96			
27	3.1			
28	2.82			
29	3.05			
30	2.94			
31	2.82			
32	3.21			
33	3.11			
34	2.9			
35	3.05			
36	2.93			
37	2.89			

◢	A	B	C	D
1	Weight		**Hypothesis Test about a Population Mean**	
2	3.15			
3	2.76			
4	3.18		Sample Size	36
5	2.77		Sample Mean	2.92
6	2.86		Sample Standard Deviation	0.170
7	2.66			
8	2.86		Hypothesized Value	3
9	2.54			
10	3.02		Standard Error	0.028
11	3.13		Test Statistic t	−2.824
12	2.94		Degrees of Freedom	35
13	2.74			
14	2.84		p value (Lower Tail)	0.0039
15	2.60		p value (Upper Tail)	0.9961
16	2.94		p value (Two Tail)	0.0078

two times the minimum of the two one-tailed p values. The value worksheet shows that the three p values are p value (lower tail) = 0.0039, p value (upper tail) = 0.9961, and p value (two tail) = 0.0078.

The development of the worksheet is now complete. Is $\bar{x} = 2.92$ small enough to lead us to reject H_0? Because this is a lower-tail test, the p value is the area under the t-distribution curve for values of $t \le -2.824$ (the value of the test statistic). Figure 6.19 depicts the p value for the Hilltop Coffee lower-tail test. This p value indicates a small probability of obtaining a sample mean of $\bar{x} = 2.92$ (and a test statistic of -2.824) or smaller when sampling from a population with $\mu = 3$. This p value does not provide much support for the null hypothesis, but is it small enough to cause us to reject H_0? The answer depends on the level of significance (α) the decision maker has selected for the test.

Note that the p value can be considered a measure of the strength of the evidence against the null hypothesis that is contained in the sample data. The greater the inconsistency between the sample data and the null hypothesis, the smaller the p value will be; thus, a smaller p value indicates that it is less plausible that the sample could have been collected from a population for which the null hypothesis is true. That is, a smaller p value indicates that the sample provides stronger evidence against the null hypothesis.

As noted previously, the director of the FTC's testing program selected a value of 0.01 for the level of significance. The selection of $\alpha = 0.01$ means that the director is willing to tolerate a probability of 0.01 of rejecting the null hypothesis when it is true as an equality ($\mu_0 = 3$). The sample of 36 coffee cans in the Hilltop Coffee study resulted in a p value of 0.0039, which means that the probability of obtaining a value of $\bar{x} = 2.92$ or less when

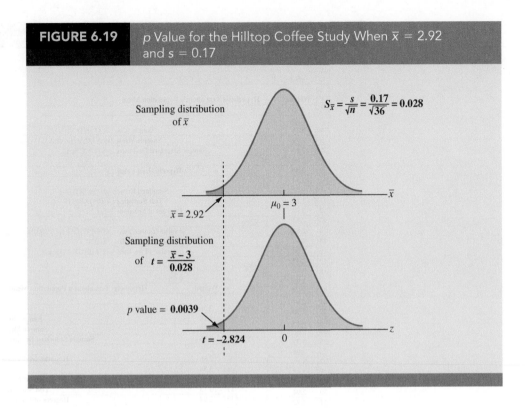

FIGURE 6.19 p Value for the Hilltop Coffee Study When $\bar{x} = 2.92$ and $s = 0.17$

the null hypothesis is true is 0.0039. Because 0.0039 is less than or equal to $\alpha = 0.01$, we reject H_0. Therefore, we find sufficient statistical evidence to reject the null hypothesis at the 0.01 level of significance.

The level of significance α indicates the strength of evidence that is needed in the sample data before we will reject the null hypothesis. If the p value is smaller than the selected level of significance α, the evidence against the null hypothesis that is contained in the sample data is sufficiently strong for us to reject the null hypothesis; that is, we believe that it is implausible that the sample data were collected from a population for which H_0: $\mu \geq 3$ is true. Conversely, if the p value is larger than the selected level of significance α, the evidence against the null hypothesis that is contained in the sample data is not sufficiently strong for us to reject the null hypothesis; that is, we believe that it is plausible that the sample data were collected from a population for which the null hypothesis is true.

We can now state the general rule for determining whether the null hypothesis can be rejected when using the p value approach. For a level of significance α, the rejection rule using the p value approach is as follows.

REJECTION RULE

Reject H_0 if p value $\leq \alpha$

In the Hilltop Coffee test, the p value of 0.0039 resulted in the rejection of the null hypothesis. Although the basis for making the rejection decision involves a comparison of the p value to the level of significance specified by the FTC director, the observed p value of 0.0039 means that we would reject H_0 for any value of $\alpha \geq 0.0039$. For this reason, the p value is also called the *observed level of significance*.

Different decision makers may express different opinions concerning the cost of making a Type I error and may choose a different level of significance. By providing the p value as part of the hypothesis testing results, another decision maker can compare the reported p value to his or her own level of significance and possibly make a different decision with respect to rejecting H_0.

At the beginning of this section, we said that one-tailed tests about a population mean take one of the following two forms:

Lower-Tail Test	Upper-Tail Test
$H_0: \mu \geq \mu_0$	$H_0: \mu \leq \mu_0$
$H_a: \mu < \mu_0$	$H_a: \mu > \mu_0$

We used the Hilltop Coffee study to illustrate how to conduct a lower-tail test. We can use the same general approach to conduct an upper-tail test. The test statistic t is still computed using equation (6.11). But, for an upper-tail test, the p value is the probability of obtaining a value for the test statistic as large as or larger than that provided by the sample. Thus, to compute the p value for the upper-tail test, we must use the t distribution to compute the probability that t is greater than or equal to the value of the test statistic. Then, according to the rejection rule, we will reject the null hypothesis if the p value is less than or equal to the level of significance α.

Let us summarize the steps involved in computing p values for one-tailed hypothesis tests.

COMPUTATION OF p VALUES FOR ONE-TAILED TESTS

1. Compute the value of the test statistic using equation (6.11).
2. **Lower-tail test:** Using the t distribution, compute the probability that t is less than or equal to the value of the test statistic (area in the lower tail).
3. **Upper-tail test:** Using the t distribution, compute the probability that t is greater than or equal to the value of the test statistic (area in the upper tail).

Two-Tailed Test In hypothesis testing, the general form for a **two-tailed test** about a population mean is as follows:

$$H_0: \mu = \mu_0$$
$$H_a: \mu \neq \mu_0$$

In this subsection we show how to conduct a two-tailed test about a population mean. As an illustration, we consider the hypothesis testing situation facing Holiday Toys.

Holiday Toys manufactures and distributes its products through more than 1,000 retail outlets. In planning production levels for the coming winter season, Holiday must decide how many units of each product to produce before the actual demand at the retail level is known. For this year's most important new toy, Holiday's marketing director is expecting demand to average 40 units per retail outlet. Prior to making the final production decision based on this estimate, Holiday decided to survey a sample of 25 retailers to gather more information about demand for the new product. Each retailer was provided with information about the features of the new toy along with the cost and the suggested selling price. Then each retailer was asked to specify an anticipated order quantity.

With μ denoting the population mean order quantity per retail outlet, the sample data will be used to conduct the following two-tailed hypothesis test:

$$H_0: \mu = 40$$
$$H_a: \mu \neq 40$$

If H_0 cannot be rejected, Holiday will continue its production planning based on the marketing director's estimate that the population mean order quantity per retail outlet will be $\mu = 40$ units. However, if H_0 is rejected, Holiday will immediately reevaluate its production plan for the product. A two-tailed hypothesis test is used because Holiday wants to reevaluate the production plan regardless of whether the population mean quantity per retail outlet is less than anticipated or is greater than anticipated. Because it's a new

DATA*file*
Orders

product and therefore, no historical data are available, the population mean μ and the population standard deviation must both be estimated using $\bar{x}$ and s from the sample data.

The sample of 25 retailers provided a mean of $\bar{x} = 37.4$ and a standard deviation of $s = 11.79$ units. Before going ahead with the use of the t distribution, the analyst constructed a histogram of the sample data in order to check on the form of the population distribution. The histogram of the sample data showed no evidence of skewness or any extreme outliers, so the analyst concluded that the use of the t distribution with $n - 1 = 24$ degrees of freedom was appropriate. Using equation (9.2) with $\bar{x} = 37.4$, $\mu_0 = 40$, $s = 11.79$, and $n = 25$, the value of the test statistic is

$$t = \frac{\bar{x} - \mu_0}{s/\sqrt{n}} = \frac{37.4 - 40}{11.79/\sqrt{25}} = -1.10$$

The sample mean $\bar{x} = 37.4$ is less than 40 and so provides some support for the conclusion that the population mean quantity per retail outlet is less than 40 units, but this could possibly be due to sampling error. We must address whether the difference between this sample mean and our hypothesized mean is sufficient for us to reject H_0 at the 0.05 level of significance. We will again reach our conclusion by calculating a p value.

Recall that the p value is a probability used to determine whether the null hypothesis should be rejected. For a two-tailed test, values of the test statistic in either tail provide evidence against the null hypothesis. For a two-tailed test the p value is the probability of obtaining a value for the test statistic *at least as unlikely* as the value of the test statistic calculated with the sample given that the null hypothesis is true. Let us see how the p value is computed for the two-tailed Holiday Toys hypothesis test.

To compute the p value for this problem, we must find the probability of obtaining a value for the test statistic at least as unlikely as $t = -1.10$ if the population mean is actually 40. Clearly, values of $t \leq -1.10$ are *at least as unlikely*. But because this is a two-tailed test, all values that are more than 1.10 standard deviations from the hypothesized value μ_0 in either direction provide evidence against the null hypothesis that is at least as strong as the evidence against the null hypothesis contained in the sample data. As shown in Figure 6.20, the two-tailed p value in this case is given by $P(t \leq -1.10) + P(t \geq 1.10)$.

To compute the tail probabilities, we apply the Excel template introduced in the Hilltop Coffee example to the Holiday Toys data. Figure 6.21 displays the formula worksheet in the background and the value worksheet in the foreground.

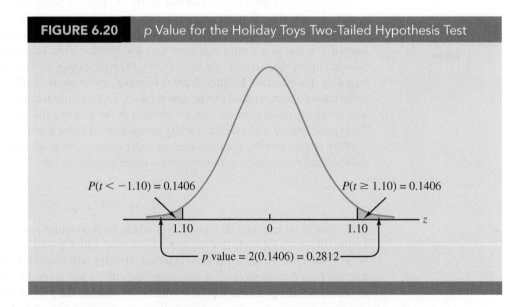

FIGURE 6.20 p Value for the Holiday Toys Two-Tailed Hypothesis Test

FIGURE 6.21	Two-Tailed Hypothesis Test for Holiday Toys

	A	B	C	D
1	Units		Hypothesis Test about a Population Mean	
2	26			
3	23			
4	32		Sample Size	=COUNT(A:A)
5	47		Sample Mean	=AVERAGE(A:A)
6	45		Sample Standard Deviation	=STDEV.S(A:A)
7	31			
8	47		Hypothesized Value	40
9	59			
10	21		Standard Error	=D6/SQRT(D4)
11	52		Test Statistic t	=(D5−D8)/D10
12	45		Degrees of Freedom	=D4−1
13	53			
14	34		p value (Lower Tail)	=T.DIST(D11,D12,TRUE)
15	45		p value (Upper Tail)	=1−D14
16	39		p value (Two Tail)	=2*MIN(D14,D15)
17	52			
18	52			
19	22			
20	22			
21	33			
22	21			
23	34			
24	42			
25	30			
26	28			

MODEL *file*

OrdersTest

Note: Rows 18–24 are hidden.

	A	B	C	D
1	Units		Hypothesis Test about a Population Mean	
2	26			
3	23			
4	32		Sample Size	25
5	47		Sample Mean	37.4
6	45		Sample Standard Deviation	11.79
7	31			
8	47		Hypothesized Value	40
9	59			
10	21		Standard Error	2.358
11	52		Test Statistic t	−1.103
12	45		Degrees of Freedom	24
13	53			
14	34		p value (Lower Tail)	0.1406
15	45		p value (Upper Tail)	0.8594
16	39		p value (Two Tail)	0.2811
17	52			

To complete the two-tailed Holiday Toys hypothesis test, we compare the two-tailed p value to the level of significance to see whether the null hypothesis should be rejected. With a level of significance of $\alpha = 0.05$, we do not reject H_0 because the two-tailed p value $= 0.2811 > 0.05$. This result indicates that Holiday should continue its production planning for the coming season based on the expectation that $\mu = 40$.

The *OrdersTest* worksheet in Figure 6.21 can be used as a template for any hypothesis tests about a population mean. To facilitate the use of this worksheet, the formulas in cells D4:D6 reference the entire column A as follows:

$$\text{Cell D4: } =COUNT(A:A)$$
$$\text{Cell D5: } =AVERAGE(A:A)$$
$$\text{Cell D6: } =STDEV.S(A:A)$$

With the A:A method of specifying data ranges, Excel's COUNT function will count the number of numeric values in column A, Excel's AVERAGE function will compute the average of the numeric values in column A, and Excel's STDEV.S function will compute the standard deviation of the numeric values in Column A. Thus, to solve a new problem it is necessary only to enter the new data in column A and enter the hypothesized value of the population mean in cell D8. Then, the standard error, the test statistic, degrees of freedom, and the three p values will be updated by the Excel formulas.

Let us summarize the steps involved in computing p values for two-tailed hypothesis tests.

COMPUTATION OF p VALUES FOR TWO-TAILED TESTS

1. Compute the value of the test statistic using equation (6.11).
2. If the value of the test statistic is in the upper tail, compute the probability that t is greater than or equal to the value of the test statistic (the upper-tail area). If the value of the test statistic is in the lower tail, compute the probability that t is less than or equal to the value of the test statistic (the lower-tail area).
3. Double the probability (or tail area) from step 2 to obtain the p value.

Summary and Practical Advice We presented examples of a lower-tail test and a two-tailed test about a population mean. Based on these examples, we can now summarize the hypothesis testing procedures about a population mean in Table 6.7. Note that μ_0 is the hypothesized value of the population mean.

The hypothesis testing steps followed in the two examples presented in this section are common to every hypothesis test.

STEPS OF HYPOTHESIS TESTING

Step 1. Develop the null and alternative hypotheses.
Step 2. Specify the level of significance.
Step 3. Collect the sample data and compute the value of the test statistic.
Step 4. Use the value of the test statistic to compute the p value.
Step 5. Reject H_0 if the $p \leq \alpha$.
Step 6. Interpret the statistical conclusion in the context of the application.

Practical advice about the sample size for hypothesis tests is similar to the advice we provided about the sample size for interval estimation in Section 6.4. In most applications, a sample size of $n \geq 30$ is adequate when using the hypothesis testing procedure described in this section. In cases in which the sample size is less than 30, the distribution of the population from which we are sampling becomes an important consideration. When the population is normally distributed, the hypothesis tests described in this section provide exact results for any sample size. When the population is not normally distributed, these procedures provide approximations. Nonetheless, we find that sample sizes of 30 or more will provide good results in most cases. If the population is approximately normal, small sample sizes (e.g., $n = 15$) can provide acceptable results. If the population is highly skewed or contains outliers, sample sizes approaching 50 are recommended.

TABLE 6.7	Summary of Hypothesis Tests About a Population Mean		
	Lower-Tail Test	**Upper-Tail Test**	**Two-Tailed Test**
Hypotheses	$H_0: \mu \geq \mu_0$ $H_a: \mu < \mu_0$	$H_0: \mu \leq \mu_0$ $H_a: \mu > \mu_0$	$H_0: \mu = \mu_0$ $H_a: \mu \neq \mu_0$
Test Statistic	$t = \dfrac{\bar{x} - \mu_0}{s/\sqrt{n}}$	$t = \dfrac{\bar{x} - \mu_0}{s/\sqrt{n}}$	$t = \dfrac{\bar{x} - \mu_0}{s/\sqrt{n}}$
p Value	=T.DIST(t,n − 1, TRUE)	=1 − T.DIST(t,n − 1, TRUE)	=2*MIN(T.DIST(t,n − 1, TRUE),1 − T.DIST(t,n − 1, TRUE))

Relationship Between Interval Estimation and Hypothesis Testing In Section 6.4 we showed how to develop a confidence interval estimate of a population mean. The $(1 - \alpha)\%$ confidence interval estimate of a population mean is given by

$$\bar{x} \pm t_{\alpha/2} \frac{s}{\sqrt{n}}$$

In this chapter we showed that a two-tailed hypothesis test about a population mean takes the following form:

$$H_0: \mu = \mu_0$$
$$H_a: \mu \neq \mu_0$$

where μ_0 is the hypothesized value for the population mean.

Suppose that we follow the procedure described in Section 6.4 for constructing a $100(1 - \alpha)\%$ confidence interval for the population mean. We know that $100(1 - \alpha)\%$ of the confidence intervals generated will contain the population mean and $100\alpha\%$ of the confidence intervals generated will not contain the population mean. Thus, if we reject H_0 whenever the confidence interval does not contain μ_0, we will be rejecting the null hypothesis when it is true ($\mu = \mu_0$) with probability α. Recall that the level of significance is the probability of rejecting the null hypothesis when it is true. So constructing a $100(1 - \alpha)\%$ confidence interval and rejecting H_0 whenever the interval does not contain μ_0 is equivalent to conducting a two-tailed hypothesis test with α as the level of significance. The procedure for using a confidence interval to conduct a two-tailed hypothesis test can now be summarized.

> **A CONFIDENCE INTERVAL APPROACH TO TESTING A HYPOTHESIS OF THE FORM**
>
> $$H_0: \mu = \mu_0$$
> $$H_a: \mu \neq \mu_0$$
>
> 1. Select a simple random sample from the population and use the value of the sample mean $\bar{x}$ to develop the confidence interval for the population mean μ.
>
> $$\bar{x} \pm t_{\alpha/2} \frac{s}{\sqrt{n}}$$
>
> 2. If the confidence interval contains the hypothesized value μ_0, do not reject H_0. Otherwise, reject[3] H_0.

For a two-tailed hypothesis test, the null hypothesis can be rejected if the confidence interval does not include μ_0.

Let us illustrate by conducting the Holiday Toys hypothesis test using the confidence interval approach. The Holiday Toys hypothesis test takes the following form:

$$H_0: \mu = 40$$
$$H_a: \mu \neq 40$$

To test these hypotheses with a level of significance of $\alpha = 0.05$, we sampled 25 retailers and found a sample mean of $\bar{x} = 37.4$ units and a sample standard deviation of $s = 11.79$ units. Using these results with $t_{0.025} = \text{T.INV}(1 - (.05/2), 25 - 1) = 2.064$, we find that the 95% confidence interval estimate of the population mean is

$$\bar{x} \pm t_{0.025} \frac{s}{\sqrt{n}}$$

$$37.4 \pm 2.064 \frac{11.79}{\sqrt{25}}$$

$$37.4 \pm 4.4$$

or

$$33.0 \text{ to } 41.8.$$

This finding enables Holiday's marketing director to conclude with 95% confidence that the mean number of units per retail outlet is between 33.0 and 41.8. Because the

---

[3]To be consistent with the rule for rejecting H_0 when $p \leq \alpha$, we would also reject H_0 using the confidence interval approach if μ_0 happens to be equal to one of the endpoints of the $100(1 - \alpha)\%$ confidence interval.

hypothesized value for the population mean, $\mu_0 = 40$, is in this interval, the hypothesis testing conclusion is that the null hypothesis, H_0: $\mu = 40$, cannot be rejected.

Note that this discussion and example pertain to two-tailed hypothesis tests about a population mean. However, the same confidence interval and two-tailed hypothesis testing relationship exists for other population parameters. The relationship can also be extended to one-tailed tests about population parameters. Doing so, however, requires the development of one-sided confidence intervals, which are rarely used in practice.

Hypothesis Test of the Population Proportion

In this section we show how to conduct a hypothesis test about a population proportion p. Using p_0 to denote the hypothesized value for the population proportion, the three forms for a hypothesis test about a population proportion are as follows:

$$H_0: p \geq p_0 \qquad H_0: p \leq p_0 \qquad H_0: p = p_0$$
$$H_a: p < p_0 \qquad H_a: p > p_0 \qquad H_a: p \neq p_0$$

The first form is called a lower-tail test, the second an upper-tail test, and the third form a two-tailed test.

Hypothesis tests about a population proportion are based on the difference between the sample proportion $\bar{p}$ and the hypothesized population proportion p_0. The methods used to conduct the hypothesis test are similar to those used for hypothesis tests about a population mean. The only difference is that we use the sample proportion and its standard error to compute the test statistic. The p value is then used to determine whether the null hypothesis should be rejected.

Let us consider an example involving a situation faced by Pine Creek golf course. Over the past year, 20% of the players at Pine Creek were women. In an effort to increase the proportion of women players, Pine Creek implemented a special promotion designed to attract women golfers. One month after the promotion was implemented, the course manager requested a statistical study to determine whether the proportion of women players at Pine Creek had increased. Because the objective of the study is to determine whether the proportion of women golfers increased, an upper-tail test with H_a: $p > 0.20$ is appropriate. The null and alternative hypotheses for the Pine Creek hypothesis test are as follows:

$$H_0: p \leq 0.20$$
$$H_a: p > 0.20$$

If H_0 can be rejected, the test results will give statistical support for the conclusion that the proportion of women golfers increased and the promotion was beneficial. The course manager specified that a level of significance of $\alpha = 0.05$ be used in carrying out this hypothesis test.

The next step of the hypothesis testing procedure is to select a sample and compute the value of an appropriate test statistic. To show how this step is done for the Pine Creek upper-tail test, we begin with a general discussion of how to compute the value of the test statistic for any form of a hypothesis test about a population proportion. The sampling distribution of $\bar{p}$, the point estimator of the population parameter p, is the basis for developing the test statistic.

When the null hypothesis is true as an equality, the expected value of $\bar{p}$ equals the hypothesized value p_0; that is, $E(\bar{p}) = p_0$. The standard error of $\bar{p}$ is given by

$$\sigma_{\bar{p}} = \sqrt{\frac{p_0(1 - p_0)}{n}}$$

In Section 6.3, we said that if $np \geq 5$ and $n(1 - p) \geq 5$, the sampling distribution of $\bar{p}$ can be approximated by a normal distribution.[4] Under these conditions, which usually apply in practice, the quantity

$$z = \frac{\bar{p} - p_0}{\sigma_{\bar{p}}} \tag{6.12}$$

---

[4] In most applications involving hypothesis tests of a population proportion, sample sizes are large enough to use the normal approximation. The exact sampling distribution of $\bar{p}$ is discrete, with the probability for each value of $\bar{p}$ given by the binomial distribution. So hypothesis testing is a bit more complicated for small samples when the normal approximation cannot be used.

has a standard normal probability distribution. With $\sigma_{\bar{p}} = \sqrt{p_0(1-p_0)/n}$, the standard normal random variable z is the test statistic used to conduct hypothesis tests about a population proportion.

TEST STATISTIC FOR HYPOTHESIS TESTS ABOUT A POPULATION PROPORTION

$$z = \frac{\bar{p} - p_0}{\sqrt{\dfrac{p_0(1-p_0)}{n}}} \qquad (6.13)$$

WomenGolf

We can now compute the test statistic for the Pine Creek hypothesis test. Suppose a random sample of 400 players was selected, and that 100 of the players were women. The proportion of women golfers in the sample is

$$\bar{p} = \frac{100}{400} = 0.25$$

Using equation (6.13), the value of the test statistic is

$$z = \frac{\bar{p} - p_0}{\sqrt{\dfrac{p_0(1-p_0)}{n}}} = \frac{0.25 - 0.20}{\sqrt{\dfrac{0.20(1-0.20)}{400}}} = \frac{0.05}{0.02} = 2.50$$

The Excel formula
= NORM.S.DIST(z, TRUE)
computes the area under
the standard normal
distribution curve that is
less than or equal to the
value z.

Because the Pine Creek hypothesis test is an upper-tail test, the p value is the probability of obtaining a value for the test statistic that is greater than or equal to $z = 2.50$; that is, it is the upper-tail area corresponding to $z \geq 2.50$ as displayed in Figure 6.22. The Excel formula $= 1 - NORM.S.DIST(2.5,TRUE)$ computes this upper-tail area of 0.0062.

Recall that the course manager specified a level of significance of $\alpha = 0.05$. A p value $= 0.0062 < 0.05$ gives sufficient statistical evidence to reject H_0 at the 0.05 level of significance. Thus, the test provides statistical support for the conclusion that the special promotion increased the proportion of women players at the Pine Creek golf course.

Using Excel Excel can be used to conduct one-tailed and two-tailed hypothesis tests about a population proportion using the p value approach. The procedure is similar to the approach used with Excel in conducting hypothesis tests about a population mean. The primary difference is that the test statistic is based on the sampling distribution of $\bar{x}$ for

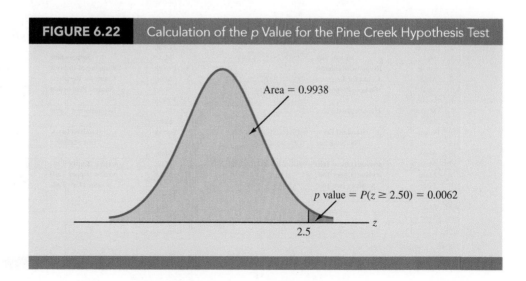

FIGURE 6.22   Calculation of the p Value for the Pine Creek Hypothesis Test

hypothesis tests about a population mean and on the sampling distribution of $\bar{p}$ for hypothesis tests about a population proportion. Thus, although different formulas are used to compute the test statistic and the p value needed to make the hypothesis testing decision, the logical process is identical.

MODEL *file*

WomenGolfTest

The worksheet in Figure 6.23 can be used as a template for hypothesis tests about a population proportion whenever $np \geq 5$ and $n(1 - p) \geq 5$. Just enter the appropriate data in column A, adjust the ranges for the formulas in cells D3 and D5, enter the appropriate response in cell D4, and enter the hypothesized value in cell D8. The standard error, the test statistic, and the three p values will then appear. Depending on the form of the hypothesis test (lower-tail, upper-tail, or two-tailed), we can then choose the appropriate p value to make the rejection decision.

We will illustrate the procedure by showing how Excel can be used to conduct the upper-tail hypothesis test for the Pine Creek golf course study. Refer to Figure 6.23 as we describe the tasks involved. The formula worksheet is on the left; the value worksheet is on the right.

The descriptive statistics needed are provided in cells D3, D5, and D6. Because the data are not numeric, Excel's COUNTA function, not the COUNT function, is used in cell D3 to determine the sample size. We entered *Female* in cell D4 to identify the response for which we wish to compute a proportion. The COUNTIF function is then used in cell D5 to determine the number of responses of the type identified in cell D4. The sample proportion is then computed in cell D6 by dividing the response count by the sample size.

The hypothesized value of the population proportion (0.20) is entered into cell D8. The standard error is obtained in cell D10 by entering the formula $=SQRT(D8*(1-D8)/D3)$. The formula $=(D6-D8)/D10$ entered into cell D11 computes the test statistic z according to equation (6.13). To compute the p value for a lower-tail test, we enter the formula $=NORM.S.DIST(D11,TRUE)$ into cell D13. The p value for an upper-tail test is tzhen computed in cell D14 as 1 minus the p value for the lower-tail test. Finally, the p value for a two-tailed test is computed in cell D15 as two times the minimum of the two one-tailed p values. The value worksheet shows that the three p values are as follows: p value (lower tail) = 0.9938, p value (upper tail) = 0.0062, and p value (two tail) = 0.0124.

The development of the worksheet is now complete. For the Pine Creek upper-tail hypothesis test, we reject the null hypothesis that the population proportion is 0.20 or less because the upper tail p value of 0.0062 is less than $\alpha = 0.05$. Indeed, with this p value we would reject the null hypothesis for any level of significance of 0.0062 or greater.

The procedure used to conduct a hypothesis test about a population proportion is similar to the procedure used to conduct a hypothesis test about a population mean. Although we illustrated how to conduct a hypothesis test about a population proportion only for an upper-tail test, similar procedures can be used for lower-tail and two-tailed tests. Table 6.8 provides a summary of the hypothesis tests about a population proportion for the case that $np \geq 5$ and $n(1 - p) \geq 5$ (and thus the normal probability distribution can be used to approximate the sampling distribution of $\bar{p}$).

FIGURE 6.23 Hypothesis Test for Pine Creek Golf Course

	A	B	C	D
1	Golfer		**Hypothesis Test about a Population Proportion**	
2	Female			
3	Male		Sample Size	=COUNTA(A2:A401)
4	Female		**Response of Interest**	Female
5	Male		Count for Response	=COUNTIF(A2:A401,D4)
6	Male		Sample Proportion	=D5/D3
7	Female			
8	Male		Hypothesized Value	0.2
9	Male			
10	Female		Standard Error	=SQRT(D8*(1−D8)/D3)
11	Male		Test Statistic z	=(D6−D8)/D10
12	Male			
13	Male		p value (Lower Tail)	=NORM.S.DIST(D11,TRUE)
14	Male		p value (Upper Tail)	=1−D13
15	Male		p value (Two Tail)	=2*MIN(D13,D14)
16	Female			
400	Male			
401	Male			
402				

	A	B	C	D	E	F
1	Golfer		**Hypothesis Test about a Population Proportion**			
2	Female					
3	Male		Sample Size	400		
4	Female		**Response of Interest**	Female		
5	Male		Count for Response	100		
6	Male		Sample Proportion	0.25		
7	Female					
8	Male		Hypothesized Value	0.20		
9	Male					
10	Female		Standard Error	0.02		
11	Male		Test Statistic z	2.5000		
12	Male					
13	Male		p value (Lower Tail)	0.9938		
14	Male		p value (Upper Tail)	0.0062		
15	Male		p value (Two Tail)	0.0124		
16	Female					
400	Male					
401	Male					
402						

TABLE 6.8	Summary of Hypothesis Tests About a Population Proportion		
	Lower-Tail Test	**Upper-Tail Test**	**Two-Tailed Test**
Hypotheses	$H_0: p \geq p_0$ $H_a: p < p_0$	$H_0: p \leq p_0$ $H_a: p > p_0$	$H_0: p = p_0$ $H_a: p \neq p_0$
Test Statistic	$z = \dfrac{\bar{p} - p_0}{\sqrt{\dfrac{p_0(1 - p_0)}{n}}}$	$z = \dfrac{\bar{p} - p_0}{\sqrt{\dfrac{p_0(1 - p_0)}{n}}}$	$z = \dfrac{\bar{p} - p_0}{\sqrt{\dfrac{p_0(1 - p_0)}{n}}}$
p Value	=NORM.S.DIST (z, TRUE)	=1 − NORM.S.DIST (z, TRUE)	2*MIN(NORM.S.DIST(z, TRUE), 1 − NORM.S.DIST(z, TRUE))

NOTES + COMMENTS

1. We have shown how to use p values. The smaller the p value, the stronger the evidence in the sample data against H_0 and the stronger the evidence in favor of H_a. Here are guidelines that some statisticians suggest for interpreting small p values:
   - Less than 0.01—overwhelming evidence to conclude that H_a is true
   - Between 0.01 and 0.05—strong evidence to conclude that H_a is true
   - Between 0.05 and 0.10—weak evidence to conclude that H_a is true
   - Greater than 0.10—insufficient evidence to conclude that H_a is true

2. The procedures for testing hypotheses about the mean that are discussed in this chapter are reliable unless the sample size is small and the population is highly skewed or contains outliers. In these cases, a nonparametric approach such as the sign test can be used. Under these conditions the results of nonparametric tests are more reliable than the hypothesis testing procedures discussed in this chapter. However, this increased reliability comes with a cost; if the sample is large or the population is relatively normally distributed, a nonparametric approach will also reject false null hypotheses less frequently.

3. We have discussed only procedures for testing hypotheses about the mean or proportion of a single population. There are many statistical procedures for testing hypotheses about multiple means or proportions. There are also many statistical procedures for testing hypotheses about parameters other than the population mean or the population proportion.

6.6 Big Data, Statistical Inference, and Practical Significance

As stated earlier in this chapter, the purpose of statistical inference is to use sample data to quickly and inexpensively gain insight into some characteristic of a population. Therefore, it is important that we can expect the sample to look like, or be representative of, the population that is being investigated. In practice, individual samples always, to varying degrees, fail to be perfectly representative of the population of interest. There are two general reasons a sample may fail to be representative of the population of interest: sampling error and nonsampling error.

Sampling Error

One reason a sample may fail to represent the population of interest is **sampling error**, or deviation of the sample from the population that results from random sampling. If repeated independent random samples of the same size are collected from the population of interest using a probability sampling techniques, on average the samples will be representative of the population from which the samples have been taken. This is the justification for collecting sample data randomly. However, the random collection of sample data does not ensure that any single sample will be perfectly representative of the population from which the sample has been taken; when collecting a sample randomly, the data in the sample cannot be expected to be perfectly representative of the population from which it has been taken. Sampling error is unavoidable when collecting a random sample; this is a risk we must accept when we chose to collect a random sample rather than incur the costs associated with taking a census of the population.

As expressed by equations (6.2) and (6.5), the standard errors of the sampling distributions of the sample mean $\bar{x}$ and the sample proportion of $\bar{p}$ reflect the potential for sampling error when using sample data to estimate the population mean μ and the population proportion p, respectively. As the sample size n increases, the potential impact of extreme values on the statistic decreases, so there is less variation in the potential values of the statistic produced by the sample and the standard errors of these sampling distributions decrease. Because these standard errors reflect the potential for sampling error when using sample data to estimate the population mean μ and the population proportion p, we see that for an extremely large sample there may be little potential for sampling error.

Nonsampling Error

Although the standard error of a sampling distribution decreases as the sample size n increases, this does not mean that we can conclude that an extremely large sample will always provide reliable information about the population of interest; this is because sampling error is not the sole reason a sample may fail to represent the target population. Deviations of the sample from the population that occur for reasons other than random sampling are referred to as **nonsampling error**. Nonsampling error can occur for a variety of reasons.

Consider the online news service PenningtonDailyTimes.com (PDT). Because PDT's primary source of revenue is the sale of advertising, the news service is intent on collecting sample data on the behavior of visitors to its web site in order to support its advertising sales. Prospective advertisers are willing to pay a premium to advertise on web sites that have long visit times, so PDT's management is keenly interested in the amount of time customers spend during their visits to PDT's web site. Advertisers are also concerned with how frequently visitors to a web site click on any of the ads featured on the web site, so PDT is also interested in whether visitors to its web site clicked on any of the ads featured on PenningtonDailyTimes.com.

From whom should PDT collect its data? Should it collect data on current visits to PenningtonDailyTimes.com? Should it attempt to attract new visitors and collect data on these visits? If so, should it measure the time spent at its web site by visitors it has attracted from competitors' web sites or visitors who do not routinely visit online news sites? The answers to these questions depend on PDT's research objectives. Is the company attempting to evaluate its current market, assess the potential of customers it can attract from competitors, or explore the potential of an entirely new market such as individuals who do not routinely obtain their news from online news services? If the research objective and the population from which the sample is to be drawn are not aligned, the data that PDT collects will not help the company accomplish its research objective. This type of error is referred to as a **coverage error**.

Nonsampling error can occur in a sample or a census.

Even when the sample is taken from the appropriate population, nonsampling error can occur when segments of the target population are systematically underrepresented or overrepresented in the sample. This may occur because the study design is flawed or because some segments of the population are either more likely or less likely to respond. Suppose PDT implements a pop-up questionnaire that opens when a visitor leaves PenningtonDailyTimes.com. Visitors to PenningtonDailyTimes.com who have installed pop-up blockers will be likely underrepresented, and visitors to PenningtonDailyTimes.com who have not installed pop-up blockers will likely be overrepresented. If the behavior of PenningtonDailyTimes.com visitors who have installed pop-up blockers differs from the behaviors of PenningtonDailyTimes.com visitors who have not installed pop-up blockers, attempting to draw conclusions from this sample about how all visitors to the PDT web site behave may be misleading. This type of error is referred to as a **nonresponse error**.

Another potential source of nonsampling error is incorrect measurement of the characteristic of interest. This type of error is referred to as a **measurement error**. For example, if PDT asks questions that are ambiguous or difficult for respondents to understand, the responses may not accurately reflect how the respondents intended to respond. For example, respondents may be unsure how to respond if PDT asks "Are the news stories on PenningtonDailyTimes.com compelling and accurate?". How should a visitor respond if she or he feels the news stories on PenningtonDailyTimes.com are compelling but erroneous? What response is appropriate if the respondent feels the news stories on PenningtonDailyTimes.com are accurate but dull? A similar issue can arise if a question is asked in a biased or leading way. If PDT asks "Many readers find the news stories on PenningtonDailyTimes.com to be compelling and accurate. Do you find the news stories on PenningtonDailyTimes.com to be compelling and accurate?", the qualifying statement PDT makes prior to the actual question will likely result in a bias toward positive responses. Incorrect measurement of the characteristic of interest can also occur when respondents provide incorrect answers; this may be due to a respondent's poor recall or unwillingness to respond honestly.

Errors that are introduced by interviewers or during the recording and preparation of the data are other types of nonsampling error. These types of error are referred to as interviewer errors and processing errors, respectively.

Nonsampling error can introduce bias into the estimates produced using the sample, and this bias can mislead decision makers who use the sample data in their decision-making processes. No matter how small or large the sample, we must contend with this limitation of sampling whenever we use sample data to gain insight into a population of interest. Although sampling error decreases as the size of the sample increases, an extremely large sample can still suffer from nonsampling error and fail to be representative of the population of interest. When sampling, care must be taken to ensure that we minimize the introduction of nonsampling error into the data collection process. This can be done by carrying out the following steps:

- Carefully define the target population before collecting sample data, and subsequently design the data collection procedure so that a probability sample is drawn from this target population.
- Carefully design the data collection process and train the data collectors.
- Pretest the data collection procedure to identify and correct for potential sources of nonsampling error prior to final data collection.
- Use stratified random sampling when population-level information about an important qualitative variable is available to ensure that the sample is representative of the population with respect to that qualitative characteristic.
- Use cluster sampling when the population can be divided into heterogeneous subgroups or clusters.
- Use systematic sampling when population-level information about an important quantitative variable is available to ensure that the sample is representative of the population with respect to that quantitative characteristic.

Finally, recognize that every random sample (even an extremely large random sample) will suffer from some degree of sampling error, and eliminating all potential sources of nonsampling error may be impractical. Understanding these limitations of sampling will enable us to be more realistic and pragmatic when interpreting sample data and using sample data to draw conclusions about the target population.

Big Data

Recent estimates state that approximately 2.5 quintillion bytes of data are created worldwide each day. This represents a dramatic increase from the estimated 100 gigabytes (GB) of data generated worldwide per day in 1992, the 100 GB of data generated worldwide per hour in 1997, and the 100 GB of data generated worldwide per second in 2002. Every minute, there is an average of 216,000 Instagram posts, 204,000,000 e-mails sent, 12 hours of footage uploaded to YouTube, and 277,000 tweets posted on Twitter. Without question, the amount of data that is now generated is overwhelming, and this trend is certainly expected to continue.

In each of these cases the data sets that are generated are so large or complex that current data processing capacity and/or analytic methods are not adequate for analyzing the data. Thus, each is an example of **big data**. There are myriad other sources of big data. Sensors and mobile devices transmit enormous amounts of data. Internet activities, digital processes, and social media interactions also produce vast quantities of data.

The amount of data has increased so rapidly that our vocabulary for describing a data set by its size must expand. A few years ago, a petabyte of data seemed almost unimaginably large, but we now routinely describe data in terms of yottabytes. Table 6.9 summarizes terminology for describing the size of data sets.

Understanding What Big Data Is

The processes that generate big data can be described by four attributes or dimensions that are referred to as the four V's:

- **Volume**—the amount of data generated
- **Variety**—the diversity in types and structures of data generated
- **Veracity**—the reliability of the data generated
- **Velocity**—the speed at which the data are generated

A high degree of any of these attributes individually is sufficient to generate big data, and when they occur at high levels simultaneously the resulting amount of data can be overwhelmingly large. Technological advances and improvements in electronic (and often automated) data collection make it easy to collect millions, or even billions, of observations in a relatively short time. Businesses are collecting greater volumes of an increasing variety of data at a higher velocity than ever.

To understand the challenges presented by big data, we consider its structural dimensions. Big data can be **tall data**; a data set that has so many observations that traditional statistical inference has little meaning. For example, producers of consumer goods collect information on the sentiment expressed in millions of social media posts each day to better understand consumer perceptions of their products. Such data consist of the sentiment expressed (the variable) in millions (or over time, even billions) of social media posts (the observations). Big data can also be **wide data**; a data set that has so many variables that simultaneous consideration of all variables is infeasible. For example, a high-resolution image can comprise millions or billions of pixels. The data used by facial recognition algorithms consider each pixel in an image when comparing an image to other images in an attempt to find a match. Thus, these algorithms make use of the characteristics of millions

TABLE 6.9	Terminology for Describing the Size of Data Sets	
Number of Bytes	**Metric**	**Name**
1000^1	kB	kilobyte
1000^2	MB	megabyte
1000^3	GB	gigabyte
1000^4	TB	terabyte
1000^5	PB	petabyte
1000^6	EB	exabyte
1000^7	ZB	zettabyte
1000^8	YB	yottabyte

or billions of pixels (the variables) for relatively few high-resolution images (the observations). Of course, big data can be both tall and wide, and the resulting data set can again be overwhelmingly large.

Statistics are useful tools for understanding the information embedded in a big data set, but we must be careful when using statistics to analyze big data. It is important that we understand the limitations of statistics when applied to big data and we temper our interpretations accordingly. Because tall data are the most common form of big data used in business, we focus on this structure in the discussions throughout the remainder of this section.

Big Data and Sampling Error

A sample of one million or more visitors might seem unrealistic, but keep in mind that amazon.com had over 91 million visitors in March of 2016 (quantcast. com, May 13, 2016).

Let's revisit the data collection problem of online news service PenningtonDailyTimes.com (PDT). Because PDT's primary source of revenue is the sale of advertising, PDT's management is interested in the amount of time customers spend during their visits to PDT's web site. From historical data, PDT has estimated that the standard deviation of the time spent by individual customers when they visit PDT's web site is $s = 20$ seconds. Table 6.10 shows how the standard error of the sampling distribution of the sample mean time spent by individual customers when they visit PDT's web site decreases as the sample size increases.

PDT also wants to collect information from its sample respondents on whether a visitor to its web site clicked on any of the ads featured on the web site. From its historical data, PDT knows that 51% of past visitors to its web site clicked on an ad featured on the web site, so it will use this value as $\bar{p}$ to estimate the standard error. Table 6.11 shows how the standard error of the sampling distribution of the proportion of the sample that clicked on any of the ads featured on PenningtonDailyTimes.com decreases as the sample size increases.

The PDT example illustrates the general relationship between standard errors and the sample size. We see in Table 6.10 that the standard error of the sample mean decreases as the sample size increases. For a sample of $n = 10$, the standard error of the sample mean is 6.32456; when we increase the sample size to $n = 100,000$, the standard error of the sample mean decreases to 0.06325; and at a sample size of $n = 1,000,000,000$, the standard error of the sample mean decreases to only 0.00063. In Table 6.11 we see that the standard error of the sample proportion also decreases as the sample size increases. For a sample of $n = 10$, the standard error of the sample proportion is 0.15808; when we increase the sample size to $n = 100,000$, the standard error of the sample proportion decreases to 0.00158; and at a sample size of $n = 1,000,000,000$, the standard error of the sample mean decreases to only 0.00002. In both Table 6.10 and Table 6.11, the standard error when $n = 1,000,000,000$ is *one ten-thousandth of the standard error when $n = 10$*.

TABLE 6.10	Standard Error of the Sample Mean $\bar{x}$ When $s = 20$ at Various Sample Sizes n
Sample Size n	**Standard Error $s_{\bar{x}} = s/\sqrt{n}$**
10	6.32456
100	2.00000
1,000	0.63246
10,000	0.20000
100,000	0.06325
1,000,000	0.02000
10,000,000	0.00632
100,000,000	0.00200
1,000,000,000	0.00063

TABLE 6.11	Standard Error of the Sample Proportion $\bar{p}$ When $p = 0.51$ at Various Sample Sizes n

Sample Size n	Standard Error $\sigma_{\bar{p}} = \sqrt{\bar{p}(1 - \bar{p})/n}$
10	0.15808
100	0.04999
1,000	0.01581
10,000	0.00500
100,000	0.00158
1,000,000	0.00050
10,000,000	0.00016
100,000,000	0.00005
1,000,000,000	0.00002

Big Data and the Precision of Confidence Intervals

We have seen that confidence intervals are powerful tools for making inferences about population parameters, but the validity of any interval estimate depends on the quality of the data used to develop the interval estimate. No matter how large the sample is, if the sample is not representative of the population of interest, the confidence interval cannot provide useful information about the population parameter of interest. In these circumstances, statistical inference can be misleading.

A review of equations (6.7) and (6.10) shows that confidence intervals for the population mean μ and population proportion p become more narrow as the size of the sample increases. Therefore, the potential sampling error also decreases as the sample size increases. To illustrate the rate at which interval estimates narrow for a given confidence level, we again consider the PenningtonDailyTimes.com (PDT) example.

Recall that PDT's primary source of revenue is the sale of advertising, and prospective advertisers are willing to pay a premium to advertise on web sites that have long visit times. Suppose PDT's management wants to develop a 95% confidence interval estimate of the mean amount of time customers spend during their visits to PDT's web site. Table 6.12 shows how the margin of error at the 95% confidence level decreases as the sample size increases when $s = 20$.

Suppose that in addition to estimating the population mean amount of time customers spend during their visits to PDT's web site, PDT would like to develop a 95% confidence interval estimate of the proportion of its web site visitors that click on an ad. Table 6.13 shows how the margin of error for a 95% confidence interval estimate of the population proportion decreases as the sample size increases when the sample proportion is $\bar{p} = 0.51$.

The PDT example illustrates the relationship between the precision of interval estimates and the sample size. We see in Tables 6.12 and 6.13 that at a given confidence level, the margins of error decrease as the sample sizes increase. As a result, if the sample mean time spent by customers when they visit PDT's web site is 84.1 seconds, the 95% confidence interval estimate of the population mean time spent by customers when they visit PDT's web site decreases from (69.79286, 98.40714) for a sample of $n = 10$ to (83.97604, 84.22396) for a sample of $n = 100,000$ to (84.09876, 84.10124) for a sample of $n = 1,000,000,000$. Similarly, if the sample proportion of its web site visitors who clicked on an ad is 0.51, the 95% confidence interval estimate of the population proportion of its web site visitors who clicked on an ad decreases from (0.20016, 0.81984) for a sample of $n = 10$ to (0.50690, 0.51310) for a sample of $n = 100,000$ to (0.50997, 0.51003) for a

TABLE 6.12	Margin of Error for Interval Estimates of the Population Mean at the 95% Confidence Level for Various Sample Sizes *n*
Sample Size *n*	**Margin of Error $t_{\alpha/2}s_{\bar{x}}$**
10	14.30714
100	3.96843
1,000	1.24109
10,000	0.39204
100,000	0.12396
1,000,000	0.03920
10,000,000	0.01240
100,000,000	0.00392
1,000,000,000	0.00124

TABLE 6.13	Margin of Error for Interval Estimates of the Population Proportion at the 95% Confidence Level for Various Sample Sizes *n*
Sample Size *n*	**Margin of Error $z_{\alpha/2}\sigma_{\bar{p}}$**
10	0.30984
100	0.09798
1,000	0.03098
10,000	0.00980
100,000	0.00310
1,000,000	0.00098
10,000,000	0.00031
100,000,000	0.00010
1,000,000,000	0.00003

sample of $n = 1,000,000,000$. In both instances, as the sample size becomes extremely large, the margin of error becomes extremely small and the resulting confidence intervals become extremely narrow.

Implications of Big Data for Confidence Intervals

Last year, the mean time spent by all visitors to PenningtonDailyTimes.com was 84 seconds. Suppose that PDT wants to assess whether the population mean time has changed since last year. PDT now collects a new sample of 1,000,000 visitors to its web site and calculates the sample mean time spent by these visitors to the PDT web site to be $\bar{x} = 84.1$ seconds. The estimated population standard deviation is $s = 20$ seconds, so the standard error is $s_{\bar{x}} = s/\sqrt{n} = 0.02000$. Furthermore, the sample is sufficiently large to ensure that the sampling distribution of the sample mean will be normally distributed. Thus, the 95% confidence interval estimate of the population mean is

$$\bar{x} \pm t_{\alpha/2}s_{\bar{x}} = 84.1 \pm 0.0392 = (84.06080, 84.13920)$$

What could PDT conclude from these results? There are three possible reasons that PDT's sample mean of 84.1 seconds differs from last year's population mean of 84 seconds: (1) sampling error, (2) nonsampling error, or (3) the population mean has changed since last year. The 95% confidence interval estimate of the population mean does not include the value for the mean time spent by all visitors to the PDT web site for last year (84 seconds), suggesting that the difference between PDT's sample mean for the new sample (84.1 seconds) and the mean from last year (84 seconds) is not likely to be exclusively a consequence of sampling error. Nonsampling error is a possible explanation and should be investigated as the results of statistical inference become less reliable as nonsampling error is introduced into the sample data. If PDT determines that it introduced little or no nonsampling error into its sample data, the only remaining plausible explanation for a difference of this magnitude is that the population mean has changed since last year.

If PDT concludes that the sample has provided reliable evidence and the population mean has changed since last year, management must still consider the potential impact of the difference between the sample mean and the mean from last year. If a 0.1 second difference in the time spent by visitors to PenningtonDailyTimes.com has a consequential effect on what PDT can charge for advertising on its site, this result could have practical business implications for PDT. Otherwise, there may be no **practical significance** of the 0.1 second difference in the time spent by visitors to PenningtonDailyTimes.com.

Confidence intervals are extremely useful, but as with any other statistical tool, they are only effective when properly applied. Because interval estimates become increasingly precise as the sample size increases, extremely large samples will yield extremely precise estimates. However, no interval estimate, no matter how precise, will accurately reflect the parameter being estimated unless the sample is relatively free of nonsampling error. Therefore, when using interval estimation, it is always important to carefully consider whether a random sample of the population of interest has been taken.

Big Data, Hypothesis Testing, and p Values

We have seen that interval estimates of the population mean μ and the population proportion p narrow as the sample size increases. This occurs because the standard error of the associated sampling distributions decrease as the sample size increases. Now consider the relationship between interval estimation and hypothesis testing that we discussed earlier in this chapter. If we construct a $100(1 - \alpha)\%$ interval estimate for the population mean, we reject $H_0: \mu = \mu_0$ if the $100(1 - \alpha)\%$ interval estimate does not contain μ_0. Thus, for a given level of confidence, as the sample size increases we will reject $H_0: \mu = \mu_0$ for increasingly smaller differences between the sample mean $\bar{x}$ and the hypothesized population mean μ_0. We can see that when the sample size n is very large, almost any difference between the sample mean $\bar{x}$ and the hypothesized population mean μ_0 results in rejection of the null hypothesis.

In this section, we will elaborate how big data affects hypothesis testing and the magnitude of p values. Specifically, we will examine how rapidly the p value associated with a given difference between a point estimate and a hypothesized value of a parameter decreases as the sample size increases.

Let us again consider the online news service PenningtonDailyTimes.com (PDT). Recall that PDT's primary source of revenue is the sale of advertising, and prospective advertisers are willing to pay a premium to advertise on web sites that have long visit times. To promote its news service, PDT's management wants to promise potential advertisers that the mean time spent by customers when they visit PenningtonDailyTimes.com is greater than last year, that is, more than 84 seconds. PDT therefore decides to collect a sample tracking the amount of time spent by individual customers when they visit PDT's web site in order to test its null hypothesis $H_0: \mu \leq 84$.

For a sample mean of 84.1 seconds and a sample standard deviation of $s = 20$ seconds, Table 6.14 provides the values of the test statistic t and the p values for the test of the null hypothesis $H_0: \mu \leq 84$. The p value for this hypothesis test is essentially 0 for all samples in Table 6.14 with at least $n = 1,000,000$.

PDT's management also wants to promise potential advertisers that the proportion of its web site visitors who click on an ad this year exceeds the proportion of its web site visitors who clicked on an ad last year, which was 0.50. PDT collects information from its sample on whether the visitor to its web site clicked on any of the ads featured on the web site, and it wants to use these data to test its null hypothesis $H_0: p \leq 0.50$.

For a sample proportion of 0.51, Table 6.15 provides the values of the test statistic z and the p values for the test of the null hypothesis $H_0: p \leq 0.50$. The p value for this hypothesis test is essentially 0 for all samples in Table 6.14 with at least $n = 100,000$.

We see in Tables 6.14 and 6.15 that the p value associated with a given difference between a point estimate and a hypothesized value of a parameter decreases as the sample size increases. As a result, if the sample mean time spent by customers when they visit PDT's web site is 84.1 seconds, PDT's null hypothesis $H_o: \mu \leq 84$ is not rejected at $\alpha = 0.01$ for samples with $n \leq 100,000$, and is rejected at $\alpha = 0.01$ for samples with $n \geq 1,000,000$. Similarly, if the sample proportion of visitors to its web site clicked on an ad featured on the web site is 0.51, PDT's null hypothesis $H_0: p \leq 0.50$ is not rejected at $\alpha = 0.01$ for samples with $n \leq 10,000$, and is rejected at $\alpha = 0.01$ for samples with $n \geq 100,000$. In both instances, as the sample size becomes extremely large the p value associated with the given difference between a point estimate and the hypothesized value of the parameter becomes extremely small.

TABLE 6.14	Values of the Test Statistic t and the p Values for the Test of the Null Hypothesis $H_0: \mu \leq 84$ for Various Sample Sizes When Sample Mean $\bar{x} = 84.1$ Seconds and Sample Standard Deviation $s = 20$	
Sample Size n	**t**	**p Value**
10	0.01581	0.49386
100	0.05000	0.48011
1,000	0.15811	0.43720
10,000	0.50000	0.30854
100,000	1.58114	0.05692
1,000,000	5.00000	2.87E-07
10,000,000	15.81139	1.30E-56
100,000,000	50.00000	0.00E+00
1,000,000,000	158.11388	0.00E+00

TABLE 6.15	Values of the Test Statistic z and the p Values for the Test of the Null Hypothesis $H_0: p \leq .50$ for Various Sample Sizes When Sample Proportion $\bar{p} = 0.51$	
Sample Size n	**z**	**p Value**
10	0.06325	0.47479
100	0.20000	0.42074
1,000	0.63246	0.26354
10,000	2.00000	0.02275
100,000	6.32456	1.27E-10
1,000,000	20.00000	0.00E+00
10,000,000	63.24555	0.00E+00
100,000,000	200.00000	0.00E+00
1,000,000,000	632.45553	0.00E+00

Implications of Big Data in Hypothesis Testing

Suppose PDT collects a sample of 1,000,000 visitors to its web site and uses these data to test its null hypotheses $H_0: \mu \leq 84$ and $H_0: p \leq 0.50$ at the 0.05 level of significance. As the sixth rows of Tables 6.14 and 6.15 show, respectively, the null hypothesis is rejected in both tests. As a result, PDT can promise potential advertisers that the mean time spent by individual customers who visit PDT's web site exceeds 84 seconds and the proportion of individual visitors to its web site who click on an ad exceeds 0.50. These results suggest that for each of these hypothesis tests, the difference between the point estimate and the hypothesized value of the parameter being tested is not likely solely a consequence of sampling error. However, the results of any hypothesis test, no matter the sample size, are only reliable if the sample is relatively free of nonsampling error. If nonsampling error is introduced in the data collection process, the likelihood of making a Type I or Type II error may be higher than if the sample data are free of nonsampling error. Therefore, when testing a hypothesis, it is always important to think carefully about whether a random sample of the population of interest has been taken.

If PDT determines that it has introduced little or no nonsampling error into its sample data, the only remaining plausible explanation for these results is that these null hypotheses are false. At this point, PDT and the companies that advertise on PenningtonDailyTimes.com should also consider whether these statistically significant differences between the point estimates and the hypothesized values of the parameters being tested are of practical significance. Although a 0.1 second increase in the mean time spent by customers when they visit PDT's web site is statistically significant, it may not be meaningful to companies that might advertise on PenningtonDailyTimes.com. Similarly, although an increase of 0.01 in the proportion of visitors to its web site that click on an ad is statistically significant, it may not be meaningful to companies that might advertise on PenningtonDailyTimes.com. One has to determine whether these statistically significant differences have meaningful implications for ensuing business decisions of PDT and its advertisers.

Ultimately, no business decision should be based solely on statistical inference. Practical significance should always be considered in conjunction with statistical significance. This is particularly important when the hypothesis test is based on an extremely large sample because even an extremely small difference between the point estimate and the hypothesized value of the parameter being tested will be statistically significant. When done properly, statistical inference provides evidence that should be considered in combination with information collected from other sources to make the most informed decision possible.

N O T E S   +   C O M M E N T S

1. Nonsampling error can occur when either a probability sampling technique or a nonprobability sampling technique is used. However, nonprobability sampling techniques such as convenience sampling and judgment sampling often introduce nonsampling error into sample data because of the manner in which sample data are collected. Therefore, probability sampling techniques are preferred over nonprobability sampling techniques.

2. When taking an extremely large sample, it is conceivable that the sample size is at least 5% of the population size; that is, $n/N \geq 0.05$. Under these conditions, it is necessary to use the finite population correction factor when calculating the standard error of the sampling distribution to be used in confidence intervals and hypothesis testing.

S U M M A R Y

In this chapter we presented the concepts of sampling and sampling distributions. We demonstrated how a simple random sample can be selected from a finite population and how a random sample can be selected from an infinite population. The data collected from such samples can be used to develop point estimates of population parameters. Different samples provide different values for the point estimators; therefore, point estimators such as $\bar{x}$ and $\bar{p}$ are random variables. The probability distribution of such a random variable is called a sampling distribution. In particular, we described in detail the sampling distributions of the sample mean $\bar{x}$ and the sample proportion $\bar{p}$. In considering the characteristics of the sampling distributions of $\bar{x}$ and $\bar{p}$, we stated that $E(\bar{x}) = \mu$ and $E(\bar{p}) = p$. After developing the standard deviation or standard error formulas for these estimators, we described the conditions necessary for the sampling distributions of $\bar{x}$ and $\bar{p}$ to follow a normal distribution.

In Section 6.4, we presented methods for developing interval estimates of a population mean and a population proportion. A point estimator may or may not provide a good estimate of a population parameter. The use of an interval estimate provides a measure of the precision of an estimate. Both the interval estimate of the population mean and the population proportion take the form: point estimate $\pm$ margin of error.

We presented the interval estimation procedure for a population mean for the practical case in which the population standard deviation is unknown. The interval estimation procedure uses the sample standard deviation s and the t distribution. The quality of the interval estimate obtained depends on the distribution of the population and the sample size. In a normally distributed population, the interval estimates will be exact in both cases, even for small sample sizes. If the population is not normally distributed, the interval estimates obtained will be approximate. Larger sample sizes provide better approximations, but the more highly skewed the population is, the larger the sample size needs to be to obtain a good approximation.

The general form of the interval estimate for a population proportion is $\bar{p} \pm$ margin of error. In practice, the sample sizes used for interval estimates of a population proportion are generally large. Thus, the interval estimation procedure for a population proportion is based on the standard normal distribution.

In Section 6.5, we presented methods for hypothesis testing, a statistical procedure that uses sample data to determine whether or not a statement about the value of a population parameter should be rejected. The hypotheses are two competing statements about a population parameter. One statement is called the null hypothesis (H_0), and the other is called the alternative hypothesis (H_a). We provided guidelines for developing hypotheses for situations frequently encountered in practice.

In the hypothesis-testing procedure for the population mean, the sample standard deviation s is used to estimate σ and the hypothesis test is based on the t distribution. The quality of results depends on both the form of the population distribution and the sample size; if the population is not normally distributed, larger sample sizes are needed. General guidelines about the sample size were provided in Section 6.5. In the case of hypothesis tests about a population proportion, the hypothesis-testing procedure uses a test statistic based on the standard normal distribution.

We also reviewed how the value of the test statistic can be used to compute a p value—a probability that is used to determine whether the null hypothesis should be rejected. If the p value is less than or equal to the level of significance α, the null hypothesis can be rejected.

In Section 6.6 we discussed the concept of big data and its implications for statistical inference. We considered sampling and nonsampling error; the implications of big data on standard errors, confidence intervals, and hypothesis testing for the mean and the proportion; and the importance of considering both statistical significance and practical significance.

GLOSSARY

Alternative hypothesis The hypothesis concluded to be true if the null hypothesis is rejected.

Big data Any set of data that is too large or too complex to be handled by standard data processing techniques and typical desktop software.

Census Collection of data from every element in the population of interest.

Central limit theorem A theorem stating that when enough independent random variables are added, the resulting sum is a normally distributed random variable. This result allows one to use the normal probability distribution to approximate the sampling distributions of the sample mean and sample proportion for sufficiently large sample sizes.

Confidence coefficient The confidence level expressed as a decimal value. For example, 0.95 is the confidence coefficient for a 95% confidence level.

Confidence interval Another name for an interval estimate.

Confidence level The confidence associated with an interval estimate. For example, if an interval estimation procedure provides intervals such that 95% of the intervals formed using the procedure will include the population parameter, the interval estimate is said to be constructed at the 95% confidence level.

Coverage error Nonsampling error that results when the research objective and the population from which the sample is to be drawn are not aligned.

Degrees of freedom A parameter of the t distribution. When the t distribution is used in the computation of an interval estimate of a population mean, the appropriate t distribution has $n - 1$ degrees of freedom, where n is the size of the sample.

Finite population correction factor The term $\sqrt{(N - n)/(N - 1)}$ that is used in the formulas for computing the (estimated) standard error for the sample mean and sample proportion whenever a finite population, rather than an infinite population, is being sampled. The generally accepted rule of thumb is to ignore the finite population correction factor whenever $n/N \leq 0.05$.

Frame A listing of the elements from which the sample will be selected.

Hypothesis testing The process of making a conjecture about the value of a population parameter, collecting sample data that can be used to assess this conjecture, measuring the strength of the evidence against the conjecture that is provided by the sample, and using these results to draw a conclusion about the conjecture.

Interval estimate An estimate of a population parameter that provides an interval believed to contain the value of the parameter. For the interval estimates in this chapter, it has the form: point estimate ± margin of error.

Interval estimation The process of using sample data to calculate a range of values that is believed to include the unknown value of a population parameter.

Level of significance The probability that the interval estimation procedure will generate an interval that does not contain the value of parameter being estimated; also the probability of making a Type I error when the null hypothesis is true as an equality.

Margin of error The ± value added to and subtracted from a point estimate in order to develop an interval estimate of a population parameter.

Nonresponse error Nonsampling error that results when some segments of the population are more likely or less likely to respond to the survey mechanism.

Nonsampling error Any difference between the value of a sample statistic (such as the sample mean, sample standard deviation, or sample proportion) and the value of the corresponding population parameter (population mean, population standard deviation, or population proportion) that are not the result of sampling error. These include but are not limited to coverage error, nonresponse error, measurement error, interviewer error, and processing error.

Null hypothesis The hypothesis tentatively assumed to be true in the hypothesis testing procedure.

One-tailed test A hypothesis test in which rejection of the null hypothesis occurs for values of the test statistic in one tail of its sampling distribution.

p value The probability, assuming that H_0 is true, of obtaining a random sample of size n that results in a test statistic at least as extreme as the one observed in the current sample. For a lower-tail test, the p value is the probability of obtaining a value for the test statistic as small as or smaller than that provided by the sample. For an upper-tail test, the p value is the probability of obtaining a value for the test statistic as large as or larger than that provided by the sample. For a two-tailed test, the p value is the probability of obtaining a value for the test statistic at least as unlikely as or more unlikely than that provided by the sample.

Parameter A measurable factor that defines a characteristic of a population, process, or system, such as a population mean μ, a population standard deviation σ, or a population proportion p.

Point estimate The value of a point estimator used in a particular instance as an estimate of a population parameter.

Point estimator The sample statistic, such as $\bar{x}$, s, or $\bar{p}$, that provides the point estimate of the population parameter.

Practical significance The real-world impact the result of statistical inference will have on business decisions.

Random sample A random sample from an infinite population is a sample selected such that the following conditions are satisfied: (1) Each element selected comes from the same population and (2) each element is selected independently.

Random variable A quantity whose values are not known with certainty.

Sample statistic A characteristic of sample data, such as a sample mean $\bar{x}$, a sample standard deviation s, or a sample proportion $\bar{p}$. The value of the sample statistic is used to estimate the value of the corresponding population parameter.

Sampled population The population from which the sample is drawn.

Sampling distribution A probability distribution consisting of all possible values of a sample statistic.

Sampling error The difference between the value of a sample statistic (such as the sample mean, sample standard deviation, or sample proportion) and the value of the corresponding population parameter (population mean, population standard deviation, or population proportion) that occurs because a random sample is used to estimate the population parameter.

Simple random sample A simple random sample of size n from a finite population of size N is a sample selected such that each possible sample of size n has the same probability of being selected.

Standard error The standard deviation of a point estimator.

Standard normal distribution A normal distribution with a mean of zero and standard deviation of one.

Statistical inference The process of making estimates and drawing conclusions about one or more characteristics of a population (the value of one or more parameters) through the analysis of sample data drawn from the population.

t distribution A family of probability distributions that can be used to develop an interval estimate of a population mean whenever the population standard deviation s is unknown and is estimated by the sample standard deviation s.

Tall data A data set that has so many observations that traditional statistical inference has little meaning.

Target population The population for which statistical inferences such as point estimates are made. It is important for the target population to correspond as closely as possible to the sampled population.

Test statistic A statistic whose value helps determine whether a null hypothesis should be rejected.

Two-tailed test A hypothesis test in which rejection of the null hypothesis occurs for values of the test statistic in either tail of its sampling distribution.

Type I error The error of rejecting H_0 when it is true.

Type II error The error of accepting H_0 when it is false.

Unbiased A property of a point estimator that is present when the expected value of the point estimator is equal to the population parameter it estimates.

Variety The diversity in types and structures of data generated.

Velocity The speed at which the data are generated.

Veracity The reliability of the data generated.

Volume The amount of data generated.

Wide data A data set that has so many variables that simultaneous consideration of all variables is infeasible.

PROBLEMS

DATA *file*

AmericanLeague

1. **Randomly Sampling American League Teams.** The American League consists of 15 baseball teams. Suppose a sample of 5 teams is to be selected to conduct player interviews. The following table lists the 15 teams and the random numbers assigned by Excel's RAND function. Use these random numbers to select a sample of size 5.

Team	Random Number	Team	Random Number
New York	0.178624	Boston	0.290197
Baltimore	0.578370	Tampa Bay	0.867778
Toronto	0.965807	Minnesota	0.811810
Chicago	0.562178	Cleveland	0.960271
Detroit	0.253574	Kansas City	0.326836
Oakland	0.288287	Los Angeles	0.895267
Texas	0.500879	Seattle	0.839071
Houston	0.713682		

2. **Randomly Sampling PGA Golfers.** The U.S. Golf Association is considering a ban on long and belly putters. This has caused a great deal of controversy among both amateur golfers and members of the Professional Golf Association (PGA). Shown below are the names of the top 10 finishers in the recent PGA Tour McGladrey Classic golf tournament.

1. Tommy Gainey	6. Davis Love III
2. David Toms	7. Chad Campbell
3. Jim Furyk	8. Greg Owens
4. Brendon de Jonge	9. Charles Howell III
5. D. J. Trahan	10. Arjun Atwal

Select a simple random sample of 3 of these players to assess their opinions on the use of long and belly putters.

3. **Monthly Sales Data.** A simple random sample of 5 months of sales data provided the following information:

Month:	1	2	3	4	5
Units Sold:	94	100	85	94	92

   a. Develop a point estimate of the population mean number of units sold per month.
   b. Develop a point estimate of the population standard deviation.

DATA *file*

MorningStar

4. **Morningstar Stock Data.** Morningstar publishes ratings data on 1,208 company stocks. A sample of 40 of these stocks is contained in the file *Morningstar*. Use the Morningstar data set to answer the following questions.
   a. Develop a point estimate of the proportion of the stocks that receive Morningstar's highest rating of 5 Stars.
   b. Develop a point estimate of the proportion of the Morningstar stocks that are rated Above Average with respect to business risk.
   c. Develop a point estimate of the proportion of the Morningstar stocks that are rated 2 Stars or less.

5. **Internet Usage by Age Group.** One of the questions in the Pew Internet & American Life Project asked adults if they used the Internet at least occasionally. The results showed that 454 out of 478 adults aged 18–29 answered Yes; 741 out of 833

adults aged 30–49 answered Yes; and 1,058 out of 1,644 adults aged 50 and over answered Yes.

  a. Develop a point estimate of the proportion of adults aged 18–29 who use the Internet.

  b. Develop a point estimate of the proportion of adults aged 30–49 who use the Internet.

  c. Develop a point estimate of the proportion of adults aged 50 and over who use the Internet.

  d. Comment on any apparent relationship between age and Internet use.

  e. Suppose your target population of interest is that of all adults (18 years of age and over). Develop an estimate of the proportion of that population who use the Internet.

EAI

6. **Point Estimates for EAI Employees.** In this chapter we showed how a simple random sample of 30 EAI employees can be used to develop point estimates of the population mean annual salary, the population standard deviation for annual salary, and the population proportion having completed the management training program.

  a. Use Excel to select a simple random sample of 50 EAI employees.

  b. Develop a point estimate of the mean annual salary.

  c. Develop a point estimate of the population standard deviation for annual salary.

  d. Develop a point estimate of the population proportion having completed the management training program.

7. **SAT Scores.** The College Board reported the following mean scores for the three parts of the SAT:

Assume that the population standard deviation on each part of the test is $\sigma = 100$.

Critical Reading	502
Mathematics	515
Writing	494

  a. For a random sample of 30 test takers, what is the sampling distribution of $\bar{x}$ for scores on the Critical Reading part of the test?

  b. For a random sample of 60 test takers, what is the sampling distribution of $\bar{x}$ for scores on the Mathematics part of the test?

  c. For a random sample of 90 test takers, what is the sampling distribution of $\bar{x}$ for scores on the Writing part of the test?

8. **Federal Income Tax Returns.** *The Wall Street Journal* reports that 33% of taxpayers with adjusted gross incomes between $30,000 and $60,000 itemized deductions on their federal income tax return. The mean amount of deductions for this population of taxpayers was $16,642. Assume that the standard deviation is $\sigma = \$2,400$.

  a. What are the sampling distributions of $\bar{x}$ for itemized deductions for this population of taxpayers for each of the following sample sizes: 30, 50, 100, and 400?

  b. What is the advantage of a larger sample size when attempting to estimate the population mean?

9. **College Graduate-Level Wages.** The Economic Policy Institute periodically issues reports on wages of entry-level workers. The institute reported that entry-level wages for male college graduates were $21.68 per hour and for female college graduates were $18.80 per hour in 2011. Assume that the standard deviation for male graduates is $2.30 and for female graduates it is $2.05.

  a. What is the sampling distribution of $\bar{x}$ for a random sample of 50 male college graduates?

  b. What is the sampling distribution of $\bar{x}$ for a random sample of 50 female college graduates?

  c. In which of the preceding two cases, part (a) or part (b), is the standard error of $\bar{x}$ smaller? Why?

10. **State Rainfalls.** The state of California has a mean annual rainfall of 22 inches, whereas the state of New York has a mean annual rainfall of 42 inches. Assume that

the standard deviation for both states is 4 inches. A sample of 30 years of rainfall for California and a sample of 45 years of rainfall for New York has been taken.
   a. Show the sampling distribution of the sample mean annual rainfall for California.
   b. Show the sampling distribution of the sample mean annual rainfall for New York.
   c. In which of the preceding two cases, part (a) or part (b), is the standard error of $\bar{x}$ smaller? Why?

11. **Orders from First-Time Customers.** The president of Doerman Distributors, Inc. believes that 30% of the firm's orders come from first-time customers. A random sample of 100 orders will be used to estimate the proportion of first-time customers. Assume that the president is correct and $p = 0.30$. What is the sampling distribution of $\bar{p}$ for this study?

12. **Ages of Entrepreneurs.** *The Wall Street Journal* reported that the age at first startup for 55% of entrepreneurs was 29 years of age or less and the age at first startup for 45% of entrepreneurs was 30 years of age or more.
   a. Suppose a sample of 200 entrepreneurs will be taken to learn about the most important qualities of entrepreneurs. Show the sampling distribution of $\bar{p}$ where $\bar{p}$ is the sample proportion of entrepreneurs whose first startup was at 29 years of age or less.
   b. Suppose a sample of 200 entrepreneurs will be taken to learn about the most important qualities of entrepreneurs. Show the sampling distribution of $\bar{p}$ where $\bar{p}$ is now the sample proportion of entrepreneurs whose first startup was at 30 years of age or more.
   c. Are the standard errors of the sampling distributions different in parts (a) and (b)?

13. **Food Waste.** People end up tossing 12% of what they buy at the grocery store. Assume this is the true population proportion and that you plan to take a sample survey of 540 grocery shoppers to further investigate their behavior. Show the sampling distribution of $\bar{p}$, the proportion of groceries thrown out by your sample respondents.

14. **Unnecessary Medical Care.** Forty-two percent of primary care doctors think their patients receive unnecessary medical care.
   a. Suppose a sample of 300 primary care doctors was taken. Show the distribution of the sample proportion of doctors who think their patients receive unnecessary medical care.
   b. Suppose a sample of 500 primary care doctors was taken. Show the distribution of the sample proportion of doctors who think their patients receive unnecessary medical care.
   c. Suppose a sample of 1,000 primary care doctors was taken. Show the distribution of the sample proportion of doctors who think their patients receive unnecessary medical care.
   d. In which of the preceding three cases, part (a) or part (b) or part (c), is the standard error of $\bar{p}$ smallest? Why?

15. **Quality Ratings of Airports.** The International Air Transport Association surveys business travelers to develop quality ratings for transatlantic gateway airports. The maximum possible rating is 10. Suppose a simple random sample of 50 business travelers is selected and each traveler is asked to provide a rating for the Miami International Airport. The ratings obtained from the sample of 50 business travelers follow.

DATA *file*
Miami

6	4	6	8	7	7	6	3	3	8	10	4	8
7	8	7	5	9	5	8	4	3	8	5	5	4
4	4	8	4	5	6	2	5	9	9	8	4	8
9	9	5	9	7	8	3	10	8	9	6		

Develop a 95% confidence interval estimate of the population mean rating for Miami.

16. **Years to Bond Maturity.** A sample containing years to maturity and yield for 40 corporate bonds is contained in the file *CorporateBonds*.
    a. What is the sample mean years to maturity for corporate bonds and what is the sample standard deviation?
    b. Develop a 95% confidence interval for the population mean years to maturity.
    c. What is the sample mean yield on corporate bonds and what is the sample standard deviation?
    d. Develop a 95% confidence interval for the population mean yield on corporate bonds.

DATA*file*

TeleHealth

17. **Telemedicine.** Health insurers are beginning to offer telemedicine services online that replace the common office visit. WellPoint provides a video service that allows subscribers to connect with a physician online and receive prescribed treatments. Wellpoint claims that users of its LiveHealth Online service saved a significant amount of money on a typical visit. The data shown below ($), for a sample of 20 online doctor visits, are consistent with the savings per visit reported by Wellpoint.

92	34	40
105	83	55
56	49	40
76	48	96
93	74	73
78	93	100
53	82	

Assuming that the population is roughly symmetric, construct a 95% confidence interval for the mean savings for a televisit to the doctor as opposed to an office visit.

18. **Automobile Insurance Premiums.** The average annual premium for automobile insurance in the United States is $1,503. The following annual premiums ($) are representative of the web site's findings for the state of Michigan.

1,905	3,112	2,312
2,725	2,545	2,981
2,677	2,525	2,627
2,600	2,370	2,857
2,962	2,545	2,675
2,184	2,529	2,115
2,332	2,442	

DATA*file*

AutoInsurance

Assume the population is approximately normal.
    a. Provide a point estimate of the mean annual automobile insurance premium in Michigan.
    b. Develop a 95% confidence interval for the mean annual automobile insurance premium in Michigan.
    c. Does the 95% confidence interval for the annual automobile insurance premium in Michigan include the national average for the United States? What is your interpretation of the relationship between auto insurance premiums in Michigan and the national average?

DATA*file*

ChildOutlook

19. **Will Our Children Be Better Off?** One of the questions on a survey of 1,000 adults asked if today's children will be better off than their parents. Representative data are shown in the file *ChildOutlook*. A response of Yes indicates that the adult surveyed did think today's children will be better off than their parents. A response of No indicates that the adult surveyed did not think today's children will be better off than their parents. A response of Not Sure was given by 23% of the adults surveyed.
    a. What is the point estimate of the proportion of the population of adults who do think that today's children will be better off than their parents?
    b. At 95% confidence, what is the margin of error?

c. What is the 95% confidence interval for the proportion of adults who do think that today's children will be better off than their parents?
d. What is the 95% confidence interval for the proportion of adults who do not think that today's children will be better off than their parents?
e. Which of the confidence intervals in parts (c) and (d) has the smaller margin of error? Why?

20. **Companies Exceeding Profit Estimates.** According to Thomson Financial, last year the majority of companies reporting profits had beaten estimates. A sample of 162 companies showed that 104 beat estimates, 29 matched estimates, and 29 fell short.
    a. What is the point estimate of the proportion that fell short of estimates?
    b. Determine the margin of error and provide a 95% confidence interval for the proportion that beat estimates.
    c. How large a sample is needed if the desired margin of error is 0.05?

21. **Internet Usage.** The Pew Research Center Internet Project conducted a survey of 857 Internet users. This survey provided a variety of statistics on them.
    a. The sample survey showed that 90% of respondents said the Internet has been a good thing for them personally. Develop a 95% confidence interval for the proportion of respondents who say the Internet has been a good thing for them personally.
    b. The sample survey showed that 67% of Internet users said the Internet has generally strengthened their relationship with family and friends. Develop a 95% confidence interval for the proportion of respondents who say the Internet has strengthened their relationship with family and friends.
    c. Fifty-six percent of Internet users have seen an online group come together to help a person or community solve a problem, whereas only 25% have left an online group because of unpleasant interaction. Develop a 95% confidence interval for the proportion of Internet users who say online groups have helped solve a problem.
    d. Compare the margin of error for the interval estimates in parts (a), (b), and (c). How is the margin of error related to the sample proportion?

22. **Employee Contributions to Health-Care Coverage.** For many years businesses have struggled with the rising cost of health care. But recently, the increases have slowed due to less inflation in health care prices and employees paying for a larger portion of health care benefits. A recent Mercer survey showed that 52% of U.S. employers were likely to require higher employee contributions for health care coverage. Suppose the survey was based on a sample of 800 companies. Compute the margin of error and a 95% confidence interval for the proportion of companies likely to require higher employee contributions for health care coverage.

23. **Hotel Guest Bills.** The manager of the Danvers-Hilton Resort Hotel stated that the mean guest bill for a weekend is $600 or less. A member of the hotel's accounting staff noticed that the total charges for guest bills have been increasing in recent months. The accountant will use a sample of future weekend guest bills to test the manager's claim.
    a. Which form of the hypotheses should be used to test the manager's claim? Explain.

$$H_0: \mu \geq 600 \quad H_0: \mu \leq 600 \quad H_0: \mu = 600$$
$$H_a: \mu < 600 \quad H_a: \mu > 600 \quad H_a: \mu \neq 600$$

    b. What conclusion is appropriate when H_0 cannot be rejected?
    c. What conclusion is appropriate when H_0 can be rejected?

24. **Bonus Plans and Automobile Sales.** The manager of an automobile dealership is considering a new bonus plan designed to increase sales volume. Currently, the mean sales volume is 14 automobiles per month. The manager wants to conduct a research study to see whether the new bonus plan increases sales volume. To collect data on the plan, a sample of sales personnel will be allowed to sell under the new bonus plan for a one-month period.

a. Develop the null and alternative hypotheses most appropriate for this situation.
b. Comment on the conclusion when H_0 cannot be rejected.
c. Comment on the conclusion when H_0 can be rejected.

25. **Filling Detergent Cartons.** A production line operation is designed to fill cartons with laundry detergent to a mean weight of 32 ounces. A sample of cartons is periodically selected and weighed to determine whether underfilling or overfilling is occurring. If the sample data lead to a conclusion of underfilling or overfilling, the production line will be shut down and adjusted to obtain proper filling.
   a. Formulate the null and alternative hypotheses that will help in deciding whether to shut down and adjust the production line.
   b. Comment on the conclusion and the decision when H_0 cannot be rejected.
   c. Comment on the conclusion and the decision when H_0 can be rejected.

26. **Process Improvement.** Because of high production-changeover time and costs, a director of manufacturing must convince management that a proposed manufacturing method reduces costs before the new method can be implemented. The current production method operates with a mean cost of $220 per hour. A research study will measure the cost of the new method over a sample production period.
   a. Develop the null and alternative hypotheses most appropriate for this study.
   b. Comment on the conclusion when H_0 cannot be rejected.
   c. Comment on the conclusion when H_0 can be rejected.

27. **Home Electricity Usage.** Duke Energy reported that the cost of electricity for an efficient home in a particular neighborhood of Cincinnati, Ohio, was $104 per month. A researcher believes that the cost of electricity for a comparable neighborhood in Chicago, Illinois, is higher. A sample of homes in this Chicago neighborhood will be taken and the sample mean monthly cost of electricity will be used to test the following null and alternative hypotheses.

$$H_0: \mu \le 104$$
$$H_a: \mu > 104$$

   a. Assume that the sample data lead to rejection of the null hypothesis. What would be your conclusion about the cost of electricity in the Chicago neighborhood?
   b. What is the Type I error in this situation? What are the consequences of making this error?
   c. What is the Type II error in this situation? What are the consequences of making this error?

28. **Orange Juice Labels.** The label on a 3-quart container of orange juice states that the orange juice contains an average of 1 gram of fat or less. Answer the following questions for a hypothesis test that could be used to test the claim on the label.
   a. Develop the appropriate null and alternative hypotheses.
   b. What is the Type I error in this situation? What are the consequences of making this error?
   c. What is the Type II error in this situation? What are the consequences of making this error?

29. **Carpet Salesperson Salaries.** Carpetland salespersons average $8,000 per week in sales. Steve Contois, the firm's vice president, proposes a compensation plan with new selling incentives. Steve hopes that the results of a trial selling period will enable him to conclude that the compensation plan increases the average sales per salesperson.
   a. Develop the appropriate null and alternative hypotheses.
   b. What is the Type I error in this situation? What are the consequences of making this error?
   c. What is the Type II error in this situation? What are the consequences of making this error?

30. **Production Operating Costs.** Suppose a new production method will be implemented if a hypothesis test supports the conclusion that the new method reduces the mean operating cost per hour.
    a. State the appropriate null and alternative hypotheses if the mean cost for the current production method is $220 per hour.
    b. What is the Type I error in this situation? What are the consequences of making this error?
    c. What is the Type II error in this situation? What are the consequences of making this error?

31. **Meal Costs.** Which is cheaper: eating out or dining in? The mean cost of a flank steak, broccoli, and rice bought at the grocery store is $13.04. A sample of 100 neighborhood restaurants showed a mean price of $12.75 and a standard deviation of $2 for a comparable restaurant meal.
    a. Develop appropriate hypotheses for a test to determine whether the sample data support the conclusion that the mean cost of a restaurant meal is less than fixing a comparable meal at home.
    b. Using the sample from the 100 restaurants, what is the p value?
    c. At $\alpha = 0.05$, what is your conclusion?

32. **CEO Tenure.** A shareholders' group, in lodging a protest, claimed that the mean tenure for a chief executive officer (CEO) was at least nine years. A survey of companies reported in *The Wall Street Journal* found a sample mean tenure of $\bar{x} = 7.27$ years for CEOs with a standard deviation of $s = 6.38$ years.
    a. Formulate hypotheses that can be used to challenge the validity of the claim made by the shareholders' group.
    b. Assume that 85 companies were included in the sample. What is the p value for your hypothesis test?
    c. At $\alpha = 0.01$, what is your conclusion?

33. **School Administrator Salaries.** The national mean annual salary for a school administrator is $90,000 a year. A school official took a sample of 25 school administrators in the state of Ohio to learn about salaries in that state to see if they differed from the national average.
    a. Formulate hypotheses that can be used to determine whether the population mean annual administrator salary in Ohio differs from the national mean of $90,000.
    b. The sample data for 25 Ohio administrators is contained in the file *Administrator*. What is the p value for your hypothesis test in part (a)?
    c. At $\alpha = 0.05$, can your null hypothesis be rejected? What is your conclusion?

34. **Time in Child Care.** The time married men with children spend on child care averages 6.4 hours per week. You belong to a professional group on family practices that would like to do its own study to determine if the time married men in your area spend on child care per week differs from the reported mean of 6.4 hours per week. A sample of 40 married couples will be used with the data collected showing the hours per week the husband spends on child care. The sample data are contained in the file *ChildCare*.
    a. What are the hypotheses if your group would like to determine if the population mean number of hours married men are spending on child care differs from the mean reported by *Time* in your area?
    b. What is the sample mean and the p value?
    c. Select your own level of significance. What is your conclusion?

35. **Per Capita Sales.** The Coca-Cola Company reported that the mean per capita annual sales of its beverages in the United States was 423 eight-ounce servings. Suppose you are curious whether the consumption of Coca-Cola beverages is higher in Atlanta, Georgia, the location of Coca-Cola's corporate headquarters. A sample of 36 individuals from the Atlanta area showed a sample mean annual consumption of 460.4 eight-ounce servings with a standard deviation of $s = 101.9$ ounces. Using $\alpha = 0.05$, do the

sample results support the conclusion that mean annual consumption of Coca-Cola beverage products is higher in Atlanta?

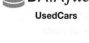

UsedCars

36. **Used Car Prices.** According to the National Automobile Dealers Association, the mean price for used cars is $10,192. A manager of a Kansas City used car dealership reviewed a sample of 50 recent used car sales at the dealership in an attempt to determine whether the population mean price for used cars at this particular dealership differed from the national mean. The prices for the sample of 50 cars are shown in the file *UsedCars*.
    a. Formulate the hypotheses that can be used to determine whether a difference exists in the mean price for used cars at the dealership.
    b. What is the p value?
    c. At $\alpha = 0.05$, what is your conclusion?

HomeState

37. **Population Mobility.** What percentage of the population live in their state of birth? According to the U.S. Census Bureau's American Community Survey, the figure ranges from 25% in Nevada to 78.7% in Louisiana. The average percentage across all states and the District of Columbia is 57.7%. The data in the file *HomeState* are consistent with the findings in the American Community Survey. The data are for a random sample of 120 Arkansas residents and for a random sample of 180 Virginia residents.
    a. Formulate hypotheses that can be used to determine whether the percentage of stay-at-home residents in the two states differs from the overall average of 57.7%.
    b. Estimate the proportion of stay-at-home residents in Arkansas. Does this proportion differ significantly from the mean proportion for all states? Use $\alpha = 0.05$.
    c. Estimate the proportion of stay-at-home residents in Virginia. Does this proportion differ significantly from the mean proportion for all states? Use $\alpha = 0.05$.
    d. Would you expect the proportion of stay-at-home residents to be higher in Virginia than in Arkansas? Support your conclusion with the results obtained in parts (b) and (c).

38. **Holiday Gifts from Employers.** Last year, 46% of business owners gave a holiday gift to their employees. A survey of business owners indicated that 35% plan to provide a holiday gift to their employees. Suppose the survey results are based on a sample of 60 business owners.
    a. How many business owners in the survey plan to provide a holiday gift to their employees?
    b. Suppose the business owners in the sample do as they plan. Compute the p value for a hypothesis test that can be used to determine if the proportion of business owners providing holiday gifts has decreased from last year.
    c. Using a 0.05 level of significance, would you conclude that the proportion of business owners providing gifts has decreased? What is the smallest level of significance for which you could draw such a conclusion?

39. **Family Stock Ownership.** Ten years ago 53% of American families owned stocks or stock funds. Sample data collected by the Investment Company Institute indicate that the percentage is now 46%.
    a. Develop appropriate hypotheses such that rejection of H_0 will support the conclusion that a smaller proportion of American families own stocks or stock funds this year than 10 years ago.
    b. Assume that the Investment Company Institute sampled 300 American families to estimate that the percent owning stocks or stock funds is 46% this year. What is the p value for your hypothesis test?
    c. At $\alpha = 0.01$, what is your conclusion?

40. **Returned Merchandise.** According to the University of Nevada Center for Logistics Management, 6% of all merchandise sold in the United States gets returned. A Houston department store sampled 80 items sold in January and found that 12 of the items were returned.

a. Construct a point estimate of the proportion of items returned for the population of sales transactions at the Houston store.

b. Construct a 95% confidence interval for the proportion of returns at the Houston store.

c. Is the proportion of returns at the Houston store significantly different from the returns for the nation as a whole? Provide statistical support for your answer.

DATA*file*

Eagle

41. **Coupon Usage.** Eagle Outfitters is a chain of stores specializing in outdoor apparel and camping gear. It is considering a promotion that involves mailing discount coupons to all its credit card customers. This promotion will be considered a success if more than 10% of those receiving the coupons use them. Before going national with the promotion, coupons were sent to a sample of 100 credit card customers.

a. Develop hypotheses that can be used to test whether the population proportion of those who will use the coupons is sufficient to go national.

b. The file *Eagle* contains the sample data. Develop a point estimate of the population proportion.

c. Use $\alpha = 0.05$ to conduct your hypothesis test. Should Eagle go national with the promotion?

DATA*file*

LawSuit

42. **Malpractice Suits.** One of the reasons health care costs have been rising rapidly in recent years is the increasing cost of malpractice insurance for physicians. Also, fear of being sued causes doctors to run more precautionary tests (possibly unnecessary) just to make sure they are not guilty of missing something. These precautionary tests also add to health care costs. Data in the file *LawSuit* are consistent with findings in a *Reader's Digest* article and can be used to estimate the proportion of physicians over the age of 55 who have been sued at least once.

a. Formulate hypotheses that can be used to see if these data can support a finding that more than half of physicians over the age of 55 have been sued at least once.

b. Use Excel and the file *LawSuit* to compute the sample proportion of physicians over the age of 55 who have been sued at least once. What is the p value for your hypothesis test?

c. At $\alpha = 0.01$, what is your conclusion?

DATA*file*

PortAuthority

43. **Value of Orders Placed.** The Port Authority sells a wide variety of cables and adapters for electronic equipment online. Last year the mean value of orders placed with the Port Authority was $47.28, and management wants to assess whether the mean value of orders placed to date this year is the same as last year. The values of a sample of 49,896 orders placed this year are collected and recorded in the file *PortAuthority*.

a. Formulate hypotheses that can be used to test whether the mean value of orders placed this year differs from the mean value of orders placed last year.

b. Use the data in the file *PortAuthority* to conduct your hypothesis test. What is the p value for your hypothesis test? At $\alpha = 0.01$, what is your conclusion?

DATA*file*

PortAuthority

44. **Customer Gender.** The Port Authority also wants to determine if the gender profile of its customers has changed since last year, when 59.4% of its orders placed were placed by males. The genders for a sample of 49,896 orders placed this year are collected and recorded in the file *PortAuthority*.

a. Formulate hypotheses that can be used to test whether the proportion of orders placed by male customers this year differs from the proportion of orders placed by male customers placed last year.

b. Use the data in the file *PortAuthority* to conduct your hypothesis test. What is the p value for your hypothesis test? At $\alpha = 0.05$, what is your conclusion?

DATA*file*

FedTaxErrors

45. **Erroneous Federal Tax Returns.** Suppose a sample of 10,001 erroneous Federal income tax returns from last year has been taken and is provided in the file *FedTaxErrors*. A positive value indicates the taxpayer underpaid and a negative value indicates that the taxpayer overpaid.

a. What is the sample mean error made on erroneous Federal income tax returns last year?

b. Using 95% confidence, what is the margin of error?

c. Using the results from parts (a) and (b), develop the 95% confidence interval estimate of the mean error made on erroneous Federal income tax returns last year.

DATA *file*

FedSickHours

46. **Federal Employee Sick Days.** According to the Census Bureau, 2,475,780 people are employed by the federal government in the United States. Suppose that a random sample of 3,500 of these federal employees was selected and the number of sick hours each of these employees took last year was collected from an electronic personnel database. The data collected in this survey are provided in the file *FedSickHours*.

a. What is the sample mean number of sick hours taken by federal employees last year?

b. Using 99% confidence, what is the margin of error?

c. Using the results from parts (a) and (b), develop the 99% confidence interval estimate of the mean number of sick hours taken by federal employees last year.

d. If the mean sick hours federal employees took two years ago was 62.2, what would the confidence interval in part (c) lead you to conclude about last year?

47. **Web Browser Preference.** Internet users were recently asked online to rate their satisfaction with the web browser they use most frequently. Of 102,519 respondents, 65,120 indicated they were very satisfied with the web browser they use most frequently.

a. What is the sample proportion of Internet users who are very satisfied with the web browser they use most frequently?

b. Using 95% confidence, what is the margin of error?

c. Using the results from parts (a) and (b), develop the 95% confidence interval estimate of the proportion of Internet users who are very satisfied with the web browser they use most frequently.

48. **Speeding Drivers.** ABC News reports that 58% of U.S. drivers admit to speeding. Suppose that a new satellite technology can instantly measure the speed of any vehicle on a U.S. road and determine whether the vehicle is speeding, and this satellite technology was used to take a sample of 20,000 vehicles at 6:00 p.m. EST on a recent Tuesday afternoon. Of these 20,000 vehicles, 9,252 were speeding.

a. What is the sample proportion of vehicles on U.S. roads that speed?

b. Using 99% confidence, what is the margin of error?

c. Using the results from parts (a) and (b), develop the 99% confidence interval estimate of the proportion of vehicles on U.S. roads that speed.

d. What does the confidence interval in part (c) lead you to conclude about the ABC News report?

DATA *file*

FedEmail

49. **Government Use of E-mail.** The Federal Government wants to determine if the mean number of business e-mails sent and received per business day by its employees differs from the mean number of e-mails sent and received per day by corporate employees, which is 101.5. Suppose the department electronically collects information on the number of business e-mails sent and received on a randomly selected business day over the past year from each of 10,163 randomly selected Federal employees. The results are provided in the file *FedEmail*. Test the Federal Government's hypothesis at $\alpha = 0.01$. Discuss the practical significance of the results.

DATA *file*

SocialNetwork

50. **CEOs and Social Networks.** CEOs who belong to a popular business-oriented social networking service have an average of 930 connections. Do other members have fewer connections than CEOs? The number of connections for a random sample of 7,515 members who are not CEOs is provided in the file *SocialNetwork*. Using this sample, test the hypothesis that other members have fewer connections than CEOs at $\alpha = 0.01$. Discuss the practical significance of the results.

51. **French Fry Purchases.** The American Potato Growers Association (APGA) would like to test the claim that the proportion of fast-food orders this year that include French fries exceeds the proportion of fast-food orders that included French fries last year. Suppose that a random sample of 49,581 electronic receipts for fast-food orders placed this year shows that 31,038 included French fries. Assuming that the proportion

of fast-food orders that included French fries last year is 0.62, use this information to test APGA's claim at $\alpha = 0.05$. Discuss the practical significance of the results.

52. **GPS Usage in Canada.** According to CNN, 55% of all U.S. smartphone users have used their GPS capability to get directions. Suppose a major provider of wireless telephone service in Canada wants to know how GPS usage by its customers compares with U.S. smartphone users. The company collects usage records for this year for a random sample of 547,192 of its Canadian customers and determines that 302,050 of these customers have used their telephone's GPS capability this year. Use this data to test whether Canadian smartphone users' GPS usage differs from U.S. smartphone users' GPS usage at $\alpha = 0.01$. Discuss the practical significance of the results.

Pedro

53. **Election Poll.** A well-respected polling agency has conducted a poll for an upcoming Presidential election. The polling agency has taken measures so that its random sample consists of 50,000 people and is representative of the voting population. The file *Pedro* contains survey data for 50,000 respondents in both a pre-election survey and a post-election poll.

a. Based on the data in the "Support Pedro in Pre-Election Poll" column, compute the 99% confidence interval on the population proportion of voters who support Pedro Ringer in the upcoming election. If Pedro needs at least 50% of the vote to win in the two-party election, should he be optimistic about winning the election?

b. Now suppose the election occurs and Pedro wins 55% of the vote. Explain how this result could occur given the sample information in part (a).

c. In an attempt to explain the election results (Pedro winning 55% of the vote), the polling agency has followed up with each of the respondents in their pre-election survey. The data in the "Voted for Pedro?" column corresponds to whether or not the respondent actually voted for Pedro in the election. Compute the 99% confidence interval on the population proportion of voters who voted for Pedro Ringer. Is this result consistent with the election results?

d. Use a PivotTable to determine the percentage of survey respondents who voted for Pedro that did not admit to supporting him in a pre-election poll. Use this result to explain the discrepancy between the pre-election poll and the actual election results. What type of error is occurring here?

CASE PROBLEM 1: YOUNG PROFESSIONAL MAGAZINE

Young Professional magazine was developed for a target audience of recent college graduates who are in their first 10 years in a business/professional career. In its two years of publication, the magazine has been fairly successful. Now the publisher is interested in expanding the magazine's advertising base. Potential advertisers continually ask about the demographics and interests of subscribers to *Young Professional*. To collect this information, the magazine commissioned a survey to develop a profile of its subscribers. The survey results will be used to help the magazine choose articles of interest and provide advertisers with a profile of subscribers. As a new employee of the magazine, you have been asked to help analyze the survey results, a portion of which are shown in the following table.

Age	Sex	Real Estate Purchases	Value of Investments ($)	Number of Transactions	Broadband Access	Household Income ($)	Children
38	Female	No	12,200	4	Yes	75,200	Yes
30	Male	No	12,400	4	Yes	70,300	Yes
41	Female	No	26,800	5	Yes	48,200	No
28	Female	Yes	19,600	6	No	95,300	No
31	Female	Yes	15,100	5	No	73,300	Yes
⋮	⋮	⋮	⋮	⋮	⋮	⋮	⋮

Some of the survey questions are as follows:

1. What is your age?
2. Are you: Male _____ Female _____
3. Do you plan to make any real estate purchases in the next two years?
   Yes_____ No_____
4. What is the approximate total value of financial investments, exclusive of your home, owned by you or members of your household?
5. How many stock/bond/mutual fund transactions have you made in the past year?
6. Do you have broadband access to the Internet at home? Yes_____ No_____
7. Please indicate your total household income last year.
8. Do you have children? Yes_____ No_____

The file *Professional* contains the responses to these questions. The table shows the portion of the file pertaining to the first five survey respondents.

Managerial Report

Prepare a managerial report summarizing the results of the survey. In addition to statistical summaries, discuss how the magazine might use these results to attract advertisers. You might also comment on how the survey results could be used by the magazine's editors to identify topics that would be of interest to readers. Your report should address the following issues, but do not limit your analysis to just these areas.

1. Develop appropriate descriptive statistics to summarize the data.
2. Develop 95% confidence intervals for the mean age and household income of subscribers.
3. Develop 95% confidence intervals for the proportion of subscribers who have broadband access at home and the proportion of subscribers who have children.
4. Would *Young Professional* be a good advertising outlet for online brokers? Justify your conclusion with statistical data.
5. Would this magazine be a good place to advertise for companies selling educational software and computer games for young children?
6. Comment on the types of articles you believe would be of interest to readers of *Young Professional*.

CASE PROBLEM 2: QUALITY ASSOCIATES, INC.

Quality Associates, Inc., a consulting firm, advises its clients about sampling and statistical procedures that can be used to control their manufacturing processes. In one particular application, a client gave Quality Associates a sample of 800 observations taken while that client's process was operating satisfactorily. The sample standard deviation for these data was 0.21; hence, with so much data, the population standard deviation was assumed to be 0.21. Quality Associates then suggested that random samples of size 30 be taken periodically to monitor the process on an ongoing basis. By analyzing the new samples, the client could quickly learn whether the process was operating satisfactorily. When the process was not operating satisfactorily, corrective action could be taken to eliminate the problem. The design specification indicated that the mean for the process should be 12. The hypothesis test suggested by Quality Associates is as follows:

$$H_0: \mu = 12$$
$$H_a: \mu \neq 12$$

Corrective action will be taken any time H_0 is rejected.

The samples listed in the following table were collected at hourly intervals during the first day of operation of the new statistical process control procedure. These data are available in the file *Quality*.

DATA *file*

Quality

Sample 1	Sample 2	Sample 3	Sample 4
11.55	11.62	11.91	12.02
11.62	11.69	11.36	12.02
11.52	11.59	11.75	12.05
11.75	11.82	11.95	12.18
11.90	11.97	12.14	12.11
11.64	11.71	11.72	12.07
11.64	11.71	11.72	12.07
11.80	11.87	11.61	12.05
12.03	12.10	11.85	11.64
11.94	12.01	12.16	12.39
11.92	11.99	11.91	11.65
12.13	12.20	12.12	12.11
12.09	12.16	11.61	11.90
11.93	12.00	12.21	12.22
12.21	12.28	11.56	11.88
12.32	12.39	11.95	12.03
11.93	12.00	12.01	12.35
11.85	11.92	12.06	12.09
11.76	11.83	11.76	11.77
12.16	12.23	11.82	12.20
11.77	11.84	12.12	11.79
12.00	12.07	11.60	12.30
12.04	12.11	11.95	12.27
11.98	12.05	11.96	12.29
12.30	12.37	12.22	12.47
12.18	12.25	11.75	12.03
11.97	12.04	11.96	12.17
12.17	12.24	11.95	11.94
11.85	11.92	11.89	11.97
12.30	12.37	11.88	12.23
12.15	12.22	11.93	12.25

Managerial Report

1. Conduct a hypothesis test for each sample at the 0.01 level of significance and determine what action, if any, should be taken. Provide the test statistic and p value for each test.
2. Compute the standard deviation for each of the four samples. Does the conjecture of 0.21 for the population standard deviation appear reasonable?
3. Compute limits for the sample mean $\bar{x}$ around $\mu = 12$ such that, as long as a new sample mean is within those limits, the process will be considered to be operating satisfactorily. If $\bar{x}$ exceeds the upper limit or if $\bar{x}$ is below the lower limit, corrective action will be taken. These limits are referred to as upper and lower control limits for quality-control purposes.
4. Discuss the implications of changing the level of significance to a larger value. What mistake or error could increase if the level of significance is increased?

Chapter 7

Linear Regression

CONTENTS

AVAILABLE IN THE MINDTAP READER:
    APPENDIX: SIMPLE LINEAR REGRESSION WITH R
    APPENDIX: MULTIPLE LINEAR REGRESSION WITH R
    APPENDIX: REGRESSION VARIABLE SELECTION PROCEDURES WITH R

ANALYTICS IN ACTION

Walmart.com*

BENTONVILLE, ARKANSAS

With more than 245 million customers per week visiting its 11,000 stores across the globe, Walmart is the world's largest retailer. In 2000, in response to increasing online shopping, Walmart launched its Internet site Walmart.com. To serve its online customers, Walmart created a network of distribution centers in the United States. One of these distribution centers, located in Carrollton, Georgia, was selected as the site for a study on how Walmart might better manage its packaging for online orders.

In its peak shipping season (November to December), the Walmart distribution center in Carrollton ships over 100,000 packages per day. The cost of fulfilling an order includes the material cost (the cost of the carton and packing material—paper that fills the empty space when the product is smaller than the volume of the box), labor for handling, and the shipping cost. The study conducted in Carrollton, called the Carton-mix Optimization Study, had as its objective to determine the number and size of cartons to have on hand for shipping Walmart's products to its online customers that would minimize raw material, labor and shipping costs.

A number of constraints limited the possibilities for the variety of cartons to have on hand. For example, management provided a minimum and maximum carton size. In addition, for boxes automatically constructed (as opposed to manually built), a line would be limited to one-size carton.

As with any study of this type, data had to be collected to build a cost model that could then be used to find the optimal carton mix. The material costs for existing cartons were known, but what about the cost of a carton in a size that is not currently used? Based on price quotes from its carton suppliers for a variety of sizes, a simple linear regression model was used to estimate the cost of any-size carton based on its volume. The following model was used to estimate the material cost of a carton in dollars per carton (y) based on the volume of the carton measured in cubic inches per carton (x):

$$y = -0.11 + 0.0014x$$

For example, for a carton with volume of 2,800 cubic inches, we have $-0.11 + 0.0014(2800) = 3.81$. Therefore, the estimated material for a carton of 2,800 cubic inches in volume is $3.81.

The simple linear regression model was imbedded into an optimization algorithm in Microsoft Excel to provide Walmart managers a recommendation on the optimal mix of carton sizes to carry at its Carrollton distribution center. The optimization model based on this regression provided documented savings of $600,000 in its first year of implementation. The model was later deployed across Walmart's other distribution centers with an estimated annual savings of $2 million.

In this chapter, we will study how to estimate a simple linear regression model, that is, a linear model in which a single variable is used to estimate the value of another variable.

*Based on S. Ahire, M. Malhotra, and J. Jensen, "Carton-Mix Optimization for Walmart.com Distribution Centers," *Interfaces*, Vol. 45, No. 4, July–August 2015, pp. 341–357.

Managerial decisions are often based on the relationship between two or more variables. For example, after considering the relationship between advertising expenditures and sales, a marketing manager might attempt to predict sales for a given level of advertising expenditures. In another case, a public utility might use the relationship between the daily high temperature and the demand for electricity to predict electricity usage on the basis of next month's anticipated daily high temperatures. Sometimes a manager will rely on intuition to judge how two variables are related. However, if data can be obtained, a statistical procedure called **regression analysis** can be used to develop an equation showing how the variables are related.

The statistical methods used in studying the relationship between two variables were first employed by Sir Francis Galton (1822–1911). Galton found that the heights of the sons of unusually tall or unusually short fathers tend to move, or "regress," toward the average height of the male population. Karl Pearson (1857–1936), a disciple of Galton, later confirmed this finding in a sample of 1,078 pairs of fathers and sons.

In regression terminology, the variable being predicted is called the **dependent variable**, or *response*, and the variables being used to predict the value of the dependent variable are called the **independent variables**, or *predictor variables*. For example, in analyzing the effect of advertising expenditures on sales, a marketing manager's desire to predict sales would suggest making sales the dependent variable. Advertising expenditure would be the independent variable used to help predict sales.

In this chapter, we begin by considering **simple linear** regression, in which the relationship between one dependent variable (denoted by y) and one independent variable (denoted by x) is approximated by a straight line. We then extend this concept to higher dimensions by introducing **multiple linear regression** to model the relationship between a dependent variable (y) and two or more independent variables ($x_1, x_2, \dots, x_q$).

7.1 Simple Linear Regression Model

Butler Trucking Company is an independent trucking company in Southern California. A major portion of Butler's business involves deliveries throughout its local area. To develop better work schedules, the managers want to estimate the total daily travel times for their drivers. The managers believe that the total daily travel times (denoted by y) are closely related to the number of miles traveled in making the daily deliveries (denoted by x). Using regression analysis, we can develop an equation showing how the dependent variable y is related to the independent variable x.

Regression Model

In the Butler Trucking Company example, a simple linear regression model hypothesizes that the travel time of a driving assignment (y) is linearly related to the number of miles traveled (x) as follows:

SIMPLE LINEAR REGRESSION MODEL

$$y = \beta_0 + \beta_1 x + \varepsilon \tag{7.1}$$

In equation (7.1), β_0 and β_1 are population parameters that describe the y-intercept and slope of the line relating y and x. The error term ε (Greek letter epsilon) accounts for the variability in y that cannot be explained by the linear relationship between x and y. The simple linear regression model assumes that the error term is a normally distributed random variable with a mean of zero and constant variance for all observations.

Estimated Regression Equation

In practice, the values of the population parameters β_0 and β_1 are not known and must be estimated using sample data. Sample statistics (denoted b_0 and b_1) are computed as estimates of the population parameters β_0 and β_1. Substituting the values of the sample statistics b_0 and b_1 for β_0 and β_1 in equation (7.1) and dropping the error term (because its expected value is zero), we obtain the **estimated regression** for simple linear regression:

ESTIMATED SIMPLE LINEAR REGRESSION EQUATION

$$\hat{y} = b_0 + b_1 x \tag{7.2}$$

Figure 7.1 provides a summary of the estimation process for simple linear regression. Using equation (7.2), $\hat{y}$ provides an estimate for the mean value of y corresponding to a given value of x.

The graph of the estimated simple linear regression equation is called the *estimated regression line*; b_0 is the estimated y-intercept, and b_1 is the estimated slope. In the next section, we show how the least squares method can be used to compute the values of b_0 and b_1 in the estimated regression equation.

The estimation of β_0 and β_1 is a statistical process much like the estimation of the population mean, μ, discussed in Chapter 6. β_0 and β_1 are the unknown parameters of interest, and b_0 and b_1 are the sample statistics used to estimate the parameters.

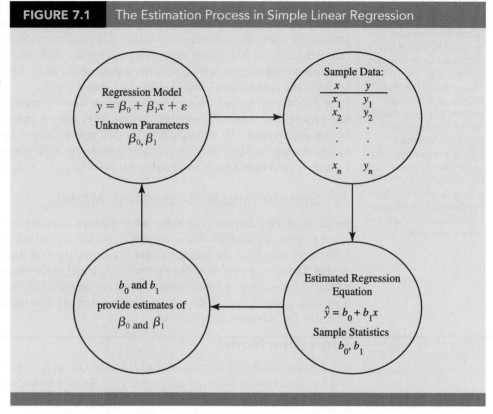

FIGURE 7.1 The Estimation Process in Simple Linear Regression

Examples of possible regression lines are shown in Figure 7.2. The regression line in Panel A shows that the estimated mean value of y is related positively to x, with larger values of $\hat{y}$ associated with larger values of x. In Panel B, the estimated mean value of y is related negatively to x, with smaller values of $\hat{y}$ associated with larger values of x. In Panel C, the estimated mean value of y is not related to x; that is, $\hat{y}$ is the same for every value of x.

In general, $\hat{y}$ is the **point estimator** of $E(y|x)$, the mean value of y for a given value of x. Thus, to estimate the mean or expected value of travel time for a driving assignment of 75 miles, Butler Trucking would substitute the value of 75 for x in equation (7.2). In some cases, however, Butler Trucking may be more interested in predicting travel time for an upcoming driving assignment of a particular length. For example, suppose Butler Trucking would like to predict travel time for a new 75-mile driving assignment the company is

A point estimator is a single value used as an estimate of the corresponding population parameter.

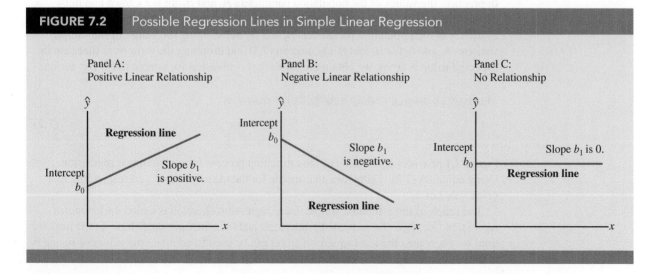

FIGURE 7.2 Possible Regression Lines in Simple Linear Regression

considering. It turns out that to predict travel time for a new 75-mile driving assignment, Butler Trucking would also substitute the value of 75 for x in equation (7.2). The value of $\hat{y}$ provides both a point estimate of $E(y|x)$ for a given value of x and a prediction of an individual value of y for a given value of x. In most cases, we will refer to $\hat{y}$ simply as the predicted value of y.

7.2 Least Squares Method

The **least squares method** is a procedure for using sample data to find the estimated regression equation. To illustrate the least squares method, suppose data were collected from a sample of 10 Butler Trucking Company driving assignments. For the ith observation or driving assignment in the sample, x_i is the miles traveled and y_i is the travel time (in hours). The values of x_i and y_i for the 10 driving assignments in the sample are summarized in Table 7.1. We see that driving assignment 1, with $x_1 = 100$ and $y_1 = 9.3$, is a driving assignment of 100 miles and a travel time of 9.3 hours. Driving assignment 2, with $x_2 = 50$ and $y_2 = 4.8$, is a driving assignment of 50 miles and a travel time of 4.8 hours. The shortest travel time is for driving assignment 5, which requires 50 miles with a travel time of 4.2 hours.

Figure 7.3 is a scatter chart of the data in Table 7.1. Miles traveled is shown on the horizontal axis, and travel time (in hours) is shown on the vertical axis. Scatter charts for regression analysis are constructed with the independent variable x on the horizontal axis and the dependent variable y on the vertical axis. The scatter chart enables us to observe the data graphically and to draw preliminary conclusions about the possible relationship between the variables.

What preliminary conclusions can be drawn from Figure 7.3? Longer travel times appear to coincide with more miles traveled. In addition, for these data, the relationship between the travel time and miles traveled appears to be approximated by a straight line; indeed, a positive linear relationship is indicated between x and y. We therefore choose the simple linear regression model to represent this relationship. Given that choice, our next task is to use the sample data in Table 7.1 to determine the values of b_0 and b_1 in the estimated simple linear regression equation. For the ith driving assignment, the estimated regression equation provides:

$$\hat{y}_i = b_0 + b_1 x_i \tag{7.3}$$

where

$\hat{y}_i$ = predicted travel time (in hours) for the ith driving assignment
b_0 = the y-intercept of the estimated regression line

DATA *file*

Butler

TABLE 7.1	Miles Traveled and Travel Time for 10 Butler Trucking Company Driving Assignments

Driving Assignment i	x = Miles Traveled	y = Travel Time (hours)
1	100	9.3
2	50	4.8
3	50	8.9
4	100	6.5
5	50	4.2
6	80	6.2
7	75	7.4
8	65	6.0
9	90	7.6
10	90	6.1

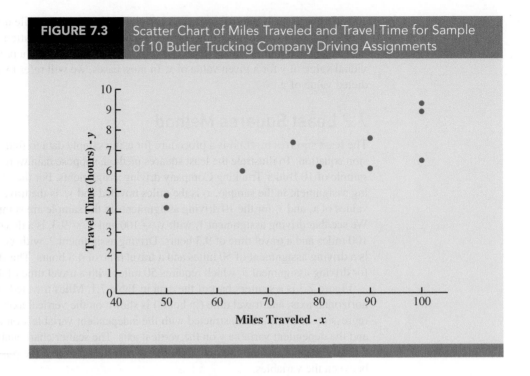

FIGURE 7.3   Scatter Chart of Miles Traveled and Travel Time for Sample of 10 Butler Trucking Company Driving Assignments

b_1 = the slope of the estimated regression line

x_i = miles traveled for the ith driving assignment

With y_i denoting the observed (actual) travel time for driving assignment i and $\hat{y}_i$ in equation (7.3) representing the predicted travel time for driving assignment i, every driving assignment in the sample will have an observed travel time y_i and a predicted travel time $\hat{y}_i$. For the estimated regression line to provide a good fit to the data, the differences between the observed travel times y_i and the predicted travel times $\hat{y}_i$ should be small.

The least squares method uses the sample data to provide the values of b_0 and b_1 that minimize the sum of the squares of the deviations between the observed values of the dependent variable y_i and the predicted values of the dependent variable $\hat{y}_i$. The criterion for the least squares method is given by equation (7.4).

LEAST SQUARES EQUATION

$$\min \sum_{i=1}^{n} (y_i - \hat{y}_i)^2 \ = \ \min \sum_{i=1}^{n} (y_1 - b_0 - b_1 x_1)^2 \tag{7.4}$$

where

y_i = observed value of the dependent variable for the ith observation

$\hat{y}_i$ = predicted value of the dependent variable for the ith observation

n = total number of observations

The error we make using the regression model to estimate the mean value of the dependent variable for the ith observation is often written as $e_i = y_i - \hat{y}_i$ and is referred to as the ith **residual**. Using this notation, equation (7.4) can be rewritten as

$$\min \sum_{i=1}^{n} e_i^2$$

and we say that we are estimating the regression equation that minimizes the sum of squared errors.

Least Squares Estimates of the Regression Parameters

Although the values of b_0 and b_1 that minimize equation (7.4) can be calculated manually with equations (see note at end of this section), computer software such as Excel is generally used to calculate b_1 and b_0. For the Butler Trucking Company data in Table 7.1, an estimated slope of $b_1 = 0.0678$ and a y-intercept of $b_0 = 1.2739$ minimize the sum of squared errors (in the next section we show how to use Excel to obtain these values). Thus, our estimated simple linear regression equation is $\hat{y} = 1.2739 + 0.0678x_1$.

We interpret b_1 and b_0 as we would the slope and y-intercept of any straight line. The slope b_1 is the estimated change in the mean of the dependent variable y that is associated with a one-unit increase in the independent variable x. For the Butler Trucking Company model, we therefore estimate that, if the length of a driving assignment were 1 mile longer, the mean travel time for that driving assignment would be 0.0678 hour (or approximately 4 minutes) longer. The y-intercept b_0 is the estimated value of the dependent variable y when the independent variable x is equal to 0. For the Butler Trucking Company model, we estimate that if the driving distance for a driving assignment was 0 units (0 miles), the mean travel time would be 1.2739 units (1.2739 hours, or approximately 76 minutes). Can we find a plausible explanation for this? Perhaps the 76 minutes represent the time needed to prepare, load, and unload the vehicle, which is required for all trips regardless of distance and which therefore does not depend on the distance traveled. However, we cautiously note that to estimate the travel time for a driving distance of 0 miles, we have to extend the relationship we have found with simple linear regression well beyond the range of values for driving distance in our sample. Those sample values range from 50 to 100 miles, and this range represents the only values of driving distance for which we have empirical evidence of the relationship between driving distance and our estimated travel time.

The estimated value of the y-intercept often results from extrapolation.

It is important to note that the regression model is valid only over the **experimental region**, which is the range of values of the independent variables in the data used to estimate the model. Prediction of the value of the dependent variable outside the experimental region is called **extrapolation** and is risky. Because we have no empirical evidence that the relationship between y and x holds true for x values outside the range of x values in the data used to estimate the relationship, extrapolation is risky and should be avoided if possible. For Butler Trucking, this means that any prediction of the travel time for a driving distance less than 50 miles or greater than 100 miles is not a reliable estimate. Thus, any interpretation of β_0 based on the Butler Trucking Company data is unreliable and likely meaningless. However, if the experimental region for a regression analysis includes zero, the y-intercept will have a meaningful interpretation.

The point estimate ŷ provided by the regression equation does not give us any information about the precision associated with the prediction. For that we must develop an interval estimate around the point estimate. In the last section of this chapter, we discuss the construction of interval estimates around the point predictions provided by a regression equation.

We can use the estimated regression equation and our known values for miles traveled for a driving assignment (x) to estimate mean travel time in hours. For example, the first driving assignment in Table 7.1 has a value for miles traveled of $x = 100$. We estimate the mean travel time in hours for this driving assignment to be

$$\hat{y}_i = 1.2739 + 0.0678(100) = 8.0539$$

Since the travel time for this driving assignment was 9.3 hours, this regression estimate would have resulted in a residual of

$$e_1 = y_1 - \hat{y}_i = 9.3 - 8.0539 = 1.2461$$

The simple linear regression model underestimated travel time for this driving assignment by 1.2461 hours (approximately 74 minutes). Table 7.2 shows the predicted mean travel times, the residuals, and the squared residuals for all 10 driving assignments in the sample data. Note the following in Table 7.2:

- The sum of predicted values $\hat{y}_i$ is equal to the sum of the values of the dependent variable y.

TABLE 7.2	Predicted Travel Time and Residuals for 10 Butler Trucking Company Driving Assignments				
Driving Assignment i	x = Miles Traveled	y = Travel Time (hours)	$\hat{y}_i = b_0 + b_1 x_i$	$e_i = y_i - \hat{y}_i$	e_i^2
1	100	9.3	8.0565	1.2435	1.5463
2	50	4.8	4.6652	0.1348	0.0182
3	100	8.9	8.0565	0.8435	0.7115
4	100	6.5	8.0565	−1.5565	2.4227
5	50	4.2	4.6652	−0.4652	0.2164
6	80	6.2	6.7000	−0.5000	0.2500
7	75	7.4	6.3609	1.0391	1.0797
8	65	6.0	5.6826	0.3174	0.1007
9	90	7.6	7.3783	0.2217	0.0492
10	90	6.1	7.3783	−1.2783	1.6341
	Totals	67.0	67.0000	0.0000	8.0288

- The sum of the residuals e_i is 0.
- The sum of the squared residuals e_i^2 has been minimized.

These three points will always be true for a simple linear regression that is determined by equation (7.5). Figure 7.4 shows the simple linear regression line $\hat{y}_i = 1.2739 + 0.0678x_i$ superimposed on the scatter chart for the Butler Trucking Company data in Table 7.1. Figure 7.4 highlights the residuals for driving assignment 3 and driving assignment 5.

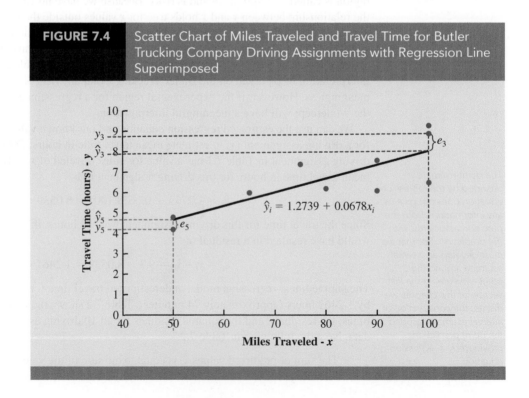

FIGURE 7.4	Scatter Chart of Miles Traveled and Travel Time for Butler Trucking Company Driving Assignments with Regression Line Superimposed

The regression model underpredicts travel time for some driving assignments ($e_3 > 0$) and overpredicts travel time for others ($e_5 < 0$), but in general appears to fit the data relatively well.

In Figure 7.5, a vertical line is drawn from each point in the scatter chart to the linear regression line. Each of these vertical lines represents the difference between the actual driving time and the driving time we predict using linear regression for one of the assignments in our data. The length of each vertical line is equal to the absolute value of the residual for one of the driving assignments. When we square a residual, the resulting value is equal to the area of the square with the length of each side equal to the absolute value of the residual. In other words, the square of the residual for driving assignment 4, ($e_4 = (-1.5565)^2 = 2.4227$), is the area of a square for which the length of each side is 1.5565. Thus, when we find the linear regression model that minimizes the sum of squared errors for the Butler Trucking example, we are positioning the regression line in the manner that minimizes the sum of the areas of the 10 squares in Figure 7.5.

Using Excel's Chart Tools to Compute the Estimated Regression Equation

Note that Excel uses y instead of ŷ to denote the predicted value of the dependent variable and puts the regression equation into slope-intercept form, whereas we use the intercept-slope form that is standard in statistics.

We can use Excel's chart tools to compute the estimated regression equation on a scatter chart of the Butler Trucking Company data in Table 7.1. After constructing a scatter chart (as shown in Figure 7.3) with Excel's chart tools, the following steps describe how to compute the estimated regression equation using the data in the worksheet:

Step 1. Right-click on any data point in the scatter chart and select **Add Trendline**
Step 2. When the **Format Trendline** task pane appears:
        Select **Linear** in the **Trendline Options** area
        Select **Display Equation on chart** in the **Trendline Options** area

The worksheet displayed in Figure 7.6 shows the original data, scatter chart, estimated regression line, and estimated regression equation.

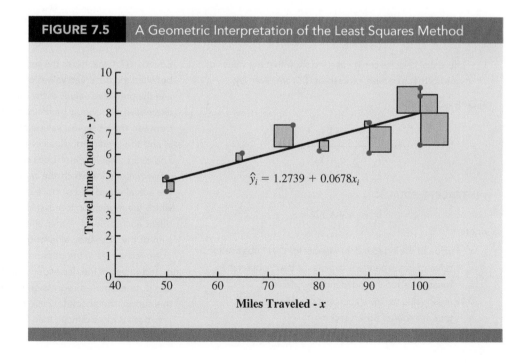

FIGURE 7.5   A Geometric Interpretation of the Least Squares Method

$$\hat{y}_i = 1.2739 + 0.0678x_i$$

FIGURE 7.6   Scatter Chart and Estimated Regression Line for Butler Trucking Company

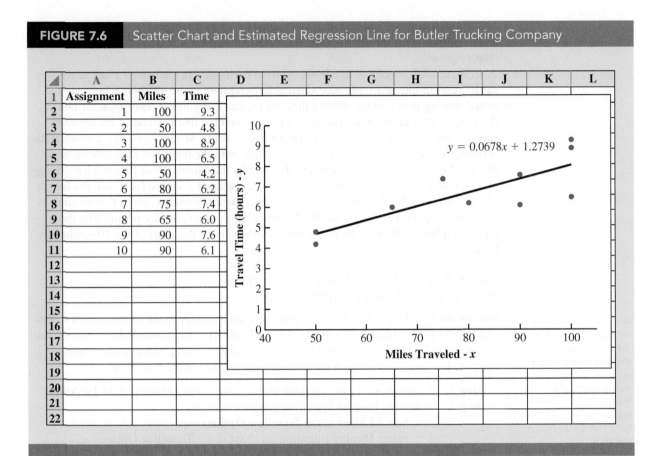

	A	B	C
1	Assignment	Miles	Time
2	1	100	9.3
3	2	50	4.8
4	3	100	8.9
5	4	100	6.5
6	5	50	4.2
7	6	80	6.2
8	7	75	7.4
9	8	65	6.0
10	9	90	7.6
11	10	90	6.1

$y = 0.0678x + 1.2739$

NOTES + COMMENTS

1. Differential calculus can be used to show that the values of b_0 and b_1 that minimize expression (7.5) are given by:

SLOPE EQUATION

$$b_1 = \frac{\sum_{i=1}^{n}(x_i - \bar{x})(y_i - \bar{y})}{\sum_{i=1}^{n}(x_i - \bar{x})^2}$$

y-INTERCEPT EQUATION

$$b_0 = \bar{y} - b_1\bar{x}$$

where

x_i = value of the independent variable for the ith observation

y_i = value of the dependent variable for the ith observation

$\bar{x}$ = mean value for the independent variable

$\bar{y}$ = mean value for the dependent variable

n = total number of observations

2. Equation (7.4) minimizes the sum of the squared deviations between the observed values of the dependent variable y_i and the predicted values of the dependent variable $\hat{y}_1$. One alternative is to simply minimize the sum of the deviations between the observed values of the dependent variable y_i and the predicted values of the dependent variable $\hat{y}_i$. This is not a viable option because then negative deviations (observations for which the regression forecast exceeds the actual value) and positive deviations (observations for which the regression forecast is less than the actual value) offset each other. Another alternative is to minimize the sum of the absolute value of the deviations between the observed values of the dependent variable y_i and the predicted values of the dependent variable $\hat{y}_i$. It is possible to compute estimated regression parameters that minimize this sum of the absolute value of the deviations, but this approach is more difficult than the least squares approach.

7.3 Assessing the Fit of the Simple Linear Regression Model

For the Butler Trucking Company example, we developed the estimated regression equation $\hat{y}_i = 1.2739 + 0.0678x_i$ to approximate the linear relationship between the miles traveled (x) and travel time in hours (y). We now wish to assess how well the estimated regression equation fits the sample data. We begin by developing the intermediate calculations, referred to as the sums of squares.

The Sums of Squares

Recall that we found our estimated regression equation for the Butler Trucking Company example by minimizing the sum of squares of the residuals. This quantity, also known as the *sum of squares due to error*, is denoted by SSE.

SUM OF SQUARES DUE TO ERROR

$$SSE = \sum_{i=1}^{n}(y_i - \hat{y}_i)^2 \tag{7.5}$$

The value of SSE is a measure of the error (in squared units of the dependent variable) that results from using the estimated regression equation to predict the values of the dependent variable in the sample.

We have already shown the calculations required to compute the sum of squares due to error for the Butler Trucking Company example in Table 7.2. The squared residual or error for each observation in the data is shown in the last column of that table. After computing and squaring the residuals for each driving assignment in the sample, we sum them to obtain $SSE = 8.0288$ hours^2. Thus, $SSE = 8.0288$ measures the error in using the estimated regression equation $\hat{y}_i = 1.2739 + 0.0678x_i$ to predict travel time for the driving assignments in the sample.

Now suppose we are asked to predict travel time in hours without knowing the miles traveled for a driving assignment. Without knowledge of any related variables, we would use the sample mean $\bar{y}$ as a predictor of travel time for any given driving assignment. To find $\bar{y}$, we divide the sum of the actual driving times y_i from Table 7.2 (67) by the number of observations n in the data (10); this yields $\bar{y} = 6.7$.

Figure 7.7 provides insight on how well we would predict the values of y_i in the Butler Trucking Company example using $\bar{y} = 6.7$. From this figure, which again highlights the residuals for driving assignments 3 and 5, we can see that $\bar{y}$ tends to overpredict travel times for driving assignments that have relatively small values for miles traveled (such as driving assignment 5) and tends to underpredict travel times for driving assignments that have relatively large values for miles traveled (such as driving assignment 3).

In Table 7.3 we show the sum of squared deviations obtained by using the sample mean $\bar{y} = 6.7$ to predict the value of travel time in hours for each driving assignment in the sample. For the ith driving assignment in the sample, the difference $y_i - \bar{y}$ provides a measure of the error involved in using $\bar{y}$ to predict travel time for the ith driving assignment. The corresponding sum of squares, called the total sum of squares, is denoted by SST.

TOTAL SUM OF SQUARES, SST

$$SST = \sum_{i=1}^{n}(y_i - \bar{y})^2 \tag{7.6}$$

The sum at the bottom of the last column in Table 7.3 is the total sum of squares for Butler Trucking Company: $SST = 23.9$ hours^2.

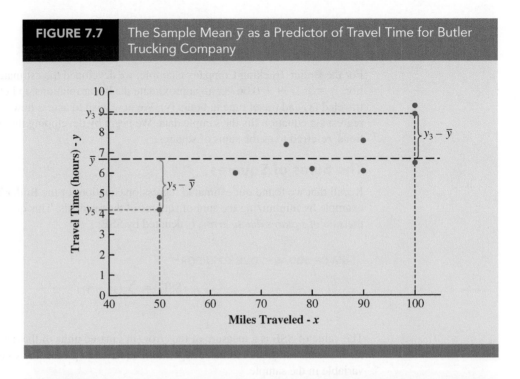

FIGURE 7.7 The Sample Mean $\bar{y}$ as a Predictor of Travel Time for Butler Trucking Company

TABLE 7.3 Calculations for the Sum of Squares Total for the Butler Trucking Simple Linear Regression

Driving Assignment i	x = Miles Traveled	y = Travel Time (hours)	$y_i - \bar{y}$	$(y_i - \bar{y})^2$
1	100	9.3	2.6	6.76
2	50	4.8	−1.9	3.61
3	100	8.9	2.2	4.84
4	100	6.5	−0.2	0.04
5	50	4.2	−2.5	6.25
6	80	6.2	−0.5	0.25
7	75	7.4	0.7	0.49
8	65	6.0	−0.7	0.49
9	90	7.6	0.9	0.81
10	90	6.1	−0.6	0.36
Totals	67.0		0	23.9

Now we put it all together. In Figure 7.8 we show the estimated regression line $\hat{y}_i = 1.2739 + 0.0678x_i$ and the line corresponding to $\bar{y} = 6.7$. Note that the points cluster more closely around the estimated regression line $\hat{y}_i = 1.2739 + 0.0678x_i$ than they do about the horizontal line $\bar{y} = 6.7$. For example, for the third driving assignment in the sample, we see that the error is much larger when $\bar{y} = 6.7$ is used to predict y_3 than when $\hat{y}_3 = 1.2739 + 0.0678(100) = 8.0539$ is used. We can think of SST as a measure of how well the observations cluster about the $\bar{y}$ line and SSE as a measure of how well the observations cluster about the $\hat{y}$ line.

To measure how much the $\hat{y}$ values on the estimated regression line deviate from y, another sum of squares is computed. This sum of squares, called the *sum of squares due to regression*, is denoted by SSR.

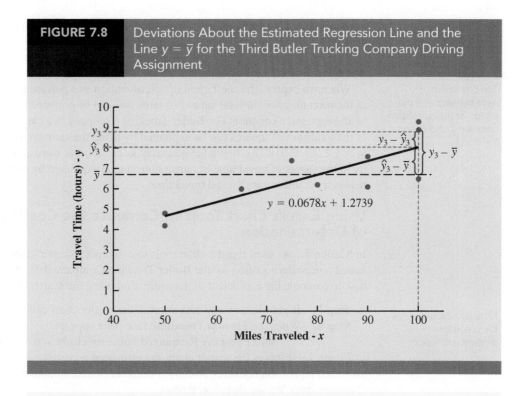

FIGURE 7.8   Deviations About the Estimated Regression Line and the Line $y = \bar{y}$ for the Third Butler Trucking Company Driving Assignment

SUM OF SQUARES DUE TO REGRESSION, SSR

$$SSR = \sum_{i=1}^{n}(\hat{y}_i - \bar{y})^2 \qquad (7.7)$$

From the preceding discussion, we should expect that SST, SSR, and SSE are related. Indeed, the relationship among these three sums of squares is

$$SST = SSR + SSE \qquad (7.8)$$

where

$$SST = \text{total sum of squares}$$
$$SSR = \text{sum of squares due to regression}$$
$$SSE = \text{sum of squares due to error}$$

The Coefficient of Determination

Now let us see how the three sums of squares, SST, SSR, and SSE, can be used to provide a measure of the goodness of fit for the estimated regression equation. The estimated regression equation would provide a perfect fit if every value of the dependent variable y_i happened to lie on the estimated regression line. In this case, $y_i - \hat{y}$ would be zero for each observation, resulting in SSE = 0. Because SST = SSR + SSE, we see that for a perfect fit SSR must equal SST, and the ratio (SSR/SST) must equal one. Poorer fits will result in larger values for SSE. Solving for SSE in equation (7.11), we see that SSE = SST − SSR. Hence, the largest value for SSE (and hence the poorest fit) occurs when SSR = 0 and SSE = SST. The ratio SSR/SST, which will take values between zero and one, is used to evaluate the goodness of fit for the estimated regression equation. This ratio is called the **coefficient of determination** and is denoted by r^2.

In simple regression, r^2 is often referred to as the simple coefficient of determination.

COEFFICIENT OF DETERMINATION

$$r^2 = \frac{SSR}{SST} \qquad (7.9)$$

For the Butler Trucking Company example, the value of the coefficient of determination is

$$r^2 = \frac{\text{SSR}}{\text{SST}} = \frac{15.8712}{23.9} = 0.6641$$

The coefficient of determination r^2 is the square of the correlation between y_i and $\hat{y}_i$, and $0 \leq r^2 \leq 1$.

When we express the coefficient of determination as a percentage, r^2 can be interpreted as the percentage of the total sum of squares that can be explained by using the estimated regression equation. For Butler Trucking Company, we can conclude that 66.41% of the total sum of squares can be explained by using the estimated regression equation $\hat{y}_i = 1.2739 + 0.0678x_i$ to predict quarterly sales. In other words, 66.41% of the variability in the values of travel time in our sample can be explained by the linear relationship between the miles traveled and travel time.

Using Excel's Chart Tools to Compute the Coefficient of Determination

In Section 7.1 we used Excel's chart tools to construct a scatter chart and compute the estimated regression equation for the Butler Trucking Company data. We will now describe how to compute the coefficient of determination using the scatter chart in Figure 7.3.

Note that Excel notates the coefficient of determination as R^2.

Step 1. Right-click on any data point in the scatter chart and select **Add Trendline**...
Step 2. When the **Format Trendline** task pane appears:
Select **Display R-squared value on chart** in the **Trendline Options** area
Figure 7.9 displays the scatter chart, the estimated regression equation, the graph of the estimated regression equation, and the coefficient of determination for the Butler Trucking Company data. We see that $r^2 = 0.6641$.

FIGURE 7.9 Scatter Chart and Estimated Regression Line with Coefficient of Determination r^2 for Butler Trucking Company

7.4 The Multiple Regression Model

We now extend our discussion to the study of how a dependent variable y is related to two or more independent variables.

Regression Model

The concepts of a regression model and a regression equation introduced in the preceding sections are applicable in the multiple regression case. We will use q to denote the number of independent variables in the regression model. The equation that describes how the dependent variable y is related to the independent variables $x_1, x_2, \ldots, x_q$ and an error term is called the multiple regression model. We begin with the assumption that the multiple regression model takes the following form:

MULTIPLE REGRESSION MODEL

$$y = \beta_0 + \beta_1 x_1 + \beta_2 x_2 + \cdots + \beta_q x_q + \varepsilon \tag{7.10}$$

In the multiple regression model, $\beta_0, \beta_1, \beta_2, \ldots, \beta_q$ are the parameters and the error term ϵ is a normally distributed random variable with a mean of zero and a constant variance across all observations. A close examination of this model reveals that y is a linear function of $x_1, x_2, \ldots, x_q$ plus the error term ϵ. As in simple regression, the error term accounts for the variability in y that cannot be explained by the linear effect of the q independent variables. The interpretation of the y-intercept β_0 in multiple regression is similar to the interpretation in simple regression; in a multiple regression model, β_0 is the mean of the dependent variable y when all of the independent variables $x_1, x_2, \ldots, x_q$ are equal to zero. On the other hand, the interpretation of the slope coefficients $\beta_1, \beta_2, \ldots, \beta_q$ in a multiple regression model differ in a subtle but important way from the interpretation of the slope β_1 in a simple regression model. In a multiple regression model the slope coefficient β_j represents the change in the mean value of the dependent variable y that corresponds to a one-unit increase in the independent variable x_j, *holding the values of all other independent variables in the model constant*. Thus, in a multiple regression model, the slope coefficient β_1 represents the change in the mean value of the dependent variable y that corresponds to a one-unit increase in the independent variable x_1, holding the values of $x_2, x_3, \ldots, x_q$ constant. Similarly, the slope coefficient β_2 represents the change in the mean value of the dependent variable y that corresponds to a one-unit increase in the independent variable x_2, holding the values of $x_1, x_3, \ldots, x_q$ constant.

Estimated Multiple Regression Equation

In practice, the values of the population parameters $\beta_0, \beta_1, \beta_2, \ldots, \beta_q$ are not known and so must be estimated from sample data. A simple random sample is used to compute sample statistics $b_0, b_1, b_2, \ldots, b_q$ that are then used as the point estimators of the parameters $\beta_0, \beta_1, \beta_2, \ldots, \beta_q$. These sample statistics provide the following estimated multiple regression equation.

ESTIMATED MULTIPLE REGRESSION EQUATION

$$\hat{y} = b_0 + b_1 x_1 + b_2 x_2 + \cdots + b_q x_q \tag{7.11}$$

where

$$b_0, b_1, b_2, \ldots, b_q = \text{the point estimates of } \beta_0, \beta_1, \beta_2, \ldots, \beta_q$$
$$\hat{y} = \text{estimated mean value of } y \text{ given values for } x_1, x_2 \ldots, x_q$$

Least Squares Method and Multiple Regression

As with simple linear regression, in multiple regression we wish to find a model that results in small errors over the sample data. We continue to use the least squares method to develop the estimated multiple regression equation; that is, we find $b_0, b_1, b_2, \ldots, b_q$ that minimize the sum of squared residuals (the squared deviations between the observed values of the dependent variable y_i and the estimated values of the dependent variable $\hat{y}$):

$$\min \sum_{i=1}^{n}(y_i - \hat{y}_i)^2 = \min \sum_{i=1}^{n}(y_i - b_0 - b_1x_1 - \cdots - b_qx_q)^2 = \min \sum_{i=1}^{n}e_i^2 \qquad \textbf{(7.12)}$$

The estimation process for multiple regression is shown in Figure 7.10.

The estimated values of the dependent variable y are computed by substituting values of the independent variables $x_1, x_2, \ldots, x_q$ into the estimated multiple regression equation (7.11).

As in simple regression, it is possible to derive formulas that determine the values of the regression coefficients that minimize equation (7.12). However, these formulas involve the use of matrix algebra and are outside the scope of this text. Therefore, in presenting multiple regression, we focus on how computer software packages can be used to obtain the estimated regression equation and other information. The emphasis will be on how to construct and interpret a regression model.

Butler Trucking Company and Multiple Regression

As an illustration of multiple regression analysis, recall that a major portion of Butler Trucking Company's business involves deliveries throughout its local area and that the

---

FIGURE 7.10   The Estimation Process for Multiple Regression managers want to estimate the total daily travel time for their drivers in order to develop better work schedules for the company's drivers.

Initially, the managers believed that the total daily travel time would be closely related to the number of miles traveled in making the daily deliveries. Based on a simple random sample of 10 driving assignments, we explored the simple linear regression model $y = \beta_0 + \beta_1 x + \varepsilon$ to describe the relationship between travel time (y) and number of miles (x). As Figure 7.9 shows, we found that the estimated simple linear regression equation for our sample data is $\hat{y}_i = 1.2739 + 0.0678x_i$. With a coefficient of determination $r^2 = 0.6641$, the linear effect of the number of miles traveled explains 66.41% of the variability in travel time in the sample data, and so 33.59% of the variability in sample travel times remains unexplained. This result suggests to Butler's managers that other factors may contribute to the travel times for driving assignments. The managers might want to consider adding one or more independent variables to the model to explain some of the remaining variability in the dependent variable.

In considering other independent variables for their model, the managers felt that the number of deliveries made on a driving assignment also contributes to the total travel time. To support the development of a multiple regression model that includes both the number of miles traveled and the number of deliveries, they augment their original data with information on the number of deliveries for the 10 driving assignments in the original data and they collect new observations over several ensuing weeks. The new data, which consist of 300 observations, are provided in the file *ButlerWithDeliveries*. Note that we now refer to the independent variables miles traveled as x_1 and the number of deliveries as x_2.

Our multiple linear regression with two independent variables will take the form $\hat{y} = b_0 + b_1 x_1 + b_2 x_2$. The SSE, SST, and SSR are again calculated using equations (7.5), (7.6), and (7.7), respectively. Thus, the coefficient of determination, which in multiple regression is denoted by R^2, is again calculated using equation (7.9). We will now use Excel's Regression tool to calculate the values of the estimates b_0, b_1, b_2, and R^2.

DATA *file*

ButlerWithDeliveries

In multiple regression, R^2 is often referred to as the multiple coefficient of determination.

Using Excel's Regression Tool to Develop the Estimated Multiple Regression Equation

When using Excel's Regression tool, the data for the independent variables must be in adjacent columns or rows. Thus, you may have to rearrange the data in order to use Excel to run a particular multiple regression.

The following steps describe how to use Excel's Regression tool to compute the estimated regression equation using the data in the worksheet.

Step 1. Click the **Data** tab in the Ribbon
Step 2. Click **Data Analysis** in the **Analysis** group
Step 3. Select **Regression** from the list of **Analysis Tools** in the **Data Analysis** tools box (shown in Figure 7.11) and click **OK**
Step 4. When the **Regression** dialog box appears (as shown in Figure 7.12):

*Selecting **New Worksheet Ply**: tells Excel to place the output of the regression analysis in a new worksheet. In the adjacent box, you can specify the name of the worksheet where the output is to be placed, or you can leave this blank and allow Excel to create a new worksheet to use as the destination for the results of this regression analysis (as we are doing here).*

> Enter *D1:D301* in the **Input Y Range:** box
> Enter *B1:C301* in the **Input X Range:** box
> Select **Labels**
> Select **Confidence Level:**
> Enter *99* in the **Confidence Level:** box
> Select **New Worksheet Ply:**
> Click **OK**

In the Excel output shown in Figure 7.13, the label for the independent variable x_1 is "Miles" (see cell A18), and the label for the independent variable x_2 is "Deliveries" (see cell A19). The estimated regression equation is

$$\hat{y} = 0.1273 = 0.0672x_1 + 0.6900x_2 \qquad (7.13)$$

If **Data Analysis** does not appear in the **Analysis** group in the **Data** tab, you will have to load the Analysis ToolPak add-in into Excel. To do so, click the **File** tab in the Ribbon, and click **Options**. When the **Excel Options** dialog box appears, click **Add-Ins** from the menu. Next to **Manage:**, select **Excel Add-ins**, and click **Go. . .** at the bottom of the dialog box. When the **Add-Ins** dialog box appears, select **Analysis ToolPak** and click **Go**. When the **Add-Ins** dialog box appears, check the box next to **Analysis ToolPak** and click **OK**.

FIGURE 7.11 Data Analysis Tools Box

FIGURE 7.12 Regression Dialog Box

The sum of squares due to error, SSE, cannot become larger (and generally will become smaller) when independent variables are added to a regression model. Therefore, because $SSR = SST - SSE$, the SSR cannot become smaller (and generally becomes larger) when an independent variable is added to a regression model. Thus, $R^2 = SSR/SST$ can never decrease as independent variables are added to the regression model.

We interpret this model in the following manner:

- For a fixed number of deliveries, we estimate that the mean travel time will increase by 0.0672 hour (about 4 minutes) when the distance traveled increases by 1 mile.
- For a fixed distance traveled, we estimate that the mean travel time will increase by 0.69 hour (about 41 minutes) when the number of deliveries increases by 1 delivery.

The interpretation of the estimated y-intercept for this model (the expected mean travel time for a driving assignment with a distance traveled of 0 miles and no deliveries) is not meaningful because it is the result of extrapolation.

This model has a multiple coefficient of determination of $R^2 = 0.8173$. By adding the number of deliveries as an independent variable to our original simple linear regression, we now explain 81.73% of the variability in our sample values of the dependent variable, travel time. Because the simple linear regression with miles traveled as the sole independent variable explained 66.41% of the variability in our sample values of travel time, we can see that adding number of deliveries as an independent variable to our regression

FIGURE 7.13	Excel Regression Output for the Butler Trucking Company with Miles and Deliveries as Independent Variables

	A	B	C	D	E	F	G	H	I
1	SUMMARY OUTPUT								
2									
3	*Regression Statistics*								
4	Multiple R	0.90407397							
5	R Square	0.817349743							
6	Adjusted R Square	0.816119775							
7	Standard Error	0.829967216							
8	Observations	300							
9									
10	ANOVA								
11		*df*	*SS*	*MS*	*F*	*Significance F*			
12	Regression	2	915.5160626	457.7580313	664.5292419	2.2419E-110			
13	Residual	297	204.5871374	0.68884558					
14	Total	299	1120.1032						
15									
16		*Coefficients*	*Standard Error*	*t Stat*	*P-value*	*Lower 95%*	*Upper 95%*	*Lower 99.0%*	*Upper 99.0%*
17	Intercept	0.127337137	0.20520348	0.620540826	0.53537766	−0.276499931	0.531174204	−0.404649592	0.659323866
18	Miles	0.067181742	0.002454979	27.36551071	3.5398E-83	0.062350385	0.072013099	0.06081725	0.073546235
19	Deliveries	0.68999828	0.029521057	23.37308852	2.84826E-69	0.631901326	0.748095234	0.613465414	0.766531147

model resulted in explaining an additional 15.32% of the variability in our sample values of travel time. The addition of the number of deliveries to the model appears to have been worthwhile.

Using this multiple regression model, we now generate an estimated mean value of y for every combination of values of x_1 and x_2. Thus, instead of a regression line, we now have created a regression plane in three-dimensional space. Figure 7.14 provides the graph of

FIGURE 7.14	Graph of the Regression Equation for Multiple Regression Analysis with Two Independent Variables

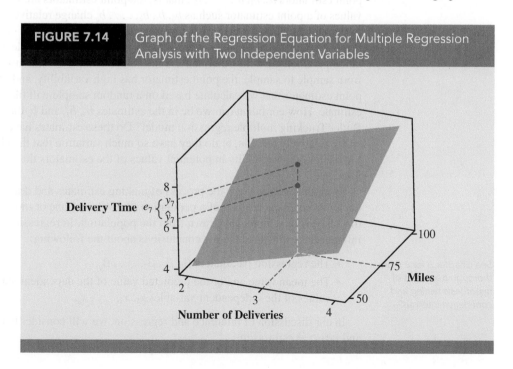

the estimated regression plane for the Butler Trucking Company example and shows the seventh driving assignment in the data. Observe that as the plane slopes upward to larger values of estimated mean travel time ($\hat{y}$) as either the number of miles traveled (x_1) or the number of deliveries (x_2) increases. Further, observe that the residual for a driving assignment when $x_1 = 75$ and $x_2 = 3$ is the difference between the observed y value and the estimated mean value of y given $x_1 = 75$ and $x_2 = 3$. Note that in Figure 7.14, the observed value lies above the regression plane, indicating that the regression model underestimates the expected driving time for the seventh driving assignment.

NOTES + COMMENTS

Although we use regression analysis to estimate relationships between independent variables and the dependent variable, it does not provide information on whether these are cause-and-effect relationships. The analyst can conclude that a cause-and-effect relationship exists between an independent variable and a dependent variable only if there is a theoretical justification that the relationship is in fact causal. In the Butler Trucking Company multiple regression, through regression analysis we have found evidence of a relationship between distance traveled and travel time and evidence of a relationship between number of deliveries and travel time. Nonetheless,

we cannot conclude from the regression model that changes in distance traveled x_1 cause changes in travel time y, and we cannot conclude that changes in number of deliveries x_2 cause changes in travel time y. The appropriateness of such cause-and-effect conclusions are left to supporting practical justification and to good judgment on the part of the analyst. Based on their practical experience, Butler Trucking's managers felt that increases in distance traveled and number of deliveries were likely causes of increased travel time. However, it is important to realize that the regression model itself provides no information about cause-and-effect relationships.

7.5 Inference and Regression

The statistics $b_0, b_1, b_2, \ldots, b_q$ are point estimators of the population parameters $\beta_0, \beta_1, \beta_2, \ldots, \beta_q$; that is, each of these $q + 1$ estimates is a single value used as an estimate of the corresponding population parameter. Similarly, we use $\hat{y}$ as a point estimator of $E(y \mid x_1, x_2, \ldots, x_q)$, the conditional mean of y given values of $x_1, x_2, \ldots, x_q$.

However, we must recognize that samples do not replicate the population exactly. Different samples taken from the same population will result in different values of the point estimators $b_0, b_1, b_2, \ldots, b_q$; that is, the point estimators are random variables. If the values of a point estimator such as $b_0, b_1, b_2, \ldots, b_q$ change relatively little from sample to sample, the point estimator has low variability, and so the value of the point estimator that we calculate based on a random sample will likely be a reliable estimate of the population parameter. On the other hand, if the values of a point estimator change dramatically from sample to sample, the point estimator has high variability, and so the value of the point estimator that we calculate based on a random sample will likely be a less reliable estimate. How confident can we be in the estimates $b_0, b_1,$ and b_2 that we developed for the Butler Trucking multiple regression model? Do these estimates have little variation and so are relatively reliable, or do they have so much variation that they have little meaning? We address the variability in potential values of the estimators through use of statistical inference.

Statistical inference is the process of making estimates and drawing conclusions about one or more characteristics of a population (the value of one or more parameters) through the analysis of sample data drawn from the population. In regression, we commonly use inference to estimate and draw conclusions about the following:

See Chapter 6 for a more thorough treatment of hypothesis testing and confidence intervals.

- The regression parameters $\beta_0, \beta_1, \beta_2, \ldots, \beta_q$.
- The mean value and/or the predicted value of the dependent variable y for specific values of the independent variables $x_1, x_2, \ldots, x_q$.

In our discussion of inference and regression, we will consider both **hypothesis testing** and **interval estimation**.

Conditions Necessary for Valid Inference in the Least Squares Regression Model

In conducting a regression analysis, we begin by making an assumption about the appropriate model for the relationship between the dependent and independent variable(s). For the case of linear regression, the assumed multiple regression model is

$$y = \beta_0 + \beta_1 x_1 + \beta_2 x_2 + \cdots + \beta_q x_q + \varepsilon$$

The least squares method is used to develop values for $b_0, b_1, b_2, \ldots, b_q$, the estimates of the model parameters $\beta_0, \beta_1, \beta_2, \ldots, \beta_p$, respectively. The resulting estimated multiple regression equation is

$$\hat{y} = b_0 + b_1 x_1 + b_2 x_2 + \cdots + b_q x_q$$

Although inference can provide greater understanding of the nature of relationships estimated through regression analysis, our inferences are valid only if the error term ε behaves in a certain way. Specifically, the validity of inferences in regression analysis depends on how well the following two conditions about the error term ε are met:

1. For any given combination of values of the independent variables $x_1, x_2, \ldots, x_q$, the population of potential error terms ϵ is normally distributed with a mean of 0 and a constant variance.
2. The values of ϵ are statistically independent.

The practical implication of normally distributed errors with a mean of zero and a constant variation for any given combination of values of $x_1, x_2, \ldots, x_q$ is that the regression estimates are unbiased (i.e., they do not tend to over- or underpredict), possess consistent accuracy, and tend to err in small amounts rather than in large amounts. This first condition must be met for statistical inference in regression to be valid. The second condition is generally a concern when we collect data from a single entity over several periods of time and must also be met for statistical inference in regression to be valid in these instances. However, inferences in regression are generally reliable unless there are marked violations of these conditions.

Figure 7.15 illustrates these model conditions and their implications for a simple linear regression; note that in this graphical interpretation, the value of $E(y|x)$ changes linearly according to the specific value of x considered, and so the mean error is zero at each value of x. However, regardless of the x value, the error term ϵ and hence the dependent variable y are normally distributed, each with the same variance.

To evaluate whether the error of an estimated regression equation reasonably meets the two conditions, the sample residuals ($e_i = y_i - \hat{y}_i$ for observations $i = 1, \ldots, n$) need to be analyzed. There are many sophisticated diagnostic procedures for detecting whether the sample errors violate these conditions, but simple scatter charts of the residuals versus the predicted values of the dependent variable and the residuals versus the independent variables are an extremely effective method for assessing whether these conditions are violated. We should review the scatter chart for patterns in the residuals indicating that one or more of the conditions have been violated. As Figure 7.16 illustrates, at any given value of the horizontal-axis variable in these residual scatter plots, the center of the residuals should be approximately zero, the spread in the errors should be similar to the spread in error for other values of the horizontal-axis variable, and the errors should be symmetrically distributed with values near zero occurring more frequently than values that differ greatly from zero. A pattern in the residuals such as this gives us little reason to doubt the validity of inferences made on the regression that generated the residuals.

While the residuals in Figure 7.16 show no discernible pattern, the residuals in the four panels of Figure 7.17 show examples of distinct patterns, each of which suggests a violation of at least one of the regression model conditions. Figure 7.17 shows plots of residuals from four different regressions, each showing a different pattern. In panel (a), the variation in the residuals (e) increases as the value of the independent variable increases, suggesting that the residuals do not have a constant variance. In panel (b), the residuals are positive for small and

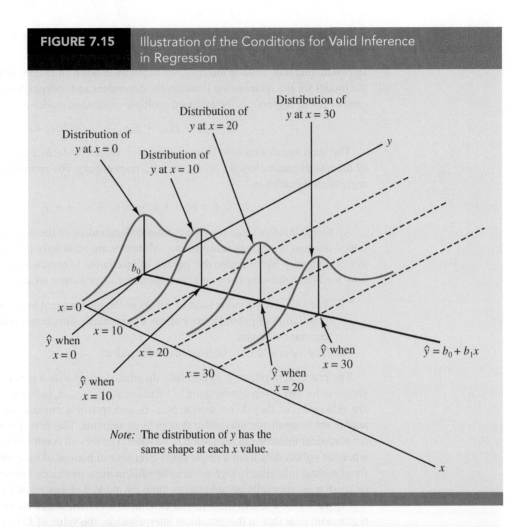

FIGURE 7.15   Illustration of the Conditions for Valid Inference in Regression

Note: The distribution of y has the same shape at each x value.

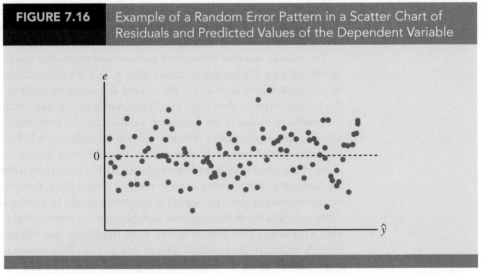

FIGURE 7.16   Example of a Random Error Pattern in a Scatter Chart of Residuals and Predicted Values of the Dependent Variable

large values of the independent variable but are negative for moderate values of the independent variable. This pattern suggests that the linear regression model underpredicts the value of the dependent variable for small and large values of the independent variable and overpredicts the value of the dependent variable for intermediate values of the independent variable. In this case, the regression model does not adequately capture the relationship between the

FIGURE 7.17   Examples of Diagnostic Scatter Charts of Residuals from Four Regressions

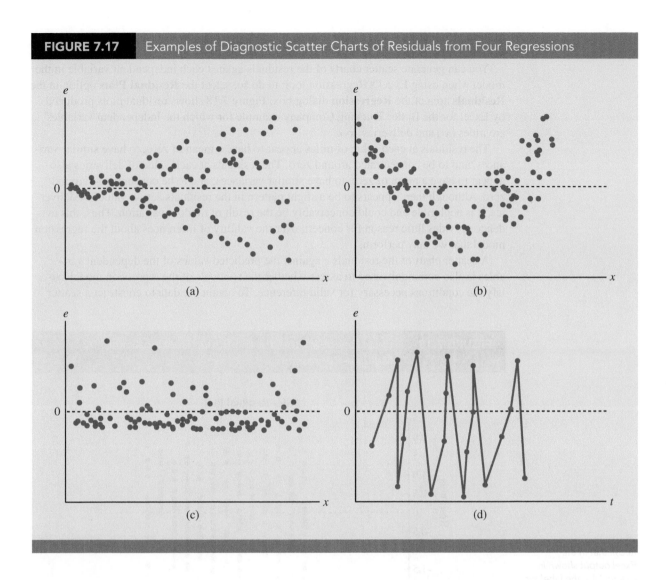

independent variable x and the dependent variable y. The residuals in panel (c) are not symmetrically distributed around 0; many of the negative residuals are relatively close to zero, while the relatively few positive residuals tend to be far from zero. This skewness suggests that the residuals are not normally distributed. Finally, the residuals in panel (d) are plotted over time t, which generally serves as an independent variable; that is, an observation is made at each of several (usually equally spaced) points in time. In this case, connected consecutive residuals allow us to see a distinct pattern across every set of four residuals; the second residual is consistently larger than the first and smaller than the third, whereas the fourth residual is consistently the smallest. This pattern, which occurs consistently over each set of four consecutive residuals in the chart in panel (d), suggests that the residuals generated by this model are not independent. A residual pattern such as this generally occurs when we have collected quarterly data and have not captured seasonal effects in the model. In each of these four instances, any inferences based on our regression will likely not be reliable.

Frequently, the residuals do not meet these conditions either because an important independent variable has been omitted from the model or because the functional form of the model is inadequate to explain the relationships between the independent variables and the dependent variable. It is important to note that calculating the values of the estimates $b_0, b_1, b_2, \ldots, b_q$ does not require the errors to satisfy these conditions. However, the errors must satisfy these conditions in order for inferences (interval estimates for predicted values of the dependent variable and confidence intervals and hypothesis tests of the regression parameters $\beta_0, \beta_1, \beta_2, \ldots, \beta_q$) to be reliable.

You can generate scatter charts of the residuals against each independent variable in the model when using Excel's Regression tool; to do so, select the **Residual Plots** option in the **Residuals** area of the **Regression** dialog box. Figure 7.18 shows residual plots produced by Excel for the Butler Trucking Company example for which the independent variables are miles (x_1) and deliveries (x_2).

The residuals at each value of miles appear to have a mean of zero, to have similar variances, and to be concentrated around zero. The residuals at each value of deliveries also appear to have a mean of zero, to have similar variances, and to be concentrated around zero. Although there appears to be a slight pattern in the residuals across values of deliveries, it is negligible and could conceivably be the result of random variation. Thus, this evidence provides little reason for concern over the validity of inferences about the regression model that we may perform.

A scatter chart of the residuals e against the predicted values of the dependent variables is also commonly used to assess whether the residuals of the regression model satisfy the conditions necessary for valid inference. To obtain the data to construct a scatter

---

FIGURE 7.18 Excel Residual Plots for the Butler Trucking Company Multiple Regression

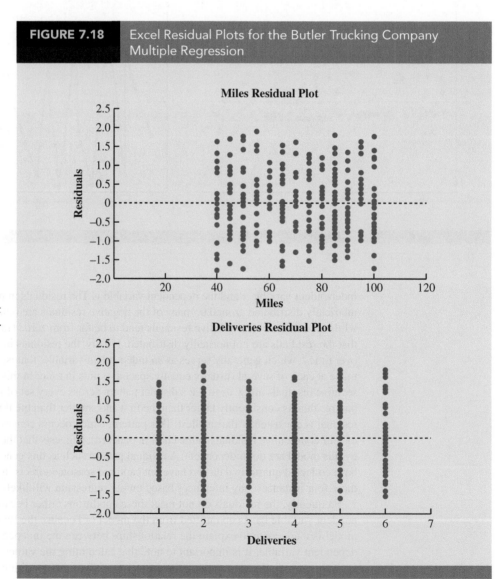

Recall that in the Excel output shown in Figure 7.13, the label for the independent variable x_1 is "Miles" and the label for the independent variable x_2 is "Deliveries".

chart of the residuals against the predicted values of the dependent variable using Excel's Regression tool, select the **Residuals** option in the **Residuals** area of the **Regression** dialog box (shown in Figure 7.12). This generates a table of predicted values of the dependent variable and residuals for the observations in the data; a partial list for the Butler Trucking multiple regression example is shown in Figure 7.19.

We can then use the Excel chart tool to create a scatter chart of these predicted values and residuals similar to the chart in Figure 7.20. The figure shows that the residuals at each predicted value of the dependent variable appear to have a mean of zero, to have similar variances, and to be concentrated around zero. Thus, the residuals provide little evidence that our regression model violates the conditions necessary for reliable inference. We can trust the inferences that we may wish to perform on our regression model.

Testing Individual Regression Parameters

Once we ascertain that our regression model satisfies the conditions necessary for reliable inference reasonably well, we can begin testing hypotheses and building confidence intervals. Specifically, we may then wish to determine whether statistically significant relationships exist between the dependent variable y and each of the independent variables x_1, x_2, . . . , x_q individually. Note that if a β_j is zero, then the dependent variable y does not change when the independent variable x_j changes, and there is no linear relationship between y and x_j. Alternatively, if a β_j is not zero, there is a linear relationship between the dependent variable y and the independent variable x_j.

See Chapter 6 for a more in-depth discussion of hypothesis testing.

We use a *t test* to test the hypothesis that a regression parameter β_j is zero. The corresponding null and alternative hypotheses are as follows:

$$H_0: \beta_j = 0$$
$$H_a: \beta_j \neq 0$$

FIGURE 7.19	Table of the First Several Predicted Values $\hat{y}$ and Residuals e Generated by the Excel Regression Tool

23	RESIDUAL OUTPUT		
24			
25	*Observation*	*Predicted Time*	*Residuals*
26	1	9.605504464	−0.305504464
27	2	5.556419081	−0.756419081
28	3	9.605504464	−0.705504464
29	4	8.225507903	−1.725507903
30	5	4.8664208	−0.6664208
31	6	6.881873062	−0.681873062
32	7	7.235932632	0.164037368
33	8	7.254143492	−1.254143492
34	9	8.243688763	−0.643688763
35	10	7.553690482	−1.453690482
36	11	6.936415641	0.063584359
37	12	7.290505212	−0.290505212
38	13	9.287776613	0.312223387
39	14	5.874146931	0.625853069
40	15	6.954596501	0.245403499
41	16	5.556419081	0.443580919

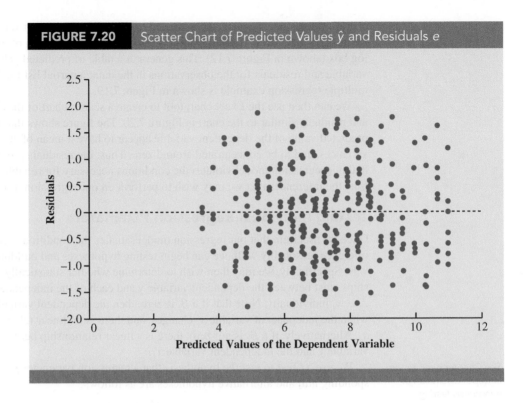

FIGURE 7.20   Scatter Chart of Predicted Values $\hat{y}$ and Residuals e

The test statistic for this t test is

$$t = \frac{b_j}{s_{b_j}} \tag{7.14}$$

where b_j is the point estimate of the regression parameter β_j and s_{b_j} is the estimated standard deviation of b_j.

As the value of b_j, the point estimate of β_j, deviates from zero in either direction, the evidence from our sample that the corresponding regression parameter β_j is not zero increases. Thus, as the magnitude of t increases (as t deviates from zero in either direction), we are more likely to reject the hypothesis that the regression parameter β_j is zero and so conclude that a relationship exists between the dependent variable y and the independent variable x_j.

Statistical software will generally report a p value for this test statistic; for a given value of t, this p value represents the probability of collecting a sample of the same size from the same population that yields a larger t statistic given that the value of β_j is actually zero. Thus, smaller p values indicate stronger evidence against the hypothesis that the value of β_j is zero (i.e., stronger evidence of a relationship between x_j and y). The hypothesis is rejected when the corresponding p value is smaller than some predetermined level of significance (usually 0.05 or 0.01).

The output of Excel's Regression tool provides the results of the t tests for each regression parameter. Refer again to Figure 7.13, which shows the multiple linear regression results for Butler Trucking with independent variables x_1 (labeled Miles) and x_2 (labeled Deliveries). The values of the parameter estimates b_0, b_1, and b_2 are located in cells B17, B18, and B19, respectively; the standard deviations s_{b_0}, s_{b_1}, and s_{b_2} are contained in cells C17, C18, and C19, respectively; the values of the t statistics for the hypothesis tests are in cells D17, D18, and D19, respectively; and the corresponding p values are in cells E17, E18, and E19, respectively.

Let's use these results to test the hypothesis that β_1 is zero. If we do not reject this hypothesis, we conclude that the mean value of y does not change when the value of x_1 changes, and so there is no relationship between driving time and miles traveled. We see in the Excel output in Figure 7.13 that the statistic for this test is 27.3655 and that the associated p value is 3.5398E-83. This p value tells us that if the value of β_1 is actually zero, the probability we could collect a random sample of 300 observations from the population of Butler Trucking driving assignments that yields a t statistic with an absolute value greater than 27.3655 is practically zero. Such a small probability represents a highly unlikely scenario; thus, the small p value allows us to reject the hypothesis that $\beta_1 = 0$ for the Butler Trucking multiple regression example at a 0.01 level of significance or even at a far smaller level of significance. Thus, this data suggests that a relationship may exist between driving time and miles traveled.

Similarly, we can test the hypothesis that β_2 is zero. If we do not reject this hypothesis, we conclude that the mean value of y does not change when the value of x_2 changes, and so there is no relationship between driving time and number of deliveries. We see in the Excel output in Figure 7.13 that the t statistic for this test is 23.3731 and that the associated p value is 2.84826E-69. This p value tells us that if the value of β_2 is actually zero, the probability we could collect a random sample of 300 observations from the population of Butler Trucking driving assignments that yields a t statistic with an absolute value greater than 23.3731 is practically zero. This is highly unlikely, and so the p value is sufficiently small to reject the hypothesis that $\beta_2 = 0$ for the Butler Trucking multiple regression example at a 0.01 level of significance or even at a far smaller level of significance. Thus, this data suggests that a relationship may exist between driving time and number of deliveries.

Finally, we can test the hypothesis that β_0 is zero in a similar fashion. If we do not reject this hypothesis, we conclude that the mean value of y is zero when the values of x_1 and x_2 are both zero, and so there is no driving time when a driving assignment is 0 miles and has 0 deliveries. We see in the Excel output that the t statistic for this test is 0.6205 and the associated p value is 0.5354. This p value tells us that if the value of β_0 is actually zero, the probability we could collect a random sample of 300 observations from the population of Butler Trucking driving assignments that yields a t statistic with an absolute value greater than 0.6205 is 0.5354. Thus, we do not reject the hypothesis that mean driving time is zero when a driving assignment is 0 miles and has 0 deliveries.

We can also execute each of these hypothesis tests through confidence intervals. A **confidence interval** for a regression parameter β_i is an estimated interval believed to contain the true value of β_i at some level of confidence. The level of confidence, or **confidence level**, indicates how frequently interval estimates based on similar-sized samples from the same population using identical sampling techniques will contain the true value of β_i. Thus, when building a 95% confidence interval, we can expect that if we took similar-sized samples from the same population using identical sampling techniques, the corresponding interval estimates would contain the true value of β_i for 95% of the samples.

See Chapter 6 for a more in-depth discussion of confidence intervals.

Although the confidence intervals for $\beta_0, \beta_1, \beta_2, \ldots, \beta_q$ convey information about the variation in the estimates $b_0, b_1, b_2, \ldots, b_q$ that can be expected across repeated samples, they can also be used to test whether each of the regression parameters $\beta_0, \beta_1, \beta_2, \ldots, \beta_q$ is equal to zero in the following manner. To test that β_j is zero (i.e., there is no linear relationship between x_j and y) at some predetermined level of significance (say 0.05), first build a confidence interval at the $(1 - 0.05)100\%$ confidence level. If the resulting confidence interval does not contain zero, we conclude that β_j differs from zero at the predetermined level of significance.

The form of a confidence interval for β_j is as follows:

$$b_j \pm t_{a/2}s_{b_j}$$

where b_j is the point estimate of the regression parameter β_j, s_{b_j} is the estimated standard deviation of b_j, and $t_{\alpha/2}$ is a multiplier term based on the sample size and specified

$100(1 - \alpha)\%$ confidence level of the interval. More specifically, $t_{\alpha/2}$ is the t value that provides an area of $\alpha/2$ in the upper tail of a t distribution with $n - q - 1$ degrees of freedom.

Most software that is capable of regression analysis can also produce these confidence intervals. For example, the output of Excel's Regression tool for Butler Trucking, given in Figure 7.13, provides confidence intervals for β_1 (the slope coefficient associated with the independent variable x_1, labeled Miles) and β_2 (the slope coefficient associated with the independent variable x_2, labeled Deliveries), as well as the y-intercept β_0. The 95% confidence intervals for β_0, β_1, and β_2 are shown in cells F17:G17, F18:G18, and F19:G19, respectively. Neither of the 95% confidence intervals for β_1 and β_2 includes zero, so we can conclude that β_1 and β_2 each differ from zero at the 0.05 level of significance. On the other hand, the 95% confidence interval for β_0 does include zero, so we conclude that β_0 does not differ from zero at the 0.05 level of significance.

The Regression tool dialog box offers the user the opportunity to generate confidence intervals for β_0, β_1, and β_2 at a confidence level other than 95%. In this example, we chose to create 99% confidence intervals for β_0, β_1, and β_2, which in Figure 7.13 are given in cells H17:I17, H18:I18, and H19:I19, respectively. Neither of the 99% confidence intervals for β_1 and β_2 includes zero, so we can conclude that β_1 and β_2 each differs from zero at the 0.01 level of significance. On the other hand, the 99% confidence interval for β_0 does include zero, so we conclude that β_0 does not differ from zero at the 0.01 level of significance.

Addressing Nonsignificant Independent Variables

If we do not reject the hypothesis that β_j is zero, we conclude that there is no linear relationship between y and x_j. This leads to the question of how to handle the corresponding independent variable. Do we use the model as originally formulated with the nonsignificant independent variable, or do we rerun the regression without the nonsignificant independent variable and use the new result? The approach to be taken depends on a number of factors, but ultimately whatever model we use should have a theoretical basis. If practical experience dictates that the nonsignificant independent variable has a relationship with the dependent variable, the independent variable should be left in the model. On the other hand, if the model sufficiently explains the dependent variable without the nonsignificant independent variable, then we should consider rerunning the regression without the nonsignificant independent variable. Note that it is possible that the estimates of the other regression coefficients and their p values may change considerably when we remove the nonsignificant independent variable from the model.

The appropriate treatment of the inclusion or exclusion of the y-intercept when b_0 is not statistically significant may require special consideration. For example, in the Butler Trucking multiple regression model, recall that the p value for b_0 is 0.5354, suggesting that this estimate of β_0 is not statistically significant. Should we remove the y-intercept from this model because it is not statistically significant? Excel provides functionality to remove the y-intercept from the model by selecting **Constant is zero** in Excel's Regression tool. This will force the y-intercept to go through the origin (when the independent variables $x_1, x_2, ..., x_q$ all equal zero, the estimated value of the dependent variable will be zero). However, doing this can substantially alter the estimated slopes in the regression model and result in a less effective regression that yields less accurate predicted values of the dependent variable. The primary purpose of the regression model is to explain or predict values of the dependent variable corresponding to values of the independent variables within the experimental region. Therefore, it is generally advised that regression through the origin should not be forced. In a situation for which there are strong *a priori* reasons for believing that the dependent variable is equal to zero when the values of all independent variables in the model are equal to zero, it is better to collect data for which the values of the independent variables are at or near zero in order to allow the regression to empirically validate this belief and avoid extrapolation. If data for which the values of the independent variables are at or near zero is not obtainable, and the regression model is intended to be used to explain or predict values of the dependent variable at or near y-intercept, then forcing the y-intercept to be zero may be a necessary action, although it results in extrapolation. A common business example of regression through the origin is a model for which output in a labor-intensive production process is the dependent variable and hours of labor is the independent variable; because the production process is labor intense, we would expect no output when the value of labor hours is zero.

Multicollinearity

We use the term *independent variable* in regression analysis to refer to any variable used to predict or explain the value of the dependent variable. The term does not mean, however, that the independent variables themselves are independent from each other in any statistical sense. On the contrary, most independent variables in a multiple regression problem are correlated with one another to some degree. For example, in the Butler Trucking example involving the two independent variables x_1 (miles traveled) and x_2 (number of deliveries), we could compute the sample correlation coefficient r_{x_1,x_2} to determine the extent to which these two variables are related. Doing so yields $r_{x_1,x_2} = 0.16$. Thus, we find some degree of linear association between the two independent variables. In multiple regression analysis, **multicollinearity** refers to the correlation among the independent variables.

DATA *file*

ButlerWithGas-Consumption

To gain a better perspective of the potential problems of multicollinearity, let us consider a modification of the Butler Trucking example. Instead of x_2 being the number of deliveries, let x_2 denote the number of gallons of gasoline consumed. Clearly, x_1 (the miles traveled) and x_2 are now related; that is, we know that the number of gallons of gasoline used depends to a large extent on the number of miles traveled. Hence, we would conclude logically that x_1 and x_2 are highly correlated independent variables and that multicollinearity is present in the model. The data for this example are provided in the file *ButlerWithGasConsumption*.

Using Excel's Regression tool, we obtain the results shown in Figure 7.21 for our multiple regression. When we conduct a t test to determine whether β_1 is equal to zero, we find a p value of 3.1544E-07, and so we reject this hypothesis and conclude that travel time is related to miles traveled. On the other hand, when we conduct a t test to determine whether β_2 is equal to zero, we find a p value of 0.6588, and so we do not reject this hypothesis. Does this mean that travel time is not related to gasoline consumption? Not necessarily.

What it probably means in this instance is that, with x_1 already in the model, x_2 does not make a significant marginal contribution to predicting the value of y. This interpretation makes sense within the context of the Butler Trucking example; if we know the miles traveled, we do not gain much new information that would be useful in predicting driving time by also knowing the amount of gasoline consumed. We can see this in the scatter chart in Figure 7.22; miles traveled and gasoline consumed are strongly related.

If any estimated regression parameters $b_1, b_2, \ldots, b_q$ or associated p values change dramatically when a new independent variable is added to the model (or an existing independent variable is removed from the model), multicollinearity is likely present. Looking for changes such as these is sometimes used as a way to detect multicollinearity.

Even though we rejected the hypothesis that β_1 is equal to zero in the model corresponding to Figure 7.21, a comparison to Figure 7.13 shows the value of the t statistic is much smaller and the p value substantially larger than in the multiple regression model that includes miles driven and number of deliveries as the independent variables. The evidence against the hypothesis that β_1 is equal to zero is weaker in the multiple regression that includes miles driven and gasoline consumed as the independent variables because of the high correlation between these two independent variables.

To summarize, in t tests for the significance of individual parameters, the difficulty caused by multicollinearity is that it is possible to conclude that a parameter associated with one of the multicollinear independent variables is not significantly different from zero when the independent variable actually has a strong relationship with the dependent variable. This problem is avoided when there is little correlation among the independent variables.

Statisticians have developed several tests for determining whether multicollinearity is strong enough to cause problems. In addition to the initial understanding of the nature of

FIGURE 7.21   Excel Regression Output for the Butler Trucking Company with Miles and Gasoline Consumption as Independent Variables

	A	B	C	D	E	F	G	H	I
1	SUMMARY OUTPUT								
2									
3	*Regression Statistics*								
4	Multiple R	0.69406354							
5	R Square	0.481724198							
6	Adjusted R Square	0.478234125							
7	Standard Error	1.398077545							
8	Observations	300							
9									
10	ANOVA								
11		*df*	*SS*	*MS*	*F*	*Significance F*			
12	Regression	2	539.5808158	269.7904079	138.0269794	4.09542E-43			
13	Residual	297	580.5223842	1.954620822					
14	Total	299	1120.1032						
15									
16		*Coefficients*	*Standard Error*	*t Stat*	*P-value*	*Lower 95%*	*Upper 95%*	*Lower 99.0%*	*Upper 99.0%*
17	Intercept	2.493095385	0.33669895	7.404523781	1.36703E-12	1.830477398	3.155713373	1.620208758	3.365982013
18	Miles	0.074701825	0.014274552	5.233216928	3.15444E-07	0.046609743	0.102793908	0.037695279	0.111708371
19	Gasoline Consumption	–0.067506102	0.152707928	–0.442060235	0.658767336	–0.368032789	0.233020584	–0.463398955	0.328386751

FIGURE 7.22   Scatter Chart of Miles and Gasoline Consumed for Butler Trucking Company

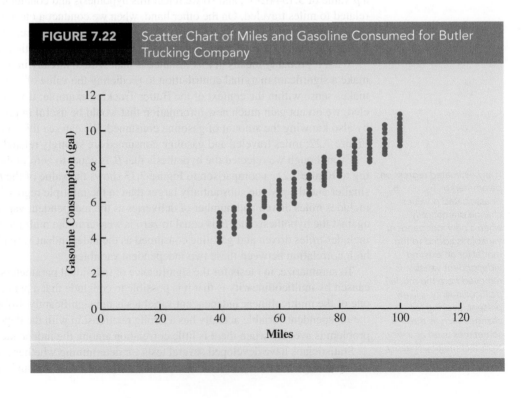

See Chapter 2 for a more in-depth discussion of correlation and how to compute it with Excel.

the relationships between the various pairs of variables that we can gain through scatter charts such as the chart shown in Figure 7.22, correlations between pairs of independent variables can be used to identify potential problems. According to a common rule-of-thumb test, multicollinearity is a potential problem if the absolute value of the sample correlation coefficient exceeds 0.7 for any two of the independent variables. We can use the Excel function

$$=CORREL(B2:B301, C2:C301)$$

to find that the correlation between Miles (in column B) and Gasoline Consumed (in column C) in the file *ButlerWithGasConsumption* is $r_{\text{Miles, Gasoline Consumed}} = 0.9572$, which supports the conclusion that Miles and Gasoline Consumed are multicollinear. Similarly, we can use the Excel function

$$=CORREL(B2:B301, D2:D301)$$

to show that the correlation between Miles (in column B) and Deliveries (in column D) for the sample data is $r_{\text{Miles, Deliveries}} = 0.0258$. This supports the conclusion that Miles and Deliveries are not multicollinear. Other tests for multicollinearity are more advanced and beyond the scope of this text.

The primary consequence of multicollinearity is that it increases the standard deviation of $b_0, b_1, b_2 \ldots, b_q$ and $\hat{y}$, and so inference based on these estimates is less precise than it should be. This means that confidence intervals for $\beta_0, \beta_1, \beta_2, \ldots, \beta_q$ and predicted values of the dependent variable are wider than they should be. Thus, we are less likely to reject the hypothesis that an individual parameter b_j is equal to zero than we otherwise would be, and multicollinearity leads us to conclude that an independent variable x_j is not related to the dependent variable y when they in fact are related. In addition, multicollinearity can result in confusing or misleading regression parameters $b_1, b_2, \ldots, b_q$. Therefore, if a primary objective of the regression analysis is inference, to explain the relationship between a dependent variable y and a set of independent variables $x_1, x_2 \ldots, x_q$, you should, if possible, avoid including independent variables that are highly correlated in the regression model. For example, when a pair of independent variables is highly correlated it is common to simply include only one of these independent variables in the regression model. When decision makers have reason to believe that substantial multicollinearity is present and they choose to retain the highly correlated independent variables in the model, they must realize that separating the relationships between each of the individual independent variables and the dependent variable is difficult (and maybe impossible). On the other hand, multicollinearity does not affect the predictive capability of a regression model, so if the primary objective is prediction or forecasting, then multicollinearity is not a concern.

NOTES + COMMENTS

1. In multiple regression we can test the null hypothesis that the regression parameters $b_1, b_2, \ldots, b_q$ are all equal to zero ($H_0: \beta_1 = \beta_2 = \cdots = \beta_q = 0$, H_a: at least one $b_j \neq 0$ for $j = 1, \ldots, q$) with an F test based on the F probability distribution. The test statistic generated by the sample data for this test is

$$F = \frac{SSR/q}{SSE/(n - q - 1)}$$

where SSR and SSE are as defined by equations (7.5) and (7.7), q is the number of independent variables in the

regression model, and n is the number of observations in the sample. If the p value corresponding to the F statistic is smaller than some predetermined level of significance (usually 0.05 or 0.01), this leads us to reject the hypothesis that the values of $b_1, b_2, \ldots, b_q$ are all zero, and we would conclude that there is an overall regression relationship; otherwise, we conclude that there is no overall regression relationship.

The output of Excel's Regression tool provides the results of the F test; in Figure 7.13, which shows the multiple linear regression results for Butler Trucking with independent variables x_1 (labeled "Miles") and x_2 (labeled "Deliveries"), the value of the F statistic and the corresponding p value are in cells E24 and F24, respectively. From the Excel output in Figure 7.13 we see that the p value for the F test is essentially 0. Thus, the p value is sufficiently small to allow us to reject the hypothesis that no overall regression relationship exists at the 0.01 level of significance.

2. Finding a significant relationship between an independent variable x_j and a dependent variable y in a linear regression does not enable us to conclude that the relationship is linear. We can state only that x_j and y are related and that a linear relationship explains a statistically significant portion of the variability in y over the range of values for x_j observed in the sample.

3. Note that a review of the correlations of pairs of independent variables is not always sufficient to entirely uncover multicollinearity. The problem is that sometimes one independent variable is highly correlated with some combination of several other independent variables. If you suspect that one independent variable is highly correlated with a combination of several other independent variables, you can use multiple regression to assess whether the sample data support your suspicion. Suppose that your original regression model includes the independent variables x_1, $x_2, \ldots, x_q$ and that you suspect that x_1 is highly correlated with a subset of the other independent variables $x_2, \ldots, x_q$. Then construct the multiple linear regression for which x_1 is the dependent variable to be explained by the subset of the independent variables $x_2, \ldots, x_q$ that you suspect

are highly correlated with x_1. The coefficient of determination R^2 for this regression provides an estimate of the strength of the relationship between x_1 and the subset of the other independent variables $x_2, \ldots, x_q$ that you suspect are highly correlated with x_1. As a rule of thumb, if the coefficient of determination R^2 for this regression exceeds 0.50, multicollinearity between x_1 and the subset of the other independent variables $x_2, \ldots, x_q$ is a concern.

4. When working with a small number of observations, assessing the conditions necessary for inference to be valid in regression can be extremely difficult. Similarly, when working with a small number of observations, assessing multicollinearity can also be difficult.

5. In some instances, the values of the independent variables to be used to estimate the value of dependent variable are not known. For example, a company may include its competitor's price as an independent variable in a regression model to be used to estimate demand for one of its products in some future period. It is unlikely that the competitor's price in some future period will be known by this company, and so the company may estimate what the competitor's price will be and substitute this estimated value into the regression equation.

In such instances, estimated values of the independent variables are sometimes substituted into the regression equation to produce an estimated value of the dependent variable. The result can be useful, but one must proceed with caution as an inaccurate estimate of the value of any independent variable can create an inaccurate estimate of the dependent variable.

7.6 Categorical Independent Variables

Thus far, the examples we have considered have involved quantitative independent variables such as the miles traveled and the number of deliveries. In many situations, however, we must work with categorical independent variables such as marital status (married, single) and method of payment (cash, credit card, check). The purpose of this section is to show how categorical variables are handled in regression analysis. To illustrate the use and interpretation of a categorical independent variable, we will again consider the Butler Trucking Company example.

Butler Trucking Company and Rush Hour

Several of Butler Trucking's driving assignments require the driver to travel on a congested segment of a highway during the afternoon rush hour. Management believes that this factor may also contribute substantially to variability in the travel times across driving assignments. How do we incorporate information on which driving assignments include travel on a congested segment of a highway during the afternoon rush hour into a regression model?

Dummy variables are sometimes referred to as indicator variables.

The previous independent variables we have considered (such as the miles traveled and the number of deliveries) have been quantitative, but this new variable is categorical and will require us to define a new type of variable called a **dummy variable**.

To incorporate a variable that indicates whether a driving assignment included travel on this congested segment of a highway during the afternoon rush hour into a model that currently includes the miles traveled (x_1) and the number of deliveries (x_2), we define the following variable:

$$x_3 = \begin{cases} 0 \text{ if an assignment did not include travel on the congested segment of highway} \\ \text{ during afternoon rush hour} \\ 1 \text{ if an assignment included travel on the congested segment of highway} \\ \text{ during afternoon rush hour} \end{cases}$$

See Chapters 2 and 3 for step-by-step descriptions of how to construct charts in Excel.

Will this dummy variable add valuable information to the current Butler Trucking regression model? A review of the residuals produced by the current model may help us make an initial assessment. Using Excel chart tools, we can create a frequency distribution and a histogram of the residuals for driving assignments that included travel on a congested segment of a highway during the afternoon rush hour period. We then create a frequency distribution and a histogram of the residuals for driving assignments that did not include travel on a congested segment of a highway during the afternoon rush hour period. The two histograms are shown in Figure 7.23.

Recall that the residual for the ith observation is $e_i = y_i - \hat{y}_i$, which is the difference between the observed and the predicted values of the dependent variable. The histograms in Figure 7.23 show that driving assignments that included travel on a congested segment of a highway during the afternoon rush hour period tend to have positive residuals, which means we are generally underpredicting the travel times for those driving assignments. Conversely, driving assignments that did not include travel on a congested segment of a highway during the afternoon rush hour period tend to have negative residuals, which means we are generally overpredicting the travel times for those driving assignments. These results suggest that the dummy variable could potentially explain a substantial proportion of the variance in travel time that is unexplained by the current model, and so we proceed by adding the dummy variable x_3 to the current Butler Trucking multiple regression model. Using Excel's Regression tool to develop the estimated regression equation on the data in the file *ButlerHighway*, we obtain the Excel output in Figure 7.24. The estimated regression equation is

DATA*file*

ButlerHighway

$$\hat{y} = -0.3302 + 0.0672x_1 + 0.6735x_2 + 0.9980x_3 \qquad \textbf{(7.15)}$$

FIGURE 7.23 Histograms of the Residuals for Driving Assignments That Included Travel on a Congested Segment of a Highway During the Afternoon Rush Hour and Residuals for Driving Assignments That Did Not

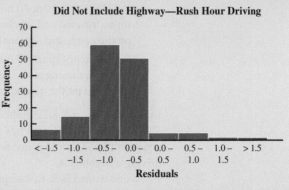

FIGURE 7.24 **FIGURE 7.24** Excel Data and Output for Butler Trucking with Miles Traveled (x_1), Number of Deliveries (x_2), and the Highway Rush Hour Dummy Variable (x_3) as the Independent Variables

	A	B	C	D	E	F	G	H	I
1	SUMMARY OUTPUT								
2									
3	*Regression Statistics*								
4	Multiple R	0.940107228							
5	R Square	0.8838016							
6	Adjusted R Square	0.882623914							
7	Standard Error	0.663106426							
8	Observations	300							
9									
10	ANOVA								
11		*df*	*SS*	*MS*	*F*	*Significance F*			
12	Regression	3	989.9490008	329.9830003	750.455757	5.7766E–138			
13	Residual	296	130.1541992	0.439710132					
14	Total	299	1120.1032						
15									
16		*Coefficients*	*Standard Error*	*t Stat*	*P-value*	*Lower 95%*	*Upper 95%*	*Lower 99.0%*	*Upper 99.0%*
17	Intercept	–0.330229304	0.167677925	–1.969426232	0.04983651	–0.66022126	–0.000237349	–0.764941128	0.104482519
18	Miles	0.067220302	0.00196142	34.27125147	4.7852E-105	0.063360208	0.071080397	0.062135243	0.072305362
19	Deliveries	0.67351584	0.023619993	28.51465081	6.74797E-87	0.627031441	0.720000239	0.612280051	0.734751629
20	Highway	0.9980033	0.076706582	13.0106605	6.49817E-31	0.847043924	1.148962677	0.799138374	1.196868226

Interpreting the Parameters

After checking to make sure this regression satisfies the conditions for inference and the model does not suffer from serious multicollinearity, we can consider inference on our results. The p values for the t tests of miles traveled (p value = 4.7852E-105), number of deliveries (p value = 6.7480E-87), and the rush hour driving dummy variable (p value = 6.4982E-31) are all extremely small, indicating that each of these independent variables has a statistical relationship with travel time. The model estimates that the mean travel time of a driving assignment increases by:

- 0.0672 hour (about 4 minutes) for every increase of 1 mile traveled, holding constant the number of deliveries and whether the driving assignment route requires the driver to travel on the congested segment of a highway during the afternoon rush hour.

- 0.6735 hour (about 40 minutes) for every delivery, holding constant the number of miles traveled and whether the driving assignment route requires the driver to travel on the congested segment of a highway during the afternoon rush hour.

- 0.9980 hour (about 60 minutes) if the driving assignment route requires the driver to travel on the congested segment of a highway during the afternoon rush hour, holding constant the number of miles traveled and the number of deliveries.

In addition, R^2 = 0.8838 indicates that the regression model explains approximately 88.4% of the variability in travel time for the driving assignments in the sample. Thus, equation (7.15) should prove helpful in estimating the travel time necessary for the various driving assignments.

To understand how to interpret the regression when a categorical variable is present, let's compare the regression model for the case when $x_3 = 0$ (the driving assignment does not include travel on congested highways) and when $x_3 = 1$ (the driving assignment does include travel on congested highways). In the case that $x_3 = 0$, we have

$$\hat{y} = -0.3302 + 0.0672x_1 + 0.6735x_2 + 0.9980(0)$$
$$= -0.3302 + 0.0672x_1 + 0.6735x_2 \tag{7.16}$$

In the case that when $x_3 = 1$, we have

$$\hat{y} = -0.3302 + 0.0672x_1 + 0.6735x_2 + 0.9980(1)$$
$$= 0.6678 + 0.0672x_1 + 0.6735x_2 \tag{7.17}$$

Comparing equations (7.16) and (7.17), we see that the mean travel time has the same linear relationship with x_1 and x_2 for both driving assignments that include travel on the congested segment of highway during the afternoon rush hour period and driving assignments that do not. However, the y-intercept is -0.3302 in equation (7.16) and 0.6678 in equation (7.17). That is, 0.9980 is the difference between the mean travel time for driving assignments that include travel on the congested segment of highway during the afternoon rush hour and the mean travel time for driving assignments that do not.

In effect, the use of a dummy variable provides two estimated regression equations that can be used to predict the travel time: One that corresponds to driving assignments that include travel on the congested segment of highway during the afternoon rush hour period, and one that corresponds to driving assignments that do not include such travel.

More Complex Categorical Variables

The categorical variable for the Butler Trucking Company example had two levels: (1) driving assignments that include travel on the congested segment of highway during the afternoon rush hour and (2) driving assignments that do not. As a result, defining a dummy variable with a value of zero indicating a driving assignment that does not include travel on the congested segment of highway during the afternoon rush hour and a value of one indicating a driving assignment that includes such travel was sufficient. However, when a categorical variable has more than two levels, care must be taken in both defining and interpreting the dummy variables. As we will show, if a categorical variable has k levels, $k - 1$ dummy variables are required, with each dummy variable corresponding to one of the levels of the categorical variable and coded as 0 or 1.

For example, suppose a manufacturer of vending machines organized the sales territories for a particular state into three regions: A, B, and C. The managers want to use regression analysis to help predict the number of vending machines sold per week. With the number of units sold as the dependent variable, they are considering several independent variables (the number of sales personnel, advertising expenditures, etc.). Suppose the managers believe that sales region is also an important factor in predicting the number of units sold. Because sales region is a categorical variable with three levels (A, B, and C), we will need $3 - 1 = 2$ dummy variables to represent the sales region. Selecting Region A to be the "reference" region, each dummy variable can be coded 0 or 1 as follows:

$$x_1 = \begin{cases} 1 \text{ if sales Region B} \\ 0 \text{ otherwise} \end{cases} \qquad x_2 = \begin{cases} 1 \text{ if sales Region C} \\ 0 \text{ otherwise} \end{cases}$$

With this definition, we have the following values of x_1 and x_2:

Region	x_1	x_2
A	0	0
B	1	0
C	0	1

The regression equation relating the estimated mean number of units sold to the dummy variables is written as

$$\hat{y} = b_0 + b_1 x_1 + b_2 x_2$$

Observations corresponding to Region A correspond to $x_1 = 0$, $x_2 = 0$, so the estimated mean number of units sold in Region A is

$$\hat{y} = b_0 + b_1(0) + b_2(0) = b_0$$

Observations corresponding to Region B are coded $x_1 = 1$, $x_2 = 0$, so the estimated mean number of units sold in Region B is

$$\hat{y} = b_0 + b_1(1) + b_2(0) = b_0 + b_1$$

Observations corresponding to Region C are coded $x_1 = 0$, $x_2 = 1$, so the estimated mean number of units sold in Region C is

$$\hat{y} = b_0 + b_1(0) + b_2(1) = b_0 + b_2$$

Dummy variables are often used to model seasonal effects in sales data. If the data are collected quarterly and we use winter as the reference season, we may use three dummy variables defined in the following manner:

$$x_1 = \begin{cases} 1 \text{ if spring} \\ 0 \text{ otherwise} \end{cases}$$

$$x_2 = \begin{cases} 1 \text{ if summer} \\ 0 \text{ otherwise} \end{cases}$$

$$x_3 = \begin{cases} 1 \text{ if fall} \\ 0 \text{ otherwise} \end{cases}$$

Thus, b_0 is the estimated mean sales for Region A, b_1 is the estimated difference between the mean number of units sold in Region B and the mean number of units sold in Region A, and b_2 is the estimated difference between the mean number of units sold in Region C and the mean number of units sold in Region A.

Two dummy variables were required because sales region is a categorical variable with three levels. But the assignment of $x_1 = 0$ and $x_2 = 0$ to indicate Region A, $x_1 = 1$ and $x_2 = 0$ to indicate Region B, and $x_1 = 0$ and $x_2 = 1$ to indicate Region C was arbitrary. For example, we could have chosen to let $x_1 = 1$ and $x_2 = 0$ indicate Region A, $x_1 = 0$ and $x_2 = 0$ indicate Region B, and $x_1 = 0$ and $x_2 = 1$ indicate Region C. In this case, b_0 is the mean or expected value of sales for Region B, b_1 is the difference between the mean number of units sold in Region A and the mean number of units sold in Region B, and b_2 is the difference between the mean number of units sold in Region C and the mean number of units sold in Region B.

The important point to remember is that when a categorical variable has k levels, $k - 1$ dummy variables are required in the multiple regression analysis. Thus, if the sales region example had a fourth region, labeled D, three dummy variables would be necessary. For example, these three dummy variables could then be coded as follows:

$$x_1 = \begin{cases} 1 \text{ if sales Region B} \\ 0 \text{ otherwise} \end{cases} \qquad x_2 = \begin{cases} 1 \text{ if sales Region C} \\ 0 \text{ otherwise} \end{cases} \qquad x_3 = \begin{cases} 1 \text{ if sales Region D} \\ 0 \text{ otherwise} \end{cases}$$

NOTES + COMMENTS

Detecting multicollinearity when a categorical variable is involved is difficult. The correlation coefficient that we used in Section 7.5 is appropriate only when assessing the relationship between two quantitative variables. However, recall that if any estimated regression parameters $b_1, b_2, \ldots, b_q$ or associated p values change dramatically when a new independent variable is added to the model (or an existing independent variable is removed from the model), multicollinearity is likely present. We can use our understanding of these ramifications of multicollinearity to assess whether there is multicollinearity that involves a dummy variable. We estimate the regression model twice; once with the dummy variable included as an independent variable and once with the dummy variable omitted from the regression model. If we see relatively little change in the estimated regression parameters $b_1, b_2, \ldots, b_q$ or associated p values for the independent variables that have been included in both regression models, we can be confident that there is not strong multicollinearity involving the dummy variable.

7.7 Modeling Nonlinear Relationships

Reynolds

Regression may be used to model more complex types of relationships. To illustrate, let us consider the problem facing Reynolds, Inc., a manufacturer of industrial scales and laboratory equipment. Managers at Reynolds want to investigate the relationship between length of employment of their salespeople and the number of electronic laboratory scales sold. The file *Reynolds* gives the number of scales sold by 15 randomly selected salespeople for the most recent sales period and the number of months each salesperson has been employed by the firm. Figure 7.25, the scatter chart for these data, indicates a possible curvilinear relationship between the length of time employed and the number of units sold.

Before considering how to develop a curvilinear relationship for Reynolds, let us consider the Excel output in Figure 7.26 for a simple linear regression; the estimated regression is

$$\text{Sales} = 113.7453 + 2.3675 \text{ Months Employed}$$

The scatter chart of residuals against the independent variable Months Employed would also suggest that a curvilinear relationship may provide a better fit to the data.

The computer output shows that the relationship is significant (p value $= 9.3954\text{E-}06$ in cell E18 of Figure 7.26 for the t test that $\beta_1 = 0$) and that a linear relationship explains a high percentage of the variability in sales ($r^2 = 0.7901$ in cell B5). However, Figure 7.27 reveals a pattern in the scatter chart of residuals against the predicted values of the dependent variable that suggests that a curvilinear relationship may provide a better fit to the data.

If we have a practical reason to suspect a curvilinear relationship between number of electronic laboratory scales sold by a salesperson and the number of months the salesperson has been employed, we may wish to consider an alternative to simple linear regression. For example, we may believe that a recently hired salesperson faces a learning curve but becomes increasingly more effective over time and that a salesperson who has been in a sales position with Reynolds for a long time eventually becomes burned out and becomes increasingly less effective. If our regression model supports this theory, Reynolds management can use the model to identify the approximate point in employment when its salespeople begin to lose their effectiveness, and management can plan strategies to counteract salesperson burnout.

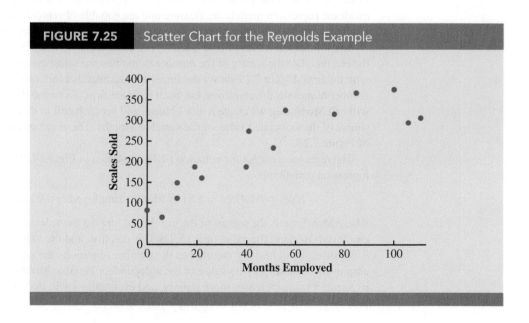

FIGURE 7.25 Scatter Chart for the Reynolds Example

FIGURE 7.26 Excel Regression Output for the Reynolds Example

	A	B	C	D	E	F	G	H	I
1	SUMMARY OUTPUT								
2									
3	*Regression Statistics*								
4	Multiple R	0.888897515							
5	R Square	0.790138792							
6	Adjusted R Square	0.773995622							
7	Standard Error	48.49087146							
8	Observations	15							
9									
10	ANOVA								
11		*df*	*SS*	*MS*	*F*	*Significance F*			
12	Regression	1	115089.1933	115089.1933	48.94570268	9.39543E–06			
13	Residual	13	30567.74	2351.364615					
14	Total	14	145656.9333						
15									
16		*Coefficients*	*Standard Error*	*t Stat*	*P-value*	*Lower 95%*	*Upper 95%*	*Lower 95.0%*	*Upper 95.0%*
17	Intercept	113.7452874	20.81345608	5.464987985	0.000108415	68.78054927	158.7100256	68.78054927	158.7100256
18	Months Employed	2.367463621	0.338396631	6.996120545	9.39543E-06	1.636402146	3.098525095	1.636402146	3.098525095

Quadratic Regression Models

To account for the curvilinear relationship between months employed and scales sold that is suggested by the scatter chart of residuals against the predicted values of the dependent variable, we could include the square of the number of months the salesperson has been employed as a second independent variable in the estimated regression equation:

$$\hat{y} = b_0 + b_1 x_1 + b_2 x_1^2 \tag{7.18}$$

Equation (7.18) corresponds to a **quadratic regression model**. As Figure 7.28 illustrates, quadratic regression models are flexible and are capable of representing a wide variety of nonlinear relationships between an independent variable and the dependent variable.

To estimate the values of b_0, b_1, and b_2 in equation (7.18) with Excel, we need to add to the original data the square of the number of months the salesperson has been employed with the firm. Figure 7.29 shows the Excel spreadsheet that includes the square of the number of months the employee has been with the firm. To create the variable, which we will call MonthsSq, we create a new column and set each cell in that column equal to the square of the associated value of the variable Months. These values are shown in Column B of Figure 7.29.

The regression output for equation (7.18) is shown in Figure 7.30. The estimated regression equation is

$$\text{Sales} = 61.4299 + 5.8198 \text{ Months Employed} - 0.0310 \text{ MonthsSq}$$

where MonthsSq is the square of the number of months the salesperson has been employed. Because the value of b_1 (5.8198) is positive, and the value of b_2 (-0.0310) is negative, $\hat{y}$ will initially increase as the number of months the salesperson has been employed increases. As the value of the independent variable Months Employed increases, its squared value increases more rapidly, and eventually $\hat{y}$ will decrease as the number of months the salesperson has been employed increases.

FIGURE 7.27 Scatter Chart of the Residuals and Predicted Values of the Dependent Variable for the Reynolds Simple Linear Regression

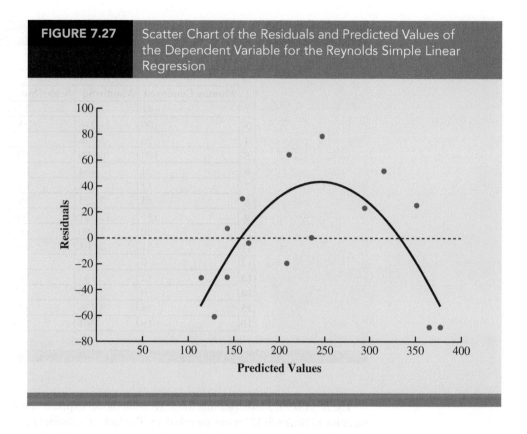

FIGURE 7.28 Relationships That Can Be Fit with a Quadratic Regression Model

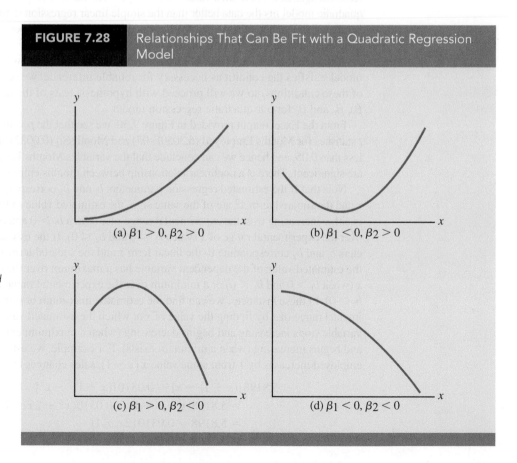

If $\beta_2 > 0$, the function is convex (bowl-shaped relative to the x-axis); if $\beta_2 < 0$, the function is concave (mound-shaped relative to the x-axis).

| FIGURE 7.29 | Excel Data for the Reynolds Quadratic Regression Model |

	A	B	C
1	**Months Employed**	**MonthsSq**	**Scales Sold**
2	41	1,681	275
3	106	11,236	296
4	76	5,776	317
5	100	10,000	376
6	22	484	162
7	12	144	150
8	85	7,225	367
9	111	12,321	308
10	40	1,600	189
11	51	2,601	235
12	0	0	83
13	12	144	112
14	6	36	67
15	56	3,136	325
16	19	361	189

The R^2 of 0.9013 indicates that this regression model explains approximately 90.1% of the variation in Scales Sold for our sample data. The lack of a distinct pattern in the scatter chart of residuals against the predicted values of the dependent variable (Figure 7.31) suggests that the quadratic model fits the data better than the simple linear regression in the Reynolds example. While not shown here, the scatter chart of residuals against the independent variable Months Employed also lack any distinct pattern.

Although it is difficult to assess from a sample as small as this whether the regression model satisfies the conditions necessary for reliable inference, we see no marked violations of these conditions, so we will proceed with hypothesis tests of the regression parameters β_0, β_1, and β_2 for our quadratic regression model.

From the Excel output provided in Figure 7.30, we see that the p values corresponding to the t statistics for Months Employed (6.2050E-05) and MonthsSq (0.0032) are both substantially less than 0.05, and hence we can conclude that the variables Months Employed and MonthsSq are significant. There is a nonlinear relationship between months employed and sales.

Note that if the estimated regression parameters b_1 and b_2 corresponding to the linear term x and the squared term x^2 are of the same sign, the estimated value of the dependent variable is either increasing over the experimental range of x (when $b_1 > 0$ and $b_2 > 0$) or decreasing over the experimental range of x (when $b_1 < 0$ and $b_2 < 0$). If the estimated regression parameters b_1 and b_2 corresponding to the linear term x and the squared term x^2 have different signs, the estimated value of the dependent variable has a maximum over the experimental range of x (when $b_1 > 0$ and $b_2 < 0$) or a minimum over the experimental range of x (when $b_1 < 0$ and $b_2 > 0$). In these instances, we can find the estimated maximum or minimum over the experimental range of x by finding the value of x at which the estimated value of the dependent variable stops increasing and begins decreasing (when a maximum exists) or stops decreasing and begins increasing (when a minimum exists). For example, we estimate that when months employed increases by 1 from some value x ($x + 1$), sales changes by

$$5.8198\,[(x + 1) - x] - 0.0310\,[(x + 1)^2 - x^2]$$
$$= 5.8198(x - x + 1) - 0.0310(x^2 + 2x + 1 - x^2)$$
$$= 5.8198 - 0.0310\,(2x + 1)$$
$$= 5.7888 - 0.0620x$$

FIGURE 7.30	Excel Output for the Reynolds Quadratic Regression Model

	A	B	C	D	E	F	G	H	I
1	SUMMARY OUTPUT								
2									
3	*Regression Statistics*								
4	Multiple R	0.949361402							
5	R Square	0.901287072							
6	Adjusted R Square	0.884834917							
7	Standard Error	34.61481184							
8	Observations	15							
9									
10	ANOVA								
11		*df*	*SS*	*MS*	*F*	*Significance F*			
12	Regression	2	131278.711	65639.35548	54.78231208	9.25218E-07			
13	Residual	12	14378.22238	1198.185199					
14	Total	14	145656.9333						
15									
16		*Coefficients*	*Standard Error*	*t Stat*	*P-value*	*Lower 95%*	*Upper 95%*	*Lower 99.0%*	*Upper 99.0%*
17	Intercept	61.42993467	20.57433536	2.985755485	0.011363561	16.60230882	106.2575605	−1.415187222	124.2750566
18	Months Employed	5.819796648	0.969766536	6.001234761	6.20497E-05	3.706856877	7.93273642	2.857606371	8.781986926
19	MonthsSq	−0.031009589	0.008436087	−3.675826286	0.003172962	−0.049390243	−0.012628935	−0.05677795	−0.005241228

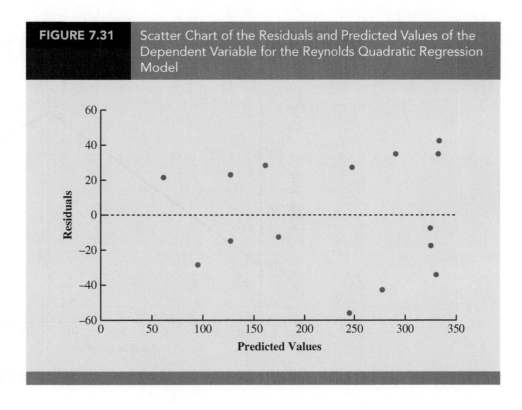

FIGURE 7.31	Scatter Chart of the Residuals and Predicted Values of the Dependent Variable for the Reynolds Quadratic Regression Model

That is, estimated Sales initially increases as Months Employed increases and then eventually decreases as Months Employed increases. Solving this result for x:

$$5.7888 - 0.0620x = 0$$
$$-0.0620x = -5.7888$$
$$x = \frac{-5.7888}{-0.0620} = 93.3387$$

tells us that estimated maximum sales occurs at approximately 93 months (in about seven years and nine months). We can then find the estimated maximum value of the dependent variable Sales by substituting this value of x into the estimated regression equation:

$$\text{Sales} = 61.58198 + 5.8198(93.3387) - 0.0310(93.3387^2) = 334.4909$$

At approximately 93 months, the maximum estimated sales of approximately 334 scales occurs.

In business analytics applications, polynomial regression models of higher than second or third order are rarely used.

Piecewise Linear Regression Models

As an alternative to a quadratic regression model, we can recognize that below some value of Months Employed, the relationship between Months Employed and Sales appears to be positive and linear, whereas the relationship between Months Employed and Sales appears to be negative and linear for the remaining observations. A **piecewise linear regression model** will allow us to fit these relationships as two linear regressions that are joined at the value of Months at which the relationship between Months Employed and Sales changes.

A piecewise linear regression model is sometimes referred to as a segment regression or a spline model.

Our first step in fitting a piecewise linear regression model is to identify the value of the independent variable Months Employed at which the relationship between Months Employed and Sales changes; this point is called the **knot**, or *breakpoint*. Although theory should determine this value, analysts often use the sample data to aid in the identification of this point. Figure 7.32 provides the scatter chart for the Reynolds data with an indication

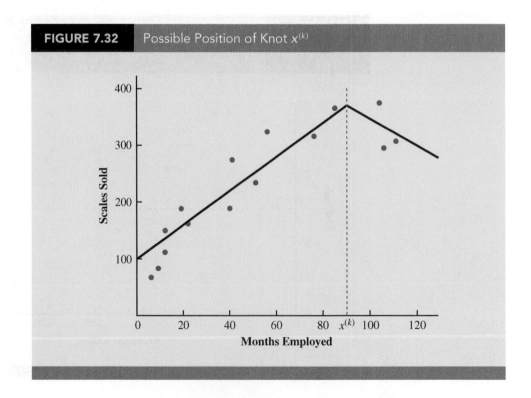

FIGURE 7.32   Possible Position of Knot $x^{(k)}$

of the possible location of the knot, which we have denoted $x^{(k)}$. From this scatter chart, it appears that the knot is at approximately 90 months.

Once we have decided on the location of the knot, we define a dummy variable that is equal to zero for any observation for which the value of Months Employed is less than or equal to the value of the knot, and equal to one for any observation for which the value of Months Employed is greater than the value of the knot:

$$x_k = \begin{cases} 0 \text{ if } x_1 \leq x^{(k)} \\ 1 \text{ if } x_1 > x^{(k)} \end{cases} \tag{7.19}$$

where

$$x_1 = \text{Months}$$
$$x^{(k)} = \text{the value of the knot (90 months for the Reynolds example)}$$
$$x_k = \text{the knot dummy variable}$$

We then fit the following estimated regression equation:

$$\hat{y} = b_0 + b_1 x_1 + b_2 (x_1 - x^{(k)}) x_k \tag{7.20}$$

The data and Excel output for the Reynolds piecewise linear regression model are provided in Figure 7.33. Because we placed the knot at $x^{(k)} = 90$, the estimated regression equation is

$$\hat{y} = 87.2172 + 3.4094 x_1 - 7.8726 (x_1 - 90) x_k$$

The output shows that the p value corresponding to the t statistic for the knot term ($p = 0.0014$) is less than 0.05, and hence we can conclude that adding the knot to the model with Months Employed as the independent variable is significant.

But what does this model mean? For any value of Months less than or equal to 90, the knot term $7.8726(x_1 - 90)x_k$ is zero because the knot dummy variable $x_k = 0$, so the regression equation is

$$\hat{y} = 87.2172 + 3.4094 x_1$$

For any value of Months Employed greater than 90, the knot term is $-7.87(x_1 - 90)$ because the knot dummy variable $x_k = 1$, so the regression equation is

$$\hat{y} = 87.2172 + 3.4094 x_1 - 7.8726(x_1 - 90)$$
$$= 87.2172 - 7.8726(-90) + (3.4094 - 7.8726)x_1 = 795.7512 - 4.4632 x_1$$

Note that if Months Employed is equal to 90, both regressions yield the same value of $\hat{y}$:

$$\hat{y} = 87.2172 + 3.4094(90) = 795.7512 - 4.4632(90) = 394.06$$

So the two regression segments are joined at the knot.

Multiple knots can be used to fit complex piecewise linear regressions.

The interpretation of this model is similar to the interpretation of the quadratic regression model. A salesperson's sales are expected to increase by 3.4094 electronic laboratory scales for each month of employment until the salesperson has been employed for 90 months. At that point the salesperson's sales are expected to decrease by 4.4632 electronic laboratory scales for each additional month of employment.

Should we use the quadratic regression model or the piecewise linear regression model? These models fit the data equally well, and both have reasonable interpretations, so we cannot differentiate between the models on either of these criteria. Thus, we must consider whether the abrupt change in the relationship between Sales and Months Employed that is suggested by the piecewise linear regression model captures the real relationship between Sales and Months Employed better than the smooth change in the relationship between Sales and Months Employed suggested by the quadratic model.

FIGURE 7.33	Data and Excel Output for the Reynolds Piecewise Linear Regression Model

	A	B	C	D	E	F	G	H	I
1	**Knot Dummy**	**Months Employed**	**Knot Dummy* Months**	**Scales Sold**					
2	0	41	0	275					
3	1	106	16	296					
4	0	76	0	317					
5	1	100	10	376					
6	0	22	0	162					
7	0	12	0	150					
8	0	85	0	367					
9	1	111	21	308					
10	0	40	0	189					
11	0	51	0	235					
12	0	0	0	83					
13	0	12	0	112					
14	0	6	0	67					
15	0	56	0	325					
16	0	19	0	189					
17									
18									
19	SUMMARY OUTPUT								
20									
21	*Regression Statistics*								
22	Multiple R	0.955796127							
23	R Square	0.913546237							
24	Adjusted R Square	0.899137276							
25	Standard Error	32.3941739							
26	Observations	15							
27									
28	ANOVA								
29		*df*	*SS*	*MS*	*F*	*Significance F*			
30	Regression	2	133064.3433	66532.17165	63.4012588	4.17545E-07			
31	Residual	12	12592.59003	1049.382502					
32	Total	14	145656.9333						
33									
34		*Coefficients*	*Standard Error*	*t Stat*	*P-value*	*Lower 95%*	*Upper 95%*	*Lower 99.0%*	*Upper 99.0%*
35	Intercept	87.21724231	15.31062519	5.696517369	9.9677E-05	53.85825572	120.5762289	40.45033153	133.9841531
36	Months Employed	3.409431979	0.338360666	10.07632484	3.2987E-07	2.67220742	4.146656538	2.375895931	4.442968028
37	Knot Dummy* Months	–7.872553259	1.902156543	–4.138751508	0.00137388	–12.01699634	–3.728110179	–13.68276572	–2.062340794

The variable Knot Dummy*Months is the product of the corresponding values of Knot Dummy and the difference between Months Employed and the knot value, that is, C2 = A2*(B2 − 90) in the Figure 7.33 spreadsheet.

Interaction Between Independent Variables

Often the relationship between the dependent variable and one independent variable is different at various values of a second independent variable. When this occurs, it is called an **interaction**. If the original data set consists of observations for y and two independent variables x_1 and x_2, we can incorporate an $x_1 x_2$ interaction into the estimated multiple linear regression equation in the following manner:

$$\hat{y} = b_0 + b_1 x_1 + b_2 x_2 + b_3 x_1 x_2 \tag{7.21}$$

To provide an illustration of an interaction and what it means, let us consider the regression study conducted by Tyler Personal Care for one of its new shampoo products. The two factors believed to have the most influence on sales are unit selling price and advertising expenditure. To investigate the effects of these two variables on sales, prices of $2.00, $2.50, and $3.00 were paired with advertising expenditures of $50,000 and $100,000 in 24 test markets.

Tyler

The data collected by Tyler are provided in the file *Tyler*. Figure 7.34 shows the sample mean sales for the six price and advertising expenditure combinations. Note that the sample mean sales corresponding to a price of $2.00 and an advertising expenditure of $50,000 is 461,000 units and that the sample mean sales corresponding to a price of $2.00 and an advertising expenditure of $100,000 is 808,000 units. Hence, with price held constant at $2.00, the difference in mean sales between advertising expenditures of $50,000 and $100,000 is $808,000 - 461,000 = 347,000$ units. When the price of the product is $2.50, the difference in mean sales between advertising expenditures of $50,000 and $100,000 is $646,000 - 364,000 = 282,000$ units. Finally, when the price is $3.00, the difference in mean sales

FIGURE 7.34	Mean Unit Sales (1,000s) as a Function of Selling Price and Advertising Expenditures

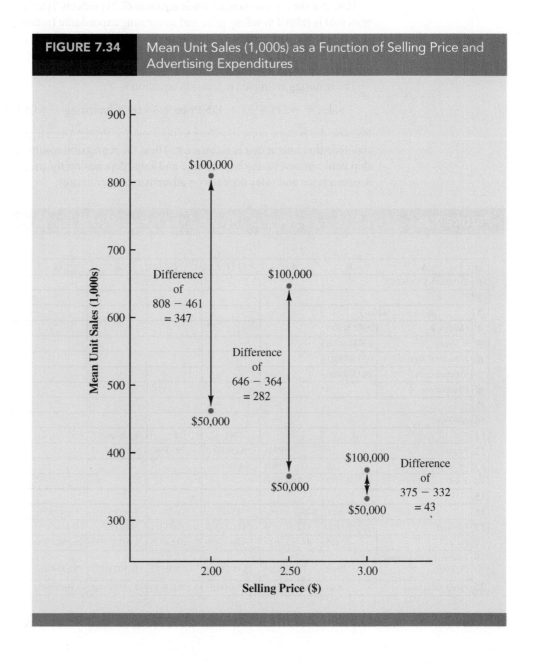

In the file Tyler, the data for the independent variable Price is in column A, the independent variable Advertising Expenditures is in column B, and the dependent variable Sales is in column D. We created the interaction variable Price*Advertising in column C by entering the function =A2*B2 in cell C2, and then copying cell C2 into cells C3 through C25.

between advertising expenditures of $50,000 and $100,000 is $375,000 - 332,000 = 43,000$ units. Clearly, the difference between mean sales for advertising expenditures of $50,000 and mean sales for advertising expenditures of $100,000 depends on the price of the product. In other words, at higher selling prices, the effect of increased advertising expenditure diminishes. These observations provide evidence of interaction between the price and advertising expenditure variables.

When interaction between two variables is present, we cannot study the relationship between one independent variable and the dependent variable y independently of the other variable. In other words, meaningful conclusions can be developed only if we consider the joint relationship that both independent variables have with the dependent variable. To account for the interaction, we use the regression equation in equation (7.21), where

$$y = \text{Unit Sales (1000s)}$$
$$x_1 = \text{Price (\$)}$$
$$x_2 = \text{Adverstising Expenditure (\$1000s)}$$

Note that the regression equation in equation (7.21) reflects Tyler's belief that the number of units sold is related to selling price and advertising expenditure (accounted for by the $\beta_1 x_1$ and $\beta_2 x_2$ terms) and an interaction between the two variables (accounted for by the $\beta_3 x_1 x_2$ term).

The Excel output corresponding to the interaction model for the Tyler Personal Care example is provided in Figure 7.35.

The resulting estimated regression equation is

$$\text{Sales} = -275.8333 + 175\,\text{Price} + 19.68\,\text{Advertising} - 6.08\,\text{Price*Advertising}$$

Because the p value corresponding to the t test for Price*Advertising is 8.6772E-10, we conclude that interaction is significant. Thus, the regression results show that the relationship between advertising expenditure and sales depends on the price (and the relationship between price and sales depends on advertising expenditure).

FIGURE 7.35 Excel Output for the Tyler Personal Care Linear Regression Model with Interaction

	A	B	C	D	E	F	G	H	I
1	SUMMARY OUTPUT								
2									
3	*Regression Statistics*								
4	Multiple R	0.988993815							
5	R Square	0.978108766							
6	Adjusted R Square	0.974825081							
7	Standard Error	28.17386496							
8	Observations	24							
9									
10	ANOVA								
11		*df*	*SS*	*MS*	*F*	*Significance F*			
12	Regression	3	709316	236438.6667	297.8692	9.25881E-17			
13	Residual	20	15875	793.7666667					
14	Total	23	5191.3333						
15									
16		*Coefficients*	*Standard Error*	*t Stat*	*P-value*	*Lower 95%*	*Upper 95%*	*Lower 99.0%*	*Upper 99.0%*
17	Intercept	−275.8333333	112.8421033	−2.444418575	0.023898351	−511.2178361	−40.44883053	−596.9074508	45.24078413
18	Price	175	44.54679188	3.928453489	0.0008316	82.07702045	267.9229796	48.24924412	301.7507559
19	Advertising Expenditure ($1,000s)	19.68	1.42735225	13.78776683	1.1263E-11	16.70259538	22.65740462	15.61869796	23.74130204
20	Price*Advertising	−6.08	0.563477299	−10.79014187	8.67721E-10	−7.255393049	−4.904606951	−7.683284335	−4.476715665

Our initial review of these results may alarm us: How can price have a positive estimated regression coefficient? With the exception of luxury goods, we expect sales to decrease as price increases. Although this result appears counterintuitive, we can make sense of this model if we work through the interpretation of the interaction. In other words, the relationship between the independent variable Price and the dependent variable Sales is different at various values of Advertising (and the relationship between the independent variable Advertising and the dependent variable Sales is different at various values of Price).

It becomes easier to see how the predicted value of Sales depends on Price by using the estimated regression equation to consider the effect when Price increases by $1:

$$\text{Sales After \$1 Price Increase} = -275.8333 + 175\,(\text{Price} + 1)$$
$$+ 19.68\,\text{Advertising} - 6.08\,(\text{Price} + 1) * \text{Advertising}$$

Thus,

$$\text{Sales After \$1 Price Increase} - \text{Sales Before \$1 Price Increase} = 175 - 6.08 * \text{Advertising}$$
$$\text{Expenditure}$$

So the change in the predicted value of sales when the independent variable Price increases by $1 depends on how much was spent on advertising.

Consider a concrete example. If Advertising Expenditures is $50,000 when price is $2.00, we estimate sales to be

$$\text{Sales} = -275.8333 + 175(2) + 19.68(50) - 6.08(2)(50) = 450.1667, \text{or } 450,167 \text{ units}$$

At the same level of Advertising Expenditures ($50,000) when price is $3.00, we estimate sales to be

$$\text{Sales} = -275.8333 + 175(3) + 19.68(50) - 6.08(3)(50) = 321.1667, \text{or } 321,167 \text{ units}$$

So when Advertising Expenditures is $50,000, a change in price from $2.00 to $3.00 results in a $450,167 - 321,167 = 129,000$ unit decrease in estimated sales. However, if Advertising Expenditures is $100,000 when price is $2.00, we estimate sales to be

$$\text{Sales} = -275.8333 + 175(2) + 19.68(100) - 6.08(2)(100) = 826.1667, \text{or } 826,167 \text{ units}$$

At the same level of Advertising Expenditures ($100,000) when price is $3.00, we estimate sales to be

$$\text{Sales} = -275.8333 + 175(3) + 19.68(100) - 6.08(3)(100) = 393.1667, \text{or } 393,167 \text{ units}$$

So when Advertising Expenditures is $100,000, a change in price from $2.00 to $3.00 results in a $826,167 - 393,167 = 433,000$ unit decrease in estimated sales. When Tyler spends more on advertising, its sales are more sensitive to changes in price. Perhaps at larger Advertising Expenditures, Tyler attracts new customers who have been buying the product from another company and so are more aware of the prices charged for the product by Tyler's competitors.

There is a second and equally valid interpretation of the interaction; it tells us that the relationship between the independent variable Advertising Expenditure and the dependent variable Sales is different at various values of Price. Using the estimated regression equation to consider the effect when Advertising Expenditure increases by $1,000:

$$\text{Sales After \$1K Advertising Increase} = -275.8333 + 175\,\text{Price} + 19.68\,(\text{Advertising} + 1)$$
$$-6.08\,\text{Price} * (\text{Advertising} + 1)$$

Thus,

$$\text{Sales After \$1K Advertising Increase} - \text{Sales Before \$1K Advertising Increase} = 19.68$$
$$- 6.08\,\text{Price}$$

So the change in the predicted value of the dependent variable that occurs when the independent variable Advertising Expenditure increases by $1,000 depends on the price.

Thus, if Price is $2.00 when Advertising Expenditures is $50,000, we estimate sales to be

$$\text{Sales} = -275.8333 + 175(2) + 19.68(50) - 6.08(2)(50) = 450.1667, \text{or } 450{,}167 \text{ units}$$

At the same level of Price ($2.00) when Advertising Expenditures is $100,000, we estimate sales to be

$$\text{Sales} = -275.8333 + 175(2) + 19.68(100) - 6.08(2)(100) = 826.1667, \text{or } 826{,}167 \text{ units}$$

So when Price is $2.00, a change in Advertising Expenditures from $50,000 to $100,000 results in a $826{,}167 - 450{,}167 = 376{,}000$ unit increase in estimated sales. However, if Price is $3.00 when Advertising Expenditures is $50,000, we estimate sales to be

$$\text{Sales} = -275.8333 + 175(3) + 19.68(50) - 6.08(3)(50) = 321.1667, \text{or } 321{,}167 \text{ units}$$

At the same level of Price ($3.00) when Advertising Expenditures is $100,000, we estimate sales to be

$$\text{Sales} = -275.8333 + 175(3) + 19.68(100) - 6.08(3)(100) = 393.1667, \text{or } 393{,}167 \text{ units}$$

So when Price is $3.00, a change in Advertising Expenditure from $50,000 to $100,000 results in a $393.167 - 321{,}167 = 72{,}000$ unit increase in estimated sales. When the price of Tyler's product is high, its sales are less sensitive to changes in advertising expenditure. Perhaps as Tyler increases its price, it must advertise more to convince potential customers that its product is a good value.

NOTES + COMMENTS

1. Just as a dummy variable can be used to allow for different y-intercepts for the two groups represented by the dummy, we can use an interaction between a dummy variable and a quantitative independent variable to allow for different relationships between independent and dependent variables for the two groups represented by the dummy. Consider the Butler Trucking example: Travel time is the dependent variable y, miles traveled and number of deliveries are the quantitative independent variables x_1 and x_2, and the dummy variable x_3 differentiates between driving assignments that included travel on a congested segment of a highway and driving assignments that did not. If we believe that the relationship between miles traveled and travel time differs for driving assignments that included travel on a congested segment of a highway and those that did not, we could create a new variable that is the interaction between miles traveled and the dummy variable $(x_4 = x_1{}^*x_3)$ and estimate the following model:

$$\hat{y} = b_0 + b_1 x_1 + b_2 x_2 + b_3 x_4$$

If a driving assignment does not include travel on a congested segment of a highway, $x_4 = x_1 {}^* x_3 = x_1 {}^* 0 = 0$ and the regression model is

$$\hat{y} = b_0 + b_1 x_1 + b_2 x_2$$

If a driving assignment does include travel on a congested segment of a highway, $x_4 = x_1 {}^* x_3 = x_1 {}^* 1 = x_1$ and the regression model is

$$\hat{y} = b_0 + b_1 x_1 + b_2 x_2 + b_3 x_1 (1)$$
$$= b_0 + (b_1 + b_3) x_1 + b_2 x_2$$

So in this regression model b_1 is the estimate of the relationship between miles traveled and travel time for driving assignments that do not include travel on a congested segment of a highway, and $b_1 + b_3$ is the estimate of the relationship between miles traveled and travel time for driving assignments that do include travel on a congested segment of a highway.

2. Multicollinearity can be divided into two types. *Data-based multicollinearity* occurs when separate independent variables that are related are included in the model, whereas *structural multicollinearity* occurs when a new independent variable is created by taking a function of one or more existing independent variables. If we use ratings that consumers give on bread's aroma and taste as independent variables in a model for which the dependent variable is the overall rating of the bread, the multicollinearity that would exist between the aroma and taste ratings is an

example of data-based multicollinearity. If we build a quadratic model for which the independent variables are ratings that consumers give on bread's aroma and the square of the ratings that consumers give on bread's aroma, the multicollinearity that would exist is an example of structural multicollinearity.

3. Structural multicollinearity occurs naturally in polynomial regression models and regression models with interactions. You can greatly reduce the structural multicollinearity in a polynomial regression by centering the independent variable x (using $x - \bar{x}$ in place of x). In a regression model with interaction, you can greatly reduce the structural multicollinearity by centering both independent variables that interact. However, quadratic regression models and regression models with interactions are frequently used only for prediction; in these instances centering independent variables is not necessary because we are not concerned with inference.

4. Note that we can combine a quadratic effect with interaction to produce a second-order polynomial model with interaction between the two independent variables. The resulting estimated regression equation is

$$y = b_0 + b_1 x_1 + b_2 x_2 + b_3 x_1^2 + b_4 x_2^2 + b_5 x_1 x_2$$

This model provides a great deal of flexibility in capturing nonlinear effects.

7.8 Model Fitting

Finding an effective regression model can be challenging. Although we rely on theory to guide us, often we are faced with a large number of potential independent variables from which to choose. In this section, we discuss common methods for building a regression model and the potential hazards of these approaches.

Variable Selection Procedures

When there are many independent variables to consider, special procedures are sometimes employed to select the independent variables to include in the regression model. These variable selection procedures include **backward elimination**, **forward selection**, **stepwise selection**, and the **best subsets** procedure. Given a data set with several possible independent variables, we can use these procedures to identify which independent variables provide a model that best satisfies some criterion. The first three procedures are iterative; at each step of the procedure a single independent variable is added or removed and the new model is evaluated. The process continues until a stopping criterion indicates that the procedure cannot find a superior model. The best subsets procedure is not a one-variable-at-a-time procedure; it evaluates regression models involving different subsets of the independent variables.

The backward elimination procedure begins with the regression model that includes all of the independent variables under consideration. At each step of the procedure, backward elimination considers the removal of an independent variable according to some criterion. One such criterion is to check if any independent variables currently in the model are not significant at a specified level of significance, and if so, then remove the least significant of these independent variables from the model. The regression model is then refit with the remaining independent variables and statistical significance is reexamined. The backward elimination procedure stops when all independent variables in the model are significant at a specified level of significance.

The forward selection procedure begins with none of the independent variables under consideration included in the regression model. At each step of the procedure, forward selection considers the addition of an independent variable according to some criterion. One such criterion is to check if any independent variables currently not in the model would be significant at a specified level of significance if included, and if so, then add the most significant of these independent variables to the model. The regression model is then refit with the additional independent variable and statistical significance is reexamined. The forward selection procedure stops when all of the independent variables not in the model would not be significant at a specified level of significance if included in the model.

The stepwise procedure requires that the criterion for an independent variable to enter the regression model is more difficult to satisfy than the criterion for an independent variable to be removed from the regression model. This requirement prevents the same independent variable from exiting and then reentering the regression model in the same step.

Similar to the forward selection procedure, the stepwise procedure begins with none of the independent variables under consideration included in the regression model. The analyst establishes both a criterion for allowing independent variables to enter the model and a criterion for allowing independent variables to remain in the model. One such criterion adds the most significant variable and removes the least significant variable at each iteration. To initiate the procedure, the most significant independent variable is added to the empty model if its level of significance satisfies the entering threshold. Each subsequent step involves two intermediate steps. First, the remaining independent variables not in the current model are evaluated, and the most significant one is added to the model if its significance satisfies the threshold to remain in the model. Then the independent variables in the resulting model are evaluated, and the least significant variable is removed if its level of significance fails to satisfy the threshold to remain in the model. The procedure stops when no independent variable not currently in the model has a level of significance that satisfies the entering threshold, and no independent variable currently in the model has a level of significance that fails to satisfy the threshold to remain in the model.

In the best subsets procedure, simple linear regressions for each of the independent variables under consideration are generated, and then the multiple regressions with all combinations of two independent variables under consideration are generated, and so on. Once a regression model has been generated for every possible subset of the independent variables under consideration, the entire collection of regression models can be compared and evaluated by the analyst.

Although these algorithms are potentially useful when dealing with a large number of potential independent variables, they do not necessarily provide useful models. Once the procedure terminates, you should deliberate whether the combination of independent variables included in the final regression model makes sense from a practical standpoint and consider whether you can create a more useful regression model with more meaningful interpretation through the addition or removal of independent variables. Use your own judgment and intuition about your data to refine the results of these algorithms.

Overfitting

The objective in building a regression model (or any other type of mathematical model) is to provide the simplest accurate representation of the population. A model that is relatively simple will be easy to understand, interpret, and use, and a model that accurately represents the population will yield meaningful results.

When we base a model on sample data, we must be wary. Sample data generally do not perfectly represent the population from which they are drawn; if we attempt to fit a model too closely to the sample data, we risk capturing behavior that is idiosyncratic to the sample data rather than representative of the population. When the model is too closely fit to sample data and as a result does not accurately reflect the population, the model is said to have been overfit.

The principle of using the simplest meaningful model possible without sacrificing accuracy is referred to as Ockham's razor, the law of parsimony, or the law of economy.

Overfitting generally results from creating an overly complex model to explain idiosyncrasies in the sample data. In regression analysis, this often results from the use of complex functional forms or independent variables that do not have meaningful relationships with the dependent variable. If a model is overfit to the sample data, it will perform better on the sample data used to fit the model than it will on other data from the population. Thus, an overfit model can be misleading with regard to its predictive capability and its interpretation.

Overfitting is a difficult problem to detect and avoid, but there are strategies that can help mitigate this problem. Use only independent variables that you expect to have real and meaningful relationships with the dependent variable. Use complex models, such as quadratic models and piecewise linear regression models, only when you have a reasonable expectation that such complexity provides a more accurate depiction of what you are modeling. Do not let software dictate your model. Use iterative modeling procedures, such as the stepwise and best-subsets procedures, only for guidance and not to generate your final model. Use your own judgment and intuition about your data and what you are modeling to refine your model. If you have access to a sufficient quantity of data, assess your model on data other than the sample data that were used to generate the model (this is referred to as **cross-validation**).

One simple cross-validation approach is the **holdout method**. In the holdout method, the sample data are randomly divided into mutually exclusive and collectively exhaustive training and validation sets. The **training set** is the data set used to build the candidate models that appear to make practical sense. The **validation set** is the set of data used to compare model performances and ultimately select a model for predicting values of the dependent variable. For example, we might randomly select half of the data for use in developing regression models. We could use these data as our training set to estimate a model or a collection of models that appear to perform well. Then we use the remaining half of the data as a validation set to assess and compare the models' performances and ultimately select the model that minimizes some measure of overall error when applied to the validation set. The advantages of the holdout method are that it is simple and quick. However, results of a holdout sample can vary greatly depending on which observations are randomly selected for the training set, the number of observations in the sample, and the number of observations that are randomly selected for the training and validation sets.

7.9 Big Data and Regression
Inference and Very Large Samples

Consider the example of a credit card company that has a very large database of information provided by its customers when they apply for credit cards. These customer records include information on the customer's annual household income, number of years of post–high school education, and number of members of the customer's household. In a second database, the company has records of the credit card charges accrued by each customer over the past year. Because the company is interested in using annual household income, the number of years of post–high school education, and the number of members of the household reported by new applicants to predict the credit card charges that will be accrued by these applicants, a data analyst links these two databases to create one data set containing all relevant information for a sample of 5,000 customers. The file *LargeCredit* contains these data, split into a training set of 3,000 observations and a validation set of 2,000 observations.

LargeCredit

The company has decided to apply multiple regression to these data to develop a model for predicting annual credit card charges for its new applicants. The dependent variable in the model is credit card charges accrued by a customer in the data set over the past year (y); the independent variables are the customer's annual household income (x_1), number of members of the household (x_2), and number of years of post–high school education (x_3). Figure 7.36 provides Excel output for the multiple regression model based on the 3,000 observations in the training set.

The model has a coefficient of determination of 0.3632 (see cell B5 in Figure 7.36), indicating that this model explains approximately 36% of the variation in credit card charges accrued by the customers in the sample over the past year. The p value for each test of the individual regression parameters is also very small (see cells E18 through E20), indicating that for each independent variable we can reject the hypothesis of no relationship with the dependent variable. The estimated slopes associated with the dependent variables are all highly significant. The model estimates the following:

- For a fixed number of household members and number of years of post–high school education, accrued credit card charges increase by $121.34 when a customer's annual household income increases by $1,000. This is shown in cell B18 of Figure 7.36.

- For a fixed annual household income and number of years of post–high school education, accrued credit card charges increase by $528.10 when a customer's household increases by one member. This is shown in cell B19 of Figure 7.36.

FIGURE 7.36	Excel Regression Output for Credit Card Company Example

▲	A	B	C	D	E	F	G	H	I
1	SUMMARY OUTPUT								
2									
3	*Regression Statistics*								
4	Multiple R	0.602663145							
5	R Square	0.363202867							
6	Adjusted R Square	0.362565219							
7	Standard Error	4834.449957							
8	Observations	3000							
9									
10	ANOVA								
11		*df*	*SS*	*MS*	*F*	*Significance F*			
12	Regression	3	39937797910	13312599303	569.5983495	6.5207E-293			
13	Residual	2996	70022231537	23371906.39					
14	Total	2999	1.0996E+11						
15									
16		*Coefficients*	*Standard Error*	*t Stat*	*P-value*	*Lower 95%*	*Upper 95%*	*Lower 99.0%*	*Upper 99.0%*
17	Intercept	2119.600282	333.0922952	6.363402314	2.27497E-10	1466.487528	2772.713036	1261.064442	2978.136122
18	Annual Income ($1000)	121.3384676	3.165148859	38.33578544	5.4905E-262	115.1323826	127.5445525	113.1803871	129.496548
19	Household Size	528.0996852	42.84154037	12.32681366	4.29401E-34	444.097873	612.1014973	417.6768433	638.522527
20	Years of Post-High School Education	-535.3593516	58.5960221	-9.136445316	1.15792E-19	-650.2518601	-420.4668432	-686.3889184	-384.3297849

- For a fixed annual household income and number of household members, accrued credit card charges decrease by $535.36 when a customer's number of years of post–high school education increases by one year. This is shown in cell B20 of Figure 7.36.

Because the *y*-intercept is an obvious result of extrapolation (no customer in the data has values of zero for annual household income, number of household members, *and* number of years of post–high school education), the estimated regression parameter β_0 is meaningless.

The small *p* values associated with a model that is fit on an extremely large sample do not imply that an extremely large sample solves all problems. Virtually all relationships between independent variables and the dependent variable will be statistically significant if the sample size is sufficiently large. That is, if the sample size is very large, there will be little difference in the b_j values generated by different random samples. Because we address the variability in potential values of our estimators through the use of statistical inference, and variability of our estimates b_j essentially disappears as the sample size grows very large, inference is of little use for estimates generated from very large samples. Thus, we generally are not concerned with the conditions a regression model must satisfy in order for inference to be reliable when we use a very large sample. Multicollinearity, on the other hand, can result in confusing or misleading regression parameters $b_1, b_2, \ldots, b_q$ and so is still a concern when we use a large data set to estimate a regression model that is to be used for explanatory purposes.

How much does sample size matter? Table 7.4 provides the regression parameter estimates and the corresponding *p* values for multiple regression models estimated on the first 50 observations, the second 50 observations, and so on for the *LargeCredit* data. Note that, even though the means of the parameter estimates for the regressions based on 50 observations are similar to the parameter estimates based on the full sample of 5,000 observations, the individual values of the estimated regression parameters in the regressions based on 50 observations show a great deal of variation. In these 10 regressions, the estimated values of b_0 range from −2,191.590 to 8,994.040, the estimated values of b_1 range from 73.207 to 155.187, the estimated values of b_2 range from −489.932 to 1,267.041, and the estimated values of b_3 range from −974.791 to 207.828. This is reflected in the *p* values

The phenomenon by which the value of an estimate generally becomes closer to the value of the parameter being estimated as the sample size grows is called the Law of Large Numbers.

TABLE 7.4	Regression Parameter Estimates and the Corresponding p Values for 10 Multiple Regression Models, Each Estimated on 50 Observations from the *LargeCredit* Data							
Observations	b_0	p Value	b_1	p Value	b_2	p Value	b_3	p Value
1–50	−805.152	0.7814	154.488	1.45E-06	234.664	0.5489	207.828	0.6721
51–100	894.407	0.6796	125.343	2.23E-07	822.675	0.0070	−355.585	0.3553
101–150	−2,191.590	0.4869	155.187	3.56E-07	674.961	0.0501	−25.309	0.9560
151–200	2,294.023	0.3445	114.734	1.26E-04	297.011	0.3700	−537.063	0.2205
201–250	8,994.040	0.0289	103.378	6.89E-04	−489.932	0.2270	−375.601	0.5261
251–300	7,265.471	0.0234	73.207	1.02E-02	−77.874	0.8409	−405.195	0.4060
301–350	2,147.906	0.5236	117.500	1.88E-04	390.447	0.3053	−374.799	0.4696
351–400	−504.532	0.8380	118.926	8.54E-07	798.499	0.0112	45.259	0.9209
401–450	1,587.067	0.5123	81.532	5.06E-04	1,267.041	0.0004	−891.118	0.0359
451–500	−315.945	0.9048	148.860	1.07E-05	1,000.243	0.0053	−974.791	0.0420
Mean	1,936.567		119.316		491.773		−368.637	

corresponding to the parameter estimates in the regressions based on 50 observations, which are substantially larger than the corresponding p values in the regression based on 3,000 observations. These results underscore the impact that a very large sample size can have on inference.

For another example, suppose the credit card company also has a separate database of information on shopping and lifestyle characteristics that it has collected from its customers during a recent Internet survey. The data analyst notes in the results in Figure 7.36 that the original regression model fails to explain almost 65% of the variation in credit card charges accrued by the customers in the data set. In an attempt to increase the variation in the dependent variable explained by the model, the data analyst decides to augment the original regression with a new independent variable, number of hours per week spent watching television (which we will designate as x_4). The analyst runs the new multiple regression and achieves the results shown in Figure 7.37.

The new model has a coefficient of determination of 0.3645 (see cell B5 in Figure 7.37), indicating the addition of number of hours per week spent watching television increased the explained variation in sample values of accrued credit card charges by less than 1%. The estimated regression parameters and associated p values for annual household income, number of household members, and number of years of post–high school education changed little after introducing into the model the number of hours per week spent watching television.

The estimated regression parameter for number of hours per week spent watching television is 12.55 (see cell B21 in Figure 7.37), suggesting that a 1-hour increase coincides with an increase of $12.55 in credit card charges accrued by each customer over the past year. The p value associated with this estimate is 0.014 (see cell E21 in Figure 7.37), so, at a 5% level of significance, we can reject the hypothesis that there is no relationship between the number of hours per week spent watching television and credit card charges accrued. However, when the model is based on a very large sample, almost all relationships will be significant whether they are real or not, and statistical significance does not necessarily imply that a relationship is meaningful or useful.

Is it reasonable to expect that the credit card charges accrued by a customer are related to the number of hours per week the consumer watches television? If not, the model that includes number of hours per week the consumer watches television as an independent variable may provide inaccurate or unreliable predictions of the credit card charges that will be accrued by new customers, even though we have found a significant relationship

FIGURE 7.37   Excel Regression Output for Credit Card Company Example After Adding Number of Hours per Week Spent Watching Television

	A	B	C	D	E	F	G	H	I
1	SUMMARY OUTPUT								
2									
3	*Regression Statistics*								
4	Multiple R	0.603724482							
5	R Square	0.36448325							
6	Adjusted R Square	0.36363448							
7	Standard Error	4830.393498							
8	Observations	3000							
9									
10	ANOVA								
11		*df*	*SS*	*MS*	*F*	*Significance F*			
12	Regression	4	40078588918	10019647230	429.4250838	8.3277E-293			
13	Residual	2995	69881440529	23332701.35					
14	Total	2999	1.0996E+11						
15									
16		*Coefficients*	*Standard Error*	*t Stat*	*P-value*	*Lower 95%*	*Upper 95%*	*Lower 99.0%*	*Upper 99.0%*
17	Intercept	1712.552073	371.7837807	4.606311953	4.26973E-06	983.5746542	2441.529492	754.2898349	2670.814311
18	Annual Income ($1000)	121.6120724	3.164453912	38.43066631	4.943E-263	115.4073492	127.8167955	113.4557814	129.7683633
19	Household Size	531.213362	42.82435656	12.40446803	1.71315E-34	447.2452317	615.1814922	420.8347874	641.5919365
20	Years of Post-High School Education	-539.8345703	58.57519443	-9.216095235	5.64208E-20	-654.6862563	-424.9828843	-690.8104864	-388.8586541
21	Hours Per Week Watching Television	12.55178379	5.109759992	2.456433142	0.014088759	2.532789303	22.57077828	-0.618478873	25.72204645

The use of out-of-sample data is common in data mining applications and is covered in detail in Chapter 9.

between these two variables. If the model is to be used to predict future amounts of credit charges, then the usefulness of including the number of hours per week the consumer watches television is best evaluated by measuring the accuracy of predictions for observations not included in the sample data used to construct the model. We demonstrate this procedure in the next subsection.

Model Selection

As we discussed in Section 7.8, various methods for identifying which independent variables to include in a regression model consider the p values of these variables in iterative procedures that sequentially add and/or remove variables. However, when dealing with a sufficiently large sample, the p value of virtually every independent variable will be small, and so variable selection procedures may suggest models with most or all the variables. Therefore, when dealing with large samples, it is often more difficult to discern the most appropriate model.

If developing a regression model for explanatory purposes, the practical significance of the estimated regression coefficients should be considered when interpreting the model and considering which variables to keep in the model. If developing a regression model to make future predictions, the selection of the independent variables to include in the regression model should be based on the predictive accuracy on observations that have not been used to train the model.

Let us revisit the example of a credit card company with a data set of customer records containing information on the customer's annual household income, number of years of post–high school education, number of members of the customer's household, and the credit card charges accrued. The file *LargeCredit* contains these data, split into a training set of 3,000 observations and a validation set of 2,000 observations.

To predict annual credit card charges for its new applicants, the company is considering two models:

- Model A—The dependent variable is credit card charges accrued by a customer in the data set over the past year (y), and the independent variables are the customer's annual household income (x_1), number of household members (x_2), and number of years of post–high school education (x_3). Figure 7.36 summarizes Model A estimated using the 3,000 observations of the training set.
- Model B—The dependent variable is credit card charges accrued by a customer in the data set over the past year (y), and the independent variables are the customer's annual household income (x_1), number of household members (x_2), number of years of post–high school education (x_3), and number of hours per week spent watching television (x_4). Figure 7.37 summarizes Model B estimated using the 3,000 observations of the training set.

Now, we would like to compare these models based on their predictive accuracy on the 2,000 observations in the validation set. For the first observation in the validation set (account number 18572870), Model A predicts annual charges of

$$\hat{y}_1^A = 2119.60 + 121.33(50.2) + 528.10(5) - 525.36(1) = \$10,315.93$$

Alternatively, Model B predicts annual charges of

$$\hat{y}_1^B = 1712.55 + 121.61(50.2) + 531.21(5) - 539.89(1) + 12.55(4) = \$9,983.92$$

Account number 18572870 has actual annual charges of \$5,472.51, so Model A's prediction of the first observation has a squared error of $(5,472.51 - 10,315.93)^2 = 23,458,721$ and Model B's prediction of the first observation has a squared error of $(5,472.51 - 9,983.92)^2 = 20,352,797$. Repeating these predictions and error calculations for each of the 2,000 observations in the validation set, Figure 7.38 shows that the sum of squared

FIGURE 7.38 Predictive Accuracy on *LargeCredit* Validation Set

	A	B	C	D	E	F	G	H	I	J	K
1							Model A (3 Variable)			Model B (4 Variable)	
2	Account Number	Annual Income ($1000)	Household Size	Years of Post-High School Education	Hours Per Week Watching Television	Annual Charges ($)	Prediction	Squared Error		Prediction	Squared Error
3	18572870	50.2	5.0	1.0	4.0	5,472.51	10,315.93	23,458,721		9,983.92	20,352,797
4	10135558	39.6	2.0	4.0	15.0	3,968.42	5,839.37	3500437.294		5,619.76	2726908.398
5	23467852	88.8	4.0	1.0	19.0	11,382.63	14,471.50	9541090.638		14,335.21	8717710.157
6	2221007	101.2	6.0	2.0	54.0	16,827.83	16,496.93	109493.0845		16,805.10	516.6005887
7	23024579	52.0	5.0	2.0	19.0	13,175.27	9,998.98	10088816.14		9,851.26	11049033.2
8	5534868	100.8	5.0	4.0	50.0	20,292.73	14,849.58	29627894.64		15,095.37	27012585.44
9	19704869	70.6	3.0	0.0	49.0	6,230.89	12,270.40	36475622.43		12,507.04	39390082.33
10	9388137	88.9	8.0	2.0	41.0	18,914.62	16,060.67	8145037.3		16,208.53	7322943.679
11	23883625	89.4	5.0	2.0	29.0	14,362.00	14,537.04	30638.65325		14,525.07	26592.06635
1991	6776616	87.6	3.0	2.0	59.0	20,541.21	13,262.43	52980632.57		13,620.30	47899053.37
1992	8695442	47.3	8.0	1.0	10.0	17,011.33	11,548.35	29844173.12		11,300.19	32617082.88
1993	5888985	82.4	4.0	1.0	48.0	9,416.69	13,694.93	18303332.35		13,920.89	20287829.66
1994	12243467	43.2	5.0	1.0	16.0	3,101.00	9,466.56	40520368.82		9,283.25	38220269.2
1995	28297658	49.9	5.0	0.0	48.0	14,538.99	10,814.89	13868933.92		11,039.55	12246101.91
1996	4605783	36.7	3.0	2.0	19.0	12,620.39	7,086.30	30626125.63		6,928.17	32401368.92
1997	21430617	54.9	1.0	5.0	27.0	3,755.45	6,632.39	8276755.445		6,559.99	7865464.344
1998	3080483	84.4	4.0	5.0	23.0	13,018.42	11,796.17	1493897.685		11,690.98	1762090.043
1999	8089356	41.6	2.0	4.0	14.0	8,740.70	6,082.04	7068459.72		5,850.43	8353673.976
2000	14223252	51.0	7.0	5.0	4.0	0.00	9,327.76	87007165.68		8,984.30	80717567.08
2001	8048637	39.0	7.0	1.0	5.0	360.73	10,013.14	93168998.76		9,696.84	87162964.44
2002	27638369	39.0	5.0	2.0	19.0	1,554.11	8,421.58	47162147.49		8,270.30	45107267.97
2003											
2004							SSE:	47,392,009,111			47,409,404,281

errors for Model A is 47,392,009,111 and the sum of squared errors for Model B is 47,409,404,281. Therefore, Model A's predictions are slightly more accurate than Model B's predictions on the validation set, as measured by squared error. Although the p value of Hours Per Week Watching Television in Model B is relatively small, these results suggest that it does not improve the accuracy of predictions.

LargeCreditValidation

7.10 Prediction with Regression

To illustrate how a regression model can be used to make predictions about new observations and support decision making, let us again consider the Butler Trucking Company. Recall from Section 7.4 that the multiple regression equation based on the 300 past routes using Miles (x_1) and Deliveries (x_2) as the independent variables to estimate travel time (y) for a driving assignment is

$$\hat{y} = 0.1273 + 0.0672x_1 + 0.6900x_2 \qquad (7.22)$$

As described by the first three columns of Table 7.5, Butler has 10 new observations corresponding to upcoming routes for which they have estimated the miles to be driven and number of deliveries. The point estimates for the travel time for each of these 10 upcoming routes can be obtained by substituting the miles driven and number of deliveries into equation (7.22). For example, the predicted travel time for Assignment 301 is

$$\hat{y}_{301} = 0.1273 + 0.0672(105) + 0.6900(3) = 9.25$$

In addition to the point estimate, there are two types of interval estimates associated with the regression equation. A confidence interval is an interval estimate of the mean y value given values of the independent variables. A **prediction interval** is an interval estimate of an individual y value given values of the independent variables.

The general form for the confidence interval on the mean y value given values of $x_1, x_2, \ldots, x_q$ is

$$\hat{y} \pm t_{\alpha/2}s_{\hat{y}} \qquad (7.23)$$

where $\hat{y}$ is the point estimate of the mean y value provided by the regression equation, $s_{\hat{y}}$ is the estimated standard deviation of $\hat{y}$, and $t_{\alpha/2}$ is a multiplier term based on the sample size and specified $100(1-\alpha)\%$ confidence level of the interval. More specifically, $t_{\alpha/2}$ is the t value that provides an area of $\alpha/2$ in the upper tail of a t distribution with $n - q - 1$ degrees of freedom. In general, the calculation of the confidence interval in equation (7.23) uses matrix algebra and requires the use of specialized statistical software.

The prediction interval on the individual y value given values of $x_1, x_2, \ldots, x_q$ is

$$\hat{y} \pm t_{\alpha/2}\sqrt{s_{\hat{y}}^2 + \frac{SSE}{n - q - 1}} \qquad (7.24)$$

where $\hat{y}$ is the point estimate of the individual y value provided by the regression equation, $s_{\hat{y}}^2$ is the estimated variance of $\hat{y}$, and $t_{\alpha/2}$ is the t value that provides an area of $\alpha/2$ in the upper tail of a t distribution with $n - q - 1$ degrees of freedom. In the term $SSE/(n - q - 1)$, n is the number of observations in the sample, q is the number of independent variables in the regression model, and SSE is the sum of squares due to error as defined by equation (7.5). In general, the calculation of the prediction interval in equation (7.24) uses matrix algebra and requires the use of specialized statistical software.

Statistical software such as JMP and R can be used to compute the confidence interval and prediction intervals on regression output.

In the Butler Trucking problem, the 95% confidence interval is an interval estimate of the mean travel time for a route assignment with the given values of Miles and Deliveries. This is the appropriate interval estimate if we are interested in estimating the mean travel time for all route assignments with specified mileage and number of deliveries. This confidence interval estimates the variability in the mean travel time.

In the Butler Trucking problem, the 95% prediction interval is an interval estimate on the prediction of travel time for an individual route assignment with the given values of Miles and Deliveries. This is the appropriate interval estimate if we are interested in

			Predicted	95% CI	95% PI
TABLE 7.5					
Assignment	Miles	Deliveries	Value	Half-Width(±)	Half-Width(±)
301	105	3	9.25	0.193	1.645
302	60	4	6.92	0.112	1.637
303	95	5	9.96	0.173	1.642
304	100	1	7.54	0.225	1.649
305	40	3	4.88	0.177	1.643
306	80	3	7.57	0.108	1.637
307	65	4	7.25	0.103	1.637
308	55	3	5.89	0.124	1.638
309	95	2	7.89	0.175	1.643
310	95	3	8.58	0.154	1.641

TABLE 7.5 Predicted Values and 95% Confidence Intervals and Prediction Intervals for 10 New Butler Trucking Routes

predicting the travel time for an individual route assignment with the specified mileage and number of deliveries. This prediction interval estimates the variability inherent in a single route's travel time.

To illustrate, consider the first observation (Assignment 301) in Table 7.5 with 105 miles and 3 deliveries. For all 105-mile routes with 3 deliveries, a 95% confidence interval on the mean travel time is 9.25 ± 0.193. That is, we are 95% confident that the true population mean travel time for 105-mile routes with 3 deliveries is between 9.06 and 9.44 hours.

Now suppose Butler Trucking is interested in predicting the travel time for a specific upcoming route assignment covering 105 miles and 3 deliveries. The best prediction for this route's travel time is still 9.25 hours, as provided by the regression equation. However, a 95% prediction interval for this travel time prediction is 9.25 ± 1.645. That is, we are 95% confident that the travel time for a single 105-mile route with 3 deliveries will be between 7.61 and 10.90 hours.

Note that the 95% prediction interval for the travel time of a single route assignment with 105 miles and 3 deliveries is wider than the 95% confidence interval for the mean travel time of all route assignments with 105 miles and 3 deliveries. The difference reflects the fact that we are able to estimate the mean y value of a group of observations with the same specified values of the independent variables more precisely than we can predict an individual y value of a single observation with specified values of the independent variables. Comparing equation (7.23) to equation (7.24), we observe the reason for the difference in the width of the confidence interval and the prediction interval. Just as the confidence interval, the prediction interval calculation includes an $s_{\hat{y}}$ term to account for the variability in estimating the mean value of y, but it also includes an additional term $SSE/(n - q - 1)$ which accounts for the variability in individual values of y about its mean value.

Finally, we point out that the width of the prediction (and confidence) intervals for the regression point estimate are not the same for each observation. Instead, the width of the interval depends on the corresponding values of the independent variables. Confidence intervals and prediction intervals are the narrowest when the values of the independent variables, $x_1, x_2, \ldots, x_q$, are closest to their respective means, $\bar{x}_1, \bar{x}_2, \ldots, \bar{x}_q$. For the 300 observations on which the regression equation model is based, the mean miles driven for a route assignment is 70.7 miles and the mean number of deliveries for a route assignment is 3.5. Assignment 307 has the mileage (65) and number of deliveries (4) that are closest to these means and correspondingly has the narrowest confidence and prediction interval. Conversely, Assignment 304 has the widest confidence and prediction intervals because it has the mileage (100) and number of deliveries (1) that are the farthest from the mean mileage and mean number of deliveries in the data.

SUMMARY

In this chapter we showed how regression analysis can be used to determine how a dependent variable y is related to an independent variable x. In simple linear regression, the regression model is $y = \beta_0 + \beta_1 x_1 + \varepsilon$. We use sample data and the least squares method to develop the estimated regression equation $\hat{y} = b_0 + b_1 x_1$. In effect, b_0 and b_1 are the sample statistics used to estimate the unknown model parameters.

The coefficient of determination r^2 was presented as a measure of the goodness of fit for the estimated regression equation; it can be interpreted as the proportion of the variation in the sample values of the dependent variable y that can be explained by the estimated regression equation. We then extended our discussion to include multiple independent variables and reviewed how to use Excel to find the estimated multiple regression equation $\hat{y} = b_0 + b_1 x_1 + b_2 x_2 + \cdots + b_q x_q$, and we considered the interpretations of the parameter estimates in multiple regression and the ramifications of multicollinearity.

The assumptions related to the regression model and its associated error term ϵ were discussed. We reviewed the t test for determining whether there is a statistically significant relationship between the dependent variable and an individual independent variable given the other independent variables in the regression model. We also showed how to use Excel to develop confidence interval estimates of the regression parameters β_0, β_1, $\beta_2 \ldots , \beta_q$.

We showed how to incorporate categorical independent variables into a regression model through the use of dummy variables, and we discussed a variety of ways to use multiple regression to fit nonlinear relationships between independent variables and the dependent variable. We discussed various automated procedures for selecting independent variables to include in a regression model and the problem of overfitting a regression model.

We discussed the implications of big data on regression analysis. Specifically, we considered the impact of very large samples on regression inference and demonstrated the use of holdout data to evaluate candidate regression models. We concluded by presenting the concepts of confidence intervals and prediction intervals related to point estimates produced by the regression model.

GLOSSARY

Backward elimination An iterative variable selection procedure that starts with a model with all independent variables and considers removing an independent variable at each step.

Best subsets A variable selection procedure that constructs and compares all possible models with up to a specified number of independent variables.

Coefficient of determination A measure of the goodness of fit of the estimated regression equation. It can be interpreted as the proportion of the variability in the dependent variable y that is explained by the estimated regression equation.

Confidence interval An estimate of a population parameter that provides an interval believed to contain the value of the parameter at some level of confidence.

Confidence level An indication of how frequently interval estimates based on samples of the same size taken from the same population using identical sampling techniques will contain the true value of the parameter we are estimating.

Cross-validation Assessment of the performance of a model on data other than the data that were used to generate the model.

Dependent variable The variable that is being predicted or explained. It is denoted by y and is often referred to as the response.

Dummy variable A variable used to model the effect of categorical independent variables in a regression model; generally takes only the value zero or one.

Estimated regression The estimate of the regression equation developed from sample data by using the least squares method. The estimated multiple linear regression equation is $\hat{y} = b_0 + b_1x_1 + b_2x_2 + \cdots + b_qx_q$.

Experimental region The range of values for the independent variables $x_1, x_2, \ldots, x_q$ for the data that are used to estimate the regression model.

Extrapolation Prediction of the mean value of the dependent variable y for values of the independent variables $x_1, x_2, \ldots, x_q$ that are outside the experimental range.

Forward selection An iterative variable selection procedure that starts with a model with no variables and considers adding an independent variable at each step.

Holdout method Method of cross-validation in which sample data are randomly divided into mutually exclusive and collectively exhaustive sets, then one set is used to build the candidate models and the other set is used to compare model performances and ultimately select a model.

Hypothesis testing The process of making a conjecture about the value of a population parameter, collecting sample data that can be used to assess this conjecture, measuring the strength of the evidence against the conjecture that is provided by the sample, and using these results to draw a conclusion about the conjecture.

Independent variable(s) The variable(s) used for predicting or explaining values of the dependent variable. It is denoted by x and is often referred to as the predictor variable.

Interaction Regression modeling technique used when the relationship between the dependent variable and one independent variable is different at different values of a second independent variable.

Interval estimation The use of sample data to calculate a range of values that is believed to include the unknown value of a population parameter.

Knot The prespecified value of the independent variable at which its relationship with the dependent variable changes in a piecewise linear regression model; also called the break-point or the joint.

Least squares method A procedure for using sample data to find the estimated regression equation.

Linear regression Regression analysis in which relationships between the independent variables and the dependent variable are approximated by a straight line.

Multicollinearity The degree of correlation among independent variables in a regression model.

Multiple linear regression Regression analysis involving one dependent variable and more than one independent variable.

Overfitting Fitting a model too closely to sample data, resulting in a model that does not accurately reflect the population.

p value The probability that a random sample of the same size collected from the same population using the same procedure will yield stronger evidence against a hypothesis than the evidence in the sample data given that the hypothesis is actually true.

Parameter A measurable factor that defines a characteristic of a population, process, or system.

Piecewise linear regression model Regression model in which one linear relationship between the independent and dependent variables is fit for values of the independent variable below a prespecified value of the independent variable, a different linear relationship between the independent and dependent variables is fit for values of the independent variable above the prespecified value of the independent variable, and the two regressions have the same estimated value of the dependent variable (i.e., are joined) at the prespecified value of the independent variable.

Prediction interval An interval estimate of the prediction of an individual y value given values of the independent variables.

Point estimator A single value used as an estimate of the corresponding population parameter.

Quadratic regression model Regression model in which a nonlinear relationship between the independent and dependent variables is fit by including the independent variable and the square of the independent variable in the model: $\hat{y} = b_o + b_1x_1 + b_2x_1^2$; also referred to as a second-order polynomial model.

Random variable A quantity whose values are not known with certainty.

Regression analysis A statistical procedure used to develop an equation showing how the variables are related.

Regression model The equation that describes how the dependent variable y is related to an independent variable x and an error term; the *multiple linear regression model* is $y = \beta_0 + \beta_1 x_1 + \beta_2 x_2 + \cdots + \beta_q x_q + \varepsilon$.

Residual The difference between the observed value of the dependent variable and the value predicted using the estimated regression equation; for the ith observation, the ith residual is $y_i - \hat{y}_i$.

Simple linear regression Regression analysis involving one dependent variable and one independent variable.

Statistical inference The process of making estimates and drawing conclusions about one or more characteristics of a population (the value of one or more parameters) through analysis of sample data drawn from the population.

Stepwise selection An iterative variable selection procedure that considers adding an independent variable and removing an independent variable at each step.

t test Statistical test based on the Student's t probability distribution that can be used to test the hypothesis that a regression parameter β_j is zero; if this hypothesis is rejected, we conclude that there is a regression relationship between the jth independent variable and the dependent variable.

Training set The data set used to build the candidate models.

Validation set The data set used to compare model forecasts and ultimately pick a model for predicting values of the dependent variable.

PROBLEMS

1. **Price and Weight of Bicycles.** *Bicycling World*, a magazine devoted to cycling, reviews hundreds of bicycles throughout the year. Its Road-Race category contains reviews of bicycles used by riders primarily interested in racing. One of the most important factors in selecting a bicycle for racing is its weight. The following data show the weight (pounds) and price ($) for 10 racing bicycles reviewed by the magazine:

DATA *file*

BicyclingWorld

Model	Weight (lb)	Price ($)
Fierro 7B	17.9	2,200
HX 5000	16.2	6,350
Durbin Ultralight	15.0	8,470
Schmidt	16.0	6,300
WSilton Advanced	17.3	4,100
bicyclette vélo	13.2	8,700
Supremo Team	16.3	6,100
XTC Racer	17.2	2,680
D'Onofrio Pro	17.7	3,500
Americana #6	14.2	8,100

a. Develop a scatter chart with weight as the independent variable. What does the scatter chart indicate about the relationship between the weight and price of these bicycles?

b. Use the data to develop an estimated regression equation that could be used to estimate the price for a bicycle, given its weight. What is the estimated regression model?

c. Test whether each of the regression parameters β_0 and β_1 is equal to zero at a 0.05 level of significance. What are the correct interpretations of the estimated regression parameters? Are these interpretations reasonable?

d. How much of the variation in the prices of the bicycles in the sample does the regression model you estimated in part (b) explain?

e. The manufacturers of the D'Onofrio Pro plan to introduce the 15-lb D'Onofrio Elite bicycle later this year. Use the regression model you estimated in part (a) to predict the price of the D'Ononfrio Elite.

f. The owner of Michele's Bikes of Nesika Beach, Oregon is trying to decide in advance whether to make room for the D'Onofrio Elite bicycle in its inventory. She is convinced that she will not be able to sell the D'Onofrio Elite for more than $7,000, and so she will not make room in her inventory for the bicycle unless its estimated price is less than $7,000. Under this condition and using the regression model you estimated in part (a), what decision should the owner of Michele's Bikes make?

2. **Production Rate and Quality Control.** In a manufacturing process the assembly line speed (feet per minute) was thought to affect the number of defective parts found during the inspection process. To test this theory, managers devised a situation in which the same batch of parts was inspected visually at a variety of line speeds. They collected the following data:

LineSpeed

Line Speed (ft/min)	No. of Defective Parts Found
20	21
20	19
40	15
30	16
60	14
40	17

a. Develop a scatter chart with line speed as the independent variable. What does the scatter chart indicate about the relationship between line speed and the number of defective parts found?

b. Use the data to develop an estimated regression equation that could be used to predict the number of defective parts found, given the line speed. What is the estimated regression model?

c. Test whether each of the regression parameters β_0 and β_1 is equal to zero at a 0.01 level of significance. What are the correct interpretations of the estimated regression parameters? Are these interpretations reasonable?

d. How much of the variation in the number of defective parts found for the sample data does the model you estimated in part (b) explain?

3. **Machine Maintenance.** Jensen Tire & Auto is deciding whether to purchase a maintenance contract for its new computer wheel alignment and balancing machine. Managers feel that maintenance expense should be related to usage, and they collected the following information on weekly usage (hours) and annual maintenance expense (in hundreds of dollars).

Jensen

Weekly Usage (hours)	Annual Maintenance Expense ($100s)
13	17.0
10	22.0
20	30.0
28	37.0
32	47.0
17	30.5
24	32.5
31	39.0
40	51.5
38	40.0

a. Develop a scatter chart with weekly usage hours as the independent variable. What does the scatter chart indicate about the relationship between weekly usage and annual maintenance expense?

b. Use the data to develop an estimated regression equation that could be used to predict the annual maintenance expense for a given number of hours of weekly usage. What is the estimated regression model?

c. Test whether each of the regression parameters β_0 and β_1 is equal to zero at a 0.05 level of significance. What are the correct interpretations of the estimated regression parameters? Are these interpretations reasonable?

d. How much of the variation in the sample values of annual maintenance expense does the model you estimated in part (b) explain?

e. If the maintenance contract costs $3,000 per year, would you recommend purchasing it? Why or why not?

4. **Absenteeism and Location.** A sociologist was hired by a large city hospital to investigate the relationship between the number of unauthorized days that employees are absent per year and the distance (miles) between home and work for the employees. A sample of 10 employees was chosen, and the following data were collected.

Absent

Distance to Work (miles)	No. of Days Absent
1	8
3	5
4	8
6	7
8	6
10	3
12	5
14	2
14	4
18	2

a. Develop a scatter chart for these data. Does a linear relationship appear reasonable? Explain.

b. Use the data to develop an estimated regression equation that could be used to predict the number of days absent given the distance to work. What is the estimated regression model?

c. What is the 99% confidence interval for the regression parameter β_1? Based on this interval, what conclusion can you make about the hypotheses that the regression parameter β_1 is equal to zero?

d. What is the 99% confidence interval for the regression parameter β_0? Based on this interval, what conclusion can you make about the hypotheses that the regression parameter β_0 is equal to zero?

e. How much of the variation in the sample values of number of days absent does the model you estimated in part (b) explain?

5. **Bus Maintenance.** The regional transit authority for a major metropolitan area wants to determine whether there is a relationship between the age of a bus and the annual maintenance cost. A sample of 10 buses resulted in the following data:

Age of Bus (years)	Annual Maintenance Cost ($)
1	350
2	370
2	480
2	520
2	590
3	550
4	750
4	800
5	790
5	950

DATA*file*

AgeCost

a. Develop a scatter chart for these data. What does the scatter chart indicate about the relationship between age of a bus and the annual maintenance cost?
b. Use the data to develop an estimated regression equation that could be used to predict the annual maintenance cost given the age of the bus. What is the estimated regression model?
c. Test whether each of the regression parameters β_0 and β_1 is equal to zero at a 0.05 level of significance. What are the correct interpretations of the estimated regression parameters? Are these interpretations reasonable?
d. How much of the variation in the sample values of annual maintenance cost does the model you estimated in part (b) explain?
e. What do you predict the annual maintenance cost to be for a 3.5-year-old bus?

DATA*file*

MktHrsPts

6. **Studying and Grades.** A marketing professor at Givens College is interested in the relationship between hours spent studying and total points earned in a course. Data collected on 156 students who took the course last semester are provided in the file *MktHrsPts*.
a. Develop a scatter chart for these data. What does the scatter chart indicate about the relationship between total points earned and hours spent studying?
b. Develop an estimated regression equation showing how total points earned is related to hours spent studying. What is the estimated regression model?
c. Test whether each of the regression parameters β_0 and β_1 is equal to zero at a 0.01 level of significance. What are the correct interpretations of the estimated regression parameters? Are these interpretations reasonable?
d. How much of the variation in the sample values of total point earned does the model you estimated in part (b) explain?
e. Mark Sweeney spent 95 hours studying. Use the regression model you estimated in part (b) to predict the total points Mark earned.
f. Mark Sweeney wants to receive a letter grade of A for this course, and he needs to earn at least 90 points to do so. Based on the regression equation developed in part (b), how many estimated hours should Mark study to receive a letter grade of A for this course?

7. **Stock Market Performance.** The Dow Jones Industrial Average (DJIA) and the Standard & Poor's 500 (S&P 500) indexes are used as measures of overall movement in the stock market. The DJIA is based on the price movements of 30 large companies; the S&P 500 is an index composed of 500 stocks. Some say the S&P 500 is a better measure of stock market performance because it is broader based. The closing price for the DJIA and the S&P 500 for 15 weeks of a previous year follow (*Barron's* web site).

DJIAS&P500

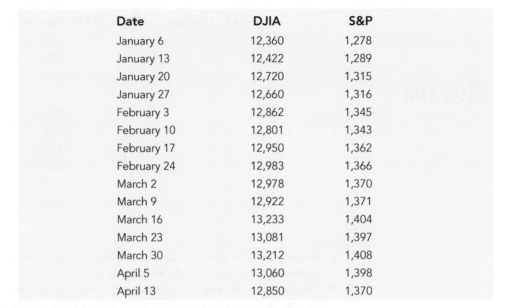

Date	DJIA	S&P
January 6	12,360	1,278
January 13	12,422	1,289
January 20	12,720	1,315
January 27	12,660	1,316
February 3	12,862	1,345
February 10	12,801	1,343
February 17	12,950	1,362
February 24	12,983	1,366
March 2	12,978	1,370
March 9	12,922	1,371
March 16	13,233	1,404
March 23	13,081	1,397
March 30	13,212	1,408
April 5	13,060	1,398
April 13	12,850	1,370

a. Develop a scatter chart for these data with DJIA as the independent variable. What does the scatter chart indicate about the relationship between DJIA and S&P 500?

b. Develop an estimated regression equation showing how S&P 500 is related to DJIA. What is the estimated regression model?

c. What is the 95% confidence interval for the regression parameter β_1? Based on this interval, what conclusion can you make about the hypotheses that the regression parameter β_1 is equal to zero?

d. What is the 95% confidence interval for the regression parameter β_0? Based on this interval, what conclusion can you make about the hypotheses that the regression parameter β_0 is equal to zero?

e. How much of the variation in the sample values of S&P 500 does the model estimated in part (b) explain?

f. Suppose that the closing price for the DJIA is 13,500. Estimate the closing price for the S&P 500.

g. Should we be concerned that the DJIA value of 13,500 used to predict the S&P 500 value in part (f) is beyond the range of the DJIA used to develop the estimated regression equation?

8. **Used Car Mileage and Price.** The Toyota Camry is one of the best-selling cars in North America. The cost of a previously owned Camry depends on many factors, including the model year, mileage, and condition. To investigate the relationship between the car's mileage and the sales price for Camrys, the following data show the mileage and sale price for 19 sales (PriceHub web site).

Miles (1,000s)	Price ($1,000s)
22	16.2
29	16.0
36	13.8
47	11.5
63	12.5
77	12.9
73	11.2
87	13.0

DATA *file*

Camry

Miles (1,000s)	Price ($1,000s)
92	11.8
101	10.8
110	8.3
28	12.5
59	11.1
68	15.0
68	12.2
91	13.0
42	15.6
65	12.7
110	8.3

a. Develop a scatter chart for these data with miles as the independent variable. What does the scatter chart indicate about the relationship between price and miles?

b. Develop an estimated regression equation showing how price is related to miles. What is the estimated regression model?

c. Test whether each of the regression parameters β_0 and β_1 is equal to zero at a 0.01 level of significance. What are the correct interpretations of the estimated regression parameters? Are these interpretations reasonable?

d. How much of the variation in the sample values of price does the model estimated in part (b) explain?

e. For the model estimated in part (b), calculate the predicted price and residual for each automobile in the data. Identify the two automobiles that were the biggest bargains.

f. Suppose that you are considering purchasing a previously owned Camry that has been driven 60,000 miles. Use the estimated regression equation developed in part (b) to predict the price for this car. Is this the price you would offer the seller?

9. **Weekly Theater Revenue.** Dixie Showtime Movie Theaters, Inc. owns and operates a chain of cinemas in several markets in the southern United States. The owners would like to estimate weekly gross revenue as a function of advertising expenditures. Data for a sample of eight markets for a recent week follow:

DATA *file*

DixieShowtime

Market	Weekly Gross Revenue ($100s)	Television Advertising ($100s)	Newspaper Advertising ($100s)
Mobile	101.3	5.0	1.5
Shreveport	51.9	3.0	3.0
Jackson	74.8	4.0	1.5
Birmingham	126.2	4.3	4.3
Little Rock	137.8	3.6	4.0
Biloxi	101.4	3.5	2.3
New Orleans	237.8	5.0	8.4
Baton Rouge	219.6	6.9	5.8

a. Develop an estimated regression equation with the amount of television advertising as the independent variable. Test for a significant relationship between television advertising and weekly gross revenue at the 0.05 level of significance. What is the interpretation of this relationship?

b. How much of the variation in the sample values of weekly gross revenue does the model in part (a) explain?

c. Develop an estimated regression equation with both television advertising and newspaper advertising as the independent variables. Test whether each of the regression parameters β_0, β_1, and β_2 is equal to zero at a 0.05 level of significance. What are the correct interpretations of the estimated regression parameters? Are these interpretations reasonable?

d. How much of the variation in the sample values of weekly gross revenue does the model in part (c) explain?

e. Given the results in parts (a) and (c), what should your next step be? Explain.

f. What are the managerial implications of these results?

10. **Ratings of Beachfront Boutique Hotels.** *Resorts & Spas*, a magazine devoted to upscale vacations and accommodations, published its Reader's Choice List of the top 20 independent beachfront boutique hotels in the world. The data shown are the scores received by these hotels based on the results from *Resorts & Spas'* annual Readers' Choice Survey. Each score represents the percentage of respondents who rated a hotel as excellent or very good on one of three criteria (comfort, amenities, and in-house dining). An overall score was also reported and used to rank the hotels. The highest ranked hotel, the Muri Beach Odyssey, has an overall score of 94.3, the highest component of which is 97.7 for in-house dining.

DATA *file*
BeachFrontHotels

Hotel	Overall	Comfort	Amenities	In-House Dining
Muri Beach Odyssey	94.3	94.5	90.8	97.7
Pattaya Resort	92.9	96.6	84.1	96.6
Sojourner's Respite	92.8	99.9	100.0	88.4
Spa Carribe	91.2	88.5	94.7	97.0
Penang Resort and Spa	90.4	95.0	87.8	91.1
Mokihana Ho-kele	90.2	92.4	82.0	98.7
Theo's of Cape Town	90.1	95.9	86.2	91.9
Cap d'Agde Resort	89.8	92.5	92.5	88.8
Spirit of Mykonos	89.3	94.6	85.8	90.7
Turismo del Mar	89.1	90.5	83.2	90.4
Hotel Iguana	89.1	90.8	81.9	88.5
Sidi Abdel Rahman Palace	89.0	93.0	93.0	89.6
Sainte-Maxime Quarters	88.6	92.5	78.2	91.2
Rotorua Inn	87.1	93.0	91.6	73.5
Club Lapu-Lapu	87.1	90.9	74.9	89.6
Terracina Retreat	86.5	94.3	78.0	91.5
Hacienda Punta Barco	86.1	95.4	77.3	90.8
Rendezvous Kolocep	86.0	94.8	76.4	91.4
Cabo de Gata Vista	86.0	92.0	72.2	89.2
Sanya Deluxe	85.1	93.4	77.3	91.8

a. Determine the estimated multiple linear regression equation that can be used to predict the overall score given the scores for comfort, amenities, and in-house dining.

b. Use the *t* test to determine the significance of each independent variable. What is the conclusion for each test at the 0.01 level of significance?

c. Remove all independent variables that are not significant at the 0.01 level of significance from the estimated regression equation. What is your recommended estimated regression equation?

d. Suppose *Resorts & Spas* has decided to recommend each of the independent beachfront boutiques in its data that achieves an estimated overall score over 90. Use the regression equation developed in part (c) to determine which of the independent beachfront boutiques will receive a recommendation from *Resorts & Spas*.

11. **Trading Stocks Electronically.** The American Association of Individual Investors (AAII) On-Line Discount Broker Survey polls members on their experiences with electronic trades handled by discount brokers. As part of the survey, members were asked to rate their satisfaction with the trade price and the speed of execution, as well as provide an overall satisfaction rating. Possible responses (scores) were no opinion (0), unsatisfied (1), somewhat satisfied (2), satisfied (3), and very satisfied (4). For each broker, summary scores were computed by computing a weighted average of the scores provided by each respondent. A portion of the survey results follow (AAII web site).

DATA *file*

Broker

Brokerage	Satisfaction with Trade Price	Satisfaction with Speed of Execution	Overall Satisfaction with Electronic Trades
Scottrade, Inc.	3.4	3.4	3.5
Charles Schwab	3.2	3.3	3.4
Fidelity Brokerage Services	3.1	3.4	3.9
TD Ameritrade	2.9	3.6	3.7
E*Trade Financial	2.9	3.2	2.9
(Not listed)	2.5	3.2	2.7
Vanguard Brokerage Services	2.6	3.8	2.8
USAA Brokerage Services	2.4	3.8	3.6
Thinkorswim	2.6	2.6	2.6
Wells Fargo Investments	2.3	2.7	2.3
Interactive Brokers	3.7	4.0	4.0
Zecco.com	2.5	2.5	2.5
Firstrade Securities	3.0	3.0	4.0
Banc of America Investment Services	4.0	1.0	2.0

a. Develop an estimated regression equation using trade price and speed of execution to predict overall satisfaction with the broker. Interpret the coefficient of determination.

b. Use the *t* test to determine the significance of each independent variable. What are your conclusions at the 0.05 level of significance?

c. Interpret the estimated regression parameters. Are the relationships indicated by these estimates what you would expect?

d. Finger Lakes Investments has developed a new electronic trading system and would like to predict overall customer satisfaction assuming they can provide satisfactory service levels (3) for both trade price and speed of execution. Use the estimated regression equation developed in part (a) to predict overall satisfaction level for Finger Lakes Investments if they can achieve these performance levels.

e. What concerns (if any) do you have with regard to the possible responses the respondents could select on the survey.

12. **NFL Winning Percentage.** The National Football League (NFL) records a variety of performance data for individuals and teams. To investigate the importance of passing on the percentage of games won by a team, the following data show the conference (Conf), average number of passing yards per attempt (Yds/Att), the number of

interceptions thrown per attempt (Int/Att), and the percentage of games won (Win%) for a random sample of 16 NFL teams for the 2011 season (NFL web site).

DATA *file*

NFLPassing

Team	Conf	Yds/Att	Int/Att	Win%
Arizona Cardinals	NFC	6.5	0.042	50.0
Atlanta Falcons	NFC	7.1	0.022	62.5
Carolina Panthers	NFC	7.4	0.033	37.5
Cincinnati Bengals	AFC	6.2	0.026	56.3
Detroit Lions	NFC	7.2	0.024	62.5
Green Bay Packers	NFC	8.9	0.014	93.8
Houston Texans	AFC	7.5	0.019	62.5
Indianapolis Colts	AFC	5.6	0.026	12.5
Jacksonville Jaguars	AFC	4.6	0.032	31.3
Minnesota Vikings	NFC	5.8	0.033	18.
New England Patriots	AFC	8.3	0.020	81.3
New Orleans Saints	NFC	8.1	0.021	81.3
Oakland Raiders	AFC	7.6	0.044	50.0
San Francisco 49ers	NFC	6.5	0.011	81.3
Tennessee Titans	AFC	6.7	0.024	56.3
Washington Redskins	NFC	6.4	0.041	31.3

a. Develop the estimated regression equation that could be used to predict the percentage of games won, given the average number of passing yards per attempt. What proportion of variation in the sample values of proportion of games won does this model explain?

b. Develop the estimated regression equation that could be used to predict the percentage of games won, given the number of interceptions thrown per attempt. What proportion of variation in the sample values of proportion of games won does this model explain?

c. Develop the estimated regression equation that could be used to predict the percentage of games won, given the average number of passing yards per attempt and the number of interceptions thrown per attempt. What proportion of variation in the sample values of proportion of games won does this model explain?

d. The average number of passing yards per attempt for the Kansas City Chiefs during the 2011 season was 6.2, and the team's number of interceptions thrown per attempt was 0.036. Use the estimated regression equation developed in part (c) to predict the percentage of games won by the Kansas City Chiefs during the 2011 season. Compare your prediction to the actual percentage of games won by the Kansas City Chiefs. (*Note*: For the 2011 season, the Kansas City Chiefs' record was 7 wins and 9 losses.)

e. Did the estimated regression equation that uses only the average number of passing yards per attempt as the independent variable to predict the percentage of games won provide a good fit?

13. **Water Filtration System Maintenance.** Johnson Filtration, Inc. provides maintenance service for water filtration systems throughout Southern Florida. Customers contact Johnson with requests for maintenance service on their water filtration systems. To estimate the service time and the service cost, Johnson's managers want to predict the repair time necessary for each maintenance request. Hence, repair time in hours is the dependent variable. Repair time is believed to be related to three factors: the number of months since the last maintenance service, the type of repair problem (mechanical or electrical), and the repairperson who performs the repair (Donna Newton or Bob Jones). Data for a sample of 10 service calls are reported in the following table:

Repair Time in Hours	Months Since Last Service	Type of Repair	Repairperson
2.9	2	Electrical	Donna Newton
3.0	6	Mechanical	Donna Newton
4.8	8	Electrical	Bob Jones
1.8	3	Mechanical	Donna Newton
2.9	2	Electrical	Donna Newton
4.9	7	Electrical	Bob Jones
4.2	9	Mechanical	Bob Jones
4.8	8	Mechanical	Bob Jones
4.4	4	Electrical	Bob Jones
4.5	6	Electrical	Donna Newton

Repair

a. Develop the simple linear regression equation to predict repair time given the number of months since the last maintenance service, and use the results to test the hypothesis that no relationship exists between repair time and the number of months since the last maintenance service at the 0.05 level of significance. What is the interpretation of this relationship? What does the coefficient of determination tell you about this model?

b. Using the simple linear regression model developed in part (a), calculate the predicted repair time and residual for each of the 10 repairs in the data. Sort the data in ascending order by value of the residual. Do you see any pattern in the residuals for the two types of repair? Do you see any pattern in the residuals for the two repairpersons? Do these results suggest any potential modifications to your simple linear regression model? Now create a scatter chart with months since last service on the x-axis and repair time in hours on the y-axis for which the points representing electrical and mechanical repairs are shown in different shapes and/or colors. Create a similar scatter chart of months since last service and repair time in hours for which the points representing repairs by Bob Jones and Donna Newton are shown in different shapes and/or colors. Do these charts and the results of your residual analysis suggest the same potential modifications to your simple linear regression model?

c. Create a new dummy variable that is equal to zero if the type of repair is mechanical and one if the type of repair is electrical. Develop the multiple regression equation to predict repair time, given the number of months since the last maintenance service and the type of repair. What are the interpretations of the estimated regression parameters? What does the coefficient of determination tell you about this model?

d. Create a new dummy variable that is equal to zero if the repairperson is Bob Jones and one if the repairperson is Donna Newton. Develop the multiple regression equation to predict repair time, given the number of months since the last maintenance service and the repairperson. What are the interpretations of the estimated regression parameters? What does the coefficient of determination tell you about this model?

e. Develop the multiple regression equation to predict repair time, given the number of months since the last maintenance service, the type of repair, and the repairperson. What are the interpretations of the estimated regression parameters? What does the coefficient of determination tell you about this model?

f. Which of these models would you use? Why?

14. **Delays in Company Audits.** A study investigated the relationship between audit delay (the length of time from a company's fiscal year-end to the date of the auditor's report) and variables that describe the client and the auditor. Some of the independent variables that were included in this study follow:

Industry   A dummy variable coded 1 if the firm was an industrial company or 0 if the firm was a bank, savings and loan, or insurance company.

Public   A dummy variable coded 1 if the company was traded on an organized
              exchange or over the counter; otherwise coded 0.
Quality   A measure of overall quality of internal controls, as judged by the auditor,
              on a 5-point scale ranging from "virtually none" (1) to "excellent" (5).
Finished   A measure ranging from 1 to 4, as judged by the auditor, where 1 indi-
              cates "all work performed subsequent to year-end" and 4 indicates "most
              work performed prior to year-end."

A sample of 40 companies provided the following data:

Delay (Days)	Industry	Public	Quality	Finished
62	0	0	3	1
45	0	1	3	3
54	0	0	2	2
71	0	1	1	2
91	0	0	1	1
62	0	0	4	4
61	0	0	3	2
69	0	1	5	2
80	0	0	1	1
52	0	0	5	3
47	0	0	3	2
65	0	1	2	3
60	0	0	1	3
81	1	0	1	2
73	1	0	2	2
89	1	0	2	1
71	1	0	5	4
76	1	0	2	2
68	1	0	1	2
68	1	0	5	2
86	1	0	2	2
76	1	1	3	1
67	1	0	2	3
57	1	0	4	2
55	1	1	3	2
54	0	0	5	2
69	1	0	3	3
82	1	0	5	1
94	1	0	1	1
74	1	1	5	2
75	1	0	4	3
69	1	0	2	2
71	1	0	4	4
79	1	0	5	2
80	1	0	1	4
91	1	0	4	1
92	1	0	1	4
46	1	1	4	3
72	1	0	5	2
85	1	0	5	1

DATA *file*

Audit

  a. Develop the estimated regression equation using all of the independent variables included in the data.

  b. How much of the variation in the sample values of delay does this estimated regression equation explain? What other independent variables could you include in this regression model to improve the fit?

  c. Test the relationship between each independent variable and the dependent variable at the 0.05 level of significance, and interpret the relationship between each of the independent variables and the dependent variable.

  d. On the basis of your observations about the relationships between the dependent variable Delay and the independent variables Quality and Finished, suggest an alternative model for the regression equation developed in part (a) to explain as much of the variability in Delay as possible.

15. **Estimating Fuel Mileage by Car Size.** The U.S. Department of Energy's *Fuel Economy Guide* provides fuel efficiency data for cars and trucks. A portion of the data for 311 compact, midsized, and large cars follows. The Class column identifies the size of the car: Compact, Midsize, or Large. The Displacement column shows the engine's displacement in liters. The FuelType column shows whether the car uses premium (P) or regular (R) fuel, and the HwyMPG column shows the fuel efficiency rating for highway driving in terms of miles per gallon. The complete data set is contained in the file *FuelData*:

DATA_file_
FuelData

Car	Class	Displacement	FuelType	HwyMPG
1	Compact	3.1	P	25
2	Compact	3.1	P	25
3	Compact	3.0	P	25
⋮	⋮	⋮	⋮	⋮
161	Midsize	2.4	R	30
162	Midsize	2.0	P	29
⋮	⋮	⋮	⋮	⋮
310	Large	3.0	R	25

  a. Develop an estimated regression equation that can be used to predict the fuel efficiency for highway driving given the engine's displacement. Test for significance using the 0.05 level of significance. How much of the variation in the sample values of HwyMPG does this estimated regression equation explain?

  b. Create a scatter chart with HwyMPG on the *y*-axis and displacement on the *x*-axis for which the points representing compact, midsize, and large automobiles are shown in different shapes and/or colors. What does this chart suggest about the relationship between the class of automobile (compact, midsize, and large) and HwyMPG?

  c. Now consider the addition of the dummy variables ClassMidsize and ClassLarge to the simple linear regression model in part (a). The value of ClassMidsize is 1 if the car is a midsize car and 0 otherwise; the value of ClassLarge is 1 if the car is a large car and 0 otherwise. Thus, for a compact car, the value of ClassMidsize and the value of ClassLarge are both 0. Develop the estimated regression equation that can be used to predict the fuel efficiency for highway driving, given the engine's displacement and the dummy variables ClassMidsize and ClassLarge. How much of the variation in the sample values of HwyMPG is explained by this estimated regression equation?

  d. Use significance level of 0.05 to determine whether the dummy variables added to the model in part (c) are significant.

e. Consider the addition of the dummy variable FuelPremium, where the value of FuelPremium is 1 if the car uses premium fuel and 0 if the car uses regular fuel. Develop the estimated regression equation that can be used to predict the fuel efficiency for highway driving given the engine's displacement, the dummy variables ClassMidsize and ClassLarge, and the dummy variable FuelPremium. How much of the variation in the sample values of HwyMPG does this estimated regression equation explain?

f. For the estimated regression equation developed in part (e), test for the significance of the relationship between each of the independent variables and the dependent variable using the 0.05 level of significance for each test.

g. An automobile manufacturer is designing a new compact model with a displacement of 2.9 liters with the objective of creating a model that will achieve at least 25 estimated highway MPG. The manufacturer must now decide if the car can be designed to use premium fuel and still achieve the objective of 25 MPG on the highway. Use the model developed in part (c) to recommend a decision to this manufacturer.

TrafficFlow

16. **Vehicle Speed and Traffic Flow.** A highway department is studying the relationship between traffic flow and speed during rush hour on Highway 193. The data in the file *TrafficFlow* were collected on Highway 193 during 100 recent rush hours.

a. Develop a scatter chart for these data. What does the scatter chart indicate about the relationship between vehicle speed and traffic flow?

b. Develop an estimated simple linear regression equation for the data. How much variation in the sample values of traffic flow is explained by this regression model? Use a 0.05 level of significance to test the relationship between vehicle speed and traffic flow. What is the interpretation of this relationship?

c. Develop an estimated quadratic regression equation for the data. How much variation in the sample values of traffic flow is explained by this regression model? Test the relationship between each of the independent variables and the dependent variable at a 0.05 level of significance. How would you interpret this model? Is this model superior to the model you developed in part (b)?

d. As an alternative to fitting a second-order model, fit a model using a piecewise linear regression with a single knot. What value of vehicle speed appears to be a good point for the placement of the knot? Does the estimated piecewise linear regression provide a better fit than the estimated quadratic regression developed in part (c)? Explain.

e. Separate the data into two sets such that one data set contains the observations of vehicle speed less than the value of the knot from part (d) and the other data set contains the observations of vehicle speed greater than or equal to the value of the knot from part (d). Then fit a simple linear regression equation to each data set. How does this pair of regression equations compare to the single piecewise linear regression with the single knot from part (d)? In particular, compare predicted values of traffic flow for values of the speed slightly above and slightly below the knot value from part (d).

f. What other independent variables could you include in your regression model to explain more variation in traffic flow?

CorporateBonds

17. **Years to Maturity and Bond Yield.** A sample containing years to maturity and (percent) yield for 40 corporate bonds is contained in the file *CorporateBonds* (*Barron's*, April 2, 2012).

a. Develop a scatter chart of the data using years to maturity as the independent variable. Does a simple linear regression model appear to be appropriate?

b. Develop an estimated quadratic regression equation with years to maturity and squared values of years to maturity as the independent variables. How much variation in the sample values of yield is explained by this regression model? Test the relationship between each of the independent variables and the dependent variable at a 0.05 level of significance. How would you interpret this model?

c. Create a plot of the linear and quadratic regression lines overlaid on the scatter chart of years to maturity and yield. Does this help you better understand the difference in how the quadratic regression model and a simple linear regression model fit the sample data? Which model does this chart suggest provides a superior fit to the sample data?

d. What other independent variables could you include in your regression model to explain more variation in yield?

18. **Cost of Renting or Purchasing a Home.** In 2011, home prices and mortgage rates fell so far that in a number of cities the monthly cost of owning a home was less expensive than renting. The following data show the average asking rent for 10 markets and the monthly mortgage on the median priced home (including taxes and insurance) for

RentMortgage

City	Rent ($)	Mortgage ($)
Atlanta	840	539
Chicago	1,062	1,002
Detroit	823	626
Jacksonville	779	711
Las Vegas	796	655
Miami	1,071	977
Minneapolis	953	776
Orlando	851	695
Phoenix	762	651
St. Louis	723	654

10 cities where the average monthly mortgage payment was less than the average asking rent (*The Wall Street Journal*, November 26–27, 2011).

a. Develop a scatter chart for these data, treating the average asking rent as the independent variable. Does a simple linear regression model appear to be appropriate?

b. Use a simple linear regression model to develop an estimated regression equation to predict the monthly mortgage on the median-priced home given the average asking rent. Construct a plot of the residuals against the independent variable rent. Based on this residual plot, does a simple linear regression model appear to be appropriate?

c. Using a quadratic regression model, develop an estimated regression equation to predict the monthly mortgage on the median-priced home, given the average asking rent.

d. Do you prefer the estimated regression equation developed in part (a) or part (c)? Create a plot of the linear and quadratic regression lines overlaid on the scatter chart of the monthly mortgage on the median-priced home and the average asking rent to help you assess the two regression equations. Explain your conclusions.

19. **Factors in Stroke Risk.** A recent 10-year study conducted by a research team at the Great Falls Medical School was conducted to assess how age, systolic blood pressure, and smoking relate to the risk of strokes. Assume that the following data are from a portion of this study. Risk is interpreted as the probability (times 100) that the patient will have a stroke over the next 10-year period. For the smoking variable, define a dummy variable with 1 indicating a smoker and 0 indicating a nonsmoker.

Risk	Age	Systolic Blood Pressure	Smoker
12	57	152	NO
24	67	163	NO
13	58	155	NO
56	86	177	YES
28	59	196	NO

Risk	Age	Systolic Blood Pressure	Smoker
51	76	189	YES
18	56	155	YES
31	78	120	NO
37	80	135	YES
15	78	98	NO
22	71	152	NO
36	70	173	YES
15	67	135	YES
48	77	209	YES
15	60	199	NO
36	82	119	YES
8	66	166	NO
34	80	125	YES
3	62	117	NO
37	59	207	YES

DATA*file*

Stroke

a. Develop an estimated multiple regression equation that relates risk of a stroke to the person's age, systolic blood pressure, and whether the person is a smoker.
b. Is smoking a significant factor in the risk of a stroke? Explain. Use a 0.05 level of significance.
c. What is the probability of a stroke over the next 10 years for Art Speen, a 68-year-old smoker who has a systolic blood pressure of 175? What action might the physician recommend for this patient?
d. An insurance company will only sell its Select policy to people for whom the probability of a stroke in the next 10 years is less than 0.01. If a smoker with a systolic blood pressure of 230 applies for a Select policy, under what condition will the company sell him the policy if it adheres to this standard?
e. What other factors could be included in the model as independent variables?

DATA*file*

RugglesCollege

20. **GPA and SAT Scores.** The Scholastic Aptitude Test (or SAT) is a standardized college entrance test that is used by colleges and universities as a means for making admission decisions. The critical reading and mathematics components of the SAT are reported on a scale from 200 to 800. Several universities believe these scores are strong predictors of an incoming student's potential success, and they use these scores as important inputs when making admission decisions on potential freshman. The file *RugglesCollege* contains freshman year GPA and the critical reading and mathematics SAT scores for a random sample of 200 students who recently completed their freshman year at Ruggles College.
a. Develop an estimated multiple regression equation that includes critical reading and mathematics SAT scores as independent variables. How much variation in freshman GPA is explained by this model? Test whether each of the regression parameters β_0, β_1, and β_2 is equal to zero at a 0.05 level of significance. What are the correct interpretations of the estimated regression parameters? Are these interpretations reasonable?
b. Using the multiple linear regression model you developed in part (a), what is the predicted freshman GPA of Bobby Engle, a student who has been admitted to Ruggles College with a 660 SAT score on critical reading and at a 630 SAT score on mathematics?
c. The Ruggles College Director of Admissions believes that the relationship between a student's scores on the critical reading component of the SAT and the student's freshman GPA varies with the student's score on the mathematics component of the SAT. Develop an estimated multiple regression equation that includes critical

reading and mathematics SAT scores and their interaction as independent variables. How much variation in freshman GPA is explained by this model? Test whether each of the regression parameters β_0, β_1, β_2, and β_3 is equal to zero at a 0.05 level of significance. What are the correct interpretations of the estimated regression parameters? Do these results support the conjecture made by the Ruggles College Director of Admissions?

d. Do you prefer the estimated regression model developed in part (a) or part (c)? Explain.

e. What other factors could be included in the model as independent variables?

21. **Consumer Credit Card Debt.** Consider again the example introduced in Section 7.5 of a credit card company that has a database of information provided by its customers when they apply for credit cards. An analyst has created a multiple regression model for which the dependent variable in the model is credit card charges accrued by a customer in the data set over the past year (y), and the independent variables are the customer's annual household income (x_1), number of members of the household (x_2), and number of years of post–high school education (x_3). Figure 7.23 provides Excel output for a multiple regression model estimated using a data set the company created.

DATAfile

ExtendedLargeCredit

a. Estimate the corresponding simple linear regression with the customer's annual household income as the independent variable and credit card charges accrued by a customer over the past year as the dependent variable. Interpret the estimated relationship between the customer's annual household income and credit card charges accrued over the past year. How much variation in credit card charges accrued by a customer over the past year is explained by this simple linear regression model?

b. Estimate the corresponding simple linear regression with the number of members in the customer's household as the independent variable and credit card charges accrued by a customer over the past year as the dependent variable. Interpret the estimated relationship between the number of members in the customer's household and credit card charges accrued over the past year. How much variation in credit card charges accrued by a customer over the past year is explained by this simple linear regression model?

c. Estimate the corresponding simple linear regression with the customer's number of years of post–high school education as the independent variable and credit card charges accrued by a customer over the past year as the dependent variable. Interpret the estimated relationship between the customer's number of years of post–high school education and credit card charges accrued over the past year. How much variation in credit card charges accrued by a customer over the past year is explained by this simple linear regression model?

d. Recall the multiple regression in Figure 7.23 with credit card charges accrued by a customer over the past year as the dependent variable and customer's annual house–hold income (x_1), number of members of the household (x_2), and number of years of post–high school education (x_3) as the independent variables. Do the estimated slopes differ substantially from the corresponding slopes that were estimated using simple linear regression in parts (a), (b), and (c)? What does this tell you about multicollinearity in the multiple regression model in Figure 7.23?

e. Add the coefficients of determination for the simple linear regression in parts (a), (b), and (c), and compare the result to the coefficient of determination for the multiple regression model in Figure 7.23. What does this tell you about multicollinearity in the multiple regression model in Figure 7.23?

f. Add age, a dummy variable for sex, and a dummy variable for whether a customer has exceeded his or her credit limit in the past 12 months as independent variables to the multiple regression model in Figure 7.23. Code the dummy variable for sex as 1 if the customer is female and 0 if male, and code the dummy variable for whether a customer has exceeded his or her credit limit in the past 12 months as 1 if the customer has exceeded his or her credit limit in the past 12 months and 0 otherwise. Do these variables substantially improve the fit of your model?

CASE PROBLEM 1: ALUMNI GIVING

Alumni donations are an important source of revenue for colleges and universities. If administrators could determine the factors that could lead to increases in the percentage of alumni who make a donation, they might be able to implement policies that could lead to increased revenues. Research shows that students who are more satisfied with their contact with teachers are more likely to graduate. As a result, one might suspect that smaller class sizes and lower student/faculty ratios might lead to a higher percentage of satisfied graduates, which in turn might lead to increases in the percentage of alumni who make a donation. The following table shows data for 48 national universities. The Graduation Rate column is the percentage of students who initially enrolled at the university and graduated. The % of Classes Under 20 column shows the percentages of classes with fewer than 20 students that are offered. The Student/Faculty Ratio column is the number of students enrolled divided by the total number of faculty. Finally, the Alumni Giving Rate column is the percentage of alumni who made a donation to the university.

DATAfile

AlumniGiving

	State	Graduation Rate	% of Classes Under 20	Student/ Faculty Ratio	Alumni Giving Rate
Boston College	MA	85	39	13	25
Brandeis University	MA	79	68	8	33
Brown University	RI	93	60	8	40
California Institute of Technology	CA	85	65	3	46
Carnegie Mellon University	PA	75	67	10	28
Case Western Reserve Univ.	OH	72	52	8	31
College of William and Mary	VA	89	45	12	27
Columbia University	NY	90	69	7	31
Cornell University	NY	91	72	13	35
Dartmouth College	NH	94	61	10	53
Duke University	NC	92	68	8	45
Emory University	GA	84	65	7	37
Georgetown University	DC	91	54	10	29
Harvard University	MA	97	73	8	46
Johns Hopkins University	MD	89	64	9	27
Lehigh University	PA	81	55	11	40
Massachusetts Institute of Technology	MA	92	65	6	44
New York University	NY	72	63	13	13
Northwestern University	IL	90	66	8	30
Pennsylvania State Univ.	PA	80	32	19	21
Princeton University	NJ	95	68	5	67
Rice University	TX	92	62	8	40
Stanford University	CA	92	69	7	34
Tufts University	MA	87	67	9	29
Tulane University	LA	72	56	12	17
University of California–Berkeley	CA	83	58	17	18
University of California–Davis	CA	74	32	19	7

	State	Graduation Rate	% of Classes Under 20	Student/ Faculty Ratio	Alumni Giving Rate
University of California–Irvine	CA	74	42	20	9
University of California– Los Angeles	CA	78	41	18	13
University of California–San Diego	CA	80	48	19	8
University of California– Santa Barbara	CA	70	45	20	12
University of Chicago	IL	84	65	4	36
University of Florida	FL	67	31	23	19
University of Illinois–Urbana Champaign	IL	77	29	15	23
University of Michigan–Ann Arbor	MI	83	51	15	13
University of North Caro- lina–Chapel Hill	NC	82	40	16	26
University of Notre Dame	IN	94	53	13	49
University of Pennsylvania	PA	90	65	7	41
University of Rochester	NY	76	63	10	23
University of Southern California	CA	70	53	13	22
University of Texas–Austin	TX	66	39	21	13
University of Virginia	VA	92	44	13	28
University of Washington	WA	70	37	12	12
University of Wisconsin–Madison	WI	73	37	13	13
Vanderbilt University	TN	82	68	9	31
Wake Forest University	NC	82	59	11	38
Washington University–St. Louis	MO	86	73	7	33
Yale University	CT	94	77	7	50

Managerial Report

1. Use methods of descriptive statistics to summarize the data.
2. Develop an estimated simple linear regression model that can be used to predict the alumni giving rate, given the graduation rate. Discuss your findings.
3. Develop an estimated multiple linear regression model that could be used to predict the alumni giving rate using Graduation Rate, % of Classes Under 20, and Student/ Faculty Ratio as independent variables. Discuss your findings.
4. Based on the results in parts (2) and (3), do you believe another regression model may be more appropriate? Estimate this model, and discuss your results.
5. What conclusions and recommendations can you derive from your analysis? What universities are achieving a substantially higher alumni giving rate than would be expected, given their Graduation Rate, % of Classes Under 20, and Student/Faculty Ratio? What universities are achieving a substantially lower alumni giving rate than would be expected, given their Graduation Rate, % of Classes Under 20, and Student/ Faculty Ratio? What other independent variables could be included in the model?

CASE PROBLEM 2: CONSUMER RESEARCH, INC.

Consumer Research, Inc., is an independent agency that conducts research on consumer attitudes and behaviors for a variety of firms. In one study, a client asked for an investigation of consumer characteristics that can be used to predict the amount charged by credit card users. Data were collected on annual income, household size, and annual credit card charges for a sample of 50 consumers. The following data are contained in the file *Consumer*.

DATA *file*

Consumer

Income ($1000s)	Household Size	Amount Charged ($)	Income ($1000s)	Household Size	Amount Charged ($)
54	3	4016	54	6	5573
30	2	3159	30	1	2583
32	4	5100	48	2	3866
50	5	4742	34	5	3586
31	2	1864	67	4	5037
55	2	4070	50	2	3605
37	1	2731	67	5	5345
40	2	3348	55	6	5370
66	4	4764	52	2	3890
51	3	4110	62	3	4705
25	3	4208	64	2	4157
48	4	4219	22	3	3579
27	1	2477	29	4	3890
33	2	2514	39	2	2972
65	3	4214	35	1	3121
63	4	4965	39	4	4183
42	6	4412	54	3	3730
21	2	2448	23	6	4127
44	1	2995	27	2	2921
37	5	4171	26	7	4603
62	6	5678	61	2	4273
21	3	3623	30	2	3067
55	7	5301	22	4	3074
42	2	3020	46	5	4820
41	7	4828	66	4	5149

Source: Consumer Research, Inc. (https://www.bbb.org/us/ny/rochester/profile/secret-shopper/consumer-research-inc-0041-45625697)

Managerial Report

1. Use methods of descriptive statistics to summarize the data. Comment on the findings.
2. Develop estimated regression equations, first using annual income as the independent variable and then using household size as the independent variable. Which variable is the better predictor of annual credit card charges? Discuss your findings.
3. Develop an estimated regression equation with annual income and household size as the independent variables. Discuss your findings.
4. What is the predicted annual credit card charge for a three-person household with an annual income of $40,000?
5. Discuss the need for other independent variables that could be added to the model. What additional variables might be helpful?

CASE PROBLEM 3: PREDICTING WINNINGS FOR NASCAR DRIVERS

Matt Kenseth won the 2012 Daytona 500, the most important race of the NASCAR season. His win was no surprise because for the 2011 season he finished fourth in the point standings with 2330 points, behind Tony Stewart (2403 points), Carl Edwards (2403 points), and Kevin Harvick (2345 points). In 2011 he earned $6,183,580 by winning three Poles (fastest driver in qualifying), winning three races, finishing in the top five 12 times, and finishing in the top ten 20 times. NASCAR's point system in 2011 allocated 43 points to the driver who finished first, 42 points to the driver who finished second, and so on down to 1 point for the driver who finished in the 43rd position. In addition any driver who led a lap received 1 bonus point, the driver who led the most laps received an additional bonus point, and the race winner was awarded 3 bonus points. But, the maximum number of points a driver could earn in any race was 48. The following table shows data for the 2011 season for the top 35 drivers (NASCAR website). These data are contained in the file *NASCAR*.

Managerial Report

1. Suppose you wanted to predict Winnings ($) using only the number of poles won (Poles), the number of wins (Wins), the number of top five finishes (Top 5), or the number of top ten finishes (Top 10). Which of these four variables provides the best single predictor of winnings?
2. Develop an estimated regression equation that can be used to predict Winnings ($) given the number of poles won (Poles), the number of wins (Wins), the number of top five finishes (Top 5), and the number of top ten finishes (Top 10). Test for individual significance and discuss your findings and conclusions.
3. Create two new independent variables: Top 2–5 and Top 6–10. Top 2–5 represents the number of times the driver finished between second and fifth place and Top 6–10

DATA *file*

NASCAR

Driver	Points	Poles	Wins	Top 5	Top 10	Winnings ($)
Tony Stewart	2403	1	5	9	19	6,529,870
Carl Edwards	2403	3	1	19	26	8,485,990
Kevin Harvick	2345	0	4	9	19	6,197,140
Matt Kenseth	2330	3	3	12	20	6,183,580
Brad Keselowski	2319	1	3	10	14	5,087,740
Jimmie Johnson	2304	0	2	14	21	6,296,360
Dale Earnhardt Jr.	2290	1	0	4	12	4,163,690
Jeff Gordon	2287	1	3	13	18	5,912,830
Denny Hamlin	2284	0	1	5	14	5,401,190
Ryan Newman	2284	3	1	9	17	5,303,020
Kurt Busch	2262	3	2	8	16	5,936,470
Kyle Busch	2246	1	4	14	18	6,161,020
Clint Bowyer	1047	0	1	4	16	5,633,950
Kasey Kahne	1041	2	1	8	15	4,775,160
A. J. Allmendinger	1013	0	0	1	10	4,825,560
Greg Biffle	997	3	0	3	10	4,318,050
Paul Menard	947	0	1	4	8	3,853,690
Martin Truex Jr.	937	1	0	3	12	3,955,560
Marcos Ambrose	936	0	1	5	12	4,750,390
Jeff Burton	935	0	0	2	5	3,807,780
Juan Montoya	932	2	0	2	8	5,020,780
Mark Martin	930	2	0	2	10	3,830,910
David Ragan	906	2	1	4	8	4,203,660

Driver	Points	Poles	Wins	Top 5	Top 10	Winnings ($)
Joey Logano	902	2	0	4	6	3,856,010
Brian Vickers	846	0	0	3	7	4,301,880
Regan Smith	820	0	1	2	5	4,579,860
Jamie McMurray	795	1	0	2	4	4,794,770
David Reutimann	757	1	0	1	3	4,374,770
Bobby Labonte	670	0	0	1	2	4,505,650
David Gilliland	572	0	0	1	2	3,878,390
Casey Mears	541	0	0	0	0	2,838,320
Dave Blaney	508	0	0	1	1	3,229,210
Andy Lally	398	0	0	0	0	2,868,220
Robby Gordon	268	0	0	0	0	2,271,890
J. J. Yeley	192	0	0	0	0	2,559,500

Source: NASCAR website, February 28, 2011. (https://www.nascar.com/)

represents the number of times the driver finished between sixth and tenth place. Develop an estimated regression equation that can be used to predict Winnings ($) using
Poles, Wins, Top 2–5, and Top 6–10. Test for individual significance and discuss your
findings and conclusions.

4. Based upon the results of your analysis, what estimated regression equation would you
recommend using to predict Winnings ($)? Provide an interpretation of the estimated
regression coefficients for this equation.

Chapter 8

Time Series Analysis and Forecasting

CONTENTS

ANALYTICS IN ACTION

ACCO Brands*

ACCO Brands Corporation is one of the world's largest suppliers of branded office and consumer products and print finishing solutions. The company's brands include AT-A-GLANCE®, Day-Timer®, Five Star®, GBC®, Hilroy®, Kensington®, Marbig®, Mead®, NOBO, Quartet®, Rexel, Swingline®, Tilibra®, Wilson Jones®, and many others.

Because it produces and markets a wide array of products with myriad demand characteristics, ACCO Brands relies heavily on sales forecasts in planning its manufacturing, distribution, and marketing activities. By viewing its relationship in terms of a supply chain, ACCO Brands and its customers (which are generally retail chains) establish close collaborative relationships and consider each other to be valued partners. As a result, ACCO Brands' customers share valuable information and data that serve as inputs into ACCO Brands' forecasting process.

In her role as a forecasting manager for ACCO Brands, Vanessa Baker appreciates the importance of this additional information. "We do separate forecasts of demand for each major customer," said Baker, "and we generally use twenty-four to thirty-six months of history to generate monthly forecasts twelve to eighteen months into the future. While trends are important, several of our major product lines, including school, planning and organizing, and decorative calendars, are heavily seasonal, and seasonal sales make up the bulk of our annual volume."

Daniel Marks, one of several account-level strategic forecast managers for ACCO Brands, adds:

The supply chain process includes the total lead time from identifying opportunities to making or procuring the product to getting the product on the shelves to align with the forecasted demand; this can potentially take several months, so the accuracy of our forecasts is critical throughout each step of the supply chain. Adding to this challenge is the risk of obsolescence. We sell many dated items, such as planners and calendars, which have a natural, built-in obsolescence. In addition, many of our products feature designs that are fashion-conscious or contain pop culture images, and these products can also become obsolete very quickly as tastes and popularity change. An overly optimistic forecast for these products can be very costly, but an overly pessimistic forecast can result in lost sales potential and give our competitors an opportunity to take market share from us.

In addition to trends, seasonal components, and cyclical patterns, there are several other factors that Baker and Marks must consider. Baker notes, "We have to adjust our forecasts for upcoming promotions by our customers." Marks agrees and adds:

We also have to go beyond just forecasting consumer demand; we must consider the retailer's specific needs in our order forecasts, such as what type of display will be used and how many units of a product must be on display to satisfy their presentation requirements. Current inventory is another factor—if a customer is carrying either too much or too little inventory, that will affect their future orders, and we need to reflect that in our forecasts. Will the product have a short life because it is tied to a cultural fad? What are the retailer's marketing and markdown strategies? Our knowledge of the environments in which our supply chain partners are competing helps us to forecast demand more accurately, and that reduces waste and makes our customers, as well as ACCO Brands, far more profitable.

---

*The authors are indebted to Vanessa Baker and Daniel Marks of ACCO Brands for providing input for this Analytics in Action.

The purpose of this chapter is to provide an introduction to time series analysis and forecasting. Suppose we are asked to provide quarterly **forecasts** of sales for one of our company's products over the upcoming one-year period. Production schedules, raw materials purchasing, inventory policies, marketing plans, and cash flows will all be affected by the quarterly forecasts we provide. Consequently, poor forecasts may result in poor planning and increased costs for the company. How should we go about providing the quarterly sales forecasts? Good judgment, intuition, and an awareness of the state of the economy may give us a rough idea, or feeling, of what is likely to happen in the future, but converting that feeling into a number that can be used as next year's sales forecast is challenging.

A forecast is simply a prediction of what will happen in the future. Managers must accept that regardless of the technique used, they will not be able to develop perfect forecasts.

Forecasting methods can be classified as qualitative or quantitative. Qualitative methods generally involve the use of expert judgment to develop forecasts. Such methods are appropriate when historical data on the variable being forecast are either unavailable or not applicable. Quantitative forecasting methods can be used when (1) past information about the variable being forecast is available, (2) the information can be quantified, and (3) it is reasonable to assume that past is prologue (i.e., that the pattern of the past will continue into the future). We will focus exclusively on quantitative forecasting methods in this chapter.

If the historical data are restricted to past values of the variable to be forecast, the forecasting procedure is called a time series method and the historical data are referred to as *time series*. The objective of time series analysis is to uncover a pattern in the time series and then extrapolate the pattern to forecast the future; the forecast is based solely on past values of the variable and/or on past forecast errors.

Causal or exploratory forecasting methods are based on the assumption that the variable we are forecasting has a cause-and-effect relationship with one or more other variables. These methods help explain how the value of one variable impacts the value of another. For instance, the sales volume for many products is influenced by advertising expenditures, so regression analysis may be used to develop an equation showing how these two variables are related. Then, once the advertising budget is set for the next period, we could substitute this value into the equation to develop a prediction or forecast of the sales volume for that period. Note that if a time series method was used to develop the forecast, advertising expenditures would not be considered; that is, a time series method would base the forecast solely on past sales.

Modern data-collection technologies have enabled individuals, businesses, and government agencies to collect vast amounts of data that may be used for causal forecasting. For example, supermarket scanners allow retailers to collect point-of-sale data that can then be used to help aid in planning sales, coupon targeting, and other marketing and planning efforts. These data can help answer important questions like, "Which products tend to be purchased together?" One of the techniques used to answer questions using such data is regression analysis. In this chapter we discuss the use of regression analysis as a causal forecasting method.

In this chapter, we discuss the various kinds of time series that a forecaster might be faced with in practice. These include a constant or horizontal pattern, a trend, a seasonal pattern, both a trend and a seasonal pattern, and a cyclical pattern. To build a quantitative forecasting model, it is also necessary to have a measurement of forecast accuracy. Different measurements of forecast accuracy, as well as their respective advantages and disadvantages, are discussed. For a horizontal or constant time series, we develop the classical moving average, weighted moving average, and exponential smoothing models. Many time series have a trend, and taking this trend into account is important; we provide regression models for finding the best model parameters when a linear trend is present, when the data show a seasonal pattern, or when the variable to be predicted has a causal relationship with other variables. Finally, we discuss considerations to be made when determining the best forecasting model to use.

NOTES + COMMENTS

Virtually all large companies today rely on enterprise resource planning (ERP) software to aid in their planning and operations. These software systems help the business run smoothly by collecting and efficiently storing company data, enabling it to be shared company-wide for planning at all levels: strategically, tactically, and operationally. Most ERP systems include a forecasting module to help plan for the future. SAP, one of the most widely used ERP systems, includes a forecasting component. This module allows the user to select from a number of forecasting techniques and/or have the system find a "best" model. The various forecasting methods and ways to measure the quality of a forecasting model discussed in this chapter are routinely available in software that supports forecasting.

8.1 Time Series Patterns

We limit our discussion to time series for which the values of the series are recorded at equal intervals. Cases in which the observations are made at unequal intervals are beyond the scope of this text.

In Chapter 2 we discussed line charts, which are often used to graph time series.

A **time series** is a sequence of observations on a variable measured at successive points in time or over successive periods of time. The measurements may be taken every hour, day, week, month, year, or at any other regular interval. The pattern of the data is an important factor in understanding how the time series has behaved in the past. If such behavior can be expected to continue in the future, we can use it to guide us in selecting an appropriate forecasting method.

To identify the underlying pattern in the data, a useful first step is to construct a *time series plot*, which is a graphical presentation of the relationship between time and the time series variable; time is represented on the horizontal axis and values of the time series variable are shown on the vertical axis. Let us first review some of the common types of data patterns that can be identified in a time series plot.

Horizontal Pattern

DATA *file*
Gasoline

A horizontal pattern exists when the data fluctuate randomly around a constant mean over time. To illustrate a time series with a horizontal pattern, consider the 12 weeks of data in Table 8.1. These data show the number of gallons of gasoline (in 1,000s) sold by a gasoline distributor in Bennington, Vermont, over the past 12 weeks. The average value, or mean, for this time series is 19.25 or 19,250 gallons per week. Figure 8.1 shows a time series plot for these data. Note how the data fluctuate around the sample mean of 19,250 gallons. Although random variability is present, we would say that these data follow a horizontal pattern.

The term **stationary time series** is used to denote a time series whose statistical properties are independent of time. In particular this means that:

1. The process generating the data has a constant mean.
2. The variability of the time series is constant over time.

For a formal definition of stationarity, see K. Ord, R. Fildes, and N. Kourentzes, Principles of Business Forecasting, 2nd ed. (Wessex, Inc., 2017).

A time series plot for a stationary time series will always exhibit a horizontal pattern with random fluctuations. However, simply observing a horizontal pattern is not sufficient evidence to conclude that the time series is stationary. More advanced texts on forecasting discuss procedures for determining whether a time series is stationary and provide methods for transforming a nonstationary time series into a stationary series.

TABLE 8.1	Gasoline Sales Time Series
Week	**Sales (1,000s of gallons)**
1	17
2	21
3	19
4	23
5	18
6	16
7	20
8	18
9	22
10	20
11	15
12	22

FIGURE 8.1	Gasoline Sales Time Series Plot

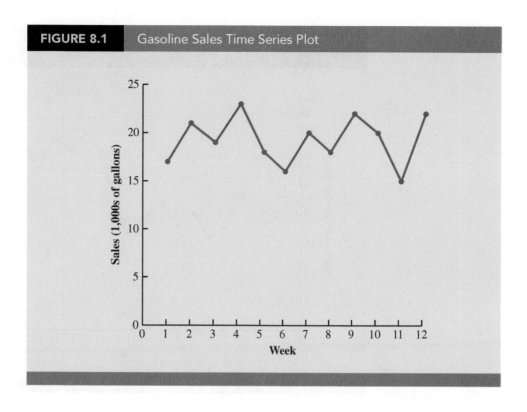

Changes in business conditions often result in a time series with a horizontal pattern that shifts to a new level at some point in time. For instance, suppose the gasoline distributor signs a contract with the Vermont State Police to provide gasoline for state police cars located in southern Vermont beginning in week 13. With this new contract, the distributor naturally expects to see a substantial increase in weekly sales starting in week 13. Table 8.2 shows the number of gallons of gasoline sold for the original time series and for the 10 weeks after signing the new contract. Figure 8.2 shows the corresponding time series plot. Note the increased level of the time series beginning in week 13. This change in the

DATA *file*

GasolineRevised

TABLE 8.2	Gasoline Sales Time Series After Obtaining the Contract with the Vermont State Police		
Week	Sales (1,000s of gallons)	Week	Sales (1,000s of gallons)
1	17	12	22
2	21	13	31
3	19	14	34
4	23	15	31
5	18	16	33
6	16	17	28
7	20	18	32
8	18	19	30
9	22	20	29
10	20	21	34
11	15	22	33

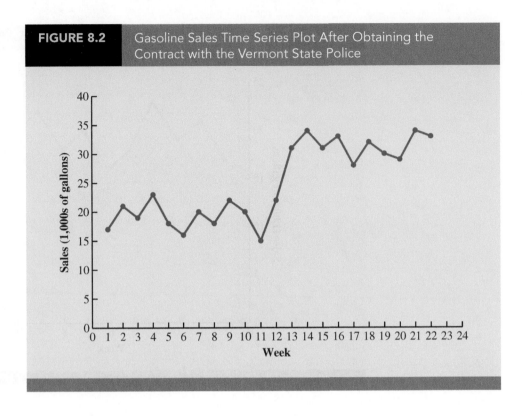

FIGURE 8.2   Gasoline Sales Time Series Plot After Obtaining the Contract with the Vermont State Police

level of the time series makes it more difficult to choose an appropriate forecasting method. Selecting a forecasting method that adapts well to changes in the level of a time series is an important consideration in many practical applications.

Trend Pattern

Although time series data generally exhibit random fluctuations, a time series may also show gradual shifts or movements to relatively higher or lower values over a longer period of time. If a time series plot exhibits this type of behavior, we say that a **trend** pattern exists. A trend is usually the result of long-term factors such as population increases or decreases, shifting demographic characteristics of the population, improving technology, changes in the competitive landscape, and/or changes in consumer preferences.

To illustrate a time series with a linear trend pattern, consider the time series of bicycle sales for a particular manufacturer over the past 10 years, as shown in Table 8.3 and Figure 8.3. Note that a total of 21,600 bicycles were sold in year 1, a total of 22,900 in year 2, and so on. In year 10, the most recent year, 31,400 bicycles were sold. Visual inspection of the time series plot shows some up-and-down movement over the past 10 years, but the time series seems also to have a systematically increasing, or upward, trend.

The trend for the bicycle sales time series appears to be linear and increasing over time, but sometimes a trend can be described better by other types of patterns. For instance, the data in Table 8.4 and the corresponding time series plot in Figure 8.4 show the sales revenue for a cholesterol drug since the company won FDA approval for the drug 10 years ago. The time series increases in a nonlinear fashion; that is, the rate of change of revenue does not increase by a constant amount from one year to the next. In fact, the revenue appears to be growing in an exponential fashion. Exponential relationships such as this are appropriate when the *percentage* change from one period to the next is relatively constant.

TABLE 8.3	Bicycle Sales Time Series
Year	**Sales (1,000s)**
1	21.6
2	22.9
3	25.5
4	21.9
5	23.9
6	27.5
7	31.5
8	29.7
9	28.6
10	31.4

DATA *file*

Bicycle

FIGURE 8.3 Bicycle Sales Time Series Plot

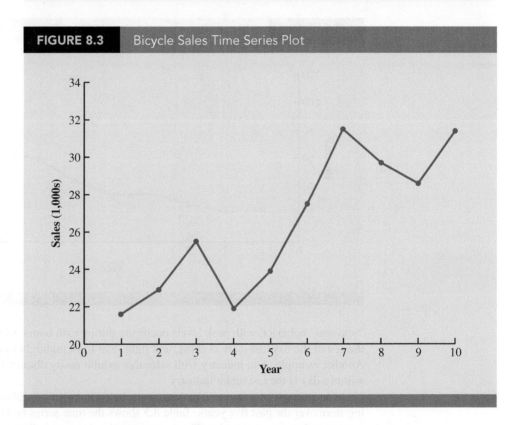

Seasonal Pattern

The trend of a time series can be identified by analyzing movements in historical data over multiple time periods. **Seasonal patterns** are recognized by observing recurring patterns over successive periods of time. For example, a retailer who sells bathing suits expects low sales activity in the fall and winter months, with peak sales in the spring and summer months to occur every year. Retailers who sell snow removal equipment and heavy clothing, however, expect the opposite yearly pattern. Not surprisingly, the pattern for a time series plot that exhibits a recurring pattern over a one-year period due to seasonal influences is called a seasonal pattern. Although we generally think of seasonal movement in a time series as occurring over one year, time series data can also exhibit seasonal patterns of less than one year in duration. For example, daily traffic volume shows within-the-day

TABLE 8.4	Cholesterol Drug Revenue Time Series
Year	**Revenue ($ Millions)**
1	23.1
2	21.3
3	27.4
4	34.6
5	33.8
6	43.2
7	59.5
8	64.4
9	74.2
10	99.3

DATA file

Cholesterol

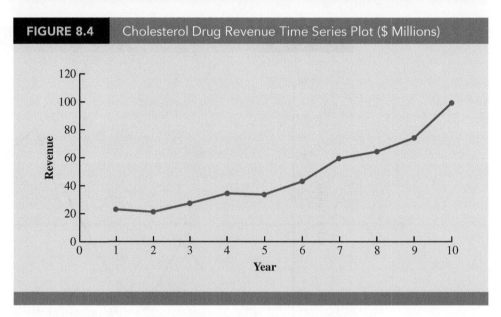

FIGURE 8.4   Cholesterol Drug Revenue Time Series Plot ($ Millions)

"seasonal" behavior, with peak levels occurring during rush hours, moderate flow during the rest of the day and early evening, and light flow from midnight to early morning. Another example of an industry with sales that exhibit easily discernible seasonal patterns within a day is the restaurant industry.

As an example of a seasonal pattern, consider the number of umbrellas sold at a clothing store over the past five years. Table 8.5 shows the time series and Figure 8.5 shows the corresponding time series plot. The time series plot does not indicate a long-term trend in sales. In fact, unless you look carefully at the data, you might conclude that the data follow a horizontal pattern with random fluctuation. However, closer inspection of the fluctuations in the time series plot reveals a systematic pattern in the data that occurs within each year. Specifically, the first and third quarters have moderate sales, the second quarter has the highest sales, and the fourth quarter has the lowest sales volume. Thus, we would conclude that a quarterly seasonal pattern is present.

Trend and Seasonal Pattern

Some time series include both a trend and a seasonal pattern. For instance, the data in Table 8.6 and the corresponding time series plot in Figure 8.6 show quarterly smartphone sales for a particular manufacturer over the past four years. Clearly an increasing trend is

TABLE 8.5	Umbrella Sales Time Series	
Year	Quarter	Sales
1	1	125
	2	153
	3	106
	4	88
2	1	118
	2	161
	3	133
	4	102
3	1	138
	2	144
	3	113
	4	80
4	1	109
	2	137
	3	125
	4	109
5	1	130
	2	165
	3	128
	4	96

DATA *file*

Umbrella

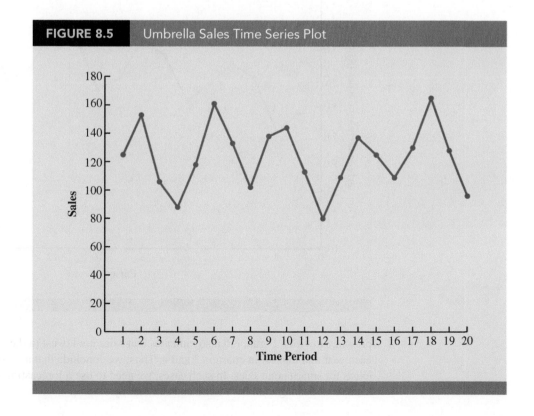

FIGURE 8.5   Umbrella Sales Time Series Plot

SmartPhoneSales

TABLE 8.6	Quarterly Smartphone Sales Time Series	
Year	**Quarter**	**Sales ($1,000s)**
1	1	4.8
	2	4.1
	3	6.0
	4	6.5
2	1	5.8
	2	5.2
	3	6.8
	4	7.4
3	1	6.0
	2	5.6
	3	7.5
	4	7.8
4	1	6.3
	2	5.9
	3	8.0
	4	8.4

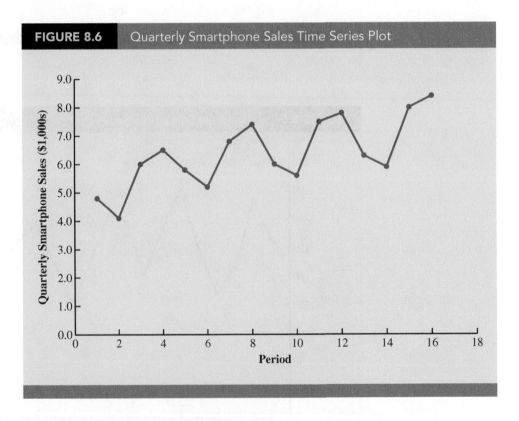

FIGURE 8.6   Quarterly Smartphone Sales Time Series Plot

present. However, Figure 8.6 also indicates that sales are lowest in the second quarter of each year and highest in quarters 3 and 4. Thus, we conclude that a seasonal pattern also exists for smartphone sales. In such cases, we need to use a forecasting method that is capable of dealing with both trend and seasonality.

Cyclical Pattern

A **cyclical pattern** exists if the time series plot shows an alternating sequence of points below and above the trendline that lasts for more than one year. Many economic time series exhibit cyclical behavior with regular runs of observations below and above the trendline. Often the cyclical component of a time series is due to multiyear business cycles. For example, periods of moderate inflation followed by periods of rapid inflation can lead to a time series that alternates below and above a generally increasing trendline (e.g., a time series of housing costs). Business cycles are extremely difficult, if not impossible, to forecast. As a result, cyclical effects are often combined with long-term trend effects and referred to as *trend-cycle effects*. In this chapter, we do not deal with cyclical effects that may be present in the time series.

Identifying Time Series Patterns

The underlying pattern in the time series is an important factor in selecting a forecasting method. Thus, a time series plot should be one of the first analytic tools employed when trying to determine which forecasting method to use. If we see a horizontal pattern, then we need to select a method appropriate for this type of pattern. Similarly, if we observe a trend in the data, then we need to use a forecasting method that is capable of handling the conjectured type of trend effectively. In the next section, we discuss methods for assessing forecast accuracy.

8.2 Forecast Accuracy

In this section, we begin by developing forecasts for the gasoline time series shown in Table 8.1 using the simplest of all the forecasting methods. We use the most recent week's sales volume as the forecast for the next week. For instance, the distributor sold 17 thousand gallons of gasoline in week 1; this value is used as the forecast for week 2. Next, we use 21, the actual value of sales in week 2, as the forecast for week 3, and so on. The forecasts obtained for the historical data using this method are shown in Table 8.7 in the Forecast column. Because of its simplicity, this method is often referred to as a **naïve forecasting method**.

TABLE 8.7	Computing Forecasts and Measures of Forecast Accuracy Using the Most Recent Value as the Forecast for the Next Period						
Week	Time Series Value	Forecast	Forecast Error	Absolute Value of Forecast Error	Squared Forecast Error	Percentage Error	Absolute Value of Percentage Error
1	17						
2	21	17	4	4	16	19.05	19.05
3	19	21	−2	2	4	−10.53	10.53
4	23	19	4	4	16	17.39	17.39
5	18	23	−5	5	25	−27.78	27.78
6	16	18	−2	2	4	−12.50	12.50
7	20	16	4	4	16	20.00	20.00
8	18	20	−2	2	4	−11.11	11.11
9	22	18	4	4	16	18.18	18.18
10	20	22	−2	2	4	−10.00	10.00
11	15	20	−5	5	25	−33.33	33.33
12	22	15	7	7	49	31.82	31.82
	Totals		5	41	179	1.19	211.69

How accurate are the forecasts obtained using this naïve forecasting method? To answer this question, we will introduce several measures of forecast accuracy. These measures are used to determine how well a particular forecasting method is able to reproduce the time series data that are already available. By selecting the method that is most accurate for the data already observed, we hope to increase the likelihood that we will obtain more accurate forecasts for future time periods. The key concept associated with measuring forecast accuracy is **forecast error**. If we denote y_t and $\hat{y}_t$ as the actual and forecasted values of the time series for period t, respectively, the forecasting error for period t is as follows:

FORECAST ERROR

$$e_t = y_t - \hat{y}_t \qquad\qquad (8.1)$$

That is, the forecast error for time period t is the difference between the actual and the forecasted values for period t.

For instance, because the distributor actually sold 21 thousand gallons of gasoline in week 2, and the forecast, using the sales volume in week 1, was 17 thousand gallons, the forecast error in week 2 is

$$e_2 = y_2 - \hat{y}_2 = 21 - 17 = 4$$

A positive error such as this indicates that the forecasting method underestimated the actual value of sales for the associated period. Next we use 21, the actual value of sales in week 2, as the forecast for week 3. Since the actual value of sales in week 3 is 19, the forecast error for week 3 is $e_3 = 19 - 21 = -2$. In this case, the negative forecast error indicates that the forecast overestimated the actual value for week 3. Thus, the forecast error may be positive or negative, depending on whether the forecast is too low or too high. A complete summary of the forecast errors for this naïve forecasting method is shown in Table 8.7 in the Forecast Error column. It is important to note that because we are using a past value of the time series to produce a forecast for period t, we do not have sufficient data to produce a naïve forecast for the first week of this time series.

A simple measure of forecast accuracy is the mean or average of the forecast errors. If we have n periods in our time series and k is the number of periods at the beginning of the time series for which we cannot produce a naïve forecast, the mean forecast error (MFE) is as follows:

MEAN FORECAST ERROR (MFE)

$$\text{MFE} = \frac{\displaystyle\sum_{t=k+1}^{n} e_t}{n - k} \qquad\qquad (8.2)$$

Table 8.7 shows that the sum of the forecast errors for the gasoline sales time series is 5; thus, the mean, or average, error is $5/11 = 0.45$. Because we do not have sufficient data to produce a naïve forecast for the first week of this time series, we must adjust our calculations in both the numerator and denominator accordingly. This is common in forecasting; we often use k past periods from the time series to produce forecasts, and so we frequently cannot produce forecasts for the first k periods. In those instances, the summation in the numerator starts at the first value of t for which we have produced a forecast (so we begin the summation at $t = k + 1$), and the denominator (which is the number of periods in our time series for which we are able to produce a forecast) will also reflect these circumstances. In the gasoline example, although the time series consists of $n = 12$ values, to compute the mean error we divided the sum of the forecast errors by 11 because there are only 11 forecast errors (we cannot generate forecast sales for the first week using this naïve forecasting method).

Also note that in the gasoline time series, the mean forecast error is positive, implying that the method is generally under-forecasting; in other words, the observed values tend to be greater than the forecasted values. Because positive and negative forecast errors tend to offset each other, the mean error is likely to be small; thus, the mean error is not a very useful measure of forecast accuracy.

The **mean absolute error (MAE)** is a measure of forecast accuracy that avoids the problem of positive and negative forecast errors offsetting each other. As you might expect given its name, MAE is the average of the absolute values of the forecast errors:

The MAE is also referred to as the mean absolute deviation (MAD).

MEAN ABSOLUTE ERROR (MAE)

$$\text{MAE} = \frac{\displaystyle\sum_{t=k+1}^{n} |e_t|}{n - k} \tag{8.3}$$

Table 8.7 shows that the sum of the absolute values of the forecast errors is 41; thus:

$$\text{MAE} = \text{average of the absolute value of the forecast errors} = \frac{41}{11} = 3.73.$$

Another measure that avoids the problem of positive and negative errors offsetting each other is obtained by computing the average of the squared forecast errors. This measure of forecast accuracy is referred to as the **mean squared error (MSE)**:

MEAN SQUARED ERROR (MSE)

$$\text{MSE} = \frac{\displaystyle\sum_{t=k+1}^{n} e_t^2}{n - k} \tag{8.4}$$

From Table 8.7, the sum of the squared errors is 179; hence

$$\text{MSE} = \text{average of the square of the forecast errors} = \frac{179}{11} = 16.27.$$

The size of the MAE or MSE depends on the scale of the data. As a result, it is difficult to make comparisons for different time intervals (such as comparing a method of forecasting monthly gasoline sales to a method of forecasting weekly sales) or to make comparisons across different time series (such as monthly sales of gasoline and monthly sales of oil filters). To make comparisons such as these we need to work with relative or percentage error measures. The **mean absolute percentage error (MAPE)** is such a measure. To calculate MAPE we use the following formula:

MEAN ABSOLUTE PERCENTAGE ERROR (MAPE)

$$\text{MAPE} = \frac{\displaystyle\sum_{t=k+1}^{n} \left| \left(\frac{e_t}{y_t} \right) 100 \right|}{n - k} \tag{8.5}$$

Table 8.7 shows that the sum of the absolute values of the percentage errors is

$$\sum_{t=k+1}^{12} \left| \left(\frac{e_t}{y_t} \right) 100 \right| = 211.69$$

Thus, the MAPE, which is the average of the absolute value of percentage forecast errors, is

$$\frac{211.69}{11} = 19.24\%$$

These measures of forecast accuracy simply measure how well the forecasting method is able to forecast historical values of the time series. Now, suppose we want to forecast sales for a future time period, such as week 13. The forecast for week 13 is 22, the actual value of the time series in week 12. Is this an accurate estimate of sales for week 13? Unfortunately, there is no way to address the issue of accuracy associated with forecasts for future time periods. However, if we select a forecasting method that works well for the historical data, and we have reason to believe the historical pattern will continue into the future, we should obtain forecasts that will ultimately be shown to be accurate.

Before concluding this section, let us consider another method for forecasting the gasoline sales time series in Table 8.1. Suppose we use the average of all the historical data available as the forecast for the next period. We begin by developing a forecast for week 2. Because there is only one historical value available prior to week 2, the forecast for week 2 is just the time series value in week 1; thus, the forecast for week 2 is 17 thousand gallons of gasoline. To compute the forecast for week 3, we take the average of the sales values in weeks 1 and 2. Thus

$$\hat{y}_3 = \frac{17 + 21}{2} = 19$$

Similarly, the forecast for week 4 is

$$\hat{y}_4 = \frac{17 + 21 + 19}{3} = 19$$

				Absolute Value	**Squared**		**Absolute Value**
	Time Series		**Forecast**	**of Forecast**	**Forecast**	**Percentage**	**of Percentage**
Week	**Value**	**Forecast**	**Error**	**Error**	**Error**	**Error**	**Error**
1	17						
2	21	17.00	4.00	4.00	16.00	19.05	19.05
3	19	19.00	0.00	0.00	0.00	0.00	0.00
4	23	19.00	4.00	4.00	16.00	17.39	17.39
5	18	20.00	−2.00	2.00	4.00	−11.11	11.11
6	16	19.60	−3.60	3.60	12.96	−22.50	22.50
7	20	19.00	1.00	1.00	1.00	5.00	5.00
8	18	19.14	−1.14	1.14	1.31	−6.35	6.35
9	22	19.00	3.00	3.00	9.00	13.64	13.64
10	20	19.33	0.67	0.67	0.44	3.33	3.33
11	15	19.40	−4.40	4.40	19.36	−29.33	29.33
12	22	19.00	3.00	3.00	9.00	13.64	13.64
		Totals	4.52	26.81	89.07	2.75	141.34

TABLE 8.8 Computing Forecasts and Measures of Forecast Accuracy Using the Average of All the Historical Data as the Forecast for the Next Period

The forecasts obtained using this method for the gasoline time series are shown in Table 8.8 in the Forecast column. Using the results shown in Table 8.8, we obtain the following values of MAE, MSE, and MAPE:

$$\text{MAE} = \frac{26.81}{11} = 2.44$$

$$\text{MSE} = \frac{89.07}{11} = 8.10$$

$$\text{MAPE} = \frac{141.34}{11} = 12.85\%$$

We can now compare the accuracy of the two forecasting methods we have considered in this section by comparing the values of MAE, MSE, and MAPE for each method.

	Naïve Method	Average of All Past Values
MAE	3.73	2.44
MSE	16.27	8.10
MAPE	19.24%	12.85%

As measured by MAE, MSE, and MAPE, the average of all past weekly gasoline sales provides more accurate forecasts for the next week than using the most recent week's gasoline sales.

Evaluating different forecasts based on historical accuracy is helpful only if historical patterns continue into the future. As we noted in Section 8.1, the 12 observations of Table 8.1 comprise a stationary time series. In Section 8.1, we also mentioned that changes in business conditions often result in a time series that is not stationary. We discussed a situation in which the gasoline distributor signed a contract with the Vermont State Police to provide gasoline for state police cars located in southern Vermont. Table 8.2 shows the number of gallons of gasoline sold for the original time series and for the 10 weeks after signing the new contract, and Figure 8.2 shows the corresponding time series plot. Note the change in level in week 13 for the resulting time series. When a shift to a new level such as this occurs, it takes several periods for the forecasting method that uses the average of all the historical data to adjust to the new level of the time series. However, in this case the simple naïve method adjusts very rapidly to the change in level because it uses only the most recent observation as the forecast.

Measures of forecast accuracy are important factors in comparing different forecasting methods, but we have to be careful not to rely too heavily on them. Good judgment and knowledge about business conditions that might affect the value of the variable to be forecast also have to be considered carefully when selecting a method. Historical forecast accuracy is not the sole consideration, especially if the pattern exhibited by the time series is likely to change in the future.

In the next section, we will introduce more sophisticated methods for developing forecasts for a time series that exhibits a horizontal pattern. Using the measures of forecast accuracy developed here, we will be able to assess whether such methods provide more accurate forecasts than we obtained using the simple approaches illustrated in this section. The methods that we will introduce also have the advantage that they adapt well to situations in which the time series changes to a new level. The ability of a forecasting method to adapt quickly to changes in level is an important consideration, especially in short-term forecasting situations.

8.3 Moving Averages and Exponential Smoothing

In this section, we discuss two forecasting methods that are appropriate for a time series with a horizontal pattern: moving averages and exponential smoothing. These methods are capable of adapting well to changes in the level of a horizontal pattern such as the one we saw with the extended gasoline sales time series (Table 8.2 and Figure 8.2). However, without modification they are not appropriate when considerable trend, cyclical, or seasonal effects are present. Because the objective of each of these methods is to smooth out random fluctuations in the time series, they are referred to as *smoothing methods*. These methods are easy to use and generally provide a high level of accuracy for short-range forecasts, such as a forecast for the next time period.

Moving Averages

The **moving average method** uses the average of the most recent k data values in the time series as the forecast for the next period. Mathematically, a moving average forecast of order k is:

MOVING AVERAGE FORECAST

$$\hat{y}_{t+1} = \frac{\Sigma\left(\text{most recent } k \text{ data values}\right)}{k} = \frac{\sum\limits_{i=t-k+1}^{t} y_i}{k}$$

$$= \frac{y_{t-k+1} + \cdots + y_{t-1} + y_t}{k} \tag{8.6}$$

where

$$\hat{y}_{t+1} = \text{forecast of the time series for period } t + 1$$
$$y_t = \text{actual value of the time series in period } t$$
$$k = \text{number of periods of time series data used to generate the forecast}$$

The term *moving* is used because every time a new observation becomes available for the time series, it replaces the oldest observation in the equation and a new average is computed. Thus, the periods over which the average is calculated change, or move, with each ensuing period.

To illustrate the moving averages method, let us return to the original 12 weeks of gasoline sales data in Table 8.1. The time series plot in Figure 8.1 indicates that the gasoline sales time series has a horizontal pattern. Thus, the smoothing methods of this section are applicable.

To use moving averages to forecast a time series, we must first select the order k, or the number of time series values to be included in the moving average. If only the most recent values of the time series are considered relevant, a small value of k is preferred. If a greater number of past values are considered relevant, then we generally opt for a larger value of k. As previously mentioned, a time series with a horizontal pattern can shift to a new level over time. A moving average will adapt to the new level of the series and continue to provide good forecasts in k periods. Thus a smaller value of k will track shifts in a time series more quickly (the naïve approach discussed earlier is actually a moving average for $k = 1$). On the other hand, larger values of k will be more effective in smoothing out random fluctuations. Thus, managerial judgment based on an understanding of the behavior of a time series is helpful in choosing an appropriate value of k.

To illustrate how moving averages can be used to forecast gasoline sales, we will use a three-week moving average ($k = 3$). We begin by computing the forecast of sales in week 4 using the average of the time series values in weeks 1 to 3:

$$\hat{y}_4 = \text{average for weeks 1 to 3} = \frac{17 + 21 + 19}{3} = 19$$

Thus, the moving average forecast of sales in week 4 is 19, or 19,000 gallons of gasoline. Because the actual value observed in week 4 is 23, the forecast error in week 4 is $e_4 = 23 - 19 = 4$.

We next compute the forecast of sales in week 5 by averaging the time series values in weeks 2 to 4:

$$\hat{y}_5 = \text{average for weeks 2 to 4} = \frac{21 + 19 + 23}{3} = 21$$

Hence, the forecast of sales in week 5 is 21 and the error associated with this forecast is $e_5 = 18 - 21 = -3$. A complete summary of the three-week moving average forecasts for the gasoline sales time series is provided in Table 8.9. Figure 8.7 shows the original time series plot and the three-week moving average forecasts. Note how the graph of the moving average forecasts has tended to smooth out the random fluctuations in the time series.

TABLE 8.9	Summary of Three-Week Moving Average Calculations						
Week	Time Series Value	Forecast	Forecast Error	Absolute Value of Forecast Error	Squared Forecast Error	Percentage Error	Absolute Value of Percentage Error
1	17						
2	21						
3	19						
4	23	19	4	4	16	17.39	17.39
5	18	21	−3	3	9	−16.67	16.67
6	16	20	−4	4	16	−25.00	25.00
7	20	19	1	1	1	5.00	5.00
8	18	18	0	0	0	0.00	0.00
9	22	18	4	4	16	18.18	18.18
10	20	20	0	0	0	0.00	0.00
11	15	20	−5	5	25	−33.33	33.33
12	22	19	3	3	9	13.64	13.64
		Totals	0	24	92	−20.79	129.21

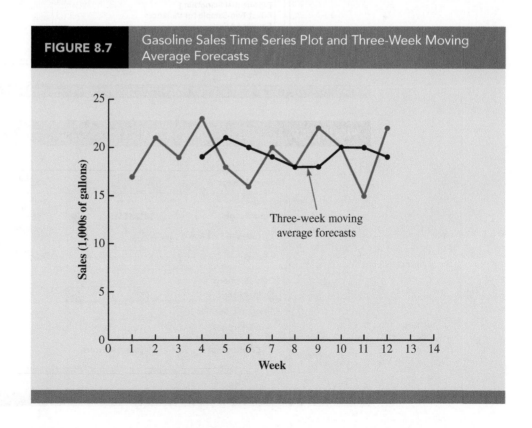

FIGURE 8.7   Gasoline Sales Time Series Plot and Three-Week Moving Average Forecasts

Gasoline

*If **Data Analysis** does not appear in your **Analyze** group in the **Data** tab, you will have to load the Analysis Toolpak add-in into Excel. To do so, click the **File** tab in the Ribbon and click **Options**. When the **Excel Options** dialog box appears, click **Add-Ins** from the menu. Next to **Manage**, select **Excel Add-ins** and click **Go...** at the bottom of the dialog box. When the **Add-Ins** dialog box appears, select **Analysis Toolpak** and click **OK**.*

To forecast sales in week 13, the next time period in the future, we simply compute the average of the time series values in weeks 10, 11, and 12:

$$\hat{y}_{13} = \text{average for weeks 10 to 12} = \frac{20 + 15 + 22}{3} = 19$$

Thus, the forecast for week 13 is 19, or 19,000 gallons of gasoline.

To show how Excel can be used to develop forecasts using the moving averages method, we develop a forecast for the gasoline sales time series in Table 8.1 and in the file *Gasoline* as displayed in Columns A and B of Figure 8.10.

The following steps can be used to produce a three-week moving average:

Step 1. Click the **Data** tab in the Ribbon
Step 2. Click **Data Analysis** in the **Analyze** group
Step 3. When the **Data Analysis** dialog box appears (Figure 8.8), select **Moving Average** and click **OK**
Step 4. When the **Moving Average** dialog box appears (Figure 8.9):
    Enter *B2:B13* in the **Input Range:** box
    Enter *3* in the **Interval:** box
    Enter *C3* in the **Output Range:** box
    Click **OK**

FIGURE 8.8   Data Analysis Dialog Box

FIGURE 8.9   Moving Average Dialog Box

FIGURE 8.10	Excel Output for Moving Average Forecast for Gasoline Data

	A	B	C
1	**Week**	**Sales (1000s of gallons)**	
2	1	17	
3	2	21	#N/A
4	3	19	#N/A
5	4	23	19
6	5	18	21
7	6	16	20
8	7	20	19
9	8	18	18
10	9	22	18
11	10	20	20
12	11	15	20
13	12	22	19
14	13		19

Once you have completed this step, the three-week moving average forecasts will appear in column C of the worksheet as shown in Figure 8.10. Note that forecasts for periods of other lengths can be computed easily by entering a different value in the **Interval:** box.

In Section 8.2 we discussed three measures of forecast accuracy: mean absolute error (MAE), mean squared error (MSE), and mean absolute percentage error (MAPE). Using the three-week moving average calculations in Table 8.9, the values for these three measures of forecast accuracy are as follows:

$$\text{MAE} = \frac{\sum_{t=4}^{12} |e_t|}{n-3} = \frac{24}{9} = 2.67$$

$$\text{MSE} = \frac{\sum_{t=4}^{12} e_t^2}{n-3} = \frac{92}{9} = 10.22$$

$$\text{MAPE} = \frac{\sum_{t=4}^{12} \left| \left(\frac{e_t}{y_t} \right) 100 \right|}{n-3} = \frac{129.21}{9} = 14.36\%$$

In Section 8.2, we showed that using the most recent observation as the forecast for the next week (a moving average of order $k = 1$) resulted in values of MAE = 3.73, MSE = 16.27, and MAPE = 19.24%. Thus, according to each of these three measures, the three-week moving average approach has provided more accurate forecasts than simply using the most recent observation as the forecast. Also note how we have revised the formulas for the MAE, MSE, and MAPE to reflect that our use of a three-week moving average leaves us with insufficient data to generate forecasts for the first three weeks of our time series.

To determine whether a moving average with a different order k can provide more accurate forecasts, we recommend using trial and error to determine the value of k that minimizes the MSE. For the gasoline sales time series, it can be shown that the minimum value of MSE corresponds to a moving average of order $k = 6$ with MSE = 6.79. If we are willing to assume that the order of the moving average that is best for the historical data will also be best for future values of the time series, the most accurate moving average forecasts of gasoline sales can be obtained using a moving average of order $k = 6$.

Exponential Smoothing

Exponential smoothing uses a weighted average of past time series values as a forecast. The exponential smoothing model is as follows:

EXPONENTIAL SMOOTHING FORECAST

$$\hat{y}_{t+1} = \alpha y_t + (1 - \alpha)\hat{y}_t \tag{8.7}$$

where

$$\hat{y}_{t+1} = \text{forecast of the time series for period } t + 1$$
$$y_t = \text{actual value of the time series in period } t$$
$$\hat{y}_t = \text{forecast of the time series for period } t$$
$$\alpha = \text{smoothing constant } (0 \le \alpha \le 1)$$

Equation (8.7) shows that the forecast for period $t + 1$ is a weighted average of the actual value in period t and the forecast for period t. The weight given to the actual value in period t is the **smoothing constant** α, and the weight given to the forecast in period t is $1 - \alpha$. It turns out that the exponential smoothing forecast for any period is actually a weighted average of all the previous actual values of the time series. Let us illustrate by working with a time series involving only three periods of data: y_1, y_2, and y_3.

To initiate the calculations, we let $\hat{y}_1$ equal the actual value of the time series in period 1; that is, $\hat{y}_1 = y_1$. Hence, the forecast for period 2 is

$$\hat{y}_2 = \alpha y_1 + (1-\alpha)\hat{y}_1$$
$$= \alpha y_1 + (1-\alpha)y_1$$
$$= y_1$$

We see that the exponential smoothing forecast for period 2 is equal to the actual value of the time series in period 1.

The forecast for period 3 is

$$\hat{y}_3 = \alpha y_2 + (1 - \alpha)\hat{y}_2 = \alpha y_2 + (1 - \alpha)y_1$$

Finally, substituting this expression for $\hat{y}_3$ into the expression for $\hat{y}_4$, we obtain

$$\hat{y}_4 = \alpha y_3 + (1 - \alpha)\hat{y}_3$$
$$= \alpha y_3 + (1 - \alpha)(\alpha y_2 + (1 - \alpha)y_1)$$
$$= \alpha y_3 + \alpha(1 - \alpha)y_2 + (1 - \alpha)^2 y_1$$

We now see that $\hat{y}_4$ is a weighted average of the first three time series values. The sum of the coefficients, or weights, for y_1, y_2, and y_3 equals 1. A similar argument can be made to show that, in general, any forecast $\hat{y}_{t+1}$ is a weighted average of all the t previous time series values.

Despite the fact that exponential smoothing provides a forecast that is a weighted average of all past observations, all past data do not need to be retained to compute the forecast for the next period. In fact, equation (8.7) shows that once the value for the smoothing constant α is selected, only two pieces of information are needed to compute the forecast for period $t + 1$: y_t, the actual value of the time series in period t; and $\hat{y}_t$, the forecast for period t.

To illustrate the exponential smoothing approach to forecasting, let us again consider the gasoline sales time series in Table 8.1. As indicated previously, to initialize the calculations we set the exponential smoothing forecast for period 2 equal to the actual value of the time series in period 1. Thus, with $y_1 = 17$, we set $\hat{y}_2 = 17$ to initiate the computations. Referring to the time series data in Table 8.1, we find an actual time series value in period 2 of $y_2 = 21$. Thus, in period 2 we have a forecast error of $e_2 = 21 - 17 = 4$.

Continuing with the exponential smoothing computations using a smoothing constant of $\alpha = 0.2$, we obtain the following forecast for period 3:

$$\hat{y}_3 = 0.2y_2 + 0.8\hat{y}_2 = 0.2(21) + 0.8(17) = 17.8$$

Once the actual time series value in period 3, $y_3 = 19$, is known, we can generate a forecast for period 4 as follows:

$$\hat{y}_4 = 0.2y_3 + 0.8\hat{y}_3 = 0.2(19) + 0.8(17.8) = 18.04$$

Continuing the exponential smoothing calculations, we obtain the weekly forecast values shown in Table 8.10. Note that we have not shown an exponential smoothing forecast or a forecast error for week 1 because no forecast was made (we used actual sales for week 1 as the forecasted sales for week 2 to initialize the exponential smoothing process). For week 12, we have $y_{12} = 22$ and $\hat{y}_{12} = 18.48$. We can we use this information to generate a forecast for week 13:

$$\hat{y}_{13} = 0.2y_{12} + 0.8\hat{y}_{12} = 0.2(22) + 0.8(18.48) = 19.18$$

Thus, the exponential smoothing forecast of the amount sold in week 13 is 19.18, or 19,180 gallons of gasoline. With this forecast, the firm can make plans and decisions accordingly.

Figure 8.11 shows the time series plot of the actual and forecasted time series values. Note in particular how the forecasts smooth out the irregular or random fluctuations in the time series.

TABLE 8.10 Summary of the Exponential Smoothing Forecasts and Forecast Errors for the Gasoline Sales Time Series with Smoothing Constant $\alpha = 0.2$

Week	Time Series Value	Forecast	Forecast Error	Squared Forecast Error
1	17			
2	21	17.00	4.00	16.00
3	19	17.80	1.20	1.44
4	23	18.04	4.96	24.60
5	18	19.03	−1.03	1.06
6	16	18.83	−2.83	8.01
7	20	18.26	1.74	3.03
8	18	18.61	−0.61	0.37
9	22	18.49	3.51	12.32
10	20	19.19	0.81	0.66
11	15	19.35	−4.35	18.92
12	22	18.48	3.52	12.39
		Totals	10.92	98.80

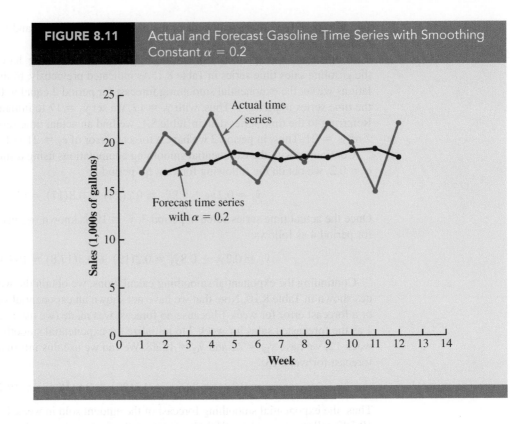

FIGURE 8.11 Actual and Forecast Gasoline Time Series with Smoothing Constant $\alpha = 0.2$

DATA*file*

Gasoline

To show how Excel can be used for exponential smoothing, we again develop a forecast for the gasoline sales time series in Table 8.1. We use the file *Gasoline,* which has the week in rows 2 through 13 of column A and the sales data for the 12 weeks in rows 2 through 13 of column B. We use $\alpha = 0.2$. The following steps can be used to produce a forecast.

Step 1. Click the **Data** tab in the Ribbon
Step 2. Click **Data Analysis** in the **Analyze** group
Step 3. When the **Data Analysis** dialog box appears (Figure 8.12), select **Exponential Smoothing** and click **OK**
Step 4. When the **Exponential Smoothing** dialog box appears (Figure 8.13):
   Enter *B2:B13* in the **Input Range:** box
   Enter *0.8* in the **Damping factor:** box
   Enter *C2* in the **Output Range:** box
   Click **OK**

Once you have completed this step, the exponential smoothing forecasts will appear in column C of the worksheet as shown in Figure 8.14. Note that the value we entered in the **Damping factor:** box is $1 - \alpha$; forecasts for other smoothing constants can be computed easily by entering a different value for $1 - \alpha$ in the **Damping factor:** box.

In the preceding exponential smoothing calculations, we used a smoothing constant of $\alpha = 0.2$. Although any value of α between 0 and 1 is acceptable, some values will yield more accurate forecasts than others. Insight into choosing a good value for α can be obtained by rewriting the basic exponential smoothing model as follows:

$$\hat{y}_{t+1} = \alpha y_t + (1 - \alpha)\hat{y}_t$$
$$= \alpha y_t + \hat{y}_t - \alpha \hat{y}_t$$
$$= \hat{y}_t + \alpha(y_t - \hat{y}_t) = \hat{y}_t + \alpha e_t$$

FIGURE 8.12	Data Analysis Dialog Box

FIGURE 8.13	Exponential Smoothing Dialog Box

FIGURE 8.14	Excel Output for Exponential Smoothing Forecast for Gasoline Data

	A	B	C
1	Week	Sales (1000s of gallons)	
2	1	17	#N/A
3	2	21	17
4	3	19	17.8
5	4	23	18.04
6	5	18	19.032
7	6	16	18.8256
8	7	20	18.2605
9	8	18	18.6084
10	9	22	18.4867
11	10	20	19.1894
12	11	15	19.3515
13	12	22	18.4812

Thus, the new forecast $\hat{y}_{t+1}$ is equal to the previous forecast $\hat{y}_t$ plus an adjustment, which is the smoothing constant α times the most recent forecast error, $e_t = y_t - \hat{y}_t$. In other words, the forecast in period $t + 1$ is obtained by adjusting the forecast in period t by a fraction of the forecast error from period t. If the time series contains substantial random variability, a small value of the smoothing constant is preferred. The reason for this choice is that if much of the forecast error is due to random variability, we do not want to overreact and adjust the forecasts too quickly. For a time series with relatively little random variability, a forecast error is more likely to represent a real change in the level of the series. Thus, larger values of the smoothing constant provide the advantage of quickly adjusting the forecasts to changes in the time series, thereby allowing the forecasts to react more quickly to changing conditions.

Nonlinear optimization can be used to identify the value of α that minimizes the MSE. Nonlinear optimization is discussed in chapter 14.

The criterion we will use to determine a desirable value for the smoothing constant α is the same as that proposed for determining the order or number of periods of data to include in the moving averages calculation; that is, we choose the value of α that minimizes the MSE. A summary of the MSE calculations for the exponential smoothing forecast of gasoline sales with $\alpha = 0.2$ is shown in Table 8.10. Note that there is one less squared error term than the number of time periods; this is because we had no past values with which to make a forecast for period 1. The value of the sum of squared forecast errors is 98.80; hence, MSE = 98.80 / 11 = 8.98. Would a different value of α provide better results in terms of a lower MSE value? Trial and error is often used to determine whether a different smoothing constant α can provide more accurate forecasts.

NOTES + COMMENTS

1. Spreadsheet packages are effective tools for implementing exponential smoothing. With the time series data and the forecasting formulas in a spreadsheet such as the one shown in Table 8.10, you can use the MAE, MSE, and MAPE to evaluate different values of the smoothing constant α.

2. Moving averages and exponential smoothing provide the foundation for much of time series analysis, and many more sophisticated refinements of these methods have been developed. These include, but are not limited to, weighted moving averages, double moving averages, Brown's method for double exponential smoothing, and Holt-Winters exponential smoothing. Appendix 8.1 explains how to implement the Holt-Winters method using Excel Forecast Sheet.

8.4 Using Regression Analysis for Forecasting

In Chapter 7, we discuss linear regression models in more detail.

Regression analysis is a statistical technique that can be used to develop a mathematical equation showing how variables are related. In regression terminology, the variable that is being predicted is called the *dependent* (or *response*) *variable*, and the variable or variables being used to predict the value of the dependent variable are called the *independent* (or *predictor*) *variables*. In this section, we will show how to use regression analysis to develop forecasts for a time series that has a trend, a seasonal pattern, and both a trend and a seasonal pattern. We will also show how to use regression analysis to develop forecast models that include causal variables.

Linear Trend Projection

We now consider forecasting methods that are appropriate for time series that exhibit trend patterns and show how regression analysis can be used to forecast a time series with a linear trend. In Section 8.1, we used the bicycle sales time series in Table 8.3 to illustrate a time series with a trend pattern. Let us now use this time series to illustrate how regression analysis can be used to forecast a time series with a linear trend. Although the time series plot in Figure 8.3 shows some up-and-down movement over the past 10 years, we might agree that a linear trendline provides a reasonable approximation of the long-run movement in the series. We can use regression analysis to develop such a linear trendline for the bicycle sales time series.

Because simple linear regression analysis yields the linear relationship between the independent variable and the dependent variable that minimizes the MSE, we can use this approach to find a best-fitting line to a set of data that exhibits a linear trend. In finding a linear trend, the variable to be forecasted (y_t, the actual value of the time series in period t) is the dependent variable and the trend variable (time period t) is the independent variable. We will use the following notation for our linear trendline:

$$\hat{y}_t = b_0 + b_1 t \qquad (8.8)$$

where

$$
\begin{aligned}
\hat{y}_t &= \text{forecast of sales in period } t \\
t &= \text{time period} \\
b_0 &= \text{the } y\text{-intercept of the linear trendline} \\
b_1 &= \text{the slope of the linear trendline}
\end{aligned}
$$

In equation (8.8), the time variable begins at $t = 1$, corresponding to the first time series observation (year 1 for the bicycle sales time series). The time variable then continues until $t = n$, corresponding to the most recent time series observation (year 10 for the bicycle sales time series). Thus, the bicycle sales time series $t = 1$ corresponds to the oldest time series value, and $t = 10$ corresponds to the most recent year.

Excel can be used to compute the estimated intercept b_0 and slope b_1. The Excel output for a regression analysis of the bicycle sales data is provided in Figure 8.15.

We see in this output that the estimated intercept b_0 is 20.4 (shown in cell B17) and the estimated slope b_1 is 1.1 (shown in cell B18). Thus,

$$\hat{y}_t = 20.4 + 1.1t \qquad (8.9)$$

is the regression equation for the linear trend component for the bicycle sales time series. The slope of 1.1 in this trend equation indicates that over the past 10 years the firm has experienced an average growth in sales of about 1,100 units per year. If we assume that the past 10-year trend in sales is a good indicator for the future, we can use equation (8.9) to project the trend component of the time series. For example, substituting $t = 11$ into equation (8.9) yields next year's trend projection, $\hat{y}_{11}$:

$$\hat{y}_{11} = 20.4 + 1.1(11) = 32.5$$

Thus, the linear trend model yields a sales forecast of 32,500 bicycles for the next year.

We can also use the trendline to forecast sales farther into the future. Using equation (8.9), we develop annual forecasts of bicycle sales for two and three years into the future as follows:

$$
\begin{aligned}
\hat{y}_{12} &= 20.4 + 1.1(12) = 33.6 \\
\hat{y}_{13} &= 20.4 + 1.1(13) = 34.7
\end{aligned}
$$

The forecasted value increases by 1,100 bicycles in each year.

Note that to produce a forecast of the value of the dependent variable y for period t in this example, we are not using values of the dependent variable from previous periods (e.g., $y_{t-1}, y_{t-2}, y_{t-3}, \ldots$) as independent variables. Thus, $k = 0$ in equations (8.3)–(8.5) to calculate the MAE, MSE, and MAPE.

We can also use more complex regression models to fit nonlinear trends. For example, to generate a forecast of a time series with a curvilinear trend, we could include t^2 and t^3 as independent variables in our model, and the estimated regression equation would become

$$\hat{y}_t = b_0 + b_1 t + b_2 t^2 + b_3 t^3$$

FIGURE 8.15   Excel Simple Linear Regression Output for Trendline Model for Bicycle Sales Data

▲	A	B	C	D	E	F	G	H	I
1	SUMMARY OUTPUT								
2									
3	*Regression Statistics*								
4	Multiple R	0.874526167							
5	R Square	0.764796016							
6	Adjusted R Square	0.735395518							
7	Standard Error	1.958953802							
8	Observations	10							
9									
10	ANOVA								
11		*df*	*SS*	*MS*	*F*	*Significance F*			
12	Regression	1	99.825	99.825	26.01302932	0.000929509			
13	Residual	8	30.7	3.8375					
14	Total	9	130.525						
15									
16		*Coefficients*	*Standard Error*	*t Stat*	*P-value*	*Lower 95%*	*Upper 95%*	*Lower 99.0%*	*Upper 99.0%*
17	Intercept	20.4	1.338220211	15.24412786	3.39989E-07	17.31405866	23.48594134	15.90975286	24.89024714
18	Year	1.1	0.215673715	5.100296983	0.000929509	0.60265552	1.59734448	0.376331148	1.823668852

Because autoregressive models typically violate the conditions necessary for inference in least squares regression, you must be careful when testing hypotheses or estimating confidence intervals in autoregressive models. There are special methods for constructing autoregressive models, but they are beyond the scope of this book.

Another type of regression-based forecasting model occurs whenever all the independent variables are previous values of the same time series. For example, if the time series values are denoted by $y_1, y_2, \ldots, y_n$, we might try to find an estimated regression equation relating y_t to the most recent time series values, y_{t-1}, y_{t-2}, and so on. If we use the actual values of the time series for the three most recent periods as independent variables, the estimated regression equation would be

$$\hat{y}_t = b_0 + b_1 y_{t-1} + b_2 y_{t-2} + b_3 y_{t-3}$$

Regression models such as this in which the independent variables are previous values of the time series are referred to as **autoregressive models.**

Seasonality Without Trend

To the extent that seasonality exists, we need to incorporate it into our forecasting models to ensure accurate forecasts. We begin by considering a seasonal time series with no trend and then, in the next section, we discuss how to model seasonality with a linear trend. Let us consider again the data from Table 8.5, the number of umbrellas sold at a clothing store over the past five years. As we see in the time series plot provided in Figure 8.5, the data do not suggest any long-term trend in sales. In fact, unless you look carefully at the data, you might conclude that the data follow a horizontal pattern with random fluctuation and that single exponential smoothing could be used to forecast sales. However, closer inspection of the time series plot reveals a pattern in the fluctuations. The first and third quarters have moderate sales, the second quarter the highest sales, and the fourth quarter the lowest sales. Thus, we conclude that a quarterly seasonal pattern is present.

Categorical variables are covered in more detail in Chapter 7.

We can model a time series with a seasonal pattern by treating the season as a dummy variable. Categorical variables are variables used to categorize observations of data, and $k - 1$ dummy variables are required to model a categorical variable that has k levels. Thus, we need three dummy variables to model four seasons. For instance, in the umbrella sales time series, the quarter to which each observation corresponds is treated as a season; it is a categorical variable with four levels: quarter 1, quarter 2, quarter 3, and quarter 4. Thus, to model the seasonal effects in the umbrella time series we need $4 - 1 = 3$ dummy variables. The three dummy variables can be coded as follows:

$$\text{Qtr}1_t = \begin{cases} 1 \text{ if period } t \text{ is quarter 1} \\ 0 \text{ otherwise} \end{cases}$$

$$\text{Qtr}2_t = \begin{cases} 1 \text{ if period } t \text{ is quarter 2} \\ 0 \text{ otherwise} \end{cases}$$

$$\text{Qtr}3_t = \begin{cases} 1 \text{ if period } t \text{ is quarter 3} \\ 0 \text{ otherwise} \end{cases}$$

Using $\hat{y}_t$ to denote the forecasted value of sales for period t, the general form of the equation relating the number of umbrellas sold to the quarter the sales take place is as follows:

$$\hat{y}_t = b_0 + b_1\text{Qtr}1_t + b_2\text{Qtr}2_t + b_3\text{Qtr}3_t \tag{8.10}$$

Note that the fourth quarter will be denoted by setting all three dummy variables to 0.

Table 8.11 shows the umbrella sales time series with the coded values of the dummy variables shown. We can use a multiple linear regression model to find the values of b_0, b_1, b_2, and b_3 that minimize the sum of squared errors. For this regression model, y_t is the dependent variable, and the quarterly dummy variables $\text{Qtr}1_t$, $\text{Qtr}2_t$, and $\text{Qtr}3_t$ are the independent variables.

Using the data in Table 8.11 and regression analysis, we obtain the following equation:

$$\hat{y}_t = 95.0 + 29.0\text{Qtr}1_t + 57.0\text{Qtr}2_t + 26.0\text{Qtr}3_t \tag{8.11}$$

We can use equation (8.11) to forecast sales of every quarter for the next year:

$$\text{Quarter 1} : \text{Sales} = 95.0 + 29.0(1) + 57.0(0) + 26.0(0) = 124$$
$$\text{Quarter 2} : \text{Sales} = 95.0 + 29.0(0) + 57.0(1) + 26.0(0) = 152$$
$$\text{Quarter 3} : \text{Sales} = 95.0 + 29.0(0) + 57.0(0) + 26.0(1) = 121$$
$$\text{Quarter 4} : \text{Sales} = 95.0 + 29.0(0) + 57.0(0) + 26.0(0) = 95$$

It is interesting to note that we could have obtained the quarterly forecasts for the next year by simply computing the average number of umbrellas sold in each quarter. Nonetheless, for more complex problem situations, such as dealing with a time series that has both trend and seasonal effects, this simple averaging approach will not work.

Seasonality with Trend

We now consider situations for which the time series contains both seasonal effects and a linear trend by showing how to forecast the quarterly sales of smartphones introduced in Section 8.1. The data for the smartphone time series are shown in Table 8.6. The time series plot in Figure 8.6 indicates that sales are lowest in the second quarter of each year and increase in quarters 3 and 4. Thus, we conclude that a seasonal pattern exists for smartphone sales. However, the time series also has an upward linear trend that will need to be accounted for in order to develop accurate forecasts of quarterly sales. This is easily done by combining the dummy variable approach for handling seasonality with the approach for handling a linear trend discussed earlier in this section.

The general form of the regression equation for modeling both the quarterly seasonal effects and the linear trend in the smartphone time series is

$$\hat{y}_t = b_0 + b_1\text{Qtr}1_t + b_2\text{Qtr}2_t + b_3\text{Qtr}3_t + b_4t \tag{8.12}$$

TABLE 8.11		Umbrella Sales Time Series with Dummy Variables				
Period	Year	Quarter	Qtr1	Qtr2	Qtr3	Sales
1	1	1	1	0	0	125
2		2	0	1	0	153
3		3	0	0	1	106
4		4	0	0	0	88
5	2	1	1	0	0	118
6		2	0	1	0	161
7		3	0	0	1	133
8		4	0	0	0	102
9	3	1	1	0	0	138
10		2	0	1	0	144
11		3	0	0	1	113
12		4	0	0	0	80
13	4	1	1	0	0	109
14		2	0	1	0	137
15		3	0	0	1	125
16		4	0	0	0	109
17	5	1	1	0	0	130
18		2	0	1	0	165
19		3	0	0	1	128
20		4	0	0	0	96

where

$\hat{y}_t$ = forecast of sales in period t

Qtr1_t = 1 if time period t corresponds to the first quarter of the year; 0 otherwise

Qtr2_t = 1 if time period t corresponds to the second quarter of the year; 0 otherwise

Qtr3_t = 1 if time period t corresponds to the third quarter of the year; 0 otherwise

t = time period (quarter)

For this regression model y_t is the dependent variable and the quarterly dummy variables Qtr1_t, Qtr2_t, and Qtr3_t and the time period t are the independent variables.

Table 8.12 shows the revised smartphone sales time series that includes the coded values of the dummy variables and the time period t. Using the data in Table 8.12 with the regression model that includes both the seasonal and trend components, we obtain the following equation that minimizes our sum of squared errors:

$$\hat{y}_t = 6.07 - 1.36\text{Qtr1}_t - 2.03\text{Qtr2}_t - 0.304\text{Qtr3}_t + 0.146t \qquad \textbf{(8.13)}$$

We can now use equation (8.13) to forecast quarterly sales for the next year. Next year is year 5 for the smartphone sales time series, that is, time periods 17, 18, 19, and 20.

Forecast for time period 17 (quarter 1 in year 5):

$$\hat{y}_{17} = 6.07 - 1.36(1) - 2.03(0) - 0.304(0) + 0.146(17) = 7.19$$

Forecast for time period 18 (quarter 2 in year 5):

$$\hat{y}_{18} = 6.07 - 1.36(0) - 2.03(1) - 0.304(0) + 0.146(18) = 6.67$$

TABLE 8.12	Smartphone Sales Time Series with Dummy Variables and Time Period					
Period	Year	Quarter	Qtr1	Qtr2	Qtr3	Sales (1,000s)
1	1	1	1	0	0	4.8
2		2	0	1	0	4.1
3		3	0	0	1	6.0
4		4	0	0	0	6.5
5	2	1	1	0	0	5.8
6		2	0	1	0	5.2
7		3	0	0	1	6.8
8		4	0	0	0	7.4
9	3	1	1	0	0	6.0
10		2	0	1	0	5.6
11		3	0	0	1	7.5
12		4	0	0	0	7.8
13	4	1	1	0	0	6.3
14		2	0	1	0	5.9
15		3	0	0	1	8.0
16		4	0	0	0	8.4

Forecast for time period 19 (quarter 3 in year 5):

$$\hat{y}_{19} = 6.07 - 1.36(0) - 2.03(0) - 0.304(1) + 0.146(19) = 8.54$$

Forecast for time period 20 (quarter 4 in year 5):

$$\hat{y}_{20} = 6.07 - 1.36(0) - 2.03(0) - 0.304(0) + 0.146(20) = 8.99$$

Thus, accounting for the seasonal effects and the linear trend in smartphone sales, the estimates of quarterly sales in year 5 are 7,190; 6,670; 8,540; and 8,990.

The dummy variables in the equation actually provide four equations, one for each quarter. For instance, if time period t corresponds to quarter 1, the estimate of quarterly sales is

Quarter 1: Sales $= 6.07 - 1.36(1) - 2.03(0) - 0.304(0) + 0.146t = 4.71 + 0.146t$

Similarly, if time period t corresponds to quarters 2, 3, and 4, the estimates of quarterly sales are as follows:

Quarter 2: Sales $= 6.07 - 1.36(0) - 2.03(1) - 0.304(0) + 0.146t = 4.04 + 0.146t$
Quarter 3: Sales $= 6.07 - 1.36(0) - 2.03(0) - 0.304(1) + 0.146t = 5.77 + 0.146t$
Quarter 4: Sales $= 6.07 - 1.36(0) - 2.03(0) - 0.304(0) + 0.146t = 6.07 + 0.146t$

The slope of the trendline for each quarterly forecast equation is 0.146, indicating a consistent growth in sales of about 146 phones per quarter. The only difference in the four equations is that they have different intercepts.

In the smartphone sales example, we showed how dummy variables can be used to account for the quarterly seasonal effects in the time series. Because there were four levels of seasonality, three dummy variables were required. However, many businesses use monthly rather than quarterly forecasts. For monthly data, season is a categorical variable with 12 levels, and thus $12 - 1 = 11$ dummy variables are required to capture monthly seasonal effects. For example, the 11 dummy variables could be coded as follows:

$$\text{Month1}_t = \begin{cases} 1 \text{ if period } t \text{ is January} \\ 0 \text{ otherwise} \end{cases}$$

$$\text{Month2}_t = \begin{cases} 1 \text{ if period } t \text{ is February} \\ 0 \text{ otherwise} \end{cases}$$

$$\vdots$$

$$\text{Month11}_t = \begin{cases} 1 \text{ if period } t \text{ is November} \\ 0 \text{ otherwise} \end{cases}$$

Other than this change, the approach for handling seasonality remains the same. Time series data collected at other intervals can be handled in a similar manner.

Using Regression Analysis as a Causal Forecasting Method

The methods discussed for estimating linear trends and seasonal effects make use of patterns in historical values of the variable to be forecast; these methods are classified as time series methods because they rely on past values of the variable to be forecast when developing the model. However, the relationship of the variable to be forecast with other variables may also be used to develop a forecasting model. Generally such models include only variables that are believed to cause changes in the variable to be forecast, such as the following:

- Advertising expenditures when sales are to be forecast.
- The mortgage rate when new housing construction is to be forecast.
- Grade point average when starting salaries for recent college graduates are to be forecast.
- The price of a product when the demand for the product is to be forecast.
- The value of the Dow Jones Industrial Average when the value of an individual stock is to be forecast.
- Daily high temperature when electricity usage is to be forecast.

Because these variables are used as independent variables when we believe they cause changes in the value of the dependent variable, forecasting models that include such variables as independent variables are referred to as **causal models**. It is important to note here that the forecasting model provides evidence only of association between an independent variable and the variable to be forecast. The model does not provide evidence of a causal relationship between an independent variable and the variable to be forecast; the conclusion that a causal relationship exists must be based on practical experience.

To illustrate how regression analysis is used as a causal forecasting method, we consider the sales forecasting problem faced by Armand's Pizza Parlors, a chain of Italian restaurants doing business in a five-state area. Historically, the most successful locations have been near college campuses. The managers believe that quarterly sales for these restaurants (denoted by y) are related positively to the size of the student population (denoted by x); that is, restaurants near campuses with a large population tend to generate more sales than those located near campuses with a small population.

Using regression analysis we can develop an equation showing how the dependent variable y is related to the independent variable x. This equation can then be used to forecast quarterly sales for restaurants located near college campuses given the size of the student population. This is particularly helpful for forecasting sales for new restaurant locations. For instance, suppose that management wants to forecast sales for a new restaurant that it is considering opening near a college campus. Because no historical data are available on sales for a new restaurant, Armand's cannot use time series data to develop the forecast. However, as we will now illustrate, regression analysis can still be used to forecast quarterly sales for this new location.

To develop the equation relating quarterly sales to the size of the student population, Armand's collected data from a sample of 10 of its restaurants located near college campuses. These data are summarized in Table 8.13. For example, restaurant 1, with $y = 58$ and $x = 2$, had \$58,000 in quarterly sales and is located near a campus with 2,000 students. Figure 8.16 shows a scatter chart of the data presented in Table 8.13, with the size of the student population shown on the horizontal axis and quarterly sales shown on the vertical axis.

What preliminary conclusions can we draw from Figure 8.16? Sales appear to be higher at locations near campuses with larger student populations. Also, it appears that the relationship between the two variables can be approximated by a straight line. In Figure 8.17, we can draw a straight line through the data that appears to provide a good linear approximation of the relationship between the variables. Observe that the relationship is not perfect. Indeed, few, if any, of the data fall exactly on the line. However, if we can develop the mathematical expression for this line, we may be able to use it to forecast the value of y corresponding to each possible value of x. The resulting equation of the line is called the estimated regression equation.

Using the least squares method of estimation, the estimated regression equation is

$$\hat{y}_i = b_0 + b_1 x_i \tag{8.14}$$

where

$\hat{y}_i$ = estimated value of the dependent variable (quarterly sales) for the ith observation
b_0 = intercept of the estimated regression equation
b_1 = slope of the estimated regression equation
x_i = value of the independent variable (student population) for the ith observation

The Excel output for a simple linear regression analysis of the Armand's Pizza data is provided in Figure 8.18.

We see in this output that the estimated intercept b_0 is 60 and the estimated slope b_1 is 5. Thus, the estimated regression equation is

$$\hat{y}_i = 60 + 5x_i$$

The slope of the estimated regression equation ($b_1 = 5$) is positive, implying that, as student population increases, quarterly sales increase. In fact, we can conclude (because sales are measured in thousands of dollars and student population in thousands) that an increase in the student population of 1,000 is associated with an increase of \$5,000 in expected

DATA *file*

Armand's

TABLE 8.13	Student Population and Quarterly Sales Data for 10 Armand's Pizza Parlors	
Restaurant	**Student Population (1,000s)**	**Quarterly Sales (\$1,000s)**
1	2	58
2	6	105
3	8	88
4	8	118
5	12	117
6	16	137
7	20	157
8	20	169
9	22	149
10	26	202

FIGURE 8.16   Scatter Chart of Student Population and Quarterly Sales for Armand's Pizza Parlors

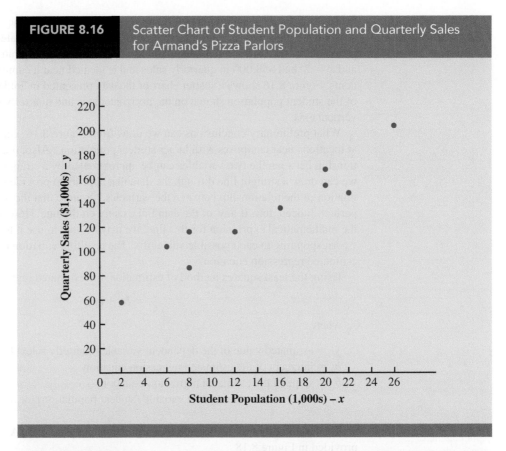

FIGURE 8.17   Graph of the Estimated Regression Equation for Armand's Pizza Parlors: $y = 60 + 5x$

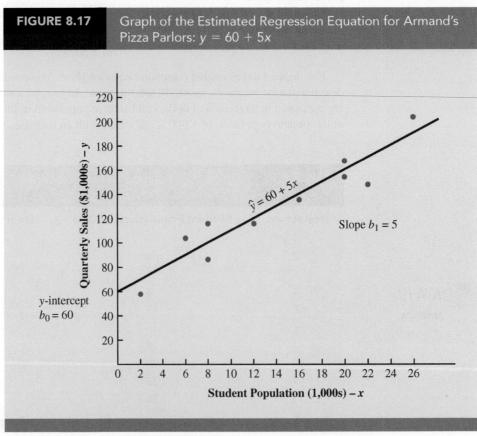

FIGURE 8.18	Excel Simple Linear Regression Output for Armand's Pizza Parlors

	A	B	C	D	E	F	G	H	I
1	SUMMARY OUTPUT								
2									
3	*Regression Statistics*								
4	Multiple R	0.950122955							
5	R Square	0.90273363							
6	Adjusted R Square	0.890575334							
7	Standard Error	13.82931669							
8	Observations	10							
9									
10	ANOVA								
11		*df*	*SS*	*MS*	*F*	*Significance F*			
12	Regression	1	14200	14200	74.24836601	2.54887E-05			
13	Residual	8	1530	191.25					
14	Total	9	15730						
15									
16		*Coefficients*	*Standard Error*	*t Stat*	*P-value*	*Lower 95%*	*Upper 95%*	*Lower 99.0%*	*Upper 99.0%*
17	Intercept	60	9.22603481	6.503335532	0.000187444	38.72472558	81.27527442	29.04307968	90.95692032
18	Student Population (1000s)	5	0.580265238	8.616749156	2.54887E-05	3.661905962	6.338094038	3.052985371	6.947014629

Note that the values of the independent variable range from 2,000 to 26,000; thus, as discussed in Chapter 7, the y-intercept in such cases is an extrapolation of the regression line and must be interpreted with caution.

quarterly sales; that is, quarterly sales are expected to increase by $5 per student. The estimated y-intercept b_0 tells us that if the student population for the location of an Armand's pizza parlor was 0 students, we would expect sales of $60,000.

If we believe that the least squares estimated regression equation adequately describes the relationship between x and y, using the estimated regression equation to forecast the value of y for a given value of x seems reasonable. For example, if we wanted to forecast quarterly sales for a new restaurant to be located near a campus with 16,000 students, we would compute as follows:

$$\hat{y} = 60 + 5(16)$$
$$= 140$$

Hence, we would forecast quarterly sales of $140,000.

Combining Causal Variables with Trend and Seasonality Effects

Regression models are very flexible and can incorporate both causal variables and time series effects. Suppose we had a time series of several years of quarterly sales data and advertising expenditures for a single Armand's restaurant. If we suspected that sales were related to advertising expenditures and that sales showed trend and seasonal effects, we could incorporate each into a single model by combining the approaches we have outlined. If we believe that the effect of advertising is not immediate, we might also try to find a relationship between sales in period t and advertising in the previous period, $t - 1$.

The value of an independent variable from the prior period is referred to as a lagged variable.

Multiple regression analysis also can be applied in these situations if additional data for other independent variables are available. For example, suppose that the management of Armand's Pizza Parlors also believes that the number of competitors near the college campus is related to quarterly sales. Intuitively, management believes that restaurants located near campuses with fewer competitors generate more sales revenue than those located near campuses with more competitors. With additional data, multiple regression analysis could be used to develop an equation relating quarterly sales to the size of the student population and the number of competitors.

Considerations in Using Regression in Forecasting

Although regression analysis allows for the estimation of complex forecasting models, we must be cautious about using such models and guard against the potential for overfitting our model to the sample data. Spyros Makridakis, a noted forecasting expert, conducted research showing that simple techniques usually outperform more complex procedures for short-term forecasting. Using a more sophisticated and expensive procedure will not guarantee better forecasts. However, many research studies, including those done by Makridakis, have also shown that quantitative forecasting models such as those presented in this chapter commonly outperform qualitative forecasts made by "experts." Thus, there is good reason to use quantitative forecasting methods whenever data are available.

Whether a regression approach provides a good forecast depends largely on how well we are able to identify and obtain data for independent variables that are closely related to the time series. Generally, during the development of an estimated regression equation, we will want to consider many possible sets of independent variables. Thus, part of the regression analysis procedure should focus on the selection of the set of independent variables that provides the best forecasting model.

NOTES + COMMENTS

Many different software packages can be used to estimate regression models. Section 7.4 in this textbook explains how Excel's Regression tool can be used to perform regression analysis. The online appendices available with this text demonstrate the use of several popular statistical packages to estimate regression models.

8.5 Determining the Best Forecasting Model to Use

Given the variety of forecasting models and approaches, the obvious question is, "For a given forecasting study, how does one choose an appropriate model?" As discussed throughout this text, it is always a good idea to get descriptive statistics on the data and graph the data so that they can be visually inspected. In the case of time series data, a visual inspection can indicate whether seasonality appears to be a factor and whether a linear or nonlinear trend seems to exist. For causal modeling, scatter charts can indicate whether strong linear or nonlinear relationships exist between the independent and dependent variables. If certain relationships appear totally random, this may lead you to exclude these variables from the model.

As in regression analysis, you may be working with large data sets when generating a forecasting model. In such cases, it is recommended to divide your data into training and validation sets. For example, you might have five years of monthly data available to produce a time series forecast. You could use the first three years of data as a training set to estimate a model or a collection of models that appear to provide good forecasts. You might develop exponential smoothing models and regression models for the training set. You could then use the last two years as a validation set to assess and compare the models' performances. Based on the errors produced by the different models for the validation set, you could ultimately pick the model that minimizes some forecast error measure, such as MAE, MSE, or MAPE. However, you must exercise caution in using the older portion of a time series for the training set and the more recent portion of the time series as the validation set; if the behavior of the time series has changed recently, the older portion of the time series may no longer show patterns similar to the more recent values of the time series, and a forecasting model based on such data will not perform well.

Some software packages try many different forecasting models on time series data (those included in this chapter and more) and report back optimal model parameters and error measures for each model tested. Although some of these software packages will even automatically select the best model to use, ultimately the user should decide which model to use going forward based on a combination of the software output and the user's managerial knowledge.

SUMMARY

This chapter provided an introduction to the basic methods of time series analysis and forecasting. First, we showed that to explain the behavior of a time series, it is often helpful to graph the time series and identify whether trend, seasonal, and/or cyclical components are present in the time series. The methods we have discussed are based on assumptions about which of these components are present in the time series.

We discussed how smoothing methods can be used to forecast a time series that exhibits no significant trend, seasonal, or cyclical effect. The moving average approach consists of computing an average of past data values and then using that average as the forecast for the next period. In the exponential smoothing method, a weighted average of past time series values is used to compute a forecast.

For time series that have only a long-term trend, we showed how regression analysis could be used to make trend projections. For time series with seasonal influences, we showed how to incorporate the seasonality for more accurate forecasts. We described how regression analysis can be used to develop causal forecasting models that relate values of the variable to be forecast (the dependent variable) to other independent variables that are believed to explain (cause) the behavior of the dependent variable. Finally, we have provided guidance on how to select an appropriate model from the models discussed in this chapter.

GLOSSARY

Autoregressive model A regression model in which a regression relationship based on past time series values is used to predict the future time series values.

Causal models Forecasting methods that relate a time series to other variables that are believed to explain or cause its behavior.

Cyclical pattern The component of the time series that results in periodic above-trend and below-trend behavior of the time series lasting more than one year.

Exponential smoothing A forecasting technique that uses a weighted average of past time series values as the forecast.

Forecast error The amount by which the forecasted value $\hat{y}_t$ differs from the observed value y_t, denoted by $e_t = y_t - \hat{y}_t$.

Forecasts A prediction of future values of a time series.

Mean absolute error (MAE) A measure of forecasting accuracy; the average of the values of the forecast errors. Also referred to as mean absolute deviation (MAD).

Mean absolute percentage error (MAPE) A measure of the accuracy of a forecasting method; the average of the absolute values of the errors as a percentage of the corresponding forecast values.

Mean squared error (MSE) A measure of the accuracy of a forecasting method; the average of the sum of the squared differences between the forecast values and the actual time series values.

Moving average method A method of forecasting or smoothing a time series that uses the average of the most recent n data values in the time series as the forecast for the next period.

Naïve forecasting method A forecasting technique that uses the value of the time series from the most recent period as the forecast for the current period.

Seasonal pattern The component of the time series that shows a periodic pattern over one year or less.

Smoothing constant A parameter of the exponential smoothing model that provides the weight given to the most recent time series value in the calculation of the forecast value.

Stationary time series A time series whose statistical properties are independent of time.

Time series A set of observations on a variable measured at successive points in time or over successive periods of time.

Trend The long-run shift or movement in the time series observable over several periods of time.

PROBLEMS

1. **Measuring the Forecast Accuracy of the Naïve Method.** Consider the following time series data:

Week	1	2	3	4	5	6
Value	18	13	16	11	17	14

Using the naïve method (most recent value) as the forecast for the next week, compute the following:
a. Mean absolute error
b. Mean squared error
c. Mean absolute percentage error
d. Forecast for week 7

2. **Measuring the Forecast Accuracy of the Average of All Historical Data.** Refer to the time series data in Problem 1. Using the average of all the historical data as a forecast for the next period, compute the following:
a. Mean absolute error
b. Mean squared error
c. Mean absolute percentage error
d. Forecast for week 7

3. **Comparing the Forecast Accuracy of the Naïve Method and the Average of All Historical Data.** Problems 1 and 2 used different forecasting methods. Which method appears to provide the more accurate forecasts for the historical data? Explain.

4. **Measuring the Forecast Accuracy for Monthly Data.** Consider the following time series data:

Month	1	2	3	4	5	6	7
Value	24	13	20	12	19	23	15

a. Compute MSE using the most recent value as the forecast for the next period. What is the forecast for month 8?
b. Compute MSE using the average of all the data available as the forecast for the next period. What is the forecast for month 8?
c. Which method appears to provide the better forecast?

5. **Forecasting Weekly Data.** Consider the following time series data:

Week	1	2	3	4	5	6
Value	18	13	16	11	17	14

a. Construct a time series plot. What type of pattern exists in the data?
b. Develop a three-week moving average for this time series. Compute MSE and a forecast for week 7.
c. Use $\alpha = 0.2$ to compute the exponential smoothing values for the time series. Compute MSE and a forecast for week 7.
d. Compare the three-week moving average forecast with the exponential smoothing forecast using $\alpha = 0.2$. Which appears to provide the better forecast based on MSE? Explain.
e. Use trial and error to find a value of the exponential smoothing coefficient α that results in a smaller MSE than what you calculated for $\alpha = 0.2$.

6. **Forecasting Monthly Data.** Consider the following time series data:

Month	1	2	3	4	5	6	7
Value	24	13	20	12	19	23	15

a. Construct a time series plot. What type of pattern exists in the data?
b. Develop a three-week moving average for this time series. Compute MSE and a forecast for week 8.

c. Use $\alpha = 0.2$ to compute the exponential smoothing values for the time series. Compute MSE and a forecast for week 8.

d. Compare the three-week moving average forecast with the exponential smoothing forecast using $\alpha = 0.2$. Which appears to provide the better forecast based on MSE?

e. Use trial and error to find a value of the exponential smoothing coefficient α that results in a smaller MSE than what you calculated for $\alpha = 0.2$.

Gasoline

7. **Forecasting Gasoline Sales with Moving Averages.** Refer to the gasoline sales time series data in Table 8.1.

a. Compute four-week and five-week moving averages for the time series.

b. Compute the MSE for the four-week and five-week moving average forecasts.

c. What appears to be the best number of weeks of past data (three, four, or five) to use in the moving average computation? Recall that the MSE for the three-week moving average is 10.22.

Gasoline

8. **Forecasting Gasoline Sales with Exponential Smoothing.** With the gasoline time series data from Table 8.1, show the exponential smoothing forecasts using $\alpha = 0.1$.

a. Applying the MSE measure of forecast accuracy, would you prefer a smoothing constant of $\alpha = 0.1$ or $\alpha = 0.2$ for the gasoline sales time series?

b. Are the results the same if you apply MAE as the measure of accuracy?

c. What are the results if MAPE is used?

9. **Comparing Gasoline Sales Forecasts with Moving Averages and Exponential Smoothing.** With a smoothing constant of $\alpha = 0.2$, equation (8.7) shows that the forecast for week 13 of the gasoline sales data from Table 8.1 is given by $\hat{y}_{13} = 0.2y_{12} + 0.8\hat{y}_{12}$. However, the forecast for week 12 is given by $\hat{y}_{12} = 0.2y_{11} + 0.8\hat{y}_{11}$. Thus, we could combine these two results to show that the forecast for week 13 can be written as

$$\hat{y}_{13} = 0.2y_{12} + 0.8(0.2y_{11} + 0.8\hat{y}_{11}) = 0.2y_{12} + 0.16y_{11} + 0.64\hat{y}_{11}$$

a. Making use of the fact that $\hat{y}_{11} = 0.2y_{10} + 0.8\hat{y}_{10}$ (and similarly for $\hat{y}_{10}$ and $\hat{y}_9$), continue to expand the expression for $\hat{y}_{13}$ until it is written in terms of the past data values $y_{12}, y_{11}, y_{10}, y_9, y_8$, and the forecast for period 8, $\hat{y}_8$.

b. Refer to the coefficients or weights for the past values $y_{12}, y_{11}, y_{10}, y_9$, and y_8. What observation can you make about how exponential smoothing weights past data values in arriving at new forecasts? Compare this weighting pattern with the weighting pattern of the moving averages method.

10. **Demand for Dairy Products.** United Dairies, Inc. supplies milk to several independent grocers throughout Dade County, Florida. Managers at United Dairies want to develop a forecast of the number of half gallons of milk sold per week. Sales data for the past 12 weeks are as follows:

UnitedDairies

Week	Sales	Week	Sales
1	2,750	7	3,300
2	3,100	8	3,100
3	3,250	9	2,950
4	2,800	10	3,000
5	2,900	11	3,200
6	3,050	12	3,150

a. Construct a time series plot. What type of pattern exists in the data?

b. Use exponential smoothing with $\alpha = 0.4$ to develop a forecast of demand for week 13. What is the resulting MSE?

Hawkins

11. **On-Time Shipments.** For the Hawkins Company, the monthly percentages of all shipments received on time over the past 12 months are 80, 82, 84, 83, 83, 84, 85, 84, 82, 83, 84, and 83.

a. Construct a time series plot. What type of pattern exists in the data?

    b. Compare a three-month moving average forecast with an exponential smoothing forecast for $\alpha = 0.2$. Which provides the better forecasts using MSE as the measure of model accuracy?

    c. What is the forecast for the next month?

TripleABond

12. **Bond Interest Rates.** Corporate triple A bond interest rates for 12 consecutive months are as follows:

    9.5　9.3　9.4　9.6　9.8　9.7　9.8　10.5　9.9　9.7　9.6　9.6

    a. Construct a time series plot. What type of pattern exists in the data?

    b. Develop three-month and four-month moving averages for this time series. Does the three-month or the four-month moving average provide the better forecasts based on MSE? Explain.

    c. What is the moving average forecast for the next month?

Alabama

13. **Building Contracts.** The values of Alabama building contracts (in millions of dollars) for a 12-month period are as follows:

    240　350　230　260　280　320　220　310　240　310　240　230

    a. Construct a time series plot. What type of pattern exists in the data?

    b. Compare a three-month moving average forecast with an exponential smoothing forecast. Use $\alpha = 0.2$. Which provides the better forecasts based on MSE?

    c. What is the forecast for the next month using exponential smoothing with $\alpha = 0.2$?

14. **Sales Forecasts.** The following time series shows the sales of a particular product over the past 12 months.

MonthlySales

Month	Sales	Month	Sales
1	105	7	145
2	135	8	140
3	120	9	100
4	105	10	80
5	90	11	100
6	120	12	110

    a. Construct a time series plot. What type of pattern exists in the data?

    b. Use $\alpha = 0.3$ to compute the exponential smoothing values for the time series.

    c. Use trial and error to find a value of the exponential smoothing coefficient α that results in a relatively small MSE.

CommodityFutures

15. **Commodity Futures Index.** Ten weeks of data on the Commodity Futures Index are as follows:

    7.35　7.40　7.55　7.56　7.60　7.52　7.52　7.70　7.62　7.55

    a. Construct a time series plot. What type of pattern exists in the data?

    b. Use trial and error to find a value of the exponential smoothing coefficient α that results in a relatively small MSE.

16. **Portfolio Composition.** The following table reports the percentage of stocks in a portfolio for nine quarters:

Portfolio

Quarter	Stock (%)
Year 1, Quarter 1	29.8
Year 1, Quarter 2	31.0
Year 1, Quarter 3	29.9
Year 1, Quarter 4	30.1
Year 2, Quarter 1	32.2
Year 2, Quarter 2	31.5
Year 2, Quarter 3	32.0
Year 2, Quarter 4	31.9
Year 3, Quarter 1	30.0

a. Construct a time series plot. What type of pattern exists in the data?
b. Use trial and error to find a value of the exponential smoothing coefficient α that results in a relatively small MSE.
c. Using the exponential smoothing model you developed in part (b), what is the forecast of the percentage of stocks in a typical portfolio for the second quarter of year 3?

17. **Using Regression for Forecasting with Five Time Periods of Data.** Consider the following time series:

t	1	2	3	4	5
y_t	6	11	9	14	15

a. Construct a time series plot. What type of pattern exists in the data?
b. Use simple linear regression analysis to find the parameters for the line that minimizes MSE for this time series.
c. What is the forecast for $t = 6$?

18. **Using Regression for Forecasting with Seven Time Periods of Data.** Consider the following time series:

t	1	2	3	4	5	6	7
y_t	120	110	100	96	94	92	88

a. Construct a time series plot. What type of pattern exists in the data?
b. Use simple linear regression analysis to find the parameters for the line that minimizes MSE for this time series.
c. What is the forecast for $t = 8$?

19. **University Enrollment.** Because of high tuition costs at state and private universities, enrollments at community colleges have increased dramatically in recent years. The following data show the enrollment for Jefferson Community College for the nine most recent years:

DATA *file*
Jefferson

Year	Period (t)	Enrollment (1,000s)
2001	1	6.5
2002	2	8.1
2003	3	8.4
2004	4	10.2
2005	5	12.5
2006	6	13.3
2007	7	13.7
2008	8	17.2
2009	9	18.1

a. Construct a time series plot. What type of pattern exists in the data?
b. Use simple linear regression analysis to find the parameters for the line that minimizes MSE for this time series.
c. What is the forecast for year 10?

20. **Administrative Expenses.** The Seneca Children's Fund (SCF) is a local charity that runs a summer camp for disadvantaged children. The fund's board of directors has been working very hard over recent years to decrease the amount of overhead expenses, a major factor in how charities are rated by independent agencies. The following data show the percentage of the money SCF has raised that was spent on administrative and fund-raising expenses over the past seven years:

DATA *file*

Seneca

Period (t)	Expense (%)
1	13.9
2	12.2
3	10.5
4	10.4
5	11.5
6	10.0
7	8.5

a. Construct a time series plot. What type of pattern exists in the data?

b. Use simple linear regression analysis to find the parameters for the line that minimizes MSE for this time series.

c. Forecast the percentage of administrative expenses for year 8.

d. If SCF can maintain its current trend in reducing administrative expenses, how long will it take for SCF to achieve a level of 5% or less?

21. **Manufacturing Costs.** The president of a small manufacturing firm is concerned about the continual increase in manufacturing costs over the past several years. The following figures provide a time series of the cost per unit for the firm's leading product over the past eight years:

DATA *file*

ManufacturingCosts

Year	Cost/Unit ($)	Year	Cost/Unit($)
1	20.00	5	26.60
2	24.50	6	30.00
3	28.20	7	31.00
4	27.50	8	36.00

a. Construct a time series plot. What type of pattern exists in the data?

b. Use simple linear regression analysis to find the parameters for the line that minimizes MSE for this time series.

c. What is the average cost increase that the firm has been realizing per year?

d. Compute an estimate of the cost/unit for the next year.

22. **Estimating Seasonal Effects.** Consider the following time series:

Quarter	Year 1	Year 2	Year 3
1	71	68	62
2	49	41	51
3	58	60	53
4	78	81	72

a. Construct a time series plot. What type of pattern exists in the data? Is there an indication of a seasonal pattern?

b. Use a multiple linear regression model with dummy variables as follows to develop an equation to account for seasonal effects in the data: Qtr1 = 1 if quarter 1, 0 otherwise; Qtr2 = 1 if quarter 2, 0 otherwise; Qtr3 = 1 if quarter 3, 0 otherwise.

c. Compute the quarterly forecasts for the next year.

23. **Estimating Trend and Seasonal Effects.** Consider the following time series data:

Quarter	Year 1	Year 2	Year 3
1	4	6	7
2	2	3	6
3	3	5	6
4	5	7	8

a. Construct a time series plot. What type of pattern exists in the data?
b. Use a multiple regression model with dummy variables as follows to develop an equation to account for seasonal effects in the data: Qtr1 = 1 if quarter 1, 0 otherwise; Qtr2 = 1 if quarter 2, 0 otherwise; Qtr3 = 1 if quarter 3, 0 otherwise.
c. Compute the quarterly forecasts for the next year based on the model you developed in part (b).
d. Use a multiple regression model to develop an equation to account for trend and seasonal effects in the data. Use the dummy variables you developed in part (b) to capture seasonal effects and create a variable t such that $t = 1$ for quarter 1 in year 1, $t = 2$ for quarter 2 in year 1, ... $t = 12$ for quarter 4 in year 3.
e. Compute the quarterly forecasts for the next year based on the model you developed in part (d).
f. Is the model you developed in part (b) or the model you developed in part (d) more effective? Justify your answer.

24. **Textbook Sales.** The quarterly sales data (number of copies sold) for a college textbook over the past three years are as follows:

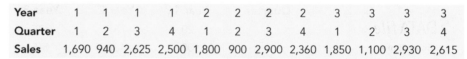

Year	1	1	1	1	2	2	2	2	3	3	3	3
Quarter	1	2	3	4	1	2	3	4	1	2	3	4
Sales	1,690	940	2,625	2,500	1,800	900	2,900	2,360	1,850	1,100	2,930	2,615

a. Construct a time series plot. What type of pattern exists in the data?
b. Use a regression model with dummy variables as follows to develop an equation to account for seasonal effects in the data: Qtr1 = 1 if quarter 1, 0 otherwise; Qtr2 = 1 if quarter 2, 0 otherwise; Qtr3 = 1 if quarter 3, 0 otherwise.
c. Based on the model you developed in part (b), compute the quarterly forecasts for the next year.
d. Let $t = 1$ refer to the observation in quarter 1 of year 1; $t = 2$ refer to the observation in quarter 2 of year 1; ... ; and $t = 12$ refer to the observation in quarter 4 of year 3. Using the dummy variables defined in part (b) and t, develop an equation to account for seasonal effects and any linear trend in the time series.
e. Based upon the seasonal effects in the data and linear trend, compute the quarterly forecasts for the next year.
f. Is the model you developed in part (b) or the model you developed in part (d) more effective? Justify your answer.

25. **Air Pollution.** Air pollution control specialists in Southern California monitor the amount of ozone, carbon dioxide, and nitrogen dioxide in the air on an hourly basis. The hourly time series data exhibit seasonality, with the levels of pollutants showing patterns that vary over the hours in the day. On July 15, 16, and 17, the following levels of nitrogen dioxide were observed for the 12 hours from 6:00 a.m. to 6:00 p.m.:

July 15	25	28	35	50	60	60	40	35	30	25	25	20
July 16	28	30	35	48	60	65	50	40	35	25	20	20
July 17	35	42	45	70	72	75	60	45	40	25	25	25

a. Construct a time series plot. What type of pattern exists in the data?
b. Use a multiple linear regression model with dummy variables as follows to develop an equation to account for seasonal effects in the data:

Hour1 = 1 if the reading was made between 6:00 a.m. and 7:00 a.m., 0 otherwise
Hour2 = 1 if the reading was made between 7:00 a.m. and 8:00 a.m., 0 otherwise
⋮
Hour11 = 1 if the reading was made between 4:00 p.m. and 5:00 p.m., 0 otherwise

Note that when the values of the 11 dummy variables are equal to 0, the observation corresponds to the 5:00 p.m. to 6:00 p.m. hour.

   c. Using the equation developed in part (b), compute estimates of the levels of nitrogen dioxide for July 18.

   d. Let $t = 1$ refer to the observation in hour 1 on July 15; $t = 2$ refer to the observation in hour 2 of July 15; . . . ; and $t = 36$ refer to the observation in hour 12 of July
17. Using the dummy variables defined in part (b) and t_s, develop an equation to
account for seasonal effects and any linear trend in the time series.

   e. Based on the seasonal effects in the data and linear trend estimated in part (d), compute estimates of the levels of nitrogen dioxide for July 18.

   f. Is the model you developed in part (b) or the model you developed in part (d) more
effective? Justify your answer.

26. **Sales of Docks and Seawalls.** South Shore Construction builds permanent docks and
seawalls along the southern shore of Long Island, New York. Although the firm has
been in business for only five years, revenue has increased from $308,000 in the first
year of operation to $1,084,000 in the most recent year. The following data show the
quarterly sales revenue in thousands of dollars:

DATAfile

SouthShore

Quarter	Year 1	Year 2	Year 3	Year 4	Year 5
1	20	37	75	92	176
2	100	136	155	202	282
3	175	245	326	384	445
4	13	26	48	82	181

   a. Construct a time series plot. What type of pattern exists in the data?

   b. Use a multiple regression model with dummy variables as follows to develop an
equation to account for seasonal effects in the data: Qtr1 = 1 if quarter 1, 0 otherwise; Qtr2 = 1 if quarter 2, 0 otherwise; Qtr3 = 1 if quarter 3, 0 otherwise.

   c. Based on the model you developed in part (b), compute estimates of quarterly sales
for year 6.

   d. Let Period = 1 refer to the observation in quarter 1 of year 1; Period = 2 refer to the
observation in quarter 2 of year 1; . . . ; and Period = 20 refer to the observation in
quarter 4 of year 5. Using the dummy variables defined in part (b) and the variable
Period, develop an equation to account for seasonal effects and any linear trend in
the time series.

   e. Based on the seasonal effects in the data and linear trend estimated in part (c), compute estimates of quarterly sales for year 6.

   f. Is the model you developed in part (b) or the model you developed in part (d) more
effective? Justify your answer.

DATAfile

IceCreamSales

27. **Sales of Frozen Treats.** Hogs & Dawgs is an ice cream parlor on the border of north-
central Louisiana and southern Arkansas that serves 43 flavors of ice creams, sherbets,
frozen yogurts, and sorbets. During the summer Hogs & Dawgs is open from 1:00 p.m. to
10:00 p.m. on Monday through Saturday, and the owner believes that sales change systematically from hour to hour throughout the day. She also believes that her sales increase as
the outdoor temperature increases. Hourly sales and the outside temperature at the start of
each hour for the last week are provided in the file *IceCreamSales*.

   a. Construct a time series plot of hourly sales and a scatter plot of outdoor temperature
and hourly sales. What types of relationships exist in the data?

   b. Use a simple regression model with outside temperature as the causal variable
to develop an equation to account for the relationship between outside temperature and hourly sales in the data. Based on this model, compute an estimate of
hourly sales for today from 2:00 p.m. to 3:00 p.m. if the temperature at 2:00 p.m.
is 93°F.

   c. Use a multiple linear regression model with the causal variable outside temperature and dummy variables as follows to develop an equation to account for both

seasonal effects and the relationship between outside temperature and hourly sales in the data:

Hour1 = 1 if the sales were recorded between 1:00 p.m. and 2:00 p.m., 0 otherwise
Hour2 = 1 if the sales were recorded between 2:00 p.m. and 3:00 p.m., 0 otherwise
⋮
Hour8 = 1 if the sales were recorded between 8:00 p.m. and 9:00 p.m., 0 otherwise

Note that when the values of the eight dummy variables are equal to 0, the observation corresponds to the 9:00-to-10:00-p.m. hour.

Based on this model, compute an estimate of hourly sales for today from 2:00 p.m. to 3:00 p.m. if the temperature at 2:00 p.m. is 93°F.

d. Is the model you developed in part (b) or the model you developed in part (c) more effective? Justify your answer.

DATA *file*

GasStation

28. **Gasoline Sales and Price.** Donna Nickles manages a gasoline station on the corner of Bristol Avenue and Harpst Street in Arcata, California. Her station is a franchise, and the parent company calls her station every day at midnight to give her the prices for various grades of gasoline for the upcoming day. Over the past eight weeks Donna has recorded the price and sales (in gallons) of regular-grade gasoline at her station as well as the price of regular-grade gasoline charged by her competitor across the street. She is curious about the sensitivity of her sales to the price of regular gasoline she charges and the price of regular gasoline charged by her competitor across the street. She also wonders whether her sales differ systematically by day of the week and whether her station has experienced a trend in sales over the past eight weeks. The data collected by Donna for each day of the past eight weeks are provided in the file *GasStation*.

a. Construct a time series plot of daily sales, a scatter plot of the price Donna charges for a gallon of regular gasoline and daily sales at Donna's station, and a scatter plot of the price Donna's competitor charges for a gallon of regular gasoline and daily sales at Donna's station. What types of relationships exist in the data?

b. Use a multiple regression model with the price Donna charges for a gallon of regular gasoline and the price Donna's competitor charges for a gallon of regular gasoline as causal variables to develop an equation to account for the relationships between these prices and Donna's daily sales in the data. Based on this model, compute an estimate of sales for a day on which Donna is charging $3.50 for a gallon of regular gasoline and her competitor is charging $3.45 for a gallon of regular gasoline.

c. Use a multiple linear regression model with the trend and dummy variables as follows to develop an equation to account for both trend and seasonal effects in the data:

Monday = 1 if the sales were recorded on a Monday, 0 otherwise
Tuesday = 1 if the sales were recorded on a Tuesday, 0 otherwise
⋮
Saturday = 1 if the sales were recorded on a Saturday, 0 otherwise

Note that when the values of the six dummy variables are equal to 0, the observation corresponds to Sunday.

Based on this model, compute an estimate of sales for Tuesday of the first week after Donna collected her data.

d. Use a multiple regression model with the price Donna charges for a gallon of regular gasoline and the price Donna's competitor charges for a gallon of regular gasoline as causal variables and the trend and dummy variables from part (c) to create an equation to account for the relationships between these prices and daily sales as well as the trend and seasonal effects in the data. Based on this model, compute an estimate of sales for Tuesday of the first week after Donna collected her data a day if Donna is charging $3.50 for a gallon of regular gasoline and her competitor is charging $3.45 for a gallon of regular gasoline.

e. Which of the three models you developed in parts (b), (c), and (d) is most effective? Justify your answer.

CASE PROBLEM 1: FORECASTING FOOD AND BEVERAGE SALES

The Vintage Restaurant, on Captiva Island near Fort Myers, Florida, is owned and operated by Karen Payne. The restaurant just completed its third year of operation. During those three years, Karen sought to establish a reputation for the restaurant as a high-quality dining establishment that specializes in fresh seafood. Through the efforts of Karen and her staff, her restaurant has become one of the best and fastest-growing restaurants on the Island.

To better plan for future growth of the restaurant, Karen needs to develop a system that will enable her to forecast food and beverage sales by month for up to one year in advance. The following table shows the value of food and beverage sales ($1,000s) for the first three years of operation:

DATA *file*

Vintage

Month	First Year	Second Year	Third Year
January	242	263	282
February	235	238	255
March	232	247	265
April	178	193	205
May	184	193	210
June	140	149	160
July	145	157	166
August	152	161	174
September	110	122	126
October	130	130	148
November	152	167	173
December	206	230	235

Managerial Report

Perform an analysis of the sales data for the Vintage Restaurant. Prepare a report for Karen that summarizes your findings, forecasts, and recommendations. Include the following:

1. A time series plot. Comment on the underlying pattern in the time series.
2. Using the dummy variable approach, forecast sales for January through December of the fourth year. How would you explain this model to Karen?

Assume that January sales for the fourth year turn out to be $295,000. What was your forecast error? If this error is large, Karen may be puzzled about the difference between your forecast and the actual sales value. What can you do to resolve her uncertainty about the forecasting procedure?

CASE PROBLEM 2: FORECASTING LOST SALES

The Carlson Department Store suffered heavy damage when a hurricane struck on August 31. The store was closed for four months (September through December), and Carlson is now involved in a dispute with its insurance company about the amount of lost sales during the time the store was closed. Two key issues must be resolved: (1) the amount of sales Carlson would have made if the hurricane had not struck and (2) whether Carlson is entitled to any compensation for excess sales due to increased business activity after the storm. More than $8 billion in federal disaster relief and insurance money came into the county, resulting in increased sales at department stores and numerous other businesses.

The following two tables give (1) Carlson's sales data for the 48 months preceding the storm and (2) the total sales for the 48 months preceding the storm for all department stores in the county, as well as the total sales in the county for the four months the Carlson Department Store was closed. Carlson's managers asked you to analyze these data and develop estimates of the lost sales at the Carlson Department Store for the months of September through December. They also asked you to determine whether a case can be made for excess storm-related sales during the same period. If such a case can be made, Carlson is entitled to compensation for excess sales it would have earned in addition to ordinary sales.

Managerial Report

Prepare a report for the managers of the Carlson Department Store that summarizes your findings, forecasts, and recommendations. Include the following:

1. An estimate of sales for Carlson Department Store had there been no hurricane.
2. An estimate of countywide department store sales had there been no hurricane.
3. An estimate of lost sales for the Carlson Department Store for September through December.

In addition, use the countywide actual department stores sales for September through December and the estimate in part (2) to make a case for or against excess storm-related sales.

Sales for Carlson Department Store ($ Millions)

Month	Year 1	Year 2	Year 3	Year 4	Year 5
January		1.45	2.31	2.31	2.56
February		1.80	1.89	1.99	2.28
March		2.03	2.02	2.42	2.69
April		1.99	2.23	2.45	2.48
May		2.32	2.39	2.57	2.73
June		2.20	2.14	2.42	2.37
July		2.13	2.27	2.40	2.31
August		2.43	2.21	2.50	2.23
September	1.71	1.90	1.89	2.09	
October	1.90	2.13	2.29	2.54	
November	2.74	2.56	2.83	2.97	
December	4.20	4.16	4.04	4.35	

DATA*file*

CarlsonSales

TABLE 17.27 Department Store Sales for the County ($ Millions)

Month	Year 1	Year 2	Year 3	Year 4	Year 5
January		46.80	46.80	43.80	48.00
February		48.00	48.60	45.60	51.60
March		60.00	59.40	57.60	57.60
April		57.60	58.20	53.40	58.20
May		61.80	60.60	56.40	60.00
June		58.20	55.20	52.80	57.00
July		56.40	51.00	54.00	57.60
August		63.00	58.80	60.60	61.80
September	55.80	57.60	49.80	47.40	69.00
October	56.40	53.40	54.60	54.60	75.00
November	71.40	71.40	65.40	67.80	85.20
December	117.60	114.00	102.00	100.20	121.80

DATA*file*

CountySales

Chapter 8 Appendix

Appendix 8.1 Using the Excel Forecast Sheet

Excel features a tool called Forecast Sheet which can automatically produce forecasts using the Holt–Winters additive seasonal smoothing model. The Holt–Winters model is an exponential smoothing approach to estimating additive linear trend and seasonal effects. It also generates a variety of other outputs that are useful in assessing the accuracy of the forecast model it produces.

We will demonstrate Forecast Sheet on the four years of quarterly smartphone sales that are provided in Table 8.6. A review of the time series plot of these data in Figure 8.6 provides clear evidence of an increasing linear trend and a seasonal pattern (sales are consistently lowest in the second quarter of each year and highest in quarters 3 and 4). We concluded in Section 8.4 that we need to use a forecasting method that is capable of dealing with both trend and seasonality when developing a forecasting model for this time series, and so it is appropriate to use Forecast Sheet to produce forecasts for these data.

We begin by putting the data into the format required by Forecast Sheet. The time series data must be collected on a consistent interval (i.e., annually, quarterly, monthly, and so on), and the spreadsheet must include two data series in contiguous columns or rows that include

- a series with the dates or periods in the time series
- a series with corresponding time series values

First, open the file *SmartPhoneSales*, then insert a column between column B ("Quarter") and Column C ("Sales (1000s)"). Enter *Period* into cell C1; this will be the heading for the column of values that will represent the periods in our data. Next enter *1* in cell C2, *2* in cell C3, *3* in cell C4, and so on, ending with *16* in Cell C17, as shown in Figure 8.19.

Now that the data are properly formatted for Forecast Sheet, the following steps can be used to produce forecasts for the next four quarters (periods 17 through 20) with Forecast Sheet:

Step 1. Highlight cells C1:D17 (the data in column C of this highlighted section is what Forecast Sheet refers to as the **Timeline Range** and the data in column D is the **Values Range**)

Step 2. Click the **Data** tab in the Ribbon

Step 3. Click **Forecast Sheet** in the **Forecast** group

Step 4. When the **Create Forecast Worksheet** dialog box appears (Figure 8.20):
Select **20** for **Forecast End**
Click **Options** to expand the **Create Forecast Worksheet** dialog box and show the options (Figure 8.20)
> Select **16** for **Forecast Start**
> Select **95%** for **Confidence Interval**
> Under **Seasonality**, click on **Set Manually** and select **4**
> Select the checkbox for **Include forecast statistics**
> Click **Create**

The results of Forecast Sheet will be output to a new worksheet as shown in Figure 8.21. The output of Forecast Sheet includes the following:

- The period for each of the 16 time series observations and the forecasted time periods in column A
- The actual time series data for periods 1 to 16 in column B

Forecast Sheet was introduced in Excel 2016; it is not available in prior versions of Excel or in Excel Online.

Excel refers to the forecasting approach used by Forecast Sheet as the AAA exponential smoothing (ETS) algorithm, where AAA stands for additive error, additive trend, and additive seasonality.

DATA *file*

SmartPhoneSales

*Forecast Sheet requires that the period selected for **Forecast Start** is one of the periods of the original time series.*

FIGURE 8.19	Smartphone Data Reformatted for Forecast Sheet

	A	B	C	D
1	**Year**	**Quarter**	**Period**	**Sales (1000s)**
2	1	1	1	4.8
3	1	2	2	4.1
4	1	3	3	6.0
5	1	4	4	6.5
6	2	1	5	5.8
7	2	2	6	5.2
8	2	3	7	6.8
9	2	4	8	7.4
10	3	1	9	6.0
11	3	2	10	5.6
12	3	3	11	7.5
13	3	4	12	7.8
14	4	1	13	6.3
15	4	2	14	5.9
16	4	3	15	8.0
17	4	4	16	8.4

- The forecasts for periods 16 to 20 in column C
- The lower confidence bounds for the forecasts for periods 16 to 20 in column D
- The upper confidence bounds for the forecasts for periods 16 to 20 in column E
- A line graph of the time series, forecast values, and forecast interval
- The values of the three parameters (alpha, beta, and gamma) used in the Holt–Winters additive seasonal smoothing model in cells H2:H4 (these values are determined by an algorithm in Forecast Sheet)
- Measures of forecast accuracy in cells H5:H8, including
  - the MASE, or mean absolute scaled error, in cell H5. MASE is defined as:

$$\text{MASE} = \frac{1}{n}\sum_{t=1}^{n}\frac{|e_t|}{\frac{1}{n-1}\sum_{t=2}^{n}|y_t - y_{t-1}|}$$

  MASE compares the forecast error, e_t, to a naïve forecast error given by $|y_t - y_{t-1}|$. If MASE > 1, then the forecast is considered inferior to a naïve forecast; if MASE < 1, the forecast is considered superior to a naïve forecast.
  - the SMAPE, or symmetric mean absolute percentage error, in cell H6. SMAPE is defined as:

$$\text{SMAPE} = \frac{1}{n}\sum_{t=1}^{n}\frac{|e_t|}{(|y_t| + |\hat{y}_t|)/2}$$

  SMAPE is similar to mean absolute percentage error (MAPE), discussed in Section 8.2; both SMAPE and MAPE measure forecast error relative to actual values.

- the MAE, or mean absolute error, (as defined in equation (8.3)) in cell H7
- the RMSE, or root mean squared error, (which is the square root of the MSE, defined in equation (8.4)) in cell H8

Figures 8.22 and 8.23 display the formula view of portions of the worksheet that Forecast Sheet generated based on the smartphone quarterly sales data. For example, in cell C18, the forecast value generated for Period 17 smartphone sales is determined by the formula:

$$=FORECAST.ETS(A18, B2:B17, A2:A17, 4, 1)$$

There is a sixth (optional) argument of the FORECAST.ETS function that addresses how to aggregate multiple observations for the same time period. Choices include AVERAGE, SUM, COUNT, COUNTA, MIN, MAX, and MEDIAN.

The first argument in this function specifies the period to be forecasted. The second argument specifies the time series data upon which the forecast is based. The third argument lists the timeline associated with the time series values. The fourth (optional) argument addresses seasonality, and the value of 4 indicates the length of the seasonal pattern. A value of 1 for the fourth argument of the FORECAST.ETS function means that Excel detects the seasonality in the data automatically. A value of 0 means that there is no seasonality in the data. The fifth (optional) argument addresses missing data, and a value of 1 means that any missing observations will be approximated as the average of the neighboring observations. A value of 0 for the fifth argument of the FORECAST.ETS function

FIGURE 8.21	Forecast Sheet Results for Quarterly Smartphone Sales

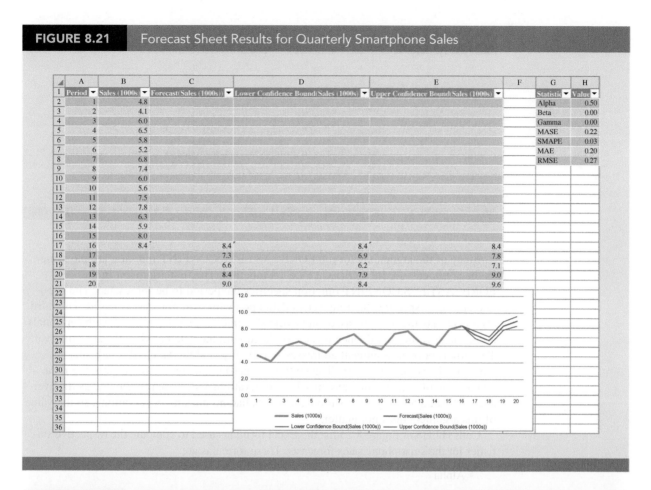

FIGURE 8.22	Formula View of Forecast Sheet Results for Quarterly Smartphone Sales

means that Excel will treat any missing observations as zeros. These data have no missing observations, so the value of this fifth argument does not matter.

Cell D18 contains the lower confidence bound for the forecast of the Period 17 smartphone sales. This lower confidence bound is determined by the formula:

$$\text{=C18-FORECAST.ETS.CONFINT(A18, B2:B17, A2:A17, 0.95, 4, 1)}$$

Similarly, cell E18 contains the upper confidence bound for the forecast of the Period 17 smartphone sales. This upper confidence bound is determined by the formula:

$$\text{=C18+FORECAST.ETS.CONFINT(A18, B2:B17, A2:A17, 0.95, 4, 1)}$$

FIGURE 8.23   Excel Formulas for Smartphone Forecast Statistics

	F	G	H
1		Statistic	Value
2		Alpha	=FORECAST.ETS.STAT($B$2:$B$17,$A$2:$A$17,1,4,1)
3		Beta	=FORECAST.ETS.STAT($B$2:$B$17,$A$2:$A$17,2,4,1)
4		Gamma	=FORECAST.ETS.STAT($B$2:$B$17,$A$2:$A$17,3,4,1)
5		MASE	=FORECAST.ETS.STAT($B$2:$B$17,$A$2:$A$17,4,4,1)
6		SMAPE	=FORECAST.ETS.STAT($B$2:$B$17,$A$2:$A$17,5,4,1)
7		MAE	=FORECAST.ETS.STAT($B$2:$B$17,$A$2:$A$17,6,4,1)
8		RMSE	=FORECAST.ETS.STAT($B$2:$B$17,$A$2:$A$17,7,4,1)

Many of the arguments for the FORECAST.ETS.CONFINT function are the same as the arguments for the FORECAST.ETS function. The first argument in the FORECAST.ETS.CONFINT function specifies the period to be forecasted. The second argument specifies the time series data upon which the forecast is based. The third argument lists the timeline associated with the time series values. The fourth (optional) argument specifies confidence level associated with the calculated confidence interval. The fifth (optional) argument addresses seasonality, and the value of 4 indicates the length of the seasonal pattern. The sixth (optional) argument addresses missing data, and a value of 1 means that any missing observations will be approximated as the average of the neighboring observations; this data had no missing observations, so the value of this argument does not matter.

Cells H2:H8 of Figure 8.23 list the Excel formulas used to compute the respective statistics for the smartphone sales forecasts. These formulas are:

- Alpha

    =FORECAST.ETS.STAT(B2:B17, A2:A17, 1, 4, 1)

- Beta

    =FORECAST.ETS.STAT(B2:B17, A2:A17, 2, 4, 1)

- Gamma

    =FORECAST.ETS.STAT(B2:B17, A2:A17, 3, 4, 1)

- MASE

    =FORECAST.ETS.STAT(B2:B17, A2:A17, 4, 4, 1)

- SMAPE

    =FORECAST.ETS.STAT(B2:B17, A2:A17, 5, 4, 1)

- MAE

    =FORECAST.ETS.STAT(B2:B17, A2:A17, 6, 4, 1)

- RMSE

    =FORECAST.ETS.STAT(B2:B17, A2:A17, 7, 4, 1)

Many of the arguments for the FORECAST.ETS.STAT function are the same as the arguments for the FORECAST.ETS function. The first argument in the FORECAST.ETS.STAT function the time series data upon which the forecast is based. The second argument lists the timeline associated with the time series values. The third argument specifies the statistic or parameter type; for example, a value of 4 corresponds to MASE statistic. The fourth (optional) argument addresses seasonality, and the value of 4 indicates the length of the seasonal pattern. The fifth (optional) argument addresses missing data, and a value of 1 means that any missing observations will be approximated as the average of the neighboring observations; this data had no missing observations, so the value of this argument does not matter.

We conclude this appendix with a few comments on the functionality of Forecast Sheet. Forecast Sheet includes an algorithm for automatically finding the number of time periods over which the seasonal pattern recurs. To use this algorithm, select the option for **Detect Automatically** under **Seasonality** in the **Create Forecast Worksheet** dialog box before clicking **Create**. We suggest using this feature only to confirm a suspected seasonal pattern as using this feature to find a seasonal effect may lead to identification of a spurious pattern that does not actually reflect seasonality. This would result in a model that is overfit on the observed time series data and would likely produce very inaccurate forecasts. A forecast model with seasonality should only be fit when the modeler has reason to suspect a specific seasonal pattern.

The **Forecast Start** parameter in the **Create Forecast Worksheet** dialog box controls both the first period to be forecasted and the last period to be used to generate the forecast model. If we had selected 15 for Forecast Start, we would have generated a forecast model for the smartphone monthly sales data based on only the first 15 periods of data in the original time series.

Forecast Sheet can accommodate multiple observations for a single period of the time series. The **Aggregate Duplicates Using** option in the **Create Forecast Worksheet** dialog box allows the user to select from several ways to deal with this issue.

Forecast Sheet allows for up to 30% of the values for the time series variable to be missing. In the smartphone quarterly sales data, the value of sales for up to 30% of the 16 periods (or 4 periods) could be missing and Forecast Sheet will still produce forecasts. The **Fill Missing Points Using** option in the **Create Forecast Worksheet** dialog box allows the user to select whether the missing values will be replaced with zero or with the result of linearly interpolating existing values in the time series.

Chapter 9

Predictive Data Mining

CONTENTS

APPENDIX: RANDOM FORESTS OF CLASSIFICATION OR REGRESSION
TREES WITH JMP PRO
APPENDIX: JMP PRO SETTINGS TO SOLVE CHAPTER 9 PROBLEMS

ANALYTICS IN ACTION

Orbitz*

Although they might not see their customers face to face, online retailers are getting to know their patrons to tailor the offerings on their virtual shelves. By mining web-browsing data collected in "cookies"—files that web sites use to track people's web-browsing behavior, online retailers identify trends that can potentially be used to improve customer satisfaction and boost online sales.

For example, consider Orbitz, an online travel agency that books flights, hotels, car rentals, cruises, and other travel activities for its customers. Tracking its patrons' online activities, Orbitz discovered that people who use Mac computers spend as much as 30% more per night on hotels. Orbitz's analytics team has uncovered other factors that affect purchase behavior, including how the shopper arrived at the Orbitz site (Did the user visit Orbitz directly or was he or she referred from another site?), previous booking history on Orbitz, and the shopper's geographic location. Orbitz can act on this and other information gleaned from the vast amount of web data to differentiate the recommendations for hotels, car rentals, flight bookings, etc.

—————

*"On Orbitz, Mac Users Steered to Pricier Hotels," *Wall Street Journal* (2012, June 26).

In Chapter 5, we describe descriptive data mining methods, such as clustering and association rules, that explore relationships between observations and/or variables.

Organizations are collecting an increasing amount of data, and one of the most pressing tasks is converting this data into actionable insights. A common challenge is to analyze these data to extract information on patterns and trends that can be used to assist decision makers in predicting future events. In this chapter, we discuss predictive methods that can be applied to leverage data to gain customer insights and to establish new business rules to guide managers.

We define an **observation**, or **record**, as the set of recorded values of **variables** associated with a single entity. An observation is often displayed as a row of values in a spreadsheet or database in which the columns correspond to the variables. For example, in direct-marketing data, an observation may correspond to a customer and contain information regarding her/his response to an e-mail advertisement as well as information regarding her/his demographic characteristics.

See Chapter 7 for a discussion of linear regression.

Supervised learning approaches to estimate a continuous outcome are also commonly referred to as regression methods. We use the language "estimation method" to avoid confusion with the term logistic regression (which is a bit of a misnomer in that it actually is a classification method).

In this chapter, we focus on data mining methods for predicting an outcome based on a set of input variables, or **features**. These methods are also referred to as **supervised learning**. Linear regression is a well-known supervised learning approach from classical statistics in which observations of a quantitative outcome (the dependent y variable) and one or more corresponding features (the independent variables $x_1, x_2, \ldots, x_q$) are used to create an equation for estimating y values. That is, in supervised learning the outcome variable "supervises" or guides the process of "learning" how to predict future outcomes. In this chapter, we focus on supervised learning methods for the **estimation** of a continuous outcome (e.g., sales revenue) and for **classification** of a binary categorical outcomes (e.g., whether or not a customer defaults on a loan).

The data mining process comprises the following steps:

Chapter 5 discusses the data-preparation process as well as clustering techniques often used to redefine variables. Chapters 2 and 3 discuss descriptive statistics and data-visualization techniques.

1. *Data sampling.* Extract a sample of data that is relevant to the business problem under consideration.
2. *Data preparation.* Manipulate the data to put it in a form suitable for formal modeling. This step includes addressing missing and erroneous data, reducing the number of variables, and defining new variables. Data exploration is an important part of this step and may involve the use of descriptive statistics, data visualization, and clustering to better understand the relationships supported by the data.
3. *Data partitioning.* Divide the sample data for the training, validation, and testing of the data mining algorithm performance.
4. *Model construction.* Apply the appropriate data mining technique (e.g., *k*-nearest neighbors) to the training data set to accomplish the desired data mining task (classification or estimation).

5. *Model assessment.* Evaluate models by comparing performance on the training and validation data sets. Apply the selected model to the test data as a final appraisal of the model's performance.

9.1 Data Sampling, Preparation, and Partitioning

Upon identifying a business problem, data on relevant variables must be obtained for analysis. Although access to large amounts of data offers the potential to unlock insight and improve decision making, it comes with the risk of drowning in a sea of data. Data repositories with millions of observations over hundreds of measured variables are now common. If the volume of relevant data is extremely large (thousands of observations or more), it is unnecessary (and computationally difficult) to use all the data in order to perform a detailed analysis. When dealing with large volumes of data (with hundreds of thousands or millions of observations), best practice is to extract a representative sample (with thousands or tens of thousands of observations) for analysis. A sample is representative if the analyst can make the same conclusions from it as from the entire population of data.

There are no definite rules to determine the size of a sample. The sample of data must be large enough to contain significant information, yet small enough to manipulate quickly. If the sample is too small, relationships in the data may be missed or spurious relationships may be suggested. Perhaps the best advice is to use enough data to eliminate any doubt about whether the sample size is sufficient; data mining algorithms typically are more effective given more data.

When obtaining a representative sample, it is also important not to carelessly discard variables. It is generally best to include as many variables as possible in the sample. In the data preparation step, the analyst can use descriptive statistics and data visualization to identify any clearly irrelevant variables that should be eliminated. Descriptive statistics and data visualization also play a role in addressing missing and erroneous data. At this stage of data preparation, clustering may be useful to define new variables based on clusters of similar observations.

Once a representative data sample has been prepared for analysis, it must be partitioned into two or three data sets to appropriately evaluate the performance of predictive data mining models. To understand the need for data partitioning, we consider a situation in which an analyst has relatively few observations from which to build a multiple regression model. To maintain the sample size necessary to obtain reliable estimates of slope coefficients, an analyst may have no choice but to use the entire data set to build a model. Even if measures such as R^2 and the standard error of the estimate suggest that the resulting linear regression model may fit the data set well, these measures only explain how well the model fits data it has "seen," and the analyst has little idea how well this model will fit other "unobserved" observations.

Multiple regression models are discussed in Chapter 7.

Classical statistics deals with scarcity of data by determining the minimum sample size needed to draw legitimate inferences about the population. In contrast, data mining applications deal with an abundance of data that simplifies the process of assessing the performance of data-based estimates of variable effects. However, the wealth of data can tempt the analyst to overfit the model. **Overfitting** occurs when the analyst builds a model that does a great job of explaining the sample of data on which it is based, but fails to accurately predict outside the sample data. We can use the abundance of data to guard against the potential for overfitting by splitting the data set into different subsets for (1) the training (or construction) of candidate models, (2) the validation (or performance comparison) of candidate models, and (3) the testing (or assessment) of future performance of a selected model.

Static Holdout Method

The most straightforward way to partition data to combat overfitting is to split the sample data into three static data sets[1]: the training set, the validation set, and the test set. The **training set** consists of the data used to build the candidate models. For example, a training set may be used to estimate the slope coefficients in a multiple regression model. We use measures of performance of these candidate models on the training set to identify a promising initial subset of models. However, since the training set consists of the data

---

[1]In this chapter's data files (.xlsx) to be used with JMP, we have preidentified the observations belonging to the training, validation, and test sets using a variable called Partition. If an observation's Partition value is "*t*" it belongs to the training set, if its value is "*v*" it belongs to the validation set, and if its value is "*s*" it belongs to the test set.

used to build the models, it cannot be used to clearly identify the best model for prediction when applied to new data (data outside the training set). We apply the promising subset of models to the **validation set** to identify which model may be the most accurate at predicting observations that were not used to build the model.

If the validation set is used to identify a "best" model through either comparison with other models or the tuning of model parameters, then the estimates of model performance are also biased (we tend to overestimate performance of the candidate model with the best performance on the validation set). Thus, the final model must be applied to the **test set** in order to conservatively estimate this model's effectiveness when applied to data that have not been used to build or select the model.

For example, suppose we have identified four models that fit the training set reasonably well. To evaluate how these models will handle predictions when applied to new data, we apply these four models to the validation set. After identifying the best of the four models, we apply this "best" model to the test set in order to obtain an unbiased estimate of this model's performance on future applications (which helps us understand how well we can expect this model to perform on new data).

For situations with relatively few observations, setting aside observations for a test set may not be possible and the analyst may resort to using only a training and validation set.

There are no definite rules for the size of the three partitions, but the training set is typically the largest. For estimation tasks, a rule of thumb is to have at least 10 times as many observations as variables. For classification tasks, a rule of thumb is to have at least $6 \times m \times q$ observations, where m is the number of outcome categories and q is the number of variables. When we are interested in predicting a rare event, such as a click-through on an advertisement posted on a web site or a fraudulent credit card transaction, it is recommended that the training set oversample the number of observations corresponding to the rare events to provide the data mining algorithm sufficient data to "learn" about the rare events. For example, if only one out of every 10,000 users clicks on an advertisement posted on a web site, we would not have sufficient information to distinguish between users who do not click-through and those who do if we constructed a representative training set consisting of one observation corresponding to a click-through and 9,999 observations with no click-through. In these cases, the training set should contain equal or nearly equal numbers of observations corresponding to the different values of the outcome variable. Note that we do not oversample the validation set and test sets; these samples should be representative of the overall population so that performance measures evaluated on these data sets appropriately reflect future performance of the data mining model.

The advantages of the static holdout method are that it is simple and quick. However, the results of the modeling procedure based on a single application of the static holdout can vary greatly depending on which observations and how many observations are selected for each of the training, validation, and test sets. That is, if we would construct another iteration of the static holdout method and split the observations differently across the three sets, we may find that a different model performs best. Motivated by this realization, we describe a more robust data partitioning method to train and validate models in the next section.

k-Fold Cross-Validation

In the holdout method, the observations that are placed into the static training, validation, and test sets can have an impact on how models are built and evaluated. In this section, we discuss a more robust procedure to train and validate models called *k*-fold cross-validation. As a pre-processing step, if an unbiased estimate of the final model is desired, we remove a desired number of observations to compose the test set. The remaining observations will be used to train and validate the model in an iterative procedure. The *k*-fold cross-validation[2] procedure randomly divides the remaining data (original data minus

---

[2]In this chapter's data files (.csv) to be used with R/Rattle, we have prepared data for *k*-fold cross-validation by creating a pair of files, e.g., *DataCV.csv* contains the observations for the training and validation and *DataTest.csv* contains the observations for the independent test set. We also have created data files (.csv) to be used with R/Rattle that reflect the static holdout method. In these cases, the observations are split into three different files called *DataTrain.csv*, *DataValidation.csv*, and *DataTest.csv*.

test set) into k equal-sized, mutually exclusive, and collectively exhaustive subsets called folds. The cross-validation procedure consists of k iterations in which a different subset is designated as the validation set at each iteration and the remaining $k-1$ subsets are combined and designated as the training set. At each iteration, a model is constructed using the respective training set data and evaluated using the respective validation set. At the end of the k iterations, the performance measures of the k models are aggregated and averaged. A common choice for the number of folds is $k=5$ or 10. The k-fold cross-validation method is more complex and time consuming than the holdout method, but the results of the k-fold cross-validation method are less sensitive to which observations are used in the training and the validation sets, respectively.

For training and validation on a set of n observations, if $k=n$, then an iteration of k-fold cross-validation consists of estimating the model on $n-1$ observations and evaluating the model on the single observation that was omitted from the training data. This procedure is repeated for n total iterations so that the model is trained on each possible combination of $n-1$ observations and evaluated on the single remaining observation in each case. This special case of k-fold cross-validation is called **leave-one-out cross-validation**.

Class Imbalanced Data

The classification of rare events (e.g., click-through on an advertisement posted on a web site or fraudulent credit card charges) presents a number of challenges. In a binary classification problem, the identification of the rare class often has greater value than identifying the frequent class. As we will discuss in the following section on performance measures, there are a variety of metrics that can be used to evaluate a classifier's effectiveness in correctly identifying observations from the rare class.

An additional approach to handle a situation with a severe imbalance between the two observation classes is to modify the sampling mechanism used to construct the training data. For example, assume we are trying to construct a classifier to identify whether or not a credit card charge is fraudulent. If 0.1% of all credit card charges are fraudulent, then a random sample of 50,000 observations would contain only approximately 50 observations corresponding to fraudulent charges. A larger random sample of 500,000 observations would contain approximately 500 fraudulent observations but would still result in a data set that potentially provides a classification method much more information on non-fraudulent observations than fraudulent observations.

There are two basic sampling approaches for modifying the class distribution of the training set. To demonstrate, we will consider a data set of 500,000 credit card charge observations; 500 of which are fraudulent and 499,500 which are not fraudulent. Instead of simply splitting the 500,000 observation randomly between the training, validation, and test sets, an **undersampling** approach reduces the size of the training set by considering fewer majority class observations in order to balance the classes. For example, a balanced training set of 800 observations would consist of 400 randomly selected fraudulent observations and 400 randomly selected non-fraudulent observations. The validation set and test set are constructed to be representative of the original data. For example, a validation set of 75,000 observations would consist of 75,925 non-fraudulent observations and 75 fraudulent observations. Similarly, a test set of 25,000 observations would consist of 24,975 non-fraudulent observations and 25 fraudulent observations.

In contrast, an **oversampling** approach maintains a larger training set size by sampling the minority class observations with replacement (effectively making copies of the minority class observations). For example, a balanced training set of 2,000 observations can be achieved by considering 1,000 randomly selected fraudulent observations (many of these duplicates) and 1,000 randomly selected non-fraudulent observations. As before, the validation set and test set are constructed to be representative of the original data. For example, a validation set of 75,000 observations would consist of 75,925 non-fraudulent observations and 75 fraudulent observations. Similarly, a test set of 25,000 observations would consist of 24,975 non-fraudulent observations and 25 fraudulent observations.

Both undersampling and oversampling have their drawbacks. By removing majority class observations, a training set constructed via undersampling is susceptible to missing importation information about the majority class. This can be addressed by performing undersampling multiple times to create multiple classifiers. By inserting copies of minority class observations, a training set constructed via oversampling may contain a lot of duplicated noise (rather than information) which may cause model overfitting. This can be addressed by careful use of a validation set to evaluate classification models.

Undersampling is often utilized when there is a lot of data from which to sample (e.g., more than 10,000 observations), while oversampling is often utilized when there is less data from which to sample (e.g., less than 10,000 observations). However, the choice of undersampling or oversampling also is affected by the degree of class imbalance.

9.2 Performance Measures

There are different performance measures for methods classifying categorical outcomes than for methods estimating continuous outcomes. We describe each of these in the context of an example from the financial services industry. Optiva Credit Union wants to better understand its personal lending process and its loan customers. The file *Optiva* contains over 40,000 customer observations with information on whether the customer defaulted on a loan, customer age, average checking account balance, whether the customer had a mortgage, the customer's job status, the customer's marital status, and the customer's level of education. We will use these data to demonstrate the use of supervised learning methods to classify customers who are likely to default and to estimate the average balance in a customer's bank accounts.

DATA *file*

Optiva

Evaluating the Classification of Categorical Outcomes

In our treatment of classification problems, we restrict our attention to problems for which we want to classify observations into one of two possible classes (e.g., loan default or no default), but the concepts generally extend to cases with more than two classes. A natural way to evaluate the performance of a classification method, or classifier, is to count the number of times that an observation is predicted to be in the wrong class. By counting the classification errors on a sufficiently large validation set and/or test set that is representative of the population, we will generate an accurate measure of classification performance of our model.

Classification error is commonly displayed in a **confusion matrix**, which displays a model's correct and incorrect classifications. Table 9.1 illustrates a confusion matrix resulting from an attempt to classify the customer observations in a subset of data from the file *Optiva*. In this table, Class 1 = loan default and Class 0 = no default. The confusion matrix is a cross-tabulation of the actual class of each observation and the predicted class of each observation. From the first row of the matrix in Table 9.1, we see that 7,479 observations corresponding to nondefaults were correctly identified and 5,244 actual nondefault observations were incorrectly classified as loan defaults. From the second row of Table 9.1, we observe that 89 actual loan defaults were incorrectly classified as nondefaults and 146 observations corresponding to loan defaults were correctly identified.

TABLE 9.1	Confusion Matrix		
		Predicted Class	
Actual Class		0	1
0		$n_{00} = 7{,}479$	$n_{01} = 5{,}244$
1		$n_{10} = 89$	$n_{11} = 146$

Many measures of classification performance are based on the confusion matrix. The percentage of misclassified observations is expressed as the **overall error rate** and is computed as

$$\text{Overall error rate} = \frac{n_{10} + n_{01}}{n_{11} + n_{10} + n_{01} + n_{00}}$$

The overall error rate of the classification in Table 9.1 is $(89 + 5{,}244)/(146 + 89 + 5{,}244 + 7{,}479) = 41.2\%$. One minus the overall error rate is often referred to as the **accuracy** of the model. The model accuracy based on Table 9.1 is 58.8%.

While overall error rate conveys an aggregate measure of misclassification, it counts misclassifying an actual Class 0 observation as a Class 1 observation (a **false positive**) the same as misclassifying an actual Class 1 observation as a Class 0 observation (a **false negative**). In many situations, the cost of making these two types of errors is not equivalent. For example, suppose we are classifying patient observations into two categories: Class 1 is cancer and Class 0 is healthy. The cost of incorrectly classifying a healthy patient observation as "cancer" will likely be limited to the expense (and stress) of additional testing. The cost of incorrectly classifying a cancer patient observation as "healthy" may result in an indefinite delay in treatment of the cancer and premature death of the patient.

In Table 9.1, n_{01} is the number of false positives and n_{10} is the number of false negatives.

To account for the asymmetric costs in misclassification, we define the error rate with respect to the individual classes:

$$\text{Class 1 error rate} = \frac{n_{10}}{n_{11} + n_{10}}$$

$$\text{Class 0 error rate} = \frac{n_{01}}{n_{01} + n_{00}}$$

The Class 1 error rate of the classification in Table 9.1 is $89/(146 + 89) = 37.9\%$. The Class 0 error rate of the classification in Table 9.1 is $(5{,}244)/(5{,}244 + 7{,}479) = 41.2\%$. That is, the model that produced the classifications in Table 9.1 is slightly better at predicting Class 1 observations than Class 0 observations.

To understand the tradeoff between Class 1 error rate and Class 0 error rate, we must be aware of the criteria generally used by classification algorithms to classify observations. Most classification algorithms first estimate an observation's probability of Class 1 membership and then classify the observation into Class 1 if this probability meets or exceeds a specified **cutoff value**. Typically, the default cutoff value for a classifier is 0.5. Modifying the cutoff value affects the likelihoods of occurrence for these two types of classification error. As we decrease the cutoff value, more observations will be classified as Class 1, thereby increasing the likelihood that a Class 1 observation will be correctly classified as Class 1; that is, Class 1 error will decrease. However, as a side effect, more Class 0 observations will be incorrectly classified as Class 1; that is, Class 0 error will rise.

To demonstrate how the choice of cutoff value affects classification error, Table 9.2 shows a list of 50 observations (11 of which are actual Class 1 members) and an estimated probability of Class 1 membership produced by the classification algorithm. Table 9.3 shows the confusion matrices and corresponding Class 1 error rates, Class 0 error rates, and overall error rates for cutoff values of 0.75, 0.5, and 0.25, respectively. As we decrease the

TABLE 9.2	Classification Probabilities		
Actual Class	**Probability of Class 1**	**Actual Class**	**Probability of Class 1**
1	1.00	0	0.66
1	1.00	0	0.65
0	1.00	1	0.64
1	1.00	0	0.62
0	1.00	0	0.60
0	0.90	0	0.51
1	0.90	0	0.49
0	0.88	0	0.49
0	0.88	1	0.46
1	0.88	0	0.46
0	0.87	1	0.45
0	0.87	1	0.45
0	0.87	0	0.45
0	0.86	0	0.44
1	0.86	0	0.44
0	0.86	0	0.30
0	0.86	0	0.28
0	0.85	0	0.26
0	0.84	1	0.24
0	0.84	0	0.22
0	0.83	0	0.21
0	0.68	0	0.04
0	0.67	0	0.04
0	0.67	0	0.01
0	0.67	0	0.00

cutoff value, more observations will be classified as Class 1, thereby increasing the likelihood that a Class 1 observation will be correctly classified as Class 1 (decreasing the Class 1 error rate). However, as a side effect, more Class 0 observations will be incorrectly classified as Class 1 (increasing the Class 0 error rate). That is, we can accurately identify more of the actual Class 1 observations by lowering the cutoff value, but we do so at a cost of misclassifying more actual Class 0 observations as Class 1 observations. Figure 9.1 shows the Class 1 and Class 0 error rates for cutoff values ranging from 0 to 1. One common approach to handling the tradeoff between Class 1 and Class 0 error is to set the cutoff value to minimize the Class 1 error rate subject to a threshold on the maximum Class 0 error rate. Specifically, Figure 9.1 illustrates that for a maximum allowed Class 0 error rate of 70%, a cutoff value of 0.45 (depicted by the vertical dashed line) achieves a Class 1 error rate of 20%.

As we have mentioned, identifying Class 1 members is often more important than identifying Class 0 members. One way to evaluate a classifier's value is to compare its effectiveness in identifying Class 1 observations as compared with random classification. To gauge a classifier's added value, a **cumulative lift chart** compares the number of actual Class 1 observations identified if considered in decreasing order of their estimated probability of being in Class 1 and compares this to the number of actual Class 1 observations identified if randomly selected. The left panel of Figure 9.2 illustrates a cumulative lift chart. The point (10, 5) on the blue curve means that if the 10 observations with the largest

---

TABLE 9.3	Confusion Matrices for Various Cutoff Values

Cutoff Value = 0.75

		Predicted Class	
Actual Class		**0**	**1**
0		$n_{00} = 24$	$n_{01} = 15$
1		$n_{10} = 5$	$n_{11} = 6$

Actual Class	No. of Cases	No. of Errors	Error Rate (%)
0	$n_{00} + n_{01} = 39$	$n_{01} = 15$	38.46
1	$n_{10} + n_{11} = 11$	$n_{10} = 5$	45.45
Overall	$n_{00} + n_{01} + n_{10} + n_{11} = 50$	$n_{01} + n_{10} = 20$	40.00

Cutoff Value = 0.50

		Predicted Class	
Actual Class		**0**	**1**
0		$n_{00} = 15$	$n_{01} = 24$
1		$n_{10} = 4$	$n_{11} = 7$

Actual Class	No. of Cases	No. of Errors	Error Rate (%)
0	39	24	61.54
1	11	4	36.36
Overall	50	28	56.00

Cutoff Value = 0.25

		Predicted Class	
Actual Class		**0**	**1**
0		$n_{00} = 6$	$n_{01} = 33$
1		$n_{10} = 1$	$n_{11} = 10$

Actual Class	No. of Cases	No. of Errors	Error Rate (%)
0	39	33	84.62
1	11	1	9.09
Overall	50	34	68.00

estimated probabilities of being in Class 1 were selected from Table 9.2, 5 of these observations correspond to actual Class 1 members. In contrast, the point (10, 2.2) on the red curve means that if 10 observations were randomly selected, only $(11/50) \times 10 = 2.2$ of these observations would be Class 1 members. Thus, the better the classifier is at identifying responders, the larger the vertical gap between points on the red and blue curves.

Another way to view how much better a classifier is at identifying Class 1 observations than random classification is to construct a **decile-wise lift chart**. For a decile-wise lift chart, observations are ordered in decreasing probability of Class 1 membership and then considered in 10 equal-sized groups. For the data in Table 9.2, the first decile group corresponds to the $0.1 \times 50 = 5$ observations most likely to be in Class 1, the second decile group corresponds to the 6th through the 10th observations most likely to be in Class 1,

A decile is one of nine values that divide ordered data into ten equal parts. The deciles determine the values for 10%, 20%, 30%, . . . , 90% of the data.

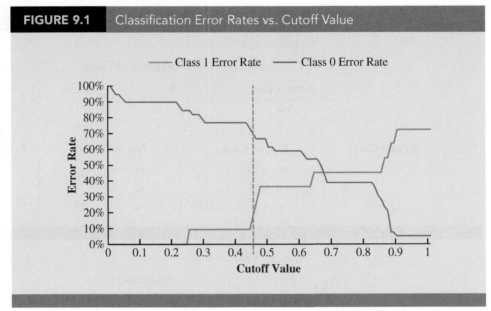

FIGURE 9.1   Classification Error Rates vs. Cutoff Value

Figure 9.1 was created using a data table that varied the cutoff value and tracked the Class 1 error rate and Class 0 error rate. For instructions on how to construct data tables in Excel, see Chapter 10.

FIGURE 9.2   Cumulative and Decile-Wise Lift Charts

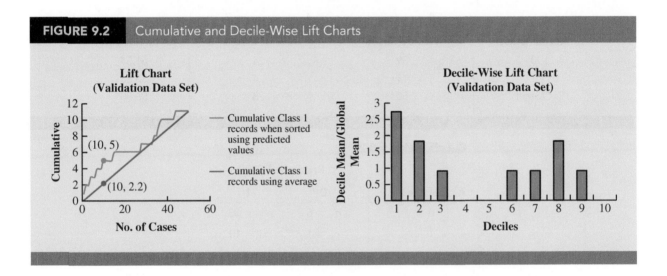

and so on. For each of these deciles, the decile-wise lift chart compares the number of actual Class 1 observations to the number of Class 1 responders in a randomly selected group of $0.1 \times 50 = 5$ observations. In the first decile group from Table 9.2 (the top 10% of observations believed by the classifier to most likely to be in Class 1), there are three Class 1 observations. A random sample of 5 observations would be expected to have $5 \times (11/50) = 1.1$ observations in Class 1. Thus, the first decile lift of this classification is $3/1.1 = 2.73$, which corresponds to the height of the first bar in the chart in the right panel of Figure 9.2. The interpretation of this ratio is that in the first decile, the model correctly predicted three observations, whereas random sampling would, on average, correctly classify only 1.1. Visually, the taller the bar in a decile-wise lift chart, the better the classifier is at identifying responders in the respective decile group. The height of the bars for the 2nd through 10th deciles is computed and interpreted in a similar manner.

Lift charts are prominently used in direct-marketing applications that seek to identify customers who are likely to respond to a direct-mail promotion. In these applications, it is common to have a fixed budget and, therefore, a fixed number of customers to target.

Lift charts identify how much better a data mining model does at identifying responders than a mailing to a random set of customers.

In addition to the overall error rate, Class 1 error rate, and Class 0 error rate, there are other measures that gauge a classifier's performance. The ability to correctly predict Class 1 (positive) observations is expressed by subtracting the Class 1 error rate from one. The resulting measure is referred to as the **sensitivity**, or **recall**, which is calculated as

$$\text{Sensitivity} = 1 - \text{Class 1 error rate} = \frac{n_{11}}{n_{11} + n_{10}}$$

Similarly, the ability to correctly predict Class 0 (negative) observations is expressed by subtracting the Class 0 error rate from one. The resulting measure is referred to as the **specificity**, which is calculated as

$$\text{Specificity} = 1 - \text{Class 0 error rate} = \frac{n_{00}}{n_{00} + n_{01}}$$

The sensitivity of the model that produced the classifications in Table 9.1 is $146/(146 + 89) = 62.1\%$. The specificity of the model that produced the classifications in Table 9.1 is $7,479/(5,244 + 7,479) = 58.8\%$.

Precision is a measure that corresponds to the proportion of observations predicted to be Class 1 by a classifier that are actually in Class 1

$$\text{Precision} = \frac{n_{11}}{n_{11} + n_{01}}$$

The **F1 Score** combines precision and sensitivity into a single measure and is defined as

$$\text{F1 score} = \frac{2n_{11}}{2n_{11} + n_{01} + n_{10}}$$

As we illustrated in Figure 9.1, decreasing the cutoff value will decrease the number of actual Class 1 observations misclassified as Class 0, but at the cost of increasing the number of Class 0 observations that are misclassified as Class 1. The **receiver operating characteristic (ROC) curve** is an alternative graphical approach for displaying this tradeoff between a classifier's ability to correctly identify Class 1 observations and its Class 0 error rate. In a ROC curve, the vertical axis is the sensitivity of the classifier, and the horizontal axis is the Class 0 error rate (which is equal to 1 – specificity).

In Figure 9.3, the blue curve depicts the ROC curve corresponding to the classification probabilities for the 50 observations in Table 9.2. The red diagonal line in Figure 9.3 represents the expected sensitivity and Class 0 error rate achieved by random classification of the 50 observations. The point (0, 0) on the blue curve occurs when the cutoff value is set so that all observations are classified as Class 0; for this set of 50 observations, a cutoff value greater than 1.0 will achieve this. That is, for a cutoff value greater than 1, for the observations in Table 9.2, sensitivity = $0/(0 + 11) = 0$ and the Class 0 error rate = $0/(0 + 39) = 0$. The point (1, 1) on the curve occurs when the cutoff value is set so that all observations are classified as Class 1; for this set of 50 observations, a cutoff value of zero will achieve this. That is, for a cutoff value of 0, sensitivity = $11/(11 + 0) = 1$ and the Class 0 error rate = $39/(39 + 0) = 1$. Repeating these calculations for varying cutoff values and recording the resulting sensitivity and Class 0 error rate values, we can construct the ROC curve in Figure 9.3.

In general, we can evaluate the quality of a classifier by computing the **area under the ROC curve**, often referred to as the AUC. The greater the area under the ROC curve, i.e., the larger the AUC, the better the classifier performs. To understand why, suppose there exists a cutoff value such that a classifier correctly identifies each observation's actual class. Then, the ROC curve will pass through the point (0, 1), which represents the case in which the Class 0 error rate is zero and the sensitivity is equal to one (which means that the Class 1 error rate is zero). In this case, the area under the ROC

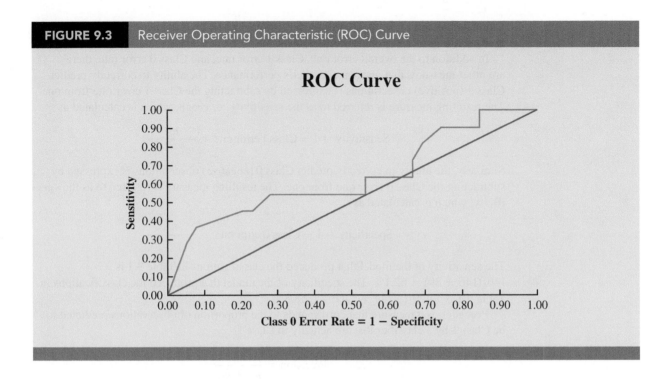

FIGURE 9.3   Receiver Operating Characteristic (ROC) Curve

curve would be equal to one as the curve would extend from (0, 0) to (0, 1) to (1, 1). In Figure 9.3, note that the area under the red diagonal line representing random classification results is 0.5. In Figure 9.3, we observe that the classifier is providing value over a random classification, as its AUC is greater than 0.5.

Evaluating the Estimation of Continuous Outcomes

In Chapter 8, we discuss additional measures, such as mean absolute error, mean absolute percentage error, and mean squared error, that also can be used to evaluate the predictions of a continuous outcome.

There are several ways to measure performance when estimating a continuous outcome variable, but each of these measures is some function of the error $e_i = y_i - \hat{y}_i$, where y_i is the actual outcome for observation i and $\hat{y}_i$ is the predicted outcome for observation i. Two common measures are the **average error** $= \sum_{i=1}^{n} e_i / n$ and the **root mean squared error** (RMSE) $= \sqrt{\sum_{i=1}^{n} e_i^2 / n}$. The average error estimates the **bias** in a model's predictions. If the average error is negative, then the model tends to overestimate the value of the outcome variable; if the average error is positive, the model tends to underestimate. The RMSE is similar to the standard error of the estimate for a regression model; it has the same units as the outcome variable predicted and provides a measure of how much the predicted value varies from the actual value.

Applying these measures (or others) to the model's predictions on the training set estimates the retrodictive performance or goodness-of-fit of the model, not the predictive performance. In estimating future performance, we are most interested in applying the performance measures to the model's predictions on the validation and test sets.

To demonstrate the computation and interpretation of average error and RMSE, we consider the challenge of predicting the average balance of Optiva Credit Union customers based on their features. Table 9.4 shows the error and squared error resulting from the predictions of the average balance for 10 observations. Using Table 9.4, we compute average error $= -80.1$ and the RMSE $= 774$. Because the average error is negative, we observe that the model overestimates the actual balance of these 10 customers. Furthermore, if the performance of the model on these 10 observations is indicative of the performance on a larger set of observations, we should investigate improvements to the estimation model, as the RMSE of 774 is 43% of the average actual balance. As a rule-of-thumb, a good estimation model should have an RMSE less than 10% of the average value of the variable being predicted.

TABLE 9.4	Computing Error in Estimates of Average Balance for 10 Customers		
Actual Average Balance	**Estimated Average Balance**	**Error (e_i)**	**Squared Error (e_i^2)**
3,793	3,784	9	81
1,800	1,460	340	115,600
900	1,381	−481	231,361
1,460	566	894	799,236
6,288	5,487	801	641,601
341	605	−264	69,696
506	760	−254	64,516
621	1,593	−972	944,784
1,442	3,050	−1,608	2,585,664
944	210	734	538,756

NOTES + COMMENTS

Lift charts analogous to those constructed for classification methods can also be applied to the continuous outcomes when using estimation methods. A lift chart for a continuous outcome variable is relevant for evaluating a model's effectiveness in identifying observations with the largest values of the outcome variable. This is similar to the way a lift chart for a categorical outcome variable helps evaluate a model's effectiveness in identifying observations that are most likely to be Class 1 members.

9.3 Logistic Regression

Similar to how multiple linear regression predicts a continuous outcome variable, y, with a collection of explanatory variables, $x_1, x_2, \ldots, x_q$, via the linear equation $\hat{y} = b_0 + b_1 x_1 + \cdots + b_q x_q$, **logistic regression** attempts to classify a binary categorical outcome ($y = 0$ or 1) as a linear function of explanatory variables. However, directly trying to explain a binary outcome via a linear function of the explanatory variables is not effective. To understand this, consider the task of predicting whether a movie wins the Academy Award for Best Picture using information on the total number of other Oscar nominations that a movie has received. Figure 9.4 shows a scatter chart of a sample of movie data found in the file *OscarsDemo*; each data point corresponds to the total number of Oscar nominations that a movie received and whether the movie won the best picture award (1 = movie won, 0 = movie lost). The diagonal line in Figure 9.4 corresponds to the simple linear regression fit. This linear function can be thought of as predicting the probability p of a movie winning the Academy Award for Best Picture via the equation $\hat{p} = -0.4054 + 0.836 \times$ total number of Oscar nominations. As Figure 9.4 shows, a linear regression model fails to appropriately explain a binary outcome variable. This model predicts that a movie with fewer than 5 total Oscar nominations has a negative probability of winning the best picture award. For a movie with more than 17 total Oscar nominations, this model predicts a probability greater than 1.0 of winning the best picture award. Furthermore, the residual plot in Figure 9.5 shows an unmistakable pattern of systematic misprediction, suggesting that the simple linear regression model is not appropriate.

As discussed in Chapter 7, if a linear regression model is appropriate, the residuals should appear randomly dispersed with no discernible pattern.

Estimating the probability p with the linear function $\hat{p} = b_0 + b_1 x_1 + \cdots + b_q x_q$ does not fit well because, although p is a continuous measure, it is restricted to the range [0, 1]; that is, a probability cannot be less than zero or larger than one. Figure 9.6 shows an

DATA *file*

OscarsDemo

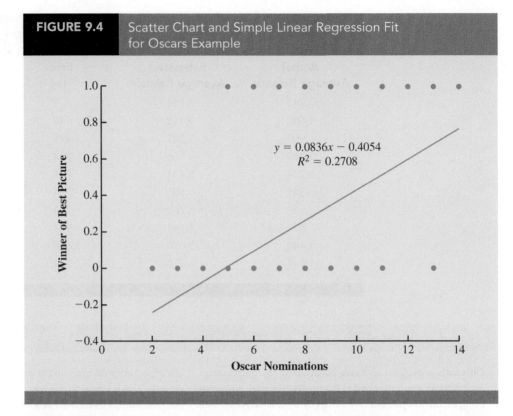

FIGURE 9.4   Scatter Chart and Simple Linear Regression Fit for Oscars Example

$y = 0.0836x - 0.4054$
$R^2 = 0.2708$

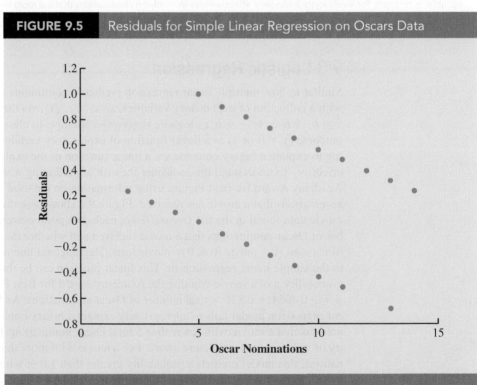

FIGURE 9.5   Residuals for Simple Linear Regression on Oscars Data

S-shaped curve that appears to better explain the relationship between the probability p of winning the best picture award and the total number of Oscar nominations. Instead of extending off to positive and negative infinity, the S-shaped curve flattens and never goes above one or below zero. We can achieve this S-shaped curve by estimating an appropriate

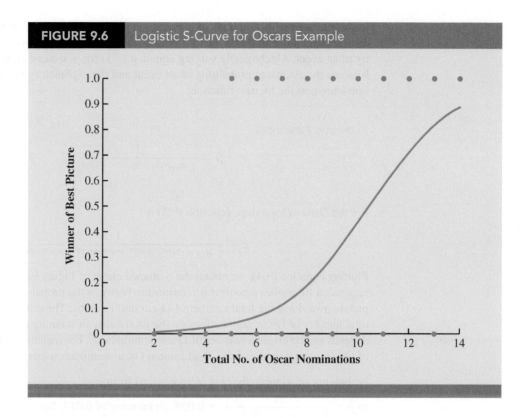

FIGURE 9.6   Logistic S-Curve for Oscars Example

function of the probability p of winning the best picture award with a linear function rather than directly estimating p with a linear function.

As a first step, we note that there is a measure related to probability known as *odds* that is very prominent in gambling and epidemiology. If an estimate of the probability of an event is $\hat{p}$ then the equivalent odds measure is $\hat{p}/(1-\hat{p})$. For example, if the probability of an event is $\hat{p} = 2/3$, then the odds measure would be $(2/3)/(1/3) = 2$, meaning that the odds are 2 to 1 that the event will occur. The odds metric ranges between zero and positive infinity, so by considering the odds measure rather than the probability $\hat{p}$, we eliminate the linear fit problem resulting from the upper bound of one on the probability $\hat{p}$. To eliminate the fit problem resulting from the remaining lower bound of zero on $\hat{p}/(1-\hat{p})$, we observe that the natural log of the odds for an event, also known as "log odds" or logit, $\ln(\hat{p}/(1-\hat{p}))$, ranges from negative infinity to positive infinity. Estimating the logit with a linear function results in a logistic regression model:

$$\ln\left(\frac{\hat{p}}{1-\hat{p}}\right) = b_0 + b_1 x_1 + \cdots + b_q x_q \qquad (9.1)$$

Given a training set of observations consisting of values for a set of explanatory variables, $x_1, x_2, \ldots, x_q$, and whether or not an event of interest occurred ($y = 0$ or 1), the logistic regression model fits values of $b_0, b_1, \ldots, b_q$ that best estimate the log odds of the event occurring. Using statistical software to fit the logistic regression model to the data in the file *OscarsDemo* results in estimates of $b_0 = -6.214$ and $b_1 = 0.596$; that is, the log odds of a movie winning the best picture award is given by

$$\ln\left(\frac{\hat{p}}{1-\hat{p}}\right) = -6.214 + 0.596 \times \text{total number of Oscar nominations} \qquad (9.2)$$

Unlike the coefficients in a multiple linear regression, the coefficients in a logistic regression do not have an intuitive interpretation. For example, $b_1 = 0.596$ means that for every additional Oscar nomination that a movie receives, its log odds of winning the best picture award increase by 0.596. In other words, the total number of Oscar nominations is linearly related to the log odds of a movie winning the best picture award. Unfortunately, a change in the log odds of an event is not as easy as to interpret as a change in the probability of an event. Algebraically solving equation (9.1) for p, we can express the relationship between the estimated probability of an event and the explanatory variables with an equation known as the logistic function:

LOGISTIC FUNCTION

$$\hat{p} = \frac{1}{1 + e^{-(b_0 + b_1 x_1 + \cdots + b_q x_q)}} \tag{9.3}$$

For the *OscarsDemo* data, equation (9.3) is

$$\hat{p} = \frac{1}{1 + e^{-(-6.214 + 0.596 \times \text{total number of Oscar nominations})}} \tag{9.4}$$

Plotting equation (9.4), we obtain the S-shaped curve of Figure 9.6. Clearly, the logistic regression fit implies a nonlinear relationship between the probability of winning the best picture award and the total number of Oscar nominations. The effect of increasing the total number of Oscar nominations on the probability of winning the best picture award depends on the original number of Oscar nominations. For instance, if the total number of Oscar nominations is four, an additional Oscar nomination increases the estimated probability of winning the best picture award from $\hat{p} = \dfrac{1}{1 + e^{-(-6.214 + 0.596 \times 4)}} = 0.021$ to $\hat{p} = \dfrac{1}{1 + e^{-(-6.214 + 0.596 \times 5)}} = 0.038$, an increase of 0.017. But if the total number of Oscar nominations is eight, an additional Oscar nomination increases the estimated probability of winning the best picture award from $\hat{p} = \dfrac{1}{1 + e^{-(-6.214 + 0.596 \times 8)}} = 0.191$ to $\hat{p} = \dfrac{1}{1 + e^{-(-6.214 + 0.596 \times 9)}} = 0.299$, an increase of 0.108.

As with other classification methods, logistic regression classifies an observation by using equation (9.3) to compute the probability of an observation belonging to Class 1 and then comparing this probability to a cutoff value. If the probability exceeds the cutoff value (a typical value is 0.5), the observation is classified as Class 1 and otherwise it is classified as Class 0. Table 9.5 shows a subsample of the predicted probabilities computed using equation (9.3) and the subsequent classification.

See Chapter 7 for an in-depth discussion of variable selection in multiple regression models.

The selection of variables to consider for a logistic regression model is similar to the approach in multiple linear regression. Especially when dealing with many variables, thorough data exploration via descriptive statistics and data visualization is essential in narrowing down viable candidates for explanatory variables. While a logistic regression model used for prediction should ultimately be judged based on its classification performance on validation and test sets, **Mallow's Cp statistic** is a measure commonly computed by statistical software

TABLE 9.5 Predicted Probabilities by Logistic Regression for Oscars Example

Total Number of Oscar Nominations	Predicted Probability of Winning	Predicted Class	Actual Class
14	0.89	Winner	Winner
11	0.58	Winner	Loser
10	0.44	Loser	Loser
6	0.07	Loser	Winner

that can be used to identify models with promising sets of variables. Models that achieve a small value of Mallow's C_p statistic tend to have smaller mean squared error and models with a value of Mallow's C_p statistic approximately equal to the number of coefficients in the model tend to have less bias (the tendency to systemically over- or under-predict).

NOTES + COMMENTS

As with multiple linear regression, strong collinearity between the independent variables $x_1, x_2, ..., x_q$ in a logistic regression model can distort the estimation of the coefficients $b_1, b_2, ..., b_q$ in equation (9.1). If we are constructing a logistic regression model to explain and quantify a relationship between the set of independent variables and the log odds of an event occurring, then it is recommended to avoid models that include independent variables that are highly correlated. However, if the purpose of a logistic regression model is to classify observations, multicollinearity does not affect predictive capability so correlated independent variables are not a concern and the model should be evaluated based on its classification performance on validation and test sets.

9.4 *k*-Nearest Neighbors

The ***k*-nearest neighbor (*k*-NN)** method can be used either to classify a categorical outcome or to estimate a continuous outcome. In a *k*-NN approach, the predicted outcome for an observation is based on the *k* most similar observations from the training set, where similarity is measured with respect to the set of input variables (features). Statistical software commonly employs Euclidean distance in the *k*-NN method to measure the similarity between observations, which is most appropriate when all features are continuous.

A critical aspect of effectively applying the *k*-NN method is the selection of the appropriate features on which to base similarity. When computing similarity with respect to too many features, Euclidean distance is less discriminating of a measure as all observations become nearly equidistant from each other. While no automated feature selection exists within the *k*-NN method, preliminary data exploration paired with experimentation can help identify promising features to include.

Classifying Categorical Outcomes with *k*-Nearest Neighbors

Unlike logistic regression, which uses a training set to generalize relationships in the data via the logistic equation and then applies this parametric model to estimate the class probabilities of observations in the validation and test sets, a nearest-neighbor classifier is a "lazy learner." That is, *k*-NN instead directly uses the entire training set to classify observations in the validation and test sets. When *k*-NN is used as a classification method, a new observation is classified as Class 1 if the proportion of Class 1 observations in its *k*-nearest neighbors from the training set is greater than or equal to a specified cutoff value (a typical value is 0.5).

The value of *k* can plausibly range from 1 to *n*, the number of observations in the training set. If $k = 1$, then the classification of a new observation is set to be equal to the class of the single most similar observation from the training set. At the other extreme, if $k = n$, then the new observation's class is naïvely assigned to the most common class in the training set. Smaller values of *k* are more susceptible to noise in the training set, while larger values of *k* may fail to capture the relationship between the features and classes of the target variable. Values of *k* from 1 to $\sqrt{n}$ are typically considered. The best value of *k* can be determined by building models for a range of *k* values and then selecting the value of k^* that results in the smallest classification error on the validation set. Note that the use of the validation set to identify k^* in this manner implies that the method should be applied to a test set with this value of k^* to accurately estimate the classification error on future data.

To illustrate, suppose that a training set consists of the 10 observations listed in Table 9.6. For this example, we will refer to an observation with Loan Default = 1 as a Class 1 observation and an observation with Loan Default = 0 as a Class 0 observation. Our task is to classify a new observation with Average Balance = 900 and Age = 28 based on its similarity to the values of Average Balance and Age of the 10 observations in the training set.

TABLE 9.6	Training Set Observations for k-NN Classifier		
Observation	Average Balance	Age	Loan Default
1	49	38	1
2	671	26	1
3	772	47	1
4	136	48	1
5	123	40	1
6	36	29	0
7	192	31	0
8	6,574	35	0
9	2,200	58	0
10	2,100	30	0
Average:	1,285	38.2	
Standard Deviation:	2,029	10.2	

In Chapter 2, we discuss z-scores.

Before computing the similarity between a new observation and the observations in the training set, it is common practice to normalize the values of all variables. By replacing the original values of each variable with the corresponding z-score, we avoid the computation of Euclidean distance being disproportionately affected by the scale of the variables. For example, the average value of the Average Balance variable in the training set is 1,285 and the standard deviation is 2,029. The average and standard deviation of the Age variable are 38.2 and 10.2, respectively. Thus, Observation 1's normalized value of Average Balance is $(49 - 1,285)/2,029 = -0.61$ and its normalized value of Age is $(38 - 38.2)/10.2 = -0.02$.

Figure 9.7 displays the 10 training-set observations and the new observation to be classified plotted according to their normalized variable values. To classify the new observation, we will use a cutoff value of 0.5. For $k = 1$, this observation is classified as a Loan Default (Class 1) because its nearest neighbor (Observation 2) is in Class 1. For $k = 2$, we

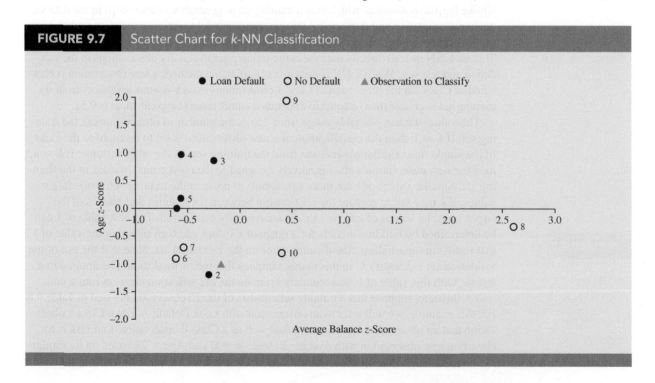

FIGURE 9.7   Scatter Chart for k-NN Classification

TABLE 9.7	Classification of Observation with Average Balance = 900 and Age = 28 for Different Values of *k*	
k	% of Class 1 Neighbors	Classification
1	1.00	1
2	0.50	1
3	0.33	0
4	0.25	0
5	0.40	0
6	0.50	1
7	0.57	1
8	0.63	1
9	0.56	1
10	0.50	1

see that the two nearest neighbors are Observation 2 (Class 1) and Observation 6 (Class 0). Because at least 0.5 of the $k = 2$ neighbors are Class 1, the new observation is classified as Class 1. For $k = 3$, the three nearest neighbors are Observation 2 (Class 1), Observation 6 (Class 0), and Observation 7 (Class 0). Because only 1/3 of the neighbors are Class 1, the new observation is classified as Class 0 (0.33 is less than the 0.5 cutoff value). Table 9.7 summarizes the classification of the new observation for values of *k* ranging from 1 to 10.

Estimating Continuous Outcomes with *k*-Nearest Neighbors

When *k*-NN is used to estimate a continuous outcome, a new observation's outcome value is predicted to be the *average* of the outcome values of its *k*-nearest neighbors in the training set. The value of *k* can plausibly range from 1 to *n*, the number of observations in the training set. If $k = 1$, then the estimation of a new observation's outcome value is set equal to the outcome value of the single most similar observation from the training set. At the other extreme, if $k = n$, then the new observation's outcome value is estimated by the average outcome value over the entire training set. Too small of a value for *k* results in predictions that are overfit to the noise in the training set, while too large of a value of *k* results in underfitting and fails to capture the relationships between the features and the outcome variable. The best value of *k* can be determined by building models over a typical range ($k = 1, \ldots, \sqrt{n}/2$) and then selecting the value of k^* that results in the smallest estimation error. Note that the use of the validation set to identify k^* in this manner implies that the method should be applied to a test set with this value of k^* to accurately estimate the estimation error on future data.

To illustrate, we again consider the training set of 10 observations listed in Table 9.6. In this case, we are interested in estimating the value of Average Balance for a new observation based on its similarity with respect to Age to the 10 observations in the training set. Figure 9.8 displays the 10 training-set observations and a new observation

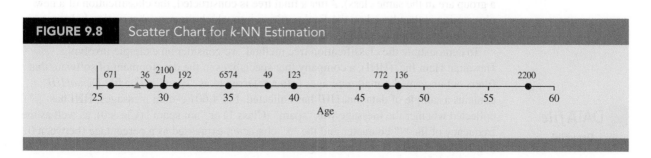

FIGURE 9.8   Scatter Chart for *k*-NN Estimation

TABLE 9.8	Estimation Average Balance for Observation with Age = 28 for Different Values of *k*
k	**Average Balance Estimate**
1	$36
2	$936
3	$936
4	$750
5	$1,915
6	$1,604
7	$1,392
8	$1,315
9	$1,184
10	$1,285

with Age = 28 for which we want to estimate the value of Average Balance. For $k = 1$, the new observation's average balance is estimated to be $36, which is the value of Average Balance for the nearest neighbor (Observation 6 in Table 9.6). For $k = 2$, we see that there is a tie between Observation 2 (Age = 26) and Observation 10 (Age = 30) for the second-closest observation to the new observation (Age = 28). While tie-breaking rules vary between statistical software packages, in this example we simply include all three observations to estimate the average balance of the new observation as (36 + 671 + 2,100)/3 = $936. Table 9.8 summarizes the estimation of the new observation's average balance for values of k ranging from 1 to 10.

9.5 Classification and Regression Trees

Classification and regression trees (CART) successively partition a data set of observations into increasingly smaller and more homogeneous subsets. At each iteration of the CART method, a subset of observations is split into two new subsets based on the values of a single variable. The CART method can be thought of as a series of questions that successively partition observations into smaller and smaller groups of decreasing **impurity**, which is the measure of the heterogeneity in a group of observations' outcome classes or outcome values. The implementation of classification and regression trees by various statistical software packages vary with respect to the metrics they employ and how they grow the tree. In this section, we present a general description of CART logic.

Classifying Categorical Outcomes with a Classification Tree

For **classification trees**, the impurity of a group of observations is based on the proportion of observations belonging to the same class (there is zero impurity if all observations in a group are in the same class). After a final tree is constructed, the classification of a new observation is then based on the final partition into which the new observation belongs (based on the variable-splitting rules).

To demonstrate the classification tree method, we consider an example involving Hawaiian Ham Inc. (HHI), a company that specializes in the development of software that filters out unwanted e-mail messages (often referred to as "spam"). The file *DemoHHI* contains a sample of data that HHI has collected. For 4,601 e-mail messages, HHI has collected whether the message was "spam" (Class 1) or "not spam" (Class 0), as well as the frequency of the "!" character and the "$" character, expressed as a percentage (between 0 and 100) of characters in the message.

DATAfile

DemoHHI

To illustrate how a classification tree categorizes observations, we consider a small training set from *DemoHHI* consisting of 46 observations. In this training set, we note that the variables Dollar and Exclamation correspond to the percentage of the "$" character and the percentage of the "!" character, respectively. The results of a classification tree analysis can be graphically displayed in a tree that explains the process of classifying a new observation. The tree outlines the values of the variables that result in an observation falling into a particular partition.

Let us consider the classification tree in Figure 9.9. At each step, the CART method identifies the split of the variable that results in the least impurity in the two resulting categories. In Figure 9.9, the number within the circle (or node) represents the value on which the variable (whose name is listed below the node) is split. The first partition is formed by splitting observations into two groups, observations with Dollar ≤ 0.0555 and observations with Dollar > 0.0555. The numbers on the left and right arcs emanating from the node denote the number of observations in the Dollar ≤ 0.0555 and Dollar > 0.0555 partitions, respectively. There are 28 e-mails that consist of less than 5.55% of the "$" character and 18 observations containing more than 5.55% of the "$" character. The split on the variable Dollar at the value 0.0555 is selected because it results in the two subsets of the original 46 observations with the least impurity. The splitting process is then repeated on these two newly created groups of observations in a manner that again results in an additional subset with the least impurity. In this tree, the second split is applied to the group of 28 observations with Dollar ≤ 0.0555 using the variable Exclamation; 21 of the 28 observations in this subset have Exclamation

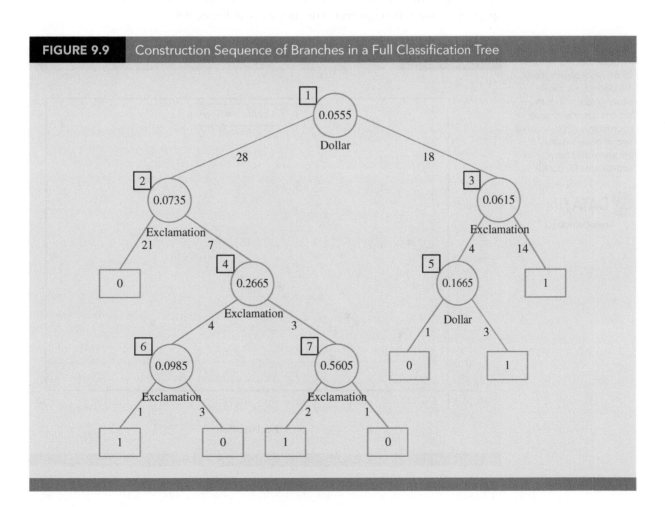

FIGURE 9.9   Construction Sequence of Branches in a Full Classification Tree

≤ 0.0735, while 7 have Exclamation > 0.0735. After this second variable splitting, there are three total partitions of the original 46 observations. There are 21 observations with values of Dollar ≤ 0.0555 and Exclamation ≤ 0.0735, 7 observations with values of Dollar ≤ 0.0555 and Exclamation > 0.0735, and 18 observations with values of Dollar > 0.0555. No further partitioning of the 21-observation group with values of Dollar ≤ 0.0555 and Exclamation ≤ 0.0735 is necessary since this group consists entirely of Class 0 (nonspam) observations (i.e., this group has zero impurity). The 7-observation group with values of Dollar ≤ 0.0555 and Exclamation > 0.0735 and 18-observation group with values of Dollar > 0.0555 are successively partitioned in the order as denoted by the boxed numbers in Figure 9.9 until subsets with zero impurity are obtained.

For example, the group of 18 observations with Dollar > 0.0555 is further split into two groups using the variable Exclamation; 4 of the 18 observations in this subset have Exclamation ≤ 0.0615, while the other 14 observations have Exclamation > 0.0615. That is, 4 observations have Dollar > 0.0555 and Exclamation ≤ 0.0615. This subset of 4 observations is further decomposed into 1 observation with Dollar ≤ 0.1665 and 3 observations with Dollar > 0.1665. At this point, there is no further branching in this portion of the tree since corresponding subsets have zero impurity. That is, the subset of 1 observation with Dollar > 0.0555, Exclamation ≤ 0.0615, and Dollar ≤ 0.1665 is a Class 0 observation (nonspam) and the subset of 3 observations with Dollar > 0.0555, Exclamation ≤ 0.0615, and Dollar > 0.1665 are all Class 1 observations. The recursive partitioning for the other branches in Figure 9.9 follows similar logic. The scatter chart in Figure 9.10 illustrates the final partitioning resulting from the sequence of variable splits. The rules defining a partition divide the variable space into eight rectangles, each corresponding to one of the eight leaf nodes in the tree in Figure 9.9.

Figure 9.10 is based on all 46 observations, but only 28 of these observations are distinct. Of the 46 observations, 18 of them are not spam and have coordinates (0,0). Another two of observations are spam and have coordinates (0, 0.210).

SpamDemoData

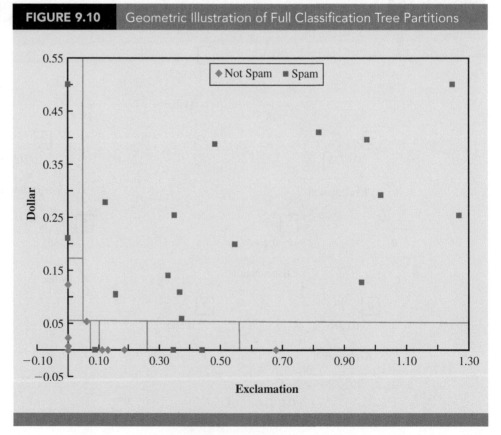

FIGURE 9.10   Geometric Illustration of Full Classification Tree Partitions

As Figure 9.10 suggests in this case, with enough variable splitting, it is possible to obtain partitions on the training set such that each partition contains either Class 1 observations or Class 0 observations, but not both. In other words, enough decomposition of this data results in a set of partitions with zero impurity, and there are no misclassifications of the training set by this full tree. In general, unless there exist observations that have identical values of all the input variables but different outcome classes, the leaf nodes of the full classification tree will have zero impurity. However, applying the entire set of partitioning rules from the full classification tree to observations in the validation set will typically result in a relatively large classification error. The degree of partitioning in the full classification tree is an example of extreme overfitting; although the full classification tree perfectly characterizes the training set, it is unlikely to classify new observations well.

To understand how to construct a classification tree that performs well on new observations, we first examine how classification error is computed. The second column of Table 9.9 lists the classification error for each stage of constructing the classification tree in Figure 9.9. The training set on which this tree is based consists of 26 Class 0 observations and 20 Class 1 observations. Therefore, with no decision rules, we can achieve a classification error of 43.5% (20/46) on the training set by simply classifying all 46 observations as Class 0. Adding the first decision node separates the observations into two groups, one group of 28 and another of 18. The group of 28 observations has values of Dollar ≤ 0.0555; 25 of these observations are Class 0 and 3 are Class 1; therefore, by the majority rule, this group would be classified as Class 0, resulting in three misclassified observations. The group of 18 observations has values of Dollar > 0.0555; 1 of these observations is Class 0, and 17 are Class 1; therefore, by the majority rule, this group would be classified as Class 1, resulting in one misclassified observation. Thus, for one decision node, the classification tree has a classification error of (3 + 1)/46 = 0.087.

When the second decision node is added, the 28 observations with values of Dollar ≤ 0.0555 are further decomposed into a group of 21 observations and a group of 7 observations. The classification tree with two decision nodes has three groups: a group of 18 observations with Dollar > 0.0555, a group of 21 observations with Dollar ≤ 0.0555 and Exclamation ≤ 0.0735, and a group of 7 observations with Dollar ≤ 0.0555 and Exclamation > 0.0735. As before, the group of 18 observations would be classified as Class 1 and misclassify a single observation that is actually Class 0. In the group of 21 observations, all of these observations are Class 0, so there is no misclassification error for this group. In the group of 7 observations, 4 are Class 0 and 3 are Class 1. Therefore, by the majority rule, this group would be classified as Class 0, resulting in three misclassified observations. Thus, for the

TABLE 9.9	Classification Error Rates on Sequence of Pruned Trees	
Number of Decision Nodes	**% Classification Error on Training Set**	**% Classification Error on Validation Set**
0	43.5	39.4
1	8.7	20.9
2	8.7	20.9
3	8.7	20.9
4	6.5	20.9
5	4.3	21.3
6	2.2	21.3
7	0	21.6

classification tree with two decision nodes (and three partitions), the classification error is $(1 + 0 + 3)/46 = 0.087$. Proceeding in a similar fashion, we can compute the classification error on the training set for classification trees with varying numbers of decision nodes to complete the second column of Table 9.9. Table 9.9 shows that the classification error on the training set decreases as we add more decision nodes and split the observations into smaller partitions.

To facilitate our explanation of how a classification tree is constructed, we split the 4,601 observations into a 46-observation training set and a validation set with 4,555 observations. In practice, the observations would be split to create a much larger (static) training set, or a k-folds cross-validation procedure would be applied using the 4,601 observations.

To evaluate how well the decision rules of the classification tree in Figure 9.9 established from the training set extend to other data, we apply it to a validation set from *DemoHHI* of 4,555 observations consisting of 2,762 Class 0 observations and 1,793 Class 1 observations. Without any decision rules, we can achieve a classification error of 39.4% (1,793/4,555) on the training set by simply classifying all 4,555 observations as Class 0. Applying the first decision node separates into a group of 3,452 observations with Dollar $\leq$ 0.0555 and 1,103 with Dollar $>$ 0.0555. In the group of 3,452 observations, 2,631 are Class 0 and 821 are Class 1; therefore, by the majority rule, this group would be classified as Class 0, resulting in 821 misclassified observations. In the group of 1,103 observations, 131 are Class 0 and 972 are Class 1; therefore, by the majority rule, this group would be classified as Class 1, resulting in 131 misclassified observations. Thus, for one decision node, the classification tree has a classification error of $(821 + 131)/4,555 = 0.209$ on the validation set. Proceeding in a similar fashion, we can apply the classification tree for varying numbers of decision nodes to compute the classification error on the validation set displayed in the third column of Table 9.9. Note that the classification error on the validation set does not necessarily decrease as more decision nodes split the observations into smaller partitions.

To identify a classification tree with good performance on new data, we "prune" the full classification tree by removing decision nodes in the reverse order in which they were added. In this manner, we seek to eliminate the decision nodes corresponding to weaker rules. Figure 9.11 illustrates the tree resulting from pruning the last variable splitting rule (Exclamation $\leq$ 0.5605 or Exclamation $>$ 0.5605) from Figure 9.9. By pruning this rule, we obtain a partition defined by Dollar $\leq$ 0.0555, Exclamation $>$ 0.0735, and Exclamation $>$ 0.2665 that contains three observations. Two of these observations are Class 1 (spam) and one is Class 0 (nonspam), so this pruned tree classifies observations in this partition as Class 1 observations, since the proportion of Class 1 observations in this partition (two-thirds) exceeds the default cutoff value of 0.5. Therefore, the classification error of this pruned tree on the training set is $1/46 = 0.022$, an increase over the zero classification error of the full tree on the training set. However, Table 9.9 shows that applying the six decision rules of this pruned tree to the validation set achieves a classification error of 0.213, which is less than the classification error of 0.216 of the full tree on the validation set. Compared to the full tree with seven decision rules, the pruned tree with six decision rules is less likely to be overfit to the training set.

Sequentially removing decision nodes, we can obtain six pruned trees. These pruned trees have one to six variable splits (decision nodes). However, while adding decision nodes at first decreases the classification error on the validation set, too many decision nodes overfits the classification tree to the training data and results in increased error on the validation set. For each of these pruned trees, each observation belongs to a single partition defined by a sequence of decision rules and is classified as Class 1 if the proportion of Class 1 observations in the partition exceeds the cutoff value and Class 0 otherwise.

One common approach for identifying the best-pruned tree is to begin with the full classification tree and prune decision rules until the classification error on the validation set increases. Following this procedure, Table 9.9 suggests that a classification tree partitioning observations into two subsets with a single decision node (Dollar $\leq$ 0.0555 or Dollar $>$ 0.0555) is just as reliable at classifying the validation data as any other tree. As Figure 9.12 shows, if the "$" character accounts for no more than 5.55% of the characters, this best-pruned tree classifies an e-mail as nonspam, otherwise this best-pruned tree classifies an e-mail as spam. This best-pruned classification tree results in a classification error of 20.9% on the validation set.

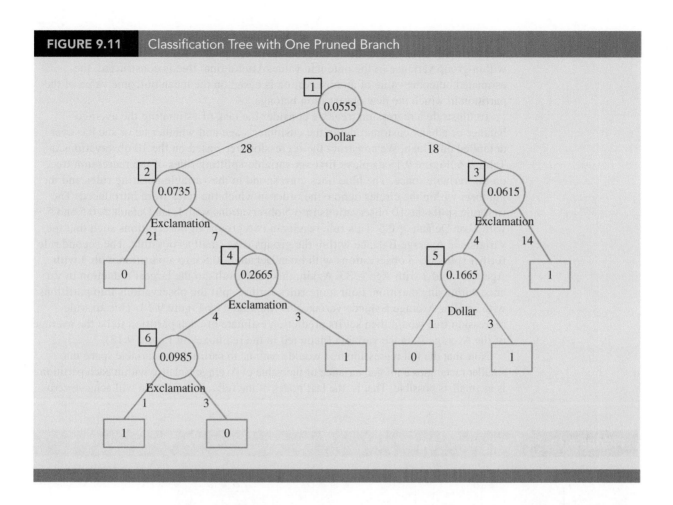

FIGURE 9.11   Classification Tree with One Pruned Branch

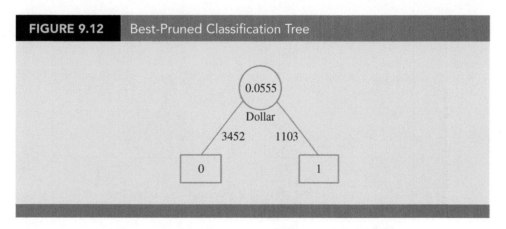

FIGURE 9.12   Best-Pruned Classification Tree

Estimating Continuous Outcomes with a Regression Tree

To estimate a continuous outcome, a **regression tree** successively partitions observations of the training set into smaller and smaller groups in a similar fashion as a classification tree. The only differences are: (1) how impurity of the partitions is measured, and (2) how a partition is used to estimate the outcome value of an observation lying in that partition. Recall that in a classification tree, the impurity of a partition is based on the proportion of incorrectly classified observations. In a regression tree, the impurity of a partition is based on the variance of the outcome value for the observations in the group. A regression tree is constructed by sequentially identifying the variable-splitting rule that results in partitions with the smallest within-group variance of the outcome value. After a final tree is constructed, the estimated outcome value of an observation is based on the mean outcome value of the partition in which the new observation belongs.

To illustrate a regression tree, we consider the task of estimating the average balance of a bank customer using the customer's age and whether he or she has ever defaulted on a loan. We construct the regression tree based on the 10 observations in Table 9.6. Figure 9.13 displays first six variable-splitting rules of the regression tree on the variable space. The blue lines correspond to the variable-splitting rules and the numbers within the circles denote the order in which the rules were introduced. The first rule splits the 10 observations into 5 observations with Loan Default $\leq$ 0.5 and 5 with Loan Default > 0.5. This rule results in two groups of observations such that the variance in Average Balance within the groups is as small as possible. The second rule further splits the 5 observations with Loan Default $\leq$ 0.5 into a partition with 3 with Age $\leq$ 33 and 2 with Age > 33. Again, this rule results in the largest reduction in variance within any partition. Four more rules further split the observations into partitions with smaller Average Balance variance as illustrated by Figure 9.13. This six-rule regression tree would then set its prediction estimate of each partition to be the average of the Average Balance variable (depicted in the red boxes in Figure 9.13).

Note that the full regression tree would continue to partition the variable space into smaller rectangles until the variance of the value of Average Balance within each partition is as small as possible. That is, the leaf nodes of the full regression tree will achieve zero

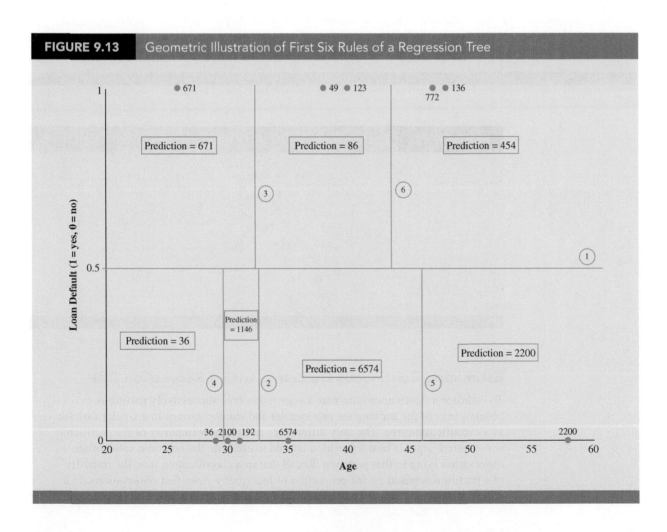

FIGURE 9.13   Geometric Illustration of First Six Rules of a Regression Tree

impurity unless there exist observations that have identical values of all the input variables but different values of the outcome variable (Average Balance). Then, similar to the classification tree, rules are pruned from this full regression tree in order to obtain the simplest tree that achieves the least amount of prediction error on the validation set.

Ensemble Methods

Up to this point, we have demonstrated the prediction of a new observation (either classification in the case of a categorical outcome or estimation in the case of a continuous outcome) based on the decision rules of a single constructed tree. In this section, we discuss the notion of ensemble methods. In an **ensemble method**, predictions are made based on the combination of a collection of models. For example, instead of basing the classification of a new observation on an individual classification tree, an ensemble method generates a collection of different classification trees and then predicts the class of a new observation based on the collective voting of this collection.

To gain an intuitive grasp of why an ensemble of prediction models may outperform, on average, any single prediction model, let's consider the task of predicting the value of the S&P 500 Index one year in the future. Suppose there are 100 financial analysts independently developing their own forecast based on a variety of information. One year from now, there certainly will be one analyst (unless there is a tie) whose forecast will prove to be the most accurate. However, identifying beforehand which of the 100 analysts will be the most accurate may be virtually impossible. Therefore, instead of trying to pick one of the analysts and depending solely on their forecast, an ensemble approach would combine their forecasts (e.g., taking an average of the 100 forecast values) and use this as the predicted value of the S&P 500 Index. The two necessary conditions for an ensemble to perform better than a single model are as follows: (1) The individual base models are constructed independently of each other (analysts don't base their forecasts on the forecasts of other analysts), and (2) the individual models perform better than just randomly guessing.

There are two primary steps to an ensemble approach: (1) the development of a committee of individual base models, and (2) the combination of the individual base models' predictions to form a composite prediction. While an ensemble can be composed of any type of individual classification or estimation model, the ensemble approach works better with an unstable prediction method. A classification or estimation method is **unstable** if relatively small changes in the training set cause its predictions to fluctuate substantially. In this section, we discuss ensemble methods using classification or regression trees, which are known to be unstable. Specifically, we discuss three different ways to construct an ensemble of classification or regression trees: bagging, boosting, and random forests.

In the **bagging** approach, the committee of individual base models is generated by first constructing multiple training sets by repeated random sampling of the n observations in the original data *with replacement*. Because the sampling is done with replacement, some observations may appear multiple times in a single training set, while other observations will not appear at all. If each generated training set consists of n observations, then the probability of an observation from the original data *not* being selected for a specific training set is $((n-1)/n)^n$. Therefore, the average proportion of a training set of size n that are unique observations from the original data is $1 - ((n-1)/n)^n$. The bagging approach then trains a predictive model on each of the m training sets and generates the ensemble prediction based on the average of the m individual predictions.

To demonstrate bagging, we consider the task of classifying customers as defaulting or not defaulting on their loan, using only their age. Table 9.10 contains the 10 observations

TABLE 9.10	Original 10-Observation Training Data									
Age	29	31	35	38	47	48	53	54	58	70
Loan default	0	0	0	1	1	1	1	0	0	0

in the original training data. Table 9.11 shows the results of generating 10 new training sets by randomly sampling from the original data with replacement. For each of these training sets, we construct a one-rule classification tree that minimizes the impurity of the resulting partition. The two partitions of each training set are illustrated with a vertical red line and accompanying decision rule.

Table 9.12 shows the results of applying this ensemble of 10 classification trees to a validation set consisting of 10 observations. The ensemble method bases its classification on the average of the 10 individual classifications trees; if at least half of the individual trees classify an observation as Class 1, so does the ensemble. Note from Table 9.12 that the 20% classification error rate of the ensemble is lower than any of the individual trees, illustrating the potential advantage of using ensemble methods.

As an alternative to using a separate validation set (as the one in Table 9.12), the predictive performance of the bagging ensemble constructed in Table 9.10 can be assessed by using **out-of-bag estimation**. Out-of-bag estimation leverages the fact that, because the training sets for each base model used in the ensemble is trained by sampling the data with replacement, each of these training sets will each be missing an average of about 36.8% of the distinct observations.[3] Each of these missing observations can be used as holdout data upon which to evaluate the subset of models which do not contain the missing observations.

To demonstrate out-of-bag estimation, consider the example in Table 9.10. Because the training sets for each respective tree in Table 9.10 are constructed by sampling the original 10 observations with replacement, these training sets do not contain all 10 original observations. For example, the training set for Tree 1 does not contain the (Age, Loan Default) observations of (53, 1); (54, 0); and (70, 0). Therefore, these three observations represent holdout data for Tree 1. In a sense, these three observations constitute a validation set for Tree 1. For each tree in the ensemble method, Table 9.13 shows how the tree classifies the observations that were missing from the respective tree's training set. For example, Tree 1's rule is to classify all observations with Age $\leq$ 36.5 as Class 0 and all observations with Age $>$ 36.5 as Class 1. Therefore, it classifies the three observations (Age = 53, Age = 54, and Age = 70) as Class 1.

After each tree predicts the observations missing from its respective training set, the classification of each of the original 10 observations is executed by aggregating the votes of the trees participating on each respective observation and classifying the observation as the majority class. For example, observation (31, 0) is classified as Class 1 by Tree 7, as Class 1 by Tree 9, and as Class 0 by Tree 10; therefore, the out-of-bag classification for this observation is Class 1 by majority vote. Based on this out-of-bag classification, an out-of-bag classification error can be computed. From Table 9.13, we see that the out-of-bag classification is incorrect on 7 of the 10 observations resulting in a 70% overall error rate. While out-of-bag estimate of the overall error rate is much higher than the 20% overall error rate observed on the validation set in Table 9.12, these values are typically much closer for larger ensembles. However, it is important to note that out-of-bag estimation does not assess performance as thoroughly as a separate validation set or a cross-validation procedure. In general, out-of-bag estimates will be more conservative than the analogous performance measures based on a validation set. That is, an out-of-bag error estimate will be larger than a validation-based error estimate, and an out-of-bag AUC estimate will be smaller than a validation-based AUC estimate. Looking down the columns of Table 9.13, we observe that the aggregate vote of each observation is based on a (different) subset of the trees.[4] Looking across the rows of Table 9.13, we observe that the trees participate in

---

[3]For a data set with n observations, the probability of an observation not being selected when randomly sampling the data set with replacement is $\left(\frac{n-1}{n}\right)^n$. For large n, $\left(\frac{n-1}{n}\right)^n$ is approximately 0.368.

[4]It is possible that an observation is included in every base model's training set. In this case (although unlikely), the observation would not contribute to the out-of-bag estimation process.

TABLE 9.11 Bagging: Generation of 10 New Training Sets and Corresponding Classification Trees

Iteration 1 — Age ≤ 36.5

Age	29	31	31	35	38	38	47	48	58	58
Loan default	0	0	0	0	1	1	1	1	0	0
Prediction	0	0	0	0	1	1	1	1	1	1

Iteration 2 — Age ≤ 50.5

Age	29	31	35	38	47	54	58	70	70	70
Loan default	0	0	0	1	1	0	0	0	0	0
Prediction	0	0	0	0	0	0	0	0	0	0

Iteration 3 — Age ≤ 36.5

Age	29	31	35	38	38	47	53	53	54	58
Loan default	0	0	0	1	1	1	1	1	0	0
Prediction	0	0	0	1	1	1	1	1	1	1

Iteration 4 — Age ≤ 34.5

Age	29	29	31	38	38	47	47	53	54	58
Loan default	0	0	0	1	1	1	1	1	0	0
Prediction	0	0	0	1	1	1	1	1	1	1

Iteration 5 — Age ≤ 39

Age	29	29	31	47	48	48	48	70	70	70
Loan default	0	0	0	1	1	1	1	0	0	0
Prediction	0	0	0	1	1	1	1	1	1	1

Iteration 6 — Age ≤ 53.5

Age	31	38	47	48	53	53	53	54	58	70
Loan default	0	1	1	1	1	1	1	0	0	0
Prediction	1	1	1	1	1	1	1	0	0	0

Iteration 7 — Age ≤ 53.5

Age	29	38	38	48	53	54	58	58	58	70
Loan default	0	1	1	1	1	0	0	0	0	0
Prediction	1	1	1	1	1	0	0	0	0	0

Iteration 8 — Age ≤ 53.5

Age	29	31	47	47	47	53	53	54	58	70
Loan default	0	0	1	1	1	1	1	0	0	0
Prediction	1	1	1	1	1	1	1	0	0	0

Iteration 9 — Age ≤ 53.5

Age	29	35	38	38	48	53	53	54	70	70
Loan default	0	0	1	1	1	1	1	0	0	0
Prediction	1	1	1	1	1	1	1	0	0	0

Iteration 10 — Age ≤ 14.5

Age	29	29	29	29	35	35	54	54	58	58
Loan default	0	0	0	0	0	0	0	0	0	0
Prediction	0	0	0	0	0	0	0	0	0	0

TABLE 9.12	Classification of 10 Observations from Validation Set with Bagging Ensemble									
Age	26	29	30	32	34	37	42	47	48	54	Overall Error Rate
Loan default	1	0	0	0	0	1	0	1	1	0	
Tree 1	0	0	0	0	0	1	1	1	1	1	30%
Tree 2	0	0	0	0	0	0	0	0	0	0	40%
Tree 3	0	0	0	0	0	1	1	1	1	1	30%
Tree 4	0	0	0	0	0	1	1	1	1	1	30%
Tree 5	0	0	0	0	0	0	1	1	1	1	40%
Tree 6	1	1	1	1	1	1	1	1	1	0	50%
Tree 7	1	1	1	1	1	1	1	1	1	0	50%
Tree 8	1	1	1	1	1	1	1	1	1	0	50%
Tree 9	1	1	1	1	1	1	1	1	1	0	50%
Tree 10	0	0	0	0	0	0	0	0	0	0	40%
Average Vote	0.4	0.4	0.4	0.4	0.4	0.7	0.8	0.8	0.8	0.4	
Bagging Ensemble	0	0	0	0	0	1	1	1	1	0	20%

TABLE 9.13	Out-of-Bag Classifications of Observations Missing from Each Tree's Training Set									
	Observation									
Tree	(29, 0)	(31, 0)	(35, 0)	(38, 1)	(47, 1)	(48, 1)	(53, 1)	(54, 0)	(58, 0)	(70, 0)
1								1	1	1
2						0	0			
3			1				1			
4				1			1			1
5			0	0				1	1	1
6	1	1								
7		1	1			1				
8			1		1	1				
9		1	1		1					
10		0		0	0	0	0			0
Aggregate Vote	1/1	2/3	4/5	1/3	2/3	3/5	2/4	2/2	2/2	3/4
Out-of-Bag Classification	1	1	1	0	1	1	1	1	1	1

varying numbers of aggregate votes.[5] In a true validation set, each observation would be predicted by each tree in the ensemble. As illustrated in Table 9.13, between two to five trees (out of the 10 trees in the ensemble) participate in the vote of the 10 original. However, in Table 9.12, each of the 10 observations in a validation set is predicted by all 10 trees from the ensemble.

---

[5]It is possible, although unlikely, that a tree's training set contains every distinct observation and therefore has no original observations missing from its training set. In this case (although unlikely), the tree would not contribute to the out-of-bag estimation process.

Similar to bagging, the **boosting** method generates its committee of individual base models by sampling multiple training sets. However, boosting differs from bagging in how it samples the multiple training sets and how it weights the resulting classification or estimation models to compute the ensemble's prediction. Boosting iteratively adapts how it samples the original data when constructing a new training set based on the prediction error of the models constructed on the previous training sets. To generate the first training set, each of the n observations in the original data is initially given equal weight of being selected. That is, each observation i has weight $w_i = 1/n$. A classification or estimation model is then trained on this training set and is used to predict the outcome of the n observations in the original data. The weight of each observation i is then adjusted based on the degree of its prediction error. For example, in a classification problem, if an observation i is misclassified by a classifier, then its weight w_i is increased, but if it is correctly classified, then its weight w_i is decreased. The next training set is then generated by sampling the observations according to the updated weights. In this manner, the next training set is more likely to contain observations that have been mispredicted in early iterations.

To combine the predictions of the m individual models from the m training sets, boosting weights the vote of each individual model based on its overall prediction error. For example, suppose that the classifier associated with the jth training set has a large prediction error and the classifier associated with the kth training set has a small prediction error. Then the classification votes of the jth classifier will be weighted less than the classification votes of the kth classifier when they are combined. Note that this method differs from bagging, in which each of the individual classifiers has an equally weighted vote.

Random forests can be viewed as a variation of bagging specifically tailored for use with classification or regression trees. As in bagging, the random forests approach generates multiple training sets by randomly sampling (with replacement) the n observations in the original data. However, when constructing a tree model for each separate training set, each tree is restricted to using only a fixed number of randomly selected input variables. For example, suppose we are attempting to classify a tax return as fraudulent or not and there are q input variables. For each of the m generated training sets, an individual classification tree is constructed based on splitting rules based on f randomly selected input variables, where f is smaller than q. The individual classification trees are referred to as "weak learners" because they are only allowed to consider a small subset of input variables. We note that these "weak learner" individual trees do not need to be pruned on a validation set as incorporating them into an ensemble reduces the likelihood of overfitting. While the best number of individual trees in the random forest depends on the data, it is not unusual for a random forest to consist of hundreds and even thousands of individual trees.

For most problems, the predictive performance of boosting ensembles exceeds the predictive performance of bagging ensembles. Boosting achieves its performance advantage because: (1) It evolves its committee of models by focusing on observations that are mispredicted, and (2) the member models' votes are weighted by their accuracy. However, boosting is more computationally expensive than bagging. Because there is no adaptive feedback in a bagging approach, all m training sets and corresponding models can be implemented simultaneously. However, in boosting, the first training set and predictive model guide the construction of the second training set and predictive model, and so on. The random forests approach has performance similar to boosting, but maintains the computational simplicity of bagging.

SUMMARY

In this chapter, we introduced the concepts and techniques in predictive data mining. Predictive data mining methods, also called supervised learning, classify a categorical outcome or estimate a continuous outcome. We described how to partition data into training, validation, and test sets in order to construct and evaluate predictive data mining models. We discussed various performance measures for classification and estimation methods. We presented three common data mining methods: logistic regression, *k*-nearest neighbors, and classification/ regression trees. We explained how logistic regression is analogous to multiple linear regression for the case when the outcome variable is binary. We demonstrated how to use logistic regression, as well as *k*-nearest neighbors and classification trees, to classify a binary categorical outcome. We also discussed the use of *k*-nearest neighbors and regression trees to estimate a continuous outcome. In our discussion of ensemble methods, we presented the concept of generating multiple prediction models and combining their predictions. We illustrated the use of ensemble methods within the context of classification trees and noted that ensemble methods based on large committees of "weak" prediction models generally outperform a single "strong" prediction model. Table 9.14 provides a comparative summary of common supervised learning approaches. We provide brief descriptions of support vector machines, the naïve Bayes method, and neural networks in the following Notes + Comments section.

TABLE 9.14	Overview of Common Supervised Learning Methods	
	Strengths	**Weaknesses**
k-**Nearest Neighbors**	Simple	Requires large amounts of data relative to number of variables
Classification and Regression Trees	Provides easy-to-interpret business rules; can handle data sets with missing data	May miss interactions between variables since splits occur one at a time; sensitive to changes in data entries
Multiple Linear Regression	Provides easy-to-interpret relationship between dependent and independent variables	Assumes linear relationship between outcome and variables
Logistic Regression	Provides interpretable effects of each variable on the log odds of an outcome	Assumes linear relationship between log odds of an outcome and variables
Support Vector Machines	Can incorporate nonlinear effects and are robust against overfitting	May be difficult to directly apply on data sets with a large number of observations and variables
Naïve Bayes	Simple and effective at classifying	Requires a large amount of data; restricted to categorical variables
Neural Networks	Flexible and often effective	Many difficult decisions to make when building the model; results cannot be easily explained, i.e., "black box"

NOTES + COMMENTS

1. A support vector machine separates observations using a hyperplane to define a boundary. When the boundary is restricted to be linear, a support vector machine is similar to the logistic equation resulting from logistic regression. However, a support vector machine can separate observations using nonlinear boundaries and capture more sophisticated relationships between variables.

2. The idea behind the naïve Bayes method is to express the likelihood that an observation belongs to Class 1 as a conditional probability that is then decomposed used Bayes' theorem. The naïve aspect comes from the assumption that each feature is conditionally independent of every other feature.

3. Neural networks are based on the biological model of brain activity. Well-structured neural networks have been shown to possess accurate classification and estimation performance in many application domains. However, the use of neural networks is a "black box" method that provides little interpretable explanation to accompany the predictions. Adjusting the parameters to tune the neural network performance is largely trial-and-error guided by rules of thumb and user experience. Neural networks form the basis of deep learning, an emerging area in machine learning with applications in image and speech recognition, among others.

GLOSSARY

Accuracy Measure of classification success defined as 1 minus the overall error rate.

Area under the ROC curve (AUC) A measure of a classification method's performance; an AUC of 0.5 implies that a method is no better than random classification while a perfect classifier has an AUC of 1.0.

Average error The average difference between the actual values and the predicted values of observations in a data set; used to detect prediction bias.

Bagging An ensemble method that generates a committee of models based on different random samples and makes predictions based on the average prediction of the set of models.

Bias The tendency of a predictive model to overestimate or underestimate the value of a continuous outcome.

Boosting An ensemble method that iteratively samples from the original training data to generate individual models that target observations that were mispredicted in previously generated models, and then bases the ensemble predictions on the weighted average of the predictions of the individual models, where the weights are proportional to the individual models' accuracy.

Class 0 error rate The percentage of Class 0 observations misclassified by a model in a data set.

Class 1 error rate The percentage of actual Class 1 observations misclassified by a model in a data set.

Classification A predictive data mining task requiring the prediction of an observation's outcome class or category.

Classification tree A tree that classifies a categorical outcome variable by splitting observations into groups via a sequence of hierarchical rules on the input variables.

Confusion matrix A matrix showing the counts of actual versus predicted class values.

Cumulative lift chart A chart used to present how well a model performs in identifying observations most likely to be in Class 1 as compared with random classification.

Cutoff value The smallest value that the predicted probability of an observation can be for the observation to be classified as Class 1.

Decile-wise lift chart A chart used to present how well a model performs at identifying observations for each of the top k deciles most likely to be in Class 1 versus a random classification.

Ensemble method A predictive data mining approach in which a committee of individual classification or estimation models are generated and a prediction is made by combining these individual predictions.

Estimation A predictive data mining task requiring the prediction of an observation's continuous outcome value.

F1 Score A measure combining precision and sensitivity into a single metric.

False negative The misclassification of a Class 1 observation as Class 0.

False positive The misclassification of a Class 0 observation as Class 1.

Features A set of input variables used to predict an observation's outcome class or continuous outcome value.

Impurity Measure of the heterogeneity of observations in a classification or regression tree.

k-fold cross-validation A robust procedure to train and validate models in which the observations to be used to train and validate the model are repeatedly randomly divided into k subsets called folds. In each iteration, one fold is designated as the validation set and the remaining $k - 1$ folds are designated as the training set. The results of the iterations are then combined and evaluated.

k-nearest neighbors A data mining method that predicts (classifies or estimates) an observation i's outcome value based on the k observations most similar to observation i with respect to the input variables.

Leave-one-out cross-validation A special case of k-fold cross validation for which the number of folds equals the number of observations in the combined training and validation data.

Logistic regression A generalization of linear regression that predicts a categorical outcome variable by computing the log odds of the outcome as a linear function of the input variables.

Mallow's C_p statistic A measure in which small values approximately equal to the number of coefficients suggest promising logistic regression models.

Observation (record) A set of observed values of variables associated with a single entity, often displayed as a row in a spreadsheet or database.

Out-of-bag estimation A measure of estimating the predictive performance of a bagging ensemble of m models (without a separate validation set) by leveraging the concept that the training of each model is only based on approximately 63.2% of the original observations (due to sampling with replacement).

Overall error rate The percentage of observations misclassified by a model in a data set.

Overfitting A situation in which a model explains random patterns in the data on which it is trained rather than just the generalizable relationships, resulting in a model with training-set performance that greatly exceeds its performance on new data.

Oversampling A technique that balances the number of Class 1 and Class 0 observations in a training set by inserting copies of minority class observations into the training set.

Precision The percentage of observations predicted to be Class 1 that actually are Class 1.

Random forests A variant of the bagging ensemble method that generates a committee of classification or regression trees based on different random samples but restricts each individual tree to a limited number of randomly selected features (variables).

Receiver operating characteristic (ROC) curve A chart used to illustrate the tradeoff between a model's ability to identify Class 1 observations and its Class 0 error rate.

Regression tree A tree that predicts values of a continuous outcome variable by splitting observations into groups via a sequence of hierarchical rules on the input variables.

Root mean squared error A performance measure of an estimation method defined as the square root of the sum of squared deviations between the actual values and predicted values of observations.

Sensitivity (recall) The percentage of actual Class 1 observations correctly identified.

Specificity The percentage of actual Class 0 observations correctly identified.

Supervised learning Category of data mining techniques in which an algorithm learns how to classify or estimate an outcome variable of interest.

Test set Data set used to compute unbiased estimate of final predictive model's performance.

Training set Data used to build candidate predictive models.

Undersampling A technique that balances the number of Class 1 and Class 0 observations in a training set by removing majority class observations from the training set.

Unstable When small changes in the training set cause a model's predictions to fluctuate substantially.

Validation set Data used to evaluate candidate predictive models.

Variable (feature) A characteristic or quantity of interest that can take on different values.

PROBLEMS

Problems 1 through 8 do not require the use of data mining software and focus on knowledge of concepts and basic calculations.

Problems 9 through 26 require the use of data mining software. If using R/Rattle to solve these problems, refer to Appendix: *R/Rattle Settings to Solve Chapter 9 Problems.* If using JMP Pro to solve these problems, refer to Appendix: *JMP Pro Settings to Solve Chapter 9 Problems.*

1. **Dating Web Site (logistic regression).** The dating web site Oollama.com requires its users to create profiles based on a survey in which they rate their interest (on a scale from 0 to 3) in five categories: physical fitness, music, spirituality, education, and alcohol consumption. A new Oollama customer, Erin O'Shaughnessy, has reviewed

the profiles of 40 prospective dates and classified whether she is interested in learning more about them.

Based on Erin's classification of these 40 profiles, Oollama has applied a logistic regression to predict Erin's interest in other profiles that she has not yet viewed. The resulting logistic regression model is as follows:

$$\text{Log Odds of Interested} = -0.920 + 0.325 \times \text{Fitness} - 3.611 \times \text{Music}$$
$$+5.535 \times \text{Education} - 2.927 \times \text{Alcohol}$$

For the 40 profiles (observations) on which Erin classified her interest, this logistic regression model generates that following probability of Interested.

Observation	Interested	Probability of Interested	Observation	Interested	Probability of Interested
35	1	1.000	13	0	0.412
21	1	0.999	2	0	0.285
29	1	0.999	3	0	0.219
25	1	0.999	7	0	0.168
39	1	0.999	9	0	0.168
26	1	0.990	12	0	0.168
23	1	0.981	18	0	0.168
33	1	0.974	22	1	0.168
1	0	0.882	31	1	0.168
24	1	0.882	6	0	0.128
28	1	0.882	20	0	0.128
36	1	0.882	15	0	0.029
16	0	0.791	5	0	0.020
27	1	0.791	14	0	0.015
30	1	0.791	19	0	0.011
32	1	0.791	8	0	0.008
34	1	0.791	10	0	0.001
37	1	0.791	17	0	0.001
40	1	0.791	4	0	0.001
38	1	0.732	11	0	0.000

a. Using a cutoff value of 0.5 to classify a profile observation as Interested or not, construct the confusion matrix for this 40-observation training set. Compute sensitivity, specificity, and precision measures and interpret them within the context of Erin's dating prospects.

b. Oollama understands that its clients have a limited amount of time for dating and therefore use decile-wise lift charts to evaluate their classification models. For the training data, what is the first decile lift resulting from the logistic regression model? Interpret this value.

c. A recently posted profile has values of Fitness = 3, Music = 1, Education = 3, and Alcohol = 1. Use the estimated logistic regression equation to compute the probability of Erin's interest in this profile.

d. Now that Oollama has trained a logistic regression model based on Erin's initial evaluations of 40 profiles, what should its next steps be in the modeling process?

2. **Cupcake Approval (*k*-NN classification).** Fleur-de-Lis is a boutique bakery specializing in cupcakes. The bakers at Fleur-de-Lis like to experiment with different combinations of four major ingredients in its cupcakes and collect customer feedback; it has data on 150 combinations of ingredients with the corresponding customer reception for each

combination classified as "thumbs up" (Class 1) or "thumbs down" (Class 0). To better anticipate the customer feedback of new recipes, Fleur-de-Lis has determined that a k-nearest neighbors classifier with $k = 10$ seems to perform well.

Using a cutoff value of 0.5 and a validation set of 45 observations, Fleur-de-Lis constructs following confusion matrix and the ROC curve for the k-nearest neighbors classifier with $k = 10$:

	Predicted Feedback	
Actual Feedback	**Thumbs Up**	**Thumbs Down**
Thumbs Up	13	1
Thumbs Down	1	30

As the confusion matrix shows, there is one observation that actually received thumbs down, but the k-nearest neighbors classifier predicts a thumbs up. Also, there is one observation that actually received a thumbs up, but the k-nearest neighbors classifier predicts a thumbs down. Specifically:

Observation ID	Actual Class	Probability of Thumbs Up	Predicted Class
A	Thumbs Down	0.5	Thumbs Up
B	Thumbs Up	0.2	Thumbs Down

a. Explain how the probability of Thumbs Up was computed for Observation A and Observation B. Why was Observation A classified as Thumbs Up and Observation B was classified as Thumbs Down?

b. Compute the values of sensitivity and specificity corresponding to the confusion matrix created using the cutoff value of 0.5. Locate the point corresponding to these values of sensitivity and specificity on the Fleur-de-Lis's ROC curve.

c. Based on what we know about Observation B, if the cutoff value is lowered to 0.2, what happens to the values of sensitivity and specificity? Explain. Use the ROC curve to estimate the values of sensitivity and specificity for a cutoff value of 0.2.

3. **Athlete Contract Negotiations (regression tree).** Casey Deesel is a sports agent negotiating a contract for Titus Johnston, an athlete in the National Football League (NFL). An important aspect of any NFL contract is the amount of guaranteed money over the life of the contract. Casey has gathered data on 506 NFL athletes who have recently signed new contracts. Each observation (NFL athlete) includes values for percentage of his team's plays that the athlete is on the field (SnapPercent), the number of awards an athlete has received recognizing on-field performance (Awards), the number of games the athlete has missed due to injury (GamesMissed), and millions of dollars of guaranteed money in the athlete's most recent contract (Money, dependent variable).

   Casey has trained a full regression tree on 304 observations and then used the validation set to prune the tree to obtain a best-pruned tree. The best-pruned tree (as applied to the 202 observations in the validation set) is:

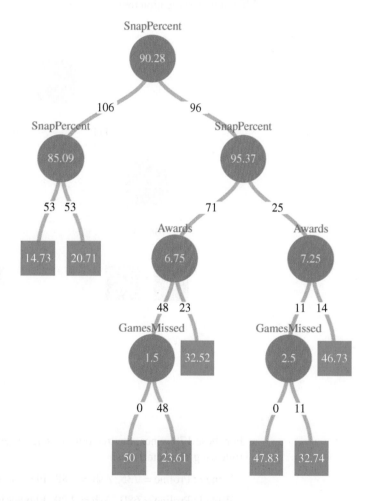

   a. Titus Johnston's variable values are: SnapPercent = 96, Awards = 7, and GamesMissed = 3. How much guaranteed money does the regression tree predict that a player with Titus Johnson's profile should earn in his contract?

   b. Casey feels that Titus was denied an additional award in the past season due to some questionable voting by some sports media. If Titus had won this additional award, how much additional guaranteed money would the regression tree predict for Titus versus the prediction in part (a)?

   c. As Casey reviews the best-pruned tree, he is confused by the leaf node corresponding to the sequence of decision rules of "SnapPercent > 90.28, SnapPercent < 95.37, Awards < 6.75, GamesMissed < 1.5." This sequence of decision rules results in an estimate of $50 million of guaranteed money, but the tree states that zero observations occur in the corresponding partition. If zero observations occur in this partition, how can the regression tree provide an estimate of $50 million? Explain this part of the regression tree to Casey by referring to how the best-pruned tree is obtained.

4. **Wine Approval (classification tree).** Sommelier4U is a company that ships its customers bottles of different types of wine and then has them rate the wines as "Like" or "Dislike." For each customer, Sommelier4U trains a classification tree based on the characteristics and customer ratings of wines that the customer has tasted. Then, Sommelier4U uses the classification tree to identify new wines that the customer may Like. Sommelier4U recommends the wines that have a greater than 50% probability of being liked. Neal Jones, a loyal customer, has provided feedback on hundreds of different wines that he has tasted. Based on this feedback, Sommelier4U trained and validated the following classification tree:

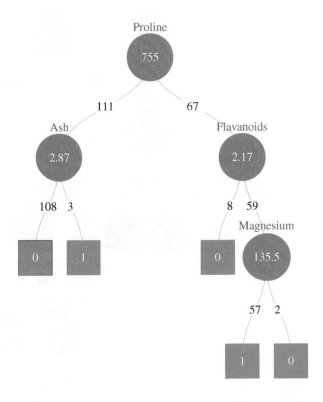

a. For these 178 wines, the tree only misclassifies two wines. These wines have the following characteristics:

Wine 1: Proline = 735, Ash = 2.88, Flavanoids = 2.69, Magnesium = 118

Wine 1: Proline = 680, Ash = 2.29, Flavanoids = 2.63, Magnesium = 103

Based on this information, construct the confusion matrix based on the 178 wines. In order to better learn Neal's preferences, what types of wines could Sommelier4U recommend to him?

b. Consider the wine with the following characteristics: Proline = 820, Ash = 2.16, Flavanoids = 3.1, and Magnesium = 87. Does Sommelier4U believe that Neal will Like this wine?

5. **Alumni Donors (random forest).** A university is applying classification methods in order to identify alumni who may be interested in donating money. The university has a database of 58,205 alumni profiles containing numerous variables. Of these 58,205 alumni, only 576 have donated in the past. The university has oversampled

the data and trained a random forest of 100 classification trees. For a cutoff value of 0.5, the following confusion matrix summarizes the performance of the random forest on a validation set:

	Predicted	
Actual	**Donation**	**No Donation**
Donation	268	20
No Donation	5375	23,439

The following table lists some information on individual observations from the validation set:

Observation ID	Actual Class	Probability of Donation	Predicted Class
A	Donation	0.8	Donation
B	No Donation	0.1	No Donation
C	No Donation	0.6	Donation

a. Explain how the probability of Donation was computed for the three observations. Why were Observations A and C classified as Donation and Observation B was classified as No Donation?

b. Compute the values of accuracy, sensitivity, specificity, and precision. Explain why accuracy is a misleading measure to consider in this case. Evaluate the performance of the random forest, particularly commenting on the precision measure.

6. **Targeted Coupon Offers.** Honey is a technology company that provides online coupons to its subscribers. Honey's analytics staff has developed a classification method to predict whether a customer who has been sent a coupon will apply the coupon toward a purchase. For a sample of customers, the following table lists the classification model's estimated coupon usage probability for a customer. For this particular campaign, suppose that when a customer uses a coupon, Honey receives $2 in revenue from the product sponsor. To target the customer with the coupon offer, Honey incurs a cost of $0.01. Honey will offer a customer a coupon as long as the expected profit of doing so is positive. Using the equation

$$\text{\textit{Expected Profit of Coupon Offer}}$$
$$= P(\textit{coupon used}) \times \textit{Profit if coupon used}$$
$$+ (1 - P(\textit{coupon used})) \times \textit{Profit if coupon not used}$$

determine which customers should be sent the coupon.

Customer	Probability of Using Coupon
1	0.49
2	0.36
3	0.27
4	0.11
5	0.04

DATA *file*
Watershed.xlsx

7. **Addressing Customer Churn.** Watershed is a media services company that provides online steaming movie and television content. As a result of the competitive market of streaming service providers, Watershed is interested in proactively identifying will

unsubscribe in the next three months based on the customer's characteristics. For a test set of customers, the file *Watershed* contains an indication of whether a customer unsubscribed in the past three months and the classification model's estimated unsubscribe probability for the customer. In an effort to prevent customer churn, Watershed wishes to offer promotions to customers who may unsubscribe. It costs Watershed $10 to offer a promotion to a customer. If offered a promotion, it successfully persuades a customer to remain a Watershed customer with probability 0.6, and the retaining the customer is worth $60 to Watershed. Assuming customers will be offered the promotion in order of decreasing estimated unsubscribe probability; determine how many customers Watershed should offer the promotion to maximize the profit of the intervention campaign. Compute the average profit from offering the top n customers a promotion as:

$$\text{Profit} = \text{Number of unsubscribing customers in top } n$$
$$\times (\text{P(unsubscribing customer persuaded to remain)} \times (60 - 10)$$
$$+ \text{P(unsubscribing customer is not persuaded)} \times (0 - 10))$$
$$+ \text{Number of customers who don't intend to unsubscribe} \times (0 - 10)$$

8. **Lift Chart for Targeted Marketing.** Mary Jay is a salesperson for a cosmetics company that relies on direct marketing to sell its products. A classification method was developed to predict whether a customer will purchase if contacted with a targeted marketing pitch. This classification method generated output to create following decile-wise lift chart on a test set of 10,000 customers, 400 of whom actually purchased the product when solicited with targeted marketing.
   a. In the top 1,000 customers deemed most likely to purchase in response to direct marketing, how many actually made a purchase?
   b. In the top 3,000 customers deemed most likely to purchase in response to direct marketing, how many actually made a purchase?

JMP: **Salmons.xlsx**
Rattle: **SalmonsTrain.csv,**
SalmonsValidation.csv,
SalmonsTest.csv

9. **Coupon Use (logistic regression).** Salmons Stores operates a national chain of women's apparel stores. Five thousand copies of an expensive four-color sales catalog have been printed, and each catalog includes a coupon that provides a $50 discount on purchases of $200 or more. Salmons would like to send the catalogs only to customers who have the highest probability of using the coupon. For each of 1,000 Salmons customers, three variables were tracked from an earlier promotional campaign: last year's total spending at Salmons (Spending), whether they have a Salmons store credit card (Card), and whether they used the promotional coupon they were sent (Coupon). Apply logistic regression to classify observations as a promotion-responder or not by using Spending and Card as input variables and Coupon as the target (or response) variable.

a. Evaluate candidate logistic regression models based on their predictive performance on the validation set. Recommend a final model and express the model as a mathematical equation relating the target variable to the input variables.

b. For the model selected in part (a), provide and interpret the lift measure on the top 10% of the test set observations most likely to use the promotional coupon.

c. What is the area under the ROC curve on the test set? To achieve a sensitivity of at least 0.80, how much Class 0 error rate must be tolerated?

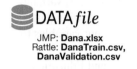

JMP: **Dana.xlsx**
Rattle: **DanaTrain.csv,
DanaValidation.csv**

10. **Student Retention (logistic regression).** Over the past few years the percentage of students who leave Dana College at the end of their first year has increased. Last year, Dana started voluntary one-credit hour-long seminars with faculty to help first-year students establish an on-campus connection. If Dana is able to show that the seminars have a positive effect on retention, college administrators will be convinced to continue funding this initiative. Dana's administration also suspects that first-year students with lower high school GPAs have a higher probability of leaving Dana at the end of the first year. Data on the 500 first-year students from last year has been collected. Each observation consists of a first-year student's high school GPA, whether they enrolled in a seminar, and whether they dropped out and did not return to Dana. Apply logistic regression to classify observations as dropped out or not dropped out by using GPA and Seminar as input variables and Dropped as the target (or response) variable.

a. Evaluate the candidate logistic regression models based on their predictive performance on the validation set. Recommend a final model and express the model as a mathematical equation relating the target variable to the input variables. What is the implication on the effectiveness of the first-year seminars on retention?

b. The data analyst team realized that they jumped directly into building a predictive model without exploring the data. Using descriptive statistics and charts, investigate any relationships in the data that may explain the unsatisfactory result in part (a). For next year's first-year class, what could Dana's administration do regarding the enrollment of the seminars to better determine whether they have an effect on retention?

JMP: **Sandhills.xlsx**
R: **Sandhills.csv**

11. **Direct Deposit Adoption (*k*-NN classification).** Sandhills Bank would like to increase the number of customers who use payroll direct deposit as part of the rollout of its new e-banking platform. Management has proposed offering an increased interest rate on a savings account if customers sign up for direct deposit into a checking account. To determine whether this proposal is a good idea, management would like to estimate how many of the 200 current customers who do not use direct deposit would accept the offer. The IT company that handles Sandhills Bank's e-banking has provided anonymized data for 1,000 customers from one of its other client banks that made a similar promotion to increase direct deposit participation. For these 1,000 customers (which correspond to the first 1,000 observations in the file *Sandhills*), each observation consists of the average monthly checking account balance and whether the customer signed up for direct deposit. Sandhills has designated the data corresponding to its 200 current customers as the test set and these customers are the last 200 observations in the file *Sandhills* (observations 1,001 to 1,200). As Sandhills has not yet launched its promotion to any of these 200 customers, it has entered an artificial value of zero (i.e., "No") for whether they have signed up for direct deposit. As some of these 200 customers will be the target of the direct-deposit promotion, Sandhills would like to estimate the likelihood of these customers signing up for direct deposit based on their average monthly balance. Classify the data using *k*-nearest neighbors for a range of values of *k*. Use Balance as the input variable and Direct as the target (or response) variable.

a. For a default cutoff value of 0.5, what value of *k* minimizes the overall error rate on a static validation set or through a 10-fold cross-validation procedure?

b. For a cutoff value of 0.5 and the value of *k* identified in part (a), how many of Sandhills Bank's 200 customers (in the test set) does *k*-nearest neighbors classify as enrolling in direct deposit?

DATA *file*

JMP: **BlueOrRed.xlsx**
R: **BlueOrRed.csv**

12. **Undecided Voters (*k*-NN classification).** Campaign organizers for both the Republican and Democratic parties are interested in identifying individual undecided voters who would consider voting for their party in an upcoming election. A non-partisan group has collected data on a sample of voters with tracked variables, including whether or not they are undecided regarding their candidate preference, age, whether they own a home, gender, marital status, household size, income, years of education, and whether they attend church. Using Undecided as the target (or response) variable, construct a series of *k*-nearest neighbor classifiers as directed by the following parts (a), (b), and (c). Evaluate a range of values of *k* and standardize the input variables to adjust for the different magnitudes of the variables.

   a. Use only the continuous variables (Age, HouseholdSize, Income, and Education) as input variables. For a default cutoff value of 0.5, what value of *k* minimizes the overall error rate on a static validation set or through a 10-fold cross-validation procedure?

   b. Use all eight variables as input variables. For a default cutoff value of 0.5, what value of *k* minimizes the overall rate on a static validation set or through a 10-fold cross-validation procedure?

   c. Generally, caution is recommended when combining continuous input variables and categorical input variables as the concept of distance differs for these two types of variables. Compare the overall error rates of models from parts (a) and (b). For these data, does combining variable types degrade performance?

DATA *file*

JMP: **BlueOrRed.xlsx**
Rattle: **BlueOrRedTrain.csv,**
BlueOrRedValidation.csv,
BlueOrRedTest.csv

13. **Undecided Voters (logistic regression).** Refer to the scenario in Problem 12 regarding the identification of undecided voters. Use logistic regression to classify observations as undecided (or decided) using Age, HomeOwner, Female, Married, HouseholdSize, Income, Education, and Church as input variables and Undecided as the target (or response) variable.

   a. Constructing models on the training set, evaluate a small set of candidate models based on their predictive performance on the validation set. Recommend a final model and express the model as a mathematical equation relating the target (or response) variable to the input variables.

   b. For the final model from part (a), increases in which variables increase the chance of a voter being undecided? Increases in which variables decrease the chance of a voter being decided?

   c. Using a default cutoff value of 0.5 for your logistic regression model, what is the overall error rate on the test set for the final model from part (a)?

DATA *file*

JMP: **BlueOrRed.xlsx**
Rattle: **BlueOrRedCV.csv,**
BlueOrRedTest.csv

14. **Undecided Voters (classification tree).** Refer to the scenario in Problem 12 regarding the identification of undecided voters. Fit an individual classification tree using Age, HomeOwner, Female, Married, HouseholdSize, Income, Education, and Church as input variables and Undecided as the target (or response) variable.

   a. For a default cutoff value of 0.5, what are the overall error rate, Class 1 error rate, and Class 0 error rate of the best-pruned tree on the test set?

   b. Consider a 50-year-old man who attends church, has 15 years of education, owns a home, is married, lives in a household of four people, and has an annual income of $150,000. Does the best-pruned tree classify this observation as Undecided?

   c. For the best-pruned tree, what is the lift on the top 30% of the test set deemed most likely to be Undecided?

DATA *file*

JMP: **BlueOrRed.xlsx**
Rattle: **BlueOrRedCV.csv**

15. **Undecided Voters (random forest classification).** Refer to scenario in Problem 12 regarding the identification of undecided voters. Apply a random forest of classification trees using Age, HomeOwner, Female, Married, HouseholdSize, Income, Education, and Church as input variables and Undecided as the target (or response) variable.

   a. Experiment with the number of trees and the number of variables per tree to recommend a random forest model (based on predictive performance on a static validation set or a cross-validation procedure).

   b. Which variable is most important in the random forest model?

16. **Cellphone Customer Retention (*k*-NN classification).** Telecommunications companies providing cell-phone service are interested in customer retention. In particular, identifying customers who are about to churn (cancel their service) is potentially worth millions of dollars if the company can proactively address the reason that customer is considering cancellation and retain the customer. Data on past customers (some of whom churned and some who did not) has been collected. The variables in this data are listed in the following table.

Variable	Description
AccountWeeks	number of weeks customer has had active account
ContractRenewal	1 if customer recently renewed contract, 0 if not
DataPlan	1 if customer has data plan, 0 if not
DataUsage	gigabytes of monthly data usage
CustServCalls	number of calls into customer service
DayMins	average daytime minutes per month
DayCalls	average number of daytime calls
MonthlyCharge	average monthly bill
OverageFee	largest overage fee in last 12 months
RoamMins	average number of roaming minutes
Churn	"Yes" if customer cancelled service, "No" if not

Classify the data using *k*-nearest neighbors for a range of values of *k*. Use Churn as the target (or response) variable and all the other variables as input variables. Standardize the input variables to adjust for the different magnitudes of the variables.

a. For a default cutoff value of 0.5, what value of *k* minimizes the overall error rate on the a static validation set or through a 10-fold cross-validation procedure?

b. What is the overall error rate, the Class 1 error rate, and the Class 0 error rate on the test set?

c. Compute and interpret the sensitivity and specificity for the test set.

d. How many false positives and false negatives did the model commit on the test set? What percentage of predicted churners were false positives? What percentage of predicted nonchurners were false negatives?

17. **Cellphone Customer Retention (classification tree).** Refer to scenario in Problem 16 regarding the identification of churning cellphone customers. Fit an individual classification tree using Churn as the target (or response) variable and all the other variables as input variables.

a. For a default cutoff value of 0.5, what is the overall rate, the Class 1 error rate, and the Class 0 error rate of the best-pruned tree on the test set?

b. List and interpret the set of rules that characterize churners in the best-pruned tree.

c. Examine the lift chart for the best-pruned tree on the test set. What is the lift for the top 10% of the test set observations deemed most likely to churn? Interpret this value.

18. **Cellphone Customer Retention (random forest classification).** Refer to scenario in Problem 16 regarding the identification of churning cellphone customers. Apply a random forest of classification trees using Churn as the target (or response) variable and all the other variables as input variables.

a. Experiment with the number of trees and the number of variables per tree to recommend a random forest model (based on predictive performance on a static validation set or a cross-validation procedure).

b. Which variable is most important in the random forest model?

19. **Cellphone Customer Retention (logistic regression).** Refer to scenario in Problem 16 regarding the identification of churning cellphone customers. Apply logistic regression using Churn as the target (or response) variable and all the other variables as input variables.

a. Evaluate several candidate models based on their predictive performance on the validation set. Recommend a final model and express the model as a mathematical equation relating the target variable to the input variables. Do the relationships suggested by the model make sense? Try to explain them.

b. What is the AUC for the ROC curve for the final model from part (a) on the test set?

JMP: **CreditScore.xlsx**
Rattle: **CreditScoreCV.csv,**
   CreditScoreTest.csv

20. **Credit Scores (regression tree).** A consumer advocacy agency, Equitable Ernest, is interested in providing a service that allows an individual to estimate his or her own credit score (a continuous measure used by banks, insurance companies, and other businesses when granting loans, quoting premiums, and issuing credit). Data from several individuals has been collected. The variables in these data are listed in the following table.

Variable	Description
BureauInquiries	number of inquiries about an individual's credit
CreditUsage	percent of an individual's credit used
TotalCredit	total amount of credit available to individual
CollectedReports	number of times an unpaid bill was reported to collection agency
MissedPayments	number of missed payments
HomeOwner	1 if individual is homeowner. 0 if not
CreditAge	average age of individual's credit
TimeOnJob	how long the individual has been continuously employed
CreditScore	score between 300 and 850 with larger number representing increased credit worthiness

Predict the individuals' credit scores using an individual regression tree. Use CreditScore as the target (or response) variable and all the other relevant variables as input variables.

a. In the construction parameters of the tree, set the minimum number of records in a terminal node to be 244. What is the RMSE of the best-pruned tree on the validation data (a static validation set or through a 10-fold cross-validation procedure) and on the test set? Discuss the implication of these calculations.

b. Consider an individual with 5 credit bureau inquiries, has used 10% of her available credit, has $14,500 of total available credit, has no collection reports or missed payments, is a homeowner, has an average credit age of 6.5 years, and has worked continuously for the past 5 years. Using the best-pruned tree from part (a), what is the predicted credit score for this individual?

c. Repeat the construction of an individual regression tree, but now set the minimum number of records in a terminal node to be 1. How does the RMSE of the best-pruned tree on the test set compare to the analogous measure from part (a)? In terms of number of decision nodes, how does the size of the best-pruned tree compare to the size of the best-pruned tree from part (a)?

JMP: **CreditScore.xlsx**
Rattle: **CreditScoreCV.csv**

21. **Credit Scores (random forest estimation).** Refer to the scenario in Problem 20 regarding the estimation of individuals' credit scores. Apply a random forest of regression trees using CreditScore as the target (or response) variable and all the other variables as input variables.

a. Experiment with the number of trees and the number of variables per tree to recommend a random forest model (based on predictive performance on a static validation set or a cross-validation procedure).

b. Which variable is most important in the random forest model?

JMP: **CreditScore.xlsx**
  R: **CreditScore.csv**

22. **Credit Scores (*k*-NN estimation).** Refer to the scenario in Problem 20 regarding the estimation of individuals' credit scores. Predict the individuals' credit scores using *k*-nearest neighbors for a range of values of *k*. Use CreditScore as the target (or response) variable and all the other variables except HomeOwner as input variables. Standardize the input variables to adjust for the different magnitudes of the variables.

a. What value of *k* minimizes the RMSE on a static validation set or through a 10-fold cross-validation procedure?

b. How does the RMSE on the test set compare to the RMSE on the validation set?

23. **Academy Awards (logistic regression).** Each year, the American Academy of Motion Picture Arts and Sciences recognizes excellence in the film industry by honoring directors, actors, and writers with awards (called "Oscars") in different categories. The most notable of these awards is the Oscar for Best Picture. Data has been collected on a sample of movies nominated for the Best Picture Oscar. The variables include total number of Oscar nominations across all award categories, number of Golden Globe awards won (the Golden Globe award show precedes the Academy Awards), whether or not the movie is a comedy, and whether or not the movie won the Best Picture Oscar award. Apply logistic regression to classify winners of the Best Picture Oscar. Use Winner as the target (or response) variable and OscarNominations, GoldenGlobeWins, and Comedy as input variables.

   a. Evaluate several candidate models based on their predictive performance on the validation set. Recommend a final model and express the model as a mathematical equation relating the target variable to the input variables. Do the relationships suggested by the model make sense? Try to explain them.

   b. Using a default cutoff value of 0.5, what is the sensitivity of the logistic regression model on the validation set? Why is this a good metric to use for this problem?

   c. Note that each year there is only one winner of the Best Picture Oscar. Knowing this, what is wrong with classifying a movie based on a cutoff value? (*Hint*: Investigate the predicted results on an annual basis.)

   d. What is the best way to use the model to predict the annual winner? For the validation set, how often is the actual winner deemed "most likely" to win out of each year's nominees?

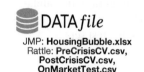

24. **Housing Price Bubble (*k*-NN estimation).** As an intern with the local home builder's association, you have been asked to analyze the state of the local housing market, which has suffered during a recent economic crisis. You have been provided two data sets: the Pre-Crisis data contains information on 1,978 single-family homes sold during the one-year period before the burst of the "housing bubble," and the Post-Crisis data contains information on 1,657 single-family homes sold during the one-year period after the burst of the housing bubble. In addition, there is a set of 2,000 observations designated as a test set corresponding to homes currently for sale. Because the homes in the test set have not yet been sold, each of these 2,000 observation has an artificial value of zero for the sale price.

   The variables in the respective data sets are listed in the following table.

Variable	Description
LandValue	assessed value for the land ($)
BuildingValue	assessed value for the building structure ($)
Acres	size of lot home sits on (acres)
AboveSpace	above ground living space (sq ft)
Basement	below ground finished living space (sq ft)
Deck	total deck space (sq ft)
Baths	number of full- or 3/4-baths
Toilets	number of 1/2-baths
Fireplaces	number of fireplaces
Beds	number of bedrooms
Rooms	number of rooms, which are not bedrooms
AC	1 if home has air conditioning for at least 1/2 of living space, 0 if not
Age	age of home at time of sale
Car	total space for parking cars in covered structures (attached garage + carport) (sq ft)
PoorCondition	1 if overall condition of home is below average, 0 if not
GoodCondition	1 if overall condition of home is above average, 0 if not
Price	price the home was sold for (seasonally adjusted $)

a. Consider the Pre-Crisis data. Predict the sale price using k-nearest neighbors with $k = 1, \ldots, 10$. Use Price as the target (or response) variable and all the other variables except AC, PoorCondition, and GoodCondition as input variables. Standardize the input variables to adjust for the different magnitudes of the variables.

   i. What value of k minimizes the RMSE on a static validation set or through a 10-fold cross-validation procedure, and what is the value of this RMSE?

   ii. Use the k-nearest neighbors with the value of k that minimizes RMSE on the validation set to predict sale prices of houses in the test set.

b. Repeat part (a) with the Post-Crisis data.

c. For each of the 2,000 houses in the test set, compare the predictions from part (a-ii) based on the pre-crisis data to those from part (b-ii) based on the post-crisis data. Specifically, compute the percentage difference in predicted price between the pre-crisis and post-crisis models, where percentage difference = (post-crisis predicted price − pre-crisis predicted price)/pre-crisis predicted price. What is the average percentage change in predicted price between the pre-crisis and post-crisis models?

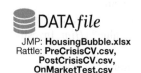

25. **Housing Price Bubble (regression tree).** Refer to the scenario in Problem 24 regarding estimating house prices.

a. Consider the Pre-Crisis data. Predict the sale price using an individual regression tree. Use Price as the target (or response) variable and all the other variables as input variables.

   i. What is the RMSE of the best-pruned tree on the validation set (a static validation set or through a 10-fold cross-validation procedure)?

   ii. Use the best-pruned tree to predict sale prices of houses in the test set.

b. Repeat part (a) with the Post-Crisis data.

c. For each of the 2,000 houses in the test set, compare the predictions from part (a-ii) based on the pre-crisis data to those from part (b-ii) based on the post-crisis data. Specifically, compute the percentage difference in predicted price between the pre-crisis and post-crisis models, where percentage difference = (post-crisis predicted price − pre-crisis predicted price)/pre-crisis predicted price. What is the average percentage change in predicted price between the pre-crisis and post-crisis models? What does this suggest about the impact of the bursting of the housing bubble?

26. **Housing Price Bubble (random forest estimation).** Refer to the scenario in Problem 24 regarding estimating house prices.

a. Consider the Pre-Crisis data. Apply a random forest of regression trees using Price as the target (or response) variable and all the other variables as input variables. Experiment with the number of trees and the number of variables per tree to recommend a random forest model (based on predictive performance on a static validation set or a cross-validation procedure). Use this random forest to predict sale prices of houses in the test set.

b. Repeat part (a) with the Post-Crisis data.

c. For each of the 2,000 houses in the test set, compare the predictions from part (a-ii) based on the pre-crisis data to those from part (b-ii) based on the post-crisis data. Specifically, compute the percentage difference in predicted price between the pre-crisis and post-crisis models, where percentage difference = (post-crisis predicted price − pre-crisis predicted price)/pre-crisis predicted price. What is the average percentage change in predicted price between the pre-crisis and post-crisis models? What does this suggest about the impact of the bursting of the housing bubble?

CASE PROBLEM: GREY CODE CORPORATION

Grey Code Corporation (GCC) is a media and marketing company involved in magazine and book publishing and in television broadcasting. GCC's portfolio of home and family magazines has been a long-running strength, but it has expanded to become a provider of a spectrum of services (market research, communications planning, web site advertising, etc.) that can enhance its clients' brands.

GCC's relational database contains over a terabyte of data encompassing 75 million customers. GCC uses the data in its database to develop campaigns for new customer acquisition, customer reactivation, and identification of cross-selling opportunities for products. For example, GCC will generate separate versions of a monthly issue of a magazine that will differ only by the advertisements they contain. It will mail a subscribing customer the version with the print ads identified by its database as being of most interest to that customer.

DATA *file*

JMP: **Grey.xlsx**
R/Rattle: **Grey.csv**

One particular problem facing GCC is how to boost the customer response rate to renewal offers that it mails to its magazine subscribers. The industry response rate is about 2%, but GCC has historically performed better than that. However, GCC must update its model to correspond to recent changes. GCC's director of database marketing, Chris Grey, wants to make sure that GCC maintains its place as one of the top achievers in targeted marketing. The file *Grey* contains 38 variables (columns) and over 40,000 rows (distinct customers). The table appended to the end of this case provides a list of the variables and their descriptions.

Play the role of Chris Grey and construct a classification model to identify customers who are likely to respond to a mailing. Write a report that documents the following steps:

1. Explore the data. Because of the large number of variables, it may be helpful to filter out unnecessary and redundant variables.

2. Appropriately partition the data set into training, validation, and test sets. Experiment with various classification methods and propose a final model for identifying customers who will respond to the targeted marketing.

3. Your report should include appropriate charts (ROC curves, lift charts, etc.) and include a recommendation on how to apply the results of your proposed model. For example, if GCC sends the targeted marketing to the top 10% of the test set that the model believes is most likely to renew, what is the expected response rate? How does that compare to the industry's average response rate?

Variable	Description
CustomerID	Customer identification number
Renewal	1 if customer renewed magazine in response to mailing, 0 otherwise
Age	Customer age (ranges from 18 to 99)
HomeOwner	Likelihood of customer owning their own home
ResidenceLength	Number of years customer has lived at current residence. Values: 1 = less than two years, 2 = two years, 3 = three years, 4 = four years, 5 = five years, 6 = six years, 7 = seven years, 8 = eight years, 9 = nine years, 10 = ten years, 11 = eleven years, 12 = twelve years, 13 = thirteen years, 14 = fourteen years, or more
DwellingType	Identifies the type of residence. S = Single family dwelling unit. M = Multi family dwelling unit, U = unknown
Gender	F = female, M = male, U = unknown
Marital	S = Single, M = Married, O = Other (divorced, widowed, etc.), U = unknown
HouseholdSize	Identifies the number of individuals in the household. Arguments are: 1 = 1 person in the household, 2 = 2 people in the household, 3 = 3 people in the household, 4 = 4 people in the household, 5 = 5 people in the household, 6 = 6 or more people in the household
ChildPresent	Indicates if children are present in the home. Y = child 21 or younger present in the home; N = no child 21 or younger present in the home; U = unknown
Child0-5	Likelihood of child 0–5 years old present in home
Child6-12	Likelihood of child 6–12 years old present in home
Child13-18	Likelihood of child 13–18 years old present in home
Income	Estimated income. Ranges from $5,000 to $500,000+
Occupation	Broad aggregation of occupations into high level categories. Arguments are: R = retired, W = professional/executive, M = sales/marketing/services/clerical, B = skilled trades/laborers (blue collar type jobs), H = at home (caregivers, unemployed, homemakers), U = unknown
HomeValue	The estimated home value in ranges. Arguments are 1–10. 1 = under $50K, 2 = $50K—under $100K, 3 = $100K—under $150K, 4 = $150K—under $200K, 5 = $200K—under $250K, 6 = $250K—under $300K, 7 = $300K—under $350K, 8 = $350K—under $400K, 9 = over $400, 10 = Unknown
MagazineStatus	Identifies the status for a customer based on their magazine business activity. A = active subscriber, B = cancelled subscription due to non-payment, C = cancelled subscription, E = subscription expired within last 3 years, N = gift subscription, O = subscription expired over 3 years ago, S = subscription suspended at request of customer, U = unknown
PaidDirectMailOrders	Number of paid direct mail orders across all magazine subscriptions
YearsSinceLastOrder	Years since last order across all business lines
TotalAmountPaid	Total dollar amount paid for all magazine subscriptions over time

Variable	Description
DollarsPerIssue	Paid Amount/Number of Issues Served. Average value per issue (takes the subscription term into account)
TotalPaidOrders	Total # of paid orders across all magazine subscriptions
MonthsSinceLastPayment	Recency - # months since most recent payment
LastPaymentType	Indicates how the customer paid on the most recent order. If it was credit order it will contain the billing effort number (how many bills were sent to collect payment). A = cash order, C = mass cancel for non-payment, D = Advanced renewal order cancelled, E = paid via collection agency, F = no billing, G = gift billed, I = online customer payment, K = payment received after order cancelled, L = extra payment, M = step-up financing, S = customer requested order cancellation, U = default paid, 0 = unpaid credit, 1 – 9 = paid credit on ith billing
UnpaidMagazines	Number of magazine titles currently in "unpaid" status for a given magazine customer
PaidCashMagazines	Number of magazine titles currently in "paid cash" status for a given magazine customer
PaidReinstateMagazines	Number of magazine titles currently in "paid reinstate" status for a given magazine customer
PaidCreditMagazines	Number of magazine titles currently in "paid credit" status for a given magazine customer
ActiveSubscriptions	Number of different magazines the customer is in "Active" status
ExpiredSubscriptions	Number of different magazines the customer is in "Expire" status
RequestedCancellations	Number of different magazines the customer is in "Cancelled via Customer Request" status
NoPayCancellations	Number of different magazines the customer is in "Cancelled for non-payment" status
PaidComplaints	Number of different magazines the customer is in "Paid Complaint" status
GiftDonor	Yes/No indicator as to whether the customer has given a magazine subscription as a gift
NumberGiftDonations	Number of subscription gift orders for this customer
MonthsSince1stOrder	Recency (in months) of 1st order for this magazine
MonthsSinceLastOrder	Recency (in months) of most recent order for this magazine
MonthsSinceExpire	Recency (in months) since the customer's subscription has expired for this magazine. Negative values represent months until an active subscription expires

Chapter 10

Spreadsheet Models

CONTENTS

ANALYTICS IN ACTION:
PROCTER & GAMBLE

ANALYTICS IN ACTION

Procter & Gamble*

Procter & Gamble (P&G) is a Fortune 500 consumer goods company headquartered in Cincinnati, Ohio. P&G produces well-known brands such as Tide detergent, Gillette razors, Swiffer cleaning products, and many other consumer goods. P&G is a global company and has been recognized for its excellence in business analytics, including supply chain analytics and market research.

With operations around the world, P&G must do its best to maintain inventory at levels that meet its high customer service requirements. A lack of on-hand inventory can result in a stockout of a product and an inability to meet customer demand. This not only results in lost revenue for an immediate sale but can also cause customers to switch permanently to a competing brand. On the other hand, excessive inventory forces P&G to invest cash in inventory when that money could be invested in other opportunities, such as research and development.

To ensure that the inventory of its products around the world is set at appropriate levels, P&G analytics personnel developed and deployed a series of spreadsheet inventory models. These spreadsheets implement mathematical inventory models to tell business units when and how much to order to keep inventory levels where they need to be in order to maintain service and keep investment as low as possible.

The spreadsheet models were carefully designed to be easily understood by the users and easy to use and interpret. Their users can also customize the spreadsheets to their individual situations.

Over 70% of the P&G business units use these models, with a conservative estimate of a 10% reduction in inventory around the world. This equates to a cash savings of nearly $350 million.

*I. Farasyn, K. Perkoz, and W. Van de Velde, "Spreadsheet Model for Inventory Target Setting at Procter & Gamble," *Interfaces* 38, no. 4 (July–August 2008): 241–250.

Numerous specialized software packages are available for descriptive, predictive, and prescriptive business analytics. Because these software packages are specialized, they usually provide the user with numerous options and the capability to perform detailed analyses. However, they tend to be considerably more expensive than a spreadsheet package such as Excel. Also, specialized packages often require substantial user training. Because spreadsheets are less expensive, often come preloaded on computers, and are fairly easy to use, they are without question the most-used business analytics tool. Every day, millions of people around the world use spreadsheet decision models to perform risk analysis, inventory tracking and control, investment planning, breakeven analysis, and many other essential business planning and decision tasks. A well-designed, well-documented, and accurate spreadsheet model can be a very valuable tool in decision making.

If you have never used a spreadsheet or have not done so recently, we suggest you first familiarize yourself with the material in Appendix A. It provides basic information that is fundamental to using Excel.

Spreadsheet models are mathematical and logic-based models. Their strength is that they provide easy-to-use, sophisticated mathematical and logical functions, allowing for easy instantaneous recalculation for a change in model inputs. This is why spreadsheet models are often referred to as **what-if models**. What-if models allow you to answer questions such as, "If the per unit cost is $4, what is the impact on profit?" Changing data in a given cell has an impact not only on that cell but also on any other cells containing a formula or function that uses that cell.

In this chapter, we discuss principles for building reliable spreadsheet models. We begin with a discussion of how to build a conceptual model of a decision problem, how to convert the conceptual model to a mathematical model, and how to implement the model in a spreadsheet. We introduce three analysis tools available in Excel: Data Tables, Goal Seek, and Scenario Manager. We discuss some Excel functions that are useful for building spreadsheet models for decision making. Finally, we present how to audit a spreadsheet model to ensure its reliability.

10.1 Building Good Spreadsheet Models

Let us begin our discussion of spreadsheet models by considering the cost of producing a single product. The total cost of manufacturing a product can usually be defined as the sum of two costs: fixed cost and variable cost. *Fixed cost* is the portion of the total cost that does not depend on the production quantity; this cost remains the same no matter how much is produced. *Variable cost*, on the other hand, is the portion of the total cost that is dependent on and varies with the production quantity. To illustrate how cost models can be developed, we will consider a manufacturing problem faced by Nowlin Plastics.

Nowlin Plastics produces a line of cell phone covers. Nowlin's best-selling cover is its Viper model, a slim but very durable black and gray plastic cover. The annual fixed cost to produce the Viper cover is $234,000. This fixed cost includes management time and other costs that are incurred regardless of the number of units eventually produced. In addition, the total variable cost, including labor and material costs, is $2 for each unit produced.

Nowlin is considering outsourcing the production of some products for next year, including the Viper. Nowlin has a bid from an outside firm to produce the Viper for $3.50 per unit. Although it is more expensive per unit to outsource the Viper ($3.50 versus $2.00), the fixed cost can be avoided if Nowlin purchases rather than manufactures the product. Next year's exact demand for Viper is not yet known. Nowlin would like to compare the costs of manufacturing the Viper in-house to those of outsourcing its production to another firm, and management would like to do that for various production quantities. Many manufacturers face this type of decision, which is known as a **make-versus-buy decision**.

Influence Diagrams

It is often useful to begin the modeling process with a conceptual model that shows the relationships between the various parts of the problem being modeled. The conceptual model helps in organizing the data requirements and provides a road map for eventually constructing a mathematical model. A conceptual model also provides a clear way to communicate the model to others. An **influence diagram** is a visual representation of which entities influence others in a model. Parts of the model are represented by circular or oval symbols called *nodes*, and arrows connecting the nodes show influence.

Figure 10.1 shows an influence diagram for Nowlin's total cost of production for the Viper. Total manufacturing cost depends on fixed cost and variable cost, which in turn depends on the variable cost per unit and the quantity required.

An expanded influence diagram that includes an outsourcing option is shown in Figure 10.2. Note that the influence diagram in Figure 10.1 is a subset of the influence diagram in Figure 10.2. Our method here—namely, to build an influence diagram for a portion of the problem and then expand it until the total problem is conceptually modeled—is usually a good way to proceed. This modular approach simplifies the process and reduces the likelihood of error. This is true not just for influence diagrams but for the construction of the mathematical and spreadsheet models as well. Next we turn our attention to using the influence diagram in Figure 10.2 to guide us in the construction of the mathematical model.

Building a Mathematical Model

The task now is to use the influence diagram to build a mathematical model. Let us first consider the cost of manufacturing the required units of the Viper. As the influence diagram shows, this cost is a function of the fixed cost, the variable cost per unit, and the quantity required. In general, it is best to define notation for every node in the influence diagram. Let us define the following:

$$q = \text{quantity (number of units) required}$$
$$FC = \text{the fixed cost of manufacturing}$$
$$VC = \text{the per-unit variable cost of manufacturing}$$
$$TMC(q) = \text{total cost to manufacture } q \text{ units}$$

FIGURE 10.1   An Influence Diagram for Nowlin's Manufacturing Cost

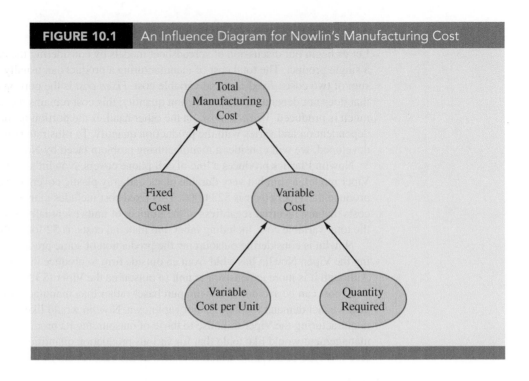

FIGURE 10.2   An Influence Diagram for Comparing Manufacturing Versus Outsourcing Cost for Nowlin Plastics

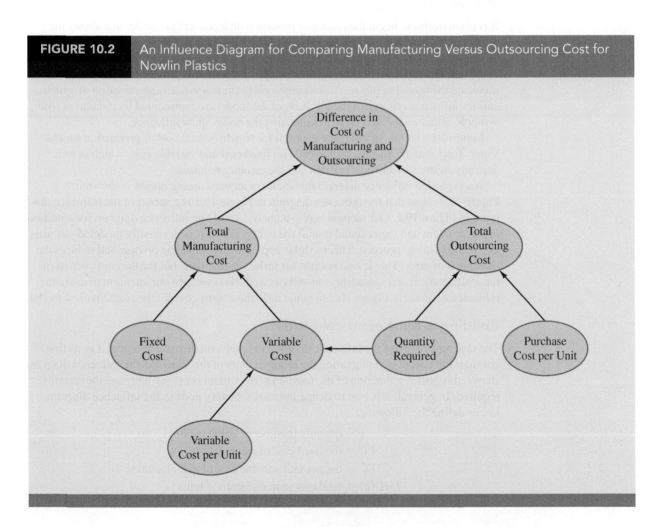

The cost-volume model for producing q units of the Viper can then be written as follows:

$$TMC(q) = FC + (VC \times q) \qquad \textbf{(10.1)}$$

For the Viper, $FC = \$234,000$ and $VC = \$2$, so that equation (10.1) becomes

$$TMC(q) = \$234,000 + \$2q$$

Once a quantity required (q) is established, equation (10.1), now populated with the data for the Viper, can be used to compute the total manufacturing cost. For example, the decision to produce $q = 10,000$ units would result in a total cost of $TMC(10,000) = \$234,000 + \$2(10,000) = \$254,000$.

Similarly, a mathematical model for purchasing q units is shown in equation (10.2). Let $P =$ the per-unit purchase cost and $TPC(q) =$ the total cost to outsource or purchase q units:

$$TPC(q) = Pq \qquad \textbf{(10.2)}$$

For the Viper, since $P = \$3.50$, equation (10.2) becomes

$$TPC(q) = \$3.5q$$

Thus, the total cost to outsource 10,000 units of the Viper is $TPC(10,000) = 3.5(10,000) = \$35,000$.

We can now state mathematically the savings associated with outsourcing. Let $S(q) =$ the savings due to outsourcing, that is, the difference between the total cost of manufacturing q units and the total cost of buying q units:

$$S(q) = TMC(q) - TPC(q) \qquad \textbf{(10.3)}$$

In summary, Nowlin's decision problem is whether to manufacture or outsource the demand for its Viper product next year. Because management does not yet know the required demand, the key question is, "For what quantities is it more cost-effective to outsource rather than produce the Viper?" Mathematically, this question is, "For what values of q is $S(q) > 0$?" Next we discuss a spreadsheet implementation of our conceptual and mathematical models that will help us answer this question.

Spreadsheet Design and Implementing the Model in a Spreadsheet

There are several guiding principles for how to build a spreadsheet so that it is easily used by others and the risk of error is mitigated. In this section, we discuss some of those principles and illustrate the design and construction of a spreadsheet model using the Nowlin Plastics make-versus-buy decision.

In the construction of a spreadsheet model, it is helpful to categorize its components. For the Nowlin Plastics problem, we have defined the following components (corresponding to the nodes of the influence diagram in Figure 10.2):

$$q = \text{number of units required}$$
$$FC = \text{the fixed cost of manufacturing}$$
$$VC = \text{the per-unit variable cost of manufacturing}$$
$$TMC(q) = \text{total cost to manufacture } q \text{ units}$$
$$P = \text{the per-unit purchase cost}$$
$$TPC(q) = \text{the total cost to purchase } q \text{ units}$$
$$S(q) = \text{the savings from outsourcing } q \text{ units}$$

Note that q, FC, VC, and P each is the beginning of a path in the influence diagram in Figure 10.2. In other words, they have no inward-pointing arrows.

Several points are in order. Some of these components are a function of other components (TMC, TPC, and S), and some are not (q, FC, VC, and P). TMC, TPC, and S will be formulas involving other cells in the spreadsheet model, whereas q, FC, VC, and P will just be entries in the spreadsheet. Furthermore, the value we can control or choose is q. In our analysis, we seek the value of q, such that $S(q) > 0$; that is, the savings associated with outsourcing is positive. The number of Vipers to make or buy for next year is Nowlin's decision. So we will treat q somewhat differently than FC, VC, and P in the spreadsheet model, and we refer to the quantity q as a **decision variable**. FC, VC, and P are measurable factors that define characteristics of the process we are modeling and so are *uncontrollable inputs* to the model, which we refer to as **parameters** of the model.

Figure 10.3 shows a spreadsheet model for the Nowlin Plastics make-versus-buy decision.

Column A is reserved for labels, including cell A1, where we have named the model "Nowlin Plastics." The input parameters (FC, VC, and P) are placed in cells B4, B5, and B7,

---

FIGURE 10.3 Nowlin Plastics Make-Versus-Buy Spreadsheet Model

	A	B	C
1	**Nowlin Plastics**		
2			
3	**Parameters**		
4	Manufacturing Fixed Cost	234000	
5	Manufacturing Variable Cost per Unit	2	
6			
7	Outsourcing Cost per Unit	3.5	
8			
9			
10	**Model**		
11	Quantity	10000	
12			
13	Total Cost to Produce	=B4+B11*B5	
14			
15	Total Cost to Outsource	=B7*B11	
16			
17	Savings due to Outsourcing	=B13–B15	
18			
19			

MODEL *file*

Nowlin

	A	B
1	**Nowlin Plastics**	
2		
3	**Parameters**	
4	Manufacturing Fixed Cost	$234,000.00
5	Manufacturing Variable Cost per Unit	$2.00
6		
7	Outsourcing Cost per Unit	$3.50
8		
9		
10	**Model**	
11	Quantity	10,000
12		
13	Total Cost to Produce	$254,000.00
14		
15	Total Cost to Outsource	$35,000.00
16		
17	Savings due to Outsourcing	$219,000.00
18		
19		

respectively. We offset *P* from *FC* and *VC* because it is for outsourcing. We have created a parameters section in the upper part of the sheet. Below the parameters section, we have created the Model section. The first entry in the Model section is the quantity *q*—the number of units of Viper produced or purchased in cell B11—and shaded it to signify that this is a decision variable. We have placed the formulas corresponding to equations (10.1) to (10.3) in cells B13, B15, and B17. Cell B13 corresponds to equation (10.1), cell B15 to (10.2), and cell B17 to (10.3).

In cell B11 of Figure 10.3, we have set the value of *q* to 10,000 units. The model shows that the cost to manufacture 10,000 units is $254,000, the cost to purchase the 10,000 units is $35,000, and the savings from outsourcing is $219,000. At a quantity of 10,000 units, we see that it is better to incur the higher variable cost ($3.50 versus $2) than to manufacture and have to incur the additional fixed cost of $234,000. It will take a value of *q* larger than 10,000 units to make up the fixed cost incurred when Nowlin manufactures the product. At this point, we could increase the value of *q* by placing a value higher than 10,000 in cell B11 and see how much the savings in cell B17 decreases, doing this until the savings are close to zero. This is called a *trial-and-error approach*. Fortunately, Excel has what-if analysis tools that will help us use our model to further analyze the problem. We will discuss these what-if analysis tools in Section 10.2. Before doing so, let us first review what we have learned in constructing the Nowlin spreadsheet model.

The general principles of spreadsheet model design and construction are as follows:

- Separate the parameters from the model.
- Document the model, and use proper formatting and color as needed.
- Use simple formulas.

Let us discuss the general merits of each of these points.

Separate the Parameters from the Model Separating the parameters from the model enables the user to update the model parameters without the risk of mistakenly creating an error in a formula. For this reason, it is good practice to have a parameters section at the top of the spreadsheet. A separate model section should contain all calculations. For a what-if model or an optimization model, some cells in the model section might also correspond to controllable inputs or decision variables (values that are not parameters or calculations but are the values we choose). The Nowlin model in Figure 10.3 is an example of this. The parameters section is in the upper part of the spreadsheet, followed by the model section, below which are the calculations and a decision cell (B11 for *q* in our model). Cell B11 is shaded to signify that it is a decision cell.

Document the Model and Use Proper Formatting and Color as Needed A good spreadsheet model is well documented. Clear labels and proper formatting and alignment facilitate navigation and understanding. For example, if the values in a worksheet are cost, currency formatting should be used. Also, no cell with content should be unlabeled. A new user should be able to easily understand the model and its calculations. If color makes a model easier to understand and navigate, use it for cells and labels.

Use Simple Formulas Clear, simple formulas can reduce errors and make it easier to maintain the spreadsheet. Long and complex calculations should be divided into several cells. This makes the formula easier to understand and easier to edit. Avoid using numbers in a formula (separate the data from the model). Instead, put the number in a cell in the parameters section of your worksheet and refer to the cell location in the formula. Building the formula in this manner avoids having to edit the formula for a simple data change. For example, equation (10.3), the savings due to outsourcing, can be calculated as follows: $S(q) = TMC(q) - TPC(q) = FC + (VC)q - Pq = FC + (VC - P)q$. Since $VC - P = 3.50 - 2 = 1.50$, we could have just entered the following formula in a single cell: $=234,000 - 1.50 * B11$. This is a very bad idea because if any of the input data change, the formula must be edited. Furthermore, the user would not know the values

As described in Appendix A, Excel formulas always begin with an equal sign.

of *VC* and *P*, only that, for the current values, the difference is 1.50. The approach in Figure 10.3 is more transparent, is simpler, lends itself better to analysis of changes in the parameters, and is less likely to contain errors.

NOTES + COMMENTS

1. Some users of influence diagrams recommend using different symbols for the various types of model entities. For example, circles might denote known inputs, ovals might denote uncertain inputs, rectangles might denote decisions or controllable inputs, triangles might denote calculations, and so forth.

2. The use of color in a spreadsheet model is an effective way to draw attention to a cell or set of cells. For example, we shaded cell B11 in Figure 10.3 to draw attention to the fact that *q* is a controllable input. However, avoid using too much color. Overdoing it may overwhelm users and actually have a negative impact on their ability to understand the model.

3. Clicking the **Formulas** tab in the Ribbon of Excel and then selecting **Show Formulas** from the **Formula Auditing** area will display all formulas used in an Excel spreadsheet.

10.2 What-If Analysis

Excel offers a number of tools to facilitate what-if analysis. In this section, we introduce three such tools, Data Tables, Goal Seek, and Scenario Manager. All of these tools are designed to rid the user of the tedious manual trial-and-error approach to analysis. Let us see how each of these tools can be used to aid with what-if analysis.

Data Tables

An Excel **Data Table** quantifies the impact of changing the value of a specific input on an output of interest. Excel can generate either a **one-way data table**, which summarizes a single input's impact on the output, or a **two-way data table**, which summarizes two inputs' impact on the output.

Let us consider how savings due to outsourcing changes as the quantity of Vipers changes. This should help us answer the question, "For which values of *q* is outsourcing more cost-effective?" A one-way data table changing the value of quantity and reporting savings due to outsourcing would be very useful. We will use the previously developed Nowlin spreadsheet for this analysis.

The first step in creating a one-way data table is to construct a sorted list of the values you would like to consider for the input. Let us investigate the quantity *q* over a range from 0 to 300,000 in increments of 25,000 units. Figure 10.4 shows the data entered in cells D5 through D17, with a column label in D4. This column of data is the set of values that Excel will use as inputs for *q*. Since the output of interest is savings due to outsourcing (located in cell B17), we have entered the formula =B17 in cell E4. In general, set the cell to the right of the label to the cell location of the output variable of interest. Once the basic structure is in place, we invoke the Data Table tool using the following steps:

Entering B11 in the **Column input cell:** *box indicates that the column of data corresponds to different values of the input located in cell B11.*

Step 1. Select cells D4:E17
Step 2. Click the **Data** tab in the Ribbon
Step 3. Click **What-If Analysis** in the **Forecast** group, and select **Data Table**
Step 4. When the **Data Table** dialog box appears, enter *B11* in the **Column input cell:** box
Click **OK**

As shown in Figure 10.5, the table will be populated with the value of savings due to outsourcing for each value of quantity of Vipers in the table. For example, when $q = 25,000$ we see that $S(25,000) = \$196,500$, and when $q = 250,000$, $S(250,000) = -\$141,000$. A negative value for savings due to outsourcing means that manufacturing is cheaper than outsourcing for that quantity.

FIGURE 10.4   The Input for Constructing a One-Way Data Table for Nowlin Plastics

	A	B	C	D	E	F	G
1	**Nowlin Plastics**						
2							
3	**Parameters**						
4	Manufacturing Fixed Cost	$234,000.00		Quantity	$219,000.00		
5	Manufacturing Variable Cost per Unit	$2.00		0			
6				25,000			
7	Outsourcing Cost per Unit	$3.50		50,000			
8				75,000			
9				100,000			
10	**Model**			125,000			
11	Quantity	10,000		150,000			
12				175,000			
13	Total Cost to Produce	$254,000.00		200,000			
14				225,000			
15	Total Cost to Outsource	$35,000.00		250,000			
16				275,000			
17	Savings due to Outsourcing	$219,000.00		300,000			
18							

Data Table dialog box:
Row input cell:
Column input cell: B11

FIGURE 10.5   Results of One-Way Data Table for Nowlin Plastics

	A	B	C	D	E	
1	**Nowlin Plastics**					
2						
3	**Parameters**					
4	Manufacturing Fixed Cost	$234,000.00		Quantity	$219,000.00	
5	Manufacturing Variable Cost per Unit	$2.00		0	$234,000	
6				25,000	$196,500	
7	Outsourcing Cost per Unit	$3.50		50,000	$159,000	
8				75,000	$121,500	
9				100,000	$84,000	
10	**Model**			125,000	$46,500	
11	Quantity	10,000		150,000	$9,000	
12				175,000	–$28,500	
13	Total Cost to Produce	$254,000.00		200,000	–$66,000	
14				225,000	–$103,500	
15	Total Cost to Outsource	$35,000.00		250,000	–$141,000	
16				275,000	–$178,500	
17	Savings due to Outsourcing	$219,000.00		300,000	–$216,000	
18						

We have learned something very valuable from this table. Not only have we quantified the savings due to outsourcing for a number of quantities, we know too that for quantities of 150,000 units or less, outsourcing is cheaper than manufacturing and for quantities of 175,000 units or more, manufacturing is cheaper than outsourcing. Depending on Nowlin's confidence in their demand forecast for the Viper product for next year, we have likely satisfactorily answered the make-versus-buy question. If, for example, management is highly confident that demand will be at least 200,000 units of Viper, then clearly they should manufacture the Viper rather than outsource. If management believes that Viper demand next year will be close to 150,000 units, they might still decide to manufacture rather than outsource. At 150,000 units, the savings due to outsourcing is only $9,000. That might not justify outsourcing if, for example, the quality assurance standards at the outsource firm are not at an acceptable level. We have provided management with valuable information that they may use to decide whether to make or buy. Next we illustrate how to construct a two-way data table.

Suppose that Nowlin has now received five different bids on the per-unit cost for outsourcing the production of the Viper. Clearly, the lowest bid provides the greatest savings. However, the selection of the outsource firm—if Nowlin decides to outsource—will depend on many factors, including reliability, quality, and on-time delivery. So it would be instructive to quantify the differences in savings for various quantities and bids. The five current bids are $2.89, $3.13, $3.50, $3.54, and $3.59. We may use the Excel Data Table to construct a two-way data table with quantity as a column and the five bids as a row, as shown in Figure 10.6.

In Figure 10.6, we have entered various quantities in cells D5 through D17, as in the one-way table. These correspond to cell B11 in our model. In cells E4 through I4, we have entered the bids. These correspond to B7, the outsourcing cost per unit. In cell D4, above the column input values and to the left of the row input values, we have entered the formula =B17, the location of the output of interest, in this case, savings due to outsourcing. Once the table inputs have been entered into the spreadsheet, we perform the following steps to construct the two-way data table.

Step 1. Select cells D4:I17
Step 2. Click the **Data** tab in the Ribbon
Step 3. Click **What-If Analysis** in the **Forecast** group, and select **Data Table**
Step 4. When the **Data Table** dialog box appears:
            Enter *B7* in the **Row input cell:** box
            Enter *B11* in the **Column input cell:** box
            Click **OK**

Figure 10.6 shows the selected cells and the Data Table dialog box. The results are shown in Figure 10.7.

We now have a table that shows the savings due to outsourcing for each combination of quantity and bid price. For example, for 75,000 Vipers at a cost of $3.13 per unit, the savings from buying versus manufacturing the units is $149,250. We can also see the range for the quantity for each bid price that results in a negative savings. For these quantities and bid combinations, it is better to manufacture than to outsource.

Using the Data Table allows us to quantify the savings due to outsourcing for the quantities and bid prices specified. However, the table does not tell us the exact number at which the transition occurs from outsourcing being cheaper to manufacturing being cheaper. For example, although it is clear from the table that for a bid price of $3.50 the savings due to outsourcing goes from positive to negative at some quantity between 150,000 units and 175,000 units, we know only that this transition occurs somewhere in that range. As we illustrate next, the what-if analysis tool Goal Seek can tell us the precise number at which this transition occurs.

Goal Seek

Excel's Goal Seek tool allows the user to determine the value of an input cell that will cause the value of a related output cell to equal some specified value (the *goal*). In the case of Nowlin Plastics, suppose we want to know the value of the quantity of Vipers at which it becomes more cost-effective to manufacture rather than outsource. For example, we see from the table in Figure 10.7 that for a bid price of $3.50 and some quantity between 150,000 units and 175,000 units, savings due to outsourcing goes from positive to negative. Somewhere in

FIGURE 10.6 The Input for Constructing a Two-Way Data Table for Nowlin Plastics

	A	B	C	D	E	F	G	H	I	J	K	L	M
1	**Nowlin Plastics**												
2													
3	**Parameters**												
4	Manufacturing Fixed Cost	$234,000.00		$219,000.00	$2.89	$3.13	$3.50	$3.54	$3.59				
5	Manufacturing Variable Cost per Unit	$2.00		0									
6				25,000									
7	Outsourcing Cost per Unit	$3.50		50,000									
8				75,000									
9				100,000									
10	**Model**			125,000									
11	Quantity	10,000		150,000									
12				175,000									
13	Total Cost to Produce	$254,000.00		200,000									
14				225,000									
15	Total Cost to Outsource	$35,000.00		250,000									
16				275,000									
17	Savings due to Outsourcing	$219,000.00		300,000									
18													
19													

Data Table

Row input cell: B7

Column input cell: B11

OK   Cancel

FIGURE 10.7 Results of a Two-Way Data Table for Nowlin Plastics

	A	B	C	D	E	F	G	H	I
1	**Nowlin Plastics**								
2									
3	**Parameters**								
4	Manufacturing Fixed Cost	$234,000.00		$219,000.00	$2.89	$3.13	$3.50	$3.54	$3.59
5	Manufacturing Variable Cost per Unit	$2.00		0	$234,000	$234,000	$234,000	$234,000	$234,000
6				25,000	$211,750	$205,750	$196,500	$195,500	$194,250
7	Outsourcing Cost per Unit	$3.50		50,000	$189,500	$177,500	$159,000	$157,000	$154,500
8				75,000	$167,250	$149,250	$121,500	$118,500	$114,750
9				100,000	$145,000	$121,000	$84,000	$80,000	$75,000
10	**Model**			125,000	$122,750	$92,750	$46,500	$41,500	$35,250
11	Quantity	10,000		150,000	$100,500	$64,500	$9,000	$3,000	–$4,500
12				175,000	$78,250	$36,250	–$28,500	–$35,500	–$44,250
13	Total Cost to Produce	$254,000.00		200,000	$56,000	$8,000	–$66,000	–$74,000	–$84,000
14				225,000	$33,750	–$20,250	–$103,500	–$112,500	–$123,750
15	Total Cost to Outsource	$35,000.00		250,000	$11,500	–$48,500	–$141,000	–$151,000	–$163,500
16				275,000	–$10,750	–$76,750	–$178,500	–$189,500	–$203,250
17	Savings due to Outsourcing	$219,000.00		300,000	–$33,000	–$105,000	–$216,000	–$228,000	–$243,000
18									

this range of quantity, the savings due to outsourcing is zero, and that is the point at which Nowlin would be indifferent to manufacturing and outsourcing. We may use Goal Seek to find the quantity of Vipers that satisfies the goal of zero savings due to outsourcing for a bid price of $3.50. The following steps describe how to use Goal Seek to find this point.

Step 1. Click the **Data** tab in the Ribbon
Step 2. Click **What-If Analysis** in the **Forecast** group, and select **Goal Seek**
Step 3. When the **Goal Seek** dialog box appears (Figure 10.8):
    Enter *B17* in the **Set cell:** box
    Enter *0* in the **To value:** box
    Enter *B11* in the **By changing cell:** box
    Click **OK**
Step 4. When the **Goal Seek Status** dialog box appears, click **OK**

The completed Goal Seek dialog box is shown in Figure 10.8.

The results from Goal Seek are shown in Figure 10.9. The savings due to outsourcing in cell B17 is zero, and the quantity in cell B11 has been set by Goal Seek to 156,000. When the annual quantity required is 156,000, it costs $564,000 either to manufacture the product or to purchase it. We have already seen that lower values of the quantity required favor outsourcing. Beyond the value of 156,000 units it becomes cheaper to manufacture the product.

Scenario Manager

As we have seen, data tables are useful for exploring the impact of changing one or two model inputs on a model output of interest. **Scenario Manager** is an Excel tool that quantifies the impact of changing multiple inputs (a setting of these multiple inputs is called a scenario) on one or more outputs of interest. That is, Scenario Manager extends the data table concept to cases when you are interested in changing more than two inputs and want to quantify the changes these inputs have on one or more outputs of interest.

FIGURE 10.8   Goal Seek Dialog Box for Nowlin Plastics

	A	B	C	D	E
1	**Nowlin Plastics**				
2					
3	**Parameters**				
4	Manufacturing Fixed Cost	$234,000.00			
5	Manufacturing Variable Cost per Unit	$2.00			
6					
7	Outsourcing Cost per Unit	$3.50			
8					
9					
10	**Model**				
11	Quantity	10,000			
12					
13	Total Cost to Produce	$254,000.00			
14					
15	Total Cost to Outsource	$35,000.00			
16					
17	Savings due to Outsourcing	$219,000.00			
18					

Goal Seek dialog box:
- Set cell: B17
- To value: 0
- By changing cell: B11
- OK / Cancel

FIGURE 10.9	Results from Goal Seek for Nowlin Plastics

▲	A	B	C	D	E	F
1	**Nowlin Plastics**					
2						
3	**Parameters**					
4	Manufacturing Fixed Cost	$234,000.00				
5	Manufacturing Variable Cost per Unit	$2.00				
6						
7	Outsourcing Cost per Unit	$3.50				
8						
9						
10	**Model**					
11	Quantity	156,000				
12						
13	Total Cost to Produce	$546,000.00				
14						
15	Total Cost to Outsource	$546,000.00				
16						
17	Savings due to Outsourcing	$0.00				
18						

Goal Seek Status dialog box:
Goal Seeking with Cell B17 found a solution.
Target value: 0
Current value: $0.00
[Step] [Pause] [OK] [Cancel]

To illustrate the use of Scenario Manager, let us consider the case of the Middletown Amusement Park. John Miller, the manager at Middletown, has developed a simple spreadsheet model of the park's daily profit. His model is shown in Figure 10.10.

On any given day, there are two types of customers in the park, those who own season passes and those who do not. Season-pass owners pay an annual membership fee during the offseason, but then pay nothing at the gate to enter the park. Those who are not season pass holders pay $35 per person to enter the park for the day. John refers to these non-season-pass holders as "admissions." On average, a season-pass holder spends $15 per person in the park on food, drinks, and novelties and an admission spends on average $45.The average daily cost of operations (including fixed costs) is $33,000 per day and the cost of goods is 50% of the price of the good. These data are reflected in John's spreadsheet model, which calculates a daily profit. As shown in Figure 10.10, for the data just described, John's model calculates the profit to be $81,500.

As you might expect, the profit generated on any given day is very dependent on the weather. As shown in Table 10.1, John has developed three weather-based scenarios: Partly Cloudy, Rain, and Sunny. The weather has a direct impact on four input parameters: the number of season-pass holders who enter the park, the number of non-season-pass holders (admissions) who enter the park, the amount each of these groups spends on average and the cost of operations. The Scenario Manager allows us to generate a report that gives an output variable or set of output variables of interest for each scenario. In this case, Scenario Manager will provide a report that gives the profit for each scenario.

The following steps describe how to use Scenario Manager to generate a scenario summary report.

Step 1. Click the **Data** tab in the Ribbon.
Step 2. Click **What-if Analysis** in the **Forecast** group and select **Scenario Manager**...

FIGURE 10.10   Middletown Amusement Park Daily Profit Model

▲	A	B	C
1	Middletown Amusement Park		
2			
3	**Parameters**		
4			
5	Admission Price	35	
6	Number of Season-Pass Holders Admitted	3000	
7	Admissions	1600	
8	Average Expenditure - Season Pass Holders	15	
9	Average Expenditure - Admissions	45	
10			
11	Cost of Operations	33000	
12	Cost of Goods %	0.5	
13			
14	**Model**		
15			
16	Admissions Revenue	=B5*B7	
17	Season Pass Holder Expenditures Revenue	=B6*B8	
18	Admissions Expenditures Revenue	=B7*B9	
19	Total Revenue	=B16+B17+B18	
20			
21	Cost of Operations	=B11	
22	Cost of Goods	=B12*(B17+B18)	
23	Total Cost	=B21+B22	
24			
25	Profit	=B19–B23	
26			

MODEL *file*

Middletown

▲	A	B	C
1	Middletown Amusement Park		
2			
3	**Parameters**		
4			
5	Admission Price	$35	
6	Number of Season-Pass Holders Admitted	3000	
7	Admissions	1600	
8	Average Expenditure - Season Pass Holders	$15	
9	Average Expenditure - Admissions	$45	
10			
11	Cost of Operations	$33,000	
12	Cost of Goods%	50%	
13			
14	**Model**		
15			
16	Admissions Revenue	$56,000	
17	Season Pass Holder Expenditures Revenue	$45,000	
18	Admissions Expenditures Revenue	$72,000	
19	Total Revenue	$173,000	
20			
21	Cost of Operations	$33,000	
22	Cost of Goods	$58,500	
23	Total Cost	$91,500	
24			
25	Profit	$81,500	
26			

Step 3.   When the **Scenario Manager** dialog box appears (Figure 10.11), click the **Add**... button

Step 4.   When the **Add Scenario** dialog box appears (Figure 10.12):
Enter *Partly Cloudy* in the **Scenario name**: box
Enter *$B$6:$B$9,$B$11* in the **Changing cells**: box
Click **OK**

TABLE 10.1	Weather Scenarios for Middletown Amusement Park		
	Scenarios		
	Partly Cloudy	**Rain**	**Sunny**
Season-pass Holders	3000	1200	8000
Admissions	1600	250	2400
Average Expenditure - Season-Pass Holders	$15	$10	$18
Average Expenditure - Admissions	$45	$20	$57
Cost of Operations	$33,000	$27,000	$37,000

FIGURE 10.11	Scenario Manager Dialog Box

Step 5. When the **Scenario Values** dialog box appears (Figure 10.13):
   Enter *3000* in the **$B$6** box
   Enter *1600* in the **$B$7** box
   Enter *15* in the **$B$8** box
   Enter *45* in the **$B$9** box
   Enter *33000* in the **$B$11** box
   Click **OK**

Step 6. When the **Scenario Manager** dialog box appears, repeat steps 3–5 for each scenario shown in Table 10.1 (Rain and Sunny)

Step 7. When all scenarios have been entered and the **Scenario Manager** dialog box appears, click **Summary...**

Step 8. When the **Scenario Summary** dialog box appears (Figure 10.14):
   Select **Scenario summary**
   Enter *B25* in the **Result Cells** box
   Click **OK**

FIGURE 10.12   Add Scenario Dialog Box

FIGURE 10.13   Scenario Values Dialog Box

FIGURE 10.14   Scenario Summary Dialog Box

FIGURE 10.15   Scenario Summary for Middletown Amusement Park

	A	B	C	D	E	F	G	H
1								
2		Scenario Summary						
3				Current Values:	Partly Cloudy	Rain	Sunny	
5		Changing Cells:						
6			SBS6	3000	3000	1200	8000	
7			SBS7	1600	1600	250	2400	
8			SBS8	$15	$15	$10	$18	
9			SBS9	$45	$45	$45	$57	
10			SBS11	$33,000	$33,000	$27,000	$37,000	
11		Result Cells:						
12			SBS25	$81,500	$81,500	−$6,625	$187,400	
13		Notes: Current Values column represents values of changing cells at						
14		time Scenario Summary Report was created. Changing cells for each						
15		scenario are highlighted in gray.						
16								

The Scenario Summary report appears on a separate worksheet as shown in Figure 10.15. The summary includes the values currently in the spreadsheet, along with the specified scenarios. We see that the profit ranges from a low of −$6,625 on a rainy day to a high of $187,400 on a sunny day.

NOTES + COMMENTS

1. We emphasize the location of the reference to the desired output in a one-way versus a two-way data table. For a one-way table, the reference to the output cell location is placed in the cell above and to the right of the column of input data so that it is in the cell just to the right of the label of the column of input data. For a two-way table, the reference to the output cell location is placed above the column of input data and to the left of the row input data.

2. Notice that in Figures 10.5 and 10.7, the tables are formatted as currency. This must be done manually after the table is constructed using the options in the **Number** group under the **Home** tab in the Ribbon. It is also a good idea to label the rows and the columns of the table.

3. For very complex functions, Goal Seek might not converge to a stable solution. Trying several different initial values

(the actual value in the cell referenced in the **By changing cell:** box) when invoking **Goal Seek** may help.

4. In Figure 10.13, we chose **Scenario summary** to generate the summary in Figure 10.14. Choosing **Scenario PivotTable report** will generate a pivot table with the relevant inputs and outputs.

5. Once all scenarios have been added to the **Scenario Manager** dialog box (Figure 10.11), there are several alternatives to choose. Scenarios can be edited via the **Edit…** button. The **Show** button allows you to look at the selected scenario settings by displaying the Scenario Values box for that scenario. The **Delete** button allows you to delete a scenario and the **Merge…** button allows you to merge scenarios from another worksheet with those of the current worksheet.

10.3 Some Useful Excel Functions for Modeling

In this section, we use several examples to introduce additional Excel functions that are useful in modeling decision problems. Many of these functions are used in spreadsheet models for simulation, optimization, and decision analysis.

SUM and SUMPRODUCT

Two very useful functions are SUM and SUMPRODUCT. The SUM function adds up all of the numbers in a range of cells. The SUMPRODUCT function returns the sum of the products of elements in a set of arrays. As we shall see in Chapter 12, SUMPRODUCT is very useful for linear optimization models.

Let us illustrate the use of SUM and SUMPRODUCT by considering a transportation problem faced by Foster Generators. This problem involves the transportation of a product from three plants to four distribution centers. Foster Generators operates plants in Cleveland, Ohio; Bedford, Indiana; and York, Pennsylvania. Production capacities for the three plants over the next three-month planning period are known.

The firm distributes its generators through four regional distribution centers located in Boston, Massachusetts; Chicago, Illinois; St. Louis, Missouri; and Lexington, Kentucky. Foster has forecasted demand for the three-month period for each of the distribution centers. The per-unit shipping cost from each plant to each distribution center is also known. Management would like to determine how much of its products should be shipped from each plant to each distribution center.

A transportation analyst developed a what-if spreadsheet model to help Foster develop a plan for how to ship its generators from the plants to the distribution centers to minimize cost. Of course, capacity at the plants must not be exceeded, and forecasted demand must be satisfied at each of the four distribution centers. The what-if model is shown in Figure 10.16.

The parameters section is rows 2 through 10. Cells B5 through E7 contain the per-unit shipping cost from each origin (plant) to each destination (distribution center). For example, it costs $2.00 to ship one generator from Bedford to St. Louis. The plant capacities are given in cells F5 through F7, and the distribution center demands appear in cells B8 through E8.

The model is in rows 11 through 20. Trial values of shipment amounts from each plant to each distribution center appear in the shaded cells, B17 through E19. The total cost of shipping for this proposed plan is calculated in cell B13 using the SUMPRODUCT function. The general form of the SUMPRODUCT function is

The arrays used as arguments in the SUMPRODUCT function must be of the same dimension. For example, in the Foster Generator model, B5:E7 is an array of three rows and four columns. B17:E19 is an array of the same dimensions.

$$=\text{SUMPRODUCT}(array1, array2)$$

The function pairs each element of the first array with its counterpart in the second array, multiplies the elements of the pairs together, and adds the results. In cell B13, =SUMPRODUCT(B5:E7,B17:E19) pairs the per-unit cost of shipping for each origin-destination pair with the proposed shipping plan for that and adds their products:

$$B5*B17 + C5*C17 + D5*D17 + E5*E17 + B6*B18 + \cdots + E7*E19$$

In cells F17 through F19, the SUM function is used to add up the amounts shipped for each plant. The general form of the SUM function is

$$=\text{SUM}(range)$$

where *range* is a range of cells. For example, the function in cell F17 is =SUM(B17:E17), which adds the values in B17, C17, D17, and E17: $5000 + 0 + 0 + 0 = 5000$. The SUM function in cells B20 through E20 does the same for the amounts shipped to each distribution center.

We will revisit the Foster Generators problem in Chapter 12, where we discuss linear optimization models.

By comparing the amounts shipped from each plant to the capacity for that plant, we see that no plant violates its capacity. Likewise, by comparing the amounts shipped to each distribution center to the demand at that center, we see that all demands are met. The total shipping cost for the proposed plan is $54,500. Is this the lowest-cost plan? It is not clear.

FIGURE 10.16   What-If Model for Foster Generators

	A	B	C	D	E	F	G
1	**Foster Generators**						
2	**Parameters**						
3	Shipping Cost/Unit		**Destination**				
4	**Origin**	Boston	Chicago	St. Louis	Lexington	Supply	
5	Cleveland	3	2	7	6	5000	
6	Bedford	6	5	2	3	6000	
7	York	2	5	4	5	2500	
8	Demand	6000	4000	2000	1500		
9							
10							
11	**Model**						
12							
13	**Total Cost**	=SUMPRODUCT(B5:E7,B17:E19)					
14							
15			**Destination**				
16	**Origin**	Boston	Chicago	St. Louis	Lexington	**Total**	
17	Cleveland	5000	0	0	0	=SUM(B17:E17)	
18	Bedford	1000	4000	1000	0	=SUM(B18:E18)	
19	York	0	0	1000	1500	=SUM(B19:E19)	
20	**Total**	=SUM(B17:B19)	=SUM(C17:C19)	=SUM(D17:D19)	=SUM(E17:E19)		
21							

MODEL *file*

Foster

	A	B	C	D	E	F	G
1	**Foster Generators**						
2	**Parameters**						
3	Shipping Cost/Unit		**Destination**				
4	**Origin**	Boston	Chicago	St. Louis	Lexington	Supply	
5	Cleveland	$3.00	$2.00	$7.00	$6.00	5000	
6	Bedford	$6.00	$5.00	$2.00	$3.00	6000	
7	York	$2.00	$5.00	$4.00	$5.00	2500	
8	Demand	6000	4000	2000	1500		
9							
10							
11	**Model**						
12							
13	**Total Cost**	$54,500.00					
14							
15			**Destination**				
16	**Origin**	Boston	Chicago	St. Louis	Lexington	**Total**	
17	Cleveland	5000	0	0	0	5000	
18	Bedford	1000	4000	1000	0	6000	
19	York	0	0	1000	1500	2500	
20	**Total**	6000	4000	2000	1500		
21							

IF and COUNTIF

Gambrell Manufacturing produces car stereos. Stereos are composed of a variety of components that the company must carry in inventory to keep production running smoothly. However, because inventory can be a costly investment, Gambrell generally likes to keep its components inventory to a minimum. To help monitor and control its inventory, Gambrell uses an inventory policy known as an *order-up-to policy*.

The order-up-to policy is as follows. Whenever the inventory on hand drops below a certain level, enough units are ordered to return the inventory to that predetermined level. If the current number of units in inventory, denoted by H, drops below M units, enough inventory is ordered to get the level back up to M units. M is called the *order-up-to point*. Stated mathematically, if Q is the amount we order, then

$$Q = M - H$$

An inventory model for Gambrell Manufacturing appears in Figure 10.17. In the upper half of the worksheet, the component ID number, inventory on hand (H), order-up-to point (M), and cost per unit are given for each of four components. Also given in this sheet is the fixed cost per order. The fixed cost is interpreted as follows: Each time a component is ordered, it costs Gambrell $120 to process the order. The fixed cost of $120 is incurred whenever an order is placed, regardless of how many units are ordered.

The model portion of the worksheet calculates the order quantity for each component. For example, for component 570, $M = 100$ and $H = 5$, so $Q = M - H = 100 - 5 = 95$. For component 741, $M = 70$ and $H = 70$ and no units are ordered because the on-hand inventory of 70 units is equal to the order-up-to point of 70. The calculations are similar for the other two components.

Depending on the number of units ordered, Gambrell receives a discount on the cost per unit. If 50 or more units are ordered, there is a quantity discount of 10% on every unit purchased. For example, for component 741, the cost per unit is $4.50, and 95 units are ordered. Because 95 exceeds the 50-unit requirement, there is a 10% discount, and the cost per unit is reduced to $4.50 - 0.1(\$4.50) = \$4.50 - \$0.45 = \$4.05$. Not including the fixed cost, the cost of goods purchased is then $4.05(95) = \$384.75$.

The Excel functions used to perform these calculations are shown in Figure 10.17 (for clarity, we show formulas for only the first three columns). The IF function is used to calculate the purchase cost of goods for each component in row 17. The general form of the IF function is

$$=\text{IF}(condition,\ result\ if\ condition\ is\ true,\ result\ if\ condition\ is\ false)$$

For example, in cell B17 we have =IF(B16 >= $B$10, $B$11*B6, B6)*B16. This statement says that if the order quantity (cell B16) is greater than or equal to minimum amount required for a discount (cell B10), then the cost per unit is B11*B6 (there is a 10% discount, so the cost is 90% of the original cost); otherwise, there is no discount, and the cost per unit is the amount given in cell B6. The cost per unit computed by the IF function is then multiplied by the order quantity (B16) to obtain the total purchase cost of component 570. The purchase cost of goods for the other components are computed in a like manner.

The total cost in cell B23 is the sum of the total fixed ordering costs (B21) and the total cost of goods (B22). Because we place three orders (one each for components 570, 578, and 755), the fixed cost of the orders is $3*120 = \$360$.

The COUNTIF function in cell B19 is used to count how many times we order. In particular, it counts the number of components having a positive order quantity. The general form of the COUNTIF function (which was discussed in Chapter 2 for creating frequency distributions) is

$$=\text{COUNTIF}(range,\ condition)$$

FIGURE 10.17	Gambrell Manufacturing Component Ordering Model

◢	A	B	C
1	**Gambrell Manufacturing**		
2	**Parameters**		
3	Component ID	**570**	**578**
4	Inventory On-Hand	5	30
5	Order-up-to Point	100	55
6	Cost per Unit	4.5	12.5
7			
8	Fixed Cost per Order	120	
9			
10	Minimum Order Size for Discount	50	
11	Discounted to	0.9	
12			
13	**Model**		
14			
15	Component ID	**=B3**	**=C3**
16	Order Quantity	=B5–B4	=C5–C4
17	Cost of Goods	=IF(B16 >= $B$10, $B$11*B6,B6)*B16	=IF(C16 >= $B$10, $B$11*C6,C6)*C16
18			
19	Total Number of Orders	=COUNTIF(B16:E16,">0")	
20			
21	Total Fixed Costs	=B19*B8	
22	Total Cost of Goods	=SUM(B17:E17)	
23	Total Cost	=SUM(B21:B22)	
24			

Notice the use of absolute references to B10 and B11 in row 17. As discussed in Appendix A, this facilitates copying cell B17 to cells C17, D17, and E17.

MODEL *file*

Gambrell

◢	A	B	C	D	E
1	**Gambrell Manufacturing**				
2	**Parameters**				
3	Component ID	**570**	**578**	**741**	**755**
4	Inventory On-Hand	5	30	70	17
5	Order-up-to Point	100	55	70	45
6	Cost per Unit	$4.50	$12.50	$3.26	$4.15
7					
8	Fixed Cost per Order	$120			
9					
10	Minimum Order Size for Discount	50			
11	Discounted to	90%			
12					
13	**Model**				
14					
15	Component ID	**570**	**578**	**741**	**755**
16	Order Quantity	95	25	0	28
17	Cost of Goods	$384.75	$312.50	$0.00	$116.20
18					
19	Total Number of Orders	3			
20					
21	Total Fixed Costs	$360.00			
22	Total Cost of Goods	$813.45			
23	Total Cost	$1,173.45			
24					

The *range* is the range to search for the *condition*. The condition is the test to be counted when satisfied. In the Gambrell model in Figure 10.17, cell B19 counts the number of cells that are greater than zero in the range of cells B16:E16 via the syntax =COUNTIF(B16:E16, ">0"). Note that quotes are required for the condition with the COUNTIF function. In the model, because only cells B16, C16, and E16 are greater than zero, the COUNTIF function in cell B19 returns 3.

As we have seen, IF and COUNTIF are powerful functions that allow us to make calculations based on a condition holding (or not). There are other such conditional functions available in Excel. In a problem at the end of this chapter, we ask you to investigate one such function, the SUMIF function. Another conditional function that is extremely useful in modeling is the VLOOKUP function, which is illustrated with an example in the next section.

VLOOKUP

The director of sales at Granite Insurance needs to award bonuses to her sales force based on performance. There are 15 salespeople, each with his or her own territory. Based on the size and population of the territory, each salesperson has a sales target for the year.

The measure of performance for awarding bonuses is the percentage achieved above the sales target. Based on this metric, a salesperson is placed into one of five bonus bands and awarded bonus points. After all salespeople are placed in a band and awarded points, each is awarded a percentage of the bonus pool, based on the percentage of the total points awarded. The sales director has created a spreadsheet model to calculate the bonuses to be awarded. The spreadsheet model is shown in Figure 10.18 (note that we have hidden rows 19–28).

As shown in cell E3 in Figure 10.18, the bonus pool is $250,000 for this year. The bonus bands are in cells A7:C11. In this table, column A gives the lower limit of the bonus band, column B the upper limit, and column C the bonus points awarded to anyone in that bonus band. For example, salespeople who achieve 56% above their sales target would be awarded 15 bonus points.

As shown in Figure 10.18, the name and percentage above the target achieved for each salesperson appear below the bonus-band table in columns A and B. In column C, the VLOOKUP function is used to look in the bonus band table and automatically assign the number of bonus points to each salesperson.

The VLOOKUP function allows the user to pull a subset of data from a larger table of data based on some criterion. The general form of the VLOOKUP function is

$$=\text{VLOOKUP}(value, \ table, \ index, \ range)$$

where

$value$ = the value to search for in the first column of the table

$table$ = the cell range containing the table

$index$ = the column in the table containing the value to be returned

$range$ = TRUE if looking for the first approximate match of *value* and FALSE if looking for an exact match of *value* (We will explain the difference between approximate and exact matches in a moment.)

VLOOKUP assumes that the first column of the table is sorted in ascending order.

The VLOOKUP function for salesperson Choi in cell C18 is as follows:

$$=\text{VLOOKUP}(B18,\$A\$7:\$C\$11,3,\text{TRUE})$$

If the range in the VLOOKUP function is FALSE, the only change is that Excel searches for an exact match of the first argument in the first column of the data.

This function uses the percentage above target sales from cell B18 and searches the first column of the table defined by A7:C11. Because the *range* is set to TRUE, indicating a search for the first approximate match, Excel searches in the first column of the table from the top until it finds a number strictly greater than the value of B18. B18 is 44%, and the first value in the table in column A larger than 44% is in cell A9 (51%). It then backs up one row (to row 8). In other words, it finds the last value in the first column less than or equal to 44%. Because a 3 is in the third argument of the VLOOKUP function, it takes the element in row 8 of the third column of the table, which is 10 bonus points. In summary, the VLOOKUP with *range* set to TRUE takes the first argument and searches the first

FIGURE 10.18 Granite Insurance Bonus Model

	A	B	C	D	E
1	Granite Insurance Bonus Awards				
2					
3	Parameters			Bonus Pool	250000
4					
5	Bonus Bands to be awarded for percentage above target sales.				
6	Lower Limit	Upper Limit	Bonus Points		
7	0	0.1	0		
8	0.11	0.5	10		
9	0.51	0.79	15		
10	0.8	0.99	25		
11	1	100	40		
12					
13	Model				
14	Last Name	% Above Target Sales	Bonus Points	% of Pool	Bonus Amount
15	Barth	0.83	=VLOOKUP(B15,$A$7:$C$11,3,TRUE)	=C15/$C$30	=D15*$E$3
16	Benson	0	=VLOOKUP(B16,$A$7:$C$11,3,TRUE)	=C16/$C$30	=D16*$E$3
17	Capel	1.18	=VLOOKUP(B17,$A$7:$C$11,3,TRUE)	=C17/$C$30	=D17*$E$3
18	Choi	0.44	=VLOOKUP(B18,$A$7:$C$11,3,TRUE)	=C18/$C$30	=D18*$E$3
29	Ruebush	0.85	=VLOOKUP(B29,$A$7:$C$11,3,TRUE)	=C29/$C$30	=D29*$E$3
30		Total	=SUM(C15:C29)	=SUM(D15:D29)	=SUM(E15:E29)

MODEL *file*

Granite

	A	B	C	D	E
1	Granite Insurance Bonus Awards				
2					
3	Parameters			Bonus Pool	$250,000
4					
5	Bonus Bands to be awarded for percentage above target sales.				
6	Lower Limit	Upper Limit	Bonus Points		
7	0%	10%	0		
8	11%	50%	10		
9	51%	79%	15		
10	80%	99%	25		
11	100%	10000%	40		
12					
13	Model				
14	Last Name	% Above Target Sales	Bonus Points	% of Pool	Bonus Amount
15	Barth	83%	25	8.5%	$21,186.44
16	Benson	0%	0	0.0%	$0.00
17	Capel	118%	40	13.6%	$33,898.31
18	Choi	44%	10	3.4%	$8,474.58
29	Ruebush	85%	25	8.5%	$21,186.44
30		Total	295	100%	$250,000.00

column of the table for the last row that is less than or equal to the first argument. It then selects from that row, the element in the column number of the third argument.

Once all salespeople are awarded bonus points based on VLOOKUP and the bonus-band table, the total number of bonus points awarded is given in cell C30 using the SUM function. Each person's bonus points as a percentage of the total awarded is calculated in column D, and in column E each person is awarded that percentage of the bonus pool. As a check, cells D30 and E30 give the total percentages and dollar amounts awarded.

Numerous mathematical, logical, and financial functions are available in Excel. In addition to those discussed here, we will introduce you to other functions, as needed, in examples and end-of-chapter problems. Having already discussed principles for building good spreadsheet models and after having seen a variety of spreadsheet models, we turn now to how to audit Excel models to ensure model integrity.

10.4 Auditing Spreadsheet Models

Excel contains a variety of tools to assist you in the development and debugging of spreadsheet models. These tools are found in the **Formula Auditing** group of the **Formulas** tab, as shown in Figure 10.19. Let us review each of the tools available in this group.

Trace Precedents and Dependents

After selecting cells, the Trace Precedents button creates arrows pointing to the selected cell from cells that are part of the formula in that cell. The Trace Dependents button, on the other hand, shows arrows pointing from the selected cell to cells that depend on the selected cell. Both of the tools are excellent for quickly ascertaining how parts of a model are linked.

An example of Trace Precedents is shown in Figure 10.20. Here we have opened the Foster Generators Excel file, selected cell B13, and clicked the **Trace Precedents** button in the **Formula Auditing** group. Recall that the cost in cell B13 is calculated as the SUMPRODUCT of the per-unit shipping cost and units shipped. In Figure 10.20, to show this relationship, arrows are drawn to these areas of the spreadsheet to cell B13. These arrows may be removed by clicking on the **Remove Arrows** button in the **Formula Auditing** group.

An example of Trace Dependents is shown in Figure 10.21. We have selected cell E18, the units shipped from Bedford to Lexington, and clicked on the **Trace Dependents** button in the **Formula Auditing** group. As shown in Figure 10.21, units shipped from Bedford to Lexington impacts the cost function in cell B13, the total units shipped from Bedford given in cell F18, as well as the total units shipped to Lexington in cell E20. These arrows may be removed by clicking on the **Remove Arrows** button in the **Formula Auditing** group.

Trace Precedents and Trace Dependents can highlight errors in copying and formula construction by showing that incorrect sections of the worksheet are referenced.

Show Formulas

The Show Formulas button does exactly that. To see the formulas in a worksheet, simply click on any cell in the worksheet and then click on **Show Formulas**. You will see the formulas residing in that worksheet. To revert to hiding the formulas, click again on the **Show Formulas** button. As we have already seen in our examples in this chapter, the use of Show Formulas allows you to inspect each formula in detail in its cell location.

FIGURE 10.19 The Formula Auditing Group

FIGURE 10.20 Trace Precedents for Foster Generator

	A	B	C	D	E	F	G
1	**Foster Generators**						
2	**Parameters**						
3	Shipping Cost/Unit		**Destination**				
4	**Origin**	Boston	Chicago	St. Louis	Lexington	Supply	
5	Cleveland	$3.00	$2.00	$7.00	$6.00	5000	
6	Bedford	$6.00	$5.00	$2.00	$3.00	6000	
7	York	$2.00	$5.00	$4.00	$5.00	2500	
8	Demand	6000	4000	2000	1500		
9							
10							
11	**Model**						
12							
13	**Total Cost**	$54,500.00					
14							
15			**Destination**				
16	**Origin**	Boston	Chicago	St. Louis	Lexington	**Total**	
17	Cleveland	5000	0	0	0	5000	
18	Bedford	1000	4000	1000	0	6000	
19	York	0	0	1000	1500	2500	
20	**Total**	6000	4000	2000	1500		
21							
22							

FIGURE 10.21 Trace Dependents for the Foster Generators Model

	A	B	C	D	E	F	G
1	**Foster Generators**						
2	**Parameters**						
3	Shipping Cost/Unit		**Destination**				
4	**Origin**	Boston	Chicago	St. Louis	Lexington	Supply	
5	Cleveland	$3.00	$2.00	$7.00	$6.00	5000	
6	Bedford	$6.00	$5.00	$2.00	$3.00	6000	
7	York	$2.00	$5.00	$4.00	$5.00	2500	
8	Demand	6000	4000	2000	1500		
9							
10							
11	**Model**						
12							
13	**Total Cost**	$54,500.00					
14							
15			**Destination**				
16	**Origin**	Boston	Chicago	St. Louis	Lexington	**Total**	
17	Cleveland	5000	0	0	0	5000	
18	Bedford	1000	4000	1000	0	6000	
19	York	0	0	1000	1500	2500	
20	**Total**	6000	4000	2000	1500		
21							
22							

Evaluate Formulas

The **Evaluate Formula** button allows you to investigate the calculations of a cell in great detail. As an example, let us investigate cell B17 of the Gambrell Manufacturing model (Figure 10.17). Recall that we are calculating cost of goods based on whether there is a quantity discount. We follow these steps:

Gambrell

Step 1. Select cell B17
Step 2. Click the **Formulas** tab in the Ribbon
Step 3. Click the **Evaluate Formula** button in the **Formula Auditing** group
Step 4. When the **Evaluate Formula** dialog box appears (Figure 10.22), click the **Evaluate** button
Step 5. Repeat Step 4 until the formula has been completely evaluated
Step 6. Click **Close**

Figure 10.23 shows the **Evaluate Formula** dialog box for cell B17 in the Gambrell Manufacturing spreadsheet model after four clicks of the **Evaluate** button.

The Evaluate Formula tool provides an excellent means of identifying the exact location of an error in a formula.

Error Checking

The **Error Checking** button provides an automatic means of checking for mathematical errors within formulas of a worksheet. Clicking on the **Error Checking** button causes Excel to check every formula in the sheet for calculation errors. If an error

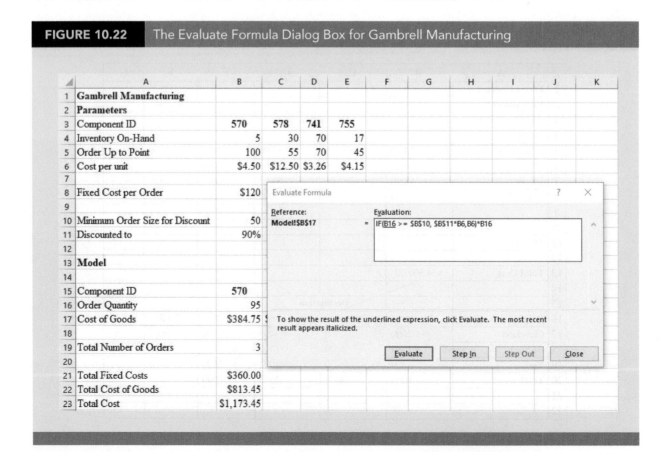

FIGURE 10.22 The Evaluate Formula Dialog Box for Gambrell Manufacturing

	A	B	C	D	E
1	**Gambrell Manufacturing**				
2	**Parameters**				
3	Component ID	570	578	741	755
4	Inventory On-Hand	5	30	70	17
5	Order Up to Point	100	55	70	45
6	Cost per unit	$4.50	$12.50	$3.26	$4.15
7					
8	Fixed Cost per Order	$120			
9					
10	Minimum Order Size for Discount	50			
11	Discounted to	90%			
12					
13	**Model**				
14					
15	Component ID	570			
16	Order Quantity	95			
17	Cost of Goods	$384.75			
18					
19	Total Number of Orders	3			
20					
21	Total Fixed Costs	$360.00			
22	Total Cost of Goods	$813.45			
23	Total Cost	$1,173.45			

Evaluate Formula dialog box:

Reference: Model!$B$17

Evaluation: IF(B16 >= $B$10, $B$11*B6, B6)*B16

To show the result of the underlined expression, click Evaluate. The most recent result appears italicized.

[Evaluate] [Step In] [Step Out] [Close]

FIGURE 10.23 The Evaluate Formula Dialog Box for Gambrell Manufacturing Cell B17 After Four Clicks of the Evaluate Button

is found, the **Error Checking** dialog box appears. An example for a hypothetical division by zero error is shown in Figure 10.24. From this box, the formula can be edited, the calculation steps can be observed (as in the previous section on Evaluate Formulas), or help can be obtained through the Excel help function. The Error Checking procedure is particularly helpful for large models where not all cells of the model are visible.

Watch Window

The **Watch Window**, located in the **Formula Auditing** group, allows the user to observe the values of cells included in the Watch Window box list. This is useful for large models when not all of the model is observable on the screen or when multiple worksheets are used. The user can monitor how the listed cells change with a change in the model without searching through the worksheet or changing from one worksheet to another.

A Watch Window for the Gambrell Manufacturing model is shown in Figure 10.25. The following steps were used to add cell B17 to the watch list:

Step 1.   Click the **Formulas** tab in the Ribbon
Step 2.   Click **Watch Window** in the **Formula Auditing** group to display the **Watch Window**
Step 3.   Click **Add Watch…**
Step 4.   Select the cell you would like to add to the watch list (in this case B17)

As shown in Figure 10.25, the list gives the workbook name, worksheet name, cell name (if used), cell location, cell value, and cell formula. To delete a cell from the watch list, click on the entry from the list, and then click on the **Delete Watch** button that appears in the upper part of the **Watch Window**.

The Watch Window, as shown in Figure 10.25, allows us to monitor the value of B17 as we make changes elsewhere in the worksheet. Furthermore, if we had other worksheets in this workbook, we could monitor changes to B17 of the worksheet even from these other worksheets. The Watch Window is observable regardless of where we are in any worksheet of a workbook.

FIGURE 10.24 The Error Checking Dialog Box for a Division by Zero Error

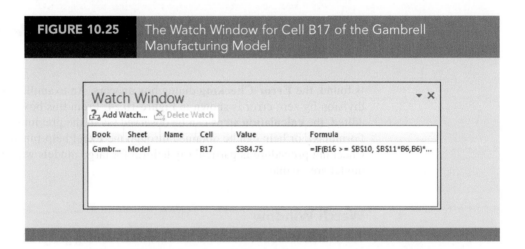

FIGURE 10.25 The Watch Window for Cell B17 of the Gambrell Manufacturing Model

10.5 Predictive and Prescriptive Spreadsheet Models

Two key phenomena that make decision making difficult are uncertainty and an overwhelming number of choices. Spreadsheet what-if models, as we have discussed thus far in this chapter, are descriptive models. Given formulas and data to populate the formulas, calculations are made based on the formulas. However, basic what-if spreadsheet models can be extended to help deal with uncertainty or the many alternatives a decision maker may face.

As we have seen in previous chapters, predictive models can be estimated from data in spreadsheets using tools provided in Excel. For example, the Excel Regression tool and other Data Analysis tools such as Exponential Smoothing and Moving Average allow us to develop predictive models based on data in the spreadsheet. These predictive models can help us deal with uncertainty by giving estimates for unknown events/quantities that serve as inputs to the decision-making process. Another important extension of what-if models that help us deal with uncertainty is simulation.

Monte Carlo simulation is discussed in detail in Chapter 11.

Monte Carlo simulation automates a manual what-if model by replacing the manual evaluation of various values of input parameters with the random generation of values for these uncertain inputs. By generating the values of the uncertain inputs with the likelihoods that the analyst believes these values may occur in the future, the simulation model allows the analyst to conduct many experiments to quantify how the uncertainty in the inputs affects the uncertainty in the output measures. Excel has built in probability functions that allow us to simulate values of uncertain inputs.

Chapters 12, 13, and 14 discuss the use optimization models for decision making and how to use Excel Solver.

To deal with the other complicating factor of decision making, namely an overwhelming number of alternatives, optimization models can be used to help make smart decisions. Optimization models are prescriptive models, characterized by having an objective to be maximized or minimized and usually have constraints that limit the options available to the decision maker. Because they yield a course of action to follow, optimization models are one type of prescriptive analytics. Excel includes a special tool called Solver that solves optimization models. Excel Solver is used to extend a what-if model to find an optimal (or best) course of action that maximizes or minimizes an objective while satisfying the constraints of the decision problem.

In this chapter, we discussed how to extend the Nowlin Plastics descriptive model to find the breakeven point by applying the Goal Seek tool to that descriptive model. Like Goal Seek, these other extensions of basic descriptive spreadsheet models to simulation and optimization models allow us to perform more advanced analytics.

SUMMARY

In this chapter we discussed the principles of building good spreadsheet models, several what-if analysis tools, some useful Excel functions, and how to audit spreadsheet models. What-if spreadsheet models are important and popular analysis tools in and of themselves, but as we shall see in later chapters, they also serve as the basis for optimization and simulation models.

We discussed how to use influence diagrams to structure a problem. Influence diagrams can serve as a guide to developing a mathematical model and implementing the model in a spreadsheet. We discussed the importance of separating the parameters from the model because it leads to simpler analysis and minimizes the risk of creating an error in a formula. In most cases, cell formulas should use cell references in their arguments rather than being "hardwired" with values. We also discussed the use of proper formatting and color to enhance the ease of use and understanding of a spreadsheet model.

We used examples to illustrate how Excel What-If Analysis tools Data Tables, Goal Seek, and Scenario Manager can be used to perform detailed and efficient what-if analysis. We also discussed a number of Excel functions that are useful for business analytics. We discussed Excel Formula Auditing tools that may be used to debug and monitor spreadsheet models to ensure that they are error-free and accurate. We ended the chapter with a brief discussion of predictive and prescriptive spreadsheet models.

GLOSSARY

Data Table An Excel tool that quantifies the impact of changing the value of a specific input on an output of interest.

Decision variable A model input the decision maker can control.

Goal Seek An Excel tool that allows the user to determine the value for an input cell that will cause the value of a related output cell to equal some specified value, called the *goal*.

Influence diagram A visual representation that shows which entities influence others in a model.

Make-versus-buy decision A decision often faced by companies that have to decide whether they should manufacture a product or outsource its production to another firm.

One-way data table An Excel Data Table that summarizes a single input's impact on the output of interest.

Parameters In a what-if model, the uncontrollable model input.

Scenario manager An Excel tool that quantifies the impact of changing multiple inputs on one or more outputs of interest.

Two-way data table An Excel Data Table that summarizes two inputs' impact on the output of interest.

What-if model A model designed to study the impact of changes in model inputs on model outputs.

PROBLEMS

1. **Profit Model for Electronics Company.** Cox Electric makes electronic components and has estimated the following for a new design of one of its products:

> Fixed cost = \$10,000
> Material cost per unit = \$0.15
> Labor cost per unit = \$0.10
> Revenue per unit = \$0.65

DATA *file*

CoxElectric

These data are given in the file *CoxElectric*. Note that fixed cost is incurred regardless of the amount produced. Per-unit material and labor cost together make up the variable cost per unit. Assuming that Cox Electric sells all that it produces, profit is calculated by subtracting the fixed cost and total variable cost from total revenue.

a. Build an influence diagram that illustrates how to calculate profit.

b. Using mathematical notation similar to that used for Nowlin Plastics, give a mathematical model for calculating profit.

c. Implement your model from part (b) in Excel using the principles of good spreadsheet design.

d. If Cox Electric makes 12,000 units of the new product, what is the resulting profit?

2. **Breakeven Volume.** Use the spreadsheet model constructed to answer Problem 1 to answer this problem.

a. Construct a one-way data table with production volume as the column input and profit as the output. Breakeven occurs when profit goes from a negative to a positive value; that is, breakeven is when total revenue = total cost, yielding a profit of zero. Vary production volume from 0 to 100,000 in increments of 10,000. In which interval of production volume does breakeven occur?

b. Use Goal Seek to find the exact breakeven point. Assign **Set cell:** equal to the location of profit, **To value:** = 0, and **By changing cell:** equal to the location of the production volume in your model.

3. **E-book Breakeven Analysis.** Eastman Publishing Company is considering publishing an electronic textbook about spreadsheet applications for business. The fixed cost of manuscript preparation, textbook design, and web site construction is estimated to be \$160,000. Variable processing costs are estimated to be \$6 per book. The publisher plans to sell single-user access to the book for \$46.

a. Build a spreadsheet model to calculate the profit/loss for a given demand. What profit can be anticipated with a demand of 3,500 copies?

b. Use a data table to vary demand from 1,000 to 6,000 in increments of 200 to assess the sensitivity of profit to demand.

c. Use Goal Seek to determine the access price per copy that the publisher must charge to break even with a demand of 3,500 copies.

d. Consider the following scenarios:

	Scenario 1	Scenario 2	Scenario 3	Scenario 4	Scenario 5
Variable Cost/ Book	\$6	\$8	\$12	\$10	\$11
Access Price	\$46	\$50	\$40	\$50	\$60
Demand	2,500	1,000	6,000	5,000	2,000

For each of these scenarios, the fixed cost remains \$160,000. Use Scenario Manager to generate a summary report that gives the profit for each of these scenarios. Which scenario yields the highest profit? Which scenario yields the lowest profit?

4. **Breakeven Analysis for a Symposium.** The University of Cincinnati Center for Business Analytics is an outreach center that collaborates with industry partners on applied research and continuing education in business analytics. One of the programs offered by the center is a quarterly Business Intelligence Symposium. Each symposium

features three speakers on the real-world use of analytics. Each corporate member of the center (there are currently 10) receives five free seats to each symposium. Nonmembers wishing to attend must pay $75 per person. Each attendee receives breakfast, lunch, and free parking. The following are the costs incurred for putting on this event:

Rental cost for the auditorium	$150
Registration processing	$8.50 per person
Speaker costs	3@$800 = $2,400
Continental breakfast	$4.00 per person
Lunch	$7.00 per person
Parking	$5.00 per person

   a. Build a spreadsheet model that calculates a profit or loss based on the number of nonmember registrants.

   b. Use Goal Seek to find the number of nonmember registrants that will make the event break even.

5. **Scenario Analysis for Profitability of a Symposium.** Consider again the scenario described in Problem 4.

   a. The Center for Business Analytics is considering a refund policy for no-shows. No refund would be given for members who do not attend, but nonmembers who do not attend will be refunded 50% of the price. Extend the model you developed in Problem 4 for the Business Intelligence Symposium to account for the fact that, historically, 25% of members who registered do not show and 10% of registered nonmembers do not attend. The center pays the caterer for breakfast and lunch based on the number of registrants (not the number of attendees). However, the center pays for parking only for those who attend. What is the profit if each corporate member registers their full allotment of tickets and 127 nonmembers register?

   b. Use a two-way data table to show how profit changes as a function of number of registered nonmembers and the no-show percentage of nonmembers. Vary the number of nonmember registrants from 80 to 160 in increments of 5 and the percentage of nonmember no-shows from 10% to 30% in increments of 2%.

   c. Consider three scenarios:

	Base Case	Worst Case	Best Case
% of Members Who Do Not Show	25.0%	50%	15%
% of Nonmembers Who Do Not Show	10.0%	30%	5%
Number of Nonmember Registrants	130	100	150

All other inputs are the same as in part (a). Use Scenario Manager to generate a summary report that gives the profit for each of these three scenarios. What is the highest profit? What is the lowest profit?

6. **Profit Maximization for an e-Book.** Consider again Problem 3. Through a series of web-based experiments, Eastman has created a predictive model that estimates demand as a function of price. The predictive model is demand $= 4,000 - 6p$, where p is the price of the e-book.

   a. Update your spreadsheet model constructed for Problem 3 to take into account this demand function.

   b. Use Goal Seek to calculate the price that results in breakeven.

   c. Use a data table that varies price from $50 to $400 in increments of $25 to find the price that maximizes profit.

7. **Retirement Planning.** Lindsay is 25 years old and has a new job in web development. She wants to make sure that she is financially sound in 30 years, so she plans to invest the same amount into a retirement account at the end of every year for the next 30 years. Note that because Lindsay invests at the end of the year, there is no interest earned on the contribution for the year in which she contributes.

a. Construct a data table that will show Lindsay the balance of her retirement account for various levels of annual investment and return.

b. Develop the two-way table for annual investment amounts of $5,000 to $20,000 in increments of $1,000 and for returns of 0% to 12% in increments of 1%.

8. **Retirement Planning with Net Present Value.** Consider again Lindsay's investment in Problem 7. The real value of Lindsay's account after 30 years of investing will depend on inflation over that period. In the Excel function =NPV(*rate, value1, value2, . . .*), *rate* is called the discount rate, and *value 1, value 2*, etc. are incomes (positive) or expenditures (negative) over equal periods of time. Update your model from Problem 7 using the NPV function to get the net present value of Lindsay's retirement fund. Construct a data table that shows the net present value of Lindsay's retirement fund for various levels of return and inflation (discount rate). Use a data table to vary the return from 0% to 12% in increments of 1% and the discount rate from 0% to 4% in increments of 1% to show the impact on the net present value. (*Hint:* Calculate the total amount added to the account each year, and discount that stream of payments using the NPV function.)

9. **Net Discounted Cash Flow.** Goal Kick Sports (GKS) is a retail chain that sells youth and adult soccer equipment. The GKS financial planning group has developed a spreadsheet model to calculate the net discounted cash flow of the first five years of operations for a new store. This model is used to assess new locations under consideration for expansion.

MODEL *file*

GoalKick

a. Use Excel's Formula Auditing tools to audit this model and correct any errors found.

b. Once you are comfortable that the model is correct, use Scenario Manager to generate a Scenario Summary report that gives Total Discounted Cash Flow for the following scenarios:

	Scenario			
	1	2	3	4
Tax Rate	33%	25%	33%	25%
Inflation Rate	1%	2%	4%	3%
Annual Growth of Sales	20%	15%	10%	12%

What is the range of values for the Total Discounted Cash Flow for these scenarios?

10. **Analyzing a Supply Chain.** Newton Manufacturing produces scientific calculators. The models are N350, N450, and N900. Newton has planned its distribution of these products around eight customer zones: Brazil, China, France, Malaysia, U.S. Northeast, U.S. Southeast, U.S. Midwest, and U.S. West. Data for the current quarter (volume to be shipped in thousands of units) for each product and each customer zone are given in the file *Newton*. Newton would like to know the total number of units going to each customer zone and also the total units of each product shipped. There are several ways to get this information from the data set. One way is to use the SUMIF function.

DATA *file*

Newton

The SUMIF function extends the SUM function by allowing the user to add the values of cells meeting a logical condition. The general form of the function is

=SUMIF(*test range, condition, range to be summed*)

The *test range* is an area to search to test the *condition*, and the *range to be summed* is the position of the data to be summed. So, for example, using the file *Newton*, we use the following function to get the total units sent to Malaysia:

=SUMIF(A3:A26, A3, C3 : C26)

Cell A3 contains the text "Malaysia"; A3:A26 is the range of customer zones; and C3:C26 are the volumes for each product for these customer zones. The SUMIF looks for matches of "Malaysia" in column A and, if a match is found, adds the volume to the total. Use the SUMIF function to get total volume by each zone and total volume by each product.

11. **Auditing a Transportation Model.** Consider the transportation model in the file *Williamson*, which is very similar to the Foster Generators model discussed in this chapter. Williamson produces a single product and has plants in Atlanta, Lexington, Chicago, and Salt Lake City and warehouses in Portland, St. Paul, Las Vegas, Tucson, and Cleveland. Each plant has a capacity, and each warehouse has a demand. Williamson would like to find a low-cost shipping plan. Mr. Williamson has reviewed the results and notices right away that the total cost is way out of line. Use the **Formula Auditing** tool under the **Formulas** tab in Excel to find any errors in this model. Correct the errors. (*Hint:* The model contains two errors. Be sure to check every formula.)

MODEL *file*

Williamson

12. **Calculating Course Grades.** Professor Rao would like to accurately calculate the grades for the 58 students in his Operations Planning and Scheduling class (OM 455). He has thus far constructed a spreadsheet, part of which follows:

MODEL *file*

OM455

	A	B	C	D	E
1	OM 455				
2	Section 001				
3	Course Grading Scale Based on Course Average:				
4		Lower	Upper	Course	
5		Limit	Limit	Grade	
6		0	59	F	
7		60	69	D	
8		70	79	C	
9		80	89	B	
10		90	100	A	
11					
12		Midterm	Final	Course	Course
13	Last Name	Score	Score	Average	Grade
14	Alt	70	56	63.0	
15	Amini	95	91	93.0	
16	Amoako	82	80	81.0	
17	Apland	45	78	61.5	
18	Bachman	68	45	56.5	
19	Corder	91	98	94.5	
20	Desi	87	74	80.5	
21	Dransman	60	80	70.0	
22	Duffuor	80	93	86.5	
23	Finkel	97	98	97.5	
24	Foster	90	91	90.5	

a. The Course Average is calculated by weighting the Midterm Score and Final Score 50% each. Use the VLOOKUP function with the table shown to generate the Course Grade for each student in cells E14 through E24.

b. Use the COUNTIF function to determine the number of students receiving each letter grade.

13. **Revenue Model with Quantity Discounts.** Richardson Ski Racing (RSR) sells equipment needed for downhill ski racing. One of RSR's products is fencing used on downhill courses. The fence product comes in 150-foot rolls and sells for $215 per roll. However, RSR offers quantity discounts. The following table shows the price per roll depending on order size:

DATA *file*

RSR

Quantity Ordered		
From	To	Price per Roll
1	50	$215
51	100	$195
101	200	$175
201	and up	$155

The file *RSR* contains 172 orders that have arrived for the coming six weeks.

  a. Use the VLOOKUP function with the preceding pricing table to determine the total revenue from these orders.

  b. Use the COUNTIF function to determine the number of orders in each price bin.

14. **European Financial Options.** A put option in finance allows you to sell a share of stock at a given price in the future. There are different types of put options. A European put option allows you to sell a share of stock at a given price, called the exercise price, at a particular point in time after the purchase of the option. For example, suppose you purchase a six-month European put option for a share of stock with an exercise price of $26. If six months later, the stock price per share is $26 or more, the option has no value. If in six months the stock price is lower than $26 per share, then you can purchase the stock and immediately sell it at the higher exercise price of $26. If the price per share in six months is $22.50, you can purchase a share of the stock for $22.50 and then use the put option to immediately sell the share for $26. Your profit would be the difference, $26 − $22.50 = $3.50 per share, less the cost of the option. If you paid $1.00 per put option, then your profit would be $3.50 − $1.00 = $2.50 per share.

  a. Build a model to calculate the profit of this European put option.

  b. Construct a data table that shows the profit per share for a share price in six months between $10 and $30 per share in increments of $1.00.

15. **Risk Analysis of European Options.** Consider again Problem 14. The point of purchasing a European option is to limit the risk of a decrease in the per-share price of the stock. Suppose you purchased 200 shares of the stock at $28 per share and 75 six-month European put options with an exercise price of $26. Each put option costs $1.

  a. Using data tables, construct a model that shows the value of the portfolio with options and without options for a share price in six months between $15 and $35 per share in increments of $1.00.

  b. Discuss the value of the portfolio with and without the European put options.

16. **Revenue with Substitutable Products.** The Camera Shop sells two popular models of digital single lens reflex (DSLR) cameras. The sales of these products are not independent; if the price of one increases, the sales of the other increases. In economics, these two camera models are called *substitutable products*. The store wishes to establish a pricing policy to maximize revenue from these products. A study of price and sales data shows the following relationships between the quantity sold (N) and price (P) of each model:

$$N_A = 195 - 0.6P_A + 0.25P_B$$
$$N_B = 301 + 0.08P_A - 0.5P_B$$

  a. Construct a model for the total revenue and implement it on a spreadsheet.

  b. Develop a two-way data table to estimate the optimal prices for each product in order to maximize the total revenue. Vary each price from $250 to $500 in increments of $10.

17. **Refinancing a Mortgage.** A few years back, Dave and Jana bought a new home. They borrowed $230,415 at an annual fixed rate of 5.49% (15-year term) with monthly payments of $1,881.46. They just made their 25th payment, and the current balance on the loan is $208,555.87.

    Interest rates are at an all-time low, and Dave and Jana are thinking of refinancing to a new 15-year fixed loan. Their bank has made the following offer: 15-year term, 3.0%, plus out-of-pocket costs of $2,937. The out-of-pocket costs must be paid in full at the time of refinancing.

    Build a spreadsheet model to evaluate this offer. The Excel function

$$=PMT(rate, nper, pv, fv, type)$$

calculates the payment for a loan based on constant payments and a constant interest rate. The arguments of this function are as follows:

$rate$ = the interest rate for the loan

$nper$ = the total number of payments

pv = present value (the amount borrowed)

fv = future value [the desired cash balance after the last payment (usually 0)]

$type$ = payment type (0 = end of period, 1 = beginning of the period)

For example, for Dave and Jana's original loan, there will be 180 payments (12 * 15 = 180), so we would use =PMT(0.0549/12, 180, 230415, 0, 0) = \$1,881.46. Note that because payments are made monthly, the annual interest rate must be expressed as a monthly rate. Also, for payment calculations, we assume that the payment is made at the end of the month.

The savings from refinancing occur over time, and therefore need to be discounted back to current dollars. The formula for converting K dollars saved t months from now to current dollars is

$$\frac{K}{(1 + r)^{t-1}}$$

where r is the monthly inflation rate. Assume that $r = 0.002$ and that Dave and Jana make their payment at the end of each month.

Use your model to calculate the savings in current dollars associated with the refinanced loan versus staying with the original loan.

18. **Mortgage Prepayment.** Consider again the mortgage refinance problem in Problem 17. Assume that Dave and Jana have accepted the refinance offer of a 15-year loan at 3% interest rate with out-of-pocket expenses of \$2,937. Recall that they are borrowing \$208,555.87. Assume that there is no prepayment penalty, so that any amount over the required payment is applied to the principal. Construct a model so that you can use Goal Seek to determine the monthly payment that will allow Dave and Jana to pay off the loan in 12 years. Do the same for 10 and 11 years. Which option for prepayment, if any, would you choose and why? (*Hint:* Break each monthly payment up into interest and principal [the amount that is deducted from the balance owed]. Recall that the monthly interest that is charged is the monthly loan rate multiplied by the remaining loan balance.)

19. **Assigning Customers to Distribution Centers.** Floyd's Bumpers has distribution centers in Lafayette, Indiana; Charlotte, North Carolina; Los Angeles, California; Dallas, Texas; and Pittsburgh, Pennsylvania. Each distribution center carries all products sold. Floyd's customers are auto repair shops and larger auto parts retail stores. You are asked to perform an analysis of the customer assignments to determine which of Floyd's customers should be assigned to each distribution center. The rule for assigning customers to distribution centers is simple: A customer should be assigned to the closest center. The file *Floyds* contains the distance from each of Floyd's 1,029 customers to each of the five distribution centers. Your task is to build a list that tells which distribution center should serve each customer. The following function will be helpful:

Floyds

=MIN(*array*)

The MIN function returns the smallest value in a set of numbers. For example, if the range A1:A3 contains the values 6, 25, and 38, then the formula =MIN(A1:A3) returns the number 6, because it is the smallest of the three numbers:

=MATCH(*lookup _ value, lookup _ array, match_type*)

The MATCH function searches for a specified item in a range of cells and returns the relative position of that item in the range. The *lookup_value* is the value to match, the *lookup_array* is the range of search, and *match_type* indicates the type of match (use 0 for an exact match).

For example, if the range A1:A3 contains the values 6, 25, and 38, then the formula =MATCH(25,A1:A3,0) returns the number 2, because 25 is the second item in the range.

$$=INDEX(array, column\_num)$$

The INDEX function returns the value of an element in a position of an array. For example, if the range A1:A3 contains the values 6, 25, and 38, then the formula =INDEX(A1: A3, 2) = 25, because 25 is the value in the second position of the array A1:A3. (*Hint:* Create three new columns. In the first column, use the MIN function to calculate the minimum distance for the customer in that row. In the second column use the MATCH function to find the position of the minimum distance. In the third column, use the position in the previous column with the INDEX function referencing the row of distribution center names to find the name of the distribution center that should service that customer.)

20. **Transportation Costs.** Refer to Problem 19. Floyd's Bumpers pays a transportation company to ship its product in full truckloads to its customers. Therefore, the cost for shipping is a function of the distance traveled and a fuel surcharge (also on a per-mile basis). The cost per mile is $2.42, and the fuel surcharge is $0.56 per mile. The file *FloydsMay* contains data for shipments for the month of May (each record is simply the customer zip code for a given truckload shipment) as well as the distance table from the distribution centers to each customer. Use the MATCH and INDEX functions to retrieve the distance traveled for each shipment, and calculate the charge for each shipment. What is the total amount that Floyd's Bumpers spends on these May shipments? (*Hint:* The INDEX function may be used with a two-dimensional array: =INDEX(*array, row_num, column_num*), where *array* is a matrix, *row_num* is the row number, and *column_num* is the column position of the desired element of the matrix.)

DATA *file*

FloydsMay

21. **Discount Price Versus Zero-Percent Financing.** An auto dealership is advertising that a new car with a sticker price of $35,208 is on sale for $25,995 if payment is made in full, or it can be financed at 0% interest for 72 months with a monthly payment of $489. Note that 72 payments × $489 per payment = $35,208, which is the sticker price of the car. By allowing you to pay for the car in a series of payments (starting one month from now) rather than $25,995 now, the dealer is effectively loaning you $25,995. If you choose the 0% financing option, what is the effective interest rate that the auto dealership is earning on your loan? (*Hint:* Discount the payments back to current dollars [see Problem 17 for a discussion of discounting], and use Goal Seek to find the discount rate that makes the net present value of the payments = $25,995.)

CASE PROBLEM: RETIREMENT PLAN

Tim is 37 years old and would like to establish a retirement plan. Develop a spreadsheet model that could be used to assist Tim with retirement planning. Your model should include the following input parameters:

Tim's current age = 37 years
Tim's current total retirement savings = $259,000
Annual rate of return on retirement savings = 4%
Tim's current annual salary = $145,000
Tim's expected annual percentage increase in salary = 2%
Tim's percentage of annual salary contributed to retirement = 6%
Tim's expected age of retirement = 65
Tim's expected annual expenses after retirement (current dollars) = $90,000
Rate of return on retirement savings after retirement = 3%
Income tax rate postretirement = 15%

Assume that Tim's employer contributes 6% of Tim's salary to his retirement fund. Tim can make an additional annual contribution to his retirement fund before taxes (tax free) up to a contribution of $16,000. Assume that he contributes $6,000 per year. Also, assume an inflation rate of 2%.

Managerial Report

Your spreadsheet model should provide the accumulated savings at the onset of retirement as well as the age at which funds will be depleted (given assumptions on the input parameters).

As a feature of your spreadsheet model, build a data table to demonstrate the sensitivity of the age at which funds will be depleted to the retirement age and additional pre-tax contributions. Similarly, consider other factors you think might be important.

Develop a report for Tim outlining the factors that will have the greatest impact on his retirement.

Chapter 11

Monte Carlo Simulation

CONTENTS

ANALYTICS IN ACTION

Evaluating Financial Risk for Loan Providers*

The so-called financial crisis of 2008 led to nearly 9 million lost jobs in 2008 and 2009 in the United States, approximately 6% of the overall workforce. The net worth of U.S. households declined by nearly $13 trillion, and the U.S. stock market fell by almost 50%. One of the major factors leading to this financial crisis was an increase in subprime mortgage defaults. A subprime mortgage is a loan granted to individuals who do not qualify for conventional loans because they have poor credit scores. These types of mortgages are exposed to considerable financial risk that was not completely understood at the time.

While the financial markets and overall economy in the United States have largely recovered from the 2008 financial crisis, many companies still face similar financial risk from large pools of loans. Even today, large banks in the United States often own more than a million mortgages. Loan servicers in the United States service up to 10 million mortgages. These types of companies face substantial financial risk in the forms of delinquency risk, meaning customers who fail to pay back their loans on time, as well as prepayment risk which is driven by customers who choose to pay off their loans early resulting in reduced cash flows for the loan providers.

Complicated closed-form equations are available for some forms of delinquency and prepayment risk for large pools of loans. However, these equations are sensitive to input parameters and often rely on strict assumptions regarding the distributions of delinquent payments and prepayments. Therefore, Monte Carlo simulation is a common tool used to quantify delinquency and prepayment risk.

In one particular study, historical data were used from 10 million subprime mortgages from across the United States across 36,000 different zip codes as well as a separate set of 16 million mortgages insured by Freddie Mac, a U.S. government sponsored agency that buys mortgages and packages them into mortgage-backed securities for investors. The data sets include loan information such as credit scores, whether or not the mortgagee is a first-time home buyer, type of mortgage, debt-to-income values for the mortgagee, and zip code of the mortgage. The data sets also include information on prepayment and default events. This historical information can then be used to create analytical models to predict delinquency and prepayments.

The predictive models then feed into a Monte Carlo simulation model that can be used to estimate future delinquency and prepayment risks based on these many different input parameters. The input parameters can be varied to estimate the sensitivity of delinquency and prepayment risks to input parameters such as the location of the mortgages in a loan pool, the number of first-time home buyers in a loan pool, etc. The goal of such models is to help companies better estimate the financial risks present in their pools of loans so that they can adequately plan for future events.

*Partially based on information from J. Sirignano and K. Giesecke, "Risk Analysis for Large Pools of Loans," *Management Science* 65, no. 1 (2019): 107–121.

Monte Carlo simulation originated during World War II as part of the Manhattan Project to develop nuclear weapons. "Monte Carlo" was selected as the code name for the classified method in reference to the famous Monte Carlo casino in Monaco and the uncertainties inherent in gambling.

Uncertainty pervades decision making in business, government, and our personal lives. This chapter introduces the use of **Monte Carlo simulation** to evaluate the impact of uncertainty on a decision. Simulation models have been successfully used in a variety of disciplines. Financial applications include investment planning, project selection, and option pricing. Marketing applications include new product development and the timing of market entry for a product. Management applications include project management, inventory ordering (especially important for seasonal products), capacity planning, and revenue management (prominent in the airline, hotel, and car rental industries). In each of these applications, uncertain quantities complicate the decision process.

As we will demonstrate, a spreadsheet simulation analysis requires a model foundation of logical formulas that correctly express the relationships between parameters and decisions to generate outputs of interest. For example, a simple spreadsheet model may compute a clothing retailer's profit, given values for the number of ski jackets ordered from the manufacturer and the number of ski jackets demanded by customers. A simulation analysis extends this model by replacing the single value used for ski jacket demand with a **probability distribution** of possible values of ski jacket demand. A probability distribution of ski jacket demand represents not only the range of possible values but also the relative likelihood of various levels of demand.

To evaluate a decision with a Monte Carlo simulation, an analyst identifies parameters that are not known with a high degree of certainty and treats these parameters as random, or uncertain, variables. The values for the **random variables** are randomly generated from the specified probability distributions. The simulation model uses the randomly generated values of the random variables and the relationships between parameters and decisions to compute the corresponding values of an output. Specifically, a simulation experiment produces a *distribution* of output values that correspond to the randomly generated values of the uncertain input variables. This probability distribution of the output values describes the range of possible outcomes, as well as the relative likelihood of each outcome. After reviewing the simulation results, the analyst is often able to make decision recommendations for the **controllable inputs** that address not only the *average* output but also the *variability* of the output.

In this chapter, we construct spreadsheet simulation models using only native Excel functionality. As we will show, practical simulation models for real-world problems can be executed in native Excel. However, there are many simulation software products that provide sophisticated simulation modeling features and automate the generation of outputs such as charts and summary statistics. Some of these software packages can be installed as Excel add-ins, including @RISK, Crystal Ball, and Analytic Solver.

11.1 Risk Analysis for Sanotronics LLC

When making a decision in the presence of uncertainty, the decision maker should be interested not only in the average, or expected, outcome, but also in information regarding the range of possible outcomes. In particular, decision makers are interested in **risk analysis**, that is, quantifying the likelihood and magnitude of an undesirable outcome. In this section, we show how to perform a risk analysis study for a medical device company called Sanotronics.

Sanotronics LLC is a start-up company that manufactures medical devices for use in hospital clinics. Inspired by experiences with family members who have battled cancer, Sanotronics's founders have developed a prototype for a new device that limits health care workers' exposure to chemotherapy treatments while they are preparing, administering, and disposing of these hazardous medications. The new device features an innovative design and has the potential to capture a substantial share of the market.

Sanotronics would like an analysis of the first-year profit potential for the device. Because of Sanotronics's tight cash flow situation, management is particularly concerned about the potential for a loss. Sanotronics has identified the key parameters in determining first-year profit: selling price per unit (p), first-year administrative and advertising costs (c_a), direct labor cost per unit (c_i), parts cost per unit (c_p), and first-year demand (d). After conducting market research and a financial analysis, Sanotronics estimates with a high level of certainty that the device's selling price will be $249 per unit and that the first-year administrative and advertising costs will total $1,000,000.

Sanotronics is not certain about the values for the cost of direct labor, the cost of parts, and the first-year demand. At this stage of the planning process, Sanotronics's base estimates of these inputs are $45 per unit for the direct labor cost, $90 per unit for the parts cost, and 15,000 units for the first-year demand. We begin our risk analysis by considering a small set of what-if scenarios.

Base-Case Scenario

Sanotronics's first-year profit is computed as follows:

$$\text{Profit} = (p - c_i - c_p) \times d - c_a \qquad \textbf{(11.1)}$$

Recall that Sanotronics is certain of a selling price of $249 per unit, and administrative and advertising costs total $1,000,000. Substituting these values into equation (11.1) yields

$$\text{Profit} = (249 - c_i - c_p) \times d - 1,000,000 \qquad \textbf{(11.2)}$$

Sanotronics's base-case estimates of the direct labor cost per unit, the parts cost per unit, and first-year demand are $45, $90, and 15,000 units, respectively. These values constitute the **base-case scenario** for Sanotronics. Substituting these values into equation (11.2) yields the following profit projection:

$$\text{Profit} = (249 - 45 - 90)(15,000) - 1,000,000 = 710,000$$

Thus, the base-case scenario leads to an anticipated profit of $710,000.

Although the base-case scenario looks appealing, Sanotronics is aware that the values of direct labor cost per unit, parts cost per unit, and first-year demand are uncertain, so the base-case scenario may not occur. To help Sanotronics gauge the impact of the uncertainty, the company may consider performing a what-if analysis. A **what-if analysis** involves considering alternative values for the random variables (direct labor cost, parts cost, and first-year demand) and computing the resulting value for the output (profit).

Sanotronics is interested in what happens if the estimates of the direct labor cost per unit, parts cost per unit, and first-year demand do not turn out to be as expected under the base-case scenario. For instance, suppose that Sanotronics believes that direct labor costs could range from $43 to $47 per unit, parts cost could range from $80 to $100 per unit, and first-year demand could range from 0 to 30,000 units. Using these ranges, what-if analysis can be used to evaluate a **worst-case scenario** and a **best-case scenario**.

Worst-Case Scenario

The worst-case scenario for the direct labor cost is $47 (the highest value), the worst-case scenario for the parts cost is $100 (the highest value), and the worst-case scenario for demand is 0 units (the lowest value). Substituting these values into equation (11.2) leads to the following profit projection:

$$\text{Profit} = (249 - 47 - 100)(0) - 1,000,000 = -1,000,000$$

So, the worst-case scenario leads to a projected *loss* of $1,000,000.

Best-Case Scenario

The best-case value for the direct labor cost is $43 (the lowest value), for the parts cost it is $80 (the lowest value), and for demand it is 30,000 units (the highest value). Substituting these values into equation (14.2) leads to the following profit projection:

$$\text{Profit} = (249 - 43 - 80)(30,000) - 1,000,000 = 2,780,000$$

So the best-case scenario leads to a projected *profit* of $2,780,000.

At this point, the what-if analysis provides the conclusion that profits may range from a loss of $1,000,000 to a profit of $2,780,000 with a base-case profit of $710,000. Although the base-case profit of $710,000 is possible, the what-if analysis indicates that either a substantial loss or a substantial profit is also possible. Sanotronics can repeat this what-if analysis for other scenarios. However, simple what-if analyses do not indicate the likelihood of the various profit or loss values. In particular, we do not know anything about the probability of a loss. To conduct a more thorough evaluation of risk by obtaining insight on the potential magnitude and probability of undesirable outcomes, we now turn to developing a spreadsheet simulation model.

Sanotronics Spreadsheet Model

The first step in constructing a spreadsheet simulation model is to express the relationship between the inputs and the outputs with appropriate formula logic. Figure 11.1 provides the formula and value views for the Sanotronics spreadsheet. Data on selling price per

FIGURE 11.1	Excel Worksheet for Sanotronics

▲	A	B
1	**Sanotronics**	
2		
3	**Parameters**	
4	Selling Price per Unit	249
5	Administrative & Advertising Cost	1000000
6	Direct Labor Cost Per Unit	45
7	Parts Cost Per Unit	90
8	Demand	15000
9		
10	**Model**	
11	Profit	=((B4-B6-B7)*B8)-B5
12		

▲	A	B
1	**Sanotronics**	
2		
3	**Parameters**	
4	Selling Price per Unit	$249.00
5	Administrative & Advertising Cost	$1,000,000
6	Direct Labor Cost Per Unit	$45.00
7	Parts Cost Per Unit	$90.00
8	Demand	15,000
9		
10	**Model**	
11	Profit	$710,000.00

DATA *file*

Sanotronics

unit, administrative and advertising cost, direct labor cost per unit, parts cost per unit, and demand are in cells B4 to B8. The profit calculation, corresponding to equation (11.1), is expressed in cell B11 using appropriate cell references and formula logic. For the values shown in Figure 11.1, the spreadsheet model computes profit for the base-case scenario. By changing one or more values for the input parameters, the spreadsheet model can be used to conduct a manual what-if analysis (e.g., the best-case and worst-case scenarios).

Manual what-if analysis is discussed in more detail in Chapter 10.

Use of Probability Distributions to Represent Random Variables

Using the what-if approach to risk analysis, we manually select values for the random variables (direct labor cost per unit, parts cost per unit, and first-year demand), and then compute the resulting profit. Instead of manually selecting the values for the random variables, a Monte Carlo simulation randomly generates values for the random variables so that the values used reflect what we might observe in practice. A probability distribution describes the possible values of a random variable and the relative likelihood of the random variable taking on these values. The analyst can use historical data and knowledge of the random variable (range, mean, mode, and standard deviation) to specify the probability distribution for a random variable. As we describe in the following paragraphs, Sanotronics researched the direct labor cost per unit, the parts cost per unit, and first-year demand to identify the respective probability distributions for these three random variables.

Probability distributions are discussed in more detail in Chapter 4.

Based on recent wage rates and estimated processing requirements of the device, Sanotronics believes that the direct labor cost will range from $43 to $47 per unit and is described by the discrete probability distribution shown in Figure 11.2. We see that there is a 0.1 probability that the direct labor cost will be $43 per unit, a 0.2 probability that the

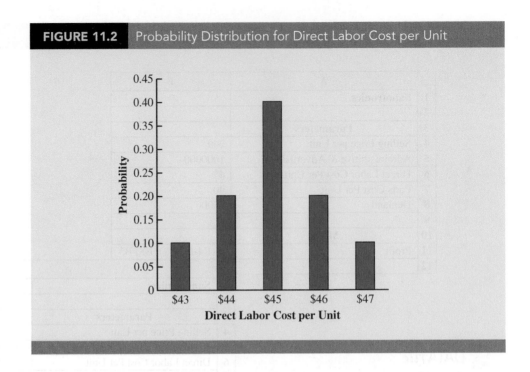

FIGURE 11.2   Probability Distribution for Direct Labor Cost per Unit

direct labor cost will be $44 per unit, and so on. The highest probability, 0.4, is associated with a direct labor cost of $45 per unit. Because we have assumed that the direct labor cost per unit is best described by a **discrete probability distribution**, the direct labor cost per unit can take on *only* the values of $43, $44, $45, $46, or $47.

Sanotronics is relatively unsure of the parts cost because it depends on many factors, including the general economy, the overall demand for parts, and the pricing policy of Sanotronics's parts suppliers. Sanotronics is confident that the parts cost will be between $80 and $100 per unit but is unsure as to whether any particular values between $80 and $100 are more likely than others. Therefore, Sanotronics decides to describe the uncertainty in parts cost with a uniform probability distribution, as shown in Figure 11.3. Costs per unit between $80 and $100 are equally likely. A uniform probability distribution is an example of a **continuous probability distribution**, which means that the parts cost can take on *any* value between $80 and $100.

Based on sales of comparable medical devices, Sanotronics believes that first-year demand is described by the normal probability distribution shown in Figure 11.4. The mean

One advantage of simulation is that the analyst can adjust the probability distributions of the random variables to determine the impact of the assumptions about the shape of the uncertainty on the output measures.

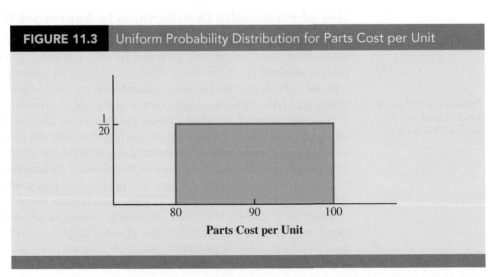

FIGURE 11.3   Uniform Probability Distribution for Parts Cost per Unit

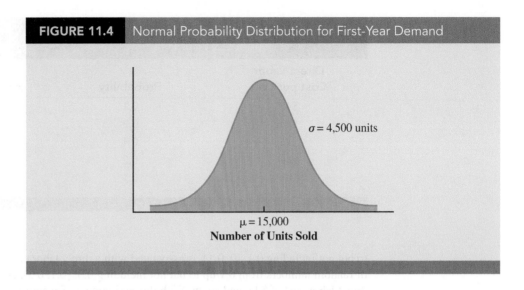

FIGURE 11.4   Normal Probability Distribution for First-Year Demand

μ of first-year demand is 15,000 units. The standard deviation σ of 4,500 units describes the variability in the first-year demand. The normal probability distribution is a continuous probability distribution in which any value is possible, but values extremely larger or smaller than the mean are increasingly unlikely.

Generating Values for Random Variables with Excel

To simulate the Sanotronics problem, we must generate values for the three random variables and compute the resulting profit. A set of values for the random variables is called a *trial*. Then we generate another trial, compute a second value for profit, and so on. We continue this process until we are satisfied that enough trials have been conducted to describe the probability distribution for profit. Put simply, simulation is the process of generating values of random variables and computing the corresponding output measures.

In the Sanotronics model, representative values must be generated for the random variables corresponding to direct labor cost per unit, the parts cost per unit, and the first-year demand. To illustrate how to generate these values, we need to introduce the concept of computer-generated random numbers.

Computer-generated random numbers[1] are randomly selected numbers from 0 up to, but not including, 1; this interval is denoted by [0, 1). All values of the computer-generated random numbers are equally likely and so the values are uniformly distributed over the interval from 0 to 1. Computer-generated random numbers can be obtained using built-in functions available in computer simulation packages and spreadsheets. For example, placing the formula =RAND() in a cell of an Excel worksheet will result in a random number between 0 and 1 being placed into that cell.

Let us show how random numbers can be used to generate values corresponding to the probability distributions for the random variables in the Sanotronics example. We begin by showing how to generate a value for the direct labor cost per unit. The approach described is applicable for generating values from any discrete probability distribution.

Table 11.1 illustrates the process of partitioning the interval from 0 to 1 into subintervals so that the probability of generating a random number in a subinterval is equal to the probability of the corresponding direct labor cost. The interval of random numbers from 0 up

---

[1]Computer-generated random numbers are formally called pseudorandom numbers because they are generated through the use of mathematical formulas and are therefore not technically random. The difference between random numbers and pseudorandom numbers is primarily philosophical, and we use the term *random numbers* even when they are generated by a computer.

TABLE 11.1	Random Number Intervals for Generating Value of Direct Labor Cost per Unit	
Direct Labor Cost per Unit	Probability	Interval of Random Numbers
$43	0.1	[0.0, 0.1)
$44	0.2	[0.1, 0.3)
$45	0.4	[0.3, 0.7)
$46	0.2	[0.7, 0.9)
$47	0.1	[0.9, 1.0)

to but not including 0.1, [0, 0.1), is associated with a direct labor cost of $43; the interval of random numbers from 0.1 up to but not including 0.3, [0.1, 0.3), is associated with a direct labor cost of $44, and so on. With this assignment of random number intervals to the possible values of the direct labor cost, the probability of generating a random number in any interval is equal to the probability of obtaining the corresponding value for the direct labor cost. Thus, to select a value for the direct labor cost, we generate a random number between 0 and 1 using the RAND function in Excel. If the random number is at least 0.0 but less than 0.1, we set the direct labor cost equal to $43. If the random number is at least 0.1 but less than 0.3, we set the direct labor cost equal to $44, and so on.

Each trial of the simulation requires a value for the direct labor cost. Suppose that on the first trial the random number is 0.9109. From Table 11.1, because 0.9109 is in the interval [0.9, 1.0), the corresponding simulated value for the direct labor cost would be $47 per unit. Suppose that on the second trial the random number is 0.2841. From Table 11.1, the simulated value for the direct labor cost would be $44 per unit.

Each trial in the simulation also requires a value of the parts cost and first-year demand. Let us now turn to the issue of generating values for the parts cost. The probability distribution for the parts cost per unit is the uniform distribution shown in Figure 11.3. Because this random variable has a different probability distribution than direct labor cost, we use random numbers in a slightly different way to generate simulated values for parts cost. To generate a value for a random variable characterized by a continuous uniform distribution, the following Excel formula is used:

$$\text{Value of uniform random variable} = \text{lower bound} + (\text{upper bound} - \text{lower bound}) \times \text{RAND()} \quad \textbf{(11.3)}$$

For Sanotronics, the parts cost per unit is a uniformly distributed random variable with a lower bound of $80 and an upper bound of $100. Applying equation (11.3) leads to the following formula for generating the parts cost:

$$\text{Parts cost} = 80 + 20 \times \text{RAND()} \quad \textbf{(11.4)}$$

By closely examining equation (11.4), we can understand how it uses random numbers to generate uniformly distributed values for parts cost. The first term of equation (11.4) is 80 because Sanotronics is assuming that the parts cost will never drop below $80 per unit. Because RAND() returns a value between 0 and 1, the second term, $20 \times$ RAND(), corresponds to how much more than the lower bound the simulated value of parts cost is. Because RAND() is equally likely to be any value between 0 and 1, the simulated value for the parts cost is equally likely to be between the lower bound ($80 + 0 = 80$) and the upper bound ($80 + 20 = 100$). For example, suppose that a random number of 0.4576 is generated by the RAND function. As illustrated by Figure 11.5, the value for the parts cost would be

$$\text{Parts cost} = 80 + 20 \times 0.4576 = 80 + 9.15 = 89.15 \text{ per unit}$$

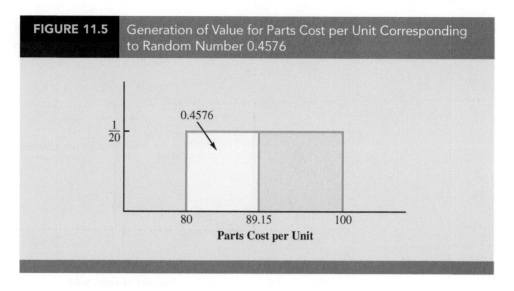

FIGURE 11.5   Generation of Value for Parts Cost per Unit Corresponding to Random Number 0.4576

Suppose that a random number of 0.5842 is generated on the next trial. The value for the parts cost would be

$$\text{Parts cost} = 80 + 20 \times 0.5842 = 80 + 11.68 = 91.68 \text{ per unit}$$

With appropriate choices of the lower and upper bounds, equation (11.3) can be used to generate values for any continuous uniform probability distribution.

Lastly, we need a procedure for generating the first-year demand from computer-generated random numbers. Because first-year demand is normally distributed with a mean of 15,000 units and a standard deviation of 4,500 units (see Figure 11.4), we need a procedure for generating random values from this normal probability distribution.

Once again we will use random numbers between 0 and 1 to simulate values for first-year demand. To generate a value for a random variable characterized by a normal distribution with a specified mean and standard deviation, the following Excel formula is used:

Equation (11.5) can be used to generate values for any normal probability distribution by changing the values specified for the mean and standard deviation, respectively.

Value of normal random variable = NORM.INV(RAND(), mean, standard deviation)   **(11.5)**

For Sanotronics, first-year demand is a normally distributed random variable with a mean of 15,000 and a standard deviation of 4,500. Applying equation (11.5) leads to the following formula for generating the first-year demand:

$$\text{Demand} = \text{NORM.INV(RAND(), 15000, 4500)} \qquad \textbf{(11.6)}$$

Suppose that the random number of 0.6026 is produced by the RAND function; applying equation (11.6) then results in Demand =NORM.INV(0.6026, 15000, 4500) = 16,170 units. To understand how equation (11.6) uses random numbers to generate normally distributed values for first-year demand, observe from Figure 11.6 that 60.26 percent of the area under the normal curve with a mean of 15,000 and a standard deviation of 4,500 lies to the left of the value of 16,170 generated by the Excel formula =NORM.INV(0.6026, 15000, 4500). Thus, the RAND function generates a percentage of the area under the normal curve, and then the NORM.INV function generates the corresponding value such that this randomly generated percentage lies to the left of this value.

Now suppose that the random number produced by the RAND function is 0.3551. Applying equation (11.6) then results in Demand =NORM.INV(0.3551, 15000, 4500) = 13,328 units. This matches intuition because half of this normal distribution lies below the mean of 15,000 and half lies above it, and so values generated by RAND() less than 0.5 result in values of first-year demand below the average of 15,000 units, and values generated by RAND() above 0.5 correspond to values of first-year demand above the average of 15,000 units.

Now that we know how to randomly generate values for the random variables (direct labor cost, parts cost, first-year demand) from their respective probability distributions, we modify the spreadsheet by adding this information. The static values in Figure 11.1 for

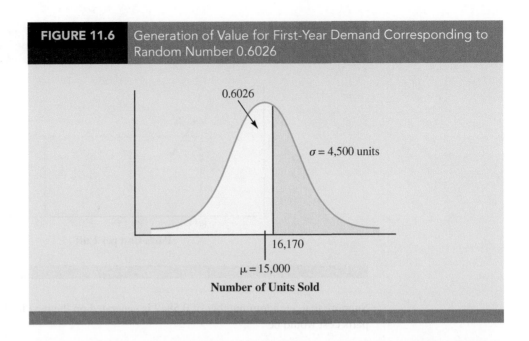

FIGURE 11.6 Generation of Value for First-Year Demand Corresponding to Random Number 0.6026

FIGURE 11.7 Formula Worksheet for Sanotronics

	A	B	C	D
1	**Sanotronics**			
2				
3	**Parameters**			
4	Selling Price per Unit	249		
5	Administrative & Advertising Cost	1000000		
6	Direct Labor Cost Per Unit	=VLOOKUP(RAND(),A15:C19,3,TRUE)		
7	Parts Cost Per Unit	=B22+(B23-B22)*RAND()		
8	Demand	=NORM.INV(RAND(),D22,D23)		
9				
10	**Model**			
11	Profit	=((B4-B6-B7)*B8)-B5		
12				
13	Direct Labor Cost			
14	Lower End of Interval	Upper End of Interval	Cost per Unit	Probability
15	0	=D15+A15	43	0.1
16	=B15	=D16+A16	44	0.2
17	=B16	=D17+A17	45	0.4
18	=B17	=D18+A18	46	0.2
19	=B18	1	47	0.1
20				
21	Parts Cost (Uniform)		Demand (Normal)	
22	Lower Bound	80	Mean	15000
23	Upper Bound	100	Standard Deviation	4500

The VLOOKUP function is discussed in more detail in Chapter 10.

these parameters in cells B6, B7, and B8 are replaced with cell formulas that will randomly generate values whenever the spreadsheet is recalculated (as shown in Figure 11.7). Cell B6 uses a random number generated by the RAND function and looks up the corresponding direct labor cost per unit by applying the VLOOKUP function to the table of intervals contained in cells A15:C19 (which corresponds to Table 11.1). Cell B7 executes equation (11.4) using references to the lower bound and upper bound of the uniform distribution of the parts cost in cells B22 and B23, respectively.[2] Cell B8 executes equation (11.6) using references to the mean and standard deviation of the normal distribution of the first-year demand in cells D22 and D23, respectively.[3]

DATA *file*

Sanotronics

Executing Simulation Trials with Excel

Each trial in the simulation involves randomly generating values for the random variables (direct labor cost, parts cost, and first-year demand) and computing profit. To facilitate the execution of multiple simulation trials, we use Excel's Data Table functionality in an unorthodox, but effective, manner. To set up the spreadsheet for the execution of 1,000 simulation trials, we structure a table as shown in cells A25 through E1025 in Figure 11.8. As Figure 11.8 shows, A26:A1025 numbers the 1,000 simulation trials (rows 47 through 1,024 are hidden). Cells B26:E26 contain references to the cells corresponding to Direct Labor Cost, Parts Cost per Unit, Demand, and Profit. To populate the table of simulation trials in cells A26 through E1025, we execute the following steps:

These steps iteratively select the simulation trial number from the range A26 through A1025 and substitute it into the blank cell selected in Step 4 (D1). This substitution has no bearing on the spreadsheet, but it forces Excel to recalculate the spreadsheet each time, thereby generating new random numbers with the RAND functions in cells B6, B7, and B8.

Step 1. Select cell range A26:E1025
Step 2. Click the **Data** tab in the Ribbon
Step 3. Click **What-If Analysis** in the **Forecast** group and select **Data Table…**
Step 4. When the **Data Table** dialog box appears, leave the **Row input cell:** box blank and enter any empty cell in the spreadsheet (e.g., *D1*) into the **Column input cell:** box
Step 5. Click **OK**

Figure 11.9 shows the results of a set of 1,000 simulation trials. After executing the simulation with the data table, each row in this table corresponds to a distinct simulation trial consisting of different values of the random variables. In Trial 1 (row 26 in the spreadsheet), we see that the direct labor cost is $45 per unit, the parts cost is $85.56 per unit, and first-year demand is 8,675 units, resulting in profit of $27,434. In Trial 2 (row 27 in the spreadsheet), we observe random variables of $47 for the direct labor cost, $86.52 for the parts cost, and 12,372 for first-year demand. These values result in a simulated profit of $428,703 on the second simulation trial. We note that every time the spreadsheet recalculates (by pressing the F9 key), new random values are generated by the RAND functions resulting in a new set of simulation trials.

Measuring and Analyzing Simulation Output

The analysis of the output observed over a set of simulation trials is a critical part of a simulation process. For the collection of simulation trials, it is helpful to compute descriptive statistics such as sample count, minimum sample value, maximum sample value, sample mean, sample standard deviation, sample proportion, and sample standard error of the proportion. To compute these statistics for the Sanotronics example, we use the following Excel functions:

DATA *file*

SanotronicsModel

Cell H26	=COUNT(E26:E1025)
Cell H27	=MIN(E26:E1025)
Cell H28	=MAX(E26:E1025)
Cell H29	=AVERAGE(E26:E1025)
Cell H30	=STDEV.S(E26:E1025)
Cell H32	=COUNTIF(E26:E1025, "<0")/COUNT(E26:E1025)
Cell H33	=SQRT(H32*(1-H32)/H26)

---

[2]Technically, random variables modeled with continuous probability distributions should be appropriately rounded to avoid modeling error. For example, the simulated values of parts cost per unit should be rounded to the nearest penny. To simplify exposition, we do not worry about the small amount of error that occurs in this case. To model these random variables more accurately, the formula in cell B7 should be =ROUND(B22+(B23−B22)*RAND(),2).

[3]In addition to being a continuous distribution that technically requires rounding when applied to discrete phenomena (like units of medical device demand), the normal distribution also allows negative values. The probability of a negative value is quite small in the case of first-year demand, and we simply ignore the small amount of modeling error for the sake of simplicity. To model first-year demand more accurately, the formula in cell B8 should be =MAX(ROUND(NORM.INV(RAND(),D22, D23),0),0).

FIGURE 11.8 Setting Up Sanotronics Spreadsheet for 1,000 Simulation Trials

	A	B	C	D	E
1	Sanotronics				
2					
3	Parameters				
4	Selling Price per Unit	249			
5	Administrative & Advertising Cost	1000000			
6	Direct Labor Cost Per Unit	=VLOOKUP(RAND(),A15:C19,3,TRUE)			
7	Parts Cost Per Unit	=B22+(B23-B22)*RAND()			
8	Demand	=NORM.INV(RAND(),D22,D23)			
9					
10	Model				
11	Profit	=((B4-B6-B7)*B8)-B5			
12					
13	Direct Labor Cost				
14	Lower End of Interval	Upper End of Interval	Cost per Unit	Probability	
15	0	=D15+A15	43	0.1	
16	=B15	=D16+A16	44	0.2	
17	=B16	=D17+A17	45	0.4	
18	=B17	=D18+A18	46	0.2	
19	=B18	1	47	0.1	
20					
21	Parts Cost (Uniform)		Demand (Normal)		
22	Lower Bound	80	Mean	15000	
23	Upper Bound	100	Standard Deviation	4500	
24					
25	Simulation Trial	Direct Labor Cost Per Unit	Parts Cost Per Unit	Demand	Profit
26	1	=B6	=B7	=B8	=B11
27	2				
28	3				
29	4				
30	5				
31	6				
32	7				
33	8				
34	9				
35	10				
36	11				
37	12				
38	13				
39	14				
40	15				
41	16				
42	17				
43	18				
44	19				
45	20				
46	21				
1025	1000				

Data Table dialog box:
- Row input cell: [blank]
- Column input cell: $D$1
- OK   Cancel

Cell H32 computes the ratio of the number of trials whose profit is less than zero over the total number of trials. By changing the value of the second argument in the COUNTIF function, the probability that the profit is less than any specified value can be computed in cell H32. Cell H33 computes the sample standard error of the proportion using the formula

FIGURE 11.9   Output from Sanotronics Simulation

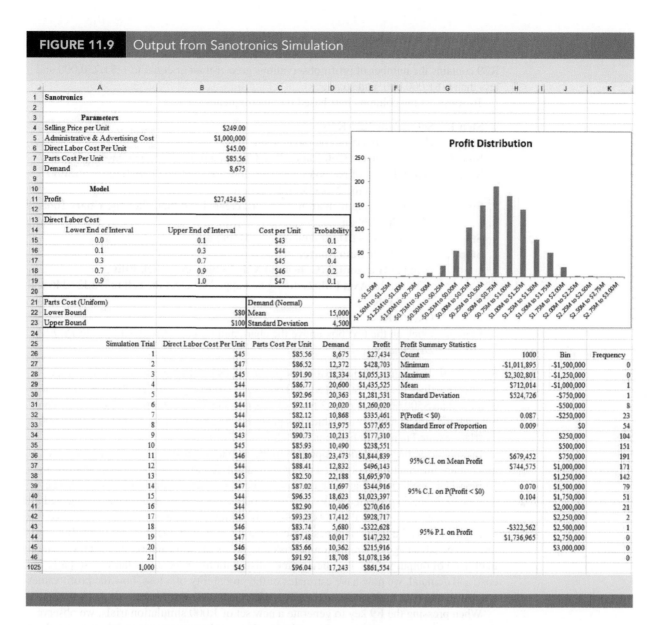

Simulation studies enable an objective estimate of the probability of a loss, which is an important aspect of risk analysis.

$\sqrt{\bar{p}(1-\bar{p})/n}$, where $\bar{p}$ is the sample proportion of observations satisfying a criterion (profit less than \$0 in this case) and n is the sample size (1,000 in this case). The sample standard error of the proportion provides a measure of how much the sample proportion P(Profit < \$0) varies across different samples of 1,000 simulation trials.

As shown in Figure 11.9, the 1,000 profit observations range from −\$1,011,895 to 2,302,801. The sample mean profit is \$712,014 and the sample standard deviation is \$524,726. There is a sample proportion of 0.087 of the observations with negative profit and the sample standard error of this estimate is 0.009.

For a detailed description of the FREQUENCY function and creating charts in Excel, see Chapters 2 and 3.

To visualize the distribution of profit on which these descriptive statistics are based, we create a histogram using the FREQUENCY function and a column chart. In Figure 11.9, the cell range J27:J44 contains the upper limits of the bins into which we wish to group the 1,000 simulated observations of profit listed in cells E26:E1025.

Step 1.   Select cells K27:K46
Step 2.   In the Formula Bar, enter the formula *=FREQUENCY(E26:E1025, J27:J45)*
Step 3.   Press **CTRL+SHIFT+ENTER** after entering the formula in Step 2

Pressing **CTRL+SHIFT+ENTER** in Excel indicates that the function should return an array of values to fill the cell range K27:K46. For example, cell K27 contains the number of profit observations less than −$1,500,000, cell K28 contains the number of profit observations greater than or equal to −$1,500,000 and less than −$1,250,000, cell K29 contains the number of profit observations greater than or equal to −$1,250,000 and less than −$1,000,000, and so on.

To construct the column chart based on this frequency data:

Step 1. Select cells K27:K46
Step 2. Click the **Insert** tab on the Ribbon
Step 3. Click the **Insert Column or Bar Chart** button ▯▮▭ in the **Charts** group
Step 4. When the list of bar chart subtypes appears, click the **Clustered Column** button ▥▦ in the **2-D Column** section
Step 5. Select the column chart that was just created and then click the **Chart Tools** tab on the Ribbon
Step 6. Click the **Select Data** button in the **Data** group
Step 7. In the **Select Data Source** dialog box:
    In the **Horizontal (Category) Axis Labels** area, click **Edit**
    When the **Axis Labels** dialog box appears, select the cell range J27:J46 and click **OK**
    Click **OK**
Step 8. Click on the text box above the chart, and replace "Chart Title" with *Profit Distribution*

Figure 11.9 shows that the distribution of profit values is fairly symmetric, with a large number of values between $0 and $1,500,000. Only 10 trials out of 1,000 resulted in a loss of more than $500,000, and only 3 trials resulted in a profit greater than $2,000,000. The bin with the largest number of values has profit ranging between $500,000 and $750,000; 91 trials resulted in a profit between $500,000 and $750,000.

In comparing the simulation approach to the manual what-if approach, we observe that much more information is obtained using simulation. Recall from the what-if analysis in Section 11.1, we learned that the base-case scenario projected a profit of $710,000. The worst-case scenario projected a loss of $1,000,000, and the best-case scenario projected a profit of $2,591,000. From the 1,000 trials of the simulation that have been run, we see that extremes such as the worst- and best-case scenarios, although possible, are unlikely. Indeed, the advantage of simulation for risk analysis is the information it provides on the likelihood of output values. For the assumed distributions of the direct labor cost, parts cost, and demand, we now have estimates of the probability of a loss, how the profit values are distributed over their range, and what profit values are most likely.

When pressing the **F9** key to generate a new set of 1,000 simulation trials, we observe that the summary statistics vary. In particular, the sample mean profit and the estimated probability of a negative profit fluctuate for each new set of simulation trials. To account for this sampling error, we can construct confidence intervals on the mean profit and proportion of observations with negative profit. Recall that the general formula for a confidence interval is point estimate +/− margin of error. To compute the confidence intervals for the Sanotronics example, we use the following Excel functions:

Confidence intervals are discussed in more detail in Chapter 6.

Cell H36	*=H29 − CONFIDENCE.T(0.05, H30, H26)*
Cell H37	*=H29 + CONFIDENCE.T(0.05, H30, H26)*
Cell H39	*=H32 − (NORM.S.INV(0.975)*H33)*
Cell H40	*=H32 + (NORM.S.INV(0.975)*H33)*

Cells H36 and H37 compute the lower and upper limits of a 95% confidence interval of the mean profit. To compute the margin of error for this interval estimate, the Excel CONFIDENCE function requires three arguments: the significance level (1 − confidence level), the sample standard deviation, and the sample size.

Recall that
=NORM.S.INV(0.975)
computes the value such
that 2.5% of the area
under the standard normal
distribution lies in the
upper tail defined by this
value.

Cells H39 and H40 compute the lower and upper limits of a 95% confidence interval of the proportion of observations with a negative profit. To compute the margin of error for this interval estimate, the sample standard error of the proportion (in cell H33) is multiplied by the z value corresponding to a 95% confidence level (as calculated by =NORM.S.INV(0.975)).

Figure 11.9 shows a 95% confidence interval on the mean profit ranging from $679,452 to $744,575 and a 95% confidence interval on the probability of a negative profit ranging from 0.070 to 0.104. A common misinterpretation is to relate the 95% confidence interval on the mean profit to the profit distribution of the 10,000 simulated profit values displayed in Figure 11.9. Looking at the profit distribution it should be clear that 95% of the values do not lie in the range [$679,452 to $744,575] suggested by the 95% confidence interval. The 95% confidence interval relates only to the confidence we have in the estimation of the mean profit, not the likelihood of an individual profit observation. If we desire an interval that contains 95% of the profit observations, we can construct this by using the Excel PERCENTILE.EXC function. For the Sanotronics example, PERCENTILE.EXC(E26:E1025,0.025) = −$322,562 and PERCENTILE.EXC(E26:E1025,0.975) = $1,736,965 provide the lower and upper limits of an interval estimating the range that is 95% likely to contain the profit outcome.

The simulation results help Sanotronics's management better understand the profit/loss potential of the new medical device. An estimated 0.070 to 0.104 probability of a loss with an estimated mean profit between $679,452 and $744,575 may be acceptable to management. On the other hand, Sanotronics might want to conduct further market research before deciding whether to introduce the product. In any case, the simulation results should be helpful in reaching an appropriate decision.

NOTES + COMMENTS

1. In the preceding section, we showed how to generate values for random variables from a generic discrete distribution, a uniform distribution, and a normal distribution. Generating values for a normally distributed random variable required the use of the NORM.INV and RAND functions. When using the Excel formula =NORM.INV(RAND( ), m, s), the RAND( ) function generates a random number r between 0 and 1 and then the NORM.INV function identifies the smallest value k such that $P(X \leq k) \geq r$, where X is a normal random variable with mean m and standard deviation s. Similarly, the RAND function can be used with the Excel functions BETA.INV, BINOM.INV, GAMMA.INV, and LOGNORM.INV to generate values for a random variable with a beta distribution, binomial distribution, gamma distribution, and lognormal distribution, respectively. Using a different probability distribution for a random variable simply changes the relative likelihood of the random variable realizing certain values. The choice of probability distribution to use for a random variable should be based on historical data and knowledge of the analyst. In Appendix 11.1, we discuss several probability distributions and how to generate them with native Excel functions.

2. We can reduce the width of the confidence intervals associated with the sample mean and the sample proportion computed from a set of simulation trials by increasing the number of trials beyond 1,000. However, increasing the number of trials can begin to tax the computational capabilities of Excel. When more than 1,000 trials are necessary to reduce the sampling error, the analyst may want to restrict Excel to only update values upon a specific command rather than updating anytime the Enter key is pressed in Excel. This can be accomplished by choosing **File** from the Ribbon, clicking **Options**, choosing **Formulas**, and then changing the **Calculation options** to **Manual**. When this change is made, Excel will update values only when the **F9** key is pressed.

11.2 Inventory Policy Analysis for Promus Corp

In this section, we demonstrate how simulation can be used to evaluate an inventory policy for a product that has an uncertain demand. In our example, we consider Promus Corp, which sells wireless routers. Each router costs Promus $75 and the company sells it for

$125. Thus, Promus realizes a gross profit of $125 − $75 = $50 for each router sold. Monthly demand for the router is uncertain, but Promus Corp has collected data to help characterize it.

Promus receives monthly deliveries from its supplier and replenishes its inventory to a predetermined level at the beginning of each month. This predetermined inventory level is referred to as the replenishment level. If monthly demand is less than the replenishment level, then Promus must hold the unsold routers in inventory. Each unsold router held by Promus results in an inventory holding cost of $15 because Promus must pay for the storage, insurance, and cost-of-capital for the inventory. However, if monthly demand is greater than the replenishment level, then a stock-out occurs which results in a shortage cost of $30 being charged for each unit of demand that cannot be satisfied. Management would like to use a simulation model to determine the average monthly net profit resulting from using different replenishment levels.

DATA file

PromusCorp

Spreadsheet Model for Promus

To evaluate different replenishment levels, we develop a simulation model that appropriately accounts for the relationships between the input parameters to compute the output measure(s) of interest. For Promus, the input parameters are the gross profit per unit (known to be $50), the unit holding cost ($15), the unit shortage cost ($30), the monthly demand (uncertain, D), and the replenishment level (a decision, Q). The output measure of interest is the monthly net profit. Having identified the input parameters and output measure, the next step is to establish computational logic that determines the output measure (monthly net profit) for given values of the input parameters. For Promus, the computation of monthly profit depends on the relative magnitude of the monthly demand and the replenishment level.

For a specified replenishment level (Q) and observed monthly demand (D), monthly net profit is calculated as follows:

$$\text{Monthly net profit} = \text{Gross profit} - \text{holding cost} - \text{shortage cost}$$
$$= 50 \times \min\{D, Q\} - 15 \times \max\{Q - D, 0\} - 30 \times \max\{D - Q, 0\} \quad \textbf{(11.7)}$$

It is informative to analyze equation (11.7) for the two cases: $D \leq Q$ and $D > Q$. When demand is less than or equal to the replenishment level ($D \leq Q$), D units are sold, and an inventory holding cost of $15 is incurred for each of the $Q - D$ units that remain in storage, and no shortage occurs. This results in:

$$\text{Monthly net profit} = 50 \times D - 15 \times (Q - D)$$

When demand is greater than replenishment level ($D > Q$), Q units are sold, no inventory remains, and a shortage of $D - Q$ occurs. This results in:

$$\text{Monthly net profit} = 50 \times Q - 30 \times (D - Q)$$

For a replenishment level of 90 and monthly demand of 100, Figure 11.10 displays the Excel implementation of equation (11.7). The gross profit per unit, holding cost per unit, and shortage cost per unit data are entered into cells B4, B5, and B6. An observed demand of 100 units is entered into cell B7. The replenishment level (a controllable input) is entered into cell B10.

Cell B11	Compute sales =*MIN(B7, B10)*
Cell B12	Calculate gross profit =*B11*B4*
Cell B13	Calculate the holding cost if demand is less than or equal to the replenishment level
	=*IF(B7<=B10, (B10−B7)*B5, 0)*
Cell B14	Calculate the shortage cost if demand is greater than the replenishment level
	=*IF(B7>B10, (B7−B10)*B6, 0)*

FIGURE 11.10	Excel Worksheet for Promus Corp

	A	B
1	**Promus Corp**	
2		
3	**Parameters**	
4	Gross Profit per Unit	50
5	Holding Cost per Unit	15
6	Shortage Cost per Unit	30
7	Demand	100
8		
9	**Model**	
10	Replenishment Level (Q)	90
11	Sales	=MIN($B$7,B10)
12	Gross Profit	=B$11*$B$4
13	Holding Cost	=IF($B$7<=B10,(B10-$B$7)*$B$5,0)
14	Shortage Cost	=IF($B$7>B10,($B$7-B10)*$B$6,0)
15	Net Profit	=B12-B13-B14

	A	B
1	**Promus Corp**	
2		
3	**Parameters**	
4	Gross Profit per Unit	$50
5	Holding Cost per Unit	$15
6	Shortage Cost per Unit	$30
7	Demand	100
8		
9	**Model**	
10	Replenishment Level (Q)	90
11	Sales	90
12	Gross Profit	$4,500
13	Holding Cost	$0
14	Shortage Cost	$300
15	Net Profit	$4,200

Generating Values for Promus Corp's Demand

With a spreadsheet model that correctly computes monthly net profit for given values of the inputs (including a specified replenishment level and an observed demand), the next step is to characterize the demand uncertainty and randomly generate values for demand in a manner that reflects the relative likelihood of future monthly demand values.

To gain a better understanding of its router business, Promus has recorded the demand for its routers for the past 60 months. Figure 11.11 plots the monthly demand over time and illustrates that, while router demand varies from month to month, there is no detectable pattern in the variation. That is, there does not appear to be any trend or seasonality in the demand. Therefore, Promus feels comfortable in treating router demands from month to month as independent quantities.

FIGURE 11.11	Router Demand Over Time

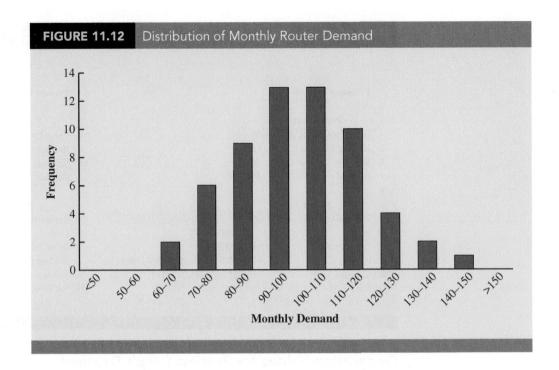

FIGURE 11.12 Distribution of Monthly Router Demand

Figure 11.12 characterizes the relative likelihood of monthly demand values with a histogram of the 60 monthly demand observations. As Figure 11.12 illustrates, the distribution of monthly demand is bell-shaped, suggesting that the normal distribution would be a good fit to these data. Due to the wide range of possible values of monthly demand, using a continuous distribution such as the normal distribution is appropriate.[4] To describe the normal distribution fitting these data, we compute the sample mean ($\bar{x} = 101$) and sample standard deviation ($s = 17$) of these 60 observations.

We can randomly generate a value for monthly demand described by a normal distribution with a mean of 101 units and a standard deviation of 17 units using the formula =NORM.INV(RAND(), 101, 17). In Figure 11.13, we modify the spreadsheet model by replacing the static value of demand in cell B7 with the formula =*NORM.INV(RAND(), E6, E7)*, where cells E6 and E7 contain the values for the sample mean and sample standard deviation, respectively (101 and 17 in this example).

Promus would like to compare the average monthly profit corresponding to a replenishment level of 90 units to the average monthly profit corresponding to a replenishment level of 110 units. To facilitate this comparison, in cells C11:C15 displayed in Figure 11.14, we implement the same logic for a replenishment level of 110 that we did for a replenishment level of 90 in cells B11:B15. We note that the computations for these two replenishment levels all use the same input data (cells B4 through B7)[5] and only differ by the replenishment level applied (cells B10 and C10). In cell B17, we compute the difference between the net profit when $Q = 110$ and the net profit when $Q = 90$ for the same value of observed demand in cell B7.

---

[4]Note that technically demand values for routers can only take integer values. The formula in Excel can be modified to require this using the Excel ROUND function, but for distributions with a relatively large mean we generally use a continuous random variable to model demand.

[5]The use of the same set of random values for demand to evaluate both replenishment levels is an example of a general technique known as common random numbers. This is not strictly required for problems such as this, but it reduces the variance in the output measures to allow for a more stable comparison of different replenishment levels. For more information on common random numbers, see Law, A.M., *Simulation Modeling and Analysis*, 5th edition, McGraw-Hill, 2014.

FIGURE 11.13	Modeling Demand as a Normal Random Variable

	A	B	C	D	E
1	**Promus Corp**				
2					
3	**Parameters**				
4	Gross Profit per Unit	50			
5	Holding Cost per Unit	15		**Demand (Normal)**	
6	Shortage Cost per Unit	30		Mean	100
7	Demand	=NORM.INV(RAND(),E6,E7)		Standard Deviation	20
8					
9	**Model**				
10	Replenishment Level (Q)	90			
11	Sales	=MIN($B$7,B10)			
12	Gross Profit	=B$11*$B$4			
13	Holding Cost	=IF($B$7<=B10,(B10-$B$7)*$B$5,0)			
14	Shortage Cost	=IF($B$7>B10,($B$7-B10)*$B$6,0)			
15	Net Profit	=B12-B13-B14			

FIGURE 11.14	Setting Up Promus Spreadsheet for Profit Comparison

	A	B	C	D	E
1	Promus Corp				
2					
3	**Parameters**				
4	Gross Profit per Unit	50			
5	Holding Cost per Unit	15		**Demand (Normal)**	
6	Shortage Cost per Unit	30		Mean	100
7	Demand	=NORM.INV(RAND(),E6,E7)		Standard Deviation	20
8					
9	**Model**				
10	Replenishment Level (Q)	90	110		
11	Sales	=MIN($B$7,B10)	=MIN($B$7,C10)		
12	Gross Profit	=B$11*$B$4	=C$11*$B$4		
13	Holding Cost	=IF($B$7<=B10,(B10-$B$7)*$B$5,0)	=IF($B$7<=C10,(C10-$B$7)*$B$5,0)		
14	Shortage Cost	=IF($B$7>B10,($B$7-B10)*$B$6,0)	=IF($B$7>C10,($B$7-C10)*$B$6,0)		
15	Net Profit	=B12-B13-B14	=C12-C13-C14		
16					
17	Profit$_{Q=110}$ - Profit$_{Q=90}$	=C15-B15			

Executing Simulation Trials and Analyzing Output

Each trial in the simulation involves randomly generating a value for the corresponding month's demand, and then computing the difference in the net profit when using a replenishment level of 110 versus a replenishment level of 90. To prepare the spreadsheet for the execution of 1,000 simulation trials, we structure the spreadsheet as in Figure 11.15. The cell range from A20 through C1019 has been prepared to hold the set of 1,000 simulation trials. Cell range A20:A1019 numbers the rows that will correspond to the 1,000 simulation trials (rows 29 through 1018 are hidden). Cells B20 and C20 contain Excel formulas referencing the random variable (monthly demand) and the output measure (difference in the net profit resulting from $Q = 110$ and $Q = 90$).

FIGURE 11.15	Setting Up the Promus Spreadsheet for 1,000 Simulation Trials

To populate the table of simulation trials in the Model worksheet, we execute the following steps:

Step 1. Select cell range A20:C1019

Step 2. Click the **Data** tab in the Ribbon

Step 3. Click **What-If Analysis** in the **Forecast** group and select **Data Table…**

Step 4. When the **Data Table** dialog box appears, leave the **Row input cell:** box blank and enter any empty cell in the spreadsheet (e.g., *D1*) into the **Column input cell:** box

Step 5. Click **OK**

Figure 11.16 shows the results of a set of 1,000 simulation trials. After executing the simulation with the Data Table, each row of this table corresponds to a distinct simulation trial consisting of different values of monthly demand. We see in the simulated month corresponding to Trial 1 that demand is 75 units and a replenishment level of 110 earns $300 less than a replenishment level of 90. In Trial 2, monthly demand is 131 and a replenishment level of 110 earns $1,600 more than a replenishment level of 90.

Similar to the Sanotronics problem in Section 11.1, we compute sample statistics and 95% confidence intervals on the mean and the proportion based on the 1,000 simulation trials. Referring to Figure 11.16:

Cell F20	$=COUNT(C20:C1019)$
Cell F21	$=MIN(C20:C1019)$
Cell F22	$=MAX(C20:C1019)$
Cell F23	$=AVERAGE(C20:C1019)$
Cell F24	$=STDEV.S(C20:C1019)$
Cell F26	$=COUNTIF(C20:C1019, ">0")/F20$
Cell F27	$=SQRT(F26*(1-F26)/F20)$

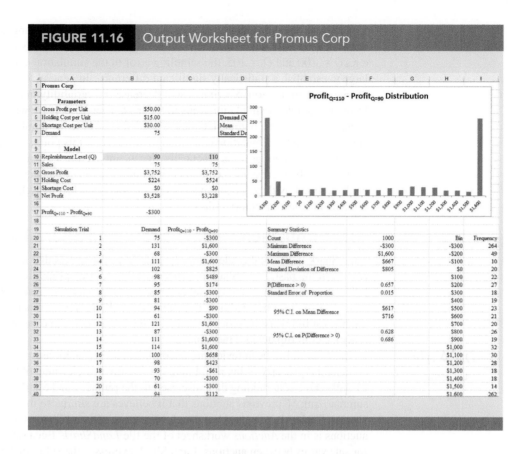

FIGURE 11.16	Output Worksheet for Promus Corp

Cell F29 $=F23 - CONFIDENCE.T(0.05, F24, F20)$
Cell F30 $=F23 + CONFIDENCE.T(0.05, F24, F20)$
Cell F32 $=F26 - NORM.S.INV(0.975)*F27$
Cell F33 $=F26 + NORM.S.INV(0.975)*F27$

Similar to the analysis for the Sanotronics problem in Section 11.1, cells H21:I40 are used to generate the frequency distribution of the returns generated from the set of 1,000 trials. Cells H21:H40 contain the upper limits of the bins for the frequency distribution and the cell range I21:I40 is populated using the FREQUENCY function.

Figure 11.16 shows that based on this set of 1,000 simulation trials, there is a mean difference of $667 between the net profit generated by a replenishment level of 110 versus a replenishment level of 90. Because the 95% confidence interval on this mean difference, [$617, $716], does not contain zero, we are assured that this difference is statistically significant. Furthermore, there is an estimated probability of 0.657 that a replenishment level of 110 will generate a larger monthly profit than a replenishment level of 90.

*To obtain a static set of values over the 1,000 simulation trials, replace the dynamic data table by selecting the range A20:C1019, **Copy** and then **Paste Values** in the same range.*

We note that a different set of 1,000 simulation trials can be generated by pressing the **F9** key, and this will result in different values of the summary statistics because these will now be based on a different sample. By pressing the **F9** key and observing how much the output statistics vary, the analyst can gauge how much sampling error exists in the output statistics. Furthermore, the 95% confidence interval on the mean difference and the 95% confidence interval on the P(Difference > 0) reflect the degree of the sampling error. Wider confidence intervals reflect more uncertainty in the accuracy of the sample mean and sample proportion. If we would press the **F9** key 100 times to create 100 different samples of 1,000 trials, we would expect 95 of the corresponding 100 confidence intervals on the mean difference to contain the true mean difference in the net profit for these two replenishment levels. Similarly, we would expect 95 of the 100 confidence intervals on the proportion of months that $Q = 110$ earns more profit than $Q = 90$ to contain the true probability that $Q = 110$ earns more than $Q = 90$ in a month.

Different pairs of replenishment levels can be compared by changing the replenishment levels in cells B10 and C10. When comparing replenishment levels that are very similar, e.g., $Q = 100$ and $Q = 105$, the sampling error in the simulation experiment may be too large to establish a statistically significant difference. In general, increasing the number of trials in a simulation experiment will decrease the variability in the summary statistics from one sample of simulation trials to the next. Therefore, if we wish to decrease the sampling error in the output statistics, we should increase the number of simulation trials and re-execute the simulation experiment. However, at this point, we must also discern if the difference in net profit is practically significant even if we can establish its statistical significance by increasing the number of simulation trials. Practical significance must be determined by the decision maker and consider such factors as how expensive it is to implement a new inventory policy.

11.3 Simulation Modeling for Land Shark Inc.

Land Shark Inc., a real estate company, purchases properties that it develops and then resells. In the past, Land Shark has successfully acquired properties via first-price sealed-bid auctions involving commercial and residential properties. In such auctions, each bidder submits a single concealed bid. The submitted bids are then compared, and the party with the highest bid wins the property and pays the bid amount. In case of a tie (a rare occurrence), a coin flip decides the winner.

DATA *file*

LandShark

Land Shark has been reviewing upcoming property auctions and has identified a commercial property of interest. Land Shark estimates the value of this property to be $1,389,000. Using bidding data disclosed to the public, Land Shark has maintained a file summarizing 56 previous auctions that it believes are similar to the upcoming property auction. Table 11.2 displays bid data for a portion of Land Shark's data. The data for all 56 auctions is in the *Auctions* worksheet of the file *LandShark*. Because the property value up for sale varies between auctions, Land Shark expresses the submitted bid amounts as fractions of the respective property's value to make the bids in different auctions comparable. These bid percentages can be converted into a bid amount (in dollars) by multiplying the bid percentage by the estimated value of the property under auction. Land Shark is considering a bid of $1,229,000 and would like to evaluate its chances of winning the upcoming auction with this bid.

TABLE 11.2	Bid Data on Commercial Property Auctions						
	Bid Amount (as a Fraction of Estimated Property Value)						
Property No.	Bid 1	Bid 2	Bid 3	Bid 4	Bid 5	Bid 6	Bid 7	Bid 8
1	0.830	0.797	0.833	0.878	0.839	0.843		
2	0.835	0.823	0.781	0.892	0.767	0.787		
3	0.763	0.862	0.814	0.895				
4	0.771	0.859	0.867	0.850	0.833			
5	0.836	0.898	0.831	0.897	0.831	0.657	0.846	
6	0.850	0.863	0.825	0.910	0.848			
7	0.890	0.820	0.874	0.877	0.818			
8	0.804	0.881	0.786	0.884	0.773	0.819	0.824	
9	0.819	0.851	0.786	0.896	0.784	0.792		
10	0.860	0.756	0.876	0.887	0.866			
11	0.880	0.834	0.831	0.871	0.857	0.759		
12	0.810	0.870						
13	0.887	0.716	0.817	0.9	0.869	0.885	0.856	0.761

Spreadsheet Model for Land Shark

To evaluate Land Shark's chances of winning the auction, we develop a simulation model for the auction. Our first step in modeling the upcoming property auction is to identify the input parameters and output measures. The next step is to develop a spreadsheet model that correctly computes the values of the output measures given static values of the input parameters. Then we prepare the spreadsheet model for simulation analysis by replacing the static values of the input parameters that Land Shark does not know with certainty with probability distributions of possible values.

The relevant input parameters for the upcoming auction are the estimated value of the property, the number of bidders competing against Land Shark, the bid amounts submitted by the competitors, and Land Shark's bid amount. Land Shark is certain about its estimate that the property is worth $1,389,000. Furthermore, Land Shark controls its bid amount and it would like to evaluate a bid amount of $1,229,000. However, Land Shark is uncertain about the number of competing bidders and the bid amounts submitted by these competitors.

The output measures in which we are interested are whether Land Shark wins the simulated auction given its specified amount and Land Shark's net return. If Land Shark wins the auction, its return is computed as the difference between the estimated value of the property and its bid amount. If Land Shark does not win the auction, its return is $0.

To understand how to construct the logic for determining whether Land Shark wins an auction and its return from the auction, let's first consider static values for the input parameters. Based on Land Shark's data on the past 56 auctions, the number of competitor bids ranges from two to eight. Therefore, there may be as many as eight different bid amounts submitted by competitors. Suppose those eight competitor bid amounts (as a percentage of the property's estimated value) are 0.887, 0.716, 0.817, 0.900, 0.869, 0.885, 0.856, and 0.761. However, it is possible that not all eight of these bid amounts will be submitted for an auction. Suppose only four competitors decide to submit bids in the auction. Then we only want to consider four of the eight bid amounts. If the bid amounts are listed in a random order (which they are in this case), we can just select the first four bid amounts and ignore the last four. In this case, the four competing bid amounts (expressed in dollars) are: $(0.887)(\$1,389,000) = \$1,232,043$; $(0.716)(\$1,389,000) = \$994,524$; $(0.817)(\$1,389,000) = \$1,134,813$; and $(0.900)(\$1,389,000) = \$1,250,100$. The largest competing bid amount is then the maximum of these four bid amounts, or $1,250,100. We compare Land Shark's bid ($1,229,000) to the largest competing bid ($1,250,100) and observe that in this scenario, Land Shark does not win the auction, so its return is $0.

In the example in the previous paragraph, we determined the largest bid from four competitors by considering only the first four competitor bids and ignoring the last four. In general, the number of competitor bids is uncertain and varies from two to eight. Therefore, we need to devise a spreadsheet model that will correctly compute the largest competing bid amount from among a varying number of bids. Figure 11.17 shows the formula view and value view of the spreadsheet implementing one way to model the problem. Cell B4 contains the estimated value of the property (Land Shark is certain of this value) and cell B5 contains a value for the number of bidders (Land Shark is uncertain of this value). Cell range B8:B15 contains the values of eight possible competing bids expressed as fractions of the property's estimated value (Land Shark is uncertain of these values). Cells C8 through C15 express the respective bid fractions in cells B8 through B15 as dollar amounts using the IF function to determine if the bid should be considered or effectively eliminated. If a bid index (from the range A8:A15) exceeds the realized number of bidders in cell B5, the corresponding bid amount in the cell range C8:C15 is set to $0, otherwise the bid amount is computed. For example, consider the formula in cell C8, =IF(A8>$B$5, 0, B8*$B$4). This formula compares the bid index in cell A8 to the number of bidders in cell B5, and if the bid index exceeds the number of bidders, a bid amount of $0 is calculated so that the bid is not considered. Otherwise, the bid amount is calculated by multiplying the bid fraction by the estimated value of the property.

The IF function is discussed in more detail in Chapter 10. Absolute cell references are discussed in Appendix A.

Cell B18 contains Land Shark's bid amount. Cell B19 computes the largest competing bid by taking the maximum value over the range C8:C15. Land Shark tracks two output measures: whether it wins the auction and the return from the auction. By comparing

FIGURE 11.17 Base Spreadsheet Model for Land Shark

	A	B	C
1	**Land Shark**		
2			
3	**Parameters**		
4	Estimated Value	1389000	
5	Number of Bidders	4	
6			
7	Bid Index	Bid Fraction	Bid Amount
8	1	0.887	=IF(A8>$B$5,0,B8*$B$4)
9	2	0.716	=IF(A9>$B$5,0,B9*$B$4)
10	3	0.818	=IF(A10>$B$5,0,B10*$B$4)
11	4	0.9	=IF(A11>$B$5,0,B11*$B$4)
12	5	0.869	=IF(A12>$B$5,0,B12*$B$4)
13	6	0.885	=IF(A13>$B$5,0,B13*$B$4)
14	7	0.856	=IF(A14>$B$5,0,B14*$B$4)
15	8	0.761	=IF(A15>$B$5,0,B15*$B$4)
16			
17	**Model**		
18	Land Shark Bid Amount	1229000	
19	Largest Competitor Bid	=MAX(C8:C15)	
20	Land Shark Win Auction?	=IF(B18>B19,1,0)	
21	Land Shark Return	=B20*(B4-B18)	

	A	B	C
1	**Land Shark**		
2			
3	**Parameters**		
4	Estimated Value	$1,389,000	
5	Number of Bidders	4	
6			
7	Bid Index	Bid Fraction	Bid Amount
8	1	0.887	$1,232,043
9	2	0.716	$994,524
10	3	0.818	$1,134,813
11	4	0.900	$1,250,100
12	5	0.869	$0
13	6	0.885	$0
14	7	0.856	$0
15	8	0.761	$0
16			
17	**Model**		
18	Land Shark Bid Amount	$1,229,000	
19	Largest Competitor Bid	$1,250,100	
20	Land Shark Win Auction?	0	
21	Land Shark Return	$0	

Land Shark's bid amount in cell B18 to the largest competitor bid in cell B19, the logic =IF(B18>B19,1,0) in cell B20 returns a value of 1 if Land Shark wins the auction and a value of 0 if Land Shark loses the auction. The value of 1 or 0 in Cell B20 to denote a Land Shark win or loss allows the simulation model to easily count the number of times Land Shark wins the auction over a set of simulation trials. The formula in cell B21, =B20*(B4−B18), computes the return from the auction; if Land Shark wins the auction, the return is equal to the estimated value minus the bid amount, otherwise the return is zero because the value of cell B20 will be zero.

Generating Values for Land Shark's Random Variables

In the Land Shark simulation model constructed in Figure 11.17, the uncertain quantities are the number of competing bidders and how much the competitors will bid (as a fraction of the property's estimated value). In this section, we discuss how to specify probability distributions for these uncertain quantities, or random variables.

Chapter 2 discusses frequency distributions in more detail.

First, consider the number of bidders. Figure 11.18 contains the frequency distribution of the number of bidders for the 56 previous auctions that Land Shark has tracked in the *Auctions* worksheet of the file *LandShark*. The number of bidders has ranged from two to eight over the past 56 auctions. Unless Land Shark has reason to believe that there may be fewer than two bids on an upcoming auction, it is probably safe to assume that there will be a minimum of two competing bids. There has not been an auction with more than eight bidders, so eight is a reasonable assumption for the maximum number of competing bids unless Land Shark's experience with the local real estate market suggests that more than eight competing bids is possible.

Figure 11.18 suggests that the relative likelihood of different values for the number of bidders appears to be equal. Thus, Land Shark decides to model the number of bidders to be 2, 3, 4, 5, 6, 7, or 8 with equal probability. In this case, the integer uniform distribution is the appropriate choice, as it is characterized by a series of equally likely consecutive integers over a specified range.

The integer uniform distribution is a special case of the discrete uniform distribution discussed in Chapter 4. In both distributions, all values are equally likely. However, in the integer uniform distribution, the possible values are consecutive integers over the defined range. In a general discrete uniform distribution, the possible values do not have to be consecutive integers (or even integers), but rather just a set of distinct, discrete values.

To generate a value for a random variable characterized by an integer uniform distribution, the following Excel formula is used:

Value of integer uniform variable
=RANDBETWEEN(lower integer value, upper integer value)   **(11.8)**

For Land Shark, the lower integer value is 2 and the upper integer value is 8. Applying equation (11.8), we enter the formula =*RANDBETWEEN(2, 8)* into cell B5.

Each competitor's bid fraction is also a random variable. From the past 56 auctions, there has been a total of 280 observations of how competitors have bid (as a fraction of the respective property's estimated value). These 280 bid amounts from the *Auctions* worksheet have been relisted in the *BidList* worksheet in the file *LandShark*. Figure 11.19 contains a histogram of the bid amount data grouped into 13 bins. We see that the bid amount distribution is negatively skewed, and that bid amounts most commonly occur in the range (0.875, 0.90).

There are several ways we could use the 280 bid amount observations as a basis for simulating bid amount values in our spreadsheet model. One way would be to use Figure 11.19 as the basis for choosing a discrete probability distribution to represent this uncertain value (in the same manner we generated values for direct labor cost per unit in the Sanotronics problem). However, such a discrete probability distribution would result in a loss of information, as only

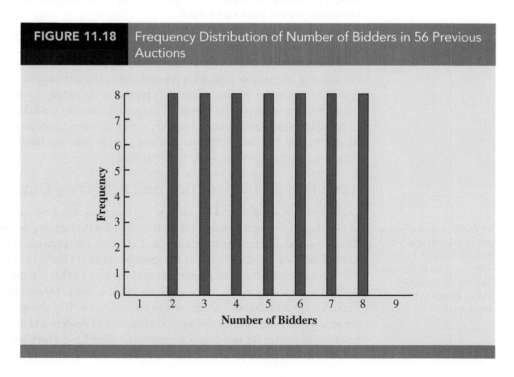

FIGURE 11.18 Frequency Distribution of Number of Bidders in 56 Previous Auctions

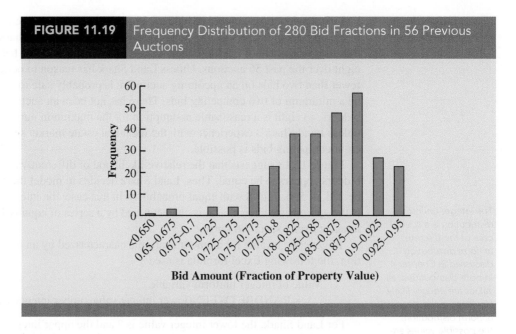

FIGURE 11.19   Frequency Distribution of 280 Bid Fractions in 56 Previous Auctions

bid percentages of, say, 0.65, 0.675, 0.70, 0.725, 0.75, 0.775, 0.80, 0.825, 0.85, 0.875, 0.90, 0.925, and 0.95 would be possible. From the 280 observations, we see that bid percentages take on many values between the minimum of 0.645 and the maximum of 0.947. Therefore, assuming a discrete probability distribution may not be preferred for generating bid percentage values.

Two other primary alternatives are to either directly sample from the 280 observations to generate values for simulation trials, or to fit a continuous probability distribution based on the 280 observations. We will describe the approach of directly sampling from the data and discuss distribution fitting later in this section.

Directly sampling from data is a good modeling choice if Land Shark believes that these 280 bid fraction values are an accurate representation of the distribution of future bids. We will simulate the bids for the upcoming auction by randomly selecting a value from one of these 280 bid fraction values. To sample a value for a bid fraction from the set of 280 possible values, we use the Excel formula:

$$=\text{VLOOKUP(RANDBETWEEN(1, 280), BidList!}\$A\$2:\$B\$281, 2, \text{FALSE})$$

When sampling values directly from sample data, we note that only values that exist in the data will be possible values for a simulation trial. Resampling empirical data is a good approach only when the data adequately represent the range of possible values and the distribution of values across this range. If the sample data do not adequately describe the set of possible values for a random variable, it may be more appropriate to identify a probability distribution that closely fits the data and sample from the fitted probability distribution rather than just sampling directly from the data.

Executing Simulation Trials and Analyzing Output

Only the output measures are strictly necessary to include table of 1,000 simulation trials, but we include the uncertain inputs as well for exposition.

Each trial in the simulation of the auction involves randomly generating values for the number of bidders and the eight possible bid fractions and then computing whether Land Shark wins the auction and its return from the auction. To prepare the spreadsheet for the execution of 1,000 simulation trials, we structure the spreadsheet as in Figure 11.20. The cell range from A24 through L1024 has been prepared to hold the set of 1,000 simulation trials. Cell range A25:A1024 numbers the rows that will correspond to the 1,000 simulation trials (rows 43 through 1023 are hidden). The first row of the table (cells B25 through L25) contains Excel formulas referencing the random variables (number of bidders and the eight possible bid amounts) as well as the two output measures (whether Land Shark wins the auction and its return from the auction).

FIGURE 11.20   Setting Up Land Shark Spreadsheet for 1,000 Simulation Trials

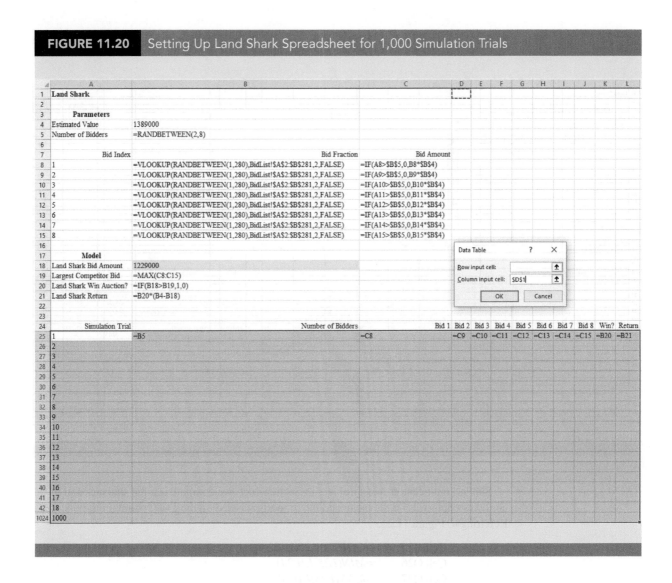

To populate the table of simulation trials in the *Model* worksheet, we execute the following steps:

Step 1. Select cell range A25:L1024

Step 2. Click the **Data** tab in the Ribbon

Step 3. Click **What-If Analysis** in the **Forecast** group and select **Data Table…**

Step 4. When the **Data Table** dialog box appears, leave the **Row input cell:** box blank and enter any empty cell in the spreadsheet (e.g., *D1*) into the **Column input cell:** box

Step 5. Click **OK**

Figure 11.21 shows the results of a set of 1,000 simulation trials. After executing the simulation with the Data Table, each row of this table corresponds to a distinct simulation trial consisting of different values of the random variables. We see that Land Shark does not win the simulated auction corresponding to Trial 1 because one of the three competing bids (Bid 1 = \$1,258,434) is larger than its bid of \$1,229,000. In Trial 4, we observe that Land Shark wins the auction because its bid of \$1,229,000 is larger than the two competing bids of \$1,091,754 and \$1,132,035.

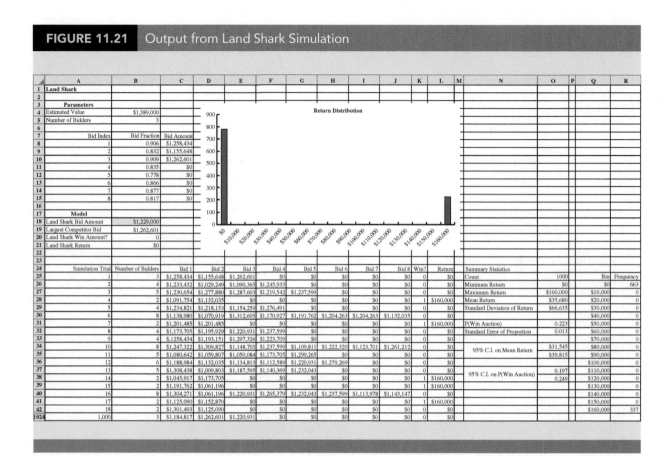

FIGURE 11.21   Output from Land Shark Simulation

Similar to the Sanotronics problem in Section 14.1, we compute sample statistics and 95% confidence intervals on the mean and the proportion based on the 1,000 simulation trials. Referring to Figure 11.21,

Cell O25	=COUNT(L25:L1024)
Cell O26	=MIN(L25:L1024)
Cell O27	=MAX(L25:L1024)
Cell O28	=AVERAGE(L25:L1024)
Cell O29	=STDEV.S(L25:L1024)
Cell O31	=AVERAGE(K25:K1024)
Cell O32	=SQRT(O31*(1−O31)/O25)
Cell O34	=O28 − CONFIDENCE.T(0.05,O29,O25)
Cell O35	=O28 + CONFIDENCE.T(0.05,O29,O25)
Cell O34	=O31 − NORM.S.INV(0.975)*O32
Cell O35	=O31 + NORM.S.INV(0.975)*O32

MODEL *file*

LandSharkResample

Again similar to our analysis for the Sanotronics problem, we compute the frequency distribution of the returns generated from the set of 1,000 trials in cells Q26:R42. Cells Q26:Q42 contain the upper limits of the bins for the frequency distribution and the cell range R26:R42 is populated by the FREQUENCY function.

Figure 11.21 shows that based on this set of 1,000 simulation trials, Land Shark's estimated mean return is $35,680 and the estimated probability that it wins the auction is 0.223. In this simulation experiment, when Land Shark bids $1,229,000, there are only two outcomes: either it wins the auction and earns a return of $160,000 or it loses the auction and earns a return of $0. Out of the 1,000 simulated auctions, the frequency table shows that Land Shark does not win the auction ($0 return) in 777 auctions and wins the auction (earns $160,000) in 223 auctions.

We note that a different set of 1,000 simulation trials can be generated by pressing the **F9** key, and this will result in different values of the summary statistics because these will now be based on a different sample. By pressing the **F9** key and observing how much the output statistics vary, the analyst can gauge how much sampling error exists in the output statistics. Furthermore, the 95% confidence interval on the mean return and the 95% confidence interval on the probability of winning the auction reflect the degree of the sampling error. Wider confidence intervals reflect more uncertainty in the accuracy of the sample mean and sample proportion. If we would press the F9 key 100 times to create 100 different samples of 1,000 trials, we would expect 95 of the corresponding 100 confidence intervals on the mean return to contain Land Shark's true mean return from the auction. Similarly, we would expect 95 of the 100 confidence intervals on the proportion of auction trials that Land Shark wins to contain the true probability of Land Shark winning the auction.

In general, increasing the number of trials in a simulation experiment will decrease the variability in the summary statistics from one sample of simulation trials to the next. Therefore, if we wish to decrease the sampling error in the output statistics, we should increase the number of simulation trials and re-execute the simulation experiment.

*When you run your LandShark simulation, the values you see will be different. This is to be expected with simulation models. Each time the simulation is executed, the values may vary because different random numbers are being used. If a set of static values is desired, you can replace the dynamic data table with a static set of trial values using the Excel functionality to **Copy** and **Paste Values**.*

Generating Bid Amounts with Fitted Distributions

In the Land Shark model represented in Figure 11.21, we generated the competing bid fractions by directly sampling from the 280 bids submitted in 56 previous auctions. The advantage of this approach is that it is relatively easy to execute, but if the 280 observations do not adequately represent the possible bid fractions for the upcoming auction, then our model may not accurately represent the future auction and Land Shark's assessment of its bid amount.

In this section, we examine another approach for using the 280 bid observations to generate bid fraction values in a simulation model. Specifically, we will use the 280 bid observations to fit a continuous probability distribution to a histogram based on the data. The advantage of fitting a distribution is that it will allow us to generate values that may not exist in the list of the original 280 observations, but still share characteristics with these data. The disadvantage of fitting a distribution is that the process is a bit more involved and requires more familiarity with probability distributions.

Specialized simulation software such as @RISK, Crystal Ball, and Analytic Solver provide automated distribution fitting functionality.

Our goal is to identify a continuous probability distribution that fits the histogram of the bid fraction data shown in Figure 11.19. Appendix 11.1 contains a description of several continuous and discrete probability distributions. For the bid fraction data, we seek a *continuous* probability distribution due to the large number of possible values for a submitted bid fraction. Furthermore, we know that the range of bid fractions has a lower bound of zero and upper bound of one; a competitor cannot bid a negative fraction and a competitor will never bid more than the property's estimated value. There are many possible continuous probability distributions that have both lower and upper bounds, but some of the most common are the uniform, triangular, and beta distributions. We will consider each of these.

Chapter 4 discusses probability distributions in more detail.

The uniform distribution assumes each value between a specified minimum value and minimum value is *equally likely*, which does not appear to be the case for bid fractions as illustrated by Figure 11.19. So, the uniform distribution does not appear to be a good choice to generate bid fraction values. Nonetheless, if we wanted to use a uniform distribution to generate bid fractions in our simulation model we only need to determine the minimum and maximum values. For these data, the minimum is 0.645 and the maximum is 0.947, but, theoretically, bid fractions could extend from 0.000 to 1.000. Setting the minimum and maximum of the distribution is a modeling choice that will affect how low and high our competitors will bid in the simulated auctions. If Land Shark believes that the observed values of 0.645 and 0.947 are likely to be the lowest and highest bid amounts placed by competitors, then these 0.645 and 0.947 should be used as the lower and upper limits of a uniform distribution. To generate a value from a continuous uniform distribution in Excel, we can use equation (11.3) as we did in the Sanotronics problem.

The triangular distribution is a unimodal distribution characterized by three input parameters: minimum (*a*), mode (*m*), and maximum (*b*). While the shape of the bid fraction distribution does not appear exactly triangular, it could be worthwhile option to explore. To determine the mode (most likely) value of the triangular distribution, we note that computing the mode of the effectively continuous bid fraction data is a bit dubious as no single value occurs frequently. Therefore, we base the mode on the histogram in Figure 11.19. We observe the most frequent bin is [0.875, 0.90) and use the midpoint of this bin, 0.8875, as the mode of the triangular distribution. Figure 11.22 provides a visualization of triangular distribution's fit to the bid fraction data. The triangle-shaped curve represents the theoretical continuous distribution from which values from the triangle distribution are generated. The blue columns correspond to one possible sample of 280 values generated from the triangular distribution. Comparing the blue curve (and blue columns) to the red columns representing the observed bid fractions, we observe that this triangular distribution appears to generate more bid fractions in the 0.645 to 0.80 range and fewer bid fractions in the 0.925 to 0.95 range. This is something to keep in mind in our simulation experiments with this distribution in the Land Shark model.

To generate a value for a random variable characterized by a triangular distribution, the following Excel formula is used:

value of triangular random variable

$$=IF(random < (m-a)/(b-a), a + SQRT((b-a)*(m-a)*random),$$
$$b - SQRT((b-a)*(b-m)*(1-random))) \tag{11.9}$$

In equation (11.9), *random* refers to a single, separate cell containing the Excel function =RAND(); a single, separate cell is necessary to make sure the same random value is used everywhere *random* appears in equation (11.9). Applying equation (11.9) for the triangular distribution fit to the 280 bid observations yields:

$$\text{bid fraction} = IF(random < (0.8875 - 0.645)/(0.947 - 0.645), 0.645 +$$
$$SQRT((0.947 - .645)*(0.8875 - 0.645)*random), 0.947 -$$
$$SQRT((0.947 - 0.645)*(0.947 - 0.8875)*(1 - random))) \tag{11.10}$$

Figure 11.23 displays the formula view of the Land Shark simulation model implementing equation (11.10) to generate bid fraction values. From Figure 11.24, we see that modeling bid fraction values with a triangular distribution results in a 95% confidence interval of $49,224 to $58,616 on the mean return and a 95% confidence interval of 0.308 to 0.366 on the probability of winning the auction. These results are significantly more optimistic for Land Shark than the results from Figure 11.21 based on generating bid fraction values by directly sampling the 280 bid observations. This can be explained by the difference in the fitted triangular distribution and observed bid fraction data. Compared to the observed bid fraction data, Figure 11.22 shows that this triangular distribution appears more likely to

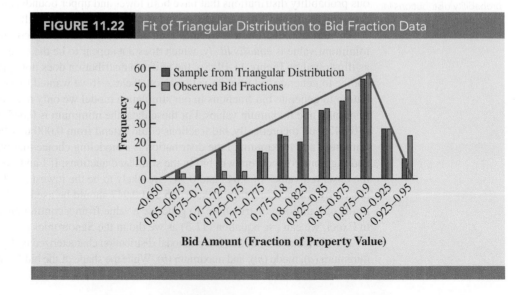

FIGURE 11.22   Fit of Triangular Distribution to Bid Fraction Data

FIGURE 11.23 Land Shark Formula Worksheet for Bid Fraction Value Generated from Triangular Distribution

	A	B	C	D	E	F	G	H
1	Land Shark							
2								
3	Parameters							
4	Estimated Value	1389000						
5	Number of Bidders	=RANDBETWEEN(2, 8)						
6								
7	Bid Index		Bid Fraction		Bid Amount	Bid % Parameters (Triangular)		Random #
8	1	=IF(H8<$F$13/$F$12,$F$8+SQRT($F$12*$F$13*H8),$F$9-SQRT($F$12*$F$14*(1-H8)))		=IF(A8>$B$5,0,B8*$B$4)	Minimum	0.645		=RAND()
9	2	=IF(H9<$F$13/$F$12,$F$8+SQRT($F$12*$F$13*H9),$F$9-SQRT($F$12*$F$14*(1-H9)))		=IF(A9>$B$5,0,B9*$B$4)	Maximum	0.9647		=RAND()
10	3	=IF(H10<$F$13/$F$12,$F$8+SQRT($F$12*$F$13*H10),$F$9-SQRT($F$12*$F$14*(1-H10)))		=IF(A10>$B$5,0,B10*$B$4)	Mode	=(0.9+0.875)/2		=RAND()
11	4	=IF(H11<$F$13/$F$12,$F$8+SQRT($F$12*$F$13*H11),$F$9-SQRT($F$12*$F$14*(1-H11)))		=IF(A11>$B$5,0,B11*$B$4)				=RAND()
12	5	=IF(H12<$F$13/$F$12,$F$8+SQRT($F$12*$F$13*H12),$F$9-SQRT($F$12*$F$14*(1-H12)))		=IF(A12>$B$5,0,B12*$B$4)	Max - Min	=F9-F8		=RAND()
13	6	=IF(H13<$F$13/$F$12,$F$8+SQRT($F$12*$F$13*H13),$F$9-SQRT($F$12*$F$14*(1-H13)))		=IF(A13>$B$5,0,B13*$B$4)	Mode - Min	=F10-F8		=RAND()
14	7	=IF(H14<$F$13/$F$12,$F$8+SQRT($F$12*$F$13*H14),$F$9-SQRT($F$12*$F$14*(1-H14)))		=IF(A14>$B$5,0,B14*$B$4)	Max - Mode	=F9-F10		=RAND()
15	8	=IF(H15<$F$13/$F$12,$F$8+SQRT($F$12*$F$13*H15),$F$9-SQRT($F$12*$F$14*(1-H15)))		=IF(A15>$B$5,0,B15*$B$4)				=RAND()
16								
17	Model							
18	Land Shark Bid Amount	1229000						
19	Largest Competitor Bid	=MAX(C8:C15)						
20	Land Shark Win Amount?	=IF(B18>B19,1,0)						
21	Land Shark Return	=B20*(B4-B18)						

FIGURE 11.24 Output from Land Shark Simulation Using Triangular Distribution to Generate Bid Fraction Values

	A	B	C	D	E	F	G	H	I	J	K	L	M	N	O	P	Q	R
1	Land Shark																	
2																		
3	Parameters																	
4	Estimated Value	$1,389,000																
5	Number of Bidders	5																
6																		
7	Bid Index	Bid Fraction	Bid Amount		Bid % Parameters (Triangular)		Random #											
8	1	0.849	$1,179,032		Minimum	0.645	0.56733423											
9	2	0.896	$1,244,931		Maximum	0.947	0.8568275											
10	3	0.817	$1,135,482		Mode	0.888	0.4062269											
11	4	0.803	$1,115,054				0.33990361											
12	5	0.824	$1,144,816		Max - Min	0.302	0.43849575											
13	6	0.753	$0		Mode - Min	0.243	0.16055478											
14	7	0.892	$0		Max - Mode	0.060	0.83394223											
15	8	0.871	$0				0.69890749											
16																		
17	Model																	
18	Land Shark Bid Amount	$1,229,000																
19	Largest Competitor Bid	$1,244,931																
20	Land Shark Win Auction?	0																
21	Land Shark Return	$0																
22																		
23																		
24	Simulation Trial	Number of Bidders	Bid 1	Bid 2	Bid 3	Bid 4	Bid 5	Bid 6	Bid 7	Bid 8	Win?	Return	Summary Statistics					
25	1	5	$1,179,032	$1,244,931	$1,135,482	$1,115,054	$1,144,816			$0	0	$0	Count		1000		Bin	Frequency
26	2	8	$1,049,329	$1,161,342	$1,162,569	$1,105,262	$1,081,620	$954,226	$1,194,310	$1,281,650	0	$0	Minimum Return		$0		$0	663
27	3	7	$1,150,016	$1,031,444	$1,220,648	$1,158,638	$1,213,327	$1,142,506	$1,271,565	$0	0	$0	Maximum Return		$160,000		$10,000	0
28	4	3	$1,235,775	$998,364	$1,143,782	$0	$0	$0	$0	$0	0	$0	Mean Return		$53,920		$20,000	0
29	5	4	$1,135,728	$1,090,066	$1,042,373	$940,721	$0	$0	$0	$0	1	$160,000	Standard Deviation of Return		$75,667		$30,000	0
30	6	7	$1,105,589	$1,232,407	$1,012,995	$1,090,354	$1,221,010	$1,215,359	$983,485	$0	0	$0					$40,000	0
31	7	2	$1,226,322	$1,258,551	$0	$0	$0	$0	$0	$0	0	$0	P(Win Auction)		0.337		$50,000	0
32	8	6	$1,227,183	$1,167,339	$1,222,031	$1,193,726	$1,040,529	$1,223,566	$0	$0	1	$160,000	Standard Error of Proportion		0.015		$60,000	0
33	9	2	$920,161	$1,170,014	$0	$0	$0	$0	$0	$0	1	$160,000					$70,000	0
34	10	4	$1,133,338	$1,205,649	$1,214,078	$1,199,552	$0	$0	$0	$0	1	$160,000	95% C.I. on Mean Return		$49,224		$80,000	0
35	11	2	$1,229,704	$1,075,628	$0	$0	$0	$0	$0	$0	0	$0			$58,616		$90,000	0
36	12	3	$998,470	$1,300,949	$1,081,719	$0	$0	$0	$0	$0	0	$0					$100,000	0
37	13	4	$1,070,679	$1,085,253	$1,108,607	$1,078,855	$0	$0	$0	$0	1	$160,000	95% C.I. on P(Win Auction)		0.308		$110,000	0
38	14	7	$1,072,458	$1,025,384	$1,210,295	$1,157,636	$1,113,508	$1,036,268	$1,126,155	$0	1	$160,000			0.366		$120,000	0
39	15	2	$1,044,975	$1,118,650	$0	$0	$0	$0	$0	$0	1	$160,000					$130,000	0
40	16	4	$1,070,444	$1,120,178	$1,054,328	$1,241,885	$0	$0	$0	$0	0	$0					$140,000	0
41	17	6	$958,575	$1,219,915	$1,143,191	$995,025	$1,241,428	$1,117,604	$0	$0	0	$0					$150,000	0
42	18	7	$1,060,230	$1,223,679	$1,111,527	$1,248,980	$1,121,966	$1,169,762	$1,223,637	$0	0	$0					$160,000	337
1024	1,000	2	$1,257,241	$1,141,695	$0	$0	$0	$0	$0	$0	0	$0						

generate smaller competing bid fractions than directly sampling from the 280 observed bid fractions.

The final alternative for modeling the bid fraction values would be to fit a beta distribution to the 280 bid observations. The beta distribution is a very flexible distribution characterized by four input parameters: alpha (α), beta (β), minimum (*A*), and maximum (*B*). A common method for estimating the α and β values in a beta distribution uses the sample mean ($\overline{x}$) and sample standard deviation (s) as shown in equations (11.11) and (11.12) below.[6]

$$\alpha = \left(\frac{\overline{x} - A}{B - A}\right)\left(\frac{\left(\frac{\overline{x} - A}{B - A}\right)\left(1 - \left(\frac{\overline{x} - A}{B - A}\right)\right)}{\frac{s^2}{(B - A)^2}} - 1\right) \tag{11.11}$$

$$\beta = \alpha \times \left(\frac{\left(1 - \left(\frac{\overline{x} - A}{B - A}\right)\right)}{\left(\frac{\overline{x} - A}{B - A}\right)}\right) \tag{11.12}$$

For the 280 bid observations, the sample mean is $\overline{x} = 0.851$, the sample standard deviation is $s = 0.056$, the minimum value is 0.645, and the maximum value is 0.947. Substituting these values first into equation (11.11) and then into equation (11.12) provides:

$$\alpha = \left(\frac{0.851 - 0.645}{0.947 - 0.645}\right)\left(\frac{\frac{0.851 - 0.645}{0.947 - 0.645}\left(1 - \left(\frac{0.851 - 0.645}{0.947 - 0.645}\right)\right)}{\frac{0.056^2}{(0.947 - 0.645)^2}} - 1\right) = 3.546$$

$$\beta = 3.546 \times \left(\frac{\left(1 - \left(\frac{0.851 - 0.645}{0.947 - 0.645}\right)\right)}{\left(\frac{0.851 - 0.645}{0.947 - 0.645}\right)}\right) = 1.655$$

To generate a value for a random variable characterized by a beta distribution, the following Excel formula is used:

value of beta random variable

$$=\text{BETA.INV}(\text{RAND}(), \alpha, \beta, A, B) \tag{11.13}$$

For the Land Shark problem, substituting the values of the parameters results in:

$$\text{bid fraction} = \text{BETA.INV}(\text{RAND}(), 3.546, 1.655, 0.645, 0.947) \tag{11.14}$$

Figure 11.25 provides a visualization of the beta distribution's fit to the bid fraction data. The blue curve represents the theoretical continuous distribution from which values from the beta distribution are generated. The blue columns correspond to one possible sample of 280 values generated from the beta distribution. Comparing the blue curve (and blue columns) to the red columns representing the observed bid fractions, we observe that this beta distribution appears to reasonably fit the observed bid fractions.

Figure 11.26 displays the formula view of the Land Shark simulation model implementing equation (11.14) to generate bid fraction values. From Figure 11.27, we see that modeling bid fraction values with a beta distribution results in a 95% confidence interval of $26,199 to $33,961 on the mean return and a 95% confidence interval of 0.164 to 0.212 on the probability of winning the auction. These results are less optimistic than the results from Figure 11.21 based on generating bid fraction values by directly sampling the 280 bid observations.

While it is impossible to discern what is the "best" way to model the uncertain bid fraction values, the exercise of testing different distributions generates insight. One benefit of using a good-fitting theoretical distribution (such as the beta distribution in this case) to generate bid fraction values is that it generates thousands of unique bid fractions.

---

[6]Estimating the parameters using equations (11.11) and (11.12) is based on a statistical method known as the "method of moments." The specifics of this method are beyond the scope of this textbook.

FIGURE 11.25   Fit of Beta Distribution to Bid Fraction Data

FIGURE 11.26   Land Shark Formula Worksheet for Bid Fraction Value Generated from Beta Distribution

	A	B	C	D	E	F
1	**Land Shark**					
2						
3	**Parameters**					
4	Estimated Value	1389000				
5	Number of Bidders	=RANDBETWEEN(2,8)				
6						
7	Bid Index	Bid Fraction	Bid Amount		Bid % Parameters (Beta)	
8	1	=BETA.INV(RAND(),$F$10,$F$11,$F$8,$F$9)	=IF(A8>$B$5,0,B8*$B$4)		Minimum	0.645
9	2	=BETA.INV(RAND(),$F$10,$F$11,$F$8,$F$9)	=IF(A9>$B$5,0,B9*$B$4)		Maximum	0.947
10	3	=BETA.INV(RAND(),$F$10,$F$11,$F$8,$F$9)	=IF(A10>$B$5,0,B10*$B$4)		Alpha	3.54618101391835
11	4	=BETA.INV(RAND(),$F$10,$F$11,$F$8,$F$9)	=IF(A11>$B$5,0,B11*$B$4)		Beta	1.6546630559593
12	5	=BETA.INV(RAND(),$F$10,$F$11,$F$8,$F$9)	=IF(A12>$B$5,0,B12*$B$4)			
13	6	=BETA.INV(RAND(),$F$10,$F$11,$F$8,$F$9)	=IF(A13>$B$5,0,B13*$B$4)			
14	7	=BETA.INV(RAND(),$F$10,$F$11,$F$8,$F$9)	=IF(A14>$B$5,0,B14*$B$4)			
15	8	=BETA.INV(RAND(),$F$10,$F$11,$F$8,$F$9)	=IF(A15>$B$5,0,B15*$B$4)			
16						
17	**Model**					
18	Land Shark Bid Amount	1229000				
19	Largest Competitor Bid	=MAX(C8:C15)				
20	Land Shark Win Auction?	=IF(B18>B19,1,0)				
21	Land Shark Return	=B20*(B4-B18)				

Conversely, sampling directly from the observed data means that the 280 values get re-used multiple times.

In general, the appropriate way to generate values for the random variables in a Monte Carlo simulation may be difficult to determine. For a well-defined situation, like rolling a fair die, it may be clear how to generate the value of the random variable (the outcome of a dice roll). In other situations, we may not know exactly how to model the uncertainty. In these situations, it is recommended that we examine any sample data available to us. The sample data can then be used by sampling directly or we can compare the sample data to common probability distributions (such as uniform, normal, triangular, and beta distributions) to determine if we can approximate the distribution of the data with an existing probability distribution.

FIGURE 11.27   Output from Land Shark Simulation Using Beta Distribution for Bid Fraction Values

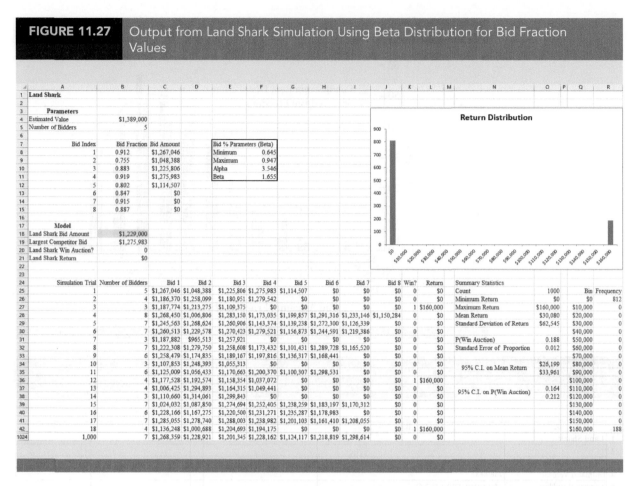

Land Shark

Parameters

Estimated Value	$1,389,000
Number of Bidders	5

Bid Index	Bid Fraction	Bid Amount		Bid % Parameters (Beta)	
1	0.912	$1,267,046		Minimum	0.645
2	0.755	$1,048,388		Maximum	0.947
3	0.883	$1,225,806		Alpha	3.546
4	0.919	$1,275,983		Beta	1.655
5	0.802	$1,114,507			
6	0.847	$0			
7	0.915	$0			
8	0.887	$0			

Model

Land Shark Bid Amount	$1,229,000
Largest Competitor Bid	$1,275,983
Land Shark Win Auction?	0
Land Shark Return	$0

Simulation Trial	Number of Bidders	Bid 1	Bid 2	Bid 3	Bid 4	Bid 5	Bid 6	Bid 7	Bid 8	Win?	Return
1	5	$1,267,046	$1,048,388	$1,225,806	$1,275,983	$1,114,507	$0	$0	$0	0	$0
2	4	$1,186,370	$1,258,099	$1,180,951	$1,279,542	$0	$0	$0	$0	0	$0
3	3	$1,187,774	$1,213,275	$1,109,375	$0	$0	$0	$0	$0	1	$160,000
4	8	$1,268,450	$1,006,806	$1,283,150	$1,173,035	$1,199,857	$1,291,316	$1,233,146	$1,150,284	0	$0
5	7	$1,245,563	$1,268,624	$1,260,906	$1,143,374	$1,139,238	$1,272,300	$1,126,339	$0	0	$0
6	7	$1,260,513	$1,229,578	$1,270,423	$1,279,521	$1,156,873	$1,244,591	$1,219,386	$0	0	$0
7	3	$1,187,882	$965,513	$1,257,921	$0	$0	$0	$0	$0	0	$0
8	7	$1,222,308	$1,279,750	$1,258,608	$1,173,432	$1,101,431	$1,289,728	$1,165,520	$0	0	$0
9	6	$1,258,479	$1,174,835	$1,189,167	$1,197,816	$1,136,317	$1,168,441	$0	$0	0	$0
10	3	$1,107,853	$1,248,393	$1,055,313	$0	$0	$0	$0	$0	0	$0
11	6	$1,125,009	$1,056,433	$1,170,663	$1,200,370	$1,100,307	$1,298,531	$0	$0	0	$0
12	4	$1,177,528	$1,192,574	$1,158,354	$1,037,072	$0	$0	$0	$0	1	$160,000
13	8	$1,006,425	$1,294,893	$1,164,315	$1,049,441	$0	$0	$0	$0	0	$0
14	3	$1,110,660	$1,314,061	$1,299,843	$0	$0	$0	$0	$0	0	$0
15	7	$1,024,032	$1,087,850	$1,274,694	$1,252,405	$1,238,259	$1,183,197	$1,170,312	$0	0	$0
16	6	$1,228,166	$1,167,275	$1,220,500	$1,231,271	$1,235,287	$1,178,983	$0	$0	0	$0
17	7	$1,285,055	$1,278,740	$1,288,003	$1,238,982	$1,201,103	$1,161,410	$1,208,055	$0	0	$0
18	4	$1,136,248	$1,000,688	$1,204,693	$1,194,175	$0	$0	$0	$0	1	$160,000
1,000	7	$1,268,359	$1,228,921	$1,201,345	$1,228,162	$1,124,117	$1,218,819	$1,298,614	$0	0	$0

Summary Statistics			Bin	Frequency
Count	1000		$0	812
Minimum Return	$0		$10,000	0
Maximum Return	$160,000		$20,000	0
Mean Return	$30,080		$30,000	0
Standard Deviation of Return	$62,545		$40,000	0
			$50,000	0
P(Win Auction)	0.188		$60,000	0
Standard Error of Proportion	0.012		$70,000	0
			$80,000	0
95% C.I. on Mean Return	$26,199		$90,000	0
	$33,961		$100,000	0
95% C.I. on P(Win Auction)	0.164		$110,000	0
	0.212		$120,000	0
			$130,000	0
			$140,000	0
			$150,000	0
			$160,000	188

In all cases, it is important to test the implications of different modeling approaches and to understand that a simulation model is not a crystal ball that allows us to perfectly see the future, but rather it helps us to understand the impact of uncertainty on our decisions.

11.4 Simulation with Dependent Random Variables

Specialized simulation software such as @RISK, Crystal Ball, and Analytic Solver provide automated procedures to incorporate dependency between random variables.

In the examples of Sections 11.1 and 11.2, we generated values of each uncertain quantity independently of each other. In other words, we treated each uncertain quantity as an independent random variable. In this section, we consider an example in which the values of some of the uncertain quantities are dependent.

Press Teag Worldwide (PTW) manufactures all of its products in the United States, but it sells the items in three different overseas markets: the United Kingdom, New Zealand, and Japan. Each of these overseas markets generates revenue in a different currency: pound sterling in the United Kingdom, New Zealand dollars in New Zealand and yen in Japan. At the end of each 13-week quarter, PTW converts the revenue from these three overseas markets back into U.S. dollars in order to pay its expenses in the United States, exposing PTW to exchange rate risk.

Spreadsheet Model for Press Teag Worldwide

To assess the degree of PTW's exposure to quarterly fluctuations in exchange rates, we develop a simulation model. The first step is to identify the input parameters and output measures. The next step is to develop a spreadsheet model that computes the values of the output measures given value of the input parameters. Then we prepare the spreadsheet model for simulation analysis by replacing the static values of the input parameters that are uncertain with probability distributions of possible values.

The relevant input parameters are: (i) the quarterly revenue generated in each of the three foreign currencies, and (ii) the end-of-quarter exchange rates between these foreign currencies and the U.S. dollar. The output measure of interest is the total end-of-quarter revenues converted into U.S. dollars.

To model the fluctuation in the exchange rate between the pound sterling and the U.S. dollar over the next quarter, PTW expresses the number of pounds sterling (£) per U.S. dollar ($) by

(end-of-quarter £/$ rate) = (start-of-quarter £/$ rate) × (1 + % change in £/$ rate) **(11.15)**

That is, equation (11.15) computes the end-of-quarter exchange rate based on the start-of-quarter exchange rate and the percent change in the exchange rate over the quarter. Analogously, the equations computing the end-of-quarter exchange rates between New Zealand dollars (NZD) per U.S. dollar and Japanese yen (¥) per U.S. dollar are as follows:

$$\begin{aligned}\text{(end-of-quarter NZD/\$ rate)} &= \text{(start-of-quarter NZD/\$ rate)}\\ &\quad \times (1 + \% \text{ change in NZD/\$ rate})\end{aligned} \quad \textbf{(11.16)}$$

(end-of-quarter ¥/$ rate) = (start-of-quarter ¥/$ rate) × (1 + % change in ¥/$ rate) **(11.17)**

To see how one would use equations (11.15), (11.16), and (11.17), suppose that the start-of-quarter exchange rates are £0.615 per U.S. dollar, NZD 1.200 per U.S. dollar, and ¥87.10 per U.S. dollar. Further, assume that there is a 4.61 percent *increase* in the £ per $ exchange rate, a 0.27 percent *decrease* in the NZD per $ exchange rate, and a 11.23 percent increase in the ¥ per $ exchange rate. Then, we would have the following:

$$\begin{aligned}\text{(end-of-quarter £/\$ rate)} &= 0.615 \times (1 + 0.0461) = £0.6436 \text{ per \$}\\ \text{(end-of-quarter NZD/\$ rate)} &= 1.200 \times (1 + (-0.0027)) = \text{NZD } 1.1968 \text{ per \$}\\ \text{(end-of-quarter ¥/\$ rate)} &= 87.10 \times (1 + 0.1123) = ¥96.8813 \text{ per \$}\end{aligned}$$

Once the end-of-quarter exchange rates are known, the quarterly revenue in pounds sterling, New Zealand dollar, and Japanese yen can be converted into U.S. dollars as follows:

(end-of-quarter $ from £) = (quarterly revenue in £) ÷ (end-of-quarter £/$ rate) **(11.18)**

$$\begin{aligned}\text{(end-of-quarter \$ from NZD)} &= \text{(quarterly revenue in NZD)}\\ &\quad \div \text{(end-of-quarter NZD/\$ rate)}\end{aligned} \quad \textbf{(11.19)}$$

(end-of-quarter $ from ¥) = (quarterly revenue in ¥) ÷ (end-of-quarter ¥/$ rate) **(11.20)**

As an illustration of these calculations, suppose the quarterly revenues generated in pounds sterling, New Zealand dollar, and the Japanese yen are £100,000, NZD 250,000, and ¥10,000,000, respectively. Then, applying equations (11.18), (11.19), and (11.20), we compute the following:

$$\begin{aligned}\text{(end-of-quarter \$ from £)} &= £100,000 \div £0.6436 \text{ per \$} = \$155,385\\ \text{(end-of-quarter \$ from NZD)} &= \text{NZD}250,000 \div \text{NZD } 1.1968 \text{ per \$} = \$208,897\\ \text{(end-of-quarter \$ from ¥)} &= ¥10,000,000 \div ¥96.8813 \text{ per \$} = \$103,219\end{aligned}$$

The total revenue in U.S. dollars is then $155,385 + $208,897 + $103,219 = $467,502 (after rounding). Figure 11.28 shows the formula view and value view of the PTW spreadsheet model for the base scenario just presented.

MODEL *file*

QuarterlyExchange

The percent change in the exchange rate between pairs of currencies from the start to the end of a quarter is uncertain. Therefore, PTW would like to use random variables to model the percent change in the £ per $ rate, the percent change in the NZD per $ rate, and the percent change in the ¥ per $ rate.

However, PTW realizes that there are dependencies between the exchange rate fluctuations. For example, if the U.S. dollar weakens against the pound sterling, it may be more likely to also weaken against the New Zealand dollar. Therefore, the percent changes in the exchange rates should not be generated independently, but instead these values should be generated

FIGURE 11.28	Base Spreadsheet Model for Press Teag Worldwide

	A	B	C	D	E
1	**Press Teag Worldwide**				
2					
3	**Parameters**				
4	Start-of-Quarter Exchange Rate (per $)	0.6152	1.2	87.1	
5	Quarterly % Change in Exchange Rate	0.0461	–0.0027	0.1123	
6	End-of-Quarter Exchange Rate (per $)	=B4*(1+B5)	=C4*(1+C5)	=D4*(1+D5)	
7	Quarterly Revenue	100000	250000	10000000	
8					
9	**Model**				Total
10	End-of-Quarter Revenue in $	=B7/B6	=C7/C6	=D7/D6	=SUM(B10:D10)

	A	B	C	D	E
1	**Press Teag Worldwide**				
2					
3	**Parameters**				
4	Start-of-Quarter Exchange Rate (per $)	£0.615	NZD 1.200	¥87.10	
5	Quarterly % Change in Exchange Rate	4.61%	–0.27%	11.23%	
6	End-of-Quarter Exchange Rate (per $)	£0.6436	NZD 1.1968	¥96.8813	
7	Quarterly Revenue	£100,000	NZD 250,000	¥10,000,000	
8					
9	**Model**				Total
10	End-of-Quarter Revenue in $	$155,385	$208,897	$103,219	$467,502

jointly (as a related collection of values). To account for these dependencies, PTW constructed a data set on the joint percent changes between the three exchange rates for 2,000 quarter-scenarios in the *Data* worksheet of the file *QuarterlyExchange*. These data are based on historical observations as well as scenarios based on expert judgment. Figure 11.29 displays these data as three scatter plots showing the pairwise relationships between the exchange rates.

Chapter 2 also discusses the concept of correlation.

Figure 11.29 indicates that the percent changes in exchange rates are correlated. Positive percentage fluctuations of £ per $ often occur with positive percentage fluctuations of NZD per $ while negative fluctuations of £ per $ often occur with negative fluctuations of NZD per $. If these values were independent, we would expect to see no pattern in this scatter plot. However, there is a clear pattern in this scatter plot suggesting positive correlation. Therefore, we conclude that the fluctuations of £ per $ and NZD per $ are not independent, but are correlated. Similarly, percent changes in £ per $ appear to be correlated with percent changes in ¥ per $. Also, percent changes in NZD per $ appear to be correlated with percent changes in ¥ per $.

To directly sample one of the 2,000 scenarios and obtain the corresponding percent change in £ per $ rate, NZD per $ rate, and ¥ per $ rate, we use the respective Excel formulas:

$$=\text{VLOOKUP(E7, Data!\$A\$3:\$D\$2002, 2, FALSE)} \qquad \textbf{(11.21)}$$

$$=\text{VLOOKUP(E7, Data!\$A\$3:\$D\$2002, 3, FALSE)} \qquad \textbf{(11.22)}$$

$$=\text{VLOOKUP(E7, Data!\$A\$3:\$D\$2002, 4, FALSE)} \qquad \textbf{(11.23)}$$

As Figure 11.30 illustrates, in equations (11.21), (11.22), and (11.23), cell E7 contains the Excel function =RANDBETWEEN(1, 2000) which randomly generates the index of one of the 2,000 quarter scenarios. The VLOOKUP function then looks up this index in the table of quarter scenarios and returns the percent change in £ per $ rate (cell B7), the percent change in NZD per $ rate (cell C7), or the percent change in ¥ per $ rate (cell D7). Note that the third argument in the VLOOKUP function corresponds to the column in the

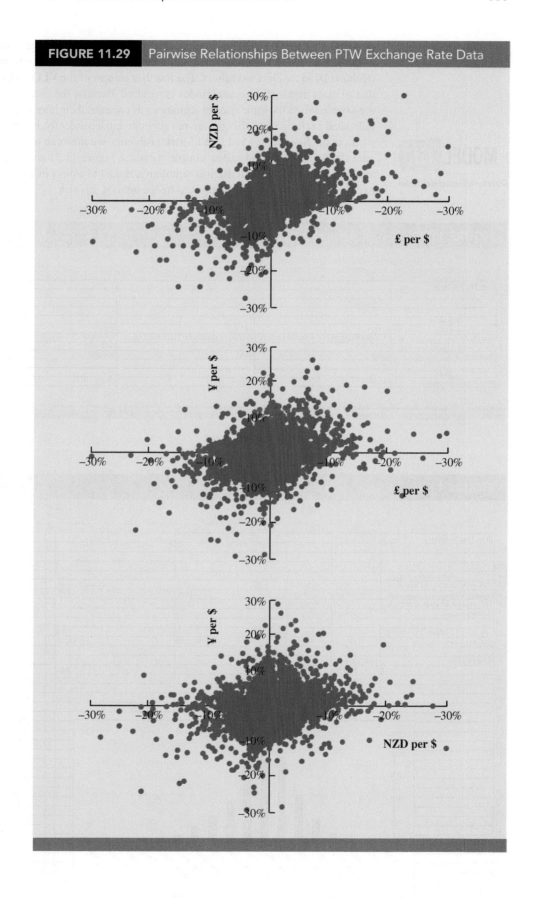

FIGURE 11.29   Pairwise Relationships Between PTW Exchange Rate Data

range Data!$A$3:$D$2002 that contains the quarterly percent change to be returned. So, =VLOOKUP(E7, Data!$A$3:$D$2002, 2, FALSE) returns the value from the second column (Column B) in the Data worksheet. The fourth argument of the VLOOKUP function specifies that an exact match of the quarter index is required. Because the exchange rate fluctuations are sampled from the same quarter scenario, this captures their inter-dependency; that is, the individual exchange rate changes are not generated independently, but rather as a collection.

QuarterlyExchangeModel

As in the Sanotronics and Land Shark problems, we now can use a Data Table to execute simulation trials and gather sample statistics. Figure 11.31 shows the results of 1,000 simulation trials. PTW can use this simulation model to assess its exposure to currency exchange rates and consider actions to hedge against this risk.

FIGURE 11.30   Formula Worksheet for PTW

	A	B	C	D	E
1	Press Teag Worldwide				
2					
3					
4					
5	**Parameters**				
6	Start-of-Quarter Exchange Rate (per $)	0.6152	1.2	87.1	Random Scenario
7	Quarterly % Change in Exchange Rate	=VLOOKUP($E$7,Data!$A$3:$D$2002,2,FALSE)	=VLOOKUP($E$7,Data!$A$3:$D$2002,2,FALSE)	=VLOOKUP($E$7,Data!$A$3:$D$2002,2,FALSE)	=RANDBETWEEN(1,2000)
8	End-of-Quarter Exchange Rate (per $)	=B6*(1+B7)	=C6*(1+C7)	=D6*(1+D7)	
9	Quarterly Revenue	100000	250000	10000000	
10					
11	**Model**				Total
12	End-of-Quarter Revenue in $	=B9/B8	=C9/C8	=D9/D8	=SUM(B12:D12)

FIGURE 11.31   Output from PTW Simulation

	A	B	C	D	E	F	G	H	I
1	Press Teag Worldwide								
2									
3									
4									
5	**Parameters**								
6	Start-of-Quarter Exchange Rate (per $)	£0.615	NZD 1.200	¥87.10	Random Scenario				
7	Quarterly % Change in Exchange Rate	1.12%	-5.53%	-13.07%	1173				
8	End-of-Quarter Exchange Rate (per $)	£0.622	NZD 1.134	¥75.72					
9	Quarterly Revenue	£100,000	NZD 250,000	¥10,000,000					
10									
11	**Model**				Total				
12	End-of-Quarter Revenue in $	$160,748	$220,529	$132,072	$513,349				
13									
14	Simulation Trial	Total $ Revenue		Summary Statistics					
15		1	$513,349	Count	1000		Bin	Frequency	Labels
16		2	$477,253	Minimum Revenue	$389,918		$420,000	5	< $420K
17		3	$501,569	Maximum Revenue	$596,365		$430,000	3	$420K - $430K
18		4	$523,797	Average Revenue	$487,087		$440,000	4	$430K - $440K
19		5	$457,771	Standard Deviation of Revenue	$22,670		$450,000	19	$440K - $450K
20		6	$474,016				$460,000	53	$450K - $460K
21							$470,000	107	$460K - $470K
22							$480,000	191	$470K - $480K
23							$490,000	213	$480K - $490K
24							$500,000	178	$490K - $500K
25							$510,000	92	$500K - $510K
26							$520,000	61	$510K - $520K
27							$530,000	37	$520K - $530K
28							$540,000	17	$530K - $540K
29							$550,000	11	$540K - $550K
30							$560,000	6	$550K - $560K
31							$570,000	2	$560K - $570K
32							$580,000	0	$570K - $580K
33								4	> $580K

Chart: **Return Distribution** — histogram with vertical axis from 0 to 250 and horizontal axis labels: < $420K, $420K–$430K, $430K–$440K, $440K–$450K, $450K–$460K, $460K–$470K, $470K–$480K, $480K–$490K, $490K–$500K, $500K–$510K, $510K–$520K, $520K–$530K, $530K–$540K, $540K–$550K, $550K–$560K, $560K–$570K, $570K–$580K, > $580K

11.5 Simulation Considerations

Verification and Validation

An important aspect of any simulation study involves confirming that the simulation model accurately describes the real system. Inaccurate simulation models cannot be expected to provide worthwhile information. Thus, before using simulation results to draw conclusions about a real system, one must take steps to verify and validate the simulation model.

Verification is the process of determining that the computer procedure that performs the simulation calculations is logically correct. Verification is largely a debugging task to make sure that there are no errors in the computer procedure that implements the simulation. In some cases, an analyst may compare computer results for a limited number of events with independent hand calculations. In other cases, tests may be performed to verify that the random variables are being generated correctly and that the output from the simulation model seems reasonable. The verification step is not complete until the user develops a high degree of confidence that the computer procedure is error free.

Validation is the process of ensuring that the simulation model provides an accurate representation of a real system. Validation requires an agreement among analysts and managers that the logic and the assumptions used in the design of the simulation model accurately reflect how the real system operates. The first phase of the validation process is done prior to, or in conjunction with, the development of the computer procedure for the simulation process. Validation continues after the computer program has been developed, with the analyst reviewing the simulation output to see whether the simulation results closely approximate the performance of the real system. If possible, the output of the simulation model is compared to the output of an existing real system to make sure that the simulation output closely approximates the performance of the real system. If this form of validation is not possible, an analyst can experiment with the simulation model and have one or more individuals experienced with the operation of the real system review the simulation output to determine whether it is a reasonable approximation of what would be obtained with the real system under similar conditions.

Verification and validation are not tasks to be taken lightly. They are key steps in any simulation study and are necessary to ensure that decisions and conclusions based on the simulation results are appropriate for the real system.

Advantages and Disadvantages of Using Simulation

The primary advantages of simulation are that it is conceptually easy to understand and that the methods can be used to model and learn about the behavior of complex systems that would be difficult, if not impossible, to deal with analytically. Simulation models are flexible; they can be used to describe systems without requiring the assumptions that are often required by other mathematical models. In general, the larger the number of random variables a system has, the more likely it is that a simulation model will provide the best approach for studying the system. Another advantage is that a simulation model provides a convenient experimental laboratory for the real system. Changing assumptions or operating policies in the simulation model and rerunning it can provide results that help predict how such changes will affect the operation of the real system. Experimenting directly with a real system is often not feasible. Simulation models frequently warn against poor decision strategies by projecting disastrous outcomes such as system failures, large financial losses, and so on.

Simulation is not without disadvantages. For complex systems, the process of developing, verifying, and validating a simulation model can be time consuming and expensive. However, the process of developing the model generally leads to a better understanding of the system, which is an important benefit. Like all mathematical models, the analyst must be conscious of the assumptions of the model in order to understand its limitations. In addition, each simulation run provides only a sample of output data. As such, the summary of the simulation data provides only estimates or approximations about the real system. Nonetheless, the danger of obtaining poor solutions is greatly mitigated if the analyst exercises good judgment in developing the simulation model and follows proper verification and validation steps. Furthermore, if a sufficiently large enough set of simulation trials is run under a wide variety of conditions, the analyst will likely have sufficient data to predict how the real system will operate.

S U M M A R Y

Simulation is a method for learning about a real system by experimenting with a model that represents the system. Some of the reasons simulation is frequently used are as follows:

1. It can be used for a wide variety of practical problems.
2. The simulation approach is relatively easy to explain and understand. As a result, management confidence is increased and the results are more easily accepted.
3. Spreadsheet software such as Excel and specialized software packages have made it easier to develop and implement simulation models for increasingly complex problems.

In this chapter, we showed how native Excel functions can be used to execute simulation models on several examples. For the Sanotronics problem, we used simulation to evaluate the risk involving the development of a new product. Then we developed a simulation model to help Land Shark Inc. estimate how varying its bid amount affects the likelihood of winning a property auction. We then demonstrated how to build a simulation model with dependent random variables using the Press Teag Worldwide example that included correlated fluctuations for currency exchange rates. With the steps below, we summarize the procedure for developing a simulation model involving controllable inputs, uncertain inputs represented by random variables, and output measures.

Summary of Steps for Conducting a Simulation Analysis

1. *Construct a spreadsheet model that computes output measures for given values of inputs.* The foundation of a good simulation model is logic that correctly relates input values to outputs. Audit the spreadsheet to ensure that the cell formulas correctly evaluate the outputs over the entire range of possible input values.
2. *Identify inputs that are uncertain, and specify probability distributions for these cells* (rather than just static numbers). Note that all inputs may not have a degree of uncertainty sufficient to require modeling with a probability distribution. Other inputs may actually be decision variables, which are not random and should not be modeled with probability distributions; rather, these are values that the decision maker can control.
3. *Select one or more outputs to record over the simulation trials.* Typical information recorded for an output includes a histogram of output values over all simulation trials and summary statistics such as the mean, standard deviation, maximum, minimum, and percentile values.
4. *Execute the simulation for a specified number of trials.* In this chapter, we have used 1,000 trials for our simulation models. The amount of sampling error can be monitored by observing how much simulation output measures fluctuate across multiple simulation runs. If the confidence intervals on the output measures are unacceptably wide, the number of trials can be increased to reduce the amount of sampling error.
5. *Analyze the outputs and interpret the implications on the decision-making process.* In addition to estimates of the mean output, simulation allows us to construct a distribution of possible output values. Analyzing the simulation results allows the decision maker to draw conclusions about the operation of the real system.

Problems 34, 35, and 36 involve small waiting-line simulation models.

In this chapter, we have focused on Monte Carlo simulation consisting of independent trials in which the results for one trial do not affect what happens in subsequent trials. Another style of simulation, called **discrete-event simulation**, involves trials that represent how a system evolves over time. One common application of discrete-event simulation is the analysis of waiting lines. In a waiting-line simulation, the random variables are the interarrival times of the customers and the service times of the servers, which together determine the waiting and completion times for the customers. Although it is possible to conduct small discrete-event simulations with native Excel functionality, discrete-event simulation modeling is best conducted with special-purpose software such as Arena®, ProModel®, and Simio®. These packages have built-in simulation clocks, simplified methods for generating random variables, and procedures for collecting and summarizing the simulation output.

GLOSSARY

Base-case scenario Output resulting from the most likely values for the random variables of a model.

Best-case scenario Output resulting from the best values that can be expected for the random variables of a model.

Continuous probability distribution A probability distribution for which the possible values for a random variable can take any value in an interval or collection of intervals. An interval can include negative and positive infinity.

Controllable input Input to a simulation model that is selected by the decision maker.

Discrete probability distribution A probability distribution for which the possible values for a random variable can take on only specified discrete values.

Discrete-event simulation A simulation method that describes how a system evolves over time by using events that occur at discrete points in time.

Monte Carlo simulation A simulation method that uses repeated random sampling to represent uncertainty in a model representing a real system and that computes the values of model outputs.

Probability distribution A description of the range and relative likelihood of possible values of a random variable (uncertain quantity).

Random variable (uncertain variable) Input to a simulation model whose value is uncertain and described by a probability distribution.

Risk analysis The process of evaluating a decision in the face of uncertainty by quantifying the likelihood and magnitude of an undesirable outcome.

Validation The process of determining that a simulation model provides an accurate representation of a real system.

Verification The process of determining that a computer program implements a simulation model as it is intended.

What-if analysis A trial-and-error approach to learning about the range of possible outputs for a model. Trial values are chosen for the model inputs (these are the what-ifs) and the value of the output(s) is computed.

Worst-case scenario Output resulting from the worst values that can be expected for the random variables of a model.

PROBLEMS

1. **Virtual Reality Goggle Inventory.** Galaxy Co. sells virtual reality (VR) goggles, particularly targeting customers who like to play video games. Galaxy procures each pair of goggles for $150 from its supplier and sells each pair of goggles for $300. Monthly demand for the VR goggles is a normal random variable with a mean of 160 units and a standard deviation of 40 units. At the beginning of each month, Galaxy orders enough goggles from its supplier to bring the inventory level up to 140 goggles. If the monthly demand is less than 140, Galaxy pays $20 per pair of goggles that remains in inventory at the end of the month. If the monthly demand exceeds 140, Galaxy sells only the 140 pairs of goggles in stock. Galaxy assigns a shortage cost of $40 for each unit of demand that is unsatisfied to represent a loss-of-goodwill among its customers. Management would like to use a simulation model to analyze this situation.
   a. What is the average monthly profit resulting from its policy of stocking 140 pairs of goggles at the beginning of each month?
   b. What is the proportion of months in which demand is completely satisfied?
   c. Use the simulation model to compare the profitability of monthly replenishment levels of 140 and 160 pairs of goggles. Use a 95% confidence interval on the difference between the average profit that each replenishment level generates to make your comparison.

2. **Dice Rolls.** Construct a spreadsheet simulation model to simulate 1,000 rolls of a die with the six sides numbered 1, 2, 3, 4, 5, and 6.

   a. Construct a histogram of the 1,000 observed dice rolls.

   b. For each roll of two dice, record the sum of the dice. Construct a histogram of the 1,000 observations of the sum of two dice.

   c. For each roll of three dice, record the sum of the dice. Construct a histogram of the 1,000 observations of the sum of three dice.

   d. For each roll of four dice, record the sum of the dice. Construct a histogram of the 1,000 observations of the sum of four dice.

   e. Compare the histograms in parts (a), (b), (c), and (d). What statistical phenomenon does this sequence of charts illustrate?

MODEL *file*

Madeira

3. **Wearable Electronic Product Launch.** The management of Madeira Computing is considering the introduction of a wearable electronic device with the functionality of a laptop computer and phone. The fixed cost to launch this new product is $300,000. The variable cost for the product is expected to be between $160 and $240, with a most likely value of $200 per unit. The product will sell for $300 per unit. Demand for the product is expected to range from 0 to approximately 20,000 units, with 4,000 units the most likely.

   a. Develop a what-if spreadsheet model computing profit for this product in the base-case, worst-case, and best-case scenarios.

   b. Model the variable cost as a uniform random variable with a minimum of $160 and a maximum of $240. Model the product demand as 1,000 times the value of a gamma random variable with an alpha parameter of 3 and a beta parameter of 2. Construct a simulation model to estimate the average profit and the probability that the project will result in a loss.

   c. What is your recommendation regarding whether to launch the product?

MODEL *file*

Brinkley

4. **Profitability of New Product.** The management of Brinkley Corporation is interested in using simulation to estimate the profit per unit for a new product. The selling price for the product will be $45 per unit. Probability distributions for the purchase cost, the labor cost, and the transportation cost are estimated as follows:

Procurement Cost ($)	Probability	Labor Cost ($)	Probability	Transportation Cost ($)	Probability
10	0.25	20	0.10	3	0.75
11	0.45	22	0.25	5	0.25
12	0.30	24	0.35		
		25	0.30		

   a. Construct a simulation model to estimate the average profit per unit. What is a 95% confidence interval around this average?

   b. Management believes that the project may not be sustainable if the profit per unit is less than $5. Use simulation to estimate the probability that the profit per unit will be less than $5. What is a 95% confidence interval around this proportion?

MODEL *file*

Statewide

5. **Estimating Auto Accident Costs.** Statewide Auto Insurance believes that for every trip longer than 10 minutes that a teenager drives, there is a 1 in 1,000 chance that the drive will result in an auto accident. Assume that the cost of an accident can be modeled with a beta distribution with an alpha parameter of 1.5, a beta parameter of 3, a minimum value of $500, and a maximum value of $20,000. Construct a simulation model to answer the following questions. (*Hint*: Review Appendix 11.1 for descriptions of various types of probability distributions to identify the appropriate way to model the number of accidents in 500 trips.)

   a. If a teenager drives 500 trips longer than 10 minutes, what is the average cost resulting from accidents? Provide a 95% confidence interval on this mean.

   b. If a teenager drives 500 trips longer than 10 minutes, what is the probability that the total cost from accidents will exceed $8,000? Provide a 95% confidence interval on this proportion.

6. **Automobile Collision Claims.** State Farm Insurance has developed the following table to describe the distribution of automobile collision claims paid during the past year.
   a. Set up a table of intervals of random numbers that can be used with the Excel VLOOKUP function to generate values for automobile collision claim payments.
   b. Construct a simulation model to estimate the average claim payment amount and the standard deviation in the claim payment amounts.
   c. Let X be the discrete random variable representing the dollar value of an automobile collision claim payment. Let, $x_1, x_2, \ldots, x_n$ represent possible values of X. Then, the mean (μ) and standard deviation (σ) of X can be computed as $\mu = x_1 \times P(X = x_1) + \cdots + x_n \times P(X = x_n)$, and $\sigma = \sqrt{(x_1 - \mu)^2 \times P(X = x_1) + \cdots + (x_n - \mu)^2 \times P(X = x_n)}$. Compare the values of sample mean and sample standard deviation in part (b) to the analytical calculation of the mean and standard deviation. How can we improve the accuracy of the sample estimates from the simulation?

Chapter 4 describes the analytical calculation of the mean and standard deviation of a random variable.

Payment($)	Probability
0	0.83
500	0.06
1,000	0.05
2,000	0.02
5,000	0.02
8,000	0.01
10,000	0.01

7. **Playoff Series in National Basketball Association.** The Dallas Mavericks and the Golden State Warriors are two teams in the National Basketball Association. Dallas and Golden State will play multiple times over the course of an NBA season. Assume that the Dallas Mavericks have a 25% probability of winning each game against the Golden State Warriors.
   a. Construct a simulation model that uses the negative binomial distribution to simulate the number of games Dallas would lose before winning four games against the Golden State Warriors.
   b. Now suppose that the Dallas Mavericks face the Golden State Warriors in a best-of-seven playoff series in which the first team to win four games out of seven wins the series. Using the simulation model from part (a), estimate that probability that the Dallas Mavericks would win a best-of-seven series against the Golden State Warriors.

8. **Tire Warranty Analysis.** Grear Tire Company has produced a new tire with an estimated mean lifetime mileage of 36,500 miles. Management also believes that the standard deviation is 5,000 miles and that tire mileage is normally distributed. To promote the new tire, Grear has offered to refund some money if the tire fails to reach 30,000 miles before the tire needs to be replaced. Specifically, for tires with a lifetime below 30,000 miles, Grear will refund a customer $1 per 100 miles short of 30,000.
   a. For each tire sold, what is the average cost of the promotion?
   b. What is the probability that Grear will refund more than $25 for a tire?

9. **Yield from Recruiting Seminars.** To generate leads for new business, Gustin Investment Services offers free financial planning seminars at major hotels in Southwest Florida. Gustin conducts seminars for groups of 25 individuals. Each seminar costs Gustin $3,500, and the commission for each new account opened is $5,000. Gustin estimates that for each individual attending the seminar, there is a 0.01 probability that he/she will open a new account.
   a. Construct a spreadsheet model that correctly computes Gustin's profit per seminar, given static values of the relevant parameters.
   b. What type of random variable is the number of new accounts opened? (*Hint*: Review Appendix 11.1 for descriptions of various types of probability distributions.)
   c. Construct a simulation model to analyze the profitability of Gustin's seminars. Would you recommend that Gustin continue running the seminars?

MODEL *file*

LandSharkBeta

MODEL *file*

NBAG

d. How many attendees (in a multiple of five, i.e., 25, 30, 35, . . .) does Gustin need before a seminar's average profit is greater than zero?

10. **Analysis of Bid Amounts.** Using the file *LandSharkBeta*, evaluate bid amounts from $1,229,000 to $1,329,000 in increments of $20,000 by building a table listing 95% confidence intervals around the average return and probability of winning the auction. Which of these bid amounts do you recommend?

11. **Point Distribution in Basketball Game.** The Iowa Wolves is scheduled to play against the Maine Red Claws in an upcoming game in the National Basketball Association (NBA) G League. Because a player in the NBA G League is still developing his skills, the number of points he scores in a game can vary substantially. Assume that each player's point production can be represented as an integer uniform random variable with the ranges provided in the following table:

Player	Iowa Wolves	Maine Red Claws
1	[5,20]	[7,12]
2	[7,20]	[15,20]
3	[5,10]	[10,20]
4	[10,40]	[15,30]
5	[6,20]	[5,10]
6	[3,10]	[1,20]
7	[2,5]	[1,4]
8	[2,4]	[2,4]

a. Develop a spreadsheet model that simulates the points scored by each team and the difference in their point totals.

b. What are the average and standard deviation of points scored by the Iowa Wolves? What is the shape of the distribution of points scored by the Iowa Wolves?

c. What are the average and standard deviation of points scored by the Maine Red Claws? What is the shape of the distribution of points scored by the Maine Red Claws?

d. Let Point Differential = Iowa Wolves points − Maine Red Claws points. What is the average Point Differential between the Iowa Wolves and Maine Red Claws? What is the standard deviation of the Point Differential? What is the shape of the Point Differential distribution?

e. What is the probability that the Iowa Wolves scores more points than the Maine Red Claws?

f. The coach of the Iowa Wolves feels that they are the underdog and is considering a riskier game strategy. The effect of this strategy is that the range of each Wolves player's point production increases symmetrically so that the new range is [0, original upper bound + original lower bound]. For example, Wolves player 1's range with the risky strategy is [0, 25]. How does the new strategy affect the average and standard deviation of the Wolves point total? How does that affect the probability of the Iowa Wolves scoring more points than the Maine Red Claws?

MODEL *file*

NYSE

12. **Simulating Stock Price.** Suppose that the price of a share of a particular stock listed on the New York Stock Exchange is currently $39. The following probability distribution shows how the price per share is expected to change over a three-month period:

Stock Price Change ($)	Probability
−2	0.05
−1	0.10
0	0.25
+1	0.20
+2	0.20
+3	0.10
+4	0.10

a. Construct a spreadsheet simulation model that computes the value of the stock price in 3 months, 6 months, 9 months, and 12 months under the assumption that the change in stock price over any three-month period is independent of the change in stock price over any other three-month period. For a current price of $39 per share, what is the average stock price per share 12 months from now? What is the standard deviation of the stock price 12 months from now?

b. Based on the model assumptions, what are the lowest and highest possible prices for this stock in 12 months? Based on your knowledge of the stock market, how valid do you think this is? Propose an alternative to modeling how stock prices evolve over three-month periods.

MODEL *file*

Overbooking

13. **Airline Overbooking.** Allegiant Airlines is considering an overbooking policy for one of its flights. The airplane has 50 seats, but Allegiant is considering accepting more reservations than seats because sometimes passengers do not show up for their flights, resulting in empty seats. The *PassengerAppearance* worksheet in the file *Overbooking* contains data on 1,000 passengers showing whether or not they showed up for their respective flights.

In addition, Allegiant has conducted a field experiment to gauge the demand for reservations for the current flight. During this experiment, they did not limit the number of reservations for the flight to observe the uncensored demand. The following table summarizes the result of the field experiment.

No. of Reservations Demanded	Probability
48	0.05
49	0.05
50	0.15
51	0.30
52	0.25
53	0.10
54	0.10

Allegiant receives a marginal profit of $100 for each passenger who books a reservation (regardless of whether they show up). Allegiant incurs a rebooking cost of $300 for each passenger who books a reservation, but is denied seating due to a full airplane; this cost results from rescheduling the passenger and any loss of goodwill.

To control its rebooking costs, Allegiant wants to set a limit on the number of reservations it will accept. Evaluate Allegiant's average net profit for reservation limits of 50, 52, and 54, respectively. Based on the 95% confidence intervals for average net profit, which reservation limit do you recommend?

14. **Project Management.** A project has four activities (A, B, C, and D) that must be performed sequentially. The probability distributions for the time required to complete each of the activities are as follows:

MODEL *file*

Project

Activity	Activity Time (Weeks)	Probability
A	5	0.25
	6	0.35
	7	0.25
	8	0.15
B	3	0.20
	5	0.55
	7	0.25
C	10	0.10
	12	0.25
	14	0.40
	16	0.20
	18	0.05
D	8	0.60
	10	0.40

FTC

a. Construct a spreadsheet simulation model to estimate the average length of the project and the standard deviation of the project length.

b. What is the estimated probability that the project will be completed in 35 weeks or less?

15. **Holiday Toy Inventory Analysis.** In preparing for the upcoming holiday season, Fresh Toy Company (FTC) designed a new doll called The Dougie that teaches children how to dance. The fixed cost to produce the doll is $100,000. The variable cost, which includes material, labor, and shipping costs, is $34 per doll. During the holiday selling season, FTC will sell the dolls for $42 each. If FTC overproduces the dolls, the excess dolls will be sold in January through a distributor who has agreed to pay FTC $10 per doll. Demand for new toys during the holiday selling season is uncertain. The normal probability distribution with an average of 60,000 dolls and a standard deviation of 15,000 is assumed to be a good description of the demand. FTC has tentatively decided to produce 60,000 units (the same as average demand), but it wants to conduct an analysis regarding this production quantity before finalizing the decision.

a. Create a what-if spreadsheet model using formulas that relate the values of production quantity, demand, sales, revenue from sales, amount of surplus, revenue from sales of surplus, total cost, and net profit. What is the profit when demand is equal to its average (60,000 units)?

b. Modeling demand as a normal random variable with a mean of 60,000 and a standard deviation of 15,000, simulate the sales of The Dougie doll using a production quantity of 60,000 units. What is the estimate of the average profit associated with the production quantity of 60,000 dolls? How does this compare to the profit corresponding to the average demand (as computed in part (a))?

c. Before making a final decision on the production quantity, management wants an analysis of a more aggressive 70,000-unit production quantity and a more conservative 50,000-unit production quantity. Run your simulation with these two production quantities. What is the average profit associated with each?

d. Besides average profit, what other factors should FTC consider in determining a production quantity? Compare the four production quantities (40,000; 50,000; 60,000; and 70,000) using all these factors. What trade-offs occur? What is your recommendation?

Contractor

16. **Project Bidding.** Jonah Arkfeld, a building contractor, is preparing a bid on a new construction project. Two other contractors will be submitting bids for the same project. Jonah has analyzed past bidding practices and the requirements of the project to determine the probability distributions of the two competing contractors. The bid from Contractor A can be described with a triangular distribution with a minimum value of $600,000, a maximum value of $800,000, and a most likely value of $725,000. The bid from Contractor B can be described with a normal distribution with a mean of $700,000 and a standard deviation of $50,000.

a. If Jonah submits a bid of $750,000, what is the probability that he will win the bid for the project?

b. What is the probability that Contractor A and Contractor B will win the bid, respectively?

Hybrid

17. **Hybrid Car Analysis.** You are considering the purchase of a new car and are weighing the choice between a Ford Fusion Hybrid sedan (which assists a gasoline engine with an electric motor powered via regenerative braking) and the Ford Fusion Non-Hybrid sedan (just a standard gasoline engine). The non-hybrid version costs $23,240 with fuel economy of 21 miles per gallon in city driving and 32 miles per gallon in highway driving. The hybrid version of the car costs $25,990 with fuel economy of 43 miles per gallon in city driving and 41 miles per gallon in highway driving.

You plan to keep the car for 10 years. Your annual mileage is uncertain; you only know that each year you will drive between 9,000 and 13,000 miles. Based on your past driving patterns, 60% of your miles are city driving and 40% of your miles are highway driving. The current gasoline price is $2.19 per gallon, but you know that gasoline prices vary unpredictably over time.

Compute the net present value (NPV) of the costs of each vehicle (purchase cost + gasoline cost) using a discount rate of 3%. Assume that you pay the entire purchase price of the vehicle immediately (Year 0) and the annual gasoline costs are incurred at the end of each year.

a. On average, what the cost savings of the hybrid vehicle over the non-hybrid?

b. Because of your concern about the maintenance needs of the hybrid vehicle, you would need to be assured of significant savings to convince you to purchase the hybrid. What is the probability that the hybrid will result in more than $2,000 in savings over the non-hybrid?

MODEL *file*

OrangeTech

18. **Product Adoption.** Orange Tech (OT) is a software company that provides a suite of programs that are essential to everyday business computing. OT has just enhanced its software and released a new version of its programs. For financial planning purposes, OT needs to forecast its revenue over the next few years. To begin this analysis, OT is considering one of its largest customers. Over the planning horizon, assume that this customer will upgrade at most once to the newest software version, but the number of years that pass before the customer purchases an upgrade varies. Up to the year that the customer actually upgrades, assume there is a 0.50 probability that the customer upgrades in any particular year. In other words, the upgrade year of the customer is a random variable. For guidance on an appropriate way to model upgrade year, refer to Appendix 11.1. Furthermore, the revenue that OT earns from the customer's upgrade also varies (depending on the number of programs the customer decides to upgrade). Assume that the revenue from an upgrade obeys a normal distribution with a mean of $100,000 and a standard deviation of $25,000. Using the template in the file *OrangeTech*, complete a simulation model that analyzes the net present value of the revenue from the customer upgrade. Use an annual discount rate of 10%.

a. What is the average net present value that OT earns from this customer? (*Hint:* Excel's NPV function computes the net present value for a sequence of cash flows that occur at the end of each period. To correctly use this function for cash flows that occur at the beginning of each period, use the formula =NPV(*discount rate, flow range*) + *initial amount*, where *discount rate* is the annual discount rate, *flow range* is the cell range containing cash flows for years 1 through *n*, and *initial amount* is the cash flow in the initial period (year 0).)

b. What is the standard deviation of net present value? How does this compare to the standard deviation of the revenue? Explain.

MODEL *file*

OuRx

19. **Flu Vaccine Ordering.** OuRx, a retail pharmacy chain, is faced with the decision of how much flu vaccine to order for the next flu season. OuRx has to place a single order for the flu vaccine several months before the beginning of the season because it takes four to five months for the supplier to create the vaccine. OuRx wants to more closely examine the ordering decision because, over the past few years, the company has ordered too much vaccine or too little. OuRx pays a wholesale price of $12 per dose to obtain the flu vaccine from the supplier and then sells the flu shot to their customers at a retail price of $20.

Because OuRx earns a profit on flu shots that it sells and it can't sell more than its supply, the appropriate profit computation depends on whether demand exceeds the order quantity or vice versa. Similarly, the number of lost sales and excess doses depends on whether demand exceeds the order quantity or vice versa. Demand for the flu vaccine is uncertain. The *VaccineDemand* worksheet in the file *OuRx* contains data produced by epidemiologists to help *OuRx* gain insight on demand for flu vaccine at their retail pharmacies.

a. Construct a base spreadsheet model that correctly computes net profit for a given level of demand and specified order quantity. For an order quantity of 500,000 doses, what is the net profit when demand is 400,000 doses and 600,000 doses, respectively?

b. To help determine how to model flu vaccine demand, construct a histogram of the data provided in the *VaccineDemand* worksheet in the file *OuRx*. In column B, compute the natural logarithm (using the Excel function LN) of each observation and construct a histogram of these logged demand observations. Based on the histograms of the non-logged demand and logged demand, respectively, what seems to be a good choice of probability distribution for (non-logged) vaccine demand? (*Hint:* Review Appendix 11.1 for descriptions of various types of probability distributions.)

c. Representing flu vaccine demand with the type of random variable you identified in part (b), complete the simulation model and determine the average net profit resulting from an order quantity of 500,000 doses. What is the 95% confidence interval on the average profit? What is the probability of running out of the flu vaccine?

SCOPE

20. **Music Concert Event Management.** At a local university, the Student Commission on Programming and Entertainment (SCOPE) is preparing to host its first music concert of the school year. To successfully produce this music concert, SCOPE has to complete several activities. The following table lists information regarding each activity. An activity's immediate predecessors are the activities that must be completed before the considered activity can begin. The table also lists duration estimates (in days) for each activity.

Activity	Immediate Predecessors	Minimum Time	Likely Time	Maximum Time
A: Negotiate contract with selected musicians	—	5	6	9
B: Reserve site	—	8	12	15
C: Logistical arrangements for music group	A	5	6	7
D: Screen and hire security personnel	B	3	3	3
E: Advertising and ticketing	B, C	1	5	9
F: Hire parking staff	D	4	7	10
G: Arrange concession sales	E	3	8	10

The following network illustrates the precedence relationships in the SCOPE project. The project begins with activities A and B, which can start immediately (time 0) because they have no predecessors. On the other hand, activity E cannot be started until activities B and C are both completed. The project is not complete until all activities are completed.

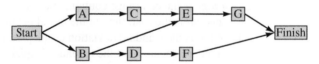

a. Using the triangular distribution to represent the duration of each activity, construct a simulation model to estimate the average amount of time to complete the concert preparations.

b. What is the likelihood that the project will be complete in 23 days or less?

TwoJets

21. **Airplane Maintenance.** Steve Austin is the fleet manager for SharePlane, a company that sells fractional ownership of private jets. SharePlane must carefully maintain their jets at all times. If a jet breaks down, it must be repaired immediately. Even if a jet functions well, it must be maintained at regularly scheduled intervals. Currently, Steve is managing two jets, Jet A and Jet B, for a collection of clients and is interested in estimating their availability in between trips to the repair shop as having both jets out-of-service due to repair or maintenance at the same time can affect its customer service. Jet A and Jet B have just completed preventive maintenance. The next maintenance is scheduled for both Jet A and Jet B in four months. It is also possible that one or both will break down before this scheduled maintenance and require repair. The amount of time to a plane's first failure is uncertain. Historical data recording the time to a plane's first failure (measured in months) is provided in the *TimeToFailData* worksheet of the file *TwoJets*. Determine an appropriate probability distribution for these data. Furthermore, once a plane enters repair (either due to a failure or as scheduled maintenance), the amount of time the plane will be in maintenance is also uncertain. Historical data recording the repair time (measured in months) is provided in the *RepairTimeData* worksheet of the file *TwoJets*. Examine the appropriateness of fitting a log-normal distribution to these data. Steve wants to develop a simulation model to estimate

the length of time that Jet A and Jet B are both out-of-service over the next few months. For simplicity, you can assume that these planes will enter repair or maintenance just once over the next few months.

    a. What is the average amount of time that the planes are both out-of-service?

    b. What is the probability that the planes are both out-of-service for longer than 1.5 months?

Blackjack

22. **Blackjack Card Game.** Blackjack, or 21, is a popular casino game that begins with each player and the dealer being dealt two cards. The value of each hand is determined by the point total of the cards in the hand. Face cards and 10s count 10 points, aces can be counted as either 1 or 11 points, and all other cards count at their face value. For instance, the value of a hand consisting of a jack and an 8 is 18; the value of a hand consisting of an ace and a two is either 3 or 13, depending on whether player counts the ace as 1 or 11 points. The goal is to obtain a hand with a value as close as possible to 21 without exceeding 21. After the initial deal, each player and the dealer may draw additional cards (called "taking a hit") in order to improve her or his hand. If a player or the dealer takes a hit and the value of the hand exceeds 21, that person "goes broke" and loses. The dealer's advantage is that each player must decide whether to take a hit before the dealer decides whether to take a hit. If a player takes a hit and goes over 21, the player loses even if the dealer later takes a hit and goes over 21. For this reason, players will often decide not to take a hit when the value of their hand is 12 or greater.

    The dealer's hand is dealt with one card up (face showing) and one card down (face hidden). The player then decides whether to take a hit based on knowledge of the dealer's up card. Suppose that you are playing blackjack and the dealer's up card is a 6 and your hand has a value of 16 for the two cards initially dealt.

    With a hand of a value of 16, if you decide to take a hit, the following cards will improve your hand: ace, 2, 3, 4, or 5. Any card with a point count greater than 5 will result in you going broke. Assume that if you have a hand with a value of 16, the following probabilities describe the ending value of your hand:

Value of Hand	17	18	19	20	21	Broke
Probability	0.0769	0.0769	0.0769	0.0769	0.0769	0.6155

A gambling professional determined that when the dealer's up card is a 6, the following probabilities describe the ending value of the dealer's hand:

Value of Hand	17	18	19	20	21	Broke
Probability	0.1654	0.1063	0.1063	0.1017	0.0972	0.4231

    a. Construct a simulation model to simulate the result of 1,000 blackjack hands when the dealer has a 6 up and you take a hit with a hand that has a value of 16. What is the probability of the dealer winning, a push (a tie), and you winning, respectively?

    b. If you have a hand with a value of 16 and don't take a hit, the only way that you can win is if the dealer goes broke. If you don't take a hit, what is the probability of the dealer winning, a push (a tie), and you winning, respectively?

    c. Based on the results from parts (a) and (b), should you take a hit or not if you have a hand of value 16 and the dealer has a 6 up?

Ginsberg

23. **Snowfall Promotion.** To boost holiday sales, Ginsberg jewelry store is advertising the following promotion: "If more than five inches of snow fall in the first three days of the year (January 1 through January 3), all purchases made between Thanksgiving and Christmas are free!" Based on historical sales records as well as experience with past promotions, the store manager believes that the total holiday sales between Thanksgiving and Christmas could range anywhere between $200,000 and $400,000 but is unsure of anything more specific. Ginsberg has collected data on snowfall from December 16 to January 18 for the past several winters in the file *Ginsberg*.

a. Construct a simulation model to assess potential refund amounts so that Ginsberg can evaluate the option of purchasing an insurance policy to cover potential losses.
b. What is the probability that Ginsberg will have to refund sales?
c. What is the average refund? Why is this a poor measure to use to assess risk?
d. In the cases when snowfall exceeds 5 inches, what is the average refund?

MODEL file
Jackpot

24. **Distribution of Money in Jackpot Soap Bars.** A creative entrepreneur has created a novelty soap called Jackpot. Inside each bar of Jackpot soap is a rolled-up bill of U.S. currency. There are 1,000 bars of soap in the initial offering of the soap. Although the denomination of the bill inside a bar of soap is unknown, the distribution of bills in these first 1,000 bars is given in the following table:

Bill Denomination	Number of Bills
$1	520
$5	260
$10	130
$20	60
$50	29
$100	1
Total	1,000

If a customer buys 40 bars of soap, the number of bars that contain a $50 or $100 bill is uncertain. On average, how many of these bars contain a $50 or $100 bill? What is the probability that at least one of the 40 bars contains a $50 or $100 bill? (*Hint:* Review Appendix 11.1 for descriptions of various types of probability distributions to identify the random variable that describes the number of bars that contain a $50 or $100 bill.)

MODEL file
Jackpot

25. **More Jackpot Soap.** Refer to the Jackpot soap scenario in Problem 24. After the sale of the original 1,000 bars of soap, Jackpot soap went viral, and the soap has become wildly popular. Production of the soap has been ramped up so that now millions of bars have been produced. However, the distribution of the bills in the soap obeys the same distribution as outlined in Problem 24. On average, how many bars of soap will a customer have to buy before purchasing three bars of soap each containing a bill of at least $20 value? (*Hint:* Review Appendix 11.1 for descriptions of various types of probability distributions.)

MODEL file
WorldSeries

26. **World Series in Major League Baseball.** Major League Baseball's World Series is a maximum of seven games, with the winner being the first team to win four games. Assume that the Atlanta Braves are playing the Minnesota Twins in the World Series and that the first two games are to be played in Atlanta, the next three games at the Twins' ballpark, and the last two games, if necessary, back in Atlanta. Taking into account the projected starting pitchers for each game and the home field advantage, the probabilities of Atlanta winning each game are as follows:

Game	1	2	3	4	5	6	7
Probability of Win	0.60	0.55	0.48	0.45	0.48	0.55	0.50

a. Set up a spreadsheet simulation model in which the outcome of each game (whether Atlanta or Minnesota wins) is a random variable.
b. What is the average number of games played regardless of the winner?
c. What is the probability that the Atlanta Braves win the World Series?

MODEL file
Anime

27. **Newsvendor Problem for Anime Magazine.** Young entrepreneur Fan Bingbing has launched a business venture in which she uses stories submitted by university students as the basis for comics in a monthly anime-style magazine. Based on market research, Fan estimates that average monthly demand will be 500 copies. She has decided to model monthly demand as normal random variable with a mean of 500 and a standard deviation of 300.

Fan must pay a publishing company $3.75 for each copy of the comic printed. She then sells the magazine for $5 each. Rather than having a store-front, Fan sells the magazines through a group of student vendors who sell the comics out of their backpacks while on campus. Fan pays a student vendor $0.35 for each magazine he/she sells. As Fan distributes a new issue each month, she only sells each issue for a month. However, the publishing company has agreed to buy back from Fan any unsold copies at the end of each month for $2.25.

a. As Fan validates the simulation model you have constructed, she observes something troublesome regarding the use of the normal distribution with a mean of 500 and a standard deviation of 300 to model monthly demand. What is it? How can you modify the simulation model to address this issue?

b. Based on the simulation model that incorporates a remedy for the validation issue observed in part (a), what is the estimate of the average profit if Fan sets the order quantity to 1,200? What is the 95% confidence interval on this estimate of average profit?

c. For an order quantity of 1,200 copies, what is the profit value such that 2.5% of the profit outcomes are smaller than this value? What is the profit value such that 2.5% of the profit outcomes are larger than this value? (*Hint:* You can use the Excel function PERCENTILE.EXC to help you determine these values.) These two values define a range which 95% of the profit outcomes lie between. Why doesn't this range correspond to the 95% confidence interval in part (b)?

28. **Product Adoption and Sales Bonus.** Bianca Peterson is a marketing engineer for Hexagon Composites, a company which sells carbon composite storage tanks. In an effort to gain product adoptions from customers, Bianca goes on sales trips (often to foreign countries). For each of 120 previous sales trips, the file *SalesTrips* lists (1) whether the trip resulted in the visited customer adopting the product, and (2) the revenue generated by the adoption.

a. Bianca has six sales trips planned over the next couple of months. What is the average revenue that Bianca expects to generate from these six trips? What is the probability that she generates $200,000 or less from these six trips?

b. Bianca receives a sales bonus if she gains three more product adoptions before the end of the year. The number of sales trips that Bianca will need to make to earn her bonus is uncertain. What is its distribution? If Bianca only has time to make 10 more sales trips before the end of the year, what is the likelihood that she earns her bonus?

29. **Financial Analysis of Restaurant.** Gorditos sells a variety of Mexican-inspired cuisine for which tortillas are often the main ingredient. Assume that each customer places an order requiring one tortilla with a 75% probability independent of other customers' orders. The other 25% of customers place orders that do not require a tortilla. Assume that the number of customers who arrive per hour has a Poisson distribution with the average number of customers in an hour time slot given in the following table:

Time of Day	Average Number of Customers
11am–noon	200
Noon–1pm	200
1pm–2pm	200
2pm–3pm	50
3pm–4pm	50
4pm–5pm	50
5pm–6pm	150
6pm–7pm	150
7pm–8pm	150
8pm–9pm	50
9pm–10pm	50

Gorditos currently prepares dough for 750 tortillas at the beginning of each day. Due to uncertain customer demand, Gorditos may run out of tortillas, which affects profit as well as customer relations. Every tortilla-based customer order generates $2.35 in profit.

Every customer who places an order requiring a tortilla but is denied (due to a tortilla stock-out) leaves Gorditos without buying anything with probability 0.13, and purchases a non-tortilla menu item (generating profit of $1.50) with probability 0.87. Create a simulation model to generate the distribution of daily lost profit due to tortilla stock-outs.

a. What is the average daily lost profit? What is the 95% confidence interval on this mean?

b. On average, which hour of the work day does Gorditos run out of tortillas? What is the 95% confidence interval on the mean?

Admissions

30. **Matriculation Yield at a University.** As admissions director for an exclusive executive MBA program which takes place on Necker Island in the Caribbean, Richard Branson must decide which applicants should receive admission offers. This is a difficult decision-making problem, as an applicant may or may not accept an admission offer. Currently, Richard is considering 30 applicants, each of which has a different probability of accepting an admission offer. Based on their academic qualifications and experience, Richard has rated each of these applicants using a value score from 1 to 10 (higher value scores represent better applicants). The file *Admissions* contains data on the 30 applicants.

Based on the capacity of their facilities, Richard would like a class of 12 students. Fewer students than 12 results in under-utilized resources (empty classroom seats), but more than 12 students results in increased marginal costs. Specifically, each attending student beyond 12 incurs a cost of 20 value points. Note that an applicant will be an attending student only if he or she is admitted and he or she accepts the admission offer.

Construct a spreadsheet model that computes the net value of offering admission to the top 20 students as ranked by value score. Compute net value as the sum of the value of attending students minus the costs of students beyond the capacity of 12 seats. What is the average net value obtained when offering admission to the top 20 students?

WeddingPlanner

31. **Wedding Attendance.** The wedding date for a couple is quickly approaching, and the wedding planner must provide the caterer an estimate of how many people will attend the reception so that the appropriate quantity of food is prepared for the buffet. The following table contains information on the number of RSVPs for the 145 invitations. Unfortunately, the number of guests who actually attend does not always correspond to the number of RSVPs.

Based on her experience, the wedding planner knows that it is extremely rare for guests to attend a wedding if they affirmed that they will not be attending. Therefore, the wedding planner will assume that no one from these 50 invitations will attend. The wedding planner estimates that each of the 25 guests planning to come alone has a 75% chance of attending alone, a 20% chance of not attending, and a 5% chance of bringing a companion. For each of the 60 RSVPs who plan to bring a companion, there is a 90% chance that she or he will attend with a companion, a 5% chance of attending alone, and a 5% chance of not attending at all. For the 10 people who have not responded, the wedding planner assumes that there is an 80% chance that each will not attend, a 15% chance that they will attend alone, and a 5% chance that they will attend with a companion.

RSVPs	No. of Invitations
0	50
1	25
2	60
No response	10

a. Assist the wedding planner by constructing a spreadsheet simulation model to estimate the average number of guests who will attend the reception.

b. To be accommodating hosts, the couple has instructed the wedding planner to use the simulation model to determine X, the minimum number of guests for which the caterer should prepare the meal, so that there is at least a 90% chance that the actual attendance is less than or equal to X. What is the best estimate for the value of X?

QuarterlyExchangeModel

32. **Hedging Currency Risk.** A European put option on a currency allows you to sell a unit of that currency at the specified strike price (exchange rate) at a particular point in time after the purchase of the option. For example, suppose Press Teag Worldwide (from Section 11.4) purchases a three-month European put option for a British pound with a strike price of £0.630 per U.S. dollar. Then, if the exchange rate in three months is such that it takes more than £0.630 to buy a U.S. dollar, for example, £0.650 per U.S. dollar, Press Teag will exercise the put option and sell its pound sterling at the strike price of £0.630 per U.S. dollar. However, if exchange rate in three months is such that it take less than £0.630 to buy a U.S. dollar, for example, £0.620 per U.S. dollar, Press Teag will not exercise its put option and sell its pound sterling at the market rate of £0.620 per U.S. dollar.

The following table lists information on the three-month European put options on pound sterling, New Zealand dollars, and Japanese yen.

Currency	Purchase Price per Option	Strike Price
Pound Sterling	$0.01 per £	£0.630 per $
New Zealand Dollar	$0.01 per NZD	NZD 1.230 per $
Japanese Yen	$0.00005 per ¥	¥90.00 per $

Modify the simulation model in the file *QuarterlyExchangeModel* to compare the strategy of hedging half of the revenue in each of three foreign currencies using European put options versus the strategy of not using put options to hedge at all. What is the average difference in revenue (hedged revenue – unhedged revenue)? What is the probability that the hedged revenue is less than the unhedged revenue?

DailyStock

33. **Modeling Stock Prices.** Over the past year, a financial analyst has tracked the daily change in the price per share of common stock for a major oil company. The financial analyst wants to develop a simulation model to analyze the stock price at the end of the next quarter. Assume 63 trading days and a current price per share of $51.60.
   a. Based on the data in the *DataToFit* worksheet of the file *DailyStock*, use the Excel formula =CORREL(B3:B313, B4:B314) to compute the correlation between the percent change in stock price on consecutive days. What do you conclude about the dependency of the percent change in stock price from day to day?
   b. Based on the data in the *DataToFit* worksheet of the file *DailyStock*, compute sample statistics and construct a histogram to visualize the distribution of the data. Select a distribution that appears to fit this data.
   c. Using the distribution that you selected in part (b) to represent the daily percent change in stock price, construct a simulation model to estimate the price per share at the end of the quarter. What is the probability that the stock price will be below $26.55?
   d. The *WhatReallyHappened* worksheet of the file *DailyStock* contains the 63 values of the daily percent change in stock price that actually occurred during the quarter. What does this reveal about the limitations of simulation modeling? What could the financial analyst do to address this limitation?

BurgerDome

34. **Wait Time Analysis at a Restaurant.** Burger Dome is a fast-food restaurant currently evaluating its customer service. In its current operation, an employee takes a customer's order, tabulates the cost, receives payment from the customer, and then fills the order. Once the customer's order is filled, the employee takes the order of the next customer waiting for service. Assume that time between each customer's arrival is an exponential random variable with a mean of 1.35 minutes. Assume that the time for the employee to complete the customer's service is an exponential random variable with a mean of 1 minute. Use the file *BurgerDome* to complete a simulation model for the waiting line at Burger Dome for a 14-hour workday. Using the summary statistics gathered at the bottom of the spreadsheet model, answer the following questions.
   a. What is the average wait time experienced by a customer?
   b. What is the longest wait time experienced by a customer?
   c. What is the probability that a customer waits more than 2 minutes?

d. Create a histogram depicting the wait time distribution.

e. By pressing the F9 key to generate a new set of simulation trials, you can observe the variability in the summary statistics from simulation to simulation. Typically, this variability can be reduced by increasing the number of trials. Why is this approach not appropriate for this problem?

35. **Effect of Service Time Distribution on Restaurant Wait Time.** One advantage of simulation is that a simulation model can be altered easily to reflect a change in the assumptions. Refer to the Burger Dome analysis in Problem 34. Assume that the service time is more accurately described by a normal distribution with a mean of 1 minute and a standard deviation of 0.2 minute. This distribution has less variability than the exponential distribution originally used. What is the impact of this change on the output measures?

MODEL *file*

BurgerDomeTwoServers

36. **Effect of Additional Server on Restaurant Wait Time.** Refer to the Burger Dome analysis in Problem 34. Burger Dome wants to consider the effect of hiring a second employee to serve customers (in parallel with the first employee). Use the file *BurgerDomeTwoServers* to complete a simulation model that accounts for the second employee. (*Hint:* The time that a customer begins service will depend on the availability of employees.) What is the impact of this change on the output measures?

CASE PROBLEM: FOUR CORNERS

What will your investment portfolio be worth in 10 years? In 20 years? When you stop working? The Human Resources Department at Four Corners Corporation was asked to develop a financial planning model that would help employees address these questions. Tom Gifford was asked to lead this effort and decided to begin by developing a financial plan for himself. Tom has a degree in business and, at the age of 40, is making $85,000 per year. Through contributions to his company's retirement program and the receipt of a small inheritance, Tom has accumulated a portfolio valued at $50,000. Tom plans to work 20 more years and hopes to accumulate a portfolio valued at $1,000,000. Can he do it?

DATA *file*

FourCorners

Tom began with a few assumptions about his future salary, his new investment contributions, and his portfolio growth rate. He assumed a 5% annual salary growth rate and plans to make new investment contributions at 6% of his salary. After some research on historical stock market performance, Tom decided that a 10% annual portfolio growth rate was reasonable. Using these assumptions, Tom developed the following Excel worksheet:

	A	B	C	D	E	F	G
1	**Four Corners**						
2							
3	Age	40					
4	Current Salary	$85,000					
5	Current Portfolio	$50,000					
6	Annual Investment Rate	6%					
7	Salary Growth Rate	5%					
8	Portfolio Growth Rate	10%					
9							
10	Year	Beginning Balance	Salary	New Investment	Earnings	Ending Balance	Age
11	1	$50,000	$85,000	$5,100	$5,255	$60,355	41
12	2	$60,355	$89,250	$5,355	$6,303	$72,013	42
13	3	$72,013	$93,713	$5,623	$7,482	$85,118	43
14	4	$85,118	$98,398	$5,904	$8,807	$99,829	44
15	5	$99,829	$103,318	$6,199	$10,293	$116,321	45
16							

The worksheet provides a financial projection for the next five years. In computing the portfolio earnings for a given year, Tom assumed that his new investment contribution would occur evenly throughout the year, and thus half of the new investment could be included in the computation of the portfolio earnings for the year. From the worksheet, we see that, at age 45, Tom is projected to have a portfolio valued at $116,321.

Tom's plan was to use this worksheet as a template to develop financial plans for the company's employees. The data in the spreadsheet would be tailored for each employee, and rows would be added to it to reflect the employee's planning horizon. After adding another 15 rows to the worksheet, Tom found that he could expect to have a portfolio of $772,722 after 20 years. Tom then took his results to show his boss, Kate Krystkowiak.

Although Kate was pleased with Tom's progress, she voiced several criticisms. One of the criticisms was the assumption of a constant annual salary growth rate. She noted that most employees experience some variation in the annual salary growth rate from year to year. In addition, she pointed out that the constant annual portfolio growth rate was unrealistic and that the actual growth rate would vary considerably from year to year. She further suggested that a simulation model for the portfolio projection might allow Tom to account for the random variability in the salary growth rate and the portfolio growth rate.

After some research, Tom and Kate decided to assume that the annual salary growth rate would vary from 0% to 5% and that a uniform probability distribution would provide a realistic approximation. Four Corners' accountants suggested that the annual portfolio growth rate could be approximated by a normal probability distribution with a mean of 10% and a standard deviation of 5%. With this information, Tom set off to redesign his spreadsheet so that it could be used by the company's employees for financial planning.

Managerial Report

Play the role of Tom Gifford, and develop a simulation model for financial planning. Write a report for Tom's boss and, at a minimum, include the following:

In Chapter 10, we discuss the details of how to use Goal Seek.

1. Without considering the random variability, extend the current worksheet to 20 years. Confirm that by using the constant annual salary growth rate and the constant annual portfolio growth rate, Tom can expect to have a 20-year portfolio of $772,722. What would Tom's annual investment rate have to increase to in order for his portfolio to reach a 20-year, $1,000,000 goal? (*Hint:* Use Goal Seek.)

2. Redesign the spreadsheet model to incorporate the random variability of the annual salary growth rate and the annual portfolio growth rate into a simulation model. Assume that Tom is willing to use the annual investment rate that predicted a 20-year, $1,000,000 portfolio in part 1. Show how to simulate Tom's 20-year financial plan. Use results from the simulation model to comment on the uncertainty associated with Tom reaching the 20-year, $1,000,000 goal.

3. What recommendations do you have for employees with a current profile similar to Tom's after seeing the impact of the uncertainty in the annual salary growth rate and the annual portfolio growth rate?

4. Assume that Tom is willing to consider working 25 more years instead of 20 years. What is your assessment of this strategy if Tom's goal is to have a portfolio worth $1,000,000?

5. Discuss how the financial planning model developed for Tom Gifford can be used as a template to develop a financial plan for any of the company's employees.

Chapter 11 Appendix

Appendix 11.1 Common Probability Distributions for Simulation

Selecting the appropriate probability distribution to characterize a random variable in a simulation model can be a critical modeling decision. In this appendix, we review several probability distributions commonly used in simulation models. We describe the native Excel functionality used to generate random values from the corresponding probability distribution.

Simulation software such as Analytic Solver, Crystal Ball, or @RISK automates the generation of random values from an even wider selection of probability distributions than is available in native Excel.

Continuous Probability Distributions

Random variables that can be many possible values (even if the values are discrete) are often modeled with a continuous probability distribution. For common continuous random variables, we provide several pieces of information. First, we list the parameters which specify the probability distribution. We then delineate the minimum and maximum values defining the range that can be realized by a random variable that follows the given distribution. We also provide a short description of the overall shape of the distribution paired with an illustration. Then, we supply an example of the application of the random variable. We conclude with the native Excel functionality for generating random values from the probability distribution.

Normal Distribution

> **Parameters:** mean (m), standard deviation (s)
>
> **Range:** $-\infty$ to $+\infty$
>
> **Description:** The normal distribution is a bell-shaped, symmetric distribution centered at its mean m. The normal distribution is often a good way to characterize a quantity that is the sum of many independent random variables.
>
> **Example:** In human resource management, employee performance is often well represented by a normal distribution. Typically, the performance of 68% of employees is within one standard deviation of the average performance, and the performance of 95% of the employees is within two standard deviations. Employees with exceptionally low or high performance are rare. For example, the performance of a pharmaceutical company's sales force may be well described by a normal distribution with a mean of 200 customer adoptions and a standard deviation of 40 customer adoptions.
>
> **Native Excel:** NORM.INV(RAND(), m, s)

$\alpha = 0.45, \beta = 0.45,$
$A = 0, B = 70$

$\alpha = 2, \beta = 5,$
$A = 0, B = 70$

Beta Distribution

> **Parameters:** alpha (α), beta (β), minimum (A), maximum (B)
>
> **Range:** A to B
>
> **Description:** Over the range specified by values A and B, the beta distribution has a very flexible shape that can be manipulated by adjusting α and β. The beta distribution is useful in modeling an uncertain quantity that has a known minimum and maximum value. To estimate the values of the alpha and beta parameters from sample data, we use the following equations (see the file *Beta* for an Excel implementation):

$$\alpha = \left(\frac{\overline{x} - A}{B - A}\right)\left(\frac{\left(\dfrac{\overline{x} - A}{B - A}\right)\left(1 - \left(\dfrac{\overline{x} - A}{B - A}\right)\right)}{\dfrac{s^2}{(B - A)^2}} - 1\right)$$

Beta

$$\beta = \alpha \times \left(\frac{\left(1 - \left(\dfrac{\overline{x} - A}{B - A} \right) \right)}{\left(\dfrac{\overline{x} - A}{B - A} \right)} \right)$$

$\alpha = 7, \beta = 2,$
$A = 0, B = 70$

Example: The boom-or-bust nature of the revenue generated by a movie from a polarizing director may be described by a beta distribution. The relevant values (in millions of dollars) are $A = 0$, $B = 70$, $\alpha = 0.45$, and $\beta = 0.45$. This particular distribution is U-shaped and extreme values are more likely than moderate values. The figures in the left margin illustrate beta distributions with different values of α and β, demonstrating its flexibility. The first figure depicts a U-shaped beta distribution. The second figure depicts a unimodal beta distribution with a positive skew. The third figure depicts a unimodal beta distribution with a negative skew.

Native Excel: BETA.INV(RAND(), α, β, A, B)

Gamma Distribution

Parameters: alpha (α), beta (β)

Range: 0 to $+\infty$

Gamma

Description: The gamma distribution has a very flexible shape controlled by the values of α and β. The gamma distribution is useful in modeling an uncertain quantity that can be as small as zero but can also realize large values. To estimate the values of the alpha and beta parameters given sample data, we use the following equations (see the file *Gamma* for an Excel implementation):

$$\alpha = \left(\frac{\overline{x}}{s} \right)^2$$

$$\beta = \frac{s^2}{\overline{x}}$$

Example: The aggregate amount (in \$100,000s) of insurance claims in a region may be described by a gamma distribution with $\alpha = 2$ and $\beta = 0.5$.

Native Excel: GAMMA.INV(RAND(), α, β)

Exponential Distribution

Parameters: mean (m)

Range: 0 to $-\infty$

Description: The exponential distribution is characterized by a mean value equal to its standard deviation and a long right tail stretching from a mode value of 0.

Example: The time between events, such as customer arrivals or customer defaults on bill payment, are commonly modeled with an exponential distribution. An exponential random variable possesses the "memoryless" property: the probability of a customer arrival occurring in the next x minutes does not depend on how long it's been since the last arrival. For example, suppose the average time between customer arrivals is 10 minutes. Then, the probability that there will be 25 or more minutes between customer arrivals if 10 minutes have passed since the last customer arrival is the same as the probability that there will be more than 15 minutes until the next arrival if a customer just arrived.

Native Excel: LN(RAND())*($-m$), or equivalently GAMMA.INV(RAND(), 1, 1/m) because the exponential distribution is a special case of the gamma distribution with $\alpha = 1$ and $\beta = 1/m$

Triangular Distribution

Parameters: minimum (a), most likely (m), maximum (b)

Range: a to b

Description: The triangular distribution is often used to subjectively assess uncertainty when little is known about a random variable besides its range, but it is thought to have a single mode. The distribution is shaped like a triangle with vertices at a, m, and b.

Triangular

Example: In corporate finance, a triangular distribution may be used to model a project's annual revenue growth in a net present value analysis if the analyst can reliably provide minimum, most likely, and maximum estimates of growth. For example, a project may have worst-case annual revenue growth of 0%, a most-likely annual revenue growth of 5%, and best-case annual revenue growth of 25%. These values would then serve as the parameters for a triangular distribution.

Native Excel: IF(*random* < (*m* − *a*)/(*b* − *a*), *a* + SQRT((*b* − *a*)*(*m* − *a*)*random), *b* − SQRT((*b* − *a*)*(*b* − *m*)*(1 − *random*))), where *random* refers to a single, separate cell containing =RAND() (see the file *Triangular* for an Excel implementation)

Uniform Distribution

Parameters: minimum (*a*), maximum (*b*)

Range: *a* to *b*

Description: The uniform distribution is appropriate when a random variable is equally likely to be any value between *a* and *b*. When little is known about a phenomenon other than its minimum and maximum possible values, the uniform distribution may be a conservative choice to model an uncertain quantity.

Example: A service technician making a house call may quote a 4-hour time window in which he will arrive. If the technician is equally likely to arrive any time during this time window, then the arrival time of the technician in this time window may be described with a uniform distribution.

Native Excel: $a + (b - a) * \text{RAND}()$

Log-Normal Distribution

Parameters: *log_mean, log_stdev*

Range: 0 to +∞

Description: The log-normal distribution is a unimodal distribution (like the normal distribution) that has a minimum value of 0 and a long right tail (unlike the normal distribution). The log-normal distribution is often a good way to characterize a quantity that is the product of many independent, positive random variables. The natural logarithm of a log-normally distributed random variable is normally distributed.

Example: The income distribution of the lower 99% of a population is often well described using a log-normal distribution. For example, for a population in which the natural logarithm of the income observations is normally distributed with a mean of 3.5 and a standard deviation of 0.5, the income observations are distributed log-normally.

Native Excel: LOGNORM.INV(RAND(), *log_mean, log_stdev*), where *log_mean* and *log_stdev* are the mean and standard deviation of the normally distributed random variable obtained when taking the logarithm of the log-normally distributed random variable.

Discrete Probability Distributions

Random variables that can be only a relatively small number of discrete values are often best modeled with a discrete distribution. The appropriate choice of discrete distribution relies on the specific situation. For common discrete random variables, we provide several pieces of information. First, we list the parameters required to specify the distribution. Then, we outline possible values that can be realized by a random variable that follows the given distribution. We also provide a short description of the distribution paired with an illustration. Then, we supply an example of the application of the random variable. We conclude with the native Excel functionality for generating random values from the probability distribution.

Integer Uniform Distribution

Parameters: lower (*l*), upper (*u*)

Possible values: $l, l + 1, l + 2, \ldots, u - 2, u - 1, u$

Description: An integer uniform random variable assumes that the integer values between l and u are equally likely.

Example: The number of philanthropy volunteers from a class of 10 students may be an integer uniform variable with values 0, 1, 2, . . . , 10.

Native Excel: RANDBETWEEN(l, u)

Discrete Uniform Distribution

Parameters: set of values $\{v_1, v_2, v_3, \ldots, v_k\}$

Possible values: $v_1, v_2, v_3, \ldots, v_k$

Description: A discrete uniform random variable is equally likely to be any of the specified set of values $\{v_1, v_2, v_3, \ldots, v_k\}$.

Example: Consider a game show that awards a contestant a cash prize from an envelope randomly selected from six possible envelopes. If the envelopes contain $1, $5, $10, $20, $50, and $100, respectively, then the prize is a discrete uniform random variable with values $\{1, 5, 10, 20, 50, 100\}$.

Native Excel: CHOOSE(RANDBETWEEN(l, k), $v_1, v_2, \ldots, v_k$)

Custom Discrete Distribution

Parameters: set of values $\{v_1, v_2, v_3, \ldots, v_k\}$ and corresponding weights $\{w_1, w_2, w_3, \ldots, w_k\}$ such that $w_1 + w_2 + \cdots + w_k = 1$

Possible values: $v_1, v_2, v_3, \ldots, v_k$

Description: A custom discrete distribution can be used to create a tailored distribution to model a discrete, uncertain quantity. The value of a custom discrete random variable is equal to the value v_i with probability w_i.

Example: Analysis of daily sales for the past 50 days at a car dealership shows that on 7 days no cars were sold, on 24 days one car was sold, on 9 days two cars were sold, on 5 days three cars were sold, on 3 days four cars were sold, and on 2 days five cars were sold. We can estimate the probability distribution of daily sales using the relative frequencies. An estimate of the probability that no cars are sold on a given day is 7/50 = 0.14, an estimate of the probability that one car is sold is 24/50 = 0.48, and so on. Daily sales may then be described by a custom discrete distribution with values of $\{0, 1, 2, 3, 4, 5\}$ with respective weights of $\{0.14, 0.48, 0.18, 0.10, 0.06, 0.04\}$.

Native Excel: Use the RAND function in conjunction with the VLOOKUP function referencing a table in which each row lists a possible value and a segment of the interval [0, 1) representing the likelihood of the corresponding value. Figure 11.32 illustrates the implementation for the car sales example.

FIGURE 11.32	Native Excel Implementation of Custom Discrete Distribution

	A	B	C	D
1	Cars Sold	=VLOOKUP(RAND(), A4:C9, 3, TRUE)		
2				
3	Lower End of Interval	Upper End of Interval	Cars Sold	Probability
4	0.00	0.14	0	0.14
5	0.14	0.62	1	0.48
6	0.62	0.80	2	0.18
7	0.80	0.90	3	0.10
8	0.90	0.96	4	0.06
9	0.96	1.00	5	0.04

Binomial Distribution

Parameters: trials (n), probability of a success (p)

Possible values: $0, 1, 2, \ldots, n$

Description: A binomial random variable corresponds to the number of times an event successfully occurs in n trials, and the probability of a success at each trial is p and independent of whether a success occurs on other trials. When $n = 1$, the binomial is also known as the Bernoulli distribution.

Example: In a portfolio of 20 similar stocks, each of which has the same probability of increasing in value of $p = 0.6$, the total number of stocks that increase in value can be described by a binomial distribution with parameters $n = 20$ and $p = 0.6$.

Native Excel: BINOM.INV(n, p, RAND())

Hypergeometric Distribution

Parameters: trials (n), population size (N), successful elements in population (s)

Possible values: $\max\{0, n + s - N\}, \ldots, \min\{n, s\}$

Description: A hypergeometric random variable corresponds to the number of times an element labeled a success is selected out of n trials in the situation where there are N total elements, s of which are labeled a success and, once selected, cannot be selected again. Note that this is similar to the binomial distribution except that now the trials are dependent because removing the selected element changes the probabilities of selecting an element labeled a success on subsequent trials.

Example: A certain company produces circuit boards to sell to computer manufacturers. Because of a quality defect in the manufacturing process, it is known that only 70 circuit boards out of a lot of 100 have been produced correctly and the other 30 are faulty. If a company orders 40 circuit boards from this lot of 100, the number of functioning circuit boards that the company will receive in their order is a hypergeometric random variable with $n = 40$, $s = 70$, and $N = 100$. Note that, in this case, between 10 ($= 40 + 70 - 100$) and 40 ($=\min\{40, 70\}$) of the 40 ordered circuit boards will be functioning. At least 10 of the 40 circuit boards will be functioning because at most 30 ($= 100 - 70$) are faulty.

Native Excel: Insert the worksheet from the file *Hypergeometric* into your Excel workbook, modify the parameters in the cell range B2:B4, and then reference cell B6 in your simulation model to obtain a value from a hypergeometric distribution. This file uses the RAND function in conjunction with the VLOOKUP function referencing a table in which each row lists a possible value and a segment of the interval [0, 1] representing the likelihood of the corresponding value; the probability of each value is computed with the HYPGEOM.DIST function. Figure 11.33 illustrates the *Hypergeometric* file with the parameter values for the circuit board example.

Negative Binomial Distribution

Parameters: required number of successes (s), probability of success (p)

Possible values: $0, 1, 2, \ldots, \infty$

Description: A negative binomial random variable corresponds to the number of times that an event fails to occur until an event successfully occurs s times, given that the probability of an event successfully occurring at each trial is p. When $s = 1$, the negative binomial is also known as the geometric distribution.

Example: Consider the research and development (R&D) division of a large company. An R&D division may invest in several projects that fail before investing in 5 projects that succeed. If each project has a probability of success of *0.50*, the number of projects that fail before 5 successful projects occur is a negative binomial random variable with parameters $s = 5$ and $p = 0.50$.

Native Excel: Insert the worksheet from the file *NegativeBinomial* into your Excel workbook, modify the parameters in the cell range B2:B3, and then reference cell B5 in your simulation model to obtain a value from a negative binomial distribution. This file uses the RAND function in conjunction with the VLOOKUP function referencing

FIGURE 11.33   Excel Template to Generate Values from a Hypergeometric Distribution

	A	B	C	D	E
1	Hypergeometric Distribution Parameters				
2	Trials (n)	40			
3	Population (N)	100			
4	Successful Elements in Population (s)	70			
5					
6	Randomly Generated Hypergeometric Value	=VLOOKUP(RAND(),$C$9:$E$109,3,TRUE)			
7					
8	Number of Successes in n Trials	Probability Mass	Lower End of Interval	Upper End of Interval	Number of Successes in n Trials
9	0	=HYPGEOM.DIST($A9,$B$2,$B$4,$B$3,FALSE)	0	=B9+C9	0
10	1	=HYPGEOM.DIST($A10,$B$2,$B$4,$B$3,FALSE)	=D9	=B10+C10	1
11	2	=HYPGEOM.DIST($A11,$B$2,$B$4,$B$3,FALSE)	=D10	=B11+C11	2
12	3	=HYPGEOM.DIST($A12,$B$2,$B$4,$B$3,FALSE)	=D11	=B12+C12	3
13	4	=HYPGEOM.DIS			
14	5	=HYPGEOM.DIS			

	A	B	C	D	E
1	Hypergeometric Distribution Parameters				
2	Trials (n)	40			
3	Population (N)	100			
4	Successful Elements in Population (s)	70			
5					
6	Randomly Generated Hypergeometric Value	29			
7					
8	Number of Successes in n Trials	Probability Mass	Lower End of Interval	Upper End of Interval	Number of Successes in n Trials
9	0	0.000	0.000	0.000	0
10	1	0.000	0.000	0.000	1
11	2	0.000	0.000	0.000	2
12	3	0.000	0.000	0.000	3
13	4	0.000	0.000	0.000	4
14	5	0.000	0.000	0.000	5
15	6	0.000	0.000	0.000	6
16	7	0.000	0.000	0.000	7
17	8	0.000	0.000	0.000	8
18	9	0.000	0.000	0.000	9
19	10	0.000	0.000	0.000	10
20	11	0.000	0.000	0.000	11
21	12	0.000	0.000	0.000	12
22	13	0.000	0.000	0.000	13
23	14	0.000	0.000	0.000	14
24	15	0.000	0.000	0.000	15
25	16	0.000	0.000	0.000	16
26	17	0.000	0.000	0.000	17
27	18	0.000	0.000	0.000	18
28	19	0.000	0.000	0.000	19
29	20	0.000	0.000	0.000	20
30	21	0.002	0.000	0.002	21
31	22	0.005	0.002	0.007	22
32	23	0.016	0.007	0.023	23
33	24	0.037	0.023	0.060	24
34	25	0.073	0.060	0.133	25
35	26	0.118	0.133	0.251	26
36	27	0.159	0.251	0.410	27
37	28	0.176	0.410	0.586	28
38	29	0.161	0.586	0.747	29
39	30	0.121	0.747	0.868	30
40	31	0.074	0.868	0.942	31
41	32	0.037	0.942	0.979	32
42	33	0.015	0.979	0.994	33
43	34	0.005	0.994	0.999	34
44	35	0.001	0.999	1.000	35

MODEL *file*

Hypergeometric

a table in which each row lists a possible value and a segment of the interval [0, 1) representing the likelihood of the corresponding value; the probability of each value is computed with the NEGBINOM.DIST function. Figure 11.34 illustrates the implementation for the R&D project example.

Poisson Distribution

Parameters: mean (m)

Possible values: 0, 1, 2, . . .

Description: A Poisson random variable corresponds to the number of times that an event occurs within a specified period of time given that m is the average number of events within the specified period of time.

Example: The number of patients arriving at a health care clinic in an hour can be modeled with a Poisson random variable with $m = 5$, if on average 5 customers arrive to the store in an hour.

Native Excel: Insert the worksheet from the file *Poisson* into your Excel workbook, modify the parameter in cell B2, and then reference cell B4 in your simulation model to obtain a value from a Poisson distribution. This file uses the RAND function in conjunction with the VLOOKUP function referencing a table in which each row lists a possible value and a segment of the interval [0, 1) representing the likelihood of the corresponding value; the probability of each value is computed with the POISSON.DIST function. Figure 11.35 illustrates the implementation for the health care clinic example.

FIGURE 11.34   Excel Template to Generate Values from a Negative Binomial Distribution

	A	B	C	D	E
1	Negative Binomial Distribution Parameters				
2	Required Number of Successes (s)	5			
3	Probability of Success (p)	0.5			
4					
5	Randomly Generated Negative Binomial Value	=VLOOKUP(RAND(),$C$8:$E$108,3,TRUE)			
6					
7	Number of Failures Before s Successes	Probability Mass	Lower End of Interval	Upper End of Interval	Number of Failures Before s Successes
8	0	=NEGBINOM.DIST($A8,$B$2,$B$3,FALSE)	0	=C8+B8	0
9	1	=NEGBINOM.DIST($A9,$B$2,$B$3,FALSE)	=D8	=C9+B9	1
10	2	=NEGBINOM.DIST($A10,$B$2,$B$3,FALSE)	=C9+B9	=C10+B10	2
11	3	=NEGBINOM.DIST($A11,$B$2,$B$3,FALSE)	=C10+B10	=C11+B11	3
12	4	=NEGBINOM.DIST($A12,$B$2,$B$3,FALSE)	=C11+B11	=C12+B12	4
13	5	=NEGBINOM.DIST($A13,$B$2,$B$3,FALSE)	=C12+B12	=C13+B13	5

	A	B	C	D	E
1	Negative Binomial Distribution Parameters				
2	Required Number of Successes (s)	5			
3	Probability of Success (p)	0.50			
4					
5	Randomly Generated Negative Binomial Value	3			
6					
7	Number of Failures Before s Successes	Probability Mass	Lower End of Interval	Upper End of Interval	Number of Failures Before s Successes
8	0	0.031	0.000	0.031	0
9	1	0.078	0.031	0.109	1
10	2	0.117	0.109	0.227	2
11	3	0.137	0.227	0.363	3
12	4	0.137	0.363	0.500	4
13	5	0.123	0.500	0.623	5
14	6	0.103	0.623	0.726	6
15	7	0.081	0.726	0.806	7
16	8	0.060	0.806	0.867	8
17	9	0.044	0.867	0.910	9
18	10	0.031	0.910	0.941	10
19	11	0.021	0.941	0.962	11
20	12	0.014	0.962	0.975	12
21	13	0.009	0.975	0.985	13
22	14	0.006	0.985	0.990	14
23	15	0.004	0.990	0.994	15
24	16	0.002	0.994	0.996	16
25	17	0.001	0.996	0.998	17
26	18	0.001	0.998	0.999	18
27	19	0.001	0.999	0.999	19
28	20	0.000	0.999	1.000	20

MODEL file

NegativeBinomial

FIGURE 11.35   Excel Template to Generate Values from a Poisson Distribution

	A	B	C	D	E
1	Poisson Distribution Parameters				
2	Mean (m)	5			
3					
4	Randomly Generated Poisson Value	=VLOOKUP(RAND(),$C$7:$E$107,3,TRUE)			
5					
6	Number of Event Occurrences	Probability Mass	Lower End of Interval	Upper End of Interval	Number of Event Occurrences
7	0	=POISSON.DIST($A7,$B$2,FALSE)	0	=C7+B7	0
8	1	=POISSON.DIST($A8,$B$2,FALSE)	=D7	=C8+B8	1
9	2	=POISSON.DIST($A9,$B$2,FALSE)	=C8	=C9+B9	2
10	3	=POISSON.DIST($A10,$B$2,FALSE)	=C9	=C10+B10	3
11	4	=POISSON.DIST($A11,$B$2,FALSE)	=C10	=C11+B11	4
12	5	=POISSON.DIST($A12,$B$2,FALSE)	=C11	=C12+B12	5

	A	B	C	D	E
1	Poisson Distribution Parameters				
2	Mean (m)	5			
3					
4	Randomly Generated Poisson Value	6			
5					
6	Number of Event Occurrences	Probability Mass	Lower End of Interval	Upper End of Interval	Number of Event Occurrences
7	0	0.007	0.000	0.007	0
8	1	0.034	0.007	0.040	1
9	2	0.084	0.040	0.125	2
10	3	0.140	0.125	0.265	3
11	4	0.175	0.265	0.440	4
12	5	0.175	0.440	0.616	5
13	6	0.146	0.616	0.762	6
14	7	0.104	0.762	0.867	7
15	8	0.065	0.867	0.932	8
16	9	0.036	0.932	0.968	9
17	10	0.018	0.968	0.986	10
18	11	0.008	0.986	0.995	11
19	12	0.003	0.995	0.998	12
20	13	0.001	0.998	0.999	13
21	14	0.000	0.999	1.000	14

MODEL file

Poisson

Chapter 12

Linear Optimization Models

CONTENTS

ANALYTICS IN ACTION: *GENERAL ELECTRIC*

ANALYTICS IN ACTION

General Electric*

With growing concerns about the environment and our ability to continue to utilize limited nonrenewable sources for energy, companies have begun to place much more emphasis on renewable forms of energy. Water, wind, and solar energy are renewable forms of energy that have become the focus of considerable investment by companies.

General Electric (GE) has products in a variety of areas within the energy sector. One such area of interest to GE is solar energy. Solar energy is a relatively new concept with rapidly changing technologies; for example, solar cells and solar power systems. Solar cells can convert sunlight directly into electricity. Concentrating solar power systems focus a larger area of sunlight into a small beam that can be used as a heat source for conventional power generation. Solar cells can be placed on rooftops and hence can be used by both commercial and residential customers, whereas solar power systems are mostly used in commercial settings. In recent years, GE has invested in several solar cell technologies.

Determining the appropriate amount of production capacity in which to invest is a difficult problem due to

the uncertainties in technology development, costs, and solar energy demand. GE uses a set of analytics tools to solve this problem. A detailed descriptive analytical model is used to estimate the cost of newly developed or proposed solar cells. Statistical models developed for new product introductions are used to estimate annual solar demand 10 to 15 years into the future. Finally, the cost and demand estimates are used in a multiperiod linear optimization model to determine the best production capacity investment plan.

The linear program finds an optimal expansion plan by taking into account inventory, capacity, production, and budget constraints. Because of the high level of uncertainty, the linear program is solved over multiple future scenarios. A solution to each individual scenario is found and evaluated in the other scenarios to assess the risk associated with that plan. GE planning analysts have used these tools to support management's strategic investment decisions in the solar energy sector.

---

*Based on B. G. Thomas and S. Bollapragada, "General Electric Uses an Integrated Framework for Product Costing, Demand Forecasting and Capacity Planning for New Photovoltaic Technology Products," *Interfaces*, 40, no. 5 (September/October 2010): 353–367.

This chapter begins our discussion of *prescriptive analytics* and how optimization models can be used to support and improve managerial decision making. Optimization problems maximize or minimize some function, called the **objective function**, and usually have a set of restrictions known as **constraints**. Consider the following typical applications of optimization:

1. A manufacturer wants to develop a production schedule and an inventory policy that will satisfy demand in future periods. Ideally, the schedule and policy will enable the company to satisfy demand and at the same time *minimize* the total production and inventory costs.
2. A financial analyst must select an investment portfolio from a variety of stock and bond investment alternatives. The analyst would like to establish the portfolio that *maximizes* the return on investment.
3. A marketing manager wants to determine how best to allocate a fixed advertising budget among alternative advertising media such as online, radio, television, and magazine. The manager would like to determine the media mix that *maximizes* advertising effectiveness.
4. A company has warehouses in a number of locations. Given specific customer demands, the company would like to determine how much each warehouse should ship to each customer so that total transportation costs are *minimized*.
5. A hospital needs to determine the work schedule of emergency room nurses for the next month. The hospital would like to minimize the amount of overtime it must pay to nurses while ensuring that the emergency room is fully staffed while also accommodating time-off requests and work rules for nurses.

Each of these examples has a clear objective. In example 1, the manufacturer wants to minimize costs; in example 2, the financial analyst wants to maximize return on investment; in example 3, the marketing manager wants to maximize advertising effectiveness; in example 4, the company wants to minimize total transportation costs; and in example 5, the hospital wants to minimize the amount of overtime it must pay to nurses.

Likewise, each problem has constraints that limit the degree to which the objective can be pursued. In example 1, the manufacturer is restricted by the constraints requiring product demand to be satisfied and limiting production capacity. The financial analyst's portfolio problem is constrained by the total amount of investment funds available and the maximum amounts that can be invested in each stock or bond. The marketing manager's media selection decision is constrained by a fixed advertising budget and the availability of the various media. In the transportation problem, the minimum-cost shipping schedule is constrained by the supply of product available at each warehouse. For the hospital, the possible schedules for nurses are constrained by how many nurses are available as well as by time-off requests and existing work rules for nurses.

Optimization models can be linear or nonlinear. We begin with linear optimization models, also known as linear programs. Linear programming is a problem-solving approach developed to help managers make better decisions. Numerous applications of linear programming can be found in today's competitive business environment. For instance, GE Capital uses linear programming to help determine optimal lease structuring, and Marathon Oil Company uses linear programming for gasoline blending and to evaluate the economics of a new terminal or pipeline.

Linear programming was initially referred to as "programming in a linear structure." In 1948, Tjalling Koopmans suggested to George Dantzig that the name was much too long: Koopman's suggestion was to shorten it to linear programming. George Dantzig agreed, and the field we now know as linear programming was named.

12.1 A Simple Maximization Problem

Par, Inc. is a small manufacturer of golf equipment and supplies whose management has decided to move into the market for medium- and high-priced golf bags. Par's distributor is enthusiastic about the new product line and has agreed to buy all the golf bags Par produces over the next three months.

After a thorough investigation of the steps involved in manufacturing a golf bag, management determined that each golf bag produced will require the following operations:

1. Cutting and dyeing the material
2. Sewing
3. Finishing (inserting umbrella holder, club separators, etc.)
4. Inspection and packaging

The director of manufacturing analyzed each of the operations and concluded that if the company produces a medium-priced standard model, each bag will require $7/10$ hour in the cutting and dyeing department, $1/2$ hour in the sewing department, 1 hour in the finishing department, and $1/10$ hour in the inspection and packaging department. The more expensive deluxe model will require 1 hour for cutting and dyeing, $5/6$ hour for sewing, $2/3$ hour for finishing, and $1/4$ hour for inspection and packaging. This production information is summarized in Table 12.1.

Par's production is constrained by a limited number of hours available in each department. After studying departmental workload projections, the director of manufacturing estimates that 630 hours for cutting and dyeing, 600 hours for sewing, 708 hours for

TABLE 12.1	Production Requirements per Golf Bag	
	Production Time (hours)	
Department	**Standard Bag**	**Deluxe Bag**
Cutting and Dyeing	$7/10$	1
Sewing	$1/2$	$5/6$
Finishing	1	$2/3$
Inspection and Packaging	$1/10$	$1/4$

finishing, and 135 hours for inspection and packaging will be available for the production of golf bags during the next three months.

The accounting department analyzed the production data, assigned all relevant variable costs, and arrived at prices for both bags that will result in a profit contribution[1] of $10 for every standard bag and $9 for every deluxe bag produced. Let us now develop a mathematical model of the Par, Inc. problem that can be used to determine the number of standard bags and the number of deluxe bags to produce in order to maximize total profit contribution.

Problem Formulation

Problem formulation, or **modeling,** is the process of translating the verbal statement of a problem into a mathematical statement. Formulating models is an art that can be mastered only with practice and experience. Even though every problem has some unique features, most problems also have common features. As a result, *some* general guidelines for optimization model formulation can be helpful, especially for beginners. We will illustrate these general guidelines by developing a mathematical model for Par, Inc.

Understand the problem thoroughly We selected the Par, Inc. problem to introduce linear programming because it is easy to understand. However, more complex problems will require much more effort to identify the items that need to be included in the model. In such cases, read the problem description to get a feel for what is involved. Taking notes will help you focus on the key issues and facts.

Describe the objective The objective is to maximize the total contribution to profit.

Describe each constraint Four constraints relate to the number of hours of manufacturing time available; they restrict the number of standard bags and the number of deluxe bags that can be produced.

- *Constraint 1:* The number of hours of cutting and dyeing time used must be less than or equal to the number of hours of cutting and dyeing time available.
- *Constraint 2:* The number of hours of sewing time used must be less than or equal to the number of hours of sewing time available.
- *Constraint 3:* The number of hours of finishing time used must be less than or equal to the number of hours of finishing time available.
- *Constraint 4:* The number of hours of inspection and packaging time used must be less than or equal to the number of hours of inspection and packaging time available.

Define the decision variables The controllable inputs for Par, Inc. are (1) the number of standard bags produced and (2) the number of deluxe bags produced. Let:

$$S = \text{number of standard bags}$$

$$D = \text{number of deluxe bags}$$

In optimization terminology, S and D are referred to as the **decision variables.**

Write the objective in terms of the decision variables Par's profit contribution comes from two sources: (1) the profit contribution made by producing S standard bags and (2) the profit contribution made by producing D deluxe bags. If Par makes $10 for every standard bag, the company will make $10S if S standard bags are produced. Also, if Par makes $9 for every deluxe bag, the company will make $9D if D deluxe bags are produced. Thus, we have

$$\text{Total profit contribution} = 10S + 9D$$

Because the objective—maximize total profit contribution—is a function of the decision variables S and D, we refer to $10S + 9D$ as the *objective function.* Using *Max* as an abbreviation for maximize, we write Par's objective as follows:

$$\text{Max } 10S + 9D$$

---

[1]From an accounting perspective, profit contribution is more correctly described as the contribution margin per bag since overhead and other shared costs are not allocated.

It is important to understand that we are maximizing profit contribution, not profit. Overhead and other shared costs must be deducted before arriving at a profit figure.

The units of measurement on the left-hand side of the constraint must match the units of measurement on the right-hand side.

Write the constraints in terms of the decision variables
Constraint 1:

$$\begin{pmatrix} \text{Hours of cutting and} \\ \text{dyeing time used} \end{pmatrix} \leq \begin{pmatrix} \text{Hours of cutting and} \\ \text{dyeing time available} \end{pmatrix}$$

Every standard bag Par produces will use $7/10$ hour cutting and dyeing time; therefore, the total number of hours of cutting and dyeing time used in the manufacture of S standard bags is $7/10\,S$. In addition, because every deluxe bag produced uses 1 hour of cutting and dyeing time, the production of D deluxe bags will use $1D$ hours of cutting and dyeing time. Thus, the total cutting and dyeing time required for the production of S standard bags and D deluxe bags is given by

$$\text{Total hours of cutting and dyeing time used} = 7/10\,S + 1D$$

The director of manufacturing stated that Par has at most 630 hours of cutting and dyeing time available. Therefore, the production combination we select must satisfy the requirement:

$$7/10\,S + 1D \leq 630 \tag{12.1}$$

Constraint 2:

$$\begin{pmatrix} \text{Hours of sewing} \\ \text{time used} \end{pmatrix} \leq \begin{pmatrix} \text{Hours of sewing} \\ \text{time available} \end{pmatrix}$$

From Table 12.1, we see that every standard bag manufactured will require $1/2$ hour for sewing, and every deluxe bag will require $5/6$ hour for sewing. Because 600 hours of sewing time are available, it follows that

$$1/2\,S + 5/6\,D \leq 600 \tag{12.2}$$

Constraint 3:

$$\begin{pmatrix} \text{Hours of finishing} \\ \text{time used} \end{pmatrix} \leq \begin{pmatrix} \text{Hours of finishing} \\ \text{time available} \end{pmatrix}$$

Every standard bag manufactured will require 1 hour for finishing, and every deluxe bag will require $2/3$ hour for finishing. With 708 hours of finishing time available, it follows that

$$1S + 2/3\,D \leq 708 \tag{12.3}$$

Constraint 4:

$$\begin{pmatrix} \text{Hours of inspection and} \\ \text{packaging time used} \end{pmatrix} \leq \begin{pmatrix} \text{Hours of inspection and} \\ \text{packaging time available} \end{pmatrix}$$

Every standard bag manufactured will require $1/10$ hour for inspection and packaging, and every deluxe bag will require $1/4$ hour for inspection and packaging. Because 135 hours of inspection and packaging time are available, it follows that

$$1/10\,S + 1/4\,D \leq 135 \tag{12.4}$$

We have now specified the mathematical relationships for the constraints associated with the four departments. Have we forgotten any other constraints? Can Par produce a negative number of standard or deluxe bags? Clearly, the answer is no. Thus, to prevent the decision variables S and D from having negative values, two constraints must be added:

$$S \geq 0 \quad \text{and} \quad D \geq 0 \tag{12.5}$$

These constraints ensure that the solution to the problem will contain only nonnegative values for the decision variables and are thus referred to as the **nonnegativity constraints**. Nonnegativity constraints are a general feature of many linear programming problems and may be written in the abbreviated form:

$$S, D \geq 0$$

Mathematical Model for the Par, Inc. Problem

The mathematical statement, or mathematical formulation, of the Par, Inc. problem is now complete. We succeeded in translating the objective and constraints of the problem into a set of mathematical relationships, referred to as a **mathematical model**. The complete mathematical model for the Par, Inc. problem is as follows:

$$\text{Max} \quad 10S + 9D$$

subject to (s.t.)

$$
\begin{array}{lll}
\tfrac{7}{10}S + 1D & \leq 630 & \text{Cutting and dyeing} \\
\tfrac{1}{2}S + \tfrac{5}{6}D & \leq 600 & \text{Sewing} \\
1S + \tfrac{2}{3}D & \leq 708 & \text{Finishing} \\
\tfrac{1}{10}S + \tfrac{1}{4}D & \leq 135 & \text{Inspection and packaging} \\
S, D & \geq 0 &
\end{array}
$$

Linear programming has nothing to do with computer programming. The use of the word programming means "choosing a course of action." Linear programming involves choosing a course of action when the mathematical model of the problem contains only linear functions.

Our job now is to find the product mix (i.e., the combination of values for S and D) that satisfies all the constraints and at the same time yields a value for the objective function that is greater than or equal to the value given by any other feasible solution. Once these values are calculated, we will have found the optimal solution to the problem.

This mathematical model of the Par, Inc. problem is a **linear programming model**, or **linear program**, because the objective function and all constraint functions (the left-hand sides of the constraint inequalities) are linear functions of the decision variables.

Mathematical functions in which each variable appears in a separate term and is raised to the first power are called **linear functions**. The objective function ($10S + 9D$) is linear because each decision variable appears in a separate term and has an exponent of 1. The amount of production time required in the cutting and dyeing department ($\tfrac{7}{10}S + 1D$) is also a linear function of the decision variables for the same reason. Similarly, the functions on the left-hand side of all the constraint inequalities (the constraint functions) are linear functions. Thus, the mathematical formulation of this problem is referred to as a linear program.

NOTES + COMMENTS

The three assumptions necessary for a linear programming model to be appropriate are proportionality, additivity, and divisibility. *Proportionality* means that the contribution to the objective function and the amount of resources used in each constraint are proportional to the value of each decision variable. *Additivity* means that the value of the objective function and the total resources used can be found by summing the objective function contribution and the resources used for all decision variables. *Divisibility* means that the decision variables are continuous. The divisibility assumption plus the nonnegativity constraints mean that decision variables can take on any value greater than or equal to zero.

12.2 Solving the Par, Inc. Problem

Now that we have modeled the Par, Inc. problem as a linear program, let us discuss how we might find the optimal solution. The optimal solution must be a feasible solution. A **feasible solution** is a setting of the decision variables that satisfies all of the constraints of the problem. The optimal solution also must have an objective function value as good as any other feasible solution. For a maximization problem like Par, Inc., this means that the solution must be feasible and achieve the highest objective function value of any feasible solution. To solve a linear program then, we must search over the **feasible region**, which is the set of all feasible solutions, and find the solution that gives the best objective function value.

Because the Par, Inc. model has two decision variables, we are able to graph the feasible region. Discussing the geometry of the feasible region of the model will help us better understand linear programming and how we are able to solve much larger problems on the computer.

The Geometry of the Par, Inc. Problem

Recall that the feasible region is the set of points that satisfies all of the constraints of the problem. When we have only two decision variables and the functions of these variables are linear, they form lines in two-dimensional space. If the constraints are inequalities, the constraint cuts the space into two, with the line and the area on one side of the line being the space that satisfies that constraint. These subregions are called *half spaces*. The *intersection* of these half spaces makes up the feasible region.

The feasible region for the Par, Inc. problem is shown in Figure 12.1. Notice that the horizontal axis corresponds to the value of S and the vertical axis to the value of D. The nonnegativity constraints define that the feasible region is in the area bounded by the horizontal and vertical axes. Each of the four constraints is graphed as equality (a line), and arrows show the direction of the half space that satisfies the inequality constraint. The intersection of the four half spaces in the area bounded by the axes is the shaded region; this is the feasible region for the Par, Inc. problem. Any point in the shaded region satisfies all four constraints of the problem and nonnegativity.

To solve the Par, Inc. problem, we must find the point in the feasible region that results in the highest possible objective function value. A contour line is a set of points on a map, all of which have the same elevation. Similar to the way contour lines are used in geography, we may define an *objective function contour* to be a set of points (in this case a line) that yield a fixed value of the objective function. By choosing a fixed value of the objective function, we may plot contour lines of the objective function over the feasible region (Figure 12.2). In this case, as we move away from the origin we see higher values of the objective function and the highest such contour is $10S + 9D = 7{,}668$, after which we leave the feasible region. The highest value contour intersects the feasible region at a single point—point ③.

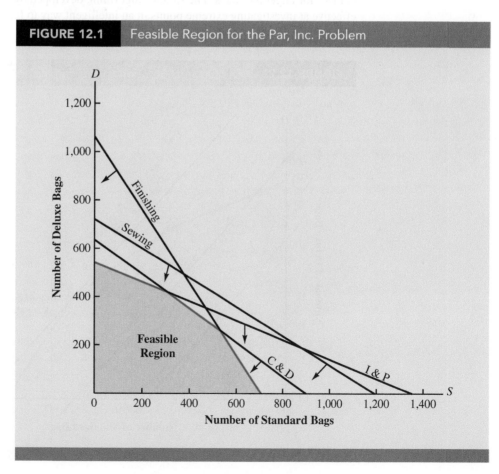

FIGURE 12.1   Feasible Region for the Par, Inc. Problem

Of course, this geometric approach to solving a linear program is limited to problems with only two variables. What have we learned that can help us solve larger linear optimization problems?

Based on the geometry of Figure 12.2, to solve a linear optimization problem we only have to search over the **extreme points** of the feasible region to find an optimal solution. The extreme points are found where constraints intersect on the boundary of the feasible region. In Figure 12.2, points ①, ②, ③, ④, and ⑤ are the extreme points of the feasible region.

Because each extreme point lies at the intersection of two constraint lines, we may obtain the values of S and D by solving simultaneously as equalities, the pair of constraints that form the given point. The values of S and D and the objective function value at points ① through ⑤ are as follows:

Point	S	D	Profit = 10S + 9D
1	0	0	10(0) + 9(0) = 0
2	708	0	10(708) + 9(0) = 7,080
3	540	252	10(540) + 9(252) = 7,080
4	300	420	10(300) + 9(420) = 6,780
5	0	540	10(0) + 9(540) = 4,860

The highest profit is achieved at point ③. Therefore, the optimal plan is to produce 540 standard bags and 252 deluxe bags, as shown in Figure 12.2.

It turns out that this approach of investigating only extreme points works well and generalizes for larger problems. The simplex algorithm, developed by George Dantzig, is quite effective at investigating extreme points in an intelligent way to find the optimal solution to even very large linear programs.

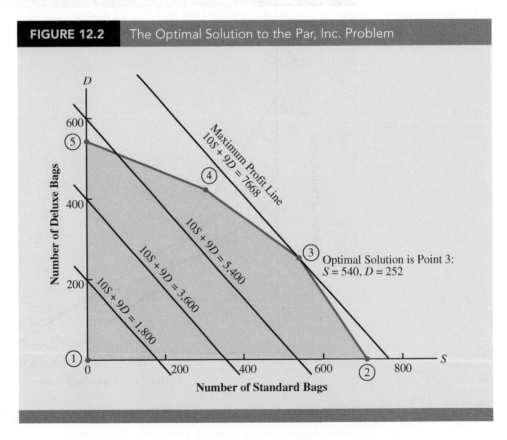

FIGURE 12.2   The Optimal Solution to the Par, Inc. Problem

Excel Solver is software that utilizes Dantzig's simplex algorithm to solve linear programs by systematically finding which set of constraints form the optimal extreme point of the feasible region. Once it finds an optimal solution, Solver then reports the optimal values of the decision variables and the optimal objective function value. Let us illustrate now how to use Excel Solver to find the optimal solution to the Par, Inc. problem.

Solving Linear Programs with Excel Solver

The first step in solving a linear optimization model in Excel is to construct the relevant what-if model. Using the principles for developing good spreadsheet models discussed in Chapter 10, a what-if model for optimization allows the user to try different values of the decision variables and see easily (a) whether that trial solution is feasible, and (b) the value of the objective function for that trial solution.

Figure 12.3 shows a spreadsheet model for the Par, Inc. problem with a trial solution of one standard bag and one deluxe bag. Rows 1 through 10 contain the parameters for the problem. Row 14 contains the decision variable cells: Cells B14 and C14 are the locations for the number of standard and deluxe bags to produce. Cell B16 calculates the objective function value for the trial solution by using the SUMPRODUCT function. The SUMPRODUCT function is very useful for linear problems. Recall how the SUMPRODUCT function works:

$$=\text{SUMPRODUCT(B9:C9,\$B\$14:\$C\$14)} = B9*B14 + C9*C14 = 10(1) + 9(1) = 19$$

Note the use of absolute referencing in the SUMPRODUCT function here. This facilitates copying this function from cell B19 to cells B20:B22 in Figure 12.3.

We likewise use the SUMPRODUCT function in cells B19:B22 to calculate the number of hours used in each of the four departments. The hours available are immediately to the right for each department. Hence, we see that the current solution is feasible, since Hours Used do not exceed Hours Available in any department.

Once the what-if model is built, we need a way to convey to Excel Solver the structure of the linear optimization model. This is accomplished through the Excel Solver dialog box as follows:

Step 1. Click the **Data** tab in the Ribbon
Step 2. Click **Solver** in the **Analyze** group
Step 3. When the **Solver Parameters** dialog box appears (Figure 12.4):
   Enter *B16* in the **Set Objective:** box
   Select **Max** for the **To:** option
   Enter *B14:C14* in the **By Changing Variable Cells:** box
Step 4. Click the **Add** button
   When the **Add Constraint** dialog box appears:
   Enter *B19:B22* in the left-hand box under **Cell Reference:**
   Select **<=** from the drop-down button
   Enter *C19:C22* in the **Constraint**: box
   Click **OK**
Step 5. Select the checkbox for **Make Unconstrained Variables Non-Negative**
Step 6. From the drop-down menu for **Select a Solving Method:**, choose **Simplex LP**
Step 7. Click **Solve**
Step 8. When the **Solver Results** dialog box appears:
   Select **Keep Solver Solution**
   In the **Reports** section, select **Answer Report**
   Click **OK**

Variable cells that are required to be integer will be discussed in Chapter 13.

The completed Solver dialog box and solution for the Par, Inc. problem are shown in Figure 12.4. The optimal solution is to make 540 standard bags and 252 deluxe bags (see cells B14 and C14) for a profit of $7,688 (see cell B16). This corresponds to point ③ in Figure 12.2. Also note that, from cells B19:B22 compared to C19:C22, we use all cutting and dyeing time as well as all finishing time. This is, of course, consistent with what we have seen in Figures 12.1 and 12.2: The cutting, dyeing, and finishing constraints intersect to form point ③ in the graph.

FIGURE 12.3   What-If Spreadsheet Model for Par, Inc.

	A	B	C	D
1	**Par, Inc.**			
2	**Parameters**			
3		**Production Time (Hours)**		**Time Available**
4	**Operation**	**Standard**	**Deluxe**	**Hours**
5	Cutting and Dyeing	=7/10	1	630
6	Sewing	=5/10	=5/6	600
7	Finishing	1	=2/3	708
8	Inspection and Packaging	=1/10	=1/4	135
9	Profit Per Bag	10	9	
10				
11	**Model**			
12				
13		**Standard**	**Deluxe**	
14	Bags Produced	1	1	
15				
16	**Total Profit**	=SUMPRODUCT(B9:C9,$B$14:$C$14)		
17				
18	**Operation**	**Hours Used**	**Hours Available**	
19	Cutting and Dyeing	=SUMPRODUCT(B5:C5,$B$14:$C$14)	=D5	
20	Sewing	=SUMPRODUCT(B6:C6,$B$14:$C$14)	=D6	
21	Finishing	=SUMPRODUCT(B7:C7,$B$14:$C$14)	=D7	
22	Inspection and Packaging	=SUMPRODUCT(B8:C8,$B$14:$C$14)	=D8	

MODEL *file*

Par

	A	B	C	D
1	**Par, Inc.**			
2	**Parameters**			
3		**Production Time (Hours)**		**Time Available**
4	**Operation**	**Standard**	**Deluxe**	**Hours**
5	Cutting and Dyeing	0.7	1	630
6	Sewing	0.5	0.83333	600
7	Finishing	1	0.66667	708
8	Inspection and Packaging	0.1	0.25	135
9	Profit Per Bag	10	9.00	
10				
11	**Model**			
12				
13		**Standard**	**Deluxe**	
14	Bags Produced	1.00	1.00	
15				
16	**Total Profit**	$19.00		
17				
18	**Operation**	**Hours Used**	**Hours Available**	
19	Cutting and Dyeing	1.7	630	
20	Sewing	1.33333	600	
21	Finishing	1.66667	708	
22	Inspection and Packaging	0.35	135	

FIGURE 12.4   Solver Dialog Box and Solution to the Par, Inc. Problem

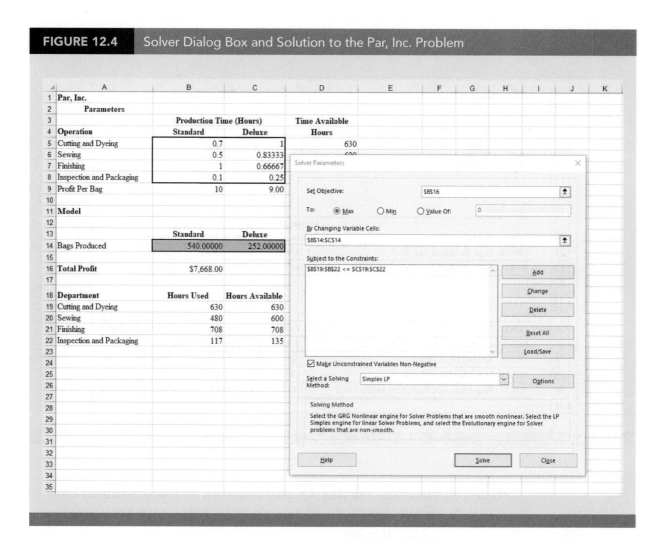

The Excel Solver Answer Report appears in Figure 12.5. The Answer Report contains three sections: Objective Cell, Variable Cells, and Constraints. In addition to some other information, each section gives the cell location, name, and value of the cell(s). The Objective Cell section indicates that the optimal (Final Value) of Total Profit is $7,668.00. In the Variable Cells section, the two far-right columns indicate the optimal values of the decision cells and whether or not the variables are required to be integer (here they are labeled "Contin" for continuous). Note that Solver generates a Name for a cell by concatenating the text to the left and above that cell. Hence, the name of cell $B$14 is created by combining the labels "Bags Produced" and "Standard" to produce the name "Bags Produced Standard."

The Constraints section gives the left-hand side value for each constraint (in this case the hours used), the formula showing the constraint relationship, the status (Binding or Not Binding), and the Slack value. A **binding constraint** is one that holds as an equality at the optimal solution. Geometrically, binding constraints intersect to form the optimal point. We see in Figure 12.5 that the cutting and dyeing and finishing constraints are designated as binding, consistent with our geometric study of this problem.

The **slack** value for each less-than-or-equal-to constraint indicates the difference between the left-hand and right-hand values for a constraint. Of course, by definition,

FIGURE 12.5 The Solver Answer Report for the Par, Inc. Problem

	A	B	C	D	E	F	G
13							
14		Objective Cell (Max)					
15		Cell	Name	Original Value	Final Value		
16		$B$16	Total Profit	$19.00	$7,668.00		
17							
18							
19		Variable Cells					
20		Cell	Name	Original Value	Final Value	Integer	
21		$B$14	Bags Produced Standard	1.000	540.000	Contin	
22		$C$14	Bags Produced Deluxe	1.000	252.000	Contin	
23							
24							
25		Constraints					
26		Cell	Name	Cell Value	Formula	Status	Slack
27		$B$19	Cutting and Dyeing Hours Used	630	$B$19<=$C$19	Binding	0
28		$B$20	Sewing Hours Used	480	$B$20<=$C$20	Not Binding	120
29		$B$21	Finishing Hours Used	708	$B$21<=$C$21	Binding	0
30		$B$22	Inspection and Packaging Hours Used	117	$B$22<=$C$22	Not Binding	18
31							

binding constraints have zero slack. Consider for example the sewing department constraint. By adding a nonnegative **slack variable**, we can make the constraint equality:

$$\tfrac{1}{2}S + \tfrac{5}{6}D \leq 600$$
$$\tfrac{1}{2}S + \tfrac{5}{6}D + \text{slack}_{\text{sewing}} = 600$$
$$\text{slack}_{\text{sewing}} = 600 - \tfrac{1}{2}(540) + \tfrac{5}{6}(252) = 600 - 270 - 210 = 120$$

The slack value for the inspecting and packaging constraint is calculated in a similar way. For resource constraints like departmental hours available, the slack value gives the amount of unused resource, in this case, time measured in hours.

NOTES + COMMENTS

1. Notice in the data section for the Par, Inc. spreadsheet, shown in Figure 12.3, that we have entered fractions in cells C6: =5/6 and C7: =2/3. We do this to make sure we maintain accuracy because rounding these values could have an impact on our solution.

2. By selecting **Make Unconstrained Variables Non-Negative** in the **Solver Parameters** dialog box, all decision variables are constrained to be nonnegative.

3. Although we have shown the Answer Report and how to interpret it, we will usually show the solution to an optimization problem directly in the spreadsheet. A well-designed spreadsheet that follows the principles discussed in Chapter 10 should make it easy for the user to interpret the optimal solution directly from the spreadsheet.

4. In addition to the Answer Report, Solver also allows you to generate two other reports. The Sensitivity Report will be discussed in Section 12.5. The Limits Report gives information on the objective function value when variables are set to their limits.

12.3 A Simple Minimization Problem

M&D Chemicals produces two products that are sold as raw materials to companies that manufacture bath soaps and laundry detergents. Based on an analysis of current inventory levels and potential demand for the coming month, M&D's management specified that the combined production for products A and B must total at least 350 gallons. Separately, a major customer's order for 125 gallons of product A must also be satisfied. Product A requires 2 hours of processing time per gallon, and product B requires 1 hour of processing time per gallon. For the coming month, 600 hours of processing time are available. M&D's objective is to satisfy these requirements at a minimum total production cost. Production costs are $2 per gallon for product A and $3 per gallon for product B.

Problem Formulation

To find the minimum-cost production schedule, we will formulate the M&D Chemicals problem as a linear program. Following a procedure similar to the one used for the Par, Inc. problem, we first define the decision variables and the objective function for the problem. Let

$$A = \text{number of gallons of product A to produce}$$
$$B = \text{number of gallons of product B to produce}$$

With production costs at $2 per gallon for product A and $3 per gallon for product B, the objective function that corresponds to the minimization of the total production cost can be written as

$$\text{Min } 2A + 3B$$

Next consider the constraints placed on the M&D Chemicals problem. To satisfy the major customer's demand for 125 gallons of product A, we know A must be at least 125. Thus, we write the constraint

$$1A \geq 125$$

For the combined production for both products, which must total at least 350 gallons, we can write the constraint

$$1A + 1B \geq 350$$

Finally, for the limitation of 600 hours on available processing time, we add the constraint

$$2A + 1B \leq 600$$

After adding the nonnegativity constraints ($A, B \geq 0$), we arrive at the following linear program for the M&D Chemicals problem:

$$
\begin{aligned}
\text{Min} \quad & 2A + 3B \\
\text{s.t.} \quad & \\
& 1A \quad\quad\; \geq 125 \quad\quad \text{Demand for product A} \\
& 1A + 1B \geq 350 \quad\quad \text{Total production} \\
& 2A + 1B \leq 600 \quad\quad \text{Processing time} \\
& A, B \quad\quad\;\; \geq 0
\end{aligned}
$$

Solution for the M&D Chemicals Problem

A spreadsheet model for the M&D Chemicals problem along with the Solver dialog box are shown in Figure 12.6. The complete linear programming model for the M&D Chemicals problem in Excel Solver is contained in the file *M&DModel*. We use the SUMPRODUCT function to calculate total cost in cell B16 and also to calculate total processing hours used in cell B23. The optimal solution, which is shown in the spreadsheet and in the Answer Report in Figure 12.7, is to make 250 gallons of product A and 100

MODEL *file*

M&DModel

FIGURE 12.6 Solver Dialog Box and Solution to the M&D Chemicals Problem

▲	A	B	C	D
1	**M&D Chemicals**			
2	**Parameters**			
3		Product A	Product B	Time Available
4	Processing Time (hours)	2	1	600
5	Production Cost	$2.00	$3.00	
6				
7	Minimum Total Production	350		
8	Product A Minimum	125		
9				
10				
11	**Model**			
12				
13		Product A	Product B	
14	Gallons Produced	250	100	
15				
16	Minimize Total Cost	$800.00		
17				
18		Provided	Required	
19	Product A	250	125	
20	Total Production	350	350	
21				
22		Hours Used	Hours Available	Unused Hours
23	Processing Time	600	600	0
24				
25				
26				
27				
28				
29				
30				

MODEL *file*

M&DModel

Solver Parameters ☒

Se_t Objective: $B$16

To: ○ Max   ◉ Min   ○ Value Of: [0]

By Changing Variable Cells:

$B$14:$C$14

Subject to the Constraints:

$B$19:$B$20 > = $C$19:$C$20
$B$23 <= $C$23

[Add]
[Change]
[Delete]
[Reset All]
[Load/Save]

☑ Ma_ke Unconstrained Variables Non-Negative

S_elect a Solving Method: [Simplex LP ▾]   [Options]

Solving Method

Select the GRG Nonlinear engine for Solver Problems that are smooth nonlinear. Select the LP Simplex engine for linear Solver Problems, and select the Evolutionary engine for Solver problems that are non-smooth.

[Help]   [Solve]   [Close]

FIGURE 12.7	The Solver Answer Report for the M&D Chemicals Problem

◢	A	B	C	D	E	F	G
13							
14	Objective Cell (Min)						
15		Cell	Name	Original Value	Final Value		
16		$B$16	Minimize Total Cost	$0.00	$800.00		
17							
18							
19	Variable Cells						
20		Cell	Name	Original Value	Final Value	Integer	
21		$B$14	Gallons Produced Product A	0	250	Contin	
22		$C$14	Gallons Produced Product B	0	100	Contin	
23							
24							
25	Constraints						
26		Cell	Name	Cell Value	Formula	Status	Slack
27		$B$19	Product A Provided	250	$B$19>=$C$19	Not Binding	125
28		$B$20	Total Production Provided	350	$B$20>=$C$20	Binding	0
29		$B$23	Processing Time Hours Used	600	$B$23<=$C$23	Binding	0
30							

gallons of product B, for a total cost of $800. Both the total production constraint and the processing time constraints are binding (350 gallons are provided, the same as required, and all 600 processing hours are used). The requirement that at least 125 gallons of Product A be produced is not binding. For greater-than-or-equal-to constraints, we can define a nonnegative variable called a surplus variable. A **surplus variable** tells how much over the right-hand side the left-hand side of a greater-than-or-equal-to constraint is for a solution. A surplus variable is subtracted from the left-hand side of the constraint. For example,

$$1A \geq 125$$
$$1A - \text{surplus}_A = 125$$
$$\text{surplus}_A = 1A - 125 = 250 - 125 = 125$$

As was the case with less-than-or-equal-to constraints and slack variables, a positive value for a surplus variable indicates that the constraint is not binding.

NOTES + COMMENTS

1. In the spreadsheet and Solver model for the M&D Chemicals problem, we separated the greater-than-or-equal-to constraints and the less-than-or-equal-to constraints. This allows for easier entry of the constraints into the **Add Constraint** dialog box.

2. In the Excel Answer Report, both slack and surplus variables are labeled "Slack."

12.4 Special Cases of Linear Program Outcomes

In this section, we discuss three special situations that can arise when we attempt to solve linear programming problems.

Alternative Optimal Solutions

From the discussion of the graphical solution procedure, we know that optimal solutions can be found at the extreme points of the feasible region. Now let us consider the special case in which the optimal objective function contour line coincides with one of the binding constraint lines on the boundary of the feasible region. We will see that this situation can lead to the case of **alternative optimal solutions**; in such cases, more than one solution provides the optimal value for the objective function.

To illustrate the case of alternative optimal solutions, we return to the Par, Inc. problem. However, let us assume that the profit for the standard golf bag (S) has been decreased to $6.30. The revised objective function becomes $6.3S + 9D$. The graphical solution of this problem is shown in Figure 12.8. Note that the optimal solution still occurs at an extreme point. In fact, it occurs at two extreme points: extreme point ④ ($S = 300$, $D = 420$) and extreme point ③ ($S = 540$, $D = 252$).

The objective function values at these two extreme points are identical; that is,

$$6.3S + 9D = 6.3(300) + 9(420) = 5,670$$

and

$$6.3S + 9D = 6.3(540) + 9(252) = 5,670$$

Furthermore, any point on the line connecting the two optimal extreme points also provides an optimal solution. For example, the solution point ($S = 420$, $D = 336$), which is halfway between the two extreme points, also provides the optimal objective function value of

$$6.3S + 9D = 6.3(420) + 9(336) = 5,670$$

A linear programming problem with alternative optimal solutions is generally a good situation for the manager or decision maker. It means that several combinations of the

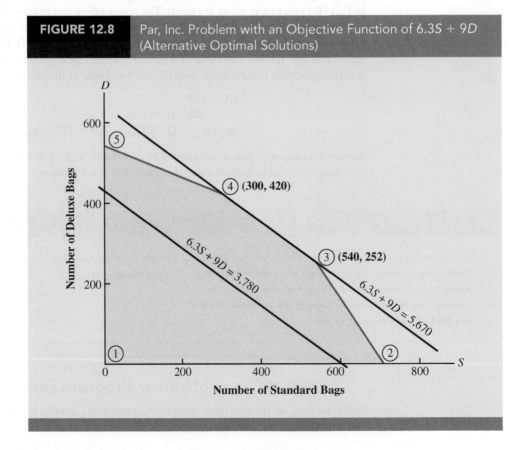

FIGURE 12.8 Par, Inc. Problem with an Objective Function of $6.3S + 9D$ (Alternative Optimal Solutions)

decision variables are optimal and that the manager can select the most desirable optimal solution. Unfortunately, determining whether a problem has alternative optimal solutions is not a simple matter. In Section 12.7, we discuss an approach for finding alternative optima.

Infeasibility

Problems with no feasible solution do arise in practice, most often because management's expectations are too high or because too many restrictions have been placed on the problem.

Infeasibility means that no solution to the linear programming problem satisfies all the constraints, including the nonnegativity conditions. Graphically, infeasibility means that a feasible region does not exist; that is, no points satisfy all the constraints and the nonnegativity conditions simultaneously. To illustrate this situation, let us look again at the problem faced by Par, Inc.

Suppose that management specified that at least 500 of the standard bags and at least 360 of the deluxe bags must be manufactured. The graph of the solution region may now be constructed to reflect these new requirements (see Figure 12.9). The shaded area in the lower left-hand portion of the graph depicts the points that satisfy the departmental constraints on the availability of time. The shaded area in the upper right-hand portion depicts the points that satisfy the minimum production requirements of 500 standard and 360 deluxe bags. But no points satisfy both sets of constraints. Thus, we see that if management imposes these minimum production requirements, no feasible region exists for the problem.

How should we interpret infeasibility in terms of this current problem? First, we should tell management that, given the resources available (i.e., production time for cutting and dyeing, sewing, finishing, and inspection and packaging), it is not possible to make 500 standard bags and 360 deluxe bags. Moreover, we can tell management exactly how much of each resource must be expended to make it possible to manufacture these numbers

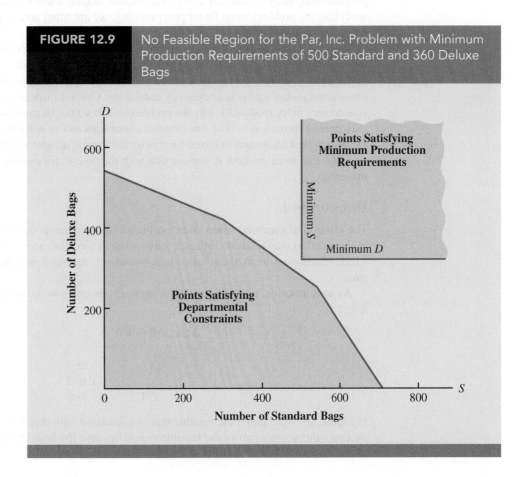

FIGURE 12.9 No Feasible Region for the Par, Inc. Problem with Minimum Production Requirements of 500 Standard and 360 Deluxe Bags

TABLE 12.2	Resources Needed to Manufacture 500 Standard Bags and 360 Deluxe Bags		
Operation	**Minimum Required Resources (hours)**	**Available Resources (hours)**	**Additional Resources Needed (hours)**
Cutting and Dyeing	$\frac{7}{10}(500) + 1(360) = 710$	630	80
Sewing	$\frac{1}{2}(500) + \frac{5}{6}(360) = 550$	600	None
Finishing	$1(500) + \frac{2}{3}(360) = 740$	708	32
Inspection and Packaging	$\frac{1}{10}(500) + \frac{1}{4}(360) = 140$	135	5

of bags. Table 12.2 shows the minimum amounts of resources that must be available, the amounts currently available, and additional amounts that would be required to accomplish this level of production. Thus, we need 80 more hours for cutting and dyeing, 32 more hours for finishing, and 5 more hours for inspection and packaging to meet management's minimum production requirements.

If after reviewing this information, management still wants to manufacture 500 standard and 360 deluxe bags, additional resources must be provided. Perhaps the resource requirements can be met by hiring another person to work in the cutting and dyeing department, transferring a person from elsewhere in the plant to work part time in the finishing department, or having the sewing people help out periodically with the inspection and packaging. As you can see, once we discover the lack of a feasible solution, many possibilities are available for corrective management action. The important thing to realize is that linear programming analysis can help determine whether management's plans are feasible. By analyzing the problem using linear programming, we are often able to point out infeasible conditions and initiate corrective action.

Whenever you attempt to solve a problem that is infeasible, Excel Solver will return a message in the Solver Results dialog box, indicating that no feasible solution exists. In this case, you know that no solution to the linear programming problem will satisfy all constraints, including the nonnegativity conditions. Careful inspection of your formulation is necessary to try to identify why the problem is infeasible. In some situations, the only reasonable approach is to drop one or more constraints and re-solve the problem. If you are able to find an optimal solution for this revised problem, you will know that the constraint(s) that were omitted, in conjunction with the others, are causing the problem to be infeasible.

Unbounded

The solution to a maximization linear programming problem is **unbounded** if the value of the solution may be made infinitely large without violating any of the constraints; for a minimization problem, the solution is unbounded if the value may be made infinitely small.

As an illustration, consider the following linear program with two decision variables, X and Y:

$$\text{Max } 20X + 10Y$$
$$\text{s.t.}$$
$$1X \qquad\qquad \geq 2$$
$$1Y \leq 5$$
$$X, Y \qquad \geq 0$$

In Figure 12.10 we graph the feasible region associated with this problem. Note that we can indicate only part of the feasible region because the feasible region extends

| FIGURE 12.10 | Example of an Unbounded Problem |

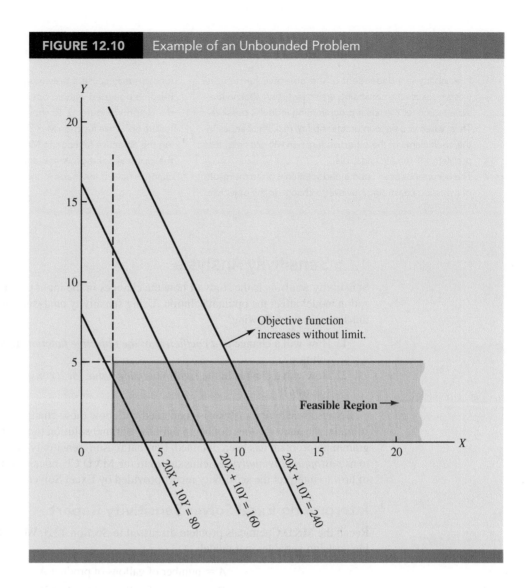

indefinitely in the direction of the *X*-axis. Looking at the objective function lines in Figure 12.10, we see that the solution to this problem may be made as large as we desire. In other words, no matter which solution we pick, we will always be able to reach some feasible solution with a larger value. Thus, we say that the solution to this linear program is *unbounded*.

Whenever you attempt to solve an unbounded problem using Excel Solver, you will receive a message in the Solver Results dialog box telling you that the "Objective Cell values do not converge." In linear programming models of real problems, the occurrence of an unbounded solution means that the problem has been improperly formulated. We know it is not possible to increase profits indefinitely. Therefore, we must conclude that if a profit maximization problem results in an unbounded solution, the mathematical model does not sufficiently represent the real-world problem. In many cases, this error is the result of inadvertently omitting a constraint during problem formulation.

The parameters for optimization models are often less than certain. In the next section, we discuss the sensitivity of the optimal solution to uncertainty in the model parameters. In addition to the optimal solution, Excel Solver can provide some useful information on the sensitivity of that solution to changes in the model parameters.

1. Infeasibility is independent of the objective function. It exists because the constraints are so restrictive that no feasible region for the linear programming model is possible. Thus, when you encounter infeasibility, making changes in the coefficients of the objective function will not help; the problem will remain infeasible.

2. The occurrence of an unbounded solution is often the result of a missing constraint. However, a change in the objective function may cause a previously unbounded problem to become bounded with an optimal solution. For example, the graph in Figure 12.10 shows an unbounded solution for the objective function Max $20X + 10Y$. However, changing the objective function to Max $-20X - 10Y$ will provide the optimal solution $X = 2$ and $Y = 0$ even though no changes have been made in the constraints.

12.5 Sensitivity Analysis

Sensitivity analysis is the study of how the changes in the input parameters of an optimization model affect the optimal solution. Using sensitivity analysis, we can answer questions such as the following:

1. How will a change *in a coefficient of the objective function* affect the optimal solution?
2. How will a change in the *right-hand-side value for a constraint* affect the optimal solution?

Because sensitivity analysis is concerned with how these changes affect the optimal solution, the analysis does not begin until the optimal solution to the original linear programming problem has been obtained. For that reason, sensitivity analysis is often referred to as *postoptimality analysis*. Let us return to the M&D Chemicals problem as an example of how to interpret the sensitivity report provided by Excel Solver.

Interpreting Excel Solver Sensitivity Report

Recall the M&D Chemicals problem discussed in Section 12.3. We had defined the following decision variables and model:

$$A = \text{number of gallons of product A}$$
$$B = \text{number of gallons of product B}$$

$$
\begin{aligned}
\text{Min} \quad & 2A + 3B \\
\text{s.t.} \quad & \\
& 1A \qquad\quad \geq 125 \quad \text{Demand for product A} \\
& 1A + 1B \geq 350 \quad \text{Total production} \\
& 2A + 1B \leq 600 \quad \text{Processing time} \\
& A, B \qquad\quad \geq 0
\end{aligned}
$$

We found that the optimal solution is $A = 250$ and $B = 100$ with objective function value $= 2(250) + 3(100) = \$800$. The first constraint is not binding, but the second and third constraints are binding because $1(250) + 1(100) = 350$ and $2(250) + 100 = 600$. After running Excel Solver, we may generate the **Sensitivity Report** by selecting **Sensitivity** from the **Reports** section of the **Solver Results** dialog box and then selecting **OK**. The Sensitivity report for the M&D Chemicals problem appears in Figure 12.11. There are two sections in this report: one for decision variables (Variable Cells) and one for Constraints.

Let us begin by interpreting the Constraints section. The cell location of the left-hand side of the constraint, the constraint name, and the value of the left-hand side of the constraint at optimality are given in the first three columns. The fourth column gives the

FIGURE 12.11	Solver Sensitivity Report for the M&D Chemicals Problem

◢	A	B	C	D	E	F	G	H
4								
5								
6		Variable Cells						
7				Final	Reduced	Objective	Allowable	Allowable
8		Cell	Name	Value	Cost	Coefficient	Increase	Decrease
9		$B$14	Gallons Produced Product A	250	0	2	1	1E + 30
10		$C$14	Gallons Produced Product B	100	0	3	1E + 30	1
11								
12		Constraints						
13				Final	Shadow	Constraint	Allowable	Allowable
14		Cell	Name	Value	Price	R.H. Side	Increase	Decrease
15		$B$19	Product A Provided	250	0	125	125	1E + 30
16		$B$20	Total Production Provided	350	4	350	125	50
17		$B$23	Processing Time Hours Used	600	−1	600	100	125
18								

shadow price for each constraint. The **shadow price** for a constraint is the change in the optimal objective function value if the right-hand side of that constraint is increased by one. Let us interpret each shadow price given in the report in Figure 12.11.

The first constraint is: $1A \geq 125$. This is a nonbinding constraint because $250 > 125$. If we change the constraint to $1A \geq 126$, there will be no change in the objective function value. The reason for this is that the constraint will remain nonbinding at the optimal solution, because $1A = 250 > 126$. Hence, the shadow price is zero. In fact, *nonbinding constraints will always have a shadow price of zero*.

The second constraint is binding and its shadow price is 4. The interpretation of the shadow price is as follows. If we change the constraint from $1A + 1B \geq 350$ to $1A + 1B \geq 351$, the optimal objective function value will increase by $4; that is, the new optimal solution will have an objective function value equal to $800 + $4 = $804.

The third constraint is also binding and has a shadow price of −1. The interpretation of the shadow price is as follows. If we change the constraint from $2A + 1B \leq 600$ to $2A + 1B \leq 601$, the objective function value will decrease by $1; that is, the new optimal solution will have an objective function value equal to $800 − $1 = $799.

Note that the shadow price for the second constraint is positive, but for the third it is negative. Why is this? The sign of the shadow price depends on whether the problem is a maximization or a minimization and the type of constraint under consideration. The M&D Chemicals problem is a cost minimization problem. The second constraint is a greater-than-or-equal-to constraint. By increasing the right-hand side, we make the constraint even *more* restrictive. This results in an increase in cost. Contrast this with the third constraint. The third constraint is a less-than-or-equal-to constraint. By increasing the right-hand side, we make more hours available. We have made the constraint less restrictive. Because we have made the constraint *less* restrictive, there are more feasible solutions from which to choose. Therefore, cost drops by $1.

Making a constraint more restrictive is often referred to as tightening the constraint. Making a constraint less restrictive is often referred to as relaxing, or loosening, the constraint.

When observing shadow prices, the following general principle holds: *Making a binding constraint more restrictive degrades or leaves unchanged the optimal objective function value, and making a binding constraint less restrictive improves or leaves unchanged the optimal objective function.* We shall see several more examples of this later in this chapter. Also, shadow prices are symmetric; so the negative of the shadow price is the change in the objective function for a *decrease* of one in the right-hand side.

In Figure 12.11, the Allowable Increase and the Allowable Decrease are the allowable changes in the right-hand side for which the current shadow price remains valid. For example, because the allowable increase in the processing time is 100, if we increase the processing time hours by 50 to $600 + 50 = 650$, we can say with certainty that the optimal objective function value will change by $(-1)50 = -50$. Hence, we know that the optimal objective function value will be $800 - \$50 = \$750$. If we increase the right-hand side of the processing time beyond the allowable increase of 100, we cannot predict what will happen. Likewise, if we decrease the right-hand side of the processing time constraint by 50, we know that the optimal objective function value will change by the negative of the shadow price: $-(-1)50 = 50$. Cost will increase by $50. If we change the right-hand side by more than the allowable increase or decrease, the shadow price is no longer valid.

Let us now turn to the Variable Cells section of the Sensitivity Report. As in the constraint section, the cell location, variable name, and final (optimal) value for each variable are given. The fourth column is Reduced Cost. The **reduced cost** for a decision variable is the shadow price of the nonnegativity constraint for that variable. In other words, the reduced cost indicates the change in the optimal objective function value that results from changing the right-hand side of the nonnegativity constraint from 0 to 1.

In the fifth column of the report, the objective function coefficient for the variable is given. The Allowable Increase and Allowable Decrease indicate the change in the objective function coefficient for which the *current optimal solution will remain optimal*. The value $1E + 30$ in the report is essentially infinity. So long as the cost of product A is greater than or equal to negative infinity and less than or equal to $2 + 1 = 3$, the current solution remains optimal. For example, if the cost of product A is really $2.50 per gallon, we do not need to re-solve the model. Because the increase in cost of $0.50 is less than the allowable increase of $1.00, the current solution of 250 gallons of product A and 100 gallons of product B remains optimal.

As we have seen, the Excel Solver Sensitivity Report can provide useful information about the sensitivity of the optimal solution to changes in the model input data. However, this type of classical sensitivity analysis is somewhat limited. Classical sensitivity analysis is based on the assumption that only one piece of input data has changed; it is assumed that all other parameters remain as stated in the original problem. In many cases, however, we are interested in what would happen if two or more pieces of input data are changed simultaneously. The easiest way to examine the effect of simultaneous changes is to make the changes and rerun the model.

NOTES + COMMENTS

We defined the reduced cost as the shadow price of the nonnegativity constraint for that variable. When there is a binding simple upper-bound constraint for a variable, the reduced cost reported by Excel Solver is the shadow price of that upper-bound constraint. Likewise, if there is a binding nonzero lower bound for a variable, the reduced cost is the shadow price for that lower-bound constraint. So to be more general, the reduced cost for a decision variable is the shadow price of the binding simple lower- or upper-bound constraint for that variable.

12.6 General Linear Programming Notation and More Examples

Earlier in this chapter, we showed how to formulate linear programming models for the Par, Inc. and M&D Chemicals problems. To formulate a linear programming model of the Par, Inc. problem, we began by defining two decision variables: S = number of standard bags and D = number of deluxe bags. In the M&D Chemicals problem, the two decision variables were defined as A = number of gallons of product A and B = number of gallons of product B. We selected decision-variable names of S and

D in the Par, Inc. problem and A and B in the M&D Chemicals problem to make it easier to recall what these decision variables represented in the problem. Although this approach works well for linear programs involving a small number of decision variables, it can become difficult when dealing with problems involving a large number of decision variables.

A more general notation that is often used for linear programs uses the letter x with a subscript. For instance, in the Par, Inc. problem, we could have defined the decision variables as follows:

$$x_1 = \text{number of standard bags}$$
$$x_2 = \text{number of deluxe bags}$$

In the M&D Chemicals problem, the same variable names would be used, but their definitions would change:

$$x_1 = \text{number of gallons of product A}$$
$$x_2 = \text{number of gallons of product B}$$

A disadvantage of using general notation for decision variables is that we are no longer able to easily identify what the decision variables actually represent in the mathematical model. However, the advantage of general notation is that formulating a mathematical model for a problem that involves a large number of decision variables is much easier. For instance, for a linear programming model with three decision variables, we would use variable names of x_1, x_2, and x_3; for a problem with four decision variables, we would use variable names of x_1, x_2, x_3, and x_4; and so on. Clearly, if a problem involved 1,000 decision variables, trying to identify 1,000 unique names would be difficult. However, using the general linear programming notation, the decision variables would be defined as $x_1, x_2, x_3, \ldots, x_{1000}$.

Using this new general notation, the Par, Inc. model would be written as follows:

$$\text{Max } 10x_1 + 9x_2$$

s.t.

$$\begin{array}{rll} \tfrac{7}{10}x_1 + 1x_2 \le 630 & \text{Cutting and dyeing} \\ \tfrac{1}{2}x_1 + \tfrac{5}{6}x_2 \le 600 & \text{Sewing} \\ 1x_1 + \tfrac{2}{3}x_2 \le 708 & \text{Finishing} \\ \tfrac{1}{10}x_1 + \tfrac{1}{4}x_2 \le 135 & \text{Inspection and packaging} \\ x_1, x_2 \ge 0 \end{array}$$

In some of the examples that follow in this section and in Chapters 13 and 14, we will use this type of subscripted notation.

Investment Portfolio Selection

In finance, linear programming can be applied in problem situations involving capital budgeting, make-or-buy decisions, asset allocation, portfolio selection, financial planning, and many more. Next, we describe a portfolio selection problem.

Portfolio selection problems involve situations in which a financial manager must select specific investments—for example, stocks and bonds—from a variety of investment alternatives. Managers of mutual funds, credit unions, insurance companies, and banks frequently encounter this type of problem. The objective function for portfolio selection problems usually is maximization of expected return or minimization of risk. The constraints usually take the form of restrictions on the type of permissible investments, state laws, company policy, maximum permissible risk, and so on. Problems of this type have been formulated and solved using a variety of optimization techniques. In this section we formulate and solve a portfolio selection problem as a linear program.

Consider the case of Welte Mutual Funds, Inc. located in New York City. Welte just obtained $100,000 by converting industrial bonds to cash and is now looking for other investment opportunities for these funds. Based on Welte's current investments, the firm's top financial analyst recommends that all new investments be made in the oil industry, steel industry, or government bonds. Specifically, the analyst identified five investment opportunities and projected their annual rates of return. The investments and rates of return are shown in Table 12.3.

The management at Welte imposed the following investment guidelines:

1. Neither industry (oil or steel) should receive more than $50,000.
2. The amount invested in government bonds should be at least 25% of the steel industry investments.
3. The investment in Pacific Oil, the high-return but high-risk investment, cannot be more than 60% of the total oil industry investment.

What portfolio recommendations—investments and amounts—should be made for the available $100,000? Given the objective of maximizing projected return subject to the budgetary and managerially imposed constraints, we can answer this question by formulating and solving a linear programming model of the problem. The solution will provide investment recommendations for the management of Welte Mutual Funds.

Let us define the following decision variables:

$$x_1 = \text{dollars invested in Atlantic Oil}$$
$$x_2 = \text{dollars invested in Pacific Oil}$$
$$x_3 = \text{dollars invested in Midwest Steel}$$
$$x_4 = \text{dollars invested in Huber Steel}$$
$$x_5 = \text{dollars invested in government bonds}$$

Using the projected rates of return shown in Table 12.3, we write the objective function for maximizing the total return for the portfolio as

$$\text{Max} \quad 0.073x_1 + 0.103x_2 + 0.064x_3 + 0.075x_4 + 0.045x_5$$

The constraint specifying investment of the available $100,000 is

$$x_1 + x_2 + x_3 + x_4 + x_5 = 100{,}000$$

The requirements that neither the oil nor steel industry should receive more than $50,000 are as follows

$$x_1 + x_2 \le 50{,}000$$
$$x_3 + x_4 \le 50{,}000$$

The requirement that the amount invested in government bonds be at least 25% of the steel industry investment is expressed as

$$x_5 \ge 0.25(x_3 + x_4)$$

Finally, the constraint that Pacific Oil cannot be more than 60% of the total oil industry investment is

$$x_2 \le 0.60(x_1 + x_2)$$

TABLE 12.3	Investment Opportunities for Welte Mutual Funds
Investment	**Projected Rate of Return (%)**
Atlantic Oil	7.3
Pacific Oil	10.3
Midwest Steel	6.4
Huber Steel	7.5
Government bonds	4.5

By adding the nonnegativity restrictions, we obtain the complete linear programming model for the Welte Mutual Funds investment problem:

$$\text{Max} \quad 0.073x_1 + 0.103x_2 + 0.064x_3 + 0.075x_4 + 0.045x_5$$

s.t.

$x_1 +$	$x_2 +$	$x_3 +$	$x_4 +$	$x_5 = 100{,}000$	Available funds
$x_1 +$	x_2			$\leq \ 50{,}000$	Oil industry maximum
		$x_3 +$	x_4	$\leq \ 50{,}000$	Steel industry maximum
$x_5 \geq 0.25\,(x_3 + x_4)$					Government bonds minimum
$x_2 \leq 0.60\,(x_1 + x_2)$					Pacific Oil restriction
$x_1, x_2, x_3, x_4, x_5 \geq 0$					

The optimal solution to this linear program is shown in Figure 12.12. Note that the optimal solution indicates that the portfolio should be diversified among all the investment opportunities except Midwest Steel. The projected annual return for this portfolio is $8,000, which is an overall return of 8%. Except for the upper bound on the Steel investment, all constraints are binding.

NOTES + COMMENTS

1. The optimal solution to the Welte Mutual Funds problem indicates that $20,000 should be spent on the Atlantic Oil stock. If Atlantic Oil sells for $75 per share, we would have to purchase exactly $266\frac{2}{3}$ shares in order to spend exactly $20,000. The difficulty of purchasing fractional shares can be handled by purchasing the largest possible integer number of shares with the allotted funds (e.g., 266 shares of Atlantic Oil). This approach guarantees that the budget constraint will not be violated. This approach, of course, introduces the possibility that the solution will no longer be optimal, but the danger is slight if a large number of securities are involved. In cases in which the analyst believes that the decision variables *must* have integer values, the problem must be formulated as an integer linear programming model (the topic of Chapter 13).

2. Financial portfolio theory stresses obtaining a proper balance between risk and return. In the Welte problem, we explicitly considered return in the objective function. Risk is controlled by choosing constraints that ensure diversity among oil and steel stocks and a balance between government bonds and the steel industry investment. In Chapter 14, we discuss investment portfolio models that control risk as measured by the variance of returns on investment.

Transportation Planning

The *transportation problem* arises frequently in planning for the distribution of goods and services from several supply locations to several demand locations. Typically, the quantity of goods available at each supply location (origin) is limited, and the quantity of goods needed at each of several demand locations (destinations) is known. The usual objective in a transportation problem is to minimize the cost of shipping goods from the origins to the destinations.

Let us revisit the transportation problem faced by Foster Generators, discussed in Chapter 10. This problem involves the transportation of a product from three plants to four distribution centers. Foster Generators operates plants in Cleveland, Ohio; Bedford, Indiana; and York, Pennsylvania. Production capacities over the next three-month planning period for one type of generator are as follows:

Origin	Plant	Three-Month Production Capacity (units)
1	Cleveland	5,000
2	Bedford	6,000
3	York	2,500
	Total	13,500

FIGURE 12.12   The Solution for the Welte Mutual Funds Problem

	A	B	C	D	E	F
1	Welte Mutual Funds Problem					
2						
3	Parameters					
4	Investment	Projected Rate of Return				
5	Atlantic Oil	0.073		Available Funds	100000	
6	Pacific Oil	0.103		Oil Max	50000	
7	Midwest Steel	0.064		Steel Max	50000	
8	Huber Steel	0.075		Pacific Oil Max	0.6	
9	Gov't Bonds	0.045		Gov't Bonds Min	0.25	
10						
11	Model					
12						
13	Investment	Amount Invested				
14	Atlantic Oil	20000				
15	Pacific Oil	30000				
16	Midwest Steel	0				
17	Huber Steel	40000				
18	Gov't Bonds	10000				
19						
20	Max Total Return	=SUMPRODUCT(B5:B9, B14:B18)				
21						
22		Funds Invested	Funds Available	Unused Funds		
23	Total	=SUM(B14:B18)	=E5	= C23–B23		
24						
25		Funds Invested	Max Allowed			
26	Oil	=SUM(B14:B15)	=E6			
27	Steel	=SUM(B16:B17)	=E7			
28	Pacific Oil	=B15	=E8*(B14+B15)			
29						
30		Funds Invested	Min Required			
31	Gov't Bonds	=B18	=E9*(B16+B17)			

MODEL *file*

Welte

	A	B	C	D	E
1	Welte Mutual Funds Problem				
2					
3	Parameters				
4	Investment	Projected Rate of Return			
5	Atlantic Oil	0.073		Available Funds	$100,000.00
6	Pacific Oil	0.103		Oil Max	$50,000.00
7	Midwest Steel	0.064		Steel Max	$50,000.00
8	Huber Steel	0.075		Pacific Oil Max	0.6
9	Gov't Bonds	0.045		Gov't Bonds Min	0.25
10					
11	Model				
12					
13	Investment	Amount Invested			
14	Atlantic Oil	$20,000.00			
15	Pacific Oil	$30,000.00			
16	Midwest Steel	$0.00			
17	Huber Steel	$40,000.00			
18	Gov't Bonds	$10,000.00			
19					
20	Max Total Return	$8,000.00			
21					
22		Funds Invested	Funds Available	Unused Funds	
23	Total	$100,000.00	$100,000.00	$0.00	
24					
25		Funds Invested	Max Allowed		
26	Oil	$50,000.00	$50,000.00		
27	Steel	$40,000.00	$50,000.00		
28	Pacific Oil	$30,000.00	$30,000.00		
29					
30		Funds Invested	Min Required		
31	Gov't Bonds	$10,000.00	$10,000.00		

The firm distributes its generators through four regional distribution centers located in Boston, Massachusetts; Chicago, Illinois; St. Louis, Missouri; and Lexington, Kentucky; the three-month forecast of demand for the distribution centers is as follows:

Destination	Distribution Center	Three-Month Demand Forecast (units)
1	Boston	6,000
2	Chicago	4,000
3	St. Louis	2,000
4	Lexington	1,500
	Total	13,500

Management would like to determine how much of its production should be shipped from each plant to each distribution center. Figure 12.13 shows graphically the 12 distribution routes Foster can use. Such a graph is called a *network*; the circles are referred to as *nodes*, and the lines connecting the nodes as *arcs*. Each origin and each destination is represented by a node, and each possible shipping route is represented by an arc. The amount of the supply is written next to each origin node, and the amount of the demand is written next to each destination node. The goods shipped from the origins to the destinations represent the flow in the network. Note that the direction of flow (from origin to destination) is indicated by the arrows.

For Foster's transportation problem, the objective is to determine the routes to be used and the quantity to be shipped via each route that will provide the minimum total transportation cost. The cost for each unit shipped on each route is given in Table 12.4 and is shown on each arc in Figure 12.13.

A linear programming model can be used to solve this transportation problem. We use *double-subscripted* decision variables, with x_{11} denoting the number of units shipped from origin 1 (Cleveland) to destination 1 (Boston), x_{12} denoting the number of units shipped from origin 1 (Cleveland) to destination 2 (Chicago), and so on. In general, the decision variables for a transportation problem having m origins and n destinations are written as follows:

$$x_{ij} = \text{number of units shipped from origin } i \text{ to destination } j$$
$$\text{where } i = 1, 2, \ldots, m \text{ and } j = 1, 2, \ldots, n$$

Because the objective of the transportation problem is to minimize the total transportation cost, we can use the cost data in Table 12.4 or on the arcs in Figure 12.13 to develop the following cost expressions:

Transportation costs for units shipped from Cleveland $= 3x_{11} + 2x_{12} + 7x_{13} + 6x_{14}$
Transportation costs for units shipped from Bedford $\ = 6x_{21} + 5x_{22} + 2x_{23} + 3x_{24}$
Transportation costs for units shipped from York $\ \ \ \ \ = 2x_{31} + 5x_{32} + 4x_{33} + 5x_{34}$

The sum of these expressions provides the objective function showing the total transportation cost for Foster Generators.

Transportation problems need constraints because each origin has a limited supply and each destination has a demand requirement. We consider the supply constraints first. The capacity at the Cleveland plant is 5,000 units. With the total number of units shipped from the Cleveland plant expressed as $x_{11} + x_{12} + x_{13} + x_{14}$, the supply constraint for the Cleveland plant is

$$x_{11} + x_{12} + x_{13} + x_{14} \leq 5{,}000 \qquad \text{Cleveland supply}$$

With three origins (plants), the Foster transportation problem has three supply constraints. Given the capacity of 6,000 units at the Bedford plant and 2,500 units at the York plant, the two additional supply constraints are as follows:

$$x_{21} + x_{22} + x_{23} + x_{24} \leq 6{,}000 \quad \text{Bedford supply}$$
$$x_{31} + x_{32} + x_{33} + x_{34} \leq 2{,}500 \quad \text{York supply}$$

With the four distribution centers as the destinations, four demand constraints are needed to ensure that destination demands will be satisfied:

$$x_{11} + x_{21} + x_{31} = 6{,}000 \quad \text{Boston demand}$$
$$x_{12} + x_{22} + x_{32} = 4{,}000 \quad \text{Chicago demand}$$
$$x_{13} + x_{23} + x_{33} = 2{,}000 \quad \text{St. Louis demand}$$
$$x_{14} + x_{24} + x_{34} = 1{,}500 \quad \text{Lexington demand}$$

FIGURE 12.13 The Network Representation of the Foster Generators Transportation Problem

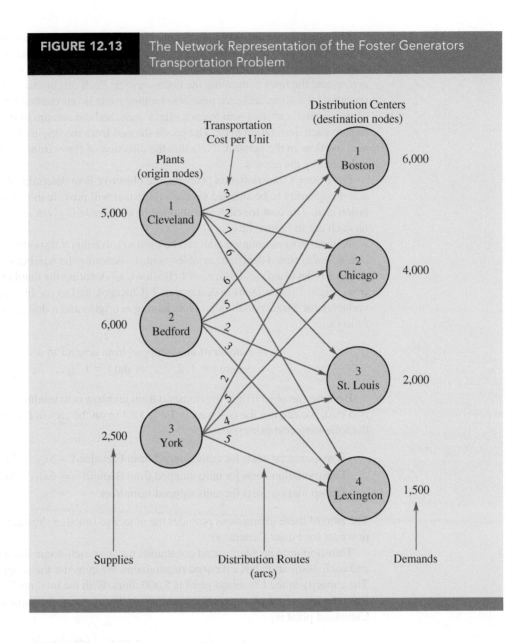

TABLE 12.4 Transportation Cost per Unit for the Foster Generators Transportation Problem ($)

	Destination			
Origin	Boston	Chicago	St. Louis	Lexington
Cleveland	3	2	7	6
Bedford	6	5	2	3
York	2	5	4	5

Combining the objective function and constraints into one model provides a 12-variable, 7-constraint linear programming formulation of the Foster Generators transportation problem:

$$\text{Min}\quad 3x_{11} + 2x_{12} + 7x_{13} + 6x_{14} + 6x_{21} + 5x_{22} + 2x_{23} + 3x_{24} + 2x_{31} + 5x_{32} + 4x_{33} + 5x_{34}$$

s.t.

$$
\begin{array}{llll}
x_{11} + x_{12} + x_{13} + x_{14} & & & \leq 5{,}000 \\
& x_{21} + x_{22} + x_{23} + x_{24} & & \leq 6{,}000 \\
& & x_{31} + x_{32} + x_{33} + x_{34} & \leq 2{,}500 \\
x_{11} \qquad\qquad + x_{21} \qquad\qquad + x_{31} & & & = 6{,}000 \\
\quad x_{12} \qquad\qquad + x_{22} \qquad\qquad + x_{32} & & & = 4{,}000 \\
\quad\; x_{13} \qquad\qquad + x_{23} \qquad\qquad + x_{33} & & & = 2{,}000 \\
\quad\;\; x_{14} \qquad\qquad + x_{24} \qquad\qquad + x_{34} & & & = 1{,}500 \\
\end{array}
$$

$$x_{ij} \geq 0 \qquad \text{for } i = 1, 2, 3 \text{ and } j = 1, 2, 3, 4$$

Comparing the linear programming formulation to the network in Figure 12.13 leads to several observations. All the information needed for the linear programming formulation is on the network. Each node has one constraint, and each arc has one variable. The sum of the variables corresponding to arcs from an origin node must be less than or equal to the origin's supply, and the sum of the variables corresponding to the arcs into a destination node must be equal to the destination's demand.

A spreadsheet model and the solution to the Foster Generators problem (Figure 12.14) show that the minimum total transportation cost is $39,500. The values for the decision variables show the optimal amounts to ship over each route. For example, 1,000 units should be shipped from Cleveland to Boston and 4,000 units should be shipped from Cleveland to Chicago. Other values of the decision variables indicate the remaining shipping quantities and routes.

Maximizing Banner Ad Revenue

Applications of linear programming to marketing are numerous. Advertising campaign mix, marketing mix, and marketing research are just a few areas of application. In this section, we consider the allocation of web site banner ads.

Content publishers such as CNN, Fox News, MSNBC, and Yahoo generate revenue by placing banner ads on their web sites. These publishers are paid based on the number of "click-throughs" on banner ads, that is, the number of times someone clicks the banner ad and goes on to the linked web site of the company that is advertising. For a given day, publishers need to determine how to allocate banner ad showings, also known as impressions, across their content pages for each advertiser so as to maximize banner ad revenue.

Let us consider the Business, Science, and Sports sections of a large content publisher, MHT. MHT has contracts for banner ads with five companies, ecommerce company Nile, management consulting company Zstar, athleticwear company Cheetah, telecommunications firm Stride, and home goods retailer Stove. Based on historical data from past contracts, MHT has determined the expected click-through rates for each of these advertisers by section of their web content. The expected click-through rates are given in Table 12.5. For example, for every 10,000 impressions of a banner ad for Nile in the Business section, $10{,}000 \times 0.0155 = 155$ click-throughs to the Nile web site are expected to occur. The other rates given in Table 12.5 are interpreted in a similar way.

MHT contracts with each of the five companies include a minimum and maximum number of impressions. The minimum and maximum number of impressions are also provided in Table 12.5.

For next Friday, MHT expects to have sufficient visitors to its web site to guarantee 2,550,000 visitors to its Business section, 2,150,000 visitors to its Science section, and 2,500,000 visitors to its Sports section. MHT receives $0.30 for each click-through achieved, regardless of company or section from which the click-through originates.

FIGURE 12.14 Spreadsheet Model and Solution for the Foster Generator Problem

	A	B	C	D	E	F
1	Foster Generators					
2	Parameters					
3	Shipping Cost/Unit		Destination			
4	Origin	Boston	Chicago	St. Louis	Lexington	Supply
5	Cleveland	3	2	7	6	5000
6	Bedford	6	5	2	3	6000
7	York	2	5	4	5	2500
8	Demand	6000	4000	2000	1500	
9						
10						
11	Model					
12						
13	Total Cost	=SUMPRODUCT(B5:E7,B17:E19)				
14						
15			Destination			
16	Origin	Boston	Chicago	St. Louis	Lexington	Total
17	Cleveland	1000	4000	0	0	=SUM(B17:E17)
18	Bedford	2500	0	2000	1500	=SUM(B18:E18)
19	York	2500	0	0	0	=SUM(B19:E19)
20	Total	=SUM(B17:B19)	=SUM(C17:C19)	=SUM(D17:D19)	=SUM(E17:E19)	
21						

MODEL *file*

Foster

	A	B	C	D	E	F	G
1	Foster Generators						
2	Parameters						
3	Shipping Cost/Unit		Destination				
4	Origin	Boston	Chicago	St. Louis	Lexington	Supply	
5	Cleveland	$3.00	$2.00	$7.00	$6.00	5000	
6	Bedford	$6.00	$5.00	$2.00	$3.00	6000	
7	York	$2.00	$5.00	$4.00	$5.00	2500	
8	Demand	6000	4000	2000	1500		
9							
10							
11	Model						
12							
13	Total Cost	$39,500.00					
14							
15			Destination				
16	Origin	Boston	Chicago	St. Louis	Lexington	Total	
17	Cleveland	1000	4000	0	0	5000	
18	Bedford	2500	0	2000	1500	6000	
19	York	2500	0	0	0	2500	
20	Total	6000	4000	2000	1500		
21							

MHT advertising planners need to determine, for next Friday, how to allocate impressions for each of the five advertisers across the three sections of the MHT web site. A linear programming model, similar to the Foster Generators problem model previously discussed, can be used to allocate impressions so as to maximize the revenue received by MHT.

Let us define decision variables as follows:

$$x_{ij} = \text{the number of impressions in section } i \text{ allocated to company } j$$

where $i = 1$ is Business, $i = 2$ is Science, $i = 3$ is Sports and $j = 1$ is Nile, $j = 2$ is Zstar, $j = 3$ is Cheetah, $j = 4$ is Stride, and $j = 5$ is Stove.

TABLE 12.5	Data for the MHT Banner Ad Allocation Problem				
	Click-Through Rates				
Section	**Nile**	**Zstar**	**Cheetah**	**Stride**	**Stove**
Business	0.0155	0.0265	0.0100	0.0170	0.0105
Science	0.0165	0.0110	0.0125	0.0265	0.0125
Sports	0.0145	0.0235	0.0190	0.0225	0.0160
	Contract Impression Limits				
	Nile	**Zstar**	**Cheetah**	**Stride**	**Stove**
Ads Lower Limit	1,500,000	1,000,000	1,100,000	1,000,000	1,500,000
Ads Upper Limit	2,000,000	2,000,000	1,800,000	2,000,000	2,000,000

The objective function is to maximize expected revenue, which can be calculated by multiplying the per-click-through revenue, the expected click-through rate and the allocated impressions. For example, for Business section impressions for Cheetah, we have $(0.30)(0.01)\,x_{13} = 0.003x_{13}$. The expected revenues from the three sections are:

$$0.3(0.0155x_{11} + 0.0265x_{12} + 0.010x_{13} + 0.0170x_{14} + 0.0105x_{15}) \quad \text{(Business)}$$
$$0.3(0.0165x_{21} + 0.0110x_{22} + 0.0125x_{23} + 0.0265x_{24} + .0125x_{25}) \quad \text{(Science)}$$
$$0.3(0.0145x_{31} + 0.0235x_{32} + 0.0190x_{33} + 0.0225x_{34} + 0.0160x_{35}) \quad \text{(Sports)}$$

The objective function is the sum of the expected revenues generated from the three sections. Multiplying and summing across the three sections we have:

$$\text{Maximize} \quad 0.0047x_{11} + 0.008x_{12} + 0.003x_{13} + 0.0051x_{14} + 0.0032x_{15} + 0.005x_{21}$$
$$+ 0.0033x_{22} + 0.0038x_{23} + 0.0008x_{24} + 0.0038x_{25} + 0.0044x_{31}$$
$$+ 0.0071x_{32} + 0.0057x_{33} + .0068x_{34} + 0.0048x_{35}$$

Now let us consider the constraints of the problem. Since each section is limited to the number of impressions that MHT can guarantee, we have the following impression availability constraints:

$$x_{11} + x_{12} + x_{13} + x_{14} + x_{15} \leq 2{,}550{,}000 \quad \text{(Business Section Impressions Available)}$$
$$x_{21} + x_{22} + x_{23} + x_{24} + x_{25} \leq 2{,}150{,}000 \quad \text{(Science Section Impressions Available)}$$
$$x_{31} + x_{32} + x_{33} + x_{34} + x_{35} \leq 2{,}500{,}000 \quad \text{(Sports Section Impressions Available)}$$

Each company has a lower limit and an upper limit on impressions received:

$$x_{11} + x_{21} + x_{31} \geq 1{,}500{,}000 \quad \text{(Lower Limit for Nile)}$$
$$x_{12} + x_{22} + x_{32} \geq 1{,}000{,}000 \quad \text{(Lower Limit for Zstar)}$$
$$x_{13} + x_{23} + x_{33} \geq 1{,}100{,}000 \quad \text{(Lower Limit for Cheetah)}$$
$$x_{14} + x_{24} + x_{34} \geq 1{,}000{,}000 \quad \text{(Lower Limit for Stride)}$$
$$x_{15} + x_{25} + x_{35} \geq 1{,}500{,}000 \quad \text{(Lower Limit for Stove)}$$

$$x_{11} + x_{21} + x_{31} \leq 2{,}000{,}000 \quad \text{(Upper Limit for Nile)}$$
$$x_{12} + x_{22} + x_{32} \leq 2{,}000{,}000 \quad \text{(Upper Limit for Zstar)}$$
$$x_{13} + x_{23} + x_{33} \leq 1{,}800{,}000 \quad \text{(Upper Limit for Cheetah)}$$
$$x_{14} + x_{24} + x_{34} \leq 2{,}000{,}000 \quad \text{(Upper Limit for Stride)}$$
$$x_{15} + x_{25} + x_{35} \leq 2{,}000{,}000 \quad \text{(Upper Limit for Stove)}$$

Adding constraints that ensure variables must be nonnegative, we have the following linear program:

Maximize $0.0047x_{11} + 0.008x_{12} + 0.003x_{13} + 0.0051x_{14} + 0.0032x_{15} + 0.005x_{21}$
$+ 0.0033x_{22} + 0.0038x_{23} + 0.0008x_{24} + 0.0038x_{25} + 0.0044x_{31}$
$+ 0.0071x_{32} + 0.0057x_{33} + 0.0068x_{34} + 0.0048x_{35}$

s.t.

$$x_{11} + x_{12} + x_{13} + x_{14} + x_{15} \leq 2{,}550{,}000 \text{ (Business Section Impressions Available)}$$
$$x_{21} + x_{22} + x_{23} + x_{24} + x_{25} \leq 2{,}150{,}000 \text{ (Science Section Impressions Available)}$$
$$x_{31} + x_{32} + x_{33} + x_{34} + x_{35} \leq 2{,}500{,}000 \text{ (Sports Impressions Available)}$$
$$x_{11} + x_{21} + x_{31} \geq 1{,}500{,}000 \quad \text{(Lower Limit for Nile)}$$
$$x_{12} + x_{22} + x_{32} \geq 1{,}000{,}000 \quad \text{(Lower Limit for Zstar)}$$
$$x_{13} + x_{23} + x_{33} \geq 1{,}100{,}000 \quad \text{(Lower Limit for Cheetah)}$$
$$x_{14} + x_{24} + x_{34} \geq 1{,}000{,}000 \quad \text{(Lower Limit for Stride)}$$
$$x_{15} + x_{25} + x_{35} \geq 1{,}500{,}000 \quad \text{(Lower Limit for Stove)}$$
$$x_{11} + x_{21} + x_{31} \leq 2{,}000{,}000 \quad \text{(Upper Limit for Nile)}$$
$$x_{12} + x_{22} + x_{32} \leq 2{,}000{,}000 \quad \text{(Upper Limit for Zstar)}$$
$$x_{13} + x_{23} + x_{33} \leq 1{,}800{,}000 \quad \text{(Upper Limit for Cheetah)}$$
$$x_{14} + x_{24} + x_{34} \leq 2{,}000{,}000 \quad \text{(Upper Limit for Stride)}$$
$$x_{15} + x_{25} + x_{35} \leq 2{,}000{,}000 \quad \text{(Upper Limit for Stove)}$$
$$x_{ij} \geq 0 \text{ for } i = 1, 2, 3 \text{ and } j = 1, 2, 3, 4, 5 \quad \text{(Nonnegativity)}$$

A spreadsheet model and an optimal solution to this linear programming problem are shown in Figure 12.15. The solution indicates that all available impressions should be used, and the resulting revenue is \$45,270. Nile impressions are split between the Business and Science sections and Stove impressions are split over the Science and Sports sections. Zstar, Cheetah and Stride are allocated exclusively to the Business, Sports and Science sections, respectively.

The sensitivity report for the MHT solution is shown in Figure 12.16. The nonzero reduced costs are all negative, indicating how much expected revenue will drop per impression that deviates from the plan. So, for example, if we use an impression for Cheetah in the Business section (row 11), then expected revenue will drop by \$0.00135. Viewed another way, if the expected revenue per impression increases by at least \$0.000135 then this alternative becomes attractive and would be in the solution. Note that the coefficient in the objective function for impressions in the Business section for Cheetah (the objective function coefficient of x_{13}) is (\$0.30)(0.01) = \$0.003. Assuming the revenue per click-through of \$0.30 is fixed, then we can interpret the reduced cost as how much the click-through rate would have to improve before that alternative becomes attractive enough to be in the solution. Hence, if a better placement, or a more attractive banner ad, could increase the click-through rate to at least 0.01 + 0.00135 = 0.01135, then it would be optimal to use that alternative. Other nonzero reduced costs are interpreted in the same way. The allowable increase and decrease in rows 9 through 23 indicate by how much the expected revenue per impression can change and the current solution remains optimal. So, for example, so long as the expected revenue per impression is between 0.00465 − 0.0003 = 0.00435 and 0.00465 + 0.0003 = 0.00495, then the current solution remains optimal.

Next, consider the Constraints section of Figure 12.16. Rows 28 through 32 correspond to the upper limit for each company's impressions. Only Zstar's upper limit is binding (the upper limit is 2,000,000 and 2,000,000 impressions are allocated). The shadow price of \$0.0003 indicates that for every increase of one in the upper limit on impressions, revenue will increase by \$0.0003. This will be true for an increase of up to 100,000 (Allowable Increase of 100,000).

Rows 33 through 37 in Figure 12.16 correspond to the lower limits on each company's impressions. Nile, Cheetah and Stove are each at their lower limit and have nonzero shadow prices. As expected, each of these shadow prices is negative, indicating that if we raise the lower limit, it will have a negative impact on revenue. For example, raising the

FIGURE 12.15	A Spreadsheet Model and the Solution to the MHT Banner Ad Problem

	A	B	C	D	E	F	G
1	MHT						
2	Parameters						
3	Section	Nile	Zstar	Cheetah	Stride	Stove	pressions Availab
4	Business	0.0155	0.0265	0.01	0.017	0.0105	2550000
5	Science	0.0165	0.011	0.0125	0.0265	0.0125	2150000
6	Sports	0.0145	0.0235	0.019	0.0225	0.016	2500000
7	Contracted Ads Lower Limit	1500000	1000000	1100000	1000000	1500000	
8	Contracted Ads Upper Limit	2000000	2000000	1800000	2000000	2000000	
9							
10	Revenue per click-through	0.3					
11							
12	Revenue per view	Nile	Zstar	Cheetah	Stride	Stove	
13	Business	=B4*$B$10	=C4*$B$10	=D4*$B$10	=E4*$B$10	=F4*$B$10	
14	Science	=B5*$B$10	=C5*$B$10	=D5*$B$10	=E5*$B$10	=F5*$B$10	
15	Sports	=B6*$B$10	=C6*$B$10	=D6*$B$10	=E6*$B$10	=F6*$B$10	
16							
17	Model						
18			Numb				
19		Nile	Zstar	Cheetah	Stride	Stove	
20	Business	550000	2000000	0	0	0	=SUM(B20:F20)
21	Science	950000	0	0	1100000	100000	=SUM(B21:F21)
22	Sports	0	0	1100000	0	1400000	=SUM(B22:F22)
23		=SUM(B20:B22)	=SUM(C20:C22)	=SUM(D20:D22)	=SUM(E20:E22)	=SUM(F20:F22)	
24							
25	Click-Through Revenue	=SUMPRODUCT(B13:F15,B20:F22)					
26							

	A	B	C	D	E	F	G	H
1	MHT							
2	Parameters							
3	Section	Nile	Zstar	Cheetah	Stride	Stove	Impressions Available	
4	Business	0.0155	0.0265	0.0100	0.0170	0.0105	2,550,000	
5	Science	0.0165	0.0110	0.0125	0.0265	0.0125	2,150,000	
6	Sports	0.0145	0.0235	0.0190	0.0225	0.0160	2,500,000	
7	Contracted Ads Lower Limit	1,500,000	1,000,000	1,100,000	1,000,000	1,500,000		
8	Contracted Ads Upper Limit	2,000,000	2,000,000	1,800,000	2,000,000	2,000,000		
9								
10	Revenue per click-through	$0.30						
11								
12	Revenue per view	Nile	Zstar	Cheetah	Stride	Stove		
13	Business	$0.0047	$0.0080	$0.0030	$0.0051	$0.0032		
14	Science	$0.0050	$0.0033	$0.0038	$0.0080	$0.0038		
15	Sports	$0.0044	$0.0071	$0.0057	$0.0068	$0.0048		
16								
17	Model							
18				Number of Banner Ads				
19		Nile	Zstar	Cheetah	Stride	Stove		
20	Business	550000	2000000	0	0	0	2550000	
21	Science	950000	0	0	1100000	100000	2150000	
22	Sports	0	0	1100000	0	1400000	2500000	
23		1500000	2000000	1100000	1100000	1500000		
24								
25	Click-Through Revenue	$45,270.00						

lower limit on Nile (row 33) from 1,500,000 to 1,500,001 will decrease revenue by $0.003. This is true for an increase of up to 100,000 (Allowable Increase). Other nonzero shadow prices in rows 33 through 37 are interpreted in the same way.

Rows 38 through 40 pertain to the limits of available impressions for each of the three sections of the MHT web site. Note that all three shadow prices are positive. This is because each of these constraints is binding, and an increase in the right-hand side allows more overall impressions. More allowed impressions will increase revenue. Of the three web site sections, the Sports section has the largest positive shadow price ($0.009), meaning that every additional impression beyond 2,500,000 up to an increase of 100,000 will increase revenue by $0.009; the shadow prices for Business and Science are interpreted in the same way.

As we have seen, the Excel Solver Sensitivity Report can provide useful information about the sensitivity of the optimal solution to changes in the model input. However, this type of classical sensitivity analysis is somewhat limited. Classical sensitivity analysis assumes that only one piece of input data has changed; it assumes that all other parameters remain as stated in the original problem. In many cases, however, we are interested in what would happen if two or more pieces of input data are changed simultaneously. The easiest way to examine the effect of simultaneous changes is to change the parameters in the model and rerun the model.

FIGURE 12.16	The Excel Sensitivity Report for the MHT Banner Ad Problem

Variable Cells

Cell	Name	Final Value	Reduced Cost	Objective Coefficient	Allowable Increase	Allowable Decrease
$B$20	Business Nile	550000	0	0.00465	0.0003	0.0003
$C$20	Business Zstar	2000000	0	0.00795	1E+30	0.0003
$D$20	Business Cheetah	0	-0.00135	0.003	0.00135	1E+30
$E$20	Business Stride	0	-0.00255	0.0051	0.00255	1E+30
$F$20	Business Stove	0	-0.0003	0.00315	0.0003	1E+30
$B$21	Science Nile	950000	0	0.00495	0.0003	0.0003
$C$21	Science Zstar	0	-0.00495	0.0033	0.00495	1E+30
$D$21	Science Cheetah	0	-0.0009	0.00375	0.0009	1E+30
$E$21	Science Stride	1100000	0	0.00795	0.0003	0.00225
$F$21	Science Stove	100000	0	0.00375	0.00165	0.0003
$B$22	Sports Nile	0	-0.00165	0.00435	0.00165	1E+30
$C$22	Sports Zstar	0	-0.00225	0.00705	0.00225	1E+30
$D$22	Sports Cheetah	1100000	0	0.0057	0.0033	0.0009
$E$22	Sports Stride	0	-0.00225	0.00675	0.00225	1E+30
$F$22	Sports Stove	1400000	0	0.0048	0.0009	0.00165

Constraints

Cell	Name	Final Value	Shadow Price	Constraint R.H. Side	Allowable Increase	Allowable Decrease
$B$23	Nile	1500000	0	2000000	1E+30	500000
$C$23	Zstar	2000000	0.0003	2000000	100000	900000
$D$23	Cheetah	1100000	0	1800000	1E+30	700000
$E$23	Stride	1100000	0	2000000	1E+30	900000
$F$23	Stove	1500000	0	2000000	1E+30	500000
$B$23	Nile	1500000	-0.003	1500000	100000	900000
$C$23	Zstar	2000000	0	1000000	1000000	1E+30
$D$23	Cheetah	1100000	-0.0033	1100000	100000	100000
$E$23	Stride	1100000	0	1000000	100000	1E+30
$F$23	Stove	1500000	-0.0042	1500000	100000	100000
$G$20	Business Impressions Available	2550000	0.00765	2550000	900000	100000
$G$21	Science Impressions Available	2150000	0.00795	2150000	900000	100000
$G$22	Sports Impressions Available	2500000	0.009	2500000	100000	100000

12.7 Generating an Alternative Optimal Solution for a Linear Program

The goal of business analytics is to provide information to management for improved decision making. If a linear program has more than one optimal solution, as discussed in Section 12.4, it would be good for management to know this. There might be factors external to the model that make one optimal solution preferable to another. For example, in a portfolio optimization problem, perhaps more than one strategy yields the maximum expected return. However, those strategies might be quite different in terms of their risk to the investor. Knowing the optimal alternatives and then assessing the risk of each, the investor could then pick the least risky alternative from the optimal solutions. In this section, we discuss how to generate an alternative optimal solution if one exists.

Let us reconsider the Foster Generators transportation problem from the previous section. If one exists, how might we generate an alternative optimal solution for this problem? From Figure 12.14 we know that the following is an optimal solution:

$$x_{11} = 1,000, \ x_{12} = 4,000, \ x_{13} = 0, \ x_{14} = 0$$
$$x_{21} = 2,500, \ x_{22} = 0, \ x_{23} = 2,000, \ x_{24} = 1,500$$
$$x_{31} = 2,500, \ x_{32} = 0, \ x_{33} = 0, \ x_{34} = 0$$

The optimal cost is \$39,500. With this information, we may revise our previous model to try to find an alternative optimal solution. We know that any alternative solution must be feasible, so it must satisfy all of the constraints of the original model. Also, to be optimal, the solution must give a total cost of \$39,500. We can enforce this by taking the objective function and making it a constraint equal to \$39,500:

$$3x_{11} + 2x_{12} + 7x_{13} + 6x_{14} + 6x_{21} + 5x_{22} + 2x_{23} + 3x_{24} + 2x_{31} + 5x_{32} + 4x_{33} + 5x_{34} = 39,500.$$

But, what should our objective function be for the revised problem? In the solution we previously found:

$$x_{13} = x_{14} = x_{22} = x_{32} = x_{33} = x_{34} = 0$$

If we maximize the sum of these variables and if the optimal objective function value of this revised problem is positive, we have found a different feasible solution that is also optimal. The revised model is as follows:

$$
\begin{array}{llllll}
\text{Max} & x_{13} + & x_{14} + & x_{22} + & x_{32} + & x_{33} + & x_{34} \\
\end{array}
$$
s.t.

$$
\begin{aligned}
x_{11} + x_{12} + x_{13} + x_{14} & & & \leq 5,000 \\
x_{21} + x_{22} + x_{23} + x_{24} & & & \leq 6,000 \\
x_{31} + x_{32} + x_{33} + x_{34} & & \leq 2,500 \\
x_{11} \qquad\qquad + x_{21} \qquad\qquad + x_{31} & & = 6,000 \\
x_{12} \qquad\qquad + x_{22} \qquad\qquad + x_{32} & & = 4,000 \\
x_{13} \qquad\qquad + x_{23} \qquad\qquad + x_{33} & & = 2,000 \\
x_{14} \qquad\qquad + x_{24} \qquad\qquad + x_{34} & & = 1,500 \\
3x_{11} + 2x_{12} + 7x_{13} + 6x_{14} + 6x_{21} + 5x_{22} + 2x_{23} + 3x_{24} + 2x_{31} + 5x_{32} + 4x_{33} + 5x_{34} & = 39,500 \\
x_{ij} & \geq 0 \\
\text{for } i = 1, 2, 3 \text{ and } j & = 1, 2, 3, 4
\end{aligned}
$$

The solution to this problem has an objective function value of $2,500$, indicating that the variables that were zero in the previous solution now add up to $2,500$. The new solution is shown in Table 12.6.

Comparing Figure 12.14 and Table 12.6, we see that in this new solution, Bedford ships 2,500 units to Chicago instead of to Boston.

What types of issues might make management prefer one of these solutions over the other? Notice that the original solution has the Boston distribution center sourced from all three plants, whereas each of the other distribution centers is sourced by one plant. This would imply that the manager in the Boston distribution center has to deal with three different plant managers, whereas each of the other distribution center managers has only one plant manager. The Boston manager might feel disadvantaged, having to spend too much time coordinating among the plants. The alternative solution provides a more balanced solution. Managers in Boston and Chicago each deal with two plants, and those in St. Louis and Lexington, which have lower total volumes, deal with only one plant. Because the alternative solution seems to be more equitable, it might be preferred. Recall that both solutions give a total cost of \$39,500.

TABLE 12.6	An Alternative Optimal Solution to the Foster Generators Transportation Problem

Total Cost 5 $39,500		Amount Shipped				
			To:			
		Boston	Chicago	St. Louis	Lexington	Total
From:	Cleveland	3,500	1,500	0	0	5,000
	Bedford	0	2,500	2,000	1,500	6,000
	York	2,500	0	0	0	2,500
	Total	6,000	4,000	2,000	1,500	

In summary, the general approach for trying to find an alternative optimal solution to a linear program is as follows:

Step 1. Solve the linear program

Step 2. Make a new objective function to be maximized. It is the sum of those variables that were equal to zero in the solution from Step 1

Step 3. Keep all the constraints from the original problem. Add a constraint that forces the original objective function to be equal to the optimal objective function value from Step 1

Step 4. Solve the problem created in Steps 2 and 3. If the objective function value is positive, you have found an alternative optimal solution

NOTES & COMMENTS

Steps 1–4 for finding an alternative optimal solution may be repeated to try to find more than one alternative optimal solution. However, the process is not guaranteed to find an alternative optimal solution when one exists. For example, alternative optimal solutions that are not an extreme point (see Figure 12.8) will not be found by this approach.

SUMMARY

We formulated linear programming models for the Par, Inc. maximization problem and the M&D Chemicals minimization problem. For the Par, Inc. problem, we showed how a graphical solution procedure could be used to solve a two-variable problem to help us better understand how the computer can solve large linear programs. We discussed how Excel Solver can be used to solve linear optimization problems. In formulating a linear programming model of the Par, Inc. and M&D problems, we developed a general definition of a linear program.

A linear program is a mathematical model with the following qualities:

1. A linear objective function that is to be maximized or minimized
2. A set of linear constraints
3. Variables restricted to nonnegative values

Slack variables may be used to write less-than-or-equal-to constraints in equality form, and surplus variables may be used to write greater-than-or-equal-to constraints in equality form. The value of a slack variable can usually be interpreted as the amount of unused resource, whereas the value of a surplus variable indicates the amount over and above some stated minimum requirement. Binding constraints have zero slack or surplus.

If the solution to a linear program is infeasible or unbounded, no optimal solution to the problem can be found. In the case of infeasibility, no feasible solutions are possible. In the case of an unbounded solution, the objective function can be made infinitely large for a maximization problem and infinitely small for a minimization problem. In the case of alternative optimal solutions, two or more optimal extreme points exist.

We also discussed sensitivity analysis and the interpretation of the Sensitivity Report generated by Excel Solver and how the impact of changes in the objective function coefficients and right-hand side values of constraints can be assessed. We showed how to write a mathematical model using general linear programming notation and presented three additional examples of linear programming applications: portfolio selection, transportation planning, and media selection. Finally, we concluded the chapter with a procedure for finding an alternative optimal solution when one exists.

GLOSSARY

Alternative optimal solutions The case in which more than one solution provides the optimal value for the objective function.

Binding constraint A constraint that holds as an equality at the optimal solution.

Constraints Restrictions that limit the settings of the decision variables.

Decision variable A controllable input for a linear programming model.

Extreme point Graphically speaking, the feasible solution points occurring at the vertices, or "corners," of the feasible region. With two-variable problems, extreme points are determined by the intersection of the constraint lines.

Feasible region The set of all feasible solutions.

Feasible solution A solution that satisfies all the constraints simultaneously.

Infeasibility The situation in which no solution to the linear programming problem satisfies all the constraints.

Linear function A mathematical function in which each variable appears in a separate term and is raised to the first power.

Linear programming model (linear program) A mathematical model with a linear objective function, a set of linear constraints, and nonnegative variables.

Mathematical model A representation of a problem in which the objective and all constraint conditions are described by mathematical expressions.

Nonnegativity constraints A set of constraints that requires all variables to be nonnegative.

Objective function The expression that defines the quantity to be maximized or minimized in a linear programming model.

Objective function coefficient allowable increase (decrease) The allowable increase/decrease of an objective function coefficient is the amount the coefficient may increase (decrease) without causing any change in the values of the decision variables in the optimal solution. The allowable increase/decrease for the objective function coefficients can be used to calculate the range of optimality.

Problem formulation (modeling) The process of translating a verbal statement of a problem into a mathematical statement called the *mathematical model*.

Reduced cost If a variable is at its lower bound of zero, the reduced cost is equal to the shadow price of the nonnegativity constraint for that variable. In general, if a variable is at its lower or upper bound, the reduced cost is the shadow price for that simple lower- or upper-bound constraint.

Right-hand side allowable increase (decrease) The amount the right-hand side may increase (decrease) without causing any change in the shadow price for that constraint. The allowable increase and decrease for the right-hand side can be used to calculate the range of feasibility for that constraint.

Sensitivity analysis The study of how changes in the input parameters of a linear programming problem affect the optimal solution.

Shadow price The change in the optimal objective function value per unit increase in the right-hand side of a constraint.

Slack The difference between the right-hand-side and the left-hand-side of a less-than-or-equal-to constraint.

Slack variable A variable added to the left-hand side of a less-than-or-equal-to constraint to convert the constraint into an equality. The value of this variable can usually be interpreted as the amount of unused resources.

Surplus variable A variable subtracted from the left-hand side of a greater-than-or-equal-to constraint to convert the constraint into an equality. The value of this variable can usually be interpreted as the amount over and above some required minimum level.

Unbounded The situation in which the value of the solution may be made infinitely large in a maximization linear programming problem or infinitely small in a minimization problem without violating any of the constraints.

PROBLEMS

1. **Sporting Goods Product Mix.** Kelson Sporting Equipment, Inc. makes two types of baseball gloves: a regular model and a catcher's model. The firm has 900 hours of production time available in its cutting and sewing department, 300 hours available in its finishing department, and 100 hours available in its packaging and shipping department. The production time requirements and the profit contribution per glove are given in the following table:

| | Production Time (hours) | | | |
Model	Cutting and Sewing	Finishing	Packaging and Shipping	Profit/Glove
Regular model	1	$\frac{1}{2}$	$\frac{1}{8}$	$5
Catcher's model	$\frac{3}{2}$	$\frac{1}{3}$	$\frac{1}{4}$	$8

Assuming that the company is interested in maximizing the total profit contribution, answer the following:

   a. What is the linear programming model for this problem?
   b. Develop a spreadsheet model and find the optimal solution using Excel Solver. How many of each model should Kelson manufacture?
   c. What is the total profit contribution Kelson can earn with the optimal production quantities?
   d. How many hours of production time will be scheduled in each department?
   e. What is the slack time in each department?

2. **Advertising Budget Allocation.** The Sea Wharf Restaurant would like to determine the best way to allocate a monthly advertising budget of $1,000 between newspaper advertising and radio advertising. Management decided that at least 25% of the budget must be spent on each type of media and that the amount of money spent on local newspaper advertising must be at least twice the amount spent on radio advertising. A marketing consultant developed an index that measures audience exposure per dollar of advertising on a scale from 0 to 100, with higher values implying greater audience exposure. If the value of the index for local newspaper advertising is 50 and the value of the index for spot radio advertising is 80, how should the restaurant allocate its advertising budget to maximize the value of total audience exposure?

   a. Formulate a linear programming model that can be used to determine how the restaurant should allocate its advertising budget in order to maximize the value of total audience exposure.
   b. Develop a spreadsheet model and solve the problem using Excel Solver.

3. **Building a Financial Portfolio.** Blair & Rosen, Inc. (B&R) is a brokerage firm that specializes in investment portfolios designed to meet the specific risk tolerances of its clients. A client who contacted B&R this past week has a maximum of $50,000 to invest. B&R's investment advisor decides to recommend a portfolio consisting of two investment funds: an Internet fund and a Blue Chip fund. The Internet fund has a projected annual return of

12%, and the Blue Chip fund has a projected annual return of 9%. The investment advisor requires that at most $35,000 of the client's funds should be invested in the Internet fund. B&R services include a risk rating for each investment alternative. The Internet fund, which is the more risky of the two investment alternatives, has a risk rating of 6 per $1,000 invested. The Blue Chip fund has a risk rating of 4 per $1,000 invested. For example, if $10,000 is invested in each of the two investment funds, B&R's risk rating for the portfolio would be $6(10) + 4(10) = 100$. Finally, B&R developed a questionnaire to measure each client's risk tolerance. Based on the responses, each client is classified as a conservative, moderate, or aggressive investor. Suppose that the questionnaire results classified the current client as a moderate investor. B&R recommends that a client who is a moderate investor limit his or her portfolio to a maximum risk rating of 240.

a. Formulate a linear programming model to find the best investment strategy for this client.
b. Build a spreadsheet model and solve the problem using Excel Solver. What is the recommended investment portfolio for this client? What is the annual return for the portfolio?
c. Suppose that a second client with $50,000 to invest has been classified as an aggressive investor. B&R recommends that the maximum portfolio risk rating for an aggressive investor is 320. What is the recommended investment portfolio for this aggressive investor?
d. Suppose that a third client with $50,000 to invest has been classified as a conservative investor. B&R recommends that the maximum portfolio risk rating for a conservative investor is 160. Develop the recommended investment portfolio for the conservative investor.

4. **Bank Loan Funds Allocation.** Adirondack Savings Bank (ASB) has $1 million in new funds that must be allocated to home loans, personal loans, and automobile loans. The annual rates of return for the three types of loans are 7% for home loans, 12% for personal loans, and 9% for automobile loans. The bank's planning committee has decided that at least 40% of the new funds must be allocated to home loans. In addition, the planning committee has specified that the amount allocated to personal loans cannot exceed 60% of the amount allocated to automobile loans.

a. Formulate a linear programming model that can be used to determine the amount of funds ASB should allocate to each type of loan to maximize the total annual return for the new funds.
b. How much should be allocated to each type of loan? What is the total annual return? What is the annual percentage return?
c. If the interest rate on home loans increases to 9%, would the amount allocated to each type of loan change? Explain.
d. Suppose the total amount of new funds available is increased by $10,000. What effect would this have on the total annual return? Explain.
e. Assume that ASB has the original $1 million in new funds available and that the planning committee has agreed to relax the requirement that at least 40% of the new funds must be allocated to home loans by 1%. How much would the annual return change? How much would the annual percentage return change?

5. **Hotel Room Reservations.** Round Tree Manor is a hotel that provides two types of rooms with three rental classes: Super Saver, Deluxe, and Business. The profit per night for each type of room and rental class is as follows:

	Rental Class		
Room	**Super Saver**	**Deluxe**	**Business**
Type I (Mountain View)	$30	$35	—
Type II (Street View)	$20	$30	$40

Round Tree's management makes a forecast of the demand by rental class for each night in the future. A linear programming model developed to maximize profit is used to determine how many reservations to accept for each rental class. The demand forecast for a particular night is 130 rentals in the Super Saver class, 60 in the Deluxe class, and 50 in the Business class. Since these are the forecasted demands, Round Tree will take no more than these amounts of each reservation for each rental class. Round Tree has a limited number of each type of room. There are 100 Type I rooms and 120 Type II rooms.

  a. Formulate and solve a linear program to determine how many reservations to accept in each rental class and how the reservations should be allocated to room types.
  b. For the solution in part (a), how many reservations can be accommodated in each rental class? Is the demand for any rental class not satisfied?
  c. With a little work, an unused office area could be converted to a rental room. If the conversion cost is the same for both types of rooms, would you recommend converting the office to a Type I or a Type II room? Why?
  d. Could the linear programming model be modified to plan for the allocation of rental demand for the next night? What information would be needed and how would the model change?

6. **Labor Allocation in a Design Project.** Industrial Designs has been awarded a contract to design a label for a new wine produced by Lake View Winery. The company estimates that 150 hours will be required to complete the project. The firm's three graphic designers available for assignment to this project are Lisa, a senior designer and team leader; David, a senior designer; and Sarah, a junior designer. Because Lisa has worked on several projects for Lake View Winery, management specified that Lisa must be assigned at least 40% of the total number of hours assigned to the two senior designers. To provide label designing experience for Sarah, the junior designer must be assigned at least 15% of the total project time. However, the number of hours assigned to Sarah must not exceed 25% of the total number of hours assigned to the two senior designers. Due to other project commitments, Lisa has a maximum of 50 hours available to work on this project. Hourly wage rates are $30 for Lisa, $25 for David, and $18 for Sarah.

  a. Formulate a linear program that can be used to determine the number of hours each graphic designer should be assigned to the project to minimize total cost.
  b. How many hours should be assigned to each graphic designer? What is the total cost?
  c. Suppose Lisa could be assigned more than 50 hours. What effect would this have on the optimal solution? Explain.
  d. If Sarah were not required to work a minimum number of hours on this project, would the optimal solution change? Explain.

7. **Component Manufacturing.** Vollmer Manufacturing makes three components for sale to refrigeration companies. The components are processed on two machines: a shaper and a grinder. The times (in minutes) required on each machine are as follows:

	Machine	
Component	Shaper	Grinder
1	6	4
2	4	5
3	4	2

The shaper is available for 120 hours, and the grinder for 110 hours. No more than 200 units of component 3 can be sold, but up to 1,000 units of each of the other components can be sold. In fact, the company already has orders for 600 units of component 1 that must be satisfied. The per unit selling price and per unit variable cost for each of the three components are as follows:

Component	Selling Price	Material Cost	Labor Cost
1	$25	$12	$5
2	$18	$8	$4
3	$27	$13	$5

a. For each component, calculate the profit margin (profit margin = selling price − material cost − labor cost). Formulate and solve for the recommended production quantities that will maximize contribution to profit.

b. What are the objective coefficient ranges for the three components? Interpret these ranges for company management.

c. What are the right-hand-side ranges? Interpret these ranges for company management.

d. If more time could be made available on the grinder, how much would it be worth?

e. If more units of component 3 can be sold by reducing the sales price by $4, should the company reduce the price?

8. **Lithium Battery Production.** Photon Technologies, Inc., a manufacturer of batteries for mobile phones, signed a contract with a large electronics manufacturer to produce three models of lithium-ion battery packs for a new line of phones. The contract calls for the following:

Battery Pack	Production Quantity
PT-100	200,000
PT-200	100,000
PT-300	150,000

Photon Technologies can manufacture the battery packs at manufacturing plants located in the Philippines and Mexico. The unit cost of the battery packs differs at the two plants because of differences in production equipment and wage rates. The unit costs for each battery pack at each manufacturing plant are as follows:

	Plant	
Product	Philippines	Mexico
PT-100	$0.95	$0.98
PT-200	$0.98	$1.06
PT-300	$1.34	$1.15

The PT-100 and PT-200 battery packs are produced using similar production equipment available at both plants. However, each plant has a limited capacity for the total number of PT-100 and PT-200 battery packs produced. The combined PT-100 and PT-200 production capacities are 175,000 units at the Philippines plant and 160,000 units at the Mexico plant. The PT-300 production capacities are 75,000 units at the Philippines plant and 100,000 units at the Mexico plant. The cost of shipping from the Philippines plant is $0.18 per unit, and the cost of shipping from the Mexico plant is $0.10 per unit.

a. Develop a linear program that Photon Technologies can use to determine how many units of each battery pack to produce at each plant to minimize the total production and shipping cost associated with the new contract.

b. Solve the linear program developed in part (a) to determine the optimal production plan.

c. Use sensitivity analysis to determine how much the production and/or shipping cost per unit would have to change to produce additional units of the PT-100 in the Philippines plant.

d. Use sensitivity analysis to determine how much the production and/or shipping cost per unit would have to change to produce additional units of the PT-200 in the Mexico plant.

9. **Promotional Budgeting.** The Westchester Chamber of Commerce periodically sponsors public service seminars and programs. Currently, promotional plans are under way for this year's program. Advertising alternatives include television, radio, and online. Audience estimates, costs, and maximum media usage limitations are as shown:

Constraint	Television	Radio	Online
Audience per advertisement	100,000	18,000	40,000
Cost per advertisement	$2,000	$300	$600
Maximum media usage	10	20	10

To ensure a balanced use of advertising media, radio advertisements must not exceed 50% of the total number of advertisements authorized. In addition, television should account for at least 10% of the total number of advertisements authorized.

a. If the promotional budget is limited to $18,200, how many commercial messages should be run on each medium to maximize total audience contact? What is the allocation of the budget among the three media, and what is the total audience reached?

b. By how much would audience contact increase if an extra $100 were allocated to the promotional budget?

10. **Production Planning.** The management of Hartman Company is trying to determine the amount of each of two products to produce over the coming planning period. The following information concerns labor availability, labor utilization, and product profitability:

	Labor-Hours Required (Hours/unit)		
Department	Product 1	Product 2	Hours Available
A	1.00	0.35	100
B	0.30	0.20	36
C	0.20	0.50	50
Profit contribution/unit	$30.00	$15.00	

a. Develop a linear programming model of the Hartman Company problem. Solve the model to determine the optimal production quantities of products 1 and 2.

b. In computing the profit contribution per unit, management does not deduct labor costs because they are considered fixed for the upcoming planning period. However, suppose that overtime can be scheduled in some of the departments. Which departments would you recommend scheduling for overtime? How much would you be willing to pay per hour of overtime in each department?

c. Suppose that 10, 6, and 8 hours of overtime may be scheduled in departments A, B, and C, respectively. The cost per hour of overtime is $18 in department A, $22.50 in department B, and $12 in department C. Formulate a linear programming model that can be used to determine the optimal production quantities if overtime is made available. What are the optimal production quantities, and what is the revised total contribution to profit? How much overtime do you recommend using in each department? What is the increase in the total contribution to profit if overtime is used?

11. **Credit Union Fund Allocation.** The employee credit union at State University is planning the allocation of funds for the coming year. The credit union makes four types of loans to its members. In addition, the credit union invests in risk-free securities to stabilize income. The various revenue-producing investments, together with annual rates of return, are as follows:

Type of Loan/Investment	Annual Rate of Return (%)
Automobile loans	8
Furniture loans	10
Other secured loans	11
Signature loans	12
Risk-free securities	9

The credit union will have $2 million available for investment during the coming year. State laws and credit union policies impose the following restrictions on the composition of the loans and investments:

- Risk-free securities may not exceed 30% of the total funds available for investment.
- Signature loans may not exceed 10% of the funds invested in all loans (automobile, furniture, other secured, and signature loans).
- Furniture loans plus other secured loans may not exceed the automobile loans.
- Other secured loans plus signature loans may not exceed the funds invested in risk-free securities.

How should the $2 million be allocated to each of the loan/investment alternatives to maximize total annual return? What is the projected total annual return?

12. **Seafood Buying Strategy.** The Atlantic Seafood Company (ASC) is a buyer and distributor of seafood products that are sold to restaurants and specialty seafood outlets throughout the Northeast. ASC has a frozen storage facility in New York City that serves as the primary distribution point for all products. One of the ASC products is frozen large black tiger shrimp, which are sized at 16 to 20 pieces per pound. Each Saturday, ASC can purchase more tiger shrimp or sell the tiger shrimp at the existing New York City warehouse market price. ASC's goal is to buy tiger shrimp at a low weekly price and sell it later at a higher price. ASC currently has 20,000 pounds of tiger shrimp in storage. Space is available to store a maximum of 100,000 pounds of tiger shrimp each week. In addition, ASC developed the following estimates of tiger shrimp prices for the next four weeks:

Week	Price/lb
1	$6.00
2	$6.20
3	$6.65
4	$5.55

ASC would like to determine the optimal buying/storing/selling strategy for the next four weeks. The cost to store a pound of shrimp for one week is $0.15, and to account for unforeseen changes in supply or demand, management also indicated that 25,000 pounds of tiger shrimp must be in storage at the end of week 4. Determine the optimal buying/storing/selling strategy for ASC. What is the projected four-week profit? (*Hint:* Define variables for buying, selling, and inventory held in each week. Then use a constraint to define the relationship between these: inventory from end of previous period + bought this period − sold this period = inventory at end of this period. This type of constraint is referred to as an inventory balance constraint.)

13. **Bicycle Production.** The Silver Star Bicycle Company will manufacture both men's and women's models for its Easy-Pedal bicycles during the next two months. Management wants to develop a production schedule indicating how many bicycles of each model should be produced in each month. Current demand forecasts call for 150 men's and 125 women's models to be shipped during the first month and 200 men's and 150 women's models to be shipped during the second month. Additional data are as follows:

Production Model	Costs	Labor Requirements (Hours) Manufacturing	Assembly	Current Inventory
Men's	$120	2.0	1.5	20
Women's	$90	1.6	1.0	30

Last month, the company used a total of 1,000 hours of labor. The company's labor relations policy will not allow the combined total hours of labor (manufacturing plus assembly) to increase or decrease by more than 100 hours from month to month. In addition, the company charges monthly inventory at the rate of 2% of the production cost based on the inventory levels at the end of the month. The company would like to have at least 25 units of each model in inventory at the end of the two months. (*Hint*: Define variables for production and inventory held in each period for each product. Then use a constraint to define the relationship between these: inventory from end of previous period + produced this period − demand this period = inventory at end of this period.)

a. Establish a production schedule that minimizes production and inventory costs and satisfies the labor-smoothing, demand, and inventory requirements. What inventories will be maintained and what are the monthly labor requirements?

b. If the company changed the constraints so that monthly labor increases and decreases could not exceed 50 hours, what would happen to the production schedule? How much will the cost increase? What would you recommend?

14. **Scheduling Police Officers.** The Clark County Sheriff's Department schedules police officers for 8-hour shifts. The beginning times for the shifts are 8:00 a.m., noon, 4:00 p.m., 8:00 p.m., midnight, and 4:00 a.m. An officer beginning a shift at one of these times works for the next 8 hours. During normal weekday operations, the number of officers needed varies depending on the time of day. The department staffing guidelines require the following minimum number of officers on duty:

Time of Day	Minimum No. of Officers on Duty
8:00 a.m.–noon	5
Noon–4:00 p.m.	6
4:00 p.m.–8:00 p.m.	10
8:00 p.m.–midnight	7
Midnight–4:00 a.m.	4
4:00 a.m.–8:00 a.m.	6

Determine the number of police officers who should be scheduled to begin the 8-hour shifts at each of the six times to minimize the total number of officers required. (*Hint*: Let x_1 = the number of officers beginning work at 8:00 a.m., x_2 = the number of officers beginning work at noon, and so on.)

15. **Fuel Production.** Bay Oil produces two types of fuel (regular and super) by mixing three ingredients. The major distinguishing feature of the two products is the octane level required. Regular fuel must have a minimum octane level of 90, whereas super must have a level of at least 100. The cost per barrel, octane levels, and available amounts (in barrels) for the upcoming two-week period appear in the following table, along with the maximum demand for each end product and the revenue generated per barrel:

Ingredient	Cost/Barrel	Octane	Available (barrels)
1	$16.50	100	110,000
2	$14.00	87	350,000
3	$17.50	110	300,000

	Revenue/Barrel	Max Demand (barrels)
Regular	$18.50	350,000
Super	$20.00	500,000

Develop and solve a linear programming model to maximize contribution to profit. What is the optimal contribution to profit?

16. **Distribution Plan to Minimize Cost.** Consider the following network representation of a transportation problem:

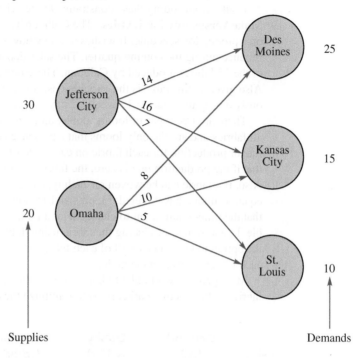

Supplies   Demands

The supplies, demands, and transportation costs per unit are shown on the network. What is the optimal (cost minimizing) distribution plan?

17. **Alternative Optimal Distribution Plan.** Refer to the transportation problem described in Problem 16. Use the procedure described in Section 12.7 to try to find an alternative optimal solution.

18. **Power Distribution.** Aggie Power Generation supplies electrical power to residential customers for many U.S. cities. Its main power generation plants are located in Los Angeles, Tulsa, and Seattle. The following table shows Aggie Power Generation's major residential markets, the annual demand in each market (in Megawatts or MW), and the cost to supply electricity to each market from each power generation plant (prices are in $/MW).

AggiePower

	Distribution Costs ($/MW)			
City	**Los Angeles**	**Tulsa**	**Seattle**	**Demand (MW)**
Seattle	$356.25	$593.75	$ 59.38	950.00
Portland	$356.25	$593.75	$178.13	831.25
San Francisco	$178.13	$475.00	$296.88	2,375.00
Boise	$356.25	$475.00	$296.88	593.75
Reno	$237.50	$475.00	$356.25	950.00
Bozeman	$415.63	$415.63	$296.88	593.75
Laramie	$356.25	$415.63	$356.25	1,187.50
Park City	$356.25	$356.25	$475.00	712.50
Flagstaff	$178.13	$475.00	$593.75	1,187.50
Durango	$356.25	$296.88	$593.75	1,543.75

a. If there are no restrictions on the amount of power that can be supplied by any of the power plants, what is the optimal solution to this problem? Which cities should be supplied by which power plants? What is the total annual power distribution cost for this solution?

b. If at most 4,000 MW of power can be supplied by any one of the power plants, what is the optimal solution? What is the annual increase in power distribution cost that results from adding these constraints to the original formulation?

19. **Make Versus Buy for Textiles.** The Calhoun Textile Mill is in the process of deciding on a production schedule. It wishes to know how to weave the various fabrics it will produce during the coming quarter. The sales department has confirmed orders for each of the 15 fabrics produced by Calhoun. These demands are given in the following table. Also given in this table is the variable cost for each fabric. The mill operates continuously during the quarter: 13 weeks, 7 days a week, and 24 hours a day.

There are two types of looms: dobby and regular. Dobby looms can be used to make all fabrics and are the only looms that can weave certain fabrics, such as plaids. The rate of production for each fabric on each type of loom is also given in the table. Note that if the production rate is zero, the fabric cannot be woven on that type of loom. Also, if a fabric can be woven on each type of loom, then the production rates are equal. Calhoun has 90 regular looms and 15 dobby looms. For this problem, assume that the time requirement to change over a loom from one fabric to another is negligible. In addition to producing the fabric using dobby and regular looms, Calhoun has the option to buy some or all of each fabric on the market. The market cost per yard for each fabric is given in the table.

Management would like to know how to allocate the looms to the fabrics and which fabrics to buy on the market so as to minimize the cost of meeting demand.

DATA *file*

Calhoun

Fabric	Demand (yd)	Dobby (yd/hr)	Regular (yd/hr)	Mill Cost ($/yd)	Market Cost ($/yd)
1	16,500	4.653	0.00	0.6573	0.80
2	52,000	4.653	0.00	0.5550	0.70
3	45,000	4.653	0.00	0.6550	0.85
4	22,000	4.653	0.00	0.5542	0.70
5	76,500	5.194	5.194	0.6097	0.75
6	110,000	3.809	3.809	0.6153	0.75
7	122,000	4.185	4.185	0.6477	0.80
8	62,000	5.232	5.232	0.4880	0.60
9	7,500	5.232	5.232	0.5029	0.70
10	69,000	5.232	5.232	0.4351	0.60
11	70,000	3.733	3.733	0.6417	0.80
12	82,000	4.185	4.185	0.5675	0.75
13	10,000	4.439	4.439	0.4952	0.65
14	380,000	5.232	5.232	0.3128	0.45
15	62,000	4.185	4.185	0.5029	0.70

20. **Alternative Optimal Plan for Make Versus Buy.** Refer to the Calhoun Textile Mill production problem described in Problem 19. Use the procedure described in Section 12.7 to try to find an alternative optimal solution. If you are successful, discuss the differences in the solution you found versus that found in Problem 19.

21. **Fitness Bracelet Distribution.** Orion Fitness produces bracelets with an embedded chip that tracks its wearer's activities. Orion has plants in Denver and Jacksonville. Bracelets produced at either plant may be shipped to either of the firm's two regional warehouses, which are located in Davenport and Cincinnati. These regional warehouses subsequently supply retail outlets in Chicago, Orlando, Houston, and Little Rock. The file *Orion* contains data on each plant's supply (number of bracelets), each retail outlet's demand (number of bracelets), and the shipping costs ($ per bracelet) for the shipping channels.

DATA *file*

Orion

Shipping Costs ($ per bracelet)

Plant	Warehouse		Supply (number of bracelets)
	Davenport	Cincinnati	
Denver	$2.00	$3.00	700
Jacksonville	$3.00	$1.00	400

Shipping Costs ($ per bracelet)

Warehouse	Retail Outlet			
	Chicago	Orlando	Houston	Little Rock
Davenport	$3.00	$7.00	$4.00	$7.00
Cincinnati	$5.00	$5.00	$7.00	$6.00
Demand (number of bracelets)	200	150	350	300

a. Construct and solve a linear optimization model that defines the supply chain strategy that meets the demand of each retail outlet at minimum total shipping cost.

b. In a separate worksheet, reformulate the problem to determine if there is an alternative optimal solution. Clearly explain your result.

22. **Scheduling Sports Equipment Production.** Brendamore Sports produces footballs and soccer balls and must plan on how many to produce each month for the next six months. The file *Brendamore* contains demand forecasts, as well as the production costs and inventory holding costs, for the next six months. Brendamore must meet the monthly demand of each product through either a combination of inventory or production during the month. Assume that demand occurs at the end of the month, so that any production during a month can meet that month's demand.

DATA *file*

Brendamore

Month	Football Demand Forecast	Soccer Ball Demand Forecast
1	15,000	10,000
2	25,000	15,000
3	20,000	10,000
4	5,000	5,000
5	2,500	5,000
6	5,000	7,500

Month	Production Cost ($ per football)	Holding Cost ($ per football)	Production Cost ($ per soccer ball)	Holding Cost ($ per soccer ball)
1	$13.80	$0.69	$10.85	$0.54
2	$13.90	$0.70	$10.55	$0.53
3	$12.95	$0.65	$10.50	$0.53
4	$12.60	$0.63	$10.50	$0.53
5	$12.55	$0.63	$10.55	$0.53
6	$12.70	$0.64	$10.00	$0.50

During each month, there is enough production capacity to produce up to 32,000 total balls (football + soccer balls), and there is enough storage capacity to store up to 20,000 total balls (football + soccer balls) at the end of the month. Brendamore wants to meet these demands on time and it currently has 7,000 footballs and 5,000 soccer balls in inventory. In anticipation of demand beyond the six-month planning horizon, Brendamore would like to have 3,000 footballs and 3,000 soccer balls in inventory at the end of the sixth month.

Brendamore wants to determine the six-month production schedule that minimizes the total production and holding cost.

23. **Developing a Risk-Averse Investment Portfolio.** An investor wishes to invest $10,000 for the coming year and anticipates that the market will be in one of four different states at the end of the year. These states affect her investments in each of three possible stocks and a bond as shown in the following table. Unfortunately, she is uncertain about which market state will occur. Because she is risk-averse, the investor would like to invest in a manner so that the return in the worst-case, no matter what market state occurs, is as good as possible. The following table provides the current price of each possible instrument as well as projected year-end prices of each instrument under each of the four possible states.

DATA *file*
MarketStates

		Possible Market States			
	Price	State 1	State 2	State 3	State 4
Stock A	$4.94	$4.58	$3.95	$5.67	$5.39
Stock B	$5.88	$5.24	$7.28	$4.82	$6.22
Stock C	$6.48	$8.27	$5.65	$7.66	$5.78
Bond D	$2.68	$2.11	$2.53	$2.80	$2.09

These data are in the file *MarketStates*. Formulate her investment problem as a linear program and solve it using Excel Solver. How much should she invest in each security? Note: It is possible to purchase fractional shares.

24. **Cash Flow Management.** A financial manager is managing a cash fund. His investment alternatives available are various certificates of deposit, also known as CDs, as listed in the following table:

Investment	Yield	Availability
1-month CD	0.5%	Beginning of each month
3-month CD	1.75%	Beginning of Months 1, 2, 3, 4
6-month CD	2.3%	Beginning of Month 1

DATA *file*
CashManagement

However, he also must ensure that sufficient funds are available to pay company expenditures over the next six months. The following table lists the net expenditures (in thousands of dollars) that the manager is obligated to cover (cash amounts in parenthesis indicate a net inflow of cash rather than outflow).

Month	Net Expenditures ($1,000s)
1	$45
2	($11)
3	$25
4	($22)
5	$43
6	($15)

The cash on hand to invest at the start of month 1 is $200,000 and the minimum cash required to be available at the end of month 6 is $100,000. Develop and solve a linear program that will recommend how to invest to maximize the amount of interest income accrued over the next six months while satisfying all financial commitments.

(*Hint*: Investment time starts at the beginning of the month and returns at the end of the month. For example, money invested in a 1-month CD in month 1 will be invested at the beginning of month 1 and returned with interest at the end of month 1. Likewise, money invested in a 3-month CD at the start of month 1 will be returned with interest at the end of month 3.)

25. **Organic Food Supply-Chain Optimization.** A produce company supplies organically grown apples to four regional specialty stores. After the apples are collected at the company's orchard, they are transported to any of three preparation centers where they are prepared for retail (by undergoing extensive cleaning and then packaging). After the apples are prepared, they are shipped to the specialty stores. Due to the fragility of the product, the cost of transporting this organic fruit is rather high.

    The company has three preparation centers available for use. The *Apple* worksheet contains the following: (i) the unit transportation costs (in $/pound) to get the apples from company's orchard to the preparation centers, (ii) the cost ($/pound) to prepare the apples in the preparation centers, (iii) the preparation centers' monthly capacities, (iv) the demand at the specialty stores, and (v) the unit costs of transporting the apples from the preparation centers to the specialty stores.

DATA*file*

Apple

Preparation Center	Transportation Cost ($/pound) (Orchard to Preparation Center)	Preparation Cost ($/pound)	Monthly Capacity (pounds)
1	$0.45	$0.15	300
2	$1.00	$0.20	500
3	$1.62	$0.18	800

| Preparation Center | Shipping Cost ($ per pound) | | | |
	Organic Orchard	Fresh & Local	Healthy Pantry	Season's Harvest
1	$0.80	$1.10	$0.70	$1.40
2	$1.20	$1.10	$0.50	$1.40
3	$0.20	$1.40	$1.30	$1.70
Monthly Demand (pounds)	300	500	400	200

   a. Construct and solve a linear optimization model to determine the number of pounds of apples to prepare at each of the three preparation centers and how much of each specialty store's demand to supply from each preparation center, to minimize the total cost of the operation.
   b. In a separate worksheet, reformulate the problem to determine if there is an alternative optimal solution. Clearly explain your result.

26. **Energy Planning.** Windsor Power can store power in a high-capacity battery. The battery has capacity to store 80 kWh (kilowatt hours). During a particular period, Windsor can buy or sell electricity at the market price known as LMP (locational marginal price). The maximum rate that power can be injected or withdrawn from the battery is 20 kWh per period. Windsor has forecasted the following LMPs for the next 10 periods:

Period:	1	2	3	4	5	6	7	8	9	10
LMP ($/kwh)	5	27	2	25	22	29	24	20	61	66

Develop a linear programming model that will assist Windsor Power in determining how to best buy, store or sell electricity for the next 10 periods based on the LMP. Assume that the battery is half full at the beginning of period 1. That is, at the start of the planning horizon, the battery contains 40 kWh of electricity. It costs $1 to hold 1 kWh in the battery per period. Be sure to define all decision variables.

27. **Ice Cream Recipes.** McKinney's Sweet Shop specializes in homemade candies and ice cream. McKinney's produces its ice cream in house, in batches of 50 pounds. The first stage in ice cream making is the blending of ingredients to obtain a mix which meets pre-specified requirements on the percentages of certain constituents of the mix. The desired composition is as follows:

Constituent	Required Percentage (%)
1. Fat	16.00
2. Serum Solids	8.00
3. Sugar Solids	16.00
4. Egg Solids	0.35
5. Stabilizer	0.25
6. Emulsifier	0.15
7. Water	59.25

The mix can be composed of ingredients from the following list:

Ingredient	Cost ($/lb)
1. 40% Cream	1.19
2. 23% Cream	0.70
3. Butter	2.32
4. Plastic Cream	2.30
5. Butter Oil	2.87
6. 4% Milk	0.25
7. Skim Condensed Milk	0.35
8. Skim Milk Powder	0.65
9. Liquid Sugar	0.25
10. Sugared Frozen Fresh Egg Yolk	1.75
11. Powdered Egg Yolk	4.45
12. Stabilizer	2.45
13. Emulsifier	1.68
14. Water	0.00

The number of pounds of a constituent found in a pound of an ingredient is shown in the following table (the rows correspond to constituents 1 through 7 and the columns correspond to ingredients 1 through 14). Note that a pound of stabilizer contributes only to the stabilizer requirement (one pound), one pound of emulsifier contributes only to the emulsifier requirement (one pound), and that water contributes only to the water requirement (one pound).

	1	2	3	4	5	6	7	8	9	10	11	12	13	14
1	0.4	0.2	0.8	0.8	0.9	0.1				0.5	0.6			
2	0.1		0.1		0.1	0.3	1							
3									0.7	0.1				
4										0.4	0.4			
5												1		
6													1	
7	0.5	0.8	0.2	0.1	0.1	0.8	0.7		0.3					1

Jack McKinney Jr. has recently acquired the shop from his father (Papa Jack). Jack's father has in the past used the following mixture: 9.73 pounds of Plastic Cream, 3.03 pounds of Skim Milk Powder, 11.37 pounds of Liquid Sugar, 0.44 pounds of Sugared Frozen Fresh Egg Yolk, 0.12 pounds of Stabilizer, 0.07 pounds of Emulsifier and 25.24 pounds of water. (The scale at McKinney's is only accurate to 100ths of a pound.)

a. Jack feels that perhaps it is possible to produce the ice cream in a more cost-effective manner. He would like to find the cheapest mix for producing a batch of ice cream, which meets the requirements specified above. How does the optimal cost compare to the cost of Papa Jack's recipe?

b. Jack is also curious about the cost effect of being a little more flexible in the requirements. He wants to know the cheapest mix if the composition meets the following tolerances:

1. Fat	15.00–17.00 %
2. Serum Solids	7.00–9.00 %
3. Sugar Solids	15.50–16.50 %
4. Egg Solids	0.30–0.40 %
5. Stabilizer	0.20–0.30 %
6. Emulsifier	0.10–0.20 %
7. Water	58.00–59.50 %

How much cost benefit is there to being more flexible?

28. **Skateboard Supply Chain.** Sports of All Sorts produces, distributes, and sells high-quality handcrafted skateboards. Its supply chain consists of three factories that produce the skateboards (located in Detroit, Los Angeles, and Austin). The Detroit and Los Angeles facilities can produce 35,000 skateboards per year, but the Austin plant is larger and can produce up to 70,000 skateboards per year. Skateboards must be shipped from the factories to one of four distribution centers, or DCs, located in Iowa, Maryland, Idaho, and Arkansas. Because of differences in labor rates, the processing and handling charge at each DC is different. These costs per skateboard are $1.34 in Iowa, $1.62 in Maryland, $1.30 in Idaho, and $1.38 in Arkansas. Each distribution center can process (repackage, mark for sale, and ship) at most 50,000 skateboards per year. Skateboards are then shipped from the distribution centers to retailers. Sports of All Sorts supplies three major U.S. retailers: Just Sports, Sports 'N Stuff, and The Sports Dude. The following tables display the per unit costs for shipping skateboards between the factories and DCs and for shipping between the DCs and the retailers.

| Shipping Costs ($ per skateboard) | | | | |
Factory/DCs	Iowa	Maryland	Idaho	Arkansas
Detroit	$25.00	$25.00	$35.00	$40.00
Los Angeles	$35.00	$45.00	$35.00	$42.50
Austin	$40.00	$40.00	$42.50	$32.50

Retailers/DC	Iowa	Maryland	Idaho	Arkansas
Just Sports	$30.00	$20.00	$35.00	$27.50
Sports 'N Stuff	$27.50	$32.50	$40.00	$25.00
The Sports Dude	$30.00	$40.00	$32.50	$42.50

DATAfile

Skateboards

This exercise assumes knowledge of concepts discussed in Chapter 8.

Sports of All Sorts needs to forecast the demand at each of its four retail locations for next year, and then plan how to produce and distribute its product from the factories through the DCs to the retailers. The file *Skateboards* contains five tabs: Plant Capacities, Transportation Costs, DC Capacities, DC Processing Costs, and Historical Demand.

a. Construct a scatter plot for the historical demand for each retailer. Use the historical demand to forecast the future demand for each retailer. For Just Sports and Sports 'N Stuff, use the average of the historical demands as the forecast for the next year. For The Sports Dude, use simple linear regression to forecast the demand for the next year. Round your forecast to the nearest one thousand units (e.g., if your forecast is 12,303, round to 12,000 for use in part (b).

b. Construct a linear programming model of the supply chain.

c. Solve the linear programming model you constructed in part (b). What is the total cost? Which plants are planned to use all of their capacity? Which distribution centers will use all of their capacity?

CASE PROBLEM: INVESTMENT STRATEGY

J. D. Williams, Inc. is an investment advisory firm that manages more than $120 million in funds for its numerous clients. The company uses an asset allocation model that recommends the portion of each client's portfolio to be invested in a growth stock fund, an income fund, and a money market fund. To maintain diversity in each client's portfolio, the firm places limits on the percentage of each portfolio that may be invested in each of the three funds. General guidelines indicate that the amount invested in the growth fund must be between 20% and 40% of the total portfolio value. Similar percentages for the other two funds stipulate that between 20% and 50% of the total portfolio value must be in the income fund and that at least 30% of the total portfolio value must be in the money market fund.

In addition, the company attempts to assess the risk tolerance of each client and adjust the portfolio to meet the needs of the individual investor. For example, Williams just contracted with a new client who has $800,000 to invest. Based on an evaluation of the client's risk tolerance, Williams assigned a maximum risk index of 0.05 for the client. The firm's risk indicators show the risk of the growth fund at 0.10, the income fund at 0.07, and the money market fund at 0.01. An overall portfolio risk index is computed as a weighted average of the risk rating for the three funds, where the weights are the fraction of the client's portfolio invested in each of the funds.

Additionally, Williams is currently forecasting annual yields of 18% for the growth fund, 12.5% for the income fund, and 7.5% for the money market fund. Based on the information provided, how should the new client be advised to allocate the $800,000 among the growth, income, and money market funds? Develop a linear programming model that will provide the maximum yield for the portfolio. Use your model to develop a managerial report.

Managerial Report

1. Recommend how much of the $800,000 should be invested in each of the three funds. What is the annual yield you anticipate for the investment recommendation?
2. Assume that the client's risk index could be increased to 0.055. How much would the yield increase, and how would the investment recommendation change?
3. Refer again to the original situation, in which the client's risk index was assessed to be 0.05. How would your investment recommendation change if the annual yield for the growth fund were revised downward to 16% or even to 14%?
4. Assume that the client expressed some concern about having too much money in the growth fund. How would the original recommendation change if the amount invested in the growth fund is not allowed to exceed the amount invested in the income fund?
5. The asset allocation model you developed may be useful in modifying the portfolios for all of the firm's clients whenever the anticipated yields for the three funds are periodically revised. What is your recommendation as to whether use of this model is possible?

Chapter 13

Integer Linear Optimization Models

CONTENTS

ANALYTICS IN ACTION: *PETROBRAS*

Petrobras*

Petrobras, one of the largest corporations in Brazil, operates approximately 80 offshore oil production and exploration platforms in the oil-rich Campos Basin. One of Petrobras's biggest challenges is planning its logistics, including how to efficiently and safely transport nearly 1,900 employees per day from its four mainland bases to the offshore platforms and then back to the mainland. Every day, planners must route and schedule the helicopters used for this purpose. This routing and scheduling problem is challenging because there are over a billion possible combinations of schedules and routes.

Petrobras uses mixed integer linear optimization to solve its helicopter transport scheduling and routing problem. The objective function of the optimization model is a weighted function designed to ensure safety, minimize unmet demand, and minimize the cost of the transport of its crews. Because offshore landings are the riskiest part of the transport, the safety objective is met by minimizing the number of offshore landings required in the schedule. Numerous constraints must be met in planning these routes and schedule. These include limiting the number of departures from a platform at certain times; ensuring no time conflicts for a given helicopter and pilot; ensuring proper breaks for pilots; and limiting the number of flights per day for a given helicopter as well as routing restrictions. The decision variables include binary variables for assigning helicopters to flights and pilots to break times, as well as variables on the number of passengers per flight.

Compared to the previously used manual approach to this problem, the new approach using the integer optimization model transports the same number of passengers but with 18% fewer offshore landings, 8% less flight time, and a reduction in cost of 14%. The annual cost savings is estimated to be approximately $24 million.

*Based on F. Menezes et al., "Optimizing Helicopter Transport of Oil Rig Crews at Petrobras," *Interfaces* 40, no. 5 (September–October 2010): 408–416.

In this chapter, we discuss a class of problems that are modeled as linear programs with the additional requirement that one or more variables must be an integer. Such problems are called **integer linear programs**.

The objective of this chapter is to provide an applications-oriented introduction to integer linear programming. We discuss the different types of integer linear programming models, the geometry of all-integer linear programs, and we show how to use Excel Solver to solve integer optimization problems. We discuss four applications of integer linear programming that make use of binary variables: capital budgeting, fixed cost, bank location, and market share optimization problems and we provide additional illustrations of the modeling flexibility provided by binary variables. We also discuss ways to generate useful alternative solutions in integer linear optimization.

13.1 Types of Integer Linear Optimization Models

The only difference between the problems in this chapter and the problems in Chapter 12 on linear programming is that one or more variables are required to be an integer. If all variables are required to be an integer, we have an **all-integer linear program**. The following is a two-variable, all-integer linear programming model:

$$\text{Max} \quad 2x_1 + 3x_2$$
$$\text{s.t.}$$
$$3x_1 + 3x_2 \leq 12$$
$$\tfrac{2}{3}x_1 + 1x_2 \leq 4$$
$$1x_1 + 2x_2 \leq 6$$
$$x_1, x_2 \geq 0 \text{ and integer}$$

If we drop the phrase *and integer* from the last line of this model, we have the familiar two-variable linear program. The linear program that results from dropping the integer requirements is called the linear programming relaxation, or **LP relaxation**, of the integer linear program.

If some, but not necessarily all, variables are required to be integer, we have a **mixed-integer linear program**. The following is a two-variable, mixed-integer linear program:

$$\text{Max} \quad 3x_1 + 4x_2$$
$$\text{s.t.}$$
$$-1x_1 + 2x_2 \leq 8$$
$$1x_1 + 2x_2 \leq 12$$
$$2x_1 + 1x_2 \leq 16$$
$$x_1, x_2 \geq 0 \text{ and } x_2 \text{ integer}$$

We obtain the LP relaxation of this mixed-integer linear program by dropping the requirement that x_2 be integer.

In some applications, the integer variables may take on only the values 0 or 1. Then we have a **binary integer linear program**. As we see later in the chapter, binary variables provide additional modeling capability.

13.2 Eastborne Realty, an Example of Integer Optimization

Eastborne Realty has $2 million available for the purchase of new rental property. After an initial screening, Eastborne reduced the investment alternatives to townhouses and apartment buildings. Each townhouse can be purchased for $282,000, and five are available. Each apartment building can be purchased for $400,000, and the developer will construct as many buildings as Eastborne wants to purchase.

Eastborne's property manager can devote up to 140 hours per month to these new properties; each townhouse is expected to require 4 hours per month, and each apartment building is expected to require 40 hours per month. The annual cash flow, after deducting mortgage payments and operating expenses, is estimated to be $10,000 per townhouse and $15,000 per apartment building. Eastborne's owner would like to determine the number of townhouses and the number of apartment buildings to purchase to maximize annual cash flow.

We begin by defining the decision variables:

$$T = \text{number of townhouses}$$
$$A = \text{number of apartment buildings}$$

The objective function for cash flow (in thousands of dollars) is

$$\text{Max } 10T + 15A$$

Three constraints must be satisfied:

$$282T + 400A \leq 2{,}000 \quad \text{Funds available (\$1,000s)}$$
$$4T + 40A \leq 140 \quad \text{Manager's time (hours)}$$
$$T \leq 5 \quad \text{Townhouses available}$$

The variables T and A must be nonnegative. In addition, the purchase of a fractional number of townhouses and/or a fractional number of apartment buildings is unacceptable. Thus, T and A must be integers. The model for the Eastborne Realty problem is the following all-integer linear program:

$$\text{Max} \quad 10T + 15A$$
$$\text{s.t.}$$
$$282T + 400A \leq 2{,}000$$
$$4T + 40A \leq 140$$
$$T \leq 5$$
$$T, A \geq 0 \text{ and integer}$$

The model for Eastborne Realty is a linear all-integer program. Next we discuss the geometry of this model.

The Geometry of Linear All-Integer Optimization

The geometry of the feasible region for the Eastborne Reality problem is shown in Figure 13.1. The lightly shaded region is the feasible region of the LP relaxation. The optimal linear programming solution is point b, which is $T = 2.479$ townhouses and $A = 3.252$ apartment buildings. The optimal value of the objective function is 73.574, which indicates an annual cash flow of \$73,574. Point b is formed by the intersection of the Manager's Time constraint and the Available Funds constraint. Unfortunately, because Eastborne cannot purchase fractional numbers of townhouses and apartment buildings, further analysis is necessary.

In many cases, a noninteger solution can be rounded to obtain an acceptable integer solution. For instance, a linear programming solution to a production scheduling problem might call for the production of 15,132.4 cases of breakfast cereal. The rounded integer solution of 15,132 cases would probably have minimal impact on the value of the objective function and the feasibility of the solution. Rounding would be a sensible approach. Indeed, whenever rounding has a minimal impact on the objective function and constraints, most managers find it acceptable; a near-optimal solution is satisfactory.

However, rounding may not always be a good strategy. When the decision variables take on small values that have a major impact on the value of the objective function or feasibility, an optimal integer solution is needed. Let us return to the Eastborne Realty problem and examine the impact of rounding. The optimal solution to the LP relaxation for

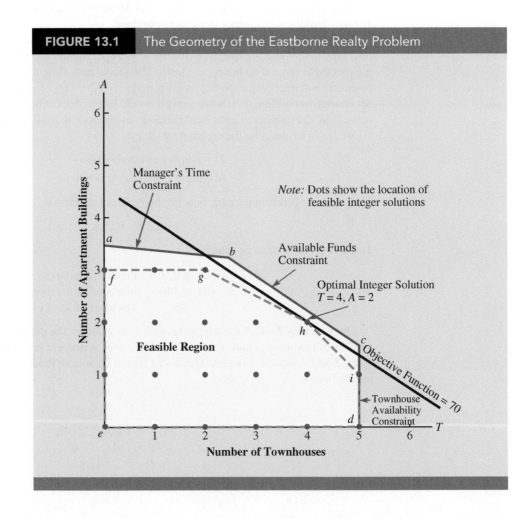

FIGURE 13.1 The Geometry of the Eastborne Realty Problem

Eastborne Realty resulted in $T = 2.479$ townhouses and $A = 3.252$ apartment buildings. Because each townhouse costs \$282,000 and each apartment building costs \$400,000, rounding to an integer solution can be expected to have a substantial economic impact on the problem.

Suppose that we round the solution to the LP relaxation to obtain the integer solution $T = 2$ and $A = 3$, with an objective function value of $10(2) + 15(3) = 65$. The annual cash flow of \$65,000 is substantially less than the annual cash flow of \$73,574 provided by the solution to the LP relaxation. Do other rounding possibilities exist? Exploring other rounding alternatives shows that the integer solution $T = 3$ and $A = 3$ is infeasible because it requires $\$282,000(3) + \$400,000(3) = \$3,738,000$, which is more than the \$2 million that Eastborne has available. The rounded solution of $T = 2$ and $A = 4$ is also infeasible for the same reason. At this point, rounding has led to two townhouses and three apartment buildings with an annual cash flow of \$65,000 as the best feasible integer solution to the problem. Unfortunately, we don't know whether this solution is the best integer solution to the problem.

Rounding to an integer solution is a trial-and-error approach. Each rounded solution must be evaluated for feasibility as well as for its impact on the value of the objective function. Even when a rounded solution is feasible, we have no guarantee that we have found the optimal integer solution. We will see shortly that the rounded solution ($T = 2$ and $A = 3$) is not optimal for Eastborne Realty.

What is the true feasible region for the Eastborne Realty problem? As shown in Figure 13.1, the feasible region is the set of integer points that lie within the feasible region of the LP relaxation. There are 20 such feasible solutions (designated by blue dots in the figure). The region bounded by the dashed lines is known as the **convex hull** of the set of feasible integer solutions. The convex hull of a set of points is the smallest intersection of linear inequalities that contain the set of points. Notice that the convex hull in Figure 13.1 has integer extreme points (points d, e, f, g, h, and i). If we knew the convex hull, we could use linear programming to find the optimal integer corner point. Unfortunately, identifying the convex hull can be very time consuming. This is somewhat counterintuitive because there are only 20 feasible solutions, but solving an integer optimization problem such as that for Eastborne Realty may require solving numerous linear programs to find the optimal integer solution. Therefore, an integer optimization problem can be much more time consuming to solve than solving a linear program of comparable size.

It is true that the optimal solution to the integer program will be an extreme point of the convex hull, so one or more of the extreme points d, e, f, g, h, and i are optimal. The objective function contour shown in Figure 13.1 with an objective function value equal to 70 shows that point h is the optimal solution. As a check, let us evaluate each of the corner points of the convex hull in Figure 13.1:

Point	T =	A =	Annual Cash Flow (\$000) =
d	5	0	10(5) + 15(0) = 50
e	0	0	10(0) + 15(0) = 0
f	0	3	10(0) + 15(3) = 45
g	2	3	10(2) + 15(3) = 65
h	4	2	10(4) + 15(2) = 70
i	5	1	10(5) + 15(1) = 65

This confirms that the optimal integer solution occurs at point h, where $T = 4$ townhouses and $A = 2$ apartment buildings. The objective function value is an annual cash flow of \$70,000. This solution is substantially better than the best solution found by rounding $T = 2, A = 3$ with an annual cash flow of \$65,000. Thus, we see that rounding would not have been the best strategy for Eastborne Realty.

1. An important observation can be made from the analysis of the Eastborne Realty problem. It has to do with the relationship between the value of the optimal integer solution and the value of the optimal solution to the LP relaxation. For integer linear programs involving maximization, the value of the optimal solution to the LP relaxation provides an upper bound on the value of the optimal integer solution. This observation is valid for the Eastborne Realty problem. The value of the optimal integer solution is $70,000, and the value of the optimal solution to the LP relaxation is $73,574. Thus, we know from the LP relaxation solution that the upper bound for the value of the objective function is $73,574. For integer linear programs involving minimization, the value of the optimal solution to the LP relaxation provides a lower bound on the value of the optimal integer solution.

2. The two popular approaches to solving integer linear optimization problems are branch-and-bound and cutting planes. Both solve a series of LP relaxations to arrive at an optimal integer solution. The *branch-and-bound approach* breaks the feasible region of the LP relaxation into subregions until the subregions have integer solutions or it is determined that the solution cannot be in the subregion. *Cutting plane* approaches try to identify the convex hull by adding a series of new constraints that do not exclude any feasible integer points. Indeed, most software for integer optimization, including Excel Solver, employs a combination of these two approaches.

13.3 Solving Integer Optimization Problems with Excel Solver

The worksheet formulation and solution for integer linear programs are similar to that for linear programming problems. Actually the worksheet formulation is exactly the same, but some additional information must be provided when setting up the Solver Parameters and Options dialog boxes. Constraints must be added in the Solver Parameters dialog box to identify the integer variables. In addition, the value for Tolerance in the Integer Options dialog box may need to be adjusted to obtain a solution.

Let us demonstrate the Excel solution of an integer linear program by showing how Excel Solver can be used to solve the Eastborne Realty problem. The worksheet with the optimal solution is shown in Figure 13.2. We will describe the key elements of the worksheet and how to obtain the solution, and then we will interpret the solution.

The parameters and descriptive labels appear in cells A1:G7 of the worksheet in Figure 13.2. The cells in the lower portion of the worksheet contain the information required by the Excel Solver (decision variables, objective function, constraint left-hand sides, and constraint right-hand sides).

Decision variables	Cells B14:C14 are reserved for the decision variables.
Objective function	The formula =SUMPRODUCT(B7:C7,B14:C14) has been placed into cell B17 to reflect the annual cash flow associated with the solution.
Left-hand sides	The left-hand sides for the three constraints are placed into cells F15:F17. Cell F15 =SUMPRODUCT(B4:C4, $B$14:$C$14) (Copy to cell F16) Cell F17 =B14
Right-hand sides	The right-hand sides for the three constraints are placed into cells G15:G17. Cell G15 =G4 (Copy to cells G16:G17)

To solve the Eastborne Realty problem, we follow these steps:

Step 1.   Click the **Data** tab in the Ribbon

Step 2.   In the **Analyze** group, click **Solver**

FIGURE 13.2	Eastborne Realty Spreadsheet Model

	A	B	C	D	E	F	G
1	Eastborne Realty Problem						
2	Parameters						
3		Townhouse	Apt. Bldg.				
4	Price (000)	282	400			Funds Avl. ($000)	2000
5	Mgr. Time	4	40			Mgr. Time Avl. (Hours)	140
6						Townhouses Avl.	5
7	Ann. Cash Flow ($000)	10	15				
8							
9							
10							
11	Model						
12		Number of					
13		Townhouses	Apt. Bldgs.				
14	Purchase Plan	4	2			Total Used	Total Available
15					Funds ($000)	=SUMPRODUCT(B4:C4,$B$14:$C$14)	=G4
16					Funds (Hours)	=SUMPRODUCT(B5:C5,$B$14:$C$14)	=G5
17	Max Cash Flow ($000)	=SUMPRODUCT(B7:C7,B14:C14)			Townhouses	=B14	=G6
18							

MODEL *file*

Eastborne

	A	B	C	D	E	F	G	H
1	Eastborne Realty Problem							
2	Parameters							
3		Townhouse	Apt. Bldg.					
4	Price (000)	$282	$400			Funds Avl. ($000)	$2,000	
5	Mgr. Time	4	40			Mgr. Time Avl. (Hours)	140	
6						Townhouses Avl.	5	
7	Ann. Cash Flow ($000)	$10	$15					
8								
9								
10								
11	Model							
12		Number of						
13		Townhouses	Apt. Bldgs.					
14	Purchase Plan	4	2			Total Used	Total Available	
15					Funds ($000)	$1,928	$2,000	
16					Time (Hours)	96	140	
17	Max Cash Flow ($000)	$70			Townhouses	4	5	
18								

Step 3. When the **Solver Parameters** dialog box appears (Figure 13.3):
  Enter *B17* in the **Set Objective:** box
    Select **Max** for the **To:** option
  Enter *B14:C14* in the **By Changing Variable Cells:** box

Step 4. Click the **Add** button
  When the **Add Constraint** dialog box appears:
  Enter *B14:C14* in the **Cell Reference:** box
  Select **int** from the drop-down menu
  When **int** is selected, the term "integer" automatically appears in the
    Constraint: box. This constraint tells Solver that the decision
  variables in cells B14 and C14 must be integers.

*Binary variables are
identified with the **bin**
designation in the Solver
Parameters dialog box.*

FIGURE 13.3 Solver Parameters Dialog Box for Eastborne Realty

Step 5. Click the **Add** button
   When the **Add Constraint** dialog box appears:
   Enter *F15:F17* in the **Cell Reference:** box
   Select ≤ from the drop-down menu
   Enter *G15:G17* in the **Constraint:** area
   Click **OK**
Step 6. Select the **Make Unconstrained Variables Non-Negative** option
   Select **Simplex LP** from the **Select a Solving Method:** drop-down menu
Step 7. Click the **Options** button
   Select the **All Methods** tab, and set the **Integer Optimality (%):** to *0*,
      as shown in Figure 13.4. This ensures that we find the optimal integer
      solution
   Click **OK** to close the **Options** dialog box
Step 8. When the **Solver Parameters** dialog box reappears, click **Solve**
Step 9. When the **Solver Results** dialog box appears, select **Answer** in the **Reports**
   area and click **OK**

EastborneModel

The completed linear integer optimization model for the Eastborne Realty problem is contained in the file *EastborneModel.*

Figure 13.5 shows the Eastborne Realty Answer Report. The structure of the Answer Report from Excel Solver for integer programs is the same as that described in Chapter 12 for linear programs. The first section gives information regarding the objective function. It shows that the objective function is located in cell B17 and that the optimal value (Final

FIGURE 13.4   Solver Options Dialog Box

Value) of the objective function is $70,000. The Variable Cells section gives the location, name, and original and optimal values (Final Value) of the decision variables, as well as an indication that the decision variables have been designated as integers. For the Eastborne problem, in Figure 13.5, we see that the optimal solution is to purchase four townhouses and two apartment buildings. Finally, the Constraints section gives us detail on the status of each constraint at optimality. We see that none of the three constraints is binding, and from the slack column, we see that we have $72,000 unused from budget and 44 unused hours and that we are under the limit of 5 townhouses by 1.

As this example illustrates, and as we have seen in Figure 13.1, unlike in a linear program, the solution to an integer program can be such that none of the constraints is binding at the optimal point.

A Cautionary Note About Sensitivity Analysis

The classical sensitivity analysis discussed in Chapter 12 for linear programs is not available for integer programs. Because of the discrete nature of integer optimization, it is not possible to easily calculate objective function coefficient ranges, shadow prices, and right-hand-side ranges. However, this does not mean that the sensitivity analysis is not important for integer programs. Sensitivity analysis is often more crucial for integer linear programming problems than for linear programming problems. A small change in one of the coefficients in the constraints can cause a relatively large change in the value of the optimal solution. To understand why, consider the following integer programming model of

FIGURE 13.5   Excel Solver Answer Report for the Eastborne Realty Problem

	A	B	C	D	E	F	G
13							
14	Objective Cell (Max)						
15		Cell	Name	Original Value	Final Value		
16		$B$17	Max Cash Flow ($000)	$0	$70		
17							
18							
19	Variable Cells						
20		Cell	Name	Original Value	Final Value	Integer	
21		$B$14	Purchase Plan Townhouses	0	4	Integer	
22		$C$14	Purchase Plan Apt. Bldgs.	0	2	Integer	
23							
24							
25	Constraints						
26		Cell	Name	Cell Value	Formula	Status	Slack
27	$F$15		Funds ($000) Total Used	$1,928	$F$15<=$G$15	Not Binding	72
28	$F$16		Time (Hours) Total Used	96	$F$16<=$G$16	Not Binding	44
29	$F$17		Townhouses Total Used	4	$F$17<=$G$17	Not Binding	1
30	$B$14:$C$14=Integer						
31							

a simple capital budgeting problem involving four projects and a budgetary constraint for a single time period:

$$\text{Max} \quad 40x_1 + 60x_2 + 70x_3 + 160x_4$$
$$\text{s.t.}$$
$$16x_1 + 35x_2 + 45x_3 + 85x_4 \leq 100$$
$$x_1, x_2, x_3, x_4 = 0, 1$$

Sensitivity reports are not available for integer optimization problems. To determine the sensitivity of the solution to changes in model inputs, you must change the data and re-solve the problem.

The optimal solution to this problem is $x_1 = 1$, $x_2 = 1$, $x_3 = 1$, and $x_4 = 0$, with an objective function value of $170. However, note that if the available budget is increased by $1 (from $100 to $101), the optimal solution changes to $x_1 = 1$, $x_2 = 0$, $x_3 = 0$, and $x_4 = 1$, with an objective function value of $200. In other words, one additional dollar in the budget would lead to a $30 increase in the return. Surely management, when faced with such a situation, would increase the budget by $1. Because of the extreme sensitivity of the value of the optimal solution to the constraint coefficients, practitioners usually recommend re-solving the integer linear program several times with variations in the coefficients before attempting to choose the best solution for implementation.

NOTES + COMMENTS

The time required to obtain an optimal solution can be highly variable for integer linear programs. If an optimal solution cannot be found within a reasonable amount of time, the **Integer Optimality (%)** can be reset to 5% or some higher value so that the search procedure may stop when a near-optimal solution (within the tolerance of being optimal) has been found.

This can shorten the solution time because, if the **Integer Optimality (%)** is set to 5%, Solver can stop when it knows it is within 5% of optimal rather than having to complete the search. In general, unless you are experiencing excessive run times, we recommend you set the **Integer Optimality (%)** to 0.

13.4 Applications Involving Binary Variables

Much of the modeling flexibility provided by integer linear programming is due to the use of binary variables. In many applications, binary variables provide selections or choices with the value of the variable equal to one if a corresponding activity is undertaken and equal to zero if the corresponding activity is not undertaken. The capital budgeting, fixed cost, bank location, and product design and market share optimization applications presented in this section make use of binary variables.

Capital Budgeting

The estimated net present value is the net cash flow discounted back to the beginning of year 1.

The Ice-Cold Refrigerator Company is considering investing in several projects that have varying capital requirements over the next four years. Faced with limited capital each year, management would like to select the most profitable projects that it can afford. The estimated net present value for each project, the capital requirements, and the available capital over the four-year period are shown in Table 13.1.

Let us define four binary decision variables:

$P = 1$ if the plant expansion project is accepted; 0 if rejected
$W = 1$ if the warehouse expansion project is accepted; 0 if rejected
$M = 1$ if the new machinery project is accepted; 0 if rejected
$R = 1$ if the new product research project is accepted; 0 if rejected

In a **capital budgeting problem**, the company's objective function is to maximize the net present value of the capital budgeting projects. This problem has four constraints: one for the funds available in each of the next four years.

A binary integer linear programming model with dollars in thousands is as follows:

$$\text{Max} \quad 90P + 40W + 10M + 37R$$
s.t.
$$15P + 10W + 10M + 15R \leq 40 \quad \text{(Year 1 capital available)}$$
$$20P + 15W \qquad\quad + 10R \leq 50 \quad \text{(Year 2 capital available)}$$
$$20P + 20W \qquad\quad + 10R \leq 40 \quad \text{(Year 3 capital available)}$$
$$15P + 5W + 4M + 10R \leq 35 \quad \text{(Year 4 capital available)}$$
$$P, W, M, R = 0, 1$$

The Ice-Cold spreadsheet model and Solver dialog box are shown in Figure 13.6. The SUMPRODUCT function is used to calculate the amount of capital used in each year as well as the net present value.

The Excel Solver Answer Report is shown in Figure 13.7. The optimal solution is $P = 1, W = 1, M = 1, R = 0$, with a total estimated net present value of $140,000. Thus,

TABLE 13.1 Project Net Present Value, Capital Requirements, and Available Capital for the Ice-Cold Refrigerator Company

	Project				
	Plant Expansion ($)	Warehouse Expansion ($)	New Machinery ($)	New Product Research ($)	Total Capital Available ($)
Present Value	90,000	40,000	10,000	37,000	
Year 1 Cap Rqmt	15,000	10,000	10,000	15,000	40,000
Year 2 Cap Rqmt	20,000	15,000		10,000	50,000
Year 3 Cap Rqmt	20,000	20,000		10,000	40,000
Year 4 Cap Rqmt	15,000	5,000	4,000	10,000	35,000

FIGURE 13.6 Ice-Cold Spreadsheet Model and Solver Dialog Box

	A	B	C	D	E	F	G
1	**Ice-Cold Refrigerator**						
2	**Parameters**						
3				Financial Data ($1000s)			
4			Plant	Warehouse	New	New Prod.	
5			Expansion	Expansion	Machinery	Research	Capital
6		Net Present Value	$90	$40	$10	$37	Available
7		Year 1 Capital	$15	$10	$10	$15	$40
8		Year 2 Capital	$20	$15		$10	$50
9		Year 3 Capital	$20	$20		$10	$40
10		Year 4 Capital	$15	$5	$4	$10	$35
11							
12							
13							
14	**Model**						
15							
16		Net Present Value ($1000s)		$140.00			
17							
18			Plant	Warehouse	New	New Prod.	
19			Expansion	Expansion	Machinery	Research	
20		Investment Plan	1	1	1	0	
21							
22		Amount ($1000s)					
23		Spent	Available				
24	Year 1	$35	$40				
25	Year 2	$35	$50				
26	Year 3	$40	$40				
27	Year 4	$24	$35				

MODEL *file*

IceCold

Solver Parameters

Se_t_ Objective: $D$16

To: ⦿ _M_ax ○ Mi_n_ ○ _V_alue Of: 0

_B_y Changing Variable Cells:

$C$20:$F$20

Subject to the Constraints:

$C$20:$F$20 = binary
$B$24:$B$27 <= $C$24:$C$27

Add
_C_hange
_D_elete
_R_eset All
_L_oad/Save

☑ _M_ake Unconstrained Variables Non-Negative

S_e_lect a Solving Method: Simplex LP

_O_ptions

Solving Method

Select the GRG Nonlinear engine for Solver Problems that are smooth nonlinear. Select the LP Simplex engine for linear Solver Problems, and select the Evolutionary engine for Solver problems that are non-smooth.

_H_elp   _S_olve   C_l_ose

the company should fund the plant expansion, warehouse expansion, and new machinery projects. The new product research project should be put on hold unless additional capital funds become available. The values of the slack variables (Figure 13.7) show that the company will have $5,000 remaining in year 1, $15,000 remaining in year 2, and $11,000 remaining in year 4. Checking the capital requirements for the new product research project, we see that enough funds are available for this project in years 2 and 4. However, the company would have to find additional capital funds of $10,000 in year 1 and $10,000 in year 3 to fund the new product research project.

FIGURE 13.7	Answer Report for Ice-Cold Refrigerator

◢	A	B	C	D	E	F	G
13							
14		Objective Cell (Max)					
15		Cell	Name	Original Value	Final Value		
16		$D$16	Net Present Value ($1000s) Expansion	$0.00	$140.00		
17							
18							
19		Variable Cells					
20		Cell	Name	Original Value	Final Value	Integer	
21		$C$20	Investment Plan Plant Expansion	0	1	Binary	
22		$D$20	Investment Plan WH Expansion	0	1	Binary	
23		$E$20	Investment Plan Machinery	0	1	Binary	
24		$F$20	Investment Plan Research	0	0	Binary	
25							
26							
27		Constraints					
28		Cell	Name	Cell Value	Formula	Status	Slack
29		$B$24	Year 1 Spent	$35	$B$24<=$C$24	Not Binding	5
30		$B$25	Year 2 Spent	$35	$B$25<=$C$25	Not Binding	15
31		$B$26	Year 3 Spent	$40	$B$26<=$C$26	Binding	0
32		$B$27	Year 4 Spent	$24	$B$27<=$C$27	Not Binding	11
33		$C$20:$F$20=Binary					
34							

Fixed Cost

In many applications, the cost of production has two components: a fixed setup cost and a variable cost directly related to the production quantity. The use of binary variables makes including the setup cost possible in a model for a production application.

As an example of a **fixed-cost problem**, consider the production problem faced by RMC Inc. Three raw materials are used to produce three products: a fuel additive, a solvent base, and a carpet cleaning fluid. The following decision variables are used:

$$F = \text{tons of fuel additive produced}$$
$$S = \text{tons of solvent base produced}$$
$$C = \text{tons of carpet cleaning fluid produced}$$

The profit contributions are $40 per ton for the fuel additive, $30 per ton for the solvent base, and $50 per ton for the carpet cleaning fluid. Each ton of fuel additive is a blend of 0.4 ton of material 1 and 0.6 ton of material 3. Each ton of solvent base requires 0.5 ton of material 1, 0.2 ton of material 2, and 0.3 ton of material 3. Each ton of carpet cleaning fluid is a blend of 0.6 ton of material 1, 0.1 ton of material 2, and 0.3 ton of material 3. RMC has 20 tons of material 1, 5 tons of material 2, and 21 tons of material 3, and management is interested in determining the optimal production quantities for the upcoming planning period.

A linear programming model of the RMC problem is as follows:

$$\text{Max } 40F + 30S + 50C$$

s.t.

$$
\begin{aligned}
0.4F + 0.5S + 0.6C &\le 20 \quad \text{Material 1} \\
0.2S + 0.1C &\le 5 \quad \text{Material 2} \\
0.6F + 0.3S + 0.3C &\le 21 \quad \text{Material 3} \\
F, S, C &\ge 0
\end{aligned}
$$

Using Excel Solver, we obtain an optimal solution consisting of 27.5 tons of fuel additive, 0 tons of solvent base, and 15 tons of carpet cleaning fluid, with a value of $1,850.

This linear programming formulation of the RMC problem does not include a fixed cost for production setup of the products. Suppose that the following data are available concerning the setup cost and the maximum production quantity for each of the three products:

Product	Setup Cost ($)	Maximum Production (tons)
Fuel additive	200	50
Solvent base	50	25
Carpet cleaning fluid	400	40

The modeling flexibility provided by binary variables can now be used to incorporate the fixed setup costs into the production model. The binary variables are defined as follows:

$$SF = 1 \text{ if the fuel additive is produced; } 0 \text{ if not}$$
$$SS = 1 \text{ if the solvent base is produced; } 0 \text{ if not}$$
$$SC = 1 \text{ if the carpet cleaning fluid is produced; } 0 \text{ if not}$$

Using these setup variables, the total setup cost is

$$200SF + 50SS + 400SC$$

We can now rewrite the objective function to include the setup cost. Thus, the net profit objective function becomes

$$\text{Max } 40F + 30S + 50C - 200SF - 50SS - 400SC$$

Next, we must write production capacity constraints so that, if a setup variable equals 0, production of the corresponding product is not permitted, and if a setup variable equals 1, production is permitted up to the maximum quantity. For the fuel additive, we do so by adding the following constraint:

$$F \leq 50SF$$

Note that, with this constraint present, production of the fuel additive is not permitted when $SF = 0$. When $SF = 1$, production of up to 50 tons of fuel additive is permitted. We can think of the setup variable as a switch. When it is off ($SF = 0$), production is not permitted; when it is on ($SF = 1$), production is permitted.

Similar production capacity constraints, using binary variables, are added for the solvent base and carpet cleaning products:

$$S \leq 25SS$$
$$C \leq 40SC$$

In summary, we have the following fixed-cost model for the RMC problem with setups:

$$\text{Max } 40F + 30S + 50C - 200SF - 50SS - 400SC$$

s.t.

$0.4F + 0.5S + 0.6C \leq 20$		Material 1
$0.2S + 0.1C \leq 5$		Material 2
$0.6F + 0.3S + 0.3C \leq 21$		Material 3
$F \leq 50SF$		Maximum Fuel Additive
$S \leq 25SS$		Maximum Solvent Base
$C \leq 40SC$		Maximum Carpet Cleaning

$$F, S, C \geq 0; SF, SS, SC = 0 \text{ or } 1$$

A spreadsheet model and Solver dialog box for the RMC problem are shown in Figure 13.8. The SUMPRODUCT function is used to calculate the material used, and cells

FIGURE 13.8   RMC with Setups Spreadsheet Model and Solver Dialog Box

◢	A	B	C	D	E
1	RMC				
2	Parameters				
3			Material Requirements (tons)		
4		Fuel	Solvent	Cleaning	Tons
5	Materials	Additive	Base	Fluid	Available
6	Material 1	0.4	0.5	0.6	20
7	Material 2		0.2	0.1	5
8	Material 3	0.6	0.3	0.3	21
9	Profit per Ton	$40	$30	$50	
10	Setup Cost	$200	$50	$400	
11	Capacity (Tons)	50	25	40	
12					
13					
14	Model				
15					
16					
17		Max Net Profit	$1,350.00		
18					
19					
20		Fuel	Solvent	Cleaning	
21	Tons Produced	25.0	20.0	0.0	
22	Setup	1	1	0	
23					
24					
25			Used	Available	
26		Material 1	20	20	
27		Material 2	4	5	
28		Material 3	21	21	
29					
30			Tons Produced	Max Tons	
31		Max F	25	50	
32		Max S	20	25	
33		Max C	0.0	0	

Solver Parameters

Se_t_ Objective: $C$17

To: ● Ma_x_   ○ Mi_n_   ○ _V_alue Of: 0

_B_y Changing Variable Cells:
$B$21:$D$22

Su_b_ject to the Constraints:
$B$22:$D$22 = binary
$C$26:$C$28 <= $D$26:$D$28
$C$31:$C$33 <= $D$31:$D$33

[Add] [Change] [Delete] [Reset All] [Load/Save]

☑ Make Unconstrained Variables Non-Negative

S_e_lect a Solving Method: Simplex LP   [Options]

Solving Method
Select the GRG Nonlinear engine for Solver Problems that are smooth nonlinear. Select the LP Simplex engine for linear Solver Problems, and select the Evolutionary engine for Solver problems that are non-smooth.

[Help]   [Solve]   [Close]

MODEL *file*

RMCSetup

D31, D32, and D33 contain the capacity multiplied by the appropriate binary variable (=B11*B22 in cell D31, =C11*C22 in cell D32, and =D11*D22 in cell D33).

The Excel Answer Report is shown in Figure 13.9. The optimal solution requires 25 tons of fuel additive and 20 tons of solvent base. The value of the objective function after deducting the setup cost is $1,350. The setup cost for the fuel additive and the solvent base is $200 + $50 = $250. The optimal solution includes $SC = 0$, which indicates that the more expensive $400 setup cost for the carpet cleaning fluid should be avoided. Thus, the carpet cleaning fluid is not produced.

The key to developing a fixed-cost model is the introduction of a binary variable for each fixed cost and the specification of an upper bound for the corresponding production variable. For a production quantity x, a constraint of the form $x \leq My$ can then be used to allow production when the setup variable $y = 1$ and not to allow production when the setup variable $y = 0$. The value of the maximum production quantity M should be large enough to allow for all reasonable levels of production, but choosing excessively large values of M will slow the solution procedure.

FIGURE 13.9 Answer Report for RMC Production Problem

◢ A	B	C	D	E	F	G
13						
14	Objective Cell (Max)					
15	Cell	Name	Original Value	Final Value		
16	$C$17	Max Net Profit	$0.00	$1,350.00		
17						
18						
19	Variable Cells					
20	Cell	Name	Original Value	Final Value	Integer	
21	$B$21	Tons Produced Fuel	0.0	25.0	Contin	
22	$C$21	Tons Produced Solvent	0.0	20.0	Contin	
23	$D$21	Tons Produced Cleaning	0.0	0.0	Contin	
24	$B$22	Setup Fuel	0	1	Binary	
25	$C$22	Setup Solvent	0	1	Binary	
26	$D$22	Setup Cleaning	0	0	Binary	
27						
28						
29	Constraints					
30	Cell	Name	Cell Value	Formula	Status	Slack
31	$C$26	Material 1 Used	20	$C$26<=$D$26	Binding	0
32	$C$27	Material 2 Used	4	$C$27<=$D$27	Not Binding	1
33	$C$28	Material 3 Used	21	$C$28<=$D$28	Binding	0
34	$C$31	Max F Tons Produced	25	$C$31<=$D$31	Not Binding	25
35	$C$32	Max S Tons Produced	20	$C$32<=$D$32	Not Binding	5
36	$C$33	Max C Tons Produced	0.0	$C$33<=$D$33	Binding	0
37	$B$22:$D$22=Binary					
38						

Bank Location

The long-range planning department for the Ohio Trust Company is considering expanding its operation into a 20-county region in northeastern Ohio (Figure 13.10). Currently, Ohio Trust does not have a principal place of business in any of the 20 counties. According to the banking laws in Ohio, if a bank establishes a principal place of business (PPB) in any county, branch banks can be established in that county and in any of the adjacent counties. However, to establish a new principal place of business, Ohio Trust must either obtain approval for a new bank from the state's superintendent of banks or purchase an existing bank.

Table 13.2 lists the 20 counties in the region and adjacent counties. For example, Ashtabula County is adjacent to Lake, Geauga, and Trumbull counties; Lake County is adjacent to Ashtabula, Cuyahoga, and Geauga counties; and so on.

As an initial step in its planning, Ohio Trust would like to determine the minimum number of PPBs necessary to do business throughout the 20-county region. A binary integer programming model can be used to solve this **location problem** for Ohio Trust. We define the variables as

$$x_i = 1 \text{ if a PPB is established in county } i; 0 \text{ otherwise}$$

To minimize the number of PPBs needed, we write the objective function as

$$\text{Min } x_1 + x_2 + \cdots + x_{20}$$

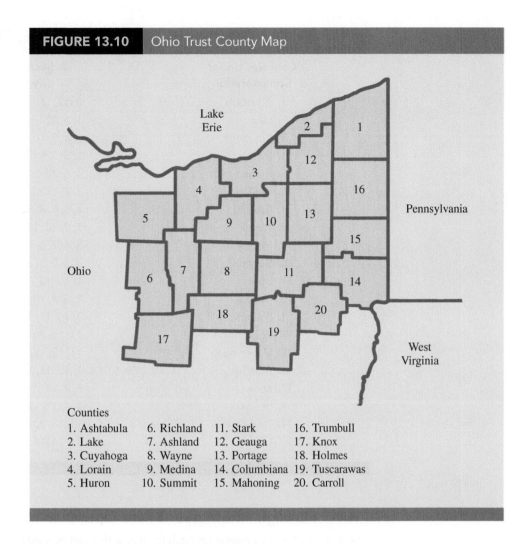

FIGURE 13.10   Ohio Trust County Map

Counties

1. Ashtabula	6. Richland	11. Stark	16. Trumbull
2. Lake	7. Ashland	12. Geauga	17. Knox
3. Cuyahoga	8. Wayne	13. Portage	18. Holmes
4. Lorain	9. Medina	14. Columbiana	19. Tuscarawas
5. Huron	10. Summit	15. Mahoning	20. Carroll

The bank may locate branches in a county if the county contains a PPB or is adjacent to another county with a PPB. Thus, the binary linear program will need one constraint for each county. For example, the constraint for Ashtabula County is

$$x_1 + x_2 + x_{12} + x_{16} \geq 1 \quad \text{Ashtabula}$$

Note that satisfaction of this constraint ensures that a PPB will be placed in Ashtabula County *or* in one or more of the adjacent counties. This constraint thus guarantees that Ohio Trust will be able to place branch banks in Ashtabula County.

The complete statement of the bank location problem is as follows:

$$
\begin{array}{lll}
\text{Min} & x_1 + x_2 + \quad \ldots \quad + x_{20} \\
\text{s.t.} \\
& x_1 + x_2 \quad\quad + x_{12} + x_{16} & \geq 1 \quad \text{Ashtabula} \\
& x_1 + x_2 + x_3 + x_{12} & \geq 1 \quad \text{Lake} \\
& \vdots & \quad\vdots \\
& \quad\quad x_{11} + x_{14} + x_{19} + x_{20} & \geq 1 \quad \text{Carroll} \\
& x_i = 0, 1 \quad i = 1, 2, \ldots, 20
\end{array}
$$

MODEL *file*

OhioTrust

In Problem 10, we ask you to solve this problem for the entire state of Ohio.

We use Excel Solver to solve this 20-variable, 20-constraint problem formulation. In Figure 13.11, we show the optimal solution. The optimal solution calls for principal places of business in Ashland, Stark, and Geauga counties. With PPBs in these three counties, Ohio Trust can place branch banks in all 20 counties. Clearly the integer programming model could be enlarged to allow for expansion into a larger area or throughout the entire state.

TABLE 13.2	Counties in the Ohio Trust Expansion Region
Counties Under Consideration	**Adjacent Counties (by Number)**
1. Ashtabula	2, 12, 16
2. Lake	1, 3, 12
3. Cuyahoga	2, 4, 9, 10, 12, 13
4. Lorain	3, 5, 7, 9
5. Huron	4, 6, 7
6. Richland	5, 7, 17
7. Ashland	4, 5, 6, 8, 9, 17, 18
8. Wayne	7, 9, 10, 11, 18
9. Medina	3, 4, 7, 8, 10
10. Summit	3, 8, 9, 11, 12, 13
11. Stark	8, 10, 13, 14, 15, 18, 19, 20
12. Geauga	1, 2, 3, 10, 13, 16
13. Portage	3, 10, 11, 12, 15, 16
14. Columbiana	11, 15, 20
15. Mahoning	11, 13, 14, 16
16. Trumbull	1, 12, 13, 15
17. Knox	6, 7, 18
18. Holmes	7, 8, 11, 17, 19
19. Tuscarawas	11, 18, 20
20. Carroll	11, 14, 19

Product Design and Market Share Optimization

Conjoint analysis is a market research technique that can be used to learn how prospective buyers of a product value the product's attributes. In this section, we will show how the results of conjoint analysis can be used in an integer programming model of a **product design and market share optimization problem**. We illustrate the approach by considering a problem facing Salem Foods, a major producer of frozen foods.

Salem Foods is planning to enter the frozen pizza market. Currently, two existing brands, Antonio's and King's, have the major share of the market. In trying to develop a sausage pizza that will capture a substantial share of the market, Salem determined that the four most important attributes when consumers purchase a frozen sausage pizza are crust, cheese, sauce, and sausage flavor. The crust attribute has two levels (thin and thick); the cheese attribute has two levels (mozzarella and blend); the sauce attribute has two levels (smooth and chunky); and the sausage flavor attribute has three levels (mild, medium, and hot).

In a typical conjoint analysis, a sample of consumers is asked to express their preference for a product with chosen levels for the attributes. Then regression analysis is used to determine the part-worth for each of the attribute levels. In essence, the **part-worth** is the utility value that a consumer attaches to each level of each attribute. Provided part-worths from regression analysis, we will show how they can be used to determine the overall value a consumer attaches to a particular product.

Table 13.3 shows the part-worths for each level of each attribute provided by a sample of eight potential Salem customers who are currently buying either King's or Antonio's pizza. For consumer 1, the part-worths for the crust attribute are 11 for thin crust and 2 for thick crust, indicating a preference for thin crust. For the cheese attribute, the part-worths

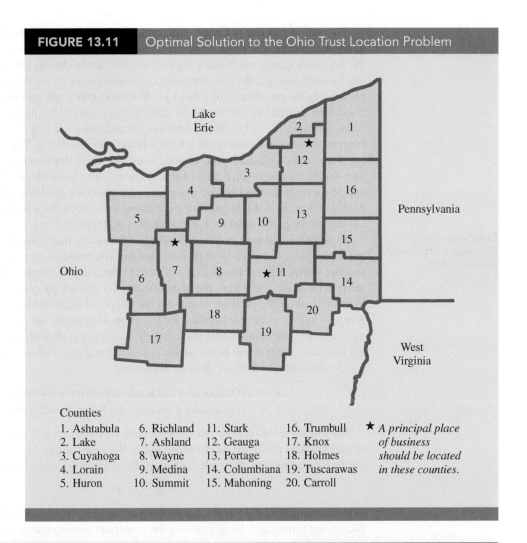

FIGURE 13.11   Optimal Solution to the Ohio Trust Location Problem

Counties

1. Ashtabula	6. Richland	11. Stark	16. Trumbull	★ *A principal place*
2. Lake	7. Ashland	12. Geauga	17. Knox	*of business*
3. Cuyahoga	8. Wayne	13. Portage	18. Holmes	*should be located*
4. Lorain	9. Medina	14. Columbiana	19. Tuscarawas	*in these counties.*
5. Huron	10. Summit	15. Mahoning	20. Carroll	

TABLE 13.3   Part-Worths for the Salem Foods Problem

	Crust		Cheese		Sauce		Sausage Flavor		
Consumer	Thin	Thick	Mozzarella	Blend	Smooth	Chunky	Mild	Medium	Hot
1	11	2	6	7	3	17	26	27	8
2	11	7	15	17	16	26	14	1	10
3	7	5	8	14	16	7	29	16	19
4	13	20	20	17	17	14	25	29	10
5	2	8	6	11	30	20	15	5	12
6	12	17	11	9	2	30	22	12	20
7	9	19	12	16	16	25	30	23	19
8	5	9	4	14	23	16	16	30	3

are 6 for the mozzarella cheese and 7 for the cheese blend; thus, consumer 1 has a slight preference for the cheese blend. From the other part-worths, we see that consumer 1 shows a strong preference for the chunky sauce over the smooth sauce (17 to 3) and has a slight preference for the medium-flavored sausage. Note that consumer 2 shows a preference for the thin crust, the cheese blend, the chunky sauce, and mild-flavored sausage. The part-worths for the other consumers are interpreted similarly.

Utility values are discussed in more detail in Chapter 15.

The part-worths can be used to determine the overall value (utility) that each consumer attaches to a particular type of pizza. For instance, consumer 1's current favorite pizza is the Antonio's brand, which has a thick crust, mozzarella cheese, chunky sauce, and medium-flavored sausage. We can determine consumer 1's utility for this particular type of pizza using the part-worths in Table 13.3. For consumer 1, the part-worths are 2 for thick crust, 6 for mozzarella cheese, 17 for chunky sauce, and 27 for medium-flavored sausage. Thus, consumer 1's utility for the Antonio's brand pizza is 2 + 6 + 17 + 27 = 52. We can compute consumer 1's utility for a King's brand pizza similarly. The King's brand pizza has a thin crust, a cheese blend, smooth sauce, and mild-flavored sausage. Because the part-worths for consumer 1 are 11 for thin crust, 7 for cheese blend, 3 for smooth sauce, and 26 for mild-flavored sausage, consumer 1's utility for the King's brand pizza is 11 + 7 + 3 + 26 = 47. In general, each consumer's utility for a particular type of pizza is the sum of the part-worths for the attributes of that type of pizza.

To be successful with its brand, Salem Foods realizes that it must entice consumers in the marketplace to switch from their current favorite brand of pizza to the Salem product. In other words, Salem must design a pizza (choose the type of crust, cheese, sauce, and sausage flavor) that will have the highest utility for enough people to ensure sufficient sales to justify making the product. Assuming the sample of eight consumers in the current study is representative of the marketplace for frozen sausage pizza, we can formulate and solve an integer programming model that can help Salem come up with such a design. In marketing literature, the problem being solved is called the *share of choice* problem.

The decision variables are defined as follows:

$$l_{ij} = 1 \text{ if Salem chooses level } i \text{ for attribute } j; 0 \text{ otherwise}$$
$$y_k = 1 \text{ if consumer } k \text{ chooses the Salem brand; 0 otherwise}$$

The objective is to choose the levels of each attribute that will maximize the number of consumers who prefer the Salem brand pizza. Because the number of consumers who prefer the Salem brand pizza is just the sum of the y_k variables, the objective function is

$$\text{Max } y_1 + y_2 + \cdots + y_8$$

One constraint is needed for each consumer in the sample. To illustrate how the constraints are formulated, let us consider the constraint corresponding to consumer 1. For consumer 1, the utility of a particular type of pizza can be expressed as the sum of the part-worths:

Utility for consumer $1 = 11l_{11} + 2l_{21} + 6l_{12} + 7l_{22} + 3l_{13} + 17l_{23} + 26l_{14} + 27l_{24} + 8l_{34}$

For consumer 1 to prefer the Salem pizza, the utility for the Salem pizza must be greater than the utility for consumer 1's current favorite. Recall that consumer 1's current favorite brand of pizza is Antonio's, with a utility of 52. Thus, consumer 1 will purchase the Salem brand only if the levels of the attributes for the Salem brand are chosen such that

$$11l_{11} + 2l_{21} + 6l_{12} + 7l_{22} + 3l_{13} + 17l_{23} + 26l_{14} + 27l_{24} + 8l_{34} > 52$$

Given the definitions of the y_k decision variables, we want $y_1 = 1$ when the consumer prefers the Salem brand and $y_1 = 0$ when the consumer does not prefer the Salem brand. Thus, we write the constraint for consumer 1 as follows:

$$11l_{11} + 2l_{21} + 6l_{12} + 7l_{22} + 3l_{13} + 17l_{23} + 26l_{14} + 27l_{24} + 8l_{34} \geq 1 + 52y_1$$

With this constraint, y_k cannot equal 1 unless the utility for the Salem design (the left-hand side of the constraint) exceeds the utility for consumer 1's current favorite by at least 1. Because the objective function is to maximize the sum of the y_k variables, the optimization will seek a product design that will allow as many y_k variables as possible to equal 1.

A similar constraint is written for each consumer in the sample. The coefficients for the l_{ij} variables in the utility functions are taken from Table 13.3, and the coefficients for the y_k

variables are obtained by computing the overall utility of the consumer's current favorite brand of pizza. The following constraints correspond to the eight consumers in the study:

$$11l_{11} + 2l_{21} + 6l_{12} + 7l_{22} + 3l_{13} + 17l_{23} + 26l_{14} + 27l_{24} + 8l_{34} \geq 1 + 52y_1$$
$$11l_{11} + 7l_{21} + 15l_{12} + 17l_{22} + 16l_{13} + 26l_{23} + 14l_{14} + 1l_{24} + 10l_{34} \geq 1 + 58y_2$$
$$7l_{11} + 5l_{12} + 8l_{12} + 14l_{22} + 16l_{13} + 7l_{23} + 29l_{14} + 16l_{24} + 19l_{34} \geq 1 + 66y_3$$
$$13l_{11} + 20l_{21} + 20l_{12} + 17l_{22} + 17l_{13} + 14l_{23} + 25l_{14} + 29l_{24} + 10l_{34} \geq 1 + 83y_4$$
$$2l_{11} + 8l_{21} + 6l_{12} + 11l_{22} + 30l_{13} + 20l_{23} + 15l_{14} + 5l_{24} + 12l_{34} \geq 1 + 58y_5$$
$$12l_{11} + 17l_{21} + 11l_{12} + 9l_{22} + 2l_{13} + 30l_{23} + 22l_{14} + 12l_{24} + 20l_{34} \geq 1 + 70y_6$$
$$9l_{11} + 19l_{21} + 12l_{12} + 16l_{22} + 16l_{13} + 25l_{23} + 30l_{14} + 23l_{24} + 19l_{34} \geq 1 + 79y_7$$
$$5l_{11} + 9l_{21} + 4l_{12} + 14l_{22} + 23l_{13} + 16l_{23} + 16l_{14} + 30l_{24} + 3l_{34} \geq 1 + 59y_8$$

Antonio's brand is the current favorite pizza for consumers 1, 4, 6, 7, and 8. King's brand is the current favorite pizza for consumers 2, 3, and 5.

Four more constraints must be added, one for each attribute. These constraints are necessary to ensure that one and only one level is selected for each attribute. For attribute 1 (crust), we must add the constraint:

$$l_{11} + l_{21} = 1$$

Because l_{11} and l_{21} are both binary variables, this constraint requires that one of the two variables equals one, and the other equals zero. The following three constraints ensure that one and only one level is selected for each of the other three attributes:

$$l_{12} + l_{22} = 1$$
$$l_{13} + l_{23} = 1$$
$$l_{14} + l_{24} + l_{34} = 1$$

Salem

The data, model, and solution for the Salem pizza problem may be found in the file *Salem*. The optimal solution to this 17-variable, 12-constraint integer linear program is $l_{11} = l_{22} = l_{23} = l_{14} = 1$ and $y_2 = y_5 = y_6 = y_7 = 1$. The value of the optimal solution is 4, indicating that if Salem makes this type of pizza, it will be preferable to the current favorite for four of the eight consumers. With $l_{21} = l_{22} = l_{23} = l_{14} = 1$, the pizza design that obtains the largest market share for Salem has a thin crust, a cheese blend, a chunky sauce, and mild-flavored sausage. Note also that with $y_2 = y_5 = y_6 = y_7 = 1$, consumers 2, 5, 6, and 7 will prefer the Salem pizza. This information may lead Salem to choose to market this type of pizza.

13.5 Modeling Flexibility Provided by Binary Variables

In Section 13.4, we presented four applications involving binary integer variables. In this section, we continue the discussion of the use of binary integer variables in modeling. First, we show how binary integer variables can be used to model multiple-choice and mutually exclusive constraints. Then we show how binary integer variables can be used to model situations in which k projects out of a set of n projects must be selected, as well as situations in which the acceptance of one project is conditional on the acceptance of another project.

Multiple-Choice and Mutually Exclusive Constraints

Recall the Ice-Cold Refrigerator capital budgeting problem introduced in Section 13.4. The decision variables were defined as follows:

$P = 1$ if the plant expansion project is accepted; 0 if rejected
$W = 1$ if the warehouse expansion project is accepted; 0 if rejected
$M = 1$ if the new machinery project is accepted; 0 if rejected
$R = 1$ if the new product research project is accepted; 0 if rejected

Suppose that, instead of one warehouse expansion project, the Ice-Cold Refrigerator Company actually has three warehouse expansion projects under consideration. One of the warehouses *must* be expanded because of increasing product demand, but new demand is not sufficient to make expansion of more than one warehouse necessary. The following variable definitions and **multiple-choice constraint** could be incorporated into the previous binary integer linear programming model to reflect this situation. Let:

W_1 = 1 if the original warehouse expansion project is accepted; 0 if rejected

W_2 = 1 if the second warehouse expansion project is accepted; 0 if rejected

W_3 = 1 if the third warehouse expansion project is accepted; 0 if rejected

The multiple-choice constraint reflecting the requirement that exactly one of these projects must be selected is

$$W_1 + W_2 + W_3 = 1$$

If W_1, W_2, and W_3 are allowed to assume only the values 0 or 1, then one and only one of these projects will be selected from among the three choices.

If the requirement that one warehouse must be expanded did not exist, the multiple-choice constraint could be modified as follows:

$$W_1 + W_2 + W_3 \leq 1$$

This modification allows for the case of no warehouse expansion ($W_1 = W_2 = W_3 = 0$) but does not permit more than one warehouse to be expanded. This type of constraint is often called a **mutually exclusive constraint**.

k Out of *n* Alternatives Constraint

An extension of the notion of a multiple-choice constraint can be used to model situations in which *k out of a set of n* projects must be selected—a *k* out of *n* **alternatives constraint**. Suppose that W_1, W_2, W_3, W_4, and W_5 represent five potential warehouse expansion projects and that two of the five projects must be accepted. The constraint that satisfies this new requirement is

$$W_1 + W_2 + W_3 + W_4 + W_5 = 2$$

If no more than two of the projects are to be selected, we would use the following less-than-or-equal-to constraint:

$$W_1 + W_2 + W_3 + W_4 + W_5 \leq 2$$

Again, each of these variables must be restricted to binary values.

Conditional and Corequisite Constraints

Sometimes the acceptance of one project is conditional on the acceptance of another. For example, suppose that for the Ice-Cold Refrigerator Company, the warehouse expansion project was conditional on the plant expansion project. In other words, suppose management will not consider expanding the warehouse unless the plant is expanded. With binary variable P representing plant expansion (1 = expand, 0 = do not expand) and W a binary variable representing warehouse expansion (1 = expand, 0 = do not expand), a conditional constraint needs to be developed to enforce the requirement the warehouse cannot be expanded unless the plant has been expanded.

When faced with this type of conditional constraint, it is often helpful to construct a **feasibility table**. A feasibility table is a table that lists all possible settings of the relevant binary variables and indicates which settings of these variables are feasible and which are not feasible. In the Ice-Cold Refrigerator case, we have the following feasibility table:

W	P	Relationship	Feasible	Rationale
0	0	$W = P$	Yes	We can choose to expand neither.
1	0	$W > P$	No	We cannot expand the warehouse if the plant is not expanded.
0	1	$W < P$	Yes	We can choose not to expand the warehouse, even if we expand the plant.
1	1	$W = P$	Yes	We can expand both the warehouse and the plant.

Notice that W is less than or equal to P for the feasible cases and W is greater than P in the infeasible case. Hence, the **conditional constraint** that enforces the restriction is

$$W \leq P$$

Let us consider another situation where the warehouse and plant expansions are dependent on each other. If the warehouse expansion project had to be accepted whenever the plant expansion project was accepted, and vice versa, we would say that we have a **corequisite constraint**. So, if we choose to expand either, the other must be expanded. In this situation, we have the following feasibility table:

W	P	Relationship	Feasible	Rationale
0	0	$W = P$	Yes	We can choose to expand neither.
1	0	$W > P$	No	We cannot expand the warehouse if the plant is not expanded.
0	1	$W < P$	No	If the warehouse is not expanded, we cannot expand the plant.
1	1	$W = P$	Yes	We can expand both the warehouse and the plant.

In this feasibility table, we see that when W and P are set to the same value, the result is feasible, but different settings of W and P are infeasible. Hence, in the corequisite situation, the following constraint enforces the restriction:

$$W = P$$

The constraint forces P and W to take on the same value.

NOTES + COMMENTS

1. As in the Ice-Cold Refrigerator examples with conditional and corequisite constraints, many restrictions will involve only two binary variables. Since in the feasibility table, we list all possible cases (settings of the binary variables), there are $2^2 = 4$ cases when there are two variables. Some conditional and corequisite constraints might involve three or more variables. For three variables, there are $2^3 = 8$ cases, for four variables there are $2^4 = 16$ cases. In general, for n variables, there will be 2^n cases. Therefore, for situations involving more than three variables, feasibility tables can become cumbersome.

2. A somewhat natural way to try to model a conditional or corequisite constraint in Excel is to use an IF function. However, since the IF function is a discontinuous function (i.e., a function with a break or jump in the function value), using an IF statement will preclude the use of the LP Simplex option as discussed in Section 13.3. While the nonlinear option in Excel Solver (discussed in Chapter 14) can sometimes find good results even with the use of an IF function, optimality cannot always be guaranteed. Therefore, we recommend you model conditional constraints in a linear way as discussed in Section 13.5.

13.6 Generating Alternatives in Binary Optimization

If alternative optimal solutions exist, it would be good for management to know this because some factors that make one alternative preferred over another might not be included in the model. Also, if the solution is a unique optimal solution, it would be good to know how much worse the second-best solution is than the unique optimal solution. If the second-best solution is very close to optimal, it might be preferred over the true optimal solution because of factors outside the model.

As an example, let us reconsider the Ohio Trust location problem presented in Section 13.4. The solution for the minimum number of principal places of business (PPBs) is three. As shown in Figure 13.11, the solution is to place PPBs in county 7 (Ashland), county 11 (Stark), and county 12 (Geauga). However, suppose when Ohio Trust tries to implement this solution, it is not possible to find a suitable location for a PPB in one of these three counties. Are there other alternative solutions of three counties, or is this a unique optimal solution? By adding a special constraint based on the current solution and then resolving the model, we may answer this question.

The current solution for Ohio Trust can be broken into two sets of variables: those that are set to one and those that are set to zero. Let the set O denote the set of variables set to one and the set Z those that are set to zero. For the Ohio Trust solution, these sets are as follows:

Set O: x_7, x_{11}, x_{12}

Set Z: $x_1, x_2, x_3, x_4, x_5, x_6, x_8, x_9, x_{10}, x_{13}, x_{14}, x_{15}, x_{16}, x_{17}, x_{18}, x_{19}, x_{20}$

We may add the following constraint:

(Sum of variables in the set O) $-$ (sum of variables in the set Z) $\leq$ (number of variables in the set O) $- 1$,

which for our current solution is

$$x_7 + x_{11} + x_{12} - x_1 - x_2 - x_3 - x_4 - x_5 - x_6 - x_8 - x_9 - x_{10} - x_{13} - x_{14} - x_{15} - x_{16} - x_{17} - x_{18} - x_{19} - x_{20} \leq 3 - 1 = 2$$

This constraint has the very special property that it makes the current solution infeasible, but keeps feasible all other solutions that are feasible to the original problem. This constraint will force (at least) one of the variables in set O to change from one to zero or will force (at least) one of the variables in set Z to change from zero to one.

When we append this new constraint to the original model, we obtain the solution displayed in Figure 13.12. Notice that the optimal objective function value has increased to

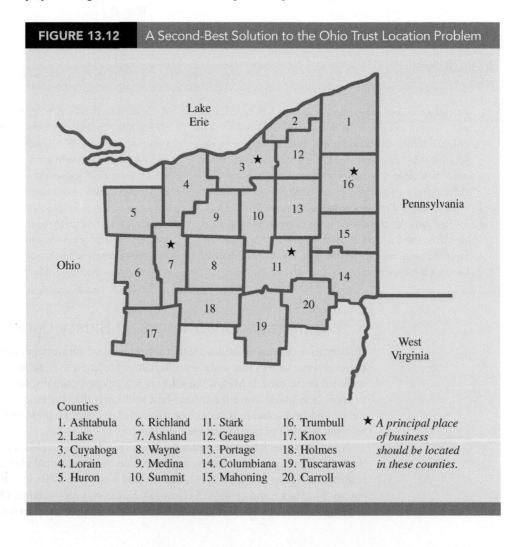

FIGURE 13.12   A Second-Best Solution to the Ohio Trust Location Problem

Counties

1. Ashtabula	6. Richland	11. Stark	16. Trumbull	★ *A principal place*
2. Lake	7. Ashland	12. Geauga	17. Knox	*of business*
3. Cuyahoga	8. Wayne	13. Portage	18. Holmes	*should be located*
4. Lorain	9. Medina	14. Columbiana	19. Tuscarawas	*in these counties.*
5. Huron	10. Summit	15. Mahoning	20. Carroll	

four. This tells us that the solution we found in Section 13.4 with objective function value equal to 3 is a unique optimal solution. Any other feasible solution will require four or more PPBs to cover the entire 20-county region. So, if for any of the three counties in the original solution we cannot find a suitable location for a PPB, the next-best solution will require PPBs in four counties and the solution in Figure 13.10 is a second-best alternative. Note that if the optimal objective functions of the new problem with constraint added had been 3, we would have found an alternative optimal solution.

We can summarize the procedure for finding an alternative solution as follows:

Step 1. Solve the original problem
Step 2. Create two sets:
    O = the set of variables equal to one in Step 1
    Z = the set of variables equal to zero in Step 1
Step 3. Add the following constraint to the original problem, and solve

$$\text{(Sum of variables in the set O)} - \text{(sum of variables in the set Z)}$$
$$\leq \text{(number of variables in the set O)} - 1 \tag{13.1}$$

If the objective function value in Step 3 is equal to the objective function value of Step 1, we have found an alternative optimal solution. If the objective function value of Step 3 is inferior to that of Step 1, we have found a next-best solution.

NOTES + COMMENTS

1. The procedure just described can be applied iteratively. In other words, we can take the second-best solution found and create the equation (13.1) based on that solution to find the next-best solution. Note that we leave all previous constraints in the problem, including the first constraint based on equation (13.1). The resulting solution could be a third-best solution or an alternative second-best solution.

   It turns out that there are numerous second-best solutions to the Ohio Trust problem using four PPBs.

2. Applying equation (13.1) iteratively and finding that the objective function value does not deteriorate, generates an alternative optimal solution. In fact applying equation (13.1) iteratively until the objective function changes ensures you have found all alternative optima.

SUMMARY

In this chapter, we introduced the important extension of linear programming referred to as integer linear programming. The only difference between the integer linear programming problems discussed in this chapter and the linear programming problems studied in the previous chapter is that one or more of the variables must be an integer. If all variables must be integer, we have an all-integer linear program. If some, but not necessarily all, variables must be an integer, we have a mixed-integer linear program. Most integer programming applications involve binary variables.

Studying integer linear programming is important for two major reasons. First, integer linear programming may be helpful when fractional values for the variables are not permitted. Rounding a linear programming solution may not provide an optimal integer solution; methods for finding optimal integer solutions are needed when the economic consequences of rounding are substantial. A second reason for studying integer linear programming is the increased modeling flexibility provided through the use of binary variables. We showed how binary variables could be used to model important managerial considerations in capital budgeting, fixed cost, facility location, and product design/market share applications. We showed how to generate second-best solutions or alternative optima if they exist by adding a constraint based on those solutions. This is important for providing alternatives for management.

The number of applications of integer linear programming continues to grow rapidly, partly because of the availability of good integer linear programming software packages. As researchers develop solution procedures capable of solving larger integer linear programs and as computer speed increases, a continuation of the growth of integer programming applications is expected.

GLOSSARY

All-integer linear program An integer linear program in which all variables are required to be integers.

Binary integer linear program An all-integer or mixed-integer linear program in which the integer variables are permitted to assume only the values 0 or 1. Also called *binary integer program*.

Capital budgeting problem A binary integer programming problem that involves choosing which possible projects or activities provide the best investment return.

Conditional constraint A constraint involving binary variables that does not allow certain variables to equal one unless certain other variables are equal to one.

Conjoint analysis A market research technique that can be used to learn how prospective buyers of a product value the product's attributes.

Convex hull The smallest intersection of linear inequalities that contain a certain set of points.

Corequisite constraint A constraint requiring that two binary variables be equal and that they are both either in or out of the solution.

Feasibility table A table that is useful in modeling conditional and corequisite constraints with binary variables. The table lists all possible settings of the relevant binary variables and indicates which settings of these variables are feasible and which are not feasible.

Fixed-cost problem A binary mixed-integer programming problem in which the binary variables represent whether an activity, such as a production run, is undertaken (variable $= 1$) or not (variable $= 0$).

Integer linear program A linear program with the additional requirement that one or more of the variables must be an integer.

***k* out of *n* alternatives constraint** An extension of the multiple-choice constraint that requires that the sum of *n* binary variables equals *k*.

Location problem A binary integer programming problem in which the objective is to select the best locations to meet a stated objective. Variations of this problem (see the bank location problem in Section 13.4) are known as *covering problems*.

LP relaxation The linear program that results from dropping the integer requirements for the variables in an integer linear program.

Mixed-integer linear program An integer linear program in which some, but not necessarily all, variables are required to be integers.

Multiple-choice constraint A constraint requiring that the sum of two or more binary variables equals one. Thus, any feasible solution makes a choice of which variable to set equal to one.

Mutually exclusive constraint A constraint requiring that the sum of two or more binary variables be less than or equal to one. Thus, if one of the variables equals one, the others must equal zero. However, all variables could equal zero.

Part-worth The utility value that a consumer attaches to each level of each attribute in a conjoint analysis model.

Product design and market share optimization problem Sometimes called the share of choice problem, the choice of a product design that maximizes the number of consumers that prefer it.

PROBLEMS

1. **Machine Tool Production Planning.** King City Inc. manufactures machine tools. The production planner who oversees the production of two of King City's machines needs to determine how many of each to produce this month. The two machines, TopLathe and BigPress, each require a certain common component. Each TopLathe requires 10 of these components and each BigPress requires 7. Only 49 components are available this month. The sales department requires that the total number of machines produced in a month must be at least 5 (the number TopLathes plus the number BigPresses must be at least 5). The profit for a TopLathe is $50,000 and $34,000 for a BigPress.

   a. Assuming that adequate labor and all other resources are available, formulate an integer programming model to determine how many of each product King City should produce to maximize profit.

   b. Solve the model formulated in part (a) without integer requirements. What is the optimal profit? What are the optimal values for TopLathe and BigPress?

   c. Round the TopLathe and BigPress values found in part (b). Is the solution feasible? Why?

   d. Truncate the TopLathe and BigPress values found in part (b) (drop the fractional part of each value). Is the solution feasible? Why?

   e. Add integer requirements to the model you constructed in part (b). What is the optimal profit and what are the optimal number of TopLathes and BigPresses?

2. **Nurse Scheduling.** Hospital administrators must schedule nurses so that the hospital's patients are provided adequate care. At the same time, careful attention must be paid to keeping costs down. From historical records, administrators can project the minimum number of nurses required to be on hand for various times of day and days of the week. The objective is to find the minimum total number of nurses required to provide adequate care.

   Nurses start work at the beginning of one of the four-hour shifts given below (except for shift 6) and work for 8 consecutive hours. Hence, possible start times are the start of shifts 1 through 5. Also, assume that the projected required number of nurses factors in time for each nurse to have a meal break.

   Formulate and solve the nurse scheduling problem as an integer program for one day for the data given below.

   Hint: Note that exceeding the minimum number of needed nurses in each shift is acceptable so long as the total number of nurses over all shifts is minimized.

DATA *file*

NurseSchedule

Shift	Time	Minimum Number of Nurses Needed
1	12:00 a.m. – 4:00 a.m.	10
2	4:00 a.m. – 8:00 a.m.	24
3	8:00 a.m. – 12:00 p.m.	18
4	12:00 p.m. – 4:00 p.m.	10
5	4:00 p.m. – 8:00 p.m.	23
6	8:00 p.m. – 12:00 a.m.	17

3. **Minimizing Scrap.** STAR Co. provides paper to smaller companies with volumes that are not large enough to warrant dealing directly with the paper mill. STAR receives 100-feet-wide paper rolls from the mill and cuts the rolls into smaller rolls of widths 12, 15, and 30 feet. The demands for these widths vary from week to week. The following cutting patterns have been established:

Pattern Number	12-ft	15-ft	30-ft	Trim Loss (ft)
1	0	6	0	10
2	0	0	3	10
3	8	0	0	4
4	2	1	2	1
5	7	1	0	1

Trim loss is the leftover paper from a pattern (e.g., for pattern 4, 2(12) + 1(15) + 2(30) = 99 feet used results in 100 − 99 = 1 foot of trim loss). Orders in hand for the coming week are 5,670 12-foot rolls, 1,680 15-foot rolls, and 3,350 30-foot rolls. Any of the three types of rolls produced in excess of the orders in hand will be sold on the open market at the selling price. No inventory is held.

a. Formulate an integer programming model that will determine how many 100-foot rolls to cut into each of the five patterns in order to minimize trim loss.

b. Solve the model formulated in part (a). What is the minimal amount of trim loss? How many of each pattern should be used and how many of each type of roll will be sold on the open market?

4. **Real Estate Project Selection.** Brooks Development Corporation (BDC) faces the following capital budgeting decision. Six real estate projects are available for investment. The net present value and expenditures required for each project (in millions of dollars) are as follows:

DATA *file*

Brooks

Project	1	2	3	4	5	6
Net Present Value ($ Millions)	$15	$5	$13	$14	$20	$9
Expenditure Required ($ Millions)	$90	$34	$81	$70	$114	$50

There are conditions that limit the investment alternatives:

- At least two of projects 1, 3, 5, and 6 must be undertaken.
- If either project 3 or 5 is undertaken, they must both be undertaken.
- Project 4 cannot be undertaken unless both projects 1 and 3 also are undertaken.

The budget for this investment period is $220 million.

a. Formulate a binary integer program that will enable BDC to find the projects to invest in to maximize net present value, while satisfying all project restrictions and not exceeding the budget.

b. Solve the model formulated in part (a). What is the optimal net present value? Which projects will be undertaken? How much of the budget is unused?

5. **Investment Net Present Value.** Spencer Enterprises is attempting to choose among a series of new investment alternatives. The potential investment alternatives, the net present value of the future stream of returns, the capital requirements, and the available capital funds over the next three years are summarized as follows:

Alternative	Net Present Value ($)	Capital Requirements ($) Year 1	Year 2	Year 3
Limited warehouse expansion	4,000	3,000	1,000	4,000
Extensive warehouse expansion	6,000	2,500	3,500	3,500
Test market new product	10,500	6,000	4,000	5,000
Advertising campaign	4,000	2,000	1,500	1,800
Basic research	8,000	5,000	1,000	4,000
Purchase new equipment	3,000	1,000	500	900
Capital funds available		10,500	7,000	8,750

a. Develop and solve an integer programming model for maximizing the net present value.

b. Assume that only one of the warehouse expansion projects can be implemented. Modify your model from part (a).

c. Suppose that if test marketing of the new product is carried out, the advertising campaign also must be conducted. Modify your formulation from part (b) to reflect this new situation.

6. **Component Ordering.** Morgan Inc. is planning the purchase of one of the component parts it needs for its finished product. The anticipated demands for the component for the next 12 periods are shown in the following table. The cost to order the component (labor, shipping, and paperwork) is $150. The cost to hold these components in inventory is $1 per component per period. The price of the component is expected to remain stable at $12 per unit for the next 12 periods, and no quantity discounts are available. The maximum order size is 1,000 units.

DATA *file*

Morgan

Period	1	2	3	4	5	6	7	8	9	10	11	12
Demand	20	20	30	40	140	360	500	540	460	80	0	20

a. Formulate a model to minimize the total cost of satisfying Morgan Inc.'s demand for this component.
b. Solve the model formulated in part (a). What is the optimal cost? How many orders are placed?

7. **Locating Police Substations.** Grave City is considering the relocation of several police substations to obtain better enforcement in high-crime areas. The locations under consideration together with the areas that can be covered from these locations are given in the following table:

Potential Locations for Substations	Areas Covered
A	1, 5, 7
B	1, 2, 5, 7
C	1, 3, 5
D	2, 4, 5
E	3, 4, 6
F	4, 5, 6
G	1, 5, 6, 7

a. Formulate an integer programming model that could be used to find the minimum number of locations necessary to provide coverage to all areas.
b. Solve the problem in part (a).

8. **Multi-product Production Planning.** Hart Manufacturing makes three products. Each product requires manufacturing operations in three departments: A, B, and C. The labor-hour requirements, by department, are as follows:

Department	Product 1	Product 2	Product 3
A	1.50	3.00	2.00
B	2.00	1.00	2.50
C	0.25	0.25	0.25

During the next production period the labor-hours available are 450 in department A, 350 in department B, and 50 in department C. The profit contributions per unit are $25 for product 1, $28 for product 2, and $30 for product 3.

a. Formulate a linear programming model for maximizing total profit contribution.
b. Solve the linear program formulated in part (a). How much of each product should be produced, and what is the projected total profit contribution?
c. After evaluating the solution obtained in part (b), one of the production supervisors noted that production setup costs had not been taken into account. She noted that setup costs are $400 for product 1, $550 for product 2, and $600 for product 3. If the solution developed in part (b) is to be used, what is the total profit contribution after taking into account the setup costs?

d. Management realized that the optimal product mix, taking setup costs into account, might be different from the one recommended in part (b). Formulate a mixed-integer linear program that takes setup costs provided in part (c) into account. Management also stated that we should not consider making more than 175 units of product 1, 150 units of product 2, or 140 units of product 3.

e. Solve the mixed-integer linear program formulated in part (d). How much of each product should be produced and what is the projected total profit contribution? Compare this profit contribution to that obtained in part (c).

9. **Carrier Selection.** Offhaus Manufacturing produces office supplies but outsources the delivery of its products to third-party carriers. Offhaus ships to 20 cities from its Dayton, Ohio, manufacturing facility and has asked a variety of carriers to bid on its business. Seven carriers have responded with bids. The resulting bids (in dollars per truckload) are shown in the table. For example, the table shows that carrier 1 bid on the business to cities 11 to 20. The right side of the table provides the number of truckloads scheduled for each destination in the next quarter.

Bid $/Truckload	Carrier 1	Carrier 2	Carrier 3	Carrier 4	Carrier 5	Carrier 6	Carrier 7	Destination	Demand (truckloads)
City 1					$2,188	$1,666	$1,790	City 1	30
City 2		$1,453			$2,602	$1,767		City 2	10
City 3		$1,534			$2,283	$1,857	$1,870	City 3	20
City 4		$1,687			$2,617	$1,738		City 4	40
City 5		$1,523			$2,239	$1,771	$1,855	City 5	10
City 6		$1,521			$1,571		$1,545	City 6	10
City 7		$2,100		$1,922	$1,938		$2,050	City 7	12
City 8		$1,800		$1,432	$1,416		$1,739	City 8	25
City 9		$1,134		$1,233	$1,181		$1,150	City 9	25
City 10		$672		$610	$669		$678	City 10	33
City 11	$724		$723	$627	$657		$706	City 11	11
City 12	$766		$766	$721	$682		$733	City 12	29
City 13	$741		$745		$682		$733	City 13	12
City 14	$815	$800	$828		$745		$832	City 14	24
City 15	$904		$880		$891		$914	City 15	10
City 16	$958		$933		$891		$914	City 16	10
City 17	$925		$929		$937		$984	City 17	23
City 18	$892		$869	$822	$829		$864	City 18	25
City 19	$927		$969		$967		$1,008	City 19	12
City 20	$963		$938		$955		$995	City 20	10
No. of Bids	10	10	10	7	20	5	18		

DATA *file*

Offhaus

Because dealing with too many carriers can be cumbersome, Offhaus would like to limit the number of carriers it uses to three. Also, for customer relationship reasons Offhaus wants each city to be assigned to only one carrier (i.e., no splitting of the demand to a given city across carriers).

a. Develop a model that will yield the three selected carriers and the city-carrier assignments that minimize the cost of shipping. Solve the model and report the solution.

b. Offhaus is not sure whether three is the correct number of carriers to select. Run the model you developed in part (a) for allowable carriers varying from one to seven. Based on results, how many carriers would you recommend and why?

10. **Manufacturing Plant Location.** The Martin-Beck Company operates a plant in St. Louis with an annual capacity of 30,000 units. Product is shipped to regional distribution centers located in Boston, Atlanta, and Houston. Because of an anticipated increase in demand, Martin-Beck plans to increase capacity by constructing a new plant in one or more of the following cities: Detroit, Toledo, Denver, or Kansas City. The estimated annual fixed cost and the annual capacity for the four proposed plants are as follows:

Proposed Plant	Annual Fixed Cost	Annual Capacity
Detroit	$175,000	10,000
Toledo	$300,000	20,000
Denver	$375,000	30,000
Kansas City	$500,000	40,000

The company's long-range planning group developed forecasts of the anticipated annual demand at the distribution centers as follows:

Distribution Center	Annual Demand
Boston	30,000
Atlanta	20,000
Houston	20,000

The shipping cost per unit from each plant to each distribution center is as follows:

	Distribution Centers		
Plant Site	Boston	Atlanta	Houston
Detroit	5	2	3
Toledo	4	3	4
Denver	9	7	5
Kansas City	10	4	2
St. Louis	8	4	3

a. Formulate a mixed-integer programming model that could be used to help Martin-Beck determine which new plant or plants to open in order to satisfy anticipated demand.
b. Solve the model you formulated in part (a). What is the optimal cost? What is the optimal set of plants to open?
c. Using equation (13.1), find a second-best solution. What is the increase in cost versus the best solution from part (b)?

11. **Cloud Services Capacity Planning.** Galaxy Cloud Services operates several data centers across the United States containing servers that store and process the data on the Internet. Suppose that Galaxy Cloud Services currently has five outdated data centers: one each in Michigan, Ohio, and California and two in New York. Management is considering increasing the capacity of these data centers to keep up with increasing demand. Each data center contains servers that are dedicated to Secure data and to

Super Secure data. The cost to update each data center and the resulting increase in server capacity for each type of server are as follows:

Data Center	Cost ($ millions)	Secure Servers	Super Secure Servers
Michigan	2.5	50	30
New York 1	3.5	80	40
New York 2	3.5	40	80
Ohio	4.0	90	60
California	2.0	20	30

The projected needs are for a total increase in capacity of 90 Secure servers and 90 Super Secure servers. Management wants to determine which data centers to update to meet projected needs and, at the same time, minimize the total cost of the added capacity.

a. Formulate a binary integer programming model that could be used to determine the optimal solution to the capacity increase question facing management.
b. Solve the model formulated in part (a) to provide a recommendation for management.

12. **Bank Location Planning.** CHB, Inc., a bank holding company, is evaluating the potential for expanding into the State of Ohio. State law permits establishing branches in any county that is adjacent to a county in which a PPB (principal place of business) is located. The following map shows the State of Ohio. The file *CHB* contains an adjacency matrix with a one in the *i*th row and *j*th column indicating that the counties represented by the *i*th row and the *j*th column share a border. A zero indicates that the two counties do not share a border.

Formulate and solve a linear binary model that will tell CHB the minimum number of PPBs required and their location in order to allow CHB to put a branch in every county in Ohio.

DATA *file*

CHB

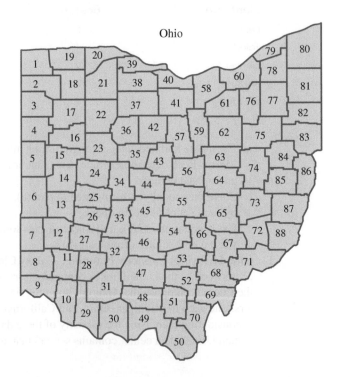

Ohio

13. **Alternative Optima for Bank Location Planning.** For Problem 12, use equation (13.1) to determine whether your solution to Problem 12 is unique. If your solution is not unique, use equation (13.1) iteratively to find all alternative optimal solutions. How many are there?

14. **Population Reach.** Consider again the CHB, Inc. problem described in Problem 12. Suppose only a limited number of PPBs can be placed. CHB would like to place this limited number of PPBs in counties so that the allowable branches can reach the maximum possible population. The file *CHBPop* contains the county adjacency matrix described in Problem 12 as well as the population of each county.

CHBPop

   a. Assume that only a fixed number of PPBs, denoted by k, can be established. Formulate a linear binary integer program that will tell CHB, Inc. where to locate the fixed number of PPBs in order to maximize the population reached. (*Hint:* Review the Ohio Trust formulation in Section 13.4. Introduce a binary variable y_i such that $y_i = 1$ if county i can be reached by a PPB (because there is a PPB in county i or in an adjacent county to county i), and $y_i = 0$ otherwise.)

   b. Suppose that two PPBs can be established. Where should they be located to maximize the population served?

   c. Solve your model from part (a) for an allowable number of PPBs ranging from 1 to 10. In other words, solve the model 10 times, k set to 1, 2, . . . , 10. Record the population reached for each value of k. Graph the results by plotting the population reached versus the number of PPBs allowed. Based on their cost calculations, CHB considers an additional PPB to be fiscally prudent only if it increases the population reached by at least 500,000 people. Based on this graph, how many PPBs do you recommend to implement?

15. **Bank Teller Scheduling.** The Northside Bank is working to develop an efficient work schedule for full-time and part-time tellers. The schedule must provide for efficient operation of the bank, including adequate customer service, employee breaks, and so on. On Fridays, the bank is open from 9:00 a.m. to 7:00 p.m. The number of tellers necessary to provide adequate customer service during each hour of operation is summarized as follows:

Time	No. of Tellers	Time	No. of Tellers
9:00 a.m. – 10:00 a.m.	6	2:00 p.m. – 3:00 p.m.	6
10:00 a.m. – 11:00 a.m.	4	3:00 p.m. – 4:00 p.m.	4
11:00 a.m. – Noon	8	4:00 p.m. – 5:00 p.m.	7
Noon – 1:00 p.m.	10	5:00 p.m. – 6:00 p.m.	6
1:00 p.m. – 2:00 p.m.	9	6:00 p.m. – 7:00 p.m.	6

Each full-time employee starts on the hour and works a 4-hour shift, followed by a 1-hour break and then a 3-hour shift. Part-time employees work one 4-hour shift beginning on the hour. Considering salary and fringe benefits, full-time employees cost the bank $15 per hour ($105 a day), and part-time employees cost the bank $8 per hour ($32 per day).

   a. Formulate an integer programming model that can be used to develop a schedule that will satisfy customer service needs at a minimum employee cost. (*Hint:* Let x_i = number of full-time employees coming on duty at the beginning of hour i and y_i = number of part-time employees coming on duty at the beginning of hour i.)

   b. Solve the LP relaxation of your model in part (a).

   c. Solve your model in part (a) for the optimal schedule of tellers. Comment on the solution.

   d. After reviewing the solution to part (c), the bank manager realized that some additional requirements must be specified. Specifically, she wants to ensure that one full-time employee is on duty at all times and that there is a staff of at least five full-time employees. Revise your model to incorporate these additional requirements, and solve for the optimal solution.

16. **Product Design.** Burnside Marketing Research conducted a study for Barker Foods on several formulations for a new dry cereal. Three attributes were found to be most influential in determining which cereal had the best taste: ratio of wheat to corn in the cereal flake, type of sweetener (sugar, honey, or artificial), and the presence or absence of flavor bits. Seven children participated in taste tests and provided the following part-worths for the attributes (see Section 13.4 for a discussion of part-worths):

DATA *file*

Burnside

	Wheat/Corn		Sweetener			Flavor Bits	
Child	Low	High	Sugar	Honey	Artificial	Present	Absent
1	15	35	30	40	25	15	9
2	30	20	40	35	35	8	11
3	40	25	20	40	10	7	14
4	35	30	25	20	30	15	18
5	25	40	40	20	35	18	14
6	20	25	20	35	30	9	16
7	30	15	25	40	40	20	11

a. Suppose that the overall utility (sum of part-worths) of the current favorite cereal is 75 for each child. What product design will maximize the number of children in the sample who prefer the new dry cereal? Note that a child will prefer the new dry cereal only if its overall utility is at least 1 part-worth larger than the utility of their current preferred cereal.

b. Assume that the overall utility of the current favorite cereal for children 1 to 4 is 70, and the overall utility of the current favorite cereal for children 5 to 7 is 80. What product design will maximize the number of children in the sample who prefer the new dry cereal? Note that a child will prefer the new dry cereal only if its overall utility is at least 1 part-worth larger than the utility of their current preferred cereal.

17. **Security System Design.** The Bayside Art Gallery is considering installing a video camera security system to reduce its insurance premiums. A diagram of Bayside's eight exhibition rooms is shown in the figure in the next page; the openings between the rooms are numbered 1 to 13. A security firm proposed that two-way cameras be installed at some room openings. Each camera has the ability to monitor the two rooms between which the camera is located. For example, if a camera were located at opening number 4, rooms 1 and 4 would be covered; if a camera were located at opening 11, rooms 7 and 8 would be covered; and so on. Management decided not to locate a camera system at the entrance to the display rooms. The objective is to provide security coverage for all eight rooms using the minimum number of two-way cameras.

a. Formulate a binary integer linear programming model that will enable Bayside's management to determine the locations for the camera systems.

b. Solve the model formulated in part (a) to determine how many two-way cameras to purchase and where they should be located.

c. Suppose that management wants to provide additional security coverage for room 7. Specifically, management wants room 7 to be covered by two cameras. How would the model you formulated in part (a) have to change to accommodate this policy restriction?

d. With the policy restriction specified in part (c), determine how many two-way camera systems will need to be purchased and where they should be located.

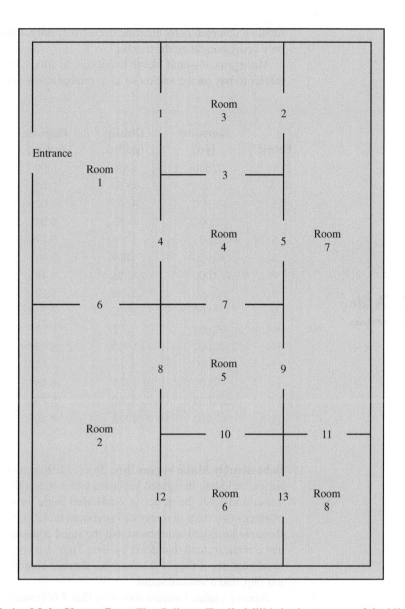

This exercise is an extension of Exercise 19 in Chapter 12.

18. **Fabrics Make Versus Buy.** The Calhoun Textile Mill is in the process of deciding on a production schedule. It wishes to know how to weave the various fabrics it will produce during the coming quarter. The sales department has confirmed orders for each of the 15 fabrics produced by Calhoun. These demands are given in the following table. Also given in this table is the variable cost for each fabric. The mill operates continuously during the quarter: 13 weeks, 7 days a week, and 24 hours a day.

There are two types of looms: dobby and regular. Dobby looms can be used to make all fabrics and are the only looms that can weave certain fabrics, such as plaids. The rate of production for each fabric on each type of loom is also given in the table. Note that if the production rate is zero, the fabric cannot be woven on that type of loom. Also, if a fabric can be woven on each type of loom, then the production rates are equal. Calhoun has 90 regular looms and 15 dobby looms. For this problem, assume that the time requirement to change over a loom from one fabric to another is negligible.

In addition to producing the fabric using dobby and regular looms, Calhoun has the option to buy each fabric on the market. The market cost per yard for each fabric is given in the table. Management wants to make sure that each fabric is sourced using exactly one of the three alternatives. That is, for a given fabric, its demand must be satisfied completely by utilizing exclusively only dobby looms, only regular looms, or only being bought on the market.

Management would like to know how to allocate the looms to the fabrics and which fabrics to buy on the market so as to minimize the cost of meeting demand.

CalhounFabrics

Fabric	Demand (yd)	Dobby (yd/hr)	Regular (yd/hr)	Mill Cost ($/yd)	Market Cost ($/yd)
1	16,500	4.653	0.00	0.6573	0.80
2	52,000	4.653	0.00	0.5550	0.70
3	45,000	4.653	0.00	0.6550	0.85
4	22,000	4.653	0.00	0.5542	0.70
5	76,500	5.194	5.194	0.6097	0.75
6	110,000	3.809	3.809	0.6153	0.75
7	122,000	4.185	4.185	0.6477	0.80
8	62,000	5.232	5.232	0.4880	0.60
9	7,500	5.232	5.232	0.5029	0.70
10	69,000	5.232	5.232	0.4351	0.60
11	70,000	3.733	3.733	0.6417	0.80
12	82,000	4.185	4.185	0.5675	0.75
13	10,000	4.439	4.439	0.4952	0.65
14	380,000	5.232	5.232	0.3128	0.45
15	62,000	4.185	4.185	0.5029	0.70

19. **Subassembly Make Versus Buy.** Roedel Electronics produces tablet computer accessories, including integrated keyboard tablet stands that connect a keyboard to a tablet device and holds the device at a preferred angle for easy viewing and typing. Roedel produces two sizes of integrated keyboard tablet stands, small and large. Each size uses the same keyboard attachment, but the stand consists of two different pieces, a top flap and a vertical stand that differ by size. Thus, a completed integrated keyboard tablet stand consists of three subassemblies that are manufactured by Roedel: a keyboard, a top flap, and a vertical stand.

Roedel's sales forecast indicates that 7,000 small integrated keyboard tablet stands and 5,000 large integrated keyboard tablet stands will be needed to satisfy demand during the upcoming Christmas season. Because only 500 hours of in-house manufacturing time are available, Roedel is considering purchasing some, or all, of the subassemblies from outside suppliers. If Roedel manufactures a subassembly in-house, it incurs a fixed setup cost as well as a variable manufacturing cost. The following table shows the setup cost, the manufacturing time per subassembly, the manufacturing cost per subassembly, and the cost to purchase each of the subassemblies from an outside supplier:

Subassembly	Setup Cost ($)	Manufacturing Time per Unit (Min)	Manufacturing Cost per Unit ($)	Purchase Cost per Unit ($)
Keyboard	1,000	0.9	0.40	0.65
Small top flap	1,200	2.2	2.90	3.45
Large top flap	1,900	3.0	3.15	3.70
Small vertical stand	1,500	0.8	0.30	0.50
Large vertical stand	1,500	1.0	0.55	0.70

a. Determine how many units of each subassembly Roedel should manufacture and how many units of each subassembly Roedel should purchase. What is the total manufacturing and purchase cost associated with your recommendation?

b. Suppose Roedel is considering purchasing new machinery to produce large top flaps. For the new machinery, the setup cost is $3,000; the manufacturing time is 2.5 minutes per unit, and the manufacturing cost is $2.60 per unit. Assuming that the new machinery is purchased, determine how many units of each subassembly Roedel should manufacture and how many units of each subassembly Roedel should purchase. What is the total manufacturing and purchase cost associated with your recommendation? Do you think the new machinery should be purchased? Explain.

20. **Television Show Planning.** John White is the program scheduling manager for the television channel CCFO. John would like to plan the schedule of television shows for next Wednesday evening.

The table below lists nine shows under consideration. John must select exactly five of these shows for the period from 8:00 p.m. to 10:30 p.m. next Wednesday evening. For each television show, the estimated advertising revenue (in $ millions) is provided. Furthermore, each show has been categorized into one or more of the categories "Public Interest," "Violent," "Comedy," and "Drama." In the following table, a 1 indicates that the show is in the corresponding category and a 0 indicates it is not.

Show	Revenue ($ Millions)	Public Interest	Violent	Comedy	Drama
Sam's Place	$6	0	0	1	1
Texas Oil	$10	0	1	0	1
Cincinnati Law	$9	1	0	0	1
Jarred	$4	0	1	0	1
Bob & Mary	$5	0	0	1	0
Chainsaw	$2	0	1	0	0
Loving Life	$6	1	0	0	1
Islanders	$7	0	0	1	0
Urban Sprawl	$8	1	0	0	0

DATA *file*

TVSchedule

John would like to determine a revenue-maximizing schedule of television shows for next Wednesday evening. However, he must be mindful of the following considerations:

- The schedule must include at least as many shows that are categorized as public interest as shows that are categorized as violent.
- If John schedules "Loving Life," then he must also schedule either "Jarred" or "Cincinnati Law" (or both).
- John cannot schedule both "Loving Life" and "Urban Sprawl."
- If John schedules more than one show in the "Violent" category, he will lose an estimated $4 million in advertising revenues from family-oriented sponsors.

a. Formulate a binary integer program that models the decisions John faces.
b. Solve the model formulated in part (a). What is the optimal revenue?

21. **Service Facility Location.** East Coast Trucking provides service from Boston to Miami using regional offices located in Boston, New York, Philadelphia, Baltimore, Washington, Richmond, Raleigh, Florence, Savannah, Jacksonville, Tampa, and Miami. The number of miles between the regional offices is provided in the following table:

	Boston	New York	Philadelphia	Baltimore	Washington	Richmond	Raleigh	Florence	Savannah	Jacksonville	Tampa	Miami
Boston	0	211	320	424	459	565	713	884	1056	1196	1399	1669
New York	211	0	109	213	248	354	502	673	845	985	1188	1458
Philadelphia	320	109	0	104	139	245	393	564	736	876	1079	1349
Baltimore	424	213	104	0	35	141	289	460	632	772	975	1245
Washington	459	248	139	35	0	106	254	425	597	737	940	1210
Richmond	565	354	245	141	106	0	148	319	491	631	834	1104
Raleigh	713	502	393	289	254	148	0	171	343	483	686	956
Florence	884	673	564	460	425	319	171	0	172	312	515	785
Savannah	1056	845	736	632	597	491	343	172	0	140	343	613
Jacksonville	1196	985	876	772	737	631	483	312	140	0	203	473
Tampa	1399	1188	1079	975	940	834	686	515	343	203	0	270
Miami	1669	1458	1349	1245	1210	1104	956	785	613	473	270	0

DATA *file*

EastCoast

The company's expansion plans involve constructing service facilities in some of the cities where regional offices are located. Each regional office must be within 400 miles of a service facility. For instance, if a service facility is constructed in Richmond, it can provide service to regional offices located in New York, Philadelphia, Baltimore, Washington, Richmond, Raleigh, and Florence. Management would like to determine the minimum number of service facilities needed and where they should be located.

a. Formulate an integer linear program that can be used to determine the minimum number of service facilities needed and their locations.

b. Solve the integer linear program formulated in part (a). How many service facilities are required, and where should they be located?

c. Suppose that each service facility can provide service only to regional offices within 300 miles. Re-solve the integer linear program with the 300-mile requirement. How many service facilities are required and where should they be located?

22. **Mutual Fund Portfolio Planning.** Dave has $100,000 to invest in 10 mutual fund alternatives with the following restrictions. For diversification, no more than $25,000 can be invested in any one fund. If a fund is chosen for investment, then at least $10,000 will be invested in it. No more than two of the funds can be pure growth funds, and at least one pure bond fund must be selected. The total amount invested in pure bond funds must be at least as much as the amount invested in pure growth funds. Using the following expected returns, formulate and solve a model that will determine the investment strategy that will maximize expected annual return. What assumptions have you made in your model? How often would you expect to run your model?

Fund	Type	Expected Return (%)
1	Growth	6.70
2	Growth	7.65
3	Growth	7.55
4	Growth	7.45
5	Growth & Income	7.50
6	Growth & Income	6.45
7	Growth & Income	7.05
8	Stock & Bond	6.90
9	Bond	5.20
10	Bond	5.90

23. **New Product Design.** Wegryn Consumer Goods (WCG) is considering entering the dish soap market with a new product it has yet to design. Using conjoint analysis, WCG has estimated part-worth utilities for 110 survey respondents for the following four attributes for dish soap:

• Surfactants—chemicals that help suspend the oils and residue on dishes (5 levels)
• Solubility—how quickly a soap dissolves in water (10 levels)
• Color—the color of the soap (5 levels)
• Scent—the aroma of the soap (4 levels)

WCG has also collected the profile of the status quo product for each of the respondents in the form of a binary vector of length 24. For example, the following vector indicates that this respondent is currently using a product comprised of level 1 of surfactants, level 6 of solubility, level 3 of color, and level 1 of scent.

DishSoap

$$[1\ 0\ 0\ 0\ 0\ 0\ 0\ 0\ 0\ 1\ 0\ 0\ 0\ 0\ 0\ 1\ 0\ 0\ 1\ 0\ 0\ 0]$$

The utility of the status quo product for each respondent can be obtained by adding up the part-worth's of the levels indicated for the status quo product.

The part-worth utilities and the status quo vector for each of the 110 respondents are given in the file *DishSoap*.

WCG wants to construct a new dish soap product so that the new product is more valuable than the status quo product for the maximum number of respondents.

24. **Clean-Sheet Manufacturing Location.** In this problem, we revisit the Martin-Beck plant location problem described in Problem 10. The management of Martin-Beck has decided to do a clean-sheet analysis. Rather than assume that the St. Louis plant is fixed as open, management wants to run a model that allows for any plant or set of plants to be open so that total cost is minimized. The annual fixed cost and the capacities of the proposed plants have been estimated (see Problem 10). The variable costs for the proposed plant locations are estimated to be the following: Detroit ($4.26), Toledo ($4.19), Denver ($4.69), and Kansas City ($4.20).

StLouisMB

We need an estimate of the fixed cost and variable cost at the current St. Louis plant. The file *StLouisMB* contains 15 observations from previous years that will allow us to estimate these.

a. Use simple linear regression, with total cost as the dependent variable (y) and volume as the independent variable (x). The model $y = b_0 + b_1 x$ will give you estimates of $b_1 =$ the per unit variable cost and $b_0 =$ annual fixed cost. Round the variable cost estimate to the nearest cent.

b. Using the data from Problem 10, the values of variable cost given above for the proposed locations and the fixed and variable costs for St. Louis estimated in part (a), build an optimization model to minimize total cost to meet demand. Which plants are open and what is the total cost to meet demand?

25. **Second Best Manufacturing Locations.** Refer to Problem 24. Find the second-best solution. How does it compare to the optimal solution found in Problem 24? Why might the second-best solution be preferred?

CASE PROBLEM: APPLECORE CHILDREN'S CLOTHING

Applecore Children's Clothing is a retailer that sells high-end clothes for toddlers (ages 1 to 3), primarily in shopping malls. Applecore also has a successful Internet-based sales division. Recently Dave Walker, vice-president of the e-commerce division, has been given the directive to expand the company's Internet sales. He commissioned a major study on the effectiveness of Internet ads placed on news web sites. The results were favorable: Current patrons who purchased via the Internet and saw the ads on news web sites spent more, on average, than did comparable Internet customers who did not see the ads.

With this new information on Internet ads, Walker continued to investigate how new Internet customers could most effectively be reached. One of these ideas involved strategically purchasing ads on news web sites prior to and during the holiday season. To determine which news sites might be the most effective for ads, Walker conducted a follow-up study. An e-mail questionnaire was administered to a sample of 1,200 current Internet customers to ascertain which of 30 news sites they regularly visit. The idea is that web sites with high proportions of current customer visits would be viable sources of future customers for Applecore products.

Walker would like to ascertain which news sites should be selected for ads. The problem is complicated because Walker does not want to count multiple exposures. So, if a respondent visits multiple sites with Applecore ads or visits a given site multiple times, that respondent should be counted as reached but not more than once. In other words, a customer is considered reached if he or she has visited at least one web site with an Applecore ad.

Data from the customer e-mail survey have begun to trickle in. Walker wants to develop a prototype model based on the current survey results. So far, 53 surveys have been returned. To keep the prototype model manageable, Walker wants to proceed with model development using the data from the 53 returned surveys and using only the first 10 news sites in the questionnaire. The costs of ads per week for the 10 web sites are given in the following table, and the budget is $10,000 per week. For each of the 53 responses received, the 10 web sites visited regularly are shown below. For a given customer–web site pair, a one indicates that the customer regularly visits that web site and a zero indicates that the customer does not regularly visit that site.

Managerial Report

1. Develop a model that will allow Applecore to maximize the number of customers reached for a budget of $10,000 for one week of promotion.
2. Solve the model. What is the maximum number of customers reached for the $10,000 budget?
3. Perform a sensitivity analysis on the budget for values from $5,000 to $35,000 in increments of $5,000. Construct a graph of percentage reach versus budget. Is the additional increase in percentage reach monotonically decreasing as the budget allocation increases? Why or why not? What is your recommended budget? Explain.

Data for Applecore Customer Visits to News Web Sites (respondents 5 to 33 hidden)

	Web Site									
	1	2	3	4	5	6	7	8	9	10
Cost/Wk ($000)	$5.0	$8.0	$3.5	$5.5	$7.0	$4.5	$6.0	$5.0	$3.0	$2.2

	Web Site									
Customer	1	2	3	4	5	6	7	8	9	10
1	0	0	0	0	0	0	0	0	0	1
2	1	0	0	1	0	0	0	0	0	0
3	1	0	0	0	0	0	0	0	0	0
4	0	0	0	0	1	1	0	0	0	0
34	0	0	0	1	1	0	0	0	0	0
35	1	0	0	0	1	1	0	0	0	0
36	1	0	1	0	0	0	0	0	0	0
37	0	0	1	0	1	0	0	1	0	0
38	0	0	1	0	0	0	0	0	0	0
39	0	1	0	0	0	0	1	0	0	0
40	0	1	0	0	0	0	1	0	0	0
41	0	0	0	0	0	0	1	0	0	0
42	0	0	0	1	1	1	0	0	0	0
43	0	0	0	0	0	0	0	0	0	0
44	0	0	0	0	1	0	0	0	0	1
45	1	1	0	0	0	0	0	0	0	0
46	0	0	0	0	0	0	1	0	0	0
47	1	0	0	0	1	0	0	0	0	1
48	0	0	1	0	0	0	0	0	0	0
49	1	0	1	1	0	0	0	0	0	0
50	0	0	0	0	0	0	0	0	0	0
51	0	1	0	0	0	1	0	0	0	0
52	0	0	0	0	0	0	0	0	0	0
53	0	1	0	0	1	0	0	1	1	1

DATA *file*

Applecore

Chapter 14

Nonlinear Optimization Models

CONTENTS

ANALYTICS IN ACTION

InterContinental Hotels*

InterContinental Hotel Group (IHG) owns, leases, or franchises over 4,500 hotels in about 100 countries around the world. It offers over 700,000 guest rooms. InterContinental Hotels, Crowne Plaza Hotels and Resorts, Holiday Inn Hotels and Resorts, and Holiday Inn Express are some of InterContinental's brands.

Like airlines and rental car companies, hotels offer a perishable good; that is, hotels have a limited time window in which to sell the product, after which the value perishes. For example, an empty seat on an airline flight is of no value, as is a hotel room that goes empty overnight. In dealing with perishable goods, how to price them in such a way as to maximize revenue is a challenge. Price the hotel room too high, and it will sit empty overnight and generate zero revenue. Price the hotel room too low, the hotel will be filled, but revenue likely will be lower than it could have been with higher pricing, even if fewer rooms

were booked. *Revenue management* (RM) is a term used to describe analytical approaches to this pricing problem.

IHG developed a novel approach to the hotel room pricing problem that uses a nonlinear optimization model to determine prices to charge for its rooms. Each day, IHG searches the Internet to acquire competitors' prices. The competitors' prices are factored into IHG's pricing optimization model, which is run daily. The model is nonlinear because the objective function is to maximize contribution (revenue − cost), but both demand and revenue are a function of the price variable. Over 2,000 IHG hotels have begun using this pricing model, and its use has led to increased revenue in excess of $145 million.

---

*Based on D. Kosuhik, J. A. Higbie, and C. Eister, "Retail Price Optimization at InterContinental Hotels Group," *Interfaces* 42, no. 1 (January–February 2012): 45–57.

Many business processes behave in a nonlinear manner. For example, the price of a bond is a nonlinear function of interest rates, and the price of a stock option is a nonlinear function of the price of the underlying stock. The marginal cost of production often decreases with the quantity produced, and the quantity demanded for a product is usually a nonlinear function of the price. These and many other nonlinear relationships are present in many business applications.

A **nonlinear optimization problem** is any optimization problem in which at least one term in the objective function or a constraint is nonlinear. In this chapter, we examine a production problem in which the objective function is a nonlinear function of the decision variables, similar to the Analytics in Action: InterContinental Hotels. We discuss issues that make nonlinear optimization very different from linear optimization. We present a nonlinear model for facility location as well as the Nobel Prize–winning Markowitz model for managing the trade-off between risk and return in the construction of an investment portfolio. We also consider a well-known model that effectively forecasts sales or adoptions of a new product.

14.1 A Production Application: Par, Inc. Revisited

We introduce constrained and unconstrained nonlinear optimization problems by considering an extension of the Par, Inc. linear program introduced in Chapter 12. We first consider the case in which the relationship between price and quantity sold causes the objective function to be nonlinear. The resulting unconstrained nonlinear program is then solved. As we shall see, the unconstrained optimal solution does not satisfy the production constraints of the original problem. Adding the production constraints back into the problem allows us to show the formulation and solution of a constrained nonlinear optimization model.

An Unconstrained Problem

Let us consider a revision of the Par, Inc. problem discussed in Chapter 12. Recall that Par, Inc. decided to manufacture standard and deluxe golf bags. In formulating the linear programming model for the Par, Inc. problem, we assumed that the company could sell all of the standard and deluxe bags it could produce. However, depending on the price of the golf bags, this assumption may not hold. An inverse relationship usually exists between price and demand. As price increases, the quantity demanded decreases. Let P_S denote the price Par, Inc. charges for each standard bag and P_D denote the price for each deluxe bag. Assume that the demand for standard bags, S, and the demand for deluxe bags, D, are given by

$$S = 2,250 - 15P_S \qquad (14.1)$$

$$D = 1,500 - 5P_D \qquad (14.2)$$

The revenue generated from standard bags is the price of each standard bag, P_S, times the number of standard bags sold, S. If the cost to produce a standard bag is \$70, then the cost to produce S standard bags is $70S$. Thus, the profit contribution for producing and selling S standard bags (revenue − cost) is

$$P_S S - 70S = (P_S - 70)S \qquad (14.3)$$

We can solve equation (14.1) for P_S to show how the price of a standard bag is related to the number of standard bags sold: $P_S = 150 - (1/15)S$. Substituting $150 - (1/15)S$ for P_S in equation (14.3), the profit contribution for standard bags is

$$(P_S - 70)S = [150 - (1/15)S - 70]S = 80S - (1/15)S^2 \qquad (14.4)$$

Suppose that the cost to produce each deluxe golf bag is \$150. Using the same logic we used to develop equation (14.4), the profit contribution for deluxe bags is

$$(P_D - 150)D = [300 - (1/5)D - 150]D = 150D - (1/5)D^2$$

Total profit contribution is the sum of the profit contribution for standard bags and the profit contribution for deluxe bags. Thus, total profit contribution is written as

$$\text{Total profit contribution} = 80S - (1/15)S^2 + 150D - (1/5)D^2 \qquad (14.5)$$

Note that the two linear demand functions, equations (14.1) and (14.2), give a nonlinear total profit contribution function, equation (14.5). This function is an example of a **quadratic function** because the nonlinear terms have an exponent of 2 (S^2 and D^2).

Details of how to use Excel Solver for nonlinear optimization are discussed in the next section.

Using Excel Solver, we find that the values of S and D that maximize the profit contribution function are $S = 600$ and $D = 375$. The corresponding prices are \$110 for standard bags and \$225 for deluxe bags, and the profit contribution is \$52,125. If all production constraints are also satisfied, these values provide the optimal solution for Par, Inc.

A Constrained Problem

In calculating the unconstrained optimal solution, we have ignored the production constraints discussed in Chapter 12. Recall that Par, Inc. has limited amounts of time available in each of four departments (cutting and dyeing, sewing, finishing, and inspection and packaging). We must enforce constraints that ensure that the amount of time used does not exceed the amount of time available in each of these departments. The problem that Par, Inc. must solve is to maximize the total profit contribution subject to all of the departmental labor hour constraints given in Chapter 12. The complete mathematical model for the Par, Inc. constrained nonlinear maximization problem is as follows:

$$\text{Max} \quad 80S - \tfrac{1}{15}S^2 + 150D - \tfrac{1}{5}D^2$$

s.t.

$$\begin{array}{lll}
\tfrac{7}{10}S + & 1D \le 630 & \text{Cutting and dyeing} \\
\tfrac{1}{2}S + & \tfrac{5}{6}D \le 600 & \text{Sewing} \\
1S + & \tfrac{2}{3}D \le 708 & \text{Finishing} \\
\tfrac{1}{10}S + & \tfrac{1}{4}D \le 135 & \text{Inspection and packaging} \\
& S, D \ge 0 &
\end{array}$$

The feasible region for the original Par, Inc. problem, along with the unconstrained optimal solution point (600, 375), is shown in Figure 14.1. The unconstrained optimum of (600, 375) is obviously outside the feasible region.

This maximization problem is exactly the same as the Par, Inc. problem in Chapter 12 except for the nonlinear objective function. The solution to this new constrained nonlinear maximization problem is shown in Figure 14.2.

In Figure 14.2 we see three profit contribution contour lines. Each point on the same contour line is a point of equal profit. Here, the contour lines show profit contributions of $45,000, $49,920.55, and $51,500. In the original Par, Inc. problem described in Chapter 12, the objective function is linear, and thus the profit contours are straight lines. However, for the Par, Inc. problem with a quadratic objective function, the profit contours are ellipses.

Because part of the $45,000 profit contour line cuts through the feasible region, we know that an infinite number of combinations of standard and deluxe bags will yield a profit of $45,000. An infinite number of combinations of standard and deluxe bags also provide a profit of $51,500. However, none of the points on the $51,500 contour profit line is in the feasible region. As the contour lines move farther out from the unconstrained optimum of (600, 375) the profit contribution associated with each contour line decreases. The contour line representing a profit of $49,920.55 intersects the feasible region at a single point. Without showing all of the details in solving for this point, the point of intersection is 459.717 standard bags and 308.198 deluxe bags. This solution provides the maximum possible profit. No contour line that has a profit contribution greater than $49,920.55 will intersect the feasible region. Because the contour lines are nonlinear, the contour line with the highest profit can touch the boundary of the feasible region at any point, not just an extreme point. In the Par, Inc. case, the optimal solution is on the cutting and dyeing constraint line partway between two extreme points.

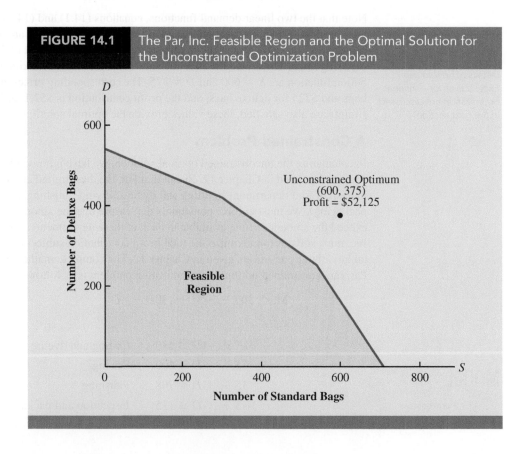

FIGURE 14.1   The Par, Inc. Feasible Region and the Optimal Solution for the Unconstrained Optimization Problem

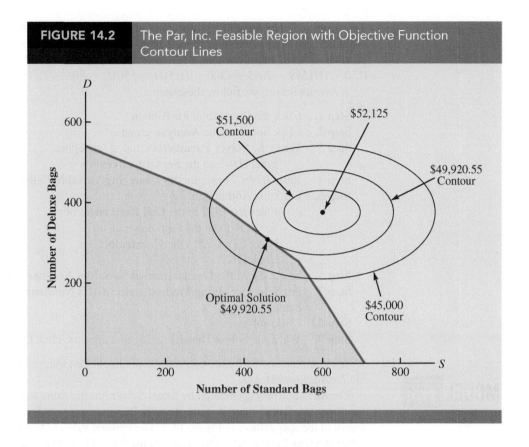

FIGURE 14.2   The Par, Inc. Feasible Region with Objective Function Contour Lines

It is also possible for the optimal solution to a nonlinear optimization problem to lie in the interior of the feasible region. For instance, if the right-hand sides of the constraints in the Par, Inc. problem were all increased by a sufficient amount, the feasible region would expand so that the optimal unconstrained solution point of (600, 375) with a profit contribution of $52,125 in Figure 14.2 would be in the interior of the feasible region.

Many linear optimization algorithms (e.g., the simplex method) optimize by examining only the extreme points and selecting the extreme point that gives the best solution value. As the solution to the constrained nonlinear problem for Par, Inc. illustrates, such a method will not work in the nonlinear case because the optimal solution is generally not an extreme-point solution. Hence, nonlinear optimization algorithms are more complex than linear optimization algorithms, and the details are beyond the scope of this text. Fortunately, we do not need to know how nonlinear algorithms work; we just need to know how to use them. Computer software such as Excel Solver and Analytic Solver are available to solve nonlinear optimization problems.

Next we discuss how to use Excel Solver to solve nonlinear optimization problems.

Solving Nonlinear Optimization Models Using Excel Solver

We use the constrained nonlinear problem for Par, Inc. to illustrate how to use Excel Solver to solve nonlinear optimization problems. The procedure for developing and entering the model in Excel is the same as for linear problems as discussed in Chapter 12, except that one or more of the functions is nonlinear.

Figure 14.3 shows the Excel model and Solver dialog box for the nonlinear Par, Inc. problem. The SUMPRODUCT function is used in cells B19 through B22 to calculate the number of hours required in each department. The price function for standard bags is entered in cell B25 as $=150-(1/15)*\$B\$14$ and similarly for deluxe bags in cell D26 as $=300-(1/5)*\$C\$14$.

MODEL *file*

ParNonlinear

The objective function in cell B16 contains the formula $=(B25-B9)*B14+(B26-C9)*C14$, which corresponds to $(150 - (1/15)S - 70)S + (300 - (1/5)D - 150)D$. As previously shown, this is mathematically equivalent to equation (14.5) because $(150 - (1/15)S - 70)S + (300 - (1/5)D - 150)D = 80S - (1/15)S^2 + 150D - (1/5)D^2$.

To invoke Solver, we follow these steps:

Step 1. Click the **Data** tab in the Ribbon
Step 2. Click **Solver** in the **Analyze** group
Step 3. When the **Solver Parameters** dialog box appears:
      Enter *B16* into the **Set Objective:** box
Step 4. Enter *B14:C14* into the **By Changing Variable Cells:** box area
Step 5. Click the **Add** button
      Enter *B19:B22* in the **Cell Reference:** box
      Select ≤ from the drop-down menu
      Enter *C19:C22* in the **Constraint:** box
      Click **OK**
Step 6. Select the **Make Unconstrained Variables Non-negative** option
Step 7. For **Select a Solving Method:** select **GRG Nonlinear** from the drop-down menu
Step 8. Click **Solve**
Step 9. When the **Solver Results** dialog box appears, click **OK**

ParNonlinearModel

The complete model for the constrained nonlinear Par, Inc. problem is contained in the file *ParNonlinearModel*.

The Answer Report generated by Excel Solver has the same structure as that of linear programs. Rather than show the Answer Report here, we refer to the optimal values shown in the spreadsheet in Figure 14.3. The optimal value of the objective function is $49,920.55, and this is achieved by producing 459.717 standard bags and 308.198 deluxe bags. This is the optimal point shown geometrically in Figure 14.2. Comparing cells C19 through C22 with cells D19 through D22 shows that only the cutting and dyeing constraint is binding, which is consistent with Figure 14.2. The optimal prices, based on the optimal quantities, are shown in cells B25 and B26. The optimal price for a standard bag is $119.35 and the optimal price for a deluxe bag is $238.36.

Sensitivity Analysis and Shadow Prices in Nonlinear Models

The Sensitivity Report for the nonlinear Par, Inc. problem is shown in Figure 14.4. As in the linear case, there are two sections: one for the variables and the other for constraints. The variables section gives the cell location, name, final (optimal) value, and **reduced gradient** for each variable. The reduced gradient is analogous to the reduced cost for linear models. It is essentially the shadow price of the nonnegativity constraint or, more generally, the shadow price of a binding simple lower or upper bound on the decision variable.

The constraint section gives the cell location, name, and final value for the left-hand side of each constraint. For the Par, Inc. problem, the final values are the amount of time in hours used in each of the four departments. The far right column gives the **Lagrangian multiplier** for each constraint. The Lagrangian multiplier is the shadow price for a constraint in a nonlinear problem. In other words, the Lagrangian multiplier is the rate of change of the objective function with respect to the right-hand side of a constraint. For the Par, Inc. example, as we increase the number of hours available in the cutting and dyeing department, we expect the profit to increase by $26.72 per hour. However, notice that no ranges are given for allowable changes to the right-hand side. This is because the allowable increase and decrease are essentially zero. Changing the right-hand side of a binding constraint by even a small amount will change the value of Lagrangian multiplier. Nonetheless, the Lagrangian multiplier does give an estimate of the importance of relieving a binding constraint.

FIGURE 14.3   Spreadsheet Model and Solver Parameters Dialog Box for the Nonlinear Par, Inc. Problem

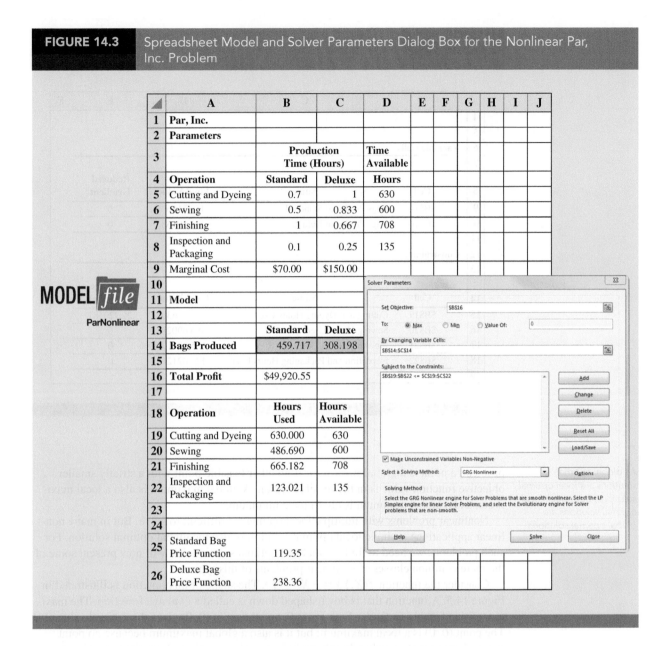

MODEL *file*

ParNonlinear

14.2 Local and Global Optima

A feasible solution is a **local optimum** if no other feasible solution with a better objective function value is found in the immediate neighborhood. For example, for the constrained Par, Inc. problem, the local optimum corresponds to a local maximum; a point is a **local maximum** if no other feasible solution with a larger objective function value is in the immediate neighborhood. Similarly, for a minimization problem, a point is a **local minimum** if no other feasible solution with a smaller objective function value is in the immediate neighborhood.

The neighborhood of a solution is a mathematical concept that refers to the set of points within a relatively close proximity of the solution. See Figure 14.7 for a graphical example of local minimums and local maximums.

Nonlinear optimization problems can have multiple local optimal solutions, which means we are concerned with finding the best of the local optimal solutions. A feasible solution is a **global optimum** if no other feasible point with a better objective function value exists in the feasible region. In the case of a maximization problem, the global optimum corresponds to a **global maximum**. A point is a global maximum if no other point in the feasible region gives a strictly larger objective function value. For a minimization

---

FIGURE 14.4 Excel Solver Sensitivity Report for the Nonlinear Par, Inc. Problem

	Cell	Name	Final Value	Reduced Gradient
Variable Cells				
	$B$14	Bags Produced Standard	459.7166	0
	$C$14	Bags Produced Deluxe	308.19838	0

	Cell	Name	Final Value	Lagrange Multiplier
Constraints				
	$B$19	Cutting and Dyeing Hours Used	630	26.720587
	$B$20	Sewing Hours Used	486.69028	0
	$B$21	Finishing Hours Used	665.18219	0
	$B$22	Inspection and Packaging Hours Used	123.02126	0

All global optimal solutions are local optimal solutions, but not all local optimal solutions are global optimal solutions.

problem, a point is a **global minimum** if no other feasible point with a strictly smaller objective function value is in the feasible region. A global maximum is also a local maximum, and a global minimum is also a local minimum.

Nonlinear problems with multiple local optima are difficult to solve. But in many nonlinear applications, a single local optimal solution is also the global optimal solution. For such problems, we need to find only a local optimal solution. We will now present some of the more common classes of nonlinear problems of this type.

Consider the function $f(X,Y) = -X^2 - Y^2$. The shape of this function is illustrated in Figure 14.5. A function that is bowl-shaped down is called a **concave function**. The maximum value for this particular function is 0, and the point (0, 0) gives the optimal value of 0. The point (0, 0) is a local maximum; but it is also a global maximum because no point gives a larger function value. In other words, no values of X and Y result in an objective function value greater than 0. Functions that are concave, such as $f(X,Y) = -X^2 - Y^2$, have a single local maximum that is also a global maximum. This type of nonlinear problem is relatively easy to maximize.

The objective function for the nonlinear Par, Inc. problem is an example of a concave function:

$$80S - \tfrac{1}{15}S^2 + 150D - \tfrac{1}{5}D^2$$

In general, if all the squared terms in a quadratic function have a negative coefficient and there are no cross-product terms, such as xy (or for the Par, Inc. problem, SD), then the function is a concave quadratic function. Thus, for the Par, Inc. problem, we are assured that the local maximum identified by Excel Solver in Figure 14.3 is the global maximum.

Let us now consider another type of function with a single local optimum that is also a global optimum. Consider the function $f(X,Y) = X^2 + Y^2$. The shape of this function is illustrated in Figure 14.6. It is bowl-shaped up and called a **convex function**. The minimum

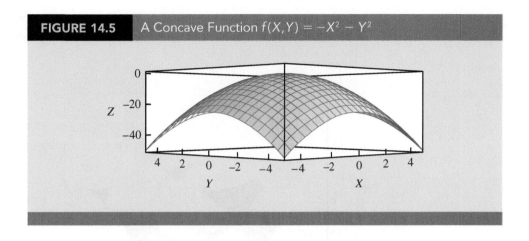

FIGURE 14.5   A Concave Function $f(X,Y) = -X^2 - Y^2$

value for this particular function is 0, and the point (0, 0) gives the minimum value of 0. The point (0, 0) is a local minimum and a global minimum because no values of X and Y give an objective function value less than 0. Convex functions, such as $f(X,Y) = X^2 + Y^2$, have a single local minimum and are relatively easy to minimize.

For a concave function, we can be assured that if our computer software finds a local maximum, it has found a global maximum. Similarly, for a convex function, we know that if our computer software finds a local minimum, it has found a global minimum. However, some nonlinear functions have multiple local optima. For example, Figure 14.7 shows the graph of the following function over the feasible regions: $0 \leq X \leq 1, 0 \leq Y \leq 1$:

$$f(X,Y) = X \sin(5\pi X) + Y \sin(5\pi Y)$$

where sin is the trigonometric sine function, and π is approximately 3.1416. The hills and valleys in this graph show that this function has a number of local maximums and local minimums.

From a technical standpoint, functions with multiple local optima pose a serious challenge for optimization software; most nonlinear optimization software methods can get stuck and terminate at a local optimum. Unfortunately, many applications can be nonlinear with multiple local optima, and the objective function value for a local optimum may be much worse than the objective function value for a global optimum. Developing algorithms capable of finding the global optimum is currently an active research area.

Next we discuss a very practical approach to dealing with local maximums and local minimums when using Excel Solver for nonlinear problems.

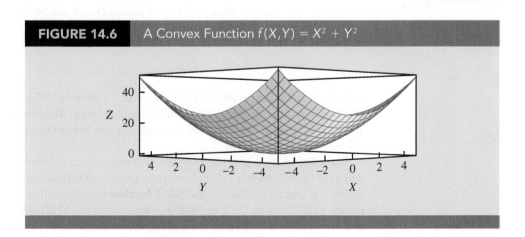

FIGURE 14.6   A Convex Function $f(X,Y) = X^2 + Y^2$

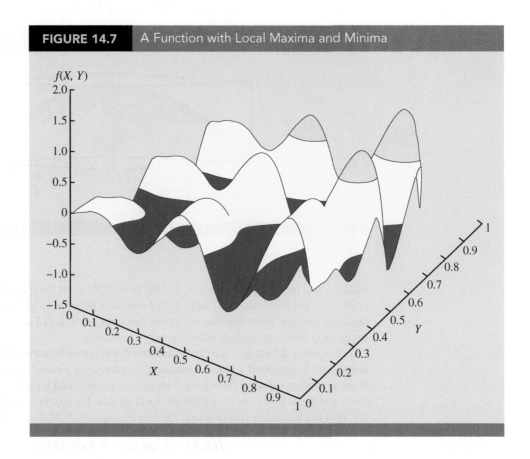

FIGURE 14.7   A Function with Local Maxima and Minima

Overcoming Local Optima with Excel Solver

How do you know when multiple local optima exist? The mathematical ways to determine this are beyond the scope of this text. From a practical point of view, if the solution obtained by optimization software depends on the starting point, then there are multiple local optima. Thus, when using Excel Solver, if the solution returned from Solver is different when starting from different values in the decision variable cells, then there are local optima. The converse is not necessarily true; that is, if the same solution is returned when starting from a different set of starting points, this does not necessarily mean that you have found the global optimal solution.

Let us consider the problem shown in Figure 14.7:

$$\text{Max } f(X, Y) = X \sin(5\pi X) + Y \sin(5\pi Y)$$

$$\text{s.t}$$

$$0 \le X \le 1$$
$$0 \le Y \le 1$$

Table 14.1 shows the results returned from Excel Solver for different starting points (values in the decision variable cells when Solver is invoked). In each of the five cases in Table 14.1, Solver returns with the message, "Solver has converged to the current solution. All constraints are satisfied."

Excel Solver does provide an option that allows you to increase the confidence that you have found a global optimal solution. Clicking **Options** on the **Solver Parameters** dialog box and then selecting the **GRG Nonlinear** tab result in the dialog box shown in Figure 14.8. Clicking the **Use Multistart** option in the **Multistart** section causes Solver to use multiple starting solutions and report the best solution found from all of the

TABLE 14.1	Solutions from Excel Solver for a Problem with Multiple Local Optima			
Starting Point		**Solution Returned**		
X	**Y**	**X**	**Y**	**Objective Function Value**
0.000	0.000	0.129	0.129	0.231
1.000	0.000	0.905	0.000	0.902
0.000	1.000	0.000	0.905	0.902
0.500	0.500	0.508	0.508	1.008
1.000	1.000	0.905	0.905	1.805

If the solution to a problem appears to depend on the starting values for the decision variables, we recommend you use the Multistart option.

starting points. The **Population Size** is the number of starting points used. Solver selects starting points randomly using the **Random Seed** (an integer value) such that the points are within the bounds specified. Although providing simple lower and upper bounds is not required (unless the **Require Bounds on the Variables** option is selected), the procedure is much more effective when bounds are provided. We recommend selecting the **Require Bounds on the Variables** checkbox and providing bounds before you use the Multistart option.

In Figure 14.8, randomly generated starting points will be used and simple bounds of 0 and 1 have been specified as constraints in the Solver dialog box. The result reported by Solver is $X = 0.90447, Y = 0.90447$, with objective function = 1.804. The message provided by Solver is "Solver converged in probability to a global solution."

FIGURE 14.8	The GRG Nonlinear Tab in Solver Options

1. The Multistart option works best with bounds specified on each decision variable. It is often easy to calculate effective upper and lower bounds for the decision variables. For example, if you have a linear less-than-or-equal-to constraint with positive coefficients, upper bounds can be calculated by simply dividing the right-hand side by the coefficient for each variable. Using the cutting and dyeing constraint from the Par, Inc. problem, $\frac{7}{10}S + 1D \leq 630$, we can deduce the following upper bounds: $S \leq 630/(7/10) = 900$ and $D \leq 630/1 = 630$.

2. In addition to GRG Nonlinear, Excel Solver provides another solution method, Evolutionary Solver, to solve nonlinear problems with local optimal solutions. Evolutionary Solver is based on a method that searches for an optimal solution by iteratively adjusting a population of candidate solutions. In this text, we limit our discussion for nonlinear problems to GRG Nonlinear, which is based on more classical optimization techniques. However, Evolutionary Solver may be useful for more complex nonlinear models that involve Excel functions such as VLOOKUP and IF.

14.3 A Location Problem

Let us consider the case of LaRosa Machine Shop (LMS). LMS is studying where to locate its tool bin facility on the shop floor. The locations of the five production stations appear in Figure 14.9. In an attempt to be fair to the workers in each of the production stations, management has decided to try to find the position of the tool bin that would *minimize the sum of the distances* from the tool bin to the five production stations. We define the following decision variables:

$$X = \text{horizontal location of the tool bin}$$
$$Y = \text{vertical location of the tool bin}$$

FIGURE 14.9   Data for the LMS Tool Bin Location Problem

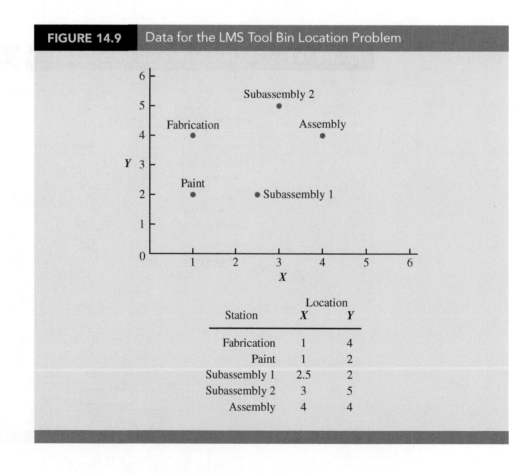

Station	Location X	Y
Fabrication	1	4
Paint	1	2
Subassembly 1	2.5	2
Subassembly 2	3	5
Assembly	4	4

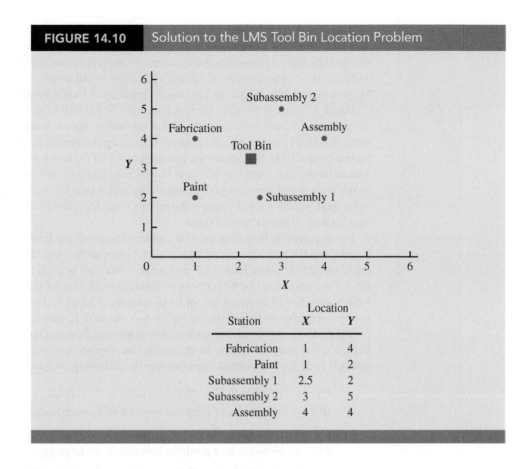

FIGURE 14.10   Solution to the LMS Tool Bin Location Problem

Station	Location X	Y
Fabrication	1	4
Paint	1	2
Subassembly 1	2.5	2
Subassembly 2	3	5
Assembly	4	4

MODEL *file*

LaRosa

We may measure the distance from a station to the tool bin located at (X, Y) by using Euclidean (straight-line) distance. For example, the distance from fabrication located at the coordinates $(1, 4)$ to the tool bin located at the coordinates (X, Y) is given by

$$\sqrt{(X - 1)^2 + (Y - 4)^2}$$

The unconstrained optimization problem is as follows:

$$\text{Min}\ \left(\sqrt{(X - 1)^2 + (Y - 4)^2} + \sqrt{(X - 1)^2 + (Y - 2)^2} + \sqrt{(X - 2.5)^2 + (Y - 2)^2}\right.$$
$$\left. + \sqrt{(X - 3)^2 + (Y - 5)^2} + \sqrt{(X - 4)^2 + (Y - 4)^2}\right)$$

The exercises at the end of this chapter provide practice in creating several different forms of location models.

Note that we do not require that the variables X or Y be nonnegative. The optimal solution found by Excel Solver is $X = 2.230$, $Y = 3.349$. The solution is shown in Figure 14.10.

Location models are used extensively for determining the optimal locations for everything from drilling holes in computer circuit boards to locating distribution centers and retail stores in supply chains. A variety of location models can be created by using different objective functions or by adding additional constraints on distances traveled.

14.4 Markowitz Portfolio Model

Harry Markowitz received the 1990 Nobel Prize for his ground-breaking work in portfolio optimization. The Markowitz mean-variance portfolio model is a classic application of nonlinear programming. In this section, we present the **Markowitz mean-variance portfolio model**. Money management firms throughout the world use numerous variations of this basic model.

A key trade-off in financial planning is that between risk and return. For a chance to earn greater returns, the investor must also accept greater risk. In most portfolio optimization models, the *return* used is the expected (or average) return of the possible outcomes, and the *risk* is some measure of variability in these possible outcomes. To illustrate the Markowitz portfolio model, let us consider the case of Hauck Investment Services.

Hauck Investment Services designs annuities, IRAs, 401(k) plans, and other investment vehicles for investors with a variety of risk tolerances. Hauck would like to develop a portfolio model that can be used to determine an optimal portfolio involving a mix of six mutual funds. Table 14.2 shows the annual return (%) for five 1-year periods for the six mutual funds. Year 1 represents a year in which all mutual funds yield good returns. Year 2 is also a good year for most of the mutual funds. But year 3 is a bad year for the small-cap value fund, year 4 is a bad year for the intermediate-term bond fund, and year 5 is a bad year for four of the six mutual funds.

It is not possible to predict the exact returns for any of the funds over the next 12 months, but the portfolio managers at Hauck Financial Services think that the returns for the five years shown in Table 14.2 are scenarios that can be used to represent the possibilities for the next year. For the purpose of building portfolios for their clients, Hauck's portfolio managers will choose a mix of these six mutual funds and assume that one of the five possible scenarios will describe the return over the next 12 months.

The portfolio construction problem is to determine how much of the portfolio to invest in each investment alternative. To determine the proportion of the portfolio that will be invested in each of the mutual funds we use the following decision variables:

FS = proportion of portfolio invested in the foreign stock mutual fund

IB = proportion of portfolio invested in the intermediate-term bond fund

LG = proportion of portfolio invested in the large-cap growth fund

LV = proportion of portfolio invested in the large-cap value fund

SG = proportion of portfolio invested in the small-cap growth fund

SV = proportion of portfolio invested in the small-cap value fund

Because the sum of these proportions must equal one, we need the following constraint:

$$FS + IB + LG + LV + SG + SV = 1$$

The other constraints are concerned with the return that the portfolio will earn under each of the planning scenarios in Table 14.2.

The portfolio return over the next 12 months depends on which of the possible scenarios (years 1 through 5) in Table 14.2 occurs. Let R_1 denote the portfolio return if the scenario represented by year 1 occurs, R_2 denote the portfolio return if the scenario represented by

TABLE 14.2   Mutual Fund Performances in Five Selected Years (Used as Planning Scenarios for the Next 12 Months)

	Annual Return (%)				
Mutual Fund	**Year 1**	**Year 2**	**Year 3**	**Year 4**	**Year 5**
Foreign Stock	10.06	13.12	13.47	45.42	−21.93
Intermediate-Term Bond	17.64	3.25	7.51	−1.33	7.36
Large-Cap Growth	32.41	18.71	33.28	41.46	−23.26
Large-Cap Value	32.36	20.61	12.93	7.06	−5.37
Small-Cap Growth	33.44	19.40	3.85	58.68	−9.02
Small-Cap Value	24.56	25.32	−6.70	5.43	17.31

year 2 occurs, and so on. The portfolio returns for the five planning years (scenarios) are as follows:

Scenario 1 return:

$$R_1 = 10.06FS + 17.64IB + 32.41LG + 32.36LV + 33.44SG + 24.56SV$$

Scenario 2 return:

$$R_2 = 13.12FS + 3.25IB + 18.71LG + 20.61LV + 19.40SG + 25.32SV$$

Scenario 3 return:

$$R_3 = 13.47FS + 7.51IB + 33.28LG + 12.93LV + 3.85SG - 6.70SV$$

Scenario 4 return:

$$R_4 = 45.42FS - 1.33IB + 41.46LG + 7.06LV + 58.68SG + 5.43SV$$

Scenario 5 return:

$$R_5 = -21.93FS + 7.36IB - 23.26LG - 5.37LV - 9.02SG + 17.31SV$$

If p_s is the probability of scenario s, among n possible scenarios, then the *expected* return for the portfolio is $\overline{R}$, where

$$\overline{R} = \sum_{s=1}^{n} p_s R_s \qquad (14.6)$$

If we assume that the five planning scenarios in the Hauck Financial Services model are equally likely to occur, then

$$\overline{R} = \sum_{s=1}^{5} \tfrac{1}{5} R_s = \tfrac{1}{5} \sum_{s=1}^{5} R_s$$

Other common risk measures in finance include semivariance, value at risk (VaR) and conditional value at risk (CVaR). One of the homework problems at the end of this chapter introduces the concept of semivariance.

Measuring risk is a bit more difficult. Entire books are devoted to the topic of risk measurement. The measure of risk most often associated with the Markowitz portfolio model is the variance of the portfolio's return. If the expected return is defined by equation (14.6), the variance of the portfolio's return is

$$Var = \sum_{s=1}^{n} p_s \left(R_s - \overline{R} \right)^2 \qquad (14.7)$$

For the Hauck Financial Services example, the five planning scenarios are equally likely, thus

$$Var = \sum_{s=1}^{5} \tfrac{1}{5} \left(R_s - \overline{R} \right)^2$$

The portfolio variance is the average of the sum of the squares of the deviations from the mean value under each scenario. The larger this number, the more widely dispersed the scenario returns are about the average value. If the portfolio variance were equal to zero, then every scenario return R_i would be equal, and there would be no risk.

Two basic ways to formulate the Markowitz model are (1) to minimize the variance of the portfolio subject to a constraint on the expected return of the portfolio and (2) to maximize the expected return of the portfolio subject to a constraint on variance. Consider the first case. Assume that Hauck clients would like to construct a portfolio from the six mutual funds listed in Table 14.2 that will minimize their risk as measured by the portfolio variance. However, the clients also require the expected portfolio return to be at least 10%. In our notation, the objective function is

$$\text{Min} \quad \tfrac{1}{5} \sum_{s=1}^{5} \left(R_s - \overline{R} \right)^2$$

The constraint on expected portfolio return is $\overline{R} \geq 10$. The complete Markowitz model involves 12 variables and 8 constraints (excluding the nonnegativity constraints).

$$\text{Min} \, \tfrac{1}{5} \sum_{s=1}^{5} \left(R_s - \overline{R} \right)^2 \qquad (14.8)$$

s.t.

$$10.06FS + 17.64IB + 32.41LG + 32.36LV + 33.44SG + 24.56SV = R_1 \quad \textbf{(14.9)}$$

$$13.12FS + {}+3.25IB + 18.71LG + 20.61LV + 19.40SG + 25.32SV = R_2 \quad \textbf{(14.10)}$$

$$13.47FS + 7.51IB + 33.28LG + 12.93LV + 3.85SG - 6.70SV = R_3 \quad \textbf{(14.11)}$$

$$45.42FS - 1.33IB + 41.46LG + 7.06LV + 58.68SG + 5.43SV = R_4 \quad \textbf{(14.12)}$$

$$-21.93FS + 7.36IB - 23.26LG - 5.37LV - 9.02SG + 17.31SV = R_5 \quad \textbf{(14.13)}$$

$$FS + IB + LG + LV + SG + SV = 1 \quad \textbf{(14.14)}$$

$$\tfrac{1}{5}\sum_{s=1}^{5} R_S = \bar{R} \quad \textbf{(14.15)}$$

$$\bar{R} \geq 10 \quad \textbf{(14.16)}$$

$$FS, IB, LG, LV, SG, SV \geq 0 \quad \textbf{(14.17)}$$

The objective for the Markowitz model is to minimize portfolio variance. Equations (14.9) through (14.13) define the return for each scenario. Equation (14.14) requires all of the money to be invested in the mutual funds; this constraint is often called the *unity constraint*. Equation (14.15) defines $\bar{R}$, which is the expected return of the portfolio. Equation (14.16) requires the portfolio return to be at least 10%. Finally, equation (14.17) requires a nonnegative investment in each Hauck mutual fund. Note that R_1, R_2, R_3, R_4, and R_5, as well as $\bar{R}$, are not required to be nonnegative. It is possible that the return in a given scenario or the expected return of the portfolio is negative.

The solution for this model using a required return of at least 10% appears in Figure 14.11. The minimum value for the portfolio variance is 27.136. This solution implies

FIGURE 14.11   Solution for the Hauck Minimum Variance Portfolio with a Required Return of At Least 10%

that the clients will get an expected return of 10% $\left(\overline{R} \geq 10\right)$ and minimize their risk as measured by portfolio variance by investing approximately 16% of the portfolio in the foreign stock fund $(FS = 0.158)$, 53% in the intermediate bond fund $(IB = 0.525)$, 4% in the large-cap growth fund $(LG = 0.042)$, and 27% in the small-cap value fund $(SV = 0.274)$.

HauckMarkowitz

The **Solver Parameters** dialog box is also shown in Figure 14.11. Note that we have selected **GRG Nonlinear** as the method and we have *not* selected **Make Unconstrained Variables Non-Negative**. Instead we have entered as an explicit constraint set that B17 through B22 must be ≥ 0.

The Markowitz portfolio model provides a convenient way for an investor to trade off risk versus return. In practice, this model is typically solved iteratively for different values of return. Figure 14.12 is a graph of the minimum portfolio variances versus required expected returns as required expected return is varied from 8% to 12% in increments of 1%. In finance, this graph is called the **efficient frontier**. Each point on the efficient frontier is the minimum possible risk (measured by portfolio variance) for the given return. By looking at the graph of the efficient frontier, investors can select the mean-variance combination with which they are most comfortable.

NOTES + COMMENTS

1. Notice that the solution given in Figure 14.11 has more than 50% of the portfolio invested in the intermediate-term bond fund. It may be unwise to allow one asset to contribute so heavily to the portfolio. Upper and lower bounds on the amount of an asset type in the portfolio can be easily modeled. Hence, upper bounds are often placed on the percentage of the portfolio invested in a single asset. Likewise, it might be undesirable to include an extremely small quantity of an asset in the portfolio. Thus, there may be constraints that require nonzero amounts of an asset to be at least a minimum percentage of the portfolio.

2. In the Hauck example, 100% of the available portfolio was invested in mutual funds. However, risk-averse investors often prefer to have some of their money in a so-called risk-free asset, such as U.S. Treasury Bills. Thus, many portfolio

optimization models allow funds to be invested in a risk-free asset.

3. In this section, portfolio variance was used to measure risk. However, variance, as it is defined, counts deviations both above and below the mean. Most investors are happy with returns above the mean but wish to avoid returns below the mean. Hence, numerous portfolio models allow for flexible risk measures. A problem at the end of this chapter illustrates the use of alternative risk measures.

4. In practice, both brokers and mutual fund companies adjust portfolios as new information becomes available. However, constantly adjusting a portfolio may lead to large transaction costs. The case problem at the end of this chapter requires you to develop a modification of the Markowitz portfolio selection problem to account for transaction costs.

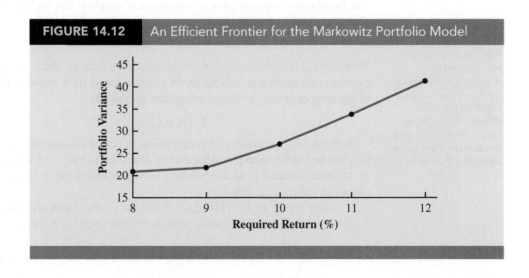

FIGURE 14.12   An Efficient Frontier for the Markowitz Portfolio Model

14.5 Adoption of a New Product: The Bass Forecasting Model

Forecasting new adoptions after a product introduction is an important marketing problem. In this section, we introduce a forecasting model developed by Frank Bass[1] that has proven to be particularly effective in forecasting the adoption of innovative and new technologies in the marketplace. Nonlinear optimization is used to estimate the parameters of the Bass forecasting model. The model has three parameters that must be estimated.

m = the number of people estimated to eventually adopt the new product

A company introducing a new product is obviously interested in the value of parameter m.

q = the coefficient of imitation

Parameter q measures the likelihood of adoption due to a potential adopter being influenced by someone who has already adopted the product. It measures the word-of-mouth or social media effect influencing purchases.

p = the coefficient of innovation

Parameter p measures the likelihood of adoption, assuming no influence from someone who has already purchased (adopted) the product. It is the likelihood of someone adopting the product because of her or his own interest in the innovation.

Using these parameters, let us now develop the forecasting model. Let S_t be the number of new adopters in period t. Let C_{t-1} denote the number of people who have adopted the product through time $t - 1$. That is, C_{t-1} is the cumulative number of adopters through period $t - 1$ ($C_{(t-1)} = \sum_{j=1}^{t-1} s_j$). Because m is the number of people estimated to eventually adopt the product, $m - C_{t-1}$ is the number of potential adopters remaining at time $t - 1$. We refer to the time interval between time $t - 1$ and time t as period t. During period t, some percentage of the remaining number of potential adopters, $m - C_{t-1}$, will adopt the product. This value depends on the likelihood of a new adoption.

Loosely speaking, the likelihood of a new adoption is the likelihood of adoption due to imitation plus the likelihood of adoption due to innovation. The likelihood of adoption due to imitation is a function of the number of people who have already adopted the product. The larger the current pool of adopters, the greater their influence through word of mouth. Because C_{t-1}/m is the fraction of the number of people estimated to adopt the product by time $t - 1$, the likelihood of adoption due to imitation is computed by multiplying this fraction by q, the coefficient of imitation. Thus, the likelihood of adoption due to imitation is

$$q(C_{t-1}/m)$$

The likelihood of adoption due to innovation is simply p, the coefficient of innovation. Thus, the likelihood of adoption is

$$p + q(C_{t-1}/m)$$

The Bass forecasting model given in equation (14.18) can be rigorously derived from statistical principles. Rather than providing such a derivation, we have emphasized the intuitive aspects of the model.

Using the likelihood of adoption we can develop a forecast of the remaining number of potential customers who will adopt the product during time period t. Thus, F_t, the forecast of the number of new adopters during time period t, is

$$F_t = (p + q[C_{t-1}/m])(m - C_{t-1}) \tag{14.18}$$

In developing a forecast of new adoptions in period t using the Bass model, the value of C_{t-1} will be known from past data. But we also need to know the values of the parameters to use in the model. Let us now see how nonlinear optimization is used to estimate the parameter values m, p, and q.

Consider Figure 14.13. This figure shows the graph of box office revenues (in $ millions) for two different films, an independent studio film and a summer blockbuster

---

[1]See Fra M. Bass, "A New Product Growth Model for Consumer Durables," *Management Science* 15 (1969).

FIGURE 14.13   Weekly Box Office Revenues for an Independent Studio Film and a Summer Blockbuster Movie

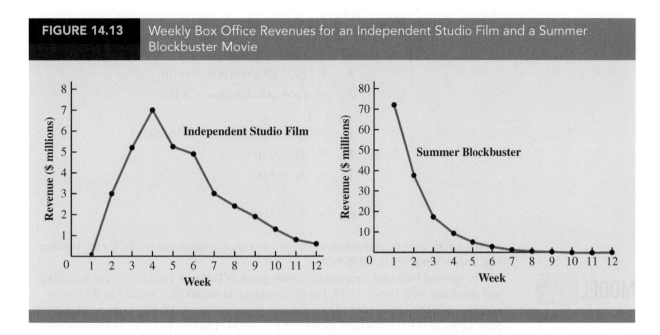

action movie, over the first 12 weeks after release. Strictly speaking, box office revenues for time period t are not the same as the number of adopters during time period t. However, the number of repeat customers is usually small, and box office revenues are a multiple of the number of moviegoers (adopters). The Bass forecasting model seems appropriate here.

These two films illustrate drastically different adoption patterns. Note that revenues for the independent studio film grow until the revenues peak in week 4 and then decline. For this film, much of the revenue is obviously due to word-of-mouth influence. In terms of the Bass model, the imitation factor dominates the innovation factor, and we expect $q > p$. However, for the summer blockbuster, revenues peak in week 1 and drop sharply afterward. The innovation factor dominates the imitation factor, and we expect $q < p$.

The forecasting model given in equation (14.18) can be incorporated into a nonlinear optimization problem to find the values of p, q, and m that give the best forecasts for a set of data. Assume that N periods of data are available. Let us denote the actual number of adopters (or a multiple of that number, such as sales) in period t as S_t for $t = 1, \ldots, N$. Then the forecast in each period and the corresponding forecast error E_t are defined by

$$F_t = \big(p + q[C_{t-1}/m]\big)(m - C_{t-1}) \text{ and } E_t = F_t - S_t$$

Notice that the forecast error is the difference between the forecast value F_t and the actual value S_t. It is common statistical practice to estimate the parameters p, q, and m by minimizing the sum of squared errors.

Doing so for the Bass forecasting model leads to the following nonlinear optimization problem:

$$\text{Min} \sum_{t=1}^{N} E_t^2 \tag{14.19}$$

s.t.

$$F_t = (p + q[C_{t-1}/m])(m - C_{t-1}) \qquad t = 1, 2, \ldots, N \tag{14.20}$$

$$E_t = F_t - S_t \qquad t = 1, 2, \ldots, N \tag{14.21}$$

Because equations (14.19) and (14.20) both contain nonlinear terms, this model is a nonlinear minimization problem.

Note that the parameters of the Bass forecasting model are the decision variables in this nonlinear optimization model.

The data in Table 14.3 provide the revenue and cumulative revenues for the independent studio film in weeks 1–12. Using these data, the nonlinear model to estimate the parameters of the Bass forecasting model for the independent studio film is as follows:

$$\text{Min} \quad E_1^2 + E_2^2 + \cdots + E_{12}^2$$

$$
\begin{aligned}
\text{s.t.} \quad F_1 &= (p)m \\
F_2 &= [p + q(0.10/m)](m - 0.10) \\
F_3 &= [p + q(3.10/m)](m - 3.10) \\
&\vdots \\
F_{12} &= [p + q(34.85/m)](m - 34.85) \\
E_1 &= F_1 - 0.10 \\
E_2 &= F_2 - 3.00 \\
&\vdots \\
E_{12} &= F_{12} - 0.60
\end{aligned}
$$

The solutions to this nonlinear model and to a similar nonlinear model for the summer blockbuster are given in Table 14.4.

Bass

The optimal forecasting parameter values given in Table 14.4 are intuitively appealing and consistent with Figure 14.13. For the independent studio film, which has the largest revenues in week 4, the value of the imitation parameter q is 0.49; this value is substantially larger than the innovation parameter $p = 0.074$. The film picks up momentum over time because of favorable word of mouth. After week 4, revenues decline as more and more of the potential market for the film has already seen it. Contrast these data with the summer blockbuster movie, which has a negative value of -0.018 for the imitation parameter q and an innovation parameter p of 0.49. The greatest number of adoptions is in week 1, and new adoptions decline afterward. Obviously the word-of-mouth influence is not favorable.

TABLE 14.3	Box Office Revenues and Cumulative Revenues in $ Millions for Independent Studio Film	
Week	**Revenues S_t**	**Cumulative Revenues C_t**
1	0.10	0.10
2	3.00	3.10
3	5.20	8.30
4	7.00	15.30
5	5.25	20.55
6	4.90	25.45
7	3.00	28.45
8	2.40	30.85
9	1.90	32.75
10	1.30	34.05
11	0.80	34.85
12	0.60	35.45

TABLE 14.4	Optimal Forecast Parameters for Independent Studio Film and Summer Blockbuster Movie	
Parameter	**Independent Studio Film**	**Summer Blockbuster**
p	0.074	0.460
q	0.490	−0.018
m	34.850	149.540

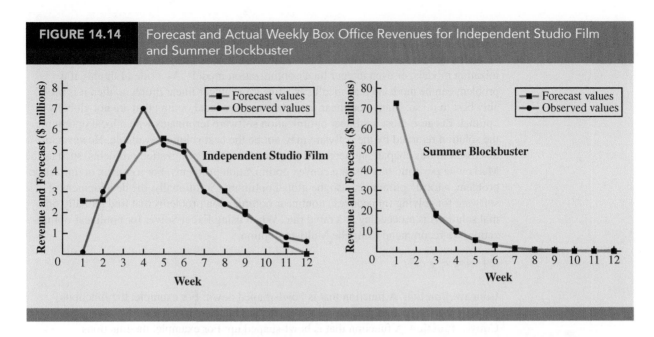

FIGURE 14.14 Forecast and Actual Weekly Box Office Revenues for Independent Studio Film and Summer Blockbuster

In Figure 14.14, we show the forecast values based on the parameters in Table 14.4 and the observed values in the same graph. The Bass forecasting model does a good job of tracking revenue for the independent small-studio film. For the summer blockbuster, the Bass model does an outstanding job; it is virtually impossible to distinguish the forecast line from the actual adoption line.

You may wonder what good a forecasting model is if we must wait until after the adoption cycle is complete to estimate the parameters. One way to use the Bass forecasting model for a new product is to assume that sales of the new product will behave in a way that is similar to a previous product for which p and q values have been calculated and to subjectively estimate m, the potential market for the new product. For example, one might assume that box office receipts for movies next summer will behave similarly to box office receipts for movies last summer. Then the p and q values used for next summer's movies would be the p and q values calculated from the actual box office receipts last summer.

A second approach is to wait until several periods of data for the new product are available. For example, if five periods of data are available, the sales data for these five periods could be used to forecast demand for period 6. Then, after six periods of sales are observed, a forecast for period 7 is made. This method is often called a *rolling-horizon* approach.

NOTES + COMMENTS

The optimization model used to determine the parameter values for the Bass forecasting model is an example of a difficult nonlinear optimization problem. It is neither convex nor concave. For such models, local optima may give values that are much worse than the global optimum. We recommend using the Multistart option in Excel Solver when solving such problems.

SUMMARY

In this chapter we introduced nonlinear optimization models. A nonlinear optimization model is a model with at least one nonlinear term in either a constraint or the objective function. Because so many applications of business analytics involve nonlinear functions, allowing nonlinear terms greatly increases the number of important applications that can be modeled as an optimization problem. Numerous problems in portfolio optimization, option pricing, marketing, economics, facility location, forecasting, and scheduling lend themselves to nonlinear models.

   Unfortunately, nonlinear optimization models are not as easy to solve as linear optimization models, or even integer linear optimization models. As a rule of thumb, if a problem can be modeled realistically as a linear or integer linear problem, then it is probably best to do so. Many nonlinear formulations have local optima that are not globally optimal. Because most nonlinear optimization software terminates with a local optimum, the solution returned by the software may not be the best solution available. However, as discussed in this chapter, numerous important classes of optimization problems, such as the Markowitz portfolio models, are convex optimization problems. For a convex optimization problem, a local optimum is also the global optimum. Additionally, the development of software for solving (nonconvex) nonlinear optimization problems that find globally optimal solutions is proceeding at a rapid rate. When using Excel Solver for nonlinear optimization, we recommend using the Multistart option.

GLOSSARY

Concave function A function that is bowl-shaped down: For example, the functions $f(x) = -5x^2 - 5x$ and $f(x, y) = -x^2 - 11y^2$ are concave functions.

Convex function A function that is bowl-shaped up: For example, the functions $f(x) = x^2 - 5x$ and $f(x, y) = x^2 + 5y^2$ are convex functions.

Efficient frontier A set of points defining the minimum possible risk (measured by portfolio variance) for a set of return values.

Global maximum A feasible solution is a global maximum if there are no other feasible points with a larger objective function value in the entire feasible region. A global maximum is also a local maximum.

Global minimum A feasible solution is a global minimum if there are no other feasible points with a smaller objective function value in the entire feasible region. A global minimum is also a local minimum.

Global optimum A feasible solution is a global optimum if there are no other feasible points with a better objective function value in the entire feasible region. A global optimum may be either a global maximum or a global minimum.

Lagrangian multiplier The shadow price for a constraint in a nonlinear problem, that is, the rate of change of the objective function with respect to the right-hand side of a constraint.

Local maximum A feasible solution is a local maximum if there are no other feasible solutions with a larger objective function value in the immediate neighborhood.

Local minimum A feasible solution is a local minimum if there are no other feasible solutions with a smaller objective function value in the immediate neighborhood.

Local optimum A feasible solution is a local optimum if there are no other feasible solutions with a better objective function value in the immediate neighborhood. A local optimum may be either a local maximum or a local minimum.

Markowitz mean-variance portfolio model An optimization model used to construct a portfolio that minimizes risk subject to a constraint requiring a minimum level of return.

Nonlinear optimization problem An optimization problem that contains at least one nonlinear term in the objective function or a constraint.

Quadratic function A nonlinear function with terms to the power of two.

Reduced gradient The value associated with a variable in a nonlinear model that is analogous to the reduced cost in a linear model; the shadow price of a binding simple lower or upper bound on the decision variable.

PROBLEMS

1. **Media Planning.** GreenLawns provides a lawn fertilizing and weed control service. The company is adding a special aeration treatment as a low-cost extra service option that it hopes will help attract new customers. Management is planning to promote this

new service in two media: radio and direct-mail advertising. A media budget of $3,000 is available for this promotional campaign. Based on past experience in promoting its other services, GreenLawns has obtained the following estimate of the relationship between sales and the amount spent on promotion in these two media:

$$S = -2R^2 - 10M^2 - 8RM + 18R + 34M$$

where

S = total sales in thousands of dollars

R = thousands of dollars spent on radio advertising

M = thousands of dollars spent on direct-mail advertising

GreenLawns would like to develop a promotional strategy that will lead to maximum sales subject to the restriction provided by the media budget.

a. What is the value of sales if $2,000 is spent on radio advertising and $1,000 is spent on direct-mail advertising?

b. Formulate an optimization problem that can be solved to maximize sales subject to the media budget of spending no more than $3,000 on total advertising.

c. Determine the optimal amount to spend on radio and direct-mail advertising. How much in sales will be generated?

2. **Estimating Economic Output.** The Cobb-Douglas production function is a classic model from economics used to model output as a function of capital and labor. It has the form

$$f(L,C) = c_0 L^{c_1} C^{c_2}$$

where c_0, c_1, and c_2 are constants. The variable L represents the units of input of labor, and the variable C represents the units of input of capital.

a. In this example, assume $c_0 = 5$, $c_1 = 0.25$, and $c_2 = 0.75$. Assume each unit of labor costs $25 and each unit of capital costs $75. With $75,000 available in the budget, develop an optimization model to determine how the budgeted amount should be allocated between capital and labor in order to maximize output.

b. Find the optimal solution to the model you formulated in part (a). (*Hint:* When using Excel Solver, use the Multistart option with bounds $0 \leq L \leq 3,000$ and $0 \leq C \leq 1,000$.)

3. **Steel Production Planning.** Let S represent the amount of steel produced (in tons). Steel production is related to the amount of labor used (L) and the amount of capital used (C) by the following function:

$$S = 20 \, L^{0.30} C^{0.70}$$

In this formula L represents the units of labor input and C the units of capital input. Each unit of labor costs $50, and each unit of capital costs $100.

a. Formulate an optimization problem that will determine how much labor and capital are needed to produce 50,000 tons of steel at minimum cost.

b. Solve the optimization problem you formulated in part (a). (*Hint:* When using Excel Solver, start with an initial $L > 0$ and $C > 0$.)

4. **Production Planning.** The profit function for two products is

$$\text{Profit} = -3x_1^2 + 42x_1 - 3x_2^2 + 48x_2 + 700$$

where x_1 represents units of production of product 1 and x_2 represents units of production of product 2. Producing one unit of product 1 requires 4 labor-hours and producing one unit of product 2 requires 6 labor-hours. Currently, 24 labor-hours are available. The cost of labor-hours is already factored into the profit function, but it is possible to schedule overtime at a premium of $5 per hour.

a. Formulate an optimization problem that can be used to find the optimal production quantity of products 1 and 2 and the optimal number of overtime hours to schedule.

b. Solve the optimization model you formulated in part (a). How much should be produced and how many overtime hours should be scheduled?

5. **Pricing Cameras.** Jim's Camera shop sells two high-end cameras, the Sky Eagle and Horizon. The demands for these two cameras are as follows: D_S = demand for the Sky Eagle, P_S is the selling price of the Sky Eagle, D_H is the demand for the Horizon, and P_H is the selling price of the Horizon.

$$D_S = 222 - 0.60P_S + 0.35P_H$$
$$D_H = 270 + 0.10P_S - 0.64P_H$$

The store wishes to determine the selling price that maximizes revenue for these two products. Develop the revenue function for these two models, and find the prices that maximize revenue.

6. **Baseball Glove Production Planning.** Heller Manufacturing has two production facilities that manufacture baseball gloves. Production costs at the two facilities differ because of varying labor rates, local property taxes, type of equipment, capacity, and so on. The Dayton plant has weekly costs that can be expressed as a function of the number of gloves produced:

$$TCD(X) = X^2 - X + 5$$

where X is the weekly production volume in thousands of units, and $TCD(X)$ is the cost in thousands of dollars. The Hamilton plant's weekly production costs are given by

$$TCH(Y) = Y^2 - 2Y + 3$$

where Y is the weekly production volume in thousands of units, and $TCH(Y)$ is the cost in thousands of dollars. Heller Manufacturing would like to produce 8,000 gloves per week at the lowest possible cost.

a. Formulate a mathematical model that can be used to determine the optimal number of gloves to produce each week at each facility.

b. Solve the optimization model to determine the optimal number of gloves to produce at each facility.

The exponential smoothing model is described in more detail in Chapter 8.

7. **Exponential Smoothing.** Many forecasting models use parameters that are estimated using nonlinear optimization. A good example is the Bass model introduced in this chapter. Another example is the exponential smoothing forecasting model which is a common forecasting model used in practice. For instance, the basic exponential smoothing model for forecasting sales is

$$\hat{y}_{t+1} = \alpha y_t + (1 - \alpha)\hat{y}_t$$

where

$$\hat{y}_{t+1} = \text{forecast of sales for period } t + 1$$
$$y_t = \text{actual sales for period } t$$
$$\hat{y}_t = \text{forecast of sales for period } t$$
$$\alpha = \text{smoothing constant, } 0 \le \alpha \le 1$$

This model is used recursively; the forecast for time period $t + 1$ is based on the forecast for period t, $\hat{y}_t$, the observed value of sales in period t, y_t, and the smoothing parameter α. The use of this model to forecast sales for 12 months is illustrated in the following table with the smoothing constant $\alpha = 0.3$. The forecast errors, $y_t - \hat{y}_t$, are calculated in the fourth column. The value of a is often chosen by minimizing the sum of squared forecast errors. The last column of the table shows the square of the forecast error and the sum of squared forecast errors.

In using exponential smoothing models, one tries to choose the value of α that provides the best forecasts.

DATA *file*
ExpSmooth

a. The file *ExpSmooth* contains the observed data shown here. Construct this table using the formula above. Note that we set the forecast in period 1 to the observed in period 1 to get started $(\hat{y}_1 = y_1 = 17)$, then the formula above for $\hat{y}_{t+1}$ is used starting in period 2. Make sure to have a single cell corresponding to α in your spreadsheet model. After confirming the values in the table below with $\alpha = 0.3$, try different values of α to see if you can get a smaller sum of squared forecast errors.

Week (t)	Observed Value (y_t)	Forecast ($\hat{y}_t$)	Forecast Error ($y_t - \hat{y}_t$)	Squared Forecast Error ($y_t - \hat{y}_t)^2$
1	17	17.00	0.00	0.00
2	21	17.00	4.00	16.00
3	19	18.20	0.80	0.64
4	23	18.44	4.56	20.79
5	18	19.81	−1.81	3.27
6	16	19.27	−3.27	10.66
7	20	18.29	1.71	2.94
8	18	18.80	−0.80	0.64
9	22	18.56	3.44	11.83
10	20	19.59	0.41	0.17
11	15	19.71	−4.71	22.23
12	22	18.30	3.70	13.69
				SUM = 102.86

   b. Use Excel Solver to find the value of α that minimizes the sum of squared forecast errors.

8. **Chair Manufacturing.** Andalus Furniture Company has two manufacturing plants, one at Aynor and another at Spartanburg. The cost in dollars of producing a kitchen chair at each of the two plants is given here. The cost of producing Q_1 chairs at Aynor is

$$75Q_1 + 5Q_1^2 + 100$$

and the cost of producing Q_2 kitchen chairs at Spartanburg is

$$25Q_2 + 2.5Q_2^2 + 150$$

Andalus needs to manufacture a total of 40 kitchen chairs to meet an order just received. How many chairs should be made at Aynor, and how many should be made at Spartanburg in order to minimize total production cost?

9. **Economic Order Quantity.** The economic order quantity (EOQ) model is a classical model used for controlling inventory and satisfying demand. Costs included in the model are holding cost per unit, ordering cost, and the cost of goods ordered. The assumptions for that model are that only a single item is considered, that the entire quantity ordered arrives at one time, that the demand for the item is constant over time, and that no shortages are allowed.

   Suppose we relax the first assumption and allow for multiple items that are independent except for a restriction on the amount of space available to store the products. The following model describes this situation:

Let

$\quad\quad D_j$ = annual demand for item j
$\quad\quad C_j$ = unit cost of item j
$\quad\quad S_j$ = cost per order placed for item j
$\quad\quad w_j$ = space required for item j
$\quad\quad W$ = the maximum amount of space available for all goods
$\quad\quad i$ = inventory carrying charge as a percentage of the cost per unit

The decision variables are Q_j, the amount of item j to order. The model is

$$\text{Minimize} \sum_{j=1}^{N} \left[C_j D_j + \frac{S_j D_j}{Q_j} + iC_j \frac{Q_j}{2} \right]$$

$$\text{s.t} \quad \sum_{j=1}^{N} w_j Q_j \leq W$$

$$Q_j \geq 0 \quad j = 1, 2, \ldots, N$$

In the objective function, the first term is the annual cost of goods, the second is the annual ordering cost (D_j/Q_j is the number of orders), and the last term is the annual inventory holding cost ($Q_i/2$ is the average amount of inventory).

Construct and solve a nonlinear optimization model for the following data:

	Item 1	Item 2	Item 3
Annual Demand	2,000	2,000	1,000
Item Cost ($)	100	50	80
Order Cost ($)	150	135	125
Space Required (sq. feet)	50	25	40
W = 5000			
i = 0.20			

10. **Product Pricing.** Phillips Inc. produces two distinct products, A and B. The products do not compete with each other in the marketplace; that is, neither cost, price, nor demand for one product will impact the demand for the other. Phillips' analysts have collected data on the effects of advertising on profits. These data suggest that, although higher advertising correlates with higher profits, the marginal increase in profits diminishes at higher advertising levels, particularly for product B. Analysts have estimated the following functions:

$$\text{Annual profit for product A} = 1.2712 LN(X_A) + 17.414$$

$$\text{Annual profit for product B} = 0.3970 LN(X_B) + 16.109$$

where X_A and X_B are the advertising amount allocated to products A and B, respectively, in thousands of dollars, profit is in millions of dollars, and LN is the natural logarithm function. The advertising budget is $500,000, and management has dictated that at least $50,000 must be allocated to each of the two products.

(*Hint:* To compute a natural logarithm for the value X in Excel, use the formula $=LN(X)$. For Solver to find an answer, you also need to start with decision variable values greater than 0 in this problem.)

a. Build an optimization model that will prescribe how Phillips should allocate its marketing budget to maximize profit.

b. Solve the model you constructed in part (a) using Excel Solver.

11. **Tool Bin Location.** Let us consider again the data from the LaRosa tool bin location problem discussed in Section 14.3.

a. Suppose we know the average number of daily trips made to the tool bin from each production station. The average number of trips per day are 12 for fabrication, 24 for Paint, 13 for Subassembly 1, 7 for Subassembly 2, and 17 for Assembly. It seems as though we would want the tool bin closer to those stations with high average numbers of trips. Develop a new unconstrained model that minimizes the sum of the *demand-weighted distance* defined as the product of the demand (measured in number of trips) and the distance to the station.

b. Solve the model you developed in part (a). Comment on the differences between the unweighted distance solution given in Section 14.3 and the demand-weighted solution.

12. **Cell Tower Location.** TN Communications provides cellular telephone services. The company is planning to expand into the Cincinnati area and is trying to determine the best location for its transmission tower. The tower transmits over a radius of 10 miles. The locations that must be reached by this tower are shown in the following figure.

DATA*file*

LaRosaDemand

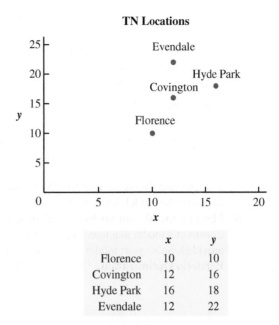

TN Locations

	x	y
Florence	10	10
Covington	12	16
Hyde Park	16	18
Evendale	12	22

TN Communications would like to find the tower location that reaches each of these cities and minimizes the sum of the distances to all locations from the new tower.

a. Formulate and solve a model to find the optimal location.

b. Formulate and solve a model that minimizes the maximum distance from the transmission tower location to the city locations.

13. **Wedding Planning.** The distance between two cities in the United States can be approximated by the following formula, where lat_1 and $long_2$ are the latitude and longitude of city 1 and lat_2 and $long_2$ are the latitude and longitude of city 2:

$$69\sqrt{(lat_1 - lat_2)^2 + (long_1 - long_2)^2}$$

Wedding

Ted's daughter is getting married, and he is inviting relatives from 15 different locations in the United States. The file *Wedding* gives the longitude, latitude, and number of relatives in each of the 15 locations. Ted would like to find a wedding location that minimizes the demand-weighted distance, where demand is the number of relatives at each location. Assuming that the wedding can occur anywhere, find the latitude and longitude of the optimal location. (*Hint:* Notice that all longitude values given for this problem are negative. Make sure that you do *not* check the option for **Make Unconstrained Variables Non-Negative** in Solver.)

14. **Markowitz Portfolio Model.** Consider the stock return scenarios for Apple Computer (APPL), Advanced Micro Devices (AMD), and Oracle Corporation (ORCL) shown in the following table:

StockReturn1

	1	2	3	4	5	6	7	8
APPL	−39.80	10.10	124.90	151.80	−58.30	14.30	−41.90	57.10
AMD	−42.50	13.60	56.90	36.70	−34.80	−67.40	183.60	6.30
ORCL	−10.20	137.90	170.60	16.60	−40.70	−30.30	15.20	−0.60

a. Develop the Markowitz portfolio model for these data with a required expected return of 25%. Assume that the eight scenarios are equally likely to occur.

b. Solve the model developed in part (a).

c. Vary the required return in 1% increments from 25% to 30% and plot the efficient frontier.

15. **Alternative Markowitz Portfolio Model.** A second version of the Markowitz portfolio model maximizes expected return subject to a constraint that the variance of the portfolio must be less than or equal to some specified amount. Consider again the Hauck Financial Service data given in Section 14.4.

DATA *file*

HauckData

	Annual Return (%)				
Mutual Fund	**Year 1**	**Year 2**	**Year 3**	**Year 4**	**Year 5**
Foreign Stock	10.06	13.12	13.47	45.42	−21.93
Intermediate-Term Bond	17.64	3.25	7.51	−1.33	7.36
Large-Cap Growth	32.41	18.71	33.28	41.46	−23.26
Large-Cap Value	32.36	20.61	12.93	7.06	−5.37
Small-Cap Growth	33.44	19.40	3.85	58.68	−9.02
Small-Cap Value	24.56	25.32	−6.70	5.43	17.31

    a. Construct this version of the Markowitz model for a maximum variance of 30.
    b. Solve the model developed in part (a).

16. **Maximizing Minimum Return of Investment.** Reconsider the data in Problem 15. Construct a model that maximizes the minimum return achieved over the five scenarios provided. Solve your model to find the optimal portfolio.

17. **Portfolio Optimization.** Consider the following stock return data:

DATA *file*

StockReturn2

	1	2	3	4	5	6
Stock 1	0.300	0.103	0.216	−0.046	−0.071	0.056
Stock 2	0.225	0.290	0.216	−0.272	0.144	0.107
Stock 3	0.149	0.260	0.419	−0.078	0.169	−0.035
	7	8	9	10	11	12
Stock 1	0.038	0.089	0.090	0.083	0.035	0.176
Stock 2	0.321	0.305	0.195	0.390	−0.072	0.715
Stock 3	0.133	0.732	0.021	0.131	0.006	0.908

    a. Construct the Markowitz portfolio model using a required expected return of 15%. Assume that the 12 scenarios are equally likely to occur.
    b. Solve the model using Excel Solver.
    c. Solve the model for various values of required expected return and plot the efficient frontier.

18. **Matching the S&P 500 Return.** Let us consider again the investment data from Hauck Financial Services used in Section 14.4 to illustrate the Markowitz portfolio model. The data are shown below, along with the return of the S&P 500 Index. Hauck would like to create a portfolio using the funds listed, so that the resulting portfolio matches the return of the S&P 500 index as closely as possible.

DATA *file*

Hauck500

Mutual Fund	**Year 1**	**Year 2**	**Year 3**	**Year 4**	**Year 5**
Foreign Stock	10.060	13.120	13.470	45.420	−21.930
Intermediate-Term Bond	17.640	3.250	7.510	−1.330	7.360
Large-Cap Growth	32.410	18.710	33.280	41.460	−23.260
Large-Cap Value	32.360	20.610	12.930	7.060	−5.370
Small-Cap Growth	33.440	19.400	3.850	58.680	−9.020
Small-Cap Value	24.560	25.320	−6.700	5.430	17.310
S&P 500 Return	25.000	20.000	8.000	30.000	−10.000

    a. Develop an optimization model that will give the fraction of the portfolio to invest in each of the funds so that the return of the resulting portfolio matches as closely as possible the return of the S&P 500 Index. (*Hint:* Minimize the sum of the squared deviations between the portfolio's return and the S&P 500 Index return for each year in the data set.)
    b. Solve the model developed in part (a).

19. **Semivariance as a Measure of Risk.** As discussed in Section 14.4, the Markowitz model uses the variance of the portfolio as the measure of risk. However, variance includes deviations both below and above the mean return. Semivariance includes only deviations below the mean and is considered by many to be a better measure of risk.

    a. Develop a model that minimizes semivariance for the Hauck Financial data given in the file *HauckData* with a required return of 10%. (*Hint:* Modify model (14.8)–(14.17). Define a variable d_s for each scenario and let $d_s \geq \bar{R} - R_s$ with $d_s \geq 0$. Then make the objective function: Min $\frac{1}{5} \sum_{s=1}^{5} d_s^2$.)

    b. Solve the model you developed in part (a) with a required expected return of 10%.

20. **Constructing an Efficient Frontier.** Refer to Problem 15. Use the model developed there to construct an efficient frontier by varying the maximum allowable variance from 20 to 60 in increments of 5 and solving for the maximum return for each. Plot the efficient frontier and compare it to Figure 14.12.

21. **Box Office Revenues.** The weekly box office revenues (in $ millions) for the summer blockbuster movie discussed in Section 14.5 follow. Use these data in the Bass forecasting model given by equations (14.19)–(14.21) to estimate the parameters p, q, and m.

Week	Revenues
1	72.39
2	37.93
3	17.58
4	9.57
5	5.39
6	3.13
7	1.62
8	0.87
9	0.61
10	0.26
11	0.19
12	0.35

The Bass forecasting model is a good example of a difficult-to-solve nonlinear program, and the answer you get may be a local optimum that is not nearly as good as the result given in Table 14.4. Solve the model using Excel Solver with the Multistart option, and see whether you can duplicate the results in Table 14.4. Use a lower bound of -1 and an upper bound of 1 on both p and q. Use a lower bound of 100 and an upper bound of 1,000 on m.

22. **Apparel Pricing.** A women's clothing retail chain has collected data on pricing and sales over the last five years at its flagship store in Charleston, SC. These data were used to estimate a regression equation that relates price to demand. The following estimated equation relates demand to the price for summer dresses:

$$Y = 1,000 - 1.89p$$

where $Y = $ the demand for summer dresses and $p = $ the price per dress.
Summer dresses cost $210. The data also show that when a summer dress is sold, on average one pair of shoes and one purse are sold with the dress. The profit on a pair of shoes is $18 and the profit on a purse is $26.

    a. What is the profit-maximizing price for dresses, ignoring the profit associated with the accompanying shoe and purse?

    b. What is the profit-maximizing price for dresses taking into account the accompanying shoe and purse purchases?

    c. Discuss the difference in prices obtained in parts (a) and (b).

23. **Constructing a Stock Portfolio.** The file *StockPrices* contains 17 observations of beginning-of-year stock prices for each of nine stocks (each in its own worksheet). The stocks are Amazon, American Express, Cracker Barrel, Disney, Exxon Mobile, JP Morgan Chase, Nike, Procter & Gamble, and Oracle.

StockPrices.xlsx

Each worksheet for the nine stocks has 17 observations including Date, Opening Price, High Price for that Day, Low Price for that Day, Closing Price for the Day, Volume Traded for the Day (number of shares traded), and Adjusted Closing Price for the Day. The adjusted closing price factors in dividends paid and stock splits.

a. Using the adjusted closing price calculate the annual returns for each of the nine stocks using the simple calculation: $(P_t - P_{t-1})/P_{t-1}$.

b. Build and solve the Markowitz model that minimizes risk as measured by variance for an expected return of 15% using each year as a scenario. Give the variance and expected return for the optimal portfolio.

c. Construct a bar chart that shows the percentage of the portfolio for each of the stocks included in the portfolio.

d. How does the optimal portfolio compare to a portfolio containing 1/9 of each of the nine stocks?

24. **Population Center of Gravity.** The file *USCities* contains the city, state, population, longitude, and latitude of 100 cities in the United States. Suppose you wish to locate a single distribution center that efficiently serves the population of these major cities. A quick estimate of a good location would be to find the center of gravity of these cities with regard to population. We can obtain the center of gravity by minimizing the weighted distance squared, where the weight for each city is its population.

USCities

Use the distance formula given in Problem 13 as a measure of distance. Minimize the sum the weighted squared distances to find the longitude and latitude of the center of gravity of these 100 cities. (*Note:* Since latitude and longitude can be negative, do not assume the decision variables will be nonnegative.)

CASE PROBLEM: PORTFOLIO OPTIMIZATION WITH TRANSACTION COSTS

Hauck Financial Services has a number of passive, buy-and-hold clients. For these clients, Hauck offers an investment account whereby clients agree to put their money into a portfolio of mutual funds that is rebalanced once a year. When the rebalancing occurs, Hauck determines the mix of mutual funds in each investor's portfolio by solving an extension of the Markowitz portfolio model that incorporates transaction costs. Investors are charged a small transaction cost for the annual rebalancing of their portfolio. For simplicity, assume the following:

- At the beginning of the time period (in this case one year), the portfolio is rebalanced by buying and selling Hauck mutual funds.

- The transaction costs associated with buying and selling mutual funds are paid at the beginning of the period when the portfolio is rebalanced, which, in effect, reduces the amount of money available to reinvest.

- No further transactions are made until the end of the time period, at which point the new value of the portfolio is observed.

- The transaction cost is a linear function of the dollar amount of mutual funds bought or sold.

Jean Delgado is one of Hauck's buy-and-hold clients. We briefly describe the model as it is used by Hauck for rebalancing her portfolio. The mix of mutual funds that are being considered for her portfolio are a foreign stock fund (*FS*), an intermediate-term bond fund (*IB*), a large-cap growth fund (*LG*), a large-cap value fund (*LV*), a small-cap growth fund (*SG*), and a small-cap value fund (*SV*). In the traditional Markowitz model, the variables are usually interpreted as the proportion of the portfolio invested in the asset represented by the variable. For example, *FS* is the proportion of the portfolio invested in the foreign stock fund.

However, it is equally correct to interpret *FS* as the dollar amount invested in the foreign stock fund. Then $FS = 25,000$ implies that \$25,000 is invested in the foreign stock fund. Based on these assumptions, the initial portfolio value must equal the amount of money spent on transaction costs plus the amount invested in all the assets after rebalancing; that is,

Initial portfolio value = amount invested in all assets after rebalancing + transaction costs

The extension of the Markowitz model that Hauck uses for rebalancing portfolios requires a balance constraint for each mutual fund. This balance constraint is

Amount invested in fund *i* = initial holding of fund *i* +

amount of fund *i* purchased − amount of fund *i* sold

Using this balance constraint requires three additional variables for each fund: one for the amount invested prior to rebalancing, one for the amount sold, and one for the amount purchased. For instance, the balance constraint for the foreign stock fund is

$$FS = FS\_START + FS\_BUY - FS\_SELL$$

Jean Delgado has \$100,000 in her account prior to the annual rebalancing, and she has specified a minimum acceptable return of 10%. Hauck plans to use the following model to rebalance Ms. Delgado's portfolio. The complete model with transaction costs is

$$\text{Min } \frac{1}{5} \sum_{s=1}^{5} (R_s - \bar{R})^2$$

s.t.

$$0.1006FS + 0.1764IB + 0.3241LG + 0.3236LV + 0.3344SG + 0.2456SV = R_1$$
$$0.1312FS + 3.2500IB + 0.1871LG + 0.2061LV + 0.1940SG + 0.2532SV = R_2$$
$$0.1347FS + 0.0751IB + 0.3328LG + 0.1293LV + 0.3850SG - 0.0670SV = R_3$$
$$0.4542FS - 0.0133IB + 0.4146LG + 0.0706LV + 0.5868SG + 0.0543SV = R_4$$
$$-0.2193FS + 0.0736IB - 0.2326LG - 0.0537LV - 0.0902SG + 0.1731SV = R_5$$

$$\frac{1}{5} \sum_{s=1}^{5} R_s = \bar{R}$$

$$\bar{R} \geq 10,000$$

$$FS + IB + LG + LV + SG + SV + TRANS\_COST = 100,000$$
$$FS\_START + FS\_BUY - FS\_SELL = FS$$
$$IB\_START + IB\_BUY - IB\_SELL = IB$$
$$LG\_START + LG\_BUY - LG\_SELL = LG$$
$$LV\_START + LV\_BUY - LV\_SELL = LV$$
$$SG\_START + SG\_BUY - SG\_SELL = SG$$
$$SV\_START + SV\_BUY - SV\_SELL = SV$$
$$TRANS\_FEE * (FS\_BUY + FS\_SELL + IB\_BUY + IB\_SELL +$$
$$LG\_BUY + LG\_SELL + LV\_BUY + LV\_SELL + SG\_BUY +$$
$$SG\_SELL + SV\_BUY + SV\_SELL) = TRANS\_COST$$
$$FS\_START = 10,000$$
$$IB\_START = 10,000$$
$$LG\_START = 10,000$$
$$LV\_START = 40,000$$
$$SG\_START = 10,000$$
$$SV\_START = 20,000$$
$$TRANS\_FEE = 0.01$$
$$FS, IB, LG, LV, SG, SV \geq 0$$

Notice that the transaction fee is set at 1% in the model (the last constraint) and that the transaction cost for buying and selling shares of the mutual funds is a linear function of the amount bought and sold. With this model, the transaction costs are deducted from the client's account at the time of rebalancing and thus reduce the amount of money invested. The solution for Ms. Delgado's rebalancing problem is shown as part of the Managerial Report.

Managerial Report

Assume that you are a financial analytics specialist newly hired by Hauck Financial Services. One of your first tasks is to review the portfolio rebalancing model in order to resolve a dispute with Jean Delgado. Ms. Delgado has had one of the Hauck passively managed portfolios for the past five years and has complained that she is not getting the rate of return of 10% that she specified. After reviewing her annual statements for the past five years, she feels that she is actually getting less than 10% on average.

1. According to the following Model Solution, $IB\_BUY = \$41,268.51$. How much in transaction costs did Ms. Delgado pay for purchasing additional shares of the intermediate-term bond fund?
2. Based on the Model Solution, what is the total transaction cost associated with rebalancing Ms. Delgado's portfolio?
3. After paying transactions costs, how much did Ms. Delgado have invested in mutual funds after her portfolio was rebalanced?
4. According to the Model Solution, $IB = \$51,268.51$. How much can Ms. Delgado expect to have in the intermediate-term bond fund at the end of the year?
5. According to the Model Solution, the expected return of the portfolio is $10,000. What is the expected dollar amount in Ms. Delgado's portfolio at the end of the year? Can she expect to earn 10% on the $100,000 she had at the beginning of the year?

MODEL SOLUTION

Optimal	Objective Value		
	27219457.356		

Variable	Value	Variable	Value
R_1	18953.280	IB_START	10000.000
$\bar{R}$	10000.000	IB_BUY	41268.510
R_2	11569.210	IB_SELL	0.000
R_3	5663.961	LG_START	10000.000
R_4	9693.921	LG_BUY	0.000
R_5	4119.631	LG_SELL	5060.688
FS	15026.860	LV_START	40000.000
IB	51268.510	LV_BUY	0.000
LG	4939.312	LV_SELL	40000.000
LV	0.000	SG_START	10000.000
SG	0.000	SG_BUY	0.000
SV	27675.000	SG_SELL	10000.000
TRANS_COST	1090.311	SV_START	20000.000
FS_START	10000.000	SV_BUY	7675.004
FS_BUY	5026.863	SV_SELL	0.000
FS_SELL	0.000	TRANS_FEE	0.010

6. It is now time to prepare a report to management to explain why Ms. Delgado did not earn 10% each year on her investment. Make a recommendation in terms of a revised portfolio model that can be used so that Jean Delgado can have an expected portfolio balance of $110,000 at the end of next year. Prepare a report that includes a modified optimization model that will give an expected return of 10% on the amount of money available at the beginning of the year before paying the transaction costs. Explain why the current model does not do this.

7. Solve the formulation in part (6) for Jean Delgado. How does the portfolio composition differ from that of the Model Solution?

Chapter 15

Decision Analysis

CONTENTS

ANALYTICS IN ACTION:
U.S. CENTERS FOR DISEASE CONTROL AND PREVENTION

ANALYTICS IN ACTION

U.S. Centers for Disease Control and Prevention*

Over the course of history, polio has been one of the most terrifying diseases known to humans. Polio is caused by the poliovirus. Wild polioviruses (WPVs) refer to polioviruses that exist in the wild, rather than viruses that are derived from vaccines. WPVs are typically transmitted when contaminated water or food is ingested by an uninfected person, which can be common in areas with poor hygiene or poor sanitation. In the 1950s, polio vaccines were developed separately by Jonas Salk and Albert Sabin. These vaccines led to the eradication of WPV transmission in the United States by 1979 and throughout the western hemisphere by 1991. However, polio remains endemic to several countries around the world, which puts all other populations at risk of infection.

The Global Polio Eradication Initiative (GPEI) seeks to eradicate polio worldwide. It is financed by a variety of public and private donors including the World Health Organization, the U.S. Centers for Disease Control and Prevention (CDC), and the Bill & Melinda Gates Foundation. The CDC collaborated with Kid Risk, Inc. to use analytics tools to evaluate the policy options available for pursuing global polio eradication in terms of benefits, risks, and costs. The researchers used a variety of decision analysis tools, including decision trees, to consider the many different options available to potentially eradicate polio around the world. These policy decisions include such options as using oral poliovirus vaccines (OPVs), inactivated poliovirus vaccines (IPVs), and whether to continue routine vaccinations after WPV transmission has been eradicated. The decision trees allowed the researchers to capture much of the complexity inherent in such a large-scale decision problem and to evaluate the relative risks, benefits, and costs of different policy options. The uncertainties in costs were modeled using 47 different probability distributions for cost inputs, and cost data were collected through extensive data collection efforts led by the Global Polio Laboratory Network.

The findings from the decision analysis model led researchers to understand that the speed with which medical professionals respond to a polio outbreak can be more effective than having extremely high rates of WPV immunity through vaccinations. The models also allowed the researchers to calculate the cost tradeoffs of eradicating polio worldwide versus responding to greater polio outbreaks. The research provided extensive evidence of the value of the GPEI by showing that net benefits of countries covered by the GPEI approach $40–50 billion. The work done by these researchers was recognized with the 2014 INFORMS Franz Edelman Award based on the enormous financial and global health impacts from these analytical models and the derived insights.

*Based on K. M. Thompson, R. J. Duintjer Tebbens, M. A. Pallansch, S. G. F. Wassilak, and S. L. Cochi, "Polio eradicators use integrated analytical models to make better decisions," *Interfaces*, 45, no. 1 (January–February 2015): 1–16.

Ultimately, business analytics is about making better decisions. The tools and techniques we have introduced previously are designed to aid a decision maker in analyzing existing data, predicting future behavior, and recommending decisions. This chapter introduces a field known as decision analysis that can be used to develop an optimal strategy when a decision maker is faced with several decision alternatives and an uncertain or risk-filled pattern of future events.

Decision analysis techniques are used widely in many different settings. The Analytics in Action for this chapter discusses how the U.S. Centers for Disease Control and Prevention used decision analysis to evaluate options for trying to eradicate polio worldwide. Other federal agencies in the United States have used decision analysis to evaluate the potential risks from terrorist attacks and to recommend counterterrorism strategies. The State of North Carolina used decision analysis in evaluating whether to implement a medical screening test to detect metabolic disorders in newborns. Decision analysis is used by many business organizations, such as Procter & Gamble, to analyze new product introductions, marketing decisions, and much more. For example, by evaluating the different naming options and understanding the potential sources of uncertainty, Procter & Gamble used decision analysis techniques to help choose the best brand name when they introduced Crest White Strips.

Even when a careful decision analysis has been conducted, uncertainty about future events means that the final outcome is not completely under the control of the decision maker. In some cases, the selected decision alternative may provide good or excellent results. In other cases, a relatively unlikely future event may occur, causing the selected decision alternative to provide only fair or even poor results. The risk associated with any decision alternative is a direct result of the uncertainty associated with the final outcome. A good decision analysis includes careful consideration of risk. Through risk analysis, the decision maker is provided with probability information about the favorable as well as the unfavorable outcomes that may occur.

We begin the study of decision analysis by considering problems that involve reasonably few decision alternatives and reasonably few possible future events. Payoff tables and decision trees are introduced to provide a structure for the decision problem and to illustrate the fundamentals of decision analysis. Decision trees are used to analyze more complex problems and to identify an optimal sequence of decisions, referred to as an *optimal decision strategy*. Sensitivity analysis shows how changes in various aspects of the problem affect the recommended decision alternative. We return to the use of Bayes' theorem for calculating the probabilities of future events and incorporating additional information about the decisions. We conclude this chapter with a discussion of utility and decision analysis that expands on different attitudes toward risk taken by decision makers.

Bayes' Theorem is introduced in Chapter 4.

15.1 Problem Formulation

The first step in the decision analysis process is problem formulation. We begin with a verbal statement of the problem. We then identify the **decision alternatives**; the uncertain future events, referred to as **chance events**; and the **outcomes** associated with each combination of decision alternative and chance event outcome. Let us begin by considering a construction project of the Pittsburgh Development Corporation.

Pittsburgh Development Corporation (PDC) purchased land that will be the site of a new luxury condominium complex. The location provides a spectacular view of downtown Pittsburgh and the Golden Triangle, where the Allegheny and Monongahela Rivers meet to form the Ohio River. PDC plans to price the individual condominium units between $300,000 and $1,400,000.

PDC commissioned preliminary architectural drawings for three different projects: one with 30 condominiums, one with 60 condominiums, and one with 90 condominiums. The financial success of the project depends on the size of the condominium complex and the chance event concerning the demand for the condominiums. The statement of the PDC decision problem is to select the size of the new luxury condominium project that will lead to the largest profit given the uncertainty concerning the demand for the condominiums.

Given the statement of the problem, it is clear that the decision is to select the best size for the condominium complex. PDC has the following three decision alternatives:

d_1 = a small complex with 30 condominiums

d_2 = a medium complex with 60 condominiums

d_3 = a large complex with 90 condominiums

A factor in selecting the best decision alternative is the uncertainty associated with the chance event concerning the demand for the condominiums. When asked about the possible demand for the condominiums, PDC's president acknowledged a wide range of possibilities but decided that it would be adequate to consider two possible chance event outcomes: a strong demand and a weak demand.

In decision analysis, the possible outcomes for a chance event are referred to as the **states of nature**. The states of nature are defined so that they are mutually exclusive (no more than one can occur) and collectively exhaustive (at least one must occur); thus, one and only one of the possible states of nature will occur. For the PDC problem, the chance event concerning the demand for the condominiums has two states of nature:

s_1 = strong demand for the condominiums

s_2 = weak demand for the condominiums

TABLE 15.1   Payoff Table for the PDC Condominium Project ($ Millions)

Decision Alternative	State of Nature	
	Strong Demand, s_1	Weak Demand, s_2
Small complex, d_1	8	7
Medium complex, d_2	14	5
Large complex, d_3	20	−9

Management must first select a decision alternative (complex size); then a state of nature follows (demand for the condominiums), and finally an outcome will occur. In this case, the outcome is PDC's profit.

Payoff Tables

Payoffs can be expressed in terms of profit, cost, time, distance, or any other measure appropriate for the decision problem being analyzed.

Given the three decision alternatives and the two states of nature, which complex size should PDC choose? To answer this question, PDC will need to know the outcome associated with each possible combination of decision alternative and state of nature. In decision analysis, we refer to the outcome resulting from a specific combination of a decision alternative and a state of nature as a **payoff**. A table showing payoffs for all combinations of decision alternatives and states of nature is a **payoff table**.

Because PDC wants to select the complex size that provides the largest profit, profit is used as the outcome. The payoff table with profits (in millions of dollars) is shown in Table 15.1. Note, for example, that if a medium complex is built and demand turns out to be strong, a profit of $14 million will be realized. We will use the notation V_{ij} to denote the payoff associated with decision alternative i and state of nature j. Using Table 15.1, $V_{31} = 20$ indicates that a payoff of $20 million occurs if the decision is to build a large complex (d_3) and the strong demand state of nature (s_1) occurs. Similarly, $V_{32} = -9$ indicates a loss of $9 million if the decision is to build a large complex (d_3) and the weak demand state of nature (s_2) occurs.

Decision Trees

A **decision tree** provides a graphical representation of the decision-making process. Figure 15.1 presents a decision tree for the PDC problem. Note that the decision tree shows the natural or logical progression that will occur over time. First, PDC must make a decision regarding the size of the condominium complex (d_1, d_2, or d_3). Then, after the decision is implemented, either state of nature s_1 or s_2 will occur. The number at each end point of the tree indicates that the payoff is associated with a particular sequence. For example, the topmost payoff of 8 indicates that an $8 million profit is anticipated if PDC constructs a small condominium complex (d_1) and demand turns out to be strong (s_1). The next payoff of 7 indicates an anticipated profit of $7 million if PDC constructs a small condominium complex (d_1) and demand turns out to be weak (s_2). Thus, the decision tree provides a graphical depiction of the sequences of decision alternatives and states of nature that provide the six possible payoffs for PDC.

The decision tree in Figure 15.1 shows four nodes, numbered 1 to 4. **Nodes** are used to represent decisions and chance events. Squares are used to depict **decision nodes**, circles are used to depict **chance nodes**. Thus, node 1 is a decision node, and nodes 2, 3, and 4 are chance nodes. The **branches** connect the nodes; those leaving the decision node correspond to the decision alternatives. The branches leaving each chance node correspond to the states of nature. The outcomes (payoffs) are shown at the end of the states-of-nature branches. We now turn to the question: How can the decision maker use the information in the payoff table or the decision tree to select the best decision alternative? Several approaches may be used and are covered in the remaining sections of this chapter.

FIGURE 15.1 Decision Tree for the PDC Condominium Project ($ Millions)

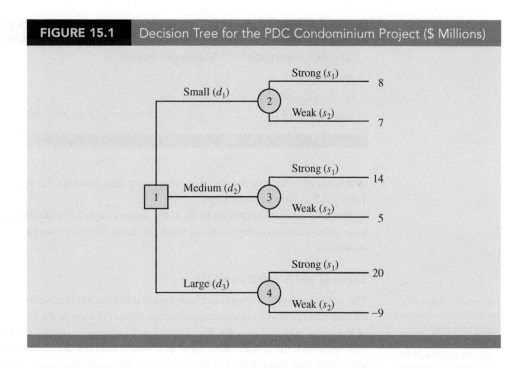

1. The first step in solving a complex problem is to decompose the problem into a series of smaller subproblems. Decision trees provide a useful way to decompose a problem and illustrate the sequential nature of the decision process.

2. People often view the same problem from different perspectives. Thus, the discussion regarding the development of a decision tree may provide additional insight into the problem.

15.2 Decision Analysis Without Probabilities

In this section, we consider approaches to decision analysis that do not require knowledge of the probabilities of the states of nature. These approaches are appropriate in situations in which a simple best-case and worst-case analysis is sufficient and in which the decision maker has little confidence in his or her ability to assess the probabilities. Because different approaches sometimes lead to different decision recommendations, the decision maker must understand the approaches available and then select the specific approach that, according to the judgment of the decision maker, is the most appropriate.

Optimistic Approach

For a maximization problem, the optimistic approach often is referred to as the maximax approach; for a minimization problem, the corresponding terminology is minimin.

The **optimistic approach** evaluates each decision alternative in terms of the *best* payoff that can occur. The decision alternative that is recommended is the one that provides the best possible payoff. For a problem in which maximum profit is desired, as in the PDC problem, the optimistic approach would lead the decision maker to choose the alternative corresponding to the largest profit. For problems involving minimization, this approach leads to choosing the alternative with the smallest payoff.

To illustrate the optimistic approach, we use it to develop a recommendation for the PDC problem. First, we determine the maximum payoff for each decision alternative; then we select the decision alternative that provides the overall maximum payoff. These steps

TABLE 15.2	Maximum Payoff for Each PDC Decision Alternative

Decision Alternative	Maximum Payoff
Small complex, d_1	8
Medium complex, d_2	14
Large complex, d_3	20 ←——— Maximum of the maximum payoff values

systematically identify the decision alternative that provides the largest possible profit. Table 15.2 illustrates these steps.

Because 20, corresponding to d_3, is the largest payoff, the decision to construct the large condominium complex is the recommended decision alternative using the optimistic approach.

Conservative Approach

For a maximization problem, the conservative approach often is referred to as the maximin approach; for a minimization problem the corresponding terminology is minimax.

The **conservative approach** evaluates each decision alternative in terms of the *worst* payoff that can occur. The decision alternative recommended is the one that provides the best of the worst possible payoffs. For a problem in which the output measure is profit, as in the PDC problem, the conservative approach would lead the decision maker to choose the alternative that maximizes the minimum possible profit that could be obtained. For problems involving minimization (e.g., when the output measure is cost instead of profit), this approach identifies the alternative that will minimize the maximum payoff.

To illustrate the conservative approach, we use it to develop a recommendation for the PDC problem. First, we identify the minimum payoff for each of the decision alternatives; then we select the decision alternative that maximizes the minimum payoff. Table 15.3 illustrates these steps for the PDC problem.

Because 7, corresponding to d_1, yields the maximum of the minimum payoffs, the decision alternative of a small condominium complex is recommended. This decision approach is considered conservative because it identifies the worst possible payoffs and then recommends the decision alternative that avoids the possibility of extremely "bad" payoffs. In the conservative approach, PDC is guaranteed a profit of at least $7 million. Although PDC may make more, it *cannot* make less than $7 million.

Minimax Regret Approach

In decision analysis, **regret** is the difference between the payoff associated with a *particular* decision alternative and the payoff associated with the decision that would yield the most desirable payoff for a given state of nature. Thus, regret represents how much potential payoff one would forgo by selecting a *particular* decision alternative, given that a specific state of nature will occur. This is why regret is often referred to as **opportunity loss**.

As its name implies, under the **minimax regret approach** to decision analysis, one would choose the decision alternative that minimizes the maximum state of regret that could occur over all possible states of nature. This approach is neither purely optimistic nor

TABLE 15.3	Minimum Payoff for Each PDC Decision Alternative

Decision Alternative	Minimum Payoff ($ millions)
Small complex, d_1	7 ←——— Maximum of the minimum payoff values
Medium complex, d_2	5
Large complex, d_3	−9

purely conservative. Let us illustrate the minimax regret approach by showing how it can be used to select a decision alternative for the PDC problem.

Suppose that PDC constructs a small condominium complex (d_1) and demand turns out to be strong (s_1). Table 15.1 showed that the resulting profit for PDC would be $8 million. However, given that the strong demand state of nature (s_1) has occurred, we realize that the decision to construct a large condominium complex (d_3), yielding a profit of $20 million, would have been the best decision. The difference between the payoff for the best decision alternative ($20 million) and the payoff for the decision to construct a small condominium complex ($8 million) is the regret or opportunity loss associated with decision alternative d_1 when state of nature s_1 occurs; thus, for this case, the opportunity loss or regret is $20 million $-$ $8 million = $12 million. Similarly, if PDC makes the decision to construct a medium condominium complex (d_2) and the strong demand state of nature (s_1) occurs, the opportunity loss, or regret, associated with d_2 would be $20 million $-$ $14 million = $6 million. Of course, if PDC chooses to construct a large complex (d_3) and demand is strong, they would have no regret.

In general, the following expression represents the opportunity loss, or regret:

REGRET (OPPORTUNITY LOSS)

$$R_{ij} = \left| V_j^* - V_{ij} \right| \tag{15.1}$$

where

R_{ij} = the regret associated with decision alternative d_i and state of nature s_j

V_j^* = the payoff value corresponding to the best decision for the state of nature s_j

V_{ij} = the payoff corresponding to decision alternative d_i and state of nature s_j

Note the role of the absolute value in equation (15.1). For minimization problems, the best payoff, V_j^*, is the smallest entry in column j. Because this value always is less than or equal to V_{ij}, the absolute value of the difference between V_j^* and V_{ij} ensures that the regret is always the magnitude of the difference.

Using equation (15.1) and the payoffs in Table 15.1, we can compute the regret associated with each combination of decision alternative d_i and state of nature s_j. Because the PDC problem is a maximization problem, V_j^* will be the largest entry in column j of the payoff table. Thus, to compute the regret, we simply subtract each entry in a column from the largest entry in the column. Table 15.4 shows the opportunity loss, or regret, table for the PDC problem.

The next step in applying the minimax regret approach is to list the maximum regret for each decision alternative; Table 15.5 shows the results for the PDC problem. Selecting the decision alternative with the *minimum* of the *maximum* regret values—hence, the name *minimax regret*—yields the minimax regret decision. For the PDC problem, the alternative to construct the medium condominium complex, with a corresponding maximum regret of $6 million, is the recommended minimax regret decision.

TABLE 15.4 Opportunity Loss, or Regret, Table for the PDC Condominium Project ($ Millions)

	State of Nature	
Decision Alternative	**Strong Demand, s_1**	**Weak Demand, s_2**
Small complex, d_1	12	0
Medium complex, d_2	6	2
Large complex, d_3	0	16

TABLE 15.5 Maximum Regret for Each PDC Decision Alternative

Decision Alternative	Maximum Regret ($ millions)
Small complex, d_1	12
Medium complex, d_2	6 ←———— Minimum of the maximum regret
Large complex, d_3	16

Note that the three approaches discussed in this section provide different recommendations, which in itself is not bad. It simply reflects the difference in decision-making philosophies that underlie the various approaches. Ultimately, the decision maker will have to choose the most appropriate approach and then make the final decision accordingly. The main criticism of the approaches discussed in this section is that they do not consider any information about the probabilities of the various states of nature. In the next section, we discuss an approach that utilizes probability information in selecting a decision alternative.

15.3 Decision Analysis with Probabilities

Expected Value Approach

In many decision-making situations, we can obtain probability assessments for the states of nature. When such probabilities are available, we can use the **expected value approach** to identify the best decision alternative. Let us first define the expected value of a decision alternative and then apply it to the PDC problem.

Let

$$N = \text{the number of states of nature}$$

$$P(s_j) = \text{the probability of state of nature } s_j$$

Because one and only one of the N states of nature can occur, the probabilities must satisfy two conditions:

$$P(s_j) \geq 0 \quad \text{for all states of nature}$$

$$\sum_{j=1}^{N} P(s_j) = P(s_1) + P(s_2) + \cdots + P(s_N) = 1$$

The **expected value (EV)** of decision alternative d_i is defined as follows:

EXPECTED VALUE OF DECISION ALTERNATIVE d_i

$$EV(d_i) = \sum_{j=1}^{N} P(s_j)V_{ij} \tag{15.2}$$

In words, the expected value of a decision alternative is the sum of weighted payoffs for the decision alternative. The weight for a payoff is the probability of the associated state of nature and therefore the probability that the payoff will occur. Let us return to the PDC problem to see how the expected value approach can be applied.

PDC is optimistic about the potential for the luxury high-rise condominium complex. Suppose that this optimism leads to an initial subjective probability assessment of 0.8 that demand will be strong (s_1) and a corresponding probability of 0.2 that demand will be weak (s_2). Thus, $P(s_1) = 0.8$ and $P(s_2) = 0.2$. Using the payoff values in Table 15.1 and equation (15.2), we compute the expected value for each of the three decision alternatives as follows:

$$EV(d_1) = 0.8(8) + 0.2(7) = 7.8$$

$$EV(d_2) = 0.8(14) + 0.2(5) = 12.2$$

$$EV(d_3) = 0.8(20) + 0.2(-9) = 14.2$$

Thus, using the expected value approach, we find that the large condominium complex, with an expected value of $14.2 million, is the recommended decision.

The calculations required to identify the decision alternative with the best expected value can be conveniently carried out on a decision tree. Figure 15.2 shows the decision tree for the PDC problem with state-of-nature branch probabilities. Working backward through the decision tree, we first compute the expected value at each chance node. In other words, at each chance node, we weight each possible payoff by its probability of occurrence. By doing so, we obtain the expected values for nodes 2, 3, and 4, as shown in Figure 15.3.

Because the decision maker controls the branch leaving decision node 1 and because we are trying to maximize the expected profit, the best decision alternative at node 1 is d_3. Thus, the decision tree analysis leads to a recommendation of d_3, with an expected value of $14.2 million. Note that this recommendation is also obtained with the expected value approach in conjunction with the payoff table.

Other decision problems may be substantially more complex than the PDC problem, but if a reasonable number of decision alternatives and states of nature are present, you can use the decision tree approach outlined here. First, draw a decision tree consisting of decision nodes, chance nodes, and branches that describe the sequential nature of the problem. If you use the expected value approach, the next step is to determine the probabilities for each of the states of nature and compute the expected value at each chance node. Then select the decision branch leading to the chance node with the best expected value. The decision alternative associated with this branch is the recommended decision.

In practice, obtaining precise estimates of the probabilities for each state of nature is often impossible. In some cases, where similar decisions have been made many times in the past, one may use historical data to estimate the probabilities for the different states of nature. However, often there are little, or no, historical data to guide the estimates of these probabilities. In these cases, we may have to rely on subjective estimates to determine the probabilities for the states of nature. When relying on subjective estimates, we often want to get more than one estimate because many studies have shown that even knowledgeable experts are often overly optimistic in their estimates. It is also particularly important when dealing with subjective probability estimates to perform risk analysis and sensitivity analysis, as we will explain.

FIGURE 15.2   PDC Decision Tree with State-of-Nature Branch Probabilities

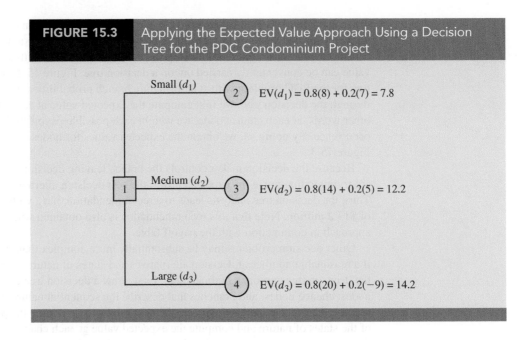

FIGURE 15.3 Applying the Expected Value Approach Using a Decision Tree for the PDC Condominium Project

Small (d_1)
② $EV(d_1) = 0.8(8) + 0.2(7) = 7.8$

Medium (d_2)
③ $EV(d_2) = 0.8(14) + 0.2(5) = 12.2$

Large (d_3)
④ $EV(d_3) = 0.8(20) + 0.2(-9) = 14.2$

Risk Analysis

Risk analysis helps the decision maker recognize the difference between the expected value of a decision alternative and the payoff that may actually occur. A decision alternative and a state of nature combine to generate the payoff associated with a decision. The **risk profile** for a decision alternative shows the possible payoffs along with their associated probabilities.

Let us demonstrate risk analysis and the construction of a risk profile by returning to the PDC condominium construction project. Using the expected value approach, we identified the large condominium complex (d_3) as the best decision alternative. The expected value of $14.2 million for d_3 is based on a 0.8 probability of obtaining a $20 million profit and a 0.2 probability of obtaining a $9 million loss. The 0.8 probability for the $20 million payoff and the 0.2 probability for the −$9 million payoff provide the risk profile for the large-complex decision alternative. This risk profile is shown graphically in Figure 15.4.

Sometimes a review of the risk profile associated with an optimal decision alternative may cause the decision maker to choose another decision alternative even though the

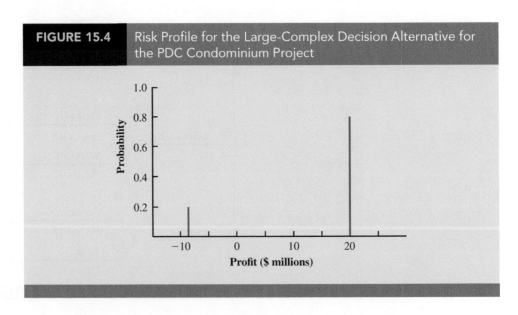

FIGURE 15.4 Risk Profile for the Large-Complex Decision Alternative for the PDC Condominium Project

Probability

Profit ($ millions)

expected value of the other decision alternative is not as good. For example, the risk profile for the medium-complex decision alternative (d_2) shows a 0.8 probability for a $14 million payoff and a 0.2 probability for a $5 million payoff. Because no probability of a loss is associated with decision alternative d_2, the medium-complex decision alternative would be judged less risky than the large-complex decision alternative. As a result, a decision maker might prefer the less risky medium-complex decision alternative even though it has an expected value of $2 million less than the large-complex decision alternative.

Sensitivity Analysis

Sensitivity analysis can be used to determine how changes in the probabilities for the states of nature or changes in the payoffs affect the recommended decision alternative. In many cases, the probabilities for the states of nature and the payoffs are based on subjective assessments. Sensitivity analysis helps the decision maker understand which of these inputs are critical to the choice of the best decision alternative. If a small change in the value of one of the inputs causes a change in the recommended decision alternative, the solution to the decision analysis problem is sensitive to that particular input. Extra effort and care should be taken to make sure the input value is as accurate as possible. On the other hand, if a modest-to-large change in the value of one of the inputs does not cause a change in the recommended decision alternative, the solution to the decision analysis problem is not sensitive to that particular input. No extra time or effort would be needed to refine the estimated input value.

One approach to sensitivity analysis is to select different values for the probabilities of the states of nature and the payoffs and then resolve the decision analysis problem. If the recommended decision alternative changes, we know that the solution is sensitive to the changes made. For example, suppose that in the PDC problem the probability for a strong demand is revised to 0.2 and the probability for a weak demand is revised to 0.8. Would the recommended decision alternative change? Using $P(s_1) = 0.2$, $P(s_2) = 0.8$, and equation (15.2), the revised expected values for the three decision alternatives are as follows:

$$\text{EV}(d_1) = 0.2(8) + 0.8(7) = 7.2$$
$$\text{EV}(d_2) = 0.2(14) + 0.8(5) = 6.8$$
$$\text{EV}(d_3) = 0.2(20) + 0.8(-9) = -3.2$$

With these probability assessments, the recommended decision alternative is to construct a small condominium complex (d_1), with an expected value of $7.2 million. The probability of strong demand is only 0.2, so constructing the large condominium complex (d_3) is the least preferred alternative, with an expected value of $-$3.2 million (a loss).

Thus, when the probability of strong demand is large, PDC should build the large complex; when the probability of strong demand is small, PDC should build the small complex. Obviously, we could continue to modify the probabilities of the states of nature and learn even more about how changes in the probabilities affect the recommended decision alternative. Sensitivity analysis calculations can also be made for the values of the payoffs. We can easily change the payoff values and resolve the problem to see if the best decision changes.

N O T E S   +   C O M M E N T S

1. The definition of expected value given in this chapter is consistent with that given in Chapter 4, but here we use the notation and terminology specific to decision analysis. In both cases, the expected value is defined as the weighted average of possible values.

2. The drawback to the sensitivity analysis approach described in this section is the numerous calculations required to evaluate the effect of several possible changes in the state-of-nature probabilities and/or payoff values. Many computer packages exist that can assist with the creation of decision trees and with the calculations required.

15.4 Decision Analysis with Sample Information

Frequently, decision makers have the ability to collect additional information about the states of nature. It is worthwhile for the decision maker to consider the potential value of this additional information and how it can affect the decision analysis process. Most often, additional information is obtained through experiments designed to provide **sample information** about the states of nature. Raw material sampling, product testing, and market research studies are examples of experiments (or studies) that may enable management to revise or update the state-of-nature probabilities.

To analyze the potential benefit of additional information, we must first introduce a few additional terms related to decision analysis. The preliminary or **prior probability** assessments for the states of nature that are the best probability values available prior to obtaining additional information. These revised probabilities after obtaining additional information are called **posterior probabilities**.

Let us return to the PDC problem and assume that management is considering a six-month market research study designed to learn more about potential market acceptance of the PDC condominium project. Management anticipates that the market research study will provide one of the following two results:

1. *Favorable report:* A substantial number of the individuals contacted express interest in purchasing a PDC condominium.
2. *Unfavorable report:* Very few of the individuals contacted express interest in purchasing a PDC condominium.

The decision tree for the PDC problem with sample information shows the logical sequence for the decisions and the chance events in Figure 15.5. By introducing the possibility of conducting a market research study, the PDC problem becomes more complex. First, PDC's management must decide whether the market research should be conducted. If it is conducted, PDC's management must be prepared to make a decision about the size of the condominium project if the market research report is favorable and, possibly, a different decision about the size of the condominium project if the market research report is unfavorable. In Figure 15.5, the squares are decision nodes and the circles are chance nodes. At each decision node, the branch of the tree that is taken is based on the decision made. At each chance node, the branch of the tree that is taken is based on probability or chance. For example, decision node 1 shows that PDC must first make the decision of whether to conduct the market research study. If the market research study is undertaken, chance node 2 indicates that both the favorable report branch and the unfavorable report branch are not under PDC's control and will be determined by chance. Node 3 is a decision node, indicating that PDC must make the decision to construct the small, medium, or large complex if the market research report is favorable. Node 4 is a decision node showing that PDC must make the decision to construct the small, medium, or large complex if the market research report is unfavorable. Node 5 is a decision node indicating that PDC must make the decision to construct the small, medium, or large complex if the market research is not undertaken. Nodes 6 to 14 are chance nodes indicating that the strong demand or weak demand state-of-nature branches will be determined by chance.

Analysis of the decision tree and the choice of an optimal strategy require that we know the branch probabilities corresponding to all chance nodes. PDC has developed the following branch probabilities:

The branch probabilities for P(favorable report) and P(unfavorable report) are calculated using Bayes' rule, first introduced in Chapter 4. We illustrate these calculations in Section 15.5.

If the market research study is undertaken:

$$P(\text{favorable report}) = 0.77$$
$$P(\text{unfavorable report}) = 0.23$$

If the market research report is favorable, the posterior probabilities are as follows:

$$P(\text{strong demand given a favorable report}) = 0.94$$
$$P(\text{weak demand given a favorable report}) = 0.06$$

FIGURE 15.5   The PDC Decision Tree Including the Market Research Study

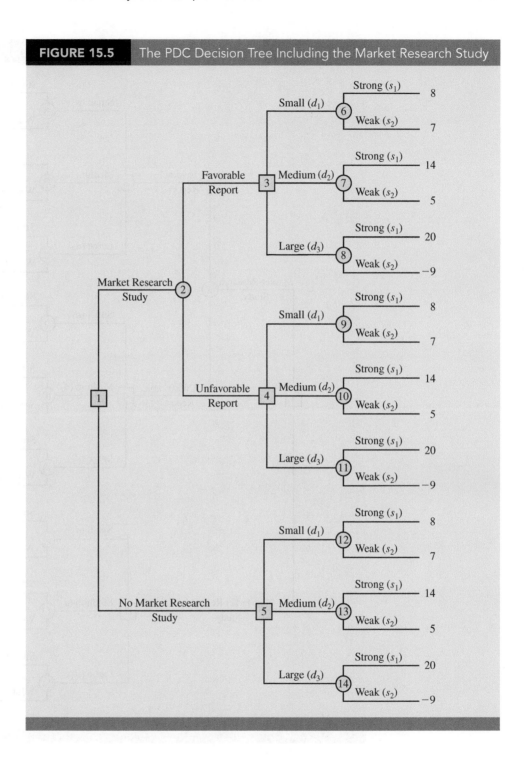

If the market research report is unfavorable, the posterior probabilities are as follows:

$$P(\text{strong demand given an unfavorable report}) = 0.35$$
$$P(\text{weak demand given an unfavorable report}) = 0.65$$

If the market research report is not undertaken, the prior probabilities are applicable:

$$P(\text{strong demand}) = 0.80$$
$$P(\text{weak demand}) = 0.20$$

FIGURE 15.6 The PDC Decision Tree with Branch Probabilities

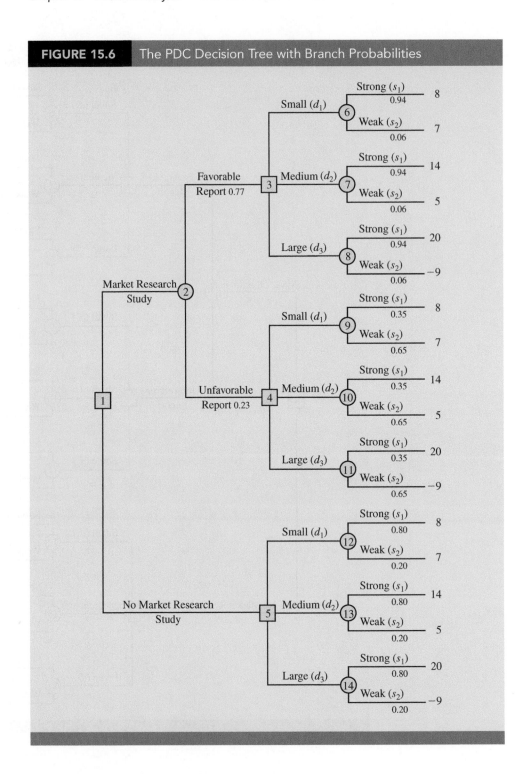

The branch probabilities are shown on the decision tree in Figure 15.6.

A **decision strategy** is a sequence of decisions and chance outcomes in which the decisions chosen depend on the yet-to-be-determined outcomes of chance events. The approach used to determine the optimal decision strategy is based on a rollback of the expected values in the decision tree using the following steps:

1. At chance nodes, compute the expected value by multiplying the payoff at the end of each branch by the corresponding branch probabilities.

2. At decision nodes, select the decision branch that leads to the best expected value. This expected value becomes the expected value at the decision node.

Starting the rollback calculations by computing the expected values at chance nodes 6 to 14 provides the following results:

$$
\begin{array}{llll}
\text{EV(Node 6)} & = & 0.94(8) + 0.06(7) & = & 7.94 \\
\text{EV(Node 7)} & = & 0.94(14) + 0.06(5) & = & 13.46 \\
\text{EV(Node 8)} & = & 0.94(20) + 0.06(-9) & = & 18.26 \\
\text{EV(Node 9)} & = & 0.35(8) + 0.65(7) & = & 7.35 \\
\text{EV(Node 10)} & = & 0.35(14) + 0.65(5) & = & 8.15 \\
\text{EV(Node 11)} & = & 0.35(20) + 0.65(-9) & = & 1.15 \\
\text{EV(Node 12)} & = & 0.80(8) + 0.20(7) & = & 7.80 \\
\text{EV(Node 13)} & = & 0.80(14) + 0.20(5) & = & 12.20 \\
\text{EV(Node 14)} & = & 0.80(20) + 0.20(-9) & = & 14.20 \\
\end{array}
$$

Figure 15.7 shows the reduced decision tree after computing expected values at these chance nodes.

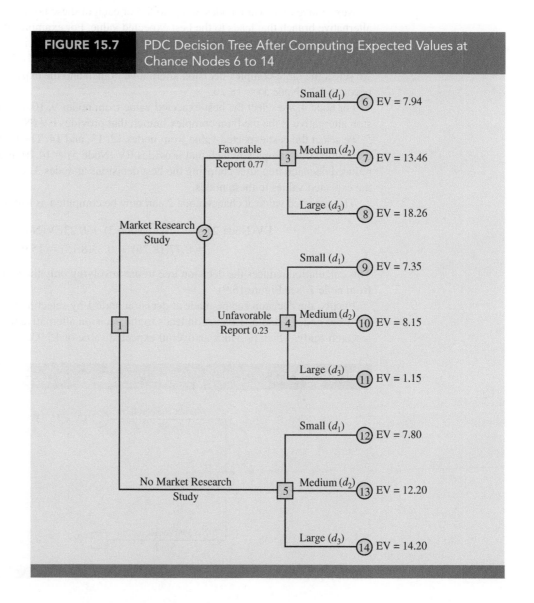

FIGURE 15.7 PDC Decision Tree After Computing Expected Values at Chance Nodes 6 to 14

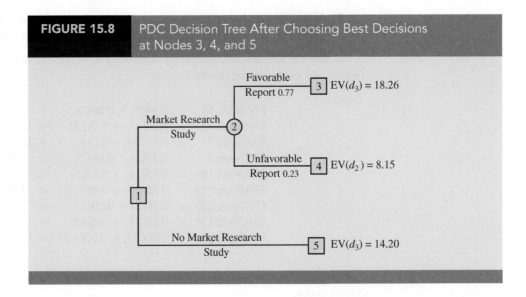

FIGURE 15.8   PDC Decision Tree After Choosing Best Decisions at Nodes 3, 4, and 5

Next, move to decision nodes 3, 4, and 5. For each of these nodes, we select the decision alternative branch that leads to the best expected value. For example, at node 3 we have the choice of the small complex branch with EV (Node 6) = 7.94, the medium complex branch with EV (Node 7) = 13.46, and the large complex branch with EV (Node 8) = 18.26. Thus, we select the large-complex decision alternative branch and the expected value at node 3 becomes EV (Node 3) = 18.26.

For node 4, we select the best expected value from nodes 9, 10, and 11. The best decision alternative is the medium complex branch that provides EV (Node 4) = 8.15. For node 5, we select the best expected value from nodes 12, 13, and 14. The best decision alternative is the large complex branch that provides EV (Node 5) = 14.20. Figure 15.8 shows the reduced decision tree after choosing the best decisions at nodes 3, 4, and 5 and rolling back the expected values to these nodes.

The expected value at chance node 2 can now be computed as follows:

$$EV(\text{Node } 2) = 0.77 EV(\text{Node } 3) + 0.23 EV(\text{Node } 4)$$
$$= 0.77(18.26) + 0.23(8.15) = 15.93$$

This calculation reduces the decision tree to one involving only the two decision branches from node 1 (see Figure 15.9).

Finally, the decision can be made at decision node 1 by selecting the best expected values from nodes 2 and 5. This action leads to the decision alternative to conduct the market research study, which provides an overall expected value of 15.93.

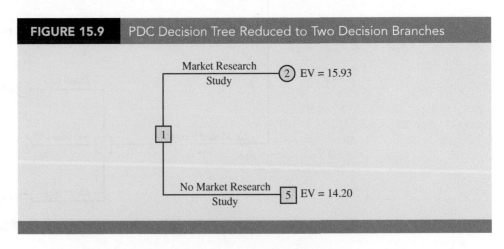

FIGURE 15.9   PDC Decision Tree Reduced to Two Decision Branches

The optimal decision for PDC is to conduct the market research study and then carry out the following decision strategy:

If the market research is favorable, construct the large condominium complex.
If the market research is unfavorable, construct the medium condominium complex.

The analysis of the PDC decision tree describes the methods that can be used to analyze more complex sequential decision problems. First, draw a decision tree consisting of decision and chance nodes and branches that describe the sequential nature of the problem. Determine the probabilities for all chance outcomes. Then, by working backward through the tree, compute expected values at all chance nodes and select the best decision branch at all decision nodes. The sequence of optimal decision branches determines the optimal decision strategy for the problem.

Expected Value of Sample Information

The EVSI = $1.73 million suggests PDC should be willing to pay up to $1.73 million to conduct the market research study.

In the PDC problem, the market research study is the sample information used to determine the optimal decision strategy. The expected value associated with the market research study is 15.93. Previously, we showed that the best expected value if the market research study is *not* undertaken is 14.20. Thus, we can conclude that the difference, $15.93 - 14.20 = 1.73$, is the **expected value of sample information (EVSI)**. In other words, conducting the market research study adds $1.73 million to the PDC expected value. In general, the expected value of sample information is as follows:

EXPECTED VALUE OF SAMPLE INFORMATION (EVSI)

$$EVSI = \left| EVwSI - EVwoSI \right| \qquad (15.3)$$

where

$EVSI$ = expected value of sample information

$EVwSI$ = expected value *with* sample information about the states of nature

$EVwoSI$ = expected value *without* sample information about the states of nature

Expected Value of Perfect Information

A special case of gaining additional information related to a decision problem is when the sample information provides **perfect information** on the states of nature. In other words, consider a case in which the marketing study undertaken by PDC would determine exactly which state of nature will occur. Clearly, such a result is highly unlikely from a marketing study, but such an analysis provides a best-case analysis of the benefit provided by the marketing study. If the investment required for the additional information exceeds the expected value of perfect information, then we would not want to invest in procuring the additional information.

To illustrate the calculation of the expected value of perfect information, we return to the PDC decision. We assume for the moment that PDC could determine with certainty, prior to making a decision, which state of nature is going to occur. To make use of this perfect information, we will develop a decision strategy that PDC should follow once it knows which state of nature will occur.

To help determine the decision strategy for PDC, we reproduce PDC's payoff table as Table 15.6. If PDC knew for sure that state of nature s_1 would occur, the best decision alternative would be d_3, with a payoff of $20 million. Similarly, if PDC knew for sure that state of nature s_2 would occur, the best decision alternative would be d_1, with a payoff of $7 million. Thus, we can state PDC's optimal decision strategy when the perfect information becomes available as follows:

If s_1, select d_3 and receive a payoff of $20 million.
If s_2, select d_1 and receive a payoff of $7 million.

TABLE 15.6	Payoff Table for the PDC Condominium Project ($ Millions)

	State of Nature	
Decision Alternative	**Strong Demand, s_1**	**Weak Demand, s_2**
Small complex, d_1	8	7
Medium complex, d_2	14	5
Large complex, d_3	20	−9

What is the expected value for this decision strategy? To compute the expected value with perfect information, we return to the original probabilities for the states of nature: $P(s_1) = 0.8$ and $P(s_2) = 0.2$. Thus, there is a 0.8 probability that the perfect information will indicate state of nature s_1, and the resulting decision alternative d_3 will provide a $20 million profit. Similarly, with a 0.2 probability for state of nature s_2, the optimal decision alternative d_1 will provide a $7 million profit. Thus, from equation (15.2) the expected value of the decision strategy that uses perfect information is $0.8(20) + 0.2(7) = 17.4$.

We refer to the expected value of $17.4 million as the *expected value with perfect information* (EVwPI).

Earlier in this section we showed that the recommended decision using the expected value approach is decision alternative d_3, with an expected value of $14.2 million. Because this decision recommendation and expected value computation were made without the benefit of perfect information, $14.2 million is referred to as the *expected value without perfect information* (EVwoPI).

The expected value with perfect information is $17.4 million, and the expected value without perfect information is $14.2; therefore, the expected value of the perfect information (EVPI) is $17.4 − $14.2 = $3.2 million. In other words, $3.2 million represents the additional expected value that can be obtained if perfect information were available about the states of nature.

In general, the **expected value of perfect information (EVPI)** is computed as follows:

It would be worth $3.2 million for PDC to learn the level of market acceptance before selecting a decision alternative. This represents the maximum that PDC should invest in any market research to provide additional information on the states of nature because no market research study can be expected to provide perfect information.

EXPECTED VALUE OF PERFECT INFORMATION (EVPI)

$$EVPI = \left| EVwPI - EVwoPI \right| \tag{15.4}$$

where

$EVPI$ = expected value of perfect information

$EVwPI$ = expected value *with* perfect information about the states of nature

$EVwoPI$ = expected value *without* perfect information about the states of nature

15.5 Computing Branch Probabilities with Bayes' Theorem

We first introduced Bayes' theorem in Chapter 4 as a means of calculating posterior probabilities as updates of prior probabilities once additional information is obtained.

In Section 15.4 the branch probabilities for the PDC decision tree chance nodes were provided in the problem description. No computations were required to determine these probabilities. In this section, we show how **Bayes' theorem** can be used to compute branch probabilities for decision trees. The branch probabilities are the posterior probabilities for demand that have been updated based on the sample information of whether the market research report is favorable or unfavorable.

The PDC decision tree is shown again in Figure 15.10. Let

$$F = \text{favorable market research report}$$
$$U = \text{unfavorable market research report}$$
$$s_1 = \text{strong demand (state of nature 1)}$$
$$s_2 = \text{weak demand (state of nature 2)}$$

At chance node 2, we need to know the branch probabilities $P(F)$ and $P(U)$. At chance nodes 6, 7, and 8, we need to know the branch probabilities $P(s_1 \mid F)$, which is read as "the probability of state of nature 1 given a favorable market research report," and $P(s_2 \mid F)$,

FIGURE 15.10   The PDC Decision Tree

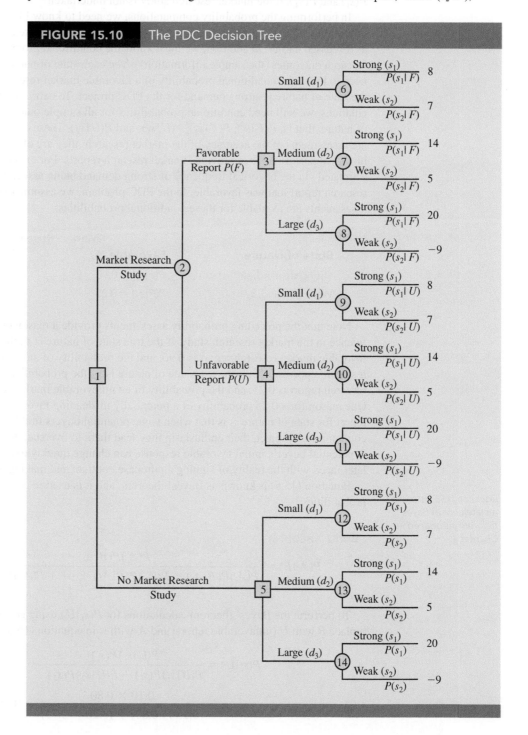

Conditional probability is introduced in Chapter 4.

which is the probability of state of nature 2 given a favorable market research report. The notation | in $P(s_1|F)$ and $P(s_2|F)$ is read as "given" and indicates a **conditional probability**, because we are interested in the probability of a particular state of nature "conditioned" on the fact that we receive a favorable market report. $P(s_1|F)$ and $P(s_2|F)$ are referred to as *posterior probabilities* because they are conditional probabilities based on the outcome of the sample information. At chance nodes 9, 10, and 11, we need to know the branch probabilities $P(s_1|U)$ and $P(s_2|U)$; note that these are also posterior probabilities, denoting the probabilities of the two states of nature *given* that the market research report is unfavorable. Finally, at chance nodes 12, 13, and 14, we need the probabilities for the states of nature, $P(s_1)$ and $P(s_2)$, if the market research study is not undertaken.

In performing the probability computations, we need to know PDC's assessment of the probabilities for the two states of nature, $P(s_1)$ and $P(s_2)$, which are the prior probabilities as discussed earlier. In addition, we must know the conditional probability of the market research outcomes (the sample information) *given* each state of nature. For example, we need to know the conditional probability of a favorable market research report given that the state of nature is strong demand for the PDC project. To carry out the probability calculations, we will need conditional probabilities for all sample outcomes given all states of nature, that is, $P(F|s_1)$, $P(F|s_2)$, $P(U|s_1)$, and $P(U|s_2)$. These conditional probabilities are assessments of the accuracy of the market research; they are often estimated using historical performance of previous market research reports. For example, $P(F|s_1)$ may be estimated via the historical frequency of strong demand being associated with a market research report that was favorable. In the PDC problem, we assume that the following assessments are available for these conditional probabilities:

	Market Research	
State of Nature	**Favorable, F**	**Unfavorable, U**
Strong demand, s_1	$P(F|s_1) = 0.90$	$P(U|s_1) = 0.10$
Weak demand, s_2	$P(F|s_2) = 0.25$	$P(U|s_2) = 0.75$

Note that the preceding probability assessments provide a reasonable degree of confidence in the market research study. If the true state of nature is s_1, the probability of a favorable market research report is 0.90, and the probability of an unfavorable market research report is 0.10. If the true state of nature is s_2, the probability of a favorable market research report is 0.25, and the probability of an unfavorable market research report is 0.75. One reason for a 0.25 probability of a potentially misleading favorable market research report for state of nature s_2 is that when some potential buyers first hear about the new condominium project, their enthusiasm may lead them to overstate their real interest in it. A potential buyer's initial favorable response can change quickly to a "no-thank-you" when later faced with the reality of signing a purchase contract and making a down payment.

Equation (15.5) is known as Bayes' theorem, and it is used to compute posterior probabilities.

Equation (15.5) is a restatement of Bayes' theorem introduced in Chapter 4.

BAYES' THEOREM

$$P(A_i|B) = \frac{P(A_i)P(B|A_i)}{P(A_1)P(B|A_1) + P(A_2)P(B|A_2) + \cdots + P(A_n)P(B|A_n)} \tag{15.5}$$

To perform the Bayes' theorem calculations for $P(s_1|U)$ using equation (15.5), we replace B with U (unfavorable report) and A_i with s_1 in equation (15.5) so that we have

$$P(s_1|U) = \frac{P(U|s_1)P(s_1)}{P(U|s_1)P(s_1) + P(U|s_2)P(s_2)}$$

$$= \frac{0.10 \times 0.80}{(0.10 \times 0.80) + (0.20 \times 0.75)} = 0.35$$

which indicates that the probability of strong demand given an unfavorable market research report is 0.35. We can also calculate the probability of weak demand given an unfavorable market research report as shown below:

$$P(s_2 | U) = \frac{P(U|s_2)P(s_2)}{P(U|s_1)P(s_1) + P(U|s_2)P(s_2)} = \frac{0.75 \times 0.20}{(0.10 \times 0.80) + (0.75 \times 0.20)} = 0.65$$

Similarly, we can calculate the posterior probabilities for strong and weak demand given a favorable market research report using equation (15.5):

$$P(s_1 | F) = \frac{P(F|s_1)P(s_1)}{P(F|s_1)P(s_1) + P(F|s_2)P(s_2)} = \frac{0.90 \times 0.80}{(0.90 \times 0.80) + (0.25 \times 0.20)} = 0.94$$

and

$$P(s_2 | F) = \frac{P(F|s_2)P(s_2)}{P(F|s_1)P(s_1) + P(F|s_2)P(s_2)} = \frac{0.25 \times 0.20}{(0.90 \times 0.80) + (0.25 \times 0.20)} = 0.06$$

This indicates that a favorable research report leads to a posterior probability of 0.94 that the demand will be strong and a posterior probability of only 0.06 that the demand will be weak.

The discussion in this section shows an underlying relationship between the probabilities on the various branches in a decision tree. It would be inappropriate to assume different prior probabilities, $P(s_1)$ and $P(s_2)$, without determining how these changes would alter $P(F)$ and $P(U)$, as well as the posterior probabilities $P(s_1 | F)$, $P(s_2 | F)$, $P(s_1 | U)$, and $P(s_2 | U)$.

15.6 Utility Theory

The decision analysis situations presented so far in this chapter expressed outcomes (payoffs) in terms of monetary values. With probability information available about the outcomes of the chance events, we defined the optimal decision alternative as the one that provides the best expected value. However, in some situations the decision alternative with the best expected value may not be the preferred alternative. A decision maker may also wish to consider intangible factors such as risk, image, or other nonmonetary criteria in order to evaluate the decision alternatives. When monetary value does not necessarily lead to the most preferred decision, expressing the value (or worth) of a consequence in terms of its utility will permit the use of expected utility to identify the most desirable decision alternative. The discussion of utility and its application in decision analysis is presented in this section.

Utility is a measure of the total worth or relative desirability of a particular outcome; it reflects the decision maker's attitude toward a collection of factors such as profit, loss, and risk. Researchers have found that as long as the monetary value of payoffs stays within a range that the decision maker considers reasonable, selecting the decision alternative with the best expected value usually leads to selection of the most preferred decision. However, when the payoffs are extreme, decision makers are often unsatisfied or uneasy with the decision that simply provides the best expected value.

As an example of a situation in which utility can help in selecting the best decision alternative, let us consider the problem faced by Swofford, Inc., a relatively small real estate investment firm located in Atlanta, Georgia. Swofford currently has two investment opportunities that require approximately the same cash outlay. The cash requirements necessary prohibit Swofford from making more than one investment at this time. Consequently, three possible decision alternatives may be considered.

The three decision alternatives, denoted by d_1, d_2, and d_3, are as follows:

$$d_1 = \text{make investment A}$$
$$d_2 = \text{make investment B}$$
$$d_3 = \text{do not invest}$$

TABLE 15.7	Payoff Table for Swofford, Inc.		
		State of Nature	
Decision Alternative	**Prices Up, s_1**	**Prices Stable, s_2**	**Prices Down, s_3**
Investment A, d_1	$30,000	$20,000	−$50,000
Investment B, d_2	$50,000	−$20,000	−$30,000
Do not invest, d_3	0	0	0

The monetary payoffs associated with the investment opportunities depend on the investment decision and on the direction of the real estate market during the next six months (the chance event). Real estate prices will go up, remain stable, or go down. Thus, the states of nature, denoted by s_1, s_2, and s_3, are as follows:

$$s_1 = \text{real estate prices go up}$$
$$s_2 = \text{real estate prices remain stable}$$
$$s_3 = \text{real estate prices go down}$$

Using the best information available, Swofford has estimated the profits, or payoffs, associated with each decision alternative and state-of-nature combination. The resulting payoff table is shown in Table 15.7.

The best estimate of the probability that real estate prices will go up is 0.3; the best estimate of the probability that prices will remain stable is 0.5; and the best estimate of the probability that prices will go down is 0.2. Thus, the expected values for the three decision alternatives are as follows:

$$\text{EV}(d_1) = 0.3(30,000) + 0.5(20,000) \quad + 0.2(-50,000) = \quad 9,000$$
$$\text{EV}(d_2) = 0.3(50,000) + 0.5(-20,000) + 0.2(-30,000) = -11,000$$
$$\text{EV}(d_3) = 0.3(0) \qquad + 0.5(0) \qquad + 0.2(0) \qquad = \qquad 0$$

Using the expected value approach, the optimal decision is to select investment A with an expected value of $9,000. Is it really the best decision alternative? Let us consider some other relevant factors that relate to Swofford's capability for absorbing the loss of $50,000 if investment A is made and prices actually go down.

Actually, Swofford's current financial position is weak. This condition is partly reflected in Swofford's ability to make only one investment. More important, however, the firm's president believes that, if the next investment results in a substantial loss, Swofford's future will be in jeopardy. Although the expected value approach leads to a recommendation for d_1, do you think the firm's president would prefer this decision? We suspect that the president would select d_2 or d_3 to avoid the possibility of incurring a $50,000 loss. In fact, a reasonable conclusion is that, if a loss of even $30,000 could drive Swofford out of business, the president would select d_3, believing that both investments A and B are too risky for Swofford's current financial position.

The way we resolve Swofford's dilemma is first to determine Swofford's utility for the various outcomes. Recall that the utility of any outcome is the total worth of that outcome, taking into account all risks and consequences involved. If the utilities for the various consequences are assessed correctly, the decision alternative with the highest expected utility is the most preferred, or best, alternative. We next show how to determine the utility of the outcomes so that the alternative with the highest expected utility can be identified.

Utility and Decision Analysis

The procedure we use to establish a utility for each of the payoffs in Swofford's situation requires that we first assign a utility to the best and worst possible payoffs. Any values will work as long as the utility assigned to the best payoff is greater than the utility assigned to the worst payoff. In this case, $50,000 is the best payoff and $-$50,000 is the worst. Suppose, then, that we arbitrarily make assignments to these two payoffs as follows:

$$\text{Utility of} - \$50,000 = U(-50,000) = 0$$
$$\text{Utility of } \$50,000 = U(50,000) = 10$$

Let us now determine the utility associated with every other payoff.

Utility values of 0 and 1 could have been selected here; we selected 0 and 10 to avoid any possible confusion between the utility value for a payoff and the probability p.

Consider the process of establishing the utility of a payoff of $30,000. First we ask Swofford's president to state a preference between a guaranteed $30,000 payoff and an opportunity to engage in the following lottery, or bet, for some probability of p that we select:

p is often referred to as the indifference probability.

Lottery: Swofford obtains a payoff of $50,000 with probability p and a payoff of $-$50,000 with probability $(1 - p)$.

Obviously, if p is very close to 1, Swofford's president would prefer the lottery to the guaranteed payoff of $30,000 because the firm would virtually ensure itself a payoff of $50,000. If p is very close to 0, Swofford's president would clearly prefer the guarantee of $30,000. In any event, as p increases continuously from 0 to 1, the preference for the guaranteed payoff of $30,000 decreases and at some point is equal to the preference for the lottery. At this value of p, Swofford's president would have equal preference for the guaranteed payoff of $30,000 and the lottery; at greater values of p, Swofford's president would prefer the lottery to the guaranteed $30,000 payoff. For example, let us assume that when $p = 0.95$, Swofford's president is indifferent between the guaranteed payoff of $30,000 and the lottery. For this value of p, we can compute the utility of a $30,000 payoff as follows:

$$U(30,000) = pU(50,000) + (1 - p)U(-50,000)$$
$$= 0.95(10) + (0.05)(0)$$
$$= 9.5$$

Obviously, if we had started with a different assignment of utilities for a payoff of $50,000 and $-$50,000, the result would have been a different utility for $30,000. For example, if we had started with an assignment of 100 for $50,000 and 10 for $-$50,000, the utility of a $30,000 payoff would be

$$U(30,000) = 0.95(100) + 0.05(10)$$
$$= 95.0 + 0.5$$
$$= 95.5$$

Hence, we must conclude that the utility assigned to each payoff is not unique but merely depends on the initial choice of utilities for the best and worst payoffs.

Before computing the utility for the other payoffs, let us consider the implication of Swofford's president assigning a utility of 9.5 to a payoff of $30,000. Clearly, when $p = 0.95$, the expected value of the lottery is

$$EV(\text{lottery}) = 0.95(\$50,000) + 0.05(-\$50,000)$$
$$= \$47,500 - \$2,500$$
$$= \$45,000$$

The difference between the expected value of the lottery and the guaranteed payoff can be viewed as the risk premium the decision maker is willing to pay.

Although the expected value of the lottery when $p = 0.95$ is $45,000, Swofford's president is indifferent between the lottery (and its associated risk) and a guaranteed payoff of $30,000. Thus, Swofford's president is taking a conservative, or risk-avoiding, viewpoint. A decision maker who would choose a guaranteed payoff over a lottery with a superior expected payoff is a **risk avoider** (or is said to be risk-averse). The president would rather have $30,000 for certain than risk anything greater than a 5% chance of incurring a loss of $50,000. In other words, the difference between the EV of $45,000 and the guaranteed payoff of $30,000 is the risk premium that Swofford's president would be willing to pay to avoid the 5% chance of losing $50,000.

To compute the utility associated with a payoff of $-$20,000, we must ask Swofford's president to state a preference between a guaranteed $-$20,000 payoff and an opportunity to engage again in the following lottery:

Lottery: Swofford obtains a payoff of $50,000 with probability p and a payoff of $-$50,000 with probability $(1 - p)$.

Note that this lottery is exactly the same as the one we used to establish the utility of a payoff of $30,000 (in fact, we can use this lottery to establish the utility for any value in the Swofford payoff table). We need to determine the value of p that would make the president indifferent between a guaranteed payoff of $-$20,000 and the lottery. For example, we might begin by asking the president to choose between a certain loss of $20,000 and the lottery with a payoff of $50,000 with probability $p = 0.90$ and a payoff of $-$50,000 with probability $(1 - p) = 0.10$. What answer do you think we would get? Surely, with this high probability of obtaining a payoff of $50,000, the president would elect the lottery. Next, we might ask whether $p = 0.85$ would result in indifference between the loss of $20,000 for certain and the lottery. Again the president might prefer the lottery. Suppose that we continue until we get to $p = 0.55$, at which point the president is indifferent between the payoff of $-$20,000 and the lottery. In other words, for any value of p less than 0.55, the president would take a loss of $20,000 for certain rather than risk the potential loss of $50,000 with the lottery; and for any value of p above 0.55, the president would choose the lottery. Thus, the utility assigned to a payoff of $-$20,000 is

$$U(-\$20,000) = pU(50,000) + (1 - p)U(-\$50,000)$$
$$= 0.55(10) + 0.45(0)$$
$$= 5.5$$

Again let us assess the implication of this assignment by comparing it to the expected value approach. When $p = 0.55$, the expected value of the lottery is

$$EV(\text{lottery}) = 0.55(\$50,000) + 0.45(-\$50,000)$$
$$= \$27,500 - \$22,500$$
$$= \$5,000$$

Thus, Swofford's president would just as soon absorb a certain loss of $20,000 as take the lottery and its associated risk, even though the expected value of the lottery is $5,000. Once again this preference demonstrates the conservative, or risk-avoiding, point of view of Swofford's president.

In these two examples, we computed the utility for the payoffs of $30,000 and $-$20,000. We can determine the utility for any payoff M in a similar fashion. First, we must find the probability p for which the decision maker is indifferent between a guaranteed payoff of M and a lottery with a payoff of $50,000 with probability p and $-$50,000 with probability $(1 - p)$. The utility of M is then computed as follows:

$$U(M) = pU(\$50,000) + (1 - p)U(-\$50,000)$$
$$= p(10) + (1 - p)0$$
$$= 10p$$

Using this procedure we developed a utility for each of the remaining payoffs in Swofford problem. The results are presented in Table 15.8.

Now that we have determined the utility of each of the possible monetary values, we can write the original payoff table in terms of utility. Table 15.9 shows the utility for the various outcomes in the Swofford problem. The notation we use for the entries in the utility table is U_{ij}, which denotes the utility associated with decision alternative d_i and state of nature s_j. Using this notation, we see that $U_{23} = 4.0$.

TABLE 15.8	Utility of Monetary Payoffs for Swofford, Inc.	
Monetary Value	**Indifference Value of p**	**Utility**
$50,000	Does not apply	10.0
30,000	0.95	9.5
20,000	0.90	9.0
0	0.75	7.5
−20,000	0.55	5.5
−30,000	0.40	4.0
−50,000	Does not apply	0

TABLE 15.9	Utility Table for Swofford, Inc.		
		State of Nature	
Decision Alternative	**Prices Up, s_1**	**Prices Stable, s_2**	**Prices Down, s_3**
Investment A, d_1	9.5	9.0	0
Investment B, d_2	10.0	5.5	4.0
Do not invest, d_3	7.5	7.5	7.5

We can now compute the **expected utility (EU)** of the utilities in Table 15.9 in a similar fashion as we computed expected value in Section 15.3. In other words, to identify an optimal decision alternative for Swofford, Inc., the expected utility approach requires the analyst to compute the expected utility for each decision alternative and then select the alternative yielding the highest expected utility. With N possible states of nature, the expected utility of a decision alternative d_i is given as follows:

EXPECTED UTILITY (EU)

$$EU(d_i) = \sum_{j=1}^{N} P(s_j)U_{ij} \qquad (15.6)$$

The expected utility for each of the decision alternatives in the Swofford problem is as follows:

$$EU(d_1) = 0.3(9.5) + 0.5(9.0) + 0.2(0) = 7.35$$
$$EU(d_2) = 0.3(10) + 0.5(5.5) + 0.2(4.0) = 6.55$$
$$EU(d_3) = 0.3(7.5) + 0.5(7.5) + 0.2(7.5) = 7.50$$

Note that the optimal decision using the expected utility approach is d_3; do not invest. The ranking of alternatives according to the president's utility assignments and the associated monetary values are as follows:

Ranking of Decision Alternatives	Expected Utility	Expected Value
Do not invest	7.50	0
Investment A	7.35	9,000
Investment B	6.55	−1,000

Note that, although investment A had the highest expected value of $9,000, the analysis indicates that Swofford should decline this investment. The rationale behind not selecting investment A is that the 0.20 probability of a $50,000 loss was considered by Swofford's president to involve a serious risk. The seriousness of this risk and its associated impact on the company were not adequately reflected by the expected value of investment A. We assessed the utility for each payoff to assess this risk adequately.

The following steps state in general terms the procedure used to solve the Swofford, Inc. investment problem:

Step 1. Develop a payoff table using monetary values
Step 2. Identify the best and worst payoff values in the table and assign each a utility, with U(best payoff) $>$ U(worst payoff)
Step 3. For every other monetary value M in the original payoff table, do the following to determine its utility:
 a. Define the lottery such that there is a probability p of the best payoff and a probability $(1 - p)$ of the worst payoff
 b. Determine the value of p such that the decision maker is indifferent between a guaranteed payoff of M and the lottery defined in Step 3(a)
 c. Calculate the utility of M as follows:

$$U(M) = pU\left(\text{best payoff}\right) + (1 - p)U\left(\text{worst payoff}\right)$$

Step 4. Convert each monetary value in the payoff table to a utility
Step 5. Apply the expected utility approach to the utility table developed in Step 4 and select the decision alternative with the highest expected utility

The procedure we described for determining the utility of monetary consequences can also be used to develop a utility measure for nonmonetary consequences. Assign the best consequence a utility of 10 and the worst a utility of 0. Then create a lottery with a probability of p for the best consequence and $(1 - p)$ for the worst consequence. For each of the other consequences, find the value of p that makes the decision maker indifferent between the lottery and the consequence. Then calculate the utility of the consequence in question as follows:

$$U(\text{consequence}) = pU(\text{best consequence}) + (1 - p)U(\text{worst consequence})$$

Utility Functions

Next, we describe how different decision makers may approach risk in terms of their assessment of utility. The financial position of Swofford, Inc. was such that the firm's president evaluated investment opportunities from a conservative, or risk-avoiding, point of view. However, if the firm had a surplus of cash and a stable future, Swofford's president might have been looking for investment alternatives that, although perhaps risky, contained a potential for substantial profit. That type of behavior would demonstrate that the president is a risk taker with respect to this decision.

A **risk taker** is a decision maker who would choose a lottery over a guaranteed payoff when the expected value of the lottery is inferior to the guaranteed payoff. In this section, we analyze the decision problem faced by Swofford from the point of view of a decision maker who would be classified as a risk taker. We then compare the conservative point of view of Swofford's president (a risk avoider) with the behavior of a decision maker who is a risk taker.

For the decision problem facing Swofford, Inc., using the general procedure for developing utilities as discussed previously, a risk taker might express the utility for the various payoffs shown in Table 15.10. As before, $U(50,000) = 10$ and $U(-50,000) = 0$. Note the difference in behavior reflected in Tables 15.10 and 15.8. In other words, in determining the value of p at which the decision maker is indifferent between a guaranteed payoff of M and a lottery in which $50,000 is obtained with probability p and $-$50,000 with probability $(1 - p)$, the risk taker is willing to accept a greater risk of incurring a loss of $50,000 in order to gain the opportunity to realize a profit of $50,000.

TABLE 15.10	Revised Utilities for Swofford, Inc., Assuming a Risk Taker	
Monetary Value	**Indifference Value of p**	**Utility**
$50,000	Does not apply	10.0
30,000	0.50	5.0
20,000	0.40	4.0
0	0.25	2.5
−20,000	0.15	1.5
−30,000	0.10	1.0
−50,000	Does not apply	0

To help develop the utility table for the risk taker, we have reproduced the Swofford, Inc. payoff table in Table 15.11. Using these payoffs and the risk taker's utilities given in Table 15.10, we can write the risk taker's utility table as shown in Table 15.12. Using the state-of-nature probabilities $P(s_1) = 0.3$, $P(s_2) = 0.5$, and $P(s_3) = 0.2$, the expected utility for each decision alternative is as follows:

$$\text{EU}(d_1) = 0.3(5.0) + 0.5(4.0) + 0.2(0) = 3.50$$
$$\text{EU}(d_2) = 0.3(10) + 0.5(1.5) + 0.2(1.0) = 3.95$$
$$\text{EU}(d_3) = 0.3(2.5) + 0.5(2.5) + 0.2(2.5) = 2.50$$

What is the recommended decision? Perhaps somewhat to your surprise, the analysis recommends investment B, with the highest expected utility of 3.95. Recall that this investment has a −$1,000 expected value. Why is it now the recommended decision? Remember that the decision maker in this revised problem is a risk taker. Thus, although the expected value of investment B is negative, utility analysis has shown that this decision maker is enough of a risk taker to prefer investment B and its potential for the $50,000 profit.

TABLE 15.11	Payoff Table for Swofford, Inc.		
		State of Nature	
Decision Alternative	**Prices Up, s_1**	**Prices Stable, s_2**	**Prices Down, s_3**
Investment A, d_1	$30,000	$20,000	−$50,000
Investment B, d_2	$50,000	−$20,000	−$30,000
Do not invest, d_3	0	0	0

TABLE 15.12	Utility Table of a Risk Taker for Swofford, Inc.		
		State of Nature	
Decision Alternative	**Prices Up, s_1**	**Prices Stable, s_2**	**Prices Down, s_3**
Investment A, d_1	5.0	4.0	0
Investment B, d_2	10.0	1.5	1.0
Do not invest, d_3	2.5	2.5	2.5

Ranking by the expected utilities generates the following order of preference of the decision alternatives for the risk taker and the associated expected values:

Ranking of Decision Alternatives	Expected Utility	Expected Value
Investment B	3.95	−$1,000
Investment A	3.50	$9,000
Do not invest	2.50	0

Comparing the utility analysis for a risk taker with the more conservative preferences of the president of Swofford, Inc., who is a risk avoider, we see that, even with the same decision problem, different attitudes toward risk can lead to different recommended decisions. The utilities established by Swofford's president indicated that the firm should not invest at this time, whereas the utilities established by the risk taker showed a preference for investment B. Note that both of these decisions differ from the best expected value decision, which was investment A.

We can obtain another perspective of the difference between behaviors of a risk avoider and a risk taker by developing a graph that depicts the relationship between monetary value and utility. We use the horizontal axis of the graph to represent monetary values and the vertical axis to represent the utility associated with each monetary value. Now, consider the data in Table 15.8, with a utility corresponding to each monetary value for the original Swofford, Inc. problem. These values can be plotted on a graph to produce the top curve in Figure 15.11. The resulting curve is the **utility function for money** for Swofford's president. Recall that these points reflected the conservative, or risk-avoiding, nature of Swofford's president. Hence, we refer to the top curve in Figure 15.11 as a utility function for a risk avoider. Using the data in Table 15.10 developed for a risk taker, we can plot these points to produce the bottom curve in Figure 15.11. The resulting curve depicts the utility function for a risk taker.

By looking at the utility functions in Figure 15.11, we can begin to generalize about the utility functions for risk avoiders and risk takers. Although the exact shape of the utility

FIGURE 15.11   Utility Function for Money for Risk-Avoider, Risk-Taker, and Risk-Neutral Decision Makers

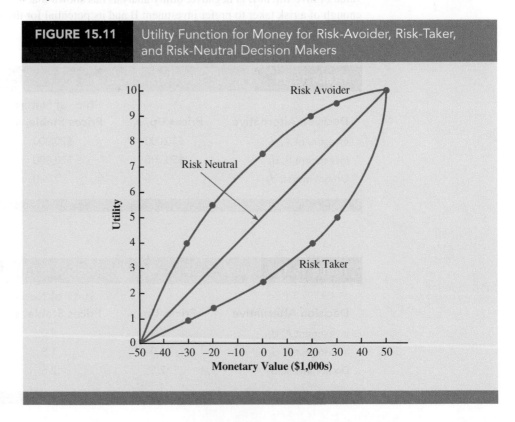

function will vary from one decision maker to another, we can see the general shape of these two types of utility functions. The utility function for a risk avoider shows a diminishing marginal return for money. For example, the increase in utility going from a monetary value of −\$30,000 to \$0 is 7.5 − 4.0 = 3.5, whereas the increase in utility in going from \$0 to \$30,000 is only 9.5 − 7.5 = 2.0.

However, the utility function for a risk taker shows an increasing marginal return for money. For example, in Figure 15.11, the increase in utility for the risk taker in going from −\$30,000 to \$0 is 2.5 − 1.0 = 1.5, whereas the increase in utility in going from \$0 to \$30,000 for the risk taker is 5.0 − 2.5 = 2.5. Note also that in either case the utility function is always increasing; that is, more money leads to more utility. All utility functions possess this property.

We concluded that the utility function for a risk avoider shows a diminishing marginal return for money and that the utility function for a risk taker shows an increasing marginal return. When the marginal return for money is neither decreasing nor increasing but remains constant, the corresponding utility function describes the behavior of a decision maker who is neutral to risk. The following characteristics are associated with a **risk-neutral** decision maker:

1. The utility function can be drawn as a straight line connecting the "best" and the "worst" points.
2. The expected utility approach and the expected value approach applied to monetary payoffs result in the same action.

The straight, diagonal line in Figure 15.11 depicts the utility function of a risk-neutral decision maker using the Swofford, Inc. problem data.

Generally, when the payoffs for a particular decision-making problem fall into a reasonable range—the best is not too good and the worst is not too bad—decision makers tend to express preferences in agreement with the expected value approach. Thus, we suggest asking the decision maker to consider the best and worst possible payoffs for a problem and assess their reasonableness. If the decision maker believes that they are in the reasonable range, the decision alternative with the best expected value can be used. However, if the payoffs appear unreasonably large or unreasonably small (e.g., a huge loss) and if the decision maker believes that monetary values do not adequately reflect her or his true preferences for the payoffs, a utility analysis of the problem should be considered.

Exponential Utility Function

Having a decision maker provide enough indifference values to create a utility function can be time consuming. An alternative is to assume that the decision maker's utility is defined by an exponential function. Figure 15.12 shows examples of different exponential utility functions. Note that all the exponential utility functions indicate that the decision maker is risk averse. The form of the exponential utility function is as follows:

In equation (15.7), the number e ≈ 2.718282... is a mathematical constant corresponding to the base of the natural logarithm. In Excel, e^x can be evaluated for any power x using the function EXP(x).

EXPONENTIAL UTILITY FUNCTION

$$U(x) = 1 - e^{-x/R} \tag{15.7}$$

The R parameter in equation (15.7) represents the decision maker's risk tolerance; it controls the shape of the exponential utility function. Larger R values create flatter exponential functions, indicating that the decision maker is less risk averse (closer to risk neutral). Smaller R values indicate that the decision maker has less risk tolerance (is more risk averse). A common method to determine an approximate risk tolerance is to ask the decision maker to consider a scenario in which he or she could win \$$R$ with probability 0.5 and lose \$$R$/2 with probability 0.5. The R value to use in equation (15.7) is the largest \$$R$ for which the decision maker would accept this gamble. For instance, if the decision maker is comfortable accepting

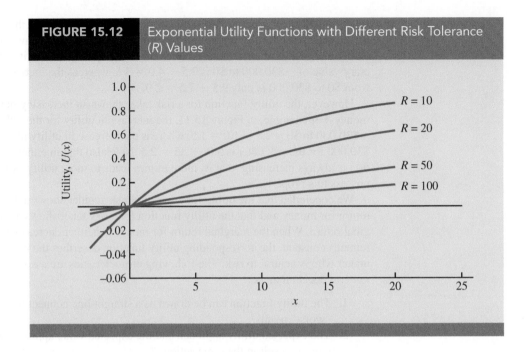

FIGURE 15.12   Exponential Utility Functions with Different Risk Tolerance (R) Values

a gamble with a 50% chance of winning $2,000 and a 50% chance of losing $1,000, but not with a gamble with a 50% chance of winning $3,000 and a 50% chance of losing $1,500, then we would use $R = \$2,000$ in equation (15.7). Determining the maximum gamble that a decision maker is willing to take and then using this value in the exponential utility function can be much less time consuming than generating a complete table of indifference probabilities. One should remember that using an exponential utility function assumes that the decision maker is risk averse; however, this is often true in practice for business decisions.

N O T E S   +   C O M M E N T S

1. In the Swofford problem, we have been using a utility of 10 for the best payoff and 0 for the worst. We could have chosen any values as long as the utility associated with the best payoff exceeds the utility associated with the worst payoff. Alternatively, a utility of 1 can be associated with the best payoff and a utility of 0 can be associated with the worst payoff. Had we made this choice, the utility for any monetary value M would have been the value of p at which the decision maker was indifferent between a guaranteed payoff of M and a lottery in which the best payoff is obtained with probability p and the worst payoff is obtained with probability $(1 - p)$. Thus, the utility for any monetary value would have been equal to the probability of earning the best payoff. Often this choice is made because of the ease in computation. We chose not to do so to emphasize the distinction between the utilities and the indifference probabilities for the lottery.

2. Circumstances often dictate whether one acts as a risk avoider or a risk taker when making a decision. For example, you may think of yourself as a risk avoider when faced with financial decisions, but if you have ever purchased

a lottery ticket, you have actually acted as a risk taker. Suppose you purchase a $1 lottery ticket for a simple lottery in which the object is to pick the six numbers that will be drawn from 50 potential numbers. Also suppose that the winner (who correctly chooses all six numbers that are drawn) will receive $1,000,000. There are 15,890,700 possible winning combinations, so your probability of winning is 1/15,890,700 = 0.000000062929889809763 (i.e., *very low*) and the expected value of your ticket is

$$\frac{1}{15{,}890{,}700}(\$1{,}000{,}000 - \$1) + \left(1 - \frac{1}{15{,}890{,}700}\right)(-\$1)$$
$$= -\$0.93707$$

or about −$0.94.

If a lottery ticket has a negative expected value, why does anyone play? The answer is in utility; most people who play lotteries associate great utility with the possibility of winning the $1,000,000 prize and relatively little utility with the $1 cost for a ticket, and so the expected value of the utility of the lottery ticket is positive even though the expected value of the ticket is negative.

SUMMARY

Decision analysis can be used to determine a recommended decision alternative or an optimal decision strategy when a decision maker is faced with an uncertain and risk-filled pattern of future events. The goal of decision analysis is to identify the best decision alternative or the optimal decision strategy, given information about the uncertain events and the possible consequences or payoffs. The "best" decision should consider the risk preference of the decision maker in evaluating outcomes.

We showed how payoff tables and decision trees could be used to structure a decision problem and describe the relationships among the decisions, the chance events, and the consequences. We presented three approaches to decision making without probabilities: the optimistic approach, the conservative approach, and the minimax regret approach. When probability assessments are provided for the states of nature, the expected value approach can be used to identify the recommended decision alternative or decision strategy.

Even though the expected value approach can be used to obtain a recommended decision alternative or optimal decision strategy, the payoff that actually occurs will usually have a value different from the expected value. A risk profile provides a probability distribution for the possible payoffs and can assist the decision maker in assessing the risks associated with different decision alternatives. Sensitivity analysis can be conducted to determine the effect changes in the probabilities for the states of nature and changes in the values of the payoffs have on the recommended decision alternative.

In cases in which sample information about the chance events is available, a sequence of decisions has to be made. First we must decide whether to obtain the sample information. If the answer is yes, an optimal decision strategy based on the specific sample information must be developed. In this situation, decision trees and the expected value approach can be used to determine the optimal decision strategy.

Bayes' theorem can be used to compute branch probabilities for decision trees. Bayes' theorem updates a decision maker's prior probabilities regarding the states of nature using sample information to compute revised posterior probabilities.

We showed how utility could be used in decision-making situations in which monetary value did not provide an adequate measure of the payoffs. Utility is a measure of the total worth of an outcome. As such, utility takes into account the decision maker's assessment of all aspects of a consequence, including profit, loss, risk, and perhaps additional nonmonetary factors. The examples showed how the use of expected utility can lead to decision recommendations that differ from those based on expected value.

A decision maker's judgment must be used to establish the utility for each consequence. We presented a step-by-step procedure to determine a decision maker's utility for monetary payoffs. We also discussed how conservative, risk-avoiding decision makers assess utility differently from more aggressive, risk-taking decision makers.

GLOSSARY

Bayes' theorem A theorem that enables the use of sample information to revise prior probabilities.

Branch Lines showing the alternatives from decision nodes and the outcomes from chance nodes.

Chance event An uncertain future event affecting the consequence, or payoff, associated with a decision.

Chance nodes Nodes indicating points at which an uncertain event will occur.

Conditional probabilities The probability of one event, given the known outcome of a (possibly) related event.

Conservative approach An approach to choosing a decision alternative without using probabilities. For a maximization problem, it leads to choosing the decision alternative that maximizes the minimum payoff; for a minimization problem, it leads to choosing the decision alternative that minimizes the maximum payoff.

Decision alternatives Options available to the decision maker.

Decision nodes Nodes indicating points at which a decision is made.

Decision strategy A strategy involving a sequence of decisions and chance outcomes to provide the optimal solution to a decision problem.

Decision tree A graphical representation of the decision problem that shows the sequential nature of the decision-making process.

Expected utility (EU) The weighted average of the utilities associated with a decision alternative. The weights are the state-of-nature probabilities.

Expected value (EV) For a chance node, the weighted average of the payoffs. The weights are the state-of-nature probabilities.

Expected value approach An approach to choosing a decision alternative based on the expected value of each decision alternative. The recommended decision alternative is the one that provides the best expected value.

Expected value of perfect information (EVPI) The difference between the expected value of an optimal strategy based on perfect information and the "best" expected value without any sample information.

Expected value of sample information (EVSI) The difference between the expected value of an optimal strategy based on sample information and the "best" expected value without any sample information.

Minimax regret approach An approach to choosing a decision alternative without using probabilities. For each alternative, the maximum regret is computed, which leads to choosing the decision alternative that minimizes the maximum regret.

Node An intersection or junction point of a decision tree.

Optimistic approach An approach to choosing a decision alternative without using probabilities. For a maximization problem, it leads to choosing the decision alternative corresponding to the largest payoff; for a minimization problem, it leads to choosing the decision alternative corresponding to the smallest payoff.

Outcome The result obtained when a decision alternative is chosen and a chance event occurs.

Payoff A measure of the outcome of a decision such as profit, cost, or time. Each combination of a decision alternative and a state of nature has an associated payoff.

Payoff table A tabular representation of the payoffs for a decision problem.

Perfect information A special case of sample information in which the information tells the decision maker exactly which state of nature is going to occur.

Posterior (revised) probabilities The probabilities of the states of nature after revising the prior probabilities based on sample information.

Prior probabilities The probabilities of the states of nature prior to obtaining sample information.

Regret (opportunity loss) The amount of loss (lower profit or higher cost) from not making the best decision for each state of nature.

Risk analysis The study of the possible payoffs and probabilities associated with a decision alternative or a decision strategy in the face of uncertainty.

Risk avoider A decision maker who would choose a guaranteed payoff over a lottery with a better expected payoff.

Risk-neutral A decision maker who is neutral to risk. For this decision maker, the decision alternative with the best expected value is identical to the alternative with the highest expected utility.

Risk profile The probability distribution of the possible payoffs associated with a decision alternative or decision strategy.

Risk taker A decision maker who would choose a lottery over a better guaranteed payoff.

Sample information New information obtained through research or experimentation that enables updating or revising the state-of-nature probabilities.

Sensitivity analysis The study of how changes in the probability assessments for the states of nature or changes in the payoffs affect the recommended decision alternative.

States of nature The possible outcomes for chance events that affect the payoff associated with a decision alternative.

Utility A measure of the total worth of a consequence reflecting a decision maker's attitude toward considerations such as profit, loss, and risk.

Utility function for money A curve that depicts the relationship between monetary value and utility.

PROBLEMS

1. **Two Decision Alternatives and Three States of Nature.** The following payoff table shows profit for a decision analysis problem with two decision alternatives and three states of nature:

	State of Nature		
Decision Alternative	s_1	s_2	s_3
d_1	250	100	25
d_2	100	100	75

   a. Construct a decision tree for this problem.
   b. If the decision maker knows nothing about the probabilities of the three states of nature, what is the recommended decision using the optimistic, conservative, and minimax regret approaches?

2. **Plant Size Decision.** Southland Corporation's decision to produce a new line of recreational products resulted in the need to construct either a small plant or a large plant. The best selection of plant size depends on how the marketplace reacts to the new product line. To conduct an analysis, marketing management has decided to view the possible long-run demand as low, medium, or high. The following payoff table shows the projected profit in millions of dollars:

	Long-Run Demand		
Plan Size	Low	Medium	High
Small	150	200	200
Large	50	200	500

   a. What is the decision to be made, and what is the chance event for Southland's problem?
   b. Construct a decision tree.
   c. Recommend a decision based on the use of the optimistic, conservative, and minimax regret approaches.

3. **Car Leases.** Amy Lloyd is interested in leasing a new Honda and has contacted three automobile dealers for pricing information. Each dealer offered Amy a closed-end 36-month lease with no down payment due at the time of signing. Each lease includes a monthly charge and a mileage allowance. Additional miles receive a surcharge on a per-mile basis. The monthly lease cost, the mileage allowance, and the cost for additional miles are as follows:

Dealer	Monthly Cost	Mileage Allowance	Cost per Additional Mile
Hepburn Honda	$299	36,000	$0.15
Midtown Motors	$310	45,000	$0.20
Hopkins Automotive	$325	54,000	$0.15

Amy decided to choose the lease option that will minimize her total 36-month cost. The difficulty is that Amy is not sure how many miles she will drive over the next three years. For purposes of this decision, she believes it is reasonable to assume that she will drive 12,000 miles per year, 15,000 miles per year, or 18,000 miles per year. With this assumption Amy estimated her total costs for the three lease options. For example, she figures that the Hepburn Honda lease will cost her $36(\$299) + \$0.15(36,000 - 36,000) = \$10,764$ if she drives 12,000 miles per year, $36(\$299) + \$0.15(45,000 - 36,000) = \$12,114$ if she drives 15,000 miles per year, or $36(\$299) + \$0.15(54,000 - 36,000) = \$13,464$ if she drives 18,000 miles per year.

a. What is the decision, and what is the chance event?
b. Construct a payoff table for Amy's problem.
c. If Amy has no idea which of the three mileage assumptions is most appropriate, what is the recommended decision (leasing option) using the optimistic, conservative, and minimax regret approaches?
d. Suppose that the probabilities that Amy drives 12,000, 15,000, and 18,000 miles per year are 0.5, 0.4, and 0.1, respectively. What option should Amy choose using the expected value approach?
e. Develop a risk profile for the decision selected in part (d). What is the most likely cost, and what is its probability?
f. Suppose that, after further consideration, Amy concludes that the probabilities that she will drive 12,000, 15,000, and 18,000 miles per year are 0.3, 0.4, and 0.3, respectively. What decision should Amy make using the expected value approach?

4. **Market Segment Investment.** Investment advisors estimated the stock market returns for four market segments: computers, financial, manufacturing, and pharmaceuticals. Annual return projections vary depending on whether the general economic conditions are improving, stable, or declining. The anticipated annual return percentages for each market segment under each economic condition are as follows:

| | Economic Condition | | |
Market Segment	Improving	Stable	Declining
Computers	10	2	-4
Financial	8	5	-3
Manufacturing	6	4	-2
Pharmaceuticals	6	5	-1

a. Assume that an individual investor wants to select one market segment for a new investment. A forecast shows improving to declining economic conditions with the following probabilities: improving (0.2), stable (0.5), and declining (0.3). What is the preferred market segment for the investor, and what is the expected return percentage?
b. At a later date, a revised forecast shows a potential for an improvement in economic conditions. New probabilities are as follows: improving (0.4), stable (0.4), and declining (0.2). What is the preferred market segment for the investor based on these new probabilities? What is the expected return percentage?

5. **Data Warehouse Operation.** Hudson Corporation is considering three options for managing its data warehouse: continuing with its own staff, hiring an outside vendor to do the managing, or using a combination of its own staff and an outside vendor. The cost of the operation depends on future demand. The annual cost of each option (in thousands of dollars) depends on demand as follows:

| | Demand | | |
Staffing Options	High	Medium	Low
Own staff	650	650	600
Outside vendor	900	600	300
Combination	800	650	500

a. If the demand probabilities are 0.2, 0.5, and 0.3, which decision alternative will minimize the expected cost of the data warehouse? What is the expected annual cost associated with that recommendation?

b. Construct a risk profile for the optimal decision in part (a). What is the probability of the cost exceeding $700,000?

6. **Two States of Nature and Two Decision Alternatives.** The following payoff table shows the profit for a decision problem with two states of nature and two decision alternatives:

	State of Nature	
Decision Alternative	s_1	s_2
d_1	10	1
d_2	4	3

a. Suppose $P(s_1) = 0.2$ and $P(s_2) = 0.8$. What is the best decision using the expected value approach?

b. Perform sensitivity analysis on the payoffs for decision alternative d_1. Assume that the probabilities are as given in part (a), and find the range of payoffs under states of nature s_1 and s_2 that will keep the solution found in part (a) optimal. Is the solution more sensitive to the payoff under state of nature s_1 or s_2?

7. **Cleveland to Myrtle Beach Air Service.** Myrtle Air Express decided to offer direct service from Cleveland to Myrtle Beach. Management must decide between a full-price service using the company's new fleet of jet aircraft and a discount service using smaller-capacity commuter planes. It is clear that the best choice depends on the market reaction to the service Myrtle Air offers. Management developed estimates of the contribution to profit for each type of service based on two possible levels of demand for service to Myrtle Beach: strong and weak. The following table shows the estimated quarterly profits (in thousands of dollars):

	Demand for Service	
Service	Strong	Weak
Full price	$960	-$490
Discount	$670	$320

a. What is the decision to be made, what is the chance event, and what is the consequence for this problem? How many decision alternatives are there? How many outcomes are there for the chance event?

b. If nothing is known about the probabilities of the chance outcomes, what is the recommended decision using the optimistic, conservative, and minimax regret approaches?

c. Suppose that management of Myrtle Air Express believes that the probability of strong demand is 0.7 and the probability of weak demand is 0.3. Use the expected value approach to determine an optimal decision.

d. Suppose that the probability of strong demand is 0.8 and the probability of weak demand is 0.2. What is the optimal decision using the expected value approach?

e. Use sensitivity analysis to determine the range of demand probabilities for which each of the decision alternatives has the largest expected value.

8. **Video Game Profitability.** Video Tech is considering marketing one of two new video games for the coming holiday season: Battle Pacific or Space Pirates. Battle Pacific is a unique game and appears to have no competition. Estimated profits (in thousands of dollars) under high, medium, and low demand are as follows:

	Demand		
Battle Pacific	High	Medium	Low
Profit	$1,000	$700	$300
Probability	0.2	0.5	0.3

Video Tech is optimistic about its Space Pirates game. However, the concern is that profitability will be affected by a competitor's introduction of a video game viewed as similar to Space Pirates. Estimated profits (in thousands of dollars) with and without competition are as follows:

Space Pirates With Competition	Demand High	Demand Medium	Demand Low
Profit	$800	$400	$200
Probability	0.3	0.4	0.3

Space Pirates Without Competition	Demand High	Demand Medium	Demand Low
Profit	$1,600	$800	$400
Probability	0.5	0.3	0.2

a. Develop a decision tree for the Video Tech problem.
b. For planning purposes, Video Tech believes there is a 0.6 probability that its competitor will produce a new game similar to Space Pirates. Given this probability of competition, the director of planning recommends marketing the Battle Pacific video game. Using expected value, what is your recommended decision?
c. Show a risk profile for your recommended decision.
d. Use sensitivity analysis to determine what the probability of competition for Space Pirates would have to be for you to change your recommended decision alternative.

9. **Chardonnay or Riesling Grapes.** Seneca Hill Winery recently purchased land for the purpose of establishing a new vineyard. Management is considering two varieties of white grapes for the new vineyard: Chardonnay and Riesling. The Chardonnay grapes would be used to produce a dry Chardonnay wine, and the Riesling grapes would be used to produce a semidry Riesling wine. It takes approximately four years from the time of planting before new grapes can be harvested. This length of time creates a great deal of uncertainty concerning future demand and makes the decision about the type of grapes to plant difficult. Three possibilities are being considered: Chardonnay grapes only; Riesling grapes only; and both Chardonnay and Riesling grapes. Seneca management decided that for planning purposes it would be adequate to consider only two demand possibilities for each type of wine: strong or weak. With two possibilities for each type of wine, it was necessary to assess four probabilities. With the help of some forecasts in industry publications, management made the following probability assessments:

Chardonnay Demand	Riesling Demand Weak	Riesling Demand Strong
Weak	0.05	0.50
Strong	0.25	0.20

Revenue projections show an annual contribution to profit of $20,000 if Seneca Hill plants only Chardonnay grapes and demand is weak for Chardonnay wine, and $70,000 if Seneca plants only Chardonnay grapes and demand is strong for Chardonnay wine. If Seneca plants only Riesling grapes, the annual profit projection is $25,000 if demand is weak for Riesling grapes and $45,000 if demand is strong for Riesling grapes. If Seneca plants both types of grapes, the annual profit projections are as shown in the following table:

Chardonnay Demand	Riesling Demand Weak	Riesling Demand Strong
Weak	$22,000	$40,000
Strong	$26,000	$60,000

a. What is the decision to be made, what is the chance event, and what is the consequence? Identify the alternatives for the decisions and the possible outcomes for the chance events.

b. Develop a decision tree.

c. Use the expected value approach to recommend which alternative Seneca Hill Winery should follow in order to maximize expected annual profit.

d. Suppose management is concerned about the probability assessments when demand for Chardonnay wine is strong. Some believe it is likely for Riesling demand to also be strong in this case. Suppose that the probability of strong demand for Chardonnay and weak demand for Riesling is 0.05 and that the probability of strong demand for Chardonnay and strong demand for Riesling is 0.40. How does this change the recommended decision? Assume that the probabilities when Chardonnay demand is weak are still 0.05 and 0.50.

e. Other members of the management team expect the Chardonnay market to become saturated at some point in the future, causing a fall in prices. Suppose that the annual profit projections fall to $50,000 when demand for Chardonnay is strong and only Chardonnay grapes are planted. Using the original probability assessments, determine how this change would affect the optimal decision.

10. **R&D Project.** Hemmingway, Inc. is considering a $5 million research and development (R&D) project. Profit projections appear promising, but Hemmingway's president is concerned because the probability that the R&D project will be successful is only 0.50. Furthermore, the president knows that even if the project is successful, it will require that the company build a new production facility at a cost of $20 million in order to manufacture the product. If the facility is built, uncertainty remains about the demand and thus uncertainty about the profit that will be realized. Another option is that if the R&D project is successful, the company could sell the rights to the product for an estimated $25 million. Under this option, the company would not build the $20 million production facility.

The decision tree follows. The profit projection for each outcome is shown at the end of the branches. For example, the revenue projection for the high demand outcome is $59 million. However, the cost of the R&D project ($5 million) and the cost of the production facility ($20 million) show the profit of this outcome to be $59 − $5 − $20 = $34 million. Branch probabilities are also shown for the chance events.

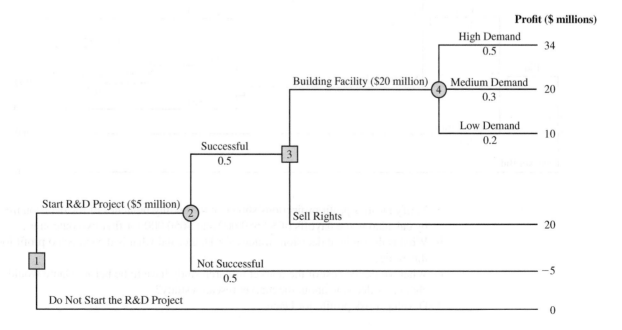

a. Analyze the decision tree to determine whether the company should undertake the R&D project. If it does, and if the R&D project is successful, what should the company do? What is the expected value of your strategy?

b. What must the selling price be for the company to consider selling the rights to the product?

c. Develop a risk profile for the optimal strategy.

11. **New Office Building Complex.** Dante Development Corporation is considering bidding on a contract for a new office building complex. The following figure shows the decision tree prepared by one of Dante's analysts. At node 1, the company must decide whether to bid on the contract. The cost of preparing the bid is $200,000. The upper branch from node 2 shows that the company has a 0.8 probability of winning the contract if it submits a bid. If the company wins the bid, it will have to pay $2 million to become a partner in the project. Node 3 shows that the company will then consider doing a market research study to forecast demand for the office units prior to beginning construction. The cost of this study is $150,000. Node 4 is a chance node showing the possible outcomes of the market research study.

Nodes 5, 6, and 7 are similar in that they are the decision nodes for Dante to either build the office complex or sell the rights in the project to another developer. The decision to build the complex will result in an income of $5 million if demand is high and $3 million if demand is moderate. If Dante chooses to sell its rights in the project to another developer, income from the sale is estimated to be $3.5 million. The probabilities shown at nodes 4, 8, and 9 are based on the projected outcomes of the market research study.

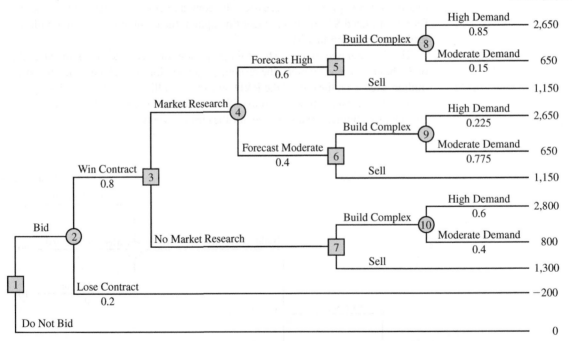

a. Verify Dante's profit projections shown at the ending branches of the decision tree by calculating the payoffs of $2,650,000 and $650,000 for first two outcomes.

b. What is the optimal decision strategy for Dante, and what is the expected profit for this project?

c. What would the cost of the market research study have to be before Dante would change its decision about the market research study?

d. Develop a risk profile for Dante.

12. **New College Textbook.** Embassy Publishing Company received a six-chapter manuscript for a new college textbook. The editor of the college division is familiar with the manuscript and estimated a 0.65 probability that the textbook will be successful. If successful, a profit of $750,000 will be realized. If the company decides to publish the textbook and it is unsuccessful, a loss of $250,000 will occur.

Before making the decision to accept or reject the manuscript, the editor is considering sending the manuscript out for review. A review process provides either a favorable (F) or unfavorable (U) evaluation of the manuscript. Past experience with the review process suggests that probabilities $P(F) = 0.7$ and $P(U) = 0.3$ apply. Let s_1 = the textbook is successful and s_2 = the textbook is unsuccessful. The editor's initial probabilities of s_1 and s_2 will be revised based on whether the review is favorable or unfavorable. The revised probabilities are as follows:

$$P(s_1|F) = 0.85 \qquad P(s_1|U) = 0.417$$
$$P(s_2|F) = 0.15 \qquad P(s_2|U) = 0.583$$

a. Construct a decision tree assuming that the company will first make the decision as to whether to send the manuscript out for review and then make the decision to accept or reject the manuscript.
b. Analyze the decision tree to determine the optimal decision strategy for the publishing company.
c. If the manuscript review costs $15,000, what is your recommendation?
d. What is the expected value of perfect information? What does this EVPI suggest for the company?

13. **Value of Perfect Information.** The following profit payoff table was presented in Problem 1:

Decision Alternative	State of Nature		
	s_1	s_2	s_3
d_1	250	100	25
d_2	100	100	75

The probabilities for the states of nature are $P(s_1) = 0.65$, $P(s_2) = 0.15$, and $P(s_3) = 0.20$.

a. What is the optimal decision strategy if perfect information were available?
b. What is the expected value for the decision strategy developed in part (a)?
c. Using the expected value approach, what is the recommended decision without perfect information? What is its expected value?
d. What is the expected value of perfect information?

14. **Lake Placid Community Center.** The Lake Placid Town Council decided to build a new community center to be used for conventions, concerts, and other public events, but considerable controversy surrounds the appropriate size. Many influential citizens want a large center that would be a showcase for the area. But the mayor feels that if demand does not support such a center, the community will lose a large amount of money. To provide structure for the decision process, the council narrowed the building alternatives to three sizes: small, medium, and large. Everybody agreed that the critical factor in choosing the best size is the number of people who will want to use the new facility. A regional planning consultant provided demand estimates under three scenarios: worst case, base case, and best case. The worst-case scenario corresponds to a situation in which tourism drops substantially; the base-case scenario corresponds to a situation in which Lake Placid continues to attract visitors at current levels; and the best-case scenario corresponds to a substantial increase in tourism. The consultant has provided probability assessments of 0.10, 0.60, and 0.30 for the worst-case, base-case, and best-case scenarios, respectively.

The town council suggested using net cash flow over a five-year planning horizon as the criterion for deciding on the best size. The following projections of net cash flow (in thousands of dollars) for a five-year planning horizon have been developed. All costs, including the consultant's fee, have been included.

	Demand Scenario		
Center Size	Worst Case	Base Case	Best Case
Small	400	500	660
Medium	−250	650	800
Large	−400	580	990

a. What decision should Lake Placid make using the expected value approach?

b. Construct risk profiles for the medium and large alternatives. Given the mayor's concern over the possibility of losing money and the result of part (a), which alternative would you recommend?

c. Compute the expected value of perfect information. Do you think it would be worth trying to obtain additional information concerning which scenario is likely to occur?

d. Suppose the probability of the worst-case scenario increases to 0.2, the probability of the base-case scenario decreases to 0.5, and the probability of the best-case scenario remains at 0.3. What effect, if any, would these changes have on the decision recommendation?

e. The consultant has suggested that an expenditure of $150,000 on a promotional campaign over the planning horizon will effectively reduce the probability of the worst-case scenario to zero. If the campaign can be expected to also increase the probability of the best-case scenario to 0.4, is it a good investment?

15. **Rezoning Property.** A real estate investor has the opportunity to purchase land currently zoned as residential. If the county board approves a request to rezone the property as commercial within the next year, the investor will be able to lease the land to a large discount firm that wants to open a new store on the property. However, if the zoning change is not approved, the investor will have to sell the property at a loss. Profits (in thousands of dollars) are shown in the following payoff table:

	State of Nature	
Decision Alternative	Rezoning Approved, s_1	Rezoning Not Approved, s_2
Purchase, d_1	600	−200
Do not purchase, d_2	0	0

a. If the probability that the rezoning will be approved is 0.5, what decision is recommended? What is the expected profit?

b. The investor can purchase an option to buy the land. Under the option, the investor maintains the rights to purchase the land anytime during the next three months while learning more about possible resistance to the rezoning proposal from area residents. Probabilities are as follows:

Let H = high resistance to rezoning

L = low resistance to rezoning

$$P(H) = 0.55 \quad P(s_1 \mid H) = 0.18 \quad P(s_2 \mid H) = 0.82$$
$$P(L) = 0.45 \quad P(s_1 \mid L) = 0.89 \quad P(s_2 \mid L) = 0.11$$

What is the optimal decision strategy if the investor uses the option period to learn more about the resistance from area residents before making the purchase decision?

c. If the option will cost the investor an additional $10,000, should the investor purchase the option? Why or why not? What is the maximum that the investor should be willing to pay for the option?

16. **Posterior Probabilities Calculation.** Suppose that you are given a decision situation with three possible states of nature: s_1, s_2, and s_3. The prior probabilities are $P(s_1) = 0.2$, $P(s_2) = 0.5$, and $P(s_3) = 0.3$. With sample information I, $P(I|s_1) = 0.1$, $P(I|s_2) = 0.05$, and $P(I|s_3) = 0.2$. Compute the revised (or posterior) probabilities: $P(s_1|I)$, $P(s_2|I)$, and $P(s_3|I)$.

17. **Carpool Route.** To save on expenses, Rona and Jerry agreed to form a carpool for traveling to and from work. Rona prefers to use the somewhat longer but more consistent Queen City Avenue. Although Jerry prefers the quicker expressway, he agreed with Rona that they should take Queen City Avenue if the expressway has a traffic jam. The following payoff table provides the one-way time estimate in minutes for traveling to or from work:

	State of Nature	
Decision Alternative	Expressway Open, s_1	Expressway Jammed, s_2
Queen City Avenue, d_1	30	30
Expressway, d_2	25	45

Based on their experience with traffic problems, Rona and Jerry agreed on a 0.15 probability that the expressway would be jammed.

In addition, they agreed that weather seemed to affect the traffic conditions on the expressway. Let

$$C = \text{clear}$$
$$O = \text{overcast}$$
$$R = \text{rain}$$

The following conditional probabilities apply:

$$P(C|s_1) = 0.8 \qquad P(O|s_1) = 0.2 \qquad P(R|s_1) = 0.0$$
$$P(C|s_2) = 0.1 \qquad P(O|s_2) = 0.3 \qquad P(R|s_2) = 0.6$$

a. Use Bayes' theorem for probability revision to compute the probability of each weather condition and the conditional probability of the expressway being open, s_1, or jammed, s_2, given each weather condition.
b. Show the decision tree for this problem.
c. What is the optimal decision strategy, and what is the expected travel time?

18. **Manufacture or Purchase.** The Gorman Manufacturing Company must decide whether to manufacture a component part at its Milan, Michigan, plant or purchase the component part from a supplier. The resulting profit is dependent on the demand for the product. The following payoff table shows the projected profit (in thousands of dollars):

	State of Nature		
	Low Demand	Medium Demand	High Demand
Decision Alternative	s_1	s_2	s_3
Manufacture, d_1	−20	40	100
Purchase, d_2	10	45	70

The state-of-nature probabilities are $P(s_1) = 0.35$, $P(s_2) = 0.35$, and $P(s_3) = 0.30$.
a. Use a decision tree to recommend a decision.
b. Use EVPI to determine whether Gorman should attempt to obtain a better estimate of demand.

c. A test market study of the potential demand for the product is expected to report either a favorable (F) or an unfavorable (U) condition. The relevant conditional probabilities are as follows:

$$P(F|s_1) = 0.10 \ P(U|s_1) = 0.90$$
$$P(F|s_2) = 0.40 \ P(U|s_2) = 0.60$$
$$P(F|s_3) = 0.60 \ P(U|s_3) = 0.40$$

Joint probabilities are discussed in Chapter 4.

What is the probability that the market research report will be favorable? [*Hint:* We can find this value by summing the joint probability values as follows: $P(F) = P(F \cap s_1) + P(F \cap s_2) + P(F \cap s_3) = P(s_1)P(F|s_1) + P(s_2)P(F|s_2) + P(s_3)P(F|s_3)$.]

d. What is Gorman's optimal decision strategy?

e. What is the expected value of the market research information?

19. **Investment Alternatives.** A firm has three investment alternatives. Payoffs are in thousands of dollars.

	Economic Conditions		
Decision Alternative	Up, s_1	Stable, s_2	Down, s_3
Investment A, d_1	100	25	0
Investment B, d_2	75	50	25
Investment C, d_3	50	50	50
Probabilities	0.40	0.30	0.30

a. Using the expected value approach, which decision is preferred?

b. For the lottery having a payoff of $100,000 with probability p and $0 with probability $(1 - p)$, two decision makers expressed the following indifference probabilities. Find the most preferred decision for each decision maker using the expected utility approach.

	Indifference Probability (p)	
Profit	Decision Maker A	Decision Maker B
$75,000	0.80	0.60
$50,000	0.60	0.30
$25,000	0.30	0.15

c. Why don't decision makers A and B select the same decision alternative?

20. **Insurance Policy for New Office Building.** Alexander Industries is considering purchasing an insurance policy for its new office building in St. Louis, Missouri. The policy has an annual cost of $10,000. If Alexander Industries doesn't purchase the insurance and minor fire damage occurs, a cost of $100,000 is anticipated; the cost if major or total destruction occurs is $200,000. The costs, including the state-of-nature probabilities, are as follows:

	Damage		
Decision Alternative	None, s_1	Minor, s_2	Major, s_3
Purchase insurance, d_1	10,000	10,000	10,000
Do not purchase insurance, d_2	0	100,000	200,000
Probabilities	0.96	0.03	0.01

a. Using the expected value approach, what decision do you recommend?

b. What lottery would you use to assess utilities? (*Note:* Because the data are costs, the best payoff is $0.)

c. Assume that you found the following indifference probabilities for the lottery defined in part (b). What decision would you recommend?

Cost	Indifference Probability
10,000	$p = 0.99$
100,000	$p = 0.60$

  d. Do you favor using expected value or expected utility for this decision problem? Why?
21. **Lottery Ticket.** In a certain state lottery, a lottery ticket costs $2. In terms of the decision to purchase or not to purchase a lottery ticket, suppose that the following payoff table applies:

	State of Nature	
Decision Alternatives	Win, s_1	Lose, s_2
Purchase lottery ticket, d_1	300,000	−2
Do not purchase lottery ticket, d_2	0	0

  a. A realistic estimate of the chances of winning is 1 in 250,000. Use the expected value approach to recommend a decision.
  b. If a particular decision maker assigns an indifference probability of 0.000001 to the $0 payoff, would this individual purchase a lottery ticket? Use expected utility to justify your answer.
22. **Risk Profiles of Decision Makers.** Three decision makers have assessed utilities for the following decision problem (payoff in dollars):

	State of Nature		
Decision Alternative	s_1	s_2	s_3
d_1	20	50	−20
d_2	80	100	−100

The indifference probabilities are as follows:

	Indifference Probability (p)		
Payoff	Decision Maker A	Decision Maker B	Decision Maker C
100	1.00	1.00	1.00
80	0.95	0.70	0.90
50	0.90	0.60	0.75
20	0.70	0.45	0.60
−20	0.50	0.25	0.40
−100	0.00	0.00	0.00

  a. Plot the utility function for money for each decision maker.
  b. Classify each decision maker as a risk avoider, a risk taker, or risk-neutral.
  c. For the payoff of 20, what is the premium that the risk avoider will pay to avoid risk? What is the premium that the risk taker will pay to have the opportunity of the high payoff?
23. **Recommended Decisions for Different Decision Makers.** In Problem 22, if $P(s_1) = 0.25$, $P(s_2) = 0.50$, and $P(s_3) = 0.25$, find a recommended decision for each of the three decision makers. (*Note:* For the same decision problem, different utilities can lead to different decisions.)
24. **Utility Calculations.** Translate the following monetary payoffs into utilities for a decision maker whose utility function is described by an exponential function with $R = 250$: −$200, −$100, $0, $100, $200, $300, $400, $500.
25. **Exponential Utility Function.** Consider a decision maker who is comfortable with an investment decision that has a 50% chance of earning $25,000 and a 50% chance of losing $12,500, but not with any larger investments that have the same relative payoffs.

a. Write the equation for the exponential function that approximates this decision maker's utility function.
b. Plot the exponential utility function for this decision maker for x values between $-20,000$ and $35,000$. Is this decision maker risk-seeking, risk-neutral, or risk-averse?
c. Suppose the decision maker decides that she would actually be willing to make an investment that has a 50% chance of earning $30,000 and a 50% chance of losing $15,000. Plot the exponential function that approximates this utility function and compare it to the utility function from part (b). Is the decision maker becoming more risk-seeking or more risk-averse?

CASE PROBLEM: PROPERTY PURCHASE STRATEGY

Glenn Foreman, president of Oceanview Development Corporation, is considering submitting a bid to purchase property that will be sold by sealed-bid auction at a county tax foreclosure. Glenn's initial judgment is to submit a bid of $5 million. Based on his experience, Glenn estimates that a bid of $5 million will have a 0.2 probability of being the highest bid and securing the property for Oceanview. The current date is June 1. Sealed bids for the property must be submitted by August 15. The winning bid will be announced on September 1.

If Oceanview submits the highest bid and obtains the property, the firm plans to build and sell a complex of luxury condominiums. However, a complicating factor is that the property is currently zoned for single-family residences only. Glenn believes that a referendum could be placed on the voting ballot in time for the November election. Passage of the referendum would change the zoning of the property and permit construction of the condominiums.

The sealed-bid procedure requires the bid to be submitted with a certified check for 10% of the amount bid. If the bid is rejected, the deposit is refunded. If the bid is accepted, the deposit is the down payment for the property. However, if the bid is accepted and the bidder does not follow through with the purchase and meet the remainder of the financial obligation within six months, the deposit will be forfeited. In this case, the county will offer the property to the next highest bidder.

To determine whether Oceanview should submit the $5 million bid, Glenn conducted some preliminary analysis. This preliminary work provided an assessment of 0.3 for the probability that the referendum for a zoning change will be approved and resulted in the following estimates of the costs and revenues that will be incurred if the condominiums are built:

Costs and Revenue Estimates	
Revenue from condominium sales	$15,000,000
Costs	
Property	$5,000,000
Construction expenses	$8,000,000

If Oceanview obtains the property and the zoning change is rejected in November, Glenn believes that the best option would be for the firm not to complete the purchase of the property. In this case, Oceanview would forfeit the 10% deposit that accompanied the bid.

Because the likelihood that the zoning referendum will be approved is such an important factor in the decision process, Glenn suggested that the firm hire a market research service to conduct a survey of voters. The survey would provide a better estimate of the likelihood that the referendum for a zoning change would be approved. The market research firm that Oceanview Development has worked with in the past has agreed to do the study for $15,000. The results of the study will be available August 1, so that Oceanview will have this information before the August 15 bid deadline. The results of the survey will be a prediction either that the zoning change will be approved or that the zoning change will be rejected. After considering the record of the market research service in previous studies conducted for Oceanview, Glenn developed the following probability estimates concerning the accuracy of the market research information:

$$P(A|s_1) = 0.9 \qquad P(N|s_1) = 0.1$$
$$P(A|s_2) = 0.2 \qquad P(N|s_2) = 0.8$$

where

A = prediction of zoning change approval

N = prediction that zoning change will not be approved

s_1 = the zoning change is approved by the voters

s_2 = the zoning change is rejected by the voters

Managerial Report

Perform an analysis of the problem facing the Oceanview Development Corporation, and prepare a report that summarizes your findings and recommendations. Include the following items in your report:

1. A decision tree that shows the logical sequence of the decision problem
2. A recommendation regarding what Oceanview should do if the market research information is not available
3. A decision strategy that Oceanview should follow if the market research is conducted
4. A recommendation as to whether Oceanview should employ the market research firm, along with the value of the information provided by the market research firm

Include the details of your analysis as an appendix to your report.

Case Problem: Capital State University Game-Day Magazines

This case draws on material from Chapters 2, 3, 7, and 11.

Capital State University (CSU) is a leading Midwest University with a strong collegiate football program. Kris Stetzel serves as CSU's Associate Athletic Director for External Affairs. His job responsibilities include negotiating with commercial vendors for services such as concessions at sporting events, event staff and security, and game-day hospitality. Kris brokers deals for corporate sponsorship of CSU athletic programs and arranges for radio and television coverage of CSU athletic events. Kris also manages CSU sports advertising and marketing and sports information-related media relations for print, radio, television, and online.

Recently, Kris has been examining CSU's business arrangement with the publishing company that prints the game-day sports magazines for CSU home football games. As part of a recent comprehensive university-wide sports media contract, CSU has a new publishing agreement with its print vendor. The magazines typically contain about 60 pages of information on the CSU football team and its opponent for that week. The magazines are sold at vendor stands positioned outside of CSU's football stadium.

Currently, CSU places one order in July, several months prior to the first home football game, that states how many magazines CSU wants for each home game of the season. The publishing company prints the magazines and ships all magazines to CSU prior to the first game of the season.

From data collected in past football seasons, Kris knows that CSU is often off by a considerable amount in their order quantities. Most weeks, CSU has many leftover magazines, but because the magazines are tailored to each home opponent, they cannot be resold in future weeks. In some weeks in previous football seasons, demand surpassed supply and CSU ran out of football magazines. Currently, CSU determines order quantities for each home game by looking at the past season's order quantities and then adjusting this amount up or down based on a gut feeling on how popular the current season's game would be in comparison to games in the previous season.

Kris believes that it should be possible to improve this ordering process. He has located data from the past nine football seasons. Kris has information on the following variables for each home game: the number of magazines sold, the year the game took place, the week that the game took place during the season, the opponent's preseason ranking, the number of preseason tickets sold for that game, the total game attendance, CSU's preseason rank, the number of the home game within CSU's season, whether or not the game was an in-conference game for CSU, whether or not the game was Homecoming for CSU, the game-day weather, the game-day kickoff temperature, the number of wins and losses for CSU's opponent in the previous season, and the number of wins and losses for CSU in the previous season. These data are in the file *MagazinesCSU*; Table 20.1 displays the data for Years 1 and 2. Kris also noted that the CSU game in Week 1 of Year 8 was somewhat of an anomaly because CSU wore special throwback uniforms to honor the players from their only National Championship season, which greatly increased attendance at that game.

DATA *file*

MagazinesCSU

| TABLE 20.1 | Portion of Data Available for Use in Determining How Many CSU Football Magazines to Order |

	Magazine Sales (Units)	Year	Week In Season	Opponent Preseason Rank	Preseason Ticket Sales	Total Game Attendance	CSU Preseason Rank	Home Game Number	Conference Game (1 = Yes; 0 = No)	Homecoming (1 = Yes; 0 = No)	Game Day Weather	Kickoff Temperature	Opponent's Previous Season Number of Wins	Opponent's Previous Season Number of Losses	CSU's Previous Season Number of Wins	CSU's Previous Season Number of Losses
Cedar Falls University	4,165	1	2	120	47,420	66,325	21	1	0	0	Sunny	70	12	2	9	3
Oklahoma A&M	3,746	1	3	58	47,420	64,893	21	2	0	0	Rain	60	4	7	9	3
Urbana College	4,943	1	5	67	47,420	70,397	21	3	1	0	Sunny	68	2	9	9	3
University of Bloomington	2,366	1	9	83	47,420	69,185	21	4	1	1	Rain	42	3	8	9	3
Indiana A&M	1,796	1	10	74	47,420	70,397	21	5	1	0	Cloudy	46	3	8	9	3
Minneapolis State University	1,979	1	13	68	47,420	64,591	21	6	1	0	Cloudy	35	4	7	9	3
Mt Pleasant College	3,866	2	1	109	46,198	58,920	57	1	0	0	Sunny	82	2	9	7	5
University of Ames	5,194	2	2	99	46,198	70,397	57	2	0	0	Sunny	86	1	10	7	5
Ann Arbor University	1,909	2	5	6	46,198	70,397	57	3	1	0	Rain	52	12	0	7	5
Evanston University	2,523	2	6	55	46,198	70,397	57	4	1	1	Sunny	62	5	7	7	5
Madison University	2,734	2	8	17	46,198	70,397	57	5	1	0	Sunny	63	8	5	7	5
Columbus University	2,034	2	11	3	46,198	69,473	57	6	1	0	Sunny	61	10	3	7	5

Kris has also done some investigation into the costs associated with ordering magazines from CSU's publisher. Under the current CSU contract with the publisher, CSU must determine order amounts for each upcoming home game by July. CSU pays $14.00 for each magazine that they order. Vendors then sell magazines at each CSU home football game for $25.00. CSU's agreement with the vendors states that CSU pays the vendor $2.50 for each magazine sold and keeps the remaining revenue. The current contract with the publisher states that the publisher must buy back any unsold magazines from CSU for $11.50.

Managerial Report

Use the concepts you have learned from Chapters 2, 3, 7, and 11 to write a report that will help Kris analyze football magazine sales in Years 1 through 9 to determine an order amount for Year 10. You should address each of the following in your report.

1. There is a considerable amount of data available in the file *MagazinesCSU*, but not all of it may be useful for your purposes here. Are there variables contained in the file *MagazinesCSU* that you would exclude from a forecast model to determine football magazine sales in Year 10? If so, why? Are there particular observations of football magazine sales from previous years that you would exclude from your forecasting model? If so, why?

2. Based on the data in the file *MagazinesCSU*, develop a regression model to forecast the average sales of football magazines for each of the seven home games in the upcoming season (Year 10). That is, you should construct a single regression model and use it to estimate the average demand for the seven home games in Year 10. In addition to the variables provided, you may create new variables based on these variables or based on observations of your analysis. Be sure to provide a thorough analysis of your final model (residual diagnostics) and provide assessments of its accuracy. What insights are available based on your regression model?

3. Use the forecasting model developed in Part 2 to create a simulation model that Kris can use to estimate the total football magazine sales amounts in Year 10. Your simulation model should have seven uncertain inputs: one input for football magazine sales at each CSU game in Year 10. Then you should sum these sales amounts for each individual game to create a total football magazine sales amount for Year 10.

4. Kris has noticed that of the typical 60 pages in a football magazine, 45 of those 60 pages are the same for every game in a season. Only the 15 pages that discuss the weekly opponent change from week-to-week. CSU's publisher has indicated that it is possible for CSU to order generic game-day football magazines in the July preceding the season. This generic magazine contains the 45 pages of material that is the same for each game. Closer to the week of each game, CSU could then tailor the generic magazine with inserts specific to that week's game, along with a book jacket cover displaying players and coaches from the two teams playing that week. The number of game-specific inserts and book jacket covers can be determined closer to the actual games in order to allow for a more accurate forecast.

   Thus, the simulation model developed in Part 3 effectively represents the sales amount for the generic magazine, and then CSU would order the game-specific inserts and book jacket covers much closer to the actual games when they have a much more accurate forecast of attendance and sales. However, Kris still is not sure how many generic magazines he should order. Should he order exactly the forecasted amount from Part 3? More? Less? Why? Based on the cost values described from the publishing contract, if Kris orders 21,500 generic magazines in July, what are the estimated expected costs of lost sales (football magazines that CSU does not sell because they run out) and unsold magazines (football magazines that CSU must send back to the publisher at the end of the season)?

5. Assuming that CSU can tailor the specific magazines for each game in Year 10 at a later date, what is the optimal order amount for Kris to place in July prior to Year 10 for the generic magazines? The optimal order amount should minimize the total expected lost sales and unsold magazines cost in Year 10? Assume that Kris must order in batches of 500 magazines.

Hanover Inc.

This case draws on material from Chapters 10, 12, and 13.

DATAfile

Hanover

Because of increasing global demand for its fiber optics products, Hanover Inc. is currently facing a decision on how to increase its production capacity. Hanover has three fiber optic products denoted by FA, FB, and FC. Hanover has two existing plants in Austin, Texas and Paris, France. Hanover plans to keep the Austin and Paris plants will open, but the production capacity at these two existing plants can be changed from their current levels (600,000 units per year). Each plant can make any mix of the three products. Seven locations are being considered for an additional new plant. These consist of two cities in the United States (Charleston, SC and Mobile, AL) and five other locations currently simply defined by country (Australia, India, Malaysia, South Africa, and Spain).

The company's customers have been aggregated onto eight customer regions (Malaysia, China, France, Brazil, US Northeast, US Southeast, US Midwest, and US West) and its Planning and Forecasting department has forecasted demand for each region five years into the future. The Planning and Forecasting department has also provided other relevant data to help with the decision on how to expand capacity given the forecasted demand. Descriptions of the available data provided in the file *Hanover* follow:

- **Duty:** This worksheet contains the duty rate charged from each plant to each customer region. This rate is multiplied by the selling price to get the cost per unit paid in duty to ship into one country from another country.
- **Fixed Cost:** This worksheet contains the fixed cost of plant operation including capital costs, insurance, management, etc. These costs depend on the capacity level of the plant, and costs for two different levels of capacity are given for each plant location. The capacities are independent of product mix.
- **Forecast:** This worksheet contains five-year-out forecasted demand for each product by customer region.
- **F&WH Cost:** This worksheet contains freight and warehousing cost per unit from each plant location to each customer region (which are independent of product type).
- **Price:** This worksheet contains the selling price of each product for each customer region.
- **Variable Cost:** This worksheet contains the variable cost of each product at each plant.

The vice president of supply chain management would like you to study this situation using the given data.

Managerial Report
Use the concepts in Chapters 10, 12, and 13 to make a recommendation to Hanover's vice president of supply chain management. In particular, make a recommendation regarding whether or not a new plant is needed and if so, at which of the seven locations under consideration it should be located. Also, your report should indicate which capacity levels should be used at each plant, and how product should be sourced.

Appendix A—Basics of Excel

CONTENTS

A.1 Using Microsoft Excel

Depending on the settings for your particular installation of Excel, you may see additional worksheets labeled Sheet2, Sheet3, and so on.

Excel stores data and calculations in a file called a **workbook**, which contains one or more **worksheets**. Figure A.1 shows the layout of a blank workbook created in Excel. The workbook is named Book1 and by default contains a worksheet named Sheet1.

The wide bar located across the top of the workbook is referred to as the Ribbon. Tabs, located at the top of the Ribbon, contain groups of related commands. By default, eight tabs are included on the Ribbon in Excel: File, Home, Insert, Page Layout, Formulas, Data, Review, and View. Loading additional packages (such as Analytic Solver or Acrobat) may create additional tabs. Each tab contains several groups of related commands. The File tab is used to Open, Save, and Print files as well as to change the Options being used by Excel and to load Add-ins. Note that the Home tab is selected when a workbook is opened. Figure A.2 displays the seven groups located in the Home tab: Clipboard, Font, Alignment, Number, Styles, Cells, and Editing. Commands are arranged within each group.

FIGURE A.1	Blank Workbook in Excel

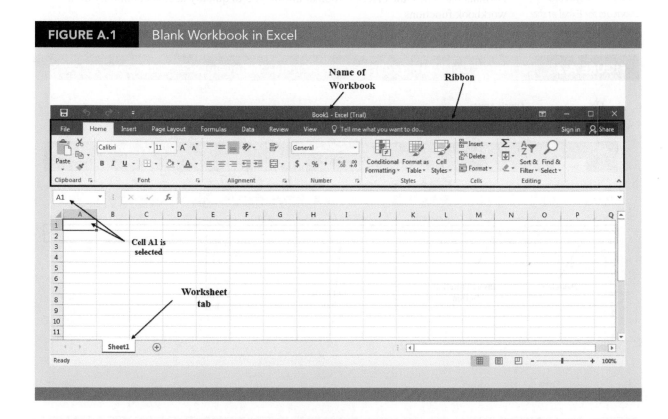

FIGURE A.2   Groups on the Home Tab in the Ribbon of an Excel Workbook

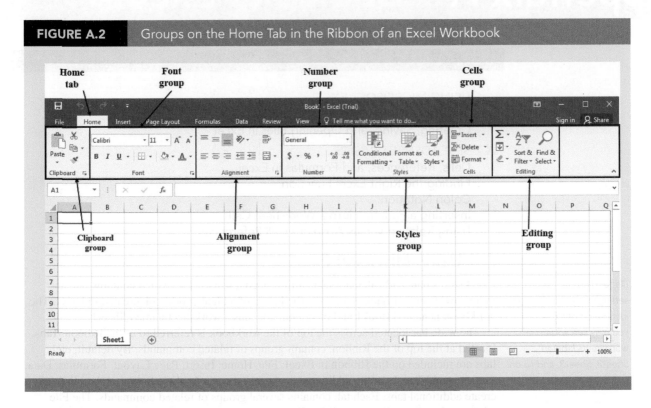

Keyboard shortcut: pressing
Ctrl-B *will change the font*
of the text in the selected
cell to bold. We include
a full list of keyboard
shortcuts for Excel at the
end of this appendix.

For example, to change selected text to boldface, click the **Home** tab and click the **Bold** button **B** in the **Font** group. The other tabs in the Ribbon are used to modify data in your spreadsheet or to perform analysis.

Figure A.3 illustrates the location of the File tab, the Quick Access toolbar, and the Formula bar. The Quick Access toolbar allows you to quickly access commonly used workbook functions.

FIGURE A.3   File Tab, Quick Access Toolbar, and Formula Bar of an Excel Workbook

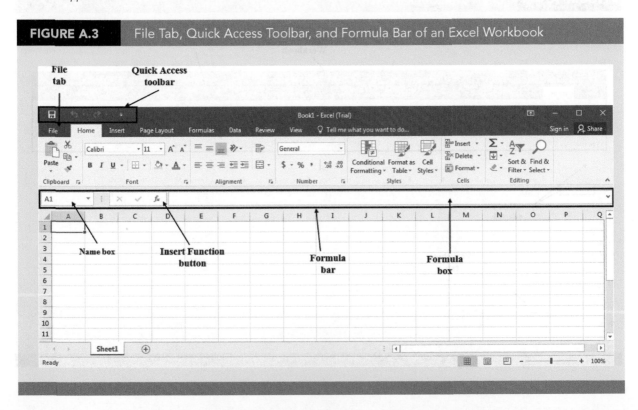

For instance, the Quick Access toolbar shown in Figure A.3 includes a **Save** button 🖫 that can be used to save files without having to first click the **File** tab. To add or remove features on the Quick Access toolbar, click the **Customize Quick Access toolbar** button ▼ on the Quick Access toolbar.

The Formula bar contains a Name box, the Insert Function button *fx*, and a Formula box. In Figure A.3, "A1" appears in the Name box because cell A1 is selected. You can select any other cell in the worksheet by using the mouse to move the cursor to another cell and clicking or by typing the new cell location in the name box and pressing the Enter key. The Formula box is used to display the formula in the currently selected cell. For instance, if you had entered $=A1+A2$ into cell A3, whenever you select cell A3, the formula $=A1+A2$ will be shown in the Formula box. This feature makes it very easy to see and edit a formula in a cell. The Insert Function button allows you to quickly access all of the functions available in Excel. Later, we show how to find and use a particular function with the Insert Function button.

Basic Spreadsheet Workbook Operations

To change the name of the current worksheet, we take the following steps:

Step 1. Right-click on the worksheet tab named **Sheet1**
Step 2. Select the **Rename** option
Step 3. Enter *Nowlin* to rename the worksheet and press **Enter**

You can create a copy of the newly renamed Nowlin worksheet by following these steps:

Step 1. Right-click the worksheet tab named **Nowlin**
Step 2. Select the **Move or Copy…** option
Step 3. When the **Move or Copy** dialog box appears, select the checkbox for **Create a Copy**, and click **OK**

The name of the copied worksheet will appear as "Nowlin (2)." You can then rename it, if desired, by following the steps outlined previously. Worksheets can also be moved to other workbooks or to a different position in the current workbook by using the Move or Copy option.

To create additional worksheets follow these steps:

New worksheets can also be created using the insert worksheet button ⊕ at the bottom of the screen.

Step 1. Right-click on the tab of any existing worksheet
Step 2. Select **Insert…**
Step 3. When the **Insert** dialog box appears, select **Worksheet** from the **General** area, and click **OK**

Worksheets can be deleted by right-clicking the worksheet tab and choosing **Delete**. After clicking **Delete**, a window may appear, warning you that any data appearing in the worksheet will be lost. Click **Delete** to confirm that you do want to delete the worksheet.

Creating, Saving, and Opening Files in Excel

To illustrate manually entering, saving, and opening a file, we will use the Nowlin Plastics make-versus-buy model from Chapter 10. The objective is to determine whether Nowlin should manufacture or outsource production for its Viper product next year. Nowlin must pay a fixed cost of $234,000 and a variable cost per unit of $2 to manufacture the product. Nowlin can outsource production for $3.50 per unit.

We begin by assuming that Excel is open and a blank worksheet is displayed. The Nowlin data can now be entered manually by simply typing the manufacturing fixed cost of $234,000, the variable cost of $2, and the outsourcing cost of $3.50 into the worksheet.

We will place the data for the Nowlin example in the top portion of Sheet1 of the new workbook. First, we enter the label *Nowlin Plastics* in cell A1 and click the **Bold** button in the **Font** group. Next, we enter the label *Parameters* and click on the **Bold** button in the **Font** group. To identify each of the three data values, we enter the label *Manufacturing*

FIGURE A.4   Nowlin Plastics Data

	A	B	C
1	**Nowlin Plastics**		
2			
3	**Parameters**		
4	Manufacturing Fixed Cost	$234,000.00	
5	Manufacturing Variable Cost per Unit	$2.00	
6			
7	Outsourcing Cost per Unit	$3.50	
8			

Fixed Cost in cell A4, the label *Manufacturing Variable Cost per Unit* in cell A5, and the label *Outsourcing Cost per Unit* in cell A7. Next, we enter the actual data into the corresponding cells in column B: the value of *$234,000* in cell B4; the value of *$2* in cell B5; and the value of *$3.50* in cell B7. Figure A.4 shows a portion of the worksheet we have just developed.

Before we begin the development of the model portion of the worksheet, we recommend that you first save the current file; this will prevent you from having to reenter the data in case something happens that causes Excel to close. To save the workbook using the filename *Nowlin*, we perform the following steps:

Step 1. Click the **File** tab on the Ribbon
Step 2. Click **Save** in the list of options
Step 3. Select **This PC** under **Save As**, and click **Browse**
Step 4. When the **Save As** dialog box appears:
             Select the location where you want to save the file
             Enter the filename *Nowlin* in the **File name:** box
             Click **Save**

*Keyboard shortcut: To save the file, press **Ctrl-S**.*

Excel's Save command is designed to save the file as an Excel workbook. As you work with and build models in Excel, you should follow the practice of periodically saving the file so that you will not lose any work. After you have saved your file for the first time, the Save command will overwrite the existing version of the file, and you will not have to perform Steps 3 and 4.

Sometimes you may want to create a copy of an existing file. For instance, suppose you change one or more of the data values and would like to save the modified file using the filename *NowlinMod*. The following steps show how to save the modified workbook using filename *NowlinMod*:

Step 1. Click the **File** tab in the Ribbon
Step 2. Click **Save As** in the list of options
Step 3. Select **This PC** under **Save As**, and click **Browse**
Step 4. When the **Save As** dialog box appears:
             Select the location where you want to save the file
             Type the filename *NowlinMod* in the **File name:** box
             Click **Save**

Once the *NowlinMod* workbook has been saved, you can continue to work with the file to perform whatever type of analysis is appropriate. When you are finished working with the file, simply click the close-window button ✕ located at the top right-hand corner of the Ribbon.

Later, you can easily access a previously saved file. For example, the following steps show how to open the previously saved *Nowlin* workbook:

Step 1. Click the **File** tab in the Ribbon
Step 2. Click **Open** in the list of options
Step 3. Select **This PC** under **Open** and click **Browse**
Step 4. When the **Open** dialog box appears:
> Find the location where you previously saved the *Nowlin* file
> Click on the filename **Nowlin** so that it appears in the **File name:** box
> Click **Open**

A.2 Spreadsheet Basics

Cells, References, and Formulas in Excel

We begin by assuming that the *Nowlin* workbook is open again and that we would like to develop a model that can be used to compute the manufacturing and outsourcing cost given a certain required volume. We develop the model based on the data in the worksheet shown in Figure A.4. The model will contain formulas that refer to the location of the data cells in the upper section of the worksheet. By putting the location of the data cells in the formula, we will build a model that can be easily updated with new data.

*To display all formulas in the cells of a worksheet, hold down the **Ctrl** key and then press the ~ key (usually located above the Tab key).*

To provide a visual reminder that the bottom portion of this worksheet will contain the model, we enter the label *Model* into cell A10 and press the **Bold** button in the **Font** group. In cell A11, we enter the label *Quantity*. Next, we enter the labels *Total Cost to Produce* in cell A13, *Total Cost to Outsource* in cell A15, and *Savings due to Outsourcing* in cell A17.

In cell B11 we enter *10000* to represent the quantity produced or outsourced by Nowlin Plastics. We will now enter formulas in cells B13, B15, and B17 that use the quantity in cell B11 to compute the values for production cost, outsourcing cost, and savings from outsourcing. The total cost to produce is the sum of the manufacturing fixed cost (cell B4) and the manufacturing variable cost. The manufacturing variable cost is the product of the production volume (cell B11) and the variable cost per unit (cell B5). Thus, the formula for total variable cost is B11*B5; to compute the value of total cost, we enter the formula *=B4+B11*B5* in cell B13. Next, total cost to outsource is the product of the outsourcing cost per unit (cell B7) and the quantity (cell B11); this is computed by entering the formula *=B7*B11* in cell B15. Finally, the savings due to outsourcing is computed by subtracting the cost of outsourcing (cell B15) from the production cost (cell B13). Thus, in cell B17 we enter the formula *=B13-B15*. Figure A.5 shows the Excel worksheet values and formulas used for these calculations.

We can now compute the savings due to outsourcing by entering a value for the quantity to be manufactured or outsourced in cell B11. Figure A.5 shows the results after entering a value of 10,000 in cell B11. We see that a quantity of 10,000 units results in a production cost of $254,000 and outsourcing cost of $35,000. Thus, the savings due to outsourcing is $219,000.

Finding the Appropriate Excel Function

Excel provides a variety of built-in formulas or functions for developing mathematical models. If we know which function is needed and how to use it, we can simply enter the function into the appropriate worksheet cell. However, if we are not sure which functions are available to accomplish a task or are not sure how to use a particular function, Excel can provide assistance.

To identify the functions available in Excel, click the **Insert Function** button *fx* on the **Formula** bar; this opens the **Insert Function** dialog box shown in Figure A.6. The **Search for a function:** box at the top of the dialog box enables us to type a brief description of what we want to do. After entering a description and clicking **Go**, Excel will search for and display the functions that may accomplish our task in the **Select a function:** box. In many situations, however, we may want to browse through an entire category of functions to see

FIGURE A.5   Nowlin Plastics Data and Model

	A	B	C
1	**Nowlin Plastics**		
2			
3	**Parameters**		
4	Manufacturing Fixed Cost	234000	
5	Manufacturing Variable Cost per Unit	2	
6			
7	Outsourcing Cost per Unit	3.5	
8			
9			
10	**Model**		
11	Quantity	10000	
12			
13	Total Cost to Produce	=B4+B11*B5	
14			
15	Total Cost to Outsource	=B7*B11	
16			
17	Savings due to Outsourcing	=B13-B15	
18			

DATA *file*

Nowlin

	A	B	C
1	**Nowlin Plastics**		
2			
3	**Parameters**		
4	Manufacturing Fixed Cost	$234,000.00	
5	Manufacturing Variable Cost per Unit	$2.00	
6			
7	Outsourcing Cost per Unit	$3.50	
8			
9			
10	**Model**		
11	Quantity	10,000	
12			
13	Total Cost to Produce	$254,000.00	
14			
15	Total Cost to Outsource	$35,000.00	
16			
17	Savings due to Outsourcing	$219,000.00	
18			

The ABS function calculates the absolute value of a number. The ACOS function calculates the arccosine of a number.

what is available. For this task, the **Or select a category:** box is helpful. It contains a drop-down list of several categories of functions provided by Excel. Figure A.6 shows that we selected the **Math & Trig** category. As a result, Excel's Math & Trig functions appear in alphabetical order in the **Select a function:** area. We see the ABS function listed first, followed by the ACOS function, and so on.

Colon Notation

Although many functions, such as the ABS function, have a single argument, some Excel functions depend on arrays. **Colon notation** provides an efficient way to convey arrays and matrices of cells to functions. For example, the colon notation B1:B5 means cell B1 "through" cell B5, namely the array of values stored in the locations (B1,B2,B3,B4,B5). Consider, for example, the following function =SUM(B1:B5). The sum function adds up

FIGURE A.6	Insert Function Dialog Box

the elements contained in the function's argument. Hence, =SUM(B1:B5) evaluates the following formula:

$$= B1 + B2 + B3 + B4 + B5$$

NowlinFinancial

To illustrate the use of colon notation, we will consider the financial data for Nowlin Plastics contained in the DATAfile *NowlinFinancial* and shown in Figure A.7. Column A contains the name of each month, column B the revenue for each month, and column C the cost data. In row 15, we compute the total revenues and costs for the year. To do this we first enter *Total:* in cell A15. Next, we enter the formula *=SUM(B2:B13)* in cell B15 and *=SUM(C2:C13)* in cell C15. This shows that the total revenues for the company are $39,319,000 and the total costs are $36,549,000.

Inserting a Function into a Worksheet Cell

Continuing with the Nowlin financial data, we will now show how to use the Insert Function and Function Arguments dialog boxes to select a function, develop its arguments, and insert the function into a worksheet cell. We wish to calculate the average monthly revenue and cost at Nowlin. To do so, we execute the following steps:

If you need additional guidance on the use of a particular function in Excel, the **Function Arguments** *dialog box contains a link,* **Help on this function***.*

Step 1.   Select cell B17 in the DATAfile *NowlinFinancial*
Step 2.   Click the **Insert Function** button *fx*.
           Select **Statistical** in the **Or select a category:** box
           Select **AVERAGE** from the **Select a function:** options
Step 3.   When the **Function Arguments** dialog box appears:
           Enter *B2:B13* in the **Number1** box
           Click **OK**
Step 4.   Repeat Steps 1 through 3 for the cost data in column C

Figure A.7 shows that the average monthly revenue is $3,276,583 and the average monthly cost is $3,045,750.

FIGURE A.7	Nowlin Plastics Monthly Revenues and Costs

	A	B	C
1	Month	Revenue	Cost
2	January	3459000	3250000
3	February	2873000	2640000
4	March	3195000	3021000
5	April	2925000	3015000
6	May	3682000	3150000
7	June	3436000	3240000
8	July	3410000	3185000
9	August	3782000	3237000
10	September	3548000	3196000
11	October	3136000	2997000
12	November	3028000	2815000
13	December	2845000	2803000
14			
15	Total:	=SUM(B2:B13)	=SUM(C2:C13)
16			
17	Average:	=AVERAGE(B2:B13)	=AVERAGE(C2:C13)

DATA *file*
NowlinFinancial

	A	B	C
1	Month	Revenue	Cost
2	January	$ 3,459,000	$ 3,250,000
3	February	$ 2,873,000	$ 2,640,000
4	March	$ 3,195,000	$ 3,021,000
5	April	$ 2,925,000	$ 3,015,000
6	May	$ 3,682,000	$ 3,150,000
7	June	$ 3,436,000	$ 3,240,000
8	July	$ 3,410,000	$ 3,185,000
9	August	$ 3,782,000	$ 3,237,000
10	September	$ 3,548,000	$ 3,196,000
11	October	$ 3,136,000	$ 2,997,000
12	November	$ 3,028,000	$ 2,815,000
13	December	$ 2,845,000	$ 2,803,000
14			
15	Total:	$39,319,000	$36,549,000
16			
17	Average:	$ 3,276,583	$ 3,045,750

DATA *file*
NowlinFinancial

*After completing Step 2, a shortcut to copying the formula to the range D3:D13 is to place the pointer in the bottom-right corner of cell D2 and then double-click. Keyboard shortcut: You can copy in Excel by pressing **Ctrl-C**. You can paste in Excel by pressing **Ctrl-V**.*

Using Relative Versus Absolute Cell References

One of the most powerful abilities of spreadsheet software such as Excel is the ability to use relative references in formulas. Use of a **relative reference** allows the user to enter a formula once into Excel and then copy and paste that formula to other places so that the formula will update with the correct data without having to retype the formula. We will demonstrate the use of relative references in Excel by calculating the monthly profit at Nowlin Plastics using the following steps:

Step 1. Enter the label *Profit* in cell D1 and press the **Bold** button in the **Font** group of the **Home** tab

Step 2. Enter the formula *=B2-C2* in cell D2

Step 3. Copy the formula from cell D2 by selecting cell D2 and clicking **Copy** from the **Clipboard** group of the **Home** tab

In some cases, you may want Excel to use relative referencing for either the column or row location and absolute referencing for the other. For instance, to force Excel to always refer to column A but use relative referencing for the row, you would enter =$A1 into, say, cell B1. If this formula is copied into cell C3, the updated formula would be =$A3 (whereas it would be updated to =B3 if relative referencing was used for both the column and the row location).

Step 4.   Select cells D3:D13
Step 5.   Paste the formula from cell D2 by clicking **Paste** from the **Clipboard** group of the **Home** tab

The result of these steps is shown in Figure A.8, where we have calculated the profit for each month. Note that even though the only formula we entered was *=B2-C2* in cell D2, the formulas in cells D3 through D13 have been updated correctly to calculate the profit of each month using that month's revenue and cost.

In some situations, however, we do not want to use relative referencing in formulas. The alternative is to use an absolute reference, which we indicate to Excel by putting "$" before the row and/or column locations of the cell location. An **absolute reference** does *not* update to a new cell reference when the formula is copied to another location. We illustrate the use of an absolute reference by continuing to use the Nowlin financial data. Nowlin calculates an after-tax profit each month by multiplying its actual monthly profit by one minus its tax rate, which is currently estimated to be 30%. Cell B19 in Figure A.9 contains this tax rate. In column E, we calculate the after-tax profit for Nowlin in each month by using the following steps:

FIGURE A.8   Nowlin Plastics Profit Calculation

	A	B	C	D
1	Month	Revenue	Cost	Profit
2	January	3459000	3250000	=B2-C2
3	February	2873000	2640000	=B3-C3
4	March	3195000	3021000	=B4-C4
5	April	2925000	3015000	=B5-C5
6	May	3682000	3150000	=B6-C6
7	June	3436000	3240000	=B7-C7
8	July	3410000	3185000	=B8-C8
9	August	3782000	3237000	=B9-C9
10	September	3548000	3196000	=B10-C10
11	October	3136000	2997000	=B11-C11
12	November	3028000	2815000	=B12-C12
13	December	2845000	2803000	=B13-C13
14				
15	Total:	=SUM(B2:B13)	=SUM(C2:C13)	
16				
17	Average:	=AVERAGE(B2:B13)	=AVERAGE(C2:C13)	

	A	B	C	D
1	Month	Revenue	Cost	Profit
2	January	$ 3,459,000	$ 3,250,000	$ 209,000
3	February	$ 2,873,000	$ 2,640,000	$ 233,000
4	March	$ 3,195,000	$ 3,021,000	$ 174,000
5	April	$ 2,925,000	$ 3,015,000	$ (90,000)
6	May	$ 3,682,000	$ 3,150,000	$ 532,000
7	June	$ 3,436,000	$ 3,240,000	$ 196,000
8	July	$ 3,410,000	$ 3,185,000	$ 225,000
9	August	$ 3,782,000	$ 3,237,000	$ 545,000
10	September	$ 3,548,000	$ 3,196,000	$ 352,000
11	October	$ 3,136,000	$ 2,997,000	$ 139,000
12	November	$ 3,028,000	$ 2,815,000	$ 213,000
13	December	$ 2,845,000	$ 2,803,000	$ 42,000
14				
15	Total:	$39,319,000	$36,549,000	
16				
17	Average:	$ 3,276,583	$ 3,045,750	

Step 1. Enter the label *After-Tax Profit* in cell E1 and press the **Bold** button in the **Font** group of the **Home** tab.

Step 2. Enter the formula *=D2*(1-$B$19)* in cell E2

Step 3. Copy the formula from cell E2 by selecting cell E2 and clicking **Copy** from the **Clipboard** group of the **Home** tab

Step 4. Select cells E3:E13

Step 5. Paste the formula from cell E2 by clicking **Paste** from the **Clipboard** group of the **Home** tab

Figure A.9 shows the after-tax profit in each month. Using $B$19 in the formula in cell E2 forces Excel to always refer to cell $B$19, even if we copy and paste this formula somewhere else in our worksheet. Notice that D2 continues to be a relative reference and is updated to D3, D4, and so on when we copy this formula to cells E3, E4, and so on, respectively.

FIGURE A.9   Nowlin Plastics After-Tax Profit Calculation Illustrating Relative Versus Absolute References

	A	B	C	D	E
1	**Month**	**Revenue**	**Cost**	**Profit**	**After-Tax Profit**
2	January	3459000	3250000	=B2-C2	=D2*(1-$B$19)
3	February	2873000	2640000	=B3-C3	=D3*(1-$B$19)
4	March	3195000	3021000	=B4-C4	=D4*(1-$B$19)
5	April	2925000	3015000	=B5-C5	=D5*(1-$B$19)
6	May	3682000	3150000	=B6-C6	=D6*(1-$B$19)
7	June	3436000	3240000	=B7-C7	=D7*(1-$B$19)
8	July	3410000	3185000	=B8-C8	=D8*(1-$B$19)
9	August	3782000	3237000	=B9-C9	=D9*(1-$B$19)
10	September	3548000	3196000	=B10-C10	=D10*(1-$B$19)
11	October	3136000	2997000	=B11-C11	=D11*(1-$B$19)
12	November	3028000	2815000	=B12-C12	=D12*(1-$B$19)
13	December	2845000	2803000	=B13-C13	=D13*(1-$B$19)
14					
15	Total:	=SUM(B2:B13)	=SUM(C2:C13)		
16					
17	Average:	=AVERAGE(B2:B13)	=AVERAGE(C2:C13)		
18					
19	Tax Rate:	0.3			

DATA *file*

NowlinFinancialComplete

	A	B	C	D	E
1	**Month**	**Revenue**	**Cost**	**Profit**	**After-Tax Profit**
2	January	$ 3,459,000	$ 3,250,000	$ 209,000	$ 146,300
3	February	$ 2,873,000	$ 2,640,000	$ 233,000	$ 163,100
4	March	$ 3,195,000	$ 3,021,000	$ 174,000	$ 121,800
5	April	$ 2,925,000	$ 3,015,000	$ (90,000)	$ (63,000)
6	May	$ 3,682,000	$ 3,150,000	$ 532,000	$ 372,400
7	June	$ 3,436,000	$ 3,240,000	$ 196,000	$ 137,200
8	July	$ 3,410,000	$ 3,185,000	$ 225,000	$ 157,500
9	August	$ 3,782,000	$ 3,237,000	$ 545,000	$ 381,500
10	September	$ 3,548,000	$ 3,196,000	$ 352,000	$ 246,400
11	October	$ 3,136,000	$ 2,997,000	$ 139,000	$ 97,300
12	November	$ 3,028,000	$ 2,815,000	$ 213,000	$ 149,100
13	December	$ 2,845,000	$ 2,803,000	$ 42,000	$ 29,400
14					
15	Total:	$39,319,000	$36,549,000		
16					
17	Average:	$ 3,276,583	$ 3,045,750		
18					
19	Tax Rate:	30%			

In Chapter 10, we give a detailed treatment of how to create more advanced business analytics models in Excel.

SUMMARY

In this appendix, we have reviewed the basics of using Microsoft Excel. We have discussed the basic layout of Excel, file creation, saving, and editing as well as how to reference cells, use formulas, and use the copy and paste functions in an Excel worksheet. We have illustrated how to find and enter Excel functions and described the difference between relative and absolute cell references. We conclude this appendix with Table A.1, which shows commonly used keyboard shortcut keys in Excel. Keyboard shortcut keys can save considerable time when entering data into Excel.

GLOSSARY

Absolute reference A reference to a cell location in an Excel worksheet formula that does not update according to its relative position when the formula copied.

Colon notation Notation used in an Excel worksheet to denote "through." For example, =SUM(B1:B4) implies sum cells B1 through B4, or equivalently, B1 + B2 + B3 + B4.

Relative reference A reference to a cell location in an Excel worksheet formula that updates according to its relative position when the formula copied.

Workbook An Excel file that contains a series of worksheets.

Worksheet A single page in an Excel workbook containing a matrix of cells defined by their column and row locations.

TABLE A.1	Keyboard Shortcut Keys in Excel
Keyboard Shortcut Key	**Task Description**
Ctrl-S	Save
Ctrl-C	Copy
Ctrl-V	Paste
Ctrl-F	Find (can be used to find text both within a cell and within a formula in Excel)
Ctrl-P	Print
Ctrl-A	Selects all cells in the current data region
Ctrl-B	Changes the selected text to/from bold font
Ctrl-I	Changes the selected text to/from italic font
Ctrl-~ (usually located above the Tab key)	Toggles between displaying values and formulas in the Worksheet.
Ctrl-↓ (down arrow key)	Moves to the bottom-most cell of the current data region
Ctrl-↑ (up arrow key)	Moves to the top-most cell of the current data region
Ctrl-→ (right arrow key)	Moves to the right-most cell of the current data region
Ctrl-← (left arrow key)	Moves to the left-most cell of the current data region
Ctrl-Home	Moves to the top-left-most cell of the current data region
Ctrl-End	Moves to the bottom-left-most cell of the current data region
Shift-↓	Selects the current cell and the cell below
Shift-↑	Selects the current cell and the cell above
Shift-→	Selects the current cell and the cell to the right
Shift-←	Selects the current cell and the cell to the left
Ctrl-Shift-↓	Selects all cells from the current cell to the bottom-most cell of the data region
Ctrl-Shift-↑	Selects all cells from the current cell to the top-most cell of the data region
Ctrl-Shift-→	Selects all cells from the current cell to the right-most cell in the data region
Ctrl-Shift-←	Selects all cells from the current cell to the left-most cell in the data region
Ctrl-Shift-Home	Selects all cells from the current cell to the top-left-most cell in the data region
Ctrl-Shift-End	Selects all cells from the current cell to the bottom-right-most cell in the data region
Ctrl-Spacebar	Selects the entire current column
Shift-Spacebar	Selects the entire current row

A data region refers to all adjacent cells that contain data in an Excel worksheet.

*Holding down the **Ctrl** key and clicking on multiple cells allows you to select multiple nonadjacent cells. Holding down the **Shift** key and clicking on two nonadjacent cells selects all cells between the two cells.*

Appendix B—Database Basics with Microsoft Access

CONTENTS

Data are the cornerstone of analytics; without accurate and timely data on relevant aspects of a business or organization, analytic techniques are useless, and the resulting analyses are meaningless (or worse yet, potentially misleading). The data used by organizations to make decisions are not static, but rather are dynamic and constantly changing, usually at a rapid pace. Every change or addition to a database represents a new opportunity to introduce errors into the data, so it is important to be capable of searching for duplicate entries or entries with errors. Furthermore, related data may be stored in different locations to simplify data entry or increase security. Because an analysis frequently requires information from several sets of data, an analyst must be able to efficiently combine information from multiple data sets in a logical manner. In this appendix, we will review tools in Microsoft Access® that can be used for these purposes.

B.1 Database Basics

A **database** is a collection of logically related data that can be retrieved, manipulated, and updated to meet a user's or organization's needs. By providing centralized access to data efficiently and consistently, a database serves as an electronic warehouse of information on some specific aspect of an organization. A database allows for the systematic accumulation, management, storage, retrieval, and analysis of the information it contains while reducing inaccuracies that routinely result from manual record keeping. Organizations of all sizes maintain databases that contain information about their customers, markets, suppliers, and employees. Before embarking on designing a database, it is important to consider what are good characteristics of a database. Foremost, the information in a database should be correct and complete so that decisions based on reports retrieved from the database will be based on accurate information. Second, a database should avoid duplicate information as much as possible in order to minimize wasted space and reduce the likelihood of errors and inconsistencies. Thus, a good database design

- divides the organization's information into subject-based tables to reduce redundant data without loss of information.
- provides the organization's database software with the information required to join information in tables together as needed.
- supports, maintains, and ensures the integrity and accuracy of the organization's information.
- avoids tables that have large numbers of entries with empty attributes.
- protects the organization's information through database security.
- accommodates the organization's data processing and reporting needs.

Throughout this appendix, we will consider issues that arise in the creation and maintenance of a database for Stinson's MicroBrew Distributor, a licensed regional independent distributor of beer and a member of the National Beer Wholesalers Association. Stinson's provides refrigerated storage, transportation, and delivery of premium beers produced by several local microbreweries, so the company's facilities include a state-of-the-art temperature-controlled warehouse and a fleet of temperature-controlled trucks. Stinson's also employs sales, receiving, warehousing/inventory, and delivery personnel. When making a delivery, Stinson's monitors the retailer's shelves, taps, and keg lines to ensure the freshness and quality of the product. Because beer is perishable and because microbreweries often do not have the capacity to store, transport, and deliver large quantities of the products they produce, Stinson's holds a critical position in this supply chain.

Stinson's needs to develop a faster, more efficient, and more accurate means of recording, maintaining, and retrieving data related to various aspects of its business. The company's management team has identified three broad key areas of data management: personnel (information on Stinson's employees); supplier (information on purchases of beer made by Stinson's from its suppliers); and retailer (information on sales to Stinson's retail customers). We will use Microsoft Access 2016 in designing Stinson's database. Access is a *relational* database management system (RDBMS), which is the most commonly used type of database system in business. Data in a relational database are stored in tables, which are the fundamental components of a database. A relational database allows the user to retrieve subsets of data from tables and retrieve and combine data that are stored in related tables.

In this section we will learn how to use Access to create a database and perform some basic database operations. In Access, a database is defined as a collection of related objects that are saved as a single file. An object in Access can be a:

- **Table**: Data arrayed in rows and columns (similar to a worksheet in an Excel spreadsheet) in which rows correspond to **records** (the individual units from which the data have been collected) and columns correspond to **fields** (the variables on which data have been collected from the records)
- **Form**: An object that is created from a table to simplify the process of entering data
- **Query**: A question posed by a user about the data in the database
- **Report**: Output from a table or a query that has been put into a specific prespecified format

We will focus on tables and queries in this appendix. You can refer to a wide variety of books on database design to learn about forms, reports, and other database objects.

Tables are the foundation of an Access database. Each field in a table has a data type. The most commonly used are as follows:

- *Short Text:* A field that contains words (such as the field *Gender* that may be used to record whether a Stinson's employee is female or male); can contain no more than 255 alphanumeric characters
- *Long Text:* A larger field that contains words and is generally used for recording lengthy descriptive entries (such as the field *Notes on Special Circumstances for a Transaction* that may be used to record detailed notes about unique aspects of specific transactions between Stinson's and its retail customers); can contain up to approximately 1 gigabyte, but controls to display a long text are limited to the first 64,000 characters.
- *Number*: A field that contains numerical values. There are several sizes of Number fields, which include:
  - *Byte:* Stores whole numbers from 0 to 255
  - *Decimal:* Stores numbers from $-10^{28} + 1$ to $10^{28} - 1$
  - *Integer:* Stores nonfractional numbers from −32,768 to 32,767
  - *Long Integer:* Stores nonfractional numbers from −2,147,483,648 to 2,147,483,647

- *Single:* Stores numbers from -3.402823×10^{38} to 3.402823×10^{38}
- *Double:* Stores numbers from $-1.79769313 \times 10^{308}$ to $1.79769313 \times 10^{308}$
- *Currency:* A field that contains monetary values (such as the field *Transaction Amount* that may be used to record payments for goods that have been ordered by Stinson's retail customers)
- *Yes/No:* A field that contains binary variables (such as the field *Sunday Deliveries?* that may be used to record whether Stinson's retail customers accept deliveries on Sundays)
- *Date/Time:* A field that contains dates and times (such as the field *Date of Order* that may be used to record the date of an order placed by Stinson's with one of its suppliers)

A Replication ID field is used for storing a globally unique identifier to prevent duplication of an identifier (such as customer number) when multiple copies of the same database are in use in different locations.

Once you create a field and set its data type, you can set additional field properties. For example, for a numerical field you can define the data size to be Byte, Integer, Long Integer, Single, Double, Replication ID, or Decimal.

A database may consist of several tables that are maintained separately for a variety of reasons. We have already mentioned that Stinson's maintains information on its personnel, its suppliers and orders and its retail customers and sales. With regard to its retail customers, Stinson's may maintain information on the company name, street address, city, state, zip code, telephone number, and e-mail address; the dates of orders placed and quantities ordered; and the dates of actual deliveries and quantities delivered. In this example, we may consider establishing a table on Stinson's retailer customers; in this table each record corresponds to a retail customer, and the fields include the retail customer's company name, street address, city, state, zip code, telephone number, and e-mail address. Maintenance of this table is relatively simple; these data likely are not updated frequently for existing retail customers, and when Stinson's begins selling to a new retail customer, it has to establish only a single new record containing the information for the new retail customer in each field.

Stinson's may maintain other tables in this database. To track purchases made by its retail customers, the company may maintain a table of retail orders that includes the retail customer's name and the dollar value, date, and number of kegs and cases of beer for each order received by Stinson's. Because this table contains one record for each order placed with Stinson's, this table must be updated much more frequently than the table of information on Stinson's retailer customers.

In addition to answering a user's questions about the data in one or more tables, a query can also be used to add a record to the end of a table, delete a record from a table, or change the values for one or more records in a table. These functions are accomplished through append, delete, and update queries. We discuss queries in more detail later in this appendix.

A user who submits a query is effectively asking a question about the information in one or more tables in a database. For example, suppose Stinson's has determined that it has surplus kegs of Fine Pembrook Ale in inventory and is concerned about potential spoilage. As a result, the Marketing Department decides to identify all retail customers who have ordered kegs of Fine Pembrook Ale during the previous three months so that Stinson's can call these retailers and offer them a discounted price on additional kegs of this beer. A query could be designed to search the Retail Orders table for retail customers who meet this criterion. When the query is run, the output of the query provides the answer.

More complex queries may require data to be retrieved from multiple tables. For these queries, the tables must be connected by a join operation that links the records of the tables by their values in some common field. The common field serves as a bridge between the two tables, and the bridged tables are then treated by the query as a large single table comprising the fields of the original tables that have been joined. In designing a database for Stinson's, we may include the customer ID as a field in both the table of retail customers and the table of retail orders; values in the field customer ID would then provide the basis for linking records in these two tables. Thus, even though the table of retail orders does not contain the information on each of Stinson's retail customers that is contained in the table of Stinson's retail customers, if the database is well designed, the information in these two tables can easily be combined whenever necessary.

For tables that do not include a primary key field, a unique identifier for each record in the table may be formed by combining two or more fields (if the combination of these two fields will yield a unique value for each record that may be included in the table); the result is called a compound primary key and is used in the same way a primary key is used.

Each table in a database generally contains a **primary key field** that has a unique value for each record in the table. A primary key field is used to identify how records from several tables in a database are logically related. In our previous example, Customer ID is the primary key field for the table of Stinson's retail customers. To facilitate the linking of records in the table of Stinson's retail customers with logically related records in the table of retail orders, the two tables must share a primary key. Thus, a field for Customer ID may be included in the table of retail orders so that information in this table can be linked to information on each of Stinson's retail customers; when a field is included in a table for the sole purpose of facilitating links with records from another table, the field is referred to as a **foreign key field**.

Considerations When Designing a Database

Before creating a new database, we should carefully consider the following issues:

- What is the purpose of this database?
- Who will use this database?
- What queries and reports do the users of this database need?
- What information or data (fields) will this database include?
- What tables must be created, and how will the fields be allocated to these tables?
- What are the relationships between these tables?
- What are the fields that will be used to link related tables?
- What forms does the organization need to create to support the use of this database?

The answers to these questions will enable us to efficiently create a more effective and useful database. Let us consider these issues within the context of designing Stinson's database. Stinson's has several reasons for developing and implementing a database. Quick access to reliable and current data will enable Stinson's to monitor inventory and place orders from the microbreweries so that it can meet the demand of the retailers it supplies, while avoiding excess quantities and potential spoilage of inventory. These data can also be used to monitor the age of the product in inventory, which is a critical issue for a perishable product. Patterns in the orders of various beers placed by Stinson's retail customers can be analyzed to determine forecasts of future demand. Employees' salaries, federal and state tax withholding, vacation and sick days taken/remaining for the current year, and contributions to retirement funds can be tracked. Orders received from retail customers and Stinson's deliveries can be better coordinated. In summary, Stinson's can use a database to utilize information about its business in numerous ways that will potentially improve the efficiency and profitability of the company.

If we were to create a database for Stinson's MicroBrew Distributor, who within the company might need to use information from the database? A quick review of Stinson's reasons for developing and implementing a database provides the answer. Warehousing/inventory can use the database to control inventory. Delivery can create efficient delivery routes for the drivers on a daily basis and assess the on-time performance of the delivery system. Receiving can anticipate and prepare to receive daily deliveries of microbrews. Human resources can administer payroll, taxes, and benefits. Marketing can identify and exploit potential sales opportunities.

By considering the users and uses for the database, we can make a preliminary determination of the queries and reports the users of this database will need and the data (fields) this database must include. At this point we can consider the tables to be created, how the fields will be allocated to the tables, and the potential relationships between these tables. We can see that we will need to incorporate data on:

- each microbrewery for which Stinson's distributes beer (Stinson's suppliers).
- each order placed with and delivery received from the microbreweries (Stinson's supplies).

- each retailer to which Stinson's distributes beer (Stinson's customers).
- each order received from and delivery made to Stinson's retail customers (Stinson's sales).
- each of Stinson's employees (Stinson's workforce).

As we design these tables and allocate fields to the tables we design, we must ensure that our database stores Stinson's data in the correct formats and is capable of outputting the queries, forms, and reports that Stinson's employees need.

With these considerations in mind, we decide to begin with the following 11 tables and associated fields in designing a database for Stinson's MicroBrew Distributor:

- TblEmployees
  - EmployeeID
  - EmpFirstName
  - EmpLastName
  - Gender
  - DOB
  - Street Address
  - City
  - State
  - Zip Code
  - Phone Number

- TblJobTitle
  - Job ID
  - Job Title

- TblEmployHist
  - EmployeeID
  - Start Date
  - End Date
  - Job ID
  - Salary
  - Hourly Rate

- TblBrewers
  - BrewerID
  - Brewery Name
  - Street Address
  - City
  - State
  - Zip Code
  - Phone Number

- TblSOrders
  - SOrder Number
  - BrewerID
  - Date of SOrder
  - EmployeeID
  - Keg or Case?
  - SQuantity Ordered

- TblSDeliveries
  - SOrder Number
  - BrewerID
  - EmployeeID
  - Date of SDelivery
  - SQuantity Delivered

- TblPurchasePrices
  - BrewerID
  - KegPurchasePrice
  - CasePurchasePrice

- TblRetailers
  - CustID
  - Name
  - Class
  - Street Address
  - City
  - State
  - Zip Code
  - Phone Number

- TblROrders
  - ROrder Number
  - Name
  - CustID
  - BrewerID
  - Date of ROrder
  - Keg or Case?
  - RQuantity Ordered
  - Rush?

- TblRDeliveries
  - CustID
  - Name
  - ROrder Number
  - EmployeeID
  - Date of RDelivery
  - RQuantity Delivered

- TblSalesPrices
  - BrewerID
  - KegSalesPrice
  - CaseSalesPrice

Note that the name of each table begins with the three letter designation Tbl; this is consistent with the Leszynski/Reddick guidelines, a common set of standards for naming database objects.

Each table contains information about a particular aspect of Stinson's business operations:

- *TblEmployees*: Information about each Stinson's employee, primarily obtained when the employee is hired
- *TblJobTitle*: Information about each type of position held by Stinson's employees
- *TblEmployHist*: Information about the employment history of each Stinson's employee
- *TblBrewers*: Information about each microbrewery that supplies Stinson's with beer
- *TblSOrders*: Information about each order that Stinson's has placed with the microbreweries that supply Stinson's with beer
- *TblSDeliveries*: Information about each delivery that Stinson's has received from the microbreweries that supply Stinson's with beer
- *TblPurchasePrices*: Information about the price charged by each microbrewery that supplies Stinson's with beer
- *TblRetailers*: Information about each retailer that Stinson's supplies with beer
- *TblROrders*: Information about each order that Stinson's has received from the retailers that Stinson's supplies with beer
- *TblRDeliveries*: Information about each delivery that Stinson's has made to the retailers that Stinson's supplies with beer
- *TblSalesPrices*: Information about the price charged to retailers by Stinson's for each of the microwbrews it distributes

The first three tables deal with personnel information, the next four with product supply/purchasing information, and the last four with demand/sales information. Figure B.1 shows how these tables are related.

The relationships among the tables define how they can be linked. For example, suppose Stinson's Shipping Manager needs information on the orders placed by Stinson's retail customers that are to be filled tomorrow so that she can solve an optimization model that provides the optimal routes for Stinson's delivery trucks. The Shipping Manager needs to generate a report that includes the amount of various beers ordered and the address of each retail customer that has placed an order. To do so, she can use the common field CustID to link records from the TblRetailers. When the delivery has been made, the relevant information is input into the TblRDeliveries table. If the Shipping Manager needs to generate a report of deliveries made by each driver for the past week, she can use the common field EmployeeID to link records from the TblEmployees table with related records from the TblRDeliveries table.

Once Stinson's is satisfied that the planned database will provide the organization with the capability to collect and manage its data, and Stinson's is also confident that the database is capable of outputting the queries, forms, and reports that its employees need, we can proceed by using Access to create the new database. However, it is important to

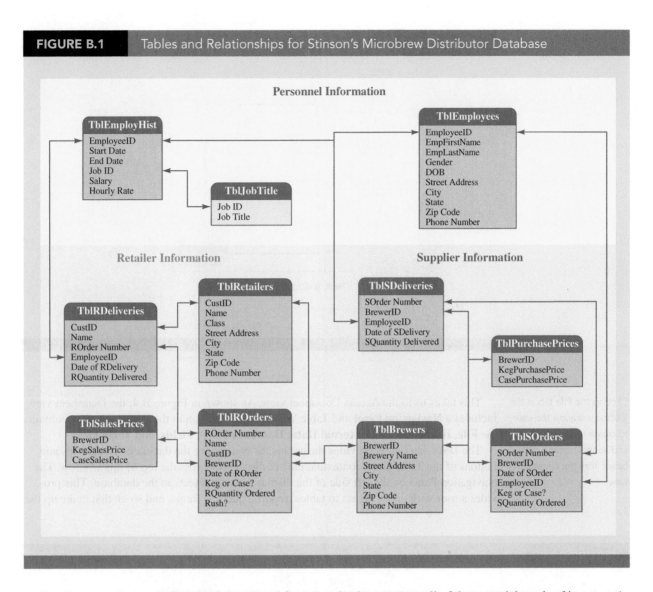

FIGURE B.1   Tables and Relationships for Stinson's Microbrew Distributor Database

realize that it is unusual for a new database to meet all of the potential needs of its users. A well-designed database allows for augmentation and revision when needs that the current database does not meet are identified.

Creating a Database in Access

When you open Access, the left pane provides links to databases you have recently opened as well as a means for opening existing database documents. The available document templates are provided in the right pane; these preinstalled templates can be used to create new databases that utilize common formats. Because we are focusing on building a fairly generic database, we will use the Blank desktop database tool. We are now ready to create a new database by following these steps:

Step 1.   Click the **Blank desktop database** icon (Figure B.2)

Step 2.   When the **Blank desktop database** dialog box (Figure B.3) appears:

Enter the name of the new database in the **File Name** box (we will call our new database *Stinsons.accdb*)

Indicate the location where the new database will be saved by clicking the **Browse** button 🗁 (we will save *Stinsons.accdb* in the folder *C:\Stinson Files*)

Step 3.   Click **Create**

FIGURE B.2 Blank Desktop Database Icon

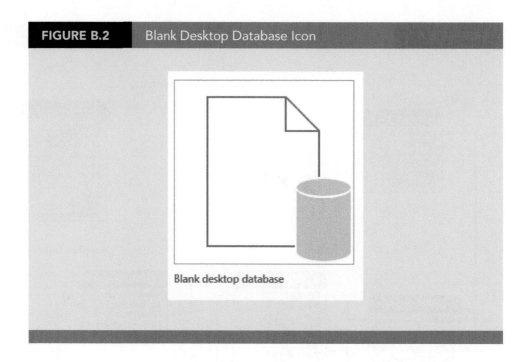

Blank desktop database

*Clicking the **File** tab in the Ribbon will allow the user to create new databases and access existing databases from the Datasheet view.*

This takes us to the Access Datasheet view. As shown in Figure B.4, the Datasheet view includes a Navigation Panel and Table Window. The Ribbon in the Datasheet view contains the **File, Home, Create, External Data, Database Tools, Fields**, and **Table** tabs.

The **Datasheet view** provides the means for controlling the database. The groups and buttons of the Table Tools contextual tab are displayed across the top of this window. The Navigation Panel on the left side of the display lists all objects in the database. This provides a user with direct access to tables, reports, queries, forms, and so on that make up the

FIGURE B.3 Blank Desktop Database Dialog Box

Blank desktop database

Should I create an Access app or an Access desktop database?

File Name

Stinsons.accdb

C:\Stinson Files\

Create

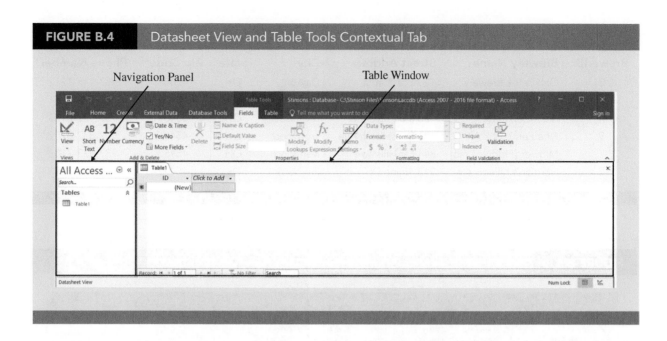

FIGURE B.4   Datasheet View and Table Tools Contextual Tab

currently open database. On the right side of the display is the Table Window; the tab in the upper left corner of the Table Window shows the name of the current table (Table1 in Figure B.4). In the Table Window, we can enter data directly into the table or modify data in an existing table.

The first step in creating a new database is to create one or more tables. Because tables store the information contained in a database, they are the foundation of a database and must be created prior to the creation of any other objects in the database. There are two options for manually creating a table: We can enter data directly in Datasheet view, or we can design a table in **Design view**. We will create our first table, TblBrewers, by entering data directly in Datasheet view. You can review an example database comprising all of the objects and relationships between the objects that we create throughout this appendix for the Stinson's database in the file *Stinsons*.

In Datasheet view the data are entered by field, one record at a time. In Figure B.1 we see that the fields for TblBrewers are BrewerID, Brewery Name, Street Address, City, State, Zip Code, and Phone Number. From Stinson's current filing system, we have been able to retrieve the information in Table B.1 on the breweries that supply Stinson's.

We can enter these data into our new database in Datasheet view by following these steps:

Step 1.   Enter the first record from Table B.1 into the first row of the **Table Window** in Access by entering a *3* in the top row next to (**New**), pressing the **Tab** key, entering *Oak Creek Brewery* in the next column, pressing the **Tab** key, entering *12 Appleton St* in the next column, pressing the **Tab** key, entering *Dayton* in the next column, pressing the **Tab** key, and so on.

Step 2.   Enter the second record from Table B.1 by repeating Step 1 for the Gonzo Microbrew data and entering these data into the second row of the **Table Window** in Access

Continue entering data for the remaining microbreweries in this manner

The completed table in Access appears in Figure B.5.

Now that we have entered all of our information on the microbreweries that supply Stinson's, we need to save this table as an object in the Stinson's database. We click on the **Save** button 🖫 in the **Quick Access Toolbar** above the Ribbon, type the table name *TblBrewers* in the **Save As** dialog box that appears (as shown in Figure B.6), and click **OK**. The name in the Table Name tab on the Table Window now reads "TblBrewers."

*You can click the **Help** button 🔲 to find detailed instructions on creating a table or using any other Access functionality.*

*When we enter 3 in Step 1, this establishes a new field with the generic name "Field1" and generates a value for the ID column. Pressing the **Tab** key moves to the next field entry box for the same record.*

TABLE B.1	Raw Data for Table TblBrewers					
BrewerID	Brewery Name	Street Address	City	State	Zip Code	Phone Number
3	Oak Creek Brewery	12 Appleton St	Dayton	OH	45455	937-445-1212
6	Gonzo Microbrew	1515 Main St	Dayton	OH	45429	937-278-2651
4	McBride's Pride	425 Mad River Rd	Miamisburg	OH	45459	937-439-0123
9	Fine Pembrook Ale	141 Dusselberg Ave	Trotwood	OH	45426	937-837-8752
7	Midwest Fiddler Crab	844 Far Hills Ave	Kettering	OH	45453	937-633-7183
2	Herman's Killer Brew	912 Airline Dr	Fairborn	OH	45442	937-878-2651

FIGURE B.5 Records for Six Microbreweries Entered into an Access Table

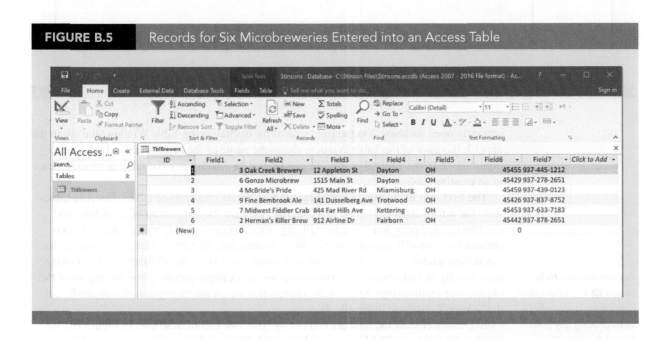

FIGURE B.6 Save as Dialog Box

We can now use the Design view to provide meaningful names for our fields and specify each field's properties. We switch to Design view by first clicking on the arrow below the **View** button ☒ in the **Views** group of the Ribbon. This will open a pull-down menu with options for various views (recall that we are currently in the Datasheet view). Clicking on

Note that Field Names used in Access cannot exceed 64 characters, cannot begin with a space, and can include any combination of letters, numbers, spaces, and special characters except for a period (.), an accent grave (`), an exclamation point (!), or square brackets ([and]).

the **Design View** option opens the Design view for the current table as shown in Figure B.7. From the Design view we can define or edit the table's fields and field properties as well as rearrange the order of the fields if we wish. The name of the current table is again identified in the Name tab, and the Table Window is replaced with two sections: the Table Design Grid on top and the Field Properties Pane on the bottom of this window.

We can now replace the generic field names (Field1, Field2, etc.) in the column on the right side of the Table Design Grid of TblBrewers with the names we established from our original database design and then move to defining the field type for each field. To change the data type for a field in design view, we follow these steps:

Step 1. Click on the cell in the **Data Type** column (the middle column) in the **Table Design Grid** in the row of the field for which you want to change the data type

Step 2. Click on the drop-down arrow in the upper right-hand corner of the selected cell

Step 3. Define the data type for the field using the drop-down menu (Figure B.8)

Notice that when you use this menu to define the data type for a field, the Field Properties Pane changes to display the properties and restrictions of the selected data type. For example, the field Brewery Name is defined as Short Text; when any row of the Table Design Grid associated with this field is selected, the Field Properties Pane shows the characteristics associated with a field of data type Short Text, including a limit of 255 characters. If we thought we might eventually do business with a brewery that has a business name that exceeds 255 characters, we may decide to select the Long Text data type for this field (Figure B.8). However, selecting a data type that allows for greater capacity will increase the size of the database and should not be used unless necessary.

A field such as State is a good candidate for reducing the field size. If we use the official U.S. Postal Service abbreviations for the states (i.e., AL for Alabama, AK for Alaska,

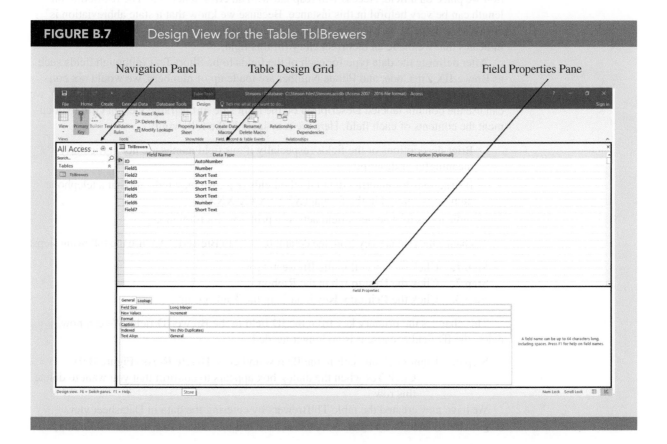

FIGURE B.7   Design View for the Table TblBrewers

FIGURE B.8   Changing the Data Type for the Brewery Name Field in the Table TblBrewers

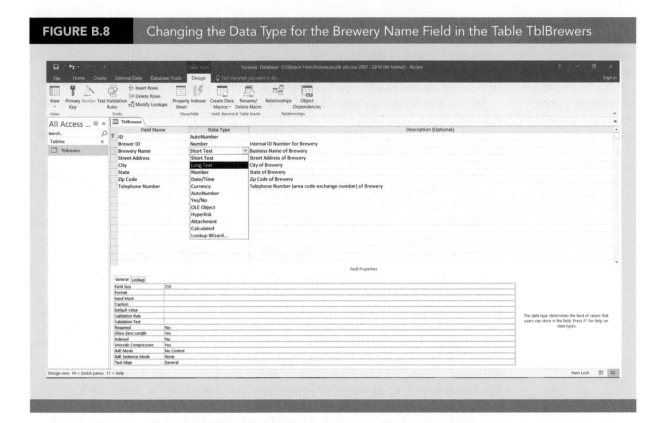

and so on), this field would always use two characters. Note that if we violate the restriction we place on a field, Access will respond with an error statement. The restriction on length can be very helpful in this instance. Because we know that a state abbreviation is always exactly two characters, an error statement regarding the length of the State field indicates that we made an incorrect entry for this field.

After defining the data type for each of the fields to be Short Text (although fields such as BrewerID, Zip Code, and Phone Number are made up of numbers, we would not consider doing arithmetic operations on these cells, so we define these fields as Short Text), we can use the column labeled Description on the right side of the Table Design Grid to document the contents of each field. Here we may include the following:

- Brief descriptions of the fields (especially if our field names are not particularly meaningful or descriptive)
- Instructions for entering data into the fields (e.g., we may indicate that a telephone number is entered in the format (XXX) XXX-XXXX)
- Indications of whether a field acts as a primary or a foreign key

To change the primary key from the default field ID to BrewerID, we use the following steps:

Step 1.   Click on any cell in the BrewerID row
Step 2.   Click the **Design** tab in the Ribbon
Step 3.   Click the **Primary Key** icon 🔑 in the **Tools** group

This changes the primary key from the ID field to the BrewerID field. We can now delete the ID field because it is no longer needed.

Step 4.   Right-click any cell in the ID row and click **Delete Rows** (Figure B.9)
Click **Yes** when the dialog box appears to confirm that you want to delete this row

We have now created the table TblBrewers by entering the data in Datasheet view (Figure B.10) and (1) changed the name of each field, (2) identified the correct data type

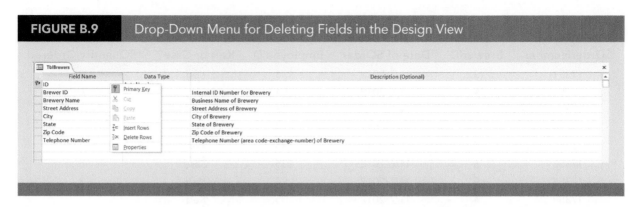

FIGURE B.9 Drop-Down Menu for Deleting Fields in the Design View

for each field, (3) revised properties for some fields, (4) added a description for each field, and (5) changed the primary key field to BrewerID in Design view. Alternatively, we could create a table in Design view. We first enter the field names, data types, and descriptions in the Table Design Grid. After saving this table as TblSOrders, we then move to the Database Window, which now has defined fields, and enter the information in the appropriate cells. Suppose we take this approach to create the table TblSOrders, which contains information on orders Stinson's places with the microbreweries. We have the following data for orders from the past week (Table B.2) that we will use to initially populate this table (new orders will be added to the table as they are placed).

The fields represent Stinson's internal number assigned to each order placed with a brewery (SOrderNumber), Stinson's internal identification number assigned to the microbrewery with which the order has been placed (BrewerID), the date on which Stinson's placed the order (Date of SOrder), the identification number of the Stinson's employee who placed the order (EmployeeID), an indication of whether the order was for kegs or cases of beer (Keg or Case?), and the quantity (in units) ordered (SQuantity Ordered). As before, we enter the information into the Field Name, Data Type, and Description columns

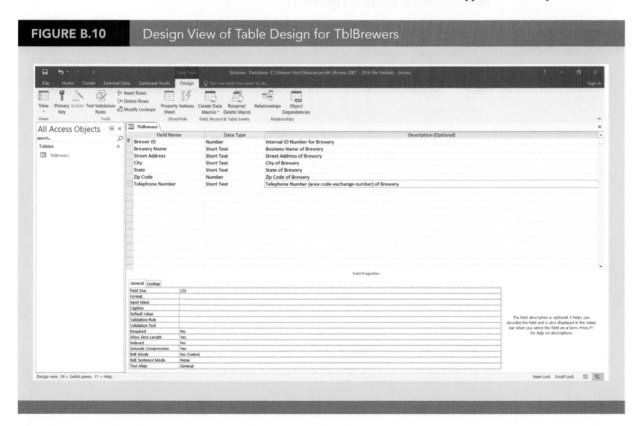

FIGURE B.10 Design View of Table Design for TblBrewers

TABLE B.2	Raw Data for Table TblSOrders				
SOrderNumber	**BrewerID**	**Date of SOrder**	**EmployeeID**	**Keg or Case?**	**SQuantity Ordered**
17351	3	11/5/2012	135	Keg	3
17352	9	11/5/2012	94	Case	6
17353	7	11/5/2012	94	Keg	2
17354	3	11/6/2012	94	Keg	3
17355	2	11/6/2012	135	Keg	2
17356	6	11/6/2012	135	Case	5
17358	9	11/7/2012	94	Keg	3
17359	4	11/7/2012	135	Keg	2
17360	3	11/8/2012	94	Case	8
17361	2	11/8/2012	94	Keg	1
17362	7	11/8/2012	94	Keg	2
17363	9	11/8/2012	135	Keg	4
17364	6	11/8/2012	94	Keg	2
17365	2	11/9/2012	135	Case	5
17366	3	11/9/2012	135	Keg	4
17367	7	11/9/2012	94	Case	4
17368	9	11/9/2012	135	Keg	4
17369	4	11/9/2012	94	Keg	3

of the Table Design Grid, remove the ID field, change the primary key field (this time to the field SOrderNumber), and revise the properties of the fields as necessary in the Field Properties area as shown in Figure B.11.

FIGURE B.11   Design View of Table Design for TblSOrders

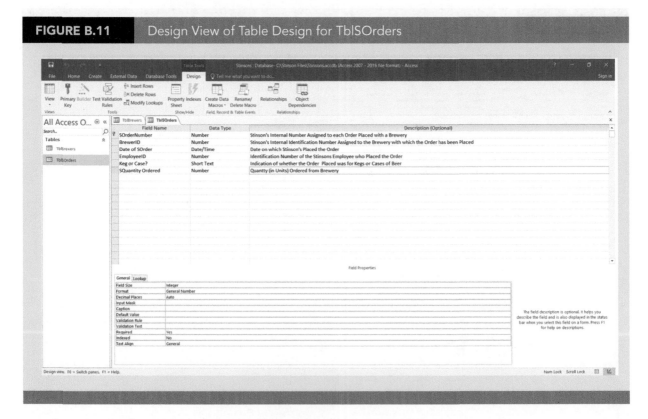

Now we return to the Database Window and manually input the data from Table B.2 into the table TblSOrders as shown in Figure B.12. Note that in both Datasheet view and Design view, we now have separate tabs with the table names TblBrewers and TblSOrders and that these two tables are listed in the Navigation Panel. We can use either Datasheet view or Design view to move between our tables.

We can also create a table by reading information from an external file. Access is capable of reading information from several types of external files. Here we demonstrate by reading data from an Excel file into a new table TblSDeliveries. The Excel file *SDeliveries.xlsx* contains the information on deliveries received by Stinson's from various microbreweries during a recent week. The fields of this table, as shown in Figure B.12, will correspond to the column headings in the Excel worksheet displayed in Figure B.13.

The columns in Figure B.13 represent the following: Stinson's internal number assigned to each order placed with a microbrewery (SOrderNumber), Stinson's internal identification number assigned to the microbrewery with which the order has been placed (BrewerID), the identification number of the Stinson's employee who received the delivery (EmployeeID), the date on which Stinson's received the delivery (Date of SDelivery), and the quantity (in units) received in the delivery (SQuantity Delivered). To import these data directly into the table TblSDeliveries, we follow these steps:

If the Excel worksheet from which we are importing the data does not contain column headings, Access will assign dummy names to the fields that can later be changed in the Table Design Grid of Design view.

Step 1. Click the **External Data** tab in the Ribbon

Step 2. Click the **Excel** icon in the **Import & Link** group (Figure B.14)

Step 3. When the **Get External Data—Excel Spreadsheet** dialog box appears (Figure B.15), click the **Browse...** button

Navigate to the location of the Excel file to be imported into Access (in this case, *SDeliveries.xlsx*), and indicate the manner in which we want to import the information in this Excel file by selecting the appropriate radio button (we are importing these data to a new table, TblSDeliveries, in the current database)

Step 4. Click **OK**

FIGURE B.12 Datasheet View for TblSOrders

FIGURE B.13   Excel Spreadsheet SDeliveries.xlsx

DATA *file*

SDeliveries

	A	B	C	D	E
1	SOrderNumber	BrewerID	EmployeeID	Date of SDelivery	SQuantity Delivered
2	17351	3	94	11/5/2012	3
3	17352	9	94	11/5/2012	6
4	17353	7	135	11/6/2012	2
5	17354	3	94	11/6/2012	3
6	17355	2	135	11/6/2012	2
7	17356	6	135	11/6/2012	5
8	17358	9	135	11/7/2012	3
9	17359	4	135	11/7/2012	2
10	17360	3	94	11/8/2012	8
11	17361	2	135	11/8/2012	1
12	17362	7	94	11/8/2012	2
13	17363	9	94	11/9/2012	4
14	17364	6	135	11/8/2012	2
15	17365	2	94	11/9/2012	5
16	17366	3	94	11/9/2012	4
17	17367	7	135	11/10/2012	4
18	17368	9	94	11/9/2012	4
19	17369	4	94	11/9/2012	3

FIGURE B.14   External Data Tab on the Access Ribbon

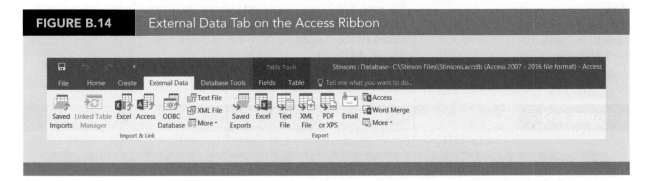

Step 5. When the **Import Spreadsheet Wizard** dialog box opens (Figure B.16), arrange the information as shown in Figure B.16

Verify that the check box for **First Row Contains Column Headings** is selected because the worksheet from which we are importing the data contains column headings

Click **Next >** to open the second screen of the **Import Spreadsheet Wizard** dialog box (Figure B.17)

Step 6. Indicate the format for the first field (in this case, SOrderNumber) and whether this field is the primary key field for the new table (it is in this case)

Click **Next >**

If your Excel file contains multiple worksheets, you will be prompted by the Import Spreadsheet Wizard to select the worksheet from which you want to import data. After you have selected a worksheet and clicked on Next, you will automatically proceed to the screen in Figure B.16.

We continue to work through the ensuing screens of the **Import Spreadsheet Wizard** dialog box, indicating the format for each field and identifying the primary key field (SOrder-Number) for the new table. When we have completed the final screen, we click **Finish** and add the table TblSDeliveries to our database. Note that in both Datasheet view (Figure B.18) and Design view, we now have separate tabs with the table names TblBrewers, TblSOrders, and TblSDeliveries, and that these three tables are listed in the Navigation Panel.

We have now created the table TblSDeliveries by reading the information from the Excel file *SDeliveries.xlsx*, and we have entered information in the fields and identified the

FIGURE B.15   Get External Data—Excel Spreadsheet Dialog Box

FIGURE B.16   First Screen of Import Spreadsheet Wizard Dialog Box

FIGURE B.17   Second Screen of Import Spreadsheet Wizard Dialog Box

FIGURE B.18   Datasheet View for TblSDeliveries

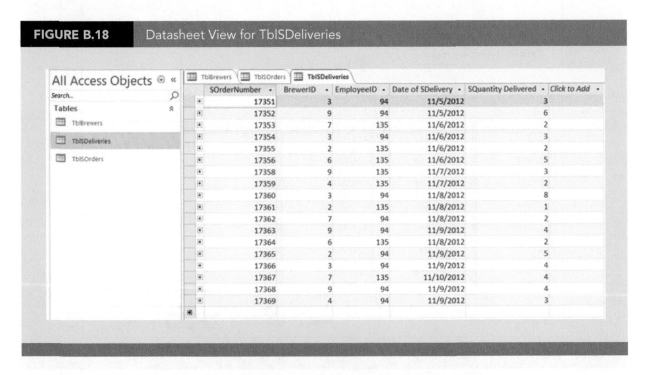

primary key field in this process. This procedure for creating a table is more convenient (and more accurate) than manually inputting the information in Datasheet view, but it requires that the data be in a file that can be imported into Access.

B.2 Creating Relationships Between Tables in Microsoft Access

One of the advantages of a database over a spreadsheet is the economy of data storage and maintenance. Information that is associated with several records can be placed in a separate table. As an example, consider that the microbreweries that supply beer to Stinson's are each associated with multiple orders for beer that have been placed by Stinson's. In this case, the names and addresses of the microbreweries do not have to be included in records of Stinson's orders, saving a great deal of time and effort in data entry and maintenance. However, the two tables, in this case the table with the information on Stinson's orders for beer and the table with information on the microbreweries that supply Stinson's with beer, must be joined (i.e., have a defined relationship) by a common field. To use the data from these two tables for a common purpose, a relationship between the two tables must be created to allow one table to share information with the other.

The first step in deciding how to join related tables is to decide what type of relationship you need to create between tables. Next we briefly summarize the three types of relationships that can exist between two tables.

One-to-Many relationships are the most common type of relationship between two tables in a relational database; these relationships are sometimes abbreviated as 1:∞.

One-to-Many This relationship occurs between two tables, which we will label as Table A and Table B, when the value in the common field for a record in Table A can match the value in the common field for multiple records in Table B, but a value in the common field for a record in Table B can match the value in the common field for at most a single record in Table A. Consider TblBrewers and TblSOrders with the common field BrewerID. In TblBrewers, each unique value of BrewerID is associated with a single record that contains contact information for a single brewer, while in TblSOrders each unique value of BrewerID may be associated with several records that contain information on various orders placed by Stinson's with a specific brewer. When these tables are linked through the common field BrewerID, each record in TblBrewers can potentially be matched with multiple records of orders in TblSOrders, but each record in TblSOrders can be matched with only one record in TblBrewers. This makes sense, as a single brewer can be matched to several orders, but each order can be matched to only a single brewer.

One-to-One relationships are the least common form of relationship between two tables in a relational database because it is often possible to include these data in a single table; these relationships are sometimes abbreviated as 1:1.

One-to-One This relationship occurs when the value in the common field for a record in Table A can match the value in the common field for at most one record in Table B, and a value in the common field for a record in Table B can match the value in the common field for at most a single record in Table A. Here we consider TblBrewers and TblPurchasePrices, which also share the common field BrewerID. In TblBrewers, each unique value of BrewerID is associated with a single record that contains contact information for a single brewer, while in TblPurchasePrices each unique value of BrewerID is associated with a single record that contains information on prices charged to Stinson's by a specific brewer for kegs and cases of beer. When these tables are linked through the common field BrewerID, each record in TblBrewers can be matched to at most a single record of prices in TblPurchasePrices, and each record in TblPurchasePrices can be matched with no more than one record in TblBrewers. This makes sense, as a single brewer can be matched only to the prices it charges, and a specific set of prices can be matched only to a single brewer.

Many-to-Many relationships are sometimes abbreviated as ∞:∞.

Many-to-Many This occurs when a value in the common field for a record in Table A can match the value in the common field for multiple records in Table B, and a value in the common field for a record in Table B can match the value in the common field for several records in Table A. Many-To-Many relationships are not directly supported by Access but can be facilitated by creating a third table, called an *associate table*, that contains a primary key and a foreign key to each of the original tables. This ultimately results in one-to-many relationships between the associate table and the two original tables. Our design for Stinson's database does not include any many-to-many relationships.

To create any of these three types of relationships between two tables, we must satisfy the rules of integrity. Recall that the primary key field for a table is a field that has (and will have throughout the life of the database) a unique value for each record. Defining a primary key field for a table ensures that the table will have **entity integrity**, which means that the table will have no duplicate records.

Note that when the primary key field for one table is a foreign key field in another table, it is possible for a value of this field to occur several times in the table for which it is a foreign key field. For example, Job ID is the primary key field in the table TblJobTitle and will have a unique value for each record in this table. But Job ID is a foreign field in the table TblEmployHist, so a value of Job ID can occur several times in TblEmployHist.

Referential integrity is the rule that establishes the relationship between two tables. For referential integrity to be established, when the foreign key field in one table (say, Table B) and the primary key field in the other table (say, Table A) are matched, each value that occurs in the foreign key field in Table B must also occur in the primary key field in Table A. For instance, to preserve referential integrity for the relationship between TblEmployHist and TblJobTitle, each employee record in TblEmployHist must have a value in the Job ID field that exactly matches a value of the Job ID field in TblJobTitle. If a record in TblEmployHist has a value for the foreign key field (Job ID) that does not occur in the primary key field (Job ID) of TblJobTitle, the record is said to be **orphaned** (in this case, this would occur if we had an employee who has been assigned a job that does not exist in our database). An orphaned record would be lost in any table that results from joining TblJobTitle and TblEmployHist. Enforcing referential integrity through Access prevents records from becoming orphaned and lost when tables are joined.

Violations of referential integrity lead to inconsistent data, which results in meaningless and potentially misleading analyses. Enforcement of referential integrity is critical not only for ensuring the quality of the information in the database but also for ensuring the validity of all conclusions based on these data.

We are now ready to establish relationships between tables in our database. We will first establish a relationship between the tables TblBrewers and TblSOrders. To establish a relationship between these two tables, take the following steps:

Step 1. Click the **Database Tools** tab in the Ribbon (Figure B.19)

Step 2. From the Navigation Panel select one of the tables for which you want to establish a relationship (we will click on **TblBrewers**)

Step 3. Click the **Relationships** icon ▫▫ in the **Relationships** group

This will open the contextual tab **Relationship Tools** in the Ribbon and a new display with a tab labeled **Relationships** in the workspace, as shown in Figure B.20.

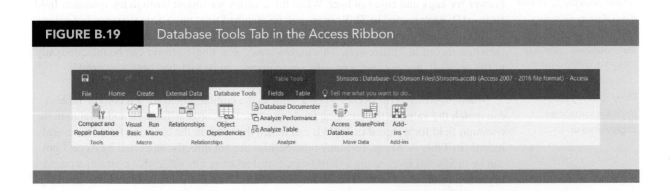

| FIGURE B.19 | Database Tools Tab in the Access Ribbon |

FIGURE B.20	Relationship Tools Contextual Tab in the Access Ribbon and Tab Labeled Relationships in the Workspace

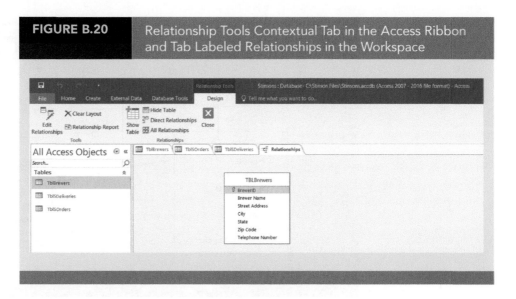

Step 4.   Click **Show Table** in the **Relationships** group

*You can select multiple tables in the **Show Table** dialog box by holding down the **Ctrl** key and selecting multiple tables.*

When the **Show Table** dialog box opens (Figure B.21), select each table for which you want to establish a relationship (in our example, **TblBrewers** and **TblSOrders**) and click **Add** to open a box listing all fields for each table you select

Click **Close**

FIGURE B.21	Show Table Dialog Box

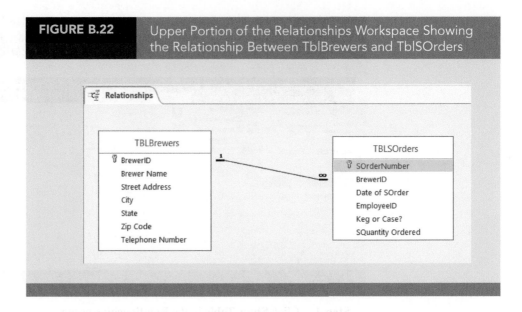

FIGURE B.22 Upper Portion of the Relationships Workspace Showing the Relationship Between TblBrewers and TblSOrders

Once we have selected the two tables (TblBrewers and TblSOrders) for which we are establishing a relationship, boxes showing the fields for the two tables will appear in the workspace. If Access can identify a common field, it will also suggest a relationship between these two tables. In our example, Access has identified BrewerID as a common field between TblBrewers and TblSOrders and is showing a relationship between these two tables based on this field (Figure B.22).

In this instance, Access has correctly identified the relationship we want to establish between TblBrewers and TblSOrders. However, if Access does not correctly identify the relationship, we can modify the relationship between these tables. If we double-click on the line connecting TblBrewers to TblSOrders, we open the relationship's **Edit Relationships** dialog box, as shown in Figure B.23.

FIGURE B.23 Edit Relationships Dialog Box

FIGURE B.24   Join Properties Dialog Box

Note here that Access has correctly identified the relationship between TblBrewers and TblSOrders to be one-to-many and that we have several options from which to select. We can use the pull-down menu under the name of each table in the relationship to select different fields to use in the relationship between the two tables.

By selecting the **Enforce Referential Integrity** option in the **Edit Relationships** dialog box, we can indicate that we want Access to monitor this relationship to ensure that it satisfies relational integrity. This means that every unique value in the BrewerID field in TblSOrders also appears in the BrewerID field of TblBrewers; that is, there is a one-to-many relationship between TblBrewers and TblSOrders, and Access will revise the display of the relationship, as shown in Figure B.22, to reflect that this is a one-to-many relationship.

Finally, we can click **Join Type..** in the **Edit Relationships** dialog box to open the **Join Properties** dialog box (Figure B.24). This dialog box allows us to specify which records are retained when the two tables are joined.

Once we have established a relationship between two tables, we can create new Access objects (tables, queries, reports, etc.) using information from both of the joined tables simultaneously. Suppose Stinson's will need to combine information from TblBrewers, TblSOrders, and TblSDeliveries. Using the same steps, we can also establish relationships among the three tables TblBrewers, TblSOrders, and TblSDeliveries, as shown in Figure B.25. Note that for each relationship shown in this figure, we have used the Enforce Referential Integrity option in the Edit Relationships dialog box to indicate that we want Access to monitor these relationships to ensure that they satisfy relational integrity. Thus, each relationship is identified in this case as a one-to-many relationship.

This set of relationships will also allow us to combine information from all three tables and create new Access objects (tables, queries, reports, etc.) using information from the three joined tables simultaneously.

B.3 Sorting and Filtering Records

As our tables inevitably grow or are joined to form larger tables, the number of records can become overwhelming. One of the strengths of relational database software such as Access is that they provide tools, such as sorting and filtering, for dealing with large quantities of data. Access provides several tools for sorting the records in a table into a desired sequence and filtering the records in a table to generate a subset of your data that meets specific criteria. We begin by considering sorting the records in a table to improve the organization of the data and increase the value of information in the table by making it easier to find records with specific characteristics. Access allows for records to be sorted on values of

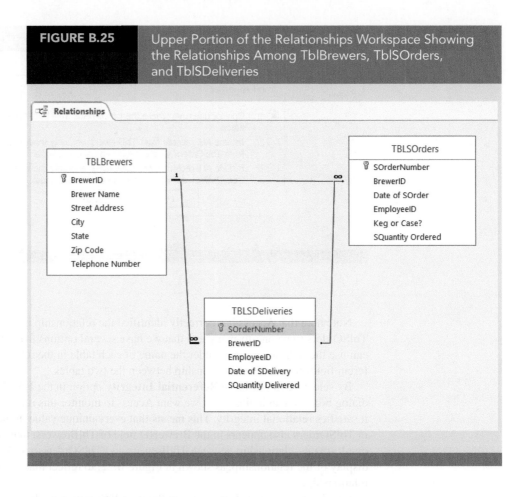

FIGURE B.25   Upper Portion of the Relationships Workspace Showing the Relationships Among TblBrewers, TblSOrders, and TblSDeliveries

one or more fields, called the *sort fields*, in either ascending or descending order. To sort on a single field, we click on the Filter Arrow in the field on which we wish to sort.

Suppose that Stinson's Manager of Receiving wants to review a list of all deliveries received by Stinson's, and she wants the list sorted by the Stinson's employee who received the orders. To accomplish this, we first open the table TblSDeliveries in Datasheet view. We then click on the **Filter Arrow** ▾ for the field EmployeeID (the sort field), as shown in Figure B.26; to sort the data in ascending order by values in the EmployeeID field, we click on ↓ **Sort Smallest to Largest** (clicking on ↑ **Sort Largest to Smallest** will sort the data in descending order by values in the EmployeeID field). By using the Filter Arrows, we can sort the data in a table on values of any of the table's fields.

We can also use this pull-down menu to filter our data to generate a subset of data in a table that satisfies specific conditions. If we want to create a display of only deliveries that were received by employee 135, we would click the **Filter Arrow** next to EmployeeID, select only the check box for **135**, and click **OK** (Figure B.27).

Note that different data types have different sort options.

Note that different data types have different filter options.

Filtering through the Filter Arrows is convenient if you want to retain records associated with several different values in a field. For example, if we want to generate a display of the records in the table TblSDeliveries associated with breweries with BrewerIDs 3, 4, and 9, we would click on the **Filter Arrow** next to BrewerID, deselect the check boxes for **2, 4, 6,** and **7**, and click **OK**.

*Clicking **Selection** in the Sort & Filter group will also filter on values of a single field.*

The **Sort & Filter** group in the **Home** tab also provides tools for sorting and filtering records in a table. To quickly sort all records in a table on values for a field, open the table to be sorted in Datasheet view, and click on any cell in the field to be sorted. Then click on ↓ **Ascending** to sort records from smallest to largest values in the sort field or on ↑ **Descending** to sort records from largest to smallest in the sort field.

FIGURE B.26   Pull-Down Menu for Sorting and Filtering Records in a Table with the Filter Arrow

Access also allows for simultaneous sorting and filtering through the Advanced function in the Sort & Filter group of the Home tab; the Advanced Filter/Sort display for the table TblSDeliveries is shown in Figure B.28. Once we have opened the table to be filtered and sorted in Datasheet view, we click on **Advanced** in the **Sort & Filter** group of the **Home** tab, as shown in Figure B.28. We then select **Advanced Filter/Sort…**. From this display, we double-click on the first field in the field list on which we wish to filter. The field we have selected will appear in the heading of the first column in the tabular display at the bottom of the screen. We can then indicate in the appropriate portion of this display the sorting and filtering to be done on this field. We continue this process for every field for which we want to apply a filter and/or sort, remembering that the sorting will be nested (the table will be sorted on the first sort field, and then the sort for the second sort field will be executed within each unique value of the first sort field, and so on).

FIGURE B.27   Top Rows of the Tabular Display of Results of Filtering

	SOrderNumber	BrewerID	EmployeeID	Date of SDelivery	SQuantity Delivered	Click to Add
⊞	17353	7	135	11/6/2012	2	
⊞	17355	2	135	11/6/2012	2	
⊞	17356	6	135	11/6/2012	5	
⊞	17358	9	135	11/7/2012	3	
⊞	17359	4	135	11/7/2012	2	
⊞	17361	2	135	11/8/2012	1	
⊞	17364	6	135	11/8/2012	2	
⊞	17367	7	135	11/10/2012	4	
*						

FIGURE B.28   Advanced Filter/Sort Display for TblSDeliveries

*We can toggle between a display of the filtered/ sorted data and a display of the original table by clicking on **Toggle Filter** in the **Sort & Filter** group of the **Home** tab.*

Suppose we wish to create a new tabular display of all records for deliveries from breweries with BrewerIDs of 4 or 7 for which fewer than 7 units were delivered, and we want the records in this display sorted in ascending order first on values of the field BrewerID and then on values of the field SQuantity Delivered. To execute these criteria, we perform the following steps:

Step 1.   Click the **Home** tab in the Ribbon

Step 2.   Click **Advanced** in the **Sort & Filter** group, and select **Advanced Filter/ Sort…**

Step 3.   In the **TblSDeliveries** box, double-click **BrewerID** to add this field to the first column in the lower pane of the screen

Select **Ascending** in the **Sort:** row of the **BrewerID** column in the lower pane

Enter *4* in the **Criteria:** row of the **BrewerID** column in the lower pane

Enter *7* in the **or:** row of the **BrewerID** column in the lower pane

Figure B.29 displays the lower pane of the Advanced Filter/Sort after Steps 1 to 4 have been completed.

Step 4.   In the **TblSDeliveries** box, double-click **SQuantity Delivered** to add this to the second column in the lower pane of the screen

Select **Ascending** in the **Sort:** row of the **SQuantity Delivered** column in the lower pane

Enter *<7* in the **Criteria:** row of the **SQuantity Delivered** column in the lower pane

Step 5.   Click **Advanced** in the **Sort & Filter** group of the **Home** tab

Click **Apply Filter/Sort**

These steps produce the tabular display shown in Figure B.30.

Note that the data, after being filtered to show only records with breweries that have values of 4 or 7 in the BrewerID field and all records with deliveries of 7 or fewer units, are sorted first in ascending order on the BrewerID field. Within each unique value in the BrewerID field, the records are sorted in ascending order on the SQuantity Delivered field.

FIGURE B.29   Tabular Display of Criteria for Simultaneous Filtering and Sorting Using Advanced Filter/Sort

Field:	BrewerID	SQuantity Delivered	
Sort:	Ascending	Ascending	
Criteria:	4	<7	
or:	7		

FIGURE B.30   Tabular Display of Filtered and Sorted Data Using Advanced Filter/Sort

	SOrderNumber	BrewerID	EmployeeID	Date of SDelivery	SQuantity Delivered	Click to Add
⊞	17359	4	135	11/7/2012	2	
⊞	17369	4	94	11/9/2012	3	
⊞	17362	7	94	11/8/2012	2	
⊞	17353	7	135	11/6/2012	2	
⊞	17367	7	135	11/10/2012	4	

TblSDeliveries   TblSDeliveriesFilter1

NOTES + COMMENTS

1. We can use wildcard symbols when filtering by substituting an asterisk symbol (*) for any portion of the value of a field you want to represent with a wildcard. For example, if we wanted to create a table of information on all Stinson's employees whose last names started with the letter B, we would filter the field EmpLastName in the table TblEmployees by entering *B** in the **Criteria:** row of the **Advanced Filter/Sort**. This filter will return all records that have the combination of the first letter "B" and any other following characters in the EmpLastName field.

B.4 Queries

Queries are a way of searching for and compiling data that meet specific criteria from one or more tables. They enable you to extract particular fields from a table or create a new table that combines information from several related tables.

Although there are similarities between queries and simple searches or filters, queries are far more powerful because they can be used to extract information from multiple tables.

For example, although you could use a search in the table TblBrewers to find the name of a brewer that supplies beer to Stinson's or a filter on the table TblSOrders to view only orders placed by Stinson's for kegs of beer, neither of those approaches would let you simultaneously view both the names of brewers and the orders placed for kegs of beer. However, you could easily run a query to create a record of every order Stinson's has placed for kegs of beer that includes the name of the brewer and the corresponding order that was placed. By taking advantage of the relationships among the tables of a database, a well-designed query can yield information that would be cumbersome or difficult to discern by examining the data in individual tables.

Access allows for several types of queries. The three most commonly used are as follows:

- **Select queries**: These are the simplest and most commonly used queries; they are used to extract the subset of data from a table that satisfy one or more criteria. For example, Stinson's Manager of Receiving may want to review a list of all deliveries received by Stinson's that includes the Stinson's employee who received each order over some period of time. A select query could be applied to the table TblSDeliveries (shown in the original database design illustrated in Figure B.1) to create the subset of this table containing only the fields SOrderNumber and EmployeeID.

Action queries are also known as Data Manipulation Language (DML) statements.

- **Action queries**: These queries are used to change data in existing tables. For example, the sales manager may want to increase the prices charged to retailers by Stinson's for the kegs of microbrews that Stinson's sells. The sales manager can quickly make this change through an action query applied to the table TblSalesPrices to quickly perform these calculations and modify these prices in the database. Action queries allow the user to modify many records quickly and efficiently. Access provides four types of action queries:
  - *Update* allows the values of one or more fields in the result set to be modified.
  - *Make table* creates a new table based on the results of the query.
  - *Append* is similar to a make table query, except that the results of the query are appended to an existing table.
  - *Delete* deletes all the records in the results of the query from the underlying table.
- **Crosstab queries**: These perform calculations on information in a table. Stinson's Manager of Receiving may be interested in how many kegs and cases of beer have been delivered to Stinson's and which Stinson's employee received the shipment. The manager could find this information by applying a crosstab query to the table TblSDeliveries (shown in the original database design in Figure B.1) to create a table that shows number of kegs and cases delivered by the Stinson's employee who received the shipment.

We next review how to execute each of these types of queries in Access.

Select Queries

We start by considering the needs of Stinson's Manager of Receiving, who wants to review a list of all deliveries received by Stinson's and the Stinson's employee who received the orders during some recent week. This requires us to perform a select query on the table TblSDeliveries to create a subset of this table that includes only the fields SOrderNumber and EmployeeID for deliveries to Stinson's during the past week (the only week for which we have data in our new database) and display this subset in Datasheet view. To execute this select query, we take the following steps:

Step 1. Click the **Create** tab in the Ribbon (Figure B.31)
Step 2. Click **Query Wizard** in the **Queries** group
Step 3. When the **New Query** dialog box appears (Figure B.32)
      Select **Simple Query Wizard**
      Click **OK**

DATA *file*

Stinsons

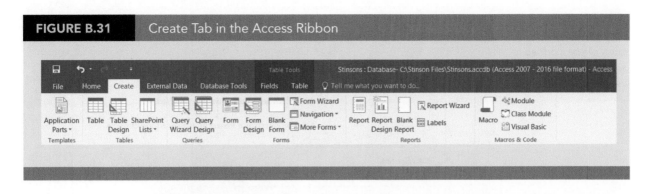

FIGURE B.31   Create Tab in the Access Ribbon

FIGURE B.32   New Query Dialog Box

New Query

Simple Query Wizard
Crosstab Query Wizard
Find Duplicates Query Wizard
Find Unmatched Query Wizard

This wizard creates a select query
from the fields you pick.

OK   Cancel

Step 4. When the next **Simple Query Wizard** dialog box appears (see Figure B.33):
Select **Table: TblSDeliveries** in the **Tables/Queries** box
Select the fields **SOrderNumber** and **EmployeeID** from the **Available Fields:** box and move these to the **Selected Fields:** box using the ⊡ button (Figure B.33)
Click **Next >**

Step 5. When the next **Simple Query Wizard** dialog box appears (Figure B.34):
Select **Detail (shows every field of every record)**
Click **Next >**

Step 6. When the final **Simple Query Wizard** dialog box appears (Figure B.35):
Name our query by entering *TblSDeliveries Employee Query* in the **What title do you want for your query?** box
Select **Open the query to view information**
Click **Finish**

The display of the query results is provided in Figure B.36. Although Step 5 offers us the option of using the Simple Query Wizard to generate a summary display of the fields

A query can be saved and used repeatedly. A saved query can be modified to suit the needs of future users.

FIGURE B.33   First Step of the Simple Query Wizard

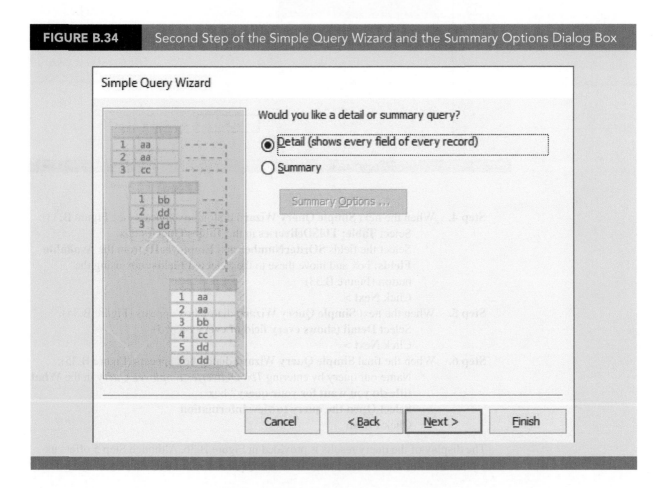

FIGURE B.34   Second Step of the Simple Query Wizard and the Summary Options Dialog Box

FIGURE B.35	Final Step of the Simple Query Wizard

Simple Query Wizard

What title do you want for your query?

TblSDeliveries Employee Query

That's all the information the wizard needs to create your query.

Do you want to open the query or modify the query's design?

◉ Open the query to view information.

○ Modify the query design.

Cancel   < Back   Next >   Finish

FIGURE B.36	Display of Results of a Simple Query

TblSDeliveries   **TblSDeliveries Employee Query**

SOrderNumber	EmployeeID
17351	94
17352	94
17353	135
17354	94
17355	135
17356	135
17358	135
17359	135
17360	94
17361	135
17362	94
17363	94
17364	135
17365	94
17366	94
17367	135
17368	94
17369	94

we selected, we use the Detailed Query option here because the Manager of Receiving wants to review a list of all deliveries received by Stinson's and the Stinson's employee who received the orders during some recent week. See Figure B.34 for displays of the dialog boxes for this step of the Simple Query Wizard and Summary Options.

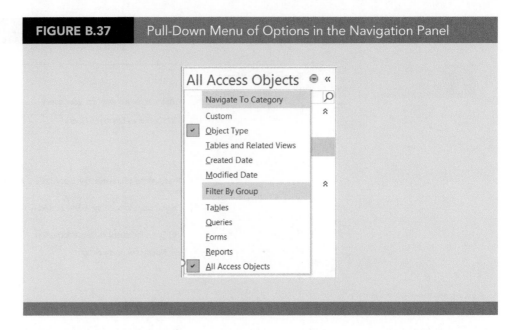

FIGURE B.37   Pull-Down Menu of Options in the Navigation Panel

Note that in both Datasheet view and Design view, we now have a new tab with the table TblSDeliveries Employee Query. We can also change the Navigation Panel so that it shows a list of all queries associated with this database by using the Navigation Panel's pull-down menu of options, as shown in Figure B.37.

Action Queries

Suppose that in reviewing the database system we are designing, Stinson's Sales Manager notices that we have made an error in the table TblSalesPrices. She shares with us that the price she charges for a keg of beer that has been produced by the Midwest Fiddler Crab microbrewery (value of 7 for BrewerID) should be $240, not $230 that we have entered in this table. We can use an action query applied to the table TblSalesPrices to quickly perform these changes. Because we want to modify all values of a field that meet some criteria, this is an update query. The Datasheet view of the table TblSalesPrices is provided in Figure B.38.

To make this pricing change, we take the following steps:

Stinsons

Step 1.   Click the **Create** tab in the Ribbon
Step 2.   Click **Query Design** in the **Queries** group. This opens the **Query Design** window and the **Query Tools** contextual tab (Figure B.39)

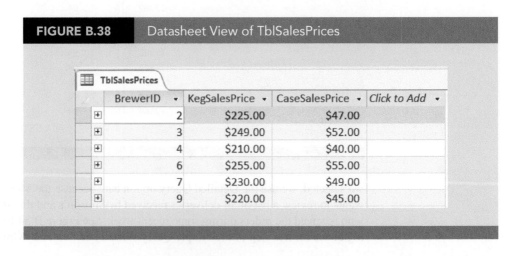

FIGURE B.38   Datasheet View of TblSalesPrices

TblSalesPrices			
BrewerID ▾	KegSalesPrice ▾	CaseSalesPrice ▾	Click to Add ▾
2	$225.00	$47.00	
3	$249.00	$52.00	
4	$210.00	$40.00	
6	$255.00	$55.00	
7	$230.00	$49.00	
9	$220.00	$45.00	

FIGURE B.39	Query Tools Contextual Tab

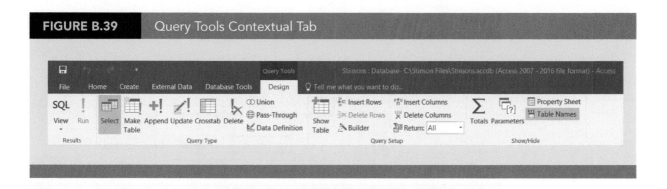

Step 3. When the **Show Table** dialog box appears, select **TblSalesPrices** and click **Add**
Click **Close**

Step 4. In the **TblSalesPrices** box, double-click on **KegSalesPrice**. This opens a column labeled "KegSalesPrice" in the **Field:** row at the bottom pane of the display
Click **Update**, ⬚, in the **Query Type** group of the **Design** tab
Enter *240* in the **Update To:** row of the **KegSalesPrice** column in the bottom pane of the display

Step 4 produces the TblSalesPrices box that contains a list of fields in this table.

Step 5. In the **TblSalesPrices** box, double-click on **BrewerID** to open a second column in the bottom pane of the display labeled "BrewerID"
Enter *7* in the **Criteria:** row of the **BrewerID** column (Figure B.40)

Step 6. Click the **Run** button ⬚ in the **Results** group of the **Design** tab
When the dialog box alerting us that we are about to update one row of the table appears, click **Yes**

Once we click **Yes** in the dialog box, the price charged to Stinson's for a keg of beer supplied by the Midwest Fiddler Crab microbrewery (BrewerID equal to 7) in the table TblSalesPrices is changed from $230.00 to $240.00.

Once saved, a query can be modified and saved again to use later.

Step 7. To save this query, click the **Save** icon ⬚ in the **Quick Access** toolbar
When the **Save As** dialog box opens (Figure B.41), enter the name *Change Price per Keg Charged by a Microbrewery* for **Query Name:**
Click **OK**

Opening the table TblSalesPrices in Datasheet view (Figure B.42) shows that the price of a keg charged to Stinson's for a keg of beer supplied by the Midwest Fiddler Crab microbrewery (BrewerID equal to 7) has been revised from $230 to $240.

Crosstab Queries

We use crosstab queries to summarize data in one field by values of one or more other fields. In our example, we will consider an issue faced by Stinson's Inventory Manager,

FIGURE B.40	Display of Information for the Update Query

Field:	KegSalesPrice	BrewerID
Table:	TblSalesPrices	TblSalesPrices
Update To:	240	
Criteria:		7
or:		

FIGURE B.41   Save as Dialog Box

Save As   ?   ✕

Query Name:

Change Price per Keg Charged by a Microbrewery

OK   Cancel

who wants to know how many kegs and cases of beer have been ordered by each Stinson's employee from each microbrewery. To provide the manager with this information, we apply a crosstab query to the table TblSOrders (shown in the original database design illustrated in Figure B.1) to create a table that shows the number of kegs and cases ordered by each Stinson's employee from each microbrewery. To create this crosstab query, we take the following steps:

DATA *file*

Stinsons

Step 3 produces the TblSOrders box in Access that contains a list of fields in this table.

Step 1.   Click the **Create** tab in the Ribbon

Step 2.   Click **Query Design** in the **Queries** group. This opens the Query Design window and the Query Tools contextual tab

Step 3.   When the **Show Table** dialog box opens, select **TblSOrders**, click **Add**, then click **Close**

Step 4.   In the **TblSOrders** box, double-click **BrewerID**, **Keg or Case?**, and **SQuantity Ordered** to add these fields to the columns in the lower pane of the window

Step 5.   In the **Query Type** group of the **Design** tab, click **Crosstab** ▦

Step 6.   In the **BrewerID** column of the window's lower pane,
Select **Row Heading** in the **Crosstab:** row
Select **Ascending** in the **Sort:** row

Step 7.   In the **Keg or Case?** column of the window's lower pane,
Select **Column Heading** in the **Crosstab:** row
Select **Ascending** in the **Sort:** row

Step 8.   In the **SQuantity Ordered** column of the window's lower pane,

FIGURE B.42   TblSalesPrices in Datasheet View After Running the Update Query

	BrewerID ▾	KegSalesPrice ▾	CaseSalesPrice ▾	Click to Add ▾
⊞	2	$225.00	$47.00	
⊞	3	$249.00	$52.00	
⊞	4	$210.00	$40.00	
⊞	6	$255.00	$55.00	
⊞	7	$240.00	$49.00	
⊞	9	$220.00	$45.00	

TblSalesPrices   Change Price per Keg Charged by a Microbrewery

FIGURE B.43   Display of Design of the Crosstab Query

Field:	BrewerID	Keg or Case?	SQuantity Ordered
Table:	TblSOrders	TblSOrders	TblSOrders
Total:	Group By	Group By	Sum
Crosstab:	Row Heading	Column Heading	Value
Sort:	Ascending	Ascending	
Criteria:			
or:			

> Select **Sum** in the **Total:** row
> Select **Value** in the **Crosstab:** row

Step 9. In the **Results** group of the **Design** tab, click the **Run** button, !, to execute the crosstab query

Figure B.43 displays the results of completing Steps 1 to 8 to create our crosstab query. In the first column, we have indicated that we want values of the field BrewerID to act as the row headings of our table (in ascending order), whereas in the second column we have indicated that we want values of the field Keg or Case? to act as the column headings of our table (again, in ascending order). In the third column, we have indicated that values of the field SQuantity Ordered will be summed for every combination of row (value of the field BrewerID) and column (value of the field Keg or Case?).

The results of the crosstab query appear in Figure B.44. From Figure B.44, we see that we have ordered 8 cases and 10 kegs of beer from the microbrewery with a value of 3 for the BrewerID field (the Oak Creek Brewery).

Step 10. To save the results of this query, click the **Save** icon, ▣, in the **Quick Access** toolbar

> When the **Save As** dialog box opens, enter *Brewer Orders Query* for
> **Query Name:**
> Click **OK**

FIGURE B.44   Results of Crosstab Query

Query1		
BrewerID	Case	Keg
2	5	3
3	8	10
4		5
6	5	2
7	4	4
9	6	11

1. Action queries permanently change the data in a database, so we suggest that you back up the database before performing an action query. After you have reviewed the results of the action query and are satisfied that the query worked as desired, you can then save the database with the results of the action query. Some cautious users save the original database under a different name so that they can revert to the original preaction query database if they later find that the action query has had an undesirable effect on the database.

2. Crosstab queries do not permanently change the data in a database.

3. The Make Table, Append, and Delete action queries work in manners similar to Update action queries and are also useful ways to modify tables to better suit the user's needs.

B.5 Saving Data to External Files

You can open the file Stinsons and follow these steps to reproduce an external Excel file of the data in TblSOrders.

Access can export data to external files in formats that are compatible with a wide variety of software. To export the information from the table TblSOrders to an external Excel file, we take the following steps:

Step 1. Click the **External Data** tab in the Ribbon (Figure B.45)
Step 2. In the **Navigation Panel**, click **TblSOrders**
Step 3. In the **Export** group of the **External Data** tab, click the **Excel** icon,
Step 4. When the **Export—Excel Spreadsheet** dialog box opens (Figure B.46), click the **Browse…** button

After we complete Step 4, another dialog box asks us if we want to save the steps we used to export the information in this table; this can be useful if we have to export similar data again.

Find the destination where you want to save your exported file and then click the **Save** button
Verify that the correct path and filename are listed in the **File Name**: box (*TblSOrders.xlsx* in this example)
Verify that the **File format:** is set to **Excel Workbook (*.xlsx)**
Select the check boxes for **Export data with formatting and layout**. and **Open the designation file after the export operation is complete**.
Click **OK**

The preceding steps export the table TblSOrders from Access into an Excel file named *TblSOrders.xlsx*. Exporting information from a relational database such as Access to Excel allows one to apply the tools and techniques covered throughout this textbook to a subset of a large data set. This can be much more efficient than using Excel to clean and filter large data sets.

FIGURE B.45 External Data Tab in Access

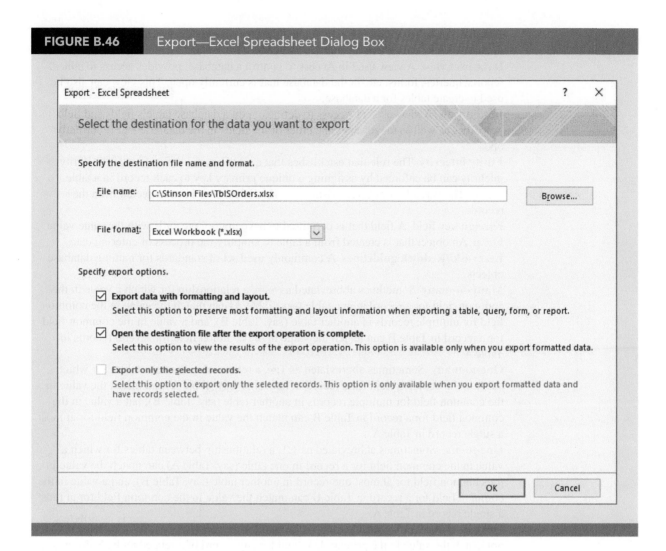

FIGURE B.46 Export—Excel Spreadsheet Dialog Box

SUMMARY

The amount of data available for analyses is increasing at a rapid rate, and this trend will not change in the foreseeable future. Furthermore, the data used by organizations to make decisions are dynamic, and they change rapidly. Thus, it is critical that a data analyst understand how data are stored, revised, updated, retrieved, and manipulated. We have reviewed tools in Microsoft Access® that can be used for these purposes.

In this appendix we have reviewed the basic concepts of database creation and management that are important to consider when using data from a database in an analysis. We have discussed several ways to create a database in Microsoft Access®, and we have demonstrated Access tools for preparing data in an existing database for analysis. These include tools for reading data from external sources into tables, creating relationships between tables, sorting and filtering records, designing and executing queries, and saving data to external files.

GLOSSARY

Action queries Queries that are used to change data in existing tables. The four types of action queries available in Access are update, make table, append, and delete.
Crosstab queries Queries that are used to summarize data in one field across the values of one or more other fields.

Database A collection of logically related data that can be retrieved, manipulated, and updated to meet a user's or organization's needs.

Datasheet view A view used in Access to control a database; provides access to tables, reports, queries, forms, etc. in the database that is currently open. This view can also be used to create tables for a database.

Design view A view used in Access to define or edit a database table's fields and field properties as well as to rearrange the order of the fields in the database that is currently open.

Entity integrity The rule that establishes that a table has no duplicate records. Entity integrity can be enforced by assigning a unique primary key to each record in a table.

Fields The variables or characteristics for which data have been collected from the records.

Foreign key field A field that is permitted to have multiple records with the same value.

Form An object that is created from a table to simplify the process of entering data.

Leszynski/Reddick guidelines A commonly used set of standards for naming database objects.

Many-to-many Sometimes abbreviated as ∞:∞, a relationship for which a value in the common field for a record in one table (say, Table A) can match the value in the common field for multiple records in another table (say, Table B), and a value in the common field for a record in Table B can match the value in the common field for several records in Table A.

One-to-many Sometimes abbreviated as 1:∞, a relationship between tables for which a value in the common field for a record in one table (say, Table A) can match the value in the common field for multiple records in another table (say, Table B), but a value in the common field for a record in Table B can match the value in the common field for at most a single record in Table A.

One-to-one Sometimes abbreviated as 1:1, a relationship between tables for which a value in the common field for a record in one table (say, Table A) can match the value in the common field for at most one record in another table (say, Table B), and a value in the common field for a record in Table B can match the value in the common field for at most a single record in Table A.

Orphaned A record in a table that has a value for the foreign key field of a table that does not match the value in the primary key field for any record of a related table. Enforcing referential integrity prevents the creation of orphaned records.

Primary key field A field that must have a unique value for each record in the table and is used to identify how records from several tables in a database are logically related.

Query A question posed by a user about the data in the database.

Records The individual units from which the data for a database have been collected.

Referential integrity The rule that establishes the proper relationship between two tables.

Report Output from a table or a query that has been put into a specific prespecified format.

Select queries Queries that are used to extract the subset of data that satisfy one or more criteria from a table.

Table Data arrayed in rows and columns (similar to a worksheet in an Excel spreadsheet) in which rows correspond to records and columns correspond to fields.

References

Data Management and Microsoft Access

Adamski, J. J., K. T. Finnegan, and S. Scollard. *New Perspectives on Microsoft® Access 2013, Comprehensive.* Cengage Learning, 2014.

Alexander, M. *The Excel Analyst's Guide to Access.* Wiley, 2010.

Alexander, M. *Access 2013 Bible*, 1st ed. Wiley, 2013.

Balter, A. *Using Microsoft Access 2010.* Que Publishing, 2010.

Carter, J., and J. Juarez. *Microsoft Office Access 2010: A Lesson Approach, Complete.* McGraw-Hill, 2011.

Conrad, J. *Microsoft Access 2013 Inside Out*, 1st ed. Microsoft Press, 2013.

Friedrichsen, L. *Microsoft® Access 2013: Illustrated Complete.* Cengage Learning, 2014.

Jennings, R. *Microsoft Access 2010 in Depth.* Que Publishing, 2010.

MacDonald. *Access 2013: The Missing Manual*, 1st ed. O'Reilly Media, 2013.

Owen, G. *Using Microsoft Excel and Access 2016 for Accounting*, 5th ed. Cengage Learning, 2017.

Pratt, P. J., and M. Z. Last. *Microsoft® Access 2013: Complete.* Cengage Learning, 2014.

Data Mining

Linoff, G. S., and M. J. Berry. *Data Mining Techniques: For Marketing, Sales, and Customer Relationship Management*, 3rd ed. Wiley, 2011.

Berthold, M., and D. J. Hand. *Intelligent Data Analysis.* Springer (Berlin), 1999.

Hand, D. J., H. Mannila, and P. Smyth. *Principles of Data Mining.* MIT Press, 2001.

Hastie, T., R. Tibshirani, and J. Friedman. *The Elements of Statistical Learning*, 2nd ed. Springer, 2009.

Schmueli, G., P. C. Bruce, M. Stephens, N. R. Patel. *Data Mining for Business Analytics: Concepts, Techniques and Applications with JMP Pro.* Wiley, 2017.

Schmueli, G., P. C. Bruce, I. Yahav, N. R. Patel, K. C. Lichtendahl Jr. *Data Mining for Business Analytics: Concepts, Techniques and Applications in R.* Wiley, 2018.

Tan, P.-N., M. Steinbach, and V. Kumar, *Introduction to Data Mining.* Pearson, 2006.

Data Visualization

Alexander, M., and J. Walkenbach. *Excel Dashboards and Reports.* Wiley, 2010.

Camm, J., M. Fry, and J. Shaffer. "A Practitioner's Guide to Best Practices in Data Visualization," *Interfaces* 47, no. 6 (November–December 2017): 473–488.

Cleveland, W. S. *Visualizing Data.* Hobart Press, 1993.

Cleveland, W. S. *The Elements of Graphing Data*, 2nd ed. Hobart Press, 1994.

Few, S. *Show Me the Numbers: Designing Tables and Graphs to Enlighten.* Analytics Press, 2004.

Few, S. *Information Dashboard Design: The Effective Visual Communication of Data.* O'Reilly Media, 2006.

Few, S. *Now You See It: Simple Visualization Techniques for Quantitative Analysis.* Analytics Press, 2009.

Longley, P. A., M. Goodchild, D. J. Maguire, and D. W. Rhind. *Geographic Information Systems and Science.* Wiley, 2010.

Milligan, J. N. *Learning Tableau 10*, 2nd ed. Packt, 2016.

Murray, D. G. *Tableau Your Data! Fast and Easy Visual Analysis with Tableau Software*, 2nd ed. Wiley, 2016.

Robbins, N. B. *Creating More Effective Graphs.* Wiley, 2004.

Telea, A. C. *Data Visualization Principles and Practice.* A. K. Peters, 2008.

Tufte, E. R. *Envisioning Information.* Graphics Press, 1990.

Tufte, E. R. *Visual and Statistical Thinking: Displays of Evidence for Making Decisions.* Graphics Press, 1997.

Tufte, E. R. *Visual Explanations: Images and Quantities, Evidence and Narrative.* Graphics Press, 1997.

Tufte, E. R. *The Visual Display of Quantitative Information*, 2nd ed. Graphics Press, 2001.

Tufte, E. R. *Beautiful Evidence.* Graphics Press, 2006.

Wexler, S., J. Shaffer, and A. Cotgreave. *The Big Book of Dashboards.* Wiley, 2017.

Wong, D. M. *The Wall Street Journal Guide to Information Graphics.* Norton, 2010.

Young, F. W., P. M. Valero-Mora, and M. Friendly. *Visual Statistics: Seeing Data with Dynamic Interactive Graphics.* Wiley, 2006.

Decision Analysis

Clemen, R. T., and T. Reilly. *Making Hard Decisions with DecisionTools.* Cengage Learning, 2004.

Golub, A. L. *Decision Analysis: An Integrated Approach.* Wiley, 1997.

Goodwin, P., and G. Wright. *Decision Analysis for Management Judgment*, 4th ed. Wiley, 2009.

Peterson, M. *An Introduction to Decision Theory.* Cambridge, 2009.

Pratt, J. W., H. Raiffa, and R. Schlaiter. *Introduction to Statistical Decision Theory.* MIT Press, 2008.

Raiffa, H. *Decision Analysis.* McGraw-Hill, 1997.

Time Series and Forecasting

Bowerman, B. L., R. T. O'Connell, and A. Koehler. *Forecasting, Time Series, and Regression*, 4th ed. Cengage Learning, 2005.

Box, G. E. P., G. M. Jenkins, and G. C. Reinsel. *Time Series Analysis: Forecasting and Control*, 5th ed. Wiley, 2015.

Hanke, J. E., and D. Wichern. *Business Forecasting*, 9th ed. Prentice Hall, 2009.

Makridakis, S. G., S. C. Wheelwright, and R. J. Hyndman. *Forecasting Methods and Applications*, 3rd ed. Wiley, 1997.

Ord, K., and R. Fildes. *Principles of Business Forecasting.* Cengage Learning, 2013.

Wilson, J. H., B. Keating, and John Galt Solutions, Inc. *Business Forecasting with Accompanying Excel-Based Forecast X™ Software*, 5th ed. McGraw-Hill/Irwin, 2007.

General Business Analytics

Ayres, I. *Super Crunchers: Why Thinking-by-Numbers Is the New Way to Be Smart.* Bantam, 2008.

Baker, S. *The Numerati.* Mariner Books, 2009.

Davenport, T. H., and J. G. Harris, *Competing on Analytics.* Harvard Business School Press, 2007.

Davenport, T. H., J. G. Harris, and R. Morrison, *Analytics at Work.* Harvard Business School Press, 2010.

Davenport, T. H., Ed. *Enterprise Analytics.* FT Press, 2012.

Fisher, M., and A. Raman. *The New Science of Retailing.* Harvard Business Press, 2010.

Lewis, M. *Moneyball: The Art of Winning an Unfair Game.* Norton, 2004.

Wind, J., P. E. Green, D. Shifflet, and M. Scarbrough. "Courtyard by Marriott: Designing a Hotel Facility with Consumer-Based Marketing Models," *Interfaces* 19, no. 1 (January–February 1989): 25–47.

Optimization

Baker, K. R. *Optimization Modeling with Spreadsheets,* 3rd ed. Wiley, 2015.

Bazaraa, M. S., H. D. Sherali, and C.M. Shetty. *Nonlinear Programming: Theory and Algorithms,* 3rd ed. Wiley, 2006.

Bazaraa, M. S., J. J. Jarvis, and H. D. Sherali. *Linear Programming and Network Flows,* 4th ed. Wiley, 2009.

Chen, D., R. G. Batson, and Y. Dang. *Applied Integer Programming.* Wiley, 2010.

Sashihara, S. *The Optimization Edge.* McGraw-Hill, 2011.

Winston, W. L. *Financial Models Using Simulation and Optimization,* 2nd ed. Palisade Corporation, 2008.

Probability

Anderson, D., D. Sweeney, T. Williams, J. Camm, J. Cochran, M. Fry, and J. Ohlman. *Modern Business Statistics with Microsoft Excel,* 7th ed. Cengage Learning, 2021.

Anderson, D., D. Sweeney, T. Williams, J. Camm, J. Cochran, M. Fry, and J. Ohlmann. *An Introduction to Statistics for Business and Economics,* 14th ed. Cengage Learning, 2020.

Ross, S. M. *An Introduction to Probability Models,* 11th ed. Academic Press, 2014.

Regression Analysis

Chatterjee, S., and A. S. Hadi. *Regression Analysis by Example,* 5th ed. Wiley, 2012.

Draper, N. R., and H. Smith. *Applied Regression Analysis,* 3rd ed. Wiley, 1998.

Graybill, F. A., and H. K. Iyer. *Regression Analysis: Concepts and Applications.* Wadsworth, 1994.

Hosmer, D. W., and S. Lemeshow. *Applied Logistic Regression,* 3rd ed. Wiley, 2013.

Kleinbaum, D. G., L. L. Kupper, A. Nizam, and E. Rosenberg. *Applied Regression Analysis and Multivariate Methods,* 5th ed. Cengage Learning, 2013.

Mendenhall, M., T. Sincich, and T. R. Dye. *A Second Course in Statistics: Regression Analysis,* 7th ed. Prentice Hall, 2011.

Montgomery, D. C., E. A. Peck, and G. G. Vining. *Introduction to Linear Regression Analysis,* 5th ed. Wiley, 2012.

Neter, J., W. Wasserman, M. H. Kutner, and C. Nashtsheim. *Applied Linear Statistical Models,* 5th ed. McGraw-Hill, 2004.

Monte Carlo Simulation

Bell, P. *Brent-Harbridge Developments, Inc.* Richard Ivey School of Business, University of Western Ontario, 1998.

Law, A. M. *Simulation Modeling and Analysis,* 4th ed. McGraw-Hill, 2006.

Ross, S. *Simulation.* Academic Press, 2013.

Savage, S. L. *Flaw of Averages.* Wiley, 2012.

Talib, N. N. *Fooled by Randomness.* Random House, 2004.

Wainer, H. *Picturing the Uncertain World.* Princeton University Press, 2009.

Winston, W. *Decision Making Under Uncertainty.* Palisade Corporation, 2007.

Spreadsheet Modeling

Leong, T., and M. Cheong. *Business Modeling with Spreadsheets: Problems, Principles, and Practice,* 2nd ed. McGraw-Hill (Asia), 2010.

Powell, S. G., and R. J. Batt. *Modeling for Insight.* Wiley, 2008.

Winston, W. *Excel 2016 Data Analysis and Business Modeling.* Microsoft Press, 2016.

Statistical Inference

Barnett, V. *Comparative Statistical Inference,* 3rd ed. Wiley, 1999.

Casella, G. and R. L. Berger. *Statistical Inference,* 2nd ed. Duxbury, 2002.

Roussas, G. G. *An Introduction to Probability and Statistical Inference,* 2nd ed. Elsevier, 2014.

Wasserman, L. *All of Statistics: A Concise Course in Statistical Inference.* Springer, 2004.

Welsh, A. H. *Aspects of Statistical Inference.* Wiley, 1996.

Young, G. A., and R. L. Smith. *Essentials of Statistical Inference.* Cambridge, 2005.

Index